VOICES Together

MennoMedia
Harrisonburg, Virginia

Voices Together

First edition
Published by MennoMedia
Harrisonburg, Virginia

24 23 22 21 20   10 9 8 7 6 5 4 3 2 1

Printed in United States of America
International Standard Book Numbers
978-1-5138-0553-5 (pew edition)
978-1-5138-0554-2 (large print edition)
978-1-5138-0555-9 (accompaniment edition)
978-1-5138-0556-6 (worship leader edition, paperback)
978-1-5138-0557-3 (worship leader edition, ebook)
978-1-5138-0574-0 (projection edition)

Cover symbol: The dove carrying an olive branch is a cherished biblical image of God's peace, originating with the story of Noah. The dove also symbolizes the presence of the Holy Spirit at the baptism of Jesus. The open circle in the symbol represents community, open to the Spirit's new life for all.

INTRODUCTION

We worship God in Christ, through the Spirit with vibrant currents of music, spoken words, visual art, and movement. Voices resound a cappella and flow through microphones and speakers. Pipe organ and electric guitar, gamelan, and hammered dulcimer, all join in a chorus of worship. Communities across Mennonite Church USA and Mennonite Church Canada are living the Psalm 150 vision: Let everything that has breath praise God!

In worship, we grow together in relationship with God and with one another. We remember, rehearse, and are shaped by the stories of God's people across time and distance. Worship invites us to bring to God our great joys, deep sorrows, offerings of time and talent, and earnest questions. Together in worship we are called and sent to live into God's vision of healing and hope not just for ourselves, but for our communities and all of creation.

A hymnal holds together stories about who God is and what God does. It shapes God's people, placing each of us in God's story as beloved individuals and members of Christian communities. This collection's title, *Voices Together*, reflects and celebrates the rich and varied expressions of worship we offer to God. Great care has been taken to assemble a collection where worshipers may find themselves and their stories honored and expressed. *Voices Together* invites us to sing one another's songs and cultivate authentic relationships within our neighborhoods and around the world.

In these pages, visual art, Scripture, spoken prayers and readings, and other supports for the practices of the church are gathered alongside songs as expansive ways to explore the rhythms of Christian faith and life.

Three symbols help leaders navigate two companion volumes and additional online resources. The worship leader edition provides theological grounding, practical guidance, and words for worship. The ⓦ symbol indicates that the worship leader edition offers specific guidance or additional words to augment the resource in this volume. The accompaniment edition features notated accompaniments ♪ and the website, VoicesTogetherHymnal.org, has reference essays ⓡ that guide leaders with context on different types of songs and traditions or musical options.

We pray that *Voices Together* will help us grow in awareness of how God is at work in the world, and help us join the activity of the Spirit. May the meanings of these words, images, and songs deepen over time and through repetition, as personal faith grows and changes with the Holy Spirit's leading, and as they find expression in changing local and global contexts.

—Bradley Kauffman, project director and general editor
on behalf of the Mennonite Worship and Song Committee

VOICES TOGETHER PERSONNEL

Project Director and General Editor
Bradley Kauffman

Mennonite Worship and Song Committee
Benjamin Bergey, music editor*
Paul Dueck
Mike Erb
Katie Graber, intercultural worship editor
Emily Grimes (2016–2018)
Tom Harder
Sarah Kathleen Johnson, worship resources editor*
Bradley Kauffman, general editor*
SaeJin Lee
Anneli Loepp Thiessen
Cynthia Neufeld Smith
Darryl Neustaedter Barg
Allan Rudy-Froese
Adam M. L. Tice, text editor*

*Editorial team

MennoMedia Staff
Steve Carpenter, director of development (2015–2019)
Russ Eanes, MennoMedia executive director (2016–2018)
Meghan Florian, managing editor
Amy Gingerich, executive director (2018–present)
Karen Gonzol, editorial assistant
Merrill Miller, senior designer

Indexers: Carl Bear, Sarah Kathleen Johnson, Ezra M. Tice, Adam M. L. Tice

Central Practices Worship Resources Committee: Irma Fast Dueck (co-chair), Sarah Kathleen Johnson (co-chair), Heidi A. Miller, Allan Rudy-Froese, Adam M. L. Tice, Isaac Villegas

Scripture Worship Resources Committee: Melanie A. Howard, Sarah Kathleen Johnson (chair), Allan Rudy-Froese, Derek Suderman

Steering Committee: Nicole Francisco Bailey, Shana Peachey Boshart, Terry Shue, (Mennonite Church USA); Irma Fast Dueck, Doug Klassen, Karen Martens Zimmerly (Mennonite Church Canada); Russ Eanes, Amy Gingerich (MennoMedia)

Additional contributions of time and expertise are listed in the acknowledgements. We wish to thank everyone named and unnamed for helping shape this extraordinary community effort.

CONTENTS

Introduction iii

Voices Together Personnel iv

GATHERING **1–67**

Welcome 1–36

God's Presence with Us 37–67

PRAISING **68–139**

Praise 68–112

Thanksgiving 113–124

Adoration 125–139

RECONCILING **140–174**

Confession of Sin 140–155

Assurance of Grace 156–174

TELLING GOD'S STORY **175–418**

Creation 175–189

Covenant 190–195

Wisdom 196–204

Prophets 205–209

Jesus' Advent 210–239

Birth of Jesus 240–269

Jesus' Epiphany 270–279

Life, Teaching, and Ministry of Jesus 280–303

Journey to the Cross 304–319

Jesus' Death 320–332

Jesus' Resurrection 333–362

Jesus' Ascension 363–366

Holy Spirit 367–385

Church 386–397

Word of God 398–406

Reign of Christ 407–418

CONFESSING FAITH **419–440**

CELEBRATING BAPTISM **441–458**

CELEBRATING COMMUNION **459–493**

Meal 459–489

Footwashing 490–493

SHARING OUR STORIES **494–672**
Morning and Evening 494–507
Child Blessing 508–510
Nurturing Faith 511–522
Family, Friendship, and Marriage 523–525
Vocation, Work, and Rest 526–535
God's Call 536–547
Conversion and New Life 548–565
Following Christ 566–584
Doubt and Faith 585–604
Suffering and Joy 605–641
Healing and Anointing 642–651
Death and Eternal Life 652–672

PRAYING **673–744**
Prayer 673–690
Lament 691–696
Gratitude 697–704
For the World 705–714
For the Church 715–722
For One Another and Ourselves 723–744

GIVING **745–760**

LIVING GOD'S STORY **761–808**
Mission 761–770
Service 771–778
Peace and Justice 779–801
Expanding our Circle 802–808

SENDING **809–849**
Commissioning 809–829
Blessing 830–849

WORSHIP RESOURCES **850–1069**

Acknowledgments 1071

Copyright Holders Index 1077

Contributors Index: *Authors, Composers, Artists, Arrangers, and Translators* 1087

Non-English Languages Index 1095

Topics and Uses in Worship Index 1096

Scriptural Allusions and References Index 1130

Metrical Index 1138

Tune Index 1142

First Lines and Common Titles Index of Worship Resources 1145

First Lines and Common Titles Index of Songs 1149

Summoned by the God Who Made Us 1

NETTLETON 8.7.8.7 D

1 Sum-moned by the God who made us rich in our di-ver-si-ty,
2 Ra-diant ris-en from the wa-ter, robed in ho-li-ness and light,
3 Trust the good-ness of cre-a-tion; trust the Spir-it strong with-in.
4 Bring the hopes of ev'-ry na-tion; bring the art of ev'-ry race.
5 Draw to-geth-er at one ta-ble all the hu-man fam-i-ly;
gath-ered in the name of Je-sus, rich-er still in u-ni-ty:
ev-'ry per-son in God's im-age, ev-'ry per-son, God's de-light.
Dare to dream the vi-sion prom-ised sprung from seed of what has been.
Weave a song of peace and jus-tice; let it sound through time and space.
shape a cir-cle ev-er wid-er and a peo-ple ev-er free.
Refrain
Let us bring the gifts that dif-fer and, in splen-did, var-ied ways,
sing a new church in-to be-ing, one in faith and love and praise.

Music: American traditional (USA), in John Wyeth's *Repository of Sacred Music, Part Second*, 1813

2 Uyai mose (Come All You People)

UYAI MOSE 5.6.5.6.5.6.7

Leader
U - ya - i mo - se, ti - na -
Come all you peo - ple, come and
E
A/E
U - ya - i mo - se, ti - na - ma - te
Come all you peo - ple, come and praise your
Ahom
Ahom
ma - te Mwa - ri; u - ya - i mo - se,
praise your Mak - er; come all you peo - ple,
E
Mwa - ri; u - ya - i mo - se,
Mak - er; come all you peo - ple,
Ahom
ti - na - ma - te Mwa - ri; u -
come and praise your Mak - er; come
B7
E
ti - na - ma - te Mwa - ri; u - ya - i
come and praise your Mak - er; come all you
Ahom
Ahom

Text: Shona; Alexander Gondo (Zimbabwe); transcr. and English paraphr. I-to Loh (Taiwan), 1986
Music: Alexander Gondo; arr. John Bell (Scotland),

ya - i mo - se, ti - na - ma - te Mwa - ri;
all you peo - ple, come and praise your Mak - er;
A/E
mo - se, ti - na - ma - te Mwa - ri;
peo - ple, come and praise your Mak - er;
Ahom
Repeat
Last time
u - ya - i mo - se zvi - no. Ti - na - ma - te Mwa-ri; no.
come now and wor-ship the Lord. Come and praise your Mak-er; Lord.
Repeat
Last time
E B E E
u - ya - i mo - se zvi - no. no.
come now and wor-ship the Lord. Lord.
Ahom Ahom Ahom Ahom

Gathered Here 3

GATHERED HERE IN THE MYSTERY Irregular

Canon

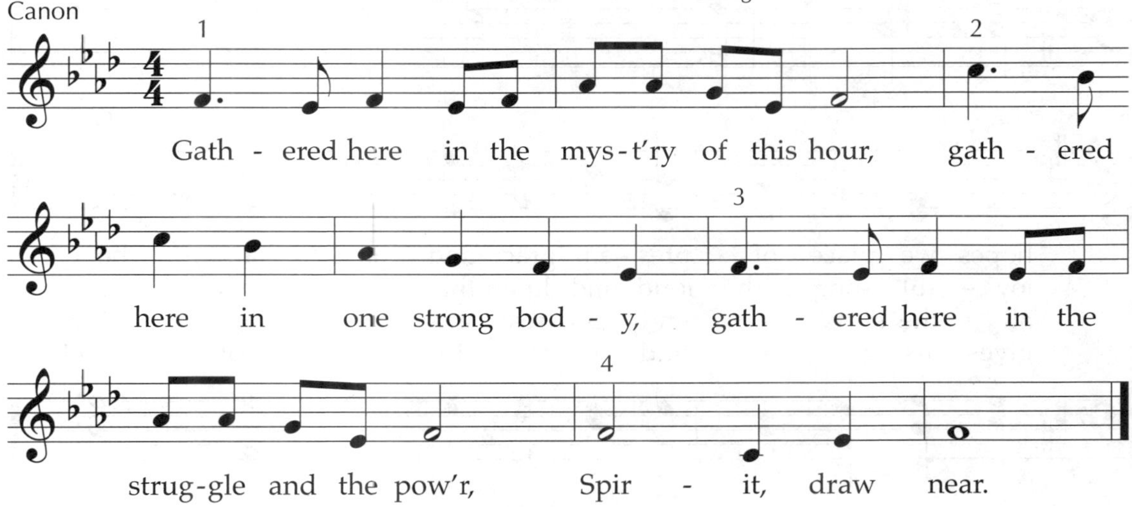
1
Gath - ered here in the mys - t'ry of this hour,
2
gath - ered here in one strong bod - y,
3
gath - ered here in the strug-gle and the pow'r,
4
Spir - it, draw near.

Text: Phil Porter (USA)
Music: Phil Porter

4 Christ Is Our Cornerstone

DARWALL'S 148th 6.6.6.6.8.8

D A Bm G A
1 Christ is our cor - ner - stone, on him a - lone we
2 Oh, then with hymns of praise these hal - low'd courts shall
3 Here may we gain from heav'n the grace which we im -
4 Praise to the God of heav'n; sing praise to Christ the
D Bm E A
build. With his true saints a - lone the courts of
ring. Our voic - es we will raise, the Three - in -
plore, and may that grace, once giv'n, be with us
Son; the Spir - it, praise be giv'n, who joins them
E7 A D G A7 Bm
heav'n are filled. On his great love our
One to sing, and thus pro - claim in
ev - er - more, un - til that day when
both as one: the ho - ly Dove, who
A G D A7 D
hopes we place of pres - ent grace and joys a - bove.
joy - ful song both loud and long that glo - rious name.
all the bless'd to end - less rest are called a - way!
gives us grace to find our place in God's great love!

Text: "Angularis fundamentum lapis" (Rome), ca. 7th c.; trans. John Chandler (England), *Hymns of the Primitive Church*, 1837, alt.
Music: John Darwall (England), *New Universal Psalmodist*, 1770

All People That on Earth Do Dwell 5

OLD HUNDREDTH LM

G D Em Bm Em D G
1 All peo - ple that on earth do dwell, sing out your
2 Know that there is one God in - deed, who fash - ions
3 En - ter the sa - cred gates with praise, with joy ap -
4 Pro - claim a - gain that God is good, whose mer - cy
D Em C G D Em D G D G
faith with cheer - ful voice; de - light in God whose
us with - out our aid, who claims us, gives us
proach the tem - ple walls. Ex - tol and bless our
is for - ev - er sure, whose truth at all times
C D G Em D Am G D G
praise you tell, whose pres - ence calls you to re - joice.
all we need, whose ten - der care will nev - er fade.
God al - ways as peo - ple whom the Spir - it calls.
firm - ly stood, and shall from age to age en - dure.

16th-century text:

1 All people that on earth do dwell,
sing to the Lord with cheerful voice.
Him serve with mirth, his praise forth tell,
come ye before him and rejoice.

2 Know that the Lord is God indeed.
Without our aid he did us make.
We are his flock, he doth us feed,
and for his sheep he doth us take.

3 Oh, enter then his gates with praise.
Approach with joy his courts unto.
Praise, laud, and bless his name always,
for it is seemly so to do.

4 For why? the Lord our God is good.
His mercy is forever sure.
His truth at all times firmly stood,
and shall from age to age endure.

Text: based on Psalm 100; William Kethe (present-day Switzerland), *Anglo-Genevan Psalter*, 1561; adapt. Thomas H. Troeger (USA), 1992
Music: Louis Bourgeois (present-day France), *Genevan Psalter*, 1551

6 Let's Walk Together

WELCOME 8.6.8.6.7.7 with refrain

E A/E B A
1 Let's walk to-geth - er for a while, and ask where
2 Let's talk to-geth - er of a time when we will
3 Let's dream to-geth - er of the day when earth and
B C♯m E A/E
we be - gin to build a world where love can grow,
share a feast, where pride and pow - er kneel to serve
heav'n are one, a cit - y built of love and light,
B A B E D
and hope can en - ter in, to be the hands of
the lone - ly and the least, and joy will set the
the new Je - ru - sa - lem, where mourn-ing turns to
C♯m F♯ B sus B
heal - ing, and to plant the seed of peace,
ta - ble as we join our hands to pray,
danc - ing, ev-'ry crea - ture lifts its voice,

Text: Laurie Zelman (USA)
Music: Mark A. Miller (USA)

Refrain
B/D♯ E A B
sing - ing wel - come, wel - come to this place. You're in -
B E A/C♯ B
vit - ed to come and know God's grace. All are
Bm9 E7 Amaj7 A B F♯/A♯ F♯
wel - come, the love of God to share, 'cause
F♯m7 A B C♯m C♯m7
all of us are wel - come here;
F♯m A E
(Last time)
all are wel - come in this place.
(Last time)

7 Come, Let Us All Unite to Sing

GOD IS LOVE 8.3.8.3.8.8.8.4 with refrain

1 Come, let us all u - nite to sing, God is love. Let heav'n and
2 O tell to earth's re - mot - est bound, God is love. In Christ we
3 What though our mor-tal flesh shall fail, God is love! Through Christ we
4 How hap-py is our por - tion here, God is love. These prom - is -
earth their prais - es bring, God is love. Let ev' - ry soul from
have re - demp-tion found, God is love. His blood has washed our
shall o'er death pre - vail, God is love! While end - less ag - es
es our spir - its cheer, God is love. God is our sun and
sin a - wake, let ev' - ry heart sweet mu - sic make, and sing with
sins a - way, his Spir - it turned our night to day, and now we
roll a - long, we'll tri-umph with the heav'n - ly throng, and this shall
shield by day, our help, our hope, our strength and stay; and will be
us for Je - sus' sake, for God is love.
can re - joice to say that God is love.
be our sweet-est song, that God is love!
with us all the way: our God is love.
Refrain
God is love! God is
God is love!

Text: anon., ca. 1812, *Millennial Praises* (USA), 1812
Music: Edmund S. Lorenz (USA), *Notes of Triumph: For the Sunday School*, 1886

D
G
D A7 D
love! Come, let us all u - nite to sing that God is love.
God is love!

Jesus A, Nahetotaetanome (Jesus Lord, How Joyful) 8

JESUS A, NAHETOTAETANOME Irregular

Je - sus A, Na - he - to - tae - ta - no - me tseh - ma - no'- ee' -
Je - sus Lord, how joy - ful you have made us to come to - geth -
to - va - tse - me - no - to, tse - 'o - noo - me - me - no - to.
er here with you now! In your mer - cy, you have called us.
"Na - nee - hoo - ve - me - o - 'o," tsex - he - še - me - no - to.
You say, "I am the way." We hear you call us.
Neh - pa - ve - a - me - otšė - še - me - no ne - me - o - ne - va!
We ask you, "Come lead us day by day." We fol - low your way.

Text: Cheyenne; John Heap of Birds (Cheyenne, USA), 20th c.; trans. David Graber (USA) and others, *Tsese-Ma'heone-Nemeotôtse (Cheyenne Spiritual Songs)*, 1982,
Music: Plains Indian traditional (USA)

ⓡ

9 Come Away from Rush and Hurry

CIVILITY 8.7.8.7 D

D A/C♯ Bm G
1 Come a - way from rush and hur - ry to the still-ness of God's peace;
2 In the pas-tures of God's good-ness we lie down to rest our soul,
D A/C♯ Bm F♯m
from our vain am-bi-tion's wor - ry, come to Christ to find re - lease.
from the wa - ters of God's mer - cy we drink deep-ly, are made whole.
A D F♯m Bm G
Come a - way from noise and clam-or, life's de-mands and fren-zied pace;
At the ta - ble of God's pres-ence all the saints are rich - ly fed.
A D A/C♯ Bm G D
come to join the peo-ple gath-ered here to seek and find God's grace.
With the oil of God's a - noint-ing in - to ser-vice we are led.

Text: Marva J. Dawn (USA), © 1999 Marva J. Dawn
Music: Gregg DeMey (USA), © 2008 Re:Create Music (admin. Faith Alive Christian Resources)

Here in This Place 10

GATHER US IN 10.9.10.10 D

1 Here in this place, the new light is stream-ing; now are the shad-ows
2 We are the young, our lives are a mys-t'ry. We are the old who
3 Here we will take the wine of com-pas-sion; here we will take the
4 Not just in build-ings, dim and con-fin-ing; not in some heav-en,

van-ished a-way. See in this space our fears and our dream-ings,
yearn for your face. We have been sung through-out all of his-t'ry,
bread of new birth. Here we be-come the peo-ple you fash-ion:
light-years a-way: here in this place, the new light is shin-ing;

brought here to you in the light of this day.
called to be light to the whole hu-man race.
chil-dren of God, to be salt for the earth.
now is the dawn-ing and now is the day.

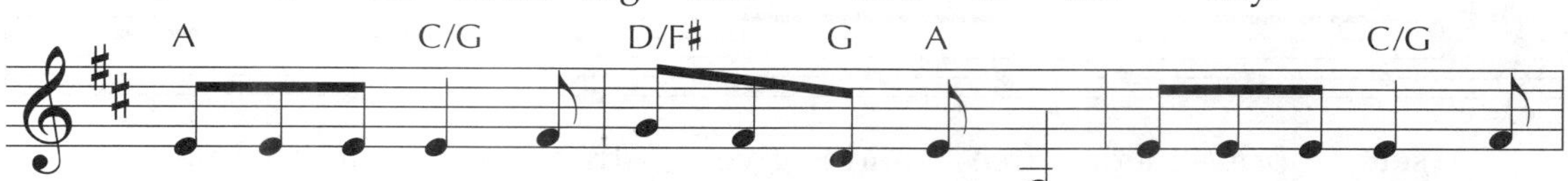

Gath-er us in, the lost and for-sak-en; gath-er us in, our
Gath-er us in, the rich and the haugh-ty; gath-er us in, the
Give us to drink the wine ev-er flow-ing, give us to eat the
Gath-er us in and hold us for-ev-er; gath-er us in and

spir-its in-flame. Call to us now, and we shall a-wak-en;
proud and the strong. Give us a heart so meek and so low-ly;
bread that is you. Nour-ish us well, and guide us in grow-ing
make us your own. Gath-er us in, all peo-ples to-geth-er,

we shall a-rise at the sound of our name.
give us the cour-age to en-ter the song.
lives that are ho-ly and hearts that are true.
fire of love in our flesh and our bone.

Text: Marty Haugen (USA), 1981, *Gather*, 1988, alt.
Music: Marty Haugen, 1981, *Gather*, 1988

11 Mountain of God

MOUNTAIN OF GOD Irregular

D D/C♯
1 Come, let us go ___ to a place that is pure, to
2 From each _ cor - ner and _ end of the earth, we'll
3 New life a-waits ___ for _ all who be-lieve; ___
G/B Asus A
learn a - bout love ___ and wipe a - way tears; ___ to
gath - er to - geth - er to sing of your worth, ___ of
all who love mer - cy, do jus - tice, walk hum - bly. With
D D/C♯
melt swords of steel and hearts made of stone, ___
blind who can see and wea - ry who rest, good
Christ as our guide u - nit - ed we'll be; ___
G/B Asus A
set pris - 'ners free and give stran - gers a home.
news for the poor, ___ free - dom for op - pressed.
liv - ing the king - dom, se - cure in God's peace.
Refrain
G D G
So come, come as you are, oh, come,
D G
from near and far, oh, come, sal-va - tion we'll
D C G D
taste as we climb the moun - tain of God.

Text: Phil Campbell-Enns (Canada)
Music: Phil Campbell-Enns; acc. Bill Derksen (Canada)

13 *Isaiah 2:3-4*

Come, let us go up
to the mountain of the LORD,
to the house of the God of Jacob;
that we may be taught God's ways,
and walk in God's paths.
For out of Zion goes forth instruction,
and the word of the LORD
from Jerusalem.
God will judge between the nations,
and will arbitrate for many peoples;
they will beat their swords
into plowshares,
and their spears into pruning hooks;
nation will not lift up sword
against nation,
neither will they learn war any more.

14 *Isaiah 55:1-2*

Come, all you who are thirsty,
come to the waters;
and you who have no money,
come, buy and eat!
Come, buy wine and milk
without money
and without cost.
Why spend money
on what is not bread,
and your labor
on what does not satisfy?
Listen to me, and eat what is good;
delight in the richest of feasts.

15 *Psalm 118:24*

This is the day that the LORD has made;
let us rejoice and be glad in it.

16 *Psalm 122:1*

I was glad when they said to me,
"Let us go to the house of the LORD!"

17 *Psalm 133:1*

How very good and pleasant it is
when kindred live together in unity!

18 *Mark 10:13-16*

Some people brought children to Jesus
for him to place his hands on them,
but the disciples scolded them.
When Jesus noticed this,
he was displeased
and said to his disciples,
"Let the children come to me,
and do not stop them,
because the reign of God
belongs to such as these.
I assure you that whoever does not
receive the reign of God like a child
will never enter it."
Then he took the children in his arms,
placed his hands on each of them,
and blessed them.

19 *Matthew 18:20*

Where two or three are gathered
in my name,
I am there among them.

20 *Psalm 100*

Make a joyful noise to the LORD,
all you lands!
Serve the LORD with gladness;
come into God's presence
with a song.
Know that the LORD is God,
our maker to whom we belong;
we are God's people
and the sheep of God's pasture.
Enter the gates of the LORD
with thanksgiving
and the courts with praise;
give thanks and bless
God's holy name.
Good indeed is the LORD,
whose steadfast love is everlasting,
whose faithfulness endures
from age to age.

21 *2 Corinthians 13:13*

May the grace of Jesus Christ,
the love of God,
and the communion of the Holy Spirit
be with you all.

Previous page: 12. *Tree of Life*, SaeJin Lee (Korea/USA), 2018, watercolor paint and colored pencils Ⓦ

What Is This Place 22

KOMT NU MET ZANG 9.8.9.8.9.6.6

C F C G F C
1 What is this place where we are meet-ing? On - ly a house, the
2 Words from a - far, stars that are fall - ing, sparks that are sown in
3 And we ac - cept bread at his ta - ble, bro - ken and shared, a
G C F C G
earth its floor, walls and a roof shel - ter - ing peo - ple,
us like seed. Names for our God, dreams, signs, and won - ders
liv - ing sign. Here in this world, dy - ing and liv - ing,
F C G C F G
win-dows for light, an o - pen door. Yet it be-comes a bod - y that
sent from the past are what we need. We in this place re - mem - ber and
we are each oth-er's bread and wine. This is the place where we can re -
C G C D7 G F G C
lives when we are gath - ered here, and know our God is near.
speak a - gain what we have heard: God's free re - deem - ing Word.
ceive what we need to in - crease: God's jus - tice and God's peace.

Text: Huub Oosterhuis (Netherlands), *Zomaar een dak boven wat hoofden*, 1968; trans. David Smith (England), © 1967 OCP Publications

Music: *Nederlandtsche Gedenckclanck*, 1626; harm. Bernard Huijbers (Netherlands), harm. © 1984 TEAM Publications, OCP Publications

23 Hamba nathi (Come, Walk with Us)

HAMBA NATHI Irregular

Leader
Ham - ba na - thi,
Ham - ba na - thi,
1 Come, walk with us,
2 Share our bur - den,
3 Come, up - lift us,
4 Give us peace,
G
C
Ham - ba na - thi mkhu - lu - li we - thu. Ham-
1 Come, walk with us, the jour - ney is long. Come,
Ham - ba na - thi,
mkhu - lu - li we - thu,
D
G
G
- ba na - thi mkhu - lu - li we - thu. Ham- lu - li we - thu, mkhu-
walk with us, the jour - ney is long. Come, jour - ney is long. The
mkhu - lu - li we - thu,
C
D
lu - li, mkhu - lu - li, mkhu - lu - li we - thu, mkhu - lu - li, mkhu-
jour - ney, the jour - ney, the jour - ney is long. The jour - ney, the

Text: Zulu; South African traditional; trans. Gerhard Cartford (USA), © Lutheran World Foundation

Music: South African traditional; arr. Anders Nyberg (Sweden), © 1984 Peace of Music Publishing AB (admin. Walton Music Corp., a division of GIA Publications, Inc.)

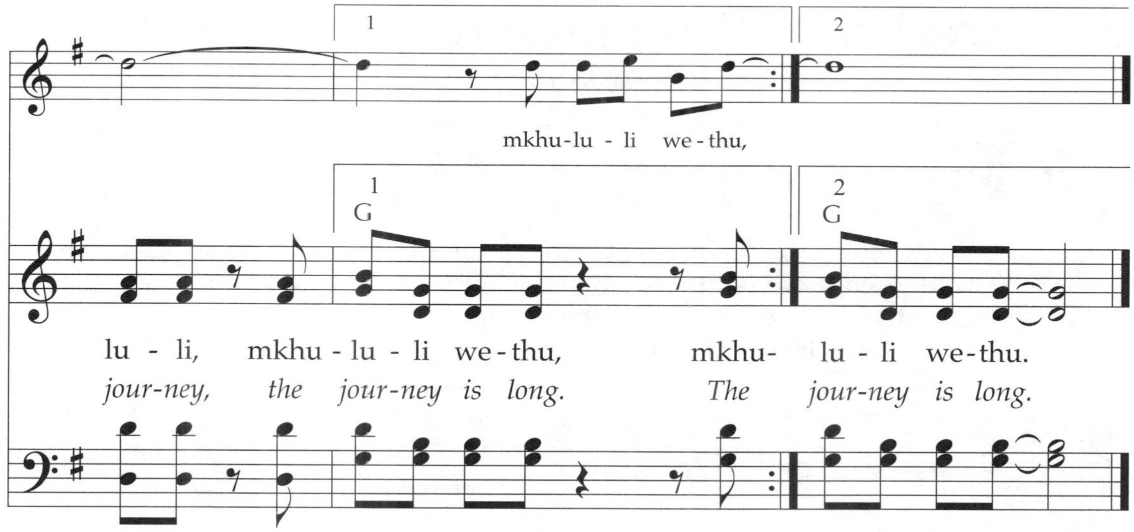
1
2
mkhu - lu - li we - thu,
1
G
2
G
lu - li, mkhu - lu - li we - thu, mkhu- lu - li we - thu.
jour-ney, the jour-ney is long. The jour-ney is long.

2 *Share our burden, and join in the song.*
3 *Come, uplift us, and bring us new life.*
4 *Give us peace when the journey is done.*

There's a River of Life 24

RIVER OF LIFE Irregular

There's a riv - er of life that's flow - ing from *his throne, a
riv - er of life that's flow - ing from *his throne. Won't you
come on in and see? This riv - er will set you free!
Way yah hey yah, way yah hey yah, high yah way.

*Alternative: "God's throne"

Text: based on Revelation 22:1; Jonathan Maracle (Mohawk, Canada)
Music: Jonathan Maracle

Ⓡ

25 Brethren, We Have Met to Worship

HOLY MANNA 8.7.8.7 D

A E A
1 Breth-ren, we have met to wor - ship; sis - ters, let us
2 Kin - dred, will you come and help us? Mo - ses' fam - 'ly
3 Is there here a trem-bling jail - er, seek - ing grace and
4 Let us love our God su - preme - ly, let us love each
E7 A E A
praise our God. Will you pray with all your pow - er?
aid - ed him. Will you help the trem-bling mourn - ers
filled with fears? Is there here a weep - ing Mar - y,
oth - er, too. Let us love and pray for sin - ners
E7 A
Will you hear and preach the word? All is vain un -
who are strug-gling hard with sin? Tell them all a -
pour - ing forth a flood of tears? Breth - ren, join your
till our God makes all things new. Christ will call us
E7 A E A
less the Spir - it of the ho - ly One comes down. Chris-tians,
bout the Sav - ior. Tell them that he will be found. Chris-tians,
cries to help them; sis - ters, let your prayers a - bound! Pray, oh
home to heav - en, at his ta - ble we'll sit down. Christ will

For a lower key, see "God, Who Stretched the Spangled Heavens" (#529).

Text: George Askins (USA), *Social and Camp-Meeting Hymns for the Pious*, 1817, alt.
Music: *The Columbian Harmony* (USA), 1825

E A E7 A
pray, and ho - ly man - na will be show-ered all a-round.
pray, and ho - ly man - na will be show-ered all a-round.
pray, that ho - ly man - na will be scat-tered all a-round.
gird him - self and serve us with sweet man - na all a-round.

Dhuh Pangeran (O Prince of Peace) 26

O PRINCE OF PEACE 10.10.10.10

1 Dhuh Pa - nge - ran ing - kang Ma - ha - su - ci. Ku - la sa - mi ma - rek te - tung - gil - an. Sa - lir bang - sa sa - lu - mah - ing bu - mi, a - me - mu - ji dha - teng as - ma Tu - wan.
2 Tu - wan tres - na mring ka - wu - la sa - mi, sa - king ki - len mi - wah sa - king we - tan. Sa - mi nung - gil pi - ta - dos ing Gus - ti, Ye - sus Kris - tus kang da - dos Pa - nut - an.
1 O Prince of peace, O ho - ly God most high, we gath - er here, your mes - sage to pro - claim. A - round the earth all na - tions join the cry to know a - gain the glo - ry of your name.
2 O God, we know you love us one and all, wheth - er from west or east we come to - day. We trust in you, and hear your sov-'reign call. O Je - sus Christ, you are our guide and stay.

Text: Javanese; Saptojoadi (Indonesia); trans. Lawrence M. Yoder (USA), *Mennonite World Conference International Songbook*, 1990, alt.
Music: Saptojoadi

27 Here to the House of God We Come

KHAO I DANG* 8.8.8.8.8.8

Dm Am7 Dm Am7 Dm
1 Here to the house of God we come, home of the
2 There is a knock - ing at our door, sound of the
3 God who is shel - ter, who is home, in bor-rowed
4 We are all ten - ants of your love; gath - er us
Am7 Dm Am7
peo - ple of the Way, here to give thanks for
home-less of the world, voice of the fright - ened
rooms you came to live, plead - ed to save the
round a com-mon fire, warm us in com - pa -
Dm Am7 Dm Am7 Dm
all we have, nam - ing our needs for ev - 'ry day,
ref - u - gee, cry of the chil-dren in the cold,
dis - pos - sessed, cru - ci - fied, lay in bor-rowed grave:
ny with Christ, give us the heart to feel, to share
Am7 Fmaj7 Cm7 G7 Am7 B♭maj7
we who have roof and rent and bread, sure of a
ask - ing the least that is their right, safe - ty and
these are no stran - gers in your eyes, this is your
ta - ble and lodg - ing with free hand, space in our
Am7 Dm Am7 Dm Am7 Dm Am7 Dm Am7 Dm
place to rest our head.
shel - ter for the night.
fam - i - ly which cries.
liv - ing, in our land.

*The name of a Cambodian refugee camp in Thailand

Chord symbols represent a simplified harmony.

Text: Shirley Erena Murray (Aotearoa New Zealand)
Music: Colin Alexander Gibson (Aotearoa New Zealand)

Come, Christians, Join to Sing 28

MADRID 6.6.6.6 D

G C G Am/C G/D D7 G
1 Come, Chris-tians, join to sing
2 Come, lift your hearts on high, Al - le - lu - ia! A - men!
3 Praise yet our Christ a - gain,
C G Am/C G/D D7 G
loud praise to Christ we bring;
let prais - es fill the sky; Al - le - lu - ia! A - men!
life shall not end the strain;
C D G Am D
let all, with heart and voice, be - fore his throne re - joice;
Christ is our guide and friend on whom we can de - pend:
on heav - en's bliss - ful shore, his good - ness we'll a - dore,
G C D G Am/C G/D D7 G
praise is his gra - cious choice.
his love shall nev - er end. Al - le - lu - ia! A - men!
sing - ing for - ev - er - more,

Text: Christian H. Bateman (Scotland), *The Sacred Song Book for Children*, 1843
Music: Spanish traditional; arr. David Evans (Wales), 1927

29 Come, Now Is the Time to Worship

COME, NOW IS THE TIME TO WORSHIP Irregular

Refrain
D G/D D A
Come, now is the time to wor - ship. Come, now is the time
Em D/F♯ G D G/D
to give your heart. Come, just as you are, to wor -
D A Em D/F♯ G D
ship. Come, just as you are, be-fore your God. Come.
Last time
G D
1 One day ev-'ry tongue will con-fess you are God;
2 Will-ing-ly we choose to sur-ren - der our lives.
G D G
one day ev-'ry knee will bow. Still, the great-est treas-ure re-mains
Will-ing-ly our knees will bow. With all our heart, soul, mind
Bm Em Asus
for those who glad - ly choose you now.
and strength, we glad - ly choose you now.

Text: Brian Doerksen (Canada)
Music: Brian Doerksen

Jesus Calls Us

30

JESUS CALLS US 8.7.8.7 D

Capo 3: (D) F (Em7) Gm7 (D) F (Em7) Gm7 (F♯m7) Am7
1 Je - sus calls us here to meet him as, through
2 Je - sus calls us to con - fess him Word of
3 Je - sus calls us to each oth - er; vast - ly
(Bm7) Dm7 (Em7) Gm7 (A) C (D) F (Em7) Gm7
word and song and prayer, we af - firm God's
Life and Lord of all, shar - er of our
dif - f'rent though we are; race and col - or,
(D) F (Em7) Gm7 (F♯m7) Am7 (Bm7) Dm7 (Em7) Gm7
prom - ised pres - ence where Christ's peo - ple live and
flesh and frail - ness, sav - ing all who fail or
class and gen - der nei - ther lim - it nor de -
(A) C (D) F (Am) Cm (D) F (Bm) Dm (Em7) Gm7
care. Praise the God who keeps each prom-ise; praise the
fall. Tell his ho - ly hu - man sto - ry; tell his
bar. Join the hand of friend and stran-ger; join the
(F♯m7) Am7 (Em7) Gm7 (A) C (D) F (Em7) Gm7 (D) F
Son who calls us friends; praise the Spir - it who, a -
tales that all may hear; tell the world that Christ in
hands of age and youth; join the faith - ful and the
(Em7) Gm7 (F♯m7) Am7 (Bm7) Dm7 (Em7) Gm7 (D) F
mong us, to our hopes and fears at - tends.
glo - ry came to earth to meet us here.
doubt - er in their com - mon search for truth.

Text: John L. Bell (Scotland) and Graham Maule (Scotland)
Music: Isle of Lewis traditional (Scotland); arr. John L. Bell

31 Come, We That Love

WE'RE MARCHING TO ZION SM extended with refrain

G D7 G D
1 Come, we that love the Lord, and let our joys be known.
2 The hill of Zi - on yields a thou-sand sa - cred sweets,
3 Then let our songs a-bound, and ev - 'ry tear be dry.
G C D A7
Join in a song with sweet ac-cord, join in a song with sweet ac -
be - fore we reach the heav'n-ly fields, be - fore we reach the heav'n-ly
We're march-ing thro' Im-man-uel's ground, we're march-ing thro' Im-man-uel's
D G D G Am G D7 G
cord, and thus sur - round the throne, and thus sur-round the throne.
fields, or walk the gol - den streets, or walk the gol - den streets.
ground, to fair - er worlds on high, to fair - er worlds on high.
and thus sur-round the throne, and thus sur-round the throne.
or walk the gol - den streets, or walk the gol - den streets.
to fair - er worlds on high, to fair - er worlds on high.

Text: Isaac Watts (England), *Hymns and Spiritual Songs*, 1707, alt; refrain Robert Lowry (USA)
Music: Robert Lowry, 1867, *The Victory*, 1869

Refrain

D
We're march - ing
We're march - ing on
to Zi - on, beau - ti-ful, beau - ti-ful Zi - on.

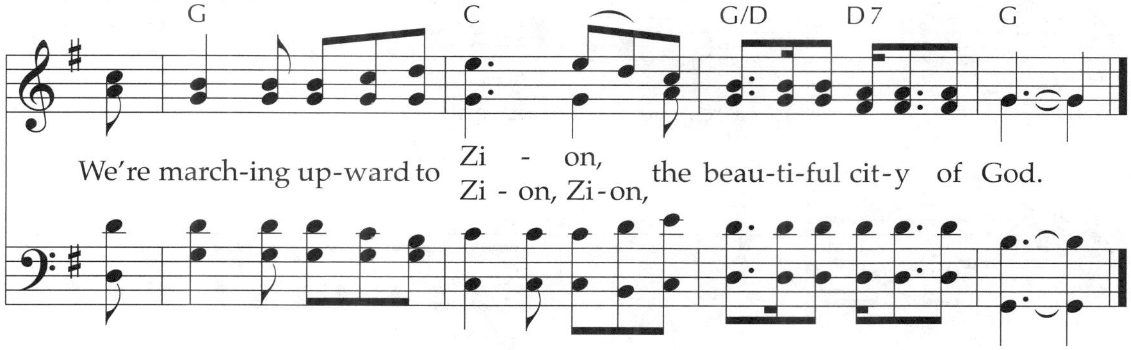
G C G/D D7 G
We're march-ing up-ward to Zi - on,
Zi - on, Zi-on,
the beau-ti-ful cit-y of God.

God Welcomes All / Amen 32

AMEN THEMBA Irregular

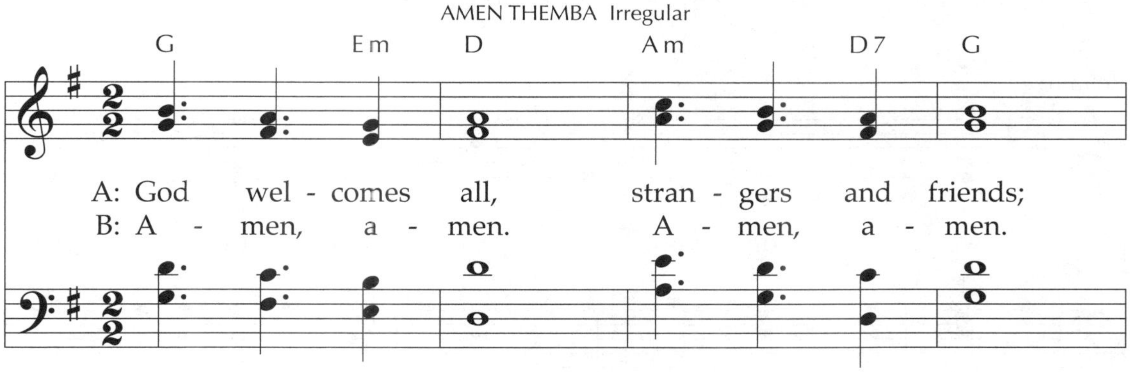
G Em D Am D7 G
A: God wel - comes all, stran - gers and friends;
B: A - men, a - men. A - men, a - men.

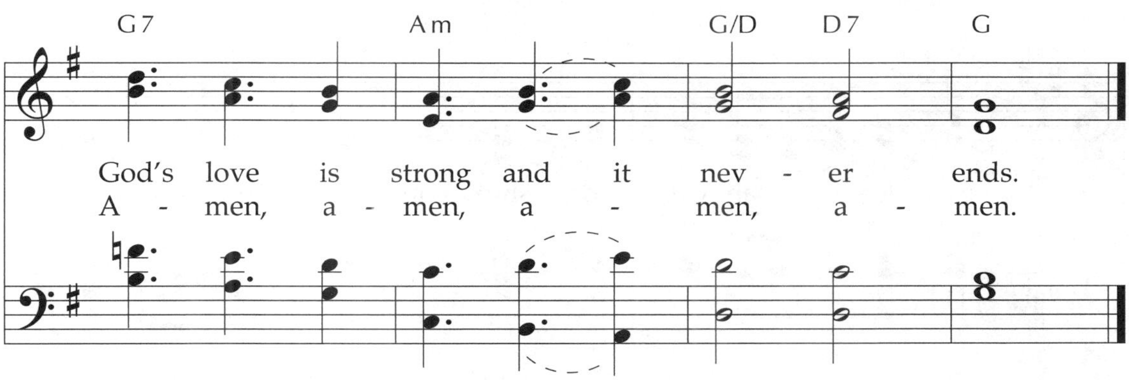
G7 Am G/D D7 G
God's love is strong and it nev - er ends.
A - men, a - men, a - men, a - men.

Text: John L. Bell (Scotland)
Music: South African traditional; transcr. John L. Bell

33 You Are Good

YOU ARE GOOD Irregular

E B/E D/E
Lord, you are good, and your mer-cy en-dur-eth for-ev - er;
A/E E B/E
Lord, you are good, and your mer-cy en-dur-eth for-
D/E A/E A B/A
ev - er. Peo-ple from ev-e - ry na-tion and
C D
tongue, from gen - er - a - tion to gen - er - a - tion,
Refrain
E B D
we wor - ship you, hal - le - lu - jah, hal-
A E B
- le - lu - jah; we wor - ship you for who you are.

Text: Israel Houghton (USA)
Music: Israel Houghton

D
A
E
B
We wor - ship you,
D
A
E/G♯
hal - le - lu - jah, hal - le - lu - jah; we wor - ship you
Bm
C
D
N.C.
for who you are: for you are good.
E5 G5 A5 E5 D5 C♯5
1
N.C. C5 B5
Bridge
2
N.C. C5 B5 E5 G5 A5
You are good all the time;
E5 D5 C♯5 N.C. C5 B5
Omit final "you are good" when returning to refrain
all the time you are good; you are good

34 We Praise You, O God, Our Redeemer

KREMSER 12.11.12.11

D Em A D
1 We praise you, O God, our Re - deem - er, Cre - a - tor;
2 We wor - ship you, God of our an - ces - tors' sto - ries,
3 With voic - es u - ni - ted, our prais - es we of - fer,
A Bm A D E7 A
in grate - ful de - vo - tion our trib - ute we bring.
through tri - al and tem - pest, com - pan - ion and guide.
and glad - ly our songs of thanks - giv - ing we raise.
A7 D Em7 A7 D
We lay it be - fore you; we kneel and a - dore you;
When per - ils o'er - take us, you will not for - sake us,
Our sins now con - fess - ing, we pray for your bless - ing,
G A D Em7 A7 D
we bless your ho - ly name: glad prais - es we sing.
but faith - ful to your prom - ise, you walk by our side.
to you, our great Re - deem - er, for - ev - er be praise!

Chord symbols represent a simplified harmony.

Text: Julia Cory (USA), *Hymns of the Living Church*, 1910, alt.
Music: *Nederlandtsche Gedenckclanck* (present-day Netherlands), 1626; adapt. Eduard Kremser (Austria), *Sechs altniederländische Volkslieder*, 1877

Come to the Water

35

DESERT ALLELUIA Irregular

N.C.
Al-le-lu-ia, Al - le-lu - ia, Al-le-lu-ia, Al-le - lu-ia.
G C/G D Am G
1 Come to the wa-ter, liv - ing wa - ter, come to the
2 Come with thanks-giv - ing, glad thanks-giv - ing, come with thanks-
3 Bring all your bur - dens, heav - y treas - ures, lay down your
4 Al - le - lu - ia, Al - le - lu - ia, Al - le -
Am/G D C/D G C/G
wa - ter, come all sing-ing, come to the wa - ter,
giv - ing, come all sing-ing, come with thanks-giv - ing,
bur - dens, come all sing-ing, bring all your bur - dens,
lu - ia, come all sing-ing, Al - le - lu - ia,
D Am G C/G D C/D
liv - ing wa - ter, come to the wa - ter, come all sing-ing.
glad thanks-giv - ing, come with thanks-giv - ing, come all sing-ing.
heav - y treas - ures, lay down your bur - dens, come all sing-ing.
Al - le - lu - ia, sing Al - le - lu - ia, Al - le - lu - ia.
D C/D D C/D C/G G
Al - le - lu - ia, Al - le - lu - ia, A - men.

Text: Carol Ann Weaver (Canada)
Music: Carol Ann Weaver

36 Let Us Build a House

TWO OAKS 9.6.8.6.8.7.10 with refrain

Capo 3: (A7) C7 (D) F (A) C (D) F (G) B♭ (A) C
1 Let us build a house where love can dwell and
2 Let us build a house where proph - ets speak, and
3 Let us build a house where love is found in
4 Let us build a house where hands will reach be -
5 Let us build a house where all are named, their
(Bm) Dm (D) F (A) C (D) F (Bm7) Dm7
all can safe - ly live, a place where saints and
words are strong and true, where all God's chil - dren
wa - ter, wine, and wheat: a ban - quet hall on
yond the wood and stone to heal and streng - then,
songs and vi - sions heard and loved and treas - ured,
(Em) Gm (A) C (Em) Gm (A7) C7 (G) B♭ (D) F
chil - dren tell how hearts learn to for - give. Built of
dare to seek to dream God's reign a - new. Here the
ho - ly ground, where peace and jus - tice meet. Here the
serve and teach, and live the Word they've known. Here the
taught and claimed as words with - in the Word. Built of
(F♯m) Am (Bm) Dm (Em) Gm (A) C (D) F
hopes and dreams and vi - sions, rock of faith and vault of
cross shall stand as wit - ness and as sym - bol of God's
love of God, through Je - sus, is re - vealed in time and
out - cast and the stran - ger bear the im - age of God's
tears and cries and laugh - ter, prayers of faith and songs of
(G) B♭ (D) F (G) B♭ (F♯7) A7 (Bm) Dm
grace; here the love of Christ shall end di - vi - sions:
grace; here as one we claim the faith of Je - sus:
space; as we share in Christ the feast that frees us:
face; let us bring an end to fear and dan - ger:
grace, let this house pro - claim from floor to raft - er:

Text: Marty Haugen (USA)
Music: Marty Haugen

Refrain
(Em) Gm (Bm) Dm (F♯m) Am (Em) Gm
all are wel - come, all are wel - come,
(D) F (Em) Gm (A7) C7 (D) F (G) B♭ (D) F
all are wel - come in this place.

Be Still and Know

37

BE STILL AND KNOW 8.8.8

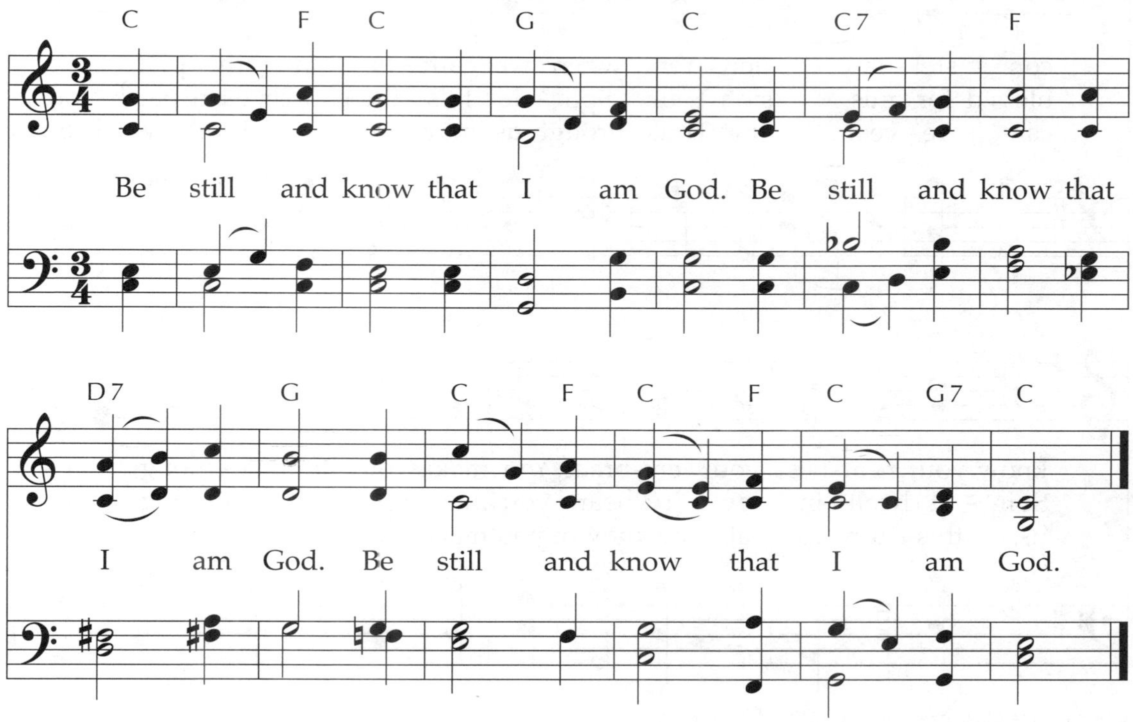
C F C G C C7 F
Be still and know that I am God. Be still and know that
D7 G C F C F C G7 C
I am God. Be still and know that I am God.

Text: Psalm 46:10
Music: anon.; arr. Jack Schrader, 1988,

38 Life-Giver, Maker, God of All

ALLEIN GOTT IN DER HÖH 8.7.8.7.8.8.7

G D G Bm Am
1 Life - giv - er, Mak - er, God of all, your breath sus - tains cre -
2 Here we be - come your liv - ing church; we learn and claim your
3 We hold your gifts in o - pen hands, to of - fer peace and
Dsus G D G Bm
a - tion. Your arms en - fold the u - ni - verse, its ev - 'ry
vi - sion: we are the hands and feet of Christ, em - pow - ered,
heal - ing. We leave this place to share our bread, your ten - der
Am Dsus G F Am F Am D
con - stel - la - tion. Yet when we gath - er in this place, we
bless'd for mis - sion. Your Spir - it fills the church, each part; your
care re - veal - ing. Thus, through us, may your love be shown; through
G D G D G Dsus G
know your near - ness, your em - brace. You make your home a - mong us!
Spir - it dwells in ev - 'ry heart: you make your home a - mong us!
us, this truth to all be known: you make your home a - mong us!

Chord symbols represent a simplified harmony.

Text: Delores Dufner, OSB (USA), 2013, alt.,
Music: Nicolaus Decius (present-day Germany), 1522, *Deutsche Evangelische Messe*, 1524

As We Rise, O God, to Meet You 39

SPIRIT, FILL US 8.7.8.7 with refrain

I
II
1 As we rise, O God, to meet you, as we o - pen wide our eyes, like the sun that fills the morn - ing, fill our bod - ies with your light.
2 As we gath - er, God, to - geth - er, as each tongue here learns to sing, like the birds that fill the for - ests, fill our bod - ies with your song.
3 As we lin - ger at your ta - ble, as we eat this com - mon bread, like the seed both sown and scat - tered, fill our bod - ies with new life.
4 As we learn, O God, to love you, as we lis - ten for your voice, like the dust from which you made us, fill our bod - ies with your breath.
5 As we go, O God, to serve you, as we o - pen wide our hands, like the wind that moves the wa - ters, spread your peace to ev - 'ry land.
Refrain
We are emp - ty, Spir - it, fill us. God, we o - pen up our lives.

Text: David Wright (USA), © 2005 David Wright
Music: James E. Clemens (USA), © 2005 James E. Clemens

40 In Thy Holy Place We Bow

IN THY HOLY PLACE WE BOW 7.7.7.7.8.7.8.7

Eb Ab/Eb Eb Bb Eb Fm/Ab F7
1 In thy ho - ly place we bow, per - fumes sweet to
2 Ho - ly light doth fill this place; Spir - it, light our
3 On thy ho - ly bread we feed, hun - ger nev - er
Bb Eb Ab Bb7 Cm Ab
heav - en rise, while our gold - en cen - sers glow with the
way to guide. In the pres - ence of thy face, sin's de -
more to know. Thou sup - pli - est all our need; Sav - ior,
Eb/Bb Bb7 Eb Bb F7 Bb
fire of sac - ri - fice. Saints low bend - ing, prayers as -
cep - tions ne'er can hide. Heav - en's gleam - ing, full - ness
whith - er shall we go? Ne'er for - sak - ing, here par -
G Cm Ab F Bb Eb Ab
cend - ing, ho - ly lips and hands im - plore, faith be - liev - ing
stream - ing, life and truth for all are found; light per - vad - ing,
tak - ing bread our souls to sat - is - fy; here a - bid - ing

Text: S. F. Coffman (USA), 1901, *Church and Sunday School Hymnal, Supplement*, 1911, alt.
Music: J. D. Brunk (USA), *Church and Sunday School Hymnal, Supplement*, 1911

B♭ Cm A♭ E♭/B♭ B♭7 E♭
and re - ceiv - ing grace from thee whom we a - dore.
nev - er fad - ing, light - ing all the world a - round.
and con - fid - ing, we shall nev - er want nor die.

For You, O God, My Soul 41

O LORD OF LIGHT 11.10.10 with refrain

Refrain
Dm(add9) Am Dm(add9) F G A
For you, O God, my soul in still-ness waits;
B♭ C Am7
To verses
Dm(add9) Am
Last time
D no3
tru - ly my hope is in you. you.
Verses
Dm(add9) Am Dm(add9) Am Dm(add9)
1 Here we will bow be - fore you, God our Mak - er,
2 Here we shall meet the Ma - ker of the heav - ens,
Am Dm(add9) Am Dm(add9) Am
Let ev-'ry heart be o - pened to you now, for we are
Cre - a - tor of the moun-tains and the seas, God of the
To refrain
Dm(add9) Am G C Am Dm(add9) Am
all the peo - ple of your hand.
stars, and pre - sent to us now.

For verses appropriate for Advent, see the accompaniment edition.

Text: based on Psalm 95:4-7; Marty Haugen (USA), alt.
Music: Marty Haugen

42 Could It Be That God Is Singing

INVITATION NEW 8.7.8.7 D

E C♯m E/B
1 Could it be that God is sing - ing and these notes are my re -
2 Have you car-ried heav-y si - lence, have you let old sor-rows
3 Hal - le - lu - jah for my Je - sus, for his life's sur-pris-ing
E C♯m
ply to the God - light warm with - in me, join - ing
win, or pro-claimed psalms of for - give - ness, but not
course! May I, too, live bold re - sist - ance to in -
E/B E B E
earth and sea and sky? Sure - ly mer - cy has a
of - fered them with - in? Oh, the Spir - it, she was
jus - tice, hate, and force. Sure - ly peace, it has a
C♯m7 B E C♯m
ca - dence— I can feel it in my soul! Sure - ly
sing - ing, e - ven when we could not hear her a -
ca - dence, ask-ing all of what we bring! And if

Text: Becca J. R. Lachman (USA), © 2004 Becca J. R. Lachman, rev. 2018
Music: *Southern Harmony* (USA), 1854; arr. Alice Parker (USA), © 2008 Alice Parker

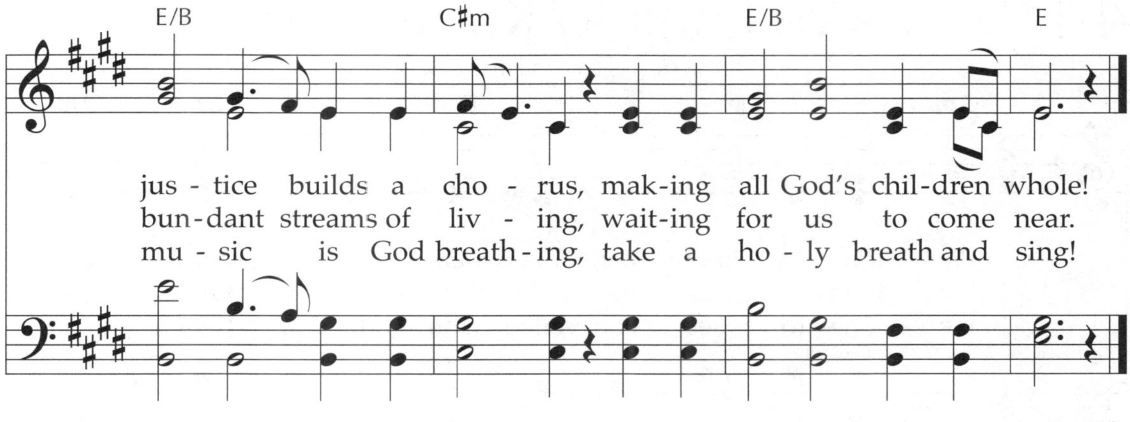
jus - tice builds a cho - rus, mak-ing all God's chil-dren whole!
bun-dant streams of liv - ing, wait-ing for us to come near.
mu - sic is God breath - ing, take a ho - ly breath and sing!

God, Be the Love 43

GREEN TYLER 9.8.9.5.5

1 God, be the love to search and keep me; God, be the prayer to move my voice; God, be the strength to now up - hold me:
2 Bind to my-self the name of Ho - ly; great cloud of wit-ness-es en - fold; proph-ets, a - pos - tles, an - gels wit - ness:
3 Bright-ness of sun and glow of moon-light; flash - ing of light-ning, strength of wind; depth of the sea to soil of plan - et:
4 Walk - ing be-hind to hem my jour - ney, go - ing a - head to light my way, and from be - neath, a - bove and al - ways,
5 Christ in the eye of all who see me; Christ in the ear that hears my voice; Christ in the hearts of all who know me:
O Christ, sur - round me, O Christ, sur - round me.

Text: based on the "Prayer of St. Patrick" (Ireland), 5th c.; Richard Bruxvoort Colligan (USA)
Music: Richard Bruxvoort Colligan

44 We Long to Know Her

STAR IN THE EAST 11.10.11.10 D

Gm Dm Cm Dm
1 We long to know her, the mak - er of heav - en,
2 We long to hear her, bold thun - der of heav - en:
3 We long to see you, veiled won - der of heav - en:
Gm Dm Gm
knit - ter of sin - ews and plant - er of grains,
voice a - mong voic - es that sum - mon the soul;
hid - den from view, be re - vealed in the light.
Dm Cm Dm
guard - ian of sheep and the found - er of vine - yards:
with - out her pres - ence, there is no com - plete - ness,
O - pen our eyes to your wis - dom a - round us;
Gm Dm Gm
she is the strong - hold who gen - tly sus - tains.
with her un - heard, heav - en can - not be whole.
au - thor of beau - ty, en - liv - en our sight.

Text: Jacque B. Jones (USA), © 2019 GIA Publications, Inc.
Music: *Southern Harmony* (USA), 1835; harm. Alice Parker (USA), © 1990 Alice Parker

Ⓡ

B♭ F Gm
She is the sculp - tor who carved earth from dark - ness,
We know her laugh - ter is pierc - ing the cos - mos;
Heart of the ho - ly and hands of the sa - cred,
B♭ F Gm Dm(no3)
ar - chi - tect build - ing cre - a - tion from dust.
we know she jud - ges in - jus - tice on earth.
god - head u - nit - ing com - pas - sion and might:
Gm Dm Cm Dm
She is the pot - ter who formed us and made us,
Shel - ter and shield of the hope - less and help - less,
bear - ing your like - ness, im - pa - tient to greet you,
Gm Dm Gm(no3)
gave us her breath, and now yearns for our trust.
from her we learn of our in - fi - nite worth.
we come to wor - ship in awe and de - light!

45 O Gott Vater (O God and Father)

AUS TIEFER NOT (HERR WIE DU WILLST) 8.7.8.7.8.8.7

G D Am D G C G Em
1 O Gott Va - ter, wir lo - ben dich, und dei - ne Gü - te
2 Öff - ne den Mund, Herr, dei - ner Knecht', gib ihn'n Weis - heit dar -
1 O God and Fa - ther of us all, we wor - ship and a -
2 A - noint the lips that read and speak, to guide their proc - lam -
D G D Am D G C G
prei - sen; die du, O Herr, so gnä - dig - lich, an uns neu
ne - ben, dass er dein Wort mög spre - chen recht, was dient zum
dore you. We gath - er now to hear your call, and bring our
a - tion. Give us the wis - dom that we seek; make good - ness
Em D G D Bm Em Am Em D
hast be - wie - sen, und hast uns Herr zu - sam - men g'führt, uns
from - men Le - ben, und nütz - lich ist zu dei - nem Preis, gib
praise be - fore you. Your good - ness comes a - new each day; teach
our vo - ca - tion. Bless us with hun - ger for this bread, your
G Am Em D G D G C D Em D G
zu er - mah - nen durch dein Wort, gib uns Gna - de zu die - sem.
uns Hun - ger nach sol - cher Speis, das ist un - ser be - geh - ren.
us to keep your nar - row way. For bless - ings we im - plore you.
Word, by which our souls are fed, the feast of cel - e - bra - tion.

Text: German; Leenaerdt Clock (present-day Germany, Netherlands), *Ausbund*, 1583; trans. Mennonite Worship and Song Committee, 2019
Music: *Theütsch kirchen ampt* (present-day France), 1525

3 Gib unserm Herzen auch Verstand,
erleuchtung hier auf Erden,
dass dein Wort in uns werd bekannt,
dass wir fromm mögen werden,
und leben in Gerechtigkeit,
achten auf dein Wort allezeit,
so bleibt man unbetrogen.

4 Dein, o Herr, ist das Reich allein,
und auch die Macht zusammen,
wir loben dich in der Gemein,
und danken deinem Namen,
und bitten dich aus Herzens Grund,
wollst bei uns sein zu dieser Stund,
durch Jesum Christum, Amen.

3 *Enlighten us to understand*
your vision, ever growing—
that we may join with heart and hand
the labor still ongoing.
With holiness prepare our way;
instill each thought and word we say
with truth beyond our knowing.

4 *O God, you sit upon the throne*
as ruler of creation.
All pow'r and might are yours alone,
beyond each earthly nation.
From humble dust, our hearts we raise,
for your name's sake, our prayer and praise,
through Christ, our true salvation.

Holy Spirit, Truth Divine 46

SONG 13 7.7.7.7

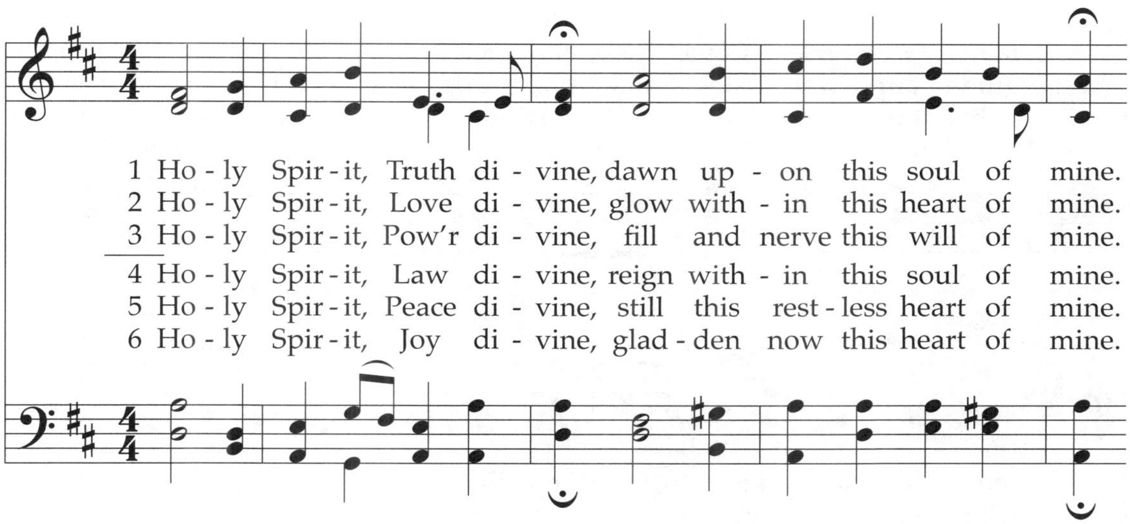
1 Ho - ly Spir - it, Truth di - vine, dawn up - on this soul of mine.
2 Ho - ly Spir - it, Love di - vine, glow with - in this heart of mine.
3 Ho - ly Spir - it, Pow'r di - vine, fill and nerve this will of mine.
4 Ho - ly Spir - it, Law di - vine, reign with - in this soul of mine.
5 Ho - ly Spir - it, Peace di - vine, still this rest - less heart of mine.
6 Ho - ly Spir - it, Joy di - vine, glad - den now this heart of mine.

Voice of God, and in - ward Light, wake my spir - it, clear my sight.
Kin - dle ev - 'ry high de - sire, pu - ri - fy me with your fire.
Bold - ly may I al - ways live, brave - ly serve and glad - ly give.
Be my law and I shall be firm - ly bound, for - ev - er free.
Speak to calm this toss - ing sea, grant me your tran - quil - i - ty.
In the de - sert ways I sing, spring, O liv - ing Wa - ter, spring!

Text: Samuel Longfellow (USA), *Hymns of the Spirit*, 1864, alt.
Music: Orlando Gibbons (England), *Hymnes and Songs of the Church*, 1623

47 God of Our Strength

GOD OF OUR STRENGTH LM with refrain

Eb Ab Eb
1 God of our strength, en-throned a - bove, the source of life, the
2 To thee we lift our joy - ful eyes, to thee on wings of
3 God of our strength, from day to day di - rect our thoughts and
4 God of our strength, on thee we call. God of our hope, our
Bb Eb Ab Eb
fount of love, O let de - vo - tion's sa - cred flame
faith we rise. Come thou, and let thy courts on earth
guide our way. Oh, may our hearts u - nit - ed be
light, our all, thy name we praise, thy love a - dore,
Refrain
Ab Eb Bb Eb Bb Eb
our souls a - wake to praise thy name.
ring out thy praise in days of mirth.
in sweet com-mun - ion, God, with thee.
our rock, our shield, for - ev - er - more.
God of our strength,
Ab Eb Ab Eb Bb7 Eb
we wait on thee, our sure de-fense for - ev - er be.

Text: Fanny J. Crosby (USA), 1882, *Baptist Hymnal*, 1883
Music: William H. Doane (USA), *Baptist Hymnal*, 1883

Come, My Way, My Truth, My Life 48

THE CALL 7.7.7.7

Capo 1: (D) E♭ (Am) B♭m (G) A♭ (Am) B♭m (D) E♭
1 Come, my Way, my Truth, my Life: such a
2 Come, my Light, my Feast, my Strength: such a
3 Come, my Joy, my Love, my Heart: such a
(Am) B♭m (G) A♭ (Am) B♭m (F) G♭ (Em) Fm (Am) B♭m
way as gives us breath; such a truth as ends all
light as shows a feast; such a feast as mends in
joy as none can move: such a love as none can
(D) E♭ (C) D♭ (D) E♭ (Em) Fm (Am) B♭m (Dsus)(D) E♭sus E♭
strife; such a life as kill - eth death.
length; such a strength as makes a guest.
part; such a heart as joys in love.

Text: George Herbert (England), *The Temple*, 1633
Music: Ralph Vaughan Williams (England), 1911, *Five Mystical Songs, No. 4*; adapt. for *Hymnal for Colleges and Schools*, 1956

49 All Who Are Thirsty

ALL WHO ARE THIRSTY Irregular

F
Am7
All who are thirst - y, all who are weak,
Bb2
Gm7 F/A
come to the foun - tain. Dip your heart in the stream of
Bb2 Bb2/C F
Am7
life. Let the pain and the sor - row be washed a - way
Bb2
Gm7 F/A
in the waves of God's mer-cy, as deep cries out to
Refrain
Bb2 F F2 Fsus F Bb2 Bb2/C
deep. We sing . . . Come, Lord Je - sus, come.
Ho - ly Spir - it, come.
Last time
F F2 Fsus F Bb2 Bb2/C F5
Come, Lord Je - sus, come.
Ho - ly Spir - it, come.

Text: Brenton Brown (USA/South Africa) and Glenn Robertson (South Africa)
Music: Brenton Brown and Glenn Robertson

Spirit, Working in Creation 50

SUN AND THUNDER 8.7.8.7

N.C.
B♭
F m
1 Spir - it, work - ing in cre - a - tion,
2 Spir - it, speak - ing through the proph - ets
3 Spir - it, breathed up - on dis - ci - ples,
4 Spir - it, wind and flame, em - pow'r - ing,
N.C.
B♭
F sus
F m
bring - ing or - der out of strife:
so the voice of God was heard,
giv - ing peace where there was fear:
fear - less wit - ness to the lost:
C m
G sus
G m
C m
A♭/C
E♭
come a - mong your gath - ered peo - ple,
come, in - spire, a - lert your peo - ple
come a - mong us, touch us, send us,
come u - nite, re - new your won - ders;
A♭
E♭
A♭
F m/A♭
C m
F5
giv - ing har - mo - ny and life.
to this day's pro - phet - ic word.
mak - ing Je - sus' pres - ence near.
give us your new Pen - te - cost.

Text: John Richards (Wales), 1978, alt., © John Richards (admin. Renewal Servicing)
Music: James E. Clemens (USA), © 2015 James E. Clemens

51 O Great Spirit

O GREAT SPIRIT Irregular

O Great Spi - rit, how I long to
hear your voice, how I long to see your face.
A - way hey ho, a - way hey ho, a - way hey hey ho.

Text: adapt. Doreen Clellamin (Nuxalk, Canada), from a song by Nuxalk young people (Canada)
Music: adapt. Doreen Clellamin, from a song by Nuxalk young people; transcr. Pablo Sosa (Argentina)

52 Confitemini Domino (Come and Fill Our Hearts)

CONFITEMINI DOMINO Irregular

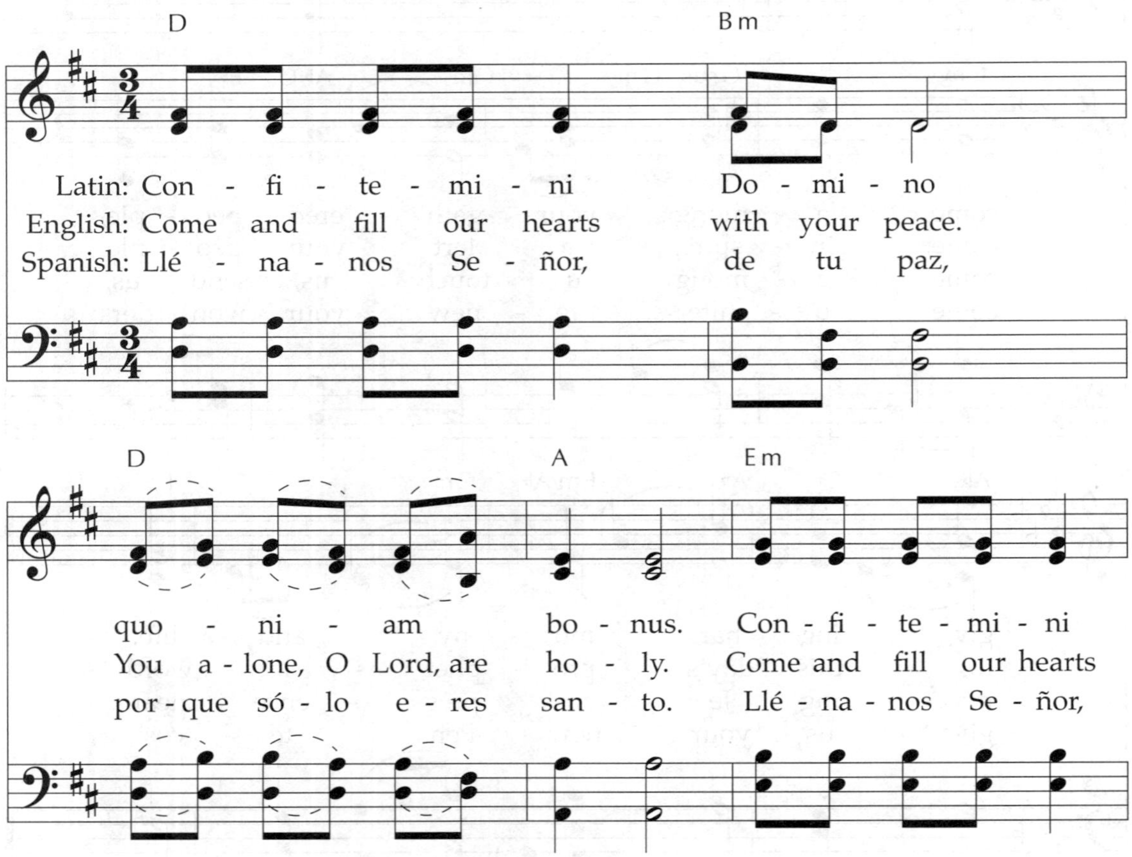
D
Bm
Latin: Con - fi - te - mi - ni Do - mi - no
English: Come and fill our hearts with your peace.
Spanish: Llé - na - nos Se - ñor, de tu paz,
D
A
Em
quo - ni - am bo - nus. Con - fi - te - mi - ni
You a - lone, O Lord, are ho - ly. Come and fill our hearts
por - que só - lo e - res san - to. Llé - na - nos Se - ñor,

Text: Latin; Psalm 136:1; English and Spanish stanzas Taizé Community (France)
Music: Jacques Berthier (France)

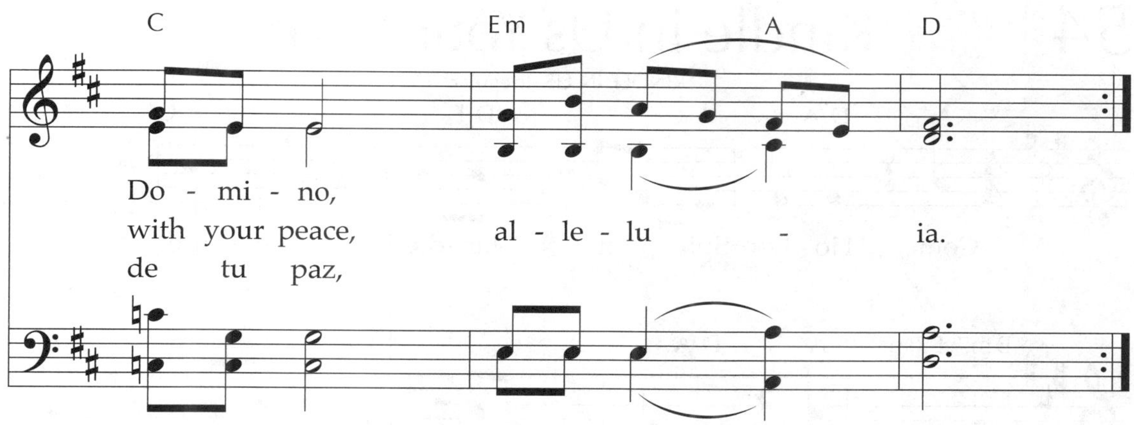
C Em A D
Do - mi - no,
with your peace, al - le - lu - ia.
de tu paz,

O Holy Spirit, by Whose Breath 53

VENI CREATOR SPIRITUS LM

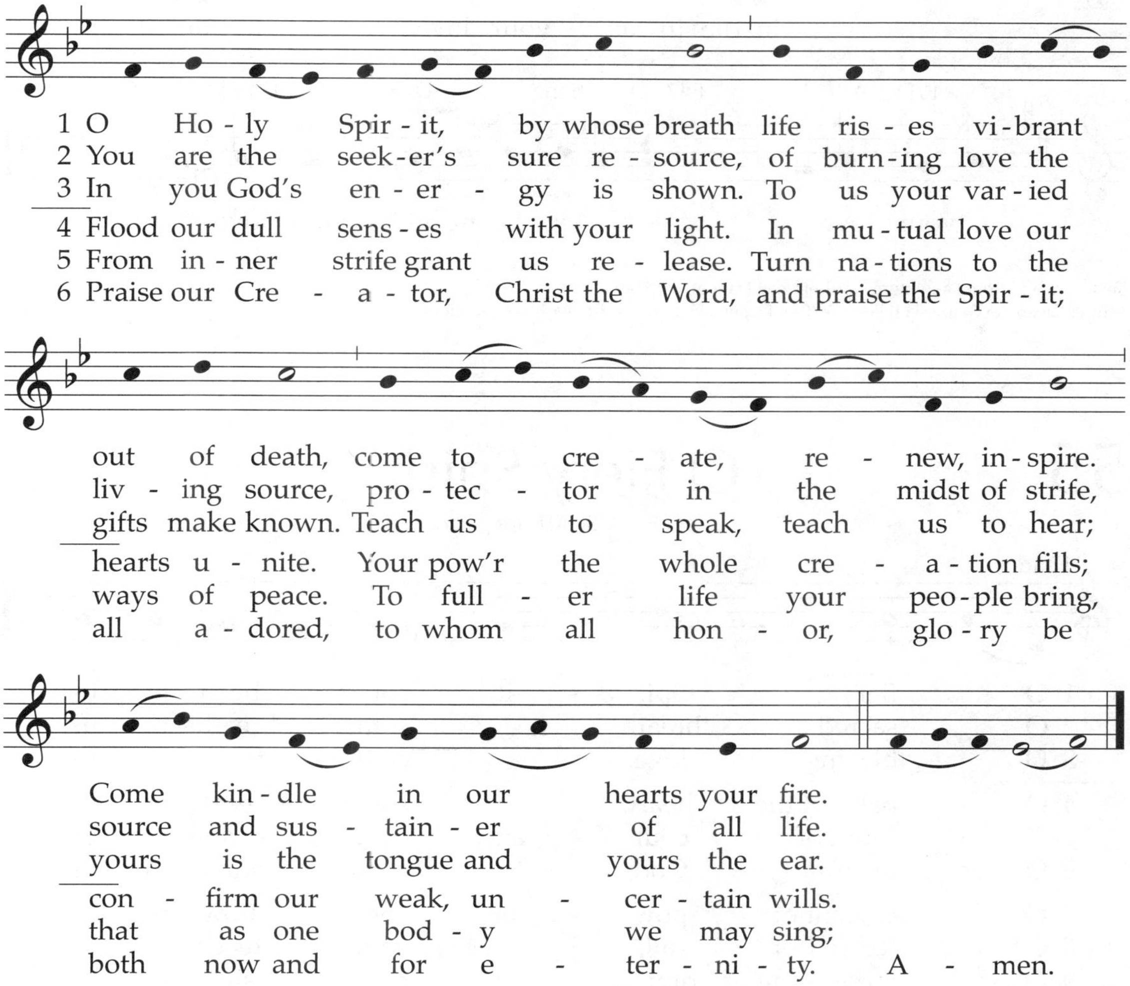
1 O Ho - ly Spir - it, by whose breath life ris - es vi - brant
2 You are the seek - er's sure re - source, of burn - ing love the
3 In you God's en - er - gy is shown. To us your var - ied
4 Flood our dull sens - es with your light. In mu - tual love our
5 From in - ner strife grant us re - lease. Turn na - tions to the
6 Praise our Cre - a - tor, Christ the Word, and praise the Spir - it;
out of death, come to cre - ate, re - new, in - spire.
liv - ing source, pro - tec - tor in the midst of strife,
gifts make known. Teach us to speak, teach us to hear;
hearts u - nite. Your pow'r the whole cre - a - tion fills;
ways of peace. To full - er life your peo - ple bring,
all a - dored, to whom all hon - or, glo - ry be
Come kin - dle in our hearts your fire.
source and sus - tain - er of all life.
yours is the tongue and yours the ear.
con - firm our weak, un - cer - tain wills.
that as one bod - y we may sing;
both now and for e - ter - ni - ty. A - men.

Text: attr. Rabanus Maurus (present-day Germany), *Veni Creator Spiritus*, 9th c.; trans. John W. Grant (Canada), *Hymn Book*, 1971, alt.,
Music: plainsong (present-day Germany), 9th c.

54 Kindle in Us Your Love

KINDLE IN US Irregular

A D/A A D/E A/C♯ F♯7(♯9)
Come, Ho-ly Spir - it, kin-dle in us the fire of
Bm7 E7sus A D/A A
your love. Come, Ho-ly Spir - it,
Repeat
D/E E A
kin-dle in us your love.
E7sus
Last time
D/E E/D A2/C♯ F♯7 Bm D/E
kin-dle in us your love, kin-dle in us
E/D A2/C♯ F♯7 Bm D/E E Fmaj7 G2 A2
your love, kin-dle in us your love.

Text: adapt. from Latin liturgy (present-day France), ca. 10th c.
Music: Deanna Witkowski (USA), © 2014 Deanna Witkowski, Tilapia Tunes (admin. BMI)

55 O Fiery Spirit

O FIERY SPIRIT Irregular

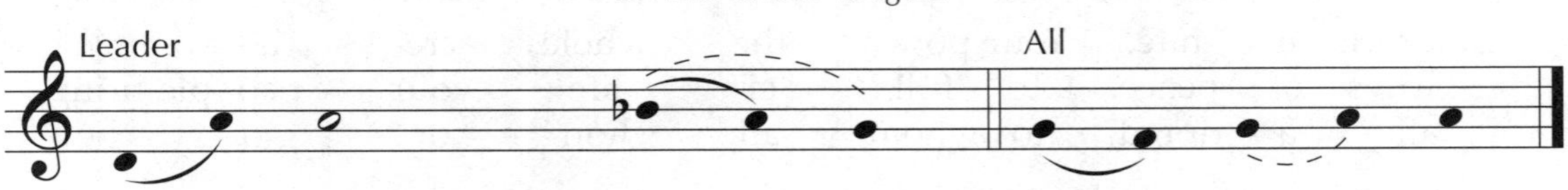
Leader
All

1 O	fiery	Spir - it,	come	burn in	us.
2 O	sacred	breath,	come	breathe in	us.
3 O	blazing	love,	come	flame in	us.
4 O	balm of the	heart,	come	heal in	us.
5 O	fount of	cour - age,	come	spring in	us.
6 O	mirror of	God,	come	shine in	us.
7 O	current of	pow - er,	come	flow in	us.
8 O	teacher of	all,	come	teach	us.
9 O	sweet song of	praise,	come	sing in	us.
10 O	delight of	life,	come	live in	us.

Text: Jody L. Caldwell (USA), after Hildegard of Bingen (present-day Germany), 12th c., © 1995 Jody L. Caldwell
Music: Kimberly A. Williams (USA), © 1995 Kimberly A. Williams

Like the Murmur of the Dove's Song 56

BRIDEGROOM 8.7.8.7.6

Capo 3: (A7) C7 (D) F (E7) G7 (A) C (A/G) C/B♭
1 Like the mur - mur of the dove's song, like the
2 To the mem - bers of Christ's bo - dy, to the
3 With the heal - ing of di - vi - sion, with the
(D) F (E7) G7 (Asus) Csus (A) C (F♯m7) Am7 (Em) Gm (C7) E♭7
chal - lenge of her flight, like the vig - or of the
branch - es of the Vine, to the church in faith as -
cease - less voice of prayer, with the pow'r to love and
(B) D (B/A) D/C (Em) Gm (D7) F7 (Em) Gm
wind's rush, like the new flame's ea - ger might:
sem - bled, to her midst as gift and sign:
wit - ness, with the peace be - yond com - pare:
(A7) C7 (F♯m7) Am (Bm7) Dm7 (Em) Gm (A) C (D) F
Come, Ho - ly Spir - it, come.

Text: Carl P. Daw Jr. (USA), *The Hymnal 1982*, 1985, © 1982 Hope Publishing Co.
Music: Peter Cutts (England), © 1969 Hope Publishing Co.; harm. Mennonite Worship and Song Committee, 2019

57 Holy Spirit, Come with Power
(Ven, Espíritu, cual viento)

BEACH SPRING 8.7.8.7 D

G Am7 G Am7 C D
1 Ho - ly Spir - it, come with pow - er, breathe in - to our
2 Ho - ly Spir - it, come with fi - re, burn us with your
3 Ho - ly Spir - it, bring your mes - sage, burn and breathe each
1 Ven, Es - pí - ri - tu, cual vien - to, so - pla en la‿os -
C G Am7 G Am7
ach - ing night. We ex - pect you this glad ho - ur, wait-ing
pres-ence new. Let us as one might - y cho - ir sing our
word a - new deep in - to our tir - ed liv - ing till we
cu - ri - dad. Es - pe - ra - mos hoy con an - sias tu gran
C D C G D
for your strength and light. We are fear - ful, we are
hymn of praise to you. Burn a - way our wast - ed
strive your work to do. Teach us love and trust-ing
luz y cla - ri - dad. A - ni - ma - dos y go -
G Em D B7 C D
ail - ing, we are weak and self - ish too. Break up -
sad - ness and en - flame us with your love. Burst up -
kind - ness, lend our hands to those who hurt. Breathe up -
zo - sos an - he - la - mos tu buen don: que des -

Text: Anne Neufeld Rupp (USA), © 1970 Anne Neufeld Rupp; Spanish trans. Barbara Mink (USA), alt., © 1988 Barbara Mink
Music: attr. B. F. White (USA), *The Sacred Harp*, 1844; harm. Joan Fyock Norris (USA), © 1989 Joan Fyock Norris

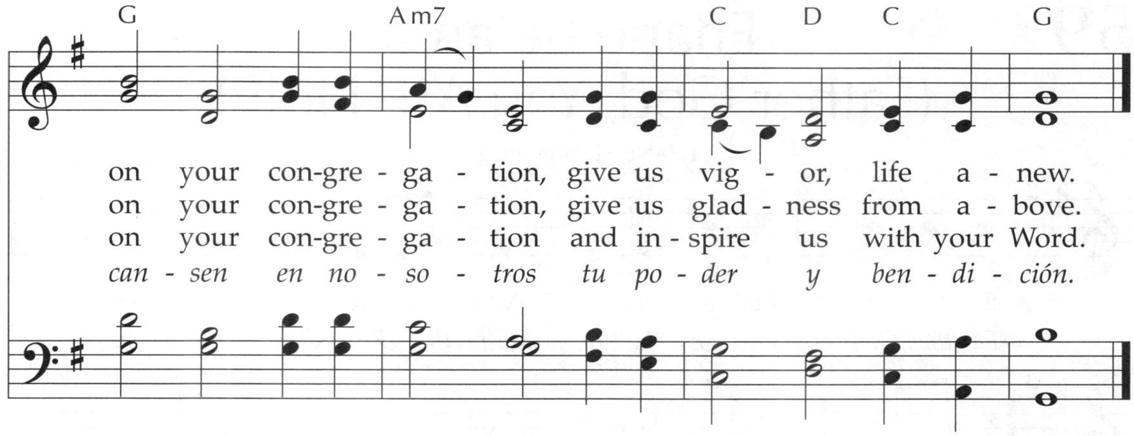
G Am7 C D C G
on your con-gre - ga - tion, give us vig - or, life a - new.
on your con-gre - ga - tion, give us glad - ness from a - bove.
on your con-gre - ga - tion and in - spire us with your Word.
can - sen en no - so - tros tu po - der y ben - di - ción.

2 *Ven, Espíritu, cual fuego y enciende nuestro ser*
y uniendo nuestras voces cantaremos tu poder.
Oh, extingue la tristeza y aumenta el amor.
Que tu chispa nos avive, que sintamos tu calor.

3 *Ven, Espíritu, cual rayo, graba tu palabra‿aquí;*
que en nuestras vidas diarias te sirvamos sólo‿a ti.
Oh, enséñanos la forma de ser cauces de amor
e infunde en nosotros tu presencia y ardor.

Holy Spirit, Come to Us 58

TUI AMORIS IGNEM Irregular

Ostinato Refrain

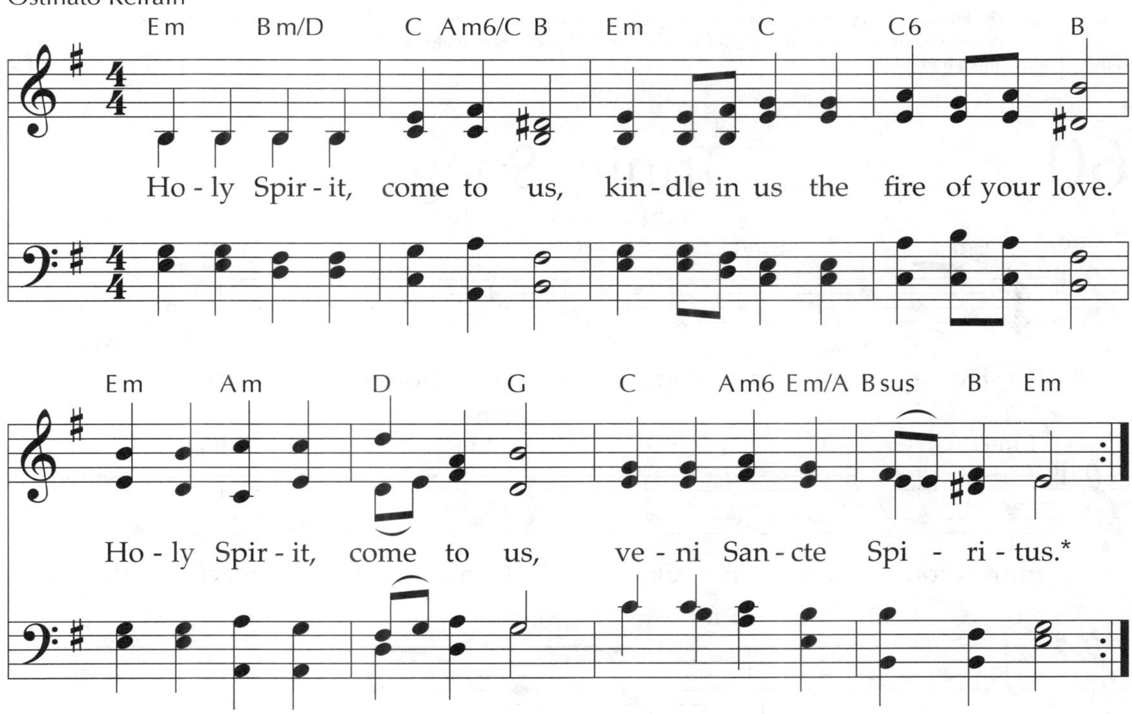
Em Bm/D C Am6/C B Em C C6 B
Ho - ly Spir - it, come to us, kin - dle in us the fire of your love.
Em Am D G C Am6 Em/A Bsus B Em
Ho - ly Spir - it, come to us, ve - ni San - cte Spi - ri - tus.*

*Latin: come, Holy Spirit

Verses can be found in the accompaniment edition.

Text: adapt. from Latin liturgy (present-day France), ca. 10th c.; John 13:35; 15:12–13; 1 John 3:16; 4:10, 16
Music: Jacques Berthier (France)

59 Ehane he'ama (Father God, You Are Holy)

EHANE HE'AMA Irregular

E - ha - ne he - 'a - ma, Vo - voa - he - to he - e!
Fa - ther God, you are ho - ly, you're the First One he - e!
Ne - 'a - nȯhenė - še - va - ta - me - na - no ne - ne -
Let your love come on down and touch your chil - dren
so - ne - ho ho - 'e - va he - e!
here on earth. Be with us he - e!
Je - sus A, ne - 'e - va - voo - me - me - no he - e!
Je - sus, we call you; watch o - ver us he - e!

Text: Cheyenne; Harvey Whiteshield (Cheyenne, USA), *Ehane He'ama Vovoaheto*; trans. David Graber (USA) and others, *Tsese-Ma'heone-Nemeotȯtse (Cheyenne Spiritual Songs)*, 1982, © 1982 Mennonite Indian Leaders' Council
Music: Plains Indian traditional

60 Trinity Song

TRINITY SONG Irregular

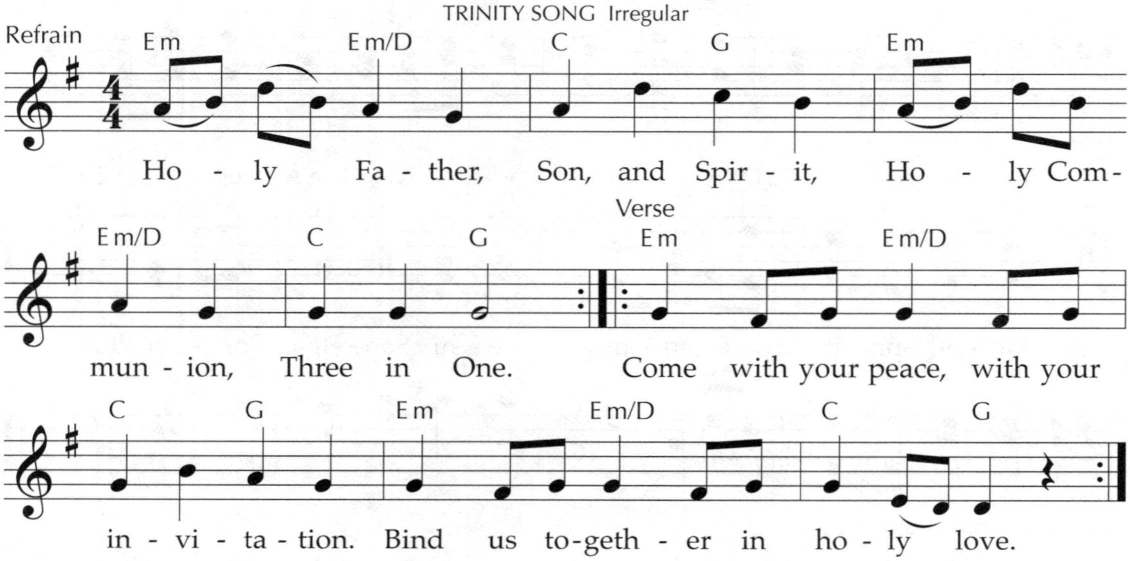
Refrain
Em
Em/D
C
G
Em
Ho - ly Fa - ther, Son, and Spir - it, Ho - ly Com -
Verse
Em/D
C
G
Em
Em/D
mun - ion, Three in One. Come with your peace, with your
C
G
Em
Em/D
C
G
in - vi - ta - tion. Bind us to - geth - er in ho - ly love.

Verse and refrain may be sung simultaneously.

Text: Sandra McCracken (USA)
Music: Sandra McCracken; acc. Zach Sprowls (USA)

You Are Holy, You Are Whole 61

DU ÄR HELIG Irregular

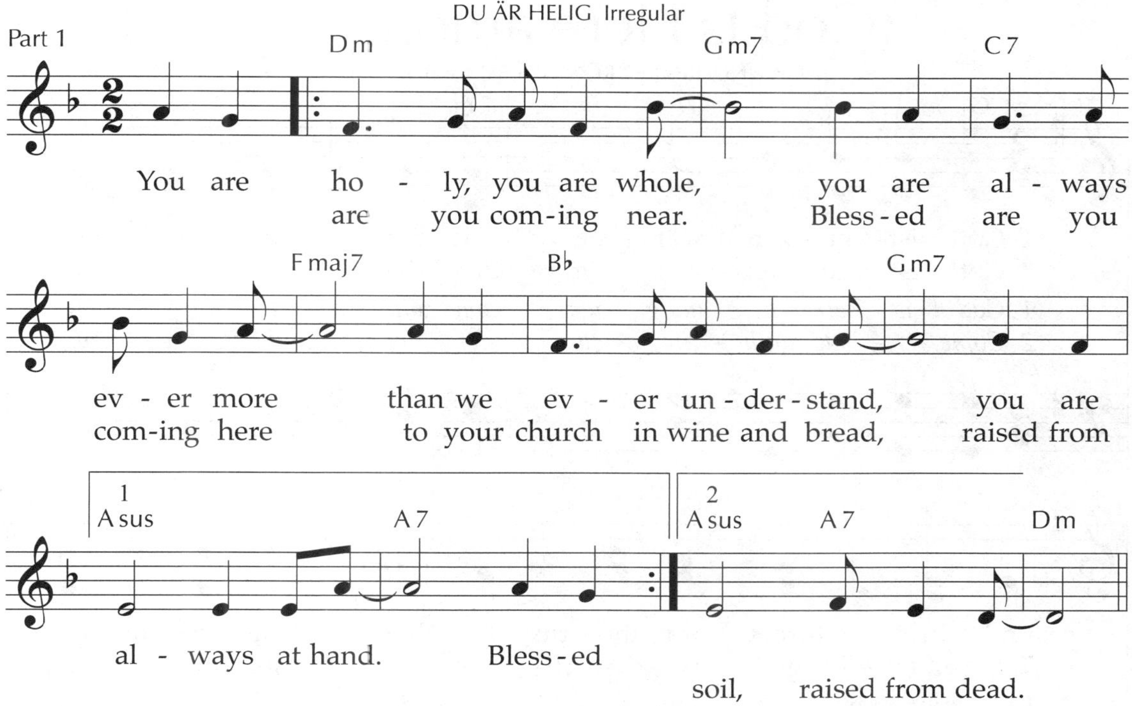
Part 1
Dm Gm7 C7
You are ho - ly, you are whole, you are al - ways
are you com-ing near. Bless - ed are you
Fmaj7 B♭ Gm7
ev - er more than we ev - er un - der - stand, you are
com-ing here to your church in wine and bread, raised from
1 Asus A7
al - ways at hand. Bless - ed
2 Asus A7 Dm
soil, raised from dead.

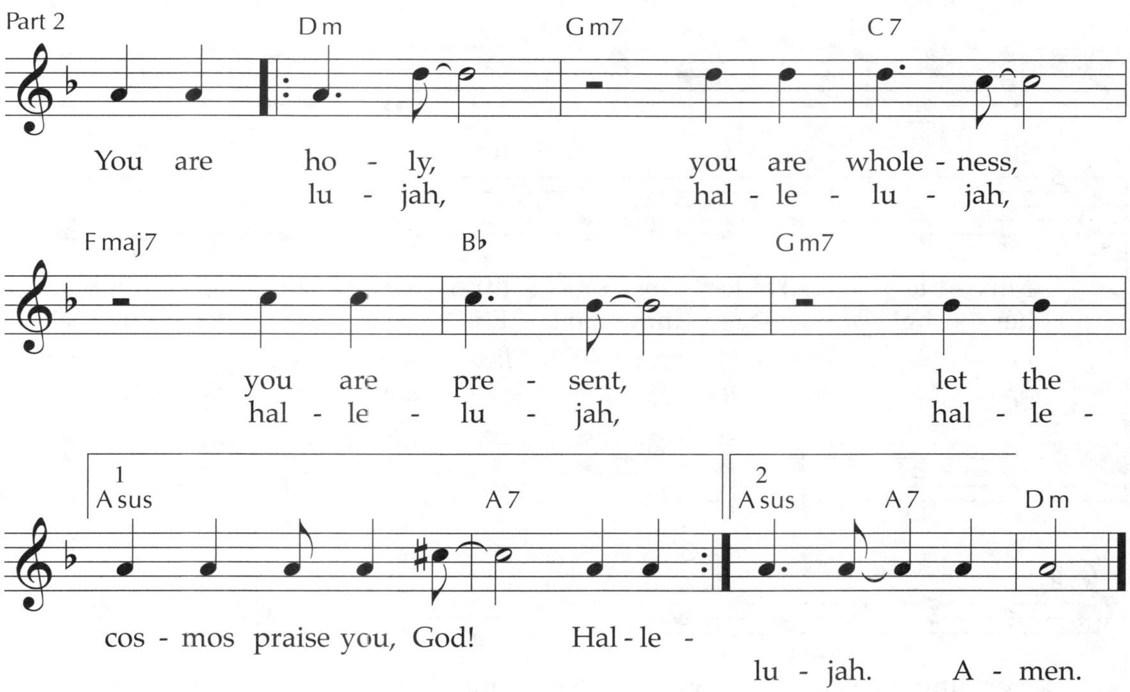
Part 2
Dm Gm7 C7
You are ho - ly, you are whole - ness,
lu - jah, hal - le - lu - jah,
Fmaj7 B♭ Gm7
you are pre - sent, let the
hal - le - lu - jah, hal - le -
1 Asus A7
cos - mos praise you, God! Hal - le -
2 Asus A7 Dm
lu - jah. A - men.

Parts 1 and 2 may be sung simultaneously.

Text: Per Harling (Sweden), 1991, alt.
Music: Per Harling, 1991

62 Gott ist gegenwärtig (God Is Here among Us)

WUNDERBARER KÖNIG 6.6.8.6.6.8.3.3.6.6

G D Em B7
1 Gott ist ge - gen - wär - tig. Las - set uns an - be - ten
2 Gott ist ge - gen - wär - tig, dem die Che - ru - bi - nen
1 God is here a - mong us: come with a - do - ra - tion,
2 Come, a - bide with - in me; let my soul, like Ma - ry,
C G D G
und in Ehr-furcht vor ihn tre - ten. Gott ist in der
Tag und Nacht ge - bü - cket die - nen. "Hei - lig, hei - lig,
fer - vent praise and ex - pec - ta - tion. God is here with -
be thine earth - ly sanc - tu - ar - y. Come, in - dwell - ing
D Em B7 C G
Mit - te. Al - les in uns schwei - ge und sich in - nigst
hei - lig!" sin - gen ihm zur Eh - re al - ler En - gel
in us: known be - yond be - liev - ing, soul in si - lent
Spir - it, with trans - fig - ured splen - dor; love and hon - or
D G C D G
vor ihm beu - ge. Wer ihn kennt, wer ihn nennt,
ho - he Chö - re. Herr, ver - nimm uns - re Stimm,
awe re - ceiv - ing. God will name and will claim
will I ren - der. Where I go here be - low,

Text: German; Gerhard Tersteegen (present-day Germany), *Geistliches Blumengärtlein*, 1729; trans. *The Hymnal*, 1940, alt.
Music: Joachim Neander (present-day Germany), *Alpha und Omega, Glaub- und Liebesübung*, 1680

schlag die Au - gen nie - der; kommt, er - gebt euch wie - der.
da auch wir Ge - rin - gen uns - re Op - fer brin - gen.
those be - held as low - ly, mak - ing all things ho - ly.
let me bow be - fore thee, know thee, and a - dore thee.

3 Herr, komm in mir wohnen;
lass mein Herz auf Erden
dir ein Heiligtum noch werden.
Komm, du nahes Wesen;
dich in mir verkläre,
dass ich dich stets lieb und ehre.
Wo ich geh, sitz und steh,
lass mich dich erblicken
und vor dir mich bücken.

3 Gladly we surrender
earth's deceitful treasures,
pride of life, and sinful pleasures.
God, we gladly offer
thine to be forever,
soul and life and each endeavor.
Thou alone shalt be known
Lord of all our being,
life's true way decreeing.

Like a Rock 63

LIKE A ROCK Irregular

Like a rock, like a rock, God is un - der our feet. Like the
star - ry night sky, God is o - ver our head. Like the
sun on the ho-ri - zon, God is ev - er be - fore. Like the riv -
- er runs to o - cean, our home is in God ev - er - more.

Text: Keri K. Wehlander (Canada), 1998
Music: Linnea Good (Canada), 1999

64 So lange Jesus bleibt der Herr (As Long as Jesus' Reign Goes On)

SO LANGE JESUS BLEIBT LM

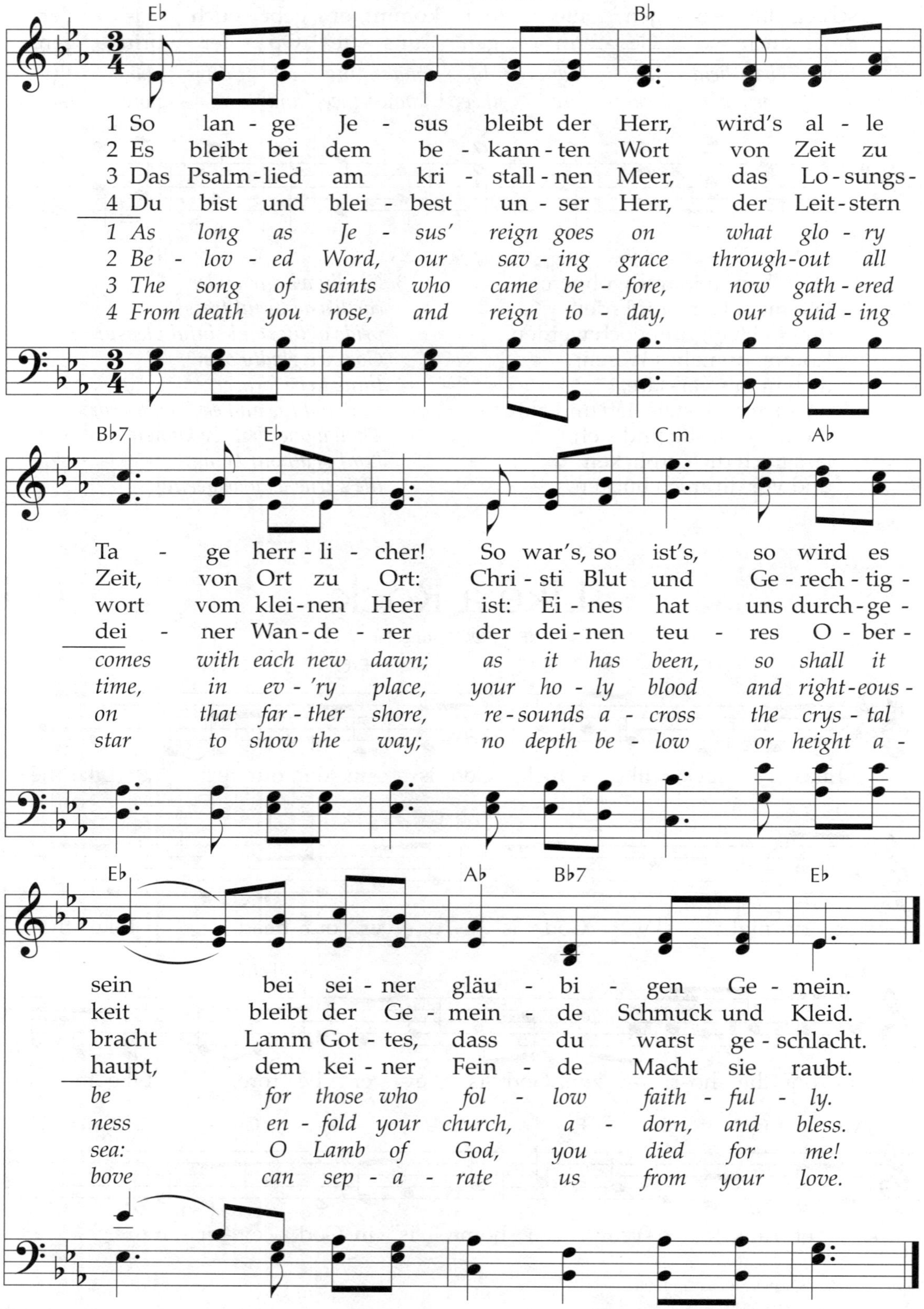
E♭
B♭
1 So lan - ge Je - sus bleibt der Herr, wird's al - le
2 Es bleibt bei dem be - kann - ten Wort von Zeit zu
3 Das Psalm - lied am kri - stall - nen Meer, das Lo - sungs -
4 Du bist und blei - best un - ser Herr, der Leit - stern
1 As long as Je - sus' reign goes on what glo - ry
2 Be - lov - ed Word, our sav - ing grace through - out all
3 The song of saints who came be - fore, now gath - ered
4 From death you rose, and reign to - day, our guid - ing
B♭7
E♭
C m
A♭
Ta - ge herr - li - cher! So war's, so ist's, so wird es
Zeit, von Ort zu Ort: Chri - sti Blut und Ge - rech - tig -
wort vom klei - nen Heer ist: Ei - nes hat uns durch - ge -
dei - ner Wan - de - rer der dei - nen teu - res O - ber -
comes with each new dawn; as it has been, so shall it
time, in ev - 'ry place, your ho - ly blood and right - eous -
on that far - ther shore, re - sounds a - cross the crys - tal
star to show the way; no depth be - low or height a -
E♭
A♭
B♭7
E♭
sein bei sei - ner gläu - bi - gen Ge - mein.
keit bleibt der Ge - mein - de Schmuck und Kleid.
bracht Lamm Got - tes, dass du warst ge - schlacht.
haupt, dem kei - ner Fein - de Macht sie raubt.
be for those who fol - low faith - ful - ly.
ness en - fold your church, a - dorn, and bless.
sea: O Lamb of God, you died for me!
bove can sep - a - rate us from your love.

Text: German; Nicolaus von Zinzendorf (present-day Germany), 1742; trans. Mennonite Worship and Song Committee, © 2019
Music: from Russian Mennonite oral tradition; transcr. *Gesangbuch*, © 1955 Gesangbuch der Mennoniten Brüdergemeinde (Canada)

Let All Mortal Flesh Keep Silence 65

PICARDY 8.7.8.7.8.7

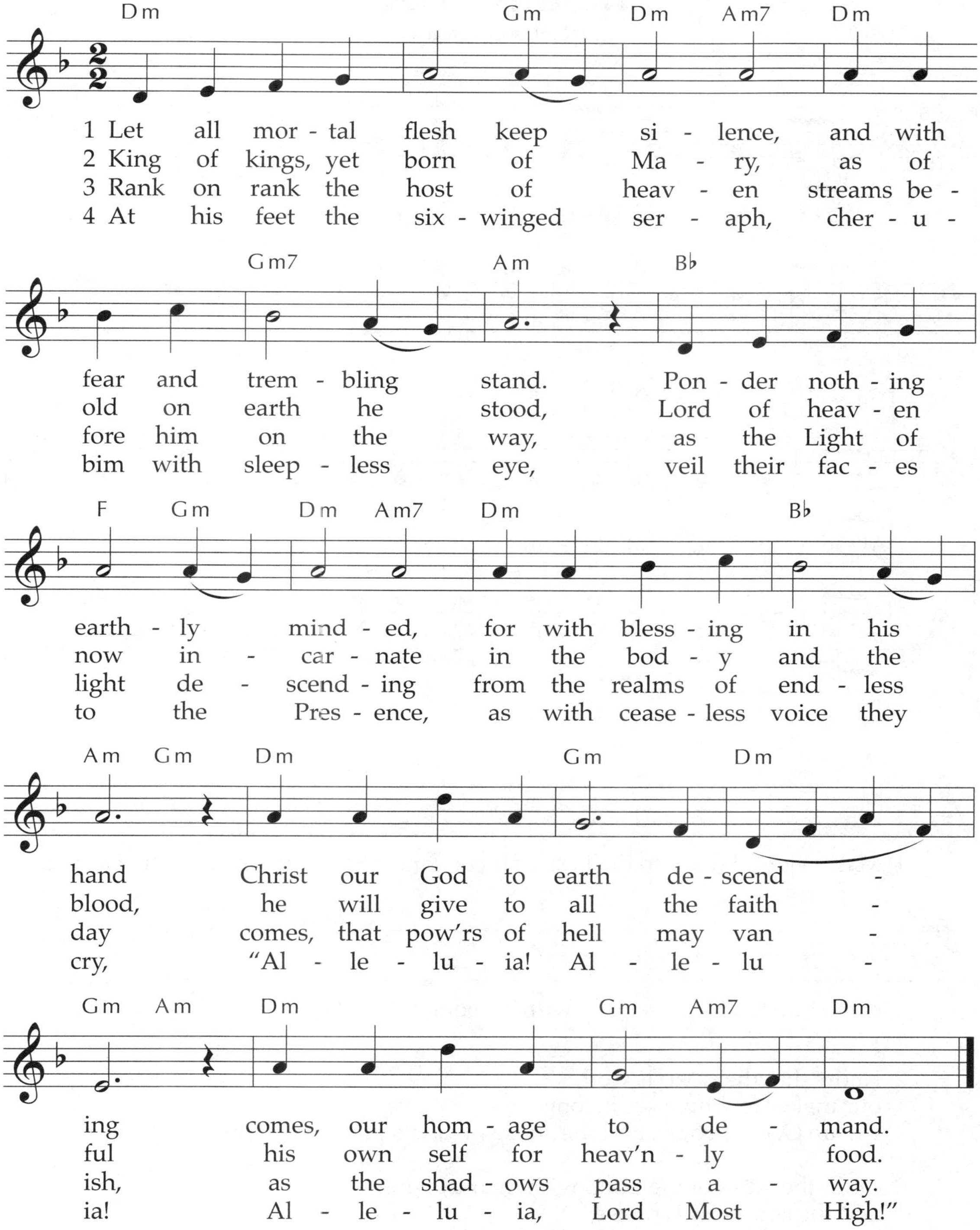
Dm Gm Dm Am7 Dm
1 Let all mor - tal flesh keep si - lence, and with
2 King of kings, yet born of Ma - ry, as of
3 Rank on rank the host of heav - en streams be -
4 At his feet the six - winged ser - aph, cher - u -
Gm7 Am B♭
fear and trem - bling stand. Pon - der noth - ing
old on earth he stood, Lord of heav - en
fore him on the way, as the Light of
bim with sleep - less eye, veil their fac - es
F Gm Dm Am7 Dm B♭
earth - ly mind - ed, for with bless - ing in his
now in - car - nate in the bod - y and the
light de - scend - ing from the realms of end - less
to the Pres - ence, as with cease - less voice they
Am Gm Dm Gm Dm
hand Christ our God to earth de - scend -
blood, he will give to all the faith -
day comes, that pow'rs of hell may van -
cry, "Al - le - lu - ia! Al - le - lu -
Gm Am Dm Gm Am7 Dm
ing comes, our hom - age to de - mand.
ful his own self for heav'n - ly food.
ish, as the shad - ows pass a - way.
ia! Al - le - lu - ia, Lord Most High!"

For an alternate chord progression, see "You, Lord, Are Both Lamb and Shepherd" (#432).

Text: from the Greek "Σιγησάτω πᾶσα σάρξ βροτεία," Liturgy of St. James of Jerusalem (Mediterranean), 5th c.; trans. Gerard Moultrie, *Lyra Eucharistica*, 2nd ed., 1864, alt.
Music: French traditional, *Chansons populaires des provinces de France*, 1860

66 Alleluia / Make a Joyful Noise (Psalm 100)

ALLELUIA 7 Irregular

Refrain
Dm F B♭ C F
Al - le - lu - ia, al - le - lu - ia, al - le - lu - ia.
Dm F Gm7 Am Dm
Al - le - lu - ia, al - le - lu - ia, al - le - lu - ia!

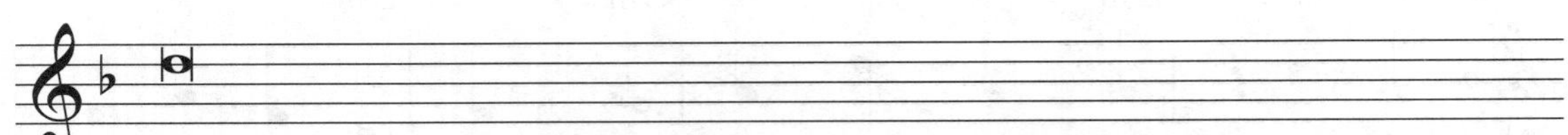
1 Make a joyful noise to the LORD, all you lands! Serve the LORD with gladness;

come into God's presence with a song. Al - le - lu - ia!

2 Know that the LORD is God,
our maker to whom we belong;
we are God's people, and the sheep of God's pasture. Alleluia! *Refrain*

3 Enter the gates of the LORD with thanksgiving
and the courts with praise;
give thanks and bless God's holy name. Alleluia! *Refrain*

4 Good indeed is the LORD,
whose steadfast love is everlasting,
whose faithfulness endures from age to age. Alleluia! *Refrain*

Text: Psalm 100; refrain Hebrew traditional; הַלְלוּ יָהּ (Hallelujah) (Mediterranean), ca. 4th c. BC, translit. Greek, ἀλληλούϊα (Alleluia) (Mediterranean), ca. 3rd c. BC; stanzas © 2006 *Evangelical Lutheran Worship* (admin. Augsburg Fortress)
Music: Jacques Berthier (France), © 1984 Les Presses de Taizé (France), (admin. GIA Publications, Inc.)

Tú estás aquí (My God Is Here) 67

TÚ ESTÁS AQUÍ Irregular

Asus D Bm
Aun-que mis o - jos no te pue - dan ver,
Aun-que mis ma - nos no pue-dan to-car
I can-not see you with my eyes a-lone,
I can-not touch you, take your hand in mine,
G
te pue-do sen - tir; sé que‿es-tás a - quí.
tu ros-tro, Se - ñor; sé que‿es-tás a - quí.
but I know you're here; I can feel you're near.
but you hold me still, and you al - ways will.
1 D 2 D A
Mi co - ra-zón
Mi co - ra-zón
My heart can feel
My heart can see
Bm G D
pue-de sen-tir tu pre-sen - cia, tú‿es-tás a - quí,
pue-de mi-rar tu‿her-mo-su - ra; tú‿es-tás a - quí,
my God is here; you are with me, here with me now.
your glo-ry shine, see your beau - ty, here with me now.
A Bm
tú‿es-tás a - quí. Pue-do sen - tir
tú‿es-tás a - quí. Pue-do sen - tir
Here with me now. I know you're here,
Here with me now. And I can feel
G D A
tu ma-jes-tad; tú‿es-tás a - quí, tú‿es-tás a - quí.
tu gran a-mor; tú‿es-tás a - quí, tú‿es-tás a - quí.
al-might-y God. My God is here. My God is here.
love with-out end. My God is here. My God is here.

Text: Spanish; Michael Rodríguez (Commonwealth of Puerto Rico, USA) and Jesús Adrián Romero (Mexico), 2004; trans. Mennonite Worship and Song Committee, 2019
Music: Michael Rodríguez and Jesús Adrián Romero, 2004

68 Akekho ofana / Hakuna wakaita (There's No One in This World like Jesus)

HAKUNA WAKAITA Irregular

G C
Zulu: A - ke - kho o - fa - na no Je - su. A -
Shona: Ha - ku - na wa-kai - ta sa Je - su, ha -
English: There's no one in this world like Je - sus, there's
G D G D G
ke - kho o - fa - na no Je - su. A - ke - kho o -
ku - na wa-kai - ta sa - ye; ha - ku - na wa -
no one in this world like him; there's no one in
C G D Em G D G
fa - na no Je - su. A - ke-kho o - fa-na na - ye.
kai - ta sa Je - su, ha - ku, ha - ku - chi - na.
this world like Je - sus, there's no one, there's no one like him.

Text: Zulu, Shona; Zimbabwean traditional; English trans. Patrick Matsikenyiri (Zimbabwe) and Daniel Charles Damon (USA)
Music: Zimbabwean traditional; arr. Patrick Matsikenyiri

G C
Sa - ha - mba, sa - ha - mba: a - ke - kho, a -
Nda - mha - nya, mha - nya, kwe - se,
I'm run - ning, run - ning, search - ing,
G
ke - kho. Sa - ji - ka, sa - ji - ka:
kwe - se. Nda - te - nde re - ra,
search - ing. I'm turn - ing, turn - ing,
D G
lu - tho, lu - tho. Sa - fu - na, sa - fu - na:
kwe - se, kwe - se. Nda - tsva - ka, tsva - ka,
search - ing, search - ing. I'm search - ing, search - ing
C G D Em G D G
lu - tho, lu - tho. A - ke - kho o - fa - na na - ye.
kwe - se, kwe - se, ha - ku, ha - ku - chi - na.
ev' - ry - where. There's no one, there's no one like him.

69 Hallelujah, Salvation, and Glory

HALLELUJAH, SALVATION, AND GLORY Irregular

Part 1
Hal-le-lu - jah, sal - va-tion, and glo-ry, hon - or and pow'r
un-to the Lord our God. For the Lord our God is might-
- y; yes, the Lord our God is om-ni-po-tent. The
Lord our God, he is won - der-ful.
Part 2
All prais - es be to the King of kings and the
Lord of lords. He is won - der-ful!
Part 3
Hal - le - lu - jah, hal-le - lu - jah, hal-le-lu-jah, hal-le-
lu-jah, hal-le-lu-jah, hal - le - lu - jah, he is won - der-ful!

Text: based on Revelation 19:1, 6, 16; A. Jeffrey LaValley (USA)
Music: A. Jeffrey LaValley

Praise God (Dedication Anthem) 70

DEDICATION ANTHEM Irregular

*Praise God from whom all bless - ings flow,
*Praise God from whom all bless-ings flow,
praise God all crea - tures here be - low,
praise God all crea-tures here be - low,
praise God all crea - tures here be - low,
praise God a - bove, praise God a - bove, praise God a -
praise God a - bove, praise God a - bove,

*Alternate phrases: Praise God from whom all blessings flow,
praise him all creatures here below, praise him above, ye heav'nly host

Text: Thomas Ken (England), *A Manual of Prayers . . .*, 1695, alt.
Music: Lowell Mason's *Boston Handel and Haydn Society Collection . . .*, 9th ed., 1830

bove, ye heav'n - ly host,
praise God a - bove, ye heav'n-ly host,
praise God a - bove,
bove, ye heav'n - ly host,
praise God a - bove, ye heav'n-ly host,
praise God a - bove, praise God a - bove, ye heav'n - ly host,
*praise Fa - ther, Son, and Ho - ly Ghost,
*praise Fa - ther, Son, and Ho - ly Ghost,
*praise Fa - ther, Son, and Ho - ly Ghost,
*praise Fa - ther, Son, and Ho - ly Ghost,
praise Fa - ther, Son, and Ho - ly Ghost, praise
Fa - ther, Son, and Ho - ly Ghost.

*Alternate phrase: O praise our God, bless'd Three in One

Hal - le - lu - jah, hal - le - lu - jah, hal - le - lu - jah, a -
men, a - men. hal - le - lu - jah, hal - le - lu - jah, hal - le-
hal - le - lu - jah,
lu - jah, hal - le - lu - jah, hal - le - lu - jah, hal - le - lu - jah, hal - le -
lu - jah, hal - le - lu - jah, a - men, a - men, hal - le -
lu - jah, a - men, hal - le - lu - jah, a - men.

71 Praise God (Doxology)

OLD HUNDREDTH LM

G D Em Bm Em D G
A: Praise God, the Source of life and birth. Praise God, the
B: Praise God from whom all bless - ings flow; praise him all
C: Praise God from whom all bless - ings flow; praise her all
D Em C G D Em D G D G C D G
Word who came to earth. Praise God the Spir - it, ho - ly Flame.
crea - tures here be - low; praise him a - bove, ye heav'n - ly host;
crea - tures here be - low; praise her a - bove, ye heavn - 'ly host;
Em D Am G D G C G
All glo - ry, hon - or to God's name.
praise Fa - ther, Son, and Ho - ly Ghost. A - men.
praise Moth - er, Son, and Ho - ly Ghost.

French

Gloire à Dieu, notre Créateur;
Gloire à Christ, notre Rédempteur;
Gloire à l'Esprit Consolateur!
Louange et gloire à Dieu, Sauveur.

Spanish

A la Divina Trinidad,
todo unidos alabad,
con alegria, y gratitud,
su amor y gracia celebrad.

German

Ehr sei dem Vater und dem Sohn
dem Heil'gen Geist in einem Thron,
der heiligen Dreieinigkeit,
sei Lob und Preis in Ewigkeit.

Text: text A Ruth Duck (USA), © 1990 The Pilgrim Press; texts B and C Thomas Ken (England), *A Manual of Prayers . . .*, 1695, alt.; Spanish trans. anon.; French trans. anon.; German trans. anon.
Music: Louis Bourgeois (present-day France), *Genevan Psalter*, 1551

Alleluia 72

DOXOLOGY REFRAIN Irregular

G C D G F C G
Al - le - lu - ia, al - le - lu - ia,
C D Em C D G
al - le - lu - ia, al - le - lu - ia!

Text: Hebrew traditional; הַלְלוּ יָהּ (Hallelujah) (Mediterranean), ca. 4th c. BC, translit. Greek, ἀλληλούϊα (Alleluia) (Mediterranean), ca. 3rd c. BC
Music: Darryl Neustaedter Barg (Canada), 2019, © 2019 Darryl Neustaedter Barg; acc. Anneli Loepp Thiessen (Canada)

Alleluia 73

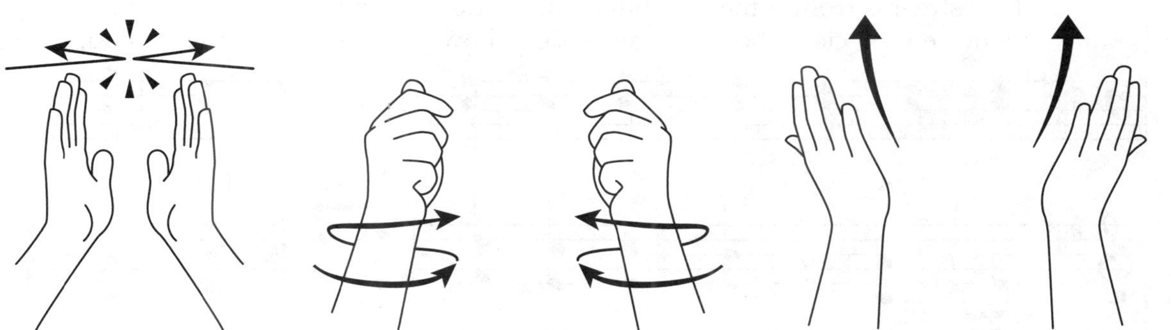

① ② ③

Text: American Sign Language; Hebrew traditional; הַלְלוּ יָהּ (Hallelujah) (Mediterranean), ca. 4th c. BC, translit. Greek, ἀλληλούϊα (Alleluia) (Mediterranean), ca. 3rd c. BC; Mennonite Worship and Song Committee, 2020; illustration by Merrill Miller (USA)

74 O Worship Our God, All Glorious Above

LYONS 10.10.11.11

A D E
1 O wor - ship our God, all glo - rious a - bove,
2 O tell of her might, O sing of her grace,
3 Your boun - ti - ful care, what tongue can re - cite?
4 Frail chil - dren of dust, and fee - ble as frail,
A A/C♯ E7 A
and joy - ful - ly laud her pow'r and her love;
whose robe is the light, whose can - o - py space.
It breathes in the air, it shines in the light,
in you do we trust, nor find you to fail;
E E7
our Shield and De - fen - der, the An - cient of Days,
Her char - iots of wrath the deep thun - der - clouds form,
it streams from the hills, it de - scends to the plain,
your mer - cies how ten - der, how firm to the end,
A A/C♯ D7 A
pa - vil - ioned in splen - dor, and gird - ed with praise.
and dark is her path on the wings of the storm.
and sweet - ly dis - tills in the dew and the rain.
our Mak - er, De - fend - er, Re - deem - er, and Friend!

Chord symbols represent a simplified harmony.

Text: based on Psalm 104; Robert H. Grant (England), *Christian Psalmody*, 1833, alt.
Music: *Sacred Melodies*, vol. 2 (England), 1815

Praise, My Soul, the King of Heaven! 75

LAUDA ANIMA 8.7.8.7.8.7

D A D G D G D G A
1 Praise, my soul, the King of heav - en! To his feet thy
2 Praise him for his grace and fa - vor to all peo - ple
3 Fa - ther - like, he tends and spares us, well our fee - ble
4 An - gels, help us to a - dore him, and be - hold him
Bm Em A F♯ Bm B7 E7sus Fdim7
trib - ute bring. Ran - somed, healed, re - stored, for - giv - en,
in dis - tress. Praise him, still the same for - ev - er,
frame he knows. In his hands he gen - tly bears us,
face to face. Sun and moon, bow down be - fore him,
F♯m E A D Bm E A D G A
ev - er - more his prais - es sing! Al - le - lu - ia!
slow to chide, and swift to bless. Al - le - lu - ia!
res - cues us from all our foes. Al - le - lu - ia!
dwell - ers all in time and space. Al - le - lu - ia!
Bm A7 Bm A G Em D A D
Al - le - lu - ia! Praise the ev - er - last - ing King.
Al - le - lu - ia! Glor - ious in his faith - ful - ness.
Al - le - lu - ia! Wide - ly yet his mer - cy flows.
Al - le - lu - ia! Praise with us the God of grace.

Text: based on Psalm 103; Henry F. Lyte (England), *The Spirit of the Psalms*, 1834, alt.
Music: John Goss (England), *The Supplemental Hymn and Tune Book*, 1869

76 Holy, Holy, Holy!

NICAEA 11.12.12.10

Descant, verse 4

4 Ho - ly, ho - ly, ho - ly! Lord God al - might - y!
D Bm A D G D
1 Ho - ly, ho - ly, ho - ly! Lord God al - might - y!
2 Ho - ly, ho - ly, ho - ly! All the saints a - dore thee,
3 Ho - ly, ho - ly, ho - ly! Though the dark-ness hide thee,
4 Ho - ly, ho - ly, ho - ly! Lord God al - might - y!
All thy works shall praise thy name,
A D Bm A E7 A
Ear - ly in the mor - ning our song shall rise to thee.
cast - ing down their gol - den crowns a - round the glass - y sea;
though the eye of sin - ful - ness thy glo - ry may not see,
All thy works shall praise thy name, in earth, and sky, and sea.
ho - ly, ho - ly, ho - ly! Mer - ci - ful and might - y!
D Bm A D G D
Ho - ly, ho - ly, ho - ly! Mer - ci - ful and might - y!
cher - u - bim and ser - a-phim fall - ing down be - fore thee,
on - ly thou art ho - ly; there is none be - side thee,
Ho - ly, ho - ly, ho - ly! Mer - ci - ful and might - y!

Text: Reginald Heber (England), *A Selection of Psalms and Hymns for the Parish Church of Banbury*, 1826
Music: John B. Dykes (England), *Hymns Ancient and Modern*, 1861; desc. Godfrey Hewitt (Canada), ca. 1971,

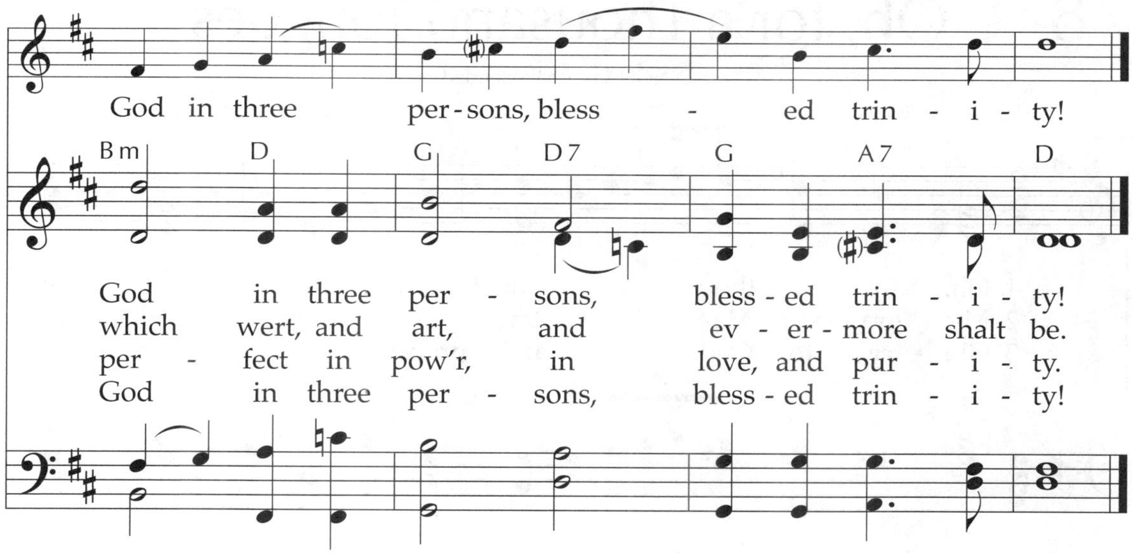
God in three per-sons, bless - ed trin - i - ty!
Bm D G D7 G A7 D
God in three per - sons, bless - ed trin - i - ty!
which wert, and art, and ev - er - more shalt be.
per - fect in pow'r, in love, and pur - i - ty.
God in three per - sons, bless - ed trin - i - ty!

Laudate Dominum (Sing, Praise, and Bless the Lord) 77

LAUDATE DOMINUM 6.6.8

Ostinato Refrain

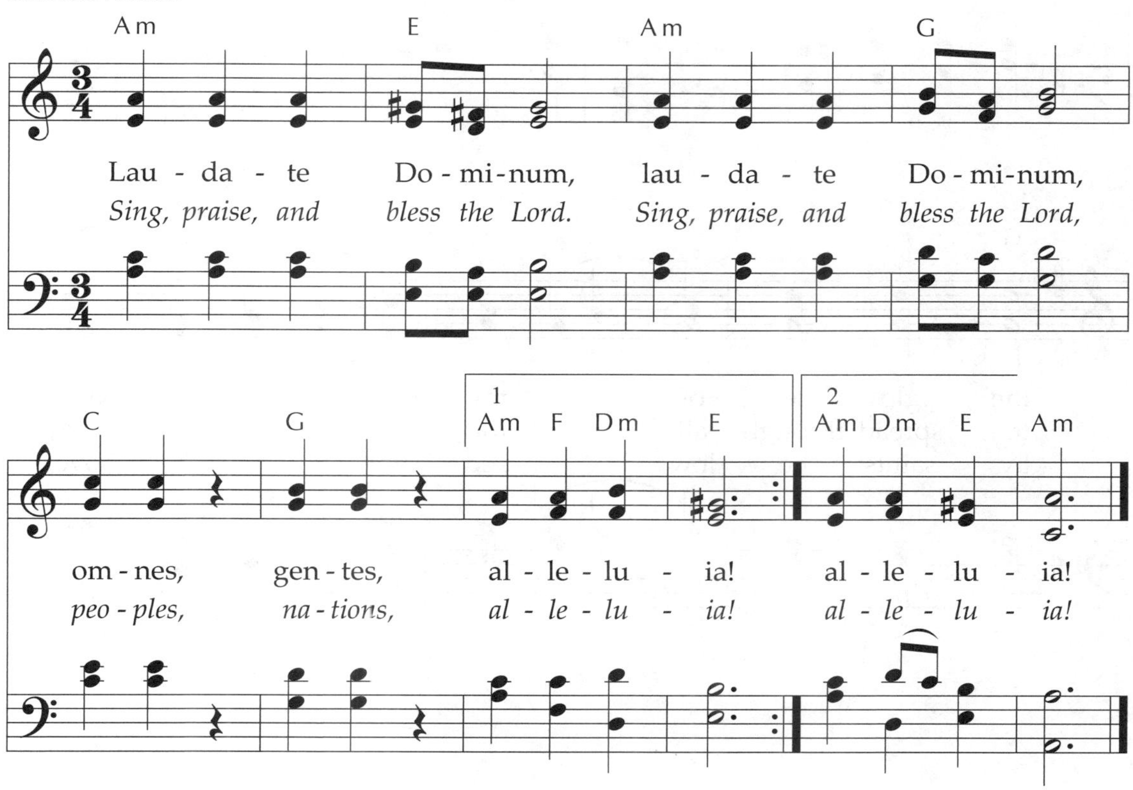
Am E Am G
Lau - da - te Do - mi - num, lau - da - te Do - mi - num,
Sing, praise, and bless the Lord. Sing, praise, and bless the Lord,
C G
1 Am F Dm E
2 Am Dm E Am
om - nes, gen - tes, al - le - lu - ia! al - le - lu - ia!
peo - ples, na - tions, al - le - lu - ia! al - le - lu - ia!

Verses can be found in the accompaniment edition.

Text: Latin; based on Psalm 117; Taizé Community (France), 1980
Music: Jacques Berthier (France), 1980

78 Oh, for a Thousand Tongues

LYNGHAM CM extended

G C G D7 G
1 Oh, for a thou - sand tongues to sing my
2 My gra - cious Mas - ter and my God, as -
3 Glo - ry to God, and praise, and love be
D7 A7 D G D/A A D
great Re-deem-er's praise, my great Re - deem - er's praise,
sist me to pro - claim, as - sist me to pro - claim,
ev - er, ev - er giv'n, be ev - er, ev - er giv'n
G D A7 D
the glo - ries of my God and King,
to spread through all the earth a - broad
by saints be - low and saints a - bove,

Text: Charles Wesley (England), 1739, *Hymns and Sacred Poems*, 1740
Music: Thomas Jarman (England), *Sacred Music*, 1803

G C
the tri - umphs of his
the hon - ors of thy
the church in earth and
the tri - umphs of his grace, the
the hon - ors of thy name, the
the church in earth and heav'n, the
G D G
grace, the tri-umphs of his grace, the
name, the hon - ors of thy name, the
heav'n, the church in earth and heav'n, the
tri-umphs of his grace, the tri-umphs of his
hon - ors of thy name, the hon - ors of thy
church in earth and heav'n, the church in earth and
C G Dsus D7 G
tri - umphs of his grace!
hon - ors of thy name.
church in earth and heav'n.
grace, the tri - umphs of his grace!
name, the hon - ors of thy name.
heav'n, the church in earth and heav'n.

79 Sanna, sannanina

SANNANINA Irregular

C G F C
San-na, san-na-ni-na, san-na, san-na, san-na.
Leader
(Ho - san - na, san-
C G F C
San-na, san-na-ni-na, san-na, san-na, san-na. San-
na.) (Ho - san - na.)
G7 C C/G G7 C
na, san-na, san - na san-na-ni-na, san-na, san-na, san-na.
G7 C
San - na, san-na, san - na, san -
(Ho - san - na.)
C/G G7 C
na - ni - na, san - na, san - na, san - na.
except last time
(Ho - san - na.)

Text meaning: Hosanna

Music: South African traditional

We Sing to You, O God

80

DARWALL'S 148th 6.6.6.6.8.8

Descant, verse 4
4 O God, e - ter - nal God, we hide with - in your wings,
D A Bm G A
1 We sing to you, O God, the Rock who gave us birth. Let
2 We wan-dered far from home out in a des-ert land. You
3 You bear us through the world, an ea - gle to her young, who
4 O God, e - ter - nal God, we hide with-in your wings, the
the ev - er - last - ing arms to whom our prais - es ring. Ah,
D Bm E A E7 A D G A7
our re-joic-ing sing your name in all the earth. To you, O
shield-ed with your love our fear-ful pil - grim band. You kept us
ris - es on her wings and bears us toward the sun. We ride the
ev - er-last-ing arms to whom our prais - es ring. Your word is
you are our God in whom we trust.
Bm A G D A7 D
God, let songs be raised, in joy - ful hymns, our feast of praise.
safe with - in your arms, and shel-tered us a - gainst the storm.
vaults of light and air, and trust in your un - fail - ing care.
true, your way is just, you are the God in whom we trust.

Chord symbols represent a simplified harmony.

Text: Gracia Grindal (USA), © 1993 Selah Publishing Co., Inc.
Music: John Darwall (England), *New Universal Psalmodist*, 1770; desc. Charles H. Webb (USA), alt., © 1980 Harold Flammer, Inc.

81 All Creatures, Worship God Most High

LASST UNS ERFREUEN LM with alleluias

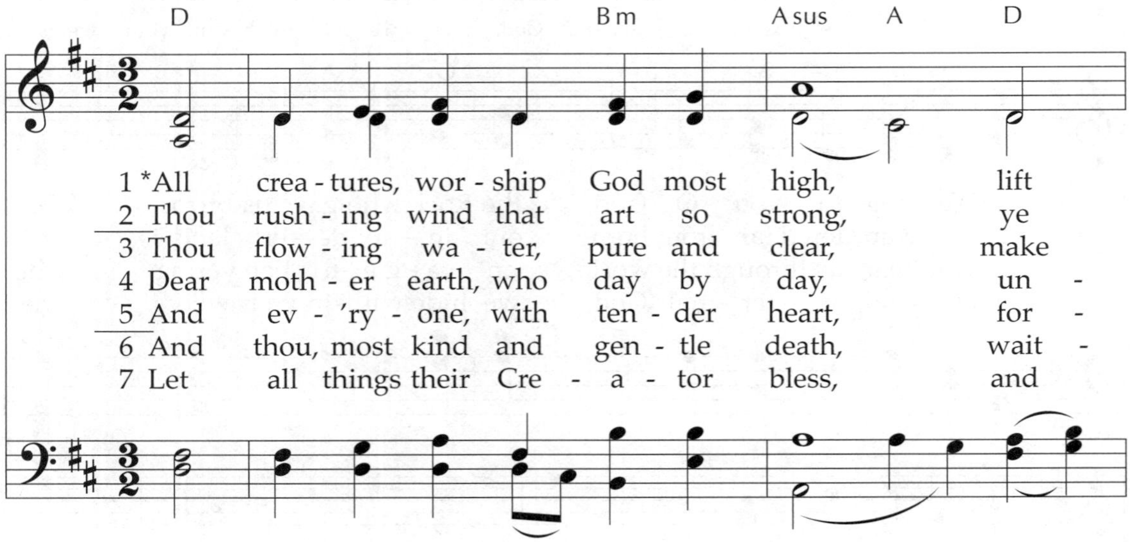
D Bm Asus A D
1 *All crea - tures, wor - ship God most high, lift
2 Thou rush - ing wind that art so strong, ye
3 Thou flow - ing wa - ter, pure and clear, make
4 Dear moth - er earth, who day by day, un -
5 And ev - 'ry - one, with ten - der heart, for -
6 And thou, most kind and gen - tle death, wait -
7 Let all things their Cre - a - tor bless, and

Bm Asus A D G D
up your voice in earth and sky,
clouds that sail in heav'n a - long,
mu - sic for thy God to hear,
fold - est bless-ings on our way, al - le - lu - ia,
giv - ing oth - ers, take your part,
ing to hush our fi - nal breath,
wor - ship God in hum - ble - ness,

*Or, "All creatures of our God and King, / lift up your voice and with us sing"

Chord symbols represent a simplified harmony.

Text: Saint Francis of Assisi (present-day Italy), "Laudato sia Dio mio Signore," 1225; trans. William H. Draper (England), *Hymns of the Spirit*, 1926, alt.
Music: *Geistliche Kirchengesäng* (present-day Germany), 1623; adapt. and harm. Ralph Vaughan Williams (England), *The English Hymnal*, 1906, simplified

E A D
Thou burn - ing sun with gold - en
Thou ris - ing morn in praise re -
Thou fire so mas - ter - ful and
al - le - lu - ia! The flow'rs and fruits that in thee
Ye who long pain and sor - row
Thou lead - est home the child of
To God all thanks and praise be -
Asus A D G D
beam, thou sil - ver moon with soft - er gleam,
joice, ye lights of eve - ning, find a voice,
bright, that giv - est all both warmth and light,
grow, let them God's glo - ry al - so show,
bear, sing praise and cast on God your care,
God, as Christ be - fore that way hath trod,
long! Join in the ev - er - last - ing song:
G A D Em A Bm
O sing ye, O sing ye, al - le -
E A Bm Em A Em Asus A7 D
lu - ia, al - le - lu - ia, al - le - lu - ia!

82 Segala puji syukur (All Our Praise)

SHOUT FOR JOY Irregular

Refrain
D G
So - rak-lah, ha - le-lu-yah! So - rak-lah, ha - le-lu-yah!
Shout for joy, hal - le-lu - jah! Shout for joy, hal - le-lu - jah!
D Bm C A D
Ha - le - lu - yah! So - rak-lah, ha - le-lu-yah!
Hal - le - lu - jah! Shout for joy, hal - le-lu - jah!
G D A D A
So - rak-lah, ha - le-lu-yah! Ha - le - lu - yah!
Shout for joy, hal - le-lu - jah! Hal - le - lu - jah!
Verse
D A G D
S'ga - la pu - ji syu - kur Han - ya bag - i - Mu, Tu - han,
All our praise and glo - ry on - ly un - to you, O God,
D Bm C A
se - bab kau lyang la - yak di - pu - ja.
You a - lone are wor - thy to be praised.
D D7/F# G D
Ka - mi mau ber - so - rak, ting - gi - kan na - ma - Mu.
We have come to - geth - er to mag - ni - fy your name.
A D A
Ha - le - lu - yah!
Hal - le - lu - jah!

Text: Indonesian; Niko Njotorahardjo (Indonesia)
Music: Niko Njotorahardjo

When in Our Music God Is Glorified 83

ENGELBERG 10.10.10.4

G D/G D7 C G
1 When in our mu - sic God is glo - ri - fied,
2 How of - ten, mak - ing mu - sic, we have found
3 So has the church, in lit - ur - gy and song,
4 And did not Je - sus sing a psalm that night
5 Let ev' - ry in - stru-ment be tuned for praise!
D7 G D A D
and ad - o - ra - tion leaves no room for pride,
a new di - men - sion in the world of sound,
in faith and love, through cen - tu - ries of wrong,
when ut - most e - vil strove a - gainst the Light?
Let all re - joice who have a voice to raise!
Dm G7 C2 Am Em Cmaj7
it is as though the whole cre - a - tion cried
as wor - ship moved us to a more pro - found
borne wit - ness to the truth in ev' - ry tongue,
Then let us sing, for whom he won the fight:
And may God give us faith to sing al - ways
1–4
Am G Dsus D
al - le - lu - ia!
5
Am G
al - le - lu - ia!

Text: Fred Pratt Green (England), 1972, *The Hymn*, 1973, © 1972 Hope Publishing Co.
Music: Charles V. Stanford (England), *Hymns Ancient and Modern*, 1904

84 To God Be the Glory

TO GOD BE THE GLORY 11.11.11.11 with refrain

Ab Eb7 Ab Eb Ab
1 To God be the glo - ry, great things he hath done: so
2 Oh, per - fect re - demp-tion, the pur-chase of blood, to
3 Great things he hath taught us, great things he hath done, and
Db Ab Bb Eb Ab Eb7
loved he the world that he gave us his Son, who yield - ed his
ev - 'ry be - liev - er the prom-ise of God. The vil - est of-
great our re - joic - ing through Je - sus the Son, but pur - er, and
Ab Eb Ab Db Ab/Eb
life an a - tone-ment for sin, and o-pened the life - gate that
fend - er who tru - ly be - lieves, that mo-ment from Je - sus a
high - er, and great - er will be our won - der, our trans-port, when
Eb7 Ab Refrain
all may go in.
par - don re - ceives. Praise the Lord, praise the Lord, let the
Je - sus we see.

Text: Fanny J. Crosby (USA), *Brightest and Best*, 1875
Music: William H. Doane (USA), *Brightest and Best*, 1875

Eb Eb7
earth hear his voice! Praise the Lord, praise the Lord, let the
Ab Eb7 Ab Eb
peo-ple re - joice! O come to the Fa-ther, through Je - sus the
Ab Db Ab/Eb Eb7 Ab
Son, and give him the glo - ry, great things he hath done.

Heleluyan

85

HELELUYAN Irregular

Canon
1 2 3 4
He - le - lu - yan,* he - le - lu - yan; he - le, he - le - lu - yan;
He - le - lu - yan, he - le - lu - yan; he - le, he - le - lu - yan.

*Translated *Hallelujah*, this song is associated with the Trail of Tears.

Text: Muscogee (Creek, USA); Hebrew traditional; הַלְלוּ יָהּ (Hallelujah) (Mediterranean), ca. 4th c. BC

Music: Muscogee (Creek) traditional; transcr. Charles H. Webb (USA), © 1989 United Methodist Publishing House (admin. Music Services)

86 You Are Exalted

HE IS EXALTED Irregular

Capo 3: (D) F (D/F♯) F/A (G) B♭
You are ex - alt - ed, for - ev - er ex - alt - ed on high. I will
(G/B) B♭/D (A) C (D) F (D/F♯) F/A
praise you. You are ex - alt - ed, for - ev - er ex - alt - ed, and
(G) B♭ (A/G) C/B♭ (G/A) B♭/C (A) C (B sus) D sus (B) D
I will praise your name!
(Em) Gm (Bm/D) Dm/F (A/C♯) C/E (A) C (D) F (D/F♯) F/A (G) B♭ (D/F♯) F/A
You are my God— for - ev - er your truth shall reign.
(Em) Gm (Bm/D) Dm/F (A/C♯) C/E (A) C (D) F (D/F♯) F/A (G) B♭ (D/F♯) F/A
Heav - en and earth re - joice in your ho - ly name.
(Em) Gm (Em/D) Gm/F (C maj7) E♭maj7 (Em7/A) Gm7/C (D) F
You are ex - alt - ed, for - ev - er ex - alt - ed on high!

Text: Twila Paris (USA), alt.
Music: Twila Paris; vocal harm. Mennonite Worship and Song Committee, 2020

O Praise the Gracious Power 87

CHRISTPRAISE RAY SM with refrain

F Bb C F Bb Gm
1 O praise the gra-cious pow'r that tum-bles walls of fear, and
2 O praise per-sis-tent truth that o-pens fist-ed minds, and
3 O praise in-clu-sive love, en-cir-cling ev-'ry race, ac-
4 O praise the word of faith that claims us as God's own, a
5 O praise the tide of grace that laps at ev-'ry shore with
6 O praise the pow'r, the truth, the love, the word, the tide. Yet
7 O praise the liv-ing Christ with faith's bright song-ful voice! An-
Bb Dm Bb A7 Gm C
gath-ers in one house of faith all stran-gers far and near:
eas-es from their anx-ious clutch the prej-u-dice that binds:
cept-ing all, with-out re-gard to gen-der, wealth, or place.
liv-ing tem-ple built on Christ, our rock and cor-ner-stone:
vi-sions of a world at peace, no long-er bled by war:
more than these, O praise their source, praise Christ the cru-ci-fied:
nounce the gos-pel to the world and with these words re-joice:
Refrain F Bb C Bb C7 F
We praise you, Christ! Your cross has made us one!
We praise

Chord symbols represent a simplified harmony and do not correspond with the keyboard accompaniment.

Text: Thomas H. Troeger (USA), 1984, *New Hymns for the Lectionary*, 1986
Music: Carol Doran (USA), 1984, *New Hymns for the Lectionary*, 1986

r

88 Lobe den Herren (Praise to the Lord, the Almighty)

LOBE DEN HERREN 14.14.4.7.8

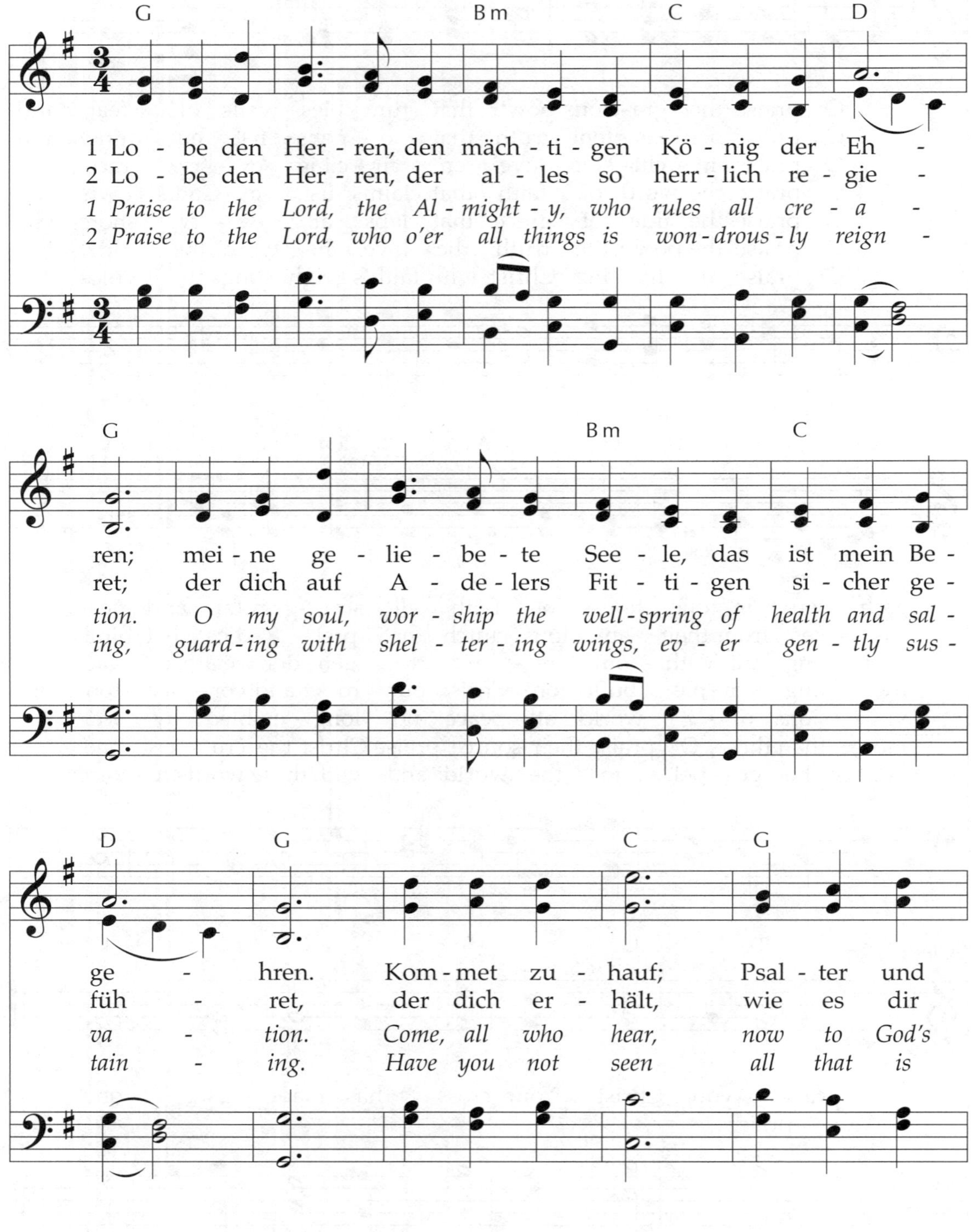
G Bm C D
1 Lo - be den Her - ren, den mäch - ti - gen Kö - nig der Eh -
2 Lo - be den Her - ren, der al - les so herr - lich re - gie -
1 Praise to the Lord, the Al - might - y, who rules all cre - a -
2 Praise to the Lord, who o'er all things is won - drous - ly reign -
G Bm C
ren; mei - ne ge - lie - be - te See - le, das ist mein Be -
ret; der dich auf A - de - lers Fit - ti - gen si - cher ge -
tion. O my soul, wor - ship the well - spring of health and sal -
ing, guard - ing with shel - ter - ing wings, ev - er gen - tly sus -
D G C G
ge - hren. Kom - met zu - hauf; Psal - ter und
füh - ret, der dich er - hält, wie es dir
va - tion. Come, all who hear, now to God's
tain - ing. Have you not seen all that is

Chord symbols represent a simplified harmony.

Text: German; Joachim Neander (present-day Germany), "Lobe den Herren, den machtigen Konig der Ehren," *Alpha und Omega, Glaub- und Liebesubung*, 1680; trans. Catherine Winkworth (England), *Choral Book for England*, 1863, alt.; stanza 4 adapt. Martin A. Seltz (USA), *Chantry Choirbook*, © 2000 Augsburg Fortress
Music: *Ernewerten Gesangbuch* (present-day Germany), 1665

D G Em Am D G
Har - fe, wacht auf. Las - set den Lob - ge - sang hö - ren.
sel - ber ge - fällt; hast du nicht die - ses ver - spü - ret?
tem - ple draw near. Join me in glad ad - o - ra - tion.
need - ed has been held in God's gra - cious or - dain - ing?

3 Lobe den Herren, der deinen Stand sichtbar gesegnet,
der aus dem Himmel mit Strömen der Liebe geregnet.
Denke daran, was der Allmächtige kann,
der dir mit Liebe begegnet.

4 Lobe den Herren; was in mir ist, lobe den Namen.
Alles, was Odem hat, lobe mit Abrahams Samen.
Er is dein Licht, Seele, vergiss es ja nicht.
Lob ihn in Ewigkeit, Amen.

3 Praise to the Lord, who will prosper our work and defend us.
Surely God's goodness and mercy shall daily attend us.
Ponder anew what the Almighty can do,
who with great love still befriends us.

4 Praise to the Lord, for in wonder my spirit is soaring!
All that has life and breath, come now with praises outpouring!
Let the "amen" sound from God's people again,
gladly forever adoring!

89 Tú eres todopoderoso (Because You're Holy)

TÚ ERES TODOPODEROSO Irregular

Bm G D
La ú-ni-ca ra-zón de mi‿a-do-ra-ción e-res tú,
Be-cause of you I raise ev'-ry song of praise; Je-sus, you
A Bm
mi Je-sús; mi ú-ni-co mo-ti-vo pa-
are my life. I find in you my mean-ing, my
G D A
ra vi-vir e-res tú, mi Se-ñor. Mi‿ú-ni-
be-ing's source; Je-sus, you are my Lord. You're the
Bm G D
ca ver-dad es-tá en ti; e-res mi luz y
Word of truth, the dawn-ing light that brings the world sal-
A Bm G
mi sal-va-ción. Mi‿ú-ni-co a-mor e-res tú, Se-ñor,
va-tion and peace. You're the source of love, and the Lord of all;
D A
y por siem-pre te a-la-ba-ré. Tú e-res
and for-ev-er, your song will not cease, be-cause you're
Refrain
Bm G D A
to-do-po-de-ro-so, e-res gran-de‿y ma-jes-tuo-so;
ho-ly, and al-might-y, full of maj-es-ty and pow'r.

Text: Spanish; Juan Salinas (USA), 1999; trans. Adam M. L. Tice (USA), 2019
Music: Juan Salinas; arr. Greg Scheer (USA), 2019

Bm G D
e - res fuer - te, in - ven - ci - ble, y no‿hay na - die co - mo tú.
Yours the glo - ry; yours the hon - or; I have noth-ing with-out you.
1, 3
A Bm G D A
Fine
(To verse)
2
A
(To refrain)
D.S. al Fine
Tú e - res
Be-cause you're

Masithi: Amen (Sing Amen) 90

AMEN SIAKUDUMISA Irregular

F C
Ma - si - thi: a - men si - a - ku - du - mi - sa. Ma - si - thi:
Sing a - men: A - men, we praise your name, O God. Sing a - men:
Gm F
a - men si - a - ku - du - mi - sa. Ma - si - thi: a - men ba - wo,
A - men, we praise your name, O God. Sing a - men: A - men, a - men,
B♭ F/A C7/G F
a - men ba - wo, a - men si - a - ku - du - mi - sa.
a - men, a - men, a - men, we praise your name, O God.

Text: Xhosa; South African traditional; trans. unknown, alt.
Music: S. C. Molefe (South Africa),

91 We Praise Thee, O God

REVIVE US AGAIN 11.11 with refrain

G
1 We praise thee, O God, for the Son of thy love,
2 We praise thee, O God, for thy Spir - it of light
3 We praise thee, O God, for the joy thou hast giv'n
4 Re - vive us a - gain, fill each heart with thy love.
C G D
for___ Je - sus who died, and is now gone a - bove.
who has shown us our Sav - ior and scat - tered our night.
to thy saints in com - mun - ion, these fore - tastes of heav'n.
May each soul be re - kin - dled with fire from a - bove.
Refrain
G C G C G D
Hal - le - lu - jah! Thine the glo - ry, hal - le - lu - jah! A - men!
G C G C G/D D7 G
Hal - le - lu - jah! Thine the glo - ry, re - vive us a - gain.

Text: William P. Mackay (Scotland), 1863, rev. *The Praise of Jesus*, 1863
Music: attr. John J. Husband (Scotland), ca. 1815, *New Praises of Jesus*, 1869

Build My Life

92

WORTHY OF EVERY SONG Irregular

E
A/E
1 Wor - thy of ev-'ry song we could ev - er sing;
2 Je - sus, the name a - bove ev - 'ry oth-er name,
wor - thy of all the praise we could ev-er bring;
Je - sus, the on - ly one who could ev - er save:
wor - thy of ev-'ry breath we could ev - er breathe.
2nd time only
We live for you. (Oh, we live for you.)
Refrain
A 2
F♯m7
C♯m7
Ho - ly, there is no one like you, there is none be - side you. O - pen up my
eyes in won-der, show me who you are, and fill me with your heart, and
lead me in your love to those a - round me.
Bridge
I will build my
B sus
E/G♯
life up - on your love; it is a firm foun - da - tion. I will
put my trust in you a - lone, and I will not be shak - en.
To refrain

Text: Brett Younker (USA), Karl Martin (Scotland), Kirby Kaple (USA), Matt Redman (England), and Pat Barret (USA)
Music: Brett Younker, Karl Martin, Kirby Kaple, Matt Redman, and Pat Barret

93 Nyanyikanlah nyanyian baru (Sing to God a New Song)

NYANYIKANLAH Irregular

Capo 3: (D) F (A) C
1 Nya - nyi-kan - lah nya - nyi - an ba - ru ba - gi Al - lah Pen-
2 Pu - ji Di - a wa - hai men - ta - ri, wa - hai bu - lan, sem-
1 Sing to God a new song; sing praise with all cre - a - tion, the
2 Hal - le - lu - jah! Sing praise to your Cre - a - tor, sun, moon, and
(D) F
cip - ta ca - kra - wa - la. Se - ga - la Se - ra -
bah - lah Di - a te - rus, dan wa - hai bin - tan
earth and heav-ens a - bove. All the ser - a - phim will
stars, and an - gels a - bove. Sing to God your Mak - er,
(A) C (D) F
fim Ke - ru - bim, pu - ji - lah Di - a, be - sar - kan - lah na - ma-Nya.
te - rang yang ge - mer lap-an, mu - li - a - kan Pen - cip - ta - Mu.
praise God, with all the hosts of cher - u - bim join - ing voic - es in praise.
all liv - ing crea - tures, all the beasts in the fields, and birds in the sky.

Text: Indonesian; based on Psalm 148; paraphr. Tilly Lubis-Nainggolan (Indonesia), 1988, © 2009 Yamuger, Indonesian Institute for Sacred Music; English trans. David J. Diephouse (USA), alt.; trans. © 2009 Faith Alive Christian Resources
Music: Batak traditional (Indonesia); arr. H. A. Pandopo (Indonesia), 1999

Refrain
(A) C (D) F
Ber - so - rak - so - rai ba - gi Ra - ja - mu! (ma - ri)
God reigns on high, let the heav - ens re - joice! (O)
(A) C (D) F
Ber - so - rak - so - rai ba - gi Ra - ja - mu!
God reigns on high, let the heav - ens re - joice!

Gloria

94

GLORIA III Irregular

Canon
Dm Gm C F Dm Gm C F
1 2
Glo - ri - a, glo - ri - a, in ex-cel - sis De - o!*
Dm Gm C F Dm Gm C F
3 4
Glo - ri - a, glo - ri - a, al - le - lu - ia, al - le - lu - ia!

*Translation: Glory to God in the highest!

Text: Latin; Luke 2:14
Music: Jacques Berthier (France),

95 Praise the Lord, Sing Hallelujah

PRAISE JEHOVAH 8.7.8.7 D with refrain

1 Praise the Lord, sing hal - le - lu - jah, from the heav-ens praise God's
2 Let them praise the Lord Cre - a - tor; they were made at God's com -
3 All you fruit - ful trees and ce - dars, ev - 'ry hill and moun-tain
name! Praise the Lord, our great cre - a - tor; all you
mand, who es - tab - lished them for - ev - er, whose de -
high, creep - ing things and beasts and cat - tle, birds that
an - gels, praise pro - claim. All you hosts, to - geth - er
cree shall ev - er stand. From the earth, O praise your
in the heav - ens fly, crowns of earth from ev - 'ry
prais - ing, sun and moon and stars on high. Praise the
mak - er, rag - ing seas, you crea - tures all, fire and
na - tion, rul - ers great, earth's judg - es all; praise to -

Text: based on Psalm 148; *The Book of Psalms* (USA), 1871; adapt. William J. Kirkpatrick (USA), ca. 1893, alt.
Music: William J. Kirkpatrick, ca. 1893

Lord, O heav'ns of heav - ens, and the floods a - bove the sky.
hail and snow and va - pors, storm-y winds that hear the call.
geth - er, all you peo - ple, a - ged ones and chil-dren small.
Refrain
God, we praise you, hal - le - lu - jah, for your
God, we praise you,
name a - lone is high. And your glo - ry is ex-
And your glo - ry
alt - ed, and your glo - ry is ex - alt - ed, and your
and your glo - ry
glo - ry is ex - alt - ed, far a - bove the earth and sky!
and your glo - ry
pp
p
ff

96 Your Love Is Amazing

YOUR LOVE IS AMAZING Irregular

C2 G2/B C2
1 Your love is a-maz - ing, stead-y and un-chang - ing.
2 Your love is sur-pris - ing, I can feel it ris - ing,
G2/D C2
Your love is a moun - tain, firm be-neath my feet.
all the joy that's grow - ing deep in-side of me.
G2/B C2
Your love is a mys - t'ry, how you gen - tly lift me.
Ev - 'ry time I see you all your good-ness shines through.
G2/D C2
When I am sur-round - ed, your love car - ries me.
I can feel this God song ris - ing up in me.
Refrain
G D Em7
Hal-le-lu - jah, hal-le-lu - jah, hal-le-lu - jah,
C G D
your love makes me sing. Hal-le-lu - jah, hal-le-lu - jah,
Em7 C
hal-le-lu - jah, your love makes me sing.

Text: Brenton Brown (USA/South Africa) and Brian Doerksen (Canada)
Music: Brenton Brown and Brian Doerksen

Magnificat

97

MAGNIFICAT Irregular

Canon 1
1 G C D7 G 2 G C D7 G
Mag-ni-fi-cat, mag-ni-fi-cat, mag-ni-fi-cat a-ni-ma me-a Do-mi-num.*
Canon 2
1 2
Mag - ni - fi - cat, mag - ni - fi - cat,
3 G C D7 G 4 G C D7 G
Mag-ni-fi-cat, mag-ni-fi-cat, mag-ni-fi-cat a-ni-ma me - a!
3 4
a - ni - ma me-a Do-mi-num, a - ni - ma me-a Do - mi-num.
Canon 3
1 2
Mag - ni - fi - cat, mag - ni - fi - cat
3 4
a - ni - ma me - a, me - a Do - mi - num.

*Translation: My soul magnifies the Lord.

Text: Latin; based on Luke 1:46
Music: Jacques Berthier (France),

98 Immortal, Invisible, God Only Wise

ST. DENIO (JOANNA) 11.11.11.11

Capo 1: (C) D♭ (D) E♭ (G) A♭
1 Im - mor - tal, in - vis - i - ble, God on - ly wise,
2 Un - rest - ing, un - hast - ing, and si - lent as light,
3 To all, life thou giv - est, to both great and small.
4 Great God of all glo - ry, great God of all light,
(C) D♭ (D) E♭ (G) A♭
in light in - ac - ces - si - ble, hid from our eyes,
nor want - ing, nor wast - ing, thou rul - est in might,
In all life thou liv - est, the true life of all.
thine an - gels a - dore thee, all veil - ing their sight.
(D) E♭
most bless - ed, most glor - ious, the An - cient of Days,
thy jus - tice like moun-tains high soar - ing a - bove
We blos - som and flour - ish as leaves on the tree,
All praise we would ren - der; O help us to see

Chord symbols represent a simplified harmony.

Text: Walter C. Smith (Scotland), *Hymns of Christ and the Christian Life*, 1867, alt.
Music: Welsh traditional, *Caniadau y Cyssegr*, 1839

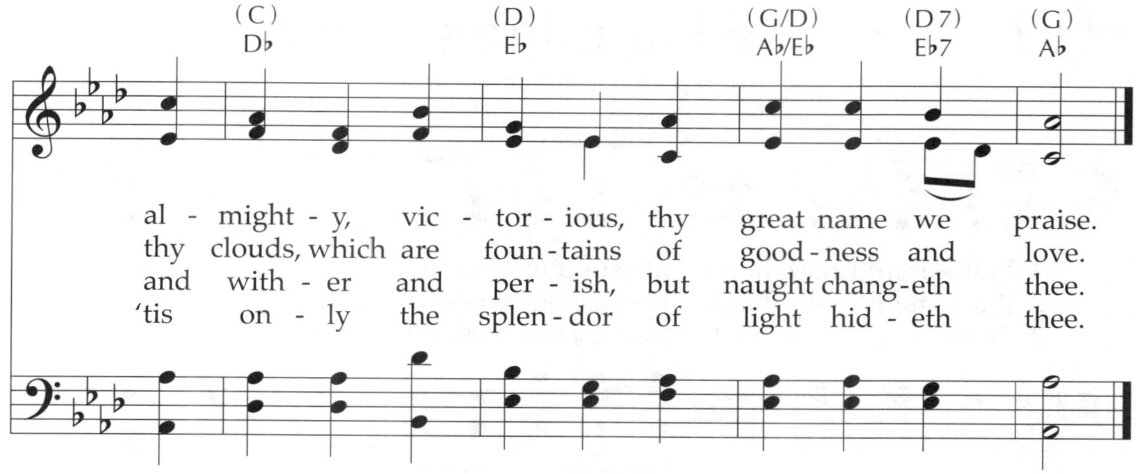
(C) D♭ (D) E♭ (G/D) A♭/E♭ (D7) E♭7 (G) A♭
al - might - y, vic - tor - ious, thy great name we praise.
thy clouds, which are foun - tains of good - ness and love.
and with - er and per - ish, but naught chang - eth thee.
'tis on - ly the splen - dor of light hid - eth thee.

Glory to God in the Highest 99

GLORIA (Mass of Creation) Irregular

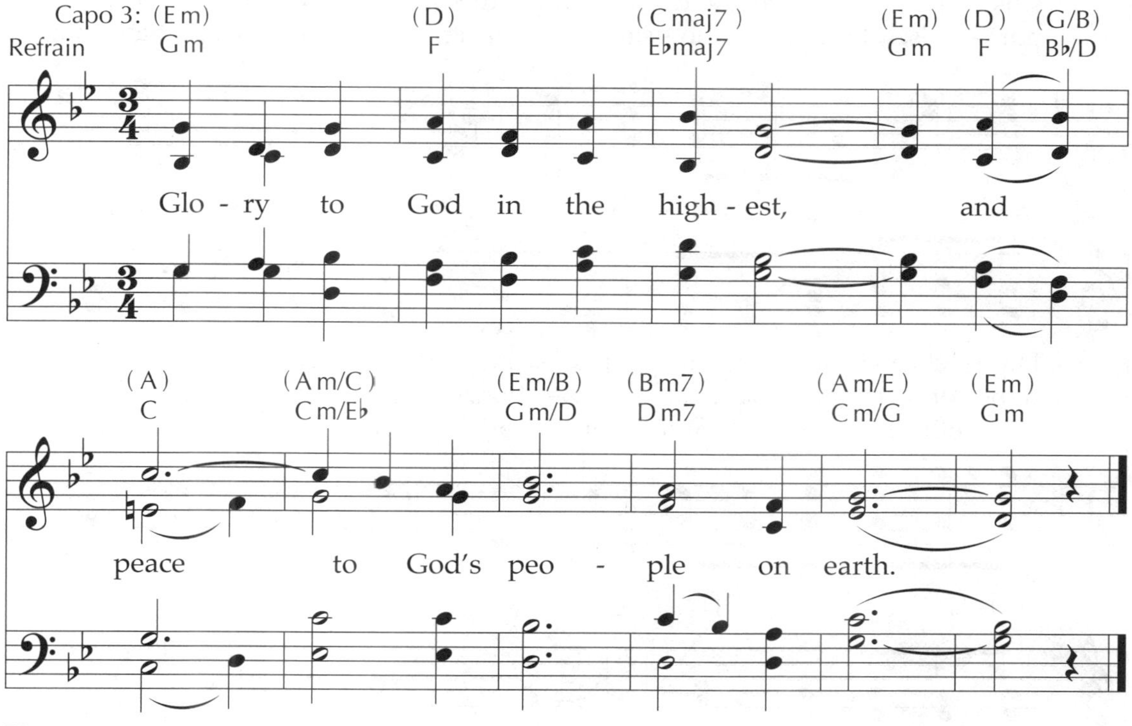
Capo 3: (Em) Gm (D) F (Cmaj7) E♭maj7 (Em) Gm (D) F (G/B) B♭/D
Refrain
Glo - ry to God in the high - est, and
(A) C (Am/C) Cm/E♭ (Em/B) Gm/D (Bm7) Dm7 (Am/E) Cm/G (Em) Gm
peace to God's peo - ple on earth.

Verses:

1 O God, heavenly One, almighty God and Sovereign, we worship you, we give you thanks, we praise you for your glory.

2 O Jesus Christ, only begotten One, true God, Lamb of God, you take away the sin of the world; have mercy on us. You are seated at the right hand of Majesty: receive our prayer.

3 For you alone are the Holy One; you alone are God, you alone are the Most High, Jesus Christ, with the Holy Spirit, in the glory of God Almighty. Amen.

Text: from the Greek "Δόξα ἐν ὑψίστοις Θεῷ" (Mediterranean), ca. 3rd c., Latin "Gloria in excelsis Deo" (Mediterranean), 4th c.; English trans. English Language Liturgical Consultation, 1988; adapt. Mennonite Worship and Song Committee, 2019
Music: Marty Haugen (USA), *Mass of Creation*, 1984, rev. 2019,

100 Praise Him, Praise Him

ALLEN 12.10.12.10.11.10 with refrain

G Am C G
1 Praise him, praise him! Je - sus, our bless-ed re - deem - er! Sing, O
2 Praise him, praise him! Je - sus, our bless-ed re - deem - er! For our
3 Praise him, praise him! Je - sus, our bless-ed re - deem - er! Heav'n-ly
Em A7 D G
earth, his won - der - ful love pro - claim! Hail him, hail him!
sins, he suf - fered, and bled, and died. He our rock, our
por - tals loud with ho - san - nas ring! Je - sus, Sav - ior,
Am C G G7 C Am
High-est arch - an - gels in glo - ry! Strength and hon - or
hope of e - ter - nal sal - va - tion, hail him, hail him!
reign-eth for - ev - er and ev - er! Crown him, crown him!
G/D D7 G D
give to his ho - ly name! Like a shep - herd,
Je - sus, the cru - ci - fied. Sound his prais - es,
proph-et, and priest, and king! Christ is com - ing,

Text: Fanny J. Crosby (USA), *Bright Jewels for the Sunday School*, 1869
Music: Chester G. Allen (USA), *Bright Jewels for the Sunday School*, 1869

G Em A7
Je - sus will guard his chil-dren. In his arms he car - ries them
Je - sus who bore our sor-rows, love un - bound-ed, won-der - ful,
o - ver the world vic - to-rious. Pow'r and glo - ry un - to the
Refrain
D G Am C
all day long.
deep, and strong. Praise him! Praise him! tell of his ex - cel-lent
Lord be - long.
G G7 C Am G/D D7 G
great - ness. Praise him! Praise him! ev - er in joy - ful song.

101 Sing Praise to God Who Reigns

MIT FREUDEN ZART 8.7.8.7.8.8.7

E♭ A♭ E♭ C7 Fm B♭
1 Sing praise to God who reigns a-bove, the God of all
2 What in al-migh - ty pow'r was made, God's gra-cious mer -
3 Our God is nev - er far a-way, through - out all grief
4 Then all my glad-some way a-long, I sing a-loud
E♭ B♭7 E♭ A♭ E♭
cre - a - tion, the God of pow'r, the God of love,
cy keep - eth. By morn-ing glow or eve-ning shade,
dis - tress - ing, an ev - er - pre - sent help and stay,
thy prais - es, that all may hear the grate-ful song
C7 Fm B♭ E♭ B♭7 E♭ Cm
the God of our sal - va - tion. With
God's watch-ful eye ne'er sleep - eth. With -
our peace, and joy, and bless - ing. As
my voice un - wea - ried rais - es: Be
Gm Cm F B♭ E♭
heal-ing balm my soul is filled, and ev-'ry faith-less
in the shel - ter of God's might, lo! all is just, and
with a moth-er's ten-der hand, God gent-ly leads the
joy-ful in your God, my heart! With soul and bod - y

Text: Johann J. Schütz (present-day Germany), "Sei Lob und Ehr dem höchsten Gut," *Christliches Gedenckbüchlein*, 1675; trans. Frances E. Cox (England), *Hymns from the German*, 1864, alt.

Music: adapt. from GENEVA 138, *Genevan Psalter* (present-day Switzerland), 1547, Bohemian Brethren's *Kirchengesänge*, 1566

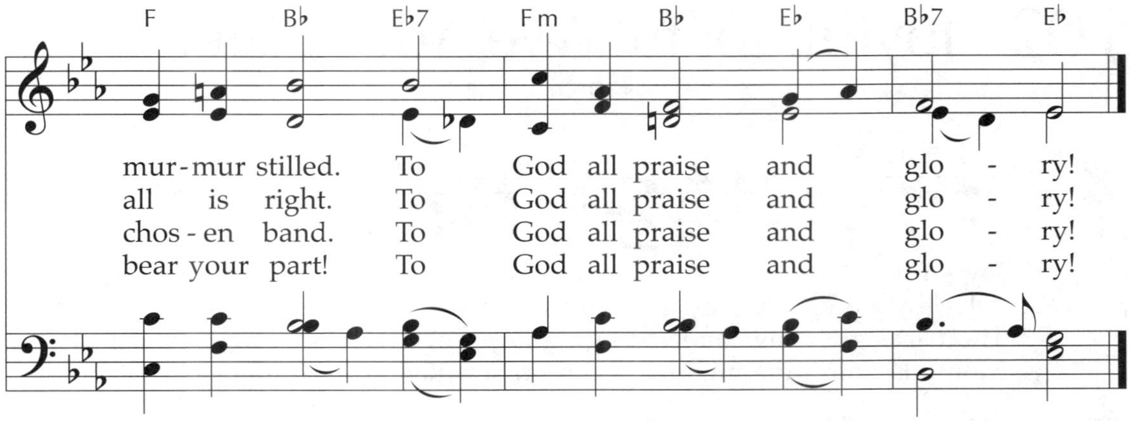
F Bb Eb7 Fm Bb Eb Bb7 Eb
mur-mur stilled. To God all praise and glo - ry!
all is right. To God all praise and glo - ry!
chos-en band. To God all praise and glo - ry!
bear your part! To God all praise and glo - ry!

Santo, santo, santo (Holy, Holy, Holy) 102

Refrain
Capo 3:
CUÉLLAR Irregular
San-to, san-to, san-to, san-to, san-to, san-to‿es nues-tro Dios, Se-ñor de to-da la tie-rra, san-to, san-to‿es nues-tro Dios.
San-to, san-to, san-to, san-to, san-to, san-to‿es nues-tro Dios, Se-ñor de to-da la‿his-to-ria, san-to, san-to‿es nues-tro Dios.
Ho-ly, ho-ly, ho-ly, ho-ly, ho-ly, ho-ly is our God, God who reigns be-yond earth's king-doms, ho-ly, ho-ly is our God.
Ho-ly, ho-ly, ho-ly, ho-ly, ho-ly, ho-ly is our God, God who reigns through all of his-t'ry, ho-ly, ho-ly is our God.
Fine
Que‿a-com-pa-ña‿a nues-tro pue-blo, que vi-ve‿en nues-tras lu-chas, del u-ni-ver-so‿en-te-ro el ú-ni-co Se-ñor.
Ben-di-tos los que‿en su nom-bre el e-van-ge-lio‿a-nun-cian, la bue-na‿y gran no-ti-cia de la li-be-ra-ción.
Walk-ing here a-mong the peo-ple and liv-ing in our strug-gles is God, who rules the heav-ens and holds the earth in love.
Who-ev-er pro-claims the gos-pel and speaks the truth to pow-er, an-nounc-ing lib-er-a-tion, will be for-ev-er blessed.
D.C.

Text: Spanish; Guillermo Cuéllar (El Salvador), ca. 1986, *Misa Salvadoreña*; refrain trans. composite; stanzas trans. Bret Hesla (USA) and William Dexheimer-Pharris (USA), alt.
Music: Guillermo Cuéllar, ca. 1986, *Misa Salvadoreña*

103 Joyful, Joyful, We Adore Thee

HYMN TO JOY 8.7.8.7 D

G D7 G D
1 Joy - ful, joy - ful, we a - dore thee, God of glo - ry, Lord of love.
2 All thy works with joy sur-round thee, earth and heav'n re - flect thy rays,
3 Thou art giv - ing and for - giv - ing, ev - er bles-sing, ev - er bless'd,
4 Mor-tals, join the might-y cho - rus, which the morn-ing stars be - gan.
G C Am G D7 G
Hearts un-fold like flow'rs be-fore thee, prais-ing thee their sun a - bove.
stars and an-gels sing a-round thee, cen-ter of un - bro-ken praise.
well-spring of the joy of liv - ing, o-cean-depth of hap-py rest!
Love di-vine is reign-ing o'er us, lead-ing us with mer-cy's hand.
D G D G D7 B Em A D G
*
Melt the clouds of sin and sad-ness; drive our fear and doubt a - way. Giv -
Field and for-est, vale and moun-tain, bloom-ing mead-ow, flash-ing sea, chant -
Known in Je-sus Christ our broth-er, all who live in love are thine. Teach
Ev - er sing-ing, march we on-ward, vic-tors in the midst of strife. Joy -
C Am G D G
- er of im - mor - tal glad-ness, fill us with the light of day!
- ing bird and flow-ing foun-tain, call us to re - joice in thee.
us how to love each oth - er, lift us to the joy di-vine.
- ful mu - sic lifts us sun-ward in the tri - umph song of life.

*Notated rhythm reflects the melody as it appears in Symphony No. 9 in D minor, Op. 125.

Text: Henry van Dyke (USA), 1907, *Poems of Henry van Dyke*, 1911, alt.
Music: Ludwig van Beethoven (Germany), 1823; adapt. Edward Hodges (England), *Trinity Collection of Church Music*, 1864, alt.

105 *Romans 12:1-2*

Dear ones, I plead with you
to give your bodies to God
because of God's mercies.
Let your bodies be a living, holy,
and acceptable sacrifice.
This is truly the way to worship God.
Do not copy the behavior and
customs of this world,
but let God transform you
into a new person
by changing the way you think.
**Then we will learn to know God's will,
which is good and pleasing
and perfect.**

106 *Isaiah 42:10-11 (excerpts)*

Sing to the LORD a new song,
sing praise from the end of the earth!
Let the sea roar and all that fills it,
**the coastlands and all
that dwell in them.**
Let the desert and its towns
lift up their voices,
**let them shout from
the tops of the mountains.**

107 *Psalm 146:1-3*

Praise the LORD!
Praise the LORD, O my soul!
**I will praise the LORD as long as I live;
I will sing praises to my God
all my life long.**
Do not put your trust in princes,
in mortals, in whom there is no help.
Praise the LORD!

108 *Psalm 47:1, 6-7*

Clap your hands, all you peoples;
shout to God with loud cries of joy.
Sing praises to God, sing praises;
sing praises to our king, sing praises.
For God is the king of all the earth;
sing praises.

109 *Psalm 121*

I lift my eyes to the hills;
where does my help come from?
**My help comes from the LORD,
the maker of heaven and earth.**
God will not let your foot slip,
your keeper will not slumber;
**the one who watches over Israel
will neither slumber nor sleep.**
The LORD watches over you
the LORD is your shade
at your right hand;
**the sun will not harm you by day,
nor the moon by night.**
The LORD will keep you from all harm;
God will watch over your life;
**the LORD will watch over
your coming and going
both now and forever.**

110 *Revelation 7:9-12*

I saw a vast crowd, too great to count,
from every nation and tribe
and people and language,
standing in front of the throne
and before the Lamb.
They were clothed in shining robes
and held palm branches in their hands.
They were shouting with a great roar,
**"Salvation comes from
our God who sits on the throne
and from the Lamb!"**
All the angels were standing
around the throne
and around the elders
and the four living beings.
And they fell before the throne
with their faces to the ground
and worshiped God.
They sang,
**"Amen!
Blessing and glory,
wisdom and thanksgiving,
honor and power and strength
belong to our God forever and ever!
Amen."**

Previous page: 104. *Sing the Goodness*, Meg Harder (Canada), 2018, ink on paper ⓦ

10,000 Reasons / Bless the Lord 111

BLESS THE LORD (TEN THOUSAND REASONS) Irregular

Capo 1:
Refrain
Bless the Lord, O my soul. Oh, my soul wor-ships your ho - ly name.
Sing like nev - er be - fore, O my soul; I'll wor-ship your ho - ly name.
Last time to coda
1 The sun comes up, it's a new day dawn-ing; it's time to sing your song a-gain. What-ev-er may pass, and what - ev-er lies be - fore me, let me be sing-ing when the eve - ning comes.
2 You're rich in love, and you're slow to an - ger. Your name is great and your heart is kind. For all your good-ness, I will keep on sing-ing ten thou-sand rea-sons for my heart to find.
3 And on that day when my strength is fail - ing, the end draws near, and my time has come, still, my soul will sing your praise un - end-ing ten thou-sand years and then for - ev - er - more!
To refrain
Coda
wor-ship your ho - ly name; wor-ship your ho - ly name.

Text: Jonas Myrin (USA) and Matt Redman (England)
Music: Jonas Myrin and Matt Redman

112 Womb of Life and Source of Being

LADUE CHAPEL 8.7.8.7 D

1 Womb of life and source of being, home of ev - 'ry rest-less heart, in your arms the worlds a - wak - ened; you have loved us from the start.
2 Word in flesh, our broth - er Je - sus, born to bring us sec - ond birth, you have come to stand be - side us, know - ing weak - ness, know - ing earth.
3 Brood - ing Spir - it, move a - mong us; be our part - ner, be our friend. When our mem - 'ry fails, re - mind us whose we are, what we in - tend.
4 Moth - er, Broth - er, ho - ly Part - ner; Fa - ther, Spir - it, On - ly Son: we would praise your name for - ev - er, one - in - three and three - in - one.
We, your chil - dren, gath - er round you, at the ta - ble you pre - pare. Shar - ing sto - ries, tears, and laugh - ter, we are nur - tured by your care.
Priest who shares our hu - man strug - gles, Life of Life, and Death of Death, ris - en Christ, come stand a - mong us, send the Spir - it by your breath.
La - bor with us; aid the birth - ing of the new world yet to be, free of ser - vant, lord, and mas - ter, free for love and u - ni - ty.
We would share your life, your pas - sion, share your word of world made new, ev - er sing - ing, ev - er prais - ing, one with all, and one with you.

Text: Ruth Duck (USA), 1986, 1990, © 1992 GIA Publications, Inc.
Music: Ronald Arnatt (USA), © 1971 Walton Music Corporation

Cantai ao Senhor (O Sing to the Lord) 113

CANTAI AO SENHOR 5.6.5.6.5.6.5.5

Em
B7
1 Can - tai ao Se - nhor um cân - ti - co no - vo, can -
1 O sing to the Lord, O sing God a new song, O
Em
tai ao Se - nhor um cân - ti - co no - vo, can -
sing to the Lord, O sing God a new song, O
E
Am
tai ao Se - nhor um cân - ti - co no - vo, can -
sing to the Lord, O sing God a new song, O
Edim7
B7
Em
tai ao Sen - hor, can - tai ao Se - nhor!
sing to the Lord, O sing to the Lord!

2 Porque ele fez,
ele faz maravilhas, *(3x)*
cantai ao Senhor, cantai ao Senhor!

3 Cantai ao Senhor,
bendizei o seu nome, *(3x)*
cantai ao Senhor, cantai ao Senhor!

4 É ele quem dá o
Espírito Santo, *(3x)*
cantai ao Senhor, cantai ao Senhor!

5 Jesus é o Senhor!
Amém, aleluia! *(3x)*
Cantai ao Senhor, cantai ao Senhor!

2 By marvelous pow'r
the Lord has done wonders, (3x)
O sing to the Lord, O sing to the Lord!

3 So dance for the Lord
and blow all the trumpets, (3x)
O sing to the Lord, O sing to the Lord!

4 O shout to the Lord,
who gave us the Spirit, (3x)
O sing to the Lord, O sing to the Lord!

5 For Jesus is Lord!
Amen, alleluia! (3x)
O sing to the Lord, O sing to the Lord!

Text: Portuguese; based on Psalm 98, Brazilian traditional
Music: Brazilian traditional; arr. Felipe Blycker (USA); harm. Samuel Pascoe (USA)

114 Nun danket alle Gott (Now Thank We All Our God)

NUN DANKET ALLE GOTT 6.7.6.7.6.6.6.6

G C G C D G
1 Nun dan - ket al - le Gott mit Her - zen, Mund und Hän - den,
2 Der e - wig - rei - che Gott woll uns bei un - serm Le - ben
3 Lob, Ehr und Preis sei Gott, dem Va - ter und dem Soh - ne
1 Now thank we all our God with heart and hands and voic - es,
2 Oh, may this boun - teous God through all our life be near us,
3 *All praise and thanks to God the Fa - ther now be giv - en,
C G C D G
der gro - ße Din - ge tut an uns und al - len En - den;
ein im - mer fröh - lich Herz und ed - len Frie - den ge - ben,
und dem, der bei - den gleich im höch - sten Him - mels - thro - ne,
who won - drous things has done, in whom this world re - joic - es,
with ev - er joy - ful hearts and bless - ed peace to cheer us,
the Son, and him who reigns with them in high - est heav - en,
D G D G A D
der uns an Leib und Seel von frü - her Kind - heit an
und uns in sei - ner Gnad er - hal - ten fort und fort
dem drei - mal ei - nen Gott, wie es ur - sprüng - lich war
who, from our moth - ers' arms, has bless'd us on our way
and keep us safe in grace, and guide us when per - plexed,
the one e - ter - nal God, whom earth and heav'n a - dore,

Chord symbols represent a simplified harmony.

Text: German; Martin Rinckart (present-day Germany), 1636; trans. Catherine Winkworth (England), *Lyra Germanica II*, 1858, alt.
Music: Johann Cruger (present-day Germany), *Praxis Pietatis Melica*, 4th ed., 1647

G C Am G D G
un - zäh - lig viel zu - gut bis hier - her hat ge - tan.
und uns aus al - ler Not er - lö - sen hier und dort.
und ist und blei - ben wird jetz - und und im - mer - dar!
with count-less gifts of love, and still is ours to - day.
and free us from all ills in this world and the next.
for thus it was, is now, and shall be ev - er - more.

*Alternative verse 3: All praise and thanks to God
who reigns in highest heaven—
Creator, living Christ,
and Spirit blest, be given—
the one eternal God,
whom earth and heav'n adore,
for thus it was, is now,
and shall be evermore.

Praise Be to God 115

SAKURA 8.7.7.7.7.8.6

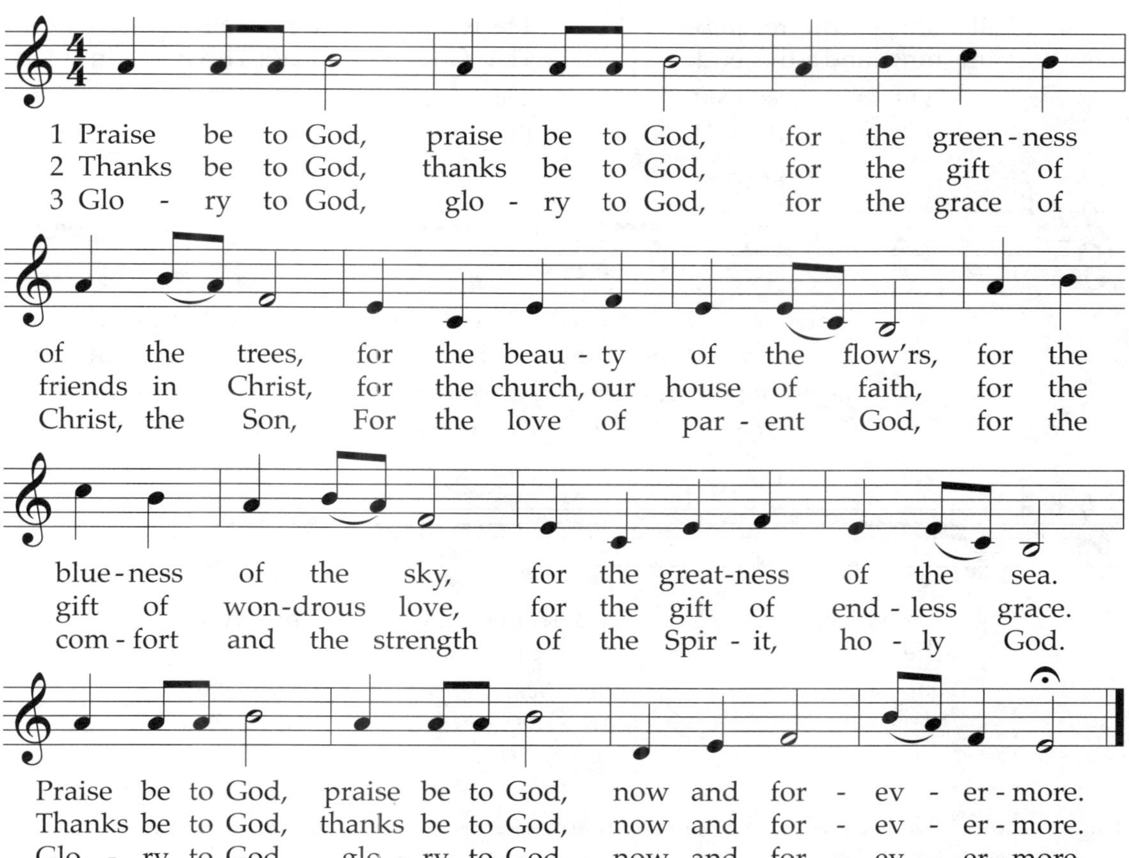
1 Praise be to God, praise be to God, for the green-ness of the trees, for the beau - ty of the flow'rs, for the blue-ness of the sky, for the great-ness of the sea.
2 Thanks be to God, thanks be to God, for the gift of friends in Christ, for the church, our house of faith, for the gift of won-drous love, for the gift of end - less grace.
3 Glo - ry to God, glo - ry to God, for the grace of Christ, the Son, For the love of par - ent God, for the com - fort and the strength of the Spir - it, ho - ly God.
Praise be to God, praise be to God, now and for - ev - er - more.
Thanks be to God, thanks be to God, now and for - ev - er - more.
Glo - ry to God, glo - ry to God, now and for - ev - er - more.

Text: Nobuaki Hanaoka (USA), *Hymns from the Four Winds*, 1983, © 1980 Nobuaki Hanaoka
Music: Japanese traditional; transcr. © 1983 Abingdon Press (admin. Music Services)

116 How Great Is Our God (Cuán grande es Dios)

HOW GREAT IS OUR GOD Irregular

A
F♯m7
1 The splen - dor of the King, clothed in maj -
2 And age to age, he stands, and time is in
1 Bri - llan - do‿el Rey es - tá, ves - ti - do‿en ma -
2 To - da la‿e - ter - ni - dad en sus ma - nos
D2
- es - ty, let all the earth re - joice, let
his hands; be - gin - ning and the end, be -
- jes - tad; se‿a - le - gra la crea - ción, se‿a -
es - tá; prin - ci - pio y fi - nal, prin -
A
all the earth re - joice. He wraps him - self in light,
gin - ning and the end. The God - head, Three in One,
le - gra la crea - ción. De luz ro - dea - do‿es - tá,
ci - pio y fi - nal. Ben - di - ta Tri - ni - dad,
F♯m7
and dark - ness tries to hide, and trem - bles at
Fa - ther, Spir - it, Son, the Li - on and
la‿os - cu - ri - dad se va, y tiem - bla‿an - te
tres en u - no son, cor - de - ro y
D2
D
his voice, and trem - bles at his voice.
the Lamb, the Li - on and the Lamb.
su voz, y tiem - bla‿an - te su voz.
le - ón, cor - de - ro y le - ón.

Text: Chris Tomlin (USA), Jesse Reeves (USA), and Ed Cash (USA); Spanish trans. Francis Castañeda (Peru), Mario Ríos, Mark Young, and Coalo Zamorano (Mexico)
Music: Chris Tomlin, Jesse Reeves, and Ed Cash

Refrain
A
How great is our God! Sing with me: how
¡Cuán gran - de es Dios! Can - ten hoy, ¡cuán
F♯m7
D
great is our God! And all will see how great, how great
gran - de es Dios! Y to - dos lo ve - rán: ¡cuán gran-
E
A
Bridge
is our God! Name a-bove all
- de es Dios! Nom - bre sin i -
F♯m7
D
names, wor - thy of all praise. My heart will sing,
gual, dig - no de‿a - do - rar. Y can - ta - ré:
E
A
Optional repeat to refrain
how great is our God!
¡cuán gran - de es Dios!

117 We Give Thanks unto You

WE GIVE THANKS UNTO YOU Irregular

Leader
Em Am7 B7
1 We give thanks un - to you, O God of might,
2 From of old you have led your peo - ple in faith,
3 You de - liv - ered the ones who called un - to you,
4 You have o - pened the sea and brought your peo - ple through,
5 You re - mem - ber your prom - ise age to age,
All
Em Am Em B7
for your love is nev - er end - ing;
Leader
B7 Em
we give thanks un - to you, the God of gods,
you have shown your com - pas - sion, strength, and love,
from bond - age to free - dom, you brought them forth,
brought them in - to a land that flows with life,
you show mer - cy on those of low de - gree,
All
G Am Em B7 Em
for your love is nev - er end - ing.

Text: based on Psalm 136; Marty Haugen (USA), *Shepherd Me, O God*, 1986
Music: Marty Haugen, *Shepherd Me, O God*, 1986

El Senyor és la meva força (In the Lord I'll Be Ever Thankful) 118

IN THE LORD I'LL BE EVER THANKFUL 9.7.8.9.9

Capo 3: (Bm) (A) (D) (G) (A) (Bm)(A) (D)
Dm C F Bb C Dm C F
El Sen - yor és la me - va for - ça, el Sen - yor el
In the Lord I'll be ev - er thank - ful, in the Lord I
(A) (G) (F♯) (Bm) (A)
C Bb A Dm C
3
meu cant. Ell m'ha‿es - tat la sal - va - ci - ó. En ell con -
will re - joice! Look to God, do not be a - fraid. Lift up your
(D) (Em/G) (A) (F♯m) (Bm) (G) (A) (D)
F Gm/Bb C Am Dm Bb C F
fi - o i no tinc por, en ell con - fi - o i no tinc por.
voic - es, the Lord is near, lift up your voic - es, the Lord is near.

Spanish

El Señor es mi fortaleza,
el Señor es mi canción.
Él nos da la salvación.
En él confío, no temeré,
en él confío, no temeré.

Text: Catalan; Taizé Community (France); English and Spanish trans. Taizé Community
Music: Jacques Berthier (France)

119 When All Thy Mercies

GENEVA CM

E♭ B♭ E♭ F
1 When all thy mer - cies, O my God, my
2 Ten thou - sand thou - sand pre - cious gifts my
3 Through ev - 'ry per - iod of my life thy
4 Through all e - ter - ni - ty, to thee a
1 When all thy mer-cies, O my God, my
2 Ten thou - sand thou-sand pre - cious gifts my
3 Through ev - 'ry per-iod of my life thy
4 Through all e - ter-ni-ty, to thee a
1 When all thy mer-cies, O my God, my
2 Ten thou-sand thou-sand pre-cious gifts my
3 Through ev-'ry per-iod of my life thy
4 Through all e-ter-ni-ty, to thee a
B♭ E♭ F7 B♭ E♭ B♭ E♭
ris - ing soul sur - veys, trans - port - ed with the
dai - ly thanks em - ploy, nor is the least a
good - ness I'll pur - sue, and af - ter death in
joy - ful song I'll raise, but, oh, e - ter - ni -
trans - port-ed with the
nor is the least a
and af - ter death in
but, oh, e - ter - ni -
A♭ B♭ E♭ Fm7 E♭/B♭ B♭7 E♭
view, I'm lost in won - der, love, and praise.
cheer - ful heart, that tastes those gifts with joy.
dis - tant worlds, The glo - rious theme re - new.
ty's too short to ut - ter all thy praise!

Chord symbols represent a simplified harmony.

Text: Joseph Addison (England), *The Spectator*, 1712
Music: John Cole (USA), *Ecclesiastical Harmony*, 1805; version from Joseph Funk and Sons' *Harmonia Sacra*, 12th ed., 1867

For the Beauty of the Earth 120

DIX 7.7.7.7.7.7

1 For the beau - ty of the earth, for the glo - ry
2 For the beau - ty of each hour of the day and
3 For the joy of ear and eye, for the heart and
4 For the joy of hu - man love, broth - er, sis - ter,
5 For each per - fect gift and sign to this world so
of the skies, for the love which from our birth
of the night, hill and vale and tree and flow'r,
mind's de - light, for the mys - tic har - mo - ny
par - ent, child, friends on earth and friends a - bove,
free - ly giv'n; grac - es hu - man and di - vine,
o - ver and a - round us lies:
sun and moon and stars of light:
link - ing sense to sound and sight: Lord of all, to
for all gen - tle thoughts and mild:
love u - nit - ing earth and heav'n:
thee we raise this our hymn of grate - ful praise.

For a lower key, see "As with Gladness" (#277).

Text: Folliott S. Pierpoint (England), *Lyra Eucharistica*, 1864, alt.
Music: Conrad Kocher (Germany), *Stimmen aus dem Reiche Gottes*, 1838; adapt. William H. Monk (England), *Hymns Ancient and Modern*, 1861

121 When at Creation's Dawn

CREATION'S DAWN 10.10.10 with alleluias

1 When at cre - a - tion's dawn there was no sound,
2 For ev - 'ry sound comes from the Mak - er's hand,
3 That mu - sic stirs in us through day and night,
4 So let our songs now ech - o na - ture's praise.
God hummed a brood - ing song of birth pro - found:
the cleans - ing rush of riv - er, drift of sand.
a u - ni - ty of soul and bod - y's light,
All strings and cords in sweet vi - bra - tion raise
the sym - pho - ny of na - ture all a - round:
Each scrap - ing in - sect sings a - cross the land:
through which our breath and voice rise in - to flight:
to glo - ri - fy our God through all our days:
Al - le - lu - ia, al - le - lu - ia.
Al - le - lu - ia.

Text: Jean Janzen (USA), 1993
Music: James E. Clemens (USA), 1993; arr. © 2019 James E. Clemens

Sing to the God of Harvest 122

WIE LIEBLICH IST DER MAIEN 7.6.7.6 D

1 Sing to the God of har - vest a song of love and praise;
2 God gives the rain and sun - shine; the des - erts bloom and spring;
3 Bring to the ho - ly ta - ble gifts God in good - ness gave:
with joy - ful hearts and voic - es your al - le - lu - ias raise.
all crea - tures leap in glad - ness; the chil - dren laugh and sing.
the wheat of gos - pel plant - ing, the world Christ died to save;
By God's com - mand the sea - sons in fruit - ful or - der move;
God fills them with a - bun - dance; all liv - ing things in - crease;
and bring the cup of bless - ing, the fruit of field and vine,
so thank the God of har - vest with hymns of heart - felt love.
the year is crowned with kind - ness, with plen - ty and with peace.
and thank the God of har - vest who calls us now to dine.

Text: Delores Dufner, OSB (USA), adapt. from "Sing to the Lord of Harvest," John S. B. Monsell (Ireland), 19th c.,
Music: Johann Steurlein (present-day Germany), 1575; harm. Healey Willan (Canada), 1958;

123 Come, Ye Thankful People

ST. GEORGE'S WINDSOR 7.7.7.7 D

G Em D G Em B
1 Come, ye thank-ful peo - ple, come! Raise the song of har - vest home.
2 All the world is God's own field, fruit un - to God's praise to yield;
3 For our God a - gain shall come, and shall take the har - vest home,
4 Then, O church tri - um - phant, come. Raise the song of har - vest home.
Em Am D G A7 D A7 D
All is safe - ly gath - ered in ere the win - ter storms be - gin.
wheat and tares to - geth - er sown, un - to joy or sor - row grown.
from the field shall in that day all of - fens - es cast a - way,
All are safe - ly gath - ered in, free from sor - row, free from sin;
G C
God, our Mak - er doth pro - vide for our need to be sup - plied.
First the blade and then the ear, then the full corn shall ap - pear.
giv - ing an - gels charge at last in the fire the tares to cast,
there for - ev - er pu - ri - fied, in God's pre - sence to a - bide.
E Am D G C G G/D D7 G
Come to God's own tem - ple, come. Raise the song of har - vest home.
God of har - vest, grant that we whole-some grain and pure may be.
but the fruit - ful ears to store in God's gar - ner ev - er - more.
Come, ten thou - sand an - gels, come! Raise the song of har - vest home.

Text: based on Psalm 103; Henry Alford (England), *Psalms and Hymns*, 1844, alt.
Music: George J. Elvey (England), *A Selection of Psalm and Hymn Tunes*, 1858

For the Fruit of All Creation 124

FIRSTFRUITS 8.4.8.4.8.8.8.4

1 For the fruit of all cre - a - tion, thanks be to God.
2 In the just re - ward of la - bor, God's will is done.
3 For the har-vest of the Spir - it, thanks be to God.
For the gifts to ev'-ry na - tion, thanks be to God. For the
In the help we give our neigh-bor, God's will is done. In our
For the good we all in - her - it, thanks be to God. For the
plow - ing, sow-ing, reap-ing, si - lent growth while we are sleep-ing,
world-wide task of car - ing for the hun - gry and de - spair-ing,
won - ders that a - stound us, for the truths that still con - found us,
fu - ture needs in earth's safe-keep-ing, thanks be to God.
in the har-vests we are shar - ing, God's will is done.
most of all, that love has found us, thanks be to God.

Alternate tune: AR HYD Y NOS (#830)

Text: Fred Pratt Green (England), *Methodist Recorder*, alt.,
Music: Bradley P. Lehman (USA),

125 Shout to the Lord (Cante al Señor)

SHOUT TO THE LORD Irregular

C Csus C G Gsus G Am G
My Je - sus, my Sav - ior, Lord, there is none like you;
Mi Cris - to, mi rey, na - die es co - mo tú;
F2 C/E F C/G Am7
all of my days, I want to praise the won - ders of your
to - da mi vi - da quie-ro‿e-xal - tar las ma - ra - vi - llas
B♭ F/A Gsus G C Csus C G Gsus G
might - y love. My com - fort, my shel - ter,
de tu‿a - mor. Con - sue - lo, re - fu - gio,
Am G F2 C/E F
tow-er of ref - uge and strength; let ev-'ry breath, all that I am,
to - rre de fuer - za‿y po - der; to - do mi ser, lo que yo soy,
C/G Am7 B♭ Dm/A Gsus G
nev - er cease to wor - ship you.
nun - ca ce - se de‿a - do - rar.
Refrain
C Am7 F F/G G
Shout to the Lord, all the earth, let us sing
Can - te‿al Se - ñor, to - da la cre - a - ción.

Text: Darlene Zschech (Australia); Spanish trans. Don Moen (USA)
Music: Darlene Zschech

C Am7 Fmaj7 G
pow - er and maj - es - ty, praise to the King.
Hon - ra, po - der, ma - jes - tad se - a‿al Rey.
Am F
Moun - tains bow down and the seas will roar at the
Mon - tes cae - rán y el mar ru - gi - rá al so -
G F/A G/B G/D C Am7
sound of your name. I sing for joy at the work
nar de su nom - bre. Can - to con go - zo‿al mi - rar
F F/G G C Am7
of your hands, for - ev - er I'll love you, for - ev -
su po - der, por siem - pre yo te a - ma - ré
Fmaj7 G Am
- er I'll stand; noth - ing com - pares to the prom -
y di - ré: in - com - pa - ra - bles pro - me -
F F/G Repeat C Csus C G Gsus G Final C
- ise I have in you. you.
- sas me das, Se - ñor. ñor.

126 Holy God, We Praise Thy Name

GROßER GOTT, WIR LOBEN DICH 7.8.7.8.7.7

G D7 G
1 Ho - ly God, we praise thy name. God of all, we
2 Hark, the loud ce - les - tial hymn, an - gel choirs a -
3 Lo! the ap - os - tol - ic train join thy sa - cred
4 Ho - ly Au - thor, Ho - ly Word, Ho - ly Spir - it,
1 Gro - ßer Gott, wir lo - ben dich! Herr, wir prei - sen
2 Al - les, was dich prei - sen kann, Che - ru - bim und
3 Hei - lig, Herr Gott Ze - ba - oth! Hei - lig, Herr der
4 Auf dem gan - zen Er-den - kreis lo - ben Gro - ße
D G D G D7 G
bow be - fore thee. All on earth your scep - ter claim;
bove are rais - ing. Cher - u - bim and ser - a - phim,
name to hal - low. Proph - ets swell the glad re - frain,
three we name thee; still, one ho - ly voice is heard:
dei - ne Stär - ke! Vor dir neigt die Er - de sich
Se - ra - phi - nen, stim - men dir ein Lob - lied an,
Him - mels - hee - re! Star - ker Hel - fer in der Not;
und auch Klei - ne; dich, Gott Va - ter; dir zum Preis
D G D
all in heav'n a - bove a - dore thee. In - fi - nite thy
in un - ceas - ing chor - us prais - ing, fill the heav'ns with
and the bless - ed mar - tyrs fol - low, and, from morn till
un - di - vid - ed God, we claim thee, and a - dor - ing
und be - wun - dert dei - ne Wer - ke. Wie du warst vor
al - le En - gel die dir die - nen, ru - fen dir stets
Him - mel, Er - de, Luft und Mee - re sind er - füllt von
singt die hei - li - ge Ge - mein - de, sie ver - ehrt auf

Chord symbols represent a simplified harmony.

Text: "Te Deum laudamus" (present-day Italy), late 4th c.; trans. Clarence A. Walworth (USA), 1853; German trans. Ignace Franz (present-day Poland), ca. 1774, alt.
Music: *Katholisches Gesangbuch* (present-day Austria), 1774

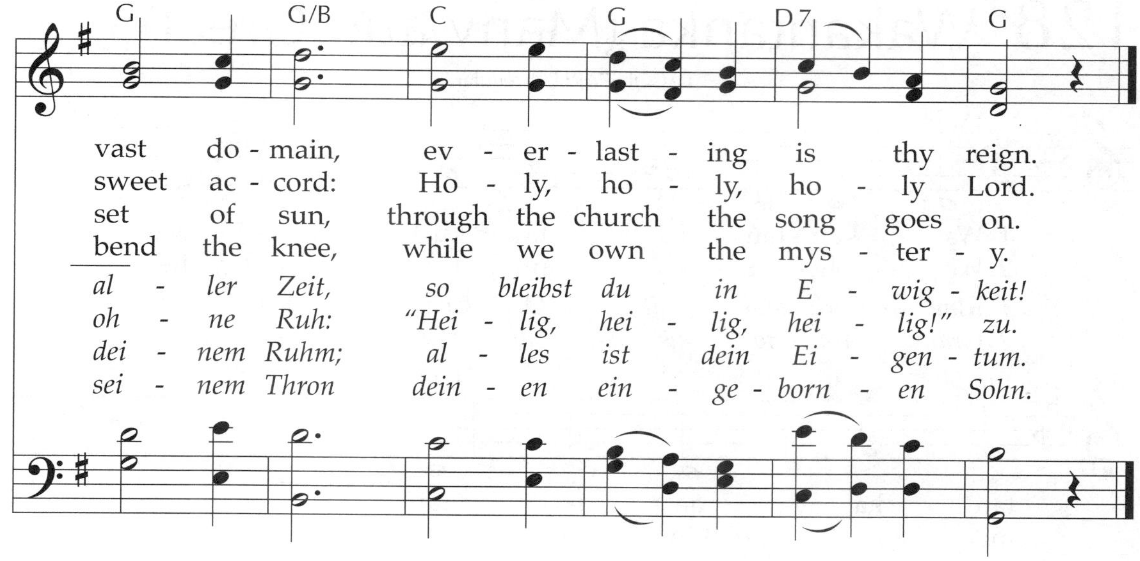
G G/B C G D7 G
vast do - main, ev - er - last - ing is thy reign.
sweet ac - cord: Ho - ly, ho - ly, ho - ly Lord.
set of sun, through the church the song goes on.
bend the knee, while we own the mys - ter - y.
al - ler Zeit, so bleibst du in E - wig - keit!
oh - ne Ruh: "Hei - lig, hei - lig, hei - lig!" zu.
dei - nem Ruhm; al - les ist dein Ei - gen - tum.
sei - nem Thron dein - en ein - ge - born - en Sohn.

Bless the Lord, My Soul (Tengo sed de ti / Bendiz o Senhor) 127

BLESS THE LORD, MY SOUL Irregular

Ostinato Refrain

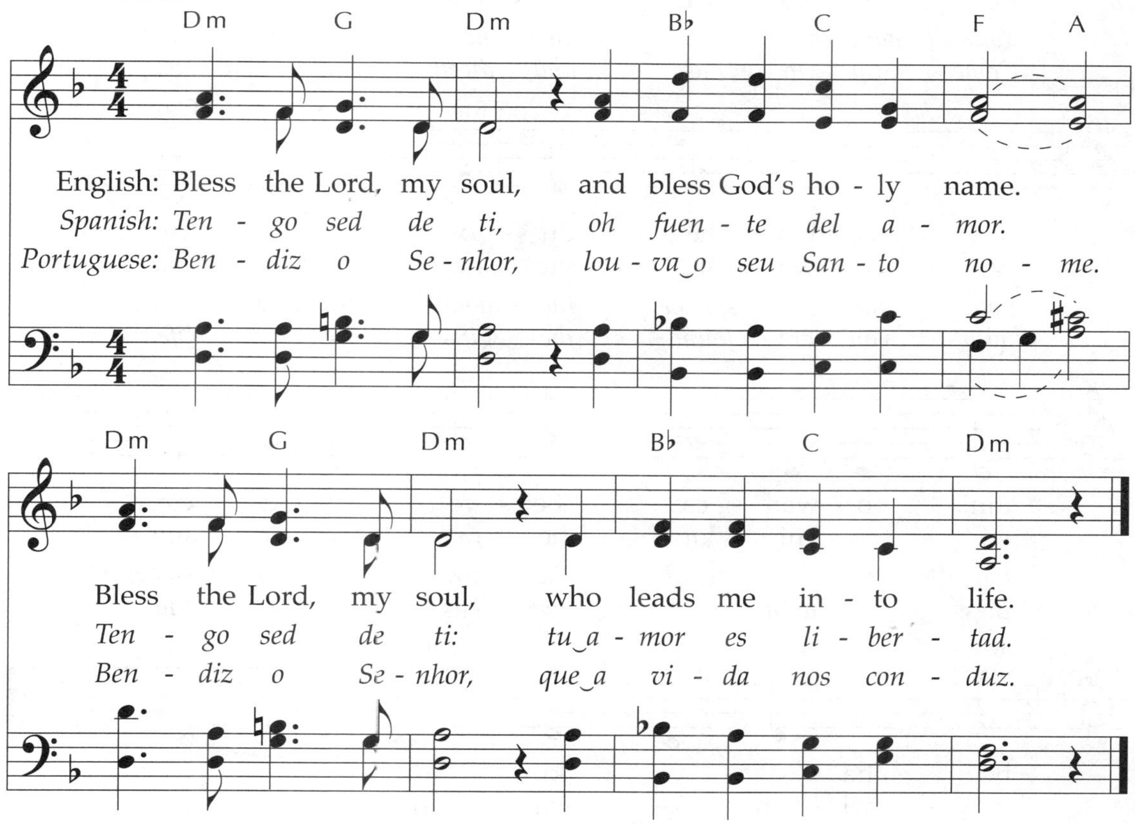
Dm G Dm B♭ C F A
English: Bless the Lord, my soul, and bless God's ho - ly name.
Spanish: Ten - go sed de ti, oh fuen - te del a - mor.
Portuguese: Ben - diz o Se - nhor, lou - va o seu San - to no - me.
Dm G Dm B♭ C Dm
Bless the Lord, my soul, who leads me in - to life.
Ten - go sed de ti: tu a - mor es li - ber - tad.
Ben - diz o Se - nhor, que a vi - da nos con - duz.

Spanish: I thirst for you, oh fount of love; your love is liberty.

Verses can be found in the accompaniment edition.

Text: based on Psalm 103:1, Taizé Community (France); Spanish text and Portuguese trans. Taizé Community
Music: Jacques Berthier (France)

128 Wakantanka (Many and Great)

LACQUIPARLE Irregular

Cm
1 Wa - kan - tan - ka ta - ku ni - ta - wa
2 Wo - eh - da - ku ni - ta - wa kin he
1 Man - y and great, O God, are your works,
2 Grant un - to us com - mun - ion with you,
Fm
Cm
tan - ka - ya qa o - ta;
mi - na - ġi kin qu wo;
mak - er of earth and sky.
O star - a - bid - ing One.
ma - hpi - ya kin e - ya - hna - ke ça,
ma - hpi - ya kin i - wan - kam ya - ti,
Your hands have set the heav - ens with stars;
Come un - to us and dwell with us;
Fm
Cm
ma - ka kin he du - o - wan - ca;
wi - co - wa - śte yu - ha nan - ka,
your fin - gers spread the moun - tains and plains.
with you are found the gifts of life.
mni - o - wan - ca śbe - ya wan - ke cin,
wi - co - ni kin he ma - ya - qu nun,
Lo, at your word the wa - ters were formed;
Bless us with life that has no end,
Fm
Cm
he - na o - ya - ki - hi.
o - wi - han - ke wa - nin.
deep seas o - bey your voice.
e - ter - nal life with you.

Text: Dakota; Joseph R. Renville (Dakota, USA), *Dakota Dowanpi Kin* (Odowan Wowapi, USA), 1846; paraphr. Philip Frazier (USA), 1929, alt.
Music: Plains Indian traditional, *Dakota Odowan*, 1879

O Worship Our God

129

BEAUTY OF HOLINESS Irregular

1–3 O wor-ship our God in the beau-ty of ho-li-ness, in the
beau-ty of ho-li-ness, in the beau-ty of ho-li-ness.
1 Mak-er of the star-light be-yond us, with-in us, from
2 Je-sus, born of Mar-y, be-fore us, be-side us, your
3 Spir-it, ev-er mov-ing, a-round us, a-mong us, breathe
si-lence, ho-ly won-der, you birth cre-a-tion's chor-us,
hum-ble love vic-to-rious has brought a great sal-va-tion,
mer-cy, flame with jus-tice, mak-ing new your whole cre-a-tion,
Refrain
oh, glo-ry hal-le-lu-jah, hal-le-lu-jah, hal-le-lu-jah, with
joy we come be-fore you and glo-ri-fy your name.

Text: Brenda Hostetler Meyer (USA), adapt. from Robert Lowry (USA), *Royal Diadem for the Sunday School*, 1873, © 2019 Brenda Hostetler Meyer

Music: Robert Lowry, *Royal Diadem for the Sunday School*, 1873

130 Schönster Herr Jesu (Beautiful Savior)

CRUSADERS' HYMN 5.6.7.5.5.8

Eb Cm Bb Eb C Fm Eb
1 Schön - ster Herr Je - su, Herr - scher al - ler En - den,
2 Schön sind die Wäl - der, schö - ner sind die Fel - der
1 Beau - ti - ful Sav - ior, rul - er of all na - ture,
2 Fair are the mea - dows, fair - er still the wood - lands,
Ab Eb Bb7 Eb Bb Eb C7 Fm
Got - tes und Ma - ri - en Sohn! Dich will ich lie - ben,
in der schö - nen Früh - lings - zeit. Je - sus ist schö - ner,
O thou of God and Mar - y's son, thee will I cher - ish,
robed in the bloom - ing garb of spring. Je - sus is fair - er,
Bb7 Eb Cm7 Eb/Bb Bb7 Eb
dich will ich eh - ren, du mei - ner See - le Freud und Kron.
Je - sus ist rei - ner, der un - ser trau - rig Herz er - freut.
thee will I hon - or, thou, my soul's glo - ry, joy, and crown.
Je - sus is pur - er, who makes the woe - ful heart to sing.
8

3 Schön leucht die Sonne,
schöner leucht der Monde
und die Sternlein allzumal;
Jesus leucht schöner,
Jesus leucht reiner
als alle Eng'l im Himmelssaal.

3 *Fair is the sunshine,*
fairer still the moonlight,
and all the twinkling starry host.
Jesus shines brighter,
Jesus shines purer
than all the angels heav'n can boast.

Chord symbols represent a simplified harmony.

Text: German; stanzas 1, 3 *Gesangbuch* (present-day Germany), 1677; stanza 2 Heinrich A. H. von Fallersleben (Germany), *Schlesische Volkslieder*, 1842; trans. anon., *Church Chorals and Choir Studies* (USA), 1850, alt.
Music: *Schlesische Volkslieder*, 1842; harm. Richard S. Willis (USA), *Church Chorals and Choir Studies*, 1850

Je louerai l'Éternel (Praise, I Will Praise You, Lord) 131

JE LOUERAI L'ÉTERNEL 6.4.10.6.6.4.11.4

F C7 Dm B♭ C7 F
1 Je loue-rai l'É - ter - nel de tout mon coeur, je
1 Praise, I will praise you, Lord,
2 Love, I will love you, Lord, with all my heart. O
3 Serve, I will serve you, Lord,
B♭ C A/C♯ Dm Gm G Csus C
ra - con - te - rai tou - tes tes mer-veilles, je chan - te - rai ton nom.
God, I will tell the won-ders of your ways, and glo - ri - fy your name.
F C7 Dm B♭ C7 F
Je loue-rai l'É - ter - nel de tout mon coeur, je
Praise, I will praise you, Lord,
Love, I will love you, Lord, with all my heart. In
Serve, I will serve you, Lord,
B♭ C A/C♯ Dm Gm/B♭ C7 F
fe - rai de toi le su - jet de ma joie. Al - lé - lu - ia!
you I will find the source of all my joy. Al - le - lu - ia!

Spanish

A Dios alabaré de todo corazón
y proclamaré sus maravillas, su nombre cantaré.
A Dios alabaré de todo corazon;
tú eres la fuente, el gozo para mí. ¡Aleluya!

For capo chords, see the accompaniment edition.

Text: French; based on Psalm 9:1–2; Claude Frayssé (France); English trans. Kenneth I. Morse (USA), 1988, English trans. © 1989 *Hymnal: A Worship Book*; Spanish trans. Pedro Stucky (Colombia), alt., Spanish trans. © 2003 Mennonite World Conference
Music: Claude Frayssé; harm. Alain Bergése (France), 1976; acc. Marilyn Houser Hamm (Canada)

132 Flow to You

FLOW TO YOU Irregular

Verse
C/G G Dsus D Em
Flow to you, flow to you, let the ri-ver of my wor-
G/D C G Dsus
-ship flow to you. Lord, I pray, in all I do,
D Em G/D C2
let the ri-ver of my wor-ship flow to you. Like
Am7 G/B C2
streams in the val-ley swell with the rain, may the songs of my heart
Dsus D C2 Dsus Em7 Dsus
rise to bless your name and flow to you, flow to you; let my
Am7 Dsus 1 G C/G G C/G 2 G D/F♯
Fine (2nd time)
wor-ship flow to you. Flow to you,
Bridge Em Cmaj7 Dsus G D/F♯ Em
I love you, Lord, and ev-'ry-thing a-bout you. I wor-ship you
Cmaj7 D Am7 Dsus D7
D.C. (to verse)
with all my heart. Let all my heart flow to you,

Text: Lynn DeShazo (USA)
Music: Lynn DeShazo

My Jesus, I Love Thee 133

GORDON 11.11.11.11

Capo 3: (D) F (G/D) B♭/F (D) F (A7) C7 (D) F
1 My Jesus, I love thee, I know thou art mine.
2 I love thee, because thou hast first loved me,
3 In mansions of glory and endless delight
(G/D) B♭/F (D) F (A7) C7 (D) F
For thee all the follies of sin I resign.
and purchased my pardon on Calvary's tree.
I'll ever adore thee in heaven so bright.
(A7) C7 (D) F (Em/G) Gm/B♭ (Asus) Csus (A) C
My gracious Redeemer, my Savior art thou.
I love thee for wearing the thorns on thy brow.
I'll sing with the glittering crown on my brow.
(D) F (G/D) B♭/F (D) F (A7) C7 (D) F
If ever I loved thee, my Jesus, 'tis now.

Text: William R. Featherstone (Canada), ca. 1862, *Primitive Methodist Magazine*, 1862
Music: Adoniram J. Gordon (USA), 1872, *The Service of Song for Baptist Churches*, 1876

134 Bring Many Names

WESTCHASE 4.5.10.6.5.5.4

Capo 1: (D) (Em7) (G2)(G) (Em) (A2)(A7) (D)
E♭ Fm7 A♭2 A♭ Fm B♭2 B♭7 E♭
1 Bring man - y names, beau - ti - ful and good, cel - e -
2 Strong moth - er God, work - ing night and day, plan - ning
3 Warm fa - ther God, bless - ing ev - 'ry child, feel - ing
4 Old, ach - ing God, grey with end - less care, calm - ly
5 Young, grow-ing God, ea - ger, on the move, say - ing
6 Great, liv - ing God, nev - er ful - ly known, joy - ful
(Em7) (D/F♯) (Em) (Asus) (A7) (D) (Em7)
Fm7 E♭/G Fm B♭sus B♭7 E♭ Fm7
brate, in par - a - ble and sto - ry, hol - i - ness in
all the won - ders of cre - a - tion, set - ting each e -
all the strains of hu - man liv - ing, car - ing and for -
pierc - ing e - vil's new dis - guis - es, glad of good sur -
no to false-hood and un - kind - ness, cry - ing out for
dark - ness far be - yond our see - ing, clos - er yet than
(G2) (G) (Em) (A2) (A7) (D) (Em) (D)
A♭2 A♭ Fm B♭2 B♭7 E♭ Fm E♭
glo - ry, liv - ing, lov - ing God. Hail and Ho -
qua - tion gen - i - us at play: Hail and Ho -
giv - ing till we're rec - on - ciled: Hail and Ho -
pris - es, wis - er than de - spair: Hail and Ho -
jus - tice, giv - ing all you have: Hail and Ho -
breath - ing, ev - er - last - ing home: Hail and Ho -
(A) (G) 1–5 (D/F♯) (Em) (Asus)(A) 6 (D/F♯) (Em)(A) (D)
B♭ A♭ E♭/G Fm B♭sus B♭ E♭/G Fm B♭ E♭
san - na! Bring man - y names!
san - na, strong moth - er God!
san - na, warm fa - ther God!
san - na, old, ach - ing God!
san - na, young, grow - ing God!
san - na, great, liv - ing God!

Alleluia 135

KIEV ALLELUIA Irregular

B♭ Cm G Cm B♭ E♭ B♭
Al - le - lu - i - a, Al - le - lu - i - a,
F B♭ F B♭
Al - le - lu - i - a.

Text: Hebrew traditional; הַלְלוּ יָהּ (Hallelujah) (Mediterranean), ca. 4th c. BC, translit. Greek, ἀλληλούϊα (Alleluia) (Mediterranean), ca. 3rd c. BC
Music: Orthodox Liturgy (Ukraine), ca. 1900

Santo (Holy) 136

ARGENTINE SANTO 6.7.9.5

C G7 Am F G7 C
¡San - to, san - to, san-to, mi co - ra-zón te a - do - ra! Mi
Ho - ly, ho - ly, ho-ly, my heart, my heart a - dores you! My
F G7 C Am F G7 C
cor - a-zón te sa - be de-cir: san - to e-res, Se - ñor.
heart is glad to say the words: you are ho - ly, Lord.

Text: Spanish; variation on traditional liturgical text (Argentina)
Music: Argentine traditional; arr. Iona Community (Scotland), based on two-part version as taught by Pablo Sosa (Argentina),

137 Heilig, heilig, heilig (Holy, Holy, Holy)

SANCTUS (Schubert) 6.5.6.5 D

1–2 Hei - lig, hei - lig, hei - lig, hei - lig ist der Herr!
1–2 Ho - ly, ho - ly, ho - ly, ho - ly is the Lord!
Hei - lig, hei - lig, hei - lig, hei - lig ist nur er!
Ho - ly, ho - ly, hol - y, ho - ly God a - lone!
1 Er, der nie be - gon - nen, er, der im - mer war,
2 All-macht, Wun-der, Lie - be, al - les rings - um - her!
1 God, the un - cre - a - ted, God who al - ways was,
2 Might-y, won-drous, lov - ing, cir - cled round with awe;
e - wig ist und wal - tet, sein wird im - mer - dar.
Hei - lig, hei - lig, hei - lig, hei - lig ist der Herr!
end - less - ly ex - al - ted, reign for - ev - er - more.
ho - ly, ho - ly, ho - ly, ho - ly is the Lord.

Text: German; Johann P. Neumann (Austria), 1826; trans. John D. Rempel (Canada), alt.,
Music: Franz Schubert (Austria), *Gesänge zur Feier des heiligen Opfer der Messe*, 1826

Christ, We Do All Adore Thee 138

ADORE THEE Irregular

C Em F G F C/E Dm7 C
Christ, we do all a - dore thee, and we do praise thee for - ev - er.
G Am Em Dm C Gsus G
Christ, we do all a - dore thee, and we do praise thee for - ev - er,
Em Am Dm B♭ F C
for on the ho - ly cross hast thou the world from sin re -
G C Em F G F
deem - ed. Christ, we do all a - dore thee, and we do
C/E Dm C Am C
praise thee for - ev - er. Christ, we do all a - dore thee.

Text: "Adoramus te Christe" (present-day France), 9th c.; trans. Theodore Baker (USA), *The Seven Last Words of Christ*, 1899
Music: Theodore Dubois (France), *The Seven Last Words of Christ*, 1867

139 This Is the Air I Breathe (Eres mi respirar)

BREATHE Irregular

A D/A A D/A
This is the air I breathe, this is the air I breathe,
E - res mi res - pi-rar, e - res mi res - pi-rar.
A E/G♯ F♯m7 E D F♯m7 E
your ho - ly pres - ence liv-ing in me.
Dios, tu pre-sen - cia vi - ve en mi.
A D/A A D/A
This is my dai - ly bread, this is my dai - ly bread,
E - res mi pan, Se-ñor, e - res mi pan, Se-ñor.
A E/G♯ F♯m7 E D F♯m7 E
your ver - y word spo-ken to me.
Dios, tus pa - la - bras son pa - ra mi.
Refrain
A E/G♯ F♯m E D F♯m7
And I, I'm des-perate for you,
Y yo te͜ an-he - lo, Se - ñor,
Esus E A E/G♯ F♯m E D
And I, I'm lost with-out you.
es-toy per - di - do sin ti.

Text: Marie Barnett (USA); Spanish trans. Ingrid Rosario (USA)
Music: Marie Barnett

Out of the Depths I Cry to You 140

AUS TIEFER NOT (DE PROFUNDIS) 8.7.8.7.8.8.7

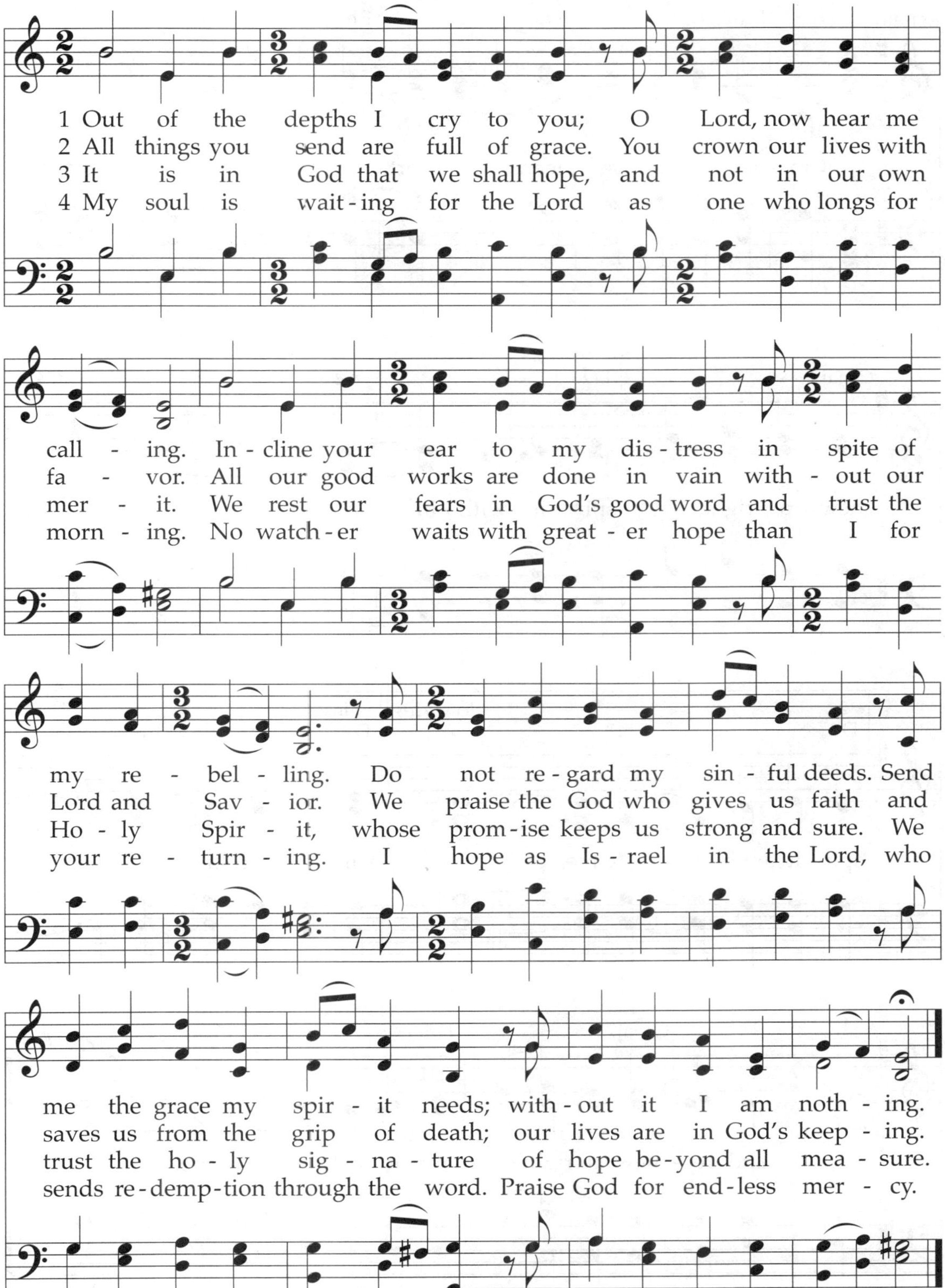
1 Out of the depths I cry to you; O Lord, now hear me
2 All things you send are full of grace. You crown our lives with
3 It is in God that we shall hope, and not in our own
4 My soul is wait-ing for the Lord as one who longs for
call - ing. In - cline your ear to my dis - tress in spite of
fa - vor. All our good works are done in vain with - out our
mer - it. We rest our fears in God's good word and trust the
morn - ing. No watch - er waits with great - er hope than I for
my re - bel - ling. Do not re - gard my sin - ful deeds. Send
Lord and Sav - ior. We praise the God who gives us faith and
Ho - ly Spir - it, whose prom - ise keeps us strong and sure. We
your re - turn - ing. I hope as Is - rael in the Lord, who
me the grace my spir - it needs; with - out it I am noth - ing.
saves us from the grip of death; our lives are in God's keep - ing.
trust the ho - ly sig - na - ture of hope be - yond all mea - sure.
sends re - demp - tion through the word. Praise God for end - less mer - cy.

Text: based on Psalm 130; Martin Luther (present-day Germany), ca. 1524, "Aus tiefer Not schrei ich zu dir," *Etlich Christlich Lieder*, 1524; trans. Gracia Grindal (USA), *Lutheran Book of Worship*, alt.,

Music: attr. Martin Luther, *Geystliche Gesangk Buchleyn* (present-day Germany), 1524; harm. *Hymnal: A Worship Book*,

141 Create in Me a Clean Heart

CLEAN HEART Irregular

Refrain
Em7 Am7 Em7
Cre - ate in me a clean heart, O God, and re -
Cmaj7
1 D2 A2 A2/F♯
new a right spir - it with - in me.
2 D2 Em7 To verses
spir - it with - in me,
Final D2 Em7
spir - it with - in me,
Cmaj7 D2 Em7 Fine
and re - new a right spir - it with - in me.

Text: based on Psalm 51:1–2; Andrew Kreider (USA)
Music: Andrew Kreider

Verses
Bm7
Solo or unison
Em7
1 Have mer - cy on me, O God,
2 I know that I have sinned.
3 You look for truth with - in me.
4 Re - store to me your joy.
Cmaj7
Bm7
B♭m7
ac - cord - ing to your stead - fast love.
For my trans - gres - sions are be - fore me.
Teach me your wis - dom in my heart.
Sus - tain in me a will - ing spir - it.
Am7
Cmaj7
G
Come wash me clean from my in - iq - ui - ty, and
F
Am7
C
D
E♭
To refrain
cleanse me from my sin, O God.

God, Grant Us Mercy 142

O PHARISEOS Irregular

Refrain
All
God, grant us mer - cy and for - give - ness.

Leader:

1 O God, you condemn the ones who boast of great deeds. *Refrain*
2 O God, your grace flows to all who humbly seek you. *Refrain*
3 For you disdain our haughty minds, our empty, prideful thoughts. *Refrain*
4 We fall before you, you who suffered in humility. *Refrain*

Text: Greek; Kassia (Greece), "Τοῦ Τελώνου καὶ τοῦ Φαρισαίου," 8th c.; trans. Katie Graber (USA), © 2019
Music: Kassia; adapt. Katie Graber (USA) © 2019, transcr. source Diane Touliatos (USA), © 1996 Hildegard Publishing Company
transcr. and adapt. © 2019 Katie Graber

143 Come Now, O God

LOST IN THE NIGHT 11.11.11 with refrain

Bm G A7 D
1 Come now, O God, when our love is for - sak - en;
2 Come when we squand - er the free - dom you gave us;
3 Come, lead us out of our self - serv - ing mad - ness;
A D Em7 D
come when our bed - rock of faith has been shak - en;
come, break the sys - tems of sin that en - slave us;
come, while the world is still shroud - ed in sad - ness;
Bm G A7 D
come when our deep - est of hopes are mis - tak - en:
come, though we won - der if you can still save us:
come, turn the tears of our mourn - ing to glad - ness:
Em7 F♯ F♯7 Bm
come, Em - man - u - el. Come, Em - man - u - el.

Text: David Bjorlin (USA),
Music: Finnish traditional

God, Give Me Time 144

SEACHRIST CMD

Dm G Dm G B♭
1 God, give me time to learn the words I find so
2 God, give me time to deal with words that threat - en
3 God, give me time to meet your Word, trans - form - ing
Am7 Dm G Dm G
hard to say: the lov - ing words, for - giv - ing words that
and de - stroy: the eas - y words of pol - i - tics that
as I go my lit - tle world, my larg - er world, by
B♭ A7 D D7 Gm C7 Am
take the sting a - way. God, give me calm to ride the
kill cre - a - tion's joy; the speech - es that pro - lif - er -
all I do and know; en - count - er - ing in oth - ers'
Dm Gm F E7 A7 Dm
storm when waves of an - ger rise, a mo - ment
ate e - con - o - mies of greed; the thieves of
faith the wis - dom and the grace that Je - sus
G Dm G B♭ Am7 Dm
when I grasp a truth my less - er self de - nies.
chil - dren's her - i - tage, the poi - son in the seed.
Christ was born to bring, and gave a hu - man face.

Chord symbols do not correspond with the keyboard harmony.

Text: Shirley Erena Murray (Aotearoa New Zealand), © 2005 Hope Publishing Co.
Music: John D. Horman (USA), © 2003 Zimbel Press

145 Touch the Earth Lightly

AI HU 5.5.10 D

F C/E Dm Am
1 Touch the earth light - ly, use the earth gen - tly,
2 We who en - dan - ger, who cre - ate hun - ger,
3 Let there be green - ing, birth from the burn - ing,
4 God of all liv - ing, God of all lov - ing,
B♭ C/B♭ F/A Gm9 C7
nour - ish the life of the world in our care:
a - gents of death for all crea - tures that live,
wa - ter that bless - es, and air that is sweet,
God of the seed - ling, the snow, and the sun,
F C/E Dm Am
gift of great won - der, ours to sur - ren - der,
we who still fos - ter clouds of dis - as - ter,
health in God's gar - den, hope in God's chil - dren,
teach us, de - flect us, Christ re - con - nect us,
B♭ C/B♭ F/A B♭/C F
trust for the chil - dren to - mor - row will bear.
God of our plan - et, fore - stall and for - give!
re - gen - er - a - tion that peace will com - plete.
us - ing us gen - tly and mak - ing us one.

Text: Shirley Erena Murray (Aotearoa New Zealand),
Music: Swee Hong Lim (Canada); arr. Tamryn Parker-Carver (USA),

Lord Jesus, Come and Overturn 146

ERHALT UNS, HERR LM

Em C G C D Em D
1 Lord Je - sus, come and o - ver - turn the pow - ers
2 You turn the ta - bles on our greed and set a
3 You cast a - side our vain de - sires and of - fer
4 Lord Je - sus, come and live in us and let your
G Am B Em C D
that cor - rupt and bind. Trans - form our tem - ples
diff' - rent kind of feast: where mer - cy an - swers
us a no - bler goal: the jus - tice that your
bless - ed truth re - sound in ev' - ry tem - ple,
Am G C Em B Em
with your love and claim our con - science with your mind.
ev - 'ry need and great ones hum - bly serve the least.
love re - quires and dig - ni - ty for ev' - ry soul.
heart, and home where char - i - ty and love are found.

Text: David Gambrell (USA), 2003, © 2015 GIA Publications, Inc.
Music: Klug's *Geistliche Lieder* (present-day Germany), 1543

147 Kyrie eleison

ORTHODOX KYRIE Irregular

E B7
Ky - ri - e e - lei - son.* Ky - ri - e e - lei - son.
E A E/B B7 E
Ky - ri - e e - lei - - - son.

*Translation: Lord, have mercy.

Text: from Greek liturgy Κύριε, ἐλέησον (Kyrie eleison) (Eastern Mediterranean), 4th c.
Music: Russian Orthodox liturgy, ca. 19th c.

148 In Words of Truth

LE CÉNACLE 11.10.11.10

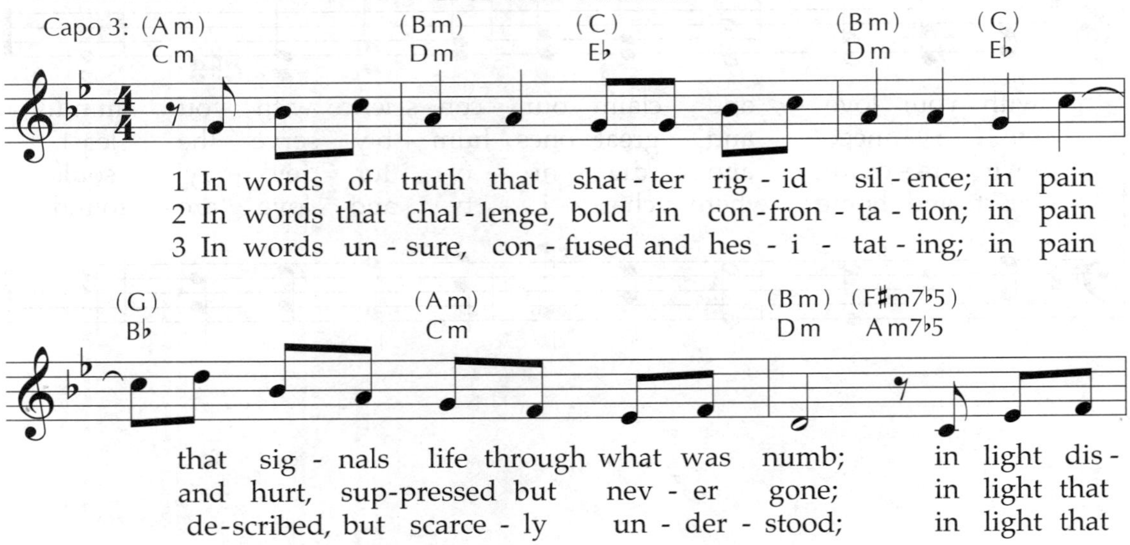
Capo 3: (Am) Cm (Bm) Dm (C) E♭ (Bm) Dm (C) E♭
1 In words of truth that shat - ter rig - id sil - ence; in pain
2 In words that chal - lenge, bold in con - fron - ta - tion; in pain
3 In words un - sure, con - fused and hes - i - tat - ing; in pain
(G) B♭ (Am) Cm (Bm) Dm (F♯m7♭5) Am7♭5
that sig - nals life through what was numb; in light dis -
and hurt, sup-pressed but nev - er gone; in light that
de-scribed, but scarce - ly un - der - stood; in light that

Chord symbols represent a simplified harmony and do not correspond to the keyboard accompaniment.

Text: Adam M. L. Tice (USA),
Music: Joseph Gelineau (France), ca. 20th c.,

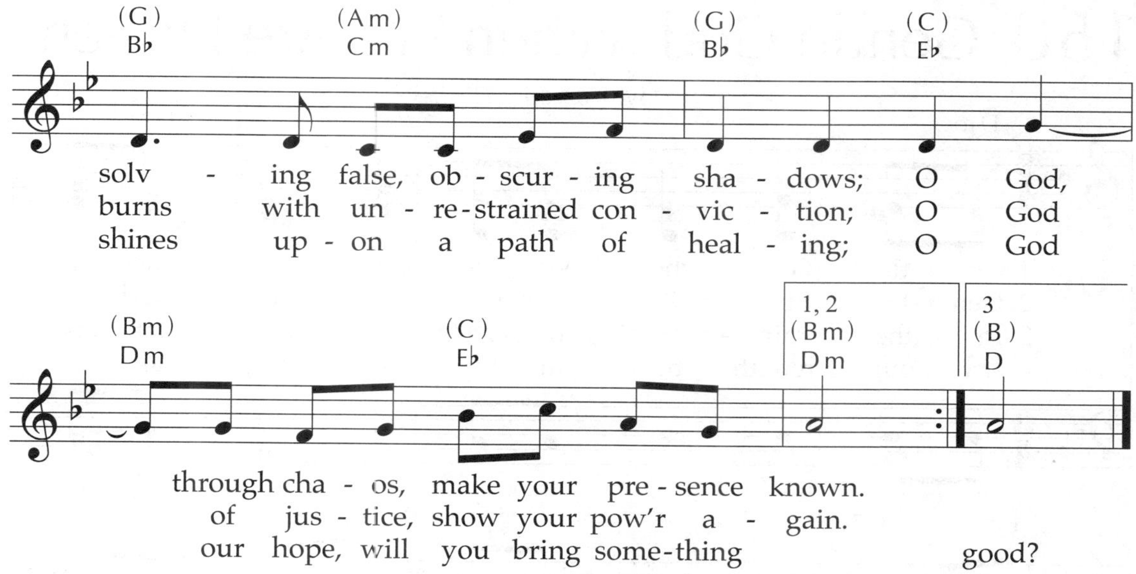
(G) Bb (Am) Cm (G) Bb (C) Eb
solv - ing false, ob - scur - ing sha - dows; O God,
burns with un - re-strained con - vic - tion; O God
shines up - on a path of heal - ing; O God
(Bm) Dm (C) Eb 1, 2 (Bm) Dm 3 (B) D
through cha - os, make your pre - sence known.
of jus - tice, show your pow'r a - gain.
our hope, will you bring some-thing good?

Forgive, Forgive Us, Holy God 149

ROUGH SEAS LM

Capo 1: (Bm) Cm (D) Eb (A/C♯) Bb/D (Bm) Cm
1 For - give, for - give us, ho - ly God! Your
2 For - give us that our souls are numb to
3 For - give the minds no long - er shocked by
4 For - give us that our house - hold gods are
5 Give us this day the bread of peace, the
(G) Ab (Bm) Cm (Em/G) Fm/Ab (F♯) G (Bm) Cm
chil - dren call on you to hear! Our blood is on each
scenes of ter - ror, screams of pain; that while we pray "Your
home - less poor, by lives a - bused; for - give us that the
self and safe - ty, pri - vate need; for - give us all our
hands to share a com - mon good, the hearts to ache for
(D) Eb (A) Bb (Em7) Fm7 (D/F♯) Eb/G (G) Ab (F♯) G (Bm) Cm
oth - er's hands, we die from hun - ger, lies and fear.
king - dom come," our world is still a bat - tle plain.
earth is stacked with weap - ons wait - ing to be used.
fit - ful prayers, the to - ken gift, the to - ken deed.
jus - tice's sake, the will to stand where Je - sus stood.

150 Gentle God, When We Are Driven

TAWA 8.7.8.7.7.7

Dm A Dm
1 Gen - tle God, when we are driv - en past the
2 Gen - tle Spir - it, when our rea - son clouds in
3 In the mir - ror of earth's mad - ness let us
4 Let our strength be in for - giv - ing as for -
F C7 F Am
lim - its of our love, when our hurt would have a
an - ger, twists in fear, when we strike in - stead of
see our rav - aged face, in the tur - moil of all
giv - en we must be, one to one in cost - ly
Dm Gm E7 A D
weap - on and the hawk de - stroy the dove, at the
sooth - ing, when we bruise and sting and smear, cool our
peo - ple let com - pas - sion find a place, touch our
lov - ing, find - ing trust and grow - ing free, gen - tle
Gm C7 F Gm A Dm
cost of seem - ing weak, help us turn the oth - er cheek.
burn - ing, take our pain, bring us to our - selves a - gain.
hearts to make a - mends, see our en - e - mies as friends.
God, be our re - lease, gen - tle Spir - it, teach us peace.

Text: Shirley Erena Murray (Aotearoa New Zealand)
Music: Jillian Bray (Aotearoa New Zealand)

Lamb of God / Cordero de Dios 151

LAMB OF GOD Irregular

Canon 1
Am Esus Em F Csus C
Lamb of God, Lamb of God,
Cor - de - ro de Dios, Cor - de - ro de Dios,
Dm Am Dm/B E Am
you take a - way the sin of the world.
que qui - tas el pe - ca - do del mun - do,
2
Esus Em F Csus C
Have mer - cy, have mer - cy,
ten pie - dad, ten pie - dad,
Dm Am Dm/B E Am
have mer - cy up - on us.
ten pie - dad de no - so - tros. Cor -

Either language may be sung alone, or the two may be sung in combination.

Text: from Latin liturgy, "Agnus Dei" (Rome), ca. 7th c., based on John 1:29; trans. anon.
Music: James E. Clemens (USA), © 2008 James E. Clemens

152 God, Whose Purpose Is to Kindle

BAPTISM BY FIRE 8.7.8.7 D

Capo 3: (Bm) Dm (Em) Gm (Bm) Dm (Em) Gm (Bm) Dm
1 God, whose pur - pose is to kin - dle, now ig - nite us
2 God, who still a sword de - liv - ers ra - ther than a
3 God, who in your ho - ly gos - pel wills that all should
(F♯m) Am (Bm) Dm (Em) Gm (Bm) Dm (Em) Gm
with your fire. While the earth a - waits your burn - ing, with your
pla - cid peace, with your sharp-ened word dis - turb us, from com -
tru - ly live, make us sense our share of fail - ure, our tran -
(Bm) Dm (F♯m) Am (Bm) Dm (D) F (Bm) Dm (G) B♭ (Bm) Dm
pas - sion us in - spire. O - ver - come our sin - ful calm - ness,
pla - cen - cy re - lease! Save us now from sat - is - fac - tion,
quil - i - ty for - give. Teach us cour - age as we strug - gle
(Em) Gm (Bm) Dm (A) C (G) B♭ (D) F
stir us with your sav - ing name. Bap - tize with your
when we pri - vate - ly are free, yet are un - dis -
in all lib - er - a - ting strife. Lift the small - ness

Chords symbols correspond to keyboard accompaniment and are intended for unison singing only.

Text: D. Elton Trueblood (USA), *The Incendiary Fellowship*, 1967, alt., © 1967 David Elton Trueblood
Music: Esther Wiebe (Canada), © 1968 Esther Wiebe

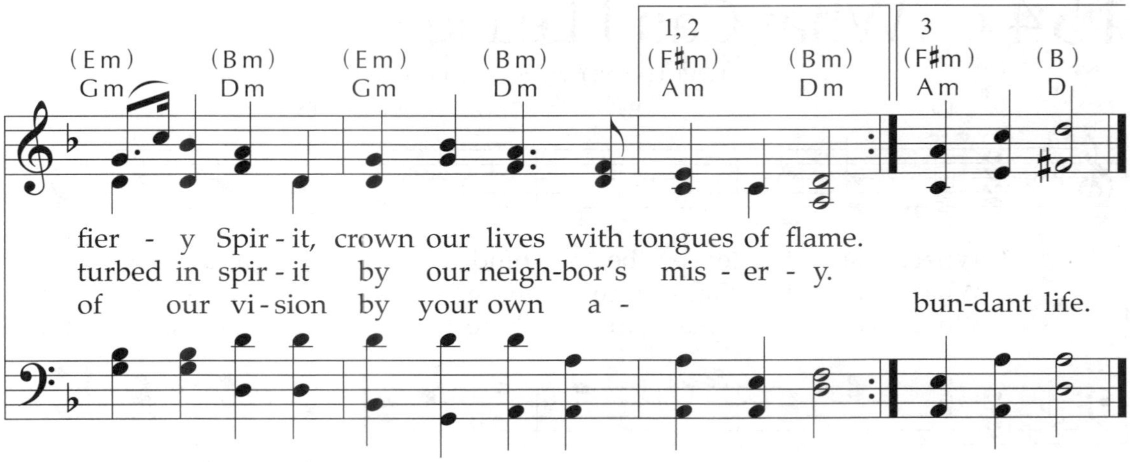
1, 2
3
(Em) (Bm) (Em) (Bm) (F♯m) (Bm) (F♯m) (B)
Gm Dm Gm Dm Am Dm Am D
fier - y Spir - it, crown our lives with tongues of flame.
turbed in spir - it by our neigh-bor's mis - er - y.
of our vi - sion by your own a - bun-dant life.

Perdón, Señor

153

CONFESIÓN 4.7.4.7.4

Refrain
All
B♭ C Dm
Fine
Leader
Fmaj7/C
All
Per - dón, Se - ñor.
1 Por tan - tas in - jus - ti - cias:
2 Por to - das nues-tras fal - tas:
3 En tu mi - se - ri - cor - dia:
1 For griev-ance and in - jus - tice,
2 For weak-ness and trans - gres-sion,
3 In your e - ter - nal mer - cy,
per -
B♭ C Dm
Leader
Gm/B♭
Dm/A
All
B♭ C Dm
To refrain
dón, Se - ñor,
por tan-ta in-di - fe - ren - cia:
por nues-tra re - bel - dí - a:
en tu di - vi - na gra - cia:
a - loof-ness and in - dif-f'rence,
re - sist-ance and re - bel - lion,
in your sus-tain-ing grace,
per - dón, Se - ñor.

Text: Spanish; Jorge Lockward (USA); trans. Raquel Mora Martínez (USA)
Music: Jorge Lockward

154 What Can I Leave Behind

LOVE UNKNOWN 6.6.6.6.4.4.8

Eb Bb7 Cm7 Bb/D Eb Gm
1 What can I leave be - hind, what old and wea - ry
2 What can I claim once more? Can life re - turn from
3 What can I take to share a neigh-bor's crush - ing
Ab Fm Gm Cm Fsus F
ways that weigh up - on my mind and strain my song of
loss? What fu - ture lies in store if I take up my
load? What burd - ens can we bear to - geth - er on the
Bb Eb Db Fm Db Ab Ab/C
praise? God, grant re - lease from bind - ing pain
cross? My burd - en raised, Christ bears it, too.
road? We walk and pray with Christ our guide,
Eb Eb/G Gm/Bb Bb7 Eb
and let me gain your hope and peace.
In all I do, may God be praised.
who, by our side, will show the way.

For capo chords, see #320.

Text: Adam M. L. Tice (USA),
Music: John N. Ireland (England), *Songs of Praise*, 1925

Lord, I Need You 155

TEACH MY SONG Irregular

Verse
E A2 E B/D♯ C♯m7 B sus
1 Lord, I come, I con - fess. Bow-ing here, I find my
(2 Where sin runs) deep, your grace is more. Where grace is found is where you
A2 E A2 E B sus
rest. And with - out you, I fall a - part. You're the one
are. And where you are, Lord, I am free. Ho - li - ness
B A2
that guides my heart.
is Christ in me.
Refrain
E A E B/D♯
Lord, I need you, oh, I need you.
C♯m7 A E B E/G♯ A E/B A/C♯
Ev' - ry hour I need you. My one de-fense, my right-eous-ness; O
E/B B E
God, how I need you.
1 A2 Fine
2 Where sin runs
2 E
So,
Bridge
A E/G♯ B sus C♯m7 A B
teach my song to rise to you when temp-ta-tion comes my
A2 A E/G♯ B sus C♯m7
way. And when I can-not stand, I'll fall on you.
A2 B sus E A E/G♯
Je-sus, you're my hope and stay. And when I can-not stand, I'll
B sus C♯m7 A2 B sus E A/E
fall on you. Je-sus, you're my hope and stay. Lord, I
To refrain

Text: Jesse Reeves (USA), Kristian Stanfill (USA), Matt Maher (Canada), Christy Nockels (USA), and Daniel Carson (USA)
Music: Jesse Reeves, Kristian Stanfill, Matt Maher, Christy Nockels, and Daniel Carson

156 There's a Wideness in God's Mercy

WELLESLEY 8.7.8.7

1 There's a wide - ness in God's mer - cy like the
2 There is wel - come for the sin - ner, and more
3 But we make God's love too nar - row by false
4 For the love of God is broad - er than the
5 If our love were but more sim - ple, we should
wide - ness of the sea. There's a kind - ness
grac - es for the good. There is mer - cy
lim - its of our own, and we mag - ni -
mea - sures of the mind, and the heart of
rest up - on God's word, and our lives would
in God's jus - tice, which is more than lib - er - ty.
with the Sav - ior, there is heal - ing in his blood.
fy its strict - ness with a zeal God will not own.
the E - ter - nal is most won - der - ful - ly kind.
be il - lu - mined by the pres - ence of our Lord.

Chord symbols represent a simplified harmony.

Text: Frederick W. Faber (England), *Hymns*, 1861
Music: Lizzie S. Tourjee (USA), *Hymnal of the Methodist Church with Tunes*, 1878

Come to Me, O Weary Traveler 157

FROM THE DEPTHS 8.7.8.7

Em B7 Em
1 Come to me, O wea - ry trav - 'ler;
2 Do not fear, my yoke is eas - y;
3 Take my yoke and leave your trou - bles;
4 Rest in me, O wea - ry trav - 'ler;
B7 Em
come to me with your dis - tress;
do not fear, my bur - den's light;
take my yoke and come with me.
rest in me and do not fear.
E Am D G
optional descant
come to me, you heav - y bur - dened;
do not fear the path be - fore you;
take my yoke, I am be - side you;
Rest in me, my heart is gen - tle;
B7 Em B7 1 Em 2 Em
come to me and find your rest; rest.
do not run from me in fright; fright.
take and learn hu - mil - i - ty; ty.
rest and cast a - way your care. care.

Text: Sylvia G. Dunstan (Canada), © 1991 GIA Publications, Inc.
Music: Russian traditional; harm. Harris J. Loewen (Canada), © 1988 Harris J. Loewen; adapt. and desc. Paul Dueck (Canada), © 2020 Paul Dueck

158 Gott ist die Liebe (I Know God Loves Me)

GOTT IST DIE LIEBE 10.9 with refrain

D G D
1 Gott ist die Lie - be, lässt mich er - lö - sen. Gott ist die
2 Ich lag in Band - en der schnö-den Sün - de, ich lag in
1 I know God loves me with love un - end - ing. I know God
2 Though sin sur-rounds me, God's love is strong - er. Though sin sur -
A D Refrain A
Lie - be, er liebt auch mich.
Band - en und konnt nicht los.
loves me, for God is love.
rounds me, God loves me still.
Drum sag ich noch ein - mal: Gott
And so I sing a - gain of
D A D
ist die Lie - be, Gott ist die Lie - be, er liebt auch mich.
how God loves me; I know God loves me, for God is love.

3 Er sandte Jesum,
den treuen Heiland,
er sandte Jesum
und macht mich los. *Refrain*

4 Jesus, mein Heiland,
gab sich zum Opfer,
Jesus, mein Heiland,
büßt meine Schuld. *Refrain*

3 *God sent us Jesus,*
our faithful savior;
God sent us Jesus
to set us free. Refrain

4 *My savior Jesus,*
you know my sorrow;
my savior Jesus,
you give new life. Refrain

Text: German; August Rische (Germany), 1852; trans. Mennonite Worship and Song Committee, 2019
Music: Thüringer traditional (Germany), ca. 1840

Kwake Yesu nasimama (Here on Christ the Rock I Will Stand) 159

KWAKE YESU NASIMAMA Irregular

G C G
Refrain: Kwa - ke Ye - su na - si - ma - ma, ndi - ye
1 Cha ku - tu - ma - i - ni si - na, i - la
2 Nji - a yan - gu i - we nde - fu, ye - ye
3 Ni - ki - i - twa hu - ku - mu - ni, ro - ho -
Refrain: Here on Christ the rock I will stand, oth - er
1 Je - sus knows the trou - bles I face; in his
2 Je - sus gives me strength when I'm weak; he's the
3 When the judg - ment comes I will be in Christ's
D G C
mwam - ba ni sa - la - ma. ndi - ye mwam - ba ni
da - mu ya - ke Ye - su si - na we - ma wa
hu - ni - pa wo - ko - vu ma - wim - bi ya - kin -
ni ni - na a - ma - ni Ni - ki - vi - kwa ha -
ground is sink - ing sand. Yes, on Christ the rock
blood flow mer - cy and grace. What he gives, I can -
sat - is - fac - tion I seek. He's my shield when trou -
pres - ence, fear - less and free, where the courts are ring -
G D G
sa - la - ma, ndi - ye mwam - ba ni sa - la - ma.
ku - to - sha, Dham - bi za - ngu ku - zi - o - zha.
- i - pi - ga, Ngu - vu za - ke ndi - zo na - nga.
- ki ya - ke, Si - na ho - fu mbe - le za - ke.
I will stand, oth - er ground is sink - ing sand.
- not re - pay, all my sin he wash - es a - way.
- bles draw near. He's my com - fort through ev - 'ry fear.
- ing with praise, crowned with right - eous - ness all my days.

Text: Swahili; anon. (Kenya), 20th c., adapt. from Edward Mote (England), "My Hope Is Built on Nothing Less," 1834; English adapt. from Swahili by Mennonite Worship and Song Committee, 2019
Music: Kenyan traditional

160 What a Fellowship / Leaning on the Everlasting Arms

SHOWALTER 10.9.10.9 with refrain

Capo 1: (G) A♭ (Am) B♭m (C) D♭ (G) A♭
1 What a fel-low-ship, what a joy di-vine, lean-ing on the ev-er-
2 Oh, how sweet to walk in this pil-grim way, lean-ing on the ev-er-
3 What have I to dread, what have I to fear, lean-ing on the ev-er-
(D) E♭ (G) A♭ (Am) B♭m (C) D♭
last-ing arms; what a bless-ed-ness, what a peace is mine,
last-ing arms. Oh, how bright the path grows from day to day,
last-ing arms? I have bless-ed peace with my Lord so near,
(G/D) A♭/E♭ (D7) E♭7 (G) A♭
Refrain
lean-ing on the ev-er-last-ing arms. Lean-ing,
lean-ing on the ev-er-last-ing arms.
lean-ing on the ev-er-last-ing arms.
Lean-ing on Je-sus,
(C) D♭ (G) A♭ (D) E♭ (G) A♭ (D) E♭ (G) A♭
lean-ing, safe and se-cure from all a-larms; lean-
lean-ing on Je-sus, lean-ing on

Text: Elisha A. Hoffman (USA), 1887
Music: Anthony J. Showalter (USA), 1887

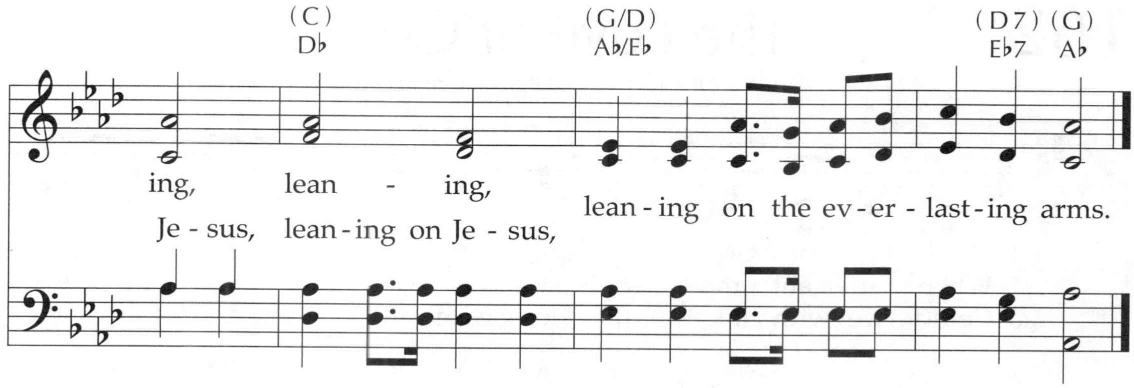
(C)
D♭
(G/D)
A♭/E♭
(D7) (G)
E♭7 A♭
ing, lean - ing,
Je - sus, lean-ing on Je - sus,
lean-ing on the ev-er-last-ing arms.

I Sought the Lord 161

FAITH 10.10.10.6

1 I sought the Lord, and af-ter-ward I knew he moved my soul to seek him, seek-ing me. It was not I that found, O Sav-ior true, no, I was found of thee.
2 Thou didst reach forth thy hand and mine en-fold, I walked and sank not on the storm-vexed sea. 'Twas not so much that I on thee took hold as thou, dear Lord, on me.
3 I find, I walk, I love, but, oh, the whole of love is but my an-swer, Lord, to thee! For thou wert long be-fore-hand with my soul, al-ways thou lov-edst me.

Text: *Holy Songs, Carols, and Sacred Ballads* (USA), 1880
Music: J. Harold Moyer (USA), 1965, *The Mennonite Hymnal*,

162 The Love of God

LOVE OF GOD 8.8.8.8.8.6.8.6 with refrain

D
1 The love of God is great - er far than tongue or
2 When an - cient time shall pass a - way, and hu - man
3 Could we with ink the o - cean fill, and were the
A D
pen can ev - er tell; it goes be - yond the high - est
thrones and king - doms fall; when those who here re - fuse to
skies of parch - ment made; were ev - 'ry stalk on earth a
A D
star, and reach - es to the low - est hell. The wan-d'ring
pray on rocks and hills and moun - tains call; God's love so
quill, and ev - 'ry - one a scribe by trade; to write the
G D A D
child is rec - on - ciled by God's be - lov - ed Son. The ach - ing
sure, shall still en - dure, all meas - ure - less and strong; grace will re -
love of God a - bove would drain the o - cean dry; nor could the

Text: F. M. Lehman (USA), ca. 1917, stanza 3 adapt. from Rabbi Meir (present-day Germany), "Haddamut," ca. 1050, and Qur'an 31:27, alt.
Music: F. M. Lehman, ca. 1917; arr. Claudia Lehman Mays (USA), alt.

G D A D
soul a - gain made whole, and price - less par - don won.
sound the whole earth round— the saints' and an - gels' song.
scroll con - tain the whole, though stretched from sky to sky.
Refrain
G D A D
O love of God, how rich and pure! How meas - ure - less and strong!
G D A7 D
It shall for - ev - er - more en - dure— the saints' and an - gels' song.

163 Amazing Grace!

NEW BRITAIN CM

G D Em G
1 A - maz - ing grace! how sweet the sound, that
2 'Twas grace that taught my heart to fear, and
3 Through man - y dan - gers, toils, and snares I
4 When we've been there ten thou - sand years, bright
A7 D7 G G7
saved a wretch like me! I once was lost, but
grace my fears re - lieved. How pre - cious did that
have al - read - y come. 'Tis grace has brought me
shin - ing as the sun, we've no less days to
C G Em G/D D7 G
now am found; was blind, but now I see.
grace ap - pear the hour I first be - lieved.
safe thus far, and grace will lead me home.
sing God's praise than when we'd first be - gun.

Text: stanzas 1–3 John Newton (England), *Olney Hymns*, 1779; stanza 4 *A Collection of Sacred Ballads* (USA), 1790, alt.
Music: American traditional (USA), *Columbian Harmony*, 1829; adapt. and harm. Edwin O. Excell (USA), 1900

Beloved, God's Chosen 164

ST. CATHERINE'S COURT 12.11.12.11

D♭ G♭ D♭
1 Be - lov - ed, God's cho - sen, put on as a gar-ment
2 With - in, call forth Wis-dom, to dwell in you rich - ly;
3 Be - lov - ed, God's cho - sen, put on as a gar-ment
B♭m D♭ E♭ A♭
com - pas - sion, for - give - ness, and good-ness of heart.
let peace rule your hearts, and that peace be of Christ.
com - pas - sion, for - give - ness, and good-ness of heart.
D♭ F B♭m
A - bove all, be - fore all, let love be your rai-ment
And from the heart's cham-ber, be - lov - ed and ho - ly,
A - bove all, be - fore all, let love be your rai-ment
D♭/A♭ D♭ A♭ D
that binds in - to one ev - 'ry dis - so - nant part.
let sing - ing thanks - giv - ing to God ev - er rise.
that binds in - to one ev - 'ry dis - so - nant part.

Chord symbols represent a simplified harmony. For a lower key and capo chords, see the accompaniment edition.

Text: based on Colossians 3:12–15; Susan Palo Cherwien (USA),
Music: Richard Strutt (England), *Jubilee Hymnbook*, 1925

165 Zisuh nih a zultu hna sinah (Peace Be with You! Jesus Told His Friends)

JEHOVAH JIREH 9.8.12.9.8.12 with refrain

E
1 Zi - suh nih a zul - tu hna si - nah deih-nak hna -
2 A - bra - ham ni Pa-thian bia-kam bang I - saac rai -
1 "Peace be with you!" Je - sus told his friends, giv - ing them
2 A - bra - ham took I - saac up a hill, fear - ing what
A E
ngam - nak kan pek hna lung rei - thei le van - sang au in
thawi - nak tuah tik - ah Je - ho - vah Ji - reh a si - nak
com - fort in their fear. "Do not be a - fraid!" he tells his
God would have him do. Why would God de - mand that he per -
C♯m B E
um ti hlah uh. Pa-thian fa - pa Zi - suh zum u
a langh-ter i, tuu - fa no - te rai - thawi - nak ca -
peo - ple to - day. Fol - low Je - sus as your friend and
form such a deed? Could he trust his con - science to de -
A E
law nan herh - mi vial - te an pek lai.
ah a sun - par - nak a langh - ter bang
guide; fol - low him on the nar - row way.
cide? Then he saw God would meet his need.
B7 E
Kan nun - nak ah khua khang - tu Je - ho - vah Ji - reh.
kan - nun - nak ah khua khang - tu Je - ho - vah Ji - reh.
We have all we need be - cause our God will pro - vide.
We can do God's will be - cause our God will pro - vide.

Text: Chin; based on John 20:19–21 and Genesis 22:1–14, attr. Evan Rohmingliana (Myanmar); trans. Mennonite Worship and Song Committee, 2018

Music: attr. Evan Rohmingliana; as taught by members of Chin Emmanuel Baptist Church, Houston, Texas, 2017

Refrain
Je - ho - vah Sha - mak kan sin a um. Je - ho - vah Sha -
Ho - ly light is shin - ing in our hearts. Ho - ly peace is
lom kan hna - ngam - nak. Je - ho - vah Ji - reh nih khua a
flow - ing in our breath. God has prom - ised us the things we
khan. Je - ho - vah Sha - bot in kan tei cang.
need, giv - ing us the vic - t'ry o - ver death.
Hal - le - lu - jah a min lian - ngan chin ko seh.
Hal - le - lu - jah, all praise and glo - ry to God.

Your Love Is Washing Over Me 166

I WON'T BE FRIGHTENED ANYMORE Irregular

Your love is wash - ing o - ver me, your love
is wash-ing o - ver me. Your love is wash-ing
o - ver me, and I won't be fright - ened an - y more.

Your mercy's washing . . .
Your peace is washing . . .
Your joy is washing . . .
Your grace is washing . . .
Your hope is washing . . .

Additional stanzas may be improvised.

Text: Jaylene Johnson (Canada), 2015
Music: Jaylene Johnson, 2015

167 Your Grace Is Enough

GREAT IS YOUR FAITHFULNESS Irregular

1 Great is your faith - ful - ness, O God.
2 Great is your love and jus - tice, God.
You wres - tle with the sin - ner's rest - less heart.
You use the weak to lead the strong.
You lead us by still wa - ters in - to mer - cy,
You lead us in the song of your sal - va - tion,
and noth - ing can keep us a - part.
and all your peo - ple sing a - long.
So re - mem - ber your peo - ple, re - mem - ber your
chil - dren, re - mem - ber your prom - ise, O God.
Refrain
Your grace is e-nough, your grace is e-nough,
your grace is e-nough for me.

Text: Matt Maher (Canada)
Music: Matt Maher

G D Em7
Your grace is e-nough, your grace is e-nough,
C2 G D C2 1
your grace is e-nough for me.
2 G D
Your grace is e-nough, heav - en reach-
grace is e-nough, I'm cov -
Em7 C2 G
- es out to us. Your grace is e-nough
- ered in your love. Your grace is e-nough
D 1 C2
for me. God, I sing, your
for me,
2 C2 G
for me.

168 Peace to You

LOCKLEY 6.5.6.5 D

1 Peace to you, my loved ones; peace to you, my friends.
2 Peace con-founds the wealth - y; peace lifts up the poor.
3 Peace is grace in ac - tion; peace is love in deeds.
Peace that Je - sus prom-ised; peace that nev - er ends.
Peace dis-rupts the might - y; peace is heav - en's door.
Peace be-comes a gar - den; peace springs up from seeds.
Peace to those who curse us; peace to those we fear.
Peace comes from the Spir - it; peace comes like a breath.
Peace to all God's crea - tures; peace to land and sea.
Peace to far - off na - tions; peace to neigh - bors here.
Peace re - veals a new world; peace does not fear death.
Peace that fills the cos - mos; peace that sets us free.

Text: Adam M. L. Tice (USA), 2017
Music: Sally Ann Morris (USA), 2017

Mercy, Mercy, Lord 169

MERCY MERCY Irregular

Mer - cy, mer-cy, Lord, your mer-cy is how
we are re-stored; mer - cy,
mer-cy, Lord, help us to show your
mer-cy, Lord.
Last time
1 You have been pa - tient with our of-fens - es,
2 Lord, you have taught us, "Love one an-oth - er,"
you have for-giv - en all of our sins;
as you have loved us, so we must love;
we were de-serv - ing on-ly your judg - ment,
al-ways for-bear - ing, al-ways for-giv - ing,
but your great mer - cy tri-umphed a - gain.
show-ing to oth - ers the mer - cy we've known.

Text: Lynn DeShazo (USA) and Gary Sadler (USA)
Music: Lynn DeShazo and Gary Sadler

170 Wonderful Grace of Jesus

WONDERFUL GRACE 7.6.7.6.7.6.12 with refrain

1 Won-der-ful grace of Je-sus, great-er than all my sin:
2 Won-der-ful grace of Je-sus, reach-ing to all the lost,
3 Won-der-ful grace of Je-sus, reach-ing the most re-viled,
how shall my tongue de-scribe it, where shall its praise be-gin?
by it I have been par-doned, saved to the ut-ter-most.
by its trans-form-ing pow-er mak-ing me God's dear child,
Tak-ing a-way my bur-den, set-ting my spir-it free,
Chains have been torn a-sun-der, giv-ing me lib-er-ty,
pur-chas-ing peace and heav-en for all e-ter-ni-ty,
for the won-der-ful grace of Je-sus reach-es me.
Refrain
the match-less grace of Je-sus,
Won-der-ful the match-less grace of Je-sus, deep-er

Text: Haldor Lillenas (USA), *Northfield Hymnal No. 3*, 1918
Music: Haldor Lillenas, *Northfield Hymnal No. 3*, 1918

the roll - ing sea, won -
than the might - y roll - ing sea, high - er than the
der - ful grace, all - suf - fi - cient for
moun - tain, spar - kling like a foun - tain, all - suf - fi - cient grace for e - ven
me, for e - ven me; broad - er than the scope of my trans -
me; trans -
gres - sions, great - er far than all my sin and shame.
gres - sions, sing it! my sin and shame.
O mag - ni - fy the pre - cious name of Je - sus, praise his name!

171 Nothing Can Separate Us

BOUND 4.4.7.5

N.C. Asus A Dm Csus C
Noth - ing, noth - ing, noth - ing, noth - ing,
F B♭ Gm7 Asus
us
noth - ing can sep - a - rate us
A B♭maj7 C D
from the
from the love of God.

Text: Romans 8:39
Music: James E. Clemens (USA), © 2008 James E. Clemens

172 God Calls You Good

BORN BELOVED 8.8.10.8.8

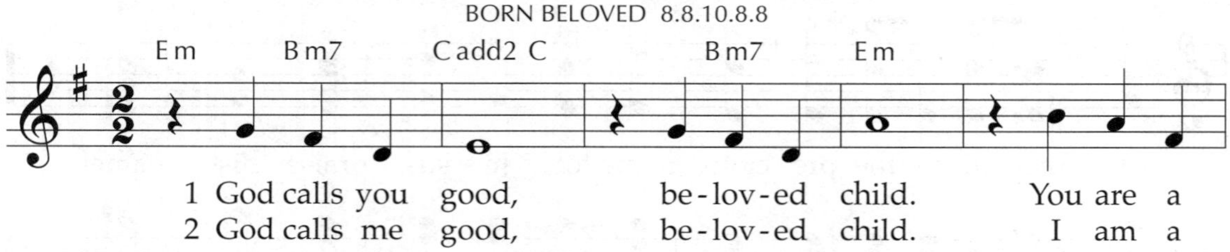
Em Bm7 Cadd2 C Bm7 Em
1 God calls you good, be-lov-ed child. You are a
2 God calls me good, be-lov-ed child. I am a

Text: Paul Vasile (USA)
Music: Paul Vasile

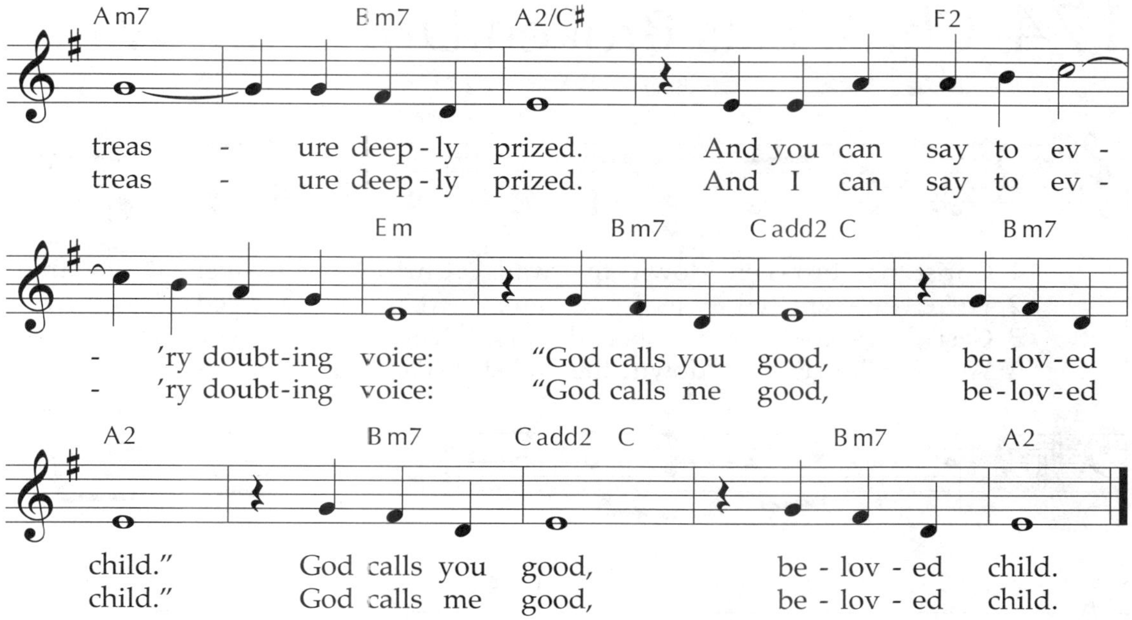
treas - ure deep - ly prized. And you can say to ev -
treas - ure deep - ly prized. And I can say to ev -
- 'ry doubt - ing voice: "God calls you good, be - lov - ed
- 'ry doubt - ing voice: "God calls me good, be - lov - ed
child." God calls you good, be - lov - ed child.
child." God calls me good, be - lov - ed child.

The Lord Your God Is with You 173

ZEPHANIAH 3:17 Irregular

The Lord your God is with you, who is might - y to
save. God will take great joy in you;
God will qui - et you with love; and
God will re - joice o - ver you with sing - ing. Al -
le - lu - ia! Al - le - lu - ia!

Text: based on Zephaniah 3:17; Nathan Stucky (USA), 1999, alt.
Music: Nathan Stucky; acc. Brian Wiebe (USA), 2020

174 Christ Has Broken Down the Wall

BROKEN WALLS 7.7.7.7

D A/C♯ D Bm7 Em7
1 Christ has bro - ken down the wall, Christ has bro - ken down the
2 We're ac - cept - ed as we are, we're ac - cept - ed as we
3 Cast a - side your doubts and fears, cast a - side your doubts and
4 We will tear down the walls! We will tear down ev - 'ry
Asus B7 Em7 D/F♯ Bm E
wall. Let us join our hearts as one,
are. Through God's love all is rec - on - ciled,
fears. Peace and love, free - ly of - fered here;
wall! God has called us, one and all;
Em7 G 1–3 G2 4 G/D D
Christ has bro - ken down the wall!
we're ac - cept - ed as we are.
cast a - side your doubts and fears.
Christ has bro - ken down the wall!

Text: Mark A. Miller (USA)
Music: Mark A. Miller

Planets Humming as They Wander 175

TREASURED 8.7.8.7 D

D G2 Asus Bm7 G D G
1 Plan - ets hum-ming as they wan - der, stars a - flame with
2 At - oms quiv-'ring deep in - side us, cells a - buzz with
3 Hu - man voic - es praise our Mak - er, part of the cre -
Asus D Bm7 Em7 A2 F♯m7 G
si - lent song: gal - ax - ies that spin on, end - less; me - lo -
en - er - gy. Par - ti - cles are chant - ing psalms in ti - ny,
at - ed choir: rum - bling tones of space be - low us, neu-tron's
D G Asus D Bm Em7 A7 Dmaj7
dies a - far but strong. God's cre - a - tion tunes its car - ol,
ho - ly syn - er - gy. All these mol - e - cules pro - vide us
des - cant ev - er higher. Hymns a - rise from all a - round us,
G Em C♯m7♭5 F♯ Bm Em7
far be - yond our mor - tal gaze. Heav'n - ly bod - ies
pat - terns of the craft of God, of - f'ring up me -
thank - ful praise our whole life long, to the One who
A7 Dmaj7 G D G A7 Dsus D
help us lis - ten to the bound - less song of praise.
lo - dic first - fruit, grate - ful hymns which leave us awed.
made us, knows us, Au - thor of the end - less song!

176 O God, Great Womb

LEAVENING LM

1 O God, great womb of won-drous love,
2 O hearth, O heart-beat of the whole,
3 O fire, O fir - ma - ment and sea,
4 O si - lent soul, O mind and strength,
5 Now come with rest, O Sab - bath sun,
your Spir - it mov - ing on the deep
your dark light dance be - gan the times,
your seeth - ing fer - ment's en - er - gy
your cen - ter did con - ceive and bear
O sanc - tu - ar - y, sa - cred home;
did wake a world with - in your - self,
the days and sea - sons, sec - onds, years,
called forth a whirl - ing waltz of life,
its male and fe - male im - age self—
we groan till all is grown com - plete,
a puls - ing, light - ed world, from sleep.
the ag - es' rhy - thms and the rhymes.
each plant and crea - ture and its seed.
all hu - man forms, one breath to share.
ful - filled, at peace, O great sha - lom.

When sung a cappella, rests should be omitted.

All Things Bright and Beautiful 177

ROYAL OAK 7.6.7.6 with refrain

Refrain
*G C D G Am D7 G
All things bright and beau - ti - ful, all crea-tures great and small,
G C D G Am D7 G
Fine
all things wise and won - der - ful, the Lord God made them all.
G C D G
1 Each lit - tle flow'r that o - pens, each lit - tle bird that sings,
2 The pur - ple - head - ed moun-tain, the riv - er run - ning by,
3 The cold wind in the win - ter, the plea - sant sum - mer sun,
4 God gave us eyes to see them, and lips that we might tell
G Em Am D G C D G
To refrain
God made their glow-ing col - ors, God made their ti - ny wings.
the sun - set, and the morn - ing that bright-ens up the sky;
the ripe fruits in the gar - den, God made them, ev - 'ry one.
how great is God Al - might - y, who has made all things well.

*Chord symbols for unison singing only

Text: Cecil F. Alexander (Ireland), *Hymns for Little children*, 1848, alt.
Music: English traditional, 17th c., *The Dancing Master*, 1686; adapt. Martin Shaw (USA), *Song Time*, 1915; harm. John Ribble (USA),

178 God of Wonders

GOD OF WONDERS Irregular

Dsus Em7 C2 Dsus Em7
1 Lord of all cre - a - tion, of wa-ter, earth, and
2 Ear - ly in the morn - ing, I will cel - e - brate the
C2 Dsus Em7 C2
sky, the heav-ens are your tab - er - nac - le.
light. When I stum - ble in the dark - ness
Dsus Em7 C2
Glo - ry to the Lord on high!
I will call your name by night.
Refrain
G Dsus D Am7
God of won - ders be-yond our gal - ax - y, you are ho - ly,
C2 G
ho - ly. The u - ni-verse de-clares your maj - es -
Dsus D Am7 C2
Last time to Coda
ty; you are ho - ly, ho - ly.

Text: Marc Byrd (USA) and Steve Hindalong (USA)
Music: Marc Byrd and Steve Hindalong

C2
1
Lord of heav-en and earth,
Lord of heav-en and earth.
2
C2
Am7
C2
Lord of heav-en and earth.
Hal-le-lu - jah to the Lord of
Am7
C2
heav-en and earth.
Hal-le-lu - jah to the Lord of heav-en and earth.
Am7
C2
To refrain
Hal-le-lu - jah to the Lord of heav-en and earth.
Coda
Am7
C2
Repeat as desired
G2
Ho - ly,
ho - ly,

179 At the Dawn of Your Creation

BEACH SPRING 8.7.8.7 D

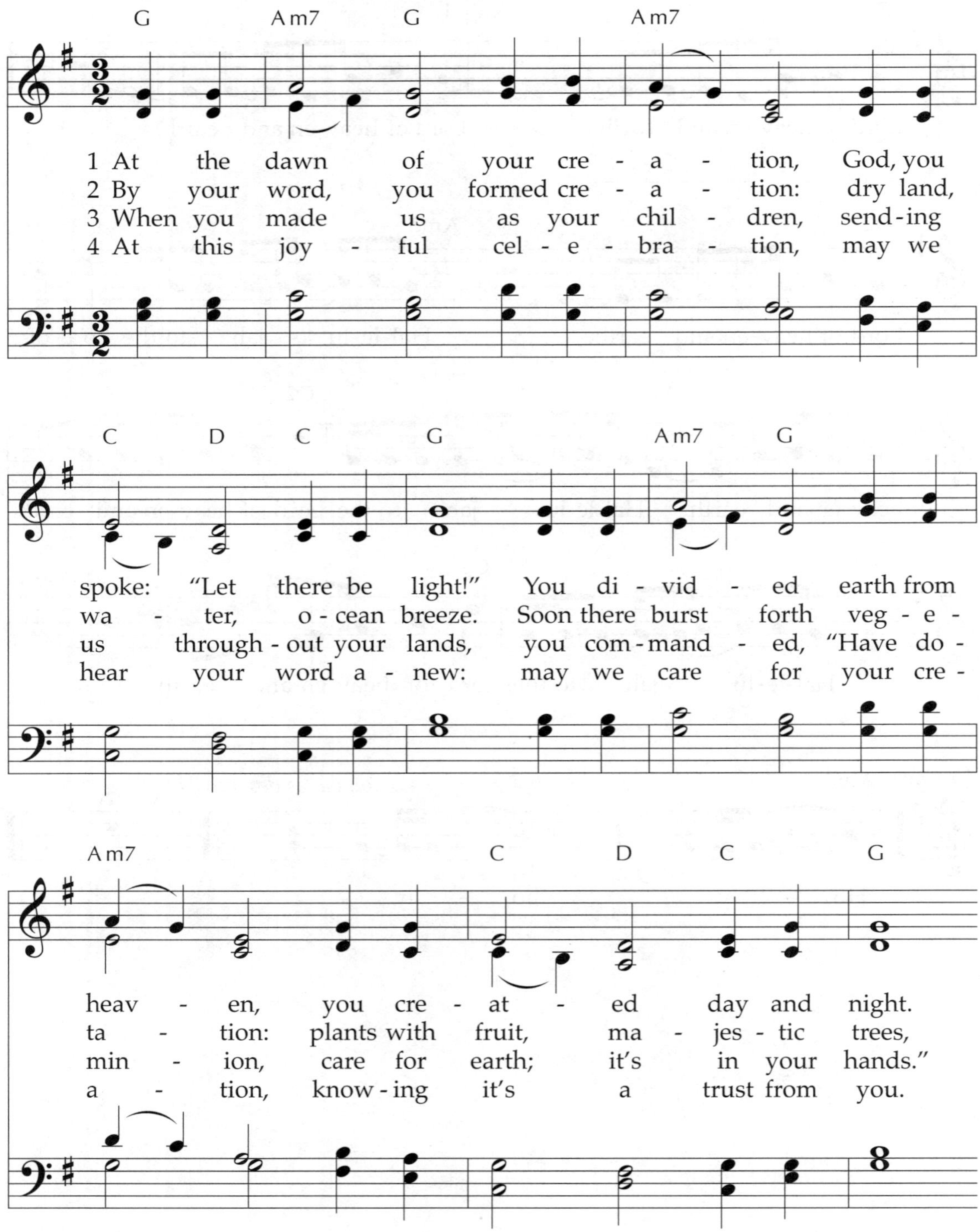
G Am7 G Am7
1 At the dawn of your cre - a - tion, God, you
2 By your word, you formed cre - a - tion: dry land,
3 When you made us as your chil - dren, send-ing
4 At this joy - ful cel - e - bra - tion, may we
C D C G Am7 G
spoke: "Let there be light!" You di - vid - ed earth from
wa - ter, o - cean breeze. Soon there burst forth veg - e -
us through - out your lands, you com - mand - ed, "Have do -
hear your word a - new: may we care for your cre -
Am7 C D C G
heav - en, you cre - at - ed day and night.
ta - tion: plants with fruit, ma - jes - tic trees,
min - ion, care for earth; it's in your hands."
a - tion, know - ing it's a trust from you.

Text: Carolyn Winfrey Gillette (USA), © 2011 Carolyn Winfrey Gillette
Music: attr. B. F. White (USA), *Sacred Harp*, 1844; harm. Joan Fyock Norris (USA), © 1989 Joan Fyock Norris

D G Em
You made sun - beams dance with shad - ows, you cre -
rain and snow and chang - ing sea - sons, crea-tures
Yet we hurt this world you've giv - en; we harm
Just as dai - ly there's a dawn - ing, bring-ing
D B7 C D G
at - ed en - er - gy! Peace - ful eve - nings, bright to -
fill - ing land and sea. God, your ver - y good cre -
earth and sky and sea. We for - get it's your cre -
light to all we see, so we dai - ly hear your
Am7 C D C G
mor - rows, all be - gan with "Let there be!"
a - tion all be - gan with "Let there be!"
a - tion, you, who once said, "Let there be!"
call - ing, you, who once said, "Let there be!"

180 This Is God's Wondrous World

TERRA BEATA SMD

Capo 1: (D) E♭ (A7) B♭7 (D) E♭ (G) A♭ (D) E♭ (A) B♭
1 This is God's won-drous world, and to my lis-t'ning ears
2 This is God's won-drous world; the birds their car - ols raise,
3 This is God's won-drous world; oh, let me ne'er for - get
(D) E♭ (F♯m) Gm (A7) B♭7 (D) E♭ (A7) B♭7 (D) E♭
all na - ture sings, and round me rings the mu - sic of the spheres.
the morn-ing light, the dark of night, de - clare their Mak-er's praise.
that though the wrong seems oft so strong, God is the ru - ler yet.
(A7) B♭7 (D) E♭ (G) A♭ (D) E♭ (G) A♭ (D) E♭
This is God's won-drous world; I rest me in the thought
This is God's won-drous world; a wand-'rer I may roam.
This is God's won-drous world; the bat - tle is not done.
(A7) B♭7 (D) E♭ (F♯m) Gm (A7) B♭7 (D) E♭ (A7) B♭7 (D) E♭
of rocks and trees, of skies and seas, the won-ders God has wrought.
What-e'er my lot, it mat-ters not, my heart is still at home.
Je - sus who died shall be glo - ri - fied, and earth and heav'n be one.

Text: Maltbie D. Babcock (USA), *Thoughts for Every-Day Living*, 1901, alt.
Music: Franklin L. Sheppard (USA), *Alleluia*, 1915, adapt. from English traditional RUSPER

Creation Is a Song / Ho'ė enemeohe 181

CREATION IS A SONG 8.6.6.6 with refrain

Refrain
Cre - a - tion is a song, a song that we can see,
Ho'ė e - ne - me-o - he. Ne - vooh - ta - no - ne.
a sa - cred gift from God, let's join the har - mo - ny.
Fine
Ma' - he - o - 'o ne - me - tae - no - ne.
1 The roll - ing of the o - ceans, the bub - bling of a spring,
2 Danc-ing prai - rie mead-ow, fruit sway - ing on the vine,
3 Ma - jes - tic sleep-ing moun-tain, for - est green and deep,
4 Ev - 'ry glow-ing sun - set, ev - 'ry out - stretched leaf
To refrain
night sky filled with jew - els, a flock of beat - ing wings.
boil - ing storm clouds ris - ing, light-ning 'cross the sky.
ev - 'ry liv - ing crea - ture in our care to keep.
is wit - ness to the glo - ry of the One who sits as Chief.

For the refrain, either language may be sung alone, or the two may be sung in combination.

Text: English and Cheyenne; based on Psalm 19; Doug Krehbiel (USA) and Jude Krehbiel (USA); inspired by the writings of Lawrence Hart (Cheyenne, USA); Cheyenne trans. Lenora Hart Holliman (Cheyenne, USA) and Wayne Leman (USA)

Music: Doug Krehbiel and Jude Krehbiel in consultation with Lenora Hart Holliman; inspired by *Cheyenne Christian Songs* given to Maude Fighting Bear (Cheyenne, USA) and *Tsese-Ma'heone-Nemeotôtse* (*Cheyenne Spiritual Songs*)

182 I Sing the Mighty Power of God

ELLACOMBE CMD

Bb Gm Bb Eb F Bb
1 I sing the might-y pow'r of God, that made the moun-tains rise,
2 I sing the good-ness of the Lord, that filled the earth with food.
3 There's not a plant or flow'r be-low, but makes thy glo-ries known,
Bb Gm Bb Eb F Bb
that spread the flow-ing seas a-broad and built the loft-y skies.
God formed the crea-tures with a word, and then pro-nounced them good.
and clouds a-rise, and tem-pests blow, by or-der from thy throne.
Bb F Bb F
I sing the wis-dom that or-dained the sun to rule the day.
Lord, how thy won-ders are dis-played, wher-e'er I turn my eye,
While all that bor-rows life from thee is ev-er in thy care,
Bb Gm Bb Eb F Bb
The moon shines full at God's com-mand and all the stars o-bey.
if I sur-vey the ground I tread, or gaze up-on the sky!
there's not a place where we can flee but God is pres-ent there.

For capo chords, see #313.

Text: Isaac Watts (England), *Divine and Moral Songs for Children*, 1715, alt.

Music: *Gesangbuch der Herzogl*, Württemberg (present-day Germany), 1784; harm. William H. Monk (England), *Appendix to Hymns Ancient and Modern*, 1868

184 *Proverbs 8:1-30 (excerpts)*

Does not Wisdom call,
and does not Understanding
raise her voice?
"In the beginning God brought me forth,
as the first act of creation.
When the foundation of the earth
was laid out,
I was the skilled artisan
beside the Almighty.
I was God's delight day after day,
always laughing with joy
in God's presence."

185 *Psalm 104 (excerpts)*

Bless the LORD, O my soul.
O LORD my God, you are very great.
You set the earth on its foundations,
so that it shall never be shaken.
You make springs
gush forth in the valleys,
giving drink to every wild animal.
You cause the grass to grow
for the cattle,
and plants for people to use.
You have made the moon
to mark the seasons;
the sun knows its time for setting.
O LORD, how manifold are your works!
In wisdom you have made them all.
The earth is full of your creatures;
they all look to you to give them
their food in due season.
When you send forth your Spirit,
they are created;
and you renew the face of the earth.

186 *Exodus 34:6-7*

The LORD is merciful and gracious,
slow to anger,
and abounding in steadfast love
and faithfulness,
keeping steadfast love
for the thousandth generation,
forgiving iniquity
and transgression and sin,
yet by no means clearing the guilty.

187 *Deuteronomy 6:4-7*

Hear, O Israel:
The LORD is our God, the LORD alone.
You shall love the LORD your God
with all your heart,
and with all your soul,
and with all your might.
Keep these words
that I am commanding you today
in your heart.
Recite them to your children
and talk about them
when you are at home
and when you are away,
when you lie down and when you rise.

188 *Psalm 85:8, 10-11*

Let me hear what the LORD God says:
Steadfast love and faithfulness
meet together;
righteousness and peace kiss each other.
Faithfulness will spring up from the earth,
and righteousness
will look down from heaven.

189 *Colossians 1:15-20*

Christ is the image of the invisible God.
Christ is the firstborn of all creation.
Everything was created in Christ,
everything in heaven and on earth,
everything seen and unseen,
including all forces and powers,
and all rulers and authorities.
All things were created through Christ,
and everything was made for Christ.
Christ is the one who was before all else,
and the one in whom everything
is held together.
Christ is the head of the body,
which is the church.
Christ is the very beginning,
the first to be raised from death,
so as to be above all others.
God was pleased to live fully in Christ.
And God was pleased for Christ
to make peace
through the blood of his cross,
so that all beings in heaven
and on earth
would be brought back to God.

Previous page: 183. *Mist, Sun, Morning*, J. Tyler Klassen (USA), 2015, color digital photograph

The God of Sarah Praise 190

LEONI 6.6.8.4 D

Capo 1: (Em) Fm (B) C (Em) Fm (Am) B♭m (G) A♭
1 The God of Sa - rah praise, the God of dreams long dead,
2 The God of A-brah'm praise, the God of all who roam,
3 The God of Ha - gar praise, the God of those op - pressed—
(D) E♭ (G) A♭ (D) E♭ (Em) Fm (G) A♭ (D7) E♭7 (G) A♭
who brings forth un - ex - pect - ed life, dis - arm - ing dread.
who guides us in - to for - eign lands and makes our home.
who sees the lost and o - ver - looked and calls them blessed.
(D) E♭ (C) D♭ (G) A♭ (Am) B♭m (B) C
Though grief lasts through the night, joy ris - es with the sun;
When dark-ness shrouds our path, the stars, as pledg-es, shine.
Though wan - der - ing a - lone through des - erts of de - spair,
(Em) Fm (G) A♭ (Am) B♭m (Em) Fm (B7) C7 (Em) Fm
God leaves us laugh-ing in sur - prise at death un - done.
God's cov - e - nant will be ful - filled by love's de - sign.
God leads us to a well of hope and meets us there.

Text: David Bjorlin (USA), © 2019 GIA Publications, Inc.
Music: Ashkenazic Yigdal, ca. 17th c.; transcr. Meyer Leoni (England), ca. 1770

191 Come, O Thou Traveler Unknown

VERNON 8.8.8.8.8.8

Dm
C
1 Come, O thou Trav - el - er un - known, whom still I hold, but
2 Wilt thou not yet to me re - veal thy new, un - ut - ter -
3 My strength is gone, my na - ture dies, I sink be - neath thy
4 Yield to me now—for I am weak, but con - fi - dent in
5 'Tis Love! 'tis Love that wres - tled me! I hear thy whis - per
Dm
can - not see! My com - pa - ny be - fore is gone, and
a - ble name? Tell me, I still be - seech thee, tell, to
weight - y hand, faint to re - vive, and fall to rise. I
self - de - spair! Speak to my heart, in bless - ing speak, be
in my heart. The morn - ing breaks, the shad - ows flee, pure,
C
Dm
F
Dm
I am left a - lone with thee. With thee all night I
know it now re - solved I am. Wres - tling, I will not
fall, and yet by faith I stand; I stand and will not
con - quered by my in - stant prayer. Speak, or thou nev - er
u - ni - ver - sal Love thou art. To me, to all, thy

Chord symbols represent a simplified harmony.

Text: based on Genesis 32:24-30; Charles Wesley (England), *Hymns and Sacred Poems*, 1742, alt.
Music: American traditional (USA), *Christian Harmony*, 1805, alt.

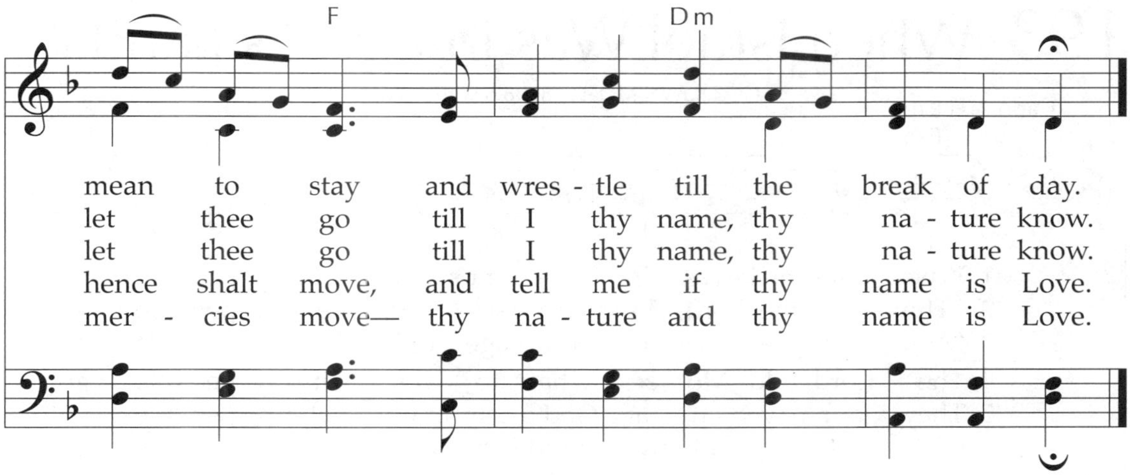
F
Dm
mean to stay and wres - tle till the break of day.
let thee go till I thy name, thy na - ture know.
let thee go till I thy name, thy na - ture know.
hence shalt move, and tell me if thy name is Love.
mer - cies move— thy na - ture and thy name is Love.

שְׁמַע Shema Yisrael 192

HEAR, O ISRAEL 5.7.5.5.5.5

G C G G7 C G/D D Em
Sh'ma Yis-ra - el, Ad - o - nai El - o - hei - nu, Ad - o -
G/D D7 G G C G G7
nai e - chad. Bar - uch shem ch' - vod, ch' -
C G/D D Em G/D D7 G
vod mal-chu - to l' - o - lam va - ed.

Hebrew:

שְׁמַע יִשְׂרָאֵל יְהוָה אֱלֹהֵינוּ יְהוָה אֶחָד
בָּרוּךְ שֵׁם כְּבוֹד מַלְכוּתוֹ לְעוֹלָם וָעֶד

Translation:

Hear, O Israel: The Lord our God, the Lord is one.

Praised be God's name, whose glorious reign is forever and ever.

Text: Hebrew; traditional prayer based on Deuteronomy 6:4 and Psalm 72:19
Music: Hebrew traditional

193 When Israel Was in Egypt's Land

GO DOWN MOSES 8.5.8.5 with refrain

Capo 1: (Em) Fm
(B7) C7
(Em) Fm
1 When Is - rael was in E - gypt's land, let my peo-ple go;
2 "Thus saith the Lord," bold Mo - ses said, "Let my peo-ple go!
3 "No more shall they in bond - age toil: let my peo-ple go!
4 The Lord told Mo - ses what to do, let my peo-ple go;
5 They jour-neyed on at God's com-mand, "Let my peo-ple go!"
6 Oh, let us all from bond - age flee; let my peo-ple go!
op - pressed so hard they could not stand, let my peo-ple go!
If not, I'll smite your first - born dead. Let my peo-ple go!"
Let them come out with E - gypt's spoil: let my peo-ple go!"
to lead the children of Is - rael through, let my peo-ple go.
and came at length to Ca - naan's land, let my peo-ple go.
And let us all in Christ be free: let my peo-ple go!
Refrain
(Am) B♭m
Go down, (go down,) Mo - ses, (Mo - ses,) way down in E - gypt's
land. Tell old Pha - raoh: Let my peo-ple go!

Text: African American spiritual (USA)
Music: African American spiritual; arr. Melva Wilson Costen (USA),

Lead On, O Cloud of Presence 194

LANCASHIRE 7.6.7.6 D

D G D G A
1 Lead on, O cloud of Pres - ence, the ex - o - dus is come.
2 Lead on, O fier - y Pil - lar, we fol - low yet with fears,
3 Lead on, O God of free - dom, and guide our pil - grim way,
D G D A E A
In wil - der - ness and de - sert our tribe shall make its home.
but we shall come re - joic - ing though joy be born of tears.
that we may trust the prom - ise through strug - gle and de - lay.
D7 G E7 A
Our slav - 'ry left be - hind us, new hopes with - in us grow.
We are not lost, though wan - d'ring, for by your light we come,
We pray that those who fol - low will live to share that land
D G D/A A7 D
We seek the land of prom - ise where milk and hon - ey flow.
and we are still God's peo - ple. The jour - ney is our home.
where jus - tice dwells with mer - cy and love is law's de - mand.

Text: Ruth Duck (USA), *Because We Are One People*, 1974, rev. 2018,
Music: Henry T. Smart (England), 1835, *Psalms and Hymns for Divine Worship*, 1867

195 No Longer Slaves to Fear

CHILD OF GOD Irregular

D
1 You un - rav - el me with a mel - o - dy. You sur -
2 From my moth-er's womb you have cho-sen me;
G A D
round me with a song of de - liv - er - ance from my
Love has called my name. I've been born a - gain in - to your
G A D
en - e-mies till all my fears are gone.
fam - i - ly; your blood flows through my veins.
Refrain
G A D Bm
I'm no long - er a slave to fear; I am a child
A D G A
of God. I'm no long - er a slave to fear;
To v. 2
To bridge
Last time
D Bm A Bm A D G Bm A D
I am a child of God.
Bridge
Bm A D G Bm
You split the sea so I could walk right through it. My fears were
A D G Bm A
drowned in per - fect love. You res-cued me so I could

Text: based on Romans 8:15 and Exodus 14:21; Brian Johnson (USA), Joel Case (USA), and Jonathan David Helser (USA)
Music: Brian Johnson, Joel Case, and Jonathan David Helser

stand and sing: I am a child of God.
To refrain
I am a child of God. I am a child of God.

Come and Seek the Ways of Wisdom 196

MADELEINE 8.7.8.7.8.7

1 Come and seek the ways of Wis-dom, she who danced when earth was new. Fol - low close - ly what she teach-es, for her words are right and true. Wis - dom clears the path to jus-tice, show - ing us what love must do.
2 Lis - ten to the voice of Wis-dom, cry - ing in the mar - ket-place. Hear the Word made flesh a - mong us, full of glo - ry, truth, and grace. When the Word takes root and rip-ens, peace and right - eous - ness em-brace.
3 Sis - ter Wis - dom, come, as-sist us; nur - ture all who seek re-birth. Spir - it-guide and close com-pan-ion, bring to life our sa - cred worth. Free us to be - come your peo-ple, ho - ly friends of God and earth.

197 God's Glory Fills the Heavens

CREATION LMD

A E A D A/E E
1 God's glo - ry fills the heav'ns with hymns; the domed sky
2 God's per - fect law re - vives the soul; its pre - cepts
3 God's ser - vant may I ev - er be: this world my
E7 Bm E7 A E A
bears the Mak - er's mark; new prais - es sound from day
make the sim - ple wise; its just com-mands re - joice
joy, that Word my guide. O cleanse me, Lord, from se -
D A/E E E7 Bm E7 A
to day and ech - o through the know - ing dark.
the heart; its truth gives light un - to the eyes.
cret sin: de - li - ver me from self - ish pride.
E A/C♯ E A A/E
With-out a word their songs roll on; in - to all
For - ev - er shall this law en - dure: un - blem - ished,
Ac - cept my thoughts and words and deeds: let them find

Text: based on Psalm 19; Carl P. Daw Jr. (USA), 1982,
Music: Franz Joseph Haydn (Austria), adapt. from *Die Schöpfung (The Creation)*, 1798

E A/E E A
lands their voic - es run. And with a champ - ion's
right - eous, true, com - plete. No gold was ev - er
fa - vor in your sight. For you a - lone can
E A Bm A/E E7 A
strength and grace from far - thest heav'n comes forth the sun.
found so fine, no hon - ey in the comb more sweet.
make me whole, O Lord, my ref - uge and my might.

Restore Our Faith, O Saving God 198

HEAVEN'S RAIN 8.6.8.6.6

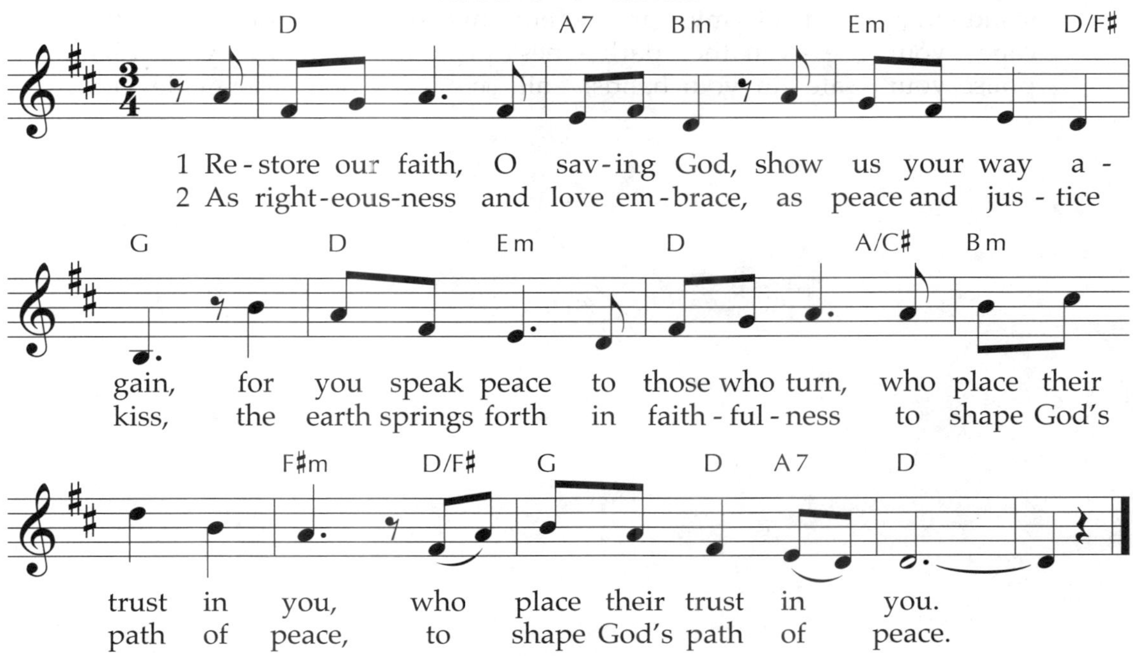
D A7 Bm Em D/F♯
1 Re - store our faith, O sav - ing God, show us your way a -
2 As right - eous - ness and love em - brace, as peace and jus - tice
G D Em D A/C♯ Bm
gain, for you speak peace to those who turn, who place their
kiss, the earth springs forth in faith - ful - ness to shape God's
F♯m D/F♯ G D A7 D
trust in you, who place their trust in you.
path of peace, to shape God's path of peace.

Text: based on Psalm 85:6–13; Jean Janzen (USA), © 2019 Jean Janzen
Music: James E. Clemens (USA), © 2008 James E. Clemens

199 O God, You Search Me

O GOD, YOU SEARCH ME 9.9.11.11

1 O God, you search me and you know me. All my thoughts lie
2 You know my rest - ing and my ris - ing. You dis - cern my
3 Be - fore a word is on my tongue, Lord, you have known its
4 Al - though your Spir - it is up - on me, still I search for
5 For you cre - at - ed me and shaped me, gave me life and

o - pen to your gaze. When I walk or lie down you are be -
pur - pose from a - far, and with love ev - er - last - ing you be -
mean - ing through and through. You are with me be - yond my un - der -
shel - ter from your light. There is no - where on earth I can es -
knit me in the womb. For the won - der of who I am, I

fore me: ev - er the mak - er and keep - er of my days.
siege me: in ev - 'ry mo - ment of life or death, you are.
stand - ing: God of my pres - ent, my past, and fu - ture, too.
cape you: e - ven the dark - ness is ra - diant in your sight.
praise you: safe in your hands, all cre - a - tion is made new.

Text: based on Psalm 139:1–16, Bernadette Farrell (England), 1992, alt.
Music: Bernadette Farrell

Darkness Is Not Dark to You, God 200

EYES CLOSED 8.7.8.7.8.7

Em
Bm7
D
Bm
1 Dark - ness is not dark to you, God, dark - ness
2 Light ob - scures the sa - cred se - crets, light makes
3 God is lo - gos, hid - den wis - dom, God is
Em
Am
is as light to you. Dark - ness is the source of
clear what should be blurred, light de - fines and sharp - ens
what we can - not see, God is shroud - ed in deep
Em
B
B7
in - sight, dark - ness leads to what is true.
bound - 'ries, light—ag - gres - sive, harsh, as - sured.
si - lence, God is ho - ly mys - ter - y,
Am
Em
B7
Am
Eyes closed, block - ing out the bril - liant,
Sit - ting in the shad - ows, wait - ing,
yet with dark, ex - plo - sive pow - er,
B
C
D
Em
(Last time E)
we be - gin to see a - new.
we are met by God the Word.
we meet our Di - vin - i - ty.

Chord symbols represent a simplified harmony.

Alternate tune: PICARDY (#65, #238, #432)

201 Hear the Turmoil of the Nations

EBENEZER 8.7.8.7 D

Em B C B Em G D
1 Hear the tur - moil of the na - tions! How earth's
2 God once set a mo - del mon - arch firm - ly
3 Lis - ten, all who gov - ern na - tions! Rul - ers
Em B7 Em B C
peo - ples sigh and groan! Voic - es call for
on a roy - al throne, there to reign with
of the earth, take heed! Trust no hu - man
B Em G D Em B7 Em
rev - o - lu - tion; fac - tions thrive, and threats are thrown.
might and wis - dom bear - ing wit - ness to God's own.
scheme or sys - tem to de - ter - mine how you lead.
G D Em B Em D
Few take time to seek God's bless - ing, which some oth - ers
When the heirs of all that great - ness took for grant - ed
Turn to God for strength and cour - age when your fears and

Chord symbols represent a simplified harmony.

Text: based on Psalm 2; Carl P. Daw Jr. (USA),
Music: Thomas J. Williams (Wales), 1890

Em D G Em B C B
false - ly claim. God, whose will a - lone is
what God gave, God ful - filled the dor - mant
doubts in - crease; in that longed - for place of
Em G D Em B7 Em
sov' - reign, soon will turn their pride to shame.
prom - ise in the One who came to save.
ref - uge, find in God your source of peace.

Peace, Be Still 202

PEACE PILGRIM'S PRAYER Irregular

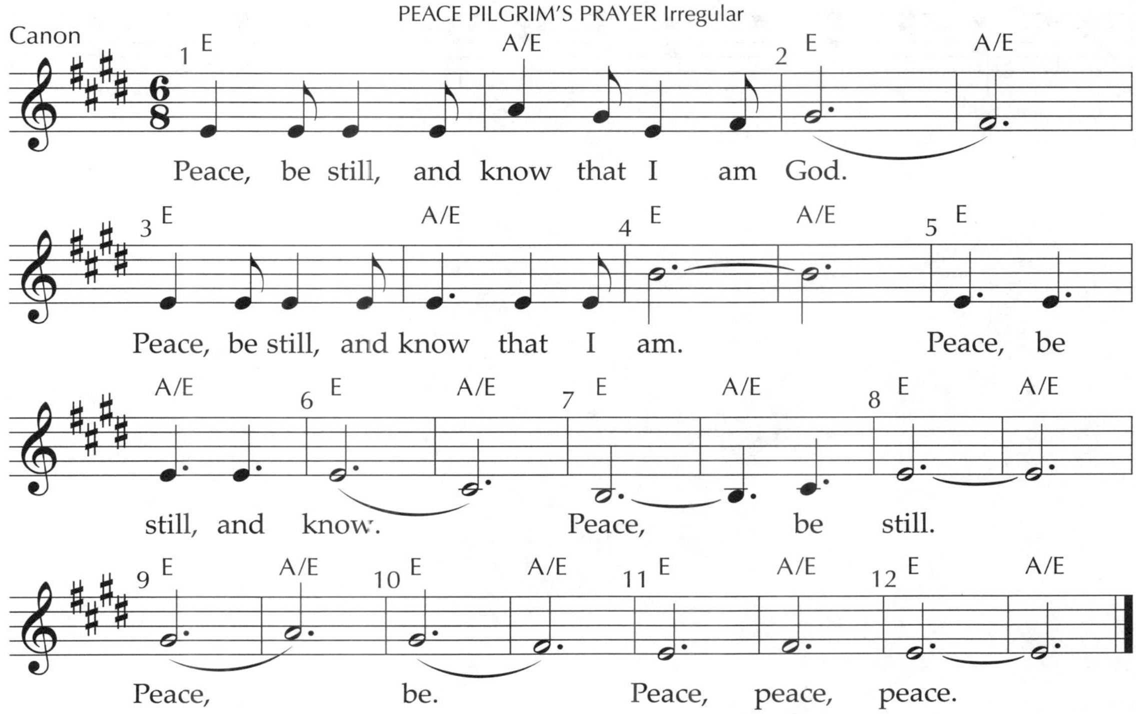
Canon
1 E A/E 2 E A/E
Peace, be still, and know that I am God.
3 E A/E 4 E A/E 5 E
Peace, be still, and know that I am. Peace, be
A/E 6 E A/E 7 E A/E 8 E A/E
still, and know. Peace, be still.
9 E A/E 10 E A/E 11 E A/E 12 E A/E
Peace, be. Peace, peace, peace.

Text: Psalm 46:10
Music: Shawn Kirchner (USA)

203 O God, Our Help in Ages Past

ST. ANNE CM

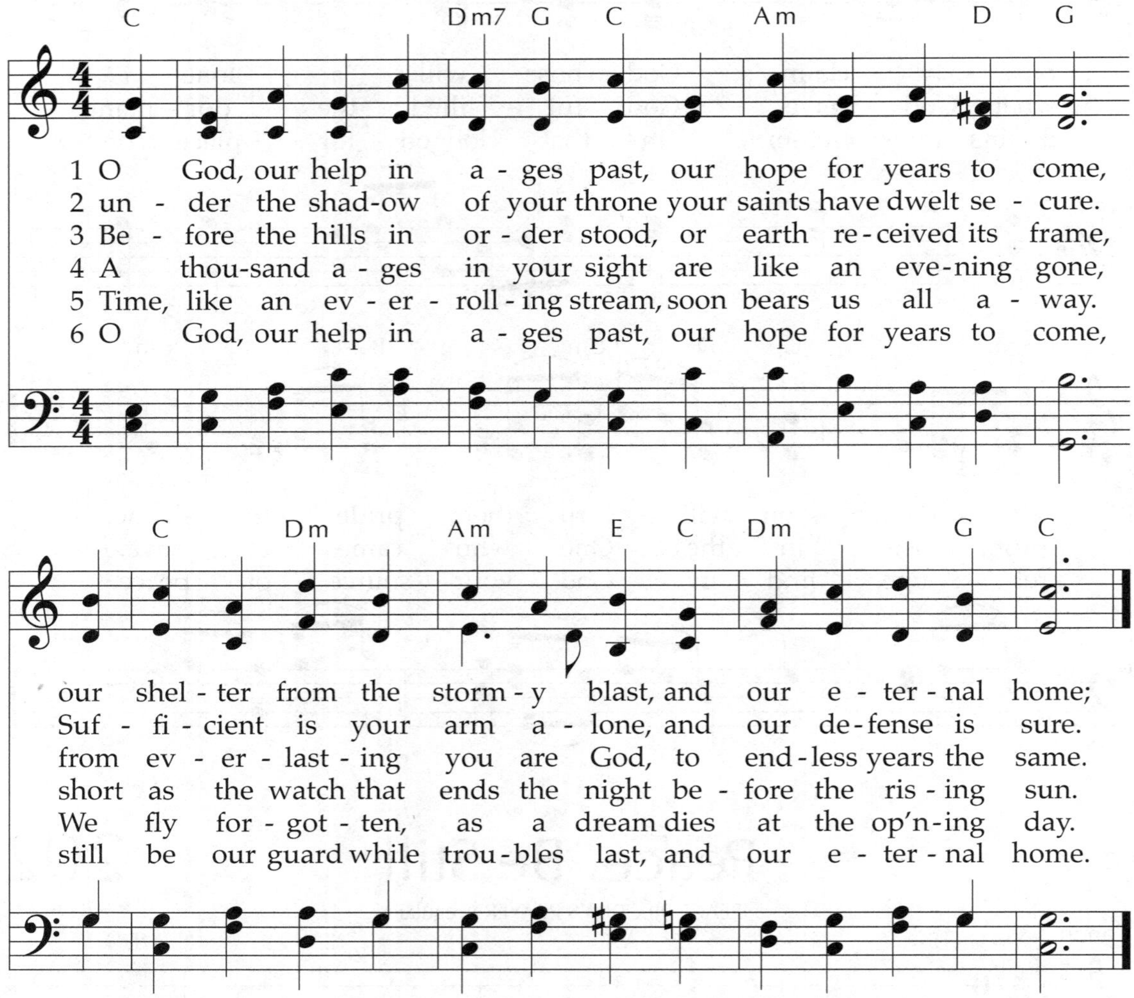
C Dm7 G C Am D G
1 O God, our help in a - ges past, our hope for years to come,
2 un - der the shad-ow of your throne your saints have dwelt se - cure.
3 Be - fore the hills in or - der stood, or earth re - ceived its frame,
4 A thou-sand a - ges in your sight are like an eve-ning gone,
5 Time, like an ev - er - roll - ing stream, soon bears us all a - way.
6 O God, our help in a - ges past, our hope for years to come,
C Dm Am E C Dm G C
our shel - ter from the storm - y blast, and our e - ter - nal home;
Suf - fi - cient is your arm a - lone, and our de - fense is sure.
from ev - er - last - ing you are God, to end - less years the same.
short as the watch that ends the night be - fore the ris - ing sun.
We fly for - got - ten, as a dream dies at the op'n-ing day.
still be our guard while trou - bles last, and our e - ter - nal home.

Text: based on Psalm 90:1–8; Isaac Watts (England), *The Psalms of David* [. . .], 1719, alt.
Music: attr. William Croft (England), *Supplement to the New Version of the Psalms by Dr. Brady and Mr. Tate*, 6th ed., 1708

Praise to the Living God 204

LEONI 6.6.8.4 D

Capo 1: (Em) Fm (B) C (Em) Fm (Am) B♭m (G) A♭
1 Praise to the liv - ing God! All prais - ed be the Name,
2 God's spir - it flow - ing free, high surg - ing where it will—
3 God plants e - ter - nal life with - in the hu - man soul.
(D) E♭ (G) A♭ (D) E♭ (Em) Fm (G) A♭ (D7) E♭7 (G) A♭
who was, and is, and is to be, is still the same;
in proph-et's word it spoke of old— is speak - ing still.
God's love shall be our strength and stay, while a - ges roll.
(D) E♭ (C) D♭ (G) A♭ (Am) B♭m (B) C
the one e - ter - nal God, ere all that now ap - pears,
Es - tab-lished is God's law, and change-less it shall stand,
Praise to the liv - ing God! All prais - ed be the Name,
(Em) Fm (G) A♭ (Am) B♭m (Em) Fm (B7) C7 (Em) Fm
the First, the Last, be - yond all thought through time-less years!
deep writ up - on the hu - man heart, on sea, or land.
who was, and is, and is to be, is still the same!

Text: Moses Maimonides (Mediterranean), 12th c.; Daniel ben Judah (Rome), *Yigdal* (Jewish doxology), 14th c.; trans. and paraphr. Max Landsberg (USA) and Newton Mann (USA), ca. 1885, alt.
Music: Ashkenazic *Yigdal*, ca. 17th c.; transcr. Meyer Leoni (England), ca. 1770

205 Light Dawns on a Weary World

TEMPLE OF PEACE 7.6.6.7.8 with refrain

G D C G C
1 Light dawns on a wea - ry world when eyes be - gin to
2 Love grows in a wea - ry world when hun - gry hearts find
3 Hope blooms in a wea - ry world when crea - tures, once for -
G D G D
see all peo - ple's dig - ni - ty. Light dawns on a
bread and chil - dren's dreams are fed. Love grows in a
lorn, find wil - der - ness re - born. Hope blooms in a
C G C G D G
wea - ry world: the prom - ised day of jus - tice comes.
wea - ry world: the prom - ised feast of plen - ty comes.
wea - ry world: the prom - ised green of E - den comes.
Refrain G C G
The trees shall clap their hands; the dry lands, gush with springs;
clap their hands; gush with
G Em D C G
the hills and moun - tains shall break forth with sing - ing!
springs;

C G
We shall go out with joy, and be led forth in peace,
out with joy, forth in
G C D G
as all the world in won-der ech-oes sha-lom.
peace,

206 Seek the Peace of the City

SEEK THE PEACE 7.5.8.5

Fm Cm7 Fm Cm7 Fm B♭m
1 Seek the peace of the cit - y; make this land your
2 Seek the peace of your neigh - bor, en - e - my or
3 Seek the peace of the ex - ile, stran - ger on the
4 Seek the peace of the Sav - ior; I will draw you
5 Seek the peace of the cit - y; find me in this
Csus C Fm A♭ Cm7 Fm D♭
home. I have set you here to pros - per;
friend. I can break the hard - est heart,
road. I will walk a - long be - side you,
near. I will bring you home for - ev - er;
place. I have brought you here to know me;
Fm/A♭ B♭m Csus Cm 1–4 F5 5 F
make this land your home.
en - e - my or friend.
stran - ger on the road.
I will draw you near.
find me in this place.

Text: based on Jeremiah 29:7; David Wright (USA), © 2004 David Wright
Music: James E. Clemens (USA), © 2004 James E. Clemens

What Does the Lord Require of You? 207

MOON Irregular

Capo 3: (G) B♭ (D) F (Em) Gm (Bm) Dm
1* What does the Lord re - quire of you?
2 Jus - tice, kind - ness,
3 To seek jus - tice and love kind - ness
(C) E♭ (G) B♭ (Am) Cm (D) F (G) B♭
Repeat as desired
What does the Lord re - quire of you?
walk hum - bly with your God.
and walk hum - bly with your God.

*The three melodic phrases may be sung consecutively, as a canon, or in any combination. One model for assigning parts is basses on line 1, altos and tenors on line 2, and sopranos on line 3.

Text: based on Micah 6:8; Jim Strathdee (USA)
Music: Jim Strathdee

208 With Mary Sing Magnificat

FOREST GREEN CMD

(D) G D Am D D7 G
1 With Ma - ry sing mag - nif - i - cat; with Mir-iam dance in praise;
2 The One who hon-ored Riz-pah's stand a - gainst a king's de - cree
3 With con - fi-dence we may pro-claim Love's lib - er - at - ing pow'r,
D G D Am D D7 G
with proph - et An - na speak a word of faith in joy a - blaze,
and bol-stered clev - er mid-wives' plans to foil bru - tal - i - ty
bear wit - ness to the sav - ing grace still with us ev - 'ry hour,
Em Bm D G D G C D
for love and mer - cy shall pre - vail; no need shall be ig - nored;
re - mains through con - flict, doubt, and fear our Ad - vo - cate and Friend;
and sing with thanks, de - light, and praise a new yet an - cient song;
D G D Am D D7 G
the lost shall find their home a - gain and ev - 'ry hope re - stored.
each grief and loss shall be re-deemed; each pain-ful wound shall mend.
to - geth - er sing mag - nif - i - cat with voic - es clear and strong.

Text: Jeannette M. Lindholm (USA),
Music: English traditional; harm. Ralph Vaughan Williams (England), *The English Hymnal*, 1906

We Dream of a Turning 209

LOCH LOMOND 11.10.13.10 with refrain

C7 F Gm/F C7
1 We dream of a turn - ing from ag - es of wrong, earth to
2 We dream of a feast where there's no one out - side, turned a -
3 We dream of a moun - tain where no harm is done, where the
F F/E Dm Dm/C B♭ C F5 Dm
E - den re-stored, and our par - don. Like Eve and Ad - am, join in a
way due to dif-f'rence or la - bel, when all the weap-ons forged to de -
wolf and the lamb lie to - geth - er. A lit - tle child shall dance, lead-ing
B♭ C7 F Dm E♭ F
sto - ry and a song as we wan - der with God through the gar - den.
stroy or to di - vide turn to rust far from God's ho - ly ta - ble.
all the crea-tures on, as we join hand to hoof, claw, and feath - er!
Refrain C7 F Dm Gm/B♭ C7
Where true peace is shin - ing as hate rolls a-way, see, God's
F Dm B♭ F B♭ C7 Dm F
bright new cre - a - tion is gleam - ing. The morn-ing rays that dawn on our
B♭ C7 F Dm C7 F
wea-ry, wak-ing day bring a hope far be-yond all our dream - ing.

Text: Adam M. L. Tice (USA), 2008, © 2009 GIA Publications, Inc.
Music: Scottish traditional; arr. Kathryn Harsha (USA), © 2019 Kathryn Harsha

210 O Come, O Come, Immanuel

VENI EMMANUEL LM with refrain

1 O come, O come, Im - man - u - el, and ran - som cap - tive
2 O come, O come, thou God of law, in cloud and maj - es -
3 O come, thou Rod of Jes - se, free thine own from Sa - tan's
4 O come, thou Day - spring, come and cheer our spir - its by thine
5 O come, thou Key of Da - vid, come and o - pen wide our
6 O come, thou Wis - dom from on high, and or - der all things
7 O come, De - sire of na - tions, bind all peo - ples in one
Is - ra - el, that mourns in lone - ly ex - ile
ty and awe. Thy pre - cepts, taught on Si - nai's
tyr - an - ny. From depths of hell thy peo - ple
ad - vent here. Dis - perse the gloom - y clouds of
heav'n - ly home. Make safe the way that leads to
far and nigh. To us the path of knowl - edge
heart and mind. Bid en - vy, strife, and quar - rels
here, un - til the Son of God ap - pear.
height, call us to lives both just and right.
save, and give them vic - t'ry o'er the grave.
night, and death's dark shad - ow put to flight.
thee and close the path to mis - er - y.
show, and cause us in thy ways to go.
cease, and fill the world with heav - en's peace.
Refrain
Re - joice! Re - joice! Im - man -
u - el shall come to thee, O Is - ra - el.

Text: anon., O Antiphons, ca. 8th-9th c.; "Veni, veni Emmanuel," 12th c.; stanzas 1–5 trans. John M. Neale (England), *Medieval Hymns and Sequences*, 1851, alt.; stanzas 6–7 trans. Henry Sloane Coffin (USA), *Hymns of the Kingdom of God*, 1916
Music: trope melody (present-day France), 15th c.

Hope Is a Candle 211

GALLOWAY TAM 11.10.11.8

1 Hope is a can - dle, once lit by the proph - ets,
2 Peace is a can - dle to show us a path - way,
3 Love is a can - dle whose light makes a cir - cle,
4 Joy is a can - dle of mys - tery and laugh - ter,
5 Christ is the light that the proph - ets a - wait - ed,

nev - er con - sumed, though it burns through the years;
threat - ened by gusts from our rage and our greed.
where ev - 'ry face is the face of a friend.
mys - tery of light that is born in the dark;
Christ is the li - on, the lamb, and the child.

dim in the day - light of pow - er and priv' - lege—
Friend, feel no en - vy for those in the shad - ows—
Wid - en the cir - cle by shar - ing and giv - ing—
laugh - ter at hear - ing the voice of an an - gel,
Christ is the love and the mys - tery and laugh - ter—

when they are gone, hope will shine on.
vio - lence and force their dead - end course.
God's ho - ly dare: love ev - 'ry - where.
ev - er so near, cast - ing out fear.
cand - les, make way! Christ is the day.

Text: Richard Leach (USA), 1994, © 1995 Selah Publishing Co., Inc.
Music: Scottish traditional; acc. James E. Clemens (USA), 2006

212 Comfort, Comfort, O My People

GENEVA 42 (FREU DICH SEHR) 8.7.8.7.7.7.8.8

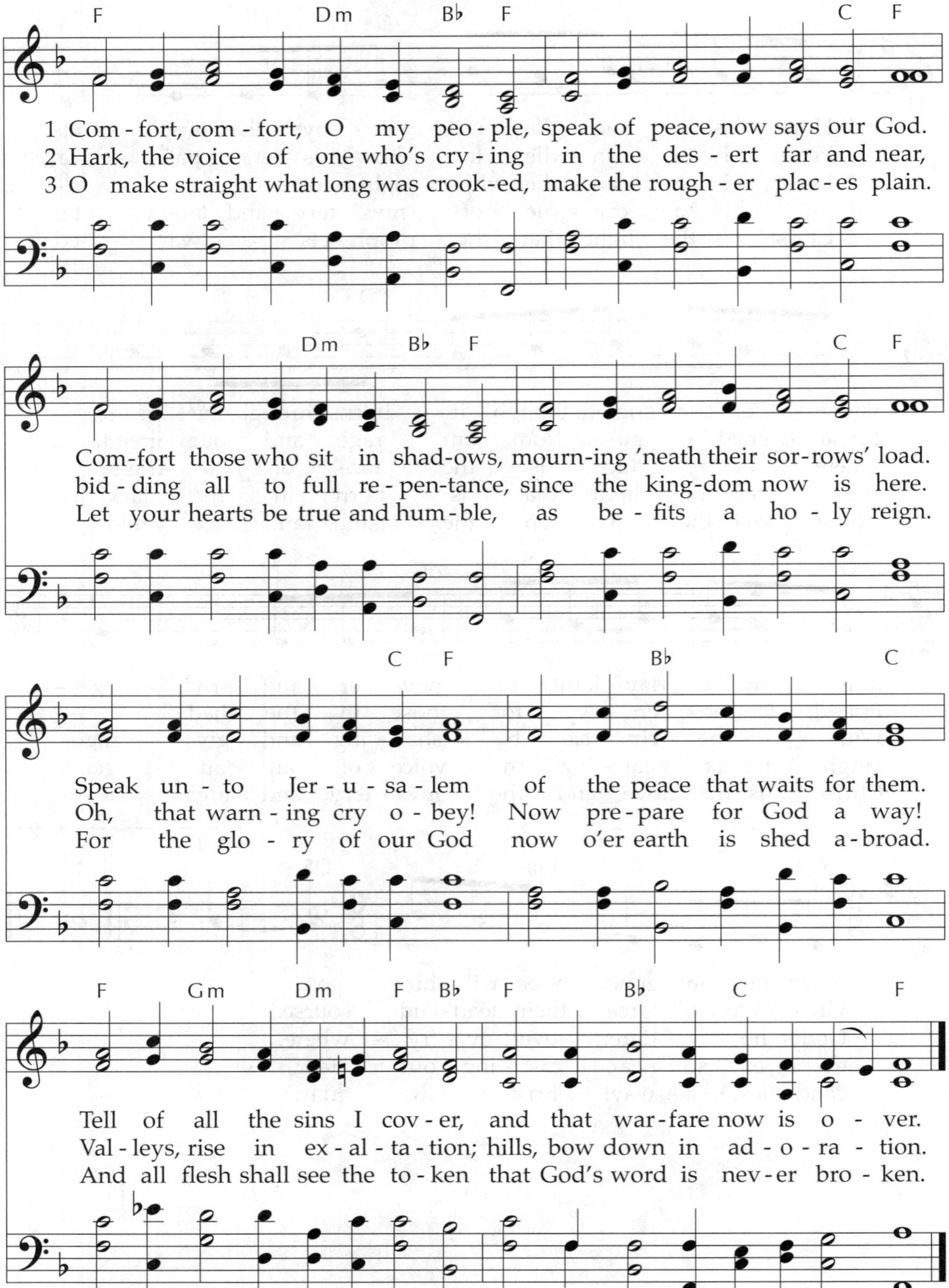
F Dm B♭ F C F
1 Com - fort, com - fort, O my peo - ple, speak of peace, now says our God.
2 Hark, the voice of one who's cry - ing in the des - ert far and near,
3 O make straight what long was crook-ed, make the rough - er plac - es plain.
Dm B♭ F C F
Com-fort those who sit in shad-ows, mourn-ing 'neath their sor-rows' load.
bid - ding all to full re - pen-tance, since the king-dom now is here.
Let your hearts be true and hum-ble, as be - fits a ho - ly reign.
C F B♭ C
Speak un - to Jer - u - sa - lem of the peace that waits for them.
Oh, that warn - ing cry o - bey! Now pre - pare for God a way!
For the glo - ry of our God now o'er earth is shed a - broad.
F Gm Dm F B♭ F B♭ C F
Tell of all the sins I cov - er, and that war-fare now is o - ver.
Val - leys, rise in ex - al - ta - tion; hills, bow down in ad - o - ra - tion.
And all flesh shall see the to - ken that God's word is nev - er bro - ken.

Chord symbols represent a simplified harmony.

Text: based on Isaiah 40:1–5; Johannes Olearius (present-day Germany), "Tröstet, tröstet, meine Lieben," *Geistliche Singe-Kunst*, 1671; trans. Catherine Winkworth (England), *Chorale Book for England*, 1863, alt.

Music: Louis Bourgeois (present-day France), Genevan Psalter, *Octante Trois Pseaumes de David*, 1551; harm. adapt. from Claude Goudimel (present-day France), *150 Pseaumes de David*, 1564

Poor of the Earth 213

WAYFARING STRANGER 9.8.9.8 D

Cm G Cm G/D Cm/E♭ C7/E
1 Poor of the earth, I am a shep-herd; in rug-ged
2 An - oth - er dawn, the sun be - fore me, an - oth - er
3 With each new day, I pause in won-der, to look at
4 This day is done, my prayers un - an - swered, once more I
Fm A♭ Gsus G Cm G Cm G/D
fields, I make my home. Yet I at - tend the words of
day to bide and watch. I trust in God and I am
Beth - le-hem a - far. From this small town will come a
sigh as dark-ness falls. Your will be done, I must be
Cm/E♭ C/E Fm G7 Fm/C
proph-ets, and I can hope. How will I know?
wait - ing. Day fol-lows day. How will I know?
sav - ior, born in our midst. How will I know?
pa - tient; I long for news. How will I know?
Cm Fm B♭7 E♭ C7/E
Sprung from the roots, the line of Jes - se, will come one
The nights are cold; I do not mind them, my lambs rest
When time is right, God, share your pur-pose; rul - ers and
My bones are tired, my soul is hun-gry, my ston - y
Fm Dm7♭5 Gsus G Cm G Cm G/D
cho - sen for us all. The proph-et's songs fore - tell a
safe with - in my care. Com - pan - ion moon is night-ly
kings, they must be told. I live a - part. I wait in
bed a - waits me now. Do not for - get your faith-ful
Cm/E♭ C7/E Fm G7 Fm/C Cm
lead - er— a vir-gin's child. How will I know?
chang-ing; my con-stant God: How will I know?
si - lence. Who will tell me? How will I know?
shep - herd. Per-haps to - night. How will I know?

For capo chords, see the accompaniment edition.

Text: Jacque B. Jones (USA), 2011, © 2014 GIA Publications, Inc.
Music: American traditional (USA); arr. Horace Clarence Boyer (USA), © 1992 Horace Clarence Boyer

214 Savior of the Nations, Come!

NUN KOMM, DER HEIDEN HEILAND 7.7.7.7

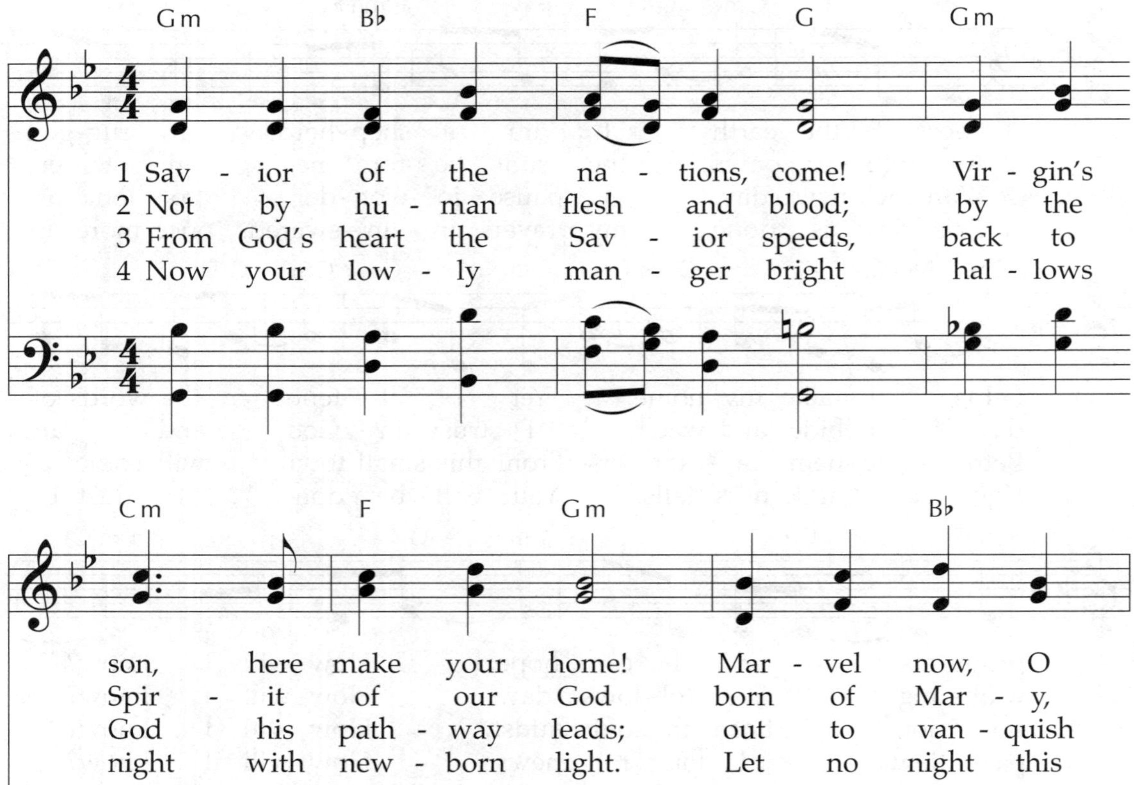
Gm Bb F G Gm
1 Sav - ior of the na - tions, come! Vir - gin's
2 Not by hu - man flesh and blood; by the
3 From God's heart the Sav - ior speeds, back to
4 Now your low - ly man - ger bright hal - lows
Cm F Gm Bb
son, here make your home! Mar - vel now, O
Spir - it of our God born of Mar - y,
God his path - way leads; out to van - quish
night with new - born light. Let no night this
Cm Gm Cm Bb Dm7 G
heav'n and earth: God has cho - sen such a birth.
moth - er blest, God in flesh is man - i - fest.
death's com - mand, back to reign at God's right hand.
light sub - due, let our faith shine ev - er new.

Chord symbols represent a simplified harmony.

Text: attr. Ambrose of Milan (present-day Italy), 4th c.; trans. Martin Luther (present-day Germany), *Nun komm, der Heiden Heiland,* 1523, *Eyn Enchiridion,* 1524; stanzas 1, 2 trans. William M. Reynolds (USA), 1851, alt.; stanzas 3, 4 Martin A. Seltz (USA), 2006; 1969, alt.; stanza 3 trans.
Music: *Geystliche Gesangk Buchleyn* (present-day Germany), 1524; harm. Melchior Vulpius (present-day Germany), ca. 1609

Oh, How Shall I Receive Thee 215

ST. THEODULPH (VALET WILL ICH DIR GEBEN) 7.6.7.6 D

C F C G F C
1 Oh, how shall I re - ceive thee, how meet thee on thy way,
2 Love caused thine in - car - na - tion; Love brought thee here to me.
3 Thou com - est, Christ, with glad - ness, in mer - cy and good will,
F C G F C
bless'd hope of ev' - ry na - tion, my soul's de - light and stay?
Thy thirst for my sal - va - tion pro - cured my lib - er - ty.
to bring an end to sad - ness and bid our fears be still.
D7 G Em Am7 D7 G
O Je - sus, Je - sus, give me now by thine own pure light
Oh, love be - yond all tell - ing, that led thee to em - brace,
We wel - come thee, our Sav - ior; come gath - er us to thee,
C F G C F G7 C
to know what - e'er is pleas - ing and wel - come in thy sight.
in love, all love ex - cel - ling, our trou - bled hu - man race.
that in thy light e - ter - nal our joy - ous home may be.

Text: Paul Gerhardt (present-day Germany), "Wie soll ich dich empfangen," *Praxis Pietatis Melica*, 1653; trans. Arthur T. Russell (England), *Psalms and Hymns*, 1851, alt.
Music: Melchior Teschner (present-day Germany), 1613, *Ein Andachtiges Gebet*, 1615

216 Lo, How a Rose E'er Blooming

ES IST EIN ROS' 7.6.7.6.6.7.6

F Bb C Dm Bb F Gm C F
1 Lo, how a Rose e'er bloom-ing from ten-der stem has sprung!
2 I - sa-iah 'twas fore-told it, the Rose I have in mind.
3 Flow - er, whose fra-grance ten - der with sweet-ness fills the air,
Bb C Dm Bb F Gm C F
Of Jes-se's lin-eage com-ing as saints of old have sung.
With Ma-ry we be-hold it, the vir-gin moth - er kind.
dis - pel in glo-rious splen-dor gloom and grief ev - 'ry - where.
Gm F G C F
It came, a flow'r-et bright, a - mid the
To show God's love a - right, she bore to
True man, yet ver - y God, from sin and
Bb C D Gm F Am C F
cold of win - ter, when half spent was the night.
us a Sav - ior, when half spent was the night.
death he saves us, and light-ens ev - 'ry load.

Text: stanzas 1–2 anon., "Es ist ein Ros' entsprungen" (present-day Germany), 15th c.; *Alte Catholische Geistliche Kirchengasäng* (present-day Germany), 1599; trans. Theodore Baker (USA), 1894; stanza 3 Friedrich Layritz (Germany), *Liederschatz*, 1832; trans. Harriet K. Spaeth (USA), *The Hymnal*, 1940, alt.

Music: German traditional, 15th c.; *Alte Catholische Geistliche Kirchengasäng*, 1599; harm. Michael Praetorius (present-day Germany), *Musae Sionae VI*, 1609

Hark! the Glad Sound! 217

COMMUNION CMD

E C♯m E/B B E
1 Hark! the glad sound! The Sav-ior comes! The Sav-ior prom-ised long!
2 He comes the pris-'ners to re-lease, in Sa-tan's bond-age held.
3 His sil-ver trum-pets pub-lish loud the day of ju-bi-lee.
C♯m E/B B E
Let ev-'ry heart pre-pare a throne, and ev'-ry voice a song.
The gates of brass be-fore him burst, the i-ron fet-ters yield.
Our debts are all re-mit-ted now; he sets the peo-ple free.
C♯m G♯m A E B E C♯m G♯m C♯m
On him the Spir-it large-ly poured ex-erts its sa-cred fire,
He comes the bro-ken heart to bind, the bleed-ing soul to cure,
Our glad ho-san-nas, Prince of Peace, thy wel-come shall pro-claim,
E C♯m E/B B E
wis-dom and might, and zeal and love, his ho-ly breast in-spire.
and with the trea-sures of his grace to en-rich the hum-ble poor.
and heav'n's e-ter-nal arch-es ring with thy be-lov-ed name.

Text: Philip Doddridge (England), 1735, *Translation and Paraphrases*, 1745, alt.
Music: "Robinson" in Wyeth's *Repository of Sacred Music, Part Second* (USA), 1813; harm. J. Harold Moyer (USA),

218 Come, Thou Long-Expected Jesus

HYFRYDOL 8.7.8.7 D

Capo 3: (D) (A) (D) (Em/D) (A) (D) (A) (D)
F C F Gm/F C F C F
1 Come, thou long - ex - pect - ed Je - sus, born to set thy
2 Come, thou u - ni - ver - sal Sav - ior; come, re - deem the
3 Born thy peo - ple to de - liv - er, born a child, and
(Em/G) (A) (D) (A) (D) (Em/D) (A)
Gm/B♭ C F C F Gm/F C
peo - ple free; from our fears and sins re - lease us,
hu - man race. Life and joy spring from thy fa - vor;
yet a king; born to reign in us for - ev - er,
(D) (A) (D) (Em/G) (A) (D) (F♯m) (Bm7) (Em7)
F C F Gm/B♭ C F Am Dm7 Gm7
let us find our rest in thee: Is - rael's strength and con - so-
cheer each soul in need of grace. Still we wait for thine ap-
now thy gra - cious king - dom bring. By thine own e - ter - nal

Text: Charles Wesley (England), *Hymns for the Nativity of Our Lord*, 1744; stanza 2 adapt. from "Light of Those Whose Dreary Dwelling" in the same collection
Music: Rowland H. Prichard (Wales), ca. 1830, *Cyfaill y Cantorion*, 1844; arr. Ralph Vaughan Williams (England), *The English Hymnal*, 1906, adapt. 1951, *BBC Hymn Book*, © Oxford University Press, London

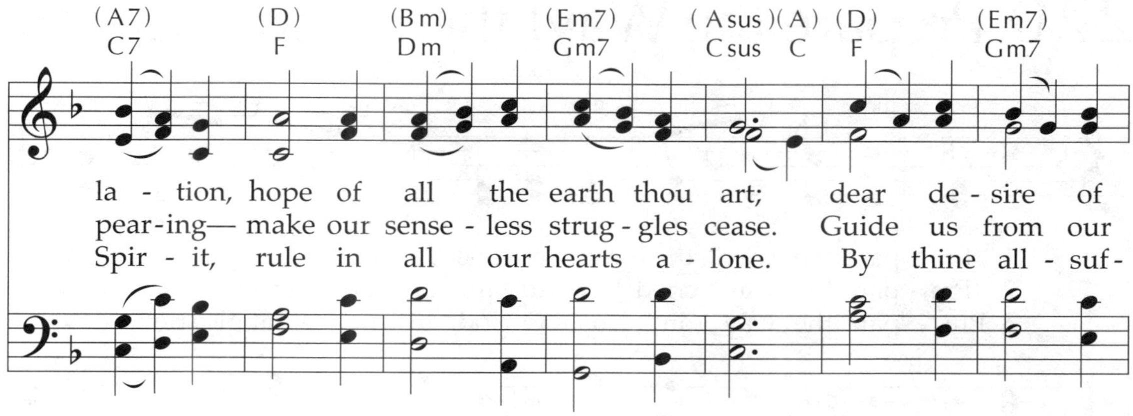
(A7) (D) (Bm) (Em7) (Asus)(A) (D) (Em7)
C7 F Dm Gm7 Csus C F Gm7
la - tion, hope of all the earth thou art; dear de - sire of
pear-ing— make our sense - less strug - gles cease. Guide us from our
Spir - it, rule in all our hearts a - lone. By thine all - suf -

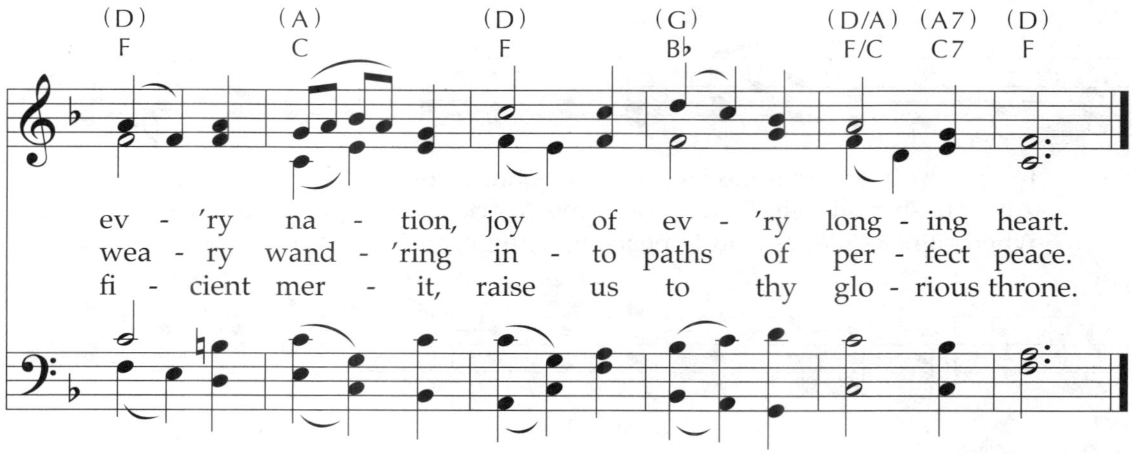
(D) (A) (D) (G) (D/A) (A7) (D)
F C F B♭ F/C C7 F
ev - 'ry na - tion, joy of ev - 'ry long - ing heart.
wea - ry wand - 'ring in - to paths of per - fect peace.
fi - cient mer - it, raise us to thy glo - rious throne.

Prepare Ye the Way of the Lord 219

PREPARE YE THE WAY 8.8

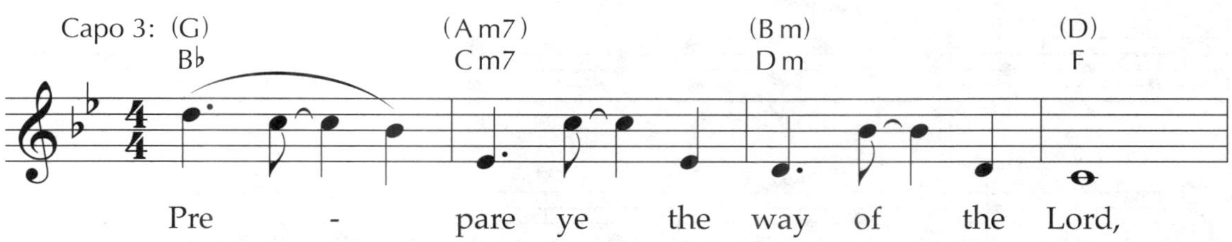
Capo 3: (G) (Am7) (Bm) (D)
B♭ Cm7 Dm F
Pre - pare ye the way of the Lord,

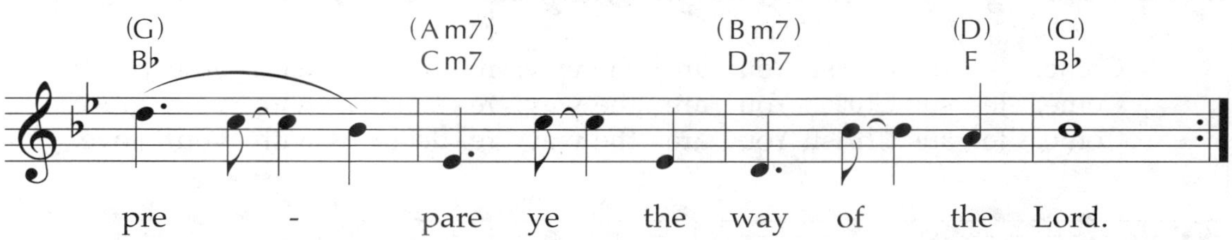
(G) (Am7) (Bm7) (D) (G)
B♭ Cm7 Dm7 F B♭
pre - pare ye the way of the Lord.

Text: Isaiah 40:3, Matthew 3:3, Mark 1:3
Music: Stephen Schwartz (USA), © 1971 Range Road Music, Inc., Quartet Music, Inc., and New Cadenza Music, Inc., dist. Hal Leonard, Inc.

220 Prepare the Way! the Prophet Called

CAROL CMD

1 "Pre - pare the way!" the proph-et called; a mes - sen-ger will come
2 "Pre - pare the way!" cried John to all be - side the Jor - dan stream.
3 Pre - pare the way in us, O God, to greet that glo-rious day
to re - af - firm God's cov - e - nant and lead the peo - ple home.
All flesh will see God's sav - ing work, the proph-ets' an - cient dream.
when right-eous-ness and peace will reign, and death will pass a - way.
The truth will shine like pur - est fire in that a-wait - ed hour.
The val - leys and the moun-tain-tops will make a lev - el place.
The ris - en one will come a - gain, de - scend - ing from a - bove.
Come, Je - sus Christ! You are the way; re - new us with your pow'r.
Come, Je - sus Christ! You are the way; re - store us with your grace.
Come, Je - sus Christ! You are the way; re - deem us with your love.

For capo chords, see #248.

Text: Edmund H. Sears (USA), *Christian Register*, 1849, alt.
Music: Richard S. Willis (USA), *Church Carols and Choir Studies*, 1850

The Angel Gabriel Called Mary Blessed 221

GABRIEL'S MESSAGE 10.10.12.7.3

Am Bdim Esus E7
1 The an - gel Ga - bri - el called Ma - ry blessed, "Re-
2 Then Ma - ry ques-tioned him, "How can this be? Why
3 From joy - ful birth to grief be - side the cross, through
Am Am/C Em Am
joice! I speak with you at God's re - quest. The
would the Ho - ly One show strength through me? Yet
fear and won - der, mir - a - cles and loss, she
C Dm D7 Gadd2 G
Might - y One now comes and in your arms will rest— for
by the Spir - it's pow'r I will serve faith - ful - ly— and
bears the ho - ly mys - ter - y of God - with - us. We
Dm Esus E Dm7 Am Em Am
you will be God's moth - er." Glo - ri - a!
I will be God's moth - er." Glo - ri - a!
cel - e-brate God's moth - er. Glo - ri - a!

Text: Sarah Kathleen Johnson (Canada), © 2019 Sarah Kathleen Johnson; inspired by Basque carol "Birjina gaztetto bat zegoen," paraphr. Sabine Baring-Gould (England), "The Angel Gabriel from Heaven Came," *University Carol Book*, 1923
Music: Basque traditional; harm. attr. C. Edgar Pettman (England), *University Carol Book*, 1923

222 My Soul Proclaims with Wonder

WALNUT 7.6.7.6 D

Refrain/Unison
G Em7 Am G Am7 D
My soul pro-claims with won - der the great-ness of the Lord,
G C Bm Am D G Bm Am7 G
re - joic - ing in God's great - ness, my spir - it is re - stored.
Fine
G C Am7 D G C
1 To me has God shown fa - vor, to one the world thought frail,
2 God's mer - cy shields the faith - ful and saves them from de - feat,
3 The might - y have been van - quished, the low - ly lift - ed up.
4 To Ab - ra-ham's de - scen - dants, the Lord will stead-fast prove,
Am E7 Am E Am Em A7 D
and ev - 'ry age will ech - o the an - gel's first "All hail."
with strength that turns to scat - ter the proud in their con - ceit.
The hun - gry find a - bun - dance, the rich, an emp - ty cup.
for God has made with Is - rael a cov - e - nant of love.
To refrain

Bless'd Be the God of Israel 223

WEBB 7.6.7.6 D

Capo 1: (A) Bb (D) Eb (A) Bb (E) F
1 Bless'd be the God of Is - rael, who comes to set us free,
2 Now from the house of Da - vid a child of grace is giv'n,
3 On all by death im - pris - oned the sun be - gins to rise,
(A) Bb (D) Eb (A) Bb (E7) F7 (A) Bb
who vis - its and re - deems us, and grants us lib - er - ty!
a Sav - ior comes a - mong us to raise us up to heav'n.
the dawn - ing of for - give - ness up - on the sin - ner's eyes,
(E) F (A) Bb (D) Eb (A/E) (E) Bb/F F
The proph - ets spoke of mer - cy, of free - dom and re - lease,
Be - fore him goes the her - ald, fore - run - ner in the way,
to guide the feet of pil - grims a - long the paths of peace.
(A) Bb (D) Eb (A) Bb (E7) F7 (A) Bb
God shall ful - fill the prom - ise to bring our peo - ple peace.
the proph - et of sal - va - tion, the har - bin - ger of day.
Oh, bless our God and Sav - ior with songs that nev - er cease!

Text: based on Luke 1:68-79; Michael A. Perry (England), *Psalm Praise*, © 1973 Hope Publishing Co.
Music: George J. Webb (USA), 1830; *The Odeon*, 1837

224 Hacia Belén (Mary Journeyed)

ALEGRÍA, ALEGRÍA, ALEGRÍA LM with refrain

D A7 D Bm7 Em A7 D
1 Ha - cia Be - lén, se͜ en - ca - mi - na Ma - ría con su͜ a - man - te͜ es - po - so, lle - van - do͜ en su com - pa - ñí - a a to - do͜ un Dios po - de - ro - so.
2 Los pa - ja - ri - llos del bos - que, al ver pa - sar los es - po - sos, les can - ta - ban me - lo - dí - as con sus tri - nos ar - mo - nio - sos.
3 En cuan - to͜ a Be - lén lle - ga - ron po - sa - da͜ al pun - to pi - die - ron, na - die les qui - so͜ hos - pe - dar por - que tan po - bres les vie - ron.
1 Ma - ry jour - neyed with her hus - band on the road to Da - vid's Cit - y. She was bear - ing Christ our Sav - ior, on - ly Son of God Al - might - y.
2 From the for - ests, at their pass - ing, all the birds came swift - ly wing - ing as they watched this lov - ing cou - ple and burst in - to hap - py sing - ing.
3 With the crowds in Da - vid's Cit - y, not a sin - gle inn was a - ble to give shel - ter to the cou - ple, but a poor and low - ly sta - ble.
Refrain
G Em7 A7 D
A - le - grí - a,͜ a - le - grí - a,͜ a - le - grí - a, A - le - grí - a,͜ a - le - grí - a͜ y pla - cer que la vir - gen va de pa - so con su͜ es - po - so͜ ha - cia Be - lén.
O what joy and what glad - ness were there when the vir - gin and her hus - band made their way to Da - vid's Cit - y.
1 A7 D
2 A7 D Last time
po - so͜ ha - cia Be - lén.
way to Beth - le - hem.

Text: unknown; trans. Mary Louise Bringle (USA)
Music: Puerto Rican traditional; arr. Ronald F. Krisman (USA)

We Come

225

WE COME Irregular

1 Our hearts are emp - ty with - out you;
2 Some - times we long for the morn - ing,
bar - ren and cold, but for the bold hope that
for a re - frain from etch - ings in pain, yet our
you your - self plant - ed with - in.
lone - li - ness draws us to you.
Refrain
In the might - y name of God, in the
sav - ing name of Je - sus, in the strong
name of the Spir - it, we come, we cry, we watch, we
wait, we look, we long for you, we come, we
cry, we watch, we wait, we look, we long for you.

Text: stanzas Jim Croegaert (USA); refrain David Adam (Scotland)
Music: Jim Croegaert; acc. Susan See (USA)

226 Sleepers, Wake

WACHET AUF 8.9.8.8.9.8.6.6.4.8.8

1 "Sleep-ers, wake!" A voice a-stounds us. The shout of ram-
2 When we hear the her-alds sing - ing, and in our hearts
3 All the heav'ns and earth a-dore you, and saints and an-
part guards sur-rounds us: "A-wake, Je-ru-sa-lem, a-rise!"
new joy is spring-ing, we wake and rise up from our gloom;
gels sing be-fore you, with harp and cym-bal's clear-est tone;
Mid-night's peace their cry has bro - ken, their ur-gent sum-
for our Friend comes down all-glo - rious, the strong in grace,
gates of gleam-ing pearl be-fore us re-sound as an-
mons clear-ly spo-ken: "The time has come, O maid-ens wise!
in truth vic - to-rious; our Star is ris'n, our Light is come!
gels sing in cho-rus and lead us to your daz-zling throne.

Text: Philipp Nicolai (present-day Germany), "Wachet auf, ruft uns die Stimme," *Appendix to Freuden-Spiegel des ewigen Lebens,* 1599; stanza 1 trans. Carl P. Daw Jr. (USA), stanzas 2, 3 trans. Catherine Winkworth (England), 1858, alt.
Music: Philipp Nicolai, *Appendix to Freuden-Spiegel des ewigen Lebens,* 1599

Rise up, and give us light. The Bride - groom is in sight.
Now come, O bless-ed One, God's own be - lov - ed Son,
No eye has seen that light, no ear the ech-oed might
Al - le - lu - ia! Your lamps pre - pare and has - ten there,
Al - le - lu - ia! Oh, hear the call! Come one, come all,
of your glo - ry; but we re - joice and sing the song,
that you the wed - ding feast may share."
and fol - low to the ban - quet hall!
Al - le - lu - ia! through ag - es long.
8

227 Here I Am to Worship (Ich will dich anbeten)

HERE I AM TO WORSHIP Irregular

E B F♯m7 A2 E
1 Light of the world, you stepped down in - to dark - ness, o - pened my
2 King of all days, oh so high - ly ex - alt - ed, glo - rious in
1 Licht die - ser Welt, du strahlst in un - s'rer Nacht auf. Leuch - test den
2 Herr al - ler Zei - ten, du bist hoch er - ha - ben, herr - lich im
B A2 E B F♯m7
eyes, let me see beau - ty that made this heart a -
heav - en a - bove, hum - bly you came to the earth you cre -
Weg, lässt mich sehn. Herr dei - ne Schön - heit lässt mich an -
Him - mel er - höht. Doch vol - ler De - mut kamst du auf die
A2 E B A2
dore you, hope of a life spent with you. So
at - ed, all for love's sake be - came poor. So
be - ten. E - wig werd' ich vor dir stehn.
Er - de. Zeigst, wor - in Lie - be be - steht.
Refrain
E B/D♯ E/G♯
here I am to wor - ship, here I am to bow down, here I am to say that
Ich will dich an - be - ten. Will mich vor dir beu - gen. Will dir sa - gen: du nur
A E B/D♯
you're my God. You're al - to - geth - er love - ly, al - to - geth - er wor - thy, al - to -
bist mein Gott, du al - lein bist herr - lich, du al - lein bist wür - dig, du nur

Text: Tim Hughes (England), 2000; German trans. Andreas Waldmann (Germany)
Music: Tim Hughes

E/G♯
1 A2 To verse 2
2 A To bridge
Last time A Fine
geth-er won-der-ful to me.
bist voll-kom-men gut zu mir.
Bridge
B E/G♯ A2
And I'll nev - er know how much it cost to see
Herr nie be-grei - fe ich die Last, die du
B E/G♯ 1–3 A2 4 A2 To refrain
my sin up-on that cross. I'll nev - that cross. So
am Kreuz ge-tra - gen hast. Herr nie - gen hast.

Wait for the Lord / Contemplaré tu vida 228

WAIT FOR THE LORD Irregular

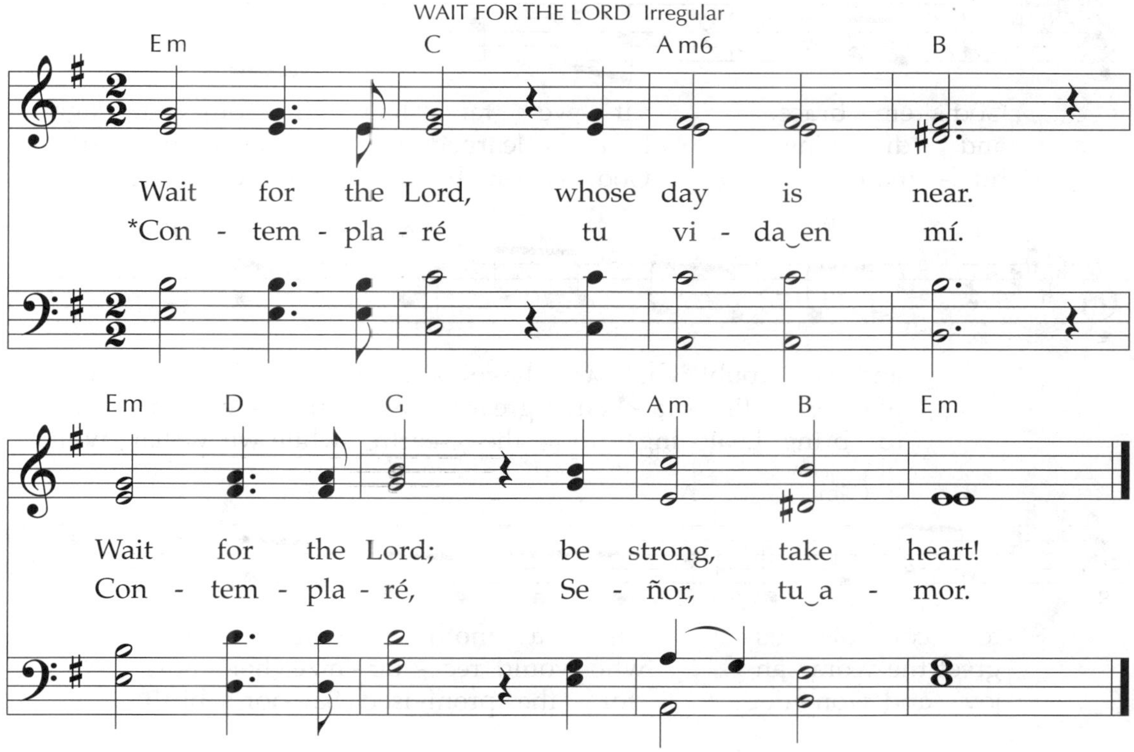
Em C Am6 B
Wait for the Lord, whose day is near.
*Con - tem - pla - ré tu vi - da en mí.
Em D G Am B Em
Wait for the Lord; be strong, take heart!
Con - tem - pla - ré, Se - ñor, tu a - mor.

*Translation: I will see your life within me. Lord, I will see your love.

Verses can be found in the accompaniment edition.

Text: based on Psalm 27:14; Taizé Community (France), 1984; Spanish text Taizé Community
Music: Jacques Berthier (France), 1984

229 Unexpected and Mysterious

ST. HELENA 8.7.8.7 D

E C♯m Amaj7 B E C♯m7 Amaj7 B E C♯m
1 Un - ex - pect - ed
2 In a mo - men -
3 We are called to
Amaj7 G♯m C♯m Amaj7 B7
and mys - te - ri - ous is the gen - tle Word of grace.
tar - y meet - ing of e - ter - ni - ty and time,
pon - der mys - te - ry and a - wait the com - ing Christ,
E C♯m7 B E
Ev - er lov - ing and sus - tain - ing is the peace of
Ma - ry learned that she would car - ry both the mor - tal
to em - bod - y God's com - pas - sion for each frag - ile
C♯m7 D A E F♯m
God's em - brace. If we fal - ter in our cour - age
and di - vine. Then she learned of God's com - pas - sion,
hu - man life. God is with us in our long - ing
D A E
and we doubt what we have known, God is faith - ful
of E - liz - a - beth's great joy, and she ran to
to bring heal - ing to the earth, while we watch with
B C♯m A B7 E
to con - sole us as a moth - er tends her own.
greet the wom - an who would rec - og - nize her boy.
joy and won - der for the prom - ised Sav - ior's birth.

Text: Jeannette M. Lindholm (USA), © 2002 Jeannette M. Lindholm (admin. Augsburg Fortress)
Music: Calvin Hampton (USA), © 1977 GIA Publications, Inc.

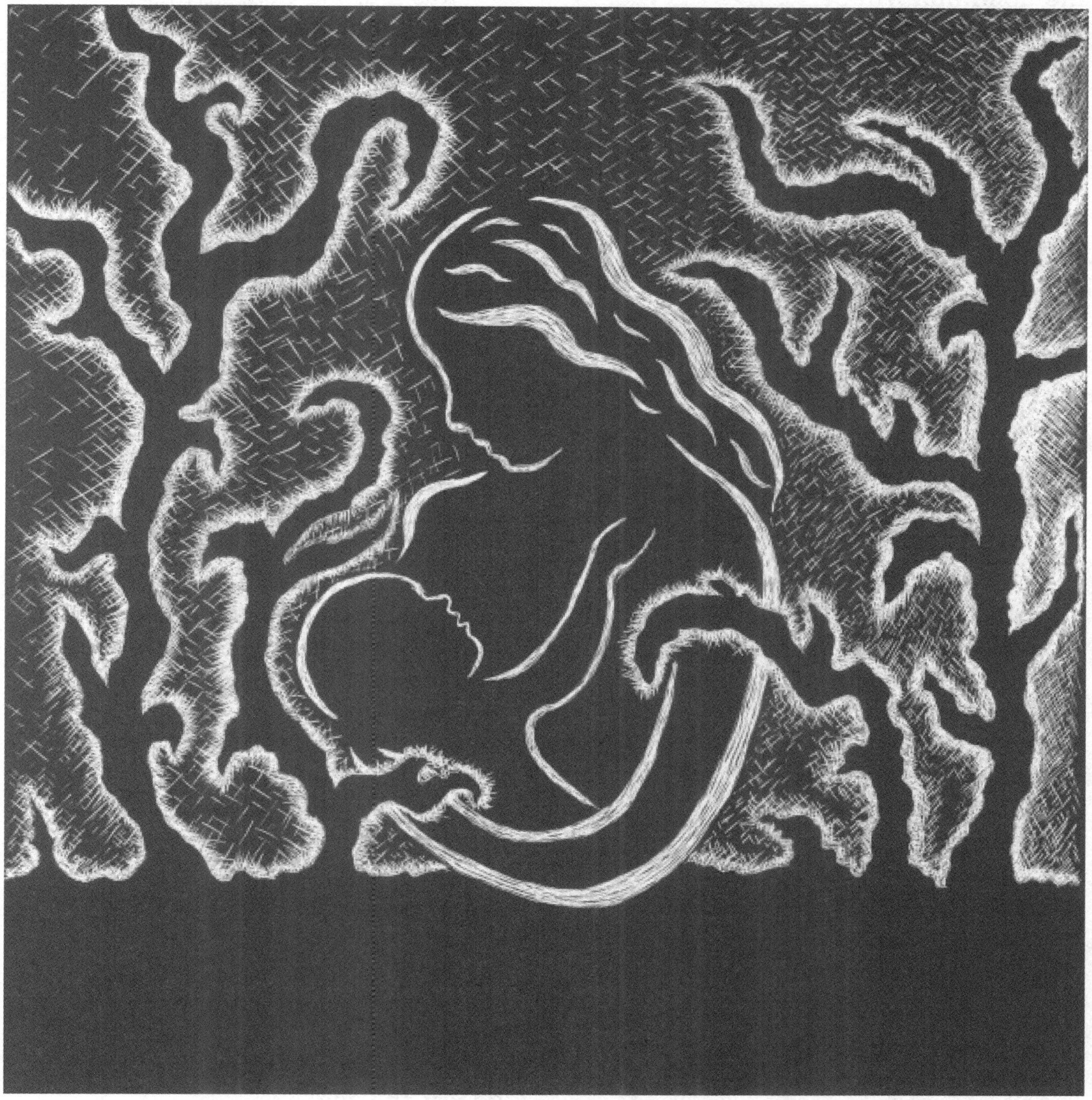

231 *Isaiah 9:2, 6*

The people walking in darkness
have seen a great light;
on those living in the land
of deep shadows
a light has shone.
For to us a child is born,
to us a son is given;
and dominion will be
upon his shoulders;
and he will be called
Wonderful Counselor,
Mighty God,
Everlasting Father,
Prince of Peace.

232 *Isaiah 11:1-4*

A shoot will come up
from the stump of Jesse;
from his roots
a branch will bear fruit,
on whom will rest
the spirit of the LORD—
the spirit of wisdom
and of understanding,
the spirit of counsel
and of might,
the spirit of the knowledge
and fear of the LORD.
This one will not judge
by what the eyes see
or decide
by what the ears hear,
but with righteousness
will judge the needy,
and with justice
will decide for the poor of the earth.

233 *Luke 1:35*

The angel said to Mary,
"The Holy Spirit will come upon you,
and the Most High will overshadow you.
Therefore, the Holy One who is born
will be called the Son of God."

234 *Luke 2:10-14 (excerpts)*

The angel said,
"Do not be afraid!
Look! I bring good news to you—
Your savior is born today
in the city of David.
He is Christ the Lord."
A great angelic assembly
was praising God, saying,
"Glory to God in the highest heaven,
and on earth peace among those
who please God."

235 *John 1:1-5, 10-14*

In the beginning was the Word.
The Word was with God
and the Word was truly God.
From the very beginning
the Word was with God.
And with this Word,
God created all things.
Nothing was made
without the Word.
From this Word,
everything that was created
received its life,
a life that gave light to everyone.
The light shines in the darkness,
and darkness has never put it out.
The Word was in the world,
but no one noticed,
even though God had made the world
with the Word.
The world belonged to the Word,
but its nations did not welcome
the Word.
Yet some people accepted the Word;
to them was given the right
to be the children of God.
They were not God's children
by nature
or because of any human desires;
God was the one
who made them children.
The Word became human
and lived here with us.
We saw the Word's true glory,
the glory of a parent's only child,
full of grace and truth.

Previous page: 230. *We Owe Them a Complicated Debt,* Rachel Epp Buller (USA) , 2017, scratchboard drawing ⓦ

Creator of the Stars of Night 236

CONDITOR ALME SIDERUM LM

1 Cre - a - tor of the stars of night, your peo - ple's
2 In sor - row that the an - cient curse should doom to
3 When this old world drew on t'ward night, you came, but
4 At your great name, O Je - sus, now all knees must
5 Come in your ho - ly might, we pray, re - deem us
6 To God Cre - a - tor, God the Son, and God the

ev - er - last - ing light, O Christ, re - deem - er
death a u - ni - verse, you came, O Sav - ior,
not in splen - dor bright, not as a mon - arch,
bend, all hearts must bow. All things on earth with
for e - ter - nal day. De - fend us while we
Spir - it, Three in One, praise, hon - or, might, and

of us all, we pray you hear us when we call.
to set free your own in glo - rious lib - er - ty.
but the child of Ma - ry, bless - ed moth - er mild.
one ac - cord, like those in heav'n, shall call you Lord.
dwell be - low from all as - saults of our dread foe.
glo - ry be from age to age e - ter - nal - ly.

Text: *Conditor alme siderum*, 9th c.; trans. John Mason Neale (England), 1851; rev. *The Hymnal*, 1940, alt.,

Music: Sarum plainsong (England), ca. 9th c.

237 Now the Heavens Start to Whisper

SUO GAN 8.7.8.7 D

D Em7 A7 Bm D/A
1 Now the heav - ens start to whis - per, as the veil is
2 Heav - y clouds that block the moon-light now be - gin to
3 Christ, e - ter - nal sun of jus - tice, Christ, the rose of
Em A7 D Bm F♯m Em/G A7
grow - ing thin. Earth from slum - ber wakes to lis - ten
drift a - way. Dia - mond bril-liance through the dark-ness
wis - dom's seed, come to bless with fire and fra-grance
Bm D/F♯ Em A7 D G
to the stir - ring, faint with - in: seed of prom - ise, deep - ly
shines the hope of com - ing day. Christ, the morn - ing star of
hours of yearn-ing, hurt, and need. In the lone - ly, in the
D Bm F♯m Em7 A7 Bm F♯m
plant - ed, child to spring from Jes - se's stem! Like the soil be -
splen - dor, gleams with-in a world grown dim. Heav - en's em - ber
strang - er, in the out - cast, hid from view: child who comes to

Text: Mary Louise Bringle (USA), 2005, © 2006 GIA Publications, Inc.
Music: Welsh traditional; harm. Alfred V. Fedak (USA), © 2011 Alfred V. Fedak

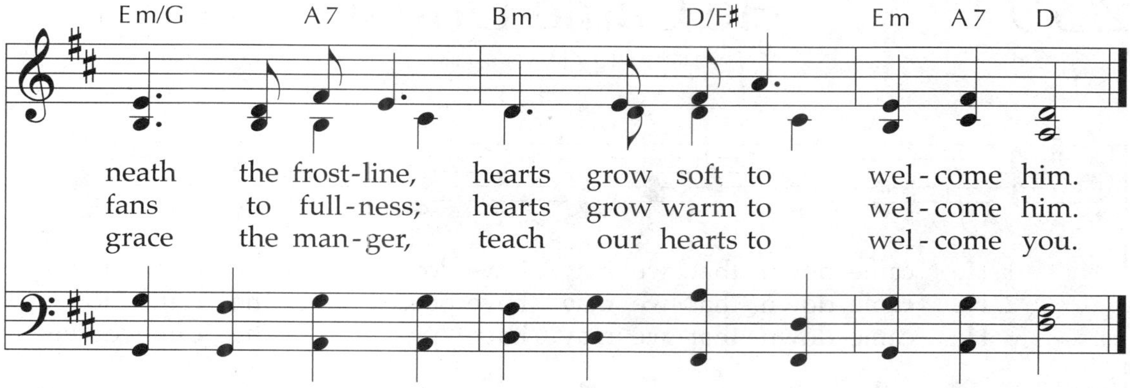
neath the frost-line, hearts grow soft to wel-come him.
fans to full-ness; hearts grow warm to wel-come him.
grace the man-ger, teach our hearts to wel-come you.

Wisdom from on High Is Dawning 238

PICARDY Irregular

1 Wis-dom from on high is dawn-ing. E-ven now a gold-en ray shines in-to a world of shad-ows from the realms of end-less day. Hid-den womb who birthed the heav-ens in the womb now hides a-way.
2 In her heart the joy of heav-en, in her hands the poor of earth, on her back all hu-man sor-row, in her laugh all hu-man mirth. God most hu-man, God most ho-ly, God in-car-nate comes to birth.
3 All cre-a-tion stands in won-der as her glo-ry fills the sky. Down in ad-o-ra-tion fall-ing, we her chil-dren raise the cry: She who is and was and ev-er-more shall be, al-le-lu-ia! God most high!

For an alternate chord progression, see "You, Lord, Are Both Lamb and Shepherd" (#432).

Text: Adam Michael Wood (USA), rev. 2017, © 2010 Adam Michael Wood
Music: French traditional, *Chansons populaires des provinces de France*, 1860

239 He Came Down

HE CAME DOWN Irregular

G D7 G G7 C Cm6 G/D D7 G
1 He came down that we may have love; he came down that we may have love; he came down that we may have love; hal-le - lu - jah for ev - er - more.
2 He came down that we may have peace; he came down that we may have peace; he came down that we may have peace; hal-le - lu - jah for ev - er - more.
3 He came down that we may have joy; he came down that we may have joy; he came down that we may have joy; hal-le - lu - jah for ev - er - more.
Leader (omit last time)
Why did he come?

Text: Cameroon traditional
Music: Cameroon traditional; arr. John L. Bell (Scotland)

Joy to the World

240

ANTIOCH CM extended

D A7 D G A
1 Joy to the world, the Lord is come! Let earth re - ceive its
2 Joy to the earth, the Sav - ior reigns! Let all their songs em -
3 No more let sins and sor - rows grow, nor thorns in - fest the
4 He rules the world with truth and grace, and makes the na - tions
D
king; let ev - 'ry heart pre - pare him room, and
ploy while fields and floods, rocks, hills, and plains, re -
ground. He comes to make his bless - ings flow far
prove the glo - ries of his right - eous - ness, and
A
heav'n and na - ture sing, and heav'n and na - ture
peat the sound - ing joy, re - peat the sound - ing
as the curse is found, far as the curse is
won - ders of his love, and won - ders of his
and heav'n and na - ture sing, and
D D/A A7 D
sing, and heav'n, and heav'n and na - ture sing.
joy, re - peat, re - peat the sound - ing joy.
found, far as, far as the curse is found.
love, and won - ders, won - ders of his love.
heav'n and na - ture sing,

Text: based on Psalm 98; Isaac Watts (England), *The Psalms of David* [. . .], 1719, alt.
Music: Lowell Mason (USA), *Occasional Psalm and Hymn Tunes*, 1836

241 O Come, All Ye Faithful

ADESTE FIDELES Irregular

Descant, verse 3
3 Sing, choirs of an - gels, sing in ex - ul - ta - tion,
G D G C G D
A - de - ste fi - de - les læ - ti tri - um - phan - tes, ve -
1 O come, all ye faith - ful, joy - ful and tri - um - phant, O
2 True God of true God, Light of light e - ter - nal,
3 Sing, choirs of an - gels, sing in ex - ul - ta - tion,
4 Yea, Lord, we greet thee, born this hap - py morn - ing,

sing, all ye cit - i - zens of heav'n a - bove;
Em D A7 D G D A7 D
ni - te, ve - ni - te in Beth - le - hem
come ye, O come ye to Beth - le - hem.
our low - ly na - ture he hath not ab - horred;
sing, all ye cit - i - zens of heav'n a - bove:
Je - sus, to thee be all glo - ry giv'n;

*Congregation sings in unison when in combination with verse 3 descant or with verse 4 alternative accompaniment.

Text: Latin; stanzas 1, 3, 4 trans. attr. John F. Wade (England), ca. 1743, "Adeste fideles læti triumphantes," *Office de St. Omer*, 1822; trans. Frederick Oakeley (England) and others, alt.; stanza 2 Etienne J. F. Borderies (France), 1822; trans. William Mercer (England), 1854

Music: attr. John F. Wade, ca. 1743, *Essay on the Church Plain Chant*, 1782; desc. David Willcocks (England), © 1961 Oxford University Press, Oxford

glo - - - ry in the high - est.
G D G D Em D
na - tum vi - de - te reg - em an - ge - lo - rum.
Come and be - hold him, born the King of an - gels.
born of a wom - an, here in flesh ap - pear - ing.
"Glo - ry to God, all glo - ry in the high - est!"
Word of the Fa - ther, be - got - ten, not cre - at - ed.
O come, O come,
Refrain
G D7 G D
Ve - ni - te a - dor - e - mus, ve - ni - te a - dor - e - mus,
O come let us a - dore him, O come let us a - dore him,
let us a - dore him, Christ the Lord.
D7 A7 D7 G C G D7 G
ve - ni - te a - dor - e - mus, Do - mi - num.
O come let us a - dore him, Christ the Lord.

242 Noche anunciada (Night Long Awaited)

EL NACIMIENTO 9.9.9.9

C G7/D C/E F C G7
1 No - che‿a-nun - cia - da, no - che de‿a - mor, Dios ha na -
2 En el pe - se - bre, mi Re - den - tor es men - sa -
3 Es - ta‿es la no - che que pro - me - tió Dios a los
1 Night long a - wait - ed, God comes to earth; bloom - ing like
2 Sleep in a man - ger, safe and a - dored. All that is
3 Now is God's prom - ise born in the night; wake to its
Am Am7 D7 Gsus G C G7/D C/E
ci - do, pé - ta - lo‿y flor. To - do‿es si - len - cio‿y
je - ro de paz y‿a - mor; cuan - do son - rí - e
pue - blos, y ya lle - gó; es No - che - bue - na,
ros - es, love giv - en birth. Still in the star - light,
bro - ken shall be re - stored. Light for our shad - ows,
full - ness; live in its light. Christ comes a - mong us;
C7 F C F G7 C
se - re - ni - dad, paz en la tie - rra, es Na - vi - dad.
se‿ha - ce la luz y‿en sus bra - ci - tos cre - ce‿un - a cruz.
no‿hay que dor - mir, Dios ha na - ci - do, Dios es - tá‿a - quí.
si - lent and clear, peace comes a - mong us; Christ - mas is here.
grace for our loss; born of our dy - ing; bear - ing our cross.
peo - ple, draw near! Come to the man - ger; Christ - mas is here.

Text: Spanish; Félix César Luna (Argentina), *Navidad Nuestra,* 1965, © Félix César Luna; trans. Adam M. L. Tice (USA), 2018
Music: Ariel Ramírez (Argentina), *Navidad Nuestra,* 1965, © Ariel Ramírez; arr. Carlos Colón (USA), 2017

Infant Holy, Infant Lowly 243

W ZLOBIE LEZY 8.7.8.7.8.8.7.7

G D G G/B C D7 G
1 In - fant ho - ly, in - fant low - ly, for his bed a cat - tle stall;
2 Flocks were sleep - ing; shep - herds keep - ing vig - il till the morn - ing new
D7 G D7 G G/B C D7 G
ox - en low - ing, lit - tle know - ing Christ the babe is Lord of all.
saw the glo - ry, heard the sto - ry, tid - ings of a gos - pel true.
C Am D Bm Em Am Dsus D
Swift - ly wing - ing an - gels sing - ing, bells are ring - ing, tid - ings bring - ing:
Thus re - joic - ing, free from sor - row, prais - es voic - ing, greet the mor - row:
G Am D7 Em Bm G/B C G/D D7 G
Christ the babe is Lord of all! Christ the babe is Lord of all!
Christ the babe was born for you! Christ the babe was born for you!

Text: Polish traditional; trans. Edith M. G. Reed (England), *Primary Education: A Monthly Journal for Primary Teachers* 28, no. 10 (December 1920)

Music: Polish traditional; harm. Arthur E. Rusbridge (England), 1962,

244 Stille Nacht, heilige Nacht (Silent Night, Holy Night / Noche de paz, noche de amor)

STILLE NACHT Irregular

Capo 3: (G) B♭ (D7) F7
German: 1 Stil - le Nacht, hei - li - ge Nacht! Al - les schläft,
English: 1 Si - lent night, ho - ly night! All is calm,
Spanish: 1 ¡No - che de paz, no - che de‿a - mor! To - do duer - me‿en
(G) B♭ (C) E♭ (G) B♭
ein - sam wacht, nur das trau - te, hoch hei - li - ge Paar.
all is bright round yon vir - gin moth - er and child!
de - rre - dor. En - tre los as - tros que‿es - par - cen su luz,
(C) E♭ (G) B♭ (D7) F7
Hold - er Knab - e im lock - ig - en Haar, schlaf in himm - li - scher
Ho - ly in - fant, so ten - der and mild, sleep in heav - en - ly
be - lla,‿a - nun - cian - do‿al ni - ñi - to Je - sús, bri - lla la‿es - tre - lla de

Text: German; Joseph Mohr (Austria), 1818, *Leipziger Gesangbuch*, 1838; English trans. John F. Young (USA), *The Sunday School Service and Tune Book*, 1863; Spanish trans. Federico Fliedner (Spain), ca. 19th c.
Music: Franz Gruber (Austria), 1818, *Leipziger Gesangbuch*, 1838

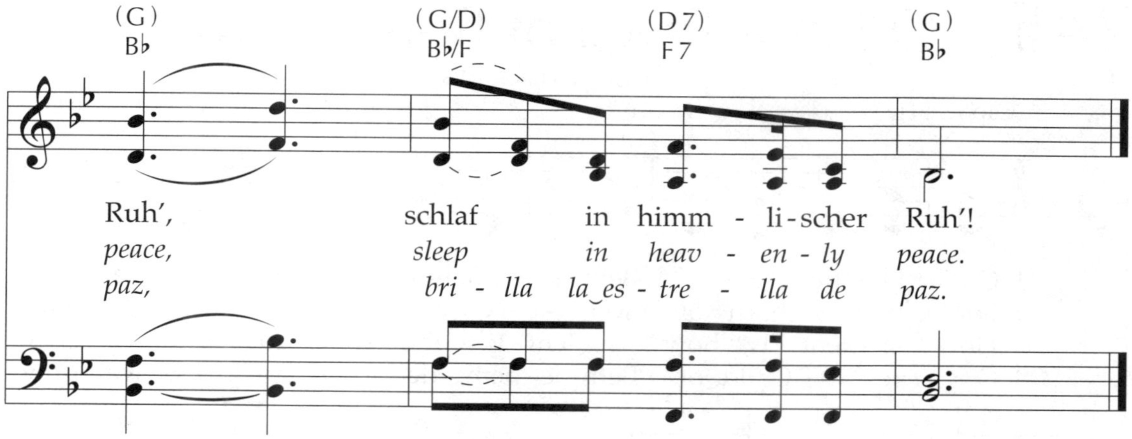
(G) B♭ (G/D) B♭/F (D7) F7 (G) B♭
Ruh', schlaf in himm - li-scher Ruh'!
peace, sleep in heav - en - ly peace.
paz, bri - lla la‿es - tre - lla de paz.

2 Stille Nacht, heilige Nacht!
Hirten erst kundgemacht
durch der Engel Halleluja,
tönt es laut von fern und nah:
Christ, der Retter, ist da!
Christ, der Retter, ist da!

3 Stille Nacht, heilige Nacht!
Gottes Sohn, o wie lacht
Lieb aus deinem göttlichen Mund,
da uns schlägt die rettende Stund',
Christ, in deiner Geburt!
Christ, in deiner Geburt!

4 Stille Nacht, heilige Nacht!
Die der Welt Heil gebracht,
aus des Himmels goldenen Höh'n,
uns der Gnaden Fülle läßt seh'n,
Jesum in Menschengestalt!
Jesum in Menschengestalt!

2 Silent night, holy night!
Shepherds quake at the sight:
glories stream from heaven afar,
heav'nly hosts sing, "Alleluia!
Christ the Savior is born,
Christ the Savior is born!"

3 Silent night, holy night!
Son of God, love's pure light,
radiant, beams from thy holy face
with the dawn of redeeming grace,
Jesus, Lord, at thy birth,
Jesus, Lord, at thy birth!

4 Silent night, holy night!
Wondrous star, lend thy light.
With the angels let us sing
"Alleluia" to our King,
"Christ the Savior is born,
Christ the Savior is born."

2 ¡Noche de paz, noche de amor!
Oye humilde el fiel pastor,
coros celestes que anuncian salud,
gracias y glorias en gran plenitud,
por nuestro buen Redentor,
por nuestro buen Redentor.

3 ¡Noche de paz, noche de amor!
Ved qué bello resplandor
luce en el rostro del niño Jesús,
en el pesebre, del mundo la luz,
astro de eterno fulgor,
astro de eterno fulgor.

245 O Little Town of Bethlehem

ST. LOUIS 8.6.8.6.7.6.7.6

Capo 3: (D) F (Em) Gm (D/A) F/C (A7) C7 (D) F
1 O lit - tle town of Beth - le - hem, how still we see thee lie!
2 For Christ is born of Ma - ry, and gath - ered all a - bove,
3 How si - lent - ly, how si - lent - ly, the won - drous gift is giv'n!
4 O ho - ly Child of Beth - le - hem, de - scend to us, we pray,
(D) F (B7) D7 (Em) Gm (D/A) F/C (A7) C7 (D) F
A - bove thy deep and dream - less sleep the si - lent stars go by.
while mor - tals sleep, the an - gels keep their watch of won - d'ring love.
So God im - parts to hu - man hearts the bless - ings of the heav'ns.
cast out our sin, and en - ter in, be born in us to - day!
(D) F (Em) Gm (F♯) A (Bm) Dm (Em) Gm (F♯) A
Yet in thy dark streets shin - eth the ev - er - last - ing light;
O morn - ing stars, to - geth - er pro - claim the ho - ly birth!
No ear may hear his com - ing, but in this world of sin,
We hear the Christ - mas an - gels the great glad tid - ings tell.
(D) F (Em) Gm (D/A) F/C (A7) C7 (D) F
the hopes and fears of all the years are met in thee to - night.
And prais - es sing—let "Glo - ry!" ring with peace to all on earth!
where meek souls will re - ceive him still the dear Christ en - ters in.
O come to us, a - bide with us, our Lord Em - man - u - el.

Text: Phillips Brooks (USA), 1868, *Sunday School Services and Hymn Book*, 1870, alt.
Music: Lewis H. Redner (USA), 1868, *The Church Porch: A Service Book and Hymnal for Sunday Schools*, 1874

Come, Join in Mary's Prophet-Song 246

SALVATION CMD

1 Come, join in Ma-ry's proph-et - song of jus - tice for the earth,
2 The "Peace on earth" which shep-herds heard is not some fan - ta - sy.
3 Em - ma - nu - el, God - with - us here, grows peace where we would dare
for right out-grows the fierc - est wrong, re - veal - ing hu - man worth—
The an - gels sang to greet the Word, whose birth is vic - to - ry.
to act de - spite our trem-bling fear and bring God's ho - ly care.
bound not with - in the wealth we crave or in the arms we bear,
The maid-en Ma - ry, not so mild, bore in - to death's do - main
The im - age God made "us" to be is al - so borne on "them."
but in the ho - ly sign God gave: the im - age that we share.
true God, and yet an in - fant child, who o - ver death would reign.
Christ bids us join our en - e - my to sing war's req - ui - em.

Text: Adam M. L. Tice (USA), 2005, © 2009 GIA Publications, Inc.
Music: Robert Boyd (USA), 1816, *Kentucky Harmony*, 1817

247 Hark! the Herald Angels Sing

MENDELSSOHN 7.7.7.7 D

Descant, verse 3
3 Hail the heav'n-born Prince of Peace! Hail the Sun of right-eous-ness! Light and life to all he brings, ris'n with heal-ing in his wings. Mild he lays his glo-ry
F C F C F B♭
1 Hark! the her-ald an-gels sing, "Glo-ry to the new-born King! Peace on earth and mer-cy mild, God and sin-ners rec-on-ciled." Joy-ful all ye na-tions,
2 Christ, by high-est heav'n a-dored; Christ, the ev-er-last-ing Lord, late in time be-hold him come, off-spring of the vir-gin's womb. Veiled in flesh the God-head
3 Hail the heav'n-born Prince of Peace! Hail the Sun of right-eous-ness! Light and life to all he brings, ris'n with heal-ing in his wings. Mild he lays his glo-ry
F/C C F F Dm G7
Am C F G7 C F C7 F

Text: Charles Wesley (England), *Hymns and Sacred Poems*, 1739, alt.
Music: Felix Mendelssohn (Germany), 1840; adapt. William H. Cummings (England), 1855, *Congregational Hymn and Tune Book*, 1857; desc. David Willcocks (England), *Carols for Choirs*,

by, born that we no more may die, born to raise us
C F C7 F C B♭
rise, join the tri-umph of the skies. With th'an-gel-ic
see, hail th'in-car-nate de-i-ty; pleased with us in
by, born that we no more may die, born to raise us
from the earth, born to give us sec-ond birth.
D7 Gm C7 F C F
host pro-claim, "Christ is born in Beth-le-hem!"
flesh to dwell, Je-sus, our Im-man-u-el!
from the earth, born to give us sec-ond birth.
Hark! the her-ald an-gels sing, "Glo-ry to the new-born King."
B♭ D Gm C7 F C7 F
Hark! the her-ald an-gels sing, "Glo-ry to the new-born King."

248 It Came upon a Midnight Clear

CAROL CMD

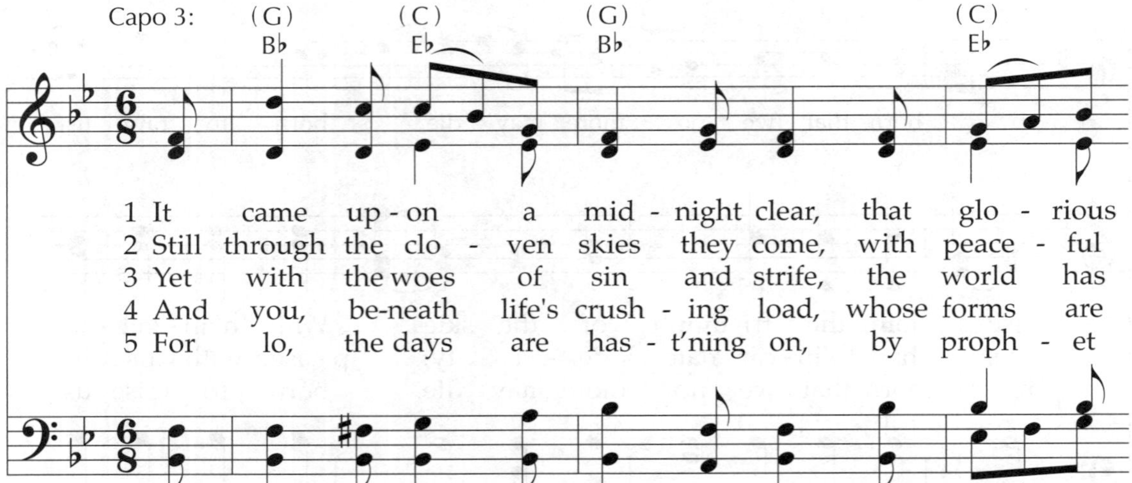
Capo 3: (G) B♭ (C) E♭ (G) B♭ (C) E♭
1 It came up - on a mid - night clear, that glo - rious
2 Still through the clo - ven skies they come, with peace - ful
3 Yet with the woes of sin and strife, the world has
4 And you, be-neath life's crush - ing load, whose forms are
5 For lo, the days are has - t'ning on, by proph - et

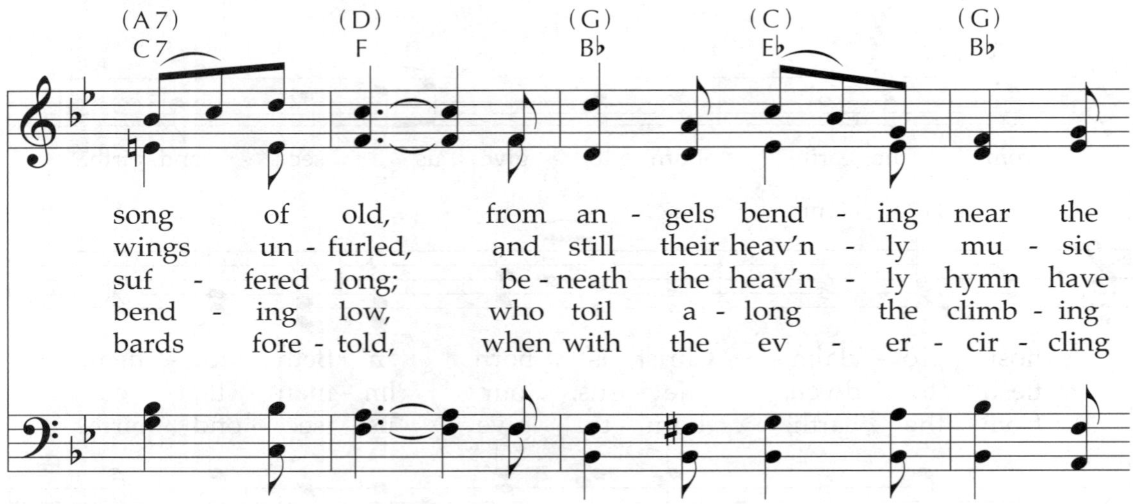
(A7) C7 (D) F (G) B♭ (C) E♭ (G) B♭
song of old, from an - gels bend - ing near the
wings un - furled, and still their heav'n - ly mu - sic
suf - fered long; be - neath the heav'n - ly hymn have
bend - ing low, who toil a - long the climb - ing
bards fore - told, when with the ev - er - cir - cling

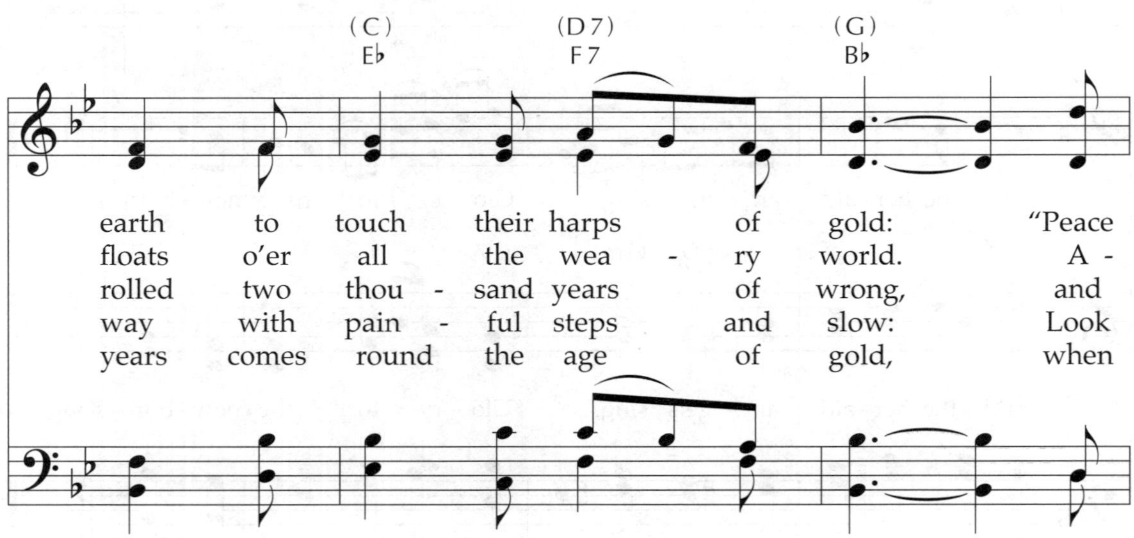
(C) E♭ (D7) F7 (G) B♭
earth to touch their harps of gold: "Peace
floats o'er all the wea - ry world. A -
rolled two thou - sand years of wrong, and
way with pain - ful steps and slow: Look
years comes round the age of gold, when

Text: Edmund H. Sears (USA), *Christian Register*, 1849, alt.
Music: Richard S. Willis (USA), *Church Carols and Choir Studies*, 1850

(B) (Em) (B) (Em) (D)
D Gm D Gm F
on the earth, good will to all from heav - en's
bove its sad and low - ly plains they bend on
war - ring hu - man - kind hears not the tid - ings
now! for glad and gold - en hours come swift - ly
peace shall o - ver all the earth its an - cient
(A7) (D) (D7) (G) (C)
C7 F F7 B♭ E♭
gra - cious King." The world in sol - emn
hov - 'ring wing, and ev - er o'er its
which they bring. O hush the noise and
on the wing. O rest be - side the
splen - dors fling, and all the world sends
(G) (C) (D7) (G)
B♭ E♭ F7 B♭
still - ness lay, to hear the an - gels sing.
Ba - bel sounds the bless - ed an - gels sing.
cease your strife and hear the an - gels sing.
wea - ry road, and hear the an - gels sing.
back the song which now the an - gels sing.

249 Angels We Have Heard on High (Les anges dans nos campagnes)

GLORIA 7.7.7.7 (English) or 8.8.8.8 (French) with refrain

Capo 3: (D) (F♯m) (A) (D) (A) (D)
F Am C F C F
1 An - gels we have heard on high, sing - ing sweet - ly through the night,
2 Shep-herds, why this ju - bi - lee? Why these songs of hap - py cheer?
3 Come to Beth - le - hem and see him whose birth the an - gels sing.
4 See him in a man - ger laid whom the an - gels praise a - bove.
(D) (F♯m) (A) (D) (A) (D)
F Am C F C F
and the moun-tains in re - ply ech - o - ing their brave de - light.
What great bright-ness did you see? What glad ti - dings did you hear?
Come, a - dore on bend - ed knee Christ the Lord, the new - born King.
Ma - ry, Jo - seph, lend your aid, while we raise our hearts in love.
(D) (Bm7) (Em7) (A7) (Dmaj7) (G) (A)
F Dm7 Gm7 C7 Fmaj7 B♭ C
Refrain
Glo - - - - - ri - a

Text: French; *Nouveau recueil de cantiques* (France), 1855; trans. anon.; alt. Earl Marlatt (USA), *New Church Hymnal*, 1937
Music: French traditional, *Nouveau recueil de cantiques*, 1855

(D) F (A) C (D) F (Bm7) Dm7 (Em7) Gm7 (A7) C7
in ex-cel-sis De-o, glo - - -
(Dmaj7) Fmaj7 (G) B♭ (A) C (D) F (D/A) F/C (A) C (D) F
- - ri-a in ex-cel-sis De - o.
French verses
1 Les an-ges dans nos cam-pa-gnes ont en-ton-né, l'hym-ne des cieux, et l'é-cho de nos mon-ta-gnes re-dit ce chant mé-lo-di-eux.
2 Ber-gers, pour qui cet-te fê-te? Quel est l'ob-jet de tous ces chants? Quel vain-queur, quel-le con-quê-te mé-ri-te ces cris tri-om-phants?
3 Cher-chons tous l'heu-reux vil-la-ge qui l'a vu naî-tre sous ses toits; of-frons-lui le ten-dre‿hom-ma-ge et de nos cœurs et de nos voix!
To refrain

250 The First Noel, the Angel Did Say

THE FIRST NOEL Irregular

D Bm A Em D/F♯ G D G D Em6
1 The first No - el the an-gel did say was to cer-tain poor
2 They look - ed up and saw a star shin-ing in the
3 And by the light of that same star three wise men
4 This star drew nigh to the north - west, o'er Beth - le -
5 Then en - tered in those wise men three, full rev - 'rent-
D G A7/E D A7 D A7 D Bm A Em D/F♯
shep-herds in fields as they lay— in fields where they lay keep-ing
east, be - yond them far, and to the earth it gave
came from coun - try far. To seek for a king was their
hem it took its rest, and there it did both stop
ly up - on the knee, and of - fered there in his
G D G D A7/E D G A7/E D A7 D
their sheep, on a cold win - ter's night that was so deep.
great light, and so it con - tin-ued both day and night.
in - tent, and to fol - low the star wher - ev - er it went.
and stay, right o - ver the place where Je - sus lay.
pres - ence, their gold and myrrh and frank - in - cense.

Text: English traditional, *Some Ancient Christmas Carols*, 2nd ed., 1823
Music: English traditional, *Christmas Carols*, 1833

Refrain
A7 D Bm F#m D G D A
No - el, No - el, No - el, No - el,
Bm D G D A7/E D A7 D
born is the King of Is - ra - el.

There Were Angels Hovering Round 251

ANGELS HOVERING ROUND Irregular

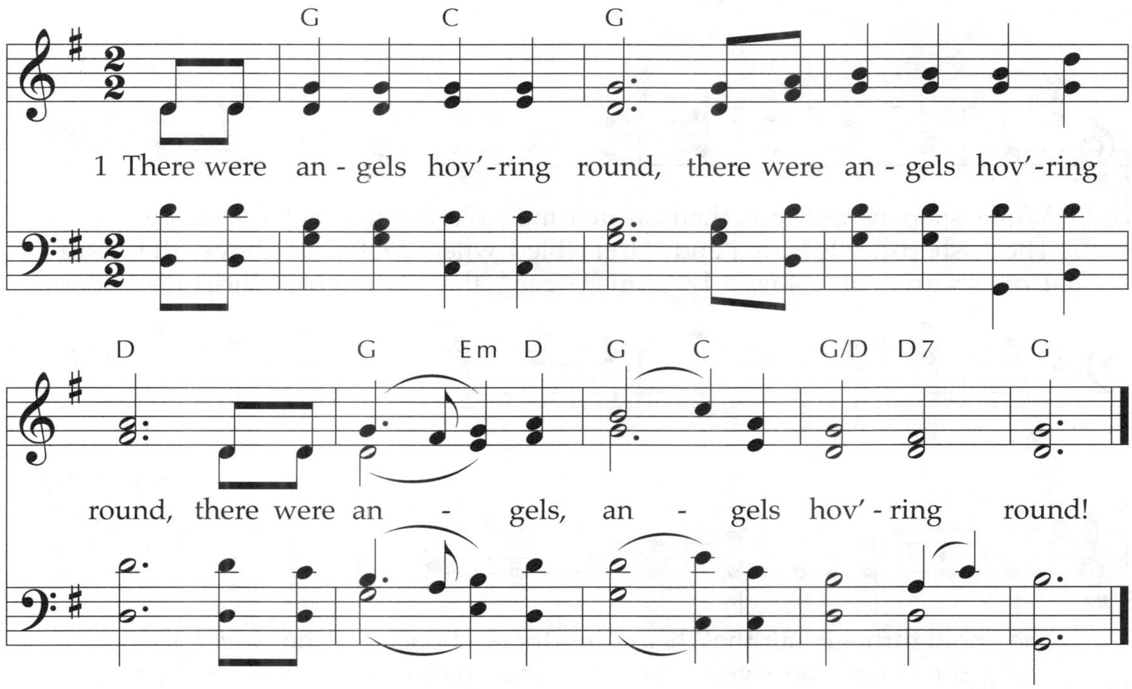
G C G
1 There were an - gels hov'-ring round, there were an - gels hov'-ring
D G Em D G C G/D D7 G
round, there were an - gels, an - gels hov' - ring round!

2 They | sing in harmony, *(x2)*
they | sing, they sing in harmony.

3 The | child in Mary's arms, *(x2)*
the | child, the child in Mary's arms.

4 The | shepherds on their knees, *(x2)*
the | shepherds, shepherds on their knees.

5 There are | angels hov'ring round, *(x2)*
there are | angels, angels hov'ring round!

Verses may be added to fill out the story.

Text: American traditional (USA), 19th c.
Music: American traditional, 19th c.

252 Go Tell It on the Mountain

GO TELL IT ON THE MOUNTAIN 7.6.7.6 with refrain

Swing:
Refrain
G Em D7 G
Go tell it on the moun-tain, o-ver the hills and ev-'ry-where;
Em G/D D7 G
go tell it on the moun-tain that Je-sus Christ is born!
D7 G
1 While shep-herds kept their watch-ing o'er si-lent flocks by night,
2 The shep-herds feared and trem-bled when lo! a-bove the earth
3 Down in a low-ly man-ger the hum-ble Christ was born,
A D7 To refrain
be-hold through-out the heav-ens there shone a ho-ly light.
rang out the an-gel cho-rus that hailed our Sav-ior's birth.
and God sent us sal-va-tion that bless-ed Christ-mas morn.

Text: African American spiritual (USA); adapt. John W. Work Jr. (USA), 1871–1925

Music: African American spiritual; arr. Valeria A. Foster (USA), alt.,

While Shepherds Watched Their Flocks 253

CHRISTMAS CM

D A G D/F♯ D
1 While shep-herds watched their flocks by night, all seat-ed
2 "Fear not," said he, for might-y dread had seized their
3 "To you, in Da-vid's town, this day is born of
4 "The heav'n-ly babe you there shall find to hu-man
5 The an-gel spoke, and sud-den-ly ap-peared a
6 "All glo-ry be to God on high and to the
G D/A A D Em A D
on the ground, the an-gel of the Lord came down,
trou-bled mind. "Glad tid-ings of great joy I bring
Da-vid's line the Sav-ior, who is Christ the Lord,
view dis-played, all hum-bly wrapped in swath-ing bands,
shin-ing throng of an-gels prais-ing God, and thus
earth be peace, good-will hence-forth from heav'n to earth
G G/D D Em D/F♯ D/A A7 D
and glo-ry shone a-round, and glo-ry shone a-round.
to you and hu-man-kind, to you and hu-man-kind.
and this shall be the sign, and this shall be the sign:
and in a man-ger laid, and in a man-ger laid."
ad-dressed their joy-ful song, ad-dressed their joy-ful song:
be-gin and ne-ver cease, be-gin and ne-ver cease!"

Text: based on Luke 2:8–14; Nahum Tate (England), 1700
Music: George F. Handel (England), 1728

254 O du fröhliche (Oh, How Joyfully)

O SANCTISSIMA 5.5.7.4.4.7

E A E A E B F♯ B
1 O du fröh-li-che, o du se-li-ge, gna-den-bring-en-de
2 O du fröh-li-che, o du se-li-ge, gna-den-bring-en-de
3 O du fröh-li-che, o du se-li-ge, gna-den-bring-en-de
1 Oh, how joy-ful-ly, oh, how hope-ful-ly, waits the earth on
2 Oh, how joy-ful-ly, oh, how peace-ful-ly, sleeps the earth on
3 Oh, how joy-ful-ly, oh, how thank-ful-ly, wakes the earth on
F♯ B E
Weih-nachts-zeit! Welt ging ver-lo-ren; Christ ist ge-
Weih-nachts-zeit! Christ ist er-schie-nen, uns zu ver-
Weih-nachts-zeit! Himm-li-sche Hee-re jauch-zen dir
Christ-mas eve! Love comes heal-ing, God re-
Christ-mas night! Sins are cov-ered, grace dis-
Christ-mas morn! God has spo-ken, death is
A E/B B7 E
bor-en: Freu-e, freu-e dich, o Chris-ten-heit!
süh-nen, Freu-e, freu-e dich, o Chris-ten-heit!
Eh-re. Freu-e, freu-e dich, o Chris-ten-heit!
veal-ing. Friends, be joy-ful and be-lieve!
cov-ered. In our dark-ness shines the light!
bro-ken. Al-le-lu-ia! Christ is born!

Text: German; stanza 1 Johann D. Falk (Germany), *Auserlesene Werke*, 1819; stanzas 2, 3 Heinrich Holzschuher (Germany); trans. Harris Loewen (Canada), re-envisioned by Brian Wren (England),

Music: Sicilian traditional, *The European Magazine and London Review*, 1792; harm. anon.

Love Came Down at Christmas 255

LOVE INCARNATE 6.7.6.7 with refrain

F C Dm C F
1 Love came down at Christ - mas, love all love - ly,
2 Wor - ship we the God - head, love in - car - nate,
3 Love shall be our to - ken, love be yours and
B♭ C F C Dm A7
love di - vine. Love was born at Christ - mas—
love di - vine. Wor - ship we our Je - sus—
love be mine, love to God and neigh - bor,
B♭ F C F
star and an - gels gave the sign.
what shall be our sa - cred sign?
love the u - ni - ver - sal sign.
Refrain
B♭
Sing no - el,
Sing no -
F B♭ F
sing no - el, sing no - el.
el, sing no - el.

Chord symbols represent a simplified harmony.

Text: Christina G. Rossetti (England), *Time Flies: A Reading Diary*, 1885; rev. in *Hymns for Today's Church*, 1987, © 1982 Jubilate Group (admin. Hope Publishing Co.)
Music: C. Edgar Pettman (England), *University Carol Book*, 1923

256 Noel

NOEL 7.7.7.8.7.7 with refrain

Capo 4: (Am)
C♯m
Love in-car-nate, love di-vine, star and an-gels gave the sign.
Bow to babe on bend-ed knee, the
(Fmaj7)
Amaj7
Sav-ior of hu-man-i-ty. Un-to us a child is born;
(Dm7)
F♯m7
he shall reign for - ev - er - more.
Refrain
(C) E (Am7) C♯m7 (F2) A2
No - el, No - el! Come and see what God has done!
(C) E (Am7) C♯m7
No - el, No - el! The
(F2) A2 (C) E
sto - ry of a - maz - ing love! The light of the world
(Gsus) Bsus (Dm7) F♯m7 (Fmaj9) Amaj9
giv-en for us. No - el!

Text: Chris Tomlin (USA), Ed Cash (USA), and Matt Redman (England)
Music: Chris Tomlin, Ed Cash, and Matt Redman

Away in a Manger 257

MUELLER 11.11.11.11

Capo 3: (D) F (G) B♭ (D) F
1 A - way in a man - ger, no crib for a bed,
2 The cat - tle are low - ing, the ba - by a - wakes,
3 Be near me, Lord Je - sus, I ask thee to stay
(A7) C7 (D) F
the lit - tle Lord Je - sus laid down his sweet head.
but lit - tle Lord Je - sus no cry - ing he makes.
close by me for - ev - er, and love me, I pray.
(G) B♭ (D) F
The stars in the bright sky looked down where he lay,
I love thee, Lord Je - sus! Look down from the sky,
Bless all the dear chil - dren in thy ten - der care,
(A7) C7 (D) F (Em/G) Gm/B♭ (A7) C7 (D) F
the lit - tle Lord Je - sus a - sleep on the hay.
and stay by my side un - til morn - ing is nigh.
and fit us for heav - en to live with thee there.

Alternate tune: CRADLE SONG (#510)

Text: stanzas 1–2 anon., *Little Children's Book* (USA), 1885; stanza 3 *Vineyard Songs*, 1892
Music: James R. Murray (USA), *Dainty Songs for Little Lads and Lasses*, 1887

258 Love Has Come

UN FLAMBEAU (BRING A TORCH) 9.9.10.9.9.8

F Gm7/B♭ C F
1 Love has come— a light in the dark - ness! Love shines forth in the
2 Love is born! Come, share in the won - der. Love is God now a -
3 Love has come and nev - er will leave us! Love is life ev - er -
Gm/B♭ C7 F F/A B♭ C7
Beth - le - hem skies. See, all heav - en has come to pro - claim it.
sleep in the hay. See the glow in the eyes of his moth - er.
last - ing and free. Love is Je - sus with - in and a - mong us.
B♭ F/A Gm7 C Dm C F
Hear how their song of joy a - ris - es: Love! Love! Born un - to
What is the name her heart is say - ing? Love! Love! Love is the
Love is the peace our hearts are seek - ing. Love! Love! Love is the
C A/C♯ Dm C F C C7 F
you, a Sav - ior! Love! Love! Glo - ry to God on high!
name she whis - pers. Love! Love! Je - sus, Em - man - u - el.
gift of Christ - mas. Love! Love! Praise to you, God on high!

Text: Ken Bible (USA)
Music: attr. Nicolas Saboly (France), 17th c.; harm. Ken Bible

To Us a Child of Hope Is Born 259

ZERAH CM extended

C G C/G G7 C
1 To us a child of hope is born, to us a son is giv'n.
2 His name shall be the Prince of peace, for - ev - er-more a - dored,
3 His pow'r, in-creas-ing, still shall spread, his reign no end shall know.
F C F C
Him shall the tribes of earth o-bey, him all the hosts of heav'n,
the Won-der-ful, the Coun-se-lor, the great and might-y Lord,
Jus - tice shall guard his throne a-bove, and peace a-bound be-low,
Am Dm G C
him shall the tribes of earth o - bey, him all the hosts of heav'n.
the Won-der - ful, the Coun-se - lor, the great and might - y Lord.
jus - tice shall guard his throne a - bove, and peace a-bound be - low.

Text: based on Isaiah 9:6–7; John Morison (Scotland), *Scottish Paraphrases*, 1781
Music: Lowell Mason (USA), *Occasional Psalm and Hymn Tunes*, 1837 or 1838, alt.

260 On This Great Day of Days

PERSONENT HODIE 6.6.6.6.6 with refrain

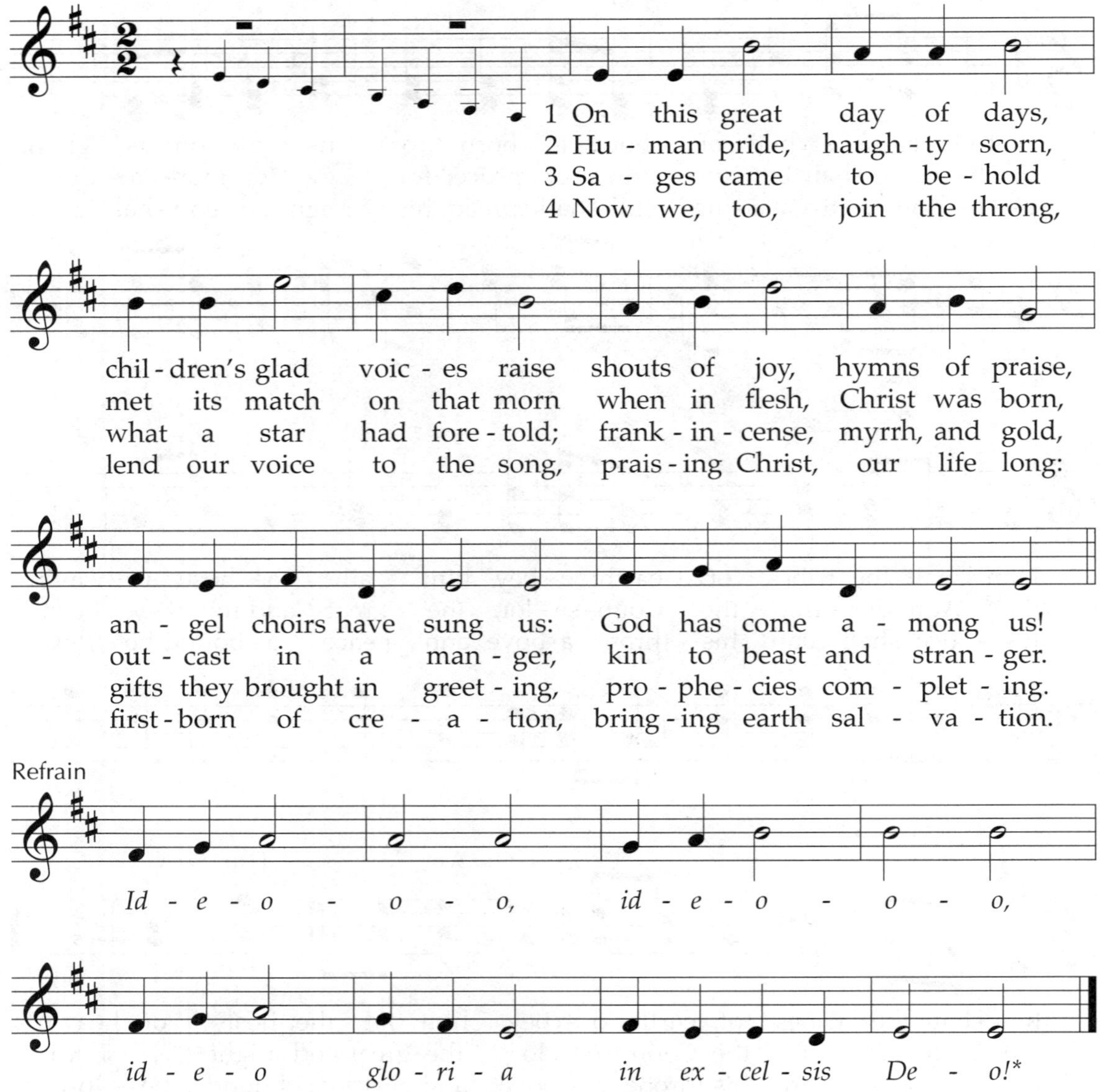
1 On this great day of days,
2 Hu - man pride, haugh - ty scorn,
3 Sa - ges came to be - hold
4 Now we, too, join the throng,
chil - dren's glad voic - es raise shouts of joy, hymns of praise,
met its match on that morn when in flesh, Christ was born,
what a star had fore - told; frank - in - cense, myrrh, and gold,
lend our voice to the song, prais - ing Christ, our life long:
an - gel choirs have sung us: God has come a - mong us!
out - cast in a man - ger, kin to beast and stran - ger.
gifts they brought in greet - ing, pro - phe - cies com - plet - ing.
first - born of cre - a - tion, bring - ing earth sal - va - tion.
Refrain
Id - e - o - o - o, id - e - o - o - o,
*id - e - o glo - ri - a in ex - cel - sis De - o!**

*Translation: Therefore, glory to God in the highest!

Text: Latin; *Piae Cantiones* . . . (modern-day Sweden), 1582; paraphr. Mary Louise Bringle (USA), © 2019 GIA Publications, Inc.
Music: German traditional, 1360, *Piae Cantiones* . . ., 1582

Good Christian Friends, Rejoice 261

IN DULCI JUBILO 6.6.7.7.7.8.5.5

F C
1 Good Chris-tian friends, re - joice, with heart and soul and voice.
2 Good Chris-tian friends, re - joice, with heart and soul and voice.
3 Good Chris-tian friends, re - joice, with heart and soul and voice.
F/A C7 F C7 F Gm/B♭ F/C C7 F
Give ye heed to what we say: Je - sus Christ is born to-day!
Now ye hear of end-less bliss; Je - sus Christ was born for this!
Now ye need not fear the grave; Je - sus Christ was born to save!
F/A C7 F C7 Dm Gm/B♭ F/C C7 F
Ox and ass be - fore him bow, and he is in the man-ger now.
He has o-pened heav-en's door, and we are bless'd for - ev - er - more.
Calls you one and calls you all, to gain his ev - er - las - ting hall.
Dm Asus A7 Dm C F Gm C F
Christ is born to - day! Christ is born to - day!
Christ was born for this! Christ was born for this!
Christ was born to save! Christ was born to save!

Text: "In dulci jubilo" (present-day Germany), 14th c.; trans. John M. Neale (England), *Carols for Christmastide*, 1853, alt.
Music: German traditional, 14th c.; *Geistliche Lieder* (present-day Germany), 1535; harm. Robert L. Pearsall (England), 1837

262 圣夜清 Sheng ye qing (Holy Night, Blessed Night)

SHENG YE JING 6.7.8.9.8

E♭ Cm Gm E♭ Fm B♭ Gm
1 圣 夜 清, 圣 夜 静 明 星
1 Sheng ye qing, sheng ye jing, ming - xing
1 Ho - ly night, bless - ed night, stars shine
2 Ho - ly night, bless - ed night, an - gels
3 Ho - ly night, bless - ed night, Christ has

Fm Gm Fm B♭7 E♭ B♭
灿 烂, 天 地 宁; 水 寂 山 眠,
can - lan tian - di ning; shui ji shan mian,
bright - ly, earth is still: hills and val - leys,
sing praise, shep - herds fear. Earth and heav - en
come down, dwells with us. Sac - ri - fice, love,

Cm E♭ Cm A♭
万 籁 无 声, 卿 云 缭 绕 拥 着 伯 利 恒,
wan - lai wu - sheng, qing yun liao - rao yong - zhe Bo - li - heng,
field and wood - lands, all sur-round the small town Beth - le - hem.
ring with prais - es: "Al - le - lu - ia," all cre - a - tion sings.
peace, and jus - tice shine up - on us like the morn - ing sun.

Text: Mandarin; Wei-yu Zhu (China) and Jing-ren Wu (China), 1921; paraphr. Kathleen Moody (England), paraph. © Kathleen Moody
Music: Qigui Shi (China), 1982; arr. I-to Loh (Taiwan), 1987

Cm Bb Cm Eb Fm Bb7 Eb
客 店 马 槽 诞 生 天 婴.
ke dian ma cao dan-sheng tian ying.
In a man - ger Christ, the child, sleeps.
Tell the good news: Christ is born now.
Grace and glo - ry bless the whole world.

2 圣夜清, 圣夜静,
天使显现, 牧人惊;
金琴玉筝, 漫天歌韵,
哈利路亚! 山海欲齐鸣,
传报佳音: 救主降生!

2 Sheng ye qing, sheng ye jing,
tian-shi xian-xian, mu-ren jing;
jin qin yu zheng, man-tian ge yun,
ha-li-lu-ya! Shan-hai yu qi ming,
chuan bao jia-yin: jiu zhu jiang-sheng!

3 圣夜清, 圣夜静,
救主耶稣今降生;
博爱,牺牲,公义,和平,
圣容赫华犹如日初升,
恩光辉耀, 照彻乾坤!

3 Sheng ye qing, sheng ye jing,
jiu zhu Ye-su jin jiang-sheng;
bo-ai, xi-sheng, gong yi, he-ping,
sheng rong he hua you ru ri chu sheng,
en guang-hui yao, zhao che qian-kun!

263 From Heaven Above to Earth I Come

VOM HIMMEL HOCH LM

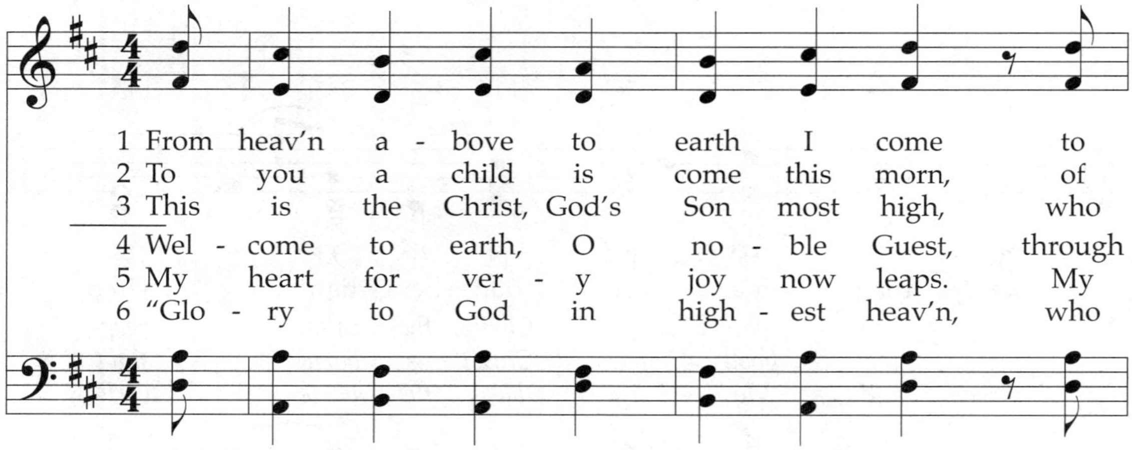
1 From heav'n a - bove to earth I come to
2 To you a child is come this morn, of
3 This is the Christ, God's Son most high, who
4 Wel - come to earth, O no - ble Guest, through
5 My heart for ver - y joy now leaps. My
6 "Glo - ry to God in high - est heav'n, who

bear good news to ev - 'ry - one. Glad tid - ings of great
Ma - ry, cho - sen maid - en, born. This lit - tle child, of
hears your sad and bit - ter cry. He will him - self your
whom this sin - ful world is bless'd! You turned not from our
voice no long - er si - lence keeps. I, too, must join the
un - to us a Son has giv'n." With an - gels sing in

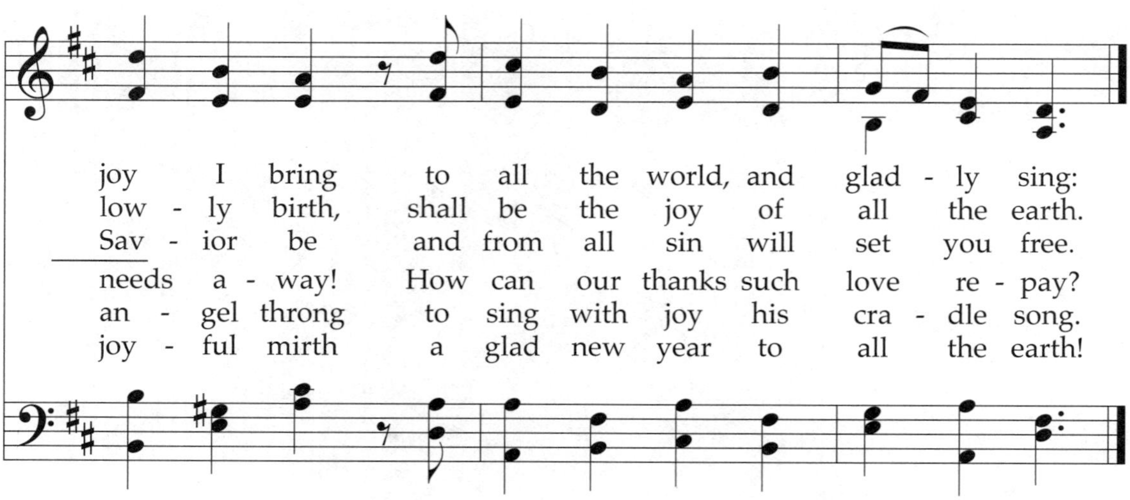
joy I bring to all the world, and glad - ly sing:
low - ly birth, shall be the joy of all the earth.
Sav - ior be and from all sin will set you free.
needs a - way! How can our thanks such love re - pay?
an - gel throng to sing with joy his cra - dle song.
joy - ful mirth a glad new year to all the earth!

Text: Martin Luther (present-day Germany), *Geistliche Lieder*, 1535; trans. Catherine Winkworth (England), *Lyra Germanica*, Series 1, 1855, composite trans. Inter-Lutheran Commission on Worship, alt., ; portions of stanzas 2, 4 George MacDonald (Scotland), *Exotics*, 1876

Music: *Geistliche Lieder* (present-day Germany), 1539

Still, Still, Still

264

STILL, STILL, STILL 3.6.9.8.3.6

Capo 1: (D) (D/C♯) (G) (D/A) (G) (A7) (D)
E♭ E♭/D A♭ E♭/B♭ A♭ B♭7 E♭
1 Still, still, still: the night is calm and still. The
2 Sleep, sleep, sleep: sweet Je - sus, soft - ly sleep, while
3 Joy, joy, joy; glad tid - ings of great joy! For
(A) (D) (A) (D)
B♭ E♭ B♭ E♭
Christ - child in his crib lies sleep - ing; an - gels round him watch are
Ma - ry sings, and gent - ly holds you, safe - ly in her arms en -
through God's ho - ly in - car - na - tion, Christ is born for our sal -
(D/C♯) (G) (D/A) (G) (A7) (D)
E♭/D A♭ E♭/B♭ A♭ B♭7 E♭
keep - ing. Still, still, still: the night is calm and still.
folds you. Sleep, sleep, sleep: sweet Je - sus, soft - ly sleep.
va - tion. Joy, joy, joy; glad tid - ings of great joy!

Text: Austrian traditional, *Salzburgische Volkslieder mit ihren Singweisen*, 1865; trans. John Rutter (England), © 1994 Oxford University Press

Music: Austrian traditional, *Salzburgische Volkslieder mit ihren Singweisen*, 1865; harm. Walter Ehret (USA), alt., © 1963, 1980 Walter Ehret (admin. Walton Music Corp.)

265 Angels, from the Realms of Glory

REGENT SQUARE 8.7.8.7.8.7

C F C
1 An - gels, from the realms of glo - ry, wing your flight o'er
2 Shep - herds, in the field a - bid - ing, watch - ing o'er your
3 Sag - es, leave your con - tem - pla - tions— bright - er vi - sions
4 Saints, be - fore the al - tar bend - ing, watch - ing long in
G7 C Am E
all the earth. As you sang cre - a - tion's sto - ry,
flocks by night, God with us is now re - sid - ing,
beam a - far. Seek the great de - sire of na - tions,
hope and fear, shall be - hold God's love un - end - ing:
Am G/D D7 G
now pro - claim Mes - si - ah's birth;
yon - der shines the in - fant light;
guid - ed by his na - tal star;
Christ will once a - gain ap - pear;
come and wor - ship,
C7 F Dm7 Gsus G7 C
come and wor - ship, wor - ship Christ, the new - born King.

For a lower key, see "For the Healing of the Nations" #705.

Text: James Montgomery (Scotland), *The Sheffield Iris*, 1816, alt.
Music: Henry Smart (England), *Psalms and Hymns for Divine Worship*, 1867

Where Is This Stupendous Stranger 266

McRAE 8.7.8.7

Em Am B Em
1 Where is this stu - pen - dous Stran - ger? Proph - ets,
2 O most Might - y, O most Ho - ly, far be -
3 Oh, the mag - ni - tude of meek - ness! worth from
4 God all bount - eous, all cre - a - tive, whom our
G D G C D G Am Bm
shep - herds, kings, ad - vise! Lead me to my Mas - ter's
yond the ser - aph's thought, are you then so mean and
worth im - mor - tal sprung! Oh, the strength of in - fant
sins could not dis - suade, you have come to be a
Am C Em/B B Em
man - ger, show me where my Sav - ior lies.
low - ly as un - heed - ed proph - ets thought?
weak - ness, if e - ter - nal is so young!
na - tive of the ver - y world you made.

Text: Christopher Smart (England), *Hymns and Spiritual Songs . . .*, 1765, alt.
Music: Joan Fyock Norris (USA),

267 What Child Is This

GREENSLEEVES 8.7.8.7.6.8.6.7

Em G D Em Am B
1 What child is this, who, laid to rest, on Ma-ry's lap is sleep - ing,
2 Why lies he in such mean es - tate where ox and ass are feed - ing?
3 So bring him in - cense, gold, and myrrh; come, peas-ant, king, to own him.
Em G D Em B Esus Em
whom an-gels greet with an-thems sweet, while shep-herds watch are keep-ing?
Good Chris-tian, fear, for sin-ners here the si - lent Word is plead-ing.
The King of kings sal - va - tion brings; let lov - ing hearts en-throne him.
Bm G D Em Am B
This, this is Christ the King, whom shep-herds guard and an - gels sing.
Nails, spear shall pierce him through, the cross be borne for me, for you.
Raise, raise the song on high; the vir - gin sings her lul - la - by.
Bm G D Em B Esus Em
Haste, haste to bring him laud, the babe, the son of Ma - ry!
Hail, hail the Word-made-flesh, the babe, the son of Ma - ry!
Joy, joy, for Christ is born, the babe, the son of Ma - ry!

Text: William C. Dix (England), *Christmas Carols New and Old*, 1871
Music: English traditional

Helpless and Hungry 268

CHILD OF THE POOR 5.4.8.5.8.5 with refrain

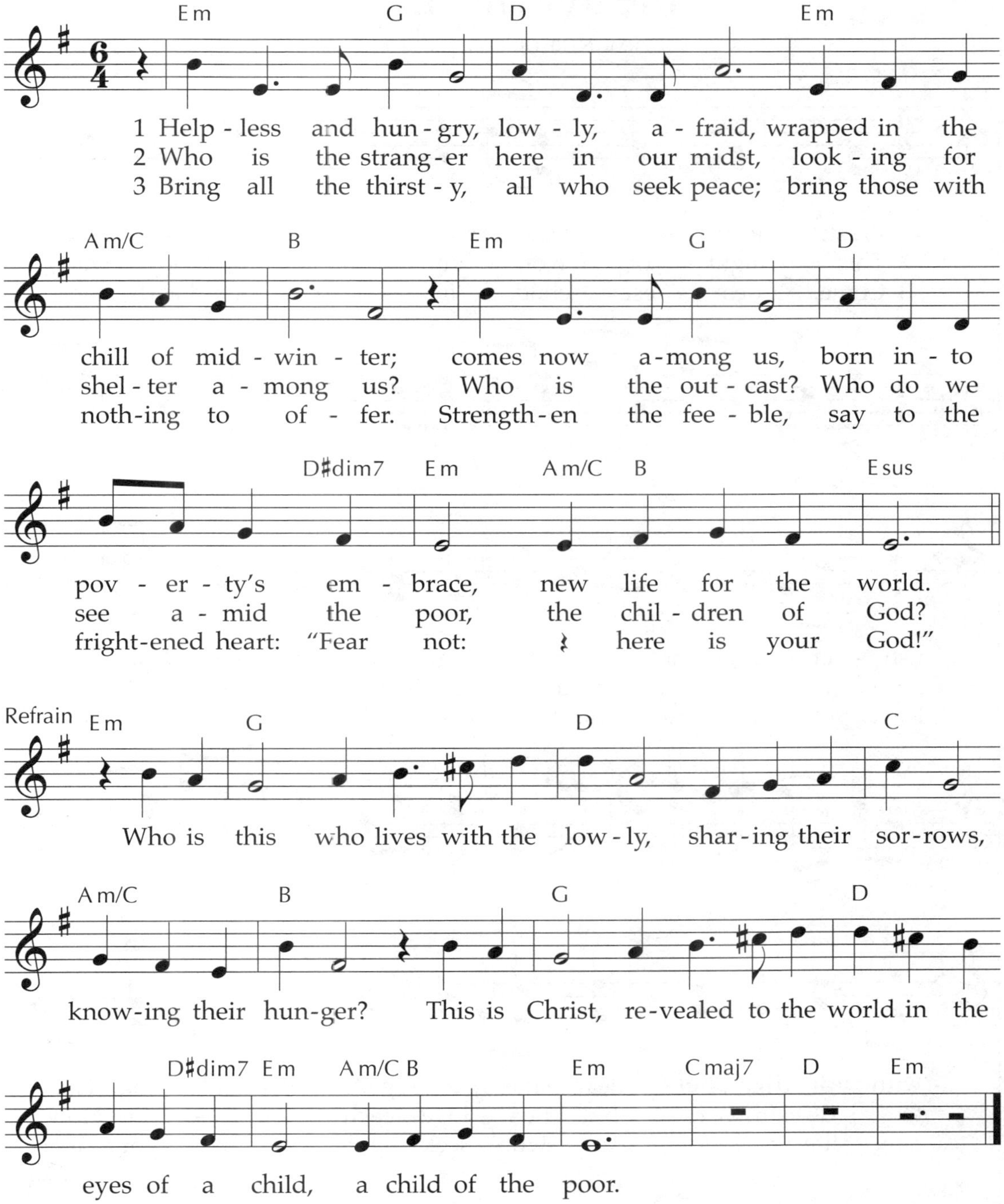
Em G D Em
1 Help - less and hun - gry, low - ly, a - fraid, wrapped in the
2 Who is the strang - er here in our midst, look - ing for
3 Bring all the thirst - y, all who seek peace; bring those with
Am/C B Em G D
chill of mid - win - ter; comes now a - mong us, born in - to
shel - ter a - mong us? Who is the out - cast? Who do we
noth - ing to of - fer. Strength - en the fee - ble, say to the
D♯dim7 Em Am/C B Esus
pov - er - ty's em - brace, new life for the world.
see a - mid the poor, the chil - dren of God?
fright - ened heart: "Fear not: here is your God!"
Refrain
Em G D C
Who is this who lives with the low - ly, shar - ing their sor - rows,
Am/C B G D
know - ing their hun - ger? This is Christ, re - vealed to the world in the
D♯dim7 Em Am/C B Em Cmaj7 D Em
eyes of a child, a child of the poor.

This hymn may be sung with "What Child Is This" (#267, melody only) as follows:

"Helpless and Hungry," verse 1, followed by "What Child Is This," verse 1;
"Helpless and Hungry," verse 2, followed by "What Child Is This," verse 2;
both sung simultaneously on verse 3.

Text: Scott Soper (USA)
Music: Scott Soper

269 Break Forth, O Beauteous Heavenly Light

ERMUNTRE DICH 8.7.8.7.8.8.7.7

1 Break forth, O beau - teous heav'n - ly light, and
2 This night of won - der, night of joy, was
3 Come, dear - est child, in - to our hearts, and
ush - er in the morn - ing. O shep - herds, shrink not
born the Christ, our broth - er. He comes, not might - y
leave your crib be - hind you! Let this be where the
with af - fright, but hear the an - gel's warn - ing. This
to de - stroy, to bid us love each oth - er. How
new life starts for all who seek and find you. To

Text: Johann von Rist (present-day Germany), "Ermuntre dich, mein schwacher Geist," *Himmlische Lieder*, 1641; stanza 1 trans. John Troutbeck (England), ca. 1885; stanzas 2–3 trans. Fred Pratt Green (England), 1986, trans. (stanzas 2–3)
Music: Johann Schop (present-day Germany), *Himmlische Lieder*, 1641; harm. J. S. Bach (present-day Germany), *Christmas Oratorio*, 1734

child, now weak in in - fan - cy, our con - fi - dence and
could he quit his high es - tate for such a world of
you be hon - or, thanks, and praise, for all your gifts this
joy shall be, the pow'r of Sa - tan
greed and hate? What deep hu - mil - i -
time of grace. Come con - quer and de -
break - ing, our peace e - ter - nal mak - ing.
a - tion se - cured the world's sal - va - tion!
liv - er this world and us for - ev - er.

270 In the Beginning

LASST UNS ERFREUEN LM with alleluias

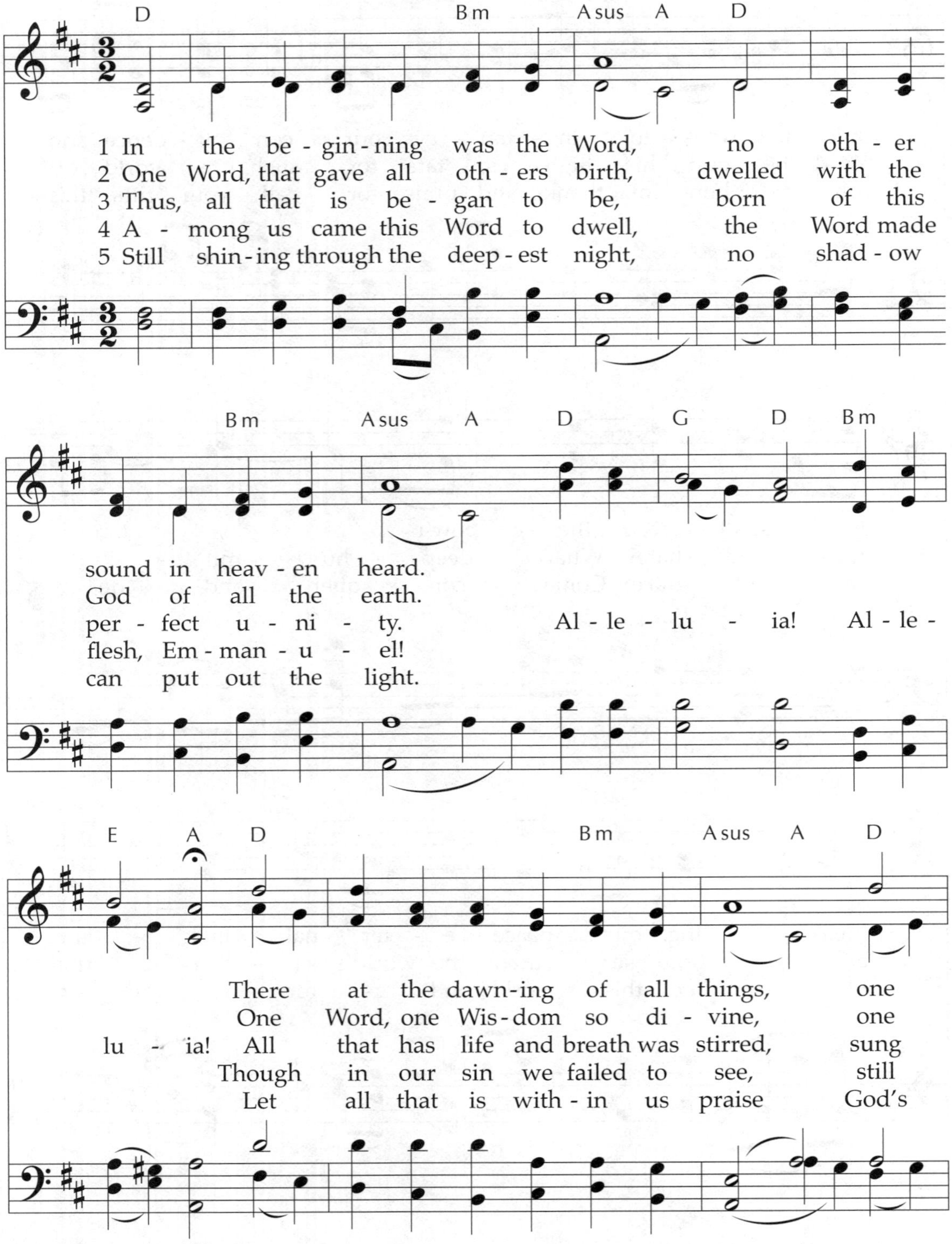
D Bm Asus A D
1 In the be - gin - ning was the Word, no oth - er
2 One Word, that gave all oth - ers birth, dwelled with the
3 Thus, all that is be - gan to be, born of this
4 A - mong us came this Word to dwell, the Word made
5 Still shin - ing through the deep - est night, no shad - ow
Bm Asus A D G D Bm
sound in heav - en heard.
God of all the earth.
per - fect u - ni - ty. Al - le - lu - ia! Al - le -
flesh, Em - man - u - el!
can put out the light.
E A D Bm Asus A D
There at the dawn - ing of all things, one
One Word, one Wis - dom so di - vine, one
lu - ia! All that has life and breath was stirred, sung
Though in our sin we failed to see, still
Let all that is with - in us praise God's

This may be sung as a call-and-response, where the congregation sings the "Alleluias" without printed music.

Text: based on John 1:1–14; Chris Shelton (USA), © 2015 GIA Publications, Inc.
Music: *Geistliche Kirchengesäng* (present-day Germany), 1623; adapt. and harm. Ralph Vaughan Williams (England), *The English Hymnal*, 1906, simplified

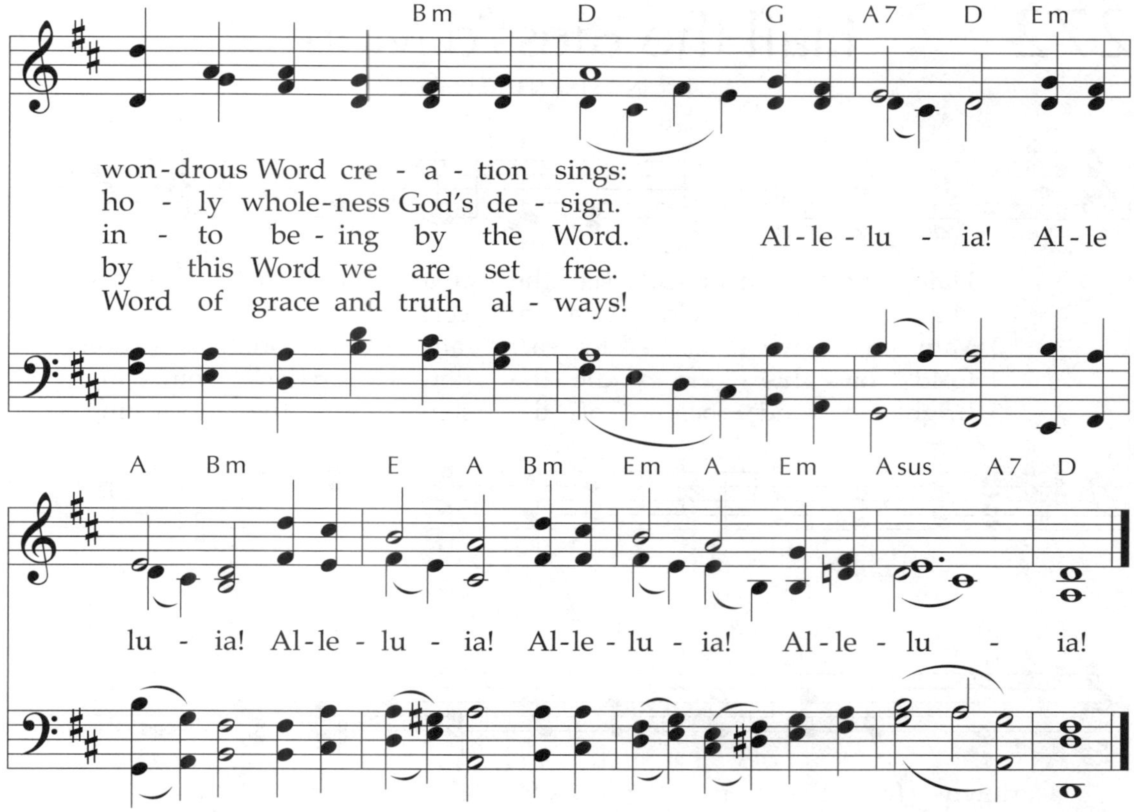
Bm D G A7 D Em
won-drous Word cre - a - tion sings:
ho - ly whole-ness God's de - sign.
in - to be - ing by the Word. Al - le - lu - ia! Al - le
by this Word we are set free.
Word of grace and truth al - ways!
A Bm E A Bm Em A Em Asus A7 D
lu - ia! Al - le - lu - ia! Al - le - lu - ia! Al - le - lu - ia!

Christe, lux mundi (Christ, You Are Light) 271

CHRISTE, LUX MUNDI Irregular

Dm Asus Am Dm Dm/C Gm/B♭ Am F
Chri - ste, lux mun - di, qui se - qui - tur te ha -
Christ, you are light for those who fol - low you. You
B♭ C Gm/B♭ Gm Dm/A Dm C
be - bit lu - men vi - tae, lu - men vi - tae.
come to bring to all the light of life.

Text: Latin; Taizé Community (France)
Music: Taizé Community

272 Hail the Bless'd Morn

MORNING STAR 11.10.11.10

A E 7/B A D/F♯ A/E E
1 Hail the bless'd morn, see the great Me - di - a - tor
2 Shall we not yield him, in cost - ly de - vo - tion,
3 Vain - ly we of - fer each am - ple ob - la - tion,
4 Cold on his cra - dle the dew - drops are shin - ing,
5 Bright - est and best of the stars of the morn - ing,
A E B 7 E E 7
down from the re - gion of glo - ry de - scend!
fra - grance of E - dom and of - f'rings di - vine,
vain - ly with gifts would his fa - vor se - cure.
low lies his head with the beasts of the stall.
dawn on our dark - ness and lend us thine aid.
A E 7/B A/C♯ D
Shep - herds, go wor - ship the babe in the man - ger;
gems of the moun - tain and pearls of the o - cean,
Rich - er by far is the heart's a - do - ra - tion,
An - gels a - dore him in slum - ber re - clin - ing,
Star of the East, the ho - ri - zon a - dorn - ing,

Chord symbols represent a simplified harmony.

Text: Reginald Heber (England), *Christian Observer*, 1811, alt.
Music: James P. Harding (England), *The Church Hymnal*, 1892

A/E Bm C♯ F♯m A/E E7 A
lo, for his guard the bright an - gels at - tend.
myrrh from the for - est or gold from the mine?
dear - er to God are the pray'rs of the poor.
Mak - er and Mon - arch and Sav - ior of all.
guide where our in - fant Re - deem - er is laid.

Arise, Your Light Is Come! 273

FESTAL SONG SM

Descant, verse 4
4 A - rise, your light is come! The moun - tains burst in song! Rise up!
A D A D B7 E
1 A - rise, your light is come! The Spir - it's call o - bey;
2 A - rise, your light is come! Fling wide the pris - on door;
3 A - rise, your light is come! All you in sor - row born,
4 A - rise your light is come! The moun-tains burst in song!
Rise up like ea - gles on the wing; God's pow'r will make us strong.
A D Bm E D Esus E7 A
show forth the glo - ry of your God, which shines on you to - day.
pro - claim the cap-tive's lib - er - ty, good tid - ings to the poor.
bind up the bro-ken-heart-ed ones and com - fort those who mourn.
Rise up like ea - gles on the wing; God's pow'r will make us strong.

Text: Ruth Duck (USA), 1974,
Music: William Henry Walter (USA), 1894; desc. Diana McLeod (Canada),

274 See Whose Glory Fills the Skies

WE'LL WALK IN THE LIGHT 7.7.7.7 with refrain

Capo 1: (D) E♭
(F♯m/A) Gm/B♭
(D) (Bm) (A7) (D) E♭ Cm B♭7 E♭
1 See whose glo - ry fills the skies:
2 Pierce the gloom of sin and grief,
3 More and more thy - self dis - play,
4 Vis - it, then, this soul of mine,
Je - sus, the light of the world!
(A) (E) (A7) (D) B♭ F B♭7 E♭
Sun of right - eous - ness, a - rise:
Scat - ter all my un - be - lief,
Shin - ing to the per - fect day,
Fill me, Ra - dian - cy di - vine!
(D aug/F♯) E♭aug/G (Bm) Cm (D/A) E♭/B♭ (A7) B♭7 (D) E♭
Je - sus, the light of the world!

Text: adapt. from Charles Wesley (England), "Christ, Whose Glory Fills the Skies," *Hymns and Sacred Poems*, 1740; additional text and refrain George D. Elderkin (USA), 1890
Music: George D. Elderkin (USA), 1890; arr. Evelyn Simpson-Curenton (USA),

Refrain
(D) Eb
We'll walk in the light! Beau-ti-ful light! Shine where the
(Bm7) Cm7 (E7) F7 (A7) Bb7 (D) Eb
dew-drops of mer-cy shine bright. Oh, shine all a-round us by
(Gmaj7) Abmaj7 (C7) Db7 (D/A) Eb/Bb (A7) Bb7 (D) Eb (A7) Bb7
Fine last time
To verses
day and by night, Je-sus, the light of the world.

275 O Beautiful Star of Bethlehem

BEAUTIFUL STAR OF BETHLEHEM 9.8.10.9.8.10 with refrain

G C
1 O beau-ti-ful star of Beth-le-hem, shi-ning a - far through shad-ows
2 O beau-ti-ful star, the hope of light, guid-ing the pil-grim through the
3 O beau-ti-ful star, the hope of rest for the re-deemed, the good, and
G Em D A/E D/F♯
dim, giv-ing a light for those who long have gone, (have gone,)
night, o - ver the moun-tain till the break of dawn; (the dawn;)
blest, yon-der in glo - ry when the crown is won; (is won,)
G C
and guid-ing the trav-'lers on their way un - to the place where Je - sus
and in - to the light of per-fect day it will give out a love - ly
for Je - sus is now that Star di-vine; bright-er and bright - er he will
G A7/E D7 G C G
lay; beau-ti-ful star of Beth - le - hem, shine on. (shine on.)
ray; beau-ti-ful star of Beth - le - hem, shine on. (shine on.)
shine; beau-ti-ful star of Beth - le - hem, shine on. (shine on.)

Text: R. Fisher Boyce (USA), ca. 1940
Music: R. Fisher Boyce, 1940; harm. Adger M. Pace (USA)

Refrain
D G C
O beau-ti-ful star of Beth-le-hem,
Beau-ti-ful, beau-ti-ful star, star of Beth-le-
G Em D A/E D/F♯
shine up-on us un-til the glo-ry dawn;
hem, shine up-on us un-til the glo-ry, glo-ry dawn;
G C
oh, give us your light to light the way in-to the land of per-fect
G A7/E D7 G C G
day; beau-ti-ful star of Beth-le-hem, shine on. (shine on.)

276 Solemn Stillness, Weary Streets

SINGING JOY TO THE WORLD 7.5.8.7.8.6 with refrain

G
1 Sol - emn still - ness— wea - ry streets strain to grasp the
2 We are shep-herds in the fields, watch - ing in the
3 Crush - ing fears are met with joy; sor - row's curse is
F C
sound. In the qui - et breathes an an - them o - ver
night. We are mor - tals, we are bear - ers, search-ing
torn. Hear the mu - sic, fling your load down, and un -
Am G C
dark and thorn - y ground. Rocks and plains re - peat the
for a per - fect light. Hur - ry, hur - ry! Sing the
bend your tir - ed form. These bright hours cir - cle
Am G D C
ech - o; splen-dor floods the star - lit morn. We are won-ders,
glo - ry! Bring the gold and bit - ter myrrh of our car - ols:
round us, let the gen - tle wings un - furl. Swift and sweet - ly
Am G D G
bless - ed won - ders, sing - ing joy to the world. (to verse 2)
Hal - le - lu - jah! Sing - ing joy to the world. (to refrain)
down the road - side, sing - ing joy to the world. (to refrain)

Text: Christopher Clymer Kurtz (USA) and Maria Clymer Kurtz (USA), 2014
Music: Christopher Clymer Kurtz and Maria Clymer Kurtz, 2014; arr. Mennonite Worship and Song Committee

Refrain
C
Am7
G
D
2 Hal-le-lu-jah! Hal-le-lu-jah! Joy to the world! We are
3 Hal-le-lu-jah! Hal-le-lu-jah! Joy to the world! Swift and
2 Joy to the world! (Joy!) Joy to the world!
3 Joy to the world! (Joy!) Joy to the world!
C
Am
G/D
D7
G
won-ders, bless-ed won-ders, sing-ing joy to the world.
sweet-ly down the road-side, sing-ing joy to the world.
Won - ders, sing - ing joy to the world.
Swift and sweet - ly joy to the world.

277 As with Gladness

DIX 7.7.7.7.7.7

G C G C G
1 As with glad - ness men of old did the guid - ing
2 As with joy - ful steps they sped, Sav - ior, to thy
3 As they of - fered gifts most rare at thy cra - dle
4 Ho - ly Je - sus, ev - 'ry day keep us in the
D G C G
star be - hold, as with joy they hailed its light,
low - ly bed, there to bend the knee be - fore
rude and bare, so may we with ho - ly joy,
nar - row way, and, when earth - ly things are past,
C G D G D G
lead - ing on - ward, beam - ing bright; so, most gra - cious
thee whom heav'n and earth a - dore; so may we with
pure and free from sin's al - loy, all our cost - liest
bring our ran - somed souls at last where they need no
D G C G D7 G
God, may we ev - er - more be led to thee.
will - ing feet ev - er seek thy mer - cy seat.
treas - ures bring, Christ, to thee, our heav'n - ly king.
star to guide, where no clouds thy glo - ry hide.

For higher key, see "For the Beauty of the Earth" #120.

Text: William C. Dix (England), ca. 1858, *Hymns of Love and Joy*, 1859

Music: Conrad Kocher (Germany), *Stimmen aus dem Reiche Gottes*, 1838; adapt. William H. Monk (England), *Hymns Ancient and Modern*, 1861

A Voice Was Heard in Ramah 278

LLANGLOFFAN 7.6.7.6 D

Gm D Gm Cm Gm D
1 A voice was heard in Ra - mah that could not be con - soled,
2 O God, we hear the cry - ing for lit - tle ones of yours;
3 O Prince of Peace, you lead us in ways of truth and grace.
E♭ F B♭ Cm E♭ D Gm
as Ra - chel wept for chil - dren she could no long - er hold.
for man - y still are dy - ing in con - flicts and in wars—
May we be brave to prac - tice your peace in ev - 'ry place—
B♭ Cm B♭ F D Gm Dsus D
For Her - od ruled the na - tion, yet feared the in - fant king.
in ev - 'ry trou - bled na - tion, on ev - 'ry vio - lent street,
to love each fear - filled na - tion, to serve each trou - bled street.
Gm D Gm E♭ D Gm
How great the dev - as - ta - tion that fear and an - ger bring!
how great the lam - en - ta - tion when fear and an - ger meet!
How great the cel - e - bra - tion when peace and jus - tice meet!

Alternate tune: HERZLICH TUT MICH VERLANGEN (#325)

Text: Carolyn Winfrey Gillette (USA),
Music: Welsh traditional, *Evans's Hymnau a Thonau*, 1865, as in *English Hymnal*, 1906

279 Jesus Entered Egypt

KING'S WESTON 6.5.6.5 D

Em D Em Am Em
1 Je-sus en-tered E-gypt flee-ing Her-od's hand,
2 Je-sus was a mi-grant liv-ing as a guest
3 Je-sus cross-es bor-ders with the wand-'ring poor,
G Bm/D Em Am
liv-ing as an al-ien in a for-eign land.
with the friends and stran-gers who could of-fer rest.
search-ing for a ref-uge, for an o-pen door.
D Bm Em D/F♯ A D
Far from home and coun-try with his fam-i-ly,
Do we hold wealth light-ly so that we can share
Do our words and ac-tions an-swer Je-sus' plea,
Em Bm G/B D Em
was there room and wel-come for this ref-u-gee?
shel-ter with the home-less, and a-bun-dant care?
"Give the low-ly wel-come, and you wel-come me"?

Text: Adam M. L. Tice (USA), 2007, © 2009 GIA Publications, Inc.
Music: Ralph Vaughan Williams (England), *Enlarged Songs of Praise*; arr. *The Hymnbook* 1955, © 1931 Oxford University Press, London

O Carpenter, Why Leave the Bench 280

CARPENTER CM

Em G D N.C.
1 O car - pen - ter, why leave the bench where
2 O car - pen - ter, why leave the tools to
3 O car - pen - ter, why leave the world of
4 O car - pen - ter, why leave re - pairs with
5 O car - pen - ter, who else could do the
Em D/F♯ D G Em Am D
wood yields to your art, and take in - stead, to
car - ry out your plans, and go in - stead to
ta - ble, bed, and house, to face the em - pire's
wood and clamp and glue, and rise from death to
work that you have done? What can we do but
G C Am Em/B B Em
try your skill, the ston - y hu - man heart?
do God's work with emp - ty, o - pen hands?
car - pen - try, to lift a Ro - man cross?
seek in - stead to make the whole world new?
sing your praise, O Sav - ior, Ma - ry's son!

281 Joyful Is the Dark

JOYFUL DARK 5.5.10.6.5.10

1 Joy - ful is the dark, ho - ly, hid - den God,
2 Joy - ful is the dark Spir - it of the deep,
3 Joy - ful is the dark, shad-owed sta - ble floor;
4 Joy - ful is the dark cool - ness of the tomb,
5 Joy - ful is the dark depth of love di - vine,
roll - ing cloud of night be - yond all nam - ing,
wing - ing wild - ly o'er the world's cre - a - tion,
an - gels flick - er, God on earth con - fess - ing,
wait - ing for the won - der of the morn - ing.
roar - ing, loom - ing thun - der - cloud of glo - ry,
maj - es - ty in dark - ness, en - er - gy of
silk - en sheen of mid - night plum-age black and
as with ex - ul - ta - tion, Mar - y, giv - ing
Nev - er was that mid - night touched by dread and
ho - ly, haunt-ing beau - ty, liv - ing, lov - ing
maj - es - ty in dark - ness, en - er - gy of love,
silk - en sheen of mid - night plum-age black and bright,
as with ex - ul - ta - tion, Mar - y, giv - ing birth,
Nev - er was that mid - night touched by dread and gloom:
ho - ly, haunt-ing beau - ty, liv - ing, lov - ing God.

Text: Brian Wren (England), 1986, *Bring Many Names,* © 1989 Hope Publishing Co.
Music: Philip K. Clemens (USA), © 1991 Philip K. Clemens

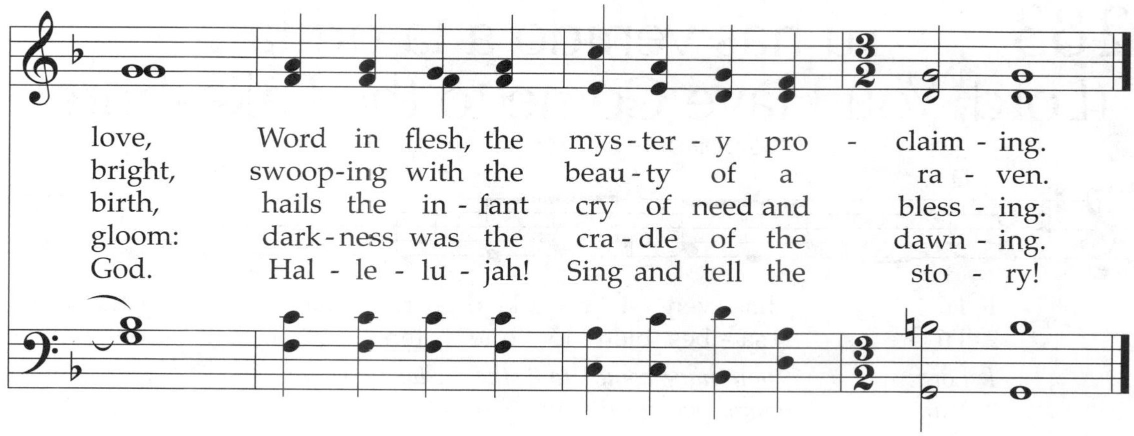
love, Word in flesh, the mys-ter-y pro - claim-ing.
bright, swoop-ing with the beau-ty of a ra-ven.
birth, hails the in-fant cry of need and bless-ing.
gloom: dark-ness was the cra-dle of the dawn-ing.
God. Hal-le-lu-jah! Sing and tell the sto-ry!

Come and See 282

COME AS A CHILD Irregular

Descant
D A G D G D
3 Chris - te, Chris - te, a - do -
Melody
1 "Come and see, come and see, I am the way and the
2, 3 Ky - ri - e, Ky - ri - e, Ky - ri - e e -
E A D A G D
ra - mus te. Al - le - lu - ia,
truth," said he. "Fol - low me, fol - low me,
le - i - son. Chris - te, Chris - te,
G D A D
Ky - ri - e e - le - i - son.*
come as a child, O come and see."
Chris - te e - le - i - son.*

*Translation: Lord, have mercy, Christ, have mercy.
Christ, we adore you, Alleluia, Lord, have mercy.

Text: Marilyn Houser Hamm (Canada), 1974, *Sing and Rejoice*, 1979; adapt. from Greek and Latin liturgies
Music: Marilyn Houser Hamm, 1974, *Sing and Rejoice*, 1979

283 Tú has venido a la orilla (Lord, You Have Come to the Lakeshore)

PESCADOR DE HOMBRES* 8.10.10 with refrain

D G A7 Bm D7
1 Tú has ven - i - do‿a la‿o - ri - lla, no‿has bus -
2 Tú sa - bes bien lo que ten - go; en mi
1 Lord, you have come to the lake - shore look - ing
2 You know so well my pos - ses - sions; my boat
G Em Em7 A7
ca - do ni‿a sa - bios, ni‿a ri - cos, tan só - lo
bar - ca no‿hay o - ro ni‿es - pa - das, tan só - lo
nei - ther for wealth - y nor wise ones. You on - ly
car - ries no gold and no wea - pons, but nets for
D F♯m G A7 D
quie - res que yo te si - ga.
re - des y mi tra - ba - jo.
asked me to fol - low hum - bly.
fish - ing, my dai - ly la - bor.
Refrain
D7 G D Em7
Se - ñor, me‿has mi - ra - do‿a los o - jos y son-
O Lord, with your eyes you have searched me, kind - ly
A7 D D7
rien - do has di - cho mi nom - bre. En la‿a-
smil - ing, have spo - ken my name. Now my
G D Em
re - na he de - ja - do mi bar - ca; jun - to‿a
boat's left on the shore-line be - hind me; by your

*Original title

Text: Spanish; Cesáreo Gabaráin (Spain); trans. composite Gertrude C. Suppe (USA), George Lockwood IV (USA), Raquel Gutiérrez-Achon (USA), Willard F. Jabusch (USA), alt.

Music: Cesáreo Gabaráin, 1979, *Dios con nosotros*

A7
D
ti, bus - ca - ré o - tro mar.
side I will seek oth - er seas.

3 Tú necesitas mis manos,
mi cansancio que a otros descanse,
amor que quiera seguir amando.
Refrain

4 Tú, pescador de otros mares,
ansia eterna de almas que esperan,
amigo bueno, que así me llamas.
Refrain

3 *You need my hands, full of caring;*
use my labors to give others rest,
with love desiring to keep on loving.
Refrain

4 *You, who have fished other oceans,*
ever longed for by souls who are waiting,
call me "beloved," and seek my friendship.
Refrain

Lo, I Am with You 284

PRESENCE 11.11.10.11

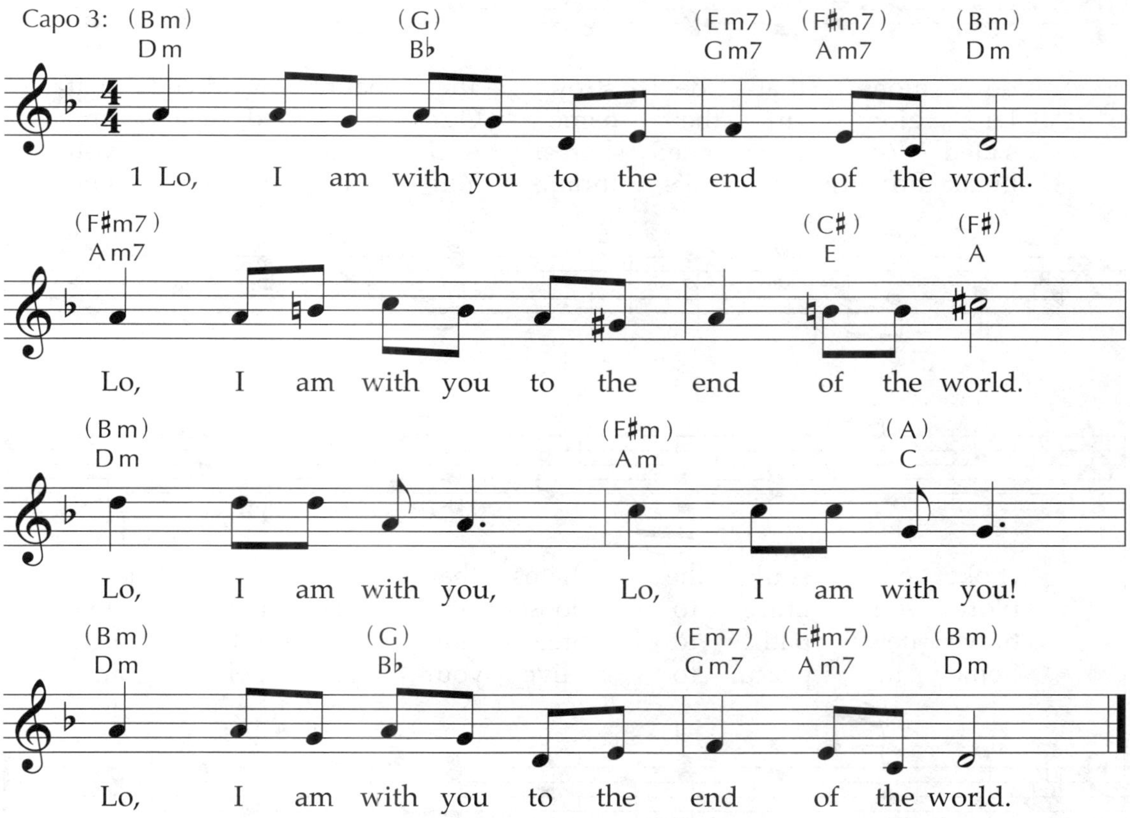
Capo 3: (Bm) Dm (G) B♭ (Em7) Gm7 (F♯m7) Am7 (Bm) Dm
1 Lo, I am with you to the end of the world.
(F♯m7) Am7 (C♯) E (F♯) A
Lo, I am with you to the end of the world.
(Bm) Dm (F♯m) Am (A) C
Lo, I am with you, Lo, I am with you!
(Bm) Dm (G) B♭ (Em7) Gm7 (F♯m7) Am7 (Bm) Dm
Lo, I am with you to the end of the world.

2 Lo, I am with you when you leave self behind . . .
3 Lo, I am with you in the struggle for peace . . .
4 Lo, I am with you when you suffer for love . . .
5 Lo, I am with you in the way of the cross . . .
6 Lo, I am with you in the darkness of death . . .
7 Lo, I am with you to the end of the world . . .

Text: stanza 1 based on Matthew 28:20, stanzas 1, 4–7 Iona Community (Scotland), 1988; stanzas 2–3 Guy Aydelott (USA), 1991
Music: John L. Bell (Scotland), 1988

285 Cast Out, O Christ

BANGOR CM

1 Cast out, O Christ, cast far a - way the
2 Our rag - ing griefs, our jeal - ous fears are
3 Once long a - go, from Gal - i - lee, you
4 Your Word breathes life and health and hope that
de - mons that de - stroy: the haunt - ing dreads that
Le - gion in their name. Our shack - led hearts im -
sailed to storm-tossed shores. And still, in pow'r, you
break through e - vil's thrall. You send us, strength - ened,
choke our souls, the hates that sti - fle joy.
plore your grace to loose our bind - ing shame.
brave new paths to breach our bolt - ed doors.
home in peace to live your gos - pel call.

Text: Mary Louise Bringle (USA), 2002, © 2006 GIA Publications, Inc.
Music: William Tans'ur (England), *Harmony of Zion*, 1734

Fierce Raged the Tempest 286

ST. AËLRED 8.8.8.3

Capo 3: (Am) Cm (E) G (Am) Cm (Dm) Fm (Am) Cm
1 Fierce raged the tem - pest, o'er the deep,
2 "Save, us, we per - ish!" was their cry.
3 The wild winds hushed; the an - gry deep
4 So, when our life is cloud - ed o'er,
(Em) Gm (F) A♭ (C) E♭ (Dm7) Fm7 (E) G (Am) Cm
anx - ious dis - ci - ples watch did keep; but you were
"Save us or we will sure - ly die!" Your word a -
fell, like a lit - tle child, to sleep; the sul - len
and storm - winds drift us from the shore, say, lest we
(G) B♭ (F) A♭ (C) E♭
wrapped in guile - less sleep, calm and still.
bove the storm rose high: "Peace! be still."
bil - lows ceased to leap, at your will.
sink to rise no more, "Peace! be still."

Text: Godfrey Thring (England), 1861, alt.
Music: John Bacchus Dykes (England), 1862

287 Jesus Christ Is Waiting

NOËL NOUVELET 11.11.10.11

E5 A Em A Em/B B Em
1 Je - sus Christ is wait - ing, wait-ing in the streets;
2 Je - sus Christ is rag - ing, rag - ing in the streets,
3 Je - sus Christ is heal - ing, heal - ing in the streets;
4 Je - sus Christ is danc - ing, danc-ing in the streets,
5 Je - sus Christ is call - ing, call - ing in the streets,
E5 A Em A Em/B B Em
no one is his neigh - bor, all a - lone he eats.
where in - jus - tice spi - rals and real hope re - treats.
cur - ing those who suf - fer, touch-ing those he greets.
where each sign of ha - tred he, with love, de - feats.
"Who will join my jour - ney? I will guide their feet."
Em B/F♯ Em/G B B/D♯ Em F♯ B B7
Lis - ten, Lord Je - sus, I am lone - ly too.
Lis - ten, Lord Je - sus, I am an - gry too.
Lis - ten, Lord Je - sus, I have pit - y too.
Lis - ten, Lord Je - sus, I should tri - umph too.
Lis - ten, Lord Je - sus, let my fears be few.

Text: John L. Bell (Scotland) and Graham Maule (Scotland), © 1988 WGRG, Iona Community (admin. GIA Publications, Inc.)
Music: French traditional, 15th c.; harm. James E. Clemens (USA), © 2001 James E. Clemens

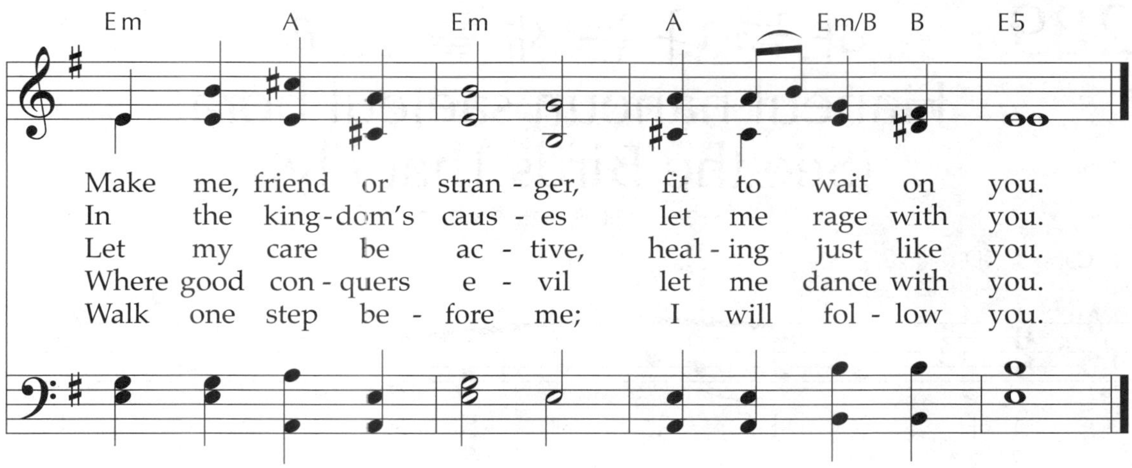
Make me, friend or stran - ger, fit to wait on you.
In the king-dom's caus - es let me rage with you.
Let my care be ac - tive, heal - ing just like you.
Where good con - quers e - vil let me dance with you.
Walk one step be - fore me; I will fol - low you.

Love the Lord Your God 288

THE GREATEST COMMANDMENT Irregular

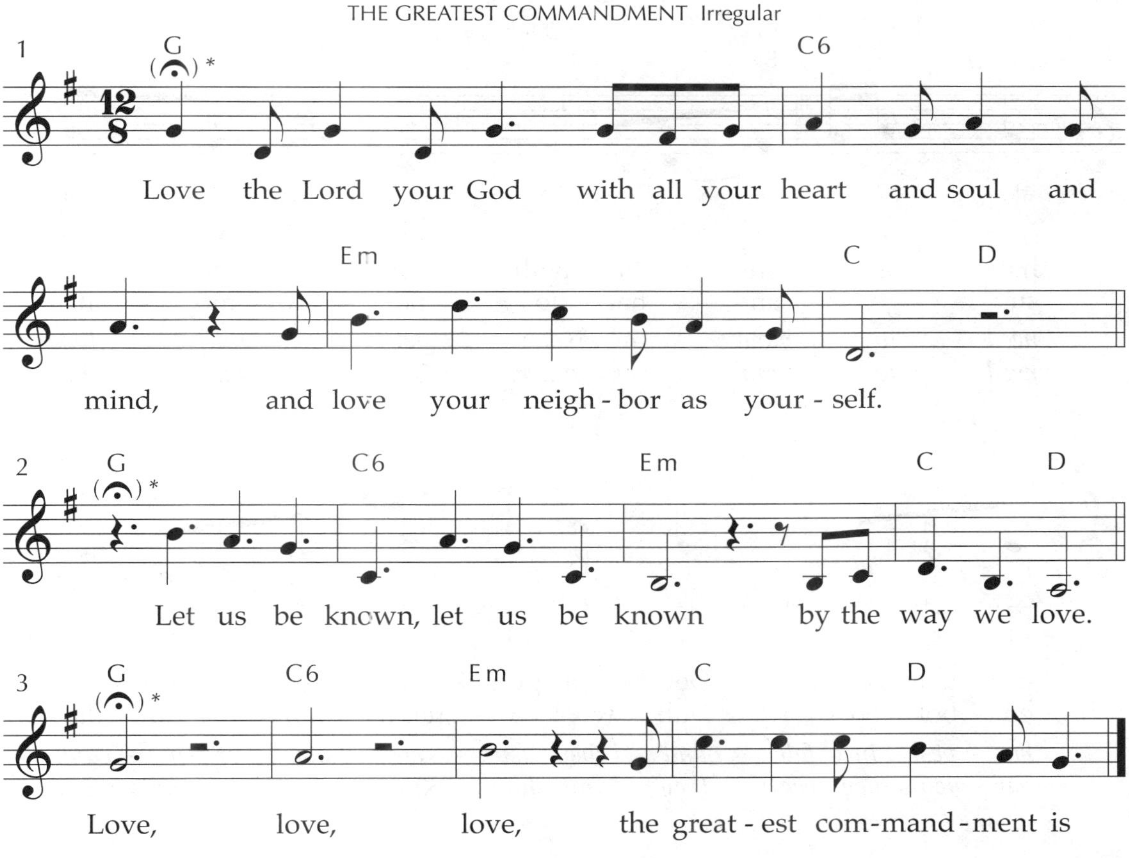
1
Love the Lord your God with all your heart and soul and mind, and love your neigh - bor as your - self.
2
Let us be known, let us be known by the way we love.
3
Love, love, love, the great - est com-mand - ment is

May be sung as a canon, or by assigning groups to repeat each section.

*Fermatas indicate the eventual ending.

Text: based on Matthew 22:37–39; Mark 12:30–31; Luke 10:27; John 13:35; Deuteronomy 6:4–5; adapt. Paul Zach (USA)
Music: Paul Zach

289 하늘나는새를보라
Haneul naneun saeleul bora (See the Birds That Fly)

SEE THE BIRDS 9.7.8.8.8.7.8.7

Capo 3: (D) F (Bm) Dm (A) C
1 하 늘 나 는 새 를 보 라 농 사
2 들 에 피 는 꽃 을 보 라 길 쌈
1 Ha - neul na - neun sae - leul bo - ra Nong - sa
2 Deu - re pi - neun ggo - cheul bo - ra Gil - ssam
1 See the birds that fly through the air, with no
2 See the flow'rs that bloom in the field, with no
(G) B♭ (D) F
하 지 않 으 며 곡 식 모 아
수 고 안 해 도 솔 로 몬 의
ha - ji an - eu - myuh Gok - shik mo - a
su - go an - hae - do So - lo - mo - nae
need to plow or sow; nev - er do they
need to spin or weave. God pro - vides the
(Bm) Dm (A) C (G) B♭ (D) F
곳 간 안 에 들 인 것 이 없 어 도
의 복 보 다 더 욱 아 름 답 도 다
got - gan a - nae Deu - lin guh - shi up - suh - do
eu - bok bo - da Duh - wook a - reum dap - do - da
har - vest in fall, and they nev - er store or pre - pare.
gar - ments they wear; they out-shine King So - lo-mon's robes.

Text: Korean; based on Matthew 6:25–34 and Luke 12:22–31, Frederick S. Miller (USA, Korea), alt.; English trans. Edward Poitras (USA), alt.; Korean trans. © 2001 The United Methodist Publishing House (admin. Music Services)
Music: Young Soo Na (Korea), © Kyung Dong Presbyterian Church

(Bm) Dm (F♯m) Am
하 늘 계 신 아 버 지 가 고 이
아 궁 속 에 던 질 풀 도 고 이
Ha - neul - gae - shin a - beo - ji - ga Go - e
A - goong so - gae dun - jil pool - do Go - e
God who reigns in heav - en a - bove feeds them
All the dry grass thrown on the fire wore green
(Bm7) Dm7 (Em7) Gm7 (A) C (D) F
먹 여 주 시 니 먹 고 마 실
입 히 시 거 든 사 랑 하 는
muh - gyuh joo - shi - ni Meok - go ma - shil
ip - he - shi - guh-deun Sa - rang - ha - neun
all with ten - der care. Do not fear, for
cloth - ing giv'n by God. God made you and
(Bm) Dm (A) C (G) B♭ (D) F
것 을 위 해 아 무 염 려 말 아 라
자 녀 들 을 입 히 시 지 않 으 랴
guh - seul we - hae A - moo yum - lyuh mal - a - ra
ja - nyuh-deul - eul Ip - he - shi - ji an - u - rya
God will pro - vide what you eat and what you wear.
God loves you still, will not God pro - vide for you?

3 너는 먼저 주의 나라
주의 의를 구하라
하나님이 모든 것을
너희에게 주시리
내일 일을 생각 하고
미리 염려 말아라
오늘 일만 생각하고
있는 힘을 다하라

3 Nuhneun meonjeo jueh nara
Jueh euleul goohara
Hananime modeun guhseul
Nuhheaegae jooshiri
Naeil ileul senggakhago
Miri yumryuh malara
Oneul ilman senggak hago
Itneun himeul dahara

3 *You who seek the kingdom of God,*
hungry for God's righteousness:
God will grant you all that you need.
Be not anxious; trust, believe;
do not worry, God will provide.
Each new day brings what it may;
set your mind on work of today.
Walk upon God's holy way.

290 Blessed Are You

REESE 7.6.7.6 D with refrain

1 Bless-ed are you, the poor ones; God calls the last and least.
Bless-ed are you, the hun-gry, for God pre-pares your feast.
Bless-ed are you who weep now, for mourn-ing turns to praise.
Bless-ed are you who suf-fer, for God will guard your ways.
2 Ru-in a-waits the wealth-y, who live to serve their greed.
Ru-in a-waits the glut-tons, who take more than they need.
Ru-in a-waits the laugh-ers, and tears will fill their eyes.
Ru-in a-waits the haugh-ty, who mock their neigh-bors' cries.
3 Bless-ed are you, the poor ones, for God is poor with you.
Bless-ed are you, the hun-gry, for God knows hun-ger too.
Bless-ed are you who weep now, for God has shared your grief.
Bless-ed are you who suf-fer, for God will bring re-lief.
Refrain
The doors of heav'n are o-pen, and glo-ry is shin-ing through—
re-joice, re-joice, God is with us, and bless-ed, bless-ed are you.
1, 2
3

Text: based on Luke 6:20–26, Adam M. L. Tice (USA), 2013
Music: Benjamin Brody (USA)

292 *Luke 4:16-19, 21 / Isaiah 61:1-2*

Jesus stood up to read
and found the place where it was written:
"The Spirit of the Lord is upon me,
because God has anointed me
to bring good news to the poor.
The Lord has sent me to proclaim
release to the captives
and recovery of sight to the blind,
to let the oppressed go free,
to proclaim the year
of God's favor."
Then Jesus began to say to them,
"Today this scripture
has been fulfilled in your hearing."

293 *Matthew 5:39-42, 44*

Do not fight back against someone
who wants to do harm to you.
If anyone hits you on the right cheek,
turn the other cheek to them also.
If anyone wants to sue you in court
and take your shirt,
let them have your coat too.
If anyone forces you to walk
with them one mile,
go two miles.
Give to anyone who asks you
for something.
Do not refuse to give to anyone
who wants to borrow from you.
Love your enemies.
Pray for those who persecute you.

294 *Matthew 13:44-46*

The reign of heaven is like a treasure
that a person discovered
hidden in a field.
In excitement, the person hid it again
and sold everything
to get enough money
to buy the field.
The reign of heaven is like a merchant
on the lookout for choice pearls.
Upon discovering a pearl
of great value,
the merchant sold everything
and bought it!

295 *Matthew 5:3-12*

Blessed are the poor in spirit,
for theirs is the kingdom of heaven.
Blessed are those who mourn,
for they shall be comforted.
Blessed are the meek,
for they shall inherit the earth.
Blessed are those who hunger
and thirst for righteousness,
for they shall be satisfied.
Blessed are the merciful,
for they shall receive mercy.
Blessed are the pure in heart,
for they shall see God.
Blessed are the peacemakers,
for they shall be called children of God.
Blessed are those who are persecuted
for righteousness' sake,
for theirs is the kingdom of heaven.
Blessed are you when others revile you
and persecute you
and utter all kinds of evil
against you falsely on my account.
Rejoice and be glad,
for your reward is great in heaven,
for so they persecuted the prophets
who were before you.

296 *Mark 14:3-9 (excerpts)*

While Jesus was in Bethany
reclining at the table,
a woman came with an alabaster jar
of very expensive perfume.
She broke the jar and poured
the perfume on Jesus' head.
Some were indignant, saying,
"Why this waste of perfume?
It could have been sold
and the money given to the poor."
And they rebuked her harshly.
But Jesus said,
"Leave her alone;
why are you bothering her?
She has done a beautiful,
good work for me.
Truly I tell to you, wherever the gospel
is preached throughout the world,
what she has done will also be told
in memory of her."

Previous page: 291. *Loaves and Fishes*, Michelle G Burkholder (USA), 2014, paper cutout ⓦ

You Are Salt for the Earth 297

BRING FORTH THE KINGDOM Irregular

Leader
1 You are salt for the earth, O peo - ple,
2 You are a light on the hill, O peo - ple,
3 You are a seed of the Word, O peo - ple,
4 We are a bless'd and a pil - grim peo - ple,
All
salt for the king - dom of God!
light for the ci - ty of God!
bring forth the king - dom of God!
bound for the king - dom of God!
Leader
Share the fla - vor of life, O peo - ple:
Shine so ho - ly and bright, O peo - ple:
Seeds of mer - cy and seeds of jus - tice,
Love our jour - ney and love our home - land:
All
life in the king - dom of God!
shine for the king - dom of God!
grow in the king - dom of God!
love is the king - dom of God!
Refrain
Bring forth the king - dom of mer - cy, bring forth the king - dom of peace.
Bring forth the king - dom of jus - tice, bring forth the cit - y of God!

Text: Marty Haugen (USA), 1985, *Gather*, 1988
Music: Marty Haugen, 1985, *Gather*, 1988

298 What Is the World Like

NEW WORLD 10.10.10.10

Capo 1: (G) A♭ (Em7) Fm7 (Am7) B♭m7 (D) E♭
1 What is the world like when God's will is done?
2 What is the world like when God's will is done?
3 What is the world like when God's will is done?
4 What is the world like when God's will is done?
5 These are the stor - ies that Je - sus im - parts,
(Em) Fm (C) D♭ (Am) B♭m (B7) C7
Mus - tard seeds grow more than we can con - ceive:
Wit - ness the wan - der - ing child com - ing home;
No more is neigh - bor just al - ly or friend;
Read - y for feast - ing, we watch through the night,
filled with the Spir - it, who joins us as one.
(Em) Fm (Am) B♭m (D) E♭ (G) A♭
roots thread the soil, branch - es reach for the sun.
watch as the par - ent breaks in - to a run.
peace thrives in plac - es where once there was none.
tend - ing our lamps till the new day's be - gun.
Born through our voic - es, our hands, and our hearts,

Text: Adam M. L. Tice (USA)
Music: Sally Ann Morris (USA)

(C) (Em7) (Am7) (D) (G)
D♭ Fm7 B♭m7 E♭ A♭
This is how God moves us each to be - lieve.
This is how God longs for us when we roam.
This is how God works when ri - val - ries end.
This is how God read - ies us for the light.
this is a new world where God's will is done.

God Lights a Lamp

299

NINA Irregular

D Em D/F♯ G
God lights a lamp, and she search-es ev' - ry - where for the
D/A G/B Asus A D Em
hid - den, lone - ly heart. God lights a lamp, and she
D/F♯ G D/A G/B Asus
search-es ev' - ry - where. When she finds you, oh, she sings:
A G D/F♯ A/C♯ D D/F♯
"I have found my treas - ure, my pre-cious sil - ver coin. I have
G Bm C A D/F♯ G D/F♯
found my love!" E-ven an - gels will
F♯/A♯ Bm G Asus D
hear the news: What once was lost is found.

Text: based on Luke 15:8–10; Katie Graber (USA), © 2020 Katie Graber
Music: Anneli Loepp Thiessen (Canada), © 2020 Anneli Loepp Thiessen

300 Far, Far Away / I Will Arise

RESTORATION (I WILL ARISE) 10.8.8.7

Capo 1: (Em) Fm
(G) A♭
1 Far, far a-way from my lov-ing fa-ther, I had been
Refrain: I will a-rise and go to Je-sus, he will em-
2 Fain had I fed on the husks a-round me, till to my-
3 I will a-rise, though faint and wea-ry, home to my
4 "Fa-ther," I'll say, "I have sinned be-fore thee, no more may
5 Then I a-rose and came to my fa-ther. Mer-cy a-
(C/G) D♭/A♭ (G/B) A♭/C (D) E♭ (G) A♭ (B7/D♯) C7/E (Em) Fm
wan-d'ring, way-ward, wild, fear-ing on-ly
brace me in his arms. In the arms of
self I came, and said, "Plen-ty have my
fa-ther I will go. Woe to me that
I be called thy son. Make me on-ly
maz-ing! Love un-known! He be-held me,
(D) E♭ (G) A♭ (Em) Fm (C) D♭ (Bm7) Cm7 (Em) Fm
lest his an-ger o-ver-take his sin-ful child.
my dear Sav-ior, oh, there are ten thou-sand charms.
fa-ther's ser-vants; per-ish I for want of bread."
e'er I wan-dered, ah, that I such need should know.
as thy ser-vant; pit-y me, a wretch un-done!"
ran, em-braced me, par-doned, wel-comed, called me "son"!

Text: based on Luke 15:1-24; vers. anon., "The Prodigal Son," *Gospel Songs* (USA), 1874
Music: American traditional (USA), *Southern Harmony*, 1835; harm. Charles H. Webb

Jesus on the Mountain Peak 301

MOUNTAIN PEAK 7.8.7.8 with alleluia

D G D G Em
1 Je - sus on the moun - tain peak stands a - lone in
2 Trem - bling at his feet we saw Mo - ses and E -
3 Swift the cloud of glo - ry came, God pro - claim - ing
4 This is God's be - lov - ed Son! Law and proph - ets
D A D A D/F♯
glo - ry blaz - ing. Let us, if we dare to speak,
li - jah speak - ing. All the proph - ets and the law
in its thun - der Je - sus as the Son by name!
sing be - fore him; first and last and on - ly One.
Gm Cm B♭ D/A A7 D
join the saints and an - gels prais - ing. Hal - le - lu - jah!
shout through them their joy - ful greet - ing. Hal - le - lu - jah!
Na - tions, cry a - loud in won - der! Hal - le - lu - jah!
All cre - a - tion shall a - dore him! Hal - le - lu - jah!

Chord symbols represent a simplified harmony.

Text: based on Matthew 17:1–8, Mark 9:2–13, Luke 9:28–36; Brian Wren (England, USA), 1962, 1988, © 1977, rev. 1995 Hope Publishing Company
Music: Bradley P. Lehman (USA), © 1984 Bradley P. Lehman

302 Unless a Grain of Wheat

NEVER THE BLADE SHALL RISE Irregular

Capo 3:
1 Un - less a grain of wheat falls to the earth, falls to the earth and dies, it re - mains on - ly a grain of wheat, and nev - er the blade shall rise.
2 The one who loves the world - ly life los - es the life so lived, while the one who hates the life in this world pre - serves it to life e - ter - nal.
3 If an - y - one would serve me, come and fol - low me; come and fol - low me; where I am, there will my ser - vant be.
Refrain
For the grain of wheat pro - duc-es much fruit, but on - ly if it dies.
Un-less a grain of wheat falls to the earth, nev-er the blade shall rise.

Text: based on John 12:24–26, Kathy Powell (USA)
Music: Kathy Powell

O Love, How Deep, How Broad 303

DEO GRACIAS LM

1 O love, how deep, how broad, how high! It
2 For us he was bap - tized and bore his
3 For us he prayed, for us he taught, for
4 For us to wick - ed hands be - trayed, scourged,
5 E - ter - nal glo - ry to our God for

fills the heart with ec - sta - sy, that
ho - ly fast, and hun - gered sore. For
us his dai - ly works he wrought, by
mocked, in pur - ple robe ar - rayed, he
love so deep, so high, so broad; the

God, the Son of God, should take our
us temp - ta - tion sharp he knew, for
words and signs and ac - tions thus still
bore the shame - ful cross and death, for
Trin - i - ty whom we a - dore for -

mor - tal form for mor - tals' sake.
us the temp - ter o - ver - threw.
seek - ing not him - self but us.
us at length gave up his breath.
ev - er and for - ev - er - more.

Text: attr. Thomas à Kempis (modern-day Netherlands), 15th c.; trans. Benjamin Webb (England), *The Hymnal Noted*, 1851, alt.
Music: English traditional, 15th c.

304 Sign Us with Ashes, Merciful God

INDIGO LM with refrain

Capo 1: (Em) (G) (D) (Bm7) (C9)
Refrain
Fm A♭ E♭ Cm7 D♭9
A: Sign us with ash - es, mer - ci - ful God, chil - dren of
B: Gath - er your peo - ple, mer - ci - ful God, gath - er the
C: Feed us and guide us, mer - ci - ful God; Light when the
(Am7) (B) (G)
B♭m7 C A♭
dust, as to dust we re - turn. Sign us with ash - es,
long - ing, the lost and un - sure. Gath - er your peo - ple,
shad - ows of life cloud our view. Feed us and guide us,
(D) (Bm7) (Am7) (Em/B)(Bm7) (Em)
E♭ Cm7 B♭m7 Fm/C Cm7 Fm
mer - ci - ful God; mark us and make us your own.
mer - ci - ful God; name us and claim us as yours.
mer - ci - ful God, peo - ple who hun - ger for you.

Text: Mary Louise Bringle (USA), © 2006, 2009 GIA Publications, Inc.
Music: Tony Alonso (USA), © 2009 GIA Publications, Inc.

305 The Glory of These Forty Days

WAREHAM LM

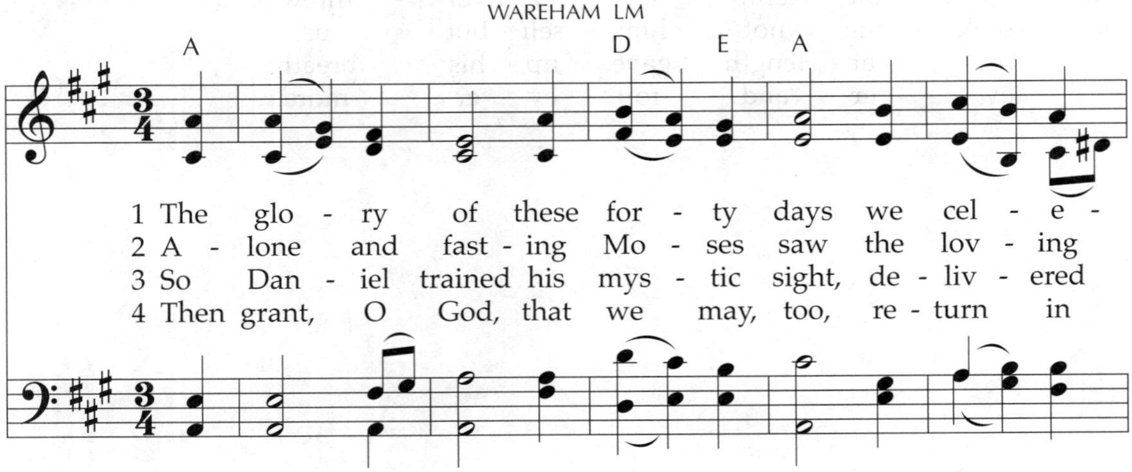
A D E A
1 The glo - ry of these for - ty days we cel - e -
2 A - lone and fast - ing Mo - ses saw the lov - ing
3 So Dan - iel trained his mys - tic sight, de - liv - ered
4 Then grant, O God, that we may, too, re - turn in

Chord symbols represent a simplified harmony.

Text: attr. Gregory the Great (Rome), 6th c.; *Clarum decus jejunii*, 11th c.; trans. Maurice F. Bell (England), *The English Hymnal*, 1906, alt.
Music: William Knapp (England), *A New Sett of Psalm-Tunes and Anthems*, 1738

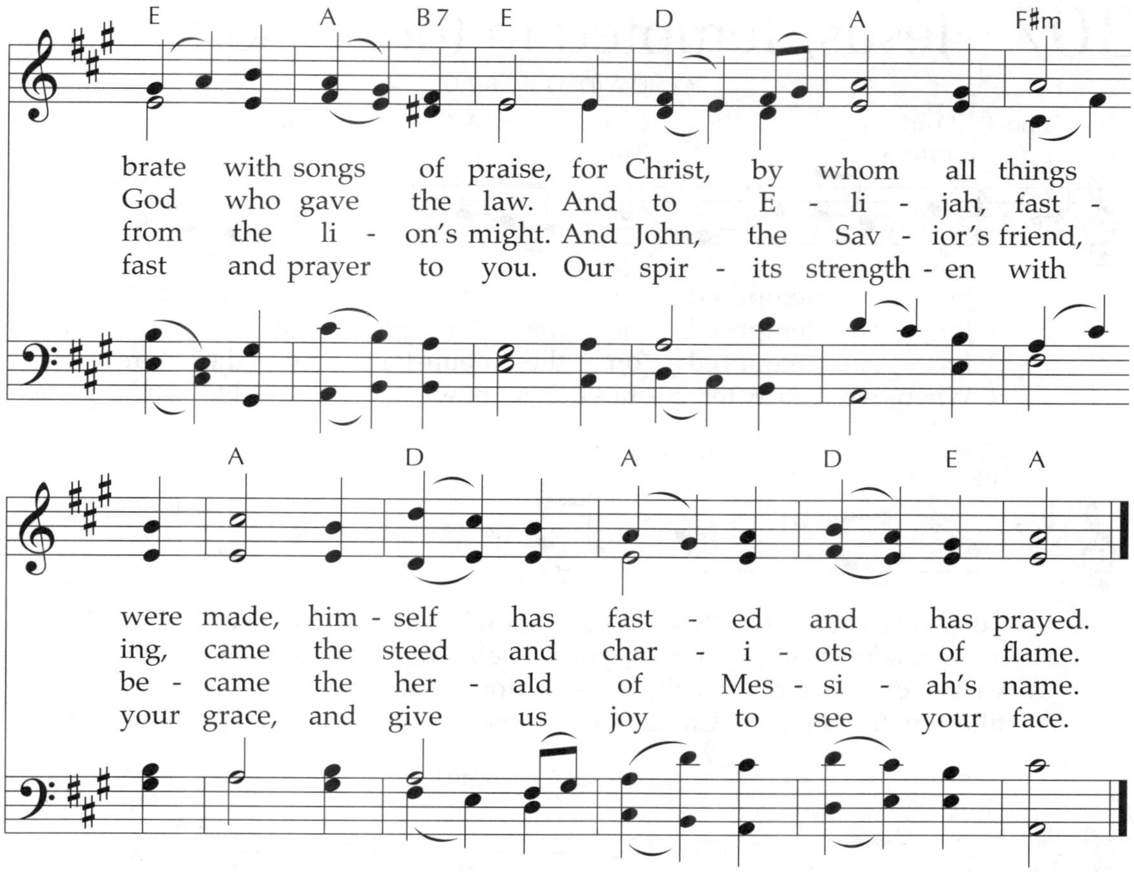
brate with songs of praise, for Christ, by whom all things
God who gave the law. And to E - li - jah, fast -
from the li - on's might. And John, the Sav - ior's friend,
fast and prayer to you. Our spir - its strength - en with
were made, him - self has fast - ed and has prayed.
ing, came the steed and char - i - ots of flame.
be - came the her - ald of Mes - si - ah's name.
your grace, and give us joy to see your face.

I Want Jesus to Walk with Me 306

SOJOURNER 8.8.8.9

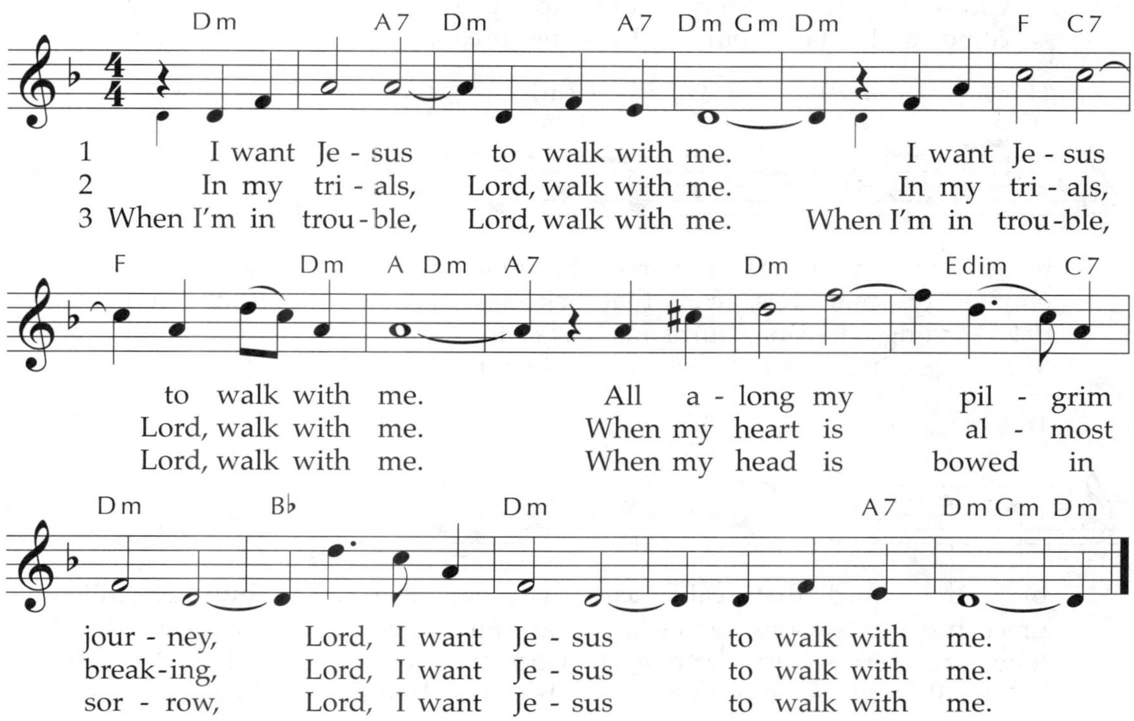
1 I want Je - sus to walk with me. I want Je - sus
2 In my tri - als, Lord, walk with me. In my tri - als,
3 When I'm in trou - ble, Lord, walk with me. When I'm in trou - ble,
to walk with me. All a - long my pil - grim
Lord, walk with me. When my heart is al - most
Lord, walk with me. When my head is bowed in
jour - ney, Lord, I want Je - sus to walk with me.
break - ing, Lord, I want Je - sus to walk with me.
sor - row, Lord, I want Je - sus to walk with me.

Text: African American spiritual (USA)
Music: African American spiritual

307 Jesus, Tempted in the Desert

GENEVA (DAY) 8.7.8.7 D

Capo 3: (Dm) Fm (Gm) B♭m (A7) C7 (Dm) Fm

1 Je - sus, tempt - ed in the de - sert, lone - ly, hun - gry,
2 Je - sus tempt - ed at the tem - ple, high a - bove its
3 Je - sus tempt - ed on the moun - tain by the lure of
4 When we face temp - ta - tion's pow - er, lone - ly strug - gling,

(Gm) B♭m (A7) C7 (Dm) Fm (Gm) B♭m (A7) C7

filled with dread: "Use your pow'r," the tempt - er tells him;
an - cient wall: "Throw your - self from loft - y tur - ret;
vast do - main: "Fall be - fore me! Be my ser - vant!
filled with dread, Christ, who knew the tempt - er's ho - ur,

(Dm) Fm (A7) C7 (Dm) Fm (D) F (Bm) Dm

"turn these bar - ren rocks to bread!" "Not a - lone by
an - gels wait to break your fall!" Je - sus shuns such
Glo - ry, fame, you're sure to gain!" Je - sus sees the
come and be our liv - ing bread. By your grace, pro -

(Em) Gm (A7) C7 (D) F (Bm) Dm (Em) Gm (A7) C7 (D) F

bread," he an - swers, "can the hu - man heart be filled. On - ly
emp - ty mar - vels, feats that fick - le crowds re - quest: "God, whose
daz - zling vi - sion, turns his eyes an - oth - er way: "God a -
tect, pre - serve us, lest we fall, your trust be - tray. Yours, a -

(Bm) Dm (Em) Gm (A7) C7 (D) F (Bm) Dm (D) F (A7) C7 (D) F

by the Word that calls us is our deep - est hun - ger stilled!"
grace pro - tects, pre - serves us, we must nev - er vain - ly test."
lone de - serves our hom - age! God a - lone will I o - bey."
bove all oth - er voic - es, be the Word we hear, o - bey.

How Can We Worship Caesar's Cross 308

LUCILE CM

1 How can we wor - ship Cae - sar's cross of
2 How can we fol - low his - t'ry's cross when
3 How can we take up fash - ion's cross worn
4 How can we find in Je - sus' cross a
tor - ture, death, and fear, a wea - pon of an
cross-marked ban - ners blaze the way for raid - ing
bold in bur - nished gold, yet borne in emp - ty
jus - tice all can see: true peace that heals, re -
un - just world, co - er - cive and se - vere?
reg - i - ments to ter - ror - ize and raze?
a - pa - thy, style swift - ly bought and sold?
stores, and builds with pas - sion fierce and free?

309 Fill Us with Your Feast

FILL US WITH YOUR FEAST 11.7.11.6 with refrain

1 Wea - ry and tempt - ed we en - ter the des - ert,
2 Deep in our dark - ness you en - ter in still - ness,
3 Seek - ing and trust - ing, we turn from de - struc - tion,
des - p'rate - ly seek - ing your face— lives that are thirst - y and
of - fer - ing com - fort so bright. Gath - ered to - geth - er with -
won - der - ing what you will bring. God of the pres - ent, the
hearts that are lone - ly, we will seek your em - brace.
in your safe shel - ter, dark - ness wel - comes the light.
past, and the fu - ture, come and do a new thing.
Refrain
Find us emp - ty and wan - der - ing: we, the lost and the least.
Find us in the wil - der - ness then fill us with your feast.

Text: Phil Campbell-Enns (Canada)
Music: Phil Campbell-Enns; acc. Marilyn Houser Hamm (Canada)

While I Keep Silence 310

SILENCE 8.6.8.6.8.6

*
1 While I keep si - lence, si - lence, si - lence, in my
2 My thirst-ing spir - it, spir - it, spir - it, wastes a -
3 All you who wan - der, wan - der, wan - der, with-out
*
flesh, my breath and bod - y fail.
way; I with - er in the sun.
hope, who know your man - y sins,
My sins grow bit - ter, bit - ter, bit - ter, in my
But as I'm turn - ing, turn - ing, turn - ing, toward the
seek out the Sav - ior, Sav - ior, Sav - ior, while he's
mouth. My bones re - turn to dust.
night, you split the si - lent skies.
found; he hides you in his hand.
*
O God, I groan both day and
O God, I stand be - neath the
O God, you hear us day and
night, be - neath your heav - y hand.
rain, be - neath the cleans - ing rain.
night; re - store us by your hand.

*These pitches may be hummed throughout the hymn, beginning at these places.

Text: based on Psalm 32:3-5; David Wright (USA), 2005, *A Field of Voices*, 2007, © 2005 David Wright
Music: James E. Clemens (USA), 2005, *A Field of Voices*, 2007, © 2005 James E. Clemens

311 We Are Often Tossed and Driven

BY AND BY 7.7.15.7.7.11

Capo 3: (D) F (G) B♭ (D) F
1 We are of - ten tossed and driv'n on the rest - less sea of time,
2 We are of - ten des - ti - tute of the things that life de - mands,
3 Temp - ta - tions, hid - den snares, of - ten take us un - a - wares,
(E) G (A) C
som - ber skies and howl - ing temp - est oft suc - ceed a bright sun - shine;
want of food and want of shel - ter, thirst - y hills and bar - ren lands;
and our hearts are made to bleed for an - y thought - less word or deed;
(D) F (G) B♭ (D) F
in that land of per - fect day, when the mists have rolled a - way,
we are trust - ing in the Lord, and ac - cord - ing to the Word,
and we won - der why the test when we try to do our best,
(D/A) F/C (Bm) Dm (E) G (A7) C7 (D) F
we will un - der - stand it bet - ter by and by.
we will un - der - stand it bet - ter by and by.
but we'll un - der - stand it bet - ter by and by.

Text: Charles A. Tindley (USA), 1905, alt.
Music: Charles A. Tindley; arr. Nolan Williams Jr. (USA)

Refrain
(G) B♭ (D) F
By and by, when the morn-ing comes, when the saints of
(E) G (A) C (D) F (G) B♭ (D) F
God are gath-ered home, we'll tell the sto - ry, how we've o-ver-come,
(D/A) F/C (Bm) Dm (E) G (A7) C7 (D) F
for we'll un - der-stand it bet-ter by and by.

312 Jesus Is Coming

PAVE THE WAY 11.8.11.8 with refrain

G
D7
Jes - us is com - ing; pave the way with branch-es.
1 G
2 G
Jes - us is com - ing. Ho - san - na! san - na! Ho-
Refrain
C G D7 G C
san - na, Je - sus is com - ing. Ho - san -
G
1 D7 G
2 D7 G
na to the Prince of Peace. Ho - Prince of Peace.

Additional verses:

Freedom for captives; pave the way with branches. Freedom for captives. Hosanna. *Refrain*
Hope for the suff'ring . . .
Debts are forgiven . . .

Additional verses may be improvised as desired.

Text: Bret Hesla (USA)
Music: Bret Hesla

Hosanna, Loud Hosanna 313

ELLACOMBE 7.6.7.6 D

Capo 3: (G) B♭ (Em) Gm (D) F (C) E♭ (D) F (G) B♭
1 Ho - san-na, loud ho - san - na, the lit - tle chil-dren sang.
2 From Ol - i - vet they fol - lowed 'mid an ex - ult - ant crowd,
3 "Ho - san-na in the high - est!" That an-cient song we sing,
(G) B♭ (Em) Gm (D) F (C) E♭ (D) F (G) B♭
Through pil-lared court and tem - ple the love-ly an-them rang.
the vic-tor palm branch wav - ing, and chant-ing clear and loud.
for Christ is our Re-deem - er, the Lord of heav'n, our King.
(G) B♭ (D) F (G) B♭ (D) F
To Je - sus, who had blessed them, close fold-ed to his breast,
The Lord of earth and heav - en rode on in low-ly state,
Oh, may we ev - er praise him with heart and life and voice,
(G) B♭ (Em) Gm (D) F (C) E♭ (D) F (G) B♭
the chil-dren sang their prais - es, the sim-plest and the best.
nor scorned that lit - tle chil - dren should on his bid-ding wait.
and in his bliss-ful pres - ence e - ter - nal - ly re - joice!

Text: Jeannette Threlfall (England), *Sunshine and Shadow*, 1873, alt.
Music: *Gesangbuch der Herzogl*, Württemberg (present-day Germany), 1784; harm. William H. Monk (England), *Appendix to Hymns Ancient and Modern*, 1868

314 Holy Lord

HOLY LORD Irregular

Refrain
G Em C D G G/B C Dsus D
Ho - ly, ho - ly, ho - ly Lord, God of pow'r and might,
G Em C D G C G
heav - en and earth of your glo - ry are full; ho - san - na, ho -
To optional final ending
C G/B C G Em7 Am/C D G
san - na, ho - san - na in the high - est!
Bridge
Em Bm/D Em B7sus Am
Bless-ed is he who comes in the name of the Lord, bless-ed is

Text: from Greek and Latin liturgy, "Sanctus" (Mediterranean), ca. 3rd–4th c., based on Isaiah 6:3 and Matthew 21:9; adapt. Steve Bell (Canada)
Music: Steve Bell

Am/G D C/D Bm/D Am/D D
To refrain
he who comes in the name of the Lord!
Optional final ending
Am/C D G C G C G/B
high - est! Ho - san - na, ho - san - na, ho -
C G Em7 Am/C D G Em7 C D G
san - na in the high - est!

315 All Glory, Laud, and Honor

ST. THEODULPH (VALET WILL ICH DIR GEBEN) 7.6.7.6 with refrain

Refrain
All glo - ry, laud, and hon - or to thee, Re - deem - er, King,
to whom the lips of chil - dren made sweet ho - san - nas ring.
Fine
1 Thou art the King of Is - rael and Da - vid's roy - al Son,
2 The peo - ple of the He - brews with palms be - fore thee went;
3 Thou didst ac - cept their prais - es, ac - cept our hymns of praise;
who in the Lord's name com - eth, the King and bless - ed One.
our praise and prayer and an - thems be - fore thee we pre - sent.
to thee, now high ex - alt - ed, our mel - o - dy we raise.
To refrain

Text: Theodulph of Orleans (present-day France), "Gloria, laus, et honor," ca. 820; trans. John M. Neale (England), *The Hymnal Noted*, 1851

Music: Melchior Teschner (present-day Germany), 1613, *Ein andächtiges Gebet . . .*, 1615

Ride On, Ride On in Majesty 316

WINCHESTER NEW LM

Capo 1: (A) (D) (E) (A) (D/F♯)
B♭ E♭ F B♭ E♭/G
1 Ride on, ride on in maj - es - ty, as all the
2 Ride on, ride on in maj - es - ty, in low - ly
3 Ride on, ride on in maj - es - ty— the an - gel
4 Ride on, ride on in maj - es - ty, in low - ly
(E) (B) (E) (A)
F C F B♭
crowds "Ho - san - na!" cry, through wav - ing branch - es
pomp ride on to die. O Christ, your tri - umph
ar - mies of the sky look down with sad and
pomp ride on to die. Bow your meek head to
(Bm) (E) (D) (A) (E) (A)
Cm F E♭ B♭ F B♭
slow - ly ride, O Sav - ior, to be cru - ci - fied.
now be - gin with cap - tured death and con - quered sin!
won - d'ring eyes to see th'ap - proach - ing sac - ri - fice.
mor - tal pain, then take, O God, your pow'r and reign.

Text: Henry H. Milman (England), *Hymns*, 1827; rev. *Hymns for Today's Church*, 1982,

Music: *Musicalisch Handbuch . . .* (present-day Germany), 1690; arr. William H. Havergal (England), *Old Church Psalmody*, 1847

317 Go to Dark Gethsemane

REDHEAD NO. 76 (GETHSEMANE) 7.7.7.7.7.7

Capo 1: (D) E♭ (A) B♭ (G) A♭ (D) E♭ (A) B♭
1 Go to dark Geth - sem - a - ne, ye that feel the
2 Fol - low to the judg - ment hall, view the Lord of
3 Cal - v'ry's mourn - ful moun - tain climb. There, a - dor - ing
(D) E♭ (A) B♭ (G) A♭ (D) E♭
tempt - er's pow'r. Your Re - deem - er's con - flict see,
life ar - raigned. Oh, the worm-wood and the gall!
at his feet, mark that mir - a - cle of time,
(A) B♭ (E7) F7 (A) B♭ (D) E♭ (A) B♭
watch with him one bit - ter hour. Turn not from his
Oh, the pangs his soul sus - tained! Shun not suff' - ring,
God's own sac - ri - fice com - plete. "It is fin - ished!"
(G) A♭ (D) E♭ (Em) Fm (A) B♭ (D) E♭
griefs a - way. Learn of Je - sus Christ to pray.
shame, or loss. Learn of him to bear the cross.
hear the cry. Learn of Je - sus Christ to die.

Chord symbols represent a simplified harmony.

Text: James Montgomery (England), *Christian Psalmist*, 1825
Music: Richard Redhead (England), *Church Hymn Tunes, Ancient and Modern*, 1853

'Tis Midnight, and on Olive's Brow 318

OLIVE'S BROW LM

Ab Db Ab/Eb Eb Ab Fm
1 'Tis mid-night, and on Ol - ive's brow the star is
2 'Tis mid-night, and from all re - moved, Im - man-uel
3 'Tis mid-night, and for oth - ers' guilt the Man of
Eb Bbm Eb Ab Eb
dimmed that late - ly shone. 'Tis mid-night; in the
wres - tles 'lone with fears. E'en that dis - ci - ple
Sor - rows weeps in blood. Yet he who hath in
Bb Eb Ab Db Ab/Eb Eb7 Ab
gar - den now the suf-f'ring Sav - ior prays a - lone.
whom he loved heeds not his Mas-ter's grief and tears.
an - guish knelt is not for - sak - en by his God.

Text: William B. Tappan (USA), *Poems*, 1822
Music: William B. Bradbury (USA), *The Shawm*, 1853

319 Stay with Me, the Night Has Come

CYSGA DI FY MHLENTYN TLWS 7.7.7.7.7

Capo 3: (Em) Gm (Bm) Dm (Em) Gm (C) E♭
1 Stay with me, the night has come, stay with me, the
(G) B♭ (Em) Gm (Bm) Dm (Em) Gm
night has come, stay with me, the night has come, and soon it
(D) F (Em) Gm (G) B♭ (Bm) Dm (E no3) G no3
will be morn - ing, and soon it will be morn - ing.

2 Pray with me . . . 3 Watch with me . . . 4 Weep with me . . .

Text: David Bjorlin (USA), © 2016 GIA Publications, Inc.
Music: Welsh traditional

320 My Song Is Love Unknown

LOVE UNKNOWN 6.6.6.6.4.4.8

Capo 1: (D) E♭ (A7) B♭7 (Bm7) Cm7 (A/C♯) B♭/D (D) E♭ (F♯m) Gm
1 My song is love un - known, my Sav - ior's love for
2 He came from heav - en's throne sal - va - tion to be -
3 Some - times they crowd his way and his sweet prais - es
4 With an - gry shouts they have my Sav - ior done a -
5 In life, no house, no home the Christ on earth might
6 Here might I sing be - lief in one my soul a -

Text: Samuel Crossman (England), *The Young Man's Meditations, or Some Few Sacred Poems . . .*, 1664; rev. *Hymns for Today's Church*, alt., © 1982 Hope Publishing Co.
Music: John N. Ireland (England), *Songs of Praise*, 1925

(G) Ab (Em) Fm (F#m) Gm (Bm) Cm (Esus) Fsus (E) F
me: love to the love - less shown that they might love - ly
stow. But they re - fused, and none the longed-for Christ would
sing, re-sound-ing all the day ho - san - nas to their
way. A mur - der - er they save, the Source of Life they
have. In death, no friend - ly tomb, but what a stran - ger
dores: nev - er was pain nor grief, nev - er was love like
(A) Bb (D) Eb (C) Db (Em) Fm (C) Db (G) Ab (G/B) Ab/C
be. But who am I, that for my sake
know. This is my friend, my friend in - deed,
king. Then "cru - ci - fy" is all their breath,
slay! Yet wil - ling - ly he bears the shame
gave. What may I say? Heav'n was his home,
yours. This is my friend in whose sweet praise
(D) Eb (D/F#) Eb/G (F#m/A) Gm/Bb (A7) Bb7 (D) Eb
my Lord should take frail flesh and die?
who at my need his life did spend.
and for his death they thirst and cry.
that through his name all might be free.
but mine the tomb where - in he lay.
I all my days could glad - ly spend.

321

يا حمل الله

Ya hamala Allah (O Lamb of God)

YA HAMALALLAH Irregular

Dm
Gm/B♭
Dm7/A
Ya ha-ma-la‿A-llah al - ha - mel kha - ta - ya -
O Lamb of God, you take a - way the
G7
E/G♯
A7
Dm
'a lam, Im - nah - na - sa - lam,
sins of the world, have mer - cy on us.
Dm/F
Gm
A7/E
Dm
Ya ha-ma-la‿A-llah al - ha - mel kha - ta - ya -
O Lamb of God, you take a - way the
G7/B
C
A7/C♯
Dm
'a lam, Im - nah - na - sa - lam, im -
sins of the world, grant us your peace, grant
B♭
Edim/G
A7
Dm
nah - na - sa - lam, im - nah - na - sa - lam.
us your peace, grant us your peace.

يا حملَ الله
يا حملَ الله الحامل خطايا العالم : ارحمنا
يا حملَ الله الحامل خطايا العالم : ارحمنا
يا حملَ الله الحامل خطايا العالم
امنحنا السلام
امنحنا السلام
امنحنا السلام

Text: Arabic; from Latin liturgy, "Agnus Dei" (Rome), ca. 7th c., based on John 1:29, Yusuf Khill (Palestine/Israel)
Music: Yusuf Khill

When I Survey the Wondrous Cross 322

SENZENINA LM

D
F♯m
(Leader)
1 When I sur - vey the won - drous cross *(on which the Prince)*
2 For - bid it, Lord, that I should boast,
3 See, from his head, his hands, his feet,
4 Were the whole realm of na - ture mine,
Em
D
A
D
on which the Prince of glo - ry died, *(my rich - est gain)*
save in the death of Christ, my God!
sor - row and love flow min - gled down!
that were an of - f'ring far too small.
A
Bm
my rich - est gain I count but loss, *(and pour con - tempt)*
All the vain things that charm me most,
Did e'er such love and sor - row meet,
Love so a - maz - ing, so di - vine,
A
G
A7
D
(When I sur - vey)
and pour con - tempt on all my pride. *(For - bid it, Lord)*
I sac - ri - fice them through his blood. *(See, from his head)*
or thorns com - pose so rich a crown? *(Were the whole realm)*
de - mands my soul, my life, my all.

Text: Isaac Watts (England), *Hymns and Spiritual Songs*, 1707
Music: South African, Zimbabwean traditional

Ⓡ

323 When I Survey the Wondrous Cross (La cruz excelsa al contemplar)

HAMBURG LM

D Em A D
1 When I sur - vey the won - drous cross on which the
2 For - bid it, Lord, that I should boast, save in the
3 See, from his head, his hands, his feet, sor - row and
1 La cruz ex - cel - sa‿al con - tem - plar do Cri - sto‿a-
2 No me per - mi - tas, Dios, glo - ri - ar, si - no‿en la
3 Ve - o‿en su ros - tro, ma - nos, pies, las mar - cas
G D A D
Prince of glo - ry died, my rich - est gain I
death of Christ, my God! All the vain things that
love flow min - gled down! Did e'er such love and
llí por mí mu - rió, na - da se pue - de
cruz de mi Se - ñor, lo que más pue - da‿am -
vi - vas del do - lor; es im - po - si - ble
Em A D A Bm G A7 D
count but loss, and pour con - tempt on all my pride.
charm me most, I sac - ri - fice them through his blood.
sor - row meet, or thorns com - pose so rich a crown?
com - pa - rar a las ri - que - zas de su a - mor.
bi - cio - nar lo sa - cri - fi - co por su a - mor.
com - pren - der tal su - fri - mien - to‿y tan - to a - mor.

4 Were the whole realm of nature mine,
that were an off'ring far too small.
Love so amazing, so divine,
demands my soul, my life, my all.

4 *El mundo‿entero no será*
dádiva digna de‿ofrecer.
Amor tan grande, sin igual,
en cambio,‿exige todo el ser.

Text: Isaac Watts (England), *Hymns and Spiritual Songs*, 1707; Spanish trans. W. T. T. Millham (Peru), alt.
Music: Lowell Mason (USA), 1824, *Boston Handel and Haydn Society Collection . . .*, 3rd. ed., 1825

The Wonderful Cross 324

WONDERFUL CROSS Irregular

G D/F♯ G
(1 pride.)
(2 blood.)
(3 crown.)
(4 all.)
Oh, the won-der-ful cross, oh, the won-der-ful cross
D/F♯ G D/F♯
bids me come and die and find that I may tru-
A G D/F♯
-ly live. Oh, the won-der-ful cross, oh, the
G D/F♯ G
won-der-ful cross; all who gath-er here by grace
D/F♯ A
To stanzas of "When I Survey"
Last time
D
draw near and bless your name.

Text: J. D. Walt (USA) and Chris Tomlin (USA)
Music: Chris Tomlin and Jesse Reeves (USA)

325 O Sacred Head, Now Wounded

HERZLICH TUT MICH VERLANGEN 7.6.7.6 D

1 O sa - cred Head, now wound - ed, with grief and shame weighed down,
2 What thou, my Lord, hast suf - fered was all for sin - ners' gain.
3 What lan-guage shall I bor - row to thank thee, dear - est Friend,
4 Be near when I am dy - ing, oh, show thy cross to me,
now scorn-ful - ly sur - round - ed with thorns, thine on - ly crown!
Mine, mine was the trans - gres - sion, but thine the dead - ly pain.
for this, thy dy - ing sor - row, thy pit - y with - out end?
and for my res - cue, fly - ing, come, Lord, and set me free!
O sa - cred Head, what glo - ry, what bliss till now was thine!
Lo, here I fall, my Sav - ior! 'Tis I de - serve thy place.
Oh, make me thine for - ev - er, and should I faint - ing be,
These eyes, new faith re - ceiv - ing, from Je - sus shall not move,
Yet, though de - spised and gor - y, I joy to call thee mine.
Look on me with thy fa - vor, and grant to me thy grace.
Lord, let me nev - er, nev - er out - live my love to thee.
for one who dies be - liev - ing dies safe - ly, through thy love.

Text: based on "Salve caput cruentatum," anon. (present-day France), 13th c.; Paul Gerhardt (present-day Germany), "O Haupt voll Blut und Wunden," *Praxis Pietatis Melica*, 1656; trans. James W. Alexander (USA), rev. *The Breaking Crucible*, 1861

Music: Hans L. Hassler (present-day Germany), *Lustgarten neuer Teutscher Gesäng*, 1601; harm. J. S. Bach (present-day Germany), *St. Matthew Passion*, 1729

How Shallow Former Shadows 326

THIRD MODE MELODY CMD

Em F E B E
1 How shal-low for-mer shad-ows seem be-side this great re-verse,
2 This is no mid-day fan-ta-sy, no flight of fe-vered brain.
3 Yet deep with-in this dark-ness lives a Love so fierce and free,
Em Dm E Am E
as dark-ness swal-lows up the light of all the u-ni-verse.
With venge-ance aw-ful, grim, and real, cha-os is come a-gain.
that arcs all voids and—risk su-preme!—em-brac-es ag-o-ny.
Em C Am Em Am Dm Am
Cre-a-tion shiv-ers at the shock, the tem-ple rends its veil.
The hands that formed us from the soil are nailed up-on the cross.
Its per-fect tes-ta-ment is etched in i-ron, blood, and wood.
C F C F Dm Am E
A pal-lid still-ness sti-fles time, and na-ture's mo-tions fail.
The Word that gave us life and breath ex-pires in ut-ter loss.
With awe we glimpse its true im-port and dare to call it good.

Text: Carl Daw (USA), *A Year of Grace*,
Music: Thomas Tallis (England), *The Whole Psalter Translated into English Metre*, 1567–1568

327 Jesus, Remember Me (Jesús, recuérdame)

REMEMBER ME Irregular

Capo 1: (D) (Em/D) (A) (D)
E♭ Fm/E♭ B♭ E♭
Je-sus, re-mem-ber me when you come in-to your king-dom.
Je-sús, re-cuér-da-me cuan-do en-tres en tu rei-no.
(Bm) (Em/G) (A) (D)
Cm Fm/A♭ B♭ E♭
Je-sus, re-mem-ber me when you come in-to your king-dom.
Je-sús, re-cuér-da-me cuan-do en-tres en tu rei-no.

Text: based on Luke 23:42; Taizé Community (France), 1981, *Music from Taizé*, vol. 1, 1981; Spanish trans. anon.
Music: Jacques Berthier (France), 1981, *Music from Taizé*, vol. 1, 1981

328 Mary, Woman Weeping

LET US STAND 6.5.6.5.7.5.6.3

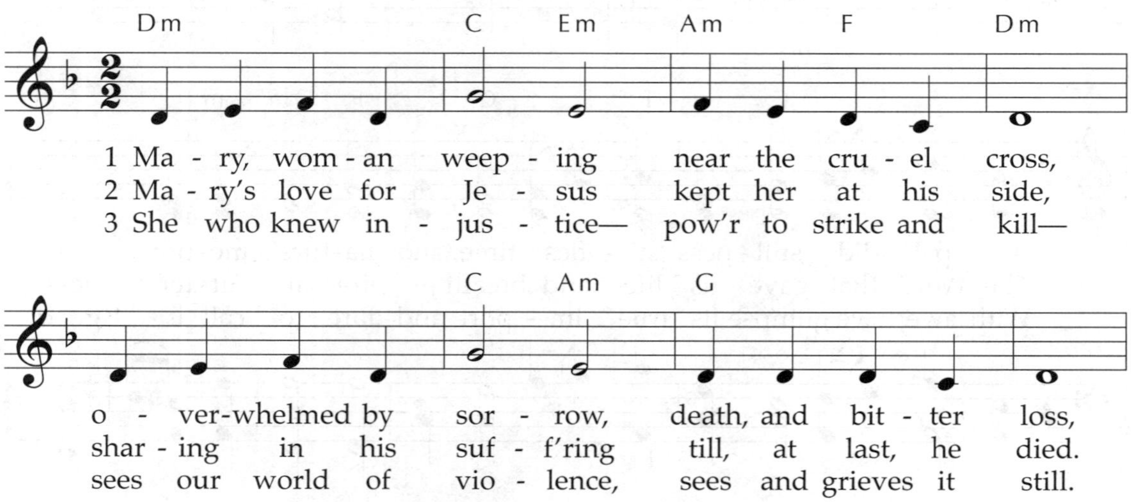
Dm C Em Am F Dm
1 Ma-ry, wom-an weep-ing near the cru-el cross,
2 Ma-ry's love for Je-sus kept her at his side,
3 She who knew in-jus-tice— pow'r to strike and kill—
C Am G
o-ver-whelmed by sor-row, death, and bit-ter loss,
shar-ing in his suf-f'ring till, at last, he died.
sees our world of vio-lence, sees and grieves it still.

Text: Delores Dufner, OSB (USA), © 2019 Sisters of St. Benedict; inspired by the *Stabat Mater* (present-day Italy), 13th c.
Music: Bradley Kauffman (USA), © 2019 Bradley Kauffman; acc. Susan See (USA)

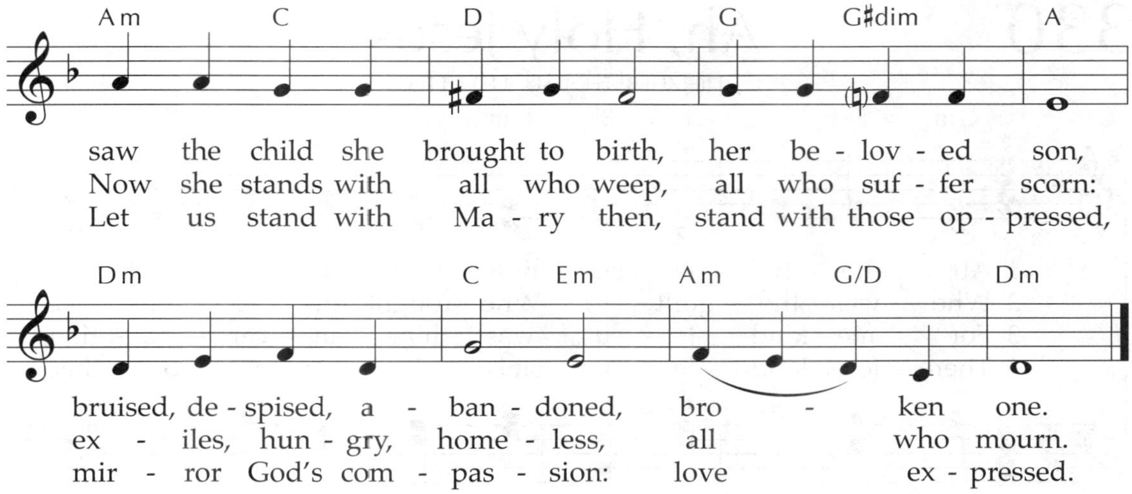
Am C D G G♯dim A
saw the child she brought to birth, her be - lov - ed son,
Now she stands with all who weep, all who suf - fer scorn:
Let us stand with Ma - ry then, stand with those op - pressed,
Dm C Em Am G/D Dm
bruised, de - spised, a - ban - doned, bro - ken one.
ex - iles, hun - gry, home - less, all who mourn.
mir - ror God's com - pas - sion: love ex - pressed.

Were You There

329

WERE YOU THERE Irregular

Capo 3: (D) F (Em) Gm (A7) C7 (D) F
1 Were you there when they cru - ci - fied my Lord? Were you
(A) C (D) F (G) B♭ (D) F
there when they cru - ci - fied my Lord? Oh!
(F♯7) A7 (Bm) Dm (G) B♭ (D) F (G) B♭ (A) C
Some-times it caus - es me to trem-ble, trem-ble, trem-ble.
(Bm) Dm (D) F (Em) Gm (A7) C7 (D) F
Were you there when they cru - ci - fied my Lord?

2 Were you there when they nailed him to the tree?
3 Were you there when the sun refused to shine?
4 Were you there when they pierced him in the side?
5 Were you there when they laid him in the tomb?
6 Were you there when he rose up from the dead?

Text: African American spiritual (USA), *Journal of American Folklore*, April–June 1897
Music: African American spiritual, *Old Plantation Hymns*, 1899

330 Ah, Holy Jesus

HERZLIEBSTER JESU 11.11.11.5

Gm Eb F Bb Gm Eb Cm D
1 Ah, ho - ly Je - sus, how hast thou of - fend - ed,
2 Who was the guilt - y? Who brought this up - on thee?
3 For me, kind Je - sus, was thine in - car - na - tion,
4 There - fore, kind Je - sus, since I can - not pay thee,
Gm Bb Eb Cm Bb F Bb Gm
that mor-tal judg-ment hath on thee de - scend - ed? By foes de -
A - las, my trea - son, Je - sus, hath un - done thee. 'Twas I, Lord
thy mor-tal sor - row, and thy life's ob - la - tion, thy death of
I do a - dore thee, and will ev - er pray thee, think on thy
Bb Cm Gm Bb Cm D Gm
rid - ed, by thine own re - ject - ed, O most af - flict - ed.
Je - sus, I it was de - nied thee; I cru - ci - fied thee.
an - guish and thy bit - ter pas - sion, for my sal - va - tion.
pit - y and thy love un - swerv-ing, not my de - serv - ing.

Chord symbols represent a simplified harmony.

Text: Johann Heermann (present-day Poland), "Herzliebster Jesu," *Devoti Musica Cordis*, 1630; trans. Robert Bridges (England), *Yattendon Hymnal*, 1899, alt.
Music: Johann Crüger (present-day Germany), *Neues vollkömliches Gesangbuch, Vol. II*, 1640

Sing, My Tongue, the Song of Triumph

331

PANGE LINGUA 8.7.8.7.8.7

1 Sing, my tongue, the song of tri - umph, tell the sto - ry
2 Thir - ty years a - mong us dwell - ing, his ap-point-ed
3 He en - dured the nails, the spit - ting, vin - e - gar and
4 Faith - ful cross, O sign of tri - umph, now for us the
5 Thus the plan of our sal - va - tion was of old in
6 Let our songs of strength and hon - or now and ev - er -

far and wide. Tell of dread and fi - nal bat - tle,
time ful - filled, born for this, he met his Pas - sion,
spear and reed. From that ho - ly bo - dy bro - ken
no - blest tree, none in fo - liage, none in blos - som,
or - der laid that the man - i - fold de - ceiv - er's
more be done: to the God who spoke cre - a - tion,

when the Christ was cru - ci - fied, how, up - on the cross a
this the Sav - ior free - ly willed. On the cross the Lamb is
blood and wa - ter both pro - ceed. Earth and stars and sky and
none in fruit can e - qual be; sweet-est wood and sweet-est
art by art might be out-weighed, and the lure the foe put
God the true be - got - ten Son, God the Spir - it, ev - er

vic - tim van-quish-ing in death, he died.
lift - ed, where his pre - cious blood he spilled.
o - cean by that flood from stain are freed.
i - ron, sweet - est weight is hung on thee.
for - ward in - to means of heal - ing made.
mov-ing, One in Three and Three in One. A - men.

Text: Venantius Fortunatus (present-day France), "Pange lingua gloriosi praelium certaminis," 569; trans. composite, John Mason Neale (England), 1851, and Percy Dearmer (England), 1905, alt.
Music: plainsong, Gallican rite (present-day France), ca. 6th–7th c.

332 In Christ Alone

IN CHRIST ALONE LMD

Capo 1: (D) (G) (D) (G) (A) (D)
E♭ A♭ E♭ A♭ B♭ E♭
1 In Christ a - lone my hope is found; he is my
2 In Christ a - lone, who took on flesh— full - ness of
3 There in the ground his bod - y lay, light of the
4 No guilt in life, no fear in death, this is the
(G) (Em7) (A7) (D) (G) (D) (G)
A♭ Fm7 B♭7 E♭ A♭ E♭ A♭
light, my strength, my song— this cor - ner - stone, this sol - id
God in help - less babe! This gift of love and right - eous -
world by dark - ness slain; then burst - ing forth in glo - rious
pow'r of Christ in me; from life's first cry to fi - nal
(A) (D) (G) (Em7) (A7) (D)
B♭ E♭ A♭ Fm7 B♭7 E♭
ground, firm through the fierc - est drought and storm.
ness, scorned by the ones he came to save,
day, up from the grave he rose a - gain!
breath, Je - sus com - mands my des - ti - ny.

Text: Keith Getty (Ireland) and Stuart Townend (England)
Music: Keith Getty and Stuart Townend; harm. and acc. Josh Holsapple (USA)

(G/B) Ab/C (D/F#) Eb/G (A) Bb (D) Eb
What heights of love, what depths of peace, when fears are
till on the cross as Je - sus died, *the wrath of
And as he stands in vic - to - ry, sin's curse has
No pow'r of hell, no hu - man plan, can ev - er
(G) Ab (D/F#) Eb/G (A) Bb (G) Ab (D) Eb (G) Ab
stilled, when striv - ings cease. My com - fort - er, my all in
God was sat - is - fied. My ev - 'ry sin on him was
lost its grip on me; for I am his and he is
pluck me from his hand; till he re - turns or calls me
(A) Bb (D) Eb (G) Ab (Em7) Fm7 (A7) Bb7 (D) Eb
all, here in the love of Christ I stand.
laid; here in the death of Christ I live.
mine, bought with the pre - cious blood of Christ.
home, here in the pow'r of Christ I'll stand!

*Alternative phrase: "the love of God was magnified"

333 Low in the Grave He Lay

CHRIST AROSE 11.10 with refrain

1 Low in the grave he lay, Je-sus, my Sav-ior! Wait-ing the com-ing day,
2 Vain-ly they watch his bed, Je-sus, my Sav-ior! Vain-ly they seal the dead,
3 Death can-not keep its prey, Je-sus, my Sav-ior! He tore the bars a-way,
Je-sus, my Lord!
Refrain: faster
Up from the grave he a-rose, he a-rose, with a might-y tri-umph o'er his foes! He a-rose!
He a-rose a vic-tor from the dark do-main, and he lives for-ev-er with his saints to reign! He a-rose! He a-rose! He a-rose! He a-rose!
Al-le-lu-ia! Christ a-rose!

Text: Robert Lowry (USA), 1874, *Brightest and Best*, 1875
Music: Robert Lowry, 1874, *Brightest and Best*, 1875

I AM MAKING ALL THINGS NEW
WE WILL ALL BE CHANGED

335 *Philippians 2:5-11*

Let the same mind be in you
that was in Christ Jesus,
who always had the nature of God,
but did not presume to remain
equal with God by force.
Instead of this,
he freely gave up all he had,
and took the nature of a servant,
becoming like a human being
and appearing in human form.
Christ was humble
and walked the path of obedience
all the way to death,
even death on the cross.
For this reason God raised Christ
to the highest place above
and gave him the name
that is greater than any other name.
And so, in honor of the name of Jesus
every knee in heaven, on earth,
and under the earth will bow,
and every tongue will confess
that Jesus Christ is Lord,
to the glory of God the Father.

336 *1 Corinthians 15:50-57 (excerpts)*

Our physical bodies cannot inherit
what will last forever.
We will not all die,
but we will all be changed.
It will happen in the blink of an eye:
those who have died will be raised
to live forever.
For our dying, mortal bodies
must be changed
into immortal bodies.
Then, when our dying bodies
have been changed,
this Scripture will be fulfilled:
"Death is swallowed up in victory.
O death, where is your victory?
O death, where is your sting?"
Thank God, who gives us victory
over sin and death
through our Savior, Jesus Christ.

337 *Romans 8:38-39*

I am convinced that
neither death, nor life,
nor angels, nor rulers,
nor things present,
nor things to come,
nor powers,
nor height, nor depth,
nor anything else in all creation,
will be able to separate us
from the love of God in Christ Jesus.

338 *John 3:16*

For God so loved the world
that he gave his only Son,
so that everyone who believes in him
may not perish
but have eternal life.

339 *Revelation 21:1-5*

I saw a new heaven and a new earth.
The first heaven and the first earth
had passed away.
Then I saw New Jerusalem,
that holy city,
coming down from God in heaven.
It was like a bride
dressed in her wedding gown
and ready to meet her spouse.
I heard a loud voice shout
from the throne:
"God's home is now
with God's people.
The Lord will live with them,
and they will be God's own."
Yes, God will make a home
among the people
and will wipe all tears from their eyes,
and there will be no more death,
suffering, crying, or pain.
These things of the past are gone forever.
And the one sitting on the throne said:
"I am making everything new."

Previous page: 334. *Alive*, Anne Hostetler Berry (USA), 2018, pen and ink ⓦ

Lift Your Glad Voices 340

RESURRECTION 10.11.11.11.12.11.10.11

1 Lift your glad voic - es in tri - umph on high,
He burst from the fet - ters of e - vil that bound him,
2 Glo - ry to God, in full an - thems of joy;
But Je - sus has cheered the deep val - ley of sor - row,
for Je - sus has ris - en and we shall not die.
re - splend - ent in glo - ry, to live and to save.
the be - ing God gave us, death can - not de - stroy.
and bade us, im - mor - tal, to heav - en as - cend.
Vain were the ter - rors that gath - ered a - round him,
Loud was the cho - rus of an - gels on high,
Sad were the life we may part with to - mor - row,
Lift then your voic - es in tri - umph on high,
and short the do - min - ion of death and the grave.
the Sav - ior has ris - en, and we shall not die.
if tears were our birth - right and death were our end.
for Je - sus has ris - en, and we shall not die.

Text: Henry Ware Jr. (USA), *Christian Disciple*, 1817, alt.
Music: John E. Gould (USA), *Methodist Hymnal with Tunes—Special Edition*, ca. 1878

341 Mfurahini, haleluya (Christ Has Arisen, Alleluia!)

MFURAHINI, HALELUYA 9.9.9.9 with refrain

F/C F C7 Dm Gm
1 M - fu - ra - hi - ni, ha - le - lu - ya, m - ko - mbo -
2 Ma - la - i - ka a - li - waam - bi - a Wa - na - wa -
3 A - me - ba - ti - lish - a She - ta - ni. A - me - wa -
1 Christ has a - ris - en, al - le - lu - ia! Re - joice and
2 The an - gel said to them, "Do not fear. You look for
3 "Go spread the news: he's not in the grave. He has a -
F C F F/C F
zi a - me - fu - fu - ka. A - me - fu - fu - ka,
ke, "M - si - og - o - pe. Sa - sa ka - bu - ri
le - te - a wo - ko - vu. Kwa hi - yo ni - nyi
praise him, al - le - lu - ia, for our re - deem - er
Je - sus who is not here. See for your - selves the
ris - en, mor - tals to save." Je - sus' re - deem - ing
C7 Dm Gm F C F
ha - le - lu - ya, m - si - fu - ni sa - sa yu ha - i.
li twa - tu - pu. Kwa - ni Ye - su a - me - fu - fu - ka."
m - tan - ga - ze, Ni ha - ki - ka, Ye - su yu ha - i.
burst from the tomb, e - ven from death, dis - pel - ling its gloom.
tomb is all bare. On - ly the grave - clothes are ly - ing there."
la - bors are done. E - ven the bat - tle with sin is won.

Text: Swahili; Bernard Kyamanywa (Tanzania), © 1968 Makumira University College (admin. Augsburg Fortress); trans. Howard S. Olson (USA), © 1977 (admin. Augsburg Fortress)
Music: Haya traditional (Tanzania)

Refrain
C C7 F C
Tu - mwi - mbi - e so - te kwa fu - ra - ha. Ye - su a -
Let us sing praise to him with end - less joy. Death's fear - ful
C7 F F/C F
me - to - ka ka - bu - ri - ni ka - shi - nda ki - fo,
sting he has come to de - stroy, our sins for - giv - ing,
C7 Dm Gm F C F
ha - le - lu - ya; Ha - le - lu - ya, Ye - su yu ha - i.
al - le - lu - ia. Christ has a - ris - en, al - le - lu - ia!

342 That Easter Morn, at Break of Day

O FILII ET FILIAE 8.8.8 with alleluias

Refrain
Fine
Al - le - lu - ia, al - le - lu - ia, al - le - lu - ia!
1 That Eas - ter morn, at break of day,
2 When Ma - ry's heart was filled with gloom
3 "Why do you weep?" his ques - tion came.
4 No lon - ger weep - ing, an - guish - bent,
5 On this most ho - ly day of days,
a faith - ful wom - an went her way to seek the
and she stood weep - ing near the tomb, a stran - ger
"Whose is the bod - y you would claim?" And then, at
but with re - joic - ing Ma - ry went, by Christ as
to God your hearts and voic - es raise in laud and
To refrain
tomb where Je - sus lay. Al - le - lu - ia!
spoke, she knew not whom. Al - le - lu - ia!
last, he spoke her name. Al - le - lu - ia!
first a - pos - tle sent. Al - le - lu - ia!
ju - bi - lee and praise. Al - le - lu - ia!

Text: based on John 20:1–18; stanzas 1, 5 Jean Tisserand (present-day France), 15th c.; trans. John Mason Neale (England), ca. 1852, alt. and adapt.; stanzas 2, 3, 4 Delores Dufner, OSB (USA),
Music: French traditional, 15th c.; harm. James E. Clemens (USA),

These Things Did Thomas Count 343

BRIGHTNESS LM

E A/E B E C♯m7
1 These things did Thom - as count as real: the warmth of
2 The vi - sion of his skep - tic mind was keen e -
3 His rea-soned cer - tain-ties de - nied that one could
4 May we, O God, by grace be - lieve and thus the
A F♯ B E/G♯
blood, the chill of steel, the grain of wood, the
nough to make him blind to an - y un - ex -
live when one had died, un - til his fin - gers
ris - en Christ re - ceive, whose raw im - print - ed
F♯ B E A/C♯ B7 E
heft of stone, the last frail twitch of blood and bone.
pect - ed act too large for his small world of fact.
read like Braille the mark-ings of the spear and nail.
hands reached out, and beck-oned Thom - as from his doubt.

Chord symbols represent a simplified harmony.

344 Seeking Warmth from Charcoal Blazing

COLUMCILLE 8.7.8.7 D

Capo 1: (Em) Fm (Bm) Cm (Em) Fm
1 Seek - ing warmth from char-coal blaz - ing, Pe - ter fought the
2 Bread and fish, a fire-side break-fast for a wea - ry
3 Ques-tions asked and an-swers giv - en, time-less fac - es
(D) E♭ (B) C (Em) Fm (Bm) Cm
chill night air. Some-one spoke, "I saw you with him." Pe - ter
fish - ing crew. Je - sus que - ried, "Do you love me?" Pe - ter
warmed by flame; bit - ter night of love's de - ni - al, with the
(F♯m) Gm (B) C (Bm) Cm (Em) Fm
said, "Not me. I swear." Two more times was Pe - ter ques-tioned,
said, "You know I do." Two more times his mas - ter ques-tioned,
dawn re - demp-tion came. We still hear these an-cient voic - es
(D) E♭ (G) A♭
two more times he an-swered "No!" Then from deep with - in the
two more times did Pe - ter vow. "Feed my lambs," was Je - sus'
and the les - son that they give. "Do you love me?" is the

shad - ows came the prom - ised roost - er crow.
bid - ding. "Tend my sheep; they need you now."
ques - tion meant to guide us as we live.

The Risen Christ 345

UPPER ROOM 10.10.10.10

1 The ris - en Christ, who walks on wound-ed feet
2 The ris - en Christ, who stands with wound-ed side,
3 The ris - en Christ, who breaks with wound-ed hand
4 May we, Christ's bod - y, walk and serve and stand

from gar - den tomb through dark-ened cit - y street,
breathes out his Spir - it on them to a - bide
the bread for those who fail to un - der - stand,
with the op-pressed in this and ev - ery land,

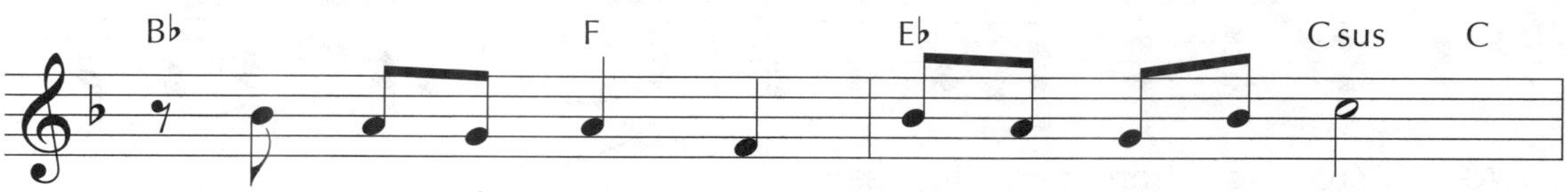

un - locks the door of grief, de - spair, and fear,
whose faith still wav - ers, who dare not be - lieve,
re - veals him - self, de - spite their lin - g'ring tears,
till all are blessed and can a bles - sing be,

and speaks a word of peace to all who hear.
new grace, new strength, new pur - pose they re - ceive.
en - flames their hearts, then quick - ly dis - ap - pears.
re - stored in Christ to true hu - man - i - ty.

Text: Nigel Weaver (Canada), © 1993 Nigel Weaver
Music: Richard VanOss (Netherlands), © 2012 Richard VanOss (admin. Faith Alive Christian Resources)

346 Christ the Lord Is Risen Today (El Señor resucitó)

EASTER HYMN 7.7.7.7 with alleluias

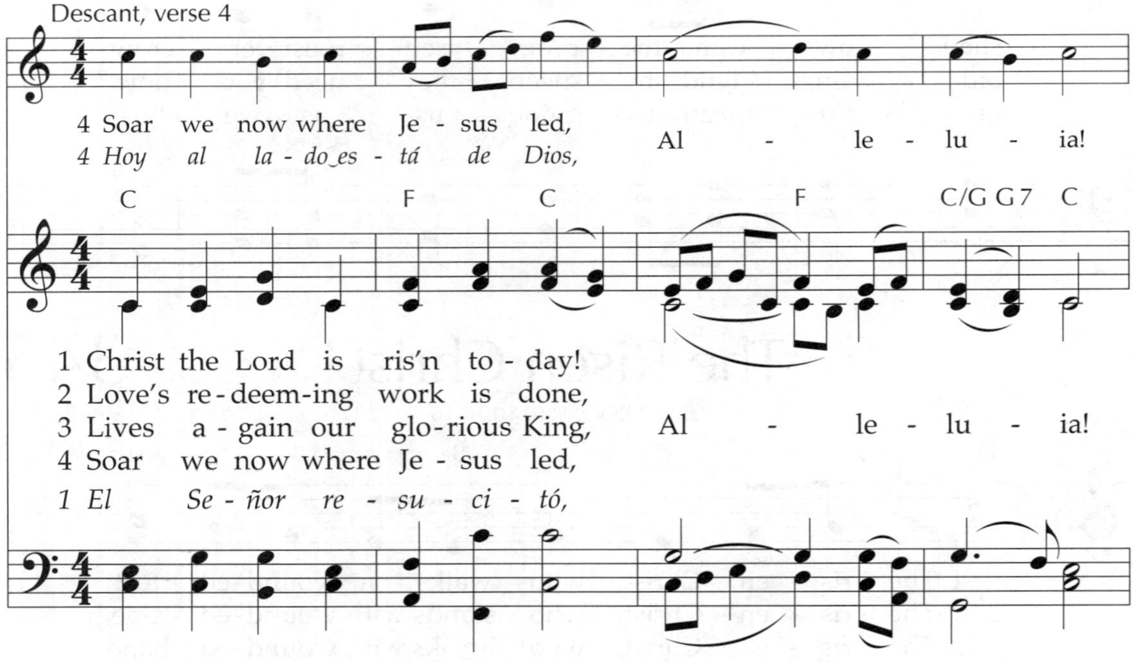
Descant, verse 4
4 Soar we now where Je - sus led, Al - le - lu - ia!
4 Hoy al la - do_es - tá de Dios,
C F C F C/G G7 C
1 Christ the Lord is ris'n to - day!
2 Love's re - deem - ing work is done,
3 Lives a - gain our glo - rious King, Al - le - lu - ia!
4 Soar we now where Je - sus led,
1 El Se - ñor re - su - ci - tó,

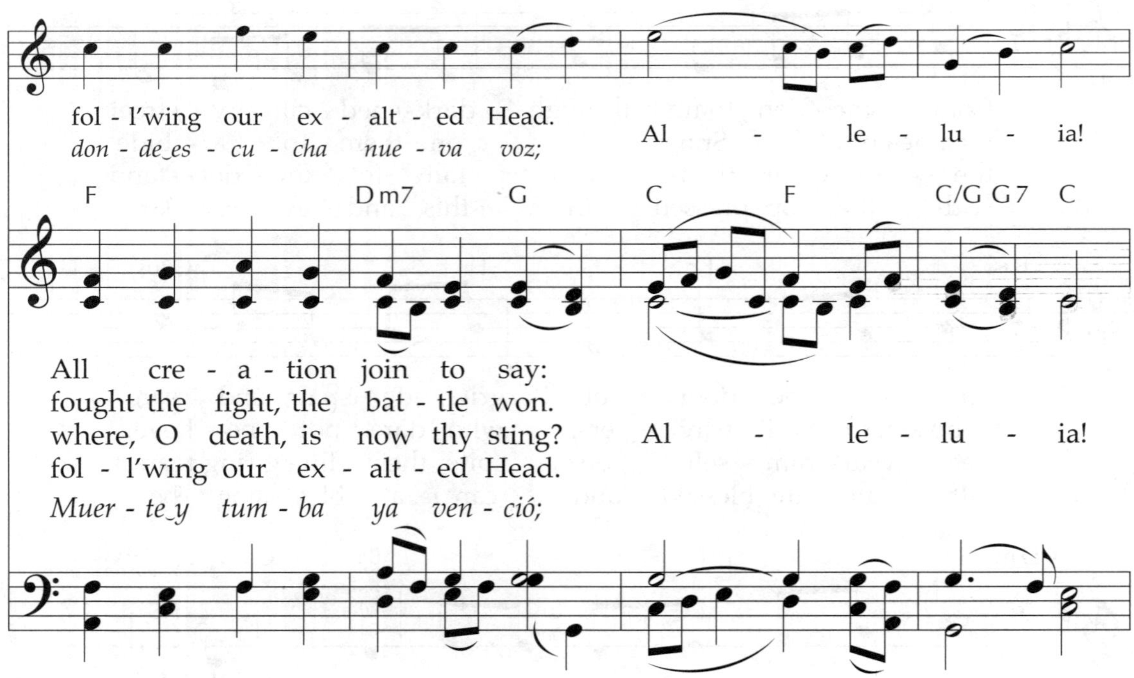
fol - l'wing our ex - alt - ed Head. Al - le - lu - ia!
don - de_es - cu - cha nue - va voz;
F Dm7 G C F C/G G7 C
All cre - a - tion join to say:
fought the fight, the bat - tle won.
where, O death, is now thy sting? Al - le - lu - ia!
fol - l'wing our ex - alt - ed Head.
Muer - te_y tum - ba ya ven - ció;

Text: Charles Wesley (England), *Hymns and Sacred Poems*, 1739, alt.; Spanish trans. Juan Bautista Cabrera (Spain)
Music: anon., *Lyra Davidica* (England), 1708; desc. Nolan Williams Jr.,

Made like Christ, we rise,
Por no - so - tros
Al - le - lu - ia!
G C G D7 G
Raise your joys and tri-umphs high:
Death in vain for - bids him rise,
Dy - ing once, he all doth save,
Made like Christ, with Christ we rise,
Con su fuer - za‿y su vir - tud,
Al - le - lu - ia!

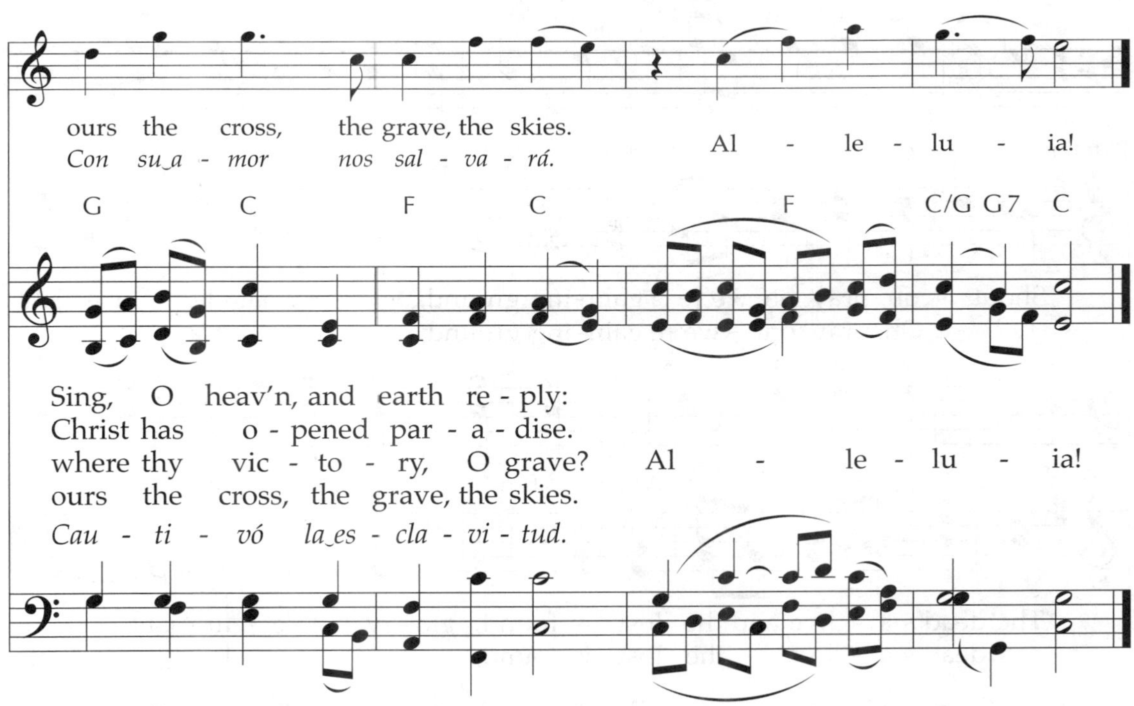
ours the cross, the grave, the skies.
Con su‿a - mor nos sal - va - rá.
Al - le - lu - ia!
G C F C F C/G G7 C
Sing, O heav'n, and earth re - ply:
Christ has o - pened par - a - dise.
where thy vic - to - ry, O grave?
ours the cross, the grave, the skies.
Cau - ti - vó la‿es - cla - vi - tud.
Al - le - lu - ia!

2 *Jesucristo se‿humilló, ¡aleluya!*
vencedor se levantó; ¡aleluya!
cante hoy la cristiandad, ¡aleluya!
su gloriosa majestad. ¡Aleluya!

3 *Cristo que la cruz sufrió, ¡aleluya!*
y‿en desolación se vio, ¡aleluya!
hoy en gloria celestial, ¡aleluya!
reina vivo e‿inmortal. ¡Aleluya!

4 *Hoy al lado‿está de Dios, ¡aleluya!*
donde‿escucha nueva voz; ¡aleluya!
por nosotros rogará, ¡aleluya!
con su‿amor nos salvará. ¡Aleluya!

347 I Know That My Redeemer Lives

SHOUT ON, PRAY ON LM extended

Em
Am Em Am Em
1 I know that my Re-deem-er lives,
2 He lives to crush the pow'rs of hell,
3 He lives, my hun-gry soul to feed,
4 He lives, all glo-ry to his name,
glo-ry, hal-le-lu-jah!
lu - jah!
Am Em Am Em
What com-fort this sweet sen-tence gives,
He lives, with-in my heart to dwell,
He lives to help in time of need,
He lives, my Sav-ior, still the same,
glo-ry, hal-le-lu-jah!
lu - jah!
Refrain
G Em G Em
Shout on, pray on, we're gain-ing ground, glo-ry, hal-le-lu-jah!
Oh, pray on, we're gain-ing ground,
Am Em Am Em Am Em
The dead's a-live and the lost is found, glo-ry, hal-le-lu-jah!
dead's a-live, the lost is found, lu - jah!

5 He lives, triumphant from the grave;
he lives, eternally to save!

6 He lives to heal and make me whole;
he lives to guard my troubled soul.

7 He lives and grants me daily breath;
he lives, and I shall conquer death!

Text: Samuel Medley (England), *Psalms and Hymns*, 1775, alt.; refrain anon.
Music: American traditional (USA), *Sacred Harp*, 2nd ed., 1850; harm. Alice Parker (USA),

Come, Ye Faithful, Raise the Strain 348

AVE VIRGO VIRGINUM (GAUDEAMUS PARITER) 7.6.7.6 D

1 Come, ye faith - ful, raise the strain of tri - um - phant glad - ness!
2 'Tis the spring of souls to - day: Christ hath burst his pris - on,
3 Nei - ther shall the gates of death, nor the tomb's dark por - tal,
God hath brought forth Is - ra - el in - to joy from sad - ness,
and from three days' sleep in death as a sun hath ris - en.
nor the watch - ers, nor the seal hold thee as a mor - tal.
loosed from Pha-raoh's bit - ter yoke Ja - cob's sons and daugh - ters,
Now re - joice, Je - ru - sa - lem, and with true af - fec - tion
But a - ris - en 'midst thy friends thou didst stand, be - stow - ing
led them with un - moist-ened foot through the Red Sea wa - ters.
wel-come in un - wea - ried strains Je - sus' res - ur - rec - tion.
thy true peace, which ev - er - more pass - es hu - man know - ing.

For chord symbols, see "We Are People of God's Peace" (#797).

Text: John of Damascus (present-day Syria), "First Ode of Canon for the Sunday after Easter," 8th c.; trans. John M. Neale (England), *Christian Remembrancer*, 1859, alt.

Music: Johann Horn (present-day Czech Republic), *Ein Gesangbuch der Bruder in Behemen und Merherm* (present-day Germany), 1544; rev. *Catholicum Hymnologium Germanicum*, 1584

349 Christ Is Risen

CHRIST IS RISEN Irregular

Refrain
Christ is ris - en from the dead, tram-pling o - ver death by death—
come a - wake, come a - wake, come and rise up from the grave.
Christ is ris - en from the dead, we are one with him a - gain—
come a - wake, come a - wake, come and rise up from the grave. (Christ is)
1st time
Fine
Bridge
O death, where is your sting? O death,
where is your vic - to - ry? O church, come stand in the light; the
glo - ry of God has de - feat - ed the night. Sing - ing:
stand in the light; our God is not dead—he's a - live, he's a - live!
To refrain
D 2
G maj7
B m7
A
D 2/F♯
G 2
A sus

Text: based on Paschal Troparion (Jerusalem), ca. 5th–6th c.; Matt Maher (Canada) and Mia Fieldes (Australia)
Music: Matt Maher and Mia Fieldes

The Strife Is O'er 350

VICTORY 8.8.8 with alleluias

E A E A E B E
*Al - le - lu - ia! Al - le - lu - ia! Al - le - lu - ia!
Verses
E A E B E
1 The strife is o'er, the bat - tle done, the vic - to -
2 The pow'rs of death have done their worst, but Christ their
3 The three sad days have quick - ly sped. He ris - es
4 Christ, by your wounds on Cal - va - ry, from death's dread
C♯m E B E A
ry of life is won. The song of tri - umph
le - gions has dis - persed. Let shouts of ho - ly
glor - ious from the dead. All glo - ry to our
sting your ser - vants free, that we may live e -
E B E B E
To verses
has be - gun: Al - le - lu - ia!
joy out - burst: Al - le - lu - ia!
ris - en Head! Al - le - lu - ia!
ter - nal - ly: Al - le - lu - ia!*

*Alleluias to be sung at the beginning and conclusion of the hymn

Text: anon., "Finita iam sunt praelia," *Symphonia Sirenum Selectarum* (present-day Germany), 1695; trans. Francis Pott (England), *Hymns Fitted to the Order of Common Prayer*, 1861

Music: Giovanni P. da Palestrina (present-day Italy), *Magnificat in the Third Mode*, 1591; adapt. William H. Monk (England), *Hymns Ancient and Modern*, 1861

351 Oh, qué bueno es Jesús (Oh, How Great Is Christ the Lord)

OH, QUÉ BUENO 7.7.7.6 with refrain

D G D A
Oh, qué bue - no es Je - sús. Que por mí mu-rió‿en la cruz.
Oh, how great is Christ the Lord! On the cross he died for me.
D G Em D/A A7 D
Mis pe - ca - dos per - do - nó. A su nom - bre, ¡glo - ria!
He has par - doned all my sin. Glo-ry be to Je - sus.
Refrain
G A7 G/D D
A su nom - bre, ¡glo - ria! A su nom - bre, ¡glo - ria!
Glo-ry be to Je - sus! Glo-ry be to Je - sus!
G Em D/A A7 D
En tres días re - su - ci - tó. A su nom - bre, ¡glo - ria!
In three days he rose a-gain. Glo-ry be to Je - sus!

Text: Spanish; Puerto Rican traditional
Music: Puerto Rican traditional; arr. James E. Clemens (USA),

This Joyful Eastertide 352

VRUECHTEN 6.7.6.7 with refrain

1 This joy-ful Eas-ter-tide a-way with sin and sor - row!
My love, the cru-ci-fied, hath sprung to life this mor - row.
2 My flesh in hope shall rest and for a sea-son slum - ber
till trum-pets east to west shall wake the dead in num - ber.
3 Death's flood hath lost its chill since Je-sus crossed the riv - er.
Lov - er of souls, from ill my pass-ing soul de - liv - er.
Refrain
Had Christ, who once was slain, ne'er burst his three-day pris - on,
our faith had been in vain. But now hath Christ a - ris - en, a -
ris - en, a - ris - en, a - ris - en.

Text: George R. Woodward (England), *Carols for Easter and Ascension*, 1894
Music: Dutch traditional, *David's Psalmen* (present-day Netherlands), 1685; harm. Alice Parker (USA),

353 Now the Green Blade Rises

NOËL NOUVELET 11.11.10.11

Eno3 A Em A Em/B B Em
1 Now the green blade ris - es from the bur - ied grain,
2 In the grave they laid him, love by ha - tred slain,
3 Forth he came at Eas - ter like the ris - en grain,
4 When our hearts are win - try, griev - ing, or in pain,
Eno3 A Em A Em/B B Em
wheat that in the dark earth man - y days has lain;
think - ing he would nev - er wake and live a - gain,
Je - sus, who for three days in the grave had lain;
Je - sus' touch can call us back to life a - gain;
Em B/F♯ Em/G B B/D♯ Em F♯ B B7
love lives a - gain, that with the dead has been;
laid in the earth like grain that sleeps un - seen;
raised from the dead, the liv - ing Christ is seen;
fields of our hearts that dead and bare have been:
Em A Em A Em/B B Eno3
love is come a - gain like wheat a - ris - ing green.

Text: John Macleod Campbell Crum (England), © 1928 Oxford University Press
Music: French traditional, 15th c.; harm. James E. Clemens (USA), © 2001 James E. Clemens

Christ Is Risen! Shout Hosanna! 354

COLBERT 8.7.8.7 D

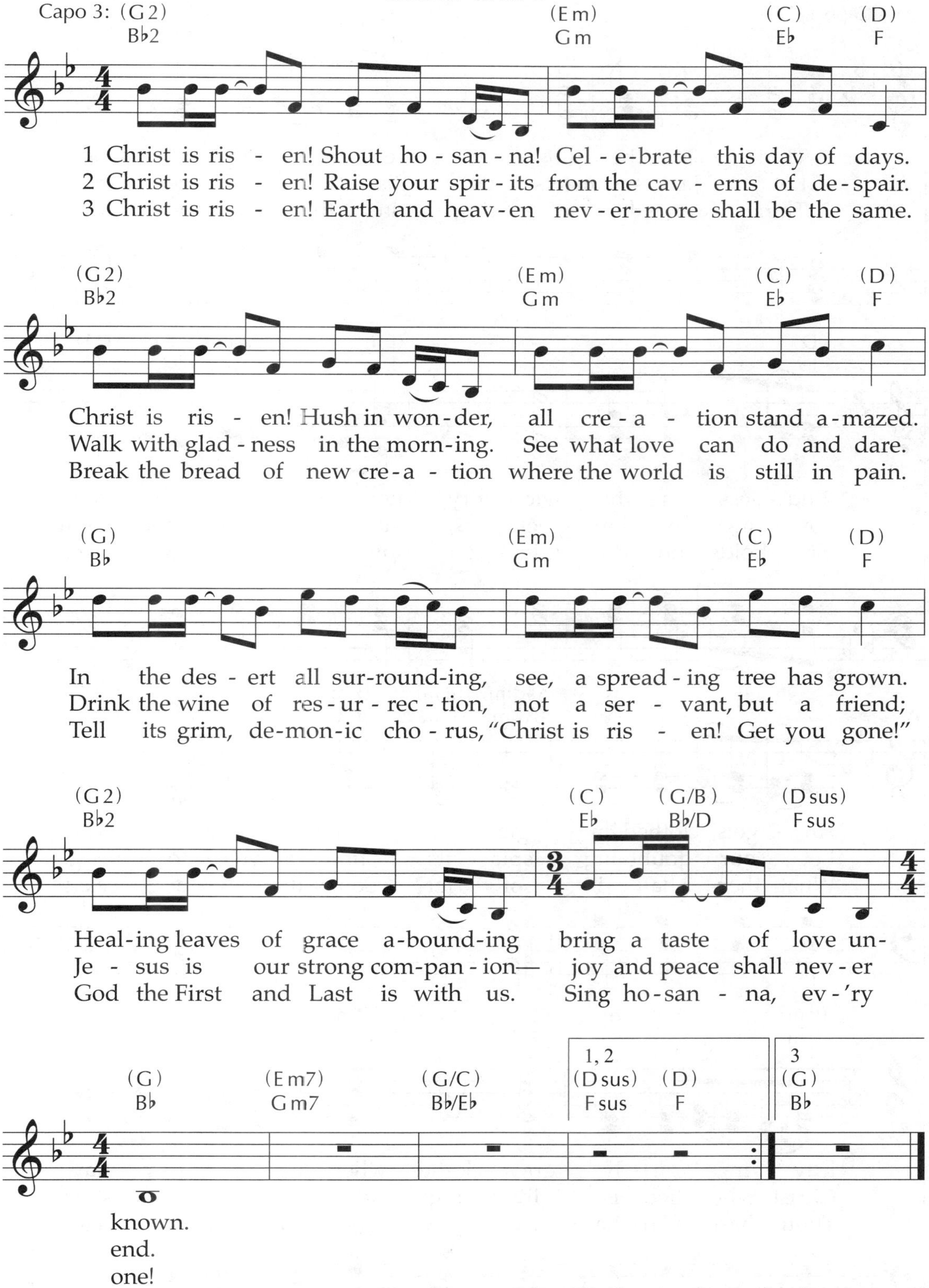
Capo 3:
1 Christ is ris - en! Shout ho - san - na! Cel - e-brate this day of days.
2 Christ is ris - en! Raise your spir - its from the cav - erns of de-spair.
3 Christ is ris - en! Earth and heav-en nev - er-more shall be the same.
Christ is ris - en! Hush in won-der, all cre - a - tion stand a-mazed.
Walk with glad - ness in the morn-ing. See what love can do and dare.
Break the bread of new cre-a - tion where the world is still in pain.
In the des - ert all sur-round-ing, see, a spread - ing tree has grown.
Drink the wine of res - ur - rec - tion, not a ser - vant, but a friend;
Tell its grim, de-mon-ic cho - rus, "Christ is ris - en! Get you gone!"
Heal-ing leaves of grace a-bound-ing bring a taste of love un-
Je - sus is our strong com-pan - ion— joy and peace shall nev - er
God the First and Last is with us. Sing ho-san - na, ev -'ry
known.
end.
one!

Text: Brian Wren (England), 1984, *Praising a Mystery*, © 1986 Hope Publishing Co.
Music: Benjamin Brody (USA), © 2011 GIA Publications, Inc.

355 Thine Is the Glory

JUDAS MACCABEUS 5.5.6.5.6.5.6.5 with refrain

Capo 1: (D) E♭ (A) B♭ (D) E♭ (A) B♭
1 Thine is the glo - ry, Res - ur - rect - ed One!
2 Lo! Je - sus meets us. Ris - en from the tomb,
3 Thine was the suf - f'ring, mine the end - less life.
(D) E♭ (Em) Fm (A sus)(A7) B♭sus B♭7 (D) E♭
End - less is the vic - t'ry now for us be - gun!
lov - ing - ly he greets us, scat - ters fear and gloom.
Sin holds no do - min - ion; love wins o - ver strife.
(A♯dim7)(Bm) Bdim7 Cm (Em) Fm (F♯) G
An - gels clothed in glo - ry rolled the stone a - way,
Let our doubt - ing spir - its find a voice to sing:
What then shall I of - fer? Songs that nev - er cease!
(Bm) Cm (E7) F7 (F♯m) Gm (E7) F7 (A) B♭
leav - ing on - ly grave - clothes where his bod - y lay.
Christ who died is liv - ing; death has lost its sting.
Thou hast won the vic - t'ry, glo - rious Prince of Peace!

Text: Edmond L. Budry (France), "A toi la gloire, O Ressuscité," *Chants Evangéliques*, 1885; trans. Mennonite Worship and Song Committee, 2018, adapt. from Richard B. Hoyle (England), *Cantate Domino*, 1925
Music: George Frederick Handel (England), *Joshua*, 1746

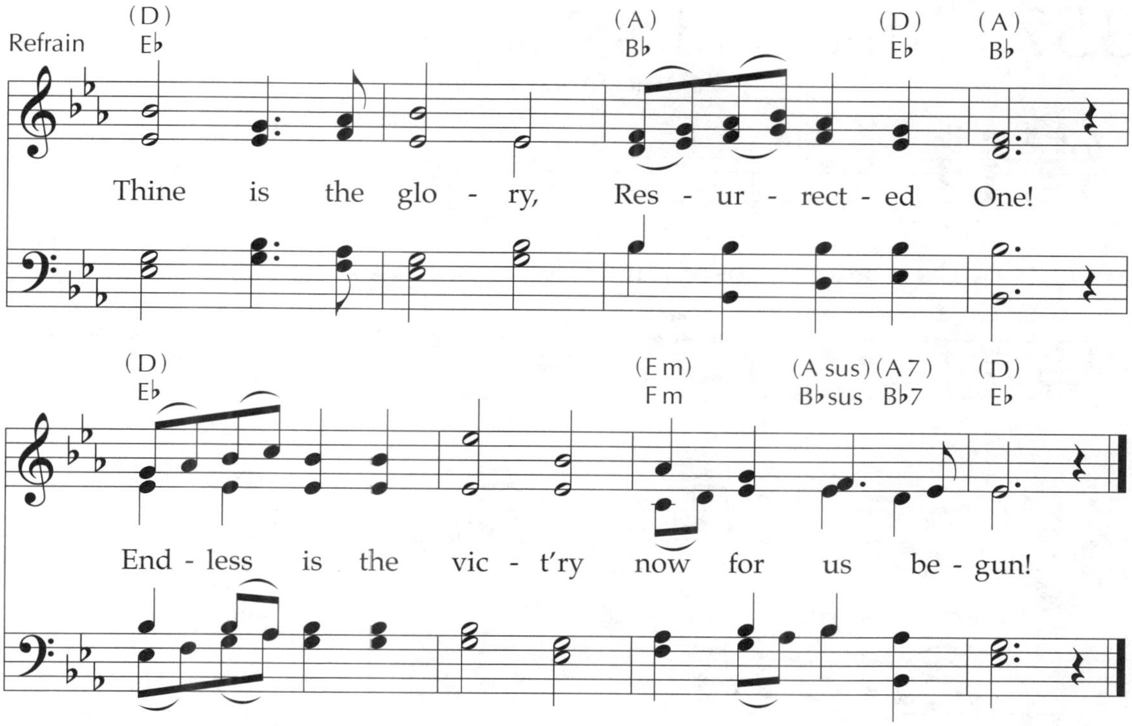
Refrain
Thine is the glo - ry, Res - ur - rect - ed One!
End - less is the vic - t'ry now for us be - gun!

Be Not Afraid 356

BE NOT AFRAID 4.4.8 D

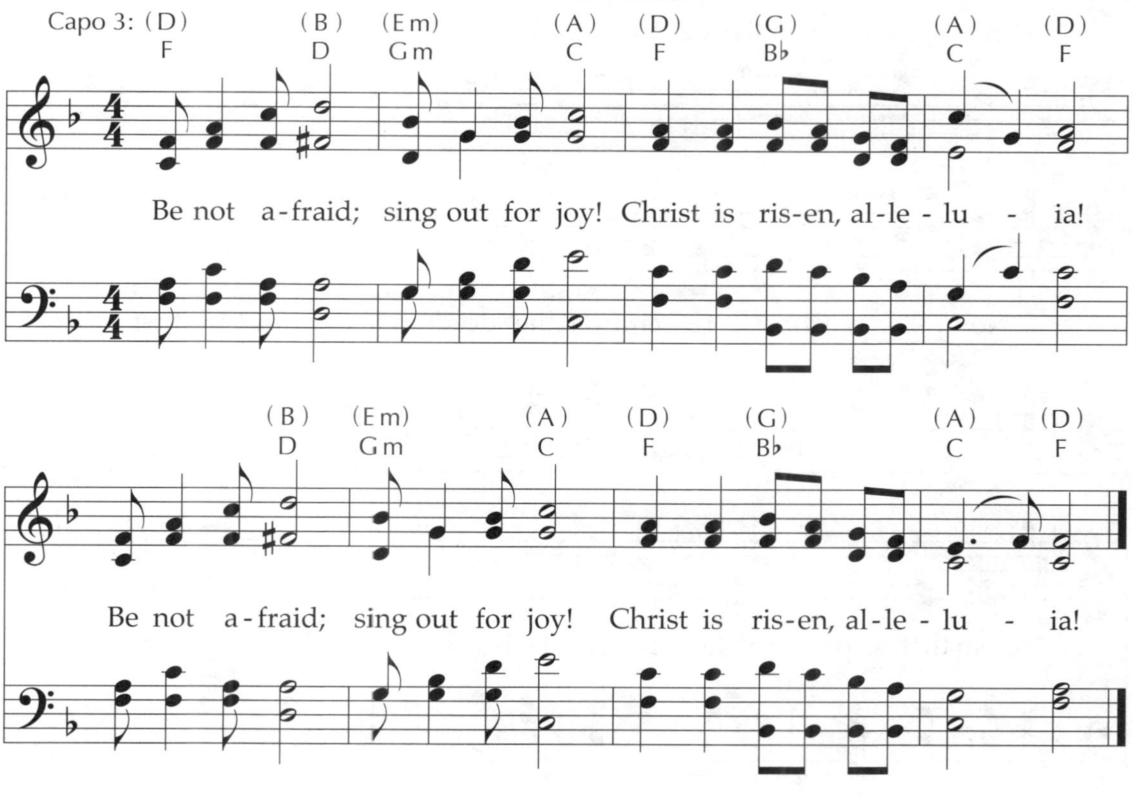
Capo 3:
Be not a-fraid; sing out for joy! Christ is ris-en, al-le-lu - ia!
Be not a-fraid; sing out for joy! Christ is ris-en, al-le-lu - ia!

Text: Taizé Community (France)
Music: Jacques Berthier (France)

357 The Lord Is Risen Indeed!

EASTER ANTHEM Irregular

The Lord is ris'n in-deed! Hal - le-lu-jah! The
Lord is ris'n in-deed! Hal - le-lu - jah!
Now is
Christ ris-en from the dead and be-come the first-fruits of them that slept.
Now is Christ ris-en from the dead and be-come the first-fruits of
them that slept. Hal-le - lu-jah, Hal-le - lu-jah, Hal-le - lu - jah.

Text: Edward Young (England), *Night Thoughts*, 1745, alt.
Music: William Billings (USA), 1787

And did he rise? And did he rise?
And did he
And did he rise? And did he rise?
And did he rise? And did he rise?
rise? Did he rise? Hear, O ye na-tions! Hear it, O ye dead!
He rose, he rose,
He rose, he rose, he rose, he rose, he burst the bars of death. He
burst the bars of death. He burst the bars of death and tri-umphed
o'er the grave. Then, then, then I rose, then I rose, then I

rose, then I rose! Then first hu - man - i - ty, tri - um - phant,
passed the crys - tal ports of light and seized e - ter - nal youth.
Thus, all im - mor - tal, hail, hail! Heav - en has lav - ished its strange
gifts to all. Thine all the glo - ry, ours the bound - less
bliss! Thine all the glo - ry, ours the bound - less bliss!

Christ Is Arisen 358

CHRIST IST ERSTANDEN Irregular

Christ is a - ris - en from death's bit - ter pris - on. We
now re - joice with glad - ness; Christ will end all sad - ness. Chri -
- ste e - lei - son.* All the world had end - ed had
Je - sus not as-cend - ed from the grave tri - um-phant-ly. For
this, Lord Christ, we hon - or thee. Chri - ste e - lei - son.
Al - le - lu - ia! Al - le - lu - ia! Al -
le - lu - ia! We now re - joice with glad - ness;
Christ will end all sad - ness. Chri - ste e - lei - son.

*Translation: Christ, have mercy.

Text: *Victimae Paschali* (present-day Germany), ca. 11th c.; "Christ ist erstanden von der Marter alle," 12th c.; trans. F. W. Herzberger (USA), *Church Hymnal for Lutheran Services*, 1911, alt.
Music: German traditional, 12th c., *Das Klugsche Gesangbuch* (Wittenberg, present-day Germany), 1529

359 Christ Is Alive! Let Christians Sing

TRURO LM

D G A D
1 Christ is a - live! Let Chris - tians sing. The cross stands
2 Christ is a - live! No long - er bound to dis - tant
3 In ev - 'ry in - sult, rift, and war, where col - or,
4 Christ is a - live, and comes to bring good news to
G D A D A E A D E
emp - ty to the sky. Let streets and homes with prais - es
years in Pal - es - tine, but sav - ing, heal - ing, here and
scorn, or wealth di - vide, Christ suf - fers still, yet loves the
this and ev - 'ry age, till earth and sky and o - cean
A D Em D/A A7 D
ring. Love, drowned in death, shall nev - er die.
now, and touch - ing ev - 'ry place and time.
more, and lives, where e - ven hope has died.
ring with joy, with jus - tice, love, and praise.

Text: Brian Wren (England), 1968, *New Church Praise*, 1975, rev. 1995,
Music: anon., *Psalmodia Evangelica, Part 2* (England), 1789

Who Are These 360

OTO SA BARANKI Irregular

Refrain
F G C/E G F G Am
Who are these who are be - liev - ers now?
F G C Am D Gsus G/F
These are they who have been shout - ing, "Al - le - lu - ia!"
C/E F Gsus G/F C/E F
They have seen the Sav - ior and have been filled with
Gsus G/F C/E G F C G7 C
splen - dor. Al - le - lu - ia, al - le - lu - ia!

Verses can be found in the accompaniment edition.

Text: based on "Ad coenam Agni" (present-day Italy), ca. 5th–6th c., refrain *Hymnal: A Worship Book*, © 1991 *Hymnal: A Worship Book*; stanzas Brenda Hostetler Meyer (USA), © 2019 Brenda Hostetler Meyer
Music: Jacek Gałuszka, OP (Poland), © 1989 Jacek Gałuszka, OP

361 Christ Who Left His Home in Glory

CHRIST IS RISEN 8.7.8.7 with refrain

1 Christ who left his home in glo - ry, and up - on the cross was slain, now is ris'n! O tell the sto - ry that the Sav - ior lives a - gain.
2 While the world in peace was sleep - ing, ear - ly on that East - er day, came the faith - ful wom - en, weep - ing, but the stone was rolled a - way.
3 Christ, our lov - ing med - i - a - tor, now with God for you and me in - ter - cedes, and our Cre - a - tor hears and an - swers ev - 'ry plea.
Refrain
Hail him! Hail him! Tell
Hail him, all hail the might - y Re - deem - er! Hail him who

Text: Abram B. Kolb (USA), 1896, *Church and Sunday School Hymnal,* 1902, alt.
Music: Abram B. Kolb, 1896, *Church and Sunday School Hymnal,* 1902

the sto - ry. Hail! all
robbed the grave of its pow'r! Tell ev - 'ry na - tion,
hail!
all is well,
Je - sus lives for - ev - er - more.

Alleluia 362

ROTHLISBERGER Irregular

Canon

1
Al - le - lu - ia, al - le - lu - ia!
2
Al - le - lu - ia, al - le - lu - ia!
3
Al - le - lu - ia, al - le - lu - ia!
4
Al - le - lu - ia, al - le - lu - ia!
(𝄐)*

*Fermatas for last time only.

Text: Hebrew traditional; הַלְלוּ יָהּ (Hallelujah) (Mediterranean), ca. 4th c. BC, translit. Greek, ἀλληλούϊα (Alleluia) (Mediterranean), ca. 3rd c. BC

Music: David J. Gonzol (USA), © 1999 David J. Gonzol

363 Sing We Triumphant Hymns

DEO GRACIAS LM

1 Sing we tri - um - phant hymns of praise! New
2 To us the shin - ing an - gels cry, "Why
3 "You see him now, as - cend - ing high a -
4 O ris - en Christ, as - cend - ed now, at
songs to heav'n ex - ult - ing raise! Christ,
stand and gaze up - on the sky? This
bove the stars, be - yond the sky. Here -
your blest name all knees shall bow; you
by a road be - fore un - trod, as -
is the Sav - ior!" Thus they say, "This
af - ter, Je - sus you shall see re -
are, while end - less a - ges run, in
cends un - to the throne of God.
is his glo - rious tri - umph day!"
turn - ing in great maj - es - ty."
Tri - une God for - ev - er One.

Text: the Venerable Bede (present-day England), "Hymnum canamus gloriae," 8th c.; trans. Benjamin Webb (England), *The Hymnal Noted,* 1851, alt.
Music: English traditional, 15th c.

All Hail the Power of Jesus' Name 364

DIADEM CM extended

1 All hail the pow'r of Je - sus' name! Let an-gels pros-trate fall, let an - gels pros-trate fall. Bring forth the roy - al di - a- dem, and crown him,
2 Let ev - 'ry kin - dred, ev - 'ry tribe, on this ter - res - trial ball, on this ter - res - trial ball, to him all maj - es - ty as- cribe,
3 Oh, that with yon - der sa - cred throng we at his feet may fall, we at his feet may fall! We'll join the ev - er - last - ing song,
and crown him, crown him, crown him, crown him,
crown
crown him, crown him, crown him, and crown him Lord of all.
him, and crown him Lord of all.

Text: Edward Perronet (England), *Gospel Magazine*, 1779-1780; rev. John Rippon (England), *Selection of Hymns*, 1789
Music: James Ellor (England), ca. 1838

365 Lord, I Lift Your Name on High (Tu nombre levantaré)

LORD I LIFT Irregular

G C/G D/G C/G G C/G
Lord, I lift your name on high; Lord, I love to sing your
Tu nom-bre le-van - ta - ré; me de-lei-to‿en a - do-
D/G C/G G C/G D/G C/G
prais - es. I'm so glad you're in my life;
rar - te. Te‿a-gra-dez - co que‿en mi vi-da‿es - tés;
G C/G D Dsus D
I'm so glad you came to save us.
que vi - nie - ras a sal - var - me.
Refrain
G C D C/D
You came from heav - en to earth to show the way,
De - jas - te‿el tro - no pa - ra mos - trar - nos la luz,
G C D C
from the earth to the cross, my debt to pay;
de tu tro - no a cruz, y mi deu - da pa - gar;

Text: Rick Founds (USA); Spanish trans. anon.
Music: Rick Founds

G C D
from the cross to the grave, from the grave
de la cruz a mo - rir, de la muer-
Em7 Am7 D G
to the sky; Lord, I lift your name on high.
- te a tu tro - no; tu nom-bre le-van - ta - ré.

Although Our Lord Has Left Us 366

CHRISTUS, DER IST MEIN LEBEN 7.6.7.6

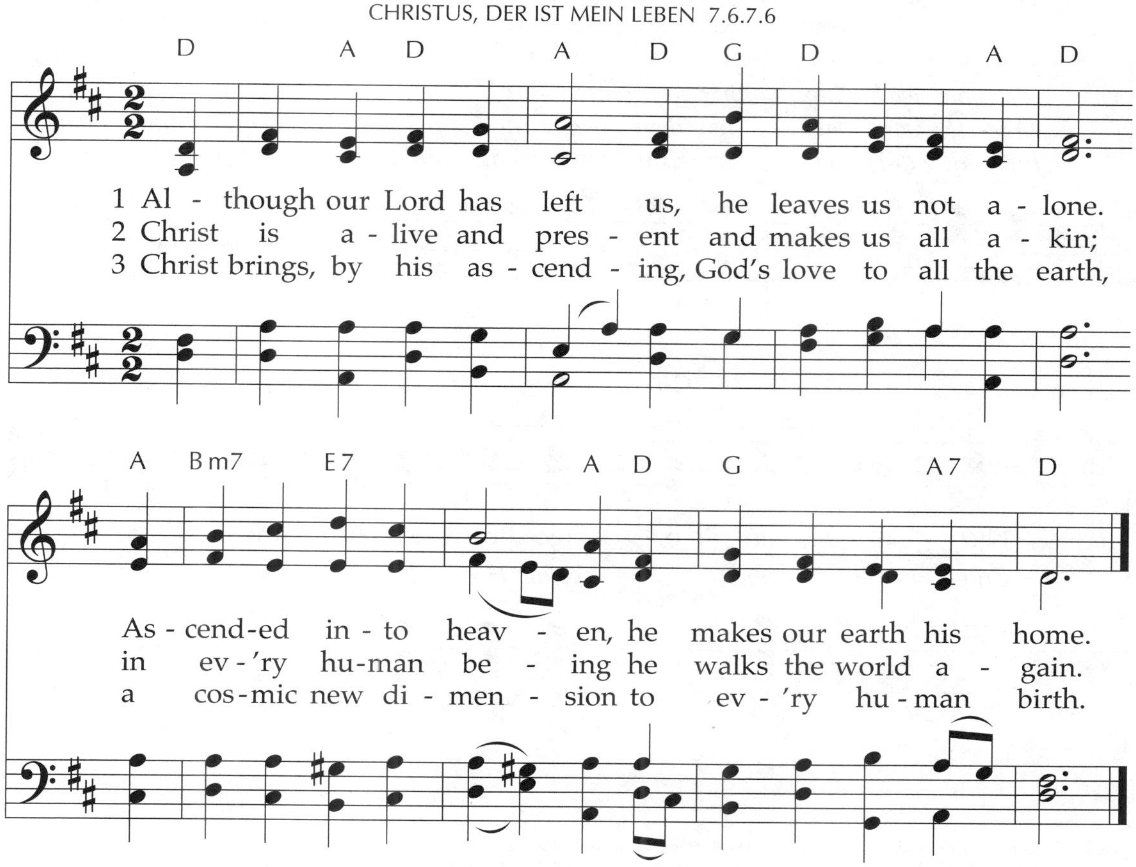
D A D A D G D A D
1 Al - though our Lord has left us, he leaves us not a - lone.
2 Christ is a - live and pres - ent and makes us all a - kin;
3 Christ brings, by his as - cend - ing, God's love to all the earth,
A Bm7 E7 A D G A7 D
As - cend-ed in - to heav - en, he makes our earth his home.
in ev - 'ry hu-man be - ing he walks the world a - gain.
a cos-mic new di - men - sion to ev - 'ry hu - man birth.

Text: Fred Kaan (England), © 1972, 1997 Hope Publishing Co.
Music: Melchior Vulpius (present-day Germany), *Ein schön geistlich Gesangbuch*, 1609

367 Njoo kwetu, Roho mwema (Gracious Spirit)

NJOO KWETU, ROHO MWEMA Irregular

G C6 G/D D G
1 Njo - o kwe - tu, Ro - ho mwe - ma, M - fa - ri - ji we - tu,
2 Kwa - nu - ru - ma tu - ba - ri - ki, tu - i - shi na we - we.
3 Ro - ho mwe - ma M - fa - ri - ji, u - tu - pe he - ki - ma;
1 Gra - cious Spir - it, heed our plead - ing, fash - ion us all a - new.
2 Guide our think - ing and our speak - ing done in your ho - ly name.
3 Not mere knowl - edge, but dis - cern - ment, nor root - less lib - er - ty;
C6 G/D D G
Tu - fu - ndi - she ya mbi - ngu - ni, tu - we wa - tu wa - pya.
Tu - ka - te - nde ki - la ki - tu ku - o - ngo - zwa na - we.
Tu - ki - wa - za na ku - te - nda, yo - te ya - we ya - ko.
It's your lead - ing that we're need - ing, help us to fol - low you.
Mo - ti - vate all in their seek - ing, free - ing from guilt and shame.
turn dis - qui - et to con - tent - ment, doubt in - to cer - tain - ty.
Refrain
G C C6 G D G
Njo - o, njo - o, njo - o, Ro - ho mwe - ma.
Come, come, come, Ho - ly Spir - it, come.

Text: Swahili; Wilson Niwagila (Tanzania), 1965; trans. Howard S. Olson (USA)
Music: Ganda traditional (Tanzania); arr. C. Michael Hawn (USA), arr. © General Board of Global Ministries

Spirit of Life

368

SPIRIT OF LIFE 8.12.8.12.8.10

C Dm7 G C Am Dm7
Spir - it of Life, come un - to me. Sing in my heart all the
G7 C F G/F Em
stir - rings of com - pas - sion. Blow in the wind, rise in the sea;
Am Dm7 G7 C F
move in the hand, giv - ing life the shape of jus - tice. Roots hold me close;
G/F Em Am Dm7 G C
wings set me free; Spir - it of Life, come to me, come to me.

Text: Carolyn McDade (USA)
Music: Carolyn McDade; harm. Grace Lewis-McLaren (USA), alt., harm. © 1992 Unitarian Universalist Association

369 There's Nothing Worth More (Nada vale más)

HOLY SPIRIT Irregular

G
1 There's noth-ing worth more that will ev - er come close.
2 I've tast - ed and seen of the sweet-est of loves,
1 Na - da va - le más que tú, mi Se - ñor.
2 He pro-ba-do, he vi - sto de tu dul - ce a - mor,
C2
Noth - ing can com-pare; you're our liv-ing hope.
where my heart be-comes free and my shame is un-done:
No hay com-pa - ra - ción, e - res nues-tro vi - vir.
don - de yo li - bre soy y ver-güen-za no hay:
G
C2
Your Pres-ence.
your Pres-ence.
Tu pre - sen - cia.
tu pre - sen - cia.
Refrain
G
C2
Ho - ly Spir-it, you are wel-come here; come flood this place and fill the
San-to Es-pí-ri-tu te in-vi-to a-quí; i - nún - da - nos, lle-na la at-
Am7
G
at - mo-sphere; your glo - ry, God, is what our hearts long for, to be
mós - fe - ra; tu glo - ria es lo que an-he - la - mos hoy, y
C2
Am7
G
o - ver - come by your Pres - ence, Lord.
ser lle - na-dos de tu pre - sen - cia.

Text: Bryan Torwalt (USA) and Katie Torwalt (USA); Spanish trans. anon.
Music: Bryan Torwalt and Katie Torwalt

C2 Am7
Last time, end on G chord
Your Pres - ence, Lord.
Tu pre - sen - cia.
Bridge C2 G/B Am7 G/B
Let us be - come more a - ware of your Pres - ence;
Dé - ja - nos ver el mo - ver de tu pre - sen - cia;
C2 G/B
To repeat
Am7 G/B
let us ex - per - i - ence the glo - ry of your good - ness.
ex - pe - ri - men - tar tu po - der y gran - de - za.
Last time
Am7 G/B C2
To refrain
ry of your good - ness, Lord.
der y gran - de - za.

Veni Sancte Spiritus

370

VENI SANCTE SPIRITUS Irregular

Ostinato
A Bm/A
Ve - ni San - cte Spi - ri - tus.

Translation: Come, Holy Spirit.

Verses can be found in the accompaniment edition.

Text: based on Latin sequence, 13th c.; Ta zé Community (France), *Music from Taizé*, vol. 1, 1978, 1980, 1981
Music: Jacques Berthier (France), 1978, *Music from Taizé*, vol. 1, 1978, 1980, 1981

371 Come, Gracious Spirit

BACA LM extended

E C♯m B
1 Come, gra-cious Spir - it, heav'n-ly Dove, with light and
2 Lead us to Christ, the liv - ing Way, nor let us
3 Lead us to heav'n, that we may share full-ness of
B7 E/B E A/E
com - fort from a - bove. Come, be our guard - ian and our
from his pas-tures stray. Lead us to hol - i - ness, the
joy for ev - er there. Lead us to our e - ter - nal
E A/E B
guide; o'er ev - 'ry thought and step pre - side,
road that we must take to dwell with God,
rest, to be with God for - ev - er bless'd,
A E/B B E
o'er ev - 'ry thought and step pre - side.
that we must take to dwell with God.
to be with God for - ev - er bless'd.

Text: Simon Browne (England), *Hymns and Spiritual Songs*, 1720, alt.
Music: William B. Bradbury (USA), *The Jubilee*, 1858

Wind Who Makes All Winds 372

FALCONE 7.7.7.7 D

1 Wind who makes all winds that blow—gusts that bend the sap-lings low,
2 Fire who fuels all fires that burn—suns a-round which plan-ets turn,
3 Ho - ly Spir - it, Wind and Flame, move with-in our mor-tal frame.
gales that heave the sea in waves, stir-rings in the mind's deep caves—
bea - cons mark-ing reefs and shoals, shin-ing truth to guide our souls—
Make our hearts an al - tar pyre. Kin-dle them with your own fire.
aim your breath with stead-y pow'r on your church, this day, this hour.
come to us as once you came; burst in tongues of sa - cred flame!
Breathe and blow up - on that blaze till our lives, our deeds, and ways
Raise, re-new the life we've lost, Spir-it God of Pen - te - cost.
Light and Pow-er, Might and Strength, fill your church, its breadth and length.
speak that tongue which ev-'ry land by your grace shall un - der - stand.

Text: Thomas H. Troeger (USA), *The Christian Ministry*, 1983
Music: Carol Doran (USA), 1985, *New Hymns for the Lectionary*, 1986; harm. Carol Doran, 1988

373 As the Wind Song through the Trees

WAIRUA TAPU Irregular

G C/G
1 As the wind song through the trees, as the stir - ring of the
2 As the rain - bow af - ter rain, as the hope that's born a -
G Em Bm Am D
breeze, so it is with the Spir - it of God; as the
gain, so it is with the Spir - it of God; as the
Em Em/D C G/B
heart made strange-ly warm, as the voice with - in the storm, so it
green in the spring, as a kite on a string, so it
Am7 D G
is with the Spir - it of God. Nev - er
is with the Spir - it of God, mak-ing
Em Bm C G
seen, ev - er known where this wind has blown, bring-ing
worlds that are new, mak - ing peace come true, bring-ing
Em Bm Am D
life, bring-ing pow'r to the world, as the
gifts, bring-ing love to the world; as the
Em Em/D C G/B
dan - cing tongues of fire, as the soul's most deep de - sire, so it
ris - ing of the yeast, as the wine at the feast, so it
Am7 D G C/G
is with the Spir - it of God.
is with the Spir - it of God.

Text: Shirley Erena Murray (Aotearoa New Zealand), 2004
Music: Lim Swee Hong (Singapore), 2004

There Are Many Gifts 374

MANY GIFTS Irregular

Refrain
There are man-y gifts, but the same Spir - it. There are
man-y works, but the same God, and the Spir-it gives each as it
choos - es. Al - le - lu - ia, praise God!
Fine
1 Now one has the gift of wis - dom, an - oth - er the call - ing to speak, one the a - bil - i - ty to com - fort, an - oth - er the call - ing to teach.
2 A bod - y has man - y mem - bers, yet all work in u - ni - ty. The church is the bod - y of Christ, his arms, ears and eyes, hands and feet.
3 Not all are called to be proph - ets, and not all are called to preach, but all should aim for the best gifts and love is the great - est of these.
To refrain

Text: based on 1 Corinthians 12:4–12; Patricia Shelly (USA), 1976, *Many Gifts*, 1977, alt.
Music: Patricia Shelly, 1976, *Many Gifts*, 1977

375 Joys Are Flowing like a River

BLESSED QUIETNESS 8.7.8.7 with refrain

Capo 1: (G) Ab
(C) Db
1 Joys are flow - ing like a riv - er since the
2 Like the rain that falls from heav - en, like the
3 See, a fruit - ful field is grow - ing, bless - ed
4 What a won - der - ful sal - va - tion, where we
(G) Ab (D) Eb (G) Ab
Com - fort - er has come, who a - bides with us for-
sun - light from the sky, so the Ho - ly Ghost is
fruit of right - eous - ness, and the streams of life are
al - ways see God's face! What a per - fect hab - i -
(C) Db (G/D) Ab/Eb (D7) Eb7 (G) Ab
ev - er, makes the trust - ing heart a home.
giv - en, com - ing on us from on high.
flow - ing in the lone - ly wil - der - ness.
ta - tion, what a qui - et rest - ing place!
Refrain
(C) Db
Bless - ed qui - et - ness, ho - ly qui - et-ness— what as -

Text: Manie P. Ferguson (USA), ca. 1897, alt.
Music: W. S. Marshall (USA), ca. 1897; adapt. James M. Kirk (USA), 1900

(G) Ab (D) Eb (G) Ab
sur - ance in my soul! On the storm - y sea speak - ing
(C) Db (G/D) Ab/Eb (D7) Eb7 (G) Ab
peace to me— how the bil - lows cease to roll!

O Holy Spirit, Root of Life 376

HILDEGARD LM

1 O Ho - ly Spir - it, Root of life, Cre - a - tor,
2 E - ter - nal Vig - or, Sav - ing One, you free us
3 O Ho - ly Wis - dom, Mov - ing Force, en - com - pass
(Hum)
Cleans - er of all things, a - noint our wounds, a -
by your liv - ing Word, be - com - ing flesh to
us with wings un - furled, and car - ry us, en -
wak - en us with lus - trous move - ment of your wings.
wear our pain, and all cre - a - tion is re - stored.
circl - ing all, a - bove, be - low, and through the world.

Text: based on the writings of Hildegard of Bingen (present-day Germany), 12th c.; Jean Janzen (USA),
Music: Anneli Loepp Thiessen (Canada),

377 New Earth, Heavens New

ALEXANDRA 5.6.5.6.5.6 with refrain

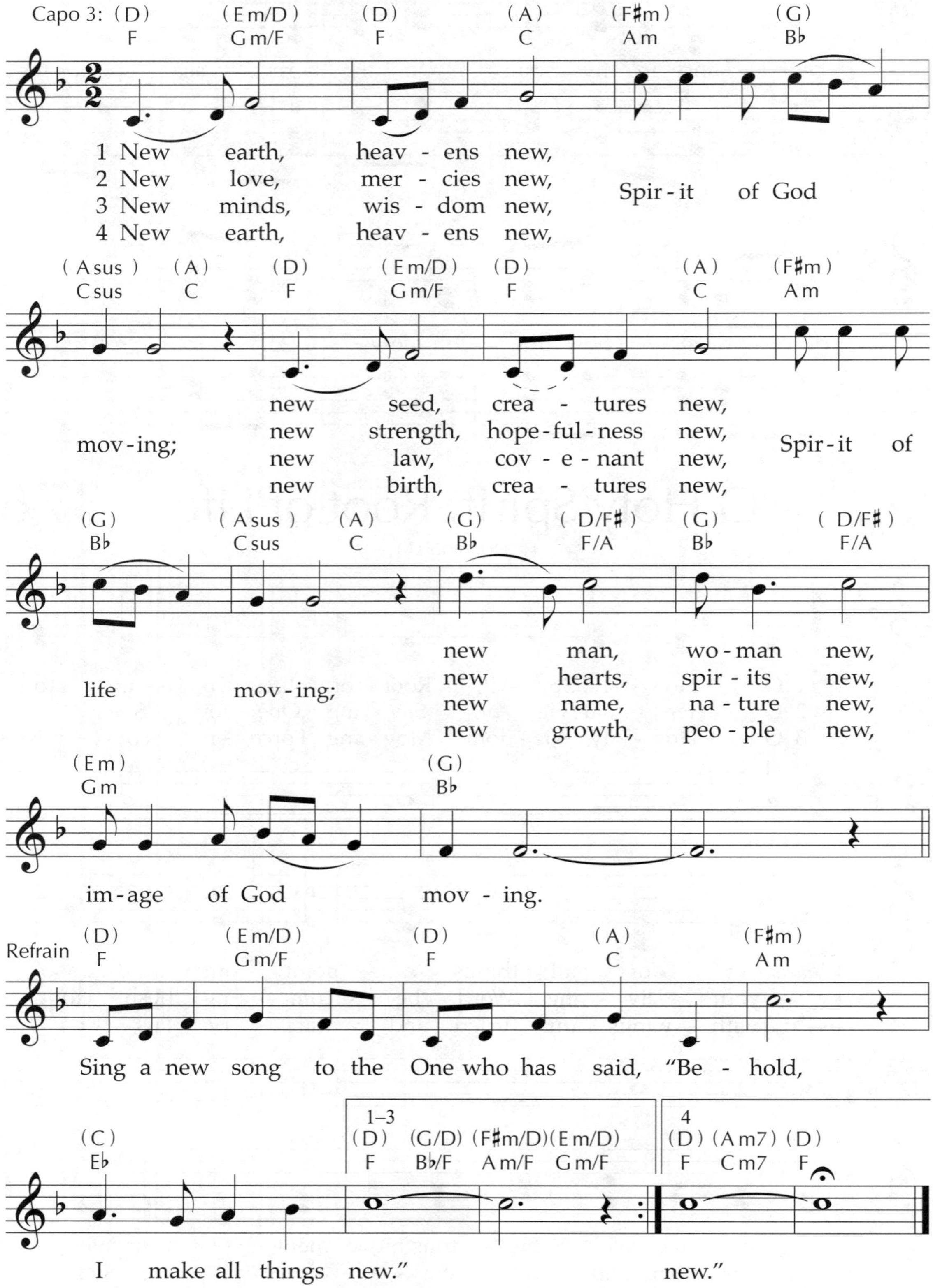
Capo 3: (D) (Em/D) (D) (A) (F♯m) (G)
F Gm/F F C Am B♭
1 New earth, heav - ens new,
2 New love, mer - cies new,
3 New minds, wis - dom new,
4 New earth, heav - ens new,
Spir - it of God
(Asus) (A) (D) (Em/D) (D) (A) (F♯m)
Csus C F Gm/F F C Am
mov - ing;
new seed, crea - tures new,
new strength, hope - ful - ness new,
new law, cov - e - nant new,
new birth, crea - tures new,
Spir - it of
(G) (Asus) (A) (G) (D/F♯) (G) (D/F♯)
B♭ Csus C B♭ F/A B♭ F/A
life mov - ing;
new man, wo - man new,
new hearts, spir - its new,
new name, na - ture new,
new growth, peo - ple new,
(Em) (G)
Gm B♭
im - age of God mov - ing.
Refrain
(D) (Em/D) (D) (A) (F♯m)
F Gm/F F C Am
Sing a new song to the One who has said, "Be - hold,
(C)
E♭
1–3
(D) (G/D) (F♯m/D)(Em/D)
F B♭/F Am/F Gm/F
4
(D) (Am7) (D)
F Cm7 F
I make all things new."
new."

Chord symbols do not correspond with the keyboard accompaniment.

Text: Harris J. Loewen (Canada), 1982, *Assembly Songs*, 1983, rev. 2019
Music: Harris J. Loewen, 1982, *Assembly Songs*, 1983; acc. Andrea Welty Peachey (USA)

379 *Acts 2:1-4*

When the day of Pentecost came,
all the believers gathered in one place.
Suddenly a sound came from heaven,
like a strong wind blowing.
It filled the whole house
where they were sitting.
They saw something that looked like fire
in the shape of tongues,
and the flames separated
and came to rest on each of them.
All were filled with the Holy Spirit.
They began to speak in languages
they had not known before,
as the Spirit gave them the ability.

380 *1 Corinthians 12:4-7*

There are different kinds of gifts,
but the same Spirit.
There are different ways
to serve the same God,
and we can each do different things.
Yet the same God works in all of us
and helps us in everything we do.
The revelation of the Spirit is given
to each for the common good.

381 *1 Peter 2:4-5, 9-10*

As you come to Christ,
the living Stone—
rejected by humans
but chosen by God
and precious to God—
you also, like living stones,
are being built into a spiritual house
to be a holy priesthood,
offering spiritual sacrifices
acceptable to God
through Jesus Christ.
You are a chosen people,
a royal priesthood,
a holy nation,
God's special possession,
that you may declare the praises
of the one who called you out of gloom
into a marvelous hope.
Once you were not a people,
but now you are God's people.

382 *Ephesians 2:19-21*

You are no longer foreigners
and outsiders
but citizens together with God's people
and members of God's family.
You are built on the foundation
of the apostles and prophets.
Jesus Christ is the cornerstone.
In Christ all the parts of the building
fit together
and grow into a holy temple in God.

383 *Ezekiel 37:11, 14*

The people say:
Our bones are dried up,
and our hope has perished
Thus says the LORD God:
I will put my spirit in you,
and you will live.
I will give you rest on your land,
and you will know
that I am the LORD.

384 *Romans 12:9-21 (excerpts)*

Be sincere in your love for others.
Hate all that is evil,
and hold tight to all that is good.
Love each other,
and honor others more than yourself.
Bless everyone who mistreats you.
Bless them and do not curse them.
When others are happy,
be happy with them;
when they are sad, be sad.
Make friends with ordinary people.
Do not mistreat someone
who has mistreated you.
But try to earn the respect of others,
and do your best to live at peace
with everyone.
Do not let evil defeat you,
but defeat evil with good.

385 *Ephesians 3:10*

Now, through the church,
the diverse wisdom of God
is made known
to the rulers and the authorities
of the heavenly places.

Previous page: 378. *When Flaming Dove Meets Rising Waters (Moment of Transformation)*, Gwen M. Stamm (USA), 2018, mixed media

One Is the Body

386

PEACOCK 10.10.12

C Csus C Csus C
1 One is the bod - y and one is the Head, one is the
2 Christ who as - cend - ed to heav - en a - bove is the same
3 Gifts have been giv - en well suit - ed to each, some to be
4 Called in - to ser - vice are wom - en and men so that this
Csus C Csus Am Cmaj7/G
Spir - it by whom we are led; one God and Moth - er, one
Je - sus whose na - ture is love, who once de - scend - ed to
proph - ets, to pas - tor or preach, some, through the gos - pel, to
bod - y might ev - er a - gain wit - ness through wor - ship, through
Fmaj7 Dm7 Gsus G C
faith, and one call for all.
bring to this earth new birth.
chal - lenge, con - vert, and teach.
deed, and through word to Christ our Lord.

Text: based on Ephesians 4:4–13, John L. Bell (Scotland)
Music: John L. Bell

387 We Are One in the Spirit

ST. BRENDAN'S 7.6.7.6.8.6 with refrain

Capo 1: (Em) Fm (Bm) Cm (Em) Fm
English: 1 We are one in the Spir-it, we are one in the Lord;
Spanish: 1 So-mos u-no en es-pí-ri-tu y en el Se-ñor,
German: 1 Wir sind ei-nig im Gei-ste, wir sind ei-nig im Herrn;
French: 1 Tous u-nis dans l'Es-prit, tous u-nis en Jé-sus;
(Am) B♭m (Em) Fm
we are one in the Spir-it, we are one in the Lord;
so-mos u-no en es-pí-ri-tu y en el Se-ñor;
wir sind ei-nig im Gei-ste, wir sind ei-nig im Herrn;
tous u-nis dans l'Es-prit, tous u-nis en Jé-sus;
(Am) B♭m (Em) Fm
and we pray that all u-ni-ty may one day be re-stored.
y ro-ga-mos que un dí-a se com-ple-te la u-nión.
lasst uns be-ten um Ein-heit durch den Geist uns-res Herrn.
nous pri-ons que bien-tôt ce qui di-vi-se ne soit plus.
Refrain
(C) D♭ (Em) Fm (Am) B♭m
And they'll know we are Chris-tians by our love, by our love,
Y que so-mos cris-tia-nos lo sa-brán, lo sa-brán,
Denn wir wer-den als Christ-en an der Lie-be er-kannt,
Et le mon-de sau-ra que nous som-mes chré-tiens
(Em) Fm (Am) B♭m (Bm) Cm (Em) Fm
and they'll know we are Chris-tians by our love.
por-que u-ni-dos es-ta-mos en a-mor.
ja, wir wer-den an der Lie-be erst er-kannt.
par l'a-mour dont nos ac-tes sont em-preints.

Text: Peter Scholtes (USA), 1966; Spanish trans. Federico J. Pagura (Argentina); German trans. Anton Schulte (Germany) and Bernd Schlottoff (Germany); French trans. Claire-Lise de Benoît (Switzerland)
Music: Peter Scholtes, 1966; arr. Richard D. Wetzel (USA)

English

2 We will walk with each other,
we will walk hand in hand; *(2x)*
and together we'll spread the news
that God is in our land. *Refrain*

3 We will work with each other,
we will work side by side. *(2x)*
And we'll guard each one's dignity
and save each one's pride. *Refrain*

Spanish

2 *Marcharemos tomados*
de la mano‿en amor; (2x)
anunciando que‿en esta
tierra vive‿y obra Dios. Refrain

3 *Trabajemos unidos*
lado‿a lado‿en amor; (2x)
restauremos a cada cuál
su dignidad y‿honor. Refrain

German

2 *Lasst uns gehn miteinander,*
lasst uns gehn Hand in Hand; (2x)
und den Menschen es sagen:
Unser Gott ist im Land. Refrain

3 *Lasst uns Seite an Seite*
an die Arbeit gehn. (2x)
Es vergeht jede Trennung,
wenn wir Jesus in uns sehn. Refrain

French

2 *Nous marchons côte à côte*
et la main dans la main; (2x)
à la table du roi nous partageons
le même pain. Refrain

3 *D'un seul coeur nous voulons*
travailler pour Jésus, (2x)
proclamer à tout homme qu'il nous
offre le salut. Refrain

388 How Can I Say

KOINONIA* Irregular

B♭/E♭ E♭ Gm7 Cm7
How can I say that I love the Lord whom I've
Fm E♭/B♭ B♭7 B♭/E♭ E♭
nev - er, ev - er seen be - fore; and for - get to say
Gm7 Cm7 Fm E♭/B♭
that I love the one whom I walk be - side each and
B♭7 Dm7♭5 Gaug Cm
ev - 'ry day? How can I look up - on your face and ig -

*Original title

For capo chords, see the accompaniment edition.

Text: V. Michael McKay (USA)
Music: V. Michael McKay

C7 Fm/C Edim7 Fm Db7 N.C. Eb/Bb
nore God's love? You I must em-brace! You're my broth-er;
Cm7 C7 Fm Eb/G Fm/Ab Am7b5 Bb
you're my sis-ter; and I love you with the love of my
1
Eb Bb/Eb Ab/Eb Bb7
Lord. How
2
Eb Bb/Eb Ab/Eb Fm7 Bb7 Eb
Lord. Love of my Lord!

389 Together

I WILL SING WITH YOU 8.5.8.5.10.12.5.5.5

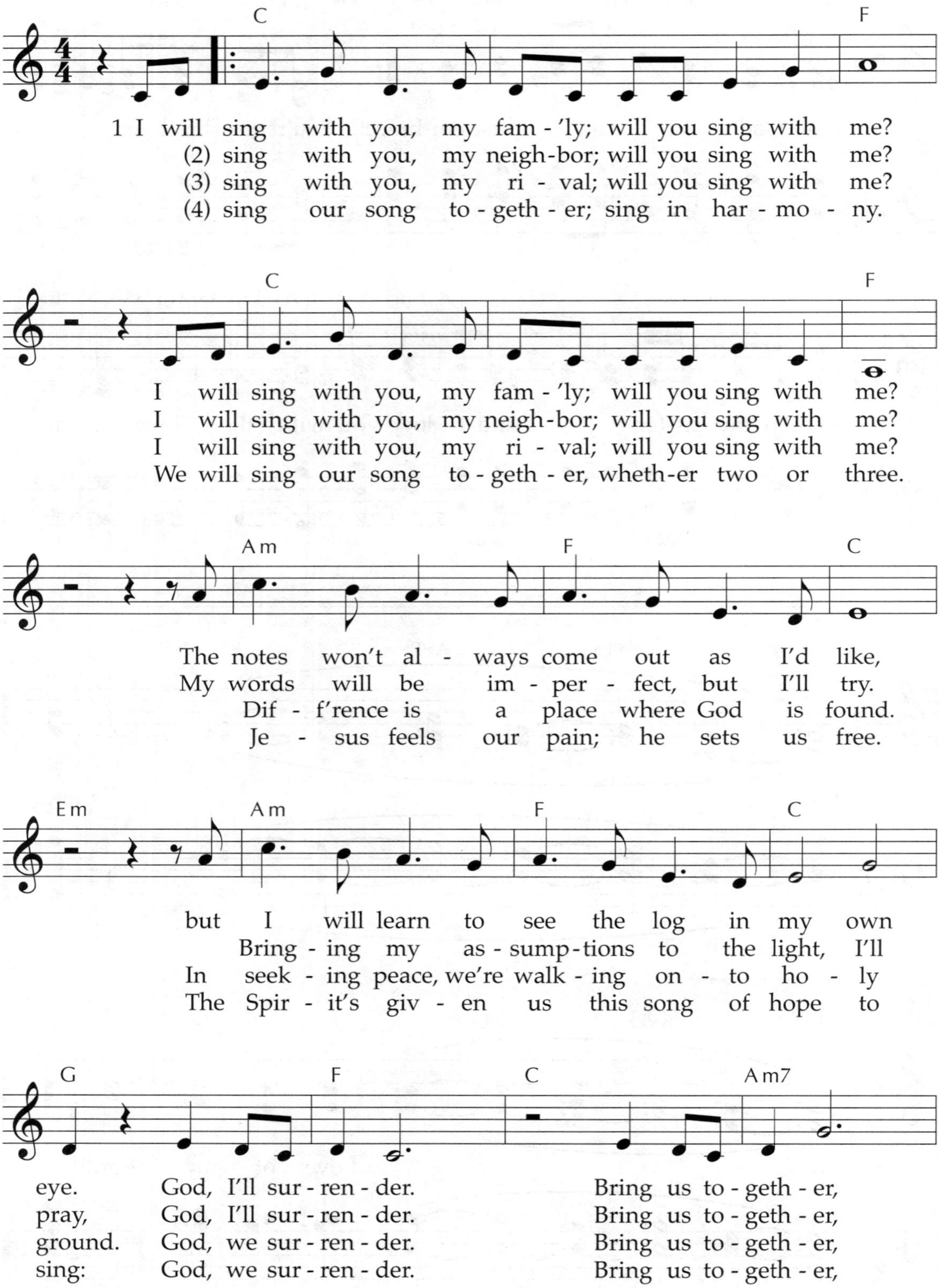
C F
1 I will sing with you, my fam - 'ly; will you sing with me?
(2) sing with you, my neigh-bor; will you sing with me?
(3) sing with you, my ri - val; will you sing with me?
(4) sing our song to - geth - er; sing in har - mo - ny.
C F
I will sing with you, my fam - 'ly; will you sing with me?
I will sing with you, my neigh-bor; will you sing with me?
I will sing with you, my ri - val; will you sing with me?
We will sing our song to - geth - er, wheth-er two or three.
Am F C
The notes won't al - ways come out as I'd like,
My words will be im - per - fect, but I'll try.
Dif - f'rence is a place where God is found.
Je - sus feels our pain; he sets us free.
Em Am F C
but I will learn to see the log in my own
Bring - ing my as - sump-tions to the light, I'll
In seek - ing peace, we're walk - ing on - to ho - ly
The Spir - it's giv - en us this song of hope to
G F C Am7
eye. God, I'll sur - ren - der. Bring us to - geth - er,
pray, God, I'll sur - ren - der. Bring us to - geth - er,
ground. God, we sur - ren - der. Bring us to - geth - er,
sing: God, we sur - ren - der. Bring us to - geth - er,

Text: Nathan Grieser (USA), 2014, rev. 2018
Music: Nathan Grieser; acc. Jonathan Landis (USA)

To verses
Last time
G F C G
bring us to-geth-er.
bring us to-geth-er.
bring us to-geth-er.
bring us to-geth-er.
2 I will
3 I will
4 We will
C Am7 G
Bring us to-geth-er, bring us to-
F C G C
geth-er.

In Christ There Is No East or West 390

ST. PETER CM

Capo 1: (D) Eb (A) Bb (D) Eb (G) Ab (A) Bb (D) Eb (A) Bb
1 In Christ there is no east or west, in him no south or north,
2 In Christ shall true hearts ev-'ry-where their high com-mun-ion find.
3 Join hands, then, peo-ple of the faith, what-e'er your race may be.
4 In Christ now meet both east and west, in him meet south and north.
(D7) Eb7 (G) Ab (D) Eb (Em) Fm (Bm) Cm (D/F♯) Eb/G (D/A) Eb/Bb (A) Bb (D) Eb
but one great fel-low-ship of love through-out the whole wide earth.
His ser-vice is the gold-en cord close bind-ing hu-man-kind.
All chil-dren of the liv-ing God are sure-ly kin to me.
All Christ-ly souls are joined as one through-out the whole wide earth.

Text: John Oxenham (England), 1908, *Bees in Amber*, 1913, alt.
Music: Alexander Robert Reinagle (England), *Psalm Tunes for the Voice and Pianoforte*, ca. 1836

391 오소서 Ososo (Come Now, O Prince of Peace)

O-SO-SO 6.5.5.6

Capo 3: (Em) Gm
(Em/D) Gm/F
(C) E♭
(B5) D5
1 오 소 서 오 소 서, 평 화 의 임 금
O - so - so o - so - so, pyong-hwa - eui im - gum.
1 Come now, O Prince of Peace, make us one bod - y.
(Am) Cm
(B5) D5
(C) E♭
(Em) Gm
우 리 가 한 몸 이 루 게 하 소 서
u - ri - ga han - mom i - ru - ge ha - so - so.
Come, O Lord Je - sus, re - con - cile your peo - ple.

2 오소서 오소서, 사랑의 임금
우리가 한몸 이루게 하소서

Ososo ososo, sarangeui imgum
uriga hanmom iruge hasoso.

3 오소서 오소서, 자유의 임금
우리가 한몸 이루게 하소서

Ososo ososo, jayueui imgum
uriga hanmom iruge hasoso.

4 오소서 오소서, 통일의 임금
우리가 한몸 이루게 하소서

Ososo ososo, tongileui imgum
uriga hanmom iruge hasoso.

2 *Come now, O God of love, make us one body.*
Come, O Lord Jesus, reconcile your people.

3 *Come now and set us free, O God, our Savior.*
Come, O Lord Jesus, reconcile all nations.

4 *Come, Hope of unity, make us one body.*
Come, O Lord Jesus, reconcile all nations.

Text: Korean; Geonyong Lee (Korea), 1988; trans. Marion Pope (Canada)
Music: Geonyong Lee, 1988

The Church of Christ Cannot Be Bound

392

MCKEE CM

C G B♭ F
1 The church of Christ can - not be bound by
2 True faith will o - pen up the door and
3 True love will not sit id - ly by when
4 If what we have we free - ly share to
5 The church of Christ can - not be bound by
G C Am C
walls of wood or stone. Where char - i - ty and
step in - to the street. True ser - vice will seek
jus - tice is de - nied. True mer - cy hears the
meet our neigh - bor's need, then we ex - tend the
walls of wood or stone. Where char - i - ty and
Em C G7 C
love are found, there can the church be known.
out the poor and ask to wash their feet.
home - less cry and wel - comes them in - side.
Spir - it's care through ev - 'ry self - less deed.
love are found, there can the church be known.

Text: Adam M. L. Tice (USA), © 2005 GIA Publications, Inc.; inspired by Menno Simons (present-day Netherlands), "True evangelical faith . . ." in *Why I Do Not Cease Teaching and Writing*, 1539, and "Ubi caritas et amor" (Latin), 8th–9th c.
Music: African American spiritual (USA), *Jubilee Songs*, 1884; adapt. Harry T. Burleigh (USA), 1940

393 Build Your Kingdom Here

BUILD YOUR KINGDOM HERE Irregular

G D G
1 Come set your rule, and reign in our hearts a -
2 We seek your king - dom first. We hun - ger and we
3 Un - leash your king - dom's pow'r, reach - ing the near and
D G D A4
gain. In - crease in us, we pray. Un - veil
thirst; re - fuse to waste our lives, for you're our
far. No force of hell can stop your beau - ty,
G D
why we're made. Come set our hearts a - blaze with hope,
joy and prize. To see the cap - tives' hearts re - leased,
chang - ing hearts. You made us for much more than this;
G D G
like wild - fire in our ver - y souls; Ho - ly Spir - it,
the hurt, the sick, the poor at peace, we lay down our
a - wake the king - dom seed in us. Fill us with the
D A4 G D
come, in - vade us now. We are your
lives for heav - en's cause. We are your
strength and love of Christ. We are your
A4 G D A4 D 1 Dsus
church; we need your pow'r in us.
church; we pray, re - vive this earth.
church; we are the hope on earth.

Text: Rend Collective (Ireland)
Music: Rend Collective

2, 3 Refrain
Dsus Bm/D A Bm7 G2 D
Build your king-dom here. Let the e-vil fear. Show your
A Bm7 G2 A D A
might-y hand. Heal our streets and land. Set your church on
Bm7 G2 D A Bm7
fire. Win your peo-ple back. Change the at-mos-phere. Build your
G2 A D Asus D Asus D Asus D
Last time, repeat refrain
Last time Fine
To v. 3
king-dom here, we pray!

God Calls Us

394

VISION: HEALING AND HOPE Irregular

D A G/B C
God calls us to be fol-low-ers of Christ, and by the
G/B D A
pow'r of the Spir-it, to grow as com-mun-i-ties of
F♯ Bm G/B D
grace, joy, and peace, so God's heal-ing and
A C G/B
hope flow through us to the world, so God's
D A G D
heal-ing and hope flow through us to the world.

Text: "Vision: Healing and Hope," Mennonite Church and General Conference Mennonite Church, 1995; adapt. Mennonite Church Canada and Mennonite Church USA, 2002; alt.
Music: Darryl Neustadter-Barg (Canada), © 2018 Darryl Neustadter-Barg

395 The Church of Christ, in Every Age

DICKINSON COLLEGE LM

D G D Bm E A F♯ Bm F♯ Bm D G A D
1 The church of Christ, in ev - 'ry age be - set by
2 Then let the ser - vant church a - rise, a car - ing
3 We have no mis - sion but to serve in full o -
change but Spir - it - led, must claim and test its her - i -
church that longs to be a part - ner in Christ's sac - ri -
be - dience to our Lord, to care for all, with - out re -
tage, and keep on ris - ing from the dead.
fice, and clothed in Christ's hu - man - i - ty.
serve, and spread his lib - er - at - ing word.

Chord symbols represent a simplified harmony.

Alternate tune: THE WATER IS WIDE (#522 or #524)

May You Be Rooted and Grounded 396

ROOTED AND GROUNDED Irregular

Swing:
Capo 3: (E5) G5
Refrain
(Am) Cm (F) A♭ (Am) Cm
May you be root-ed and ground-ed in love,
(C) E♭ (Am) Cm (E7) G7 (Am) Cm
strength-ened in the Spir-it through faith, to know the height and
(F) A♭ (Am) Cm (F7) A♭7 (Am) Cm (E7) G7 (Am) Cm
Last time
depth and length and breadth of God's un-der-stand-ing and grace.
(C) E♭ (G/B) B♭/D (Am) Cm (F7) A♭7
1 Paul said we're all one bod - y, though
2 Let all you do be done in love, and
3 So when you feel like wor-ry - ing, turn
(Am) Cm (G) B♭ (F) A♭ (Em) Gm (Am) Cm (C) E♭ (G/B) B♭/D
each has dif - f'rent gifts, each giv - en for the
o - pen your heart wide. If you live by the
ev - 'ry - thing to prayer, and God will search your
(Am) Cm (F7) A♭7 (B7) D7 (E7) G7
To refrain
com-mon good; to - geth-er we are lift - ed up, and
Spir - it, let the Spir - it be your guide, and keep you
heart and soul, and hope will find you there. You will be

Text: based on Ephesians 3:17–18, Romans 12:4–5, 1 Corinthians 16:14, Galatians 5:25, Philippians 4:6; Lisa Hubbell (USA), rev. 2019
Music: Lisa Hubbell, acc. Morgan Kusmer (USA)

397 The Church's One Foundation

AURELIA 7.6.7.6 D

Capo 1: (D) E♭ (A) B♭ (G) A♭ (A) B♭ (D) E♭
1 The chur-ch's one foun - da - tion is Je - sus Christ, our Lord;
2 The church in ev - 'ry na - tion is one through all the earth;
3 Still, schis-ms, trib - u - la - tion, and ha - tred fuel our war;
4 Yet we on earth have un - ion with God, the Three in One,
(F♯) G (G) A♭ (D) E♭ (A) B♭
we are a new cre - a - tion by wa - ter and the Word.
our char - ter of sal - va - tion, one God, one faith, one birth;
we wait the con - sum - ma - tion of peace for - ev - er - more.
and mys - tic, sweet com - mu - nion with those whose rest is won.
(D) E♭ (G) A♭ (D) E♭ (Bm) Cm (Em) Fm
From heav'n he came and taught us what per - fect love can be;
one name to - geth - er bless - ing, one ho - ly food we share,
The saints their watch are keep - ing; their cry goes up, "How long?"
Oh, hap - py ones and ho - ly! God, give us grace that we,
(D) E♭ (Gmaj7) A♭maj7 (Em7) Fm7 (Asus) B♭sus (A) B♭ (D) E♭
through life and death he sought us, and rose to set us free.
to one hope ev - er press - ing, at one in work and prayer.
And soon the night of weep - ing shall be the morn of song.
like them, the meek and low - ly, may live e - ter - nal - ly.

Text: Samuel J. Stone (England), *Lyra Fidelium*, 1866, alt.
Music: Samuel S. Wesley (England), *Selection of Psalms and Hymns*, 1864

Thy Word Is a Lamp 398

THY WORD Irregular

Refrain
G D/F♯ G C/E D G
Thy word is a lamp un-to my feet and a light un-to my path.
D/F♯ G C/E D G
Fine
Thy word is a lamp un-to my feet and a light un-to my path.
D Am Em Bm
1 When I feel a-fraid, and I think I've lost my way,
2 I will not for-get your love for me, and yet my
C D C/G G D Am
still you're there right be-side me. Noth-ing will I fear as
heart for-ev-er is wan-der-ing. Je-sus, be my guide and
Em Bm C D D/E E Dsus D
To refrain
long as you are near. Please be near me to the end.
hold me to your side; I will love you to the end.

Text: Amy Grant (USA) and Michael W. Smith (USA); refrain based on Psalm 119:105
Music: Amy Grant and Michael W. Smith

399 The Word of God Is Solid Ground

THE WORD OF GOD 8.7.8.7 D Iambic

Em Am Bm Em
1 The word of God is sol - id ground, our con - stant
2 What pow - ers can our faith con - strain? What i - ron -
3 What God - word brings, may we em - brace; suc - cess and
Bm Em Am
firm con - fes - sion, no source of free - dom more pro - found, no
clad re - stric - tions? No self - de - ceiv - ing rule can chain our
suf - f'ring greet us; con - front - ing e - vil face to face, as
Em D G Em C Am
pur - er a pro - fes - sion. All stead - fast strength, all breadth and
con - science and con - vic - tions. Our God a - lone is on the
scorn and an - ger meet us. For free - dom's sake we bend, we
D Bm Em Am G C Bm
length of truth, from God's word spring - ing shall we em - ploy to
throne, and we are sub - jects will - ing. Our lives o - bey God's
break, a sign to ev - 'ry na - tion that we have found a

Text: anon., ca. 1550, *Ausbund* (present-day Germany), 1583; adapt. Harris J. Loewen (Canada), *Assembly Songs*,

Music: J. Harold Moyer (USA), *Assembly Songs*,

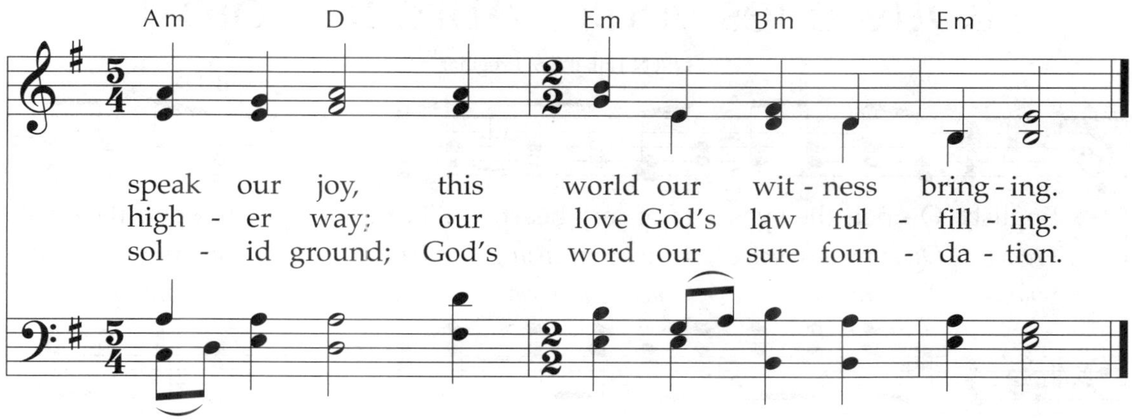
Am D Em Bm Em
speak our joy, this world our wit - ness bring - ing.
high - er way; our love God's law ful - fill - ing.
sol - id ground; God's word our sure foun - da - tion.

Dawk'yah towgyah thawy báht-awm 400
(Take the Saving Word of God)

DAWK'YAH TOWGYAH Irregular

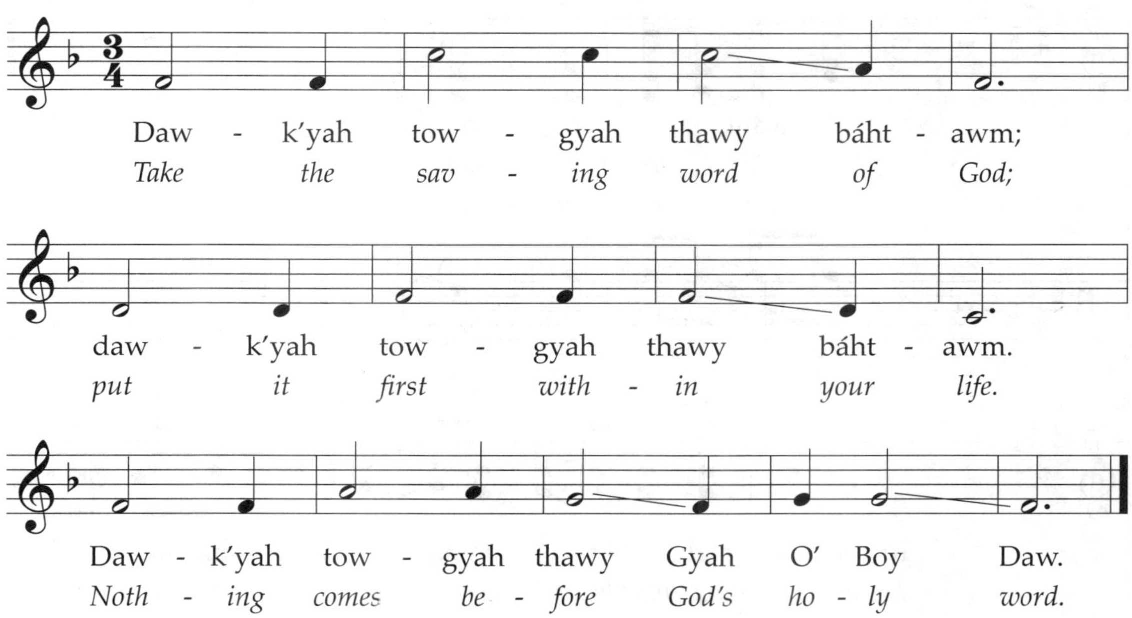
Daw - k'yah tow - gyah thawy báht - awm;
Take the sav - ing word of God;
daw - k'yah tow - gyah thawy báht - awm.
put it first with - in your life.
Daw - k'yah tow - gyah thawy Gyah O' Boy Daw.
Noth - ing comes be - fore God's ho - ly word.

Text: Kiowa; Pawltay (Kiowa, USA); English trans. John Thornburg (USA), English stanza © 2008 General Board of Global Ministries
Music: Kiowa traditional; transcr. Carlton R. Young (USA), 2008

401 Open the Eyes of My Heart (Ouvre les yeux / Abre mis ojos)

OPEN THE EYES Irregular

E2
B/D♯
English: O - pen the eyes of my heart, Lord, o - pen the eyes
French: Ou - vre les yeux de mon coeur, Père, ou - vre les yeux
Spanish: A - bre mis o - jos, oh Cris - to; a - bre mis o -
A2/C♯
of my heart; I want to see you,
de mon coeur; je dé - sire te voir,
- jos te pi - do. Yo quie - ro ver - te,
A2
E2
1
E sus
I want to see you.
je dé - sire te voir.
yo quie - ro ver - te.
Refrain
2
E
B
C♯m
A2
To see you high and lift - ed up, shin-ing in the
É - le - vé au plus haut des cieux ray - on-nant de
Y con-tem - plar tu ma - jes-tad, y el res-plan-

Text: Paul Baloche (USA), 1997; French trans. unknown; Spanish trans. unknown
Music: Paul Baloche, 1997

B sus
B
light of your glo - ry. Pour out your pow-er and love
l'é - lat de ta gloire, ré-pands ton a-mour, ta force
dor de tu glo - ria. De-rra-ma tu‿a-mor y po-der
C♯m
F♯m
B sus
as we sing ho-ly, ho - ly, ho - ly.
a-lors que nous chan-tons: Tu es Saint.
cuan-do can - ta-mos: san - to, san - to.
Coda
E
B/D♯
Ho-ly, ho - ly, ho - ly, ho-ly, ho - ly, ho - ly,
Tu es Saint, Tu es Saint, Tu es Saint, Tu es Saint,
San-to, san - to, san - to, san-to, san - to, san-to,
A/C♯
A
F♯m/E
E
ho - ly, ho - ly, ho - ly, I want to see you.
Tu es Saint, Tu es Saint. Je dé - sire te voir.
san - to, san - to, san - to; yo quie - ro ver - te.

402 Rejoice, Rejoice Forevermore

AWFUL MAJESTY CM

E A E
1 Re - joice, re - joice for - ev - er - more, all Chris - tians
2 O peo - ple ev - 'ry - where, ac - cept the truth that
3 O Je - sus Christ, the Son of God, our friend, the
4 Praise God, praise God for - ev - er - more, all Chris - tians
5 God's word will stand e - ter - nal - ly; in that we
B E
ev - 'ry - where, for now in na - tions
Scrip - ture brings. A - ban - don self - made
liv - ing Word, don't let us turn a -
ev - 'ry - where. The word of Love has
are se - cure. So now we all sing
B C♯m E A B7 E
far and wide rings out God's might - y word.
ways; re - ly on God the faith - ful guide.
way from you, but from this tempt - ing world.
spread a - broad. We trust that Love a - lone.
joy - ful - ly: A - men! God's love is sure.

Chord symbols represent a simplified harmony.

Text: Balthasar Hubmaier (present-day Germany), ca. 1520; trans. Ruth Naylor (USA), alt.,
Music: attr. S.M. McFarland (USA) c. 1814; adapt. Joseph Funk (USA), *Harmonia Sacra*, 4th ed., 1847; arr. Alice Parker (USA),

Comme un souffle fragile (As a Sigh Great with Yearning) 403

COMME UN SOUFFLE FRAGILE 7.6.7.6 with refrain

Refrain
Em Am B7 Em
Comme un souf - fle fra - gi - le, ta pa - ro - le se don-ne;
As a sigh great with yearn-ing, God, your Word comes up - on us;
Cmaj7 Am6 B7 Em Fine
comme un va - se d'ar - gi - le, ton a - mour nous fa - çon - ne.
as the clay shapes in turn - ing, ho - ly love forms a - mong us.
Instrumental interlude
Em Am7 D Gmaj7 Cmaj7 Am B7 Em
Em Am D Gmaj7
1 Ta pa - role est mur - mu - re comme un se - cret d'a - mour,
2 Ta pa - role est nais - san - ce comme on sort de pri - son,
3 Ta pa - role est par - ta - ge comme on cou - pe du pain,
1 Your Word is a mur - m'ring of a love's se - cret ways;
2 Your Word is a know - ing, a de - liv - 'rance, a birth;
3 Your Word is a break - ing, like the of - f'ring of bread;
To refrain
Cmaj7 Am B7 Em
ta pa - role est bles - su - re qui nous ou - vre le jour.
ta pa - role est se - men - ce qui pro - met la mois - son.
ta pa - role est pas - sa - ge qui nous dit un che - min.
your Word is a wound - ing, giv - ing birth to new days.
your Word is a sow - ing in the wel - com - ing earth.
your Word is a bea - con to a safe path a - head.

Text: French; Pierre Jacob (France), © SECLI, Soeur Marie-Christine Messin; English adapt. Andrew Donaldson (Canada), © 2017 Andrew Donaldson

Music: Gaëtan de Courrèges (France); harm. Didier Godel (Switzerland), harm. © FEEPR

404 We Praise the Word of God

WORD OF GOD 6.6.8.4 D

1 We praise the Word of God, made flesh in Je - sus Christ:
2 We learn the Word of God in sto - ries of the faith:
3 We live the Word of God when good news we pro - claim,
the well-spring of un - dy - ing love, the bread of life;
the Scrip-tures' liv - ing wit-ness to God's truth and grace;
when cap - tives find their lib - er - ty and lose their chains;
who spoke with hu - man lips, yet taught with heav - en's voice;
where proph - ets cry for peace, a - pos - tles preach and pray,
when mourn-ers sing with joy, the Word of God re - sounds,
in whom we put our hope and trust, and still re - joice.
and saints of all the ag - es seek God's ho - ly way.
the Spir - it of the Lord still speaks, and grace a - bounds.

Listen to the Word That God Has Spoken 405

LISTEN 10.10.11.10

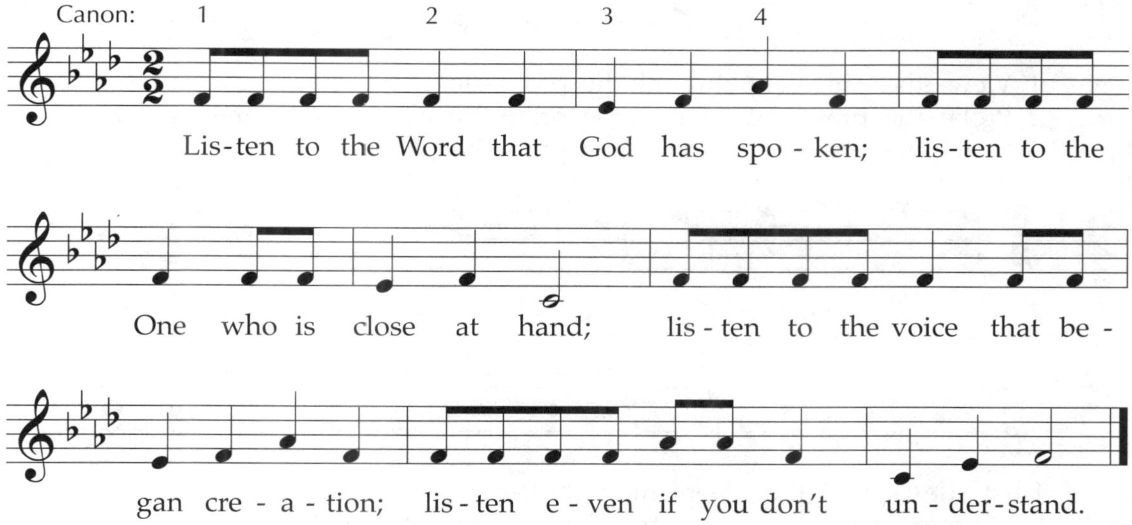
Canon: 1 2 3 4
Lis-ten to the Word that God has spo - ken; lis-ten to the
One who is close at hand; lis - ten to the voice that be -
gan cre - a - tion; lis - ten e - ven if you don't un - der - stand.

Text: anon. (Canada), alt.
Music: anon. (Canada); adapt. *Church Hymnary*, 4th ed., 2005

Because the Words We Wait to Hear 406

DISTURB Irregular

Capo 3: (Em)
Gm
Be - cause the words we wait to hear could shake us to the
(Cmaj7) (F♯dim) (Em) (Cmaj7) (D) (E)
E♭maj7 A dim Gm E♭maj7 F G
core, be with us, God; be with us, God.

Chord symbols represent a simplified harmony and do not correspond to the keyboard accompaniment.

Text: John Thornburg (USA)
Music: Jane Marshall (USA)

407 View the Present

FRANKLIN PARK 8.5.8.5.8.8.8.5

G C Am7 D7sus D7
1 View the pres - ent through the prom - ise,
2 Probe the pres - ent with the prom - ise, Christ will come a - gain.
3 Match the pres - ent to the prom - ise,
Em C Am7 D Em Cmaj7 Dsus D
Trust de - spite the deep-'ning dark - ness,
Let your dai - ly ac - tions wit - ness, Christ will come a - gain.
Make this hope your guid - ing prem - ise,
Am G Am Em Am7 Bm C
Lift the world a - bove its griev-ing through your watch-ing and be - liev-ing
Let your lov - ing and your giv - ing and your just - ice and for - giv-ing
Pat - tern all your cal - cu - lat - ing and the world you are cre - at - ing
G Cmaj7 Am C Am7 D7 G
in the hope past hope's con - ceiv - ing:
be a sign to all the liv - ing: Christ will come a - gain.
to the ad - vent you are wait - ing:

Text: Thomas H. Troeger (USA),
Music: Roy Hopp (USA),

Crown Him with Many Crowns 408

DIADEMATA SMD

E C♯m A E B7/F♯ E B
1 Crown him with man - y crowns, the Lamb up - on the throne.
2 Crown him the Lord of life, who tri-umphed o'er the grave
3 Crown him the Lord of love; be - hold his hands and side.
4 Crown him the Lord of peace, whose pow'r a scep - ter sways
5 Crown him the Lord of years, the po - ten - tate of time,
E C♯m F♯ B E F♯ B
Hark! how the heav'n-ly an-them drowns all mu - sic but its own.
and rose vic - to - rious in the strife for those he came to save.
Rich wounds, yet vis - i - ble a - bove, in beau - ty glo - ri - fied.
from pole to pole that wars may cease, ab-sorbed in prayer and praise.
cre - a - tor of the roll - ing spheres, in - ef - fa - bly sub - lime.
E A C♯7 F♯ B B7
A - wake, my soul, and sing of him who died for thee, and
His glo - ries now we sing who died, and rose on high, who
No an - gels in the sky can ful - ly bear that sight, but
His reign shall know no end; and round his pierc - ed feet fair
All hail, Re - deem - er, hail! for thou hast died for me. Thy
E A F♯m7 E A Bsus B7 E
hail him as the match-less king, through all e - ter - ni - ty.
died, e - ter - nal life to bring, and lives that death may die.
down-ward bend their burn - ing eyes at mys - ter - ies so bright.
flow'rs of par - a - dise ex - tend their fra-grance ev - er sweet.
praise shall nev - er, nev - er fail through-out e - ter - ni - ty.
8

Text: stanzas 1, 3–5 Matthew Bridges (England), *Hymns of the Heart*, 2nd ed., 1851; stanza 2 Godfrey Thring (England), *Hymns and Sacred Lyrics*, 1874
Music: George J. Elvey (England), *Appendix to Hymns Ancient and Modern*, 1868

409 For We Are Strangers No More

STRANGERS NO MORE 11.10.11.10 with refrain

Refrain
G Am C F C C7
For we are strang-ers no more, but mem-bers of one
F C F E7 Am D7
fam - i - ly; strang-ers no more, but part of one hu -
G C C7 F Dm E7 Am
man - i - ty; strang-ers no more, we're neigh-bors to each oth - er
A♭ C G7 G7 C
now; strang-ers no more, we're bound to one an - oth - er now.
Fine

Text: Kenneth I. Morse (USA), 1979, alt., © 1979 Church of the Brethren General Board
Music: Dianne Huffman Morningstar (USA), © 1979 Dianne Huffman Morningstar

C G Am C F D7 G
1 Come, walk with me, we'll wor - ship God to - geth - er,
2 Where dif - f'ring cul - tures meet, we'll serve to - geth - er.
3 There is a love that binds the world to - geth - er,
C G Am C D7 G F
as we join song to song, and prayer to prayer. Come,
Where ha - tred ra - ges, we will strive for peace. Come,
a love that seeks the last, the lost, the least. One
Dm E7 Am Dm
take my hand, and we will work to - geth - er by lift - ing
take my hand, and we will pray to - geth - er that jus - tice
day that love will bring us all to - geth - er in Christ, from
G7 C C7 F G7
D.S.
all the bur - dens we can share.
come, and strife and war - fare cease. For we are
South and North, from West and East.

410 Christ Is King! Let Earthly Powers

IRBY 8.7.8.7.8.7

G D7 G D7 G Em G
1 Christ is King! Let earth - ly pow - ers, wealth, do - min - ion,
2 Christ is King! O saints, be joy - ful; grace and jus - tice
3 Christ is King! Death's pow'r is end - ed; now there is no
C D G D7 G A7 D7 G Em
state, and crown, here be - fore the Ser - vant Sav - ior praise and
will be shown, weak-ness lift - ed in - to glo - ry, pride and
need for fear. Love and love a - lone re - deems us, wipes a -
G C D G C G D7
wor - ship and kneel down. Je - sus reigns, a cross ex -
greed cast from their throne. Je - sus reigns, the once - re -
way our guilt and tears. Je - sus reigns, the Lamb once -
G C G C D G
alts him; suf - f'ring is the roy - al gown.
ject - ed has be - come the Cor - ner - stone.
slaugh-tered in a - bun - dant life ap - pears.

Text: Sylvia G. Dunstan (Canada),
Music: Henry T. Smart (England), 1866

All Hail the Power of Jesus' Name 411

CORONATION CM extended

G D D7
1 All hail the pow'r of Je - sus' name! Let an - gels pros - trate
2 Let ev - 'ry kin - dred, ev - 'ry tribe, on this ter - res - trial
3 Oh, that with yon - der sa - cred throng we at his feet may
G D G D
fall. Bring forth the roy - al di - a - dem, and
ball, to him all maj - es - ty as - cribe, and
fall! We'll join the ev - er - last - ing song, and
G D/F♯ Em A D G
crown him Lord of all! Bring forth the roy - al
crown him Lord of all! To him all maj - es -
crown him Lord of all! We'll join the ev - er -
D7 G C G/D D7 G
di - a - dem, and crown him Lord of all!
ty as - cribe, and crown him Lord of all!
last - ing song, and crown him Lord of all!

Text: Edward Perronet (England), *Gospel Magazine*, 1779-1780; rev. John Rippon (England), *Selection of Hymns*, 1789
Music: Oliver Holden (USA), 1792, *Union Harmony*, 1793

412 My Soul Cries Out

STAR OF THE COUNTY DOWN 9.8.10.8 D with refrain

Em C D
1 My soul cries out with a joy - ful shout that the
2 Though I am small, my God, my all, you
3 From the halls of power to the for - tress tower, not a
4 Though the na - tions rage from age to age, we re -
Em C D Em
God of my heart is great, and my spir - it sings of the
work great things in me, and your mer - cy will last from the
stone will be left on stone. Let the king be - ware for your
mem - ber who holds us fast: God's mer - cy must de -
G D Em C Em
won - drous things that you bring to the ones who wait. You
depths of the past to the end of the age to be. Your
jus - tice tears ev - 'ry ty - rant from his throne. The
liv - er us from the con - quer - or's crush - ing grasp. This
G D Em
fixed your sight on your ser - vant's plight, and my weak - ness you
ver - y name puts the proud to shame, and to those who would
hun - gry poor shall weep no more for the food they can
sav - ing word that our fore - bears heard is the prom - ise which
C D Em
did not spurn, so from east to west shall my
for you yearn, you will show your might, put the
nev - er earn; there are ta - bles spread, ev - 'ry
holds us bound, till the spear and rod can be

Original title: "Canticle of the Turning"

Text: based on Luke 1:46–55; Rory Cooney (USA)
Music: Irish traditional; arr. Rory Cooney

G D Em C Em
name be blest. Could the world be a - bout to turn?
strong to flight, for the world is a - bout to turn.
mouth be fed, for the world is a - bout to turn.
crushed by God, who is turn - ing the world a - round.
Refrain
G D Em
My heart shall sing of the day you bring. Let the fires of your
My heart shall sing of the day you bring. Let the fires
C D Em
jus - tice burn. Wipe a - way all tears, for the
of your jus - tice burn. Wipe a - way all tears, for the
C D Em C Em
dawn draws near, and the world is a-bout to turn!
dawn draws near, and the world is a - bout to turn.

413 Na nzela na lola (As Long as We Follow)

MALEMBE 6.8.8 with refrain

Capo 3: (D) F (G) B♭ (D) F
1 Na nze-la na lo - la to-ko-tam-bo-la ma-lem-be, ma-
1 As long as we fol - low in the way that God is lead-ing, we
2 As long as we hope there is a fu-ture for cre-a-tion, a
(G) B♭ (D) F Refrain
lem - be to-ko-tam-bo-la. Ma-lem - be, ma-
know God's reign will sure-ly come. We know this, we
fu - ture for the un-i-verse.
(G/D) B♭/F (D) F (G) B♭ (D) F
lem - be, ma-lem - be, to-ko-tam-bo - la.
know this. We know God's reign will sure - ly come.

Text: Lingala; Joseph Kabemba (Democratic Republic of the Congo); stanza 1 and refrain trans. S. T. Kimbrough (USA); stanza 2 trans. Carolyn Kappauf (Germany)
Music: Joseph Kabemba

Jesus Shall Reign 414

DUKE STREET LM

D G D E A D
1 Je - sus shall reign wher - e'er the sun does its suc -
2 For him shall end - less prayer be made, and prais - es
3 Peo - ple and realms of ev - 'ry tongue dwell on his
4 Bless-ings a - bound wher - e'er Christ reigns; and pris-'ners
5 Let ev - 'ry crea - ture rise and bring each its pe -
G D Em D A D A D
ces - sive jour - neys run. His realm shall stretch from
throng to crown his head. His name, like sweet per -
love with sweet - est song, and in - fant voic - es
leap to loose their chains, the wea - ry find e -
cu - liar praise to sing; an - gels de - scend with
G D A D G D Em D/A A7 D
shore to shore, till moons shall wax and wane no more.
fume, shall rise with ev - 'ry morn - ing sac - ri - fice.
shall pro - claim their ear - ly bless - ings on his name.
ter - nal rest, and all who suf - fer want are bless'd.
songs a - gain, and earth re - peat the loud a - men!

Text: based on Psalm 7; Isaac Watts (England), *Psalms of David*, 1719, alt.
Music: attr. John Hatton (England), *Psalm and Hymn Tunes*, 1793

415 Revelation Song (Digno y santo)

REVELATION SONG Irregular

Verse 1
1 Wor - thy is the Lamb who was slain,
1 Dig - no y san - to el Cor - de - ro
ho - ly, ho - ly is he. Sing a new song
in - mo - la - do en la cruz. Nue - vo can - to
to him who sits on heav - en's mer - cy seat.
le - van - ta - re - mos al que en Su tro - no es - tá.
Refrain
Ho - ly, ho - ly, ho - ly is the Lord God Al - might - y,
San - to, san - to, san - to Dios to - do - po - de - ro - so
who was and is and is to come. With all cre -
quien fue, quien es y quien ven - drá. La cre - a -
a - tion I sing praise to the King of kings; you are my
ción te can - ta ho - sa - na, el gran Yo Soy. Tú e - res

Text: based on Revelation 4 and 5, Jennie Lee Riddle (USA); Spanish trans. Alejandro Allen (USA)
Music: Jennie Lee Riddle

ev-'ry-thing, and I will a-dore you.
mi to-do y yo te a-do-ra-ré.
To verses Last time
Verse 2
2 Clothed in rain-bows of liv-ing col-or, flash-es of light-ning, rolls of thun-der; bless-ing and hon-or, strength and glo-ry, and pow-er be to you, the on-ly wise King.
2 De‿un ar-co‿i-ris, es-tás ves-ti-do, tu voz re-sue-na, co-mo los true-nos; re-ci-be‿ho-nor y glo-ria, po-der y ma-jes-tad: a ti, el ú-ni-co Rey.
To refrain
Verse 3
3 Filled with won-der, awe-struck won-der, at the men-tion of your name; Je-sus, your name is pow-er, breath, and liv-ing wa-ter, such a mar-v'lous mys-ter-y.
3 Tan gran-dio-so, a-som-bro-so, con so-lo de-cir Je-sús; Cris-to, tu nom-bre‿es gran-de, fuen-te‿i-na-go-ta-ble; tu mis-te-rio glo-rio-so‿es.
To refrain

416 Beyond a Dying Sun

ENGLE 14.10.14.10 with refrain

D G Em7 A
1 Be - yond a dy - ing sun I saw a vi - sion on the sea
2 For God at last shall wipe a - way the tears from ev' - ry eye.
3 Though ha - tred rag - es on the wind and wars de - file the land,
D Bm E A
of gold - en sails full bil - lowed on the wind. (on the wind.)
The sting of death shall pierce the heart no more. (heart no more.)
I see those gold - en sails still com - ing strong, (com - ing strong,)
D G Em7 A
And ech - o - ing a - bove the waves a voice called af - ter me,
When griev - ing turns to laugh - ter all the pain from us shall fly,
for through the eyes of faith still shines the vi - sion of the Lamb,
D Em7 A7 D
"God's dwell - ing place is with you till the end." (till the end.)
and form - er ways lie bleached up - on the shore. (on the shore.)
and o'er a wea - ry earth there rings this song. (rings this song.)

Text: Steve Engle (USA), 1970; rev. 1984
Music: Steve Engle, 1970; harm. Steve Engle and Don Frederick (USA)

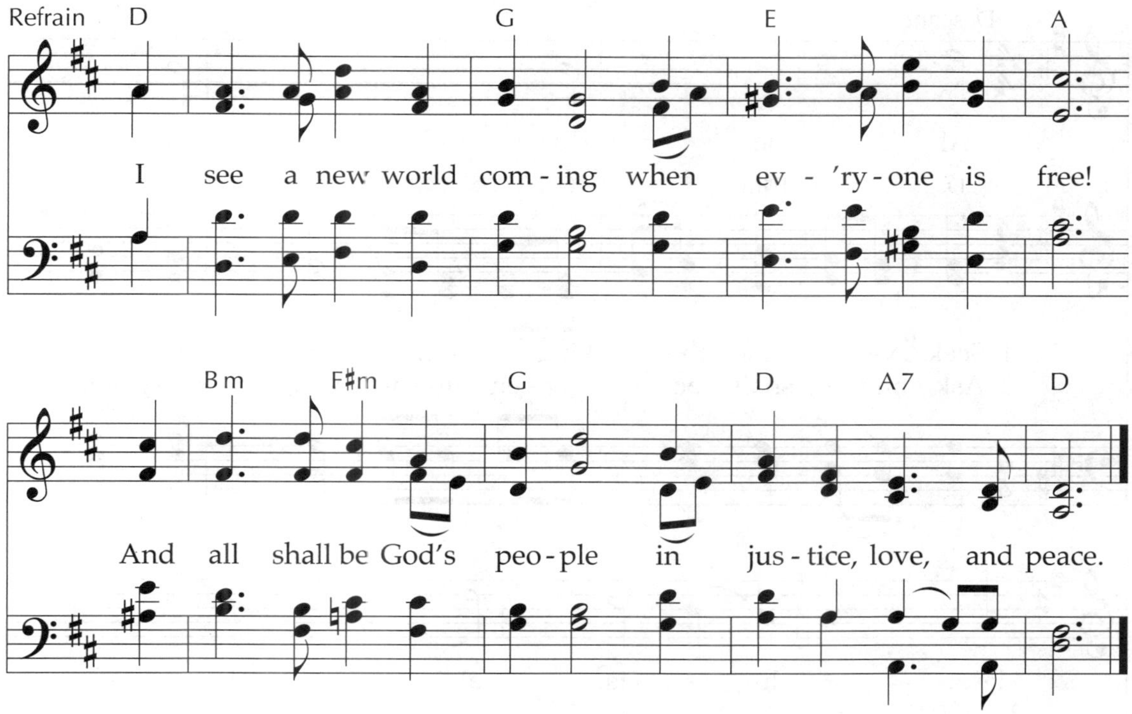
Refrain
D G E A
I see a new world com-ing when ev-'ry-one is free!
Bm F♯m G D A7 D
And all shall be God's peo-ple in jus-tice, love, and peace.

417 Seek Ye First

LAFFERTY Irregular

Descant
Al - le - lu - ia, al - le - lu - ia, al - le - lu - ia, al - le - lu, al - le - lu - ia!
D F♯m G D G D Em7 A7 D F♯m G D G D Em7 A D
1 Seek ye first the king - dom of God and its right - eous - ness, and all these things shall be add - ed un - to you. Al - le - lu, al - le - lu - ia!
2 Ask, and it shall be giv - en un - to you; seek, and ye shall find; knock, and the door shall be o - pened un - to you. Al - le - lu, al - le - lu - ia!

Text: based on Matthew 6:33, 7:7, Luke 11:9, 12:31; Karen Lafferty (USA), 1972
Music: Karen Lafferty, 1972

From the Parent's Heart, the Firstborn 418
(Corde natus ex parentis)

DIVINUM MYSTERIUM Irregular

Cor - de na - tus ex pa - ren - tis An - te
1 From the Par - ent's heart, the first - born when no
2 Word who or - dered and cre - at - ed, by whose
3 Here is One whom seers and sag - es longed to
4 Let the high - est heav - ens ring out with an -
mun - di ex - or - di - um A et O co - gno -
worlds had been be - gun, this is Al - pha and
word all came to be, call - ing forth three - fold
know in an - cient days, One fore - told by faith -
gel - ic mel - o - dy. All who have the pow'r
mi - na - tus, i - pse fons et clau - su - la
O - me - ga, source and end that join as one
cre - a - tion: heav - en, earth, en - cir - cling sea,
ful proph - ets, sing - ing with their hearts a - blaze.
to praise God, sing, wher - ev - er you may be.
O - mni - um quae sunt, fu - e - runt,
all that is now, ev - er has been,
filled with life that shares the moon's glow
So shines forth the One long prom - ised,
Let no mor - tal tongue keep si - lent;
quae - que post fu - tu - ra sunt.
and in fu - ture will be done,
and the sun's warm en - er - gy,
who in - spires all crea - tures' praise,
voic - es, blend in har - mo - ny,
Sae - cu - lo - rum sae - cu - lis.
1–4 ev - er - more and ev - er - more.

Text: Latin; Aurelius Clemens Prudentius (present-day Spain), "Corde natus ex parentis," 4th–5th c.; trans. Carl P. Daw Jr. (USA),

Music: plainsong "Sanctus trope," 10th–13th c.; adapt. *Piae Cantiones* (present-day Finland), 1582

419 Great Is Thy Faithfulness

FAITHFULNESS 11.10.11.10 with refrain

Capo 1: (D) E♭ (G) A♭ (A7) B♭7 (D) E♭
1 Great is thy faith - ful-ness, O God my Fa - ther.*
2 Sum - mer and win - ter, and spring-time and har - vest,
3 Par - don for sin and a peace that en - dur - eth,
(G) A♭ (D) E♭ (E7) F7 (A) B♭
There is no shad - ow of turn - ing with thee.
sun, moon, and stars in their cours - es a - bove,
thine own dear pres - ence to cheer and to guide,
(A7) B♭7 (D) E♭ (G) A♭
Thou chang - est not, thy com - pas - sions, they fail not.
join with all na - ture in man - i - fold wit - ness
strength for to - day and bright hope for to - mor - row;
(G♯dim7) A dim7 (D/A) E♭/B♭ (A7) B♭7 (D) E♭
As thou hast been thou for - ev - er wilt be.
to thy great faith - ful - ness, mer - cy, and love.
bless - ings all mine, with ten thou - sand be - side!

*Alternative texts: "O God my Mother" or "O God Creator"

Text: Thomas O. Chisholm (USA), *Songs of Salvation and Service,* 1923
Music: William M. Runyan (USA), *Songs of Salvation and Service,* 1923

Refrain
(A) B♭ (D) E♭ (B7) C7 (Em) Fm
Great is thy faith-ful-ness! Great is thy faith-ful-ness!
(A7) B♭7 (D) E♭ (Dm) E♭m (A/E) B♭/F (E7) F7 (A) B♭
Morn-ing by morn-ing new mer-cies I see.
(A7) B♭7 (D) E♭ (G) A♭
All I have need-ed thy hand hath pro-vid-ed.
(G♯dim7) Adim7 (D/A) E♭/B♭ (A7) B♭7 (D) E♭
Great is thy faith-ful-ness, Lord, un-to me!

420 God of the Bible

FRESH AS THE MORNING 5.5.5.4.5.5.5.4 with refrain

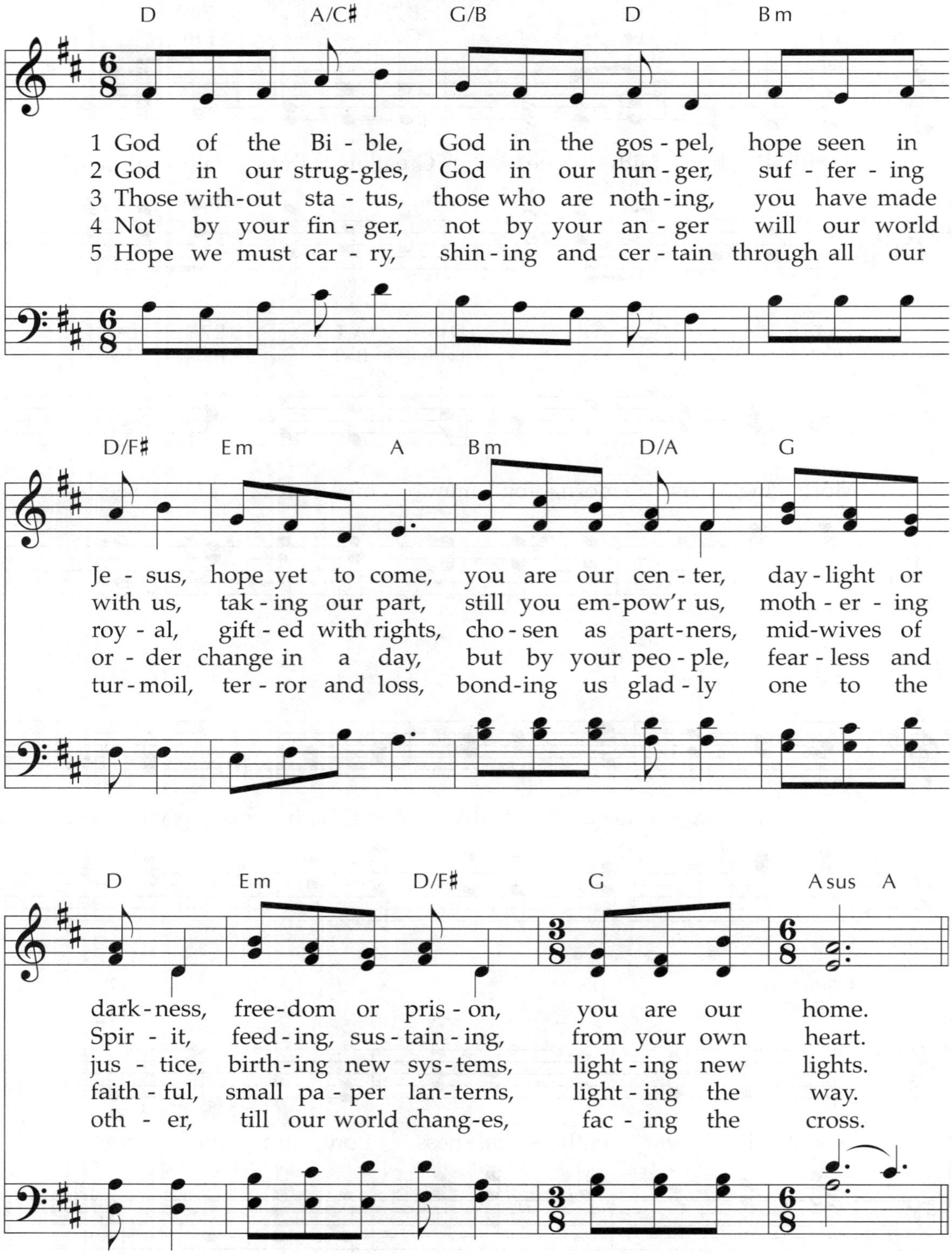
D A/C♯ G/B D Bm
1 God of the Bi - ble, God in the gos - pel, hope seen in
2 God in our strug-gles, God in our hun - ger, suf - fer - ing
3 Those with-out sta - tus, those who are noth - ing, you have made
4 Not by your fin - ger, not by your an - ger will our world
5 Hope we must car - ry, shin - ing and cer - tain through all our
D/F♯ Em A Bm D/A G
Je - sus, hope yet to come, you are our cen - ter, day - light or
with us, tak - ing our part, still you em - pow'r us, moth - er - ing
roy - al, gift - ed with rights, cho - sen as part - ners, mid-wives of
or - der change in a day, but by your peo - ple, fear - less and
tur - moil, ter - ror and loss, bond - ing us glad - ly one to the
D Em D/F♯ G Asus A
dark - ness, free - dom or pris - on, you are our home.
Spir - it, feed - ing, sus - tain - ing, from your own heart.
jus - tice, birth - ing new sys - tems, light - ing new lights.
faith - ful, small pa - per lan - terns, light - ing the way.
oth - er, till our world chang - es, fac - ing the cross.

Refrain
Soprano (Melody)
D A/D G/D D Em D/F#
Fresh as the morn - ing, sure as the sun - rise, God al-ways faith-ful,
Alto
Fresh as the sun - rise, al - ways faith-ful,
Tenor/Bass
Em A D A/D G/D D
you do not change. Fresh as the morn-ing, sure as the sun - rise,
you do not change. Fresh as the sun - rise,
Em D/F# G/A D A/D
God al - ways faith - ful, you do not change.
al - ways faith - ful, you do not change.
G/D D A/D G/D D

421 A Mighty Fortress Is Our God

EIN FESTE BURG 8.7.8.7.6.6.6.6.7

1 A mighty - y for - tress is our God, a bul - wark
2 If we in our own strength con - fide, our striv - ing
3 And though this world, with dev - ils filled, should threat - en
4 That Word be - yond all earth - ly pow'rs, no thanks to
nev - er fail - ing. Our pres - ent help a - mid the flood of
would be los - ing, but there is one who takes our side, the
to un - do us, we trem - ble not, for God has willed that
them, is sound - ing. The Spir - it and the gifts are ours, by
mor - tal ills pre - vail - ing. For still our an - cient foe
one of God's own choos - ing. You ask who that may be:
truth will tri - umph through us. Though Sa - tan rant and rage
God's good grace a - bound - ing. Lay down all earth - ly fame,
does seek to work us woe with craft and cun - ning great, and
Christ Je - sus, it is he! The Lord of hosts by name, from
and fierc - est war en - gage, such wrath we can en - dure, for
wealth, fam' - ly, life, and name. The bod - y they may kill; God's

Text: based on Psalm 46; Martin Luther (present-day Germany), 1527–1529, "Ein feste Burg ist unser Gott," 1529, 1531; trans. Frederick H. Hedge (USA), 1852, alt.
Music: Martin Luther, 1529, *Geistliche Lieder*, 1529, 1531

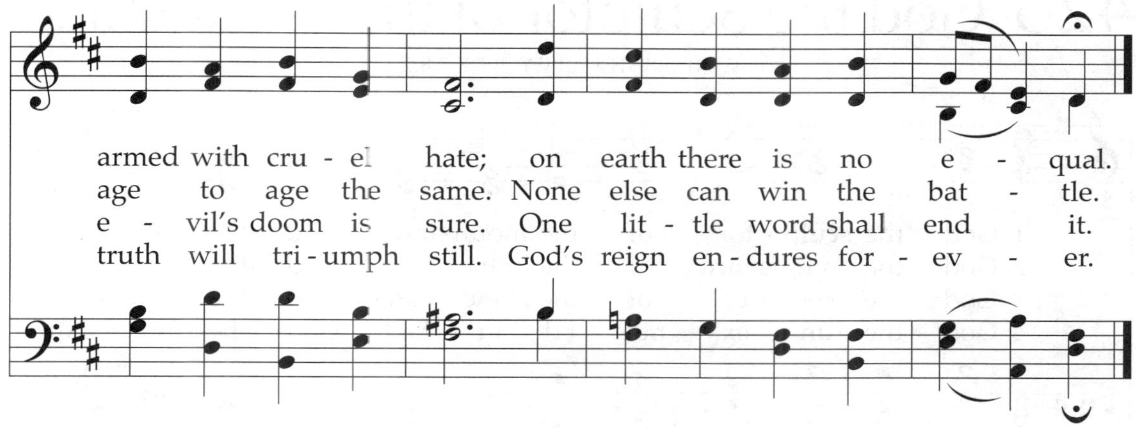
armed with cru - el hate; on earth there is no e - qual.
age to age the same. None else can win the bat - tle.
e - vil's doom is sure. One lit - tle word shall end it.
truth will tri - umph still. God's reign en - dures for - ev - er.

Called or Not Called, God Is There 422

JUNG'S LINTEL Irregular

Swing:
C Gm F Abmaj7 Bb C Gm
Called or not called, God is there. Called or not
F Ab Bb C Gm F Ab
called, God is there. Called or not called, God is
Bb C Gm F Ab Bb C
there; the hand of the Mak - er is ev - 'ry - where.

Additional stanzas: Known or unknown . . . Seen or unseen . . . Named or unnamed . . .

Text: Shawn Kirchner (USA); desc. Ryan Harrison (USA); inspired by Carl Jung (Switzerland), 20th c.
Music: Shawn Kirchner; desc. Ryan Harrison

423 God the Sculptor of the Mountains

WESTMINSTER ABBEY 8.7.8.7.8.7

G C D G
1 God the sculp - tor of the moun - tains, God the mill - er
2 God the nui - sance of the Pha - raoh, God the cleav - er
3 God the dress - er of the vine - yard, God the plant - er
4 God the un - ex - pect - ed in - fant, God the calm, de -
D/A A D G
of the sand, God the jewel - er of the heav - ens,
of the sea, God the pil - lar in the dark - ness,
of the wheat, God the reap - er of the har - vest,
ter - mined youth, God the ta - ble - turn - ing proph - et,
C Am B Em E A
God the pot - ter of the land: you are womb of
God the bea - con of the free: you are fount of
God the source of all we eat: you are host at
God the res - ur - rect - ed truth: you are pres - ent
D G C2 D C D7 G
all cre - a - tion; we are form - less; shape us now.
all de - li - v'rance; we are aim - less; lead us now.
ev - 'ry ta - ble; we are hun - gry; feed us now.
ev - 'ry mo - ment; we are search - ing; meet us now.

Text: John Thornburg (USA), 1993, alt.,
Music: Henry Purcell (England), ca. 1680, alt.

We Worship God the Rock 424

GENEVA 124 (OLD 124th) 10.10.10.10.10

1 We wor-ship God the Rock, un-moved, se - cure, like moun-tains
2 We wor-ship God the Riv - er, flow - ing fast, with life - re -
3 We wor-ship God the Rock and Riv - er, one; with - out the
which from ag - es past en - dure, a strong foun - da - tion
new - ing wa - ters sweep-ing past, a stream cre - at - ing
wa - ter, life had not be - gun; with - out the rock, the
for our faith and life, our rock of con - fi - dence in storm and
good to bless the earth, and bring-ing beau - ty in new forms to
riv - er could not flow; we find both true, when God we ful - ly
strife. We wor-ship God the Rock, un-moved, se - cure.
birth. We wor-ship God the Riv - er, flow - ing fast.
know. We wor-ship God the Rock and Riv - er, one.

Text: Albert F. Bayly (England), 20th c., © Oxford University Press
Music: Louis Bourgeois (present-day France), Genevan Psalter, 1551; harm. Claude Goudimel (present-day France), *Les Pseaumes . . .*, 1565

425 మార్గం, సత్యం, జీవం నీవె
Margam, Satyam, Jivam nive
(Living, Moving, End and Beginning)

MARGAM, SATYAM, JIVAM NIVE Irregular

Refrain
Mar - gam, Sa - tyam, Ji - vam ni - ve,
Liv - ing, mov - ing, End and Be - gin - ning,
A - di, A - dha - ram, An - tam ni - ve.
you are Love, ho - ly; you are, shall be.
1 Pa - la - na, po - sha - na, pra - nam, ni - ve. Pu - ni - tam,
2 Ru - pam, dee - pam, gop - yam, ni - ve. Hru - da - yam,
3 Ho - mam, kshe - mam, shan - tam, ni - ve. Nit - yam,
1 Breath - giv - er, heal - er, you are light and ra - diance; you are all
2 You are the cher - ished one, source of our be - ing, mer - ci - ful,
3 You are the truth and the way for our walk - ing. You are life:
puj - yam, pur - ham, ni - ve. Pre - mam, dha - mam, dhya - nam,
stha - nam pra - dha - mam, ni - ve vak - yam, bha - vam jna - nam
sat - yam, su - gu - nam, ni - ve. Bhag - yam, bho - gam, sauk - yam,
jus - tice, fair - ness, pa - tience. In you all souls flow - er,
faith - ful, shel - t'ring, heal - ing. You are mu - sic, you are
wak - ing, death's pow'r break - ing. Thun - der, whirl - wind, si - lence,
ni - ve. Pra - bha - lam, pha - li - tam pun - yam ni - ve.
ni - ve gee - tam, ga - nam ra - gam ni - ve.
ni - ve. Dhar - mam, mar - mam, pa - ra - mam ni - ve.
o - pen: in - tel - lect, ho - li - ness, ten - der - ness, de - vo - tion.
rhy - thm, mel - o - dy, po - e - try, har - mo - ny, and wis - dom.
mys - t'ry, sac - ri - fice, nour - ish - ment; you are, shall be.

Text: Telugu; author unknown (India); English paraphr. Andrew Donaldson (Canada), from a literal trans. by Peniel Jesudason Rufus Rajkumar (India), © Andrew Donaldson
Music: Ravela Joseph (India), as taught by Vinita Manchala (Switzerland)

Refrain మార్గం, సత్యం, జీవం నీవె
ఆది, ఆధారం, అంతం నీవె

1 పాలన, పోషణ, ప్రాణం, నీవె
పునీతం, పూజ్యం, పూర్ణం, నీవె
ప్రేమం, ధామం, ధ్యానం, నీవె
ప్రభలం, ఫలితం పుణ్యం నీవె

2 రూపం, దీపం, గోప్యం, నీవె
హ్రుదయం, స్థానం ప్రధమం, నీవె
వాక్యం, భావం జ్ఞానం నీవె
గీతం, గానం రాగం నీవె

3 హోమం, క్షెమం, షాంతం, నీవె
నిత్యం, సత్యం, సుగుణం, నీవె
భాగ్యం, భోగం, సౌక్యం, నీవె
ధర్మం, మర్మం, పరమం నీవె

Mothering God, You Gave Me Birth 426

ARMS OF PATIENCE LM

G* D C G
1 Moth - er-ing God, you gave me birth in the bright
2 Moth - er-ing Christ, you took my form, of - fer - ing
3 Moth - er-ing Spir - it, nur - t'ring one, in arms of
D Em Am G/B D Bm Em
morn - ing of this world. Cre - a - tor, Source of
me your food of light, grain of ___ life and
pa - tience hold me close so that in faith I
G/B C Am9 Bm7 Cadd2 G
ev - 'ry breath, you are my rain, my wind, my sun.
grape of love, your ver - y bod - y for my peace.
root and grow un - til I flow'r, un - til I know.

*Chord symbols for unison singing only; they do not correspond with the vocal harmonies.

Text: based on the writings of Julian of Norwich (England), 14th c.; Jean Janzen (USA),
Music: James E. Clemens (USA), 2004,

427 Creating God, Your Fingers Trace

PUER NOBIS NASCITUR LM

D Bm D D/A A D
1 Cre - at - ing God, your fin - gers trace the bold de -
2 Sus - tain - ing God, your hands up - hold earth's mys - t'ries
3 Re - deem - ing God, your arms em - brace all now op -
4 In - dwell - ing God, your gos - pel claims one fam - 'ly
A/C♯ D Bm A
signs of far - thest space. Let sun and moon and
known or yet un - told. Let wa - ter's frag - ile
pressed for creed or race. Let peace, de - scend - ing
with a bil - lion names. Let ev - 'ry life be
G D A/C♯ A G A D
stars and light and what lies hid - den praise your might.
blend with air, en - a - bling life, pro - claim your care.
like a dove, make known on earth your heal - ing love.
touched by grace un - til we praise you face to face.

Text: Jeffery W. Rowthorn (England), 1974, © 1979 The Hymn Society
Music: Trier manuscript (present-day Germany), 15th c.; adapt. Michael Praetorius (present-day Germany), 1609; harm. George Ratcliffe Woodward (England), 1910

Praise with Joy the World's Creator 428

LAUDA ANIMA 8.7.8.7.8.7

D A D A G D G D G A
1 Praise with joy the world's Cre - a - tor, God of jus - tice,
2 Praise to Christ who feeds the hun - gry, frees the cap - tive,
3 Praise the Spir - it sent a - mong us, lib - at - ing
4 Praise the Mak - er, Christ, and Spir - it, o in com -
Bm Em A F♯ Bm B7 E7sus F♯dim7
love, and peace, source and end of hu - man knowl - edge,
finds the lost, heals the sick, up - sets re - li - gion,
truth from pride, forg - ing bonds where race or gen - der,
mu - ni - ty, call - ing Chris - tians to em - bod - y
F♯m E A D Bm E A D G A
God whose grace shall nev - er cease. Cel - e - brate the
fear - less both of fate and cost. Cel - e - brate Christ's
age or na - tion dare di - vide. Cel - e - brate the
one - ness and di - ver - si - ty. This the world shall
Bm A7 Bm A G Em D A D
Mak - er's glo - ry— pow'r to res - cue and re - lease.
con - stant pres - ence—friend and strang - er, guest and host.
Spir - it's trea - sure— fool - ish - ness none dare de - ride.
see re - flect - ed: God is One and One in Three.

Alternate tune: REGENT SQUARE (#265 or #705)

Text: Iona Community (Scotland), 1985, alt.,
Music: John Goss (England), *The Supplemental Hymn and Tune Book*, 1869

429 Glory to God, Whose Goodness Shines on Me

GLORY TO GOD (Vasile) Irregular

Capo 3: (D) F (G) B♭ (D) F (G) B♭ (D) F (Em) Gm (D) F
1 Gl to God, whose good-ness shines on me,
2 World ith-out end, with-out end, A - men.
(G) B♭ (C) E♭ (G) B♭ (Em7) Gm7 (A7) C7
and to the Son, whose grace has par - doned me,
World with - out end, with - out end, A - men.
(D) F (F♯) A (Bm) Dm
and to the Spir - it, whose love has set me free.
World with - out end, with - out end. A - men.
(Bm7) Dm7 (D) F (Bm7♭5) Dm7♭5
As it was in the be - gin - ning, is
(Em7) Gm7 (Dm) Fm (A7) C7 (D) F (Em7) Gm7 (D) F (Em7) Gm7
Last time
now and ev - er shall be, A - men.

Text: early Christian doxology "Gloria Patri" (Latin, Rome); adapt. Paul Vasile (USA)
Music: Paul M. Vasile

Sing with Joy to the Author / Glory Be to the Father 430

GREATOREX 7.4.6.8.8.8

Capo 1: (D) E♭ (A7) B♭7 (D) E♭ (A) B♭
A: Sing with joy to the Au - thor, the Spo - ken
B: Glo - ry be to the Fa - ther, and to the
(D) E♭ (A/E) B♭/F (E) F (A) B♭ (D) E♭
Word, and to the Breath of Love: From be - fore the
Son, and to the Ho - ly Ghost. As it was in
(G) A♭ (A) B♭ (D) E♭
first be - gin - ning to the end of ev' - ry end - ing,
the be - gin - ning, is now and ev - er shall be,
(A7) B♭7 (D) E♭ (A7) B♭7 (D) E♭
Three ev - er One: A - men, a - men.
world with - out end: A - men, a - men.

Text: text A Brian Wren (England), © 2009 Hope Publishing Company; inspired by early Christian doxology "Gloria Patri" (Latin; Rome); text B early Christian doxology "Gloria Patri" (Latin; Rome); trans. traditional
Music: Henry W. Greatorex (USA), 1851

431 Wij geloven één voor één (We Believe, as One by One)

KLEIN CREDO 7.4.8.4

D G D Bm F♯m
1 Wij ge - lo - ven één voor één en ook sa - men:
1 We be - lieve, as one by one and to - geth - er;
2 We be - lieve in Je - sus' name, Christ a - mong us,
3 We be - lieve that e - ven now God the Spir - it
D G D A D A D
de Heer is God en an - ders geen. A - men, a - men.
the Lord is God, there is none else, a - men, a - men.
con-demned to death, but raised to life: Al - le - lu - ia!
will heal the world and heal us all: Peace be with us!

2 Wij geloven in de naam
Jezus Christus,
gestorven en weer opgestaan.
Halleluja!

3 Wij geloven dat de Geest
ook nog heden
de wereld en onzelf geneest.
Vrede, vrede.

Text: Dutch; Joke Ribbers (Netherlands),1988; trans. Fred Kaan (England)
Music: Bernard Smilde (Netherlands), 1988

You, Lord, Are Both Lamb and Shepherd 432

PICARDY 8.7.8.7.8.7

1 You, Lord, are both Lamb and Shep-herd. You, Lord, are both
2 Clothed in light up - on the moun-tain, stripped of might up -
3 You, who walk each day be - side us, sit in pow - er
4 Wor - thy is our earth - ly Je - sus! Wor - thy is our

prince and slave. You, peace-mak - er and sword - bring - er
on the cross, shin - ing in e - ter - nal glo - ry,
at God's side. You, who preach a way that's nar - row,
cos - mic Christ! Wor - thy your de - feat and vic - t'ry;

of the way you took and gave. You, the ev - er - last - ing
beg-gar'd by a sol-dier's toss, you, the ev - er - last - ing
have a love that reach - es wide. You, the ev - er - last - ing
wor - thy still your peace and strife. You, the ev - er - last - ing

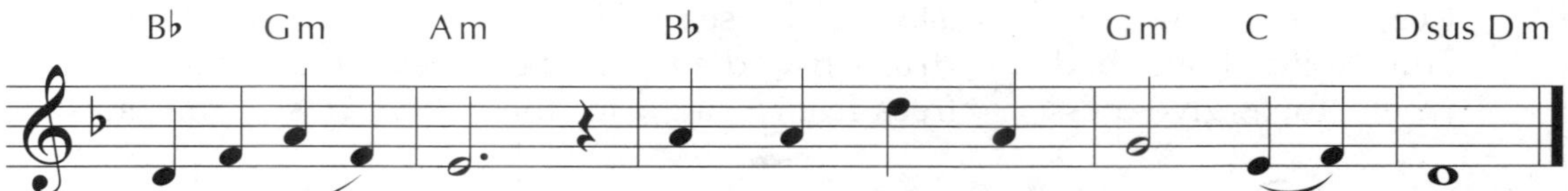

in - stant; you, whom we both scorn and crave.
in - stant; you who are both gift and cost.
in - stant; you, who are our pil - grim guide.
in - stant; you, who are our death and life.

For an alternate chord progression, see "Let All Mortal Flesh Keep Silence" (#65) or "Wisdom from on High Is Dawning" (#238).

Text: Sylvia G. Dunstan (Canada),
Music: French traditional, *Chansons populaires des provinces de France*, 1860

433 I Believe in God Almighty

PLEADING SAVIOR 8.7.8.7 D
G C G D G C
1 I be - lieve in God Al - might - y, Au - thor of all
2 I be - lieve that Je - sus suf - fered, scourged and scorned and
3 I be - lieve in God's own Spir - it, bond - ing all the
D G C G D
things that be, Mak - er of the earth and heav - ens,
cru - ci - fied; tak - en from the cross, was bur - ied—
saints with - in one Church, cath - o - lic and ho - ly,
G C D G C
Keep - er of the sky and sea. I be - lieve in God's Son,
True Life there had tru - ly died. I be - lieve that on the
where for - give - ness frees from sin; in the bod - y's re - sur -
D G C D G
Je - sus, now for us both Lord and Christ, of the
third day Christ was raised up from the grave, then as -
rec - tion, for the break - ing of death's chain gives the

Text: based on Apostles' Creed (Mediterranean), ca. 4th c.; Sylvia G. Dunstan (Canada), *In Search of Hope and Grace*, alt., © 1991 GIA Publications, Inc.
Music: American traditional (USA), *Christian Lyre*, 1831; harm. Ralph Vaughan Williams, *The English Hymnal*, 1906

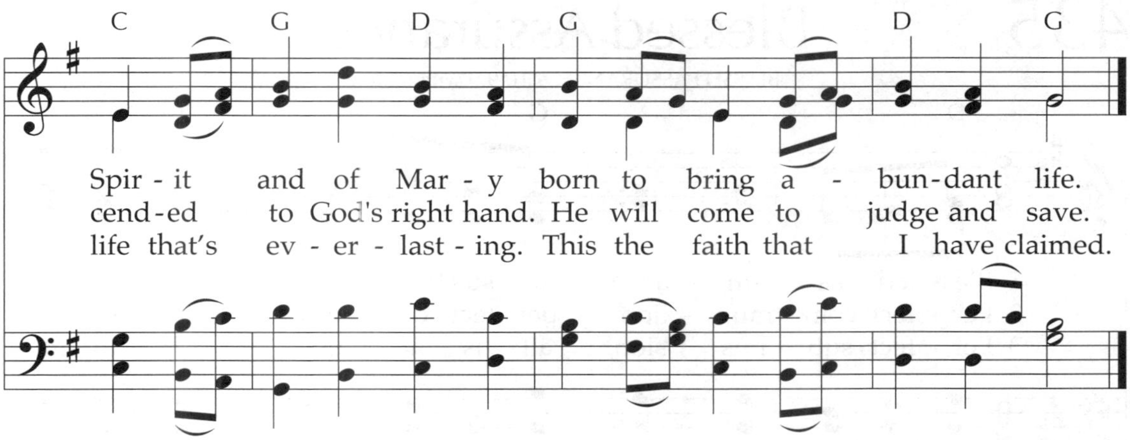
C G D G C D G
Spir - it and of Mar - y born to bring a - bun - dant life.
cend - ed to God's right hand. He will come to judge and save.
life that's ev - er - last - ing. This the faith that I have claimed.

O God, Our Refuge 434

OUR REFUGE LM

C Am G C
1 O God, our re - fuge is your love, where
2 In love we do the work of faith, for
3 When ty - rants taunt with shame and fear your
4 O God, our ref - uge is your love; no
F C G F C
truth and spir - it bid us stand; through hum - ble crea - tures
jus - tice' sake we share our bread; as Ma - ry chose the
joy - ful com - fort guides our speech; and e - ven hemmed by
fear can take us cap - tive when we fol - low your cou -
G Am F C G C
you re - veal the might and won - der of your hand.
bet - ter part, we search and stu - dy what you've said.
pris - on walls, we find your strength with - in our reach.
ra - geous Lamb, then leap the walls. A - men, a - men.

Text: Brenda Hostetler Meyer (USA), © 2019 Brenda Hostetler Meyer; inspired by the writings and recorded testimonies of Anabaptist martyrs in the 16th c., particularly Anna Jansz of Rotterdam (present-day Netherlands), Martha Baert (present-day Belgium); both in *Profiles of Anabaptist Women . . .*, ed. C. Arnold Snyder (Canada) and Linda A. Huebert Hecht (Canada), 1996; and Lisjken Dircks (present-day Netherlands) and six unnamed women, in *Elizabeth's Manly Courage: Testimonials and Songs . . .*, ed. and trans. Hermina Joldersma (Canada) and Louis Peter Grijp (Netherlands), 2001

Music: The Walking Roots Band (USA), © 2019 The Walking Roots Band; acc. Susan See (USA), 2020

435 Blessed Assurance

BLESSED ASSURANCE 9.10.9.9 with refrain

D G D
1 Bless - ed as - sur - ance, Je - sus is mine! Oh, what a
2 Per - fect com - mun - ion, per - fect de - light, vi - sions of
3 Per - fect sub - mis - sion, all is at rest. I in my
A E7 A D
fore - taste of glo - ry di - vine! Heir of sal - va - tion,
rap - ture now burst on my sight. An - gels de - scend - ing
Sav - ior am hap - py and bless'd, watch - ing and wait - ing,
G D Em A7 D
pur - chase of God, born of his Spir - it, washed in his blood.
bring from a - bove ech - oes of mer - cy, whis - pers of love.
look - ing a - bove, filled with his good - ness, lost in his love.
Refrain
G D
This is my sto - ry, this is my song, prais - ing my

Text: Fanny J. Crosby (USA), *Gems of Praise*, 1873, alt.
Music: Phoebe P. Knapp (USA), *Gems of Praise*, 1873

G A/E A A7 D G
Sav - ior all the day long. This is my sto - ry, this is my
D Em A7 D
song, prais - ing my Sav - ior all the day long.

436 O Lord My God / How Great Thou Art

HOW GREAT THOU ART 11.10.11.10 with refrain

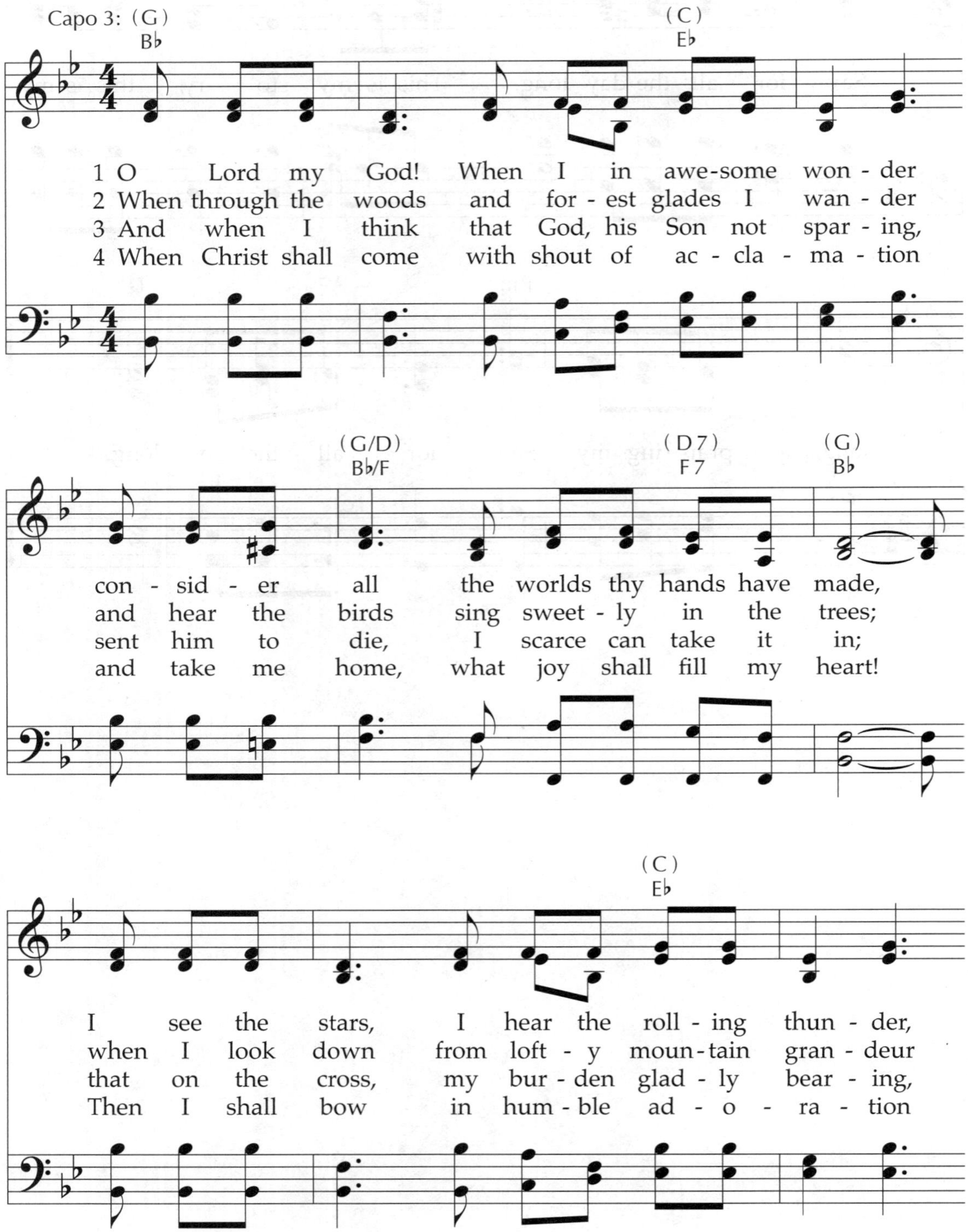
Capo 3: (G) B♭
(C) E♭
(G/D) B♭/F
(D7) F7
(G) B♭
(C) E♭
1 O Lord my God! When I in awe-some won - der
2 When through the woods and for - est glades I wan - der
3 And when I think that God, his Son not spar - ing,
4 When Christ shall come with shout of ac - cla - ma - tion
con - sid - er all the worlds thy hands have made,
and hear the birds sing sweet - ly in the trees;
sent him to die, I scarce can take it in;
and take me home, what joy shall fill my heart!
I see the stars, I hear the roll - ing thun - der,
when I look down from loft - y moun - tain gran - deur
that on the cross, my bur - den glad - ly bear - ing,
Then I shall bow in hum - ble ad - o - ra - tion

Text: Stuart K. Hine (England), 1949, alt.
Music: Swedish traditional

(G/D) B♭/F (D7) F7 (G) B♭
thy pow'r through - out the un - i - verse dis - played:
and hear the brook and feel the gen - tle breeze:
he bled and died to take a - way my sin:
and there pro - claim, "My God, how great thou art!"
Refrain
(C) E♭ (G) B♭ (D7) F7
Then sings my soul, my Sav - ior God, to thee: How great thou
(G) B♭ (C) E♭
art, how great thou art! Then sings my soul, my Sav - ior God, to
(G) B♭ (Am7) Cm7 (D7) F7 (G) B♭
thee: How great thou art, how great thou art!

437 The Lord Is My Light

THE LORD IS MY LIGHT Irregular

1 The Lord is my light and my sal - va - tion, the Lord is my
3 Wait on the Lord and be of good cour - age, O wait on the
light and my sal - va - tion, the Lord is my light and
Lord, and be of good cour - age, wait on the Lord and
my sal - va - tion; whom shall I fear?
be of good cour - age; he shall strength - en thine heart.
Refrain
Whom shall I fear, whom shall I fear? The Lord is the strength

Text: based on Psalm 27:1, 5, 14, Lillian Bouknight (USA)
Music: Lillian Bouknight; arr. Stephen Key (USA), arr. © 2000 GIA Publications, Inc.

G Am C/G G7 C
Fine
of my life; whom shall I fear? (to v. 2) 2 In the time of trou-ble,
(to v. 3)
Dm C G C Dm C
he shall hide me, in the time of trou-ble, he shall hide me,
Dm C C/G G7 C
To refrain
in the time of trou-ble, he shall hide me, whom shall I fear?

Christ Has Died, Christ Is Risen 438

ACCLAMATION (Henry) Irregular

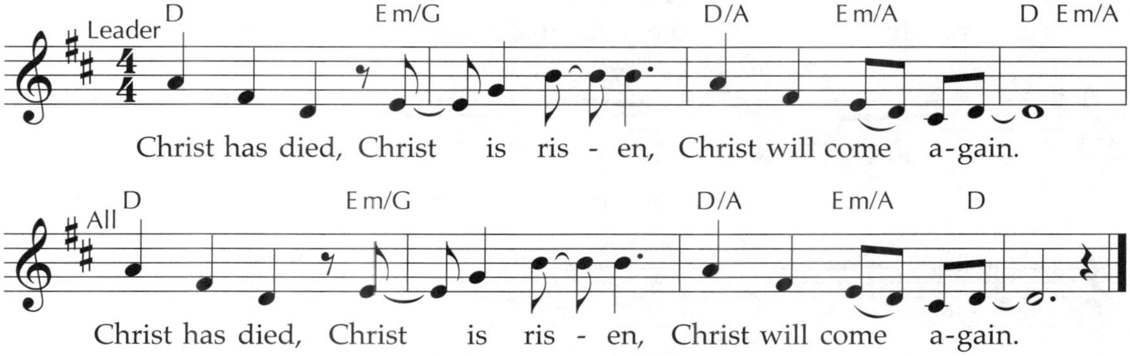
Leader
D Em/G D/A Em/A D Em/A
Christ has died, Christ is ris - en, Christ will come a-gain.
All
D Em/G D/A Em/A D
Christ has died, Christ is ris - en, Christ will come a-gain.

Text: from Eastern Eucharistic prayer liturgies, *Memorial Acclamation*
Music: Jackson Henry (USA), © 2011 Jackson Henry

439 True Evangelical Faith

WE WILL WALK Irregular

Em7 Am7 Bm7 Em7 Am7 Bm7
1 True e-van-gel-i-cal faith can't lie dor - mant.
2 True e-van-gel-i-cal faith tends cre - a - tion.
3 True e-van-gel-i-cal faith works for jus - tice.
Em7 Am7 Bm7 Em7 Am7 Bm7
True e-van-gel-i-cal faith is prov-en by love.
True e-van-gel-i-cal faith gives to the poor.
True e-van-gel-i-cal faith prays for its foes.
Em7 Am7 Bm7 Em7 Am7 Bm7
True e-van-gel-i-cal faith dies to its old self.
True e-van-gel-i-cal faith binds up the wound-ed.
True e-van-gel-i-cal faith coun-ters op-press-ion.
Em7 Am7 Bm7 Em7 E7
True e-van-gel-i-cal faith says "Je - sus is Lord."
True e-van-gel-i-cal faith loves and serves all.
True e-van-gel-i-cal faith shakes e - vil with good.
Refrain
Am7 Em7
If we tru - ly be-lieve that we're born of God, and
Am7 Em7 Am7
care-ful-ly walk the path that's good, and bur-y our sin
Em7 Am7
in the death of Christ, we'll be walk-ing to-geth -
F♯ B7 Em7
- er in the new-ness of a bap - tized life.

Text: Jeremy Kempf (USA); adapt. from Menno Simons (present-day Netherlands), *Why I Do Not Cease Teaching and Writing*, 1539
Music: Jeremy Kempf

Ask the Complicated Questions 440

McRAE 8.7.8.7

Em Am B Em
1 Ask the com - pli - cat - ed ques - tions; do not
2 Seek the dis - con - cert - ing an - swers; fol - low
3 Knock on doors of new i - de - as, test as -
4 For in strug - gle we dis - cov - er truth both
G D G C D G Am Bm
fear to be found out, for our God makes strong our
where the Spir - it blows, test com - pet - ing truths for
sump - tions long grown stale, for Christ calls from shores of
sim - ple and pro - found: in the knock - ing, ask - ing,
Am C Em/B B Em
weak - ness, forg - ing faith in fires of doubt.
wis - dom, for in ten - sion new life grows.
won - der, dar - ing us to try and fail.
seek - ing, we are o - pened, an - swered, found.

441 Crashing Waters at Creation

RESTORATION (I WILL ARISE) 8.7.8.7

Fm Ab
1 Crash - ing wa - ters at cre - a - tion, or - dered
2 Part - ing wa - ter stood and trem - bled as the
3 Cleans - ing wa - ter once at Jor - dan closed a -
4 Liv - ing wa - ter, nev - er end - ing, quench the
Db/Ab Ab/C Eb Ab C7/E Fm
by the Spir - it's breath, first to wit - ness
cap - tives passed on through, wash - ing off the
round the One fore - told, o - pened to re -
thirst and flood the soul. Well - spring, source of
Eb Ab Fm Db Cm7 Fm
day's be - gin - ning from the bright - ness of night's death.
chains of bond - age— chan - nel to a life made new.
veal the glo - ry ev - er new and ev - er old.
life e - ter - nal, drench our dry - ness, make us whole.

For capo chords, see #300.

Text: Sylvia G. Dunstan (Canada),
Music: American traditional (USA), *Southern Harmony*, 1835; harm. Charles H. Webb

From the Waters I Will Rise 442

RISE 7.5.7.5

D D/F♯ G A
1 From the wa - ters I will rise— I will rise and
2 From my kneel - ing I will stand— I will stand and
3 From my won-d'ring I will know— I will know and
4 From my death I'm born a - new— born a - new, I
Bm D/A G D/F♯ Bm7
walk. Wipe the wa - ter from my eyes— walk with
sing. Reach for me and take my hand— sing with
dream. Shar - ing wis - dom, we will grow— dream with
live. Come and see what God will do— live with
1–3
Em Em7/D Cadd9 G6/B A
(Sop. 1–3) me in Christ.
me, walk with me.
me, sing with me.
me, dream with me.
4
Em Em7/D A/C♯
me in Christ,
A G/B A D D/A A7 D
live with me in Christ.

443 I Have Decided to Follow Jesus

ASSAM 5.5.5.5.5.5.4.4

Text: anon. (India); adapt. Paul B. Smith (Canada); Navajo, Cantonese, Thai trans. anon.
Music: Indian traditional; adapt. Paul B. Smith; harm. Norman Johnson (USA)

Cantonese

1
我已經決定要跟隨耶穌,
我已經決定要跟隨耶穌,
我已經決定要跟隨耶穌,
永不回頭,永不回頭!

2
十架在前面世界在背後,
十架在前面世界在背後,
十架在前面世界在背後,
永不回頭,永不回頭!

3
雖無人同走我仍要跟隨,
雖無人同走我仍要跟隨,
雖無人同走我仍要跟隨,
永不回頭,永不回頭!

Cantonese transliteration

1
Ngo ji ging kyut ding jiu gan ceoi je sou,
ngo ji ging kyut ding jiu gan ceoi je sou,
ngo ji ging kyut ding jiu gan ceoi je sou,
wing bat wui tau, wing bat wui tau!

2
Sap gaa zoi cin min sai gaai zoi bui hau,
sap gaa zoi cin min sai gaai zoi bui hau,
sap gaa zoi cin min sai gaai zoi bui hau,
wing bat wui tau, wing bat wui tau!

3
Seoi mou jan tung zau ngo jing jiu gan ceoi,
seoi mou jan tung zau ngo jing jiu gan ceoi,
seoi mou jan tung zau ngo jing jiu gan ceoi,
wing bat wui tau, wing bat wui tau!

Thai

1
ฉันตัดสินใจแล้ว จะตามพระเยซู
ฉันตัดสินใจแล้ว จะตามพระเยซู
ฉันตัดสินใจแล้ว จะตามพระเยซู
ไม่หันกลับเลย ไม่หันกลับเลย

2
กางเขนอยู่เบื้องหน้า ทิ้งโลกไว้เบื้องหลัง
กางเขนอยู่เบื้องหน้า ทิ้งโลกไว้เบื้องหลัง
กางเขนอยู่เบื้องหน้า ทิ้งโลกไว้เบื้องหลัง
ไม่หันกลับเลย ไม่หันกลับเลย

3
แม้ใครไม่ไปด้วย ฉันก็จะตามไป
แม้ใครไม่ไปด้วย ฉันก็จะตามไป
แม้ใครไม่ไปด้วย ฉันก็จะตามไป
ไม่หันกลับเลย ไม่หันกลับเลย

Thai transliteration

1
C̄hạn tạds̄inci læ̂w ca tāmph ra yesū,
c̄hạn tạds̄inci læ̂w ca tāmph ra yesū,
c̄hạn tạds̄inci læ̂w ca tāmph ra yesū,
mị̀ h̄ạn klạb ley mị̀ h̄ạn klạb ley.

2
Kāngk̄hen xyū̀ beụ̄xngh̄n̂ā thîng lok wị̂ beụ̄xngh̄lạng,
kāngk̄hen xyū̀ beụ̄xngh̄n̂ā thîng lok wị̂ beụ̄xngh̄lạng,
kāngk̄hen xyū̀ beụ̄xngh̄n̂ā thîng lok wị̂ beụ̄xngh̄lạng,
mị̀ h̄ạn klạb ley mị̀ h̄ạn klạb ley.

3
Mæ̂ khır mị̀ pị d̂wy c̄hạn k̆ ca tām pị,
mæ̂ khır mị̀ pị d̂wy c̄hạn k̆ ca tām pị,
mæ̂ khır mị̀ pị d̂wy c̄hạn k̆ ca tām pị,
mị̀ h̄ạn klạb ley mị̀ h̄ạn klạb ley.

444 I Sing with Exultation

NUN WEND IHR HÖREN SAGEN 7.5.7.5.7.6.7.6

D G D Bm D E A
1 I sing with ex - ul - ta - tion! All my heart's de - light
2 God sends him as ex - am - ple, light and liv - ing guide.
3 Sing praise to Christ our Sav - ior, who, in grace in - clined,
4 Christ bids us, none com - pel - ling, to his glo - rious throne—
D G D Bm D E A
is God who brings sal - va - tion, frees from death's dread might.
Be - fore my end he bids me in God's realm a - bide,
to us re - veals his na - ture: pa - tient, lov - ing, kind.
they on - ly who are will - ing Christ as Lord to own.
D Bm D E A
I praise you, Christ of heav - en, who ev - er shall en - dure,
that I may love and cher - ish his right - eous - ness di - vine,
His love di - vine out - pour - ing, dis - played to ev - 'ry - one,
They are as - sured of heav - en who will right faith pur - sue.
D Bm D A G A D
who takes a - way my sor - row, keeps me safe and se - cure.
that I with him for - ev - er bliss e - ter - nal may find.
is fash - ioned like his Fa - ther's as no oth - er has done.
With hearts made pure do pen - ance, sealed in bap - tis - m true.

Text: Felix Manz (present-day Switzerland), ca. 1526, "Mit Lust so will ich singen," *Ausbund*, 1583; trans. Marion Wenger (USA), 1966, *The Mennonite Hymnal*, 1969, © 1966 Marion Wenger; alt. Harris J. Loewen (Canada), © 1990 Harris J. Loewen
Music: *Im Bentzenauer Ton* (present-day Germany), 1540

ϹΥΕΙΟΥΙΟϹΜΟΥΟΑΓΑΠΗΤΟϹ

446 *Ephesians 4:1-6*

Lead a life worthy of the calling
to which you have been called.
Be humble and gentle in every way.
Be patient with each other
and lovingly accept each other.
Through the peace that ties you together,
do your best to maintain the unity
that the Spirit gives.
There is one body and one Spirit.
In the same way we were called
to share one hope.
There is one Lord,
one faith,
one baptism,
one God and Creator of all,
who is over all,
and through all,
and in all.

447 *Luke 3:21-22*

While everyone was being baptized,
Jesus was also baptized.
While he was praying,
heaven was opened
and the Holy Spirit came down on him
in bodily form like a dove.
And there was a voice from heaven:
"You are my Son,
whom I dearly love;
in you I delight."

448 *Isaiah 42:1-3*

Here is my servant,
the one I uphold,
my chosen,
in whom I delight.
I have put my spirit upon my servant
to bring justice to the nations;
who will not shout or cry out,
or be heard in the street;
who will not break a bruised reed,
or put out a smoldering wick.
In faithfulness, my servant
will bring forth justice.

449 *Romans 6:3-4, 10-11*

Do you not know
that all who were baptized into Christ
were baptized into Jesus' death?
Therefore, we were buried together
through baptism into Christ's death,
so that just as Christ was raised
from the dead
through the glory of God,
we too can walk in newness of life.
In dying, the Messiah died to sin
once and for all,
but the life Christ lives is with God.
In the same way,
you also should consider yourselves
dead to sin
but alive for God in Christ Jesus.

450 *Galatians 3:26-28*

In Christ Jesus
you are all children of God
through faith.
For all of you
who were baptized into Christ
have clothed yourselves with Christ.
There is no longer Jew or Greek,
no longer slave or free,
no longer male and female;
for all of you are one in Christ Jesus.

451 *Matthew 28:16, 18-20*

Jesus' eleven disciples
went to a mountain in Galilee,
where Jesus had told them to meet.
Jesus came to them and said:
I have been given all authority
in heaven and on earth.
Make disciples,
going to the people of all nations,
baptizing them
in the name of the Father,
the Son,
and the Holy Spirit,
and teaching them
to do everything I have told you.
I will be with you always,
even until the end of the world.

Previous page: 445. *From the River to the Wilderness*, Matthew C. Regier (USA), 2018, linocut ⓦ

With Water Freely Flowing 452

OPEN HEART 7.6.7.6 D

G Am7 G/B Am7 D G
1 With wa - ter free - ly flow-ing we cel - e - brate new birth,
2 The Spir - it, swift - ly soar-ing, de - scend-ing as a dove,
3 By wa - ter and the Spir - it bap - tized in Christ, we rise
C D/C G Em A A7 D
in sa - cred sign ex - press-ing God's love for all on earth.
con - veys the star-t'ling pres-ence on all whose vow is love.
to walk new paths un - fold - ing be - fore our o - pened eyes.
Am7 D Bm Em Am7 C D
The well of liv - ing wa - ter springs up for us this day;
The breath of God with - in us en - liv - ens and sus - tains,
We jour-ney from this mo-ment, faith's pil-grim-age em - brace.
G Am7 C D Em Am7 D7 G
en - gulfed by love's ac - cept - ance, our fears are washed a - way.
be - yond this rite of pas - sage with us al-ways re - mains.
By Spir - it and by wa - ter we feel and sense God's grace.

Text: Larry E. Schultz (USA), 2008, © 2010 Celebrating Grace, Inc.
Music: Amanda Husberg (USA), © 2005 Wayne Leupold Editions, Inc.

453 As I Went Down to the River to Pray

AS I WENT DOWN TO THE RIVER Irregular

Refrain
As I went down to the riv-er to pray, stud-y-in' a-bout that good old way, and who shall wear the star-ry crown, good Lord, show me the way.
Fine
1 Oh, sis-ters, let's go down, let's go down, come on down.
Oh, sis-ters, let's go down, down to the riv-er to pray.
To refrain

2 Oh, brothers, . . .
3 Oh, children, . . .
4 Oh, sinners, . . .

Text: African American spiritual (USA)
Music: African American spiritual

454 Wade in the Water

WADE IN THE WATER Irregular

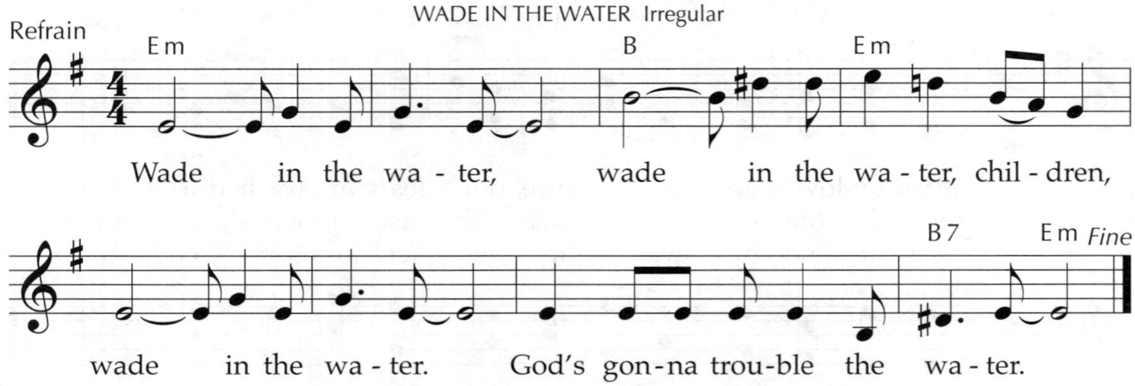
Refrain
Wade in the wa-ter, wade in the wa-ter, chil-dren,
wade in the wa-ter. God's gon-na trou-ble the wa-ter.
Fine

Text: African American spiritual (USA)
Music: African American spiritual

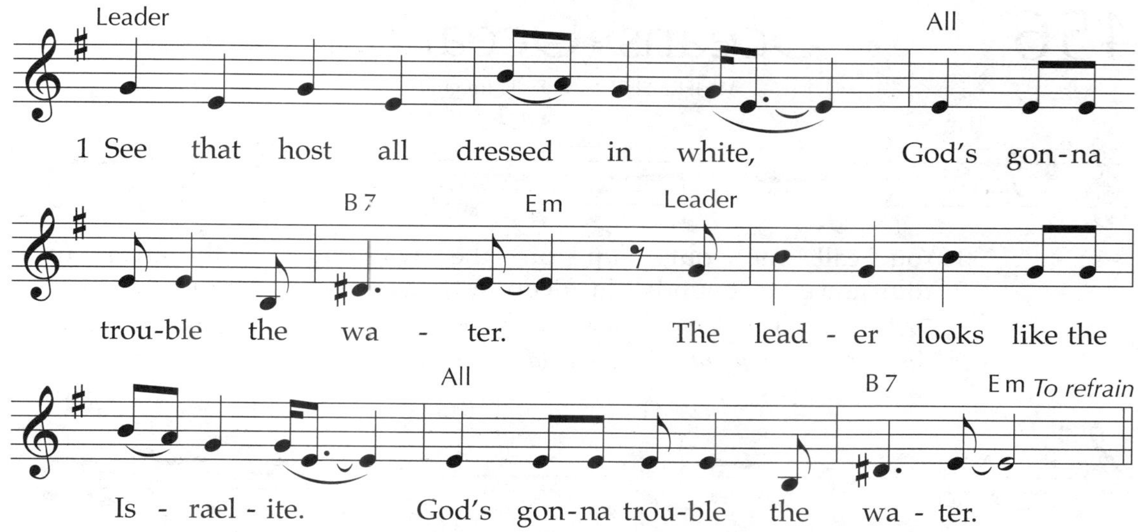
Leader
1 See that host all dressed in white,
All
God's gon-na trou-ble the wa - ter.
B7
Em
Leader
The lead - er looks like the Is - rael - ite.
All
God's gon-na trou-ble the wa - ter.
B7
Em To refrain

Leader:

2 See that band all | dressed in red, . . . | Looks like the band that | Moses led.

3 If you don't believe I've | been redeemed, . . . Just | follow me down to | Jordan's stream.

Make Us One 455

HINCKS Irregular

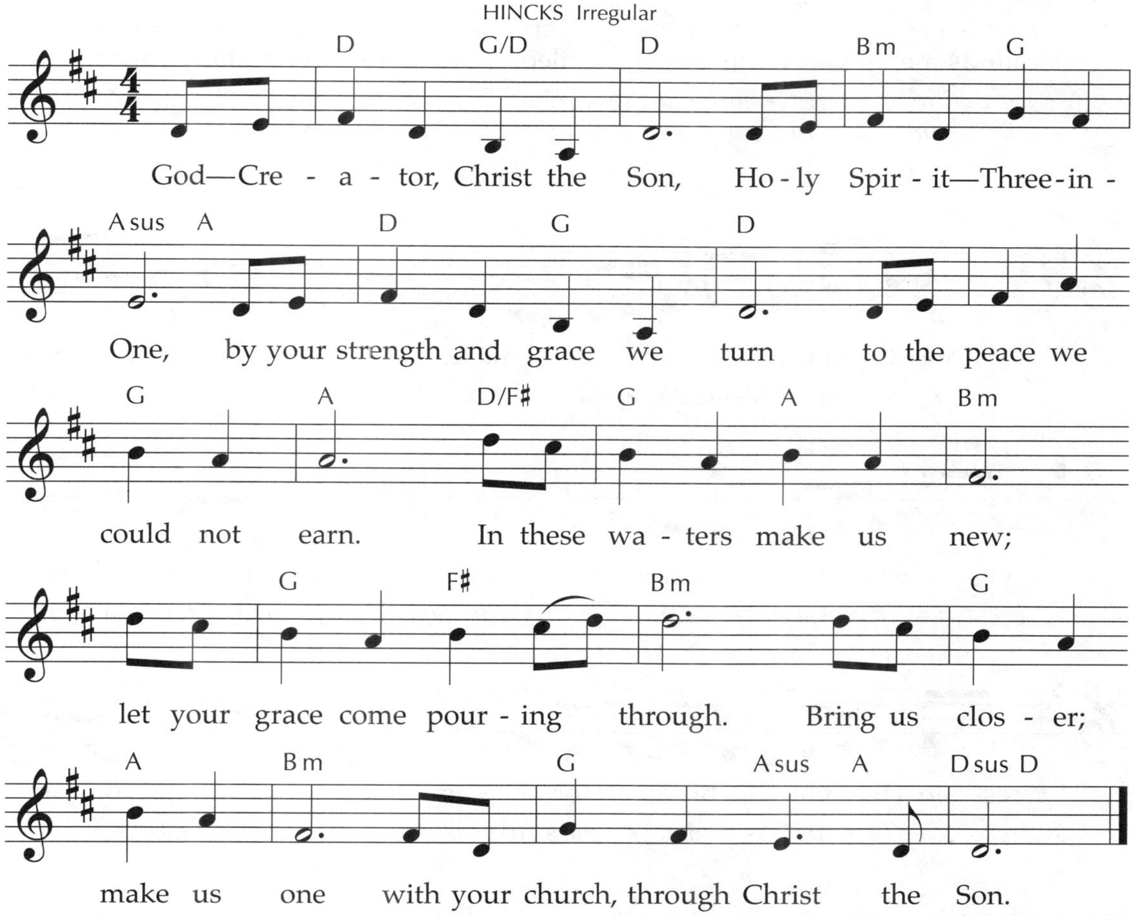
D G/D D Bm G
God—Cre - a - tor, Christ the Son, Ho - ly Spir - it—Three-in -
Asus A D G D
One, by your strength and grace we turn to the peace we
G A D/F♯ G A Bm
could not earn. In these wa - ters make us new;
G F♯ Bm G
let your grace come pour - ing through. Bring us clos - er;
A Bm G Asus A Dsus D
make us one with your church, through Christ the Son.

Text: Anneli Loepp Thiessen (Canada)
Music: Anneli Loepp Thiessen

456 Oceans (Océanos)

WHERE FEET MAY FAIL Irregular

Bm A/C♯ D
1 You call me out up - on the wa - ters, the great un -
2 Your grace a - bounds in deep - est wa - ters, your sov - 'reign
1 Tu voz me lla - ma a las a - guas, don - de mis
2 Tu gra - cia‿a - bun - da‿en la tor - men - ta, tu ma - no,
A G Bm A/C♯
- known where feet may fail. And there I find you in the
hand will be my guide. Where feet may fail and fear sur -
pies pue - den fa - llar. Y‿a - hí te‿en-cuen-tro en lo‿in-
Dios, me gui - a - rá. Cuan-do‿hay te - mor en mi ca -
D A G
mys - t'ry, in o - ceans deep my faith will stand.
rounds me, you've nev - er failed, and you won't start now.
cier - to, ca - mi - na - ré so - bre el mar.
mi - no, tú er - es fiel y no cam - bia - rás.
Refrain
G D A G
And I will call up-on your name and keep my
Y a tu nom - bre cla - ma - ré en ti mis
D A G
eyes a-bove the waves. When o - ceans rise, my soul will
o - jos fi - ja - ré. En tem - pe - stad, des - can - sa -
D A G A
rest in your em - brace, for I am yours and you are
ré en tu po - der, pues tu - yo soy ha - sta‿el fi -

Text: Joel Houston (USA), Matt Crocker (USA), and Salomon Ligthelm (USA); Spanish trans. Armando Sanchez (Commonwealth of Puerto Rico, USA) and Toni Romero (Argentina)
Music: Joel Houston, Matt Crocker, and Salomon Ligthelm

1st time to verse 2
2nd time to bridge
Last time Fine
Bm A/C♯ D D/F♯ A A/C♯ G6
mine.
- nal.
Bridge
Bm G D A Bm G D A
Spir - it, lead me where my trust is with - out bor - ders, let me walk up-on the wa - ters wher - ev - er you would call me. Take me deep - er than my feet could ev - er wan - der, and my faith will be made strong - er in the pres - ence of my Sav - ior.
Que tu Es - pí - ri - tu me guí - e sin fron - te - ras, más a - llá de las ba - rre - ras a don - de tú me lla - mes. Tú me lle - vas más a - llá de lo so - ña - do, don - de pue - do es - tar con - fia - do al es - tar en tu pre - sen - cia.
To refrain

You Have Put On Christ 457

BAPTIZED IN CHRIST Irregular

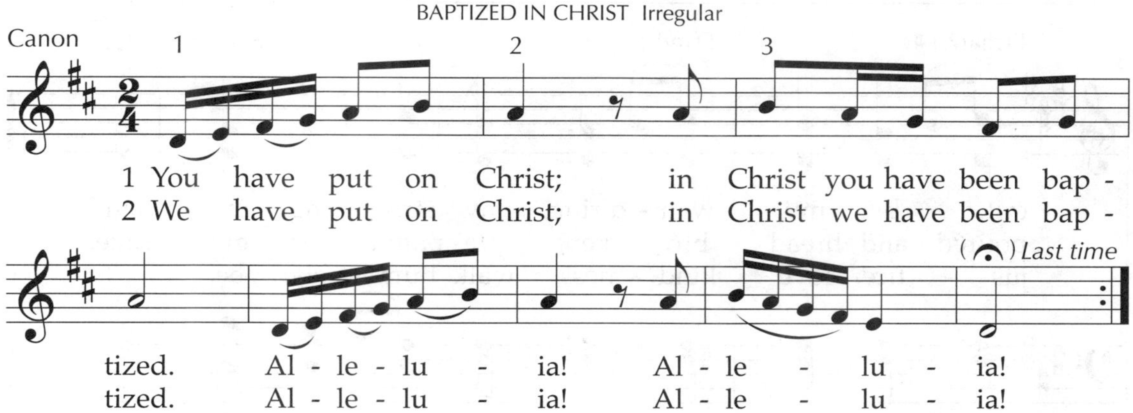
Canon
1 2 3
1 You have put on Christ; in Christ you have been bap - tized. Al - le - lu - ia! Al - le - lu - ia!
2 We have put on Christ; in Christ we have been bap - tized. Al - le - lu - ia! Al - le - lu - ia!
( ) Last time

Text: from the Rite of Baptism, based on Galatians 3:27,
Music: Howard Hughes, SM (USA),

458 The Water Is Ready

STILLWATER 6.6.6.5 D

A D/A E/G♯ E7/G♯ A A/G♯
1 The wa - ter is read - y; how can I be worth - y? Yet
2 The ta - ble is read - y; how can I be wel - come? Yet
3 A call - ing is read - y; how can I be cho - sen? Yet
F♯m F♯m7 D A/C♯ A A2/E E7sus E7
God has in - vit - ed, so I will step in. The
God has for - giv - en, so I will par - take. The
God is more gra - cious than I can con - ceive. A
A D/A E/G♯ E7/G♯ A/G A2/G
wa - ter is wait - ing, and my soul is thirst - y— dried
ta - ble is spa - cious, and my soul is hun - gry—wine
call - ing is of - fered, and my soul has heard it: do
Dmaj7/F♯ Dm/F A/E Asus/E 1, 2 A
out by my wan - d'ring, my striv - ing, my sin.
poured and bread bro - ken, pre - pared for my sake.
jus - tice, love kind - ness, walk hum - bly; be -

Text: Adam M. L. Tice (USA), 2016
Music: Lee Dengler (USA), 2016

3
A
Dmaj7/F♯
Dm/F
A/E
Asus/E
A
lieve. Do jus - tice, love kind - ness, walk hum - bly; be - lieve.

Let the Hungry Come to Me 459

ADORO TE DEVOTE 12.12.11.11

1 "Let the hun - gry come to me, let the poor be fed.
2 "I my - self am liv - ing bread; feed on me and live.
3 "Here a - mong you shall I dwell, mak - ing all things new.
4 Hail, O Word In - car - nate, born from Ma - ry's womb;
5 Now with glad thanks - giv - ing, praise Christ glo - ri - fied;

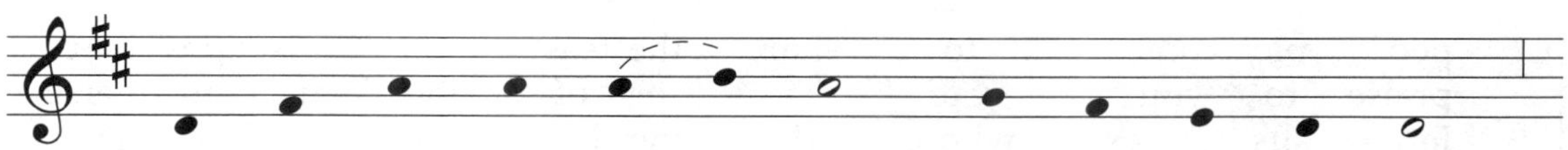

Let the thirst - y come to drink, share my wine and bread.
In this cup my blood for you; drink the wine I give.
You shall be my ver - y own, I, your God with you.
hail, O Strength im - mor - tal, ris - en from the tomb.
he in us is pres - ent, we in him a - bide.

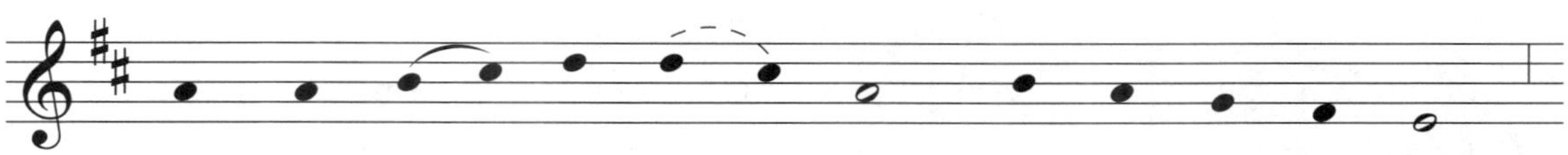

Though you have no mon - ey, come to me and eat.
All who eat my bod - y, all who drink my blood,
Blest are you in - vit - ed to my wed - ding feast.
Share with us your vic - to - ry, Sav - ior ev - er blest:
Mem - bers of his bod - y, we in him are one;

Drink the cup I of - fer, feed on fin - est wheat.
shall have joy for - ev - er, share the life of God.
You shall live for - ev - er, all your joys in - creased."
live more ful - ly in our hearts; be our con - stant guest.
hail the sa - cred un - ion, heav'n on earth be - gun!

Text: stanzas 1–3 Delores Dufner, OSB (USA), © 1985 Sisters of St. Benedict; stanzas 4–5 "Adoro te devote," attr. Thomas Aquinas (present-day Italy), 13th c.; trans. Omer Westendorf (USA), © World Library Publications
Music: plainsong, 13th c., *Processionale* (present-day France), 1697

460 From North and South, from East and West

THREE IN ONE CMD

G Am C G Am
1 From north and south, from east and west, O faithful
2 We lift our hearts, O liv - ing God, with thanks and
3 We thank you for your Word made flesh, our Sav - ior,
4 Pour out your Spir - it now, to bless these gifts of
G D G Am C G
peo - ple, come to share the feast that Christ pre - pares,
praise to you. Cre - a - tor of the u - ni - verse,
Je - sus Christ, whose dy - ing has de - stroyed our death,
bread and wine, and let them be a feast for us,
C Am G Bm D
where heav'n and earth are one. Come, all who hun - ger,
your love makes all things new. "Most ho - ly, ho - ly,
whose ris - ing gives us life. With grate - ful hearts we
your cov' - nant seal and sign. As Christ is pres - ent

Alternate tune: ELLACOMBE (#182 or #313).

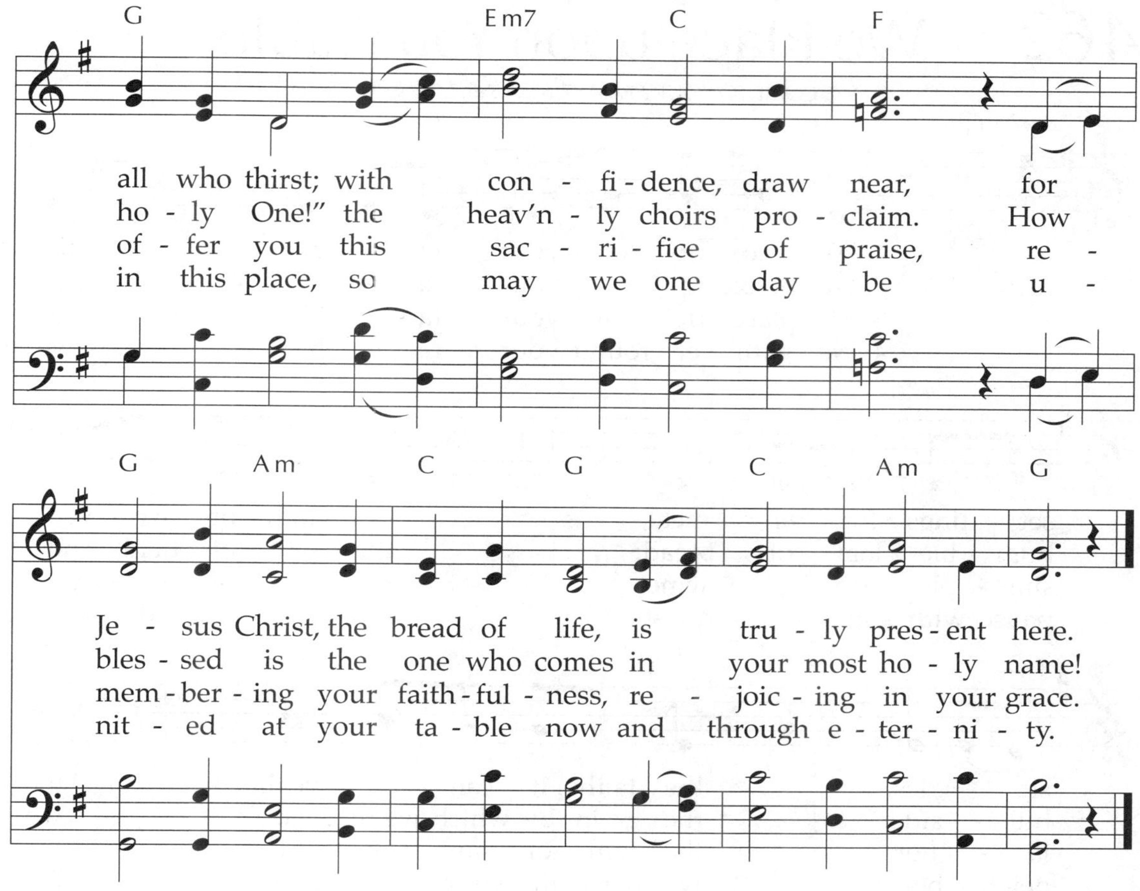
G Em7 C F
all who thirst; with con - fi - dence, draw near, for
ho - ly One!" the heav'n - ly choirs pro - claim. How
of - fer you this sac - ri - fice of praise, re -
in this place, so may we one day be u -
G Am C G C Am G
Je - sus Christ, the bread of life, is tru - ly pres - ent here.
bles - sed is the one who comes in your most ho - ly name!
mem - ber - ing your faith - ful - ness, re - joic - ing in your grace.
nit - ed at your ta - ble now and through e - ter - ni - ty.

Come to the Table of Grace 461

TABLE OF GRACE 7.7.10.7

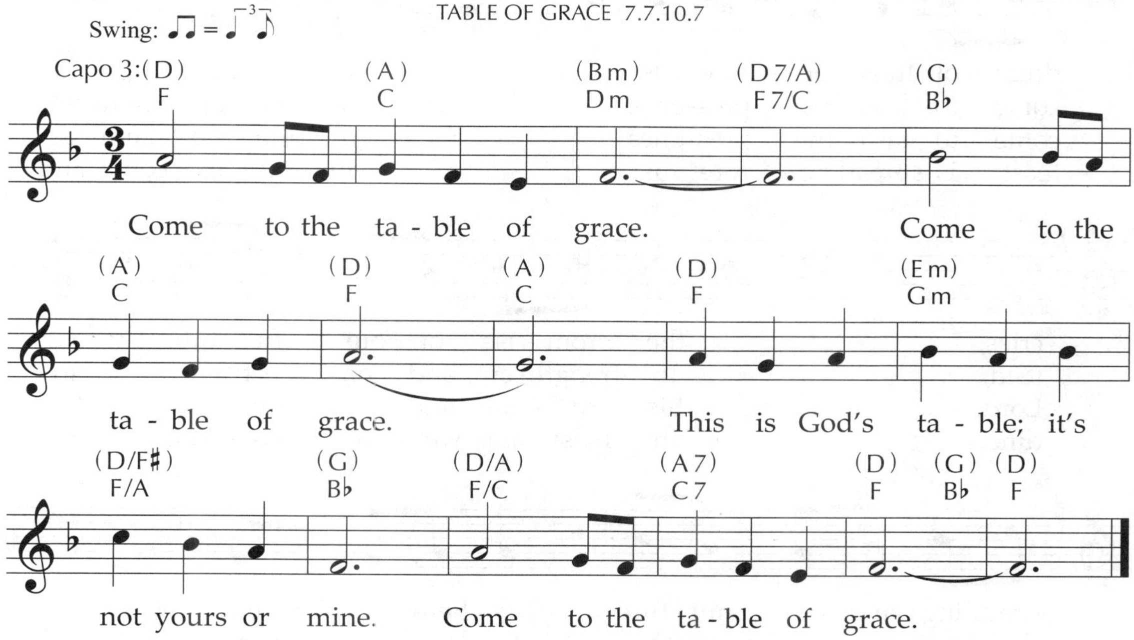
Swing:
Capo 3:(D) F (A) C (Bm) Dm (D7/A) F7/C (G) B♭
Come to the ta - ble of grace. Come to the
(A) C (D) F (A) C (D) F (Em) Gm
ta - ble of grace. This is God's ta - ble; it's
(D/F♯) F/A (G) B♭ (D/A) F/C (A7) C7 (D) F (G) B♭ (D) F
not yours or mine. Come to the ta - ble of grace.

2 Come to the table of peace . . .
3 Come to the table of love . . .
4 Come to the table of hope . . .
5 Come to the table of joy . . .

Text: Barbara Hamm (USA)
Music: Barbara Hamm

462 We Place upon Your Table

WE COME TO YOUR FEAST 7.6.7.6.7.6.7.7.6 with refrain

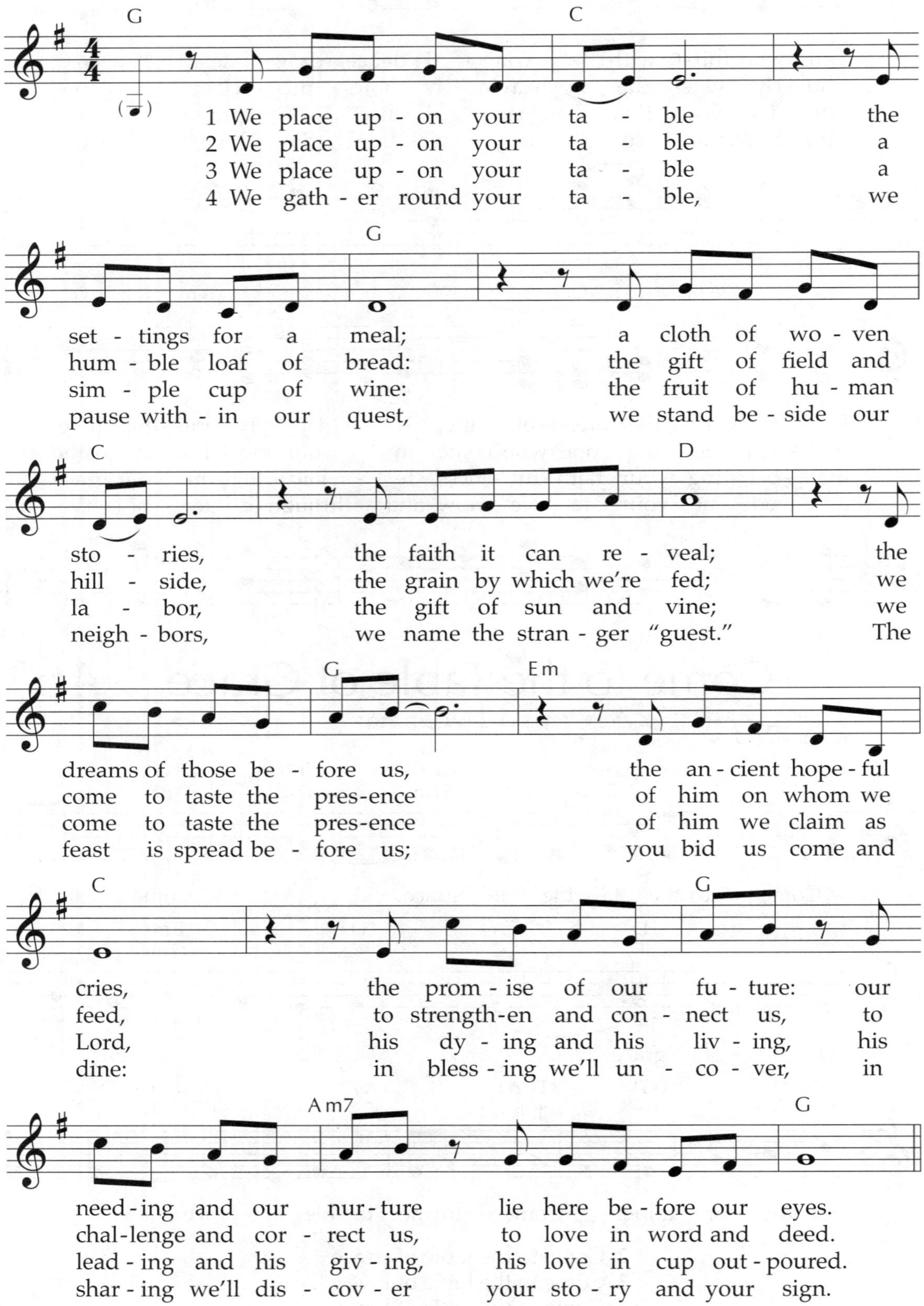
G C
1 We place up - on your ta - ble the
2 We place up - on your ta - ble a
3 We place up - on your ta - ble a
4 We gath - er round your ta - ble, we
G
set - tings for a meal; a cloth of wo - ven
hum - ble loaf of bread: the gift of field and
sim - ple cup of wine: the fruit of hu - man
pause with - in our quest, we stand be - side our
C D
sto - ries, the faith it can re - veal; the
hill - side, the grain by which we're fed; we
la - bor, the gift of sun and vine; we
neigh - bors, we name the stran - ger "guest." The
G Em
dreams of those be - fore us, the an - cient hope - ful
come to taste the pres - ence of him on whom we
come to taste the pres - ence of him we claim as
feast is spread be - fore us; you bid us come and
C G
cries, the prom - ise of our fu - ture: our
feed, to strength - en and con - nect us, to
Lord, his dy - ing and his liv - ing, his
dine: in bless - ing we'll un - co - ver, in
Am7 G
need - ing and our nur - ture lie here be - fore our eyes.
chal - lenge and cor - rect us, to love in word and deed.
lead - ing and his giv - ing, his love in cup out - poured.
shar - ing we'll dis - cov - er your sto - ry and your sign.

Text: Michael Joncas (USA), alt.
Music: Michael Joncas

Refrain
Melody
Harmony
C G Em A A7 D C G Am7 Am7/D G
We come to your feast, we come to your feast:
the young and the old, the fright-ened, the bold, the
great-est and the least.
We come to your feast, we come to your feast
with the fruit of our lands and the work of our hands,
we come to your feast.

463 Christ Jesus Lay

CHRIST LAG IN TODESBANDEN 8.7.8.7.7.8.7.4

1 Christ Je - sus lay in death's strong bands for our of - fens - es
2 It was a strange and dread-ful strife when life and death con -
3 Then let us keep this feast to - day that God has free - ly
giv - en, but now at God's right hand he stands and
tend - ed. The vic - to - ry re - mained with life, the
giv - en. The word of grace has swept a - way the
brings us life from heav - en. There - fore let us
reign of death is end - ed. So the scrip - ture
old and e - vil leav - en. Christ to - day will
all re - joice and sing to God with heart and voice loud
makes it plain that death by death's own sword is slain. Its
meet his own and faith will feed on him a - lone; the

Text: *Victimae Paschali*, (present-day Germany), ca. 11th c.; trans. Martin Luther (present-day Germany), "Christ lag in Todesbanden," *Eyn Enchiridion*, 1524; English trans. composite Richard Massie (England), *Martin Luther's Spiritual Songs*, 1854, Catherine Winkworth (England), *Lyra Germanica I*, 1855, and Johann Christian Jacobi (present-day Germany), *Psalmodia Germanica*, 1722

Music: medieval traditional; adapt. Johann Walther (present-day Germany), CHRIST IST ERSTANDEN, *Gesangbuchlein*, 1524; harm. J. S. Bach (present-day Germany), from Cantata No. 4, *Christ lag in Todesbanden*, ca. 1708

songs of hal - le - lu - jah!
sting is lost for - ev - er. Hal - le - lu - jah!
liv - ing bread of heav - en.

Somos pueblo que camina (We Are People on a Journey) 464

SOMOS PUEBLO 8.7 with refrain

E B B7 E
1 So - mos pue-blo que ca - mi - na por la sen-da del do - lor.
2 Los hu - mil-des y los po-bres in - vi - ta-dos son de Dios.
3 Los se-dien-tos de jus - ti - cia bus-can su li - be - ra - ción.
1 We are peo - ple on a jour-ney; pain is with us all the way.
2 God has sent the in - vi - ta - tion to the hum-ble and the poor.
3 All who tru - ly thirst for jus - tice seek their lib - er - a - tion here.

Refrain
E A E B7 E
A - cu - da-mos ju - bi - lo - sos a la san - ta co - mu - nión.
Joy - ful - ly we come to - geth - er at the ho - ly feast of God.

4 Este pan que Dios nos brinda alimenta nuestra‿unión.
5 Cristo‿aquí se‿hace presente; al reunirnos en su‿amor.

4 This is bread that God provides us, nourishing our unity.
5 Christ is ever present with us to unite us all in love.

Text: Spanish; Manuel Dávila (Nicaragua), *La Misa Popular Nicaragüense*, 20th c.; trans. Carolyn Jennings (USA),
Music: Manuel Dávila, *La Misa Popular Nicaragüense*, 20th c.

465 Prepare a Room for Me

SOUTHWELL SM

Capo 1: (Em) Fm (B) C (Em) Fm
1 "Pre - pare a room for me, your Sav - ior,
2 This room we have pre - pared; the ta - ble
3 "Where e - ven two or three have come the
4 Lord Christ, we seek the food your grace a -
5 "My prom - ise I will keep; your hun - ger
6 All thanks and praise to you, our Sav - ior,
(D) E♭ (G) A♭ (D) E♭ (D7) E♭7
Host and Priest, where I may gath - er
now is set. We wait your prom - ised
meal to share, un - seen, but liv - ing,
lone can give. We come with emp - ty,
will be fed, for in this meal I
Lord and Friend, that through this loaf and
(G) A♭ (D) E♭ (Am) B♭m (B) C (Em) Fm
you, my friends, to cel - e - brate the feast."
pres - ence, Lord, where we once more are met.
lov - ing still, I sure - ly will be there!"
hung'r - ing hearts that we may eat and live.
of - fer you my - self, the liv - ing bread!"
cup you share your love that has no end!

Chord symbols represent a simplified harmony.

The verses of this hymn may be sung in alternation between a soloist and the congregation.

Text: Herman G. Stuempfle Jr. (USA),
Music: W. Damon (England), *Psalmes of David*, 1579

The Bread We Break Is Telling 466

JONATHAN'S TUNE 7.6.7.6 D

G C2 D G D
1 The bread we break is tell - ing a great - er bro - ken - ness:
2 The bread we break is tell - ing a mend - ing that will come,
3 As light breaks in - to rain - bows to show the storm is past,
G C2 D G
the bro - ken hu - man na - ture that dared to build a cross,
sur - pas - sing all the break - ing that hu - man hands have done.
when bread broke, the dis - ci - ples could see the Lord at last.
C D G/B Am7 G/B Am7 D
and cru - ci - fy the Sav - ior who came to heal and mend;
For ho - ly love has shat - tered the tomb where Je - sus lay,
O Je - sus, wel - come, wel - come! The burn - ing hearts were true;
G C2 D G
un - til he comes in glo - ry, we break the bread a - gain.
and he was known when shar - ing the bread at close of day.
the bread and cup of bless - ing will make us one with you.

467 Taste and See

TASTE AND SEE Irregular

Refrain
F C/F B♭/F F F/A B♭9 F/A Gm11 C7
Taste and see, taste and see the good-ness of the Lord. O
F C/F B♭/F F B♭9 F/A Gm7 C7 F
Fine
taste and see, taste and see the good-ness of the Lord, of the Lord.
B♭/F F Csus C7 F2 Am7
3
1 I will bless the Lord at all
2 Glo - ri - fy the Lord with
3 Wor - ship the Lord, all you
B♭maj7 F/A Gm11 F/A
3
times. Praise shall al-ways be on my
me. To-geth-er let us all praise God's
peo-ple. You'll want for noth-ing if you
C9sus C7 F A7 A/C♯ Dm2
lips; my soul shall glo-ry in the Lord,
name. I called the Lord who an - swered me;
ask. Taste and see that the Lord is good;
Dm7/C B♭9 F/A Gm7 C7
3
To refrain
for God has been so good to me.
from all my trou-bles I was set free.
in God we need put all our trust.

Text: based on Psalm 34:1-10; James E. Moore (USA)
Music: James E. Moore

469 *1 Corinthians 11:23-26*

For I received from the Lord
what I also handed on to you,
that the Lord Jesus on the night
when he was betrayed
took a loaf of bread,
and when he had given thanks,
he broke it and said,
"This is my body that is for you.
Do this in remembrance of me."
In the same way he took the cup also,
after supper, saying,
"This cup is the new covenant
in my blood.
Do this, as often as you drink it,
in remembrance of me."
For as often as you eat this bread
and drink the cup,
you proclaim the Lord's death
until he comes.

470 *Luke 24:13-35 (excerpts)*

Two disciples were traveling
to a village called Emmaus.
While they were discussing
everything that had happened,
Jesus arrived and joined them
on their journey.
They were prevented from
recognizing him.
When they came to Emmaus,
Jesus went in to stay with them.
After taking a seat at the table,
Jesus took the bread,
blessed and broke it,
and gave it to them.
Their eyes were opened
and they recognized him,
but he disappeared from their sight.
They said to each other,
"Were not our hearts on fire when Jesus
spoke with us along the road?"
They got up and returned to Jerusalem,
where the eleven and their companions
were gathered together and saying,
"Christ really has risen!
He appeared to Simon!"
Then the two disciples described
what had happened along the road
and how Jesus was made known
to them in the breaking of bread.

471 *John 6:30-35*

The crowd said to Jesus,
"You must show us more miracles
if you want us to believe
you are the Messiah.
Give us bread every day,
as our ancestors had
while they journeyed
through the wilderness!
As the Scriptures say,
'Moses gave them bread
from heaven.'"
Jesus said,
"Truly, Moses did not give them
bread from heaven.
God gives you true bread
from heaven.
The true bread is sent by God
from heaven,
and gives life to the world."
They said,
"Give us that bread
every day of our lives!"
Jesus replied,
"I am the bread of life.
No one who comes to me
will ever be hungry again.
Those who believe in me
will never thirst."

472 *John 15:1-5*

Jesus said,
"I am the true vine.
God is the gardener.
God trims every branch
that bears fruit
so that it will bear even more fruit.
Remain in me,
just as I also remain in you.
No branch can bear fruit by itself.
It must remain in the vine.
In the same way, you cannot bear fruit
unless you remain in me.
I am the vine.
You are the branches.
If you remain in me,
and I in you,
you will bear much fruit."

Previous page: 468. *Communion*, Dona Park (Canada), 2018, digital illustration ⓦ

Haleluya! Pelo tsa rona (Hallelujah! We Sing Your Praises) 473

HALELUYA! PELO TSA RONA Irregular

Am G C G D
Ha - le - lu - ya! Pe - lo tsa ro - na, di tha - bi - le ka - o -
Hal - le - lu - jah! We sing your prais-es! All our hearts are filled with
Am G G7 Am G Em D
fe - la. Ha - le - lu - ya! Pe - lo tsa ro - na, di tha - bi - le
glad - ness! Hal - le - lu - jah! We sing your prais-es! All our hearts are
D7 G Am G C G D Am
Fine
ka - o - fe - la. Ke Mo - re - na Je - so, ya re du me - let -
filled with glad - ness! Je - sus Christ to us said: "I am wine, I am
G G7 Am G Em D D7 G
D.C.
seng, ya re du - me - let - seng ko tsa - mai - sa e - van - ge - di.
bread, I am wine, I am bread, give to all who thirst and hun - ger!"

Text: Sotho; South African traditional; trans. Anders Nyberg (Sweden)
Music: South African traditional; arr. Anders Nyberg

474 All Who Hunger, Gather Gladly

ALL WHO HUNGER 8.7.8.7 D

G2 D/G C/G G G/B
1 All who hun - ger, gath - er glad - ly; ho - ly
2 All who hun - ger, nev - er stran - gers, seek - er,
3 All who hun - ger, sing to - geth - er; Je - sus
C Am7 Dsus D G2 D/G
man - na is our bread. Come from wil - der -
be a wel - come guest. Come from rest - less -
Christ is liv - ing bread. Come from lone - li -
C/G G G/B C Am7
ness and wan - d'ring. Here, in truth, we will be
ness and roam - ing. Here, in joy, we keep the
ness and long - ing. Here, in peace, we have been
Dsus D F Em7 F Cmaj7
fed. You that yearn for days of full - ness,
feast. We that once were lost and scat - tered
led. Blest are those who from this ta - ble
Am7 G/B C Dsus D Am7/D
all a - round us is our food.
in com - mun - ion's love have stood.
live their days in grat - i - tude.
Refrain G D/G C/G Gsus G G/B G
Taste and see the grace e - ter - nal. Taste and
F Am7 Am7/D G D/G C/G C/D G
see that God is good.

Spirit, Do Your Work in Us 475

MARPECK 7.6.7.6

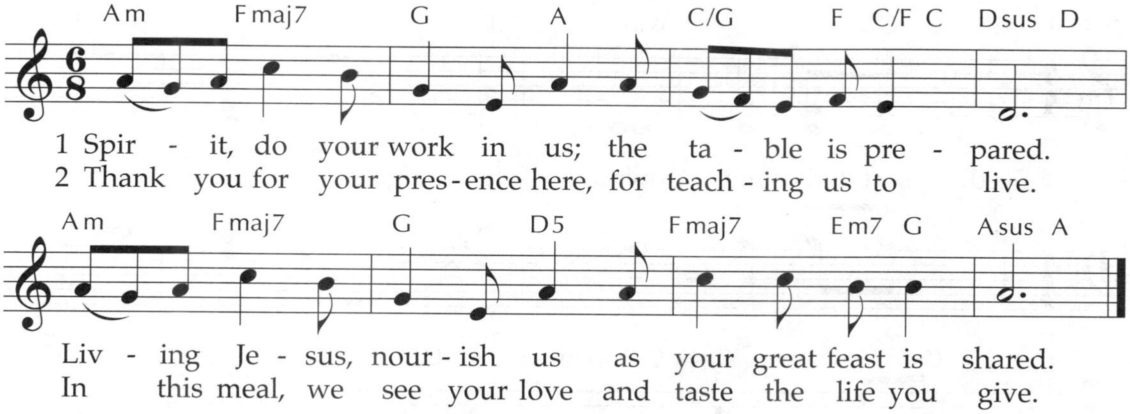
Am Fmaj7 G A C/G F C/F C Dsus D
1 Spir - it, do your work in us; the ta - ble is pre - pared.
2 Thank you for your pres - ence here, for teach - ing us to live.
Am Fmaj7 G D5 Fmaj7 Em7 G Asus A
Liv - ing Je - sus, nour - ish us as your great feast is shared.
In this meal, we see your love and taste the life you give.

Text: Adam M. L. Tice (USA), 2004, © 2015 GIA Publications, Inc.
Music: Chris Ángel (USA), © 2015, GIA Publications, Inc.

Eat This Bread (Coman de este pan) 476

EAT THIS BREAD Irregular

G C Am D
Eat this bread, drink this cup,
Co - man de es - te pan, be - ban de es - te cá - liz,
Bm Em Dsus D G D
come to me and nev - er be hun - gry. Eat this bread,
ven - gan y no ten - drán ham - bre. Co - man de es - te pan,
Em Bm C D G
drink this cup, trust in me and you will not thirst.
be - ban de es - te cá - liz, cre - an y no ten - drán sed.

Text: based on John 6:35; Robert J. Batastini (USA) and the Taizé Community (France), 1983, *Music from Taizé*, vol. 2, 1984; Spanish trans. anon.
Music: Jacques Berthier (France), *Music from Taizé*, vol. 2, 1984

477 Seed, Scattered and Sown

EKKLESIA Irregular

Refrain
Seed, scat-tered and sown, wheat, gath-ered and grown,
bread, bro-ken and shared as one, the liv-ing Bread of God.
Vine, fruit of the land, wine, work of our hands, one cup that is
shared by all, the liv-ing Cup, the liv-ing Bread of God.
Fine
1 Is not the bread we break a shar-ing in our Lord?
2 The seed which falls on rock will with-er and will die.
3 As wheat up-on the hills was gath-ered and was grown,

Text: based on *Didache* (Mediterranean), ca. 1st–2nd c.; Dan Feiten (USA), 1987, *Gather*, 1988
Music: Dan Feiten, 1987, *Gather*, 1988

E Am F G G7 *To refrain*

Is not the cup we bless the blood of Christ out - poured?
The seed with - in good ground will flow - er and have life.
so may the church of God be gath - ered in - to one.

I Come with Joy 478

DOVE OF PEACE CM extended

Capo 3: (D) F (Em) Gm (F♯m) Am (Em) Gm (D) F

1 I come with joy, a child of God, for - giv - en,
2 I come with Chris - tians far and near to find, as
3 As Christ breaks bread, and bids us share, each proud di -
4 The Spir - it of the ris - en Christ, un - seen, but
5 To - geth - er met, to - geth - er bound by all that

(Bm) Dm (A) C (D) F (Gmaj7) B♭maj7 (F♯m) Am (Bm) Dm (D) F

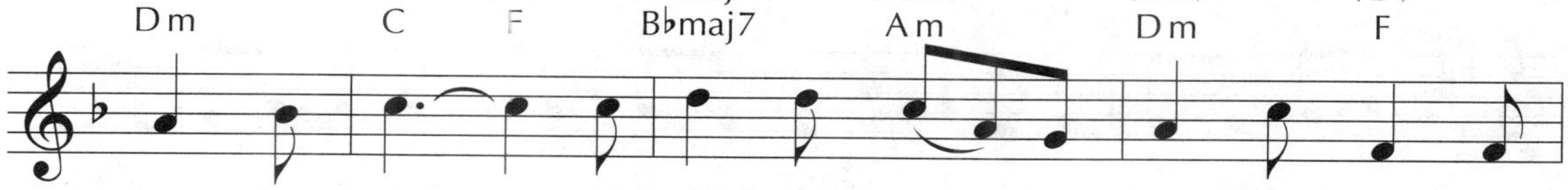

loved and free, the life of Je - sus to re - call, in
all are fed, the new com - mu - ni - ty of love in
vi - sion ends. The love that made us, makes us one, and
ev - er near, is in such friend - ship bet - ter known, a -
God has done, we'll go with joy, to give the world the

(Em7) Gm7 (F♯m) Am (G) B♭ (Gmaj7) B♭maj7 (A) C (A7) C7 (D) F

love laid down for me, in love laid down for me.
Christ's com - mun - ion bread, in Christ's com - mun - ion bread.
stran - gers now are friends, and stran - gers now are friends.
live a - mong us here, a - live a - mong us here.
love that makes us one, the love that makes us one.

Text: Brian Wren (England), 1968, rev. 1993, © 1971, rev. 1995 Hope Publishing Company
Music: American traditional (USA), *Southern Harmony*, 1854

479 Remembrance

OH HOW COULD IT BE Irregular

D Dmaj7
1 Oh, how could it be that my God would wel-come
(2 See his) bod - y, his blood; know that he has o - ver -
G/D Em9
me in - to this mys - te - ry, say, "Take this
come ev-'ry tri - al we will face. And none too
D Dmaj7
bread, take this wine"? Now the sim - ple made di - vine for
lost to be saved, none too bro - ken or a-shamed: all are
G/D Em9 D/F♯
an - y to re - ceive. By your mer - cy we come
wel-come in this place.
G2 A Em9 D/F♯
to your ta - ble. By your grace you are mak - ing us faith-
Refrain
G2 D Bm7 A
- ful. So we re - mem - ber you, and re-mem-
G2 D A D Bm7
- brance leads us to wor - ship. And as we wor - ship you,
A G2 D A
our wor - ship leads to com-mun - ion. We re-spond

Text: Matt Maher (Canada) and Matt Redman (England)
Music: Matt Maher and Matt Redman

Em7 D/F♯ Last time to Coda 1 G2 A
to your in - vi - ta - tion. We re-mem - ber
D Dmaj7 G/D Em9
you. 2 See his
2 G2 A D
- tion. We re-mem-ber you. Dy - ing, you de -
Bridge G A D G A
stroyed our death. Ris-ing, you re - stored our
Bm7 A
life. O Je-sus, come in glo - ry. O Je-sus, come in
G D A
glo - ry. O Je - sus, come in glo - ry.
G G2 To refrain
O Je-sus, come in glo - ry. So we re -
Coda G2 Em7 D/F♯ G2 Bm7 A
- tion. We re-spond to your in-vi-ta - tion. We re-mem-ber
D Dmaj7 G/D Em9 D
you.

480 I Am the Bread of Life (Yo soy el pan de vida)

I AM THE BREAD OF LIFE Irregular

English verses
A C♯m D
1 I am the bread of life. You who come to me
2 The bread that I will give is my flesh for the
3 Un - less you eat of the flesh of the
4 I am the res - ur - rec - tion, I
5 Yes, Lord, I be - lieve that you
E A C♯m D
shall not hun - ger, and who be - lieve in me shall not thirst.
life of the world, and if you eat of this bread,
Son of Man and drink of his blood, and
am the life. If you be - lieve in me,
are the Christ, the Son of God,
A D Bm E
No one can come to me un - less the Fa - ther beck - ons.
you shall live for - ev - er, you shall live for - ev - er.
drink of his blood, you shall not have life with - in you.
e - ven though you die, you shall live for - ev - er.
who has come in - to the world.
Refrain
A E A D E
And I will raise you up, and I will raise you up,
Yo los re - su - ci - ta - ré, Yo los re - su - ci - ta - ré,

Text: based on John 6:35–58 and 11:24–27; Suzanne Toolan (USA), *Music for the Requiem Mass*, 1966; Spanish trans. unknown, rev. Ronald F. Krisman (USA)
Music: Suzanne Toolan, *Music for the Requiem Mass*

A/C♯ D A E A
and I will raise ___ you up on the last ___ day.
Yo los re - su - ci - ta - ré en el dí - a fi - nal.

Spanish verses
A C♯m D
1 Yo soy el pan de ___ vi - da. A mí ven-gan: ___ no ten-drán
2 El pan que ___ yo da - ré ___ es mi car - ne, la vi - da del
3 Si us - te - des no co - men la ___ car - ne del Hi - jo del
4 Yo soy la ___ re - su - rrec - ción, ___ Yo ___ soy ___ la ___
5 Sí, Se - ñor, cre - e - mos que ___ tú‿e - res ___ el ___ Me -
E A C♯m D
ham - bre. En mí cre - an: no ten - drán sed. ___
mun - do. Los que co - men de‿es - te pan ___
Hom - bre, y no be - ben de ___ su san - gre, no
vi - da. Si en mí us - te - des cre - en, ___
sí - as, el ___ Hi - jo ___ de Dios, ___ que
A D Bm E Al estribillo
Na - die vie - ne‿a mí ___ si mi Pa - dre no lo‿a - tra - e.
vi - vi - rán por siem - pre, ___ vi - vi - rán por siem - pre.
be - ben de su san - gre, no po - drán te - ner mi vi - da.
aun - que ha - yan muer - to, ___ vi - vi - rán por siem - pre.
has ve - ni - do‿al mun - do ___ pa - ra re - di - mir - nos.

481 In the Singing, in the Silence

CHUNG CHI 8.8.8.8 with refrain

1 In the sing - ing, in the si - lence, in the
1 在 歌 唱 中, 在 静 默 中, 伸 雙
1 Zai ge - chang zhong, zai jing - mo zhong, shen shuang-
2 In the ques - tion, in the an - swer, in the
hands ex - pec - tant o - pen, in the bless - ing, in the
手 正 迫 切 期 待, 祝 謝 餅 杯, 犧 牲
shou zheng po - qie qi - dai, zhu xie bing bei, xi - sheng
mo - ment of ac - cept - ance, in the heart's cry, in the
break - ing, in the Pres - ence at this ta - ble,
擘 開, 主 於 聖 桌 親 自 臨 在,
bo kai, Zhu yu sheng zhuo qin - zi lin zai,
heal - ing, in the cir - cle of your peo - ple,
Refrain
Je - sus Christ, Je - sus Christ, be the wine of grace:
主 耶 穌, 主 基 督, 做 我 救 恩 聖 杯:
Zhu Ye - su, Zhu Ji - du, zuo wo jiu - en sheng bei:
Je - sus Christ, Je - sus Christ, be the bread of peace.
主 耶 穌, 主 基 督, 世 界 和 平 聖 餅.
Zhu Ye - su, Zhu Ji - du, shi - jie he - ping sheng bing.

2 在疑惑中, 在答案中,
相接納, 互安慰時刻,
療傷醫治, 悲傷哭泣,
或在主內温馨團契, Refrain

2 *Zai yihuo zhong, zai daan zhong,*
xiang jiena, hu anwei shike,
liaoshang yizhi, beishang kuqi,
huo zai Zhu nei wenxin tuanqi, Refrain

Text: Shirley Erena Murray (Aotearoa New Zealand), 1994, ; Mandarin trans. I-to Loh (Taiwan),
Music: I-to Loh,

Let Us Break Bread Together 482

BREAK BREAD TOGETHER 10.10 with refrain

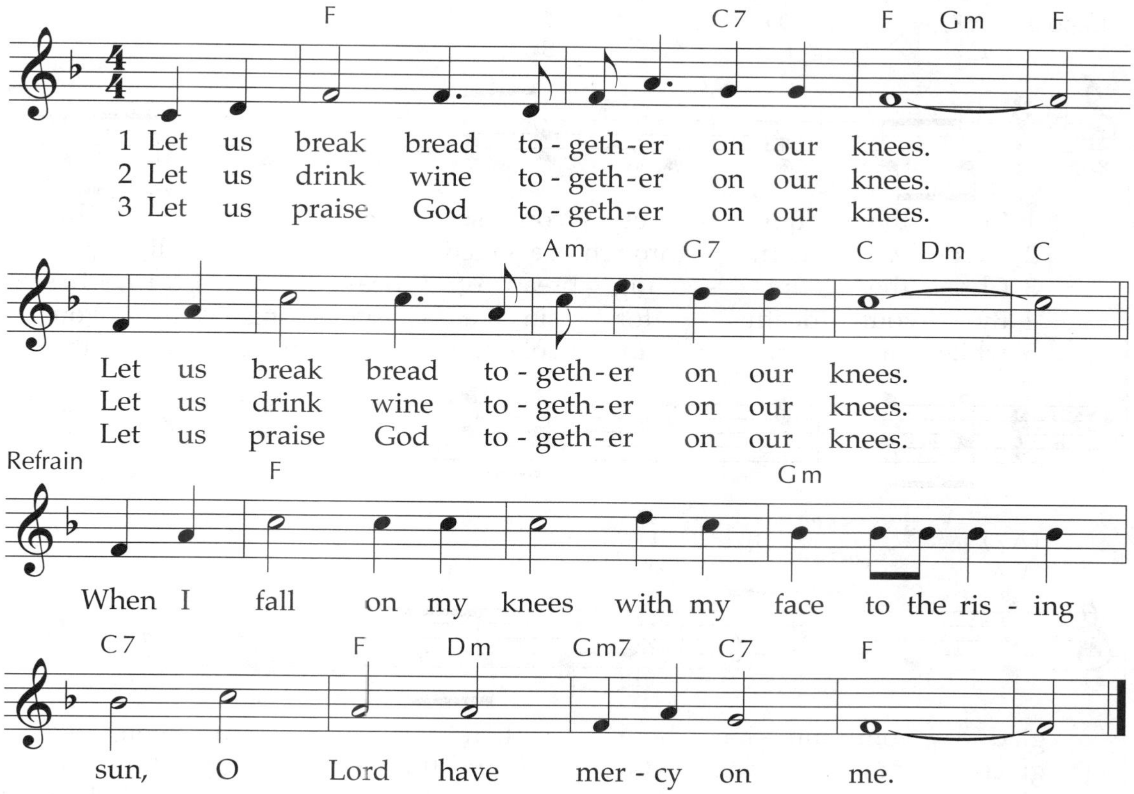
1 Let us break bread to-geth-er on our knees.
2 Let us drink wine to-geth-er on our knees.
3 Let us praise God to-geth-er on our knees.
Let us break bread to-geth-er on our knees.
Let us drink wine to-geth-er on our knees.
Let us praise God to-geth-er on our knees.
Refrain
When I fall on my knees with my face to the ris-ing
sun, O Lord have mer-cy on me.

Text: African American spiritual (USA)
Music: African American spiritual

Word and Sign 483

LYDIA 3.3.3.3.3.3.3.3

Word and sign; pulse and breath; bread and wine; life and death;
hear the call: calm your fear. Through it all, Christ is here.

484 In the Quiet Consecration

STENKA RAZIN 8.7.8.7

Capo 3: (A7) C7 (D) F (G) B♭ (A) C
1 In the qui - et con - se - cra - tion of this
2 Here we learn through sa - cred sym - bol all your
3 Christ, the liv - ing bread of heav - en, Christ, whose
4 By your death for sin a - ton - ing, by your
5 while a - far in sol - emn ra - diance shines the
(A7) C7 (D) F (G) B♭
glad com - mun - ion hour, here we rest in you, O
grace can be and do by this won - der - ful in -
blood is drink in - deed, here by faith and with thanks -
res - ur - rec - tion life, hold us fast in joy - ful
feast that is to come— af - ter con - flict, heav - en's
(D) F (Bm7) Dm7 (Em) Gm (A7) C7 (D) F
Je - sus, taste your love and touch your pow'r.
dwell - ing— you in us, and we in you.
giv - ing in our hearts on you we feed.
un - ion, strength - en us to face the strife;
glo - ry, your great feast of love and home.

Text: Constance Coote (England), 1910, *At His Table*, 1913
Music: Russian traditional; harm. Cynthia Neufeld Smith (USA),

Put Peace into Each Other's Hands 485

ST. COLUMBA 8.7.8.7 Iambic

Capo 3: (C) E♭ (G) B♭ (C) E♭
1 Put peace in - to each oth - er's hands and like a
2 Put peace in - to each oth - er's hands with lov - ing
3 Put peace in - to each oth - er's hands like bread we
4 Put Christ in - to each oth - er's hands to share love's
(F) A♭ (C) E♭ (G) B♭ (Am) Cm (C) E♭
treas - ure hold - it, pro - tect it like a
ex - pec - ta - tion; be gen - tle in your
break for shar - ing; look peo - ple warm - ly
deep - est meas - ure; in love make peace, give
(Em7) Gm7 (Am) Cm (C) E♭ (G) B♭ (C) E♭
can - dle flame, with ten - der - ness en - fold it.
words and ways, in touch with God's cre - a - tion.
in the eye: our life is meant for car - ing.
peace a chance, and share it like a treas - ure.

For communion:
As at communion, shape your hands
into a waiting cradle;
the gift of Christ receive, revere,
united round the table.

Text: Fred Kaan (England),
Music: Irish traditional, *Irish Church Hymnal*, ca. 1873; harm. Charles Villiers Stanford (England), *The English Hymnal*, 1906

486 Great God, the Giver of All Good

RETREAT LM

C F C G7
Great God, the giv - er of all good, ac - cept our thanks and
C G C G
bless this food. Grace, health, and strength to us af - ford, through
C F G7 C F Dm7 C
Je - sus Christ, our ris - en Lord. A - men.

Text: John Skinner (England), ca. 1867, *A Book of Praise for Home and School*, 1872, alt.
Music: Thomas Hastings (USA), *Juvenile Songs*, 1841

487 Gracias, Señor (Thank You, O God)

GRACIAS SEÑOR Irregular

D A7 Bm D7 G A7
Gra - cias, Se - ñor, por el pan, y da pan a los que tie - nen
Thank you, O God, for this bread. And give food to ev - 'ry - one who
F♯m Bm7 Em A7
ham - bre, y ham - bre de jus - ti - cia a los que te - ne - mos
hun - gers, and hun - ger for your jus - tice to those who_ have their
D Bm A7 D
pan. Gra - cias, Se - ñor, por el pan.
food. Thank you, O God, for this bread.

Text: Spanish; Latin American traditional; English trans. J. Nelson Kraybill (USA), 2011,
Music: Latin American traditional; acc. Marilyn Houser Hamm, 2020

God Is Great and God Is Good 488

HENDON 7.7.7.7.7

G D G Em C Am
God is great and God is good— we give thanks and
G D7 G D G C G
share our food. By your hands we all are fed; give us, God, our
D G D Em D G C G/D D G C G
dai - ly bread, give us, God, our dai - ly bread. A - men.

Text: anon., ca. 19th c.; adapt. Mennonite Worship and Song Committee, 2019
Music: Henri Abraham César Malan (Switzerland), 1827; harm. Lowell Mason (USA), *Carmina Sacra*, 1841

Bless This Food and Bless Your People 489

TABLE GRACE 8.6

Canon

1 2 3 4
Bless this food and bless your peo - ple. God, be with us. A - men.

Text: James E. Clemens (USA), 2008
Music: James E. Clemens, 2008

490 Jesus Took a Towel

JESUS TOOK A TOWEL Irregular

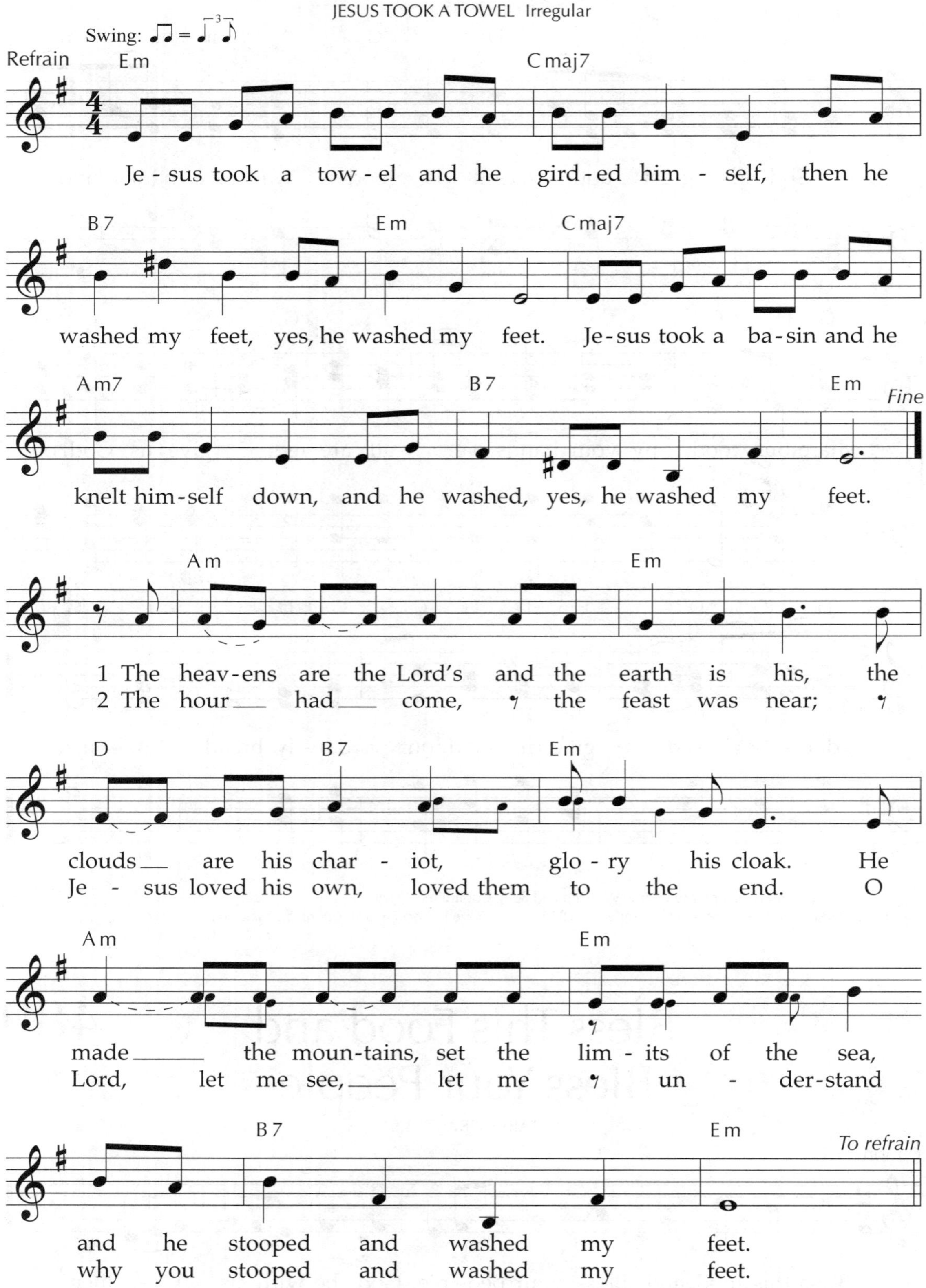
Swing:
Refrain
Em
Cmaj7
Je - sus took a tow - el and he gird - ed him - self, then he
B7
Em
Cmaj7
washed my feet, yes, he washed my feet. Je - sus took a ba - sin and he
Am7
B7
Em
Fine
knelt him - self down, and he washed, yes, he washed my feet.
Am
Em
1 The heav - ens are the Lord's and the earth is his, the
2 The hour had come, the feast was near;
D
B7
Em
clouds are his char - iot, glo - ry his cloak. He
Je - sus loved his own, loved them to the end. O
Am
Em
made the moun - tains, set the lim - its of the sea,
Lord, let me see, let me un - der - stand
B7
Em
To refrain
and he stooped and washed my feet.
why you stooped and washed my feet.

Text: based on John 13; Chrysogonus Waddell, OCSO (USA), *Worship III*, 1986
Music: Chrysogonus Waddell, OCSO, *Worship III*, 1986; acc. Randall L. Spaulding (USA), 1992

Christ, on the Night He Was Betrayed 491

ROCKINGHAM OLD LM

E♭ B♭7 E♭ A♭ E♭
1 Christ, on the night he was be - trayed, for us a
2 Be - fore he suf - fered, he de - sired to show us
3 Such gen - tle kind - ness did he show with towel and
4 "If I have done this un - to you, you ought to
A♭ E♭ B♭ E♭ B♭ F B♭
plain ex - am - ple made. The Pas - chal feast had
all what love re - quired. The hon - ored teach - er
ba - sin, stoop - ing low! When all were washed, he
serve each oth - er, too. And if my ser - vants
E♭ F7 B♭ E♭ Fm E♭ B♭ Cm A♭ B♭7 E♭
been pre - pared, and with his friends he free - ly shared.
left his seat and knelt to wash his ser - vant's feet.
stood to ask that they re - peat this hum - ble task.
you would be, o - bey my word and fol - low me."

Text: *A Selection of Psalms, Hymns, and Spiritual Songs* (Mennonite, USA), 1847, alt.
Music: *Supplement to Psalmody*, ca. 1780; adapt. Edward Miller (England), 1790

Ubi caritas (Where True Love) 492

UBI CARITAS 12.12.12.12 with refrain

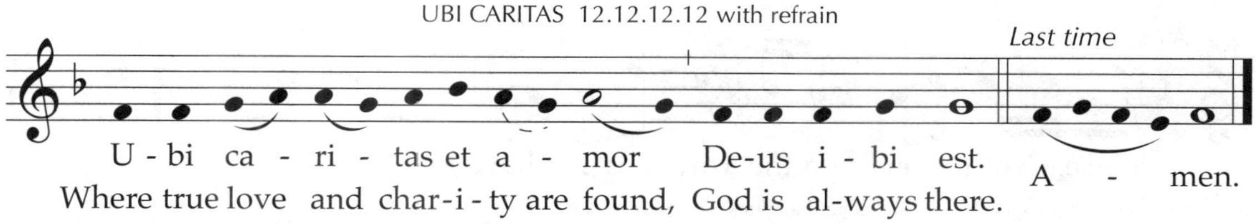
Last time
U - bi ca - ri - tas et a - mor De-us i - bi est.
Where true love and char-i - ty are found, God is al-ways there.
A - men.

Verses can be found in the accompaniment edition.

Text: Latin; 8th–9th c.; trans. Richard Proulx (USA), 1975
Music: chant, mode VI, 8th–9th c.

493 All the Room Was Hushed and Still

LOVE EACH OTHER Irregular

1 All the room was hushed and still,
2 Let the room be hushed and still,
and when the bowl was filled he stooped to wash their
let us go to where he kneels and join him as he
feet. And when it was com - plete, he said,
serves, and learn his ways of love. He said,
"This is what I'm ask-ing you to do; this is why I'm kneel-ing here be-
side you; this is what I want my church to be; this is what I
want the world to see— who it is you fol - low."
Refrain
Love each oth - er, one an-oth - er. Love each oth - er in the
way that I have loved you. Walk to-geth - er, and what-ev - er comes,
love each oth - er in the way that I have loved you.

Text: based on John 13:1–17, 34–35; Graham Kendrick (England)
Music: Graham Kendrick

Gravity of Love

494

GRAVITY OF LOVE 8.10.8.10 with refrain

G/B C D Em
1 I lift my eyes up to the hills. This my
2 We lift our eyes up to the hills. When will
C D C/E D/F♯
morn - ing song, where my strength comes from.
our help come? God, we cry, "How long?"
G/B C D Em
I lift my eyes up to the hills. This my
We lift our eyes up to the hills. E - ven
C D C/E D/F♯
eve - ning song, where my help comes from.
as we run, hope is chas - ing us.
Refrain
G Dsus Em C
This is the grav - i - ty of love; just as the moon fol-lows the
G Dsus G/B C Dsus D
sun, you're all a - round me, you're hold - ing ev - 'ry - thing.
G Dsus D Em C
This is the hope of ev - 'ry land; just as the u - ni - verse ex-
G/D Dsus D G/B C Dsus
pands, your love is reach - ing, you're hold - ing ev - 'ry - thing.
G D Em C2 G/D D C2

Text: John Arndt (USA), David Gungor (USA), and Matt Maher (Canada)
Music: John Arndt, David Gungor, and Matt Maher

495 Morning Has Broken

BUNESSAN 5.5.5.4 D

C
Dm/F G
F C
1 Morn-ing has bro - ken like the first morn - ing; black-bird has
2 Sweet the rain's new fall, sun-lit from heav - en, like the first
3 Mine is the sun - light, mine is the morn - ing, born of the
C/E F C
G7
C
Am F C
spo - ken like the first bird. Praise for the sing - ing, praise for the
dew - fall on the first grass. Praise for the sweet - ness of the wet
one light E - den saw play. Praise with e - la - tion, praise ev - 'ry
Am D C
Em Am Dm/F G
C
morn - ing, praise for them, spring - ing fresh from the Word.
gar - den, sprung in com - plete - ness where God's feet pass.
morn - ing, God's re - cre - a - tion of the new day.

Text: Eleanor Farjeon (England), *Enlarged Songs of Praise*, 1931, alt.,

Music: Scottish Gaelic traditional, *Songs and Hymns of the Gael*, 1888; harm. Martin Shaw (England), 1931, alt.,

I Owe the Lord a Morning Song 496

GRATITUDE CM

G C G/D G D
1 I owe the Lord a morn - ing song of
2 God kept me safe an - oth - er night; I
3 Keep me from dan - ger and from sin, help
4 Keep me un - til you call me hence, where
G A7 D G D G C
grat - i - tude and praise, for the kind mer - cy
see an - oth - er day. Now, Ho - ly Spir - it,
me your will to do, so that my heart be
nev - er night can be, and save me, God, for
G/D G G7 C G/D D7 G
free - ly shown in length - 'ning out my days.
as the light, di - rect me in your way.
pure with - in, and I your good - ness know.
Je - sus' sake; he shed his blood for me.

Chord symbols represent a simplified harmony.

Text: Amos Herr (USA), *Hymns and Tunes . . .*, 1890, alt.
Music: Amos Herr, *Hymns and Tunes . . .*, 1890

497 Hallelujah! schöner Morgen (Hallelujah! Fairest Morning!)

HARWELL 8.7.8.7.7.7 with refrain

G D
Hal - le - lu - jah! schö - ner Mor - gen, schö - ner,
1 Hal - le - lu - jah! fair - est morn - ing! Fair - er
2 In the glad - ness of God's wor - ship we will
3 Let the day with you be end - ed, as with
G D7 G
als man den - ken mag! Heu - te fühl ich kei - ne
than our words can say! Down we lay the heav - y
seek our joy to - day. It is then we learn the
you it has be - gun; and your bless - ing, God, be
D G D7 G
Sor - gen, denn das ist ein lie - ber Tag,
bur - den of our toil and care to - day,
full - ness of the grace for which we pray,
grant - ed, till earth's days and weeks are done;

Text: German; Jonathan Krause (present-day Poland), 1732; trans. Jane Borthwick (Scotland), 1853
Music: Lowell Mason (USA), 1840

D7
der durch sei - ne Lieb - lich - keit
1 while this morn of joy and love
2 when the word of life is giv'n,
3 that at last your ser - vants may
der durch sei - ne Lieb - lich - keit recht das
1 while this morn of joy and love brings fresh
2 when the word of life is giv'n, like the
3 that at last your ser - vants may keep e -
G
recht das In - ner - ste er - freut.
brings fresh vig - or from a - bove.
like the Sav - ior's voice from heav'n.
keep e - ter - nal Sab - bath day.
Hal - le-
In - ner - ste er - freut.
vig - or from a - bove.
Sav - ior's voice from heav'n.
ter - nal Sab - bath day.
D G D7 G
lu - jah! Hal - le - lu - jah! Hal - le - lu - jah! A - men!

498 清早起來看 Qing zao qi lai kan (Golden Breaks the Dawn)

LE P'ING 5.5.5.5 D

Capo 3: (D) (A) (Bm) (D) (Bm7) (D) (A7) (D) (A)
F C Dm F Dm7 F C7 F C
清 早 起 來 看, 紅 日 出 東 方,
懇 求 聖 天 父, 時 常 保 守 我,
1 Qing zao qi lai kan, hong ri chu dong fang;
2 Ken qiu sheng Tian Fu, jiang wo tuo bao cun,
1 Gold - en breaks the dawn; comes the east - ern sun
2 Ho - ly, liv - ing God, keep me safe to - day;
(D) (A) (Bm) (D) (Bm7) (D) (A) (Bm)(Em) (Dsus) (D)
F C Dm F Dm7 F C Dm Gm Fsus F
雄 壯 像 勇 士, 美 好 像 新 郎;
行 為 能 良 善, 顏 色 會 和 溫,
xiong zhuang xiang yong shi, mei hao xiang xin lang;
xing wei neng liang shan, yan se hui he wen,
like a rid - er strong, set the course to run.
though I wea - ry plod, make me kind, I pray.
(Em) (Bm) (Em) (A) (D) (A)
Gm Dm Gm C F C
天 高 飛 鳥 過, 地 闊 野 花 香;
樂 得 布 衣 暖, 不 嫌 麥 飯 粗,
tian gao fei niao guo, di kuo ye hua xiang;
le de bu yi nuan, bu xian mai fan cu,
Birds a - bove me fly; flow - ers bloom be - low;
Give me dai - ly bread, while I do my part;
(A7) (D) (G) (D) (Bm) (A) (D)
C7 F B♭ F Dm C F
照 我 勤 工 作, 天 父 有 恩 光。
千 千 萬 萬 事, 樣 樣 主 幫 扶。
cu wo qin gong zuo, Tian Fu you en guang.
qian qian wan wan shi, yang yang Zhu bang fu.
through the earth and sky God's great mer - cies flow.
bright skies o - ver - head, glad - ness in my heart.

Text: Mandarin; Tzu-chen Chao (China), 1931; paraphr. Frank W. Price (USA), 1953, alt.
Music: Te-ngai Hu (China), 1934; arr. Bliss Wiant (USA), 1934

In the Morning When I Rise 499

GIVE ME JESUS 6.6.6.4 with refrain

Capo 1: (G9) A♭9 (C) D♭ (G9) A♭9 (C) D♭ (G) A♭ (C) D♭
1 In the morn-ing when I rise, in the morn-ing when I
2 Dark mid-night was my cry, dark mid-night was my
3 I heard the mourn-er say, I heard the mourn-er
4 Oh, when I come to die, oh, when I come to
(G7) A♭7 (C) D♭ (Am) B♭m (D7) E♭7 (G7) A♭7 (C) D♭ (F) G♭ (C) D♭
rise, in the morn-ing when I rise, give me Je - sus.
cry, dark mid-night was my cry, give me Je - sus.
say, I heard the mourn-er say, give me Je - sus.
die, oh, when I come to die, give me Je - sus.
Refrain
(G) A♭ (G7) A♭7 (C) D♭ (C7) D♭7 (E7) F7
Give me Je - sus, give me Je - sus. You may
(F) G♭ (C) D♭ (G7) A♭7 (C) D♭ (F) G♭ (C) D♭
have all this world, give me Je - sus.

Text: African American spiritual (USA)
Music: African American spiritual; arr. Wendell Whalum (USA),

500 O Splendor of God's Glory Bright

SPLENDOR PATERNAE LM

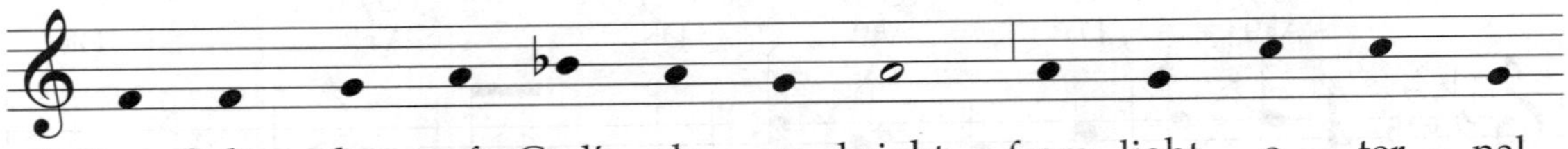

1 O Splen - dor of God's glo - ry bright, from light e - ter - nal
2 Come, ver - y Sun of heav - en's love, in last - ing ra - diance
3 Con - firm our will to do the right, and keep our hearts from
4 Be hal - low'd this and ev - 'ry day; let meek - ness be our
5 O Christ, with each re - turn - ing morn, thine im - age to our

bring - ing light, light's foun - tain and e - ter - nal spring,
from a - bove, and pour the Ho - ly Spir - it's ray
en - vy's blight. Let faith its ea - ger fires re - new,
morn - ing ray, and faith - ful love our noon - day light,
hearts is borne. Oh, may we ev - er clear - ly see

true Day, all days il - lu - min - ing.
on all we think or do to - day.
and hate the false and love the true.
our hope, our sun - set, calm and bright.
our Sav - ior and our God in thee. A - men.

Text: Ambrose of Milan (present-day Italy), "Splendor paternae gloriae," 4th c.; trans. composite
Music: Sarum plainsong (England), *Sarum Antiphonal*, 13th c.

501 Ngayong nagdadapit hapon (When Twilight Comes)

DAPIT HAPON Irregular

1 Nga - yong nag - da - da - pit ha - pon at lu -
2 No - on din ay da - pit ha - pon at nag -
3 Nga - yong nag - da - da - pit ha - pon at lu -

1 When twi - light comes and the sun sets, moth - er
2 Je - sus, our sav - ior and rab - bi, called the
3 So gath - er round once a - gain, friends, touched by

Text: Filipino; Moises Andrade (Philippines); trans. and paraphr. James Minchin (Australia), © 1990 (admin. Asian Institute for Liturgy and Music)
Music: Francisco Feliciano (Philippines), © 1990 Francisco Feliciano (admin. Asian Institute for Liturgy and Music); arr. © 2006 Augsburg Fortress

B7 Em C
mu - lu - bog ang a - raw, hu - ma - ha - pon
wa - wa - kas ang a - raw, nag ha - pu - nan
mu - lu - bog ang a - raw, ang mga ma - gu -
hen pre - pares for night's rest. As her brood shel - ters
twelve to share his last meal. As the hen tends her
fad - ing glow of sun's gold, and re - count all our
Em
ang i - na - hin at ang kan - yang ma - nga i - na -
ang gu - ro at pa - ti kan - yang ma - nga a - la -
lang at ang mga a - nak ay nag - ha - ha - pu -
un - der her wings, she gives the love of God to her
young, so for them he spent him - self to seek and to
frail hu - man hopes: the dreams of young and sto - ries of
B7 G Em Am
kay. Ti - ni - ti - pon u - pang mag - sa - lo
gad. Nag - ti - pon si - la at nag - sa - lo
nan, Nag - ti - ti - pon at nag - sa - sa - lo
nest. Oh! what joy to feel her warm heart - beat
heal. Oh! what joy to be with Christ Je - sus,
old. Oh, what joy to pray close to - geth - er,
B7 Em
sa a - lab ng pag - ma - ma - hal, sa pag -
sa ti - na - pay at sa a - lak, sa pi -
sa li - ga - ya't pag - di - ri - wang, Sa A -
and be near her all night long; so the
hear his voice, oh! sheer de - light, and re -
kneel - ing as one fam - i - ly, by a
Am6 B7 Em
lu - kob ng pak - pak ng ma - pag - pa - lang ka - may.
ging ng bu - hay n'yang i - ni - a - lay sa la - hat.
ma't A - nak na Diyos, Diyos E - spi - ri - tung Ba - nal.
young can find re - pose, then re - new to - mor - row's song.
ceive his ser - vant care: all be - fore the com - ing night.
moth - er's love em - braced in the bless - ed Trin - i - ty.

502 Abide with Me

EVENTIDE 10.10.10.10

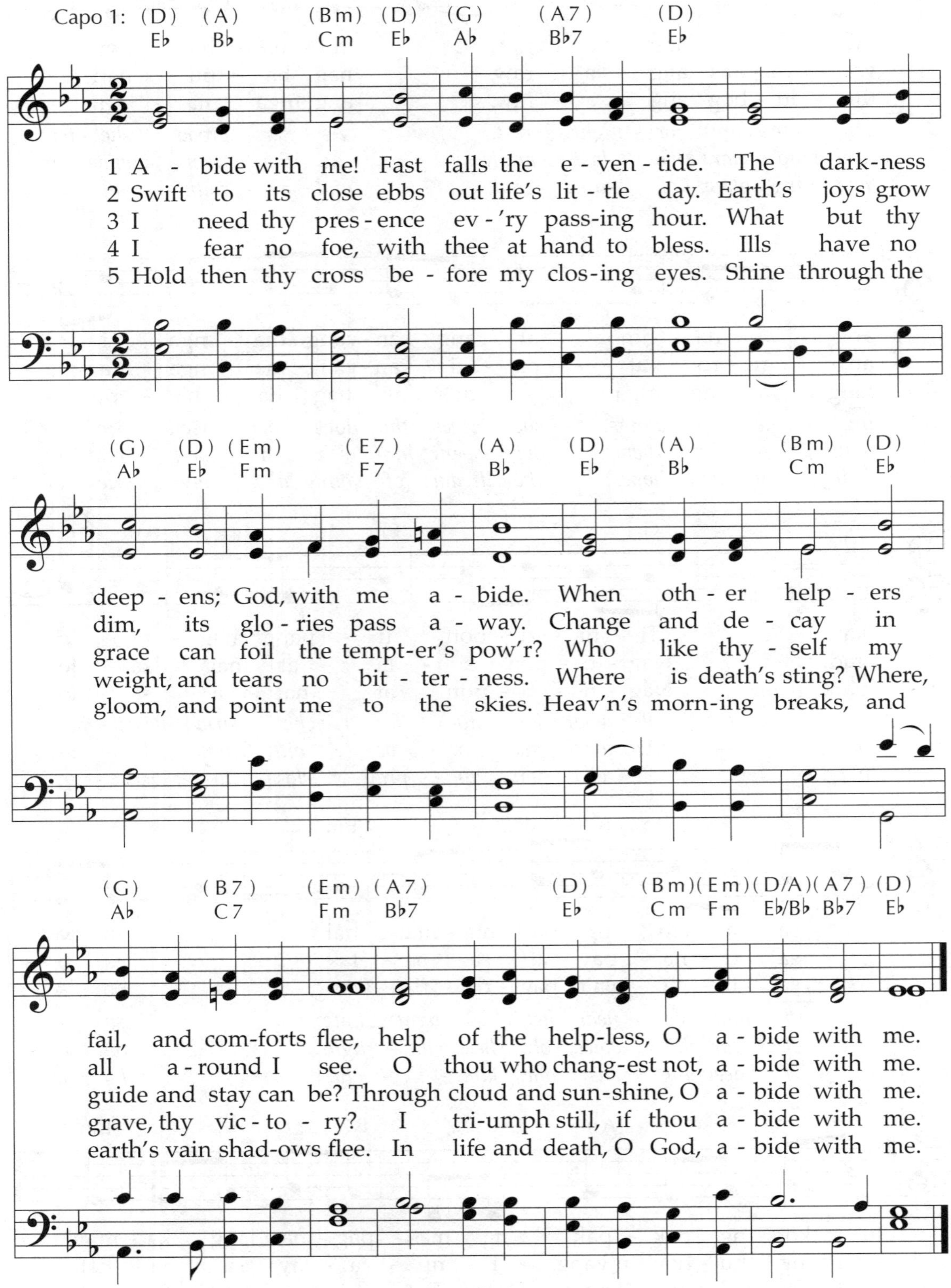
Capo 1: (D) (A) (Bm) (D) (G) (A7) (D)
Eb Bb Cm Eb Ab Bb7 Eb
1 A - bide with me! Fast falls the e - ven - tide. The dark-ness
2 Swift to its close ebbs out life's lit - tle day. Earth's joys grow
3 I need thy pres - ence ev - 'ry pass-ing hour. What but thy
4 I fear no foe, with thee at hand to bless. Ills have no
5 Hold then thy cross be - fore my clos-ing eyes. Shine through the
(G) (D) (Em) (E7) (A) (D) (A) (Bm) (D)
Ab Eb Fm F7 Bb Eb Bb Cm Eb
deep - ens; God, with me a - bide. When oth - er help - ers
dim, its glo - ries pass a - way. Change and de - cay in
grace can foil the tempt-er's pow'r? Who like thy - self my
weight, and tears no bit - ter - ness. Where is death's sting? Where,
gloom, and point me to the skies. Heav'n's morn-ing breaks, and
(G) (B7) (Em) (A7) (D) (Bm)(Em)(D/A)(A7) (D)
Ab C7 Fm Bb7 Eb Cm Fm Eb/Bb Bb7 Eb
fail, and com-forts flee, help of the help-less, O a - bide with me.
all a - round I see. O thou who chang-est not, a - bide with me.
guide and stay can be? Through cloud and sun-shine, O a - bide with me.
grave, thy vic - to - ry? I tri-umph still, if thou a - bide with me.
earth's vain shad-ows flee. In life and death, O God, a - bide with me.

Text: Henry F. Lyte (Scotland), 1847, *Remains of Henry Francis Lyte*, 1850, alt.
Music: William H. Monk (England), *Hymns Ancient and Modern*, 1861

Now, on Land and Sea Descending 503

VESPER HYMN 8.7.8.7.8.6.8.7

1 Now, on land and sea de-scend-ing, brings the night its peace pro-found.
2 Soon as dies the sun-set glo - ry, stars of heav'n shine out a - bove,
3 Now, our wants and bur-dens leav-ing to our God who cares for all,
4 As the dark-ness deep-ens o'er us, lo! E - ter - nal stars a - rise.
Let our ves - per hymn be blend-ing with the ho - ly calm a - round.
tell - ing still the an-cient sto - ry— their Cre - a - tor's end - less love.
cease we fear-ing, cease we griev-ing; touched by God our bur-dens fall.
Hope and faith and love rise glo-rious, shin-ing in the Spir - it's skies.
Ju - bi - la - te! Ju - bi - la - te! Ju - bi - la - te! A - men!
Let our ves-per hymn be blend-ing with the ho - ly calm a-round.
Tell - ing still the an - cient sto-ry— their Cre - a - tor's change-less love.
Cease we fear-ing, cease we griev-ing; touched by God our bur-dens fall.
Hope and faith and love rise glo-rious, shin - ing in the Spir-it's skies.

Chord symbols represent a simplified harmony.

Text: Samuel Longfellow (USA), *Vespers*, 1859
Music: John A. Stevenson (Ireland), *A Selection of Popular National Airs*, 1818

504 Joyous Light of Heavenly Glory

JOYOUS LIGHT 8.7.8.7 D

1 Joy-ous light of heav'n-ly glo - ry, lov-ing glow of God's own face,
2 In the stars that grace the dark-ness, in the blaz - ing sun of dawn,
3 You who made the heav-en's splen-dor, ev'-ry danc-ing star of night,
you who sing cre - a-tion's sto - ry, shine on ev-'ry land and race.
in the light of peace and wis-dom, we can hear your qui-et song.
make us shine with gen-tle jus - tice, let us each re-flect your light.
Now as eve - ning falls a - round us, we shall raise our songs to you.
Love that fills the night with won-der, love that warms the wear-y soul,
Might-y God of all cre - a - tion, gen-tle Christ who lights our way,
God of day-break, God of shad-ows, come and light our hearts a - new.
love that bursts all chains a - sun - der, set us free and make us whole.
lov - ing Spir - it of sal - va - tion, lead us on to end - less day.

Text: based on Greek Φῶς Ἱλαρόν (Phos hilaron) (Eastern Mediterranean), ca. 3rd c.; Marty Haugen (USA), 1987
Music: Marty Haugen, 1987

All Praise to Thee, My God 505

TALLIS' CANON LM

G D Em D G
1* 2 3
1 All praise to thee, my God, this night, for
2 For - give me, God, for this I pray, the
†3 Praise God from whom all bless - ings flow; in
Am G D7 G Am G
4
all the bless - ings of the light. Keep me, kind mak - er
wrong that I have done this day. May peace with God and
heav'n a - bove and earth be - low; one God, three per - sons
D7 G Am G D7 G
of all things, be - neath thine own al - might - y wings.
neigh - bor be be - fore I sleep, re - stored to me.
we a - dore. To God be praise for - ev - er more.

*Unison when sung in canon. Chord symbols represent a simplified harmony.

†For additional options for this stanza, see "Praise God (Doxology)" (#71).

Text: stanzas 1–2 Thomas Ken (England), 1694, appendix to *A Manual of Prayers*, 1695, alt.; stanza 3 *Hymns for Today's Church*, 1982,
Music: Thomas Tallis (England), *The Whole Psalter Translated into English Metre*, 1561–1567

506 The Day You Gave Us

ST. CLEMENT 9.8.9.8

Capo 1: (G) A♭ (D) E♭ (Em) Fm (D) E♭
1 The day you gave us, God, is end - ed; the
2 We thank you that your church, un - sleep - ing while
3 As o - ver con - ti - nent and is - land each
4 So be it, God, your throne shall nev - er, like
(G) A♭ (Em) Fm (A) B♭ (D) E♭ (G) A♭ (D) E♭
dark - ness falls at your re - quest. To you our morn - ing
earth rolls on - ward in - to light, through all the world its
dawn leads on an - oth - er day, the voice of prayer is
earth's proud em - pires, pass a - way. Your reign en - dures and
(Em) Fm (D) E♭ (G) A♭ (Em) Fm (Am) B♭m (D7) E♭7 (G) A♭
hymns as - cend - ed; your praise shall sanc - ti - fy our rest.
watch is keep - ing, and nev - er rests by day or night.
nev - er si - lent, nor do the prais - es die a - way.
grows for - ev - er, un - til there dawns your glo - rious day.

Chord symbols represent a simplified harmony.

Text: John Ellerton (England), 1870, *Church Hymns*, 1871, alt.
Music: Clement C. Scholefield (England), *Church Hymns with Tunes*, 1874

Time Propels Us like a Current 507

ST. HELENA 8.7.8.7 D

E C♯m Amaj7 G♯m C♯m
1 Time pro-pels us like a cur - rent, yet it turns, a
2 At our ends and our be - gin - nings, the E - ter - nal
3 Yet we fear, O God of Ag - es: still old e - vils
4 Teach us all the steps of kind - ness; lead us in your
Amaj7 B7 E C♯m7 B
spin - ning sphere; now a mo - ment, then it pass -
One is there, si - lent Voice, in - vit - ing Pres -
wound and rage. Fear-some voic - es, gain-ing pow -
ho - ly dance, keep-ing time with love e - ter -
E C♯m7 D A
es, gone like breath on fro - zen air. Time is ours to
ence, say - ing, "Now. The time is here. Mor - tal one, you
er, shout their hate from ev - 'ry stage. You sang peace on
nal, liv - ing in your pres - ent tense. Be for us the
E F♯m D A
mark and mea-sure, not to grasp, or un - der-stand. Ho - ly
are be - lov - ed. I would walk this while with you. Do not
waves of cha - os, or - dered rhy-thms: nights and days. Hone in
turn - ing cen - ter, pres-ent Part-ner, stead - y Friend. Love, com -
E B C♯m A B7 E
Pres - ence, we re - ceive it, gift and mys-t'ry, from your hand.
fear; stir up your spir - it: I am mak-ing all things new."
us the skills of jus - tice, sing in us your song of grace.
pel us, lead us, joy - ful; faith-ful till the ag - es end.

Text: Andrew Donaldson (Canada),
Music: Calvin Hampton (USA),

508 Child of Blessing, Child of Promise

KINGDOM 8.7.8.7

G C D C
1 Child of bless - ing, child of prom - ise, love's cre -
2 Child of joy, our dear - est treas - ure, God's you
3 Child of God, your lov - ing Par - ent, learn to
Em G A D B7 Em D7
a - tion, loved in - deed! Fresh from God, re - fresh our
are, from God you came. Back to God we hum - bly
lis - ten for God's call. Grow to laugh and sing and
G D G Dsus D7 G
spir - its; in - to joy and laugh - ter lead.
give you, bless - ing you in Je - sus' name.
wor - ship, trust and love God more than all.

Text: Ronald S. Cole-Turner (USA), *Everflowing Streams,* alt., © 1981 Ronald S. Cole-Turner
Music: V. Earle Copes (USA), © 1960, renewed 1988 Hope Publishing Co.

See the Children Here before Us 509

DEANNA 8.7.8.7 D

G C D G C D
1 See the chil-dren here be-fore us, fresh ex-pres-sions of God's love,
2 Price-less gifts be-yond all meas-ure are the chil-dren in our care.
3 Now the church has come to-geth-er with a prom-ise we must share:
G C D G C D G
each young life a pre-cious prom-ise, sent from heav-en's realm a-bove.
At this hour of ded-i-ca-tion, God, please hear our hum-ble prayer:
to be faith-ful to the chil-dren you en-trust-ed to our care.
D7 G Em C D
God, we ask you now to bless them as they learn and grow each day.
bless these par-ents on their jour-ney through a vast, un-chart-ed land;
Let us see your love re-flect-ed in each small and pre-cious face;
G C D G C D G
Help us teach en-dur-ing les-sons that will guide them on their way.
help them fol-low as you lead them with a gen-tle guid-ing hand.
help us show them all the won-ders of your end-less love and grace.

Alternate tune: NETTLETON (#1 or #563)

Text: Jan McGuire (USA), 2008
Music: Pepper Choplin (USA), 2008

510 Today Earth Is Singing

CRADLE SONG 11.11.11.11

Capo 3: (D) F (Bm) Dm (Em) Gm
To - day earth is sing - ing with stars up a - bove,
(A) C (D) F (Em) Gm (A) C
our arms wide in wel - come for God's gift of love;
(D) F (Bm) Dm (Em) Gm
we greet you, dear ________, we're glad you are here;
(A) C (D) F (Em) Gm (A7) C7 (D) F
your new - ness re - news us and heav - en comes near.

Text: Brenda Hostetler Meyer (USA), © 2019 Brenda Hostetler Meyer
Music: William J. Kirkpatrick (USA), *Around the World with Christmas*, 1895; harm. Joan Fyock Norris (USA), © 1989 Joan Fyock Norris

Come On, Children, to the Gospel Feast 511

OWEN Irregular

Capo 3: (D) F
Leader
Come on, chil-dren, to the gos-pel feast.
(G) B♭ (D/A) F/C (A7) C7 (D) F
All
Gath-er round, gath-er round!
Leader
All are wel-come at the gos-pel feast.
(G) B♭ (D/A) F/C (A7) C7 (D) F
All
Gath-er round, gath-er round!
(A) C (D) F (G) B♭ (A7) C7
This is where we sing and pray, read God's word on this glad day.
(D) F (G) B♭ (E7) G7 (G) B♭ (D/A) F/C (A7) C7 (D) F
Come on, chil-dren, to the gos-pel feast. Gath-er round, gath-er round!

Text: Mark Morgan (USA)
Music: Mark Morgan

512 Let the Children Come to Me

LET THE CHILDREN COME Irregular

Refrain
D
"Let the chil-dren come to me;
"Let the chil-dren come to
G A7 D A7
let the chil-dren come. Nev-er hin-der them; nev-er
me; let them come. Nev-er hin-der; never
D Em A7
To verses
D
stop them. Oh, let the chil-dren come."
stop them. Oh, let the chil-dren come."
Last time
D Em G D/A A7 D
come."
come. Oh, let the chil-dren come, let them come."
come. Oh, let the chil-dren come."

Verses can be found in the accompaniment edition.

Text: James V. Marchionda (USA)
Music: James V. Marchionda; arr. Michael K. Runyan (USA), alt.

When Hands Reach Out 513

ALSACE LM

G D G D G
1 When hands reach out and fin - gers trace the beau - ty
2 When fin - gers spell and signs ex - press our prayer and
3 When bro - ken bo - dies will not mend, we thank you,
4 And when the ways we learn and grow are not the
5 Your Spir - it gives us dif - f'ring ways to serve you
D G D A7 D G
of a loved one's face, we thank you, God, that
praise and thank - ful - ness, we thank you, God, that
God, for Christ our friend. In him, our heal - ing
ways that oth - ers know, we thank you, God, that
well and of - fer praise. When all are joined as
D7 G D7 G
love re - lies on gifts of grace not seen with eyes.
hands can sing; you bless the si - lent songs we bring.
can be - gin: he wel - comes all the wound - ed in.
we have learned your love's a gift, and nev - er earned.
one, we'll be your a - ble, strong com - mu - ni - ty.

Music: Ludwig van Beethoven (Germany), adapt. from Symphony no. 2, 1802

514 I Saw a Tree by the Riverside

TREE SONG* Irregular

D G/D A/D G/D D G
1 I saw a tree by the
2 I saw a tree in the
3 I saw a tree in the
A F♯m Em A D
riv - er - side one day as I walked a - long,
win - ter - time when snow lay on the ground,
cit - y streets where build - ings blocked the sun;
D G A F♯m
straight as an ar - row and point-ing to the sky,
straight as an ar - row and point-ing to the sky; and
green and love - ly, I could see it gave
Em A D G/D D G C
grow - ing tall and strong. "How do you grow so
win-ter winds blew all a - round. "How do you stay so
joy to ev - 'ry - one. "How do you grow in the
D Bm Am7 D G A7
tall and strong?" I said to the riv - er - side tree.
tall and strong?" I said to the win-ter-time tree.
cit - y streets?" I said to the down - town tree.
D G A A7 D G/D
This is the song that my tree friend sang to me:

*Original title

Text: Ken Medema (USA)
Music: Ken Medema

Refrain
"I've got roots grow-ing down to the wa - ter, I've got
leaves grow-ing up to the sun-shine, and the fruit that I bear is a
sign of the life in me. I am shade from the
hot sum-mer sun-down, I am nest for the birds of the heav - en.
I'm be - com-ing what the Lord of trees has meant me to
be— a strong young tree.
Last time

515 O Little Children, Gather

BEAUTIFUL FLOWER 8.7.12.7

G D7 G D7
1 O lit - tle chil - dren, gath - er near and learn of Je - sus'
2 Let Je - sus Christ your teach - er be, your thoughts to him ad -
3 O chil - dren, fol - low in his ways, and pray - ing, read - ing,
G
glo - ry. Now come and of his good - ness hear, his
dress - ing. He calls: "O come now un - to me and
sing - ing, seek heav - en all your earth - ly days, and
Em D Em G D7 G
love and pow'r; come lis - ten to his sto - ry.
joy - ful be. I'll give you ev - 'ry bless - ing."
shout his praise, to him all hon - or bring - ing.

Text: Christopher Dock (present-day USA), *Ach Kinder, wollt ihr lieben*, ca. 1770; trans. Alice Parker (USA), 1962, *Come Let Us Join*, 1966, alt.
Music: *The Philharmonia* (USA),1875; arr. Alice Parker, *Come Let Us Join*, 1966

Jesus Loves Me 516

JESUS LOVES ME 7.7.7.7 with refrain

D G D
Je - sus loves me! this I know, for the Bi - ble tells me so.
G D A D
Lit - tle ones to him be - long, *they are weak, but he is strong.
G D A
Yes, Je - sus loves me. Yes, Je - sus loves me.
D G D A7 D
Yes, Je - sus loves me, the Bi - ble tells me so.

*Alternate phrase: "in my weakness, he is strong"

Text: Anna B. Warner (USA), 1859
Music: William B. Bradbury (USA), *The Golden Shower*, 1862

517 Children of the Heavenly Father

SANDELL LM

D A
1 Chil - dren of the heav'n - ly Fa - ther safe - ly
2 God his own doth tend and nour - ish, in his
3 Nei - ther life nor death shall ev - er from the
4 Though he giv - eth or he tak - eth, God his
A7 D G
in his bos - om gath - er. Nest-ling bird nor star in
ho - ly courts they flour - ish. From all e - vil things he
Lord his chil - dren sev - er. Un - to them his grace he
chil - dren ne'er for - sak - eth. His the lov - ing pur - pose
D B7 Em A A7 D
heav - en such a ref - uge e'er was giv - en.
spares them, in his might - y arms he bears them.
show - eth, and their sor - rows all he know - eth.
sole - ly to pre - serve them safe and ho - ly.

Text: Caroline V. S. Berg (Sweden), *Tryggare kan ingen vara, Andeliga Daggdroppar*, 1855; trans. Ernst W. Olson (USA), *The Hymnal*, 1925, alt.
Music: Swedish traditional, *Song Book for Sunday School*, 1871

Like a Mother Who Has Borne Us 518

AUSTIN 8.7.8.7

D G A D
1 Like a moth - er who has borne us, held us
2 Like a fa - ther who has taught us, grasped our
3 Though as chil - dren we have wan - dered, placed our
4 When we of - fer food and com - fort, grasp our
A D A Bm G Em
close in her de - light, fed us free - ly from her
hand and been our guide, lift - ed us and healed our
trust in pow'r and might, left be - hind our friends and
neigh - bor's hand in love, tread the path of peace and
Bm A G D A D
bod - y, God has called us in - to life.
sor - rows, God has walked with us in life.
fam' - ly, God still calls us in - to life.
jus - tice, God still walks with us in life.

Text: Daniel Bechtel (USA), © 1986 Daniel Bechtel
Music: William P. Rowan (USA), 1992, © 1993 Selah Publishing Co., Inc.

519 God, Give Me Faith like a Child

EZRA D 7.7.7.7.7.7

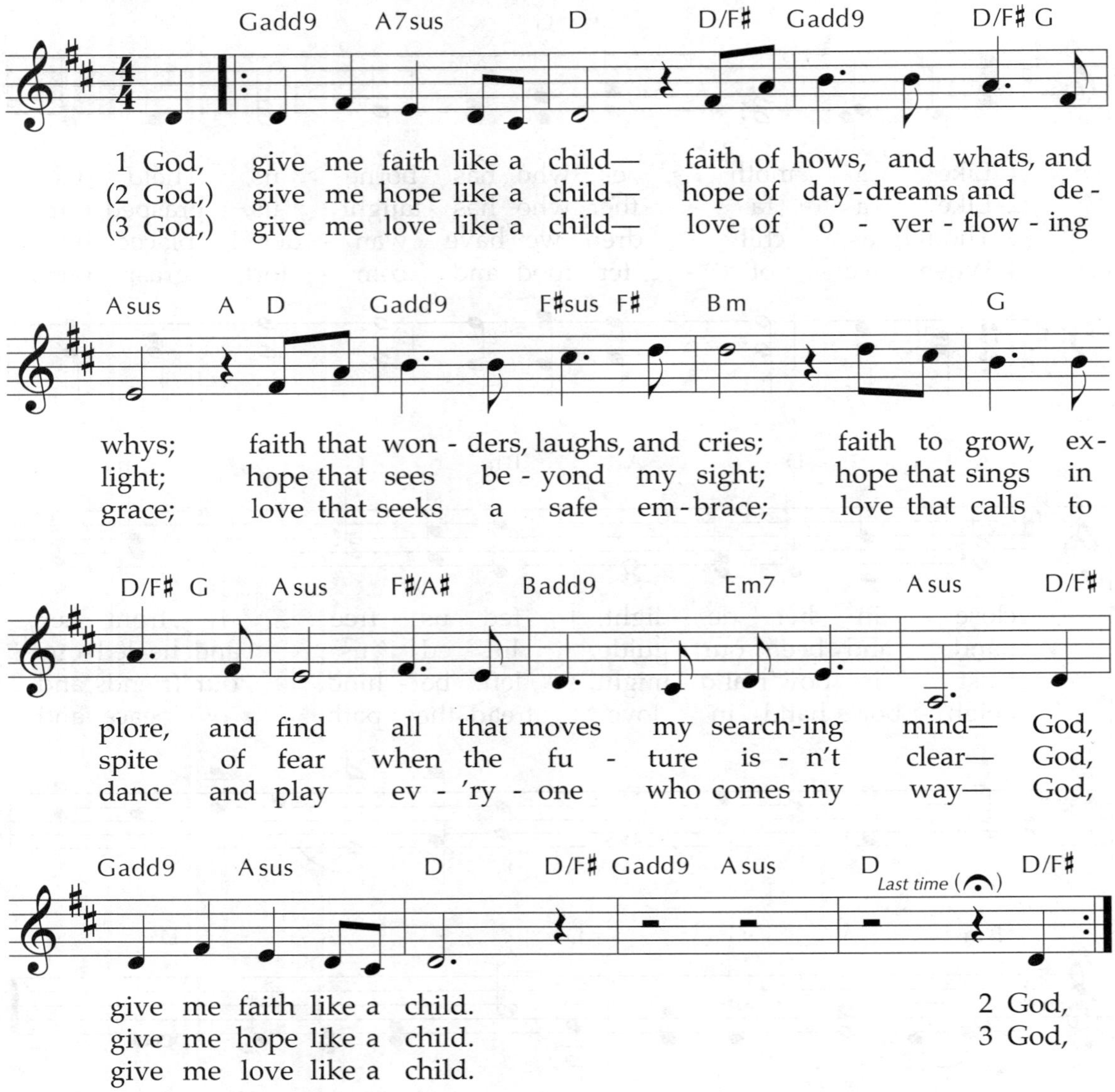
Gadd9 A7sus D D/F♯ Gadd9 D/F♯ G
1 God, give me faith like a child— faith of hows, and whats, and
(2 God,) give me hope like a child— hope of day-dreams and de-
(3 God,) give me love like a child— love of o - ver - flow - ing
Asus A D Gadd9 F♯sus F♯ Bm G
whys; faith that won - ders, laughs, and cries; faith to grow, ex-
light; hope that sees be - yond my sight; hope that sings in
grace; love that seeks a safe em - brace; love that calls to
D/F♯ G Asus F♯/A♯ Badd9 Em7 Asus D/F♯
plore, and find all that moves my search-ing mind— God,
spite of fear when the fu - ture is - n't clear— God,
dance and play ev - 'ry - one who comes my way— God,
Gadd9 Asus D D/F♯ Gadd9 Asus D D/F♯
Last time
give me faith like a child. 2 God,
give me hope like a child. 3 God,
give me love like a child.

Text: Adam M. L. Tice (USA), 2012
Music: Sally Ann Morris (USA)

When Aging Takes Its Toll 520

MIKTAM SM extended

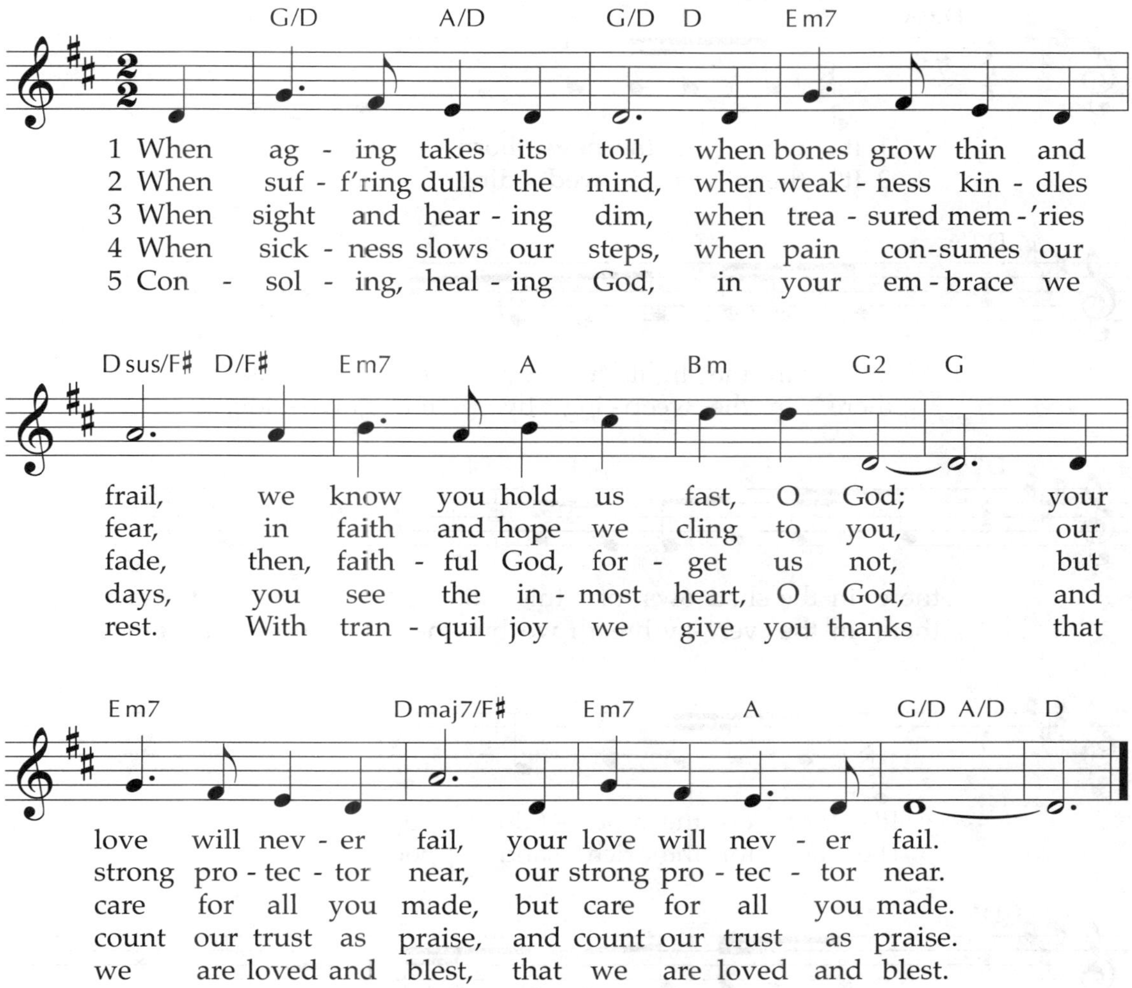
G/D A/D G/D D Em7
1 When ag - ing takes its toll, when bones grow thin and
2 When suf - f'ring dulls the mind, when weak - ness kin - dles
3 When sight and hear - ing dim, when trea - sured mem - 'ries
4 When sick - ness slows our steps, when pain con-sumes our
5 Con - sol - ing, heal - ing God, in your em - brace we
Dsus/F♯ D/F♯ Em7 A Bm G2 G
frail, we know you hold us fast, O God; your
fear, in faith and hope we cling to you, our
fade, then, faith - ful God, for - get us not, but
days, you see the in - most heart, O God, and
rest. With tran - quil joy we give you thanks that
Em7 Dmaj7/F♯ Em7 A G/D A/D D
love will nev - er fail, your love will nev - er fail.
strong pro - tec - tor near, our strong pro - tec - tor near.
care for all you made, but care for all you made.
count our trust as praise, and count our trust as praise.
we are loved and blest, that we are loved and blest.

Alternate tune: GOLDEN HILL (#589).

Text: Delores Dufner, OSB (USA), 2013, 2015,
Music: Larry Visser (USA),

521 Your Grace Finds Me

YOUR GRACE FINDS ME Irregular

1 It's there in the new - born cry,
2 It's there on a wed - ding day,
there in the light of ev - 'ry sun - rise,
there in the weep - ing by the grave - side,
there in the shad - ows of this life: your great grace.
there in the ver - y breath we breathe: your great grace.
It's there on the moun - tain - top,
The same for the rich and poor,
there in the ev - 'ry - day and the mun - dane,
the same for the saint and for the sin - ner,
there in the sor - row and the danc - ing:
e - nough for this whole wide world:
Your great grace, oh, such grace.
your great grace, oh, such grace.

Text: Matt Redman (England) and Jonas Myrin (USA)
Music: Matt Redman and Jonas Myrin

Refrain
A
E/G♯
From the cre - a - tion to the cross,
F♯m7
D
A/C♯
there from the cross in - to e - ter - ni - ty, your grace
D2
A
1
finds me, yes, your grace finds me.
Bridge
2
D
A
D2/A
Oh, oh, oh,
A
1
D2/A
2
D2/A
oh, oh, oh. So I'm
A
D2/A
breath - ing in your grace and breath - ing out your praise. I'm
A
To repeat
D2/A
breath - ing in your grace and breath - ing out your praise. I'm
Last time
D2/A
D
breath - ing out your praise. Yes, your grace
A
D
A
finds me, yes, your grace finds me.

522 O Blessed Spring

THE WATER IS WIDE LM

Dsus D G C G Dsus D7
1 O bless-ed spring, where word and sign em-brace us
2 Through sum-mer heat of youth-ful years, un-cer-tain
3 When au-tumn cools and youth is cold, when limbs their
4 As win-ter comes, as win-ter must, we breathe our
5 Christ, ho-ly Vine, Christ, liv-ing Tree, be praised for
Em Am Dsus D G/B D7/A G/B
in-to Christ the Vine: here Christ en-joins each
faith, re-bel-lious tears, sus-tained by Christ's in-
heav-y har-vest hold, then through us, warm, the
last, re-turn to dust; still held in Christ, our
this blest mys-ter-y; that work and wa-ter
G Em Bm Am/C G
one to be a branch of this life-giv-ing Tree.
fus-ing rain, the boughs will shout for joy a-gain.
Christ will move with gifts of beau-ty, wis-dom, love.
souls take wing and trust the prom-ise of the spring.
thus re-vive and join us to your Tree of life.

Text: Susan Palo Cherwien (USA), © 1993 Susan Palo Cherwien (admin. Augsburg Fortress)
Music: English traditional, ca. 19th c., transcr. as "O Waly, Waly" in *Folk Songs from Somerset* (England), 1906; harm. James E. Clemens (USA), © 2004 James E. Clemens

God Made from One Blood 523

GOD MADE 11.11.11.11

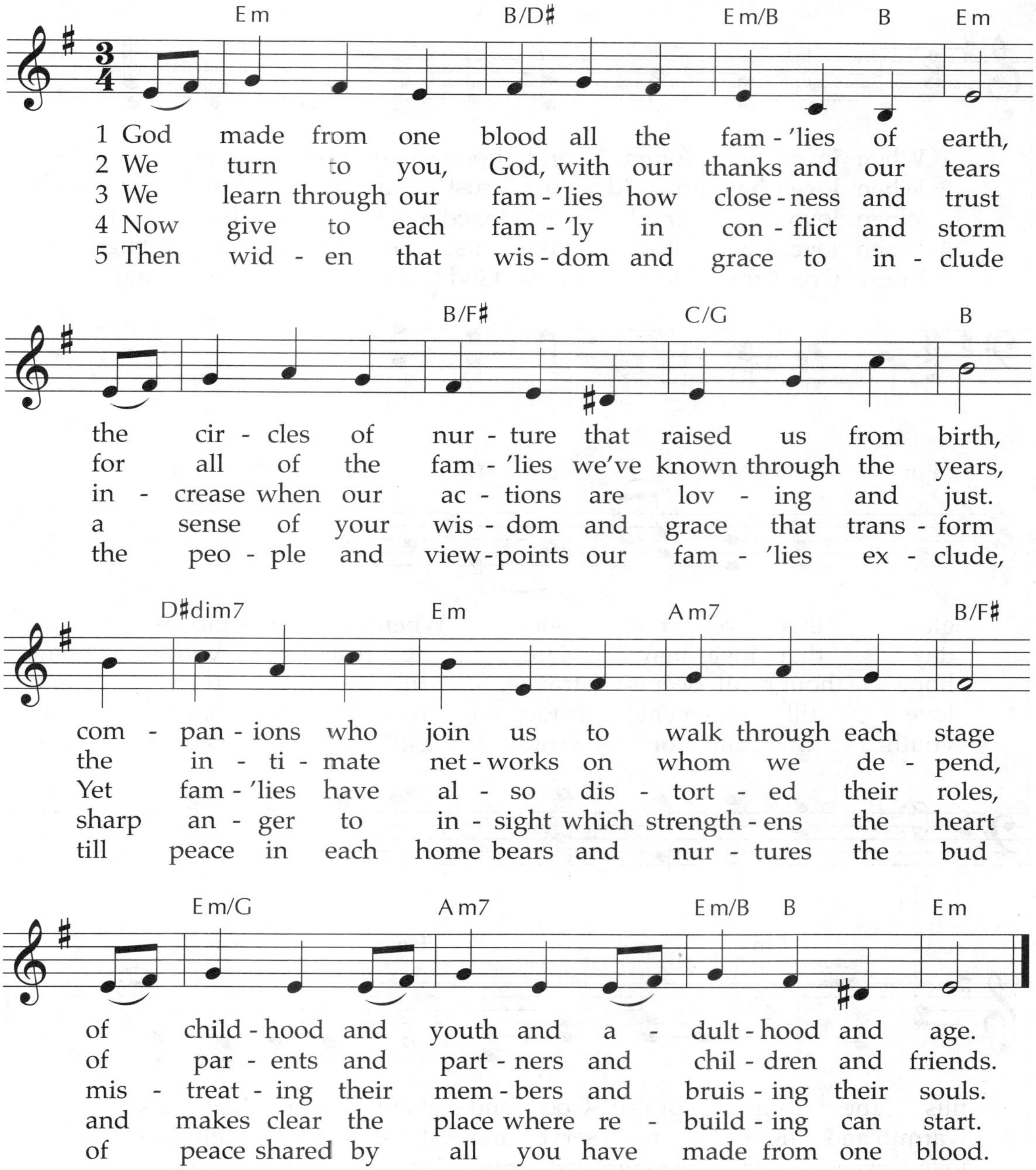
Em B/D♯ Em/B B Em
1 God made from one blood all the fam - 'lies of earth,
2 We turn to you, God, with our thanks and our tears
3 We learn through our fam - 'lies how close - ness and trust
4 Now give to each fam - 'ly in con - flict and storm
5 Then wid - en that wis - dom and grace to in - clude
B/F♯ C/G B
the cir - cles of nur - ture that raised us from birth,
for all of the fam - 'lies we've known through the years,
in - crease when our ac - tions are lov - ing and just.
a sense of your wis - dom and grace that trans - form
the peo - ple and view - points our fam - 'lies ex - clude,
D♯dim7 Em Am7 B/F♯
com - pan - ions who join us to walk through each stage
the in - ti - mate net - works on whom we de - pend,
Yet fam - 'lies have al - so dis - tort - ed their roles,
sharp an - ger to in - sight which strength - ens the heart
till peace in each home bears and nur - tures the bud
Em/G Am7 Em/B B Em
of child - hood and youth and a - dult - hood and age.
of par - ents and part - ners and chil - dren and friends.
mis - treat - ing their mem - bers and bruis - ing their souls.
and makes clear the place where re - build - ing can start.
of peace shared by all you have made from one blood.

Text: Thomas H. Troeger (USA), 1986, alt., © 1986 Oxford University Press
Music: Gregory A. Smucker (USA), © 2019 Gregory A. Smucker

524 When Love Is Found

THE WATER IS WIDE LM

Dsus D G C G Dsus D7
1 When love is found and hope comes home, sing and be
2 When love has flower'd in trust and care, build both each
3 When love is tried as loved ones change, hold still to
4 When love is torn and trust be - trayed, pray strength to
5 Praise God for love, praise God for life, in age or
Em Am Dsus D G/B D7/A G/B
glad that two are one. When love ex - plodes and
day that love may dare to reach be - yond home's
hope though all seems strange, till ease re - turns and
love till tor - ments fade, till lov - ers keep no
youth, in calm or strife. Lift up your hearts! Let
G Em Bm Am/C G
fills the sky, praise God and share our Mak - er's joy.
warmth and light, to serve and strive for truth and right.
love grows wise through list' - ning ears and o - pened eyes.
score of wrong, but hear through pain love's Eas - ter song.
love be fed through death and life in bro - ken bread.

Text: Brian Wren (England), 1978, *Faith Looking Forward*, © 1983 Hope Publishing Co.
Music: English traditional, ca. 19th c., transcr. as "O Waly, Waly" in *Folk Songs from Somerset* (England), 1906; harm. James E. Clemens (USA), © 2004 James E. Clemens

ໂອ ພີ່ ນ້ອງ ເອີຍ O phi nong oei 525

(Dear Friends, We're One)

O PHI NONG OEI Irregular

C G Am G Dm7 Em C Em Am Fmaj7 C Dm G C
ໂອ້ ພີ່ ນ້ອງ ເອີຍ ພຣະ ເຢ ຊູ ຮັກ
O phi nong oei pra Ye - su hak
Dear friends, we're one in Je - sus' love,
ຖະ ຫວາຍ ຕົນ ເອງ ເປັນ ເຄື່ອງ ບູ ຊາ ໄຖ່
tha waiih ton eng Pen khueng bou sa thaih
who gave him - self as sac - ri - fice to
ໂທດ ຄົນ ບາບ ໃຫ້ ທຸກ ຊົນ ຊາດ ໃຫ້ ມີ ຄວາມ
thoad khon barb hai thouk xon sard Hai mee khuam
save the sin - ners of this world and set all
ຫວັງ ໃນ ພຣະ ເຢ ຊູ ທຸກ ວັນ ເວ ລາ ໂອ້ ພີ່ ນ້ອງ
wungh nai pra Ye - su thouk wun weh la O phi nong
peo - ples free to find new life in him. Dear friends, we're
ເອີຍ ພຣະ ເຢ ຊູ ຮັກ ທຸກ ວັນ ເວ ລາ
oei pra Ye - su hak thouk wun weh la
one in Je - sus' love, re - stored to hope,
ຈົ່ງ ເຊື່ອ ສຸດ ໃຈ ໃນ ພຣະ ເຢ ຊູ ໃດ ພີ່ ນ້ອງ ເອີຍ
Jong seua sout jai nai pra Ye - su daih phi nong oei
so trust him ful - ly; he's the Lord who calls us friends.

Text: Laotian; anon.; trans. anon.
Music: Laotian traditional; sometimes YESU HAK; acc. Matthew Boutda (Canada), 2019

526 En medio de la vida (You Are the God within Life)

BOLIVIANO 7.6.7.6 D with refrain

1 En me - dio de la vi - da es - tás pre - sen - te, oh
2 Es - tás en el tra - ba - jo del cam - po o la ciu -
3 Es - tás en la a - le - grí - a y es - tás en el do -
4 Es - tás en la fa - mi - lia, hués - ped de ca - da ho -

1 You are the God with - in life, pres - ent where - e'er we
2 There with us in the of - fice; there when we're till - ing
3 With us in joy and sor - row, you raise us when we
4 With us in friends and fam - 'ly, so - journ - er, stran - ger,

Dios, más cer - ca que mi a - lien - to, sus - ten - to
dad, y es him - no de la vi - da el dia - rio
lor, com - par - tes con tu pue - blo, la lu - cha
gar, o - yen - te in - vi - si - ble de nues - tro

live, clos - er than all our sigh - ing, sus - tain - ing
soil; cit - y, or town, or coun - try, God joins us
fall; you join us in our strug - gles, seek - ing the
guest, you join us at our ta - ble, break - ing the

de mi ser. Im - pul - sas en mis ve - nas
tra - ji - nar. El gol - pe del mar - ti - llo,
por el bien. En Cris - to tú has ve - ni - do
con - ver - sar. Ben - di - ces nues - tra me - sa

pow'r you give. In - side our ver - y bod - ies,
in our toil. Hear how the ring - ing ham - mer
good of all. In Christ you brought re - demp - tion,
bread you've blessed. With us as child and el - der,

Text: Spanish; Mortimer Arias (Bolivia); stanza 1 and refrain trans. George Lockwood (USA); stanzas 2–4 trans. Adam M. L. Tice (USA)
Music: Antonio Auza (Bolivia); arr. Homero Perera (Uruguay)

(F) A♭ (E) G (F) A♭
mi san-gre‿al pal - pi - tar y‿el rit - mo de la
la te - cla‿al es - cri - bir en - to - nan su‿a - la -
la vi - da‿a re - di - mir y‿en pren - da de tu
y no nos fal - ta‿el pan, cui - das de nues - tros
you pump the blood of life; rhy - thm in ev - 'ry
joins with the key - board's clack— ech - oes of God's good
bind - ing all things to you— show - ing us life's a -
through all of life's brief course, your love gives us our
(Am/E) Cm/G (E7) G7 (Am) Cm
vi - da vas dan - do‿al co - ra - zón.
ban - za al Dios de la cre‿a - ción.
rei - no, el mun - do‿a con - ver - tir.
hi - jos, fru - tos de nues - tro‿a - mor.
heart - beat drums out the pulse of life.
la - bor, giv - ing our an - swer back!
bun - dance, mak - ing cre - a - tion new.
be - ing, our cen - ter, and our source.
Estribillo / Refrain
(G) B♭ (C) E♭
O Dios de cie - lo‿y tie - rra, te sir - vo des - de‿a -
O God of earth and heav - en, we serve you where we
(F) A♭ (Am/E) Cm/G
quí: te‿a - mo‿en mis her - ma - nos,*
are. We love you in all peo - ple,
(E7) G7 (Am) Cm (Dm) Fm (Am) Cm
te‿a - do - ro‿en la cre‿a - ción.
we praise you in your world!

*Or *hermanas*

527 Bless the Arms That Comfort

CRANHAM 6.5.6.5 D

Capo 3: (D) F (Bm) Dm (Em7) Gm7 (A7) C7
1 Bless the arms that com - fort, strong to shoul-der care,
2 Bless the ears that lis - ten, shar - ing joys and fears—
3 Bless the feet that fol - low, like Na - o - mi's Ruth—
(D) F (Bm) Dm (Em7) Gm7 (A7) C7 (D) F
gen - tle in their heal - ing, reach - ing through des - pair.
laugh - ing in our tri - umphs, weep - ing with our tears.
con - stant friend through sor - row, speak - ing ho - ly truth:
(G) B♭ (Bm) Dm (D) F (G) B♭ (A) C
Bless the hands that la - bor Mar - tha's dai - ly deeds;
Bless the eyes whose wis - dom sees through pride's fa - çade,
Though our jour - neys lead us far in time and space,
(D) F (Bm) Dm (Em7) Gm7 (A7) C7 (D) F
Ma - ry's pre - cious oint - ment, balm for dif - f'rent needs.
cher - ish - ing our weak - ness with the heart of God.
God a - noints com - pan - ions, min - i - sters of grace.

Text: Mary Louise Bringle (USA),
Music: Gustav Holst (England), 1906

God, Bless the Work Your People Do 528

SARAH-ELIZABETH CMD

Capo 3: (D) F (F♯m7) Am7 (Bm) Dm (F♯m) Am (Em7) Gm7
1 God, bless the work your peo - ple do through-out each
2 For all who have no res - pite, God, from la - bor
3 We pray for those who can - not work, or seek for
4 As you a - chieved cre - a - tion's work, then rest - ed
(A) C (G) B♭ (A7) C7 (D) F (Bm) Dm
work - ing day, the con - tri - bu - tions that they make, the
with - out ease, for those for whom their work is filled with
work in vain; great God, we pray your mer - cy shall en -
from your task, God, bless the work your peo - ple do, and
(Em) Gm (A7) C7 (D) F (G) B♭
tal - ents they dis - play. God, bless the work your
dan - ger or dis - ease, for all who la - bor
cour - age them, a - gain! We pray for those whose
call it good, we ask! Grant un - to each a
(D) F (Bm) Dm (Em7) Gm7 (A) C (D) F
peo - ple do, with minds and hands and hearts, to ben - e -
with - out gain, or have no rest this day, for all who
work is hard, on bod - y, spir - it, soul, the un - der -
day de - signed for wor - ship, joy, and rest; a Sab - bath
(F♯m7) Am7 (Bm) Dm (F♯m) Am (Em) Gm (A) C (D) F
fit the com - mon good, the sci - enc - es and arts.
la - bor with - out hope, O God, we hum - bly pray.
paid, un - der - em - ployed, who fill a vi - tal role.
time of ho - li - ness, in which they may be blessed.

Text: John A. Dalles (USA),
Music: Amanda Husberg (USA), 1996,

529 God, Who Stretched the Spangled Heavens

HOLY MANNA 8.7.8.7 D

G D G
1 God, who stretched the span-gled heav - ens, in - fi - nite in
2 We have ven-tured worlds un-dreamed of since the child-hood
3 As each far ho - ri - zon beck - ons, may it chal-lenge
D7 G D G
time and place, flung the suns in burn - ing ra - diance
of our race, known the ec - sta - sy of wing - ing
us a - new, chil - dren of cre - a - tive pur - pose
D7 G
through the si - lent fields of space; we, your chil - dren
through un - trav - eled realms of space, probed the se - crets
serv - ing oth - ers, hon-'ring you. May our dreams prove
D7 G D G
in your like-ness, share in - ven - tive pow'rs with you. Great Cre -
of the at - om, yield-ing un - im - ag - ined pow'r, fac - ing
rich with prom-ise, each en - deav - or well be - gun. Great Cre -

Text: Catherine Cameron (USA), 1967, *Contemporary Worship I*, 1969, alt., © 1967 Hope Publishing Co.
Music: *The Columbian Harmony* (USA), 1825

D G D7 G
a - tor still cre - a - ting, show us what we yet may do.
us with life's de - struc - tion or our most tri - um - phant hour.
a - tor, give us guid - ance till our goals and yours are one.

In the Heartbeat of the City 530

OLD YEAVERING 8.8.8.7

Capo 3: (D) F (Em7) Gm7 (A) C (G) B♭ (D) F (C♯m) Em
1 In the heart - beat of the cit - y, through its
2 To its life of noise and clam - or, in the
3 In our mu - sic and our trou - ble, through the
4 Through the streets that make us wea - ry, in the
5 In the wel - come and the wash - ing, at the
(Bm) Dm (E7) G7 (A) C (D) F (Am7) Cm7 (D7) F7
rhy - thm and its beau - ty, for the low - ly and the
smooth - ness or the squal - or, in the hope of grace and
rest - less hours of trav - el, to the bus - y and the
bur - dens we must car - ry, by the cross of Christ our
bread and wine for shar - ing, by the word of God for
(Gmaj7) B♭maj7 (G) B♭ (G♯dim) Bdim (D) F (A) C (D) F
might - y comes the gra - cious peace of God.
val - or comes the gen - tle peace of God.
brit - tle comes the heal - ing peace of God.
glo - ry comes the last - ing peace of God.
hear - ing comes the per - fect peace of God.

Text: Christopher M. Idle (England), © 1988 (admin. Hope Publishing Co.)
Music: Noël Tredinnick (England), © 1982 Noël Tredinnick (admin. Jubilate Hymns)

531 Holy Presence, Holy Teacher

RUSTINGTON 8.7.8.7 D

Capo 3: (D) F (G) B♭ (Em) Gm (A) C (D) F (G) B♭
1 Ho - ly Pres - ence, Ho - ly Teach - er, Light il - lu - min -
2 By our nur - ture and by cul - ture ev - 'ry life is
3 Yours the world of pow'r and beau - ty, ours the task to
4 God, we pray for un - der - stand - ing in our stud - y,
(Em) Gm (D) F (A) C (Bm) Dm (E7) G7 (A) C (D) F
ing our lives, in the com - pass of your wis - dom all our
shaped to grow, fed by long tra - di - tion's learn - ing, formed by
tend its needs, day by day in cheer - ful ser - vice grow - ing
in our goals, con - cepts that will change and chal - lenge, vi - sion
(F♯m) Am (E7) G7 (A) C (D7) F7 (G) B♭ (Em7) Gm7
work and wor - ship thrives: lead us when we sense your
men - tors as we go; tune our ears to hear the
faith like mus - tard seeds, striv - ing in un - like - ly
to in - spire our souls, that this place for mind's re -

Chord symbols for unison singing.

Text: Shirley Erena Murray (Aotearoa New Zealand), alt., © 2008 Hope Publishing Co.
Music: C. Hubert H. Parry (England), 1897

(A) C (F♯m) Am (Bm) Dm (Em) Gm (A) C
call - ing till we find our chos - en field, fol - low -
gos - pel ques - tion - ing ac - cept - ed thought, read - y
pla - ces, stand - ing where in - deed we must, act - ing
flec - tion, faith ex - am - ined, Word ad - dressed, be a
(D7) F7 (G) B♭ (Em) Gm (D) F (G) B♭ (A7) C7 (D) F
ing your hand's di - rec - tion, hon - or - ing your truth re - vealed.
to re - spect each oth - er, see the gifts that each has brought.
from com - pel - ling con-science, work-ing for what's fair and just.
wit - ness to your teach - ing and our faith - ful search be blessed.

Be at Rest

532

BE AT REST Irregular

D G
Be at rest once more, O my soul. Be at
D A Bm
rest once more, O my soul, for the Lord
G D A Bm G D
has been good, oh, the Lord has been
A Bm G D A D
good, oh, the Lord has been good, to you.

Text: based on Psalm 116:7; Gord Johnson (Canada)
Music: Gord Johnson

533 Quietly, Peacefully

NEW WORLD (Dvořák) Irregular

Refrain
C
Dm7/C
G/C
Qui - et - ly, peace - ful - ly let me rest in you.
Am
Fmaj7
Dm7
Gsus
G7
C
Qui - et - ly, peace - ful - ly lead me back to you.
Verses
F
G/F
F
Fmaj7
G/F
F
1 Lov - ing wis - dom, you a - lone, know all I can be.
2 In the night I call to you; can you hear my cry?
3 Heal - ing grace, take my pain, guard me night and day.
4 Breathe your law deep in me, plant it in my soul.
F
G/F
Fmaj7
F
G/F
F
To refrain
You, the hope my spir - it seeks, come and set me free.
Sad and fear - ful, still I plead: do not pass me by.
Show - er me with your love, wash my tears a - way.
Let your jus - tice be my song, kind - ness be my goal.

Text: Lori True (USA)
Music: Antonín Dvořák (present-day Czech Republic/USA), 1893; adapt. Lori True

God the Spirit, Guide and Guardian 534

TREASURED 8.7.8.7 D

D G2 Asus Bm7 G D G
1 God the Spir - it, guide and guard - ian, wind - sped flame and
2 Christ our Sav - ior, sov - 'reign, shep - herd, Word made flesh, Love
3 Great Cre - a - tor, life be - stow - er, truth be - yond all
4 Tri - une God, mys - ter - ious be - ing, un - di - vid - ed
Asus D Bm7 Em7 A2 F♯m7 G
hov - 'ring dove, breath of life and voice of proph - ets, sign of
cru - ci - fied, teach - er, heal - er, suf - f'ring ser - vant, friend of
thought's re - call, fount of wis - dom, womb of mer - cy, giv - ing
and di - verse, deep - er than our minds can fath - om, great - er
D G Asus D Bm Em7 A7 Dmaj7
bless - ing, pow'r of love: Give to those who lead your peo - ple
sin - ners, foe of pride: In your tend - ing may all lead - ers
and for - giv - ing all: As you know our strength and weak - ness,
than our creeds re - hearse: Help us in our var - ied call - ings
G Em C♯m7 F♯ Bm Em7 A7
fresh a - noint - ing of your grace. Send them forth as bold a -
learn and live a shep - herd's care. Grant them cour - age and com -
so may those the church ex - alts o - ver - see its life stead -
your full im - age to pro - claim, that our min - i - stries u -
Dmaj7 G D G A7 Dsus D
pos - tles to your church in ev - 'ry place.
pas - sion shown through word and deed and prayer.
fast - ly, yet not o - ver - look its faults.
nit - ing may give glo - ry to your name.

Alternate tune: HYFRYDOL (#218 or #745)

Text: Carl P. Daw Jr. (USA), 1987, *The United Methodist Hymnal*, © 1989 Hope Publishing Co.
Music: Sally Ann Morris (USA), 2009, © 2016 GIA Publications, Inc.

535 Today We Sing with Thankfulness

JONES CMD

G D G C
1 To - day we sing with thank - ful - ness for those who
2 To - day we sing of ho - li - ness, of heal - ing
3 To - day we sing with rest - less - ness, we ev - er
4 To - day we sing with hope - ful - ness that we may
Am7 D G D G
turned the tide. Con - fined by nar - row bound - a - ries, they
touch and word; of dis - ap - point - ment deep - ly felt, con-
look to you. In - fuse us with your Spir - it, then, give
car - ry on, to hon - or past ac - com - plish - ments, the
Am7 D G Am7 D
knew your call was wide. De - mand - ing change, they
vic - tions un - der - stood; of grace that lets for -
us your work to do. Fill us with cour - age
steps we build up - on. And what of those who

Chord symbols represent a simplified harmony.

Text: Jacque B. Jones (USA), 2006
Music: Amanda Husberg (USA)

G Em Am7 D G Am7
led the way, with pas-sion and with pain. They touch our
give-ness flow with-in com-mu-ni - ty; of love that
and re-solve, and grant hu-mil-i - ty, as we em-
fol-low us? Your jus-tice be their theme! A gift-ed
D B Em Am7 Em7 D7 G
lives a - cross the years, their leg - a - cy our gain.
seeks to rec - on - cile, re - stor - ing u - ni - ty.
ploy our minds and hearts to right the wrongs we see.
gen - er - a - tion poised— God, chal-lenge them to dream!

536 I Heard the Voice of Jesus Say

KINGSFOLD CMD
Em C G D G Am Dsus D
1 I heard the voice of Je - sus say, "Come un - to me and rest.
2 I heard the voice of Je - sus say, "Be - hold, I free - ly give
3 I heard the voice of Je - sus say, "I am the dawn-ing light.
Em Am Em D G Am Em
Lay down, O wea - ry one, lay down your head up - on my breast."
the liv - ing wa - ter, thirst-y one; stoop down and drink and live."
Look un - to me, your morn shall rise, and all your day be bright."
Bm Em Am G Bm Em Dsus D
I came to Je - sus as I was, so wea-ry, worn, and sad.
I came to Je - sus, and I drank of that life - giv - ing stream.
I looked to Je - sus, and I found in him my star, my sun,
C Am Em D G/B Am Em
I found in him a rest-ing place, and he has made me glad.
My thirst was quenched, my soul re - vived, and now I live in him.
and in that light of life I'll walk till tra-v'ling days are done.

Text: Horatius N. Bonar (Scotland), *Hymns Original and Selected*, 1846, alt.
Music: English traditional, *English Country Songs*, 1893; adapt. and harm. Ralph Vaughan Williams (England), *The English Hymnal*, 1906, alt.

Lord, You Sometimes Speak 537

CLEVELAND 8.7.8.7.9

Capo 3: (C9) E♭9
(Am9) Cm9
1 Lord, you some-times speak in won - ders,
2 Lord, you some-times speak in whis - pers,
3 Lord, you some-times speak in si - lence,
4 Lord, you sure - ly speak in Scrip - ture
5 Lord, you al - ways speak in Je - sus,
(F) A♭ (G7) B♭7 (F♯7sus) A7sus (F♯7) A7
un - mis - tak - a - ble and clear; might - y
still and small and scarce - ly heard; on - ly
through our loud and nois - y day. We can
words that sum - mon from the page, shown and
al - ways new yet still the same. Teach us
(Bm) Dm (F♯7/A♯) A7/C♯ (Bm/A) Dm/C (Gmaj7) B♭maj7
signs to prove your pres - ence, o - ver - com - ing doubt and fear.
those who want to lis - ten catch the all im - por - tant word.
know and trust you bet - ter when we quiet - ly wait and pray.
taught us by your Spir - it with fresh light for ev - 'ry age.
now more of our Sav - ior; make our lives dis - play his name.
(F♯m) Am (D/F♯) F/A (Gmaj7) B♭maj7 1–4 (Bm9) Dm9
O Lord, you some-times speak in won - ders.
O Lord, you some-times speak in whis - pers.
O Lord, you some-times speak in si - lence.
O Lord, you sure - ly speak in Scrip - ture.
O Lord, you al - ways speak in
(F) A♭ (Bm9) Dm9 (Dm7) Fm7 (G7) B♭7 5 (B9) D9
Je - sus.

Text: Christopher Idle (England), 1966, *Youth Praise 2*, 1969
Music: Christopher Johnson (England), 1987, *New Songs of Praise 4*, 1988

538 Ikke ved makt (Not by Your Might)

IKKE VED MAKT 4.11.5.11

1 Ik - ke ved makt— ik - ke ved vold og ved
2 Ik - ke ved sverd— ik - ke ved ild og ved
1 Not by your might, no, not by vio - lence or
2 Not with a sword, no, not with fire or a
3 Not us - ing fear, no, not by ter - ror or
4 Not with a threat, no, not by men - ace or

makt vil du rå - de, nei, ved din nå - de,
sverd du oss bøy - e! Nei, ved ditt øy - e,
might do you rule us, but by your mer - cy,
sword do you force us, but with your vi - sion,
fear do you drive us, but by your glad - ness,
threat do you sway us. Urge us to seek you,

ja, ved din kjær - li - ge hånd og din nå - de!
ja, ved et fa - der - lig blikk fra ditt øy - e.
yes, by your mer - ci - ful hand and com - pas - sion.
yes, with the gaze of your love do you draw us.
yes, by our souls filled with joy do you lead us.
fill - ing our hearts with your hope and your long - ing.

3 Ikke ved frykt—
ikke ved redsel og frykt vil du lede,
nei, ved din glede,
ja, ved det sinn som du fyller med glede!

4 Ikke ved dom—
ikke forstøt oss til trelldom og trengsel!
Nei, gi oss lengsel!
Styr våre hjerter ved håp og ved lengsel!

Text: Norwegian; Sverre Therkelsen (Norway); trans. Maggie Hamilton (England), alt.
Music: Knut Nystedt (Norway),

God Speaks to Us in Bird and Song 539

EVENING LIGHT 8.8.8.6

Dm F G Am Dm B♭ Am
1 God speaks to us in bird and song, in winds that
2 God speaks to us in far and near, in peace of
3 God speaks to us in dark - est night, by qui - et
4 O Voice di - vine, speak un - to me, be - yond the
Dm G A B♭ F
drift the clouds a - long, a - bove the din and
home and friends most dear, from fad - ed past and
ways through morn - ings bright, when shad - ows fall with
earth, be - yond the sea, and let me ech - o
C/E Dm A B♭ C Dsus G/D D
toil of wrong, a mel - o - dy of love.
pre - sent clear, a mel - o - dy of love.
eve - ning light, a mel - o - dy of love.
joy - ful - ly a mel - o - dy of love.

Text: Joseph Johnson (England), 1888, alt.
Music: Pax Ressler (USA), © 2016 Pax Ressler

540 Will You Come and Follow Me

KELVINGROVE 7.6.7.6.7.7.7.6

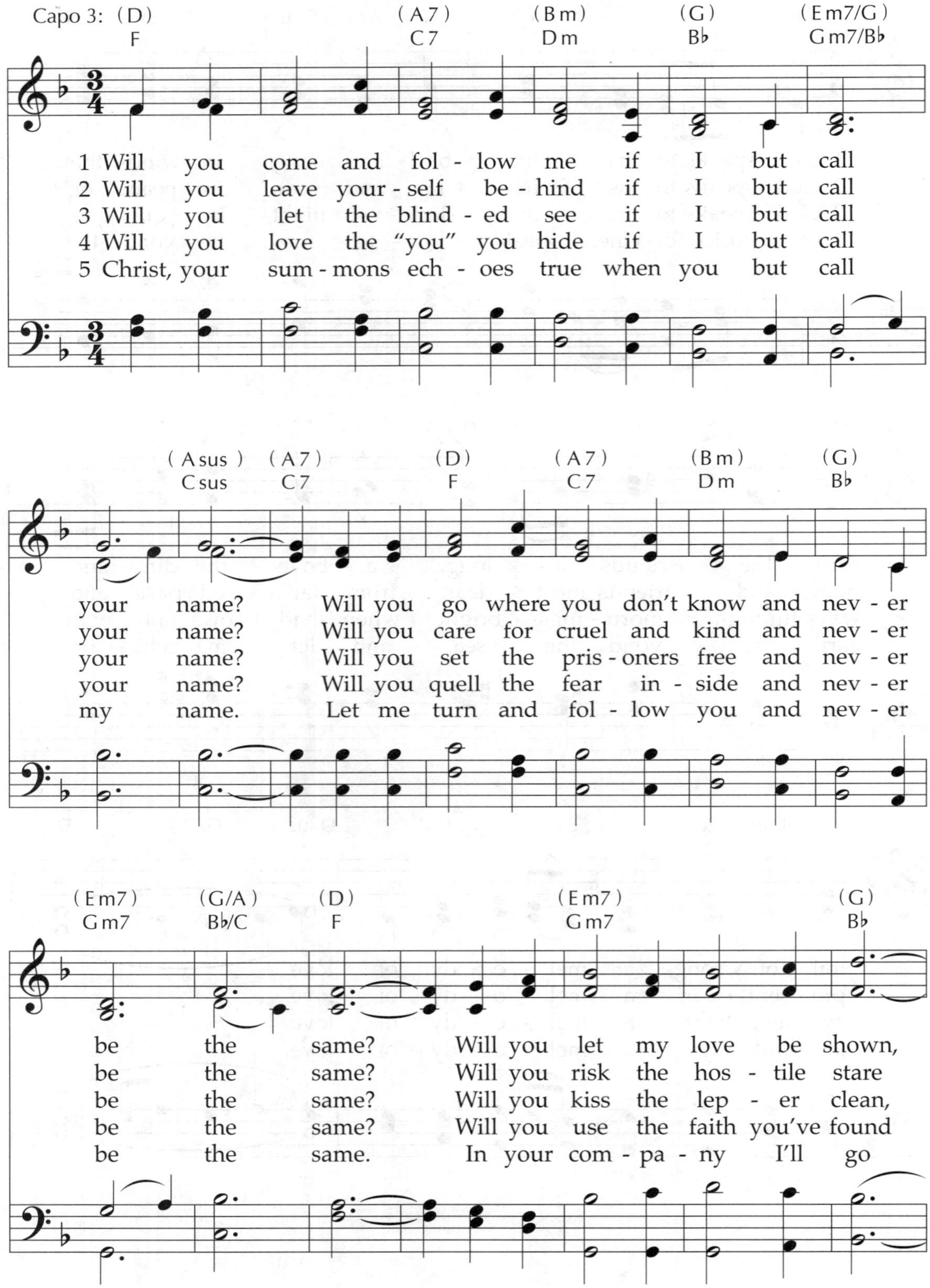
Capo 3: (D) F
(A7) C7
(Bm) Dm
(G) B♭
(Em7/G) Gm7/B♭
1 Will you come and fol - low me if I but call
2 Will you leave your - self be - hind if I but call
3 Will you let the blind - ed see if I but call
4 Will you love the "you" you hide if I but call
5 Christ, your sum - mons ech - oes true when you but call
(Asus) Csus
(A7) C7
(D) F
(A7) C7
(Bm) Dm
(G) B♭
your name? Will you go where you don't know and nev - er
your name? Will you care for cruel and kind and nev - er
your name? Will you set the pris - oners free and nev - er
your name? Will you quell the fear in - side and nev - er
my name. Let me turn and fol - low you and nev - er
(Em7) Gm7
(G/A) B♭/C
(D) F
(Em7) Gm7
(G) B♭
be the same? Will you let my love be shown,
be the same? Will you risk the hos - tile stare
be the same? Will you kiss the lep - er clean,
be the same? Will you use the faith you've found
be the same. In your com - pa - ny I'll go

Text: John L. Bell (Scotland) and Graham Maule (Scotland)
Music: Scottish traditional; arr. Lloyd Kauffman (USA), arr. © 2015 Lilly Chapel Press, LLC

(Em) Gm (F♯m) Am (G) B♭ (A7) C7 (D) F
will you let my name be known, will you let my
should your life at - tract or scare? Will you let me
and do such as this un - seen, and ad - mit to
to re - shape the world a - round, through my sight and
where your love and foot - steps show. Thus I'll move and
(A7) C7 (Bm) Dm (Em) Gm (A7) C7 (D) F
life be grown in you and you in me?
an - swer prayer in you and you in me?
what I mean in you and you in me?
touch and sound in you and you in me?
live and grow in you and you in me.

Listen in the Silence 541

LISTEN IN THE SILENCE Irregular

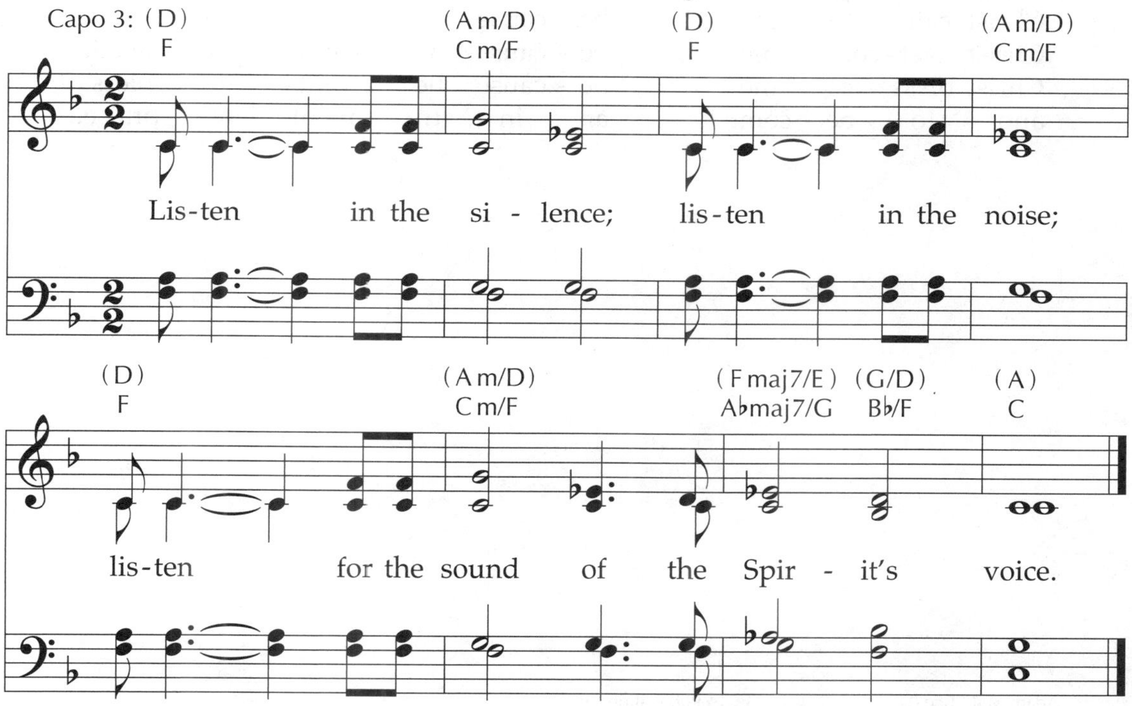
Capo 3: (D) F (Am/D) Cm/F (D) F (Am/D) Cm/F
Lis-ten in the si - lence; lis-ten in the noise;
(D) F (Am/D) Cm/F (Fmaj7/E) A♭maj7/G (G/D) B♭/F (A) C
lis-ten for the sound of the Spir - it's voice.

Text: Linnea Good (Canada)
Music: Linnea Good

542 Christ Calls to Me

TAKE UP THE SONG 10.10.10.10

G
B♭
Am7
Dno3
1 Christ calls to me, but not be - cause I seek,
2 Christ wel - comes me, but not be - cause I trust,
3 Christ bless - es me, but not be - cause I serve,
4 I seek, I trust, I serve, be - cause of grace,
G
B♭
Am7
D
and not be - cause of an - y words I pray,
and not be - cause of mer - it, work, or deed,
and not be - cause I share all I pos - sess,
a grace that tunes my heart to ho - ly ways,
G
B♭
Am7
Dno3
or times that I con - fess that I am weak;
or an - y claims that I am good and just;
and seek no more than what I might de - serve;
to live and love with - in Christ's broad em - brace,
G
Christ calls to me be - cause I of - ten stray.
Christ wel - comes me be - cause he knows my need.
Christ bless - es me be - cause he wants to bless.
and to be - come an in - stru - ment of praise.

De noche iremos (By Night, We Hasten)

543

DE NOCHE IREMOS LM

Ostinato Refrain
Dm
Bb
De no - che͜ i - re - mos, de no - che, que
By night, we has - ten in dark - ness, to
Am Gm Asus A Dm C
pa - ra͜ en - con - trar la fuen - te, só - lo la sed nos a -
search for the liv - ing wa - ter, on - ly our thirst leads us
F A Bb A
Last time
lum - bra, só - lo la sed nos a - lum - bra.
on - wards, on - ly our thirst leads us on - wards.
Last time

Verses appear in the accompaniment edition.

Text: Spanish; (verses Psalm 42:2, 6, 8); Luis Rosales (Spain); trans. Taizé Community (France)
Music: Jacques Berthier (France), *Music from Taizé*

544 Softly and Tenderly Jesus Is Calling

THOMPSON 11.7.11.7 with refrain

Capo 1: (G) Ab (C) Db (G) Ab
1 Soft - ly and ten - der - ly Je - sus is call - ing,
2 Why should we tar - ry when Je - sus is plead - ing,
3 O for the won - der - ful love he has prom - ised,
(A7) Bb7 (D) Eb (G) Ab
call - ing for you and for me; see, on the por - tals he's
plead - ing for you and for me? Why should we lin - ger and
prom - ised for you and for me! Though we have sinned, he has
(C) Db (G) Ab (D) Eb (G) Ab
wait - ing and watch - ing, watch - ing for you and for me.
heed not his mer - cies, mer - cies for you and for me?
mer - cy and par - don, par - don for you and for me.
Refrain
(D) Eb (G) Ab
"Come home, come home!
come home, Come home!

Text: Will L. Thompson (USA), *Sparkling Gems Nos. 1 & 2 Combined,* 1880
Music: Will L. Thompson, *Sparkling Gems Nos. 1 & 2 Combined,* 1880

(D) (E7) (A) (D) (A7)(D7) (G)
Eb F7 Bb Eb Bb7 Eb7 Ab
You who are wea-ry, come home." Ear-nest-ly, ten-der-ly,
(C) (G) (D7) (G)
Db Ab Eb7 Ab
Je-sus is call-ing, call-ing, *"O sin-ner, come home!"

*or, "Beloved, come home!"

545 Here I Am, Lord

HERE I AM, LORD 7.7.7.4 D with refrain

1 I, the Lord of sea and sky, I have heard my peo-ple cry. All who dwell in deep-est sin my hand will save. I who made the stars of night, I will make the dark-ness bright. Who will bear my light to them? Whom shall I send?
2 I, the Lord of snow and rain, I have borne my peo-ple's pain. I have wept for love of them. They turn a-way. I will break their hearts of stone, give them hearts for love a-lone. I will speak my word to them. Whom shall I send?
3 I, the Lord of wind and flame, I will call the poor by name. I will set a feast for them. My hand will save. Fin-est bread I will pro-vide till their hearts be sat-is-fied. I will give my life to them. Whom shall I send?
Refrain
Here I am, Lord. Is it I, Lord?

Text: Daniel L. Schutte (USA), 1980, *Lord of Light*, 1981, alt.
Music: Daniel L. Schutte; arr. Michael Pope, SJ (USA), and John Weissrock (USA)

Am7 G/B Am/C C D
I have heard you call-ing in the night.
G Gsus G C/E G
I will go, Lord, if you lead me.
Am7 D G Gsus G
I will hold your peo-ple in my heart.

546 There Is a Line of Women

CLIMBING VINE 7.6.7.6 D

Capo 1: (D) E♭ (G) A♭
1 There is a line of wom-en ex - tend - ing back to
2 There is a line of wom-en who took on pow'r - ful
3 There is a line of wom-en who stood by Je - sus'
(D) E♭ (A) B♭ (D) E♭
Eve whose role in shap - ing hist' - ry God
men, de - fy - ing laws and scru - ples to
side, who housed him while he mini-stered and
(A) B♭ (G) A♭
on - ly could con - ceive; and though through end - less
let life live a - gain; and though, de - spite their
held him when he died; and though they claimed he'd
(Bm) Cm (Bm/A) Cm/B♭ (G) A♭ (F♯m) Gm
ag - es their wit - ness was re - pressed, God
tri - umph, their sto - ries stayed un - told, God
ris - en, their news was deemed sus - pect till
(Em) Fm (Bm) Cm (G) A♭ (A) B♭
val - ued and in - spired them through whom the world was
kept their num - ber grow - ing, cre - a - tive, strong, and
Je - sus stood a - mong them, his wo - man - ly e -
(D) E♭ (G/A) A♭/B♭ (A) B♭ (D) E♭
bless'd. So sing a song of Sa - rah— to
bold. So sing a song of Shiph-rah with
lect. So sing a song of An - na who

Text: John L. Bell (Scotland), © 2002 WGRG, Iona Community (admin. GIA Publications, Inc.)
Music: Charlene Nafziger (Canada), © 2019 Charlene Nafziger

(G) A♭ (D) E♭
laugh - ter she gave birth; and sing a song of
Pu - ah close at hand: en - gaged to kill male
saw Christ's in - fant face; and sing a song of
(E) F (A) B♭
Ta - mar who stood for wo-men's worth; and
chil - dren, they foiled the king's com - mand; and
Mar - tha who gave him food and space; and
(G) A♭ (D) E♭ (Bm) Cm (D/A) E♭/B♭
sing a song of Han-nah who bar - gained with her
sing a song of Ra - hab who shel - tered spies and
sing of all the Ma - rys who heed - ed his re -
(G) A♭ (G/F♯) A♭/G (Em) Fm (D/F♯) E♭/G
Lord; and sing a song of Ma - ry who
lied; and sing a song of Es - ther pre -
quests and now at heav - en's ban-quet are
(G) A♭ (A) B♭ (D) E♭ (G/A) A♭/B♭ (A) B♭
Last time
bore and bred God's Word.
vent - ing gen - o - cide.
Je - sus' fond - est guests.

547 How Clear Is Our Vocation

REPTON 8.6.8.8.6.6

Capo 1: (D) E♭ (A) B♭ (Bm) Cm
1 How clear is our vo - ca - tion, Lord, when
2 But if, for - get - ful, we should find your
3 We mar - vel how your saints be - come in
4 In what you give us, Lord, to do, to -
(G) A♭ (A) B♭ (D) E♭ (A) B♭ (Em) Fm (A) B♭
once we heed your call: to live ac - cord - ing to your
yoke is hard to bear; if world - ly pres - sures fray the
hin - dranc - es more sure, whose joy - ful vir - tues put to
ge - ther or a - lone, in old rou - tines and ven - tures
(Bm) Cm (G) A♭ (A) B♭
word, and dai - ly learn, re - freshed, re - stored, that
mind, and love it - self can - not un - wind its
shame the cas - ual way we wear your name, and
new, may we not cease to look to you. The
(D) E♭ (A7) B♭7 (Em) Fm (A7) B♭7 (D) E♭
you are Lord of all, and will not let us fall.
tan - gled skein of care, our in - ward life re - pair.
by our faults ob - scure your pow'r to cleanse and cure.
cross you hung up - on— all you en - deav - ored done.

Chord symbols represent a simplified harmony.

Music: Charles H. H. Parry (England), *Judith*, 1888

Open, Lord, My Inward Ear 548

WHISPER 7.6.7.6.7.7.7.6

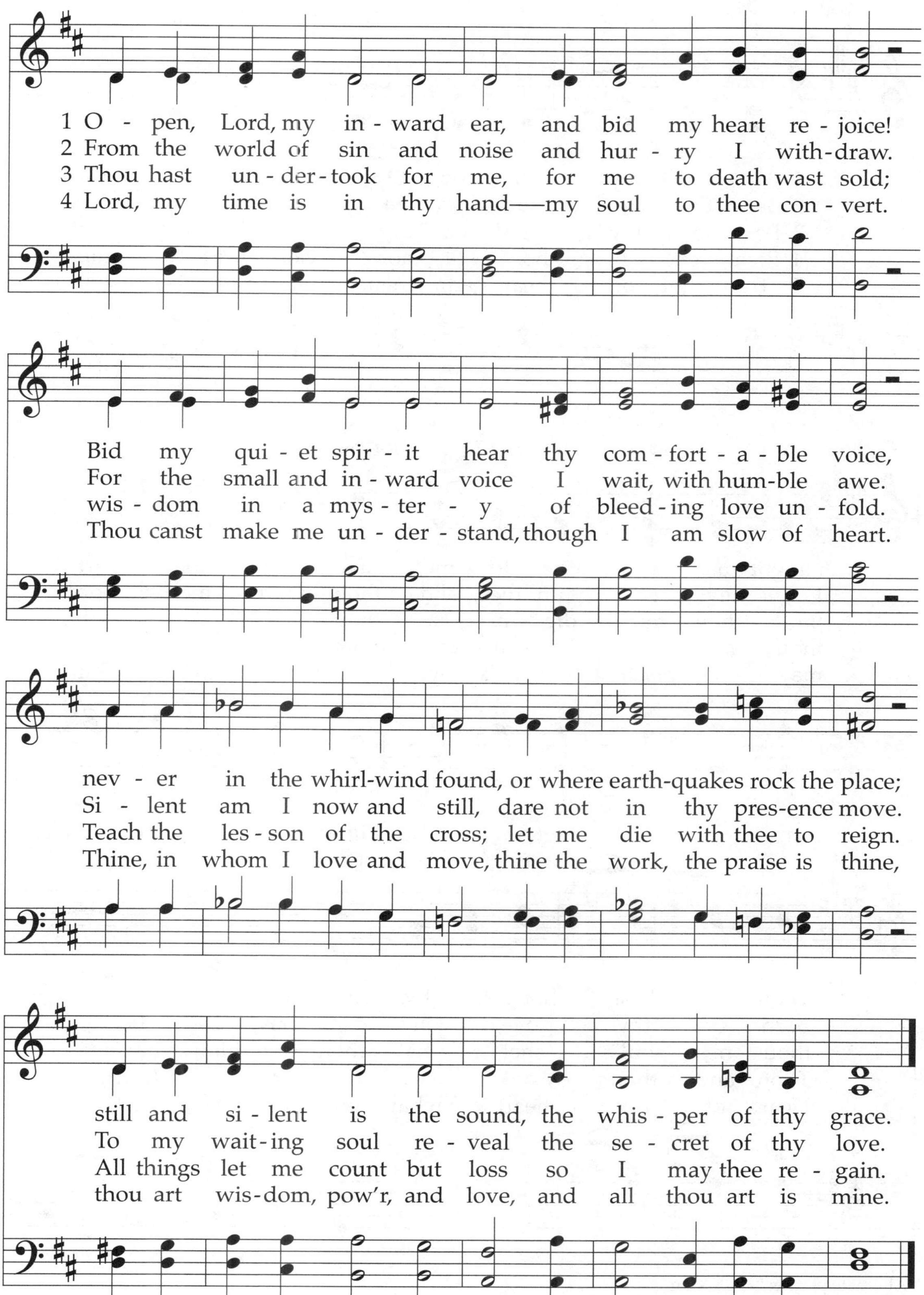
1 O - pen, Lord, my in - ward ear, and bid my heart re - joice!
2 From the world of sin and noise and hur - ry I with-draw.
3 Thou hast un - der - took for me, for me to death wast sold;
4 Lord, my time is in thy hand—my soul to thee con - vert.
Bid my qui - et spir - it hear thy com - fort - a - ble voice,
For the small and in - ward voice I wait, with hum-ble awe.
wis - dom in a mys - ter - y of bleed - ing love un - fold.
Thou canst make me un - der - stand, though I am slow of heart.
nev - er in the whirl-wind found, or where earth-quakes rock the place;
Si - lent am I now and still, dare not in thy pres-ence move.
Teach the les - son of the cross; let me die with thee to reign.
Thine, in whom I love and move, thine the work, the praise is thine,
still and si - lent is the sound, the whis - per of thy grace.
To my wait - ing soul re - veal the se - cret of thy love.
All things let me count but loss so I may thee re - gain.
thou art wis - dom, pow'r, and love, and all thou art is mine.

Text: Charles Wesley (England), *Hymns and Spiritual Songs*, 1742
Music: Bradley P. Lehman (USA),

549 Be Thou My Vision

SLANE 10.10.9.10

Capo 2: (D) E (G) A (D) E (Bm) C♯m (A) B (D) E
1 Be thou my vi - sion, O Lord of my heart;
2 Be thou my wis - dom, be thou my true word;
3 Be thou my buck - ler, my sword for the fight.
4 Rich - es I heed not, nor vain emp - ty praise;
5 *True Light of heav - en, when vic - t'ry is won

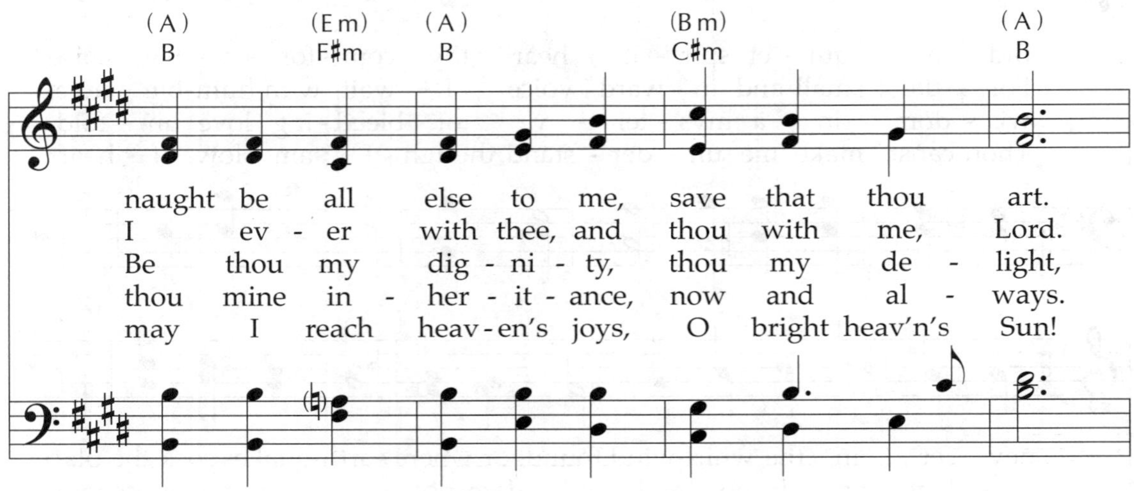
(A) B (Em) F♯m (A) B (Bm) C♯m (A) B
naught be all else to me, save that thou art.
I ev - er with thee, and thou with me, Lord.
Be thou my dig - ni - ty, thou my de - light,
thou mine in - her - it - ance, now and al - ways.
may I reach heav - en's joys, O bright heav'n's Sun!

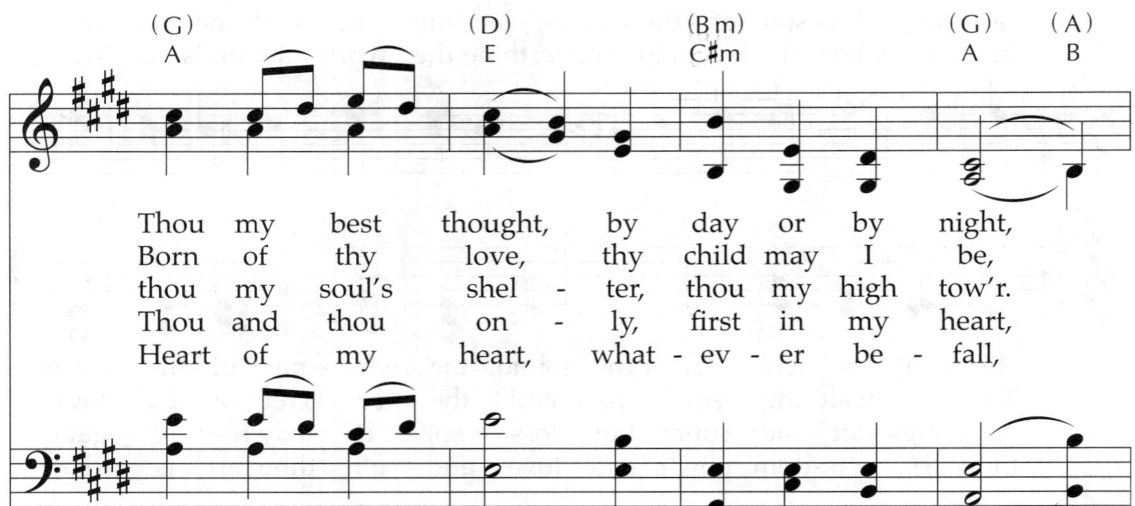
(G) A (D) E (Bm) C♯m (G) A (A) B
Thou my best thought, by day or by night,
Born of thy love, thy child may I be,
thou my soul's shel - ter, thou my high tow'r.
Thou and thou on - ly, first in my heart,
Heart of my heart, what - ev - er be - fall,

*Alternate phrase: "High King"

Text: Irish traditional, "Rob tu mo bhoile, a Comdi cride," ca. 8th c.; trans. Mary Elizabeth Byrne (Ireland), *Ériu*, Vol. 2, 1905, alt.
Music: Irish traditional, *Old Irish Folk Music and Songs*, 1909; harm. Martin Shaw (England), *Enlarged Songs of Praise*, 1931, alt.,

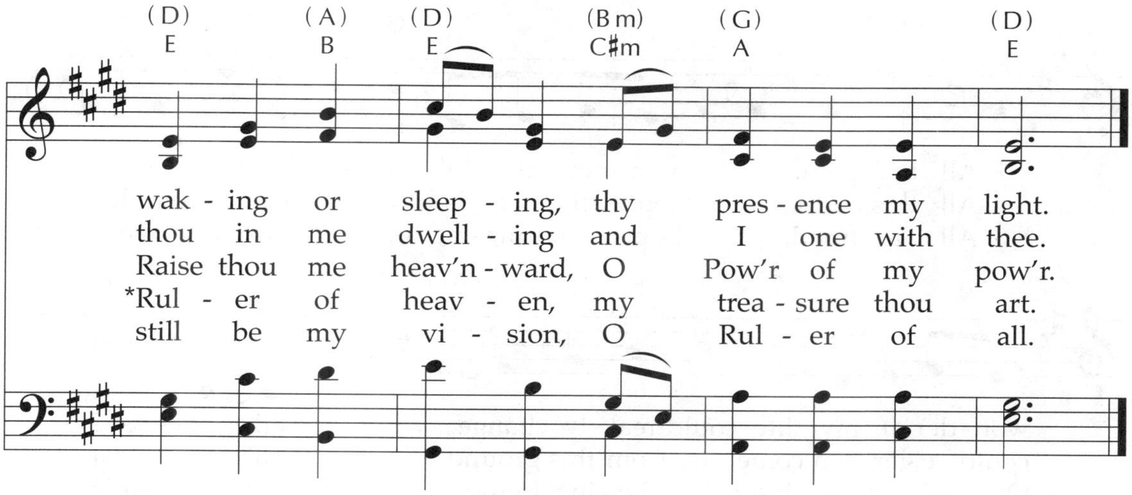
(D) (A) (D) (Bm) (G) (D)
E B E C♯m A E
wak - ing or sleep - ing, thy pres - ence my light.
thou in me dwell - ing and I one with thee.
Raise thou me heav'n - ward, O Pow'r of my pow'r.
*Rul - er of heav - en, my trea - sure thou art.
still be my vi - sion, O Rul - er of all.

God Who Touches Earth with Beauty 550

EARTHRISE 8.5.8.5

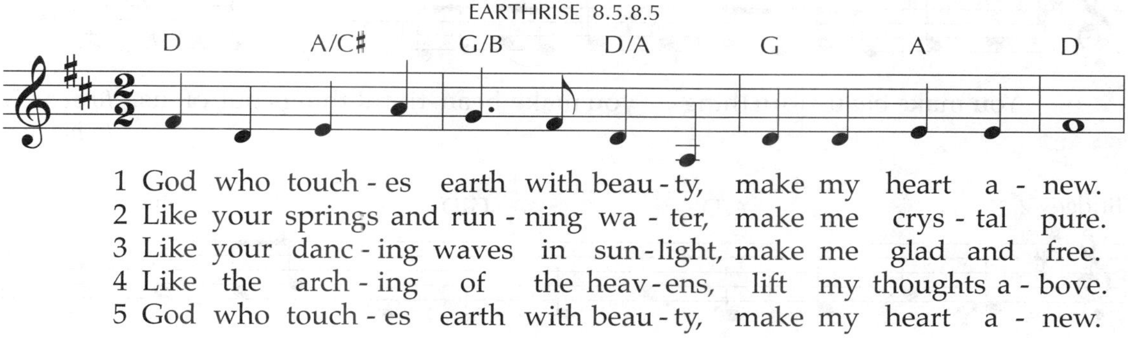
D A/C♯ G/B D/A G A D
1 God who touch - es earth with beau - ty, make my heart a - new.
2 Like your springs and run - ning wa - ter, make me crys - tal pure.
3 Like your danc - ing waves in sun - light, make me glad and free.
4 Like the arch - ing of the heav - ens, lift my thoughts a - bove.
5 God who touch - es earth with beau - ty, make my heart a - new.

Bm D/A G D/F♯ Em A7 D
With your Spir - it re - cre - ate me pure and strong and true.
Like your rocks of tow - 'ring gran - deur, make me strong and sure.
Like the straight - ness of the pine trees, let me up - right be.
Turn my dreams to no - ble ac - tion, min - is - tries of love.
Keep me ev - er, by your Spi - rit, pure and strong and true.

Text: Mary S. Edgar (Canada), 1925, alt.
Music: Alfred V. Fedak (USA), 1988, © 1989 Sacred Music Press

551 Beautiful Things

BEAUTIFUL THINGS Irregular

G A/G D G A/G D
1 All this pain. I won-der if I'll ev - er find my way; I
2 All this earth. Could all that is lost ev - er be found;
3 All a - round, hope is spring-ing up from this old ground.
G A/G Bm7 Asus G A/G D
won-der if my life could real - ly change at all. to verse 2
could a gar-den come up from this ground at all? to refrain
Out of cha-os, life is be - ing found in you. to refrain
Refrain
D A/D G/D D
You make beau-ti-ful things, you make beau-ti - ful things out of the dust.
D A/D G/D D
You make beau-ti-ful things, you make beau-ti - ful things out of us. to verse 3
to bridge
Bridge
D A/D G/D D
You make me new, you are mak - ing me new.
D A/D G/D D
You make me new, you are mak - ing me new.

Text: Michael Gungor (USA) and Lisa Gungor (USA)
Music: Michael Gungor and Lisa Gungor

As a Deer in Want of Water 552

GENEVA 42 (FREU DICH SEHR) 8.7.8.7.7.7.8.8

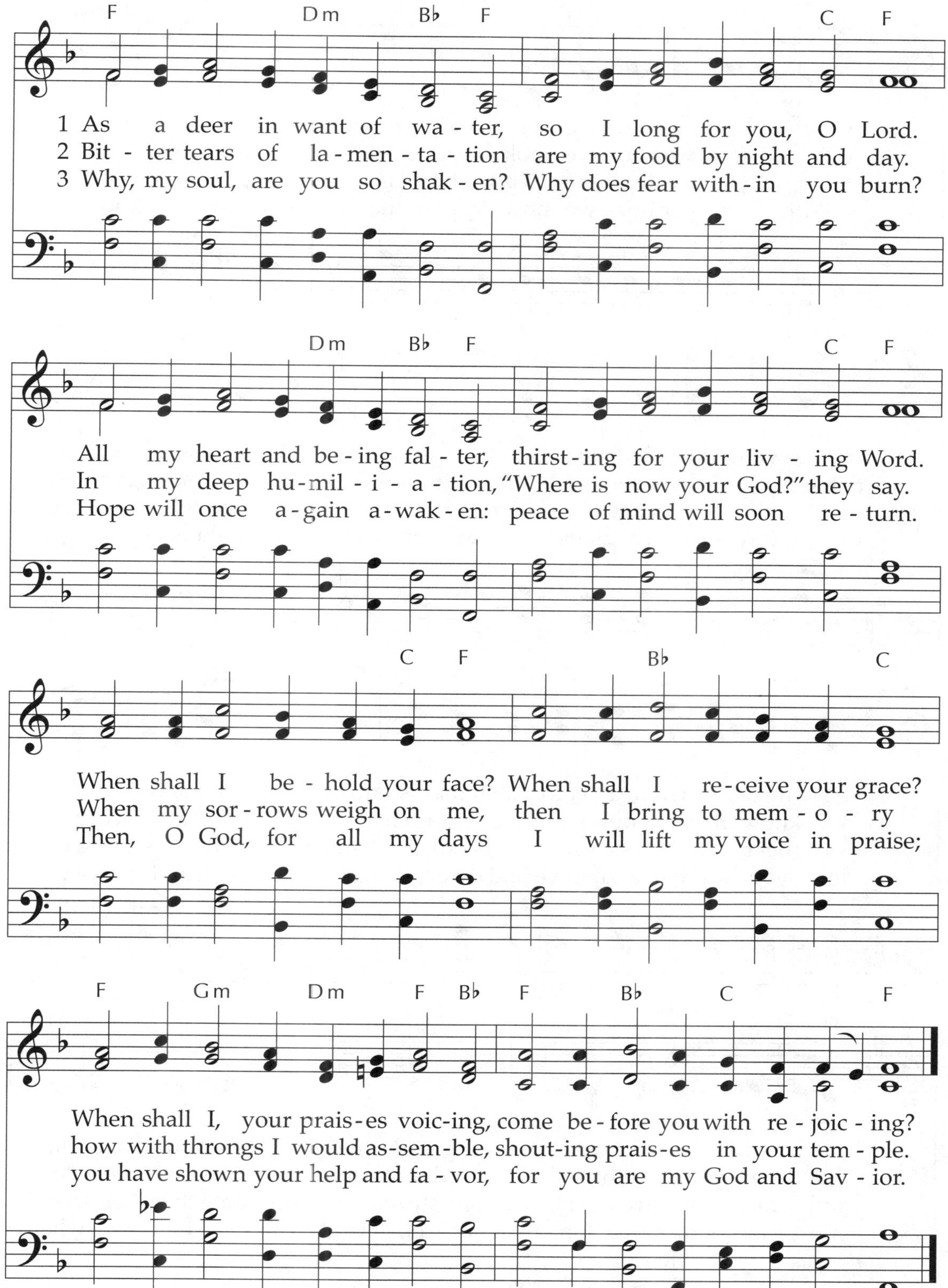
F Dm B♭ F C F
1 As a deer in want of wa - ter, so I long for you, O Lord.
2 Bit - ter tears of la - men - ta - tion are my food by night and day.
3 Why, my soul, are you so shak - en? Why does fear with - in you burn?
Dm B♭ F C F
All my heart and be - ing fal - ter, thirst - ing for your liv - ing Word.
In my deep hu - mil - i - a - tion, "Where is now your God?" they say.
Hope will once a - gain a - wak - en: peace of mind will soon re - turn.
C F B♭ C
When shall I be - hold your face? When shall I re - ceive your grace?
When my sor - rows weigh on me, then I bring to mem - o - ry
Then, O God, for all my days I will lift my voice in praise;
F Gm Dm F B♭ F B♭ C F
When shall I, your prais - es voic - ing, come be - fore you with re - joic - ing?
how with throngs I would as - sem - ble, shout - ing prais - es in your tem - ple.
you have shown your help and fa - vor, for you are my God and Sav - ior.

Text: based on Psalm 42; stanzas 1–2 *Psalter Hymnal* (USA), 1987, alt., © 1987 Faith Alive Christian Resources; stanza 3 Mennonite Worship and Song Committee

Music: Louis Bourgeois (present-day France), Genevan Psalter, *Octante Trois Pseaumes de David*, 1551; harm. adapt. from Claude Goudimel (present-day France), *150 Pseaumes de David*, 1564

553 How Many Times We Start Again

THE ROWAN TREE CMD

D G D
1 How man-y times we start a-gain on faith's un-wind-ing way;
2 Be - fore we go, we look a-round, sur-vey-ing where we are.
3 But great-er than the cost we find is our ex-pand-ed view
4 With ea-ger hope we now de-part the plac-es that we know,
G D A D
we want, dear God, to set-tle in, to build a home and stay,
Some ask, why leave fa - mil-iar ground for some-where strange and far?
of what it means, with heart and mind, to trust and fol - low you:
to trav - el re-gions in your heart where you would have us go.
G D
but then a dream, a voice, a light dis - turbs our peace and rest
We know from all our start-ings out each jour - ney has its cost:
we hear a mu - sic nev - er heard, a dif - f'rent light de - scends,
In you we live and move and dwell, as close as breath and prayer,
D G D A D
and sets be-fore our strain-ing sight new stag - es on our quest.
that some - times faith gives way to doubt and some-times we get lost.
and meet - ing stran-gers, we are stirred to wel-come them as friends.
you are our home: Em - man - u - el, God-with-us ev - 'ry-where.

Text: Thomas H. Troeger (USA), © 2009 Oxford University Press
Music: Scottish traditional; harm. Bradley Kauffman (USA), © 2020 Bradley Kauffman

Eternal Light, Shine in My Heart 554

SERENA LM

F Gm Am Gm7 F
1 E - ter - nal Light, shine in my heart. E - ter - nal
2 E - ter - nal Life, raise me from death. E - ter - nal
3 un - til by your most cost - ly grace, in - vit - ed
Gm Am C/G B♭ F/A
Hope, lift up my eyes. E - ter - nal Pow'r, be
Bright-ness, help me see. E - ter - nal Spir - it,
by your ho - ly word, at last I come be -
Gm7 C B♭ Csus C
1, 2
F
my sup - port. E - ter - nal Wis-dom, make me wise.
give me breath. E - ter - nal Sav - ior, come to me,
fore your face to know you, my e - ter - nal
3
Dm B♭ Csus C F
God, to know you, my e - ter - nal God.

Text: based on a prayer by Alcuin (England), 8th c.; Christopher Idle (England), 1977, *Hymns for Today's Church*,
Music: Irene Zacharias Moon (USA),

555 Lord, I Am Fondly, Earnestly Longing

OPEN THE WELLS 10.9.10.9 with refrain

1 Lord, I am fond - ly, ear - nest - ly long - ing in - to thy ho - ly like - ness to grow, thirst - ing for more and deep - er com - mun - ion, yearn - ing thy love more ful - ly to know.
2 Dead to the world would I be, O Sav - ior, dead un - to sin, a - live un - to thee. Cru - ci - fy all the earth - ly with - in me, emp - tied of sin and self may I be.
3 I would be thine and serve thee for - ev - er, filled with thy Spir - it, lost in thy love. Come to my heart, Lord, come with a - noint - ing, show - ers of grace send down from a - bove.
Refrain
O - pen the wells of grace and sal - va - tion, pour the rich streams
O - pen the wells of grace and sal - va - tion, pour the rich

Text: Elisha A. Hoffman (USA), *Church and Sunday School Hymnal*, 1902, alt.
Music: Charles E. Pollock (USA), *Church and Sunday School Hymnal*, 1902

G
deep in - to my heart. Cleanse and re - fine my
streams deep in - to my heart. Cleanse and re - fine my
Am D7 G
thought and af - fec-tion, seal me and make me pure as thou art.
thought and af - fec-tion, seal me and make me pure as thou art.

I Bind My Heart This Tide 556

UNION 6.7.7.7

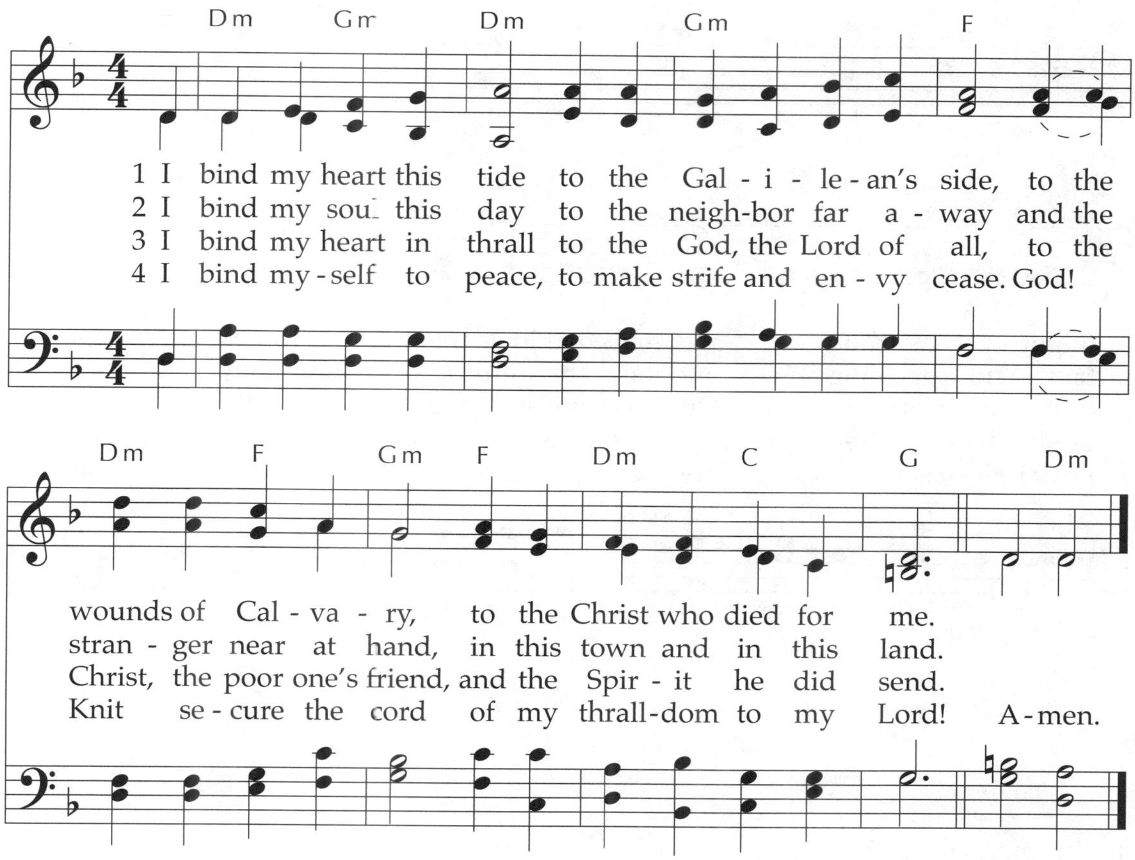
Dm Gm Dm Gm F
1 I bind my heart this tide to the Gal - i - le - an's side, to the
2 I bind my soul this day to the neigh-bor far a - way and the
3 I bind my heart in thrall to the God, the Lord of all, to the
4 I bind my - self to peace, to make strife and en - vy cease. God!
Dm F Gm F Dm C G Dm
wounds of Cal - va - ry, to the Christ who died for me.
stran - ger near at hand, in this town and in this land.
Christ, the poor one's friend, and the Spir - it he did send.
Knit se - cure the cord of my thrall-dom to my Lord! A-men.

Text: Lauchlan M. Watt (Scotland), *The Tryst: A Book of the Soul*, 1907, alt.
Music: J. Randall Zercher (USA), 1965, *The Mennonite Hymnal*, 1969,

557 Spirit of God! Descend

MORECAMBE 10.10.10.10

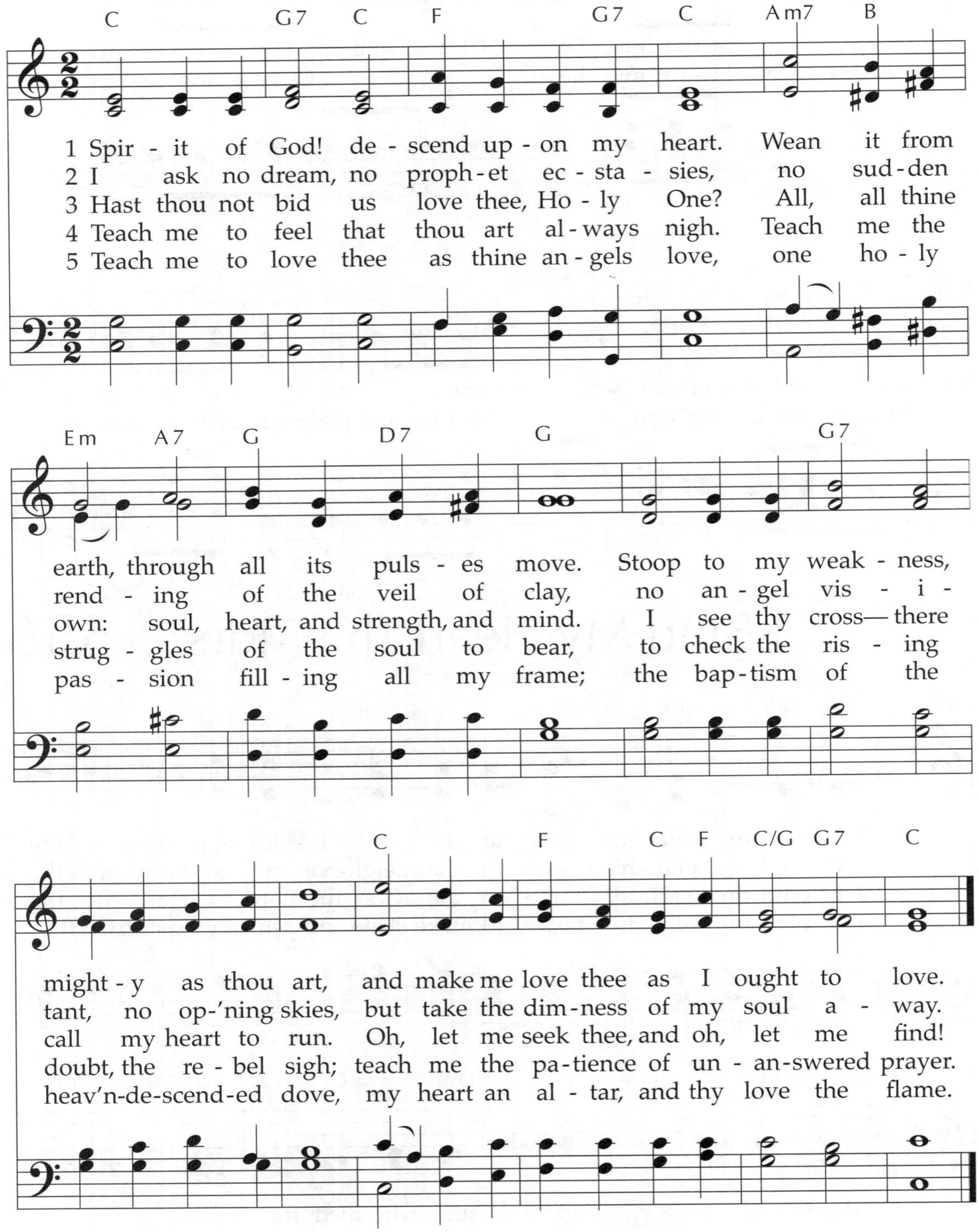
C G7 C F G7 C Am7 B
1 Spir - it of God! de - scend up - on my heart. Wean it from
2 I ask no dream, no proph - et ec - sta - sies, no sud - den
3 Hast thou not bid us love thee, Ho - ly One? All, all thine
4 Teach me to feel that thou art al - ways nigh. Teach me the
5 Teach me to love thee as thine an - gels love, one ho - ly
Em A7 G D7 G G7
earth, through all its puls - es move. Stoop to my weak - ness,
rend - ing of the veil of clay, no an - gel vis - i -
own: soul, heart, and strength, and mind. I see thy cross— there
strug - gles of the soul to bear, to check the ris - ing
pas - sion fill - ing all my frame; the bap - tism of the
C F C F C/G G7 C
might - y as thou art, and make me love thee as I ought to love.
tant, no op-'ning skies, but take the dim - ness of my soul a - way.
call my heart to run. Oh, let me seek thee, and oh, let me find!
doubt, the re - bel sigh; teach me the pa - tience of un - an - swered prayer.
heav'n - de - scend - ed dove, my heart an al - tar, and thy love the flame.

Text: George Croly (England), *Lyra Britannica*, 1867, alt.
Music: Frederick C. Atkinson (England), 1870, *Congregational Church Hymnal*, 1887

Lord, I Want to Be a Christian 558

LORD, I WANT TO BE A CHRISTIAN Irregular

D G D
1 Lord, I want to be a Chris-tian in my heart, in my heart.
A Bm G D G D
Lord, I want to be a Chris-tian in my heart.
G D Bm
In my heart, in my heart,
In my heart, in my heart,
D A7 Bm G D
Lord, I want to be a Chris-tian in my heart.

2 Lord, I want to be more loving . . .
3 Lord, I want to be more holy . . .
4 Lord, I want to be like Jesus . . .

Text: African American spiritual (USA), *Folk Songs of the American Negro*, 1907
Music: African American spiritual, *Folk Songs of the American Negro*, 1907; harm. anon.

559 Agneau de Dieu (O Lamb of God)

AGNEAU DE DIEU Irregular

Capo 3: (D) F (G) B♭ (Em) Gm (A7) C7
1 Ag-neau de Dieu, je viens, Ag-neau de Dieu, je viens, (à toi)
2 Si je vis, c'est pour toi, si je vis, c'est pour toi, (pour toi)
3 Al - le - lu - ia, a - men, al - le - lu - ia, a - men, (a - men)
1 O Lamb of God, I come, O Lamb of God, I come, (to you)
2 I give my life to you, I give my life to you, (to you)
3 Al - le - lu - ia, a - men, al - le - lu - ia, a - men, (a - men)
(D) F (Em) Gm (D/A) F/C (A7) C7 (D) F
Ag-neau de Dieu, je viens, (à toi) Ag-neau de Dieu, je viens.
si je vis, c'est pour toi, (pour toi) si je vis, c'est pour toi.
al - le - lu - ia, a - men, (a - men) al - le - lu - ia, a - men.
O Lamb of God, I come, (to you) O Lamb of God, I come.
I give my life to you, (to you) I give my life to you.
al - le - lu - ia, a - men, (a - men) al - le - lu - ia, a - men.

Text: French; Abraham Arpellet (Côte d'Ivoire)
Music: unknown (West Africa)

Just As I Am, without One Plea 560

WOODWORTH LM

D A D A
1 Just as I am, with - out one plea, but that thy blood was
2 Just as I am, though tossed a - bout with man - y‿a con - flict,
3 Just as I am, thou wilt re - ceive, wilt wel - come, par - don,
4 Just as I am, thy love un-known hath bro - ken ev - 'ry
G/D D G
shed for me, and that thou bidst me come to thee,
man - y‿a doubt, fight - ings and fears with - in, with - out,
cleanse, re - lieve; be - cause thy prom - ise I be - lieve,
bar - rier down. Now to be thine, yea, thine a - lone,
D A D
O Lamb of God, I come, I come!

Alternate tune: THE WATER IS WIDE (#522 or #524)

Text: Charlotte Elliott (England), 1834, *Invalid's Hymn Book,* 1836
Music: William B. Bradbury (USA), *The Mendelssohn Collection, or . . . Third Book of Psalmody,* 1849

561 Here's My Life, I Lay It Down

LAY IT DOWN Irregular

G C2 G
1 Here's my life, I lay it down; here's my
C2 Dsus D
life, I lay it down, I lay it down.
Refrain
D C2 Dsus
I sur-ren-der it all to you; I sur-ren-der it all
Em7 D/F♯ G C2
to you; I sur-ren-der it all to you;
Dsus C2 Csus2 C2
I let go and give it to you.
2 Here's my pride … 3 Here's my fear …

Text: Dave Lubben (USA)
Music: Dave Lubben

562 Dooládó' Shi Diyinda (What a Wonderful Savior)

DOOLÁDÓ' SHI DIYINDA Irregular

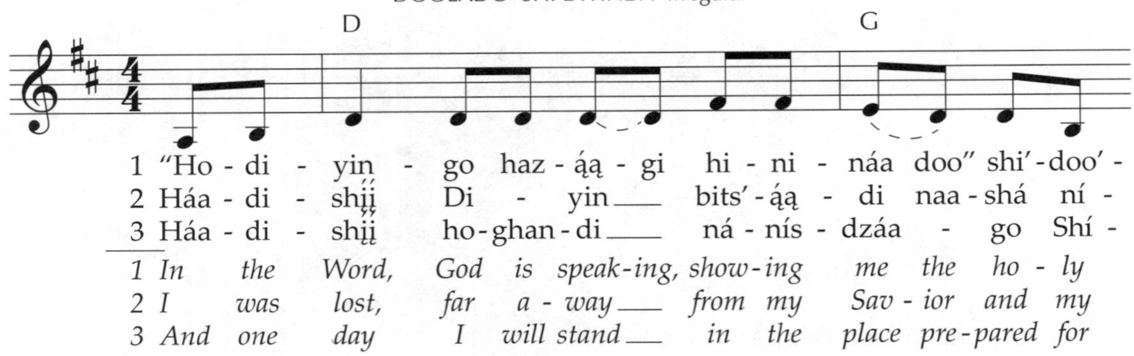
D G
1 "Ho - di - yin - go haz - ą́ą - gi hi - ni - náa doo" shi'-doo' -
2 Háa - di - shįį Di - yin___ bits'-ą́ą - di naa-shá ní -
3 Háa - di - shįį ho-ghan-di___ ná - nís - dzáa - go Shí -
1 In the Word, God is speak-ing, show-ing me the ho - ly
2 I was lost, far a - way___ from my Sav - ior and my
3 And one day I will stand___ in the place pre-pared for

Text: Navajo; Daniel Smiley (Navajo, USA)
Music: Daniel Smiley

D
A
niid. "Háá - lá ná a - hóó - t'i' - go ná'‿ál - yaa" Níł-ch'i
t'ę́ę́ Tsí - dá yée - go á - deesh - chxo' ní - t'ę́ę́ Je - sus
éí Je - sus shi - zéé - doo - chił - go "She' - a -
way, for the path has been o - pened to me. Ho - ly
friend. I had was - ted my life, walked in shame. Je - sus
me, And I'll hear Je - sus say, "Wel-come home! Well
D
D7
G
D
Di - yin - ii éí Shi - k'i hoo - le' go shił hóz -
éí shi - dáá - dóó yii - zi' go hash - íí dziiz shił hóz -
wéé' shaa - néín dzáá - lá" di - doo - niił, shił hóz -
Spir - it of God, sanc - ti - fy my soul. With
came, washed me clean, saved my soul, set me free. With
done, my child, come to me, find your rest." With
A7
D
Refrain
hǫ́ǫ - go ho - ghan - góó dah dii yá.
hǫ́ǫ - go ho - ghan - góó dah dii - yá. Dool - á - dó' Shi Di-
hǫ́ǫ - go yá' - aa - dee - sháál.
joy in my heart I'm head - ed home.
joy in my heart I'm head - ed home. What a won - der - ful
joy in my heart I'll en - ter home.
A
yin - da, ay - óó - 'at' - éi éí yee á - kás - zaaz. T'áa-doo
Sav - ior, he is might - y and a - ble to save! In his
D
D7
G
D
bą́ą́ nish - łį́į - nii éi - dí shaa - yii léh. Ay - óó' -
mer - cy and grace he has giv - en all we need, And his
A
D
a - shóo' - níi - go éí á - dí - shóól - ł'ąh'.
heart o - ver - flows with love for me.

563 Come, Thou Fount

NETTLETON 8.7.8.7 D

A7 D A D G A7 D
1 Come, thou fount of ev-'ry bless-ing, tune my heart to sing thy grace.
2 Here I raise my Eb-en-e-zer, hith-er by thy help I'm come,
3 Oh, to grace how great a debt-or dai-ly I'm con-strained to be!
A7 D A D G A7 D
Streams of mer-cy, nev-er ceas-ing, call for songs of loud-est praise.
and I hope, by thy good plea-sure, safe-ly to ar-rive at home.
Let that grace now, like a fet-ter, bind my wan-d'ring heart to thee.
A7 D G D A7 D G D
Teach me some me-lo-dious son-net, sung by flam-ing tongues a-bove.
Je-sus sought me when a stran-ger, wan-d'ring from the fold of God.
Prone to wan-der, Lord, I feel it, prone to leave the God I love.
A7 D A D G A7 D
Praise the mount, I'm fixed up-on it, mount of God's un-chang-ing love.
He, to res-cue me from dan-ger, in-ter-posed his pre-cious blood.
Here's my heart, O take and seal it, seal it for thy courts a-bove.

Text: Robert Robinson (England), 1758, *A Collection of Hymns* [. . .], 1759
Music: American traditional (USA), in John Wyeth's *Repository of Sacred Music, Part Second*, 1813

What Wondrous Love Is This 564

WONDROUS LOVE 12.9.12.12.9

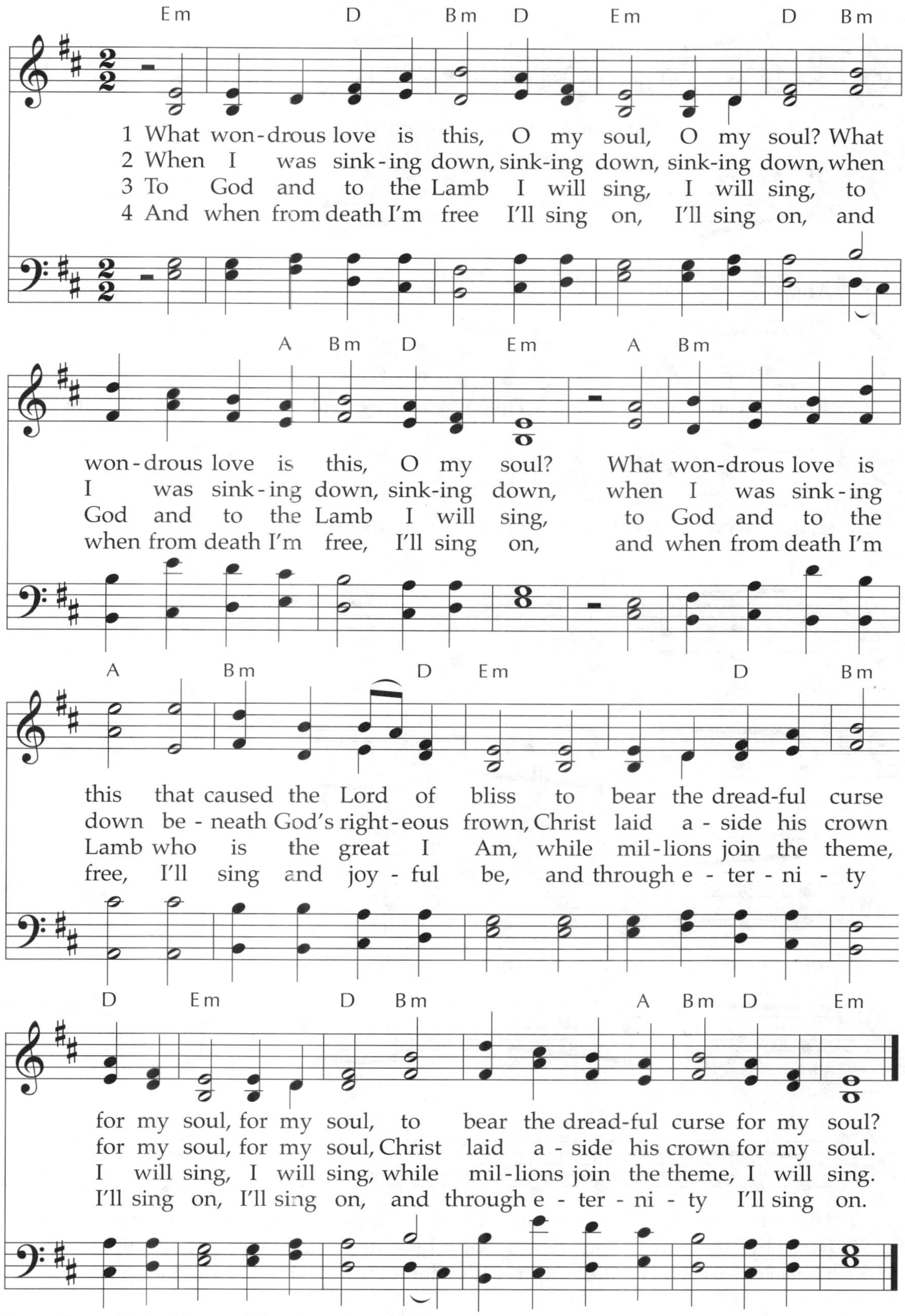
Em D Bm D Em D Bm
1 What won-drous love is this, O my soul, O my soul? What
2 When I was sink-ing down, sink-ing down, sink-ing down, when
3 To God and to the Lamb I will sing, I will sing, to
4 And when from death I'm free I'll sing on, I'll sing on, and
A Bm D Em A Bm
won-drous love is this, O my soul? What won-drous love is
I was sink-ing down, sink-ing down, when I was sink-ing
God and to the Lamb I will sing, to God and to the
when from death I'm free, I'll sing on, and when from death I'm
A Bm D Em D Bm
this that caused the Lord of bliss to bear the dread-ful curse
down be-neath God's right-eous frown, Christ laid a-side his crown
Lamb who is the great I Am, while mil-lions join the theme,
free, I'll sing and joy-ful be, and through e-ter-ni-ty
D Em D Bm A Bm D Em
for my soul, for my soul, to bear the dread-ful curse for my soul?
for my soul, for my soul, Christ laid a-side his crown for my soul.
I will sing, I will sing, while mil-lions join the theme, I will sing.
I'll sing on, I'll sing on, and through e-ter-ni-ty I'll sing on.

Text: *Cluster of Spiritual Songs*, 3rd ed. (USA), 1823
Music: American traditional (USA), *Southern Harmony*, 1840; harm. Alice Parker (USA),

565 Christ Is Alive, and Goes Before Us

CHRIST IS ALIVE 9.8.9.8 with refrain

Refrain
Christ is a - live, and goes be-fore us to show and share what
show and
love can do. This is a day of new be - gin-nings;
share what love can do. This day new be - gin - nings;
our God is mak - ing all things new,
our God is mak - ing all things new.
Fine
1 This is a day of new be - gin-nings, time to re - mem - ber
2 For by the life and death of Je - sus, love's might - y Spir - it,
3 Then let us, with the Spir - it's dar - ing, step from the past and

Text: Brian Wren (England), © 1983 Hope Publishing Co.
Music: Lori True (USA), © 2003 GIA Publications, Inc.

Am Dsus D G C/G G F Em7
and move on, time to be - lieve what love is bring - ing,
now as then, can make for us a world of dif - f'rence,
leave be - hind our dis - ap - point - ment, guilt, and griev - ing,
Am7 G/B Cm7 Dsus D
To refrain
lay - ing to rest the pain that's gone.
as faith and hope are born a - gain.
seek - ing new paths, and sure to find.

Somlandela (We Will Follow) 566

SOMLANDELA 10.9.10.10

G C G
Som - lan - de - la, som-lan-del' u - Je - su. Som - lan - de - la
We will fol - low, we will fol - low Je - sus. We will fol - low,
D G C
yo - nke in - da - wo. Som - lan - de - la, som-lan-del' u - Je - su.
ev - 'ry-where he goes. We will fol - low, we will fol - low Je - sus.
G/D Em D C G
La - pho e - ya - kho - na som - lan - de - la.
Ev - 'ry - where he goes we will fol - low.

Text: Zulu; Zimbabwean traditional; trans. anon.
Music: Zimbabwean traditional; harm. anon.

567 Prabhoo Lay lay (Savior Jesus, Enfold Me)

PRABHOO LAY LAY Irregular

Refrain
Am Dm G E Fine
Pra-bhoo Lay lay muj-hay Too Ba-hoñ Meñ Ka heen gir na jaa-un gu naa hon meñ.
Sav-ior Je-sus, en-fold me in your arms, let me nev-er be part-ed from your love.
Verses
Am Em Am Am E Am Dm G E E
To refrain
1 Me-ra tan man aur dhan te-ray lee-ay, me-ra sa-ra jee-van te-ray lee-ay. ay. Mu-jay lay chal tu ap nee ra-hon May, ka heen gir na jaa un gu naa hon meñ. Mu-jay meñ.
2 Me-ray dil ko too ap-nay ruh say bhar; me-ray dil ho se-raf te-ra ni ghar, ghar, Too he too ho me-ree ni-gaa-hon may, ka heen gir na jaa-un gu naa hon meñ. Too he meñ.
3 Paa-pe e-on ko main laau te-ray pass Ab-di ku-shi pa-en jo hain ud aas aas Vo bhee jaa-en te-ray ga-vaa-hon may. Ka heen gir na jaa-un gu naa hon meñ. Vo bhee meñ.
1 All my be-ing and all that I pos-sess, all my life is com-mit-ted un-to you, you, come and turn all my foot-steps to your way, let me nev-er be part-ed from your love, come and love.
2 Let your Spir-it be al-ways in my heart, and let on-ly your Spir-it live with-in, in, come and turn all my foot-steps to your way, let me nev-er be part-ed from your love, come and love.
3 Let me bring to you oth-ers who are lost, in their sad-ness, may they dis-cov-er joy, joy, in be-liev-ing, they'll wit-ness to your truth, let me nev-er be part-ed from your love, in be-love.

Text: Urdu; Samuel Paul (Pakistan); trans. Shirley Erena Murray (Aotearoa New Zealand), alt., trans. © 1990 Hope Publishing Co.
Music: Samuel Paul

Christ Has No Body Here but Ours 568

WITH KINDNESS Irregular

D Dsus D
1 Christ has no bod - y here but ours; no hands, no
2 Ours are the hands through which he works, ours are the
F♯m G
feet here on earth but ours. Ours are the eyes through
feet on which he moves, ours are the voic - es through
D A D
which he looks on this world with kind - ness.
which he speaks to this world with kind - ness.
A 1 D G 2 D G 3
Through our touch, our smile, our
F♯m G Bm A
list-'ning ear, em-bod-ied in us, Je-sus is liv-ing here.
D Dsus D
So let us go now, filled with the Spir - it,
A D
in - to this world with kind - ness.

Text: based on a prayer attr. Teresa of Ávila (present-day Spain), 16th c.; paraphr. Brian McLaren (USA)
Music: Brian McLaren; acc. Benjamin Bergey (USA), 2019

569 We Read the Cross

SHEPHERD'S PIPES CMD

Gm F Cm Dm E♭ Dm Gm
1 We read the cross so man - y ways: a sac - ri - fice, a sign,
2 Our hearts will nev - er com-pre - hend the mean-ing of the cross,
3 To bear the cross and fol-low Christ brings then both joy and tears,
Cm Dm Cm B♭ Gm Dm Gm
a cause for grief, a cause for praise, a par - a - dox to mine,
if all our def - i - ni - tions end at on - ly death and loss.
brings life re - born and sac - ri - fice, brings hope a - long with fears,
Cm Gm Dm Gm D
a judg-ment on our lives of sin, a tool of death and pain,
The cross that made the sun grow dim at reach-ing noon-day's height
brings all the am - bi - gu - i - ty of be - ing dust and clay,
Gm Dm Cm Dm Cm Dm Gm
a junc-tion where new lives be - gin, where grace and mer - cy reign.
stands emp - ty when the Eas - ter hymn greets morn-ing's wel-come light.
yet brings as well the clar - i - ty of love's e - ter - nal way.

When We Walk with the Lord 570

TRUST AND OBEY 6.6.9 D with refrain

1 When we walk with the Lord in the light of his word, what a
2 Ev - 'ry bur - den we bear, ev - 'ry sor - row we share, all our
3 But we nev - er can prove the de - lights of his love, un - til
4 Then in fel - low - ship sweet we will sit at his feet, or we'll
glo - ry he sheds on our way! While we do his good will, he a -
toil he doth rich - ly re - pay. E - ven grief, pain, and loss as we
all on the al - tar we lay, for the fa - vor he shows, and the
walk by his side in the way. What he says we will do, where he
bides with us still, and with all who will trust and o - bey.
car - ry a cross will be blessed as we trust and o - bey.
joy he be - stows, are for them who will trust and o - bey.
sends we will go, nev - er fear, on - ly trust and o - bey.
Refrain
Trust and o - bey, for there's no oth - er way to be
hap - py in Je - sus, but to trust and o - bey.

Text: John H. Sammis (USA), *Hymns Old and New*, 1887, alt.
Music: Daniel B. Towner (USA), *Hymns Old and New*, 1887

571 O God, We Read the Holy Law

EIN FESTE BURG 8.7.8.7.6.6.6.6.7

1 O God, we read the ho - ly law to shape our
2 All peo - ple born of God a - bove will live as
3 So let our love for God be known in how we
ways of liv - ing like those who first in fear
Je - sus taught us: God's cho - sen chil - dren prac -
treat cre - a - tion— true love in word and ac -
and awe re - ceived it with thanks - giv - ing.
- tice love, for God in love has sought us.
- tion shown to ev - 'ry tongue and na - tion.
These laws that Je - sus knew he sum - ma - rized with
We know love nev - er fails; and through love, good pre -
If we would heed this call and of - fer love to

Text: Michael Schneider (present-day Germany), *Christliche Gesäng wie dieselbigen zu Passau von den Schweizer Brüdern . . .* (precursor to the *Ausbund*), 1564; trans. Scott R. Troyer (USA); vers. Mennonite Worship and Song Committee
Music: Martin Luther (present-day Germany), *Geistliche Lieder*, 1529, 1531

two that cap - ture best the whole: "With heart, mind, strength, and
vails. When all else turns to dust, in this we place our
all, then we must sure - ly praise our source of love al -
soul, love God, and love your neigh - bor."
trust: God's love en - dures for - ev - er.
ways: to God a - lone be glo - ry!

Let This Mind Be in You 572

SERVANT 6.6.6.7

D Bm A D Em/D D A
Let this mind be in you, let this mind be in you,
D/F♯ Em/G D/G A Bm Bm7 G D/A A Em/D D
let this mind be in you that is al - so in Je - sus.

Text: Philippians 2:5
Music: James E. Clemens (USA), 2008;

573 Strong, Peaceful Man of Galilee

MELITA 8.8.8.8.8.8

C F C D7 G
1 Strong, peace - ful man of Gal - i - lee, robed with your strength we
2 Strong, right - eous man of Gal - i - lee, dressed with your peace we
3 Strong, suf - f'ring man of Gal - i - lee, clad in your grace we
4 God's peace - ful man of Gal - i - lee, Love's tri - umph, we at
D G G7 C A7 D
long to be— not to re - venge; to heal and pray, to
long to be— in tem - ple court, your cleans - ing rod; on
hope to be—love at the well, share Mar - tha's loss, for -
last will see— to crum - ble ev - 'ry bound - 'ry wall, build
Em Am Em/B B Em C7 F
turn the cheek, and trib - ute pay. Robed with your strength we
greed and lies, the wrath of God. Dressed with your peace we
give the nails, and take the cross. Clad in your grace we
high - ways to the hearts of all. Love's tri - umph, we at
D7 G C G7 C
long to be, strong, peace - ful man of Gal - i - lee.
long to be, strong, right - eous man of Gal - i - lee.
hope to be, strong, suf - f'ring man of Gal - i - lee.
last will see, God's peace - ful man of Gal - i - lee.

Text: Harry W. Farrington (USA), 1921, *The Hymnal for Boys and Girls*, 1935, alt.
Music: John B. Dykes (England), *Hymns Ancient and Modern*, 1861

We Shall Walk through the Valley 574

WE SHALL WALK THROUGH THE VALLEY IN PEACE Irregular

G7 C Dm G7
1 We shall walk through the val - ley of the shad - ow of death,
2 There will be no sor - row - ing there,
3 (Hum)
(melody)
(melody) C Am Gsus G
we shall walk through the val - ley in peace!
there will be no sor - row - ing there.
(Hum)
C C7 Am Fm
And if Je - sus him - self will be our lead - er,
C G7 C
(melody)
we shall walk through the val - ley in peace!

Text: African American spiritual (USA)
Music: African American spiritual; adapt. Wi liam Appling (USA), © 1970 World Library Publications, Inc.

575 Faith of the Martyrs

ST. CATHERINE LM with refrain

1 *Faith of the mar - tyrs, liv - ing still in spite of dun - geon, fire, and sword; oh, how our hearts beat high with joy when - e'er we hear that glo - rious word!
2 The mar-tyrs chained in pris - on cells were still in heart and con - science free, and bless'd would be their chil - dren's fate if they, like them, should die for thee!
3 Faith of the mar - tyrs, we will love both friend and foe in all our strife, and preach thee, too, as love knows how, by sav - ing word and faith - ful life!
Refrain
Faith of the mar - tyrs, ho - ly faith, we will be true to thee till death.

*Alternate phrases: "Faith of our fathers" or "Faith of our mothers"

Text: Frederick W. Faber (England), *Jesus and Mary*, 1849, alt.
Music: Henri F Hemy (England), *Crown of Jesus Music*, 1864; adapt. James G. Walton (England), *Plainsong Music for the Holy Communion Office*, 1874

Who Now Would Follow Christ 576

WARUM BETRÜBST DU DICH, MEIN HERZ 8.8.6.8.6

1 Who now would fol - low Christ in life must scorn the
2 Christ's ser - vants fol - low him to death and give their
3 Re - nounc - ing all, they choose the cross, and claim - ing
world's in - sult and strife, and bear the cross each day.
bod - y, life, and breath on cross and rack and pyre.
it, count all as loss, e'en hus - band, child, and wife.
For this a - lone leads to the throne; Christ is the on - ly way.
As gold is tried and pu - ri - fied, they stand the test of fire.
For - sak - ing gain, for - get - ting pain, they en - ter in - to life.

Text: "Wer Christo jetzt will folgen nach," *Ausbund* (present-day Germany), 1583; trans. David Augsburger (USA), 1962, *The Mennonite Hymnal*, 1969, rev. 1983.

Music: Bartholomeus Monoetius (present-day Germany), 1565; harm. J. Harold Moyer (USA), 1965, *The Mennonite Hymnal*,

577 Count Well the Cost

MACH'S MIT MIR / EISENACH 8.7.8.7.8.8

1 "Count well the cost," Christ Je - sus says, "when you lay
2 In - to Christ's death be bur - ied now through bap-tism's
3 With - in the chur - ch's warm em - brace the child of
4 In Chris - tian growth we are ma - tured, of fruit - ful
the foun - da - tion." Are you re - solved, though all seem lost,
joy - ous un - ion. No self - ish claim should you al - low
God is mold - ed. God's Spir - it lights the in - fant face,
vines a tok - en. That this good growth may be as - sured
to risk your rep - u - ta - tion, your self, your wealth, for
if you de - sire com - mun - ion when Christ's re - deemed to -
and in God's grace is fold - ed. With child - like steps, Christ's
oft - times to us is brok - en the bread of fel - low -
Christ the Lord, as you now give your sol - emn word?
geth - er meet, the bread of fel - low - ship to eat.
plan we trace, till we grow up in god - ly grace.
ship re - plete when Christ's re - deemed to - geth - er meet.

Text: Alexander Mack Sr. (present-day Germany), "Überschlag die Kost," *Geistreiches Gesang-Buch...*, 1720; trans. Ora W. Graber (USA), *European Origins of the Brethren,* 1958, alt.
Music: Bartholomäus Gesius (present-day Germany), ca. 1600; adapt. Johann H. Schein (present-day Germany), 1628

Balaacoolwe (Blessed Are the Persecuted) 578

TONGA MELODY Irregular

1 Ba - laa - cool - we ba - pen - zeg - wa nkaa - mbo ka - Je - su mum - yo - yo ya - bo.
2 Ba - laa - cool - we ba - fwa nza - la ya - ku - mu - u - ya mum - yo - yo ya - bo.
1 Bless - ed are the per - se - cut - ed, for Je - sus Christ is liv - ing with - in them.
2 Bless - ed are they who are hun - gry in spir - it, for the Lord lives with - in them.
Refrain
Ba - ya ku - ta - mbu - la mu - syi - ni wa - buu - mi a - ku - boo - la i - Mwa - mi Je - su.
Great will be their re - ward, they shall be giv'n a crown when the Lord comes from heav'n to meet them.

3 Balaacoolwe basalala nkaambo
kaJesu mumyoyo yabo.

4 Balaacoolwe bafwa nyota
yakumuuya mumyoyo yabo.

3 Blessed are the pure in heart,
for Jesus Christ is living within them.

4 Blessed are they who are thirsty
in spirit, for the Lord lives within them.

Text: Tonga; based on Matthew 5; anon. (Zambia); adapt. Esther C. Bergen (USA),
Music: Tonga traditional (Zambia)

579 With Astonishment, Fear, and Wonder

COMO PODEN PER SAS CULPAS 9.9.9.9 D with refrain

1 With as - ton - ish - ment, fear, and won - der, we are
As the le - gions of fear and pow - er are ap -
2 We're sur - round - ed by glad com - pan - ions, ho - ly
Here is Mir - i - am, with her tim - brel; here is
walk - ing the road with Je - sus; we are walk-ing the peace - ful
proach-ing with sword and ar - mor, with Em - man - u - el we are
com - pa - ny, great and awe-some: all our an - ces - tors sing - ing
Josh - u - a, with the sho - fars; here are Si - las and Paul, from
path - way; we are sing - ing the com - ing king - dom.
march - ing, with no sword but a song: Ho - san - na! To refrain
wit - ness to the Ho - ly One, work - ing a - mong us.
pris - on; they are sing - ing God's reign, Ho - san - na! To refrain
Refrain
Leader
All
Come and help us, O God, Ho - san - na! Come de - liv - er, O God, Ho - san - na!
Give us cour-age and joy, Ho - san - na! For your song is our strength, Ho -
san - na! With as - ton - ish - ment, fear, and won - der, we are walk-ing the
road with Je - sus: we are walk-ing the peace - ful path - way; we are
sing-ing the com - ing king-dom.
Fine
Interlude (omit final time)

Text: Andrew Donaldson (Canada), © 2015 Andrew Donaldson
Music: Spanish traditional, "Como poden per sas culpas," 13th c.

To Leave the Stones Unthrown 580

MARIANNE SMD

C Am7 F
1 To leave the stones un - thrown, to turn the oth - er
2 Not on - ly in ex - tremes, in mo - ments stark and
3 New cross - es wait each day, new chal - leng - es to
G C F C Am
cheek, to bear a load an ex - tra mile, to
clear, in dark - night wres - tling grim and fierce, or
meet, new sign - posts for the way of life, new
D7 G E♭ F B♭
lis - ten more than speak: such are the marks of love,
ag - o - ny se - vere, but in some faith - ful act,
marks of death's de - feat: yet, be they great or small,
D♭ E♭ A♭ C F
the tes - ta - ments of grace, the dai - ly glimps - es
some scarce - ly con - scious choice, we find the grace to
u - nique or com - mon - place, they help us look be -
C Am Dm7 G7 Csus C C2 C
of the cross Christ calls us to em - brace.
hear and heed the bid - ding of Christ's voice.
yond our - selves to see and know Christ's face.

Alternate tune: TERRA BEATA (#180)

Text: Carl P. Daw Jr. (USA), © 2005 Hope Publishing Co.
Music: Sally Ann Morris (USA), 2009, © 2016 GIA Publications, Inc.

581 Jésus, je voudrais te chanter (Lord Jesus, You Shall Be My Song)

LES PETITES SOEURS 12.14.12.12

D A Bm7 A7/C♯ G/D D
1 Jé - sus, je vou - drais te chan - ter sur ma rou - te; Jé -
2 Jé - sus, je vou - drais te lou - er sur ma rou - te; Jé -
1 Lord Je - sus, you shall be my song as I jour - ney; I'll
2 Lord Je - sus, I'll praise you as long as I jour - ney. May
Gsus9 G/F♯ Em Em/D A/C♯ Em/D A/C♯ A/B
sus, je vou - drais t'an-non - cer à mes voi - sins par - tout,
sus, je vou - drais que ma voix soit l'é - cho de ta joie,
tell ev-'ry - bo - dy a - bout you wher - ev - er I go:
all of my joy be a faith - ful re - flec - tion of you.
A A/G D/F♯ D Gsus9 B7/D♯ Em Em/D A/C♯
car toi seul es la vie et la paix et l'a-mour: Jé -
et que chan - te la terre et que chan - te le ciel; Jé -
you a - lone are our life and our peace and our love. Lord
May the earth and the sea and the sky join my song. Lord

Text: French; les Petites Soeurs de Jesus (France) and L'Arche Community (France), 1961; stanzas 1–3 trans. Stephen Somerville (Canada), stanzas 1–3 trans. © 1970 Estate of Stephen Sommerville; stanza 4 trans. Mennonite Worship and Song Committee
Music: Les Petites Souers de Jesus and L'Arche Community

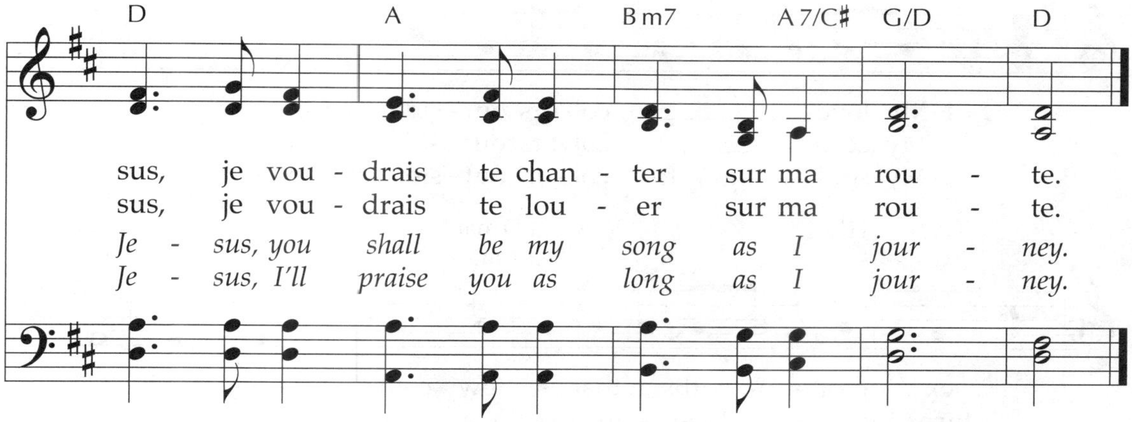
D
A
Bm7
A7/C♯
G/D
D
sus, je vou - drais te chan - ter sur ma rou - te.
sus, je vou - drais te lou - er sur ma rou - te.
Je - sus, you shall be my song as I jour - ney.
Je - sus, I'll praise you as long as I jour - ney.

3 Jésus, je voudrais te servir sur ma route,
Jésus, je voudrais partager les souffrances de ta croix,
car tu livres pour moi et ton corps et ton sang;
Jésus, je voudrais te servir sur ma route.

4 Jésus, je voudrais tout au long de ma route,
entendre tes pas résonner dans la nuit près de moi,
jusqu'à l'aube du jour où ton peuple sauvé,
Jésus, chantera ton retour sur ma route.

3 *As long as I live, Jesus, make me your servant*
to carry your cross and to share all your burdens and tears.
For you saved me by giving your body and blood.
As long as I live, Jesus, make me your servant.

4 *Lord Jesus, stay with me wherever I journey.*
I listen at night as the sound of your steps leads the way.
Till your new day shall dawn on the people you saved,
Lord Jesus, we'll sing your return on our journey.

582 My Love Colors Outside the Lines

MY LOVE COLOURS OUTSIDE THE LINES Irregular

Capo 3:
1 My love colors outside the lines,
2 My Lord colors outside the lines,
3 My soul longs to color outside the lines,
explor-ing paths that few could ever find;
turns wounds to bless-ings, wa-ter into wine;
tear back the cur-tains, sun, come in and shine!
and takes me into plac-es where I've
and takes me into plac-es where I've
I want to walk be-yond the bound-'ries where I've
nev-er been be-fore, and o-pens doors to
nev-er been be-fore, and o-pens doors to
nev-er been be-fore, throw o-pen doors to
worlds out-side the lines.
worlds out-side the lines.
worlds out-side the lines.
1
2, 3

Text: Gordon Light (Canada), 1995
Music: Gordon Light, 1995; arr. Andrew Donaldson (Canada), arr. © Andrew Donaldson; acc. Benjamin Bergey (USA), 2019

Refrain
(G) B♭ (A) C (D) F (A/C♯) C/E
We'll nev-er walk on wa-ter if we're not pre-pared to drown:
(Bm) Dm (F♯m7) Am7 (G) B♭ (A7) C7
bod-y and soul need a soak-ing from
(D) F (Am7) Cm7 (D7) F7 (G) B♭
time to time. And we'll nev-er move the grave-
(A) C (D) F (A/C♯) C/E (Bm) Dm (F♯m7) Am7
-stones if we're not pre-pared to die, and re-al-ize
(G) B♭ (A7) C7 (D) F
there are worlds out-side the lines.

583 O Christ, Impart Your Teaching True

MARYTON LM

E♭ A♭ Fm B♭
1 O Christ, im - part your teach - ing true and gath - er
2 O Christ, like gold our hearts re - fine, and fill our
3 O Christ, your peo - ple tru - ly keep, who fol - low
E♭ F7 B♭ B♭7 E♭
in your faith - ful few. Now grant that each with
lives with joy di - vine to fol - low you for -
dai - ly as your sheep; and if through bit - ter
A♭ B♭7 E♭ Fm B♭ E♭
pa - tient care their cross of love should dai - ly bear.
ev - er - more: your Word, your will, your truth a - dore.
death we pass, your grace will keep us to the last.

Text: Michael Sattler (present-day Germany), 1527; *Ausbund,* 1583; trans. Myron Augsburger (USA), 1965, ; adapt. Mennonite Worship and Song Committee
Music: H. Percy Smith (England), *Church Hymns with Tunes,* 1874

Jesus, Be the Center 584

BE THE CENTRE Irregular

Verses
1 Je - sus, be the cen - ter, be my source, be my light, Je - sus.
2 Je - sus, be the cen - ter, be my hope, be my song, Je - sus.
3 Je - sus, be my vi - sion, be my path, be my guide, Je - sus.
4 Je - sus, be the cen - ter, be my source, be my light, Je - sus.
Last time to Coda
Refrain
Be the fire in my heart. Be the wind in these sails. Be the rea - son that I live, Je - sus, Je - sus.
To verses
Coda
Be my source, be my light, Je - sus. Je - sus. Je - sus.

Text: Michael Frye (England)
Music: Michael Frye

585 Faith Begins by Letting Go

FIDES INCIPIT 7.7.7.7.7.7

1 Faith be - gins by let - ting go, giv - ing up what had seemed sure,
2 Faith en - dures by hold - ing on, keep - ing mem'-ry's roots a - live
3 Faith ma - tures by reach - ing out, stretch - ing minds, en - larg - ing hearts,
tak - ing risks and press - ing on, though the way feels less se - cure:
so that hope may bear its fruit; pro - mise - fed, our souls will thrive,
shar - ing strug - gles, liv - ing prayer, bind - ing up the bro - ken parts;
pil - grim - age both right and odd, trust - ing all our life to God.
not through mer - it we pos - sess but by God's great faith - ful - ness.
till we find the com - mon - place ripe with wit - ness to God's grace.

Text: Carl P. Daw Jr. (USA), 1995, © 1996 Hope Publishing Company
Music: David J. Gonzol (USA), © 2019 David J. Gonzol

586 All Will Be Well

Ostinato Refrain

OUR LORD SAID THAT ALL WOULD BE WELL Irregular

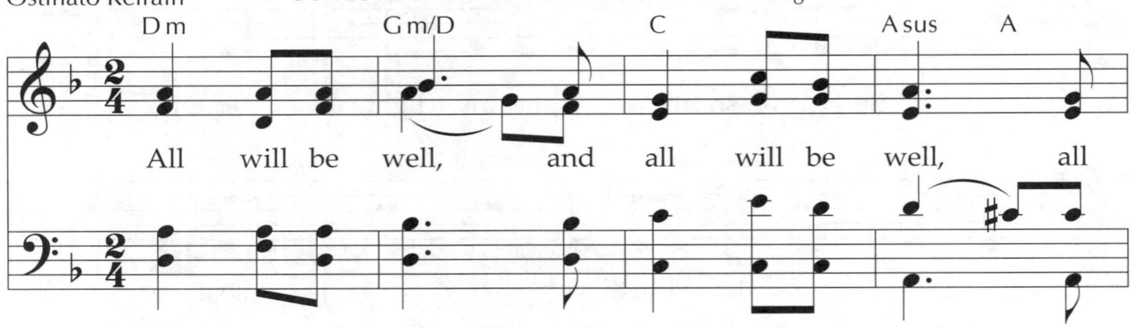
All will be well, and all will be well, all

Verses that may be sung over the refrain are included in the accompaniment edition.

Text: Julian of Norwich (England), *The Revelation of Divine Love,* 14th c.; adapt. Steven C. Warner (USA)
Music: Steven C. Warner

Repeat
Last time
B♭ C G
man - ner of things will be well.
G B♭ D
well, will be well, will be well.

In the Quiet Curve of Evening 587

YOU ARE THERE 8.7.8.3.8.7.8.3 with refrain

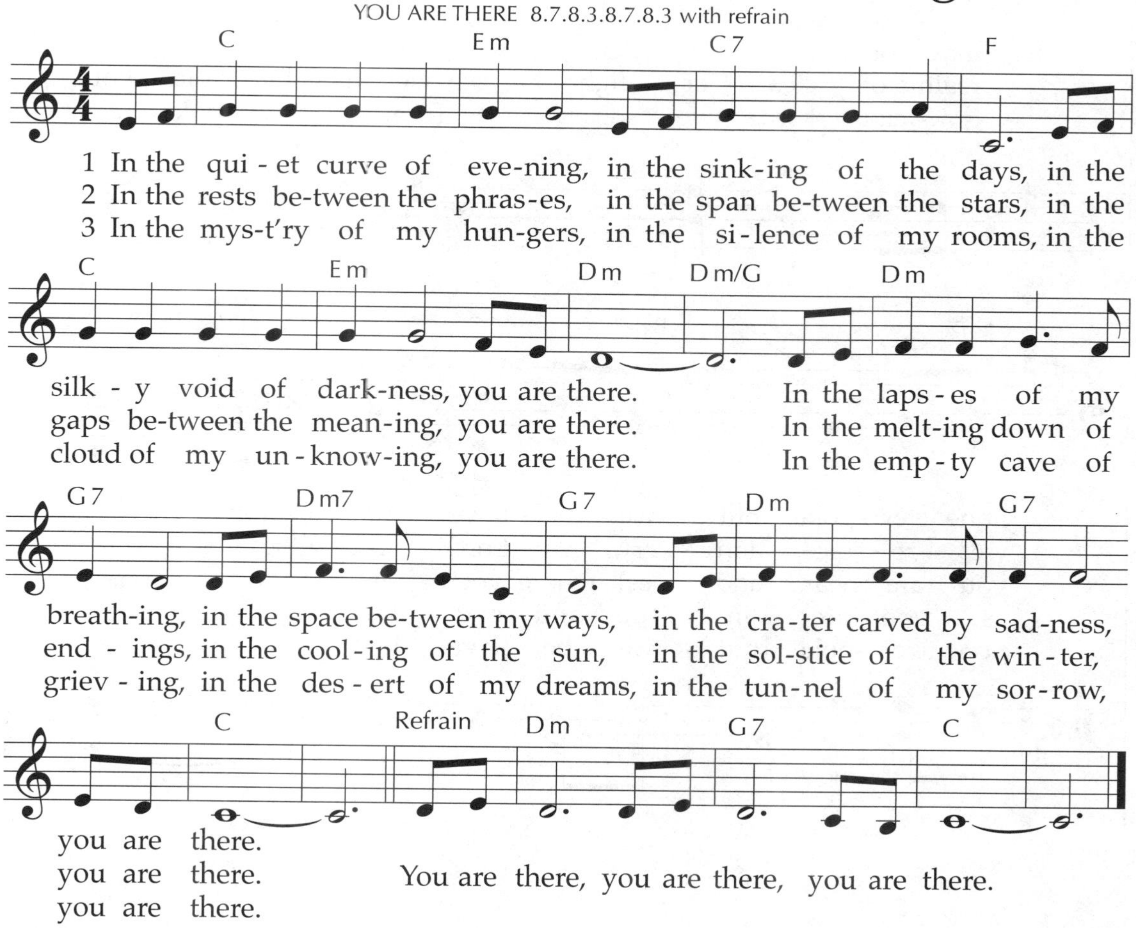
C Em C7 F
1 In the qui - et curve of eve-ning, in the sink-ing of the days, in the
2 In the rests be-tween the phras-es, in the span be-tween the stars, in the
3 In the mys-t'ry of my hun-gers, in the si-lence of my rooms, in the
C Em Dm Dm/G Dm
silk - y void of dark-ness, you are there. In the laps - es of my
gaps be-tween the mean-ing, you are there. In the melt-ing down of
cloud of my un-know-ing, you are there. In the emp - ty cave of
G7 Dm7 G7 Dm G7
breath-ing, in the space be-tween my ways, in the cra-ter carved by sad-ness,
end - ings, in the cool-ing of the sun, in the sol-stice of the win-ter,
griev - ing, in the des - ert of my dreams, in the tun-nel of my sor-row,
C Refrain Dm G7 C
you are there.
you are there.
you are there.
You are there, you are there, you are there.

Text: Juliana Howard (USA)
Music: Juliana Howard; acc. Vera Lyons (USA), alt.

588 We Walk by Faith

SHANTI CM

E A D E
1 We walk by faith, and not by sight; no
2 We may not touch his hands and side, nor
3 Help then, O Lord, our un - be - lief, and
4 that when our life of faith is done, in
5 We walk by faith, and not by sight; no
F♯m Dmaj7 Bm7/E E F♯m
gra - cious words we hear from one who spoke as
fol - low where he trod, yet in his prom - ise
may our faith a - bound to call on you when
realms of clear - er light we may be - hold you
gra - cious words we hear from one who spoke as
C♯m7 Bm7 E7 A D/A E A
none e'er spoke, but we be - lieve him near.
we re - joice, and cry, "My Lord and God!"
you are near, and seek where you are found:
as you are in full and end - less sight.
none e'er spoke, but we be - lieve him near.

Text: Henry Alford (England), *Psalms and Hymns*, 1844, alt.
Music: Marty Haugen (USA), 1983, *Mass of Creation*,

山路こえて Yamaji koete (In Lonely Mountain Ways) 589

GOLDEN HILL SM

1 Ya - ma - ji ko - e - te hi - to - ri
2 Mi - chi ke - wa - shi - ku yu - ku - te
3 Hi mo ku - re - na - ba i - shi no
1 In lone - ly moun - tain ways of this world's
2 My jour - ney may be long, the path - way
3 And though when eve - ning falls, a stone my
yu - ke - do shu no te ni su -
to - o - shi ko - ko - ro - za - su
ma - ku - ra, ka - ri - ne no yu -
trial and care, my heart knows naught of
rough and steep. Suf - fi - cient for each
pil - low shapes, the vi - sion of our
ga - re - ru mi wa ya - su - ke - shi
ka - ta ni i - tsu - ka tsu - ku - ran
me ni mo mi - ku - ni shi - no ban
fear - scarred days; the Mas - ter's hand is there!
day my song; my way the Lord does keep.
king - dom calls and here a Beth - el makes.

1 山路こえて ひとりゆけど、
主の手にすがれる 身はやすけし。

2 みちけわしく ゆくてとおし、
こころざすかたに いつか着くらん。

3 日もくれなば、石のまくら
かりねの夢にも み国しのばん。

Text: Japanese; Sugao Nishimura (Japan), 1903; trans. Paul R. Gregory (USA), © 1983 Paul R. Gregory
Music: attr. variously to Amzi Chapin (USA). Lucius Chapin (USA), Aaron Chapin (USA), and Ananias Davisson (USA), published as "Thirtieth," *Patterson's Church Music*, 1813

590 I Know Not Why God's Wondrous

EL NATHAN CM with refrain

Capo 1: (D) E♭ (G) A♭ (D) E♭ (G) A♭ (D) E♭ (A) B♭
1 I know not why God's won-drous grace to me is dai-ly shown,
2 I know not how this sav-ing faith to me he did im-part,
3 I know not how the Spir-it moves, con-vinc-ing us of sin,
4 I know not when my Lord may come, at night or noon-day fair,
(D) E♭ (G) A♭ (D) E♭ (G) A♭ (D) E♭ (A) B♭ (A7) B♭7 (D) E♭
nor why, with mer-cy, Christ in love re-deemed me for his own.
nor how be-liev-ing in his word wrought peace with-in my heart.
re-veal-ing Je-sus through the Word, cre-at-ing faith in him.
nor if I'll walk the vale with him, or meet him in the air.
Refrain
(G) A♭ (D) E♭ (A7) B♭7 (D) E♭
But "I know whom I have be-liev-ed, and am per-suad-ed that he is a-ble
(G) A♭ (D) E♭ (A7) B♭7 (D) E♭
to keep that which I've com-mit-ted un-to him a-gainst that day."

Text: stanzas Daniel W. Whittle (USA); refrain 2 Timothy 1:12 (KJV); *Gospel Hymns, No. 5*, 1887, alt.
Music: James McGranahan (USA), *Gospel Hymns, No. 5*, 1887

When I Can't Find My Way 591

TO THE ONE Irregular

Capo 2: (G) A (Em) F♯m (C) D (Em) F♯m (D) E
1 When I can't find my way in the mist and the gray, I find
an - ger with-in me is strong-er than love, I find
(Em) F♯m (C) D (D) E (Em) F♯m (C) D
faith in the rus - tling leaves. When life dis - ap-pears and love
peace in the crash - ing of waves. When grief numbs my sens - es and
(Em) F♯m (D) E (Em) F♯m (C) D (D) E
gives way to fear, I find hope in the cool sil - ver breeze.
with - ers my trust, I find strength in the wind on my face.
Refrain
(Em) F♯m (C) D (D) E (Em) F♯m
And I stand all a-lone in the night; and I cry out with
(C) D (D) E (G) A (D) E
all of my might. And I sing to the One who turns tears in - to rain
(Em) F♯m (C) D (D) E
that wa - ters the seeds that will bring a-bout change. And I
(G) A (D) E (Em) F♯m
sing to the One who gives growth out of pain, so through ev-'ry trag - e - dy,
(C) D (D) E (Am/E) Bm/F♯ (D) E (Em) F♯m (C) D (Em) F♯m (D) E (C2) D2 Fine last time
hope will re - main— and I sing.
2 When

Text: Jessica Hedrick Miller (USA)
Music: Jessica Hedrick Miller; acc. Anneli Loepp Thiessen (Canada), 2020

592 How Firm a Foundation

FOUNDATION (BELLEVUE) 11.11.11.11

1 How firm a foun - da - tion, you saints of the Lord,
2 "Fear not, I am with you; O be not dis - mayed,
3 "When through the deep wa - ters I call you to go,
4 "When through fier - y tri - als your path - way shall lie,
5 "The soul that on Je - sus still leans for re - pose,
is laid for your faith in his ex - cel - lent Word!
for I am your God, and will still give you aid.
the riv - ers of sor - row shall not o - ver - flow,
my grace, all suf - fi - cient, shall be your sup - ply.
I will not, I will not de - sert to its foes.
What more can he say than to you he has said,
I'll strength - en you, help you, and cause you to stand,
for I will be with you, your trou - bles to bless,
The flames shall not hurt you. I on - ly de - sign
That soul, though all hell should en - deav - or to shake,
to you who for ref - uge to Je - sus have fled?
up - held by my right - eous, om - ni - po - tent hand.
and sanc - ti - fy to you the deep - est dis - tress.
your dross to con - sume, and your gold to re - fine.
I'll nev - er, no nev - er, no nev - er for - sake!"

Text: "K" in Rippon's *Selection of Hymns* (England), 1787, alt.
Music: American traditional (USA), in Joseph Funk's *Genuine Church Music*, 1st ed., 1832

Si tuvieras fe (If You Only Had Faith) 593

SI TUVIERAS FE Irregular

Am F E7
Spanish: "Si tu-vie - ras fe co-mo‿un gra-ni - to de mos - ta - za,"
English: "If you on-ly had faith, just like a lit - tle seed of mus-tard,"
French: "Si tu a - vais foi comme u - ne grai-ne de mou - tar - de,"
1
Am E
e - so lo di - ce‿el Se - ñor, "si tú-vie - ras
this is what Je - sus has said, "if you on-ly had
ain - si di - sait le Sei - gneur, "si to a - vais
2
Am Dm G7 Am Fmaj7
ñor, tú - le di - rí - as a‿e-sa mon - ta - ña: ¡Mué-ve-
said, "you would be a - ble to tell this moun-tain: Move a-
gneur, "tu pour-rais di - re à cette mon - ta - gne: Pous - se-
1
Bdim E7 Am A
te! ¡Mué-ve - te! Tú le di - te!
way! Move a - way! You would be way!
toi! Pous - se - toi! Tu pour-rais toi!
2
Bdim E7
¡Mué-ve -
Move a -
Pous - se -
Am E7
te!" Y la mon-ta - ña se mo-ve - rá, se mo-ve-rá, se mo-ve-
way!" And then the moun - tain will move a - way, will move a-way, will move a -
toi!" Et la mon - ta - gne se pous-se - ra, se pous-se-ra, se pous-se-
Repeat ad lib
Am
rá. Y la mon-ta - ña se mo - ve - rá.
way. And then the moun - tain will move a - way.
ra. Et la mon - ta - gne se pous - se - ra.
Final
Am

Text: Spanish; based on Matthew 17:20; English trans. Pablo Sosa (Argentina), English trans. © GIA Publications, Inc.; French trans. Sida Hodoroaba-Roberts (USA), French trans. © 2013 Community of Christ

Music: traditional Caribbean; transc. Jorge Lockward (USA)

594 Over My Head

OVER MY HEAD Irregular

Refrain
G D7 G
O-ver my head, I hear mu-sic in the air; o-ver my
D7 G D7 G
head, I hear mu-sic in the air; o-ver my head, I hear
D7 Em Am G/D D7 G
mu-sic in the air; there must be a God some-where.
Fine
Solo
1 Oh, when the world is si-lent,
2 And when I'm feel-ing lone-ly,
3 Now when I think on Je-sus,
G D7 G
(Hum) I hear mu-sic in the air;

Text: African American spiritual (USA)
Music: African American spiritual; arr. John L. Bell (Scotland), alt.

oh, when the world is si - lent,
and when I'm feel - ing lone - ly,
now when I think on Je - sus,
D7 G D7 G
(Hum) I hear mu - sic in the air;
oh, when the world is si - lent,
and when I'm feel - ing lone - ly,
now when I think on Je - sus,
D7 Em
(Hum) I hear mu - sic in the air;
To refrain
there must be a God some - where.
Am G/D D7 G
To refrain
there must be a God some - where.

595 When the Storms of Life Are Raging

STAND BY ME 8.3.8.3.7.7.8.3

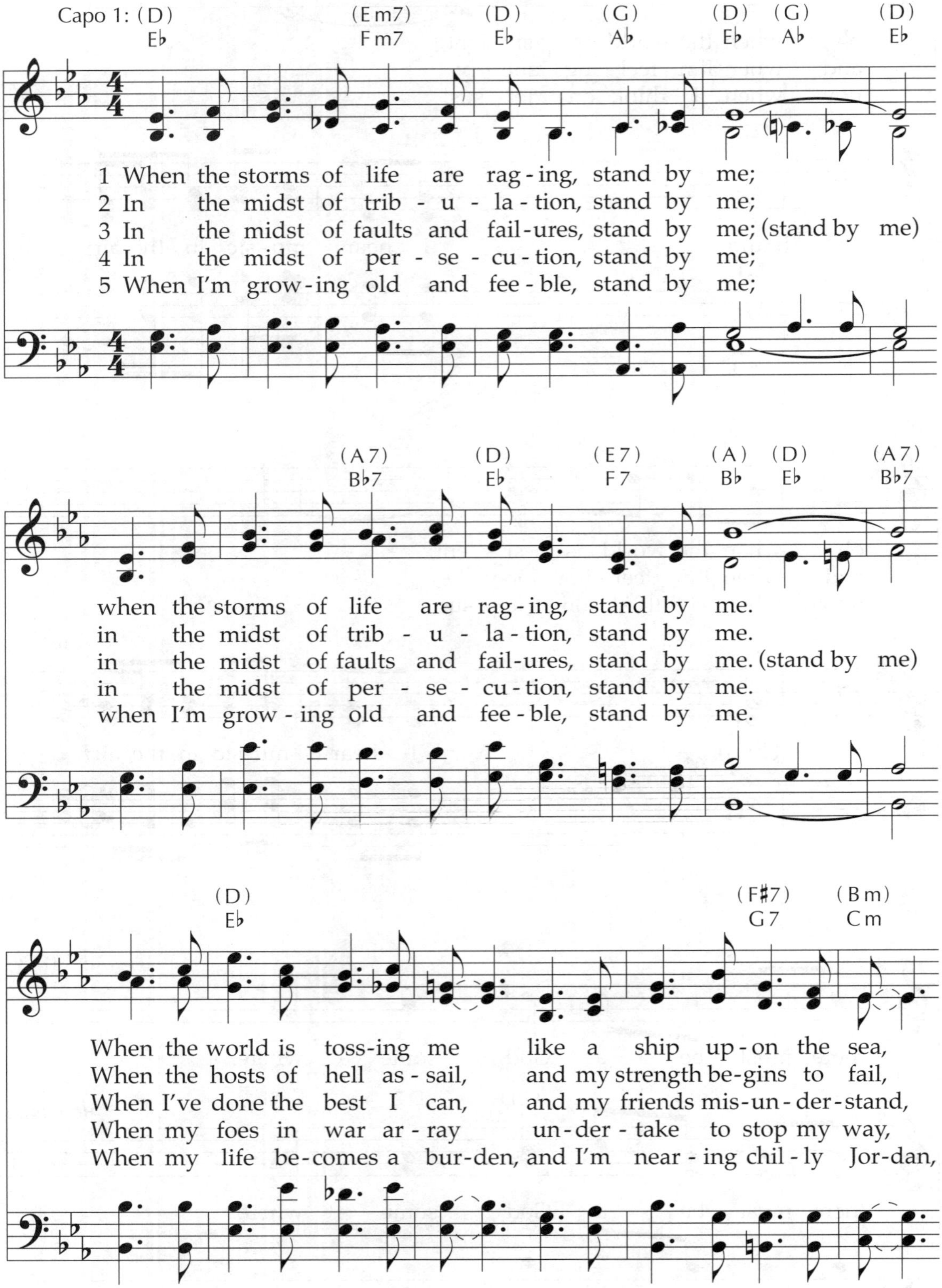
Capo 1: (D) E♭ (Em7) Fm7 (D) E♭ (G) A♭ (D) E♭ (G) A♭ (D) E♭
1 When the storms of life are rag-ing, stand by me;
2 In the midst of trib-u-la-tion, stand by me;
3 In the midst of faults and fail-ures, stand by me; (stand by me)
4 In the midst of per-se-cu-tion, stand by me;
5 When I'm grow-ing old and fee-ble, stand by me;
(A7) B♭7 (D) E♭ (E7) F7 (A) B♭ (D) E♭ (A7) B♭7
when the storms of life are rag-ing, stand by me.
in the midst of trib-u-la-tion, stand by me.
in the midst of faults and fail-ures, stand by me. (stand by me)
in the midst of per-se-cu-tion, stand by me.
when I'm grow-ing old and fee-ble, stand by me.
(D) E♭ (F♯7) G7 (Bm) Cm
When the world is toss-ing me like a ship up-on the sea,
When the hosts of hell as-sail, and my strength be-gins to fail,
When I've done the best I can, and my friends mis-un-der-stand,
When my foes in war ar-ray un-der-take to stop my way,
When my life be-comes a bur-den, and I'm near-ing chil-ly Jor-dan,

Text: Charles A.Tindley (USA), ca. 1906
Music: Charles A. Tindley, ca 1906; arr. William F. Smith (USA), *The United Methodist Hymnal*,

ⓡ

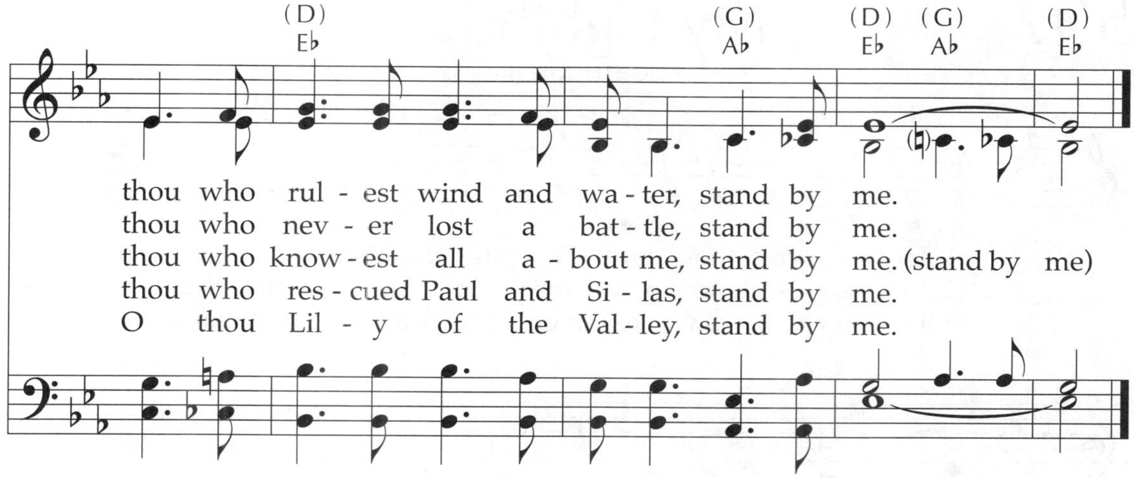
(D) Eb (G) Ab (D) Eb (G) Ab (D) Eb
thou who rul - est wind and wa - ter, stand by me.
thou who nev - er lost a bat - tle, stand by me.
thou who know - est all a - bout me, stand by me. (stand by me)
thou who res - cued Paul and Si - las, stand by me.
O thou Lil - y of the Val - ley, stand by me.

Don't Be Afraid

596

DON'T BE AFRAID Irregular

C G Dm G7 C F/A
Don't be a-fraid. My love is strong-er, my love is
Dm7 Gsus G C G Dm G7
strong-er than your fear. Don't be a-fraid. My love is
C Am F C/E Dm7 Gsus G7 C
strong-er and I have prom-ised, prom-ised to be al - ways near.

Text: John L. Bell (Scotland)
Music: John L. Bell, alt.

597 My Lighthouse

MY LIGHTHOUSE Irregular

B E2 B E2 B
1 In my wres-tling, and in my doubts, in my fail - ures,
2 In the si - lence, you won't let go. In the ques-tions,
3 I won't fear what to - mor - row brings. With each morn - ing,
F♯sus B E2
you won't walk out. Your great love will lead me
your truth will hold. Your great love will lead me
I'll rise and sing. My God's love will lead me
B E2 B/D♯ F♯sus B
through: you are the peace in my trou - bled sea, whoa, oh,
through: you are the peace in my trou - bled sea, whoa, oh,
through: you are the peace in my trou - bled sea, whoa, oh,
E2 B/D♯ F♯sus B
you are the peace in my trou - bled sea. To verse 2
you are the peace in my trou - bled sea. To refrain
you are the peace in my trou - bled sea. To refrain
Refrain
E2 B G♯m7 F♯sus E2
My Light-house, my Light-house shin-ing in the dark-
B G♯m7 F♯sus E2 B
- ness, I will fol-low you! Oh, my Light-house,
G♯m7 F♯sus E2 B G♯m7
my Light-house, I will trust the prom - ise: you will car-ry me

Text: Rend Collective (Ireland)
Music: Rend Collective

F♯sus E2 B F♯ E2 B
safe to shore, safe to shore,
F♯ E2 B F♯ B
Fine
safe to shore, safe to shore.
To verse 3
To bridge
Bridge
E2 B G♯m7 F♯ E2
Fire be-fore us, you're the bright-est. You will
B
1–3
G♯m7 F♯
4
G♯m7 F♯
To refrain
lead us through the storms. through the storms.

More Than You Know 598

NEW HOPE Irregular

D D2 D2/F♯ G2 F♯m
More than you know, more than you know, God's love is
Em7 D F♯m Bm
with you. More than you know, more than you
Gmaj7 Em7 Asus A A/F♯ Em7
know God cares for you. And more than you know,
F♯m G Bm G2 D
more than you know God's love is in you,
Em7 A G/E D Em/D D
walk-ing with you, hold - ing you, liv - ing with you.

Text: Connie Johnson-Evers (USA), 2008
Music: Connie Johnson-Evers, 2008; acc. Marilyn Houser Hamm (Canada), 2019

599 We've Come This Far by Faith

DON'T BE DISCOURAGED WHEN TROUBLE'S IN YOUR LIFE Irregular

Refrain
E B7 E F♯m B7
We've come this far by faith, lean-ing on the
A/E E C7
Lord; trust - ing in his ho - ly Word,
E/B B7 E B7
he's nev - er failed me yet. Oh,
E7 C♯7 F♯m E/B B E
can't turn a - round, we've come this far by faith.
Fine

Text: Albert A. Goodson (USA)
Music: Albert A. Goodson; arr. James Abbington (USA), arr. © 2000 GIA Publications, Inc.

A
E
F♯m7
B7
Don't be dis - cour - aged when trou - ble's in your
E
A
A♯dim
E
G♯7
C♯m
life, he'll bear your bur - dens and
F♯m
E/B
E
3
D.S.
move all mis - er - y and strife. That's why we've

600 O Thou, in Whose Presence

ZION'S PILGRIM 11.8.11.8 D

Am
Dm
Am/E
1 O thou, in whose pres - ence my soul takes de - light, on whom in af -
2 Oh, why should I wan - der an al - ien from thee or cry in the
Em
Am
Dm
flic - tion I call, my com - fort by day, and my song in the night,
des - ert for bread? Thy foes will re - joice when my sor - rows they see
Am/E
Em
Am
G
my hope, my sal - va - tion, my all: where dost thou, dear Shep - herd, re -
and smile at the tears I have shed. Yet speak, and ten thou - sands of
C
Dm
Em
Am
Dm
Em
Am
sort with thy sheep to feed in the pas - tures of love? Say, why in the
an - gels re - joice; thy soul - cheer - ing wis - dom im - part. E - ter - ni - ty
Dm
Am/E
Em
Am
val - ley of death should I weep or lone in the wil - der - ness rove?
ech - oes the sound of thy voice that reach - es my des - o - late heart.

Text: Joseph Swain (England), *Sacred Poetry: Comprising an Entire System of Divine Truth*, 1790, alt.
Music: *Christian Lyre* (USA), 1831; harm. J. Harold Moyer (USA), 1965, *The Mennonite Hymnal*,

Lead Me, Guide Me 601

Swing:
LEAD ME, GUIDE ME Irregular
Capo 1: (D)
Refrain
Eb (E7) F7 (A) Bb (E7) F7 (A) Bb (D7) Eb7 (G) Ab
Lead me, guide me, a - long the way, for if you
(F♯m) Gm (Em) Fm (D) Eb (A7) Bb7 (D) Eb (D/A) Eb/Bb
lead me, I can - not stray. Lord, let me walk each
(D) Eb (C7) Db7 (B7) C7 (Em) Fm (D) Eb (E7) F7 (A) Bb (D) Eb (G) Ab (D) Eb
day with thee. Lead me, O Lord, lead me.
Fine
(Am/C) Bbm/Db (B7) C7 (Em) Fm (A7) Bb7
1 I am weak and I need thy strength and pow'r
2 Help me tread in the paths of right - eous - ness.
3 I am lost if you take your hand from me.
(Em) Fm (A7) Bb7 (D) Eb (A7) Bb7 (D) Eb
to help me o - ver my weak - est hour.
Be my aid when Sa - tan and sin op - press.
I am blind with - out thy light to see.
(A7) Bb7 (D7) Eb7 (Em) Fm (B7) C7 (Em) Fm
Help me through the dark-ness thy face to see.
I am put - ting all my trust in thee.
Lord, just al - ways let me thy ser - vant be.
(D) Eb (E7) F7 (A7) Bb7 (G) Ab (A7) Bb7 (D) Eb
Lead me, O Lord, lead me.
To refrain

Text: Doris M. Akers (USA)
Music: Doris M. Akers

602 I to the Hills Will Lift My Eyes

DUNDEE CM

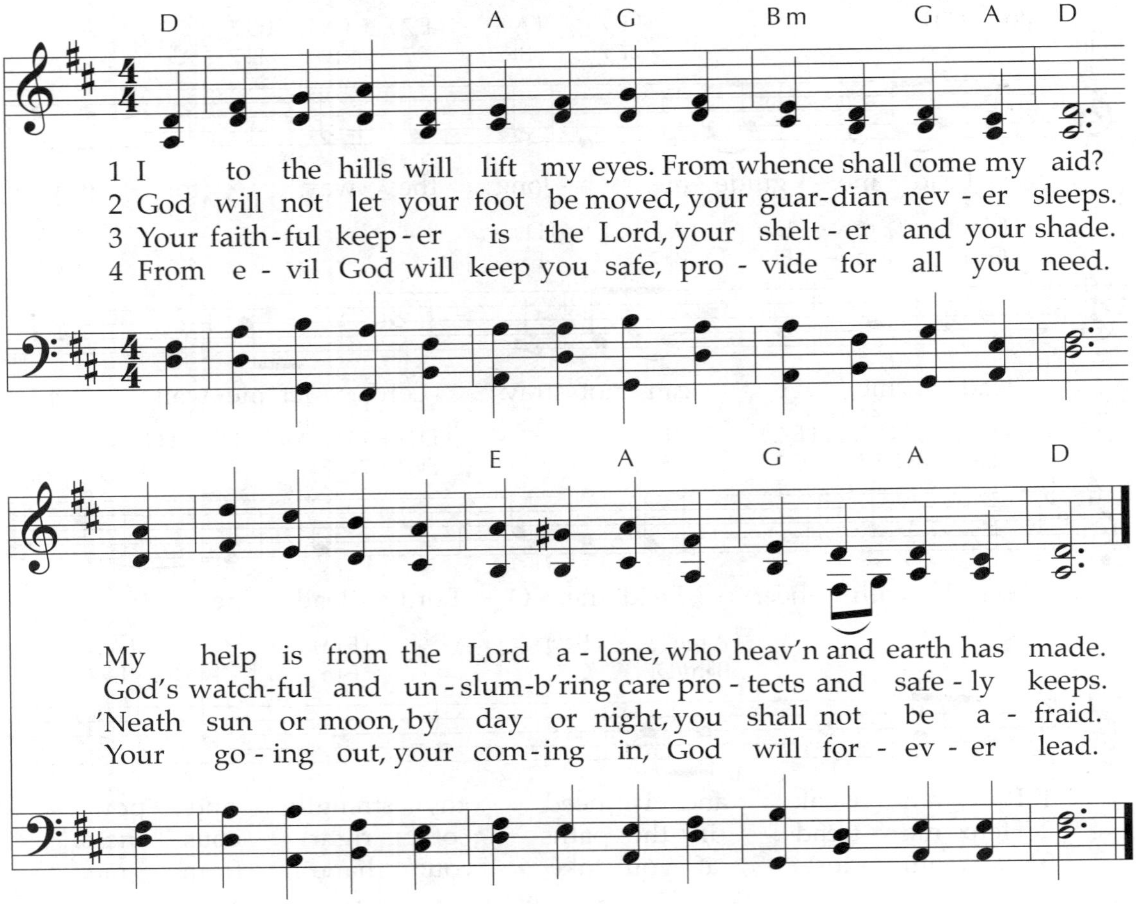
D A G Bm G A D
1 I to the hills will lift my eyes. From whence shall come my aid?
2 God will not let your foot be moved, your guar-dian nev - er sleeps.
3 Your faith-ful keep - er is the Lord, your shelt - er and your shade.
4 From e - vil God will keep you safe, pro - vide for all you need.
E A G A D
My help is from the Lord a - lone, who heav'n and earth has made.
God's watch-ful and un - slum-b'ring care pro - tects and safe - ly keeps.
'Neath sun or moon, by day or night, you shall not be a - fraid.
Your go - ing out, your com-ing in, God will for - ev - er lead.

Chord symbols represent a simplified harmony.

Text: based on Psalm 121; *The New Metrical Version of the Psalms* (Canada and USA), 1912, alt.
Music: *The CL. Psalmes of David* (Scotland), 1615

603 Still My Soul

UNRAVELED 8.8.8.8.8.8.7.8

B♭ D aug E♭maj7
Still my soul, calm my roam - ing mind. Give me peace; may my
E♭m(maj7) B♭/F D aug(♯9)
heart un-wind. Let me stay, your be - lov - ed guest. Take my

Text: Katie Graber (USA), © 2019 Katie Graber
Music: Charlene Nafziger (Canada), © 2017 Charlene Nafziger

E♭maj9 E♭m(maj7) B♭/F Daug
fear, make my wor - ry rest. What I hold, let me give to you. Aid my
E♭ E♭m(maj7) B♭/F
strength when my storms drive through. When my thoughts won't
Gm7 Cm7 E♭/F F7 E♭/B♭ B♭
let me go, I'll sing to you: oh, still my soul.

Nada te turbe 604

NADA TE TURBE Irregular

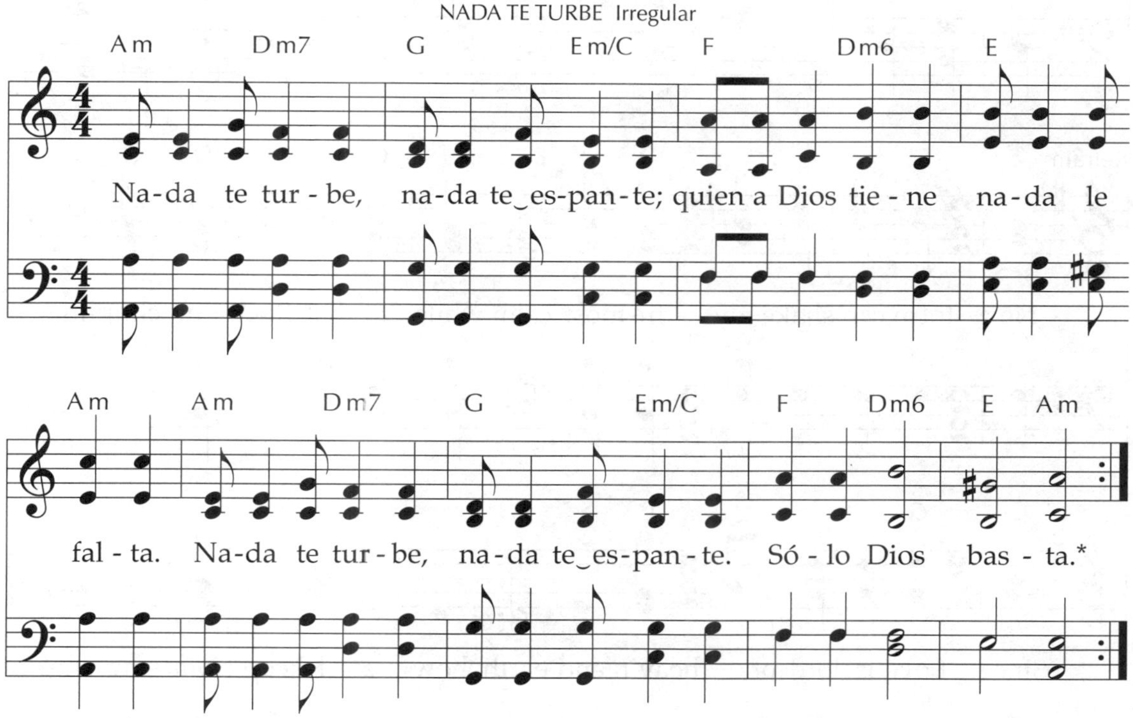
Am Dm7 G Em/C F Dm6 E
Na-da te tur - be, na-da te‿es-pan - te; quien a Dios tie - ne na-da le
Am Am Dm7 G Em/C F Dm6 E Am
fal - ta. Na-da te tur - be, na-da te‿es-pan - te. Só - lo Dios bas - ta.*

*Translation: Let nothing trouble you. Let nothing frighten you. Whoever has God lacks nothing.

Verses can be found in the accompaniment edition.

Text: Spanish; attr. Teresa of Ávila (Spain), 16th c.; paraphr. Taizé Community (France), 1986
Music: Jacques Berthier (France), 1986

605 My Life Flows On

HOW CAN I KEEP FROM SINGING 8.7.8.7 with refrain

G C G D
1 My life flows on in end-less song, a-bove earth's lam-en-ta-tion.
2 Through all the tu-mult and the strife, I hear that mu-sic ring-ing.
3 What though my joys and com-forts die, I know my Sav-ior liv-eth.
4 The peace of Christ makes fresh my heart, a foun-tain ev-er spring-ing!
G C G D G
I catch the sweet, though far-off hymn that hails a new cre-a-tion.
It finds an ech-o in my soul. How can I keep from sing-ing?
What though the dark-ness gath-er round? Songs in the night he giv-eth.
All things are mine since I am his! How can I keep from sing-ing?
Refrain
G D Em G D G
No storm can shake my in-most calm while to that Rock I'm cling-ing.
G C G D G
Since Love is lord of heav'n and earth, how can I keep from sing-ing?

Text: Robert Lowry's *Bright Jewels for the Sunday School* (USA), 1869, alt.
Music: Robert Lowry's *Bright Jewels for the Sunday School*, 1869, refrain arr. © 1989 *Hymnal: A Worship Book*, alt.

Guide Me, O Thou Great Jehovah 606

CWM RHONDDA 8.7.8.7.8.7 extended

1 Guide me, O thou great Je - ho - vah, pil - grim through this bar - ren
2 O - pen now the crys - tal foun - tain whence the heal - ing wa - ters
3 When I tread the verge of Jor - dan, bid my anx - ious fears sub-
land. I am weak, but thou art might - y; hold me with thy
flow. Let the fier - y, cloud - y pil - lar lead me all my
side. Death of death and hell's de - struc - tion, land me safe on
pow'r - ful hand. Bread of heav - en, bread of hea - ven, feed me till I
jour - ney through. Strong De - liv - 'rer, strong De - liv - 'rer, be thou still my
Ca - naan's side. Songs of prais - es, songs of prais - es, I will ev - er
want no more, (want no more,) feed me till I want no more.
strength and shield, (strength and shield,) be thou still my strength and shield.
give to thee, (give to thee,) I will ev - er give to thee.

Text: William Williams (Wales), "Arglwydd arwain trwy'r anialwch," *Alleluia*, 1745; trans. Peter Williams (Wales) and William Williams, *Hymns on Various Subjects*, 1771
Music: John Hughes (Wales), 1905 or 1907, *The Voice of Thanksgiving, No. 4*, 1928

607 Onyame wo mu o (In Your Sickness)

ONYAME WO MU Irregular

Capo 3:
O-nya-me wo mu‿o, wo mu‿o, wo mu‿o. Bi-ri-
In your sick-ness, your suf-f'rings, your trials, and pains, God is
bia-ra be-ye yie. O-nya-me wo mu‿o, wo mu‿o,
with you all the time. Per-se-cu-tion, temp-ta-tions, and
wo mu‿o. Bi-ri-bia-ra be-ye yie.
lone-li-ness, God is with you all the time.
O-nya-me wo mu‿o, O-nya-me wo mu‿o. Bi-ri-
God is there with you, al-ways there with you, God is
bia-ra be-ye yie. O-nya-me wo mu‿o, O-nya-
with you all the time. God is there with you, al-ways
me wo mu‿o. Bi-ri-bia-ra be-ye yie.
there with you, God is with you all the time.

Text: Twi; Ghanaian traditional, *Asempa Hymns*, alt.
Music: Ghanaian traditional, *Ghana Praise*

O Love That Will Not Let Me Go 608

ST. MARGARET 8.8.8.8.8.6

G Dsus D D7
1 O Love that will not let me go, I rest my
2 O Light that fol-lows all my way, I yield my
3 O Joy that seek-est me through pain, I can - not
4 O Cross that lift - est up my head, I dare not
G B
wea - ry soul in thee. I give thee back the life I
flick-'ring torch to thee. My heart re - stores its bor - rowed
close my heart to thee. I trace the rain - bow through the
ask to fly from thee. I lay in dust, life's glo - ry
Em A7
owe, that in thine o - cean depths its
ray, that in thy sun - shine's blaze its
rain, and feel the prom - ise is not
dead, and from the ground there blos - soms
G/D D G/D D7 G
flow may rich - er, full - er be.
day may bright - er, fair - er be.
vain, that morn shall tear - less be.
red, life that shall end - less be.

*An adaptation of this tune (ST. MARGARET) is available in the accompaniment edition.

Text: George Matheson (Scotland), 1882, *Life and Work . . .*, 1883
Music: Albert L. Peace (England), 1884, *Scottish Hymnal*, 1885

*r

609 Lord, You've Searched Me

LORD, YOU'VE SEARCHED ME Irregular

Refrain
G C G
Lord, you've searched me and you know me.
C D C G C
You know when I sit and rise. Love lives in
G F C
my heart most ful - ly when you, Lord,
G D F C G
you, Lord, you, Lord in me a-bide.
Fine
Am G/B C D
1 Lord, you have cho - sen me; you know my soul,
2 Lord, you watch o - ver me. You guide my way.
Am G/B C D
each word that leaves my tongue. You al - read - y know
With ev - 'ry step I take both night and day,
Em D/F♯ C D
each song of joy and pain - ful mel - o - dy;
En - light - en ev - 'ry turn and help me be
C D C
knowl-edge too won - der - ful for me.
with - in your truth that sets me free.
To refrain

Text: based on Psalm 139:1–12, Camps with Meaning (Canada), 2000
Music: Camps with Meaning, 2000; acc. Anneli Loepp Thiessen (Canada), 2019

Precious Lord, Take My Hand 610

Swing:

PRECIOUS LORD Irregular

Capo 1: (G) A♭
(G7/D) A♭7/E♭
(C) D♭
1 Pre - cious Lord, take my hand, lead me on, help me stand,
2 When my way grows drear, pre-cious Lord, lin-ger near,
3 When the dark - ness ap-pears and the night draws near,
(G) A♭ (D7/F♯) E♭7/G (Em) Fm (A9) B♭9 (D) E♭ (D7) E♭7
I am tired, I am weak, I am worn. Through the
when my life is al - most gone, hear my
and the day is past and gone, at the
(G) A♭ (D7/A) E♭7/B♭ (G7) A♭7 (Am/C) B♭m/D♭ (C) D♭ (C♯dim) D dim
storm, through the night, lead me on to the light,
cry, hear my call, hold my hand lest I fall.
riv - er I stand, guide my feet, hold my hand.
(G) A♭ (D7) E♭7 (G) A♭
take my hand, pre-cious Lord, lead me home.

611 Lift Every Voice and Sing

ANTHEM 6.6.10.6.6.10.14.14.6.6.10

D G B7 Em G B7 Em
1 Lift ev - 'ry voice and sing, till earth and heav - en ring,
2 Ston - y the road we trod, bit - ter the chas - t'ning rod,
3 God of our wea - ry years, God of our si - lent tears,
Am B7 C G/D D
ring with the har - mo - nies of lib - er - ty.
felt in the days when hope un - born had died;
thou who hast brought us thus far on the way,
G B7 E Am B7 C
Let our re - joic - ing rise high as the lis - t'ning skies,
yet with a stead - y beat, have not our wea - ry feet
thou who hast by thy might led us in - to the light,
C♯dim7 G/D D7 G
let it re - sound loud as the roll - ing sea.
come to the place for which our peo - ple sighed?
keep us for - ev - er in the path, we pray.

Text: James W. Johnson (USA), 1900
Music: J. Rosamund Johnson (USA), 1905

Em D
Sing a song full of the faith that the dark past has taught us.
We have come o - ver a way that with tears has been wa - tered.
Lest our feet stray from the plac - es, our God, where we met thee;
G Cm G
Sing a song full of the hope that the pres - ent has brought
We have come, tread - ing our path thro' the blood of the slaugh -
lest our hearts, drunk with the wine of the world, we for - get
D7 G B7 E Am B7
us. Fac - ing the ris - ing sun of our new day be -
tered, out from the gloom - y past, till now we stand at
thee; shad - owed be - neath thy hand, may we for - ev - er
C C♯dim7 G/D D7 G
gun, let us march on till vic - to - ry is won.
last where the bright gleam of our bright star is cast.
stand, true to our God, true to our na - tive land.

612 When Pain or Sorrow / Hold On

ERB 10.10.11.8 with refrain

Capo 3: (C) Eb (F/C) Ab/Eb (F) Ab (C/E) Eb/G
1 When pain or sor - row is
2 If God is si - lent when
3 And when it looks like there's
(F) Ab (G) Bb (Am) Cm (F) Ab
too much to bear; when your heart feels
you need to hear that you're not a -
no end in sight, know all that is
(C/E) Eb/G (Dm7) Fm7 (Gsus) Bbsus (G) Bb (Am) Cm
numb, un - a - ble to care, when faith seems so
lone, that com - fort is near; if you are a -
wrong can still be made right. You're nev - er a -
(Em/G) Gm/Bb (F) Ab (Fm) Abm (C/E) Eb/G
point - less that you can - not pray, when
ban - doned when you need a friend, when
lone; God has prom - ised to be with
(Dm) Fm (C/E) Eb/G (F) Ab (D/F#) F/A (G7sus) Bb7sus (G7) Bb7 (C) Eb
no one knows quite what to say, then
all good things come to an end, then
us e - ven when we can't see, so
Refrain
(Fmaj7) Abmaj7 (C/E) Eb/G (E7sus) G7sus (E7) G7 (Am) Cm (F) Ab
hold on, hold on, to find a

Text: Adam M. L. Tice (USA)
Music: Adam M. L. Tice; acc. Sally Ann Morris (USA)

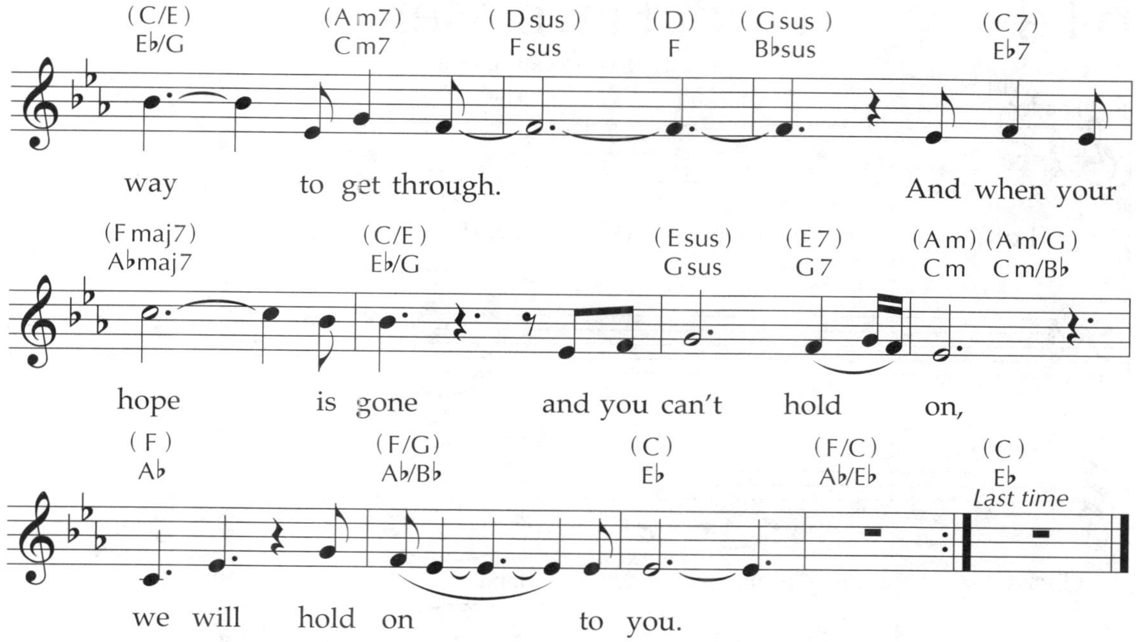
(C/E) Eb/G (Am7) Cm7 (Dsus) Fsus (D) F (Gsus) Bbsus (C7) Eb7
way to get through. And when your
(Fmaj7) Abmaj7 (C/E) Eb/G (Esus) Gsus (E7) G7 (Am) Cm (Am/G) Cm/Bb
hope is gone and you can't hold on,
(F) Ab (F/G) Ab/Bb (C) Eb (F/C) Ab/Eb (C) Eb
Last time
we will hold on to you.

God, Be with Us 613

JOURNEY 8.7.10

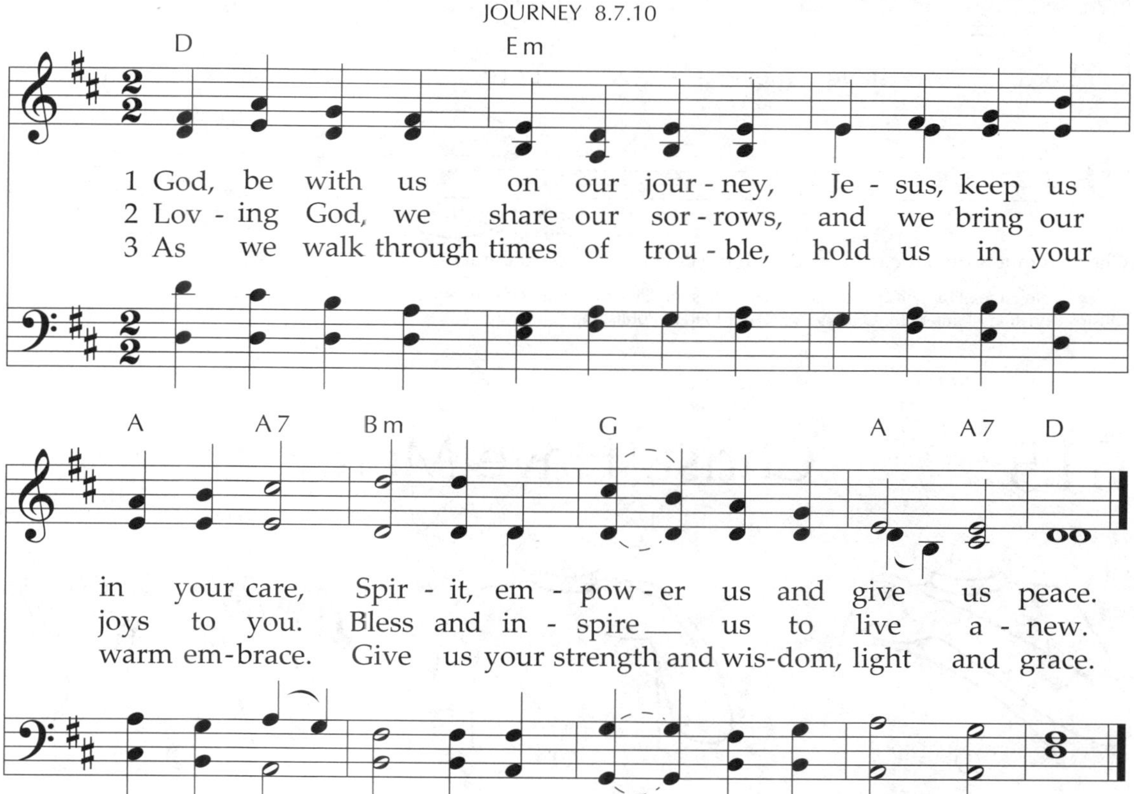
D Em
1 God, be with us on our jour-ney, Je-sus, keep us
2 Lov-ing God, we share our sor-rows, and we bring our
3 As we walk through times of trou-ble, hold us in your
A A7 Bm G A A7 D
in your care, Spir-it, em-pow-er us and give us peace.
joys to you. Bless and in-spire us to live a-new.
warm em-brace. Give us your strength and wis-dom, light and grace.

Text: Joanne Bender (Canada)
Music: Joanne Bender

614 Lord, Have Mercy

MANDERFELD KYRIE Irregular

Am
Leader
Lord, have mer - cy.
All
G C Am
Lord, have mer - cy.
Dm
Leader
Christ, have mer - cy.
All
Gm Dm Bb C Dm
Christ, have mer - cy.
Am
Leader
Lord, have mer - cy.
All
G C Am
Lord, have mer - cy.

Chord symbols do not correspond with the keyboard accompaniment.

Text: from Greek liturgy Κύριε, ἐλέησον (Kyrie eleison) (Eastern Mediterranean), 4th c.
Music: Christine Manderfeld, OSB (USA), © 2014 Hope Publishing Company

615 Christ, Have Mercy

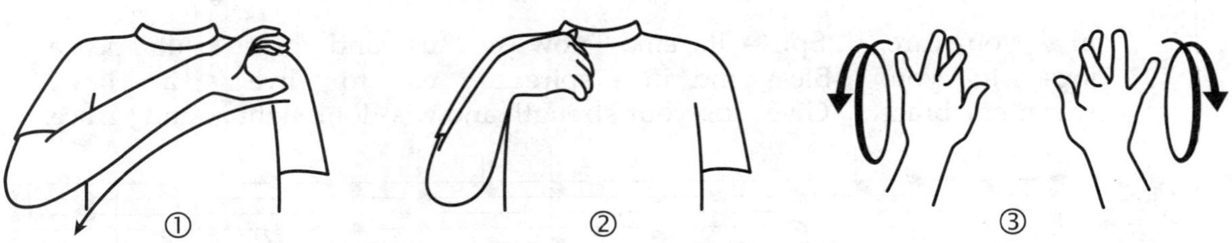
①
②
③

Text: American Sign Language; Mennonite Worship and Song Committee, 2020; illustration by Merrill Miller (USA)

Cast Thy Burden upon the Lord 616

BIRMINGHAM (MENDELSSOHN) Irregular

Eb Ab Bb Eb* Ab Bb7 Eb
Cast thy burden up - on the Lord, who ev - er sus - tains thee,
Cm Bb Fm G Cm Gm Ab
who nev - er will suf - fer the right-eous to fall, and is at thy
Bb7 Eb Bb Fm Cm F Bb
right hand. Thy mer - cy, Lord, is great, and far a - bove the heav'ns.
Eb Ab Eb/G Ab Bb7 Eb
Let none be made a - sham - ed, that wait up - on thee.

*Fermatas for use with keyboard accompaniment.

Text: Julius Schubring (Germany), 1846, *Wirf dein Anliegen auf den Herrn*; trans. William Bartholomew (England), *Elijah*, 1846, alt.
Music: *Neu-vermehrtes Gesangbuch* (present-day Germany), 1693; adapt. Felix Mendelssohn (Germany), *Elijah*, 1846

617 When Peace like a River

VILLE DU HAVRE 11.8.11.9 with refrain

Capo 1: (C) D♭
(G7) A♭7
(C) D♭
1 When peace like a river attendeth my way, when sorrows like sea billows roll, whatever my lot, thou hast taught me to say, "It is well, it is well with my soul."
2 Though Satan should buffet, though trials should come, let this blest assurance control, that Christ hath regarded my helpless estate, and hath shed his own blood for my soul.
3 Redeemed! Oh, the bliss of this glorious thought: My sin— not in part, but the whole—is nailed to his cross, and I bear it no more, praise the Lord, praise the Lord, O my soul!
4 And, Lord, haste the day when my faith shall be sight, the clouds be rolled back as a scroll, the trumpet shall sound, and the Lord shall descend, even so, it is well with my soul.
(Am) B♭m
(D) E♭
(G) A♭
(C) D♭
(F) G♭
(Dm) E♭m
(G) A♭
(C) D♭
(G) A♭
(C) D♭
Refrain
(G) A♭
(G7) A♭7
(C) D♭
It is well with my soul,
It is well with my soul,

Text: Horatio G. Spafford (USA), *Gospel Hymns, No. 2*, 1876, alt.
Music: Philip P. Bliss (USA), *Gospel Hymns, No. 2*, 1876

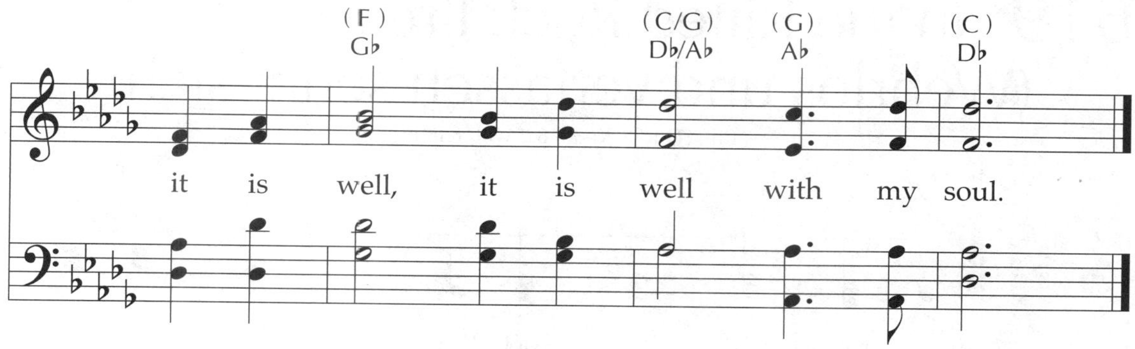
(F) Gb (C/G) Db/Ab (G) Ab (C) Db
it is well, it is well with my soul.

Sometimes a Light Surprises 618

SALLY GARDENS 7.6.7.6 D

C G C F C F Dm7 C
1 Some - times a light sur - pris - es the child of God who sings:
2 In ho - ly con - tem - pla - tion with joy we shall pur - sue
3 It can bring with it noth - ing but God will bear us through.
4 Though vine and fig tree neith - er their year - ly fruit should bear,
G C F C Dm7 C
the light of one who ris - es with gen - tle, heal - ing wings.
the theme of God's sal - va - tion, and find it ev - er new.
Who gives the lil - ies cloth - ing will clothe the peo - ple, too.
though all the fields should with - er, nor flocks nor herds be there,
Am Em F Am F
When com - forts are de - clin - ing, God grants the soul a - gain
Set free from pres - ent sor - row, we cheer - ful - ly can say,
Be - neath the spread - ing heav - ens no crea - ture but is fed:
yet God, the same a - bid - ing, through praise shall tune my voice,
C7 F C Dm7 C
a sea - son of clear shin - ing, to cheer it af - ter rain.
let the un - known to - mor - row bring with it what it may.
the One who feeds the ra - vens will give the chil - dren bread.
for while in love con - fid - ing I can - not but re - joice.

Text: William Cowper (England), *Olney Hymns, Book III*, 1779, alt.
Music: Irish traditional, 19th c.; arr. Alfred V. Fedak (USA), © 2011 Alfred V. Fedak

619 In the Rifted Rock I'm Resting (Wehrlos und verlassen sehnt sich)

RIFTED ROCK 8.7.8.7 with refrain

Capo 4: (C) E (F) A
1 In the rift - ed Rock I'm rest - ing, safe - ly
2 Long pur - sued by sin and Sa - tan, wea - ry,
1 Wehr - los und ver - las - sen sehnt sich oft mein
2 Drückt mich Kum - mer, Müh' und Sor - ge, mei - ne
(C) E (G) B (C) E
shel - tered, I a - bide. There no foes nor storms as -
sad, I longed for rest. Then I found this heav'n - ly
Herz nach stil - ler Ruh'; doch du de - ckest mit dem
Zu - flucht bist nur du, ret - test mich aus al - len
(F) A (C/G) E/B (G7) B7 (C) E
sail me, while with - in the cleft I hide.
shel - ter, o - pened in my Sav - ior's breast.
Fit - tich dei - ner Lie - be sanft mich zu.
Äng - sten, trö - stest mich und deckst mich zu.

Text: Mary Dagworthy James (USA), *Christian Songs for the Sunday School*, 1872, rev. *Crystal Notes: A Choice Collection*, 1878; German stanzas Carl Röhl (Germany), *Evangelisches Gesangbuch*, 1895
Music: W. Warren Bentley (USA), *Beulah Songs: A Choice Collection*, 1879

Refrain
Now I'm rest - ing, sweet - ly rest - ing, in the
Un - ter dei - nem sanf - ten Fit - tich find' ich
(G) (C) (G) (C)
B E B E
cleft once made for me. Je - sus, bless - ed Rock of
Frie - den, Trost und Ruh'; denn du schir - mest mich so
(F) (C/G) (G7) (C)
A E/B B7 E
ag - es, I will hide my - self in thee.
freund - lich, schü - tzest mich und deckst mich zu.

3 Peace which passeth understanding,
joy the world can never give,
now in Jesus, I am finding;
in his smiles of love I live.

4 In the rifted Rock I'll hide me,
till the storms of life are past,
all secure in this blest refuge,
heeding not the fiercest blast.

3 Sicher bin ich und geborgen,
denn bei dir ist süße Ruh';
mag es auch im Leben stürmen,
Herr, dein Fittich deckt mich zu.

4 Kommt dann meine letzte Stunde,
geh' ich ein zur ew'gen Ruh';
und du deckst mit deinen Flügeln
ewiglich dein Kindlein zu.

620 Oré poriajú verekó (Kyrie eleison)

ORÉ PORIAJÚ VEREKÓ (KYRIE ELEISON) Irregular

C F
Guarani: O - ré po - ria - jú ve - re -
Greek: Ky - ri - e e - le - i - son, Ky - ri -
Spanish: Se - ñor, ten pie - dad. Se -
French: Sei - gneur, prends pi - tié. Sei -
G C A
kó Ñan - de - ya - ra. O - ré po - ria -
e e - le - i - son, Ky - ri - e e - le - i -
ñor, ten pie - dad. Se - ñor, ten pie -
gneur, prends pi - tié. Sei - gneur, prends pi -
Dm G C
jú ve - re - kó, Ñan - de - ya - ra.
son, Ky - ri - e e - le - i - son.
dad. Se - ñor, ten pie - dad.
tié. Sei - gneur, prends pi - tié.

Translation: Lord, have mercy.

Text: Guarani; from Greek liturgy Κύριε, ελέησον (Kyrie eleison) (Eastern Mediterranean), 4th c.; Spanish and French trans. traditional

Music: Guarani traditional (Paraguay); arr. *More Voices* (Canada) 2005,

My Hope Is Built

621

SOLID ROCK LM with refrain

G D C
1 My hope is built on noth-ing less than Je-sus' blood and
2 In ev-'ry rough and storm-y gale, my an-chor holds with-
3 Not earth, nor hell, my soul can move; I rest up-on un-
4 When he shall come with trum-pet sound, oh, may I then in
D G D C
right-eous-ness. I dare not trust the sweet-est frame but whol-ly
in the vale. When all a-round my soul gives way, he then is
chang-ing love. I trust his right-eous char-ac-ter, his coun-sel,
him be found, dressed in his right-eous-ness a-lone, fault-less to
D G Refrain C
lean on Je-sus' name.
all my hope and stay.
prom-ise, and his pow'r.
stand be-fore the throne.
On Christ, the sol-id rock, I stand; all
G D G D G
oth-er ground is sink-ing sand, all oth-er ground is sink-ing sand.

Text: Edward Mote (England), ca. 1834, *Hymns of Praise: A New Selection of Gospel Hymns,* 1836, alt.
Music: William B. Bradbury (USA), 1863, *Devotional Hymn and Tune Book,* 1864

622 Jesus, Rock of Ages

JESUS, ROCK OF AGES Irregular

Refrain
F C Gm
Je - sus, Rock of ag - es, let me hide
Dm Bb F C
my-self in thee. Je - sus, liv-ing Wa - ter,
Gm Dm D m/C
Last time to Coda
let me drink from your flow-ing stream.
Bb C F C/E
1 Your love comes pour - ing in my life,
2 Your love has been a firm foun - da - tion,
Dm Eb Bb C
fills my heart till it o - ver-flows.
a sol - id rock that nev - er moves.
Bb C F
You re-vive my dy - ing spir - it till it
Your words of wis - dom will pro-tect me and

Text: Jerry Derstine (JD Martin) (USA), 1973
Music: Jerry Derstine (JD Martin), 1973; arr. Marilyn Houser Hamm (Canada); harm. © 1991 Marilyn Houser Hamm and Jerry Derstine (JD Martin)

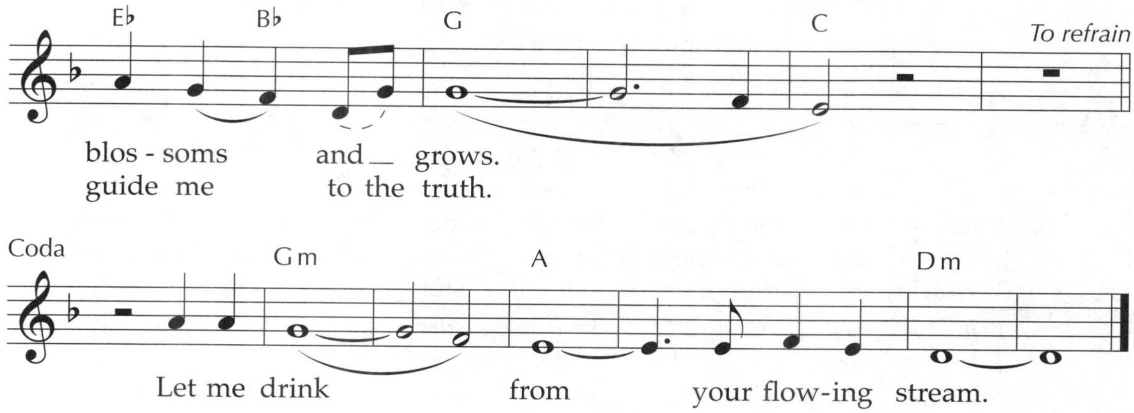
E♭ B♭ G C
To refrain
blos - soms and _ grows.
guide me to the truth.
Coda
Gm A Dm
Let me drink from your flow-ing stream.

What Comfort Can Our Worship Bring 623

MORNING SONG (CONSOLATION) CM

Gm Dm Gm E♭ B♭
1 What com-fort can our wor-ship bring on bleak and emp-ty days
2 What sor-row can we dare to own, what an - ger, loss, and fears?
3 O God, hear ev - 'ry long-ing sigh as voic-es rise and strain,
F Dm Gm Dm Gm
to those who can-not bear to sing when pain is missed in praise?
Not just in joy is God made known, but al - so in our tears.
and meet us in that hon-est cry where praise is voiced in pain.

Chord symbols represent a simplified harmony.

Text: Adam M. L. Tice (USA), © 2009 GIA Publications, Inc.
Music: anon., *Wyeth's Repository of Sacred Music, Part Second* (USA), 1813; arr. *Hymnal: A Worship Book*, alt. © 1992 *Hymnal: A Worship Book*

624 Jesu, meine Freude (Jesus, Priceless Treasure)

JESU MEINE FREUDE 6.6.5.6.6.5.7.8.6

1 Je - su, mei - ne Freu - de, mei - nes Her - zens
2 Un - ter dei - nem Schir - men bin ich vor den
3 Weicht, ihr Trau - er - gei - ster; denn mein Freu - den -
1 Je - sus, price - less trea - sure, source of pur - est
2 In thine arm I rest me; foes who have op -
3 Hence, all thoughts of sad - ness! for the Lord of
Wei - de, Je - su, mei - ne Zier! Ach, wie lang, ach
Stür - men al - ler Fein - de frei. Lass den Sa - tan
mei - ster, Je - sus, tritt he - rein. De - nen, die Gott
plea - sure, tru - est friend to me, long my heart hath
pressed me can - not reach me here. Though the earth be
glad - ness, Je - sus, en - ters in. Those who love the
lan - ge ist dem Her - zen ban - ge und ver - langt nach
wet - tern, lass die Welt er - zit - tern, mir steht Je - sus
lie - ben, muss auch ihr Be - trü - ben lau - ter Freu - de
pant - ed, till it well - nigh faint - ed, thirst - ing af - ter
shak - ing, ev - 'ry heart be quak - ing, Je - sus calms my
Sav - ior, though the storms may gath - er, still have peace with-

Text: German; Johann Franck (present-day Germany), *Praxis pietatis melica*, 5th ed., 1653; trans. Catherine Winkworth (England), *Chorale Book for England*, 1863, alt.

Music: Johann Crüger (present-day Germany), 1653, *Praxis pietatis melica*, 5th ed.; harm. J. S. Bach (present-day Germany), Motet no. 3, 1723

dir! Got - tes Lamm, mein Bräu - ti - gam, au - ßer dir soll
bei. Ob es jetzt gleich kracht und blitzt, ob gleich Sünd und
sein. Duld ich schon hier Spott und Hohn, den - noch bleibst du
thee. Thine I am, O spot - less Lamb; I will suf - fer
fear. Sin and hell in con - flict fell with their heav - iest
in. Yea, what - e'er we here must bear, still in thee lies
mir auf Er - den nichts sonst Lie - bers wer - den.
Höl - le schre - cken, Je - sus will mich de - cken.
auch im Lei - de, Je - su, mei - ne Freu - de.
naught to hide thee, ask for naught be - side thee.
storms as - sail me; Je - sus will not fail me.
pur - est plea - sure, Je - sus, price - less trea - sure!

625 Far Above the Noise of Life

GENTLE VOICE Irregular

C G F/A F/G
1 Far a - bove the noise of life, there's a voice that is gen-tly
(2 Gen-tle) voice, so meek and mild; gen - tle words of un-der-
F C G F/A F/G
call - ing. "Leave be-hind your cares and strife. Come to me. I will give you
stand-ing. "You are my be - lov - ed child. Come to me. I will give you
C C/E F2 F C2/E C/E
rest. Bring your fear and bring your pain. Bring your
rest. Bring your grief and bring your cares. Bring your
Dm7 F/G C C/E F2 F
an - ger and bring your wor - ry." Do you hear the voice of
heart-aches and bring your sor-row." Do you hear the voice of

Text: Susan Naus Dengler (USA), 2006
Music: Lee Dengler (USA), 2006

C/E Dm7 F/G 1 C
Je-sus, gen-tly call-ing, "Come un-to me"? 2 Gen-tle
Je-sus, gen-tly call-ing, "Come un-to
2 C C/E F2 F C C/E
me"? Gen-tle voice, so full of love. Gen-tle
F2 F C/E Fmaj7 C/G G C/G C
words so rich in mer-cy. "You are my be-lov-ed
G F/A F/G C
child. Come to me. I will give you rest."

626 A Wonderful Savior Is Jesus

KIRKPATRICK 11.8.11.8 with refrain

D G D
1 A won - der-ful Sav - ior is Je - sus my Lord, a
2 A won - der-ful Sav - ior is Je - sus my Lord; he
3 With num - ber-less bless-ings each mo - ment he crowns, and
4 When clothed in his bright-ness, trans - port - ed I rise to
A D
won - der-ful Sav - ior to me. He hid - eth my soul in the
tak - eth my bur-den a - way. He hold - eth me up, and I
filled with his full-ness di - vine, I sing in my rap-ture, "Oh,
meet him in clouds of the sky, his per - fect sal - va - tion, his
G D/A A7 D
cleft of the rock, where riv - ers of pleas - ure I see.
shall not be moved; he giv - eth me strength as my day.
glo - ry to God for such a Re - deem - er as mine!"
won - der-ful love, I'll shout with the mil - lions on high.
Refrain
A7 D A7
He hid - eth my soul in the cleft of the rock that shad-ows a dry, thirst-y

Text: Fanny J. Crosby (USA), *The Finest of the Wheat No. 1*, 1890
Music: William J. Kirkpatrick (USA), *The Finest of the Wheat No. 1*, 1890

D G D/A
land. He hid - eth my life in the depths of his love, and cov - ers me
A D D/A A7 D
there with his hand, and cov - ers me there with his hand.

Bleibet hier (Stay with Me) 627

BLEIBET HIER Irregular

Dm Gm Dm Gm Dm C
German: Blei - bet hier und wa - chet mit mir. Wa - chet und
English: Stay with me, re - main here with me, watch and
Spanish: Ve - la - ré con - ti - go, Se - ñor, mien - tras yo
F C Dm Asus A
be - tet, wa - chet und be - tet.
pray, watch and pray.
vi - va, mien - tras yo vi - va.

Verses can be found in the accompaniment edition.

Text: German; based on Matthew 26:38–42, Mark 14:32–36, Luke 22:39–46), *Music from Taizé*, vol. 2; English and Spanish trans. Taizé Community (France)
Music: Jacques Berthier (France), *Music from Taizé*, vol. 2

628 What a Friend We Have in Jesus

CONVERSE 8.7.8.7 D

Capo 3: (D)
1 What a friend we have in Je - sus, all our sins and griefs to bear!
2 Have we tri - als and temp-ta - tions? Is there trou-ble an - y-where?
3 Are we weak and heav-y la - den, 'cum-bered with a load of care?
What a priv - i - lege to car - ry ev - 'ry-thing to God in prayer!
We should nev - er be dis - cour-aged— take it to the Lord in prayer!
Pre - cious Sav - ior, still our ref - uge, take it to the Lord in prayer!
Oh, what peace we of - ten for - feit, oh, what need-less pain we bear,
Can we find a friend so faith-ful, who will all our sor-rows share?
Do thy friends de-spise, for-sake thee? Take it to the Lord in prayer!
all be-cause we do not car - ry ev - 'ry-thing to God in prayer.
Je - sus knows our ev-'ry weak-ness— take it to the Lord in prayer!
Je - sus' arms will take and shield thee— thou wilt find a sol-ace there.

For a French translation, see the accompaniment edition.

Text: Joseph M. Scriven (Canada), 1855, *Spirit Minstrel: A Collection of Hymns and Music*, 1857, alt.; Lao trans. anon.; Hmong trans. anon.

Music: Charles C. Converse (USA), 1868, *Silver Wings*, 1870

Lao

1 ມິດ ສະຫາຍເຮົາຄື ພຣະເຢ ຊູ
ຊົງ ແບກເອົາຜິດບາບໃຫ້ຫາຍ
ເຮົາຈຶ່ງ ມີ ສິດເຂົ້າມາເຝົ້າ ຢູ່
ດ້ວຍ ບໍ່ ຢ້ານຈະ ຖືກຂັບ ໄລ່
ສຸກ ສໍາລານໄດ້ຫວິດໄປ ຫຼາຍ ທີ່
ເກີດລໍາບາກຈິນ ຕືອຫືອ ອ່ອນ
ການໜັກ ໃຈ ຝູງ ນີ້ ບັງເກີດ ມີ
ເພາະໝູ່ ເຮົາຖິ້ມການໄຫອ້ອອນ

2 ານທຸກໃຫຍ່ການລອງໃຈມີ ມາ
ການລໍາ ບາກມາເຖິງເມື່ອໃດ
ໃຫ້ ເຮົາມີຄວາມເຊື່ອແລະໝັ້ນມາ
ຫາ ພຣະເຈົ້າປົງ ທຸກອາງໃຈ
ຜູ້ ຮັກເໝືອນພຣະອົງຫາ ບໍ່ ໄດ້
ພຣະອົງ ຊົງແບກຄວາມໂສກເສົ້າ
ຊົງ ຮູ້ ຈັກ ໃຈເຮົາຈຶ່ງບອກ ໄອ້ ອ່າ
ຈົ່ງຮິບໄຫອ້ອອນພຣະເຈົ້າ

3 ເມື່ອອິດອອນໜັກ ອິກ ໜັກໃຈນັ້ນ
ມີ ທຸກ ໃຫຍ່ບໍ່ ແພ້ ອິດເອົາ
ໂອ້ ຜູ້ ຊ່ອຍຂໍ ໃຫ້ ໝູ່ ເຮົາຫັ່ນ
ໄຫອ້ອອນ ຂໍ ຈິນ ໄດ້ບັນເທົາ
ເມື່ອໝູ່ ຄູ່ ໝ່◌າຍ ຊົງພາກອອກໄປ
ຄວນອອກປາກເປັນຄໍາອ້ອນວອນ
ພຣະເຢ ຊູ ຈະຊົງ ອຸ້ມເຮົາ ໄປ
ນໍາ ພຣະອົງຈະ ໄດ້ ຮັບພອນ

Lao transliteration

1 Mid sahaihaokheu phrayesu,
song baebaophid haihai,
haoching mee sidkhaomafao yu,
duai bo yancha theukkhap lai.
suk samlan dai hewpai lai thi
koed lambakchon tuaeet on,
kannak chai fung nee bangkoed mee
phomu haothimkanvaivvon.

2 Kanthukhyaikanlongchaimee ma,
kanlambak mathoengmeuodai,
hai haomikhuaamseulaemanma ha
phrachaopok thukvangchai.
phu hakmeuonphraongha bodai
phraong songbaebkhuaamosoksao,
song hu chakchaihaochingbok vai va
chongbibhaivvonphrachao.

3 Meuidonak oak nakchainan
mee thuk yai bo paeh od aow,
o phu soykhohai mu haomun
haivuaon kho chon daibanthao.
meuomu khu hai sang phakoakpai
khuan oakpak pen khamonuaon,
phrayesu chasong umhaopai
nam phraongcha dai habphon.

Hmong

1 Kuv tug kwvluag yog Tswv Yesxus,
nwg tsi tso kuv tseg ib txhis.
Leejtwg hlub kuv npaum le Yesxus?
Tsi muaj ib tug hlub le nwg.
Nwg paab kuv dlim dlaab le xibteg
lug nyob huv nwg lub xubndlag.
Kuv yuav muab sab rau ntseeg Yesxus,
leejtwg yuav ua kuas kuv ntshai?

2 Tej kev txomnyem huv nplajteb nuav
txawj ua kuas kuv lub sab ntxhuv.
Kuv raug kev txhawj xeeb ua luaj nua,
leejtwg yuav has kuv ib lus?
Kuav yuav nrhav ib tug ua kwvluag,
nrhav huv nplajteb ntshai tsi muaj.
Yesxus tuab leeg yuav paab kuv dlim,
kuv txhaj tau txujsa ib txhis.

3 Tej kev txhawj xeeb tej kev quaj ntsuag
tej ua kuas kuv ntshai ua luaj.
Kuv muab txhua yaam tso rua Yesxus,
ca sab ntsoov nwg yuav paab kuv.
Kuv yuav qha tej kws kuv ntxhuv sab,
kuv tsi xaav khaws tej nuav ca.
Muab taagnrho rua Yesxus saib xyuas,
naj nub nyob kuv tso sab plhuav.

629 Here by the Water

SOFT FIELD OF CLOVER Irregular

Capo 2:
1 Soft field of clo - ver, moon shin-ing o - ver the val - ley, join - ing the song of the riv - er to the great Giv - er of the great good. As it en - folds me some-how it holds me to-geth - er. I re - al - ize I've been sing - ing. Still, it comes ring - ing clear - er than clear.
2 I think how a yearn - ing kept on re - turn - ing to move me down roads I'd nev - er have cho - sen, half the time fro - zen, too numb to feel. I know it was storm - y; hope it was for me a learn - ing. Blood on the road was - n't mine, though. Some-one that I know walked here be - fore.
Refrain
And here by the wa - ter I'll build an al - tar to praise

Text: Jim Croegaert (USA)
Music: Jim Croegaert

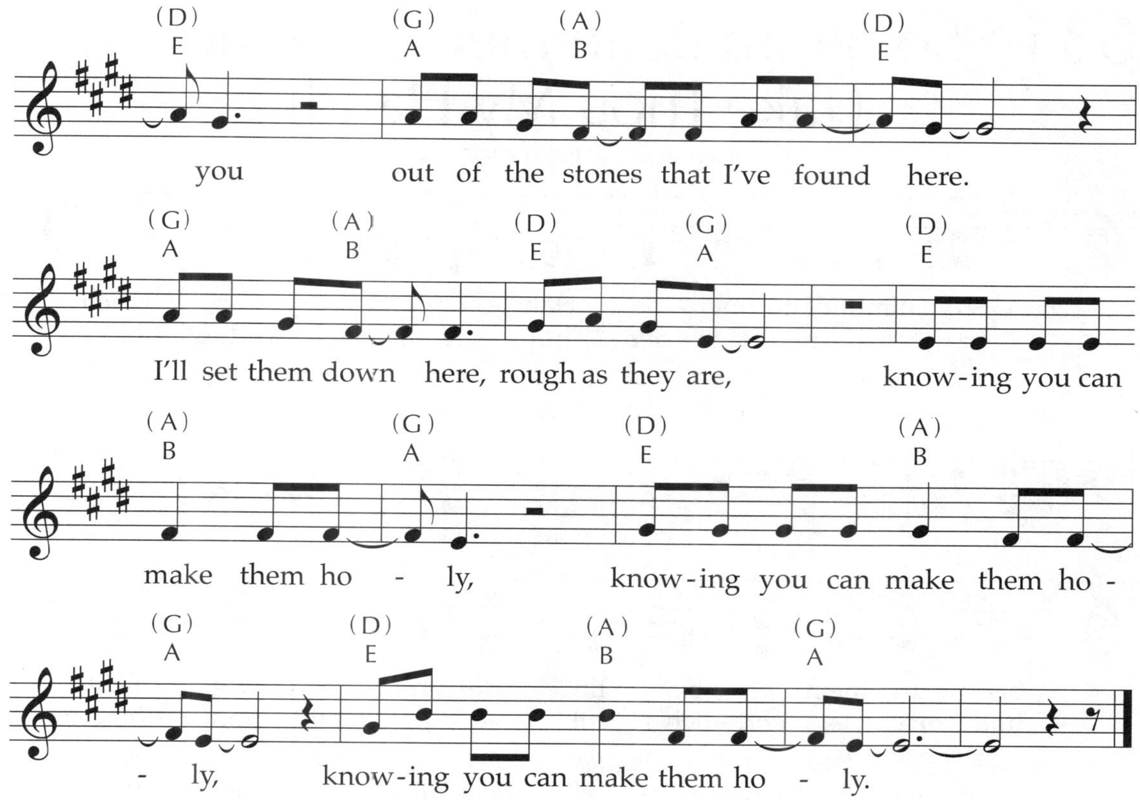
(D) E (G) A (A) B (D) E
you out of the stones that I've found here.
(G) A (A) B (D) E (G) A (D) E
I'll set them down here, rough as they are, know-ing you can
(A) B (G) A (D) E (A) B
make them ho - ly, know-ing you can make them ho -
(G) A (D) E (A) B (G) A
- ly, know-ing you can make them ho - ly.

Everlasting God, On You I Call 630

ANNELEIN'S PRAYER 9.8.8.8

Cmaj7 Am9 Dm7 Gsus G Cmaj7
1 Ev - er - last - ing God, on you I call. Oh, may I
2 Un - to you I raise my wear - y soul. In tri - als,
3 When I walk through death, I am sus - tained. I know you'll
Am9 Dm7 Gsus G E E/G♯ Am
nev - er turn from you; and keep me in your
I am in your care. In sor - row, tor - ture,
al - ways be my guide. E - ter - nal God, I
C/G F C/E Dm7 Fdim7 C
grace and truth, my strength and shield till life is through.
fear, and want, still I'm as - sured that you are there.
cry to you. For - ev - er keep me by your side.

Text: based on the writings of Annelein of Freiburg (present-day Germany), 16th c. (published in the *Ausbund*, 1583); Susan Naus Dengler (USA), © 2019 Susan Naus Dengler
Music: Anneli Loepp Thiessen (Canada), © 2019 Anneli Loepp Thiessen

631 So nimm denn meine Hände (Take Thou My Hand)

SO NIMM DENN MEINE HÄNDE 7.4.7.4 D

1 So nimm denn mei - ne Hän - de und füh - re mich
2 In dei - ner Gna - den hül - le mein schwa - ches Herz,
1 Take thou my hand and lead me; stay by my side
2 O cov - er with thy mer - cy my poor, weak heart!
bis an mein se - lig En - de und e - wig - lich!
und mach es end - lich stil - le in Freud und Schmerz.
till in thy joy e - ter - nal I may a - bide.
Let ev - 'ry thought re - bel - lious from me de - part.
Ich kann al - lein nicht ge - hen, nicht ei - nen Schritt;
Lass ruhn zu dei - nen Fü - ßen dein schwa - ches Kind;
A - lone I will not wan - der one sin - gle day.
Per - mit thy child to lin - ger here at thy feet,
wo du wirst gehn und ste - hen, da nimm mich mit.
es will die Au - gen schlie - ßen und fol - gen blind.
Be thou my true com - pan - ion and with me stay.
and ful - ly trust thy good - ness with faith com - plete.

Text: German; Julie K. Hausmann (present-day Estonia), "So nimm denn meine Hände," *Maiblumen, Lieder einer Stillen im Lande*, vol. 1, 1862; trans. Herman Brüchner (USA), *Wartburg Hymnal for Church, School, and Home*, 1918, alt.
Music: Friedrich Silcher (Germany), *Kinderlieder*, vol. 3, 1842

3 Wenn ich auch gar nichts fühle
von deiner Macht,
du bringst mich doch zum Ziele
auch durch die Nacht.
So nimm denn meine Hände
und führe mich
bis an mein selig Ende
und ewiglich!

3 *Though naught of thy great power*
may move my soul,
with thee through night and darkness
I reach the goal.
Take, then, my hand and lead me,
stay by my side,
and in thy joy eternal
I shall abide.

Dans nos obscurités (Within Our Darkest Night) 632

DANS NOS OBSCURITÉS Irregular

B Em D
Dans nos obs-cu-ri - tés al-lu-me le feu qui ne s'é-teint ja -
With - in our dark-est night, you kin-dle the fire that nev-er dies a -
G C G D G Em C Am
mais, ne s'é-teint ja - mais. Dans nos obs-cu-ri - tés al-lu-me le
way, nev-er dies a - way. With - in our dark-est night, you kin - dle the
B Em Am B Em Am B
(𝄐) Last time
feu qui ne s'é-teint ja - mais, ne s'é-teint ja - mais. Dans nos obs-cu - ri -
fire that nev-er dies a - way, nev-er dies a - way. With - in our dark-est
(𝄑) Last time

Text: French; Taizé Community (France), 1991; trans. Taizé Community
Music: Jacques Berthier (France), 1991

633 Total Praise

TOTAL PRAISE Irregular

Lord, I will lift mine eyes to the hills,
know - ing my help is com - ing from you.
Your peace you give me in time of the storm.
You are the source of my strength.
You are the strength of my life.

For chord symbols, see the accompaniment edition.

Text: Richard Smallwood (USA)
Music: Richard Smallwood; arr. Stephen Key (USA)

1
I lift my hands in to - tal praise to you.
2
A - men.
A -
you. A - men, a - men.
A - men.
A -
men, a - men.
A - men, a -
men, a - men. A - men.
A - men, a -
A - men.
men. A - men, a - men.
men.

634 Rain, Come Down

NO WORDS 7.5.8.8 with refrain

Capo 3: (D) (G) (D) (Em/G) (A7) (D/A)(A7) (D)
Refrain F B♭ F Gm/B♭ C7 F/C C7 F
Come, rain, come down. Come, rain, come down.
Rain, come down, come rain, come down. Heav-en's
(Bm7) (Em) (A7) (D/A)(A7) (D)
Dm7 Gm C7 F/C C7 F
Fine
Heav-en's tears of mer - cy, come run - ning down.
tears of mer - cy a - run - ning down.
(D) (G) (D) (Em) (A7) (D/A)(A7) (D)
F B♭ F Gm C7 F/C C7 F
1 Say no words, it is too soon, say no words out loud.
2 Come wash a - way this aw - ful stain; let this place be clean.
(Bm7) (Em) (A7) (D/A)(A7) (D)
Dm7 Gm C7 F/C C7 F
But wrap your qui - et arms a - round, hide us in your cloud.
And bring the fair - est flow'rs to meet *the sor - rows we have seen.

*Originally: the evil we have seen

Text: Shawn Kirchner (USA), 2002, alt.
Music: Shawn Kirchner, 2002

Alleluia

635

AUTUMN 4.4.8.4.4.4 D

Text: Hebrew traditional; הַלְלוּ יָהּ (Hallelujah) (Mediterranean), ca. 4th c. BC; translit. Greek, ἀλληλούϊα (Alleluia) (Mediterranean), ca. 3rd c. BC

Music: James E. Clemens (USA), © 2008 James E. Clemens

636 Spirit, Open My Heart

WILD MOUNTAIN THYME 7.8.6.8 with refrain

Capo 3: (G/A) (D) (G/D) (D) (G) (A)
Refrain
B♭/C F B♭/F F B♭ C
Spir - it, o - pen my heart to the joy and pain of
(D) (G) (A) (Bm)
F B♭ C Dm
liv - ing. As you love, may I love, in re -
(G) (D/F♯) (Em7) (G/A) (D) (G/D) (D)
B♭ F/A Gm7 B♭/C F B♭/F F
Fine
ceiv - ing and in giv-ing; Spir - it, o - pen my heart.
(G/A) (D) (G/D) (D)
B♭/C F B♭/F F
1 God, re - place my ston - y heart with a
2 Write your love up - on my heart as my
3 May I weep with those who weep, share the

Text: Ruth Duck (USA), 1996, rev. 2019, © 1996 The Pilgrim Press
Music: Irish traditional, 20th c., based on composite of 19th c. Scottish tunes; arr. Daniel Charles Damon (USA), © 2014 Hope Publishing Co.

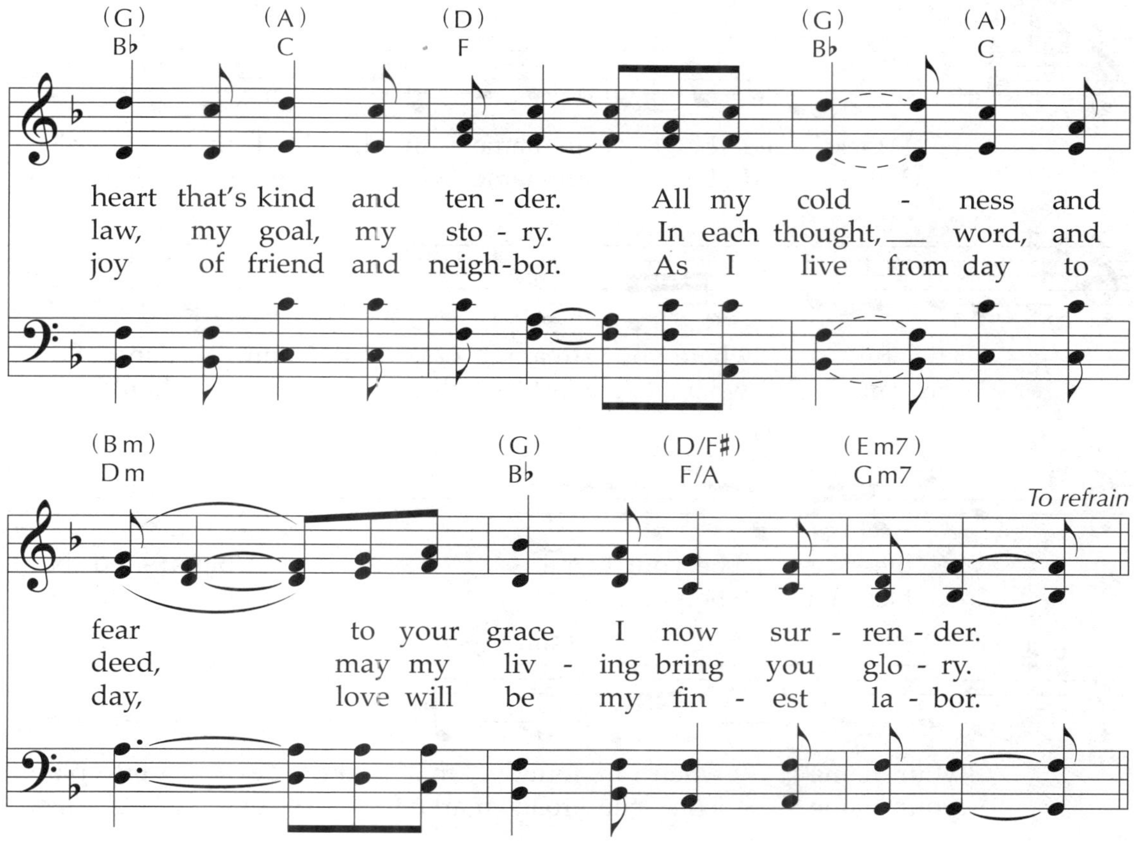
(G) Bb (A) C (D) F (G) Bb (A) C
heart that's kind and ten - der. All my cold - ness and
law, my goal, my sto - ry. In each thought, word, and
joy of friend and neigh-bor. As I live from day to
(Bm) Dm (G) Bb (D/F#) F/A (Em7) Gm7
To refrain
fear to your grace I now sur - ren - der.
deed, may my liv - ing bring you glo - ry.
day, love will be my fin - est la - bor.

637 Blessed Be Your Name

BLESSED BE YOUR NAME Irregular

A2 E F♯m7
1 Bless - ed be your name in the land that is plen-
2 Bless - ed be your name when the sun's shin - ing down
D D2 A2 E
- ti - ful, where your streams of a - bun - dance flow,
on me, when the world's all as it should be,
D D2 A2
bless-ed be your name. Bless - ed be
bless-ed be your name. Bless - ed be
E F♯m7 D D2
your name when I'm found in the des - ert place,
your name on the road marked with suf - fer - ing,
A2 E
though I walk through the wil - der-ness, bless-ed
though there's pain in the of - fer - ing, bless-ed
D D2 A2 E
be your name.
be your name.
Ev-'ry bless-ing you pour out I'll
F♯m7 D D2 A2
turn back to praise. When the storm clouds
E F♯m7 D
gath - er in, Lord, still I will say, "Blessed be the

Text: Matt Redman (England) and Beth Redman (England)
Music: Matt Redman and Beth Redman

Refrain
A E F♯m7 D
name of the Lord, bless-ed be your name.
A E
Bless-ed be the name of the Lord, bless-ed be your
F♯m7 E D D2 D2
To verse 2
To bridge
Fine
Bridge
glo - ri - ous name." You
A E E2 F♯m7
give and take a - way, you give and take a -
D D2 A E E2
way. My heart will choose to say, "Lord,
F♯m7
Repeat as desired
D D2
Last time
D
To refrain
bless-ed be your name." You name." Bless-ed be the

638 Love Divine, All Loves Excelling

BEECHER 8.7.8.7 D

B♭ F7 B♭ E♭ B♭/F F B♭
1 Love di-vine, all loves ex-cel-ling, joy of heav'n, to earth come down,
2 Breathe, O breathe thy lov-ing Spir-it in-to ev-'ry trou-bled breast.
3 Come, Al-might-y, to de-liv-er, let us all thy life re-ceive.
4 Fin-ish, then, thy new cre-a-tion; true and spot-less let us be.
F7 Gm E♭ B♭/F F7 B♭
fix in us thy hum-ble dwell-ing, all thy faith-ful mer-cies crown.
Let us all in thee in-her-it, let us find the prom-ised rest.
Sud-den-ly re-turn, and nev-er, nev-er-more thy tem-ples leave.
Let us see thy great sal-va-tion per-fect-ly re-stored in thee.
Gm D7 Gm D B♭ F/C C F F7
Je-sus, thou art all com-pas-sion, pure, un-bound-ed love thou art.
Take a-way the love of sin-ning; Al-pha and O-me-ga be.
Thee we would be al-ways bless-ing, serve thee as thy hosts a-bove,
Changed from glo-ry in-to glo-ry, till in heav'n we take our place,
B♭ F7 Gm E♭ B♭/F F7 B♭
Vis-it us with thy sal-va-tion; en-ter ev-'ry trem-bling heart.
End of faith, as its be-gin-ning, set our hearts at lib-er-ty.
pray, and praise thee with-out ceas-ing, glo-ry in thy per-fect love.
till we cast our crowns be-fore thee, lost in won-der, love, and praise.

Text: Charles Wesley (England), *Hymns for Those That Seek . . .*, 1747
Music: John Zundel (USA), *Christian Heart Songs*, 1870

Jesu, Joy of Our Desiring 639

WERDE MUNTER 8.7.8.7.8.8.7.7

(8)*
1 Je - su, joy of our de - sir - ing, ho - ly wis - dom, love most bright, drawn by thee, our souls as - pir - ing soar to un - cre - at - ed light. Word of God, our flesh that fash-ioned, with the fire of life im - pas-sioned, striv - ing still to truth un - known, soar - ing, dy - ing round thy throne.
2 Through the way, where hope is guid-ing, hark, what peace - ful mu - sic rings, where the flock, in thee con - fid - ing, drink of joy from death - less springs. Theirs is beau - ty's fair - est pleas-ure. Theirs is wis - dom's ho - liest treas-ure. Thou dost ev - er lead thine own in the love of joys un - known.
(1) (6) (1) (7) (2) (2) (1) (11)

*Numbers in parentheses indicate measures of rest when Bach's accompaniment is used.

Text: Martin Janus (present-day Germany), "Jesu, meiner Seelen Wonne," *Christlich Herzens Andach*, 1665; trans. and paraphr. Robert Bridges (England), 1927

Music: Johann Schop (present-day Germany), *Das Dritte Zehn*, 1642; harm. J. S. Bach (present-day Germany), Cantata 147, *Herz und Mund und Tat und Leben*, 1716

640 My Shepherd Will Supply My Need

RESIGNATION CMD

D Bm D
1 My Shep-herd will sup-ply my need; most ho-ly
2 When I walk through the shades of death, your pres-ence
3 The sure pro-vi-sions of my God at-tend me
D/A A D Bm D
is your name. In pas-tures fresh you make me feed, be-
is my stay. One word of your sup-port-ing breath drives
all my days. Oh, may your house be my a-bode, and
D/A A D G Em
side the liv-ing stream. You bring my wan-d'ring spir-it
all my fears a-way. Your hand, in sight of all my
all my work be praise. There would I find a set-tled
D Bm G Em Bm D
back, when I for-sake your ways, and lead me
foes, does still my ta-ble spread. My cup with
rest, while oth-ers go and come, no more a

Text: based on Psalm 23; Isaac Watts (England), *Psalms of David . . .*, 1719, alt.
Music: American traditional (USA), early 19th c., version from Joseph Funk's *Genuine Church Music*, 1st ed., 1832; harm. J. Harold Moyer (USA), 1965,

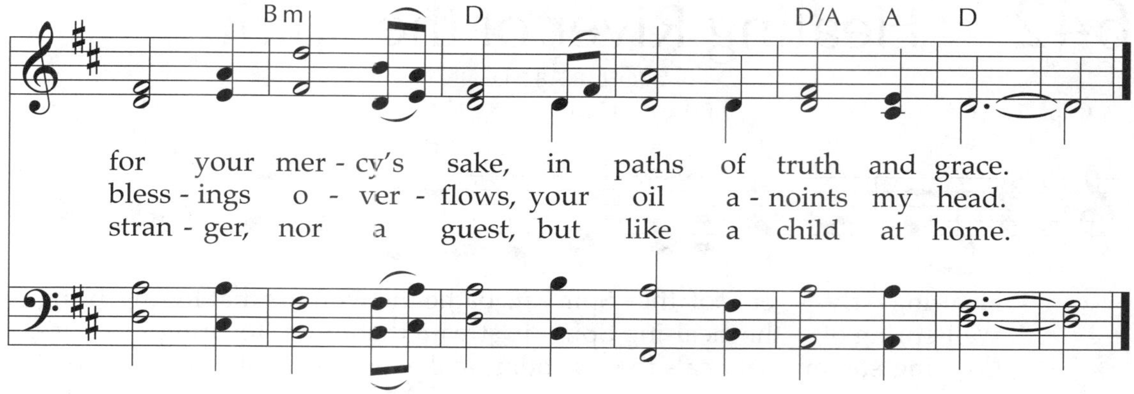
Bm D D/A A D
for your mer - cy's sake, in paths of truth and grace.
bless - ings o - ver - flows, your oil a - noints my head.
stran - ger, nor a guest, but like a child at home.

And I Will Raise You Up 641

ON EAGLE'S WINGS Irregular

A7 D
"And I will raise you up on ea - gle's wings,
Em A7 D D7
bear you on the breath of dawn, make you to shine like the
G Em A Bm F♯m Em A7 D
sun, and hold you in the palm of my hand."

Verses can be found in the accompaniment edition.

Text: based on Psalm 91; Michael Joncas (USA), alt.
Music: Michael Joncas

642 Healing River of the Spirit

JOEL 8.7.8.7 D

Capo 3: (G) (C) (D) (Em) (C) (B) (Em)
B♭ E♭ F Gm E♭ D Gm
1 Heal-ing riv - er of the Spir - it, bathe the wounds that liv-ing brings.
2 Well-spring of the heal-ing Spir - it, stream that flows to bring re - lease,
3 Liv - ing stream that heals the na - tions, make us chan-nels of your pow'r.
(C) (Bm7) (Gmaj7) (F♯m7) (E)
E♭ Dm7 B♭maj7 Am7 G
Plunge our pain, our sin, our sad-ness deep be-neath your sa-cred springs.
as we gain our selves, our sens - es, may our lives re-flect your peace.
All the world is torn by con-flict; wars are rag-ing at this hour.
(C) (Em) (C) (B)
E♭ Gm E♭ D
Wea - ry from the rest-less search-ing that has lured us from your side,
Grate-ful for the flood that heals us, may your church en-act your grace.
Sav - ing Spir - it, move a - mong us; guide our wind-ing hu - man course,
(Em) (D) (G) (C) (D) (G)
Gm F B♭ E♭ F B♭
we dis - cov - er in your pres-ence peace the world can-not pro - vide.
As we meet both friend and stran-ger, may we see our Sav-ior's face.
till we find our way to - geth - er, flow-ing home-ward to our Source.

Text: Ruth C. Duck (USA), 1994,
Music: Sally Ann Morris (USA), 1991,

Come, Ye Disconsolate 643

CONSOLATOR (CONSOLATION) 11.10.11.10

C F/C C F G7 C
1 Come, ye dis - con - so - late, wher - e'er ye lan - guish,
2 Joy of the des - o - late, light of the stray - ing,
3 Here see the Bread of life; see wa - ters flow - ing
F G/D D7 G
come to the mer - cy seat, fer - vent - ly kneel.
hope of the pen - i - tent, fade - less and pure!
forth from the throne of God, pure from a - bove.
C F/C C F C
Here bring your wound - ed hearts, here tell your an - guish.
Here speaks the Com - fort - er, ten - der - ly say - ing,
Come to the feast of love, come, ev - er know - ing
F C/G G7 C
Earth has no sor - rows that Heav'n can - not heal.
"Earth has no sor - rows that Heav'n can - not cure."
earth has no sor - rows but Heav'n can re - move.

Chord symbols do not correspond with keyboard accompaniment.

Text: stanzas 1–2 Thomas Moore (Ireland), *Sacred Songs, Duets and Trios*, 1816, alt.; stanza 3 Thomas Hastings (USA), *Spiritual Songs for Social Worship*, 1831
Music: Samuel Webbe Sr. (England), *A Collection of Motetts and Antiphons*, 1792; acc. Alice Parker (USA), 1977

644 Healer of Our Every Ill

HEALER OF OUR EVERY ILL Irregular

Refrain
D Em7/D G/D A/D D Bm Bm7/A G A F♯m7
Heal-er of our ev-'ry ill, light of each to - mor - row, give us
Bm Em7 F♯7 G Em A D
Fine
peace be - yond our fear, and hope be-yond our sor - row.
Bm F♯m/A G
1 You who know our fears and sad - ness, grace us with your
2 In the pain and joy be-hold - ing how your grace is
3 You who know each thought and feel - ing, teach us all your
F Em D/F♯ G Bm A/C♯ G/B A
To refrain
peace and glad-ness. Spir - it of all com-fort, fill our hearts.
still un - fold - ing, Spir - it of all kind-ness, be our guide.
way of heal - ing. Spir - it of com-pas - sion, fill each heart.

Text: Marty Haugen (USA), 1986, *Gather*, 1988
Music: Marty Haugen, 1986, *Gather*, 1988

Anointing Fall on Me 645

ANOINTING FALL ON ME Irregular

G13 Em7 Am7 Dm G13 Bm7♭5/F
A - noint - ing fall on me. A -
Em7 Am7 Dm G13
noint - ing fall on me. Let the
Gm7 C7 Fmaj9 B♭9
pow - er of the Ho - ly Ghost fall on me.
Dm11 Cmaj7 Dm7 G13 C
A - noint - ing fall on me.

Text: Donn C. Thomas (USA)
Music: Donn C. Thomas; arr. Evelyn Simpson-Curenton (USA), arr. © 2000 GIA Publications, Inc.

646 O God, to You I Cry in Pain

AFFLICTION CM

Am7 Dm E Am Dm Esus E A7 Dm B7 E Am E Am
1 O God, to you I cry in pain when sick - ness makes me weak, when mind and bod - y out of tune bring fears I can - not speak.
2 Give me the strength to face my ill, to trust in skill and care, to bless the hands that help me heal, and find your Spir - it there.
3 Re - mind me I am not a - lone, when suf - f'ring makes its mark; be pres - ent at my pil - low's side, and help me through the dark.
4 With - in the com - fort and the love that hu - man touch can give, re - store in me a larg - er sense of what it is to live.
5 Al - low my mind to rest in you, and let your peace per - vade to hold me in your great - er pow'r, and not to be a - fraid.

Text: Shirley Erena Murray (Aotearoa New Zealand), © 2006 Hope Publishing Co.
Music: Jillian Bray (Aotearoa New Zealand), © 2008 Hope Publishing Co.

647 There Is a Balm in Gilead

BALM IN GILEAD Irregular

Refrain D7 G D7 G G/D D7 G
There is a balm in Gil-e-ad to make the wound-ed whole, there is a balm in Gil-e-ad to heal the sin - sick soul.
Fine
1 Some - times I feel dis -
2 If you can - not preach like

Text: African American spiritual (USA)
Music: African American spiritual

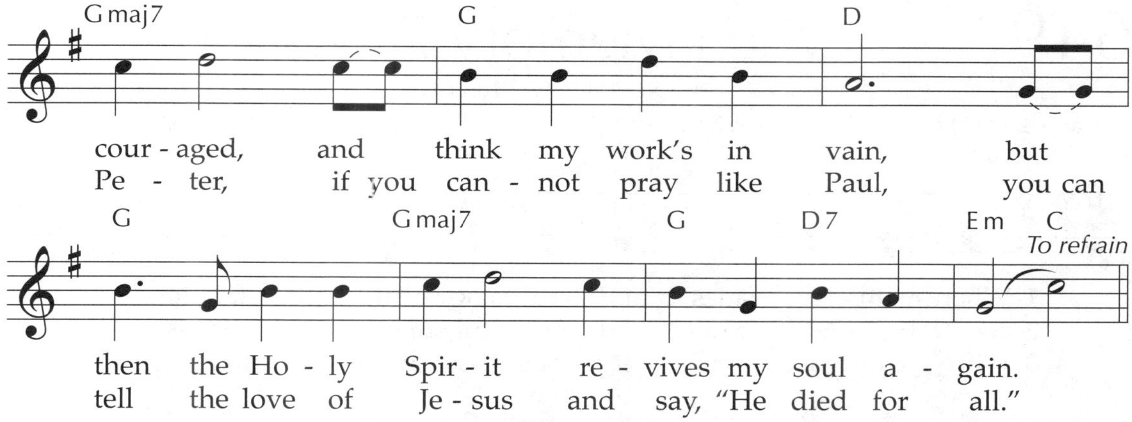
Gmaj7 G D
cour - aged, and think my work's in vain, but
Pe - ter, if you can - not pray like Paul, you can
G Gmaj7 G D7 Em C
To refrain
then the Ho - ly Spir - it re - vives my soul a - gain.
tell the love of Je - sus and say, "He died for all."

Kombo na Yesu (The Name of Jesus) 648

KOMBO NA YESU Irregular

Refrain
All C Dm
Kom-bo na Ye - su, kom-bo na ngu-ya, nkom-bo n'el-on-ga-
The name of Je - sus, the name with pow-er, the pow-er of vic-
G C Fine
- a, kom-bo na Ye - su, en - ton-da na-ngu - ya.
- t'ry, the name of Je - sus, the name a-bove all names.
Leader Dm
To - ku - mi - sa ye to-san-jo-la Ye - su. Ye nko-lo
When we need heal-ing, we call up-on Je - sus. When we need
All G C Last time to refrain
na bi-ka-mua kom-bo na Ye-su en - ton-da na-ngu - ya.
won-ders to come, we pray to Je-sus, the name a-bove all names.

Text: Lingala; Stockwell Massamba (USA), 2012; trans. Mennonite Worship and Song Committee, 2019
Music: Stockwell Massamba; acc. Thierry Nkwansambu (USA)

649 When Memory Fades

FINLANDIA 11.10.11.10.11.10

Capo 3: (D) F (A7/E) C7/G (D) F (G) B♭ (A) C (D) F
1 When mem - 'ry fades and re - cog - ni - tion fal - ters,
2 As frail - ness grows, and youth - ful strengths di - min - ish
3 With - in your Spir - it, good-ness lives un - fad - ing.
(A7/E) C7/G (D) F (G) B♭ (D) F
when eyes we love grow dim, and minds con - fused,
in wea - ry arms, which worked their ear - nest fill,
The past and fu - ture min - gle in - to one.
(Bm) Dm (D) F (A) C (Em) Gm
speak to our souls of love that nev - er al - ters;
your ag - ing ser - vants la - bor now to fin - ish
All joys re - main, un - shad-owed light per - vad - ing.
(D/A) F/C (G) B♭ (F♯) A
speak to our hearts by pain and fear a - bused.
their earth - ly tasks, as fits your mys - t'ry's will.
No val - ued deed will ev - er be un - done.

*For alternate tune (HEGER), see the accompaniment edition.

Text: Mary Louise Bringle (USA),
Music: Jean Sibelius (Finland), 1899; arr. *The Hymnal*, 1933

*ⓡ

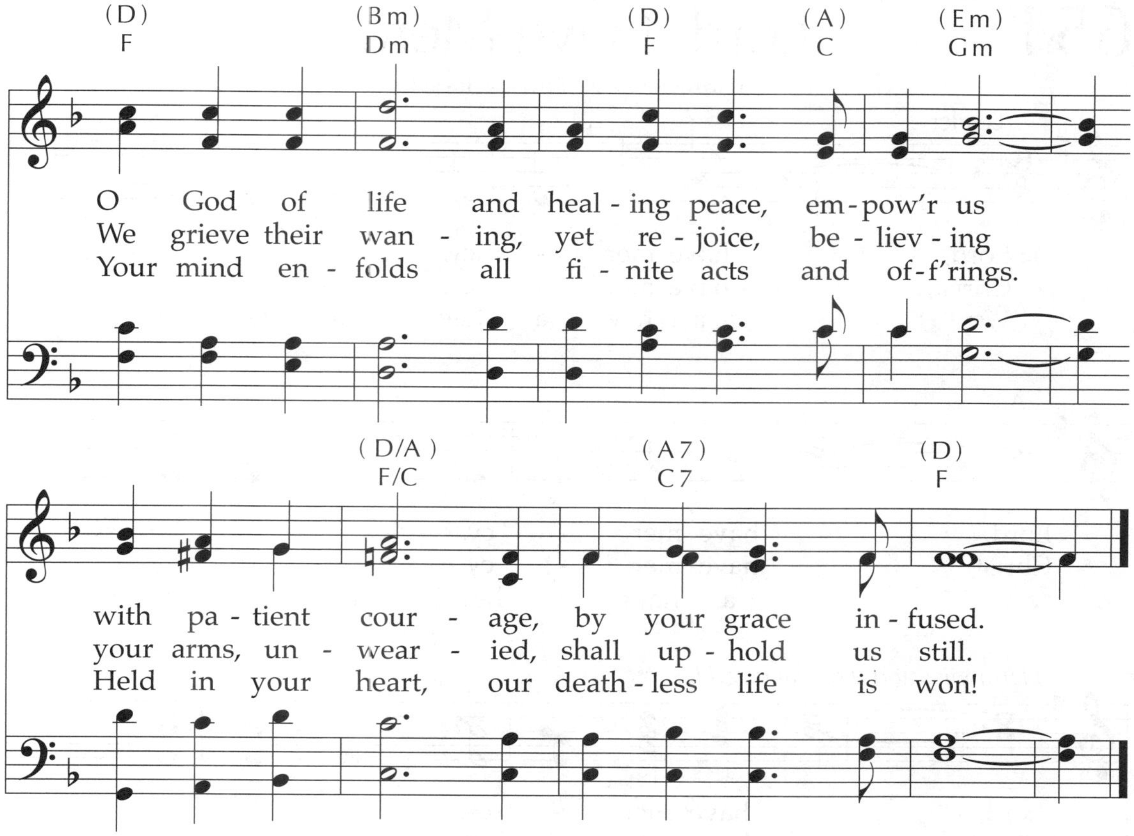
(D) F (Bm) Dm (D) F (A) C (Em) Gm
O God of life and heal - ing peace, em - pow'r us
We grieve their wan - ing, yet re - joice, be - liev - ing
Your mind en - folds all fi - nite acts and of - f'rings.
(D/A) F/C (A7) C7 (D) F
with pa - tient cour - age, by your grace in - fused.
your arms, un - wear - ied, shall up - hold us still.
Held in your heart, our death - less life is won!

Alleluia

650

ALLELUIA SOUTH AFRICA 8.8.8.8

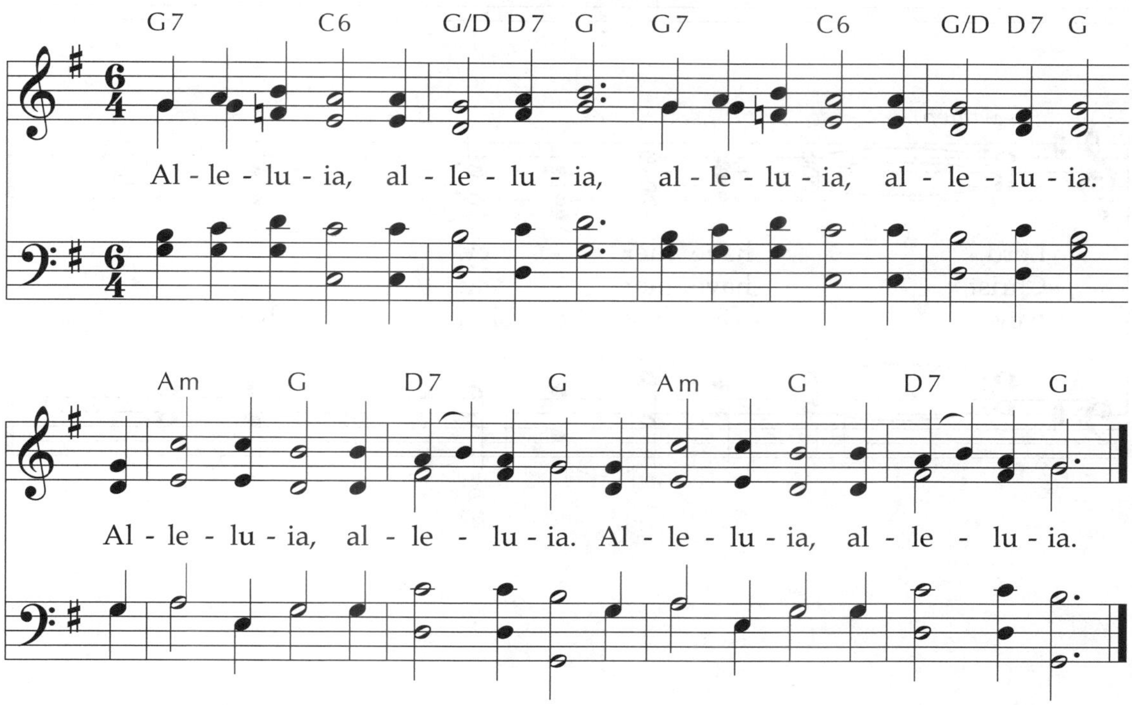
G7 C6 G/D D7 G G7 C6 G/D D7 G
Al - le - lu - ia, al - le - lu - ia, al - le - lu - ia, al - le - lu - ia.
Am G D7 G Am G D7 G
Al - le - lu - ia, al - le - lu - ia. Al - le - lu - ia, al - le - lu - ia.

Text: Hebrew traditional; הַלְלוּ יָהּ (Halleluja) (Mediterranean), ca. 4th c. BC; translit. Greek, ἀλληλούϊα (Alleluia) (Mediterranean), ca. 3rd c. BC

Music: from the singing of George Mxadana (South Africa); transcr. John L. Bell (Scotland), transcr. © 1990 WGRG, Iona Community (admin. GIA Publications, Inc.)

651 Lord, Have Mercy

THE MOOSONEE SERVICE Irregular

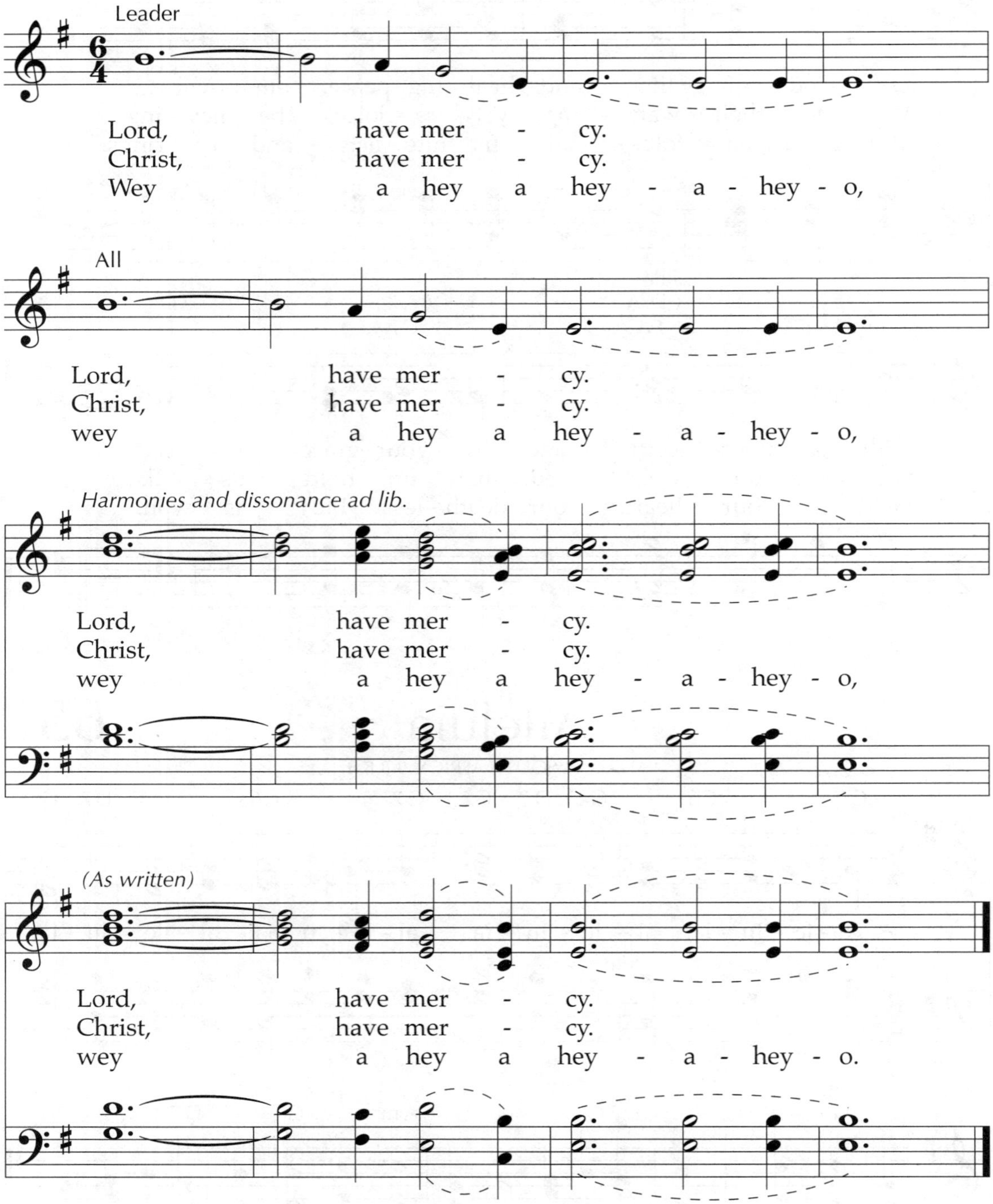
Leader
Lord, have mer - cy.
Christ, have mer - cy.
Wey a hey a hey - a - hey - o,
All
Lord, have mer - cy.
Christ, have mer - cy.
wey a hey a hey - a - hey - o,
Harmonies and dissonance ad lib.
Lord, have mer - cy.
Christ, have mer - cy.
wey a hey a hey - a - hey - o,
(As written)
Lord, have mer - cy.
Christ, have mer - cy.
wey a hey a hey - a - hey - o.

Text: from Greek liturgy Κύριε, ἐλέησον (Kyrie eleison) (Eastern Mediterranean), 4th c.; English trans. traditional; vocable stanza traditional (Cree, Ontario)

Music: David Buley (Canada), composed for the consecration of Bishop Tom Corston (Chapleau Cree, Ontario) as bishop of the Anglican Diocese of Moosonee,

Before the Waters Nourished Earth 652

ST. COLUMBA 8.7.8.7 Iambic

E♭ B♭ E♭
1 Be - fore the wa - ters nour - ished earth or night im -
2 This Love re - mained as time re - vealed the loss of
3 De - spair, so deep it bears no name, or sor - rows
4 The Love that called cre - a - tion good all good - ness
B♭ Cm E♭
ag - ined morn - ing, a Love con - ceived the
E - den's glo - ry and, griev - ing, holds in
par - a - lyz - ing can - not re - voke Love's
still is bring - ing. This Love turns death a -
Gm7 Cm E♭ B♭ E♭
u - ni - verse and rev - eled in its form - ing.
mem - o - ry each tra - gic hu - man sto - ry.
faith - ful claim to dwell with - in our dy - ing.
gain to life and si - lence in - to sing - ing.

For capo chords, see #485.

Text: Jeannette M. Lindholm (USA), © 1996 Jeannette M. Lindholm (admin. Augsburg Fortress)
Music: Irish traditional, *Irish Church Hymnal*, ca. 1873; harm. Charles Villiers Stanford (England), *The English Hymnal*, 1906

653 Nothing Is Lost on the Breath of God

GREEN LANE Irregular

A E F♯m A/C♯ D
1 Noth-ing is lost on the breath of God, noth-ing is
2 Noth-ing is lost to the eyes of God, noth-ing is
3 Noth-ing is lost to the heart of God, noth-ing is
B m/D E sus E A E F♯m
lost for - ev - er; God's breath is love, and that love will re -
lost for - ev - er. God sees with love, and that love will re -
lost for - ev - er; God's heart is love, and that love will re -
A/C♯ D B m/D E sus E A
main, hold-ing the world for - ev - er. No feath-er too
main, hold-ing the world for - ev - er. No jour-ney too
main, hold-ing the world for - ev - er. No im-pulse of
E/G♯ D/F♯ A/E B 7/D♯ B 7
light, no hair too fine, no flow - er too brief in its
far, no dis-tance too great, no val - ley of dark-ness too
love, no of - fice of care, no mo-ment of life in its

Text: Colin Gibson (New Zealand)
Music: Colin Gibson

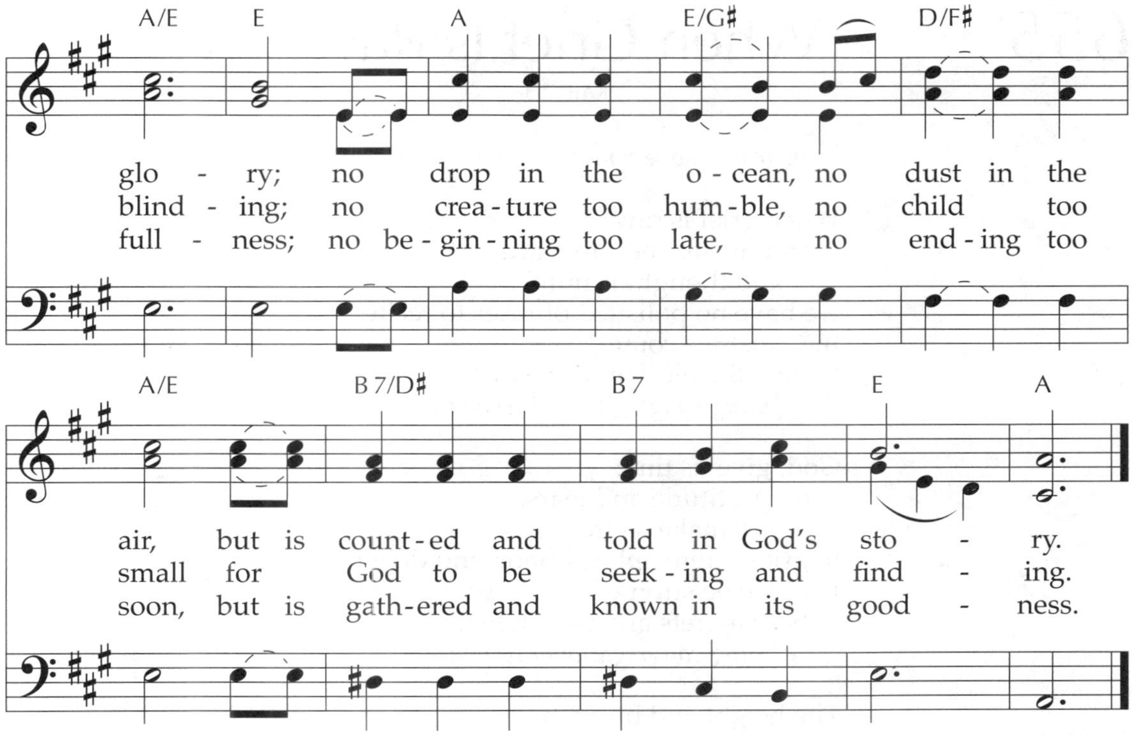
A/E E A E/G♯ D/F♯
glo - ry; no drop in the o - cean, no dust in the
blind - ing; no crea - ture too hum - ble, no child too
full - ness; no be - gin - ning too late, no end - ing too
A/E B7/D♯ B7 E A
air, but is count - ed and told in God's sto - ry.
small for God to be seek - ing and find - ing.
soon, but is gath - ered and known in its good - ness.

Nothing Can Ever Come between Us 654

NOTHING CAN EVER Irregular

Refrain
Noth - ing can ev - er come be - tween us and the love of God,
the love of God re - vealed to us in Christ Je - sus.
Last time
Verses
Ooh
Ooh
Last time

Verses can be found in the accompaniment edition.

Text: Romans 8:38–39, Taizé Community (France)
Music: Taizé Community

655 When Grief Is Raw

KAB 7.3

To be read by one voice:

When grief is raw
and music goes unheard
and thought is numb,
we have no polished phrases to recite.
In Christ we come
to hear the old familiar words:
**Sung congregational response*

God, give us time
for gratitude and tears,
and make us free
to grieve, remember, honor, and delight.
Let love be strong
to bear regrets and banish fears:
**Sung congregational response*

The height and breadth
of all that love prepares
soar out of time,
beyond our speculation and our sight.
The cross remains
to ground the promise that it bears:
**Sung congregational response*

All shall be judged,
the greatest and the least,
and all be loved,
till every hurt is healed, all wrong set right.
In bread and wine
we taste the great homecoming feast,
and in the midst of death we are in life.
**Sung congregational response*

*Sung congregational response

"I am the re - sur - rec - tion. I am life."

Text: Brian Wren (England), 1976, *Faith Looking Forward*, © 1983 Hope Publishing
Music: Benjamin Bergey (USA), © 2019 Benjamin Bergey

God Weeps with Us 656

MOSHIER CMD

Capo 3: (Am) Cm (F) Ab (Am) Cm (F) Ab (G) Bb (C) Eb
1 God weeps with us who weep and mourn; God's
2 Through tears and sor - row, God, we share a
3 And yet be-cause, like us, you weep, we
(Am) Cm (Dm) Fm (Esus) Gsus (E) G (C) Eb (F) Ab (Am) Cm
tears flow down with ours, and God's own heart is
sense of your vast grief: the weight of bear - ing
trust you will re - ceive and in your ten - der
(F) Ab (G) Bb (C) Eb (Am) Cm (Dm) Fm (G7) Bb7 (C) Eb
bruised and worn from all the heav - y hours
ev - 'ry prayer for heal - ing and re - lief,
heart will keep the ones for whom we grieve,
(F) Ab (Am) Cm (F) Ab (C) Eb
of watch - ing while the soul's bright fire burned
the bur - den of our ques - tions why, the
while with your tears our hearts will taste the
(Am) Cm (C) Eb (D) F (Esus) Gsus (E) G (C) Eb (F) Ab (Am) Cm
low - er day by day, and pulse and breath and
doubts that they en - gage, and as our friends and
deep, dear core of things from which both life and
(F) Ab (C) Eb (Dm) Fm (Esus) Gsus (E) G (Am) Cm
love's de - sire dimmed down to ash and clay.
loved ones die, our hope - less - ness and rage.
death are graced by love's re - new - ing springs.

Chord symbols do not correspond with keyboard accompaniment.

657 Go, Silent Friend

LONDONDERRY AIR 11.10.11.10 D

G C F
1 Go, si-lent friend, your life has found its end - ing; to dust re -
2 Go, si-lent friend, for-give us if we grieved you; safe now in
C/G Em D7 G C
turns your wea-ry mor-tal frame. Be-fore your birth, God called you in - to
heav - en, kind-ly say our name. Your life has touched us, that is why we
F C/G G7 C
be - ing. God calls a - gain with ac-cents still the same.
mourn you; our lives with - out you can-not be the same.
G7 C F G C G7
Go, si-lent friend, your life in Christ is bur - ied; for you he
Go, si-lent friend, we do not grudge you glo - ry; sing, sing with

Text: John L. Bell (Scotland), alt., © 1996 WGRG, Iona Community (admin. GIA Publications, Inc.)
Music: Irish traditional, 19th c.; harm. Dean McIntyre (USA), © 1997 Dean McIntyre

C F C D7 G7 C7 F
lived and died and rose a - gain. Close by his side your prom - ised
joy deep prais-es to your Lord. You, who be - lieved that Christ would
C Am F C/G G7 C
place is wait - ing where, ful - ly known, you shall with God re - main.
come back for you, now cel - e - brate that Je - sus keeps his word.

658 Nearer, My God, to Thee

BETHANY 6.4.6.4.6.6.4

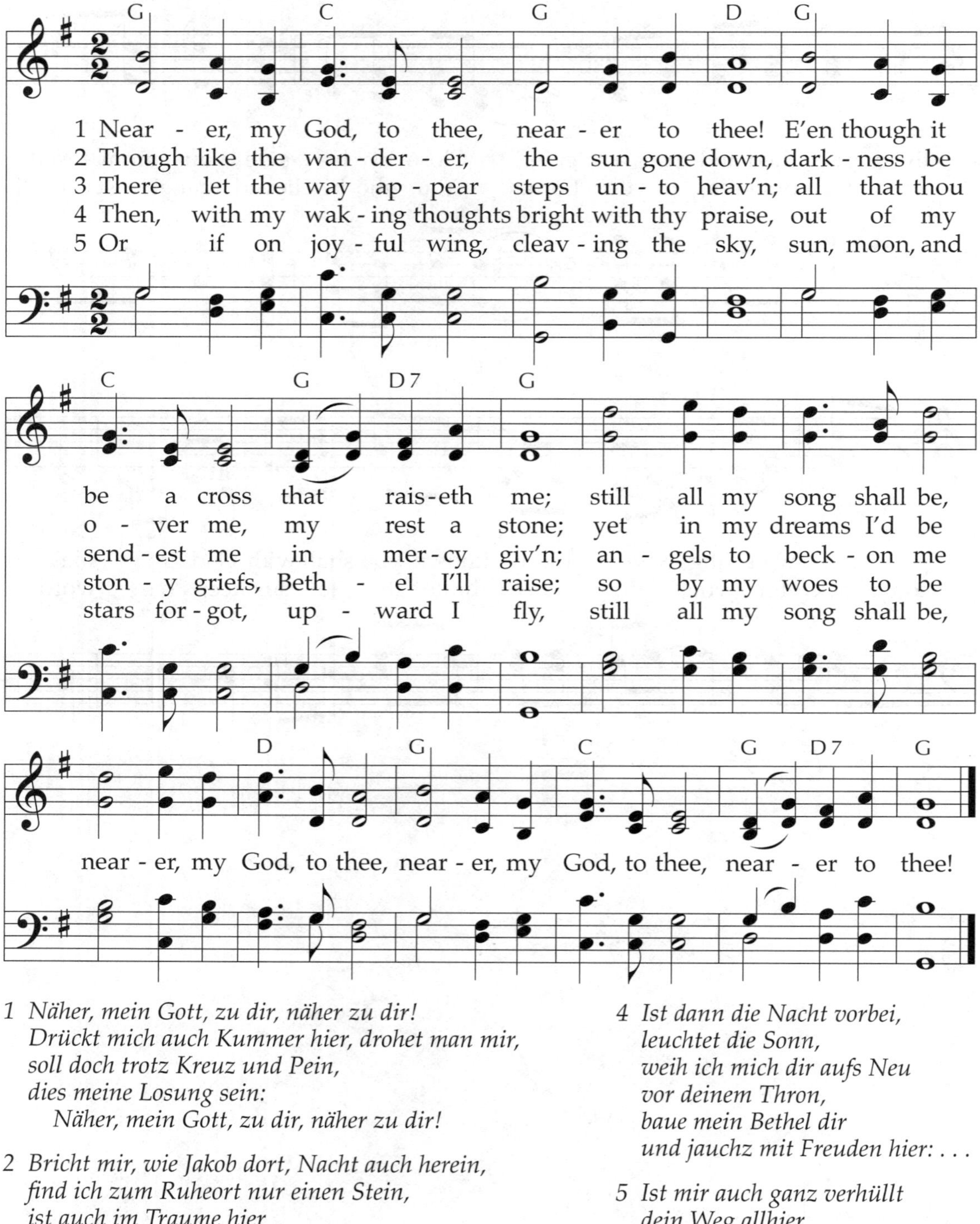
G C G D G
1 Near - er, my God, to thee, near - er to thee! E'en though it
2 Though like the wan - der - er, the sun gone down, dark - ness be
3 There let the way ap - pear steps un - to heav'n; all that thou
4 Then, with my wak - ing thoughts bright with thy praise, out of my
5 Or if on joy - ful wing, cleav - ing the sky, sun, moon, and
C G D7 G
be a cross that rais - eth me; still all my song shall be,
o - ver me, my rest a stone; yet in my dreams I'd be
send - est me in mer - cy giv'n; an - gels to beck - on me
ston - y griefs, Beth - el I'll raise; so by my woes to be
stars for - got, up - ward I fly, still all my song shall be,
D G C G D7 G
near - er, my God, to thee, near - er, my God, to thee, near - er to thee!

1 *Näher, mein Gott, zu dir, näher zu dir!*
Drückt mich auch Kummer hier, drohet man mir,
soll doch trotz Kreuz und Pein,
dies meine Losung sein:
Näher, mein Gott, zu dir, näher zu dir!

2 *Bricht mir, wie Jakob dort, Nacht auch herein,*
find ich zum Ruheort nur einen Stein,
ist auch im Traume hier
mein Sehnen für und für: . . .

3 *Geht auch die schmale Bahn aufwärts gar steil,*
führt sie doch himmelan zu unserm Heil.
Engel, so licht und schön,
winken aus selgen Höhn. . . .

4 *Ist dann die Nacht vorbei,*
leuchtet die Sonn,
weih ich mich dir aufs Neu
vor deinem Thron,
baue mein Bethel dir
und jauchz mit Freuden hier: . . .

5 *Ist mir auch ganz verhüllt*
dein Weg allhier,
wird nur mein Wunsch erfüllt:
näher zu dir!
Schließt dann mein Pilgerlauf,
schwing ich mich freudig auf, . . .

Chord symbols represent a simplified harmony.

Text: Sarah Flower Adams (England), 1841; German trans. Erhardt Friedrich Wunderlich (Germany), 1875
Music: Lowell Mason (USA), 1856

Jesus, Lover of My Soul 659

ABERYSTWYTH 7.7.7.7 D

Em B7 Em B7 Em B
1 Je - sus, lov - er of my soul, let me to thy bos - om fly,
2 Oth - er ref - uge have I none; hangs my help-less soul on thee.
3 Plen-teous grace with thee is found, grace to cov - er all my sin.
Em B7 Em B G Em B7 Em
while the near - er wa-ters roll, while the tem-pest still is high.
Leave, ah, leave me not a - lone, still sup - port and com-fort me.
Let the heal - ing streams a - bound, make and keep me whole with - in.
C G Em D G F# Bm
Hide me, O my Sav - ior, hide, till the storm of life is past;
All my trust on thee is stayed, all my help from thee I bring.
Thou of life the foun-tain art, free - ly let me take of thee.
C G Em A B Em B7 Em
safe in - to the ha - ven guide, O re - ceive my soul at last.
Cov - er my de - fense-less head with the shad - ow of thy wing.
Spring thou up with - in my heart, rise to all e - ter - ni - ty.

Text: Charles Wesley (England), *Hymns and Sacred Poems*, 1740, alt.
Music: Joseph Parry (Wales), *Ail Llyfr Tonau ac Emynau*, 1879

660 The Lord's My Shepherd

CRIMOND CM

Capo 3: (D) F (G) B♭ (D) F (G) B♭ (D/A) F/C (A) C (D) F
1 The Lord's my shep - herd, I'll not want. He
2 My soul he doth re - store a - gain, and
3 Yea, though I walk in death's dark vale, yet
4 My ta - ble thou hast fur - nish - ed in
5 Good - ness and mer - cy all my life shall
(E7) G7 (A) C (D) F (A) C
1 makes me down to lie in pas - tures green; he
2 me to walk doth make with - in the paths of
3 will I fear none ill, for thou art with me
4 pres - ence of my foes. My head thou dost with
5 sure - ly fol - low me, and in God's house for -
(A7) C7 (D) F (Em) Gm (D/A) F/C (A) C (D) F
1 lead - eth me the qui - et wa - ters by.
2 right - eous - ness, e'en for his own name's sake.
3 and thy rod and staff me com - fort still.
4 oil a - noint, and my cup o - ver - flows.
5 ev - er - more my dwell - ing place shall be.

Text: based on Psalm 23; *The Psalms of David in Meeter* (Scotland), 1650
Music: Jessie S. Irvine (Scotland), 1872; harm. and adapt. David Grant (England), *The Northern Psalter*, 1872

On Jordan's Stormy Banks I Stand 661

BOUND FOR THE PROMISED LAND CM with refrain

Em Am B Em B
1 On Jor-dan's storm-y banks I stand, and cast a wish-ful eye
2 There gen-'rous fruits that nev-er fail on trees im-mor-tal grow.
3 All o'er those wide ex-tend-ed plains shines one e-ter-nal day.
4 Filled with de-light, my rap-tured soul can here no long-er stay.
Em Em/B B Em
to Ca-naan's fair and hap-py land, where my pos-ses-sions lie.
There rocks and hills and brooks and vales with milk and hon-ey flow.
There God the sun for-ev-er reigns, and scat-ters night a-way.
Though Jor-dan's waves a-round me roll, fear-less I'd launch a-way.
Refrain
Am B Em B
I'm bound for the prom-ised land, I'm bound for the prom-ised land.
Em Em/B B Em
Oh, who will come and go with me? I'm bound for the prom-ised land.

Text: Samuel Stennett (England), *A Selection of Hymns from the Best Authors*, 1787
Music: American traditional (USA), *Southern Harmony*, 1835; harm. J. Harold Moyer (USA), 1965, *The Mennonite Hymnal*,

662 My Latest Sun Is Sinking Fast

ANGEL BAND CM with refrain

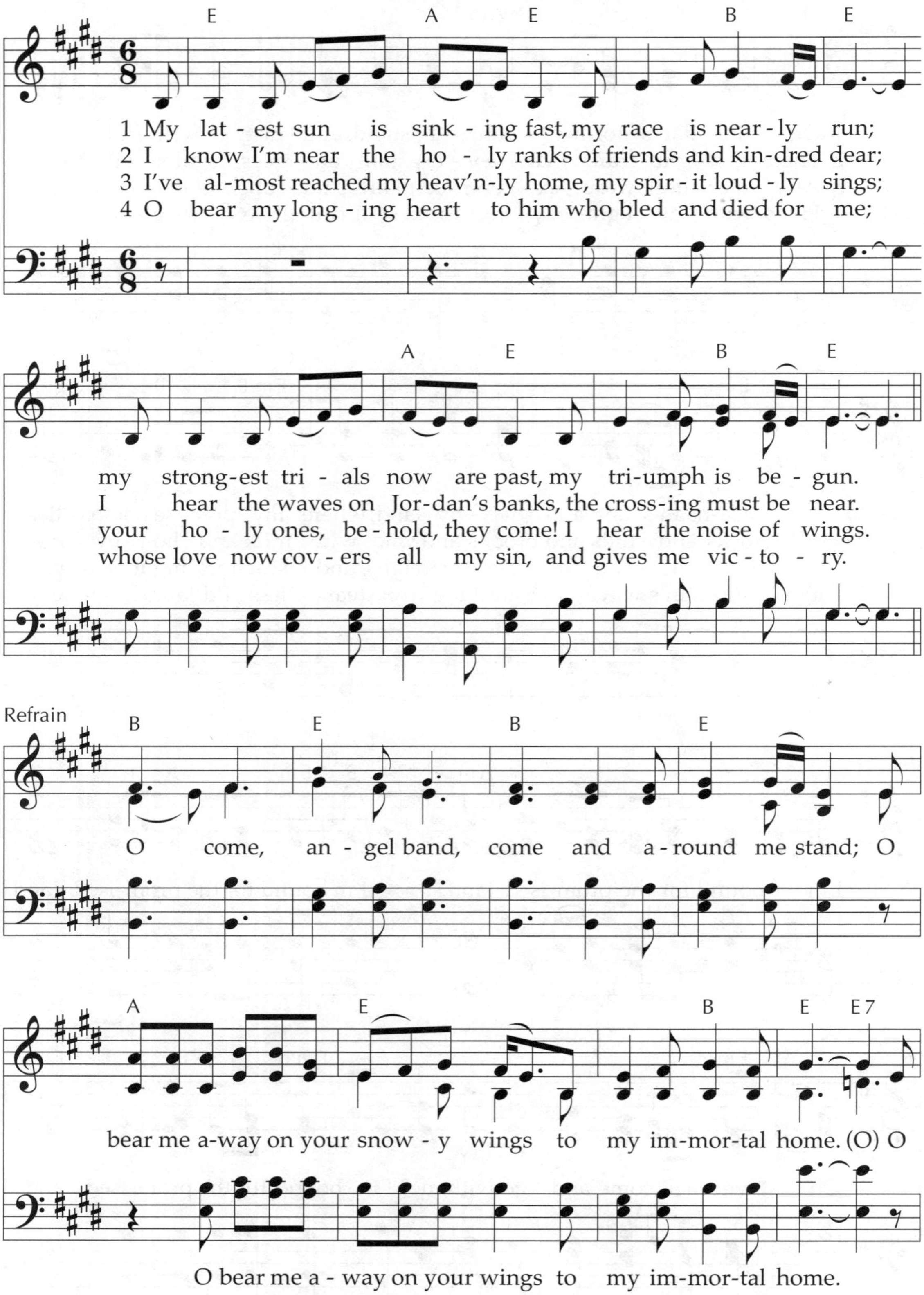
E A E B E
1 My lat - est sun is sink - ing fast, my race is near - ly run;
2 I know I'm near the ho - ly ranks of friends and kin-dred dear;
3 I've al-most reached my heav'n-ly home, my spir - it loud - ly sings;
4 O bear my long - ing heart to him who bled and died for me;
A E B E
my strong-est tri - als now are past, my tri-umph is be - gun.
I hear the waves on Jor-dan's banks, the cross-ing must be near.
your ho - ly ones, be - hold, they come! I hear the noise of wings.
whose love now cov - ers all my sin, and gives me vic - to - ry.
Refrain
B E B E
O come, an - gel band, come and a - round me stand; O
A E B E E7
bear me a-way on your snow - y wings to my im-mor-tal home. (O) O
O bear me a - way on your wings to my im-mor-tal home.

Text: Jefferson Hascall (USA), 1860, alt.
Music: William Bradbury (USA), *The New Golden Shower*, 1862; arr. Bradley Kauffman, 2002, alt., © 2019 Bradley Kauffman; inspired by the Stanley Brothers

A E B E
bear me a-way on your snow - y wings to my im-mor-tal home.
O bear me a - way on your wings to my im-mor-tal home.

I Am That Great and Fiery Force 663

DE SPIRITU SANCTO LM

1 I am that great and fier - y force spar - kling in ev - 'ry - thing that lives; in shin - ing of the riv - er's course, in green - ing grass that glo - ry gives.
2 I shine and glit - ter on the seas, in burn - ing sun, in moon and stars. In un - seen wind, in ver - dant trees I breathe with - in, both near and far.
3 And where I breathe there is no death, and mead - ows glow with beau - ties rife. I am in all, the spir - it's breath, the thun - dered word, for I am Life.

Text: Hildegard of Bingen (present-day Germany), *Liber Divinorum Operum* (The Book of Divine Works), 12th c.; trans. *Singing the Living Tradition*, 1993

Music: based on chant "Spiritus sanctus vivificans," Hildegard of Bingen, 12th c.; arr. Benjamin Bergey (USA),

ⓡ

664 Be Still, My Soul

FINLANDIA 10.10.10.10.10.10

F C7/G F B♭ C F
1 Be still, my soul! for God is on your side;
2 Be still, my soul! for God will un - der - take
3 Be still, my soul! the hour is has - t'ning on
C7/G F B♭ F
bear pa - tient - ly the cross of grief or pain:
to guide the fu - ture sure - ly as the past.
when we shall be for - ev - er in God's peace;
Dm F C Gm
leave to your God to or - der and pro - vide,
Your hope, your con - fi - dence, let noth - ing shake;
when dis - ap - point - ment, grief, and fear are gone,
F/C B♭ A
who through all chang - es faith - ful will re - main.
all now mys - te - rious shall be clear at last.
love's joys re - stored, our striv - ings all shall cease.

For capo chords, see #649.

Text: Catharina A. D. von Schlegel (present-day Germany), 1752, *Stille, mein Wille*; trans. Jane Laurie Borthwick (Scotland), 1855, alt.
Music: Jean Sibelius (Finland); arr. *The Hymnal*, © 1933, 1961 Presbyterian Board of Christian Education

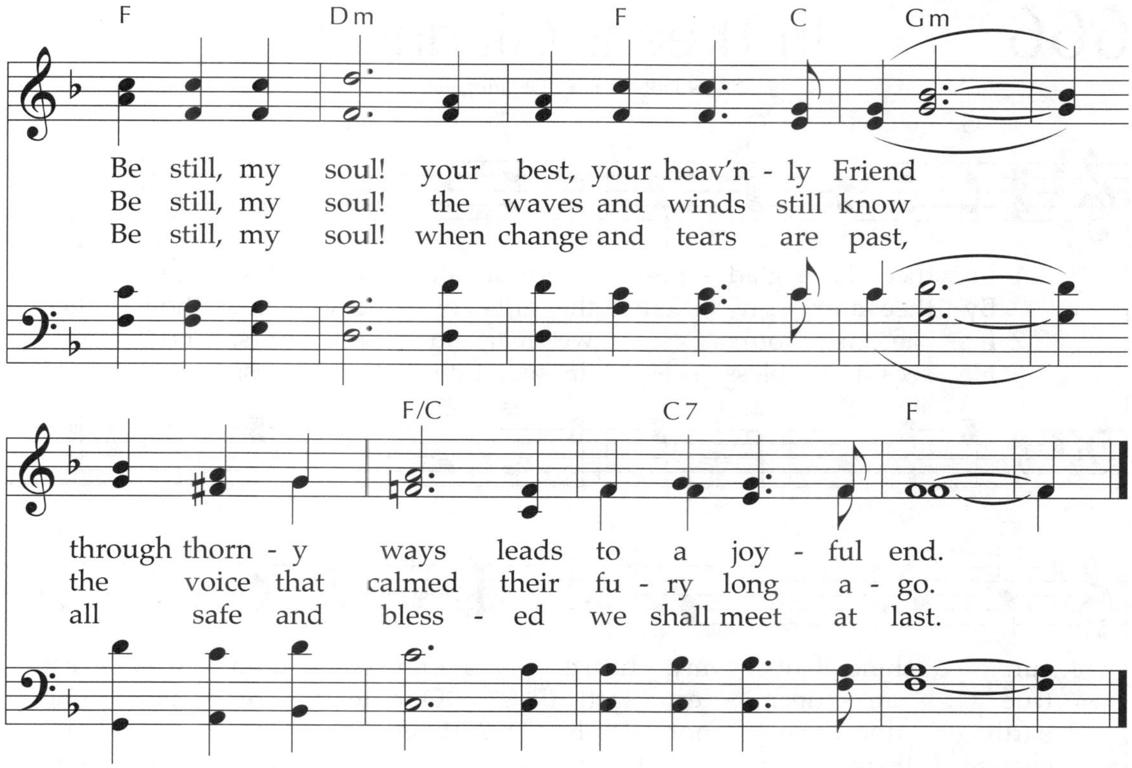
F Dm F C Gm
Be still, my soul! your best, your heav'n - ly Friend
Be still, my soul! the waves and winds still know
Be still, my soul! when change and tears are past,
F/C C7 F
through thorn - y ways leads to a joy - ful end.
the voice that calmed their fu - ry long a - go.
all safe and bless - ed we shall meet at last.

El cielo canta alegría (Heaven Is Singing for Joy) 665

ALEGRÍA (Sosa) 7.4.6.8 with refrain

Capo 3: (Am) Cm (C/G) E♭/B♭ (F) A♭ (G) B♭ (C) E♭ (E7) G7
1–3 El cie - lo can - ta‿a - le - grí - a, ¡a - le - lu - ya!,
1–3 Heav - en is sing - ing for joy, al - le - lu - ia,
(Am) Cm (E) G (Am) Cm
1 por - que‿en tu vi - da‿y la mí - a bri - lla la glo - ria de Dios.
2 por - que‿a tu vi - da‿y la mí - a las u - ne‿el a - mor de Dios.
3 por - que tu vi - da‿y la mí - a pro - cla - ma - rán al Se - ñor.
1 for your life and mine shine out with the glo - ry of God.
2 for your life and mine u - nite in the love of our God.
3 for your life and mine will al - ways bear wit - ness to God.
Refrain
(G7) B♭7 (C) E♭ (G7) B♭7 (C) E♭ (G7) B♭7 (C) E♭ (F) A♭ (Em7) Gm7 (Am) Cm
¡A - le - lu - ya, a - le - lu - ya! ¡A - le - lu - ya, a - le - lu - ya!

Text: Spanish; Pablo Sosa (Argentina); trans. Pablo Sosa, © 1958 GIA Publications, Inc.
Music: Pablo Sosa, © 1958 GIA Publications, Inc.; arr. © 2010 GIA Publications, Inc.

666 In Thee Is Gladness

IN DIR IST FREUDE Irregular

G C G C G
1 In thee is glad - ness a - mid all sad - ness, Je - sus,
By thee are giv - en the gifts of heav - en, thou the
2 If he is ours we fear no pow - ers, nor of
He sees and bless - es in worst dis - tress - es; he can
G D G C
1 sun - shine of my heart! 1 Our souls thou wak - est,
true re - deem - er art! Our hearts are pin - ing
2 earth, nor sin, nor death. 2 Where-fore the sto - ry,
change them with a breath. We shout for glad - ness,
G D C
1 our bonds thou break - est, who trusts thee sure - ly hath built se -
to see thy shin - ing, dy - ing or liv - ing to thee are
2 tell of his glo - ry, with heart and voic - es all heav'n re -
tri - umph o'er sad - ness, love thee and praise thee, and still shall
D G C D G D G
1 cure - ly, and stands for - ev - er: Hal - le - lu - jah!
cleav - ing, naught can us sev - er: Hal - le - lu - jah!
2 joic - es in him for - ev - er: Hal - le - lu - jah!
raise thee glad hymns for - ev - er: Hal - le - lu - jah!

Chord symbols represent a simplified harmony. For a lower key, see the accompaniment edition.

Text: Johann Lindemann (present-day Germany), "In dir ist Freude," *Decades Amorum Filii Dei*, 1594, 1596; trans. Catherine Winkworth (England), *Lyra Germanica*, Series II, 1858
Music: adapt. from Giovanni G. Gastoldi (Italy), *Balletti*, 1591

Shall We Gather at the River 667

BEAUTIFUL RIVER 8.7.8.7 with refrain

Capo 1: (D) E♭
(A) B♭
1 Shall we gath-er at the riv-er, where bright an-gel feet have trod,
2 On the mar-gin of the riv-er, wash-ing up its sil-ver spray,
3 Ere we reach the shin-ing riv-er, lay we ev-'ry bur-den down.
4 Soon we'll reach the shin-ing riv-er, soon our pil-grim-age will cease,
(D) E♭
(A) B♭
(D) E♭
with its crys-tal tide for-ev-er flow-ing by the throne of God?
we will walk and wor-ship ev-er, all the hap-py gold-en day.
Grace our spir-its will de-liv-er, and pro-vide a robe and crown.
soon our hap-py hearts will quiv-er with the mel-o-dy of peace.
Refrain
(G) A♭
(D) E♭
(A) B♭
(D) E♭
Yes, we'll gath-er at the riv-er, the beau-ti-ful, the beau-ti-ful riv-er,
(G) A♭
(D) E♭
(A) B♭
(D) E♭
gath-er with the saints at the riv-er that flows by the throne of God.

Text: Robert Lowry (USA), 1864, *Happy Voices*, 1865
Music: Robert Lowry, *Happy Voices*, 1865

668 Oh, Have You Not Heard (Ich weiß einen Strom)

THE BEAUTIFUL RIVER 11.7.11.7 with refrain

Capo 1: (G) A♭ (D7) E♭7 (G) A♭
1 Oh, have you not heard of that beau - ti - ful stream
2 Its foun - tains are deep and its wa - ters are pure,
1 Ich weiß ei - nen Strom, des - sen herr - li - che Flut
2 Wo - hin die - ser Strom sich nur im - mer er - gießt,
(D) E♭
that flows through the prom - ised land?
and sweet to the wea - ry soul.
fließt wun - der - bar stil - le durchs Land,
da ju - belt und jauch - zet das Herz,
(G) A♭ (D) E♭ (G) A♭
Its wa - ters gleam bright in the heav - en - ly light,
It flows from the throne of Je - ho - vah a - lone!
doch strah - let und glänzt er wie feu - ri - ge Glut,
das nun - mehr den köst - lich - sten Se - gen ge - nießt,
(Em) Fm (D) E♭ (G) A♭
and rip - ple o'er gold - en sand.
O come where its bright ___ waves roll.
wem ist die - ses Was - ser be - kannt?
er - lös - et von Sor - gen und Schmerz.

Chord symbols represent a simplified harmony.

Text: Richard Torrey Jr. (USA), *Sabbath School Gems* (England), 1864; German trans. Ernst H. Gebhardt (Germany), *Frohe Botschaft*, 1875
Music: Asa Hull (USA), *Sabbath School Gems*, 1864

Refrain
(D) E♭
O seek that beau-ti-ful stream, O seek that
O See-le, ich bit-te dich: Komm! und such die-sen
(G) A♭ (C) D♭
beau-ti-ful stream. Its wa-ters, so free, are
herr-lich-en Strom! Sein Was-ser fließt frei und
(D) E♭ (G) A♭ (D7) E♭7 (G) A♭
flow-ing for thee, O seek that beau-ti-ful stream.
mäch-tig-lich, O Glaub's, es flie-ßet für dich!

3 This beautiful stream is the river of life!
It flows for all nations free!
A balm for each wound in its water is found;
O sinner, it flows for thee! *Refrain*

4 Oh, will you not drink of this beautiful stream,
and dwell on its peaceful shore?
The Spirit says: Come, all ye weary ones home,
and wander in sin no more. *Refrain*

3 *Der Strom ist gar tief und sein Wasser ist klar,*
es schmecket so lieblich und fein;
es heilet die Kranken und stärkt wunderbar,
ja machet die Unreinsten rein. Refrain

4 *Wen dürstet, der komme und trinke sich satt,*
so rufet der Geist und die Braut,
nur wer in dem Strome gewaschen sich hat,
das Angesicht Gottes einst schaut. Refrain

669 Soon and Very Soon

SOON AND VERY SOON Irregular

Text: Andrae Crouch (USA)
Music: Andrae Crouch

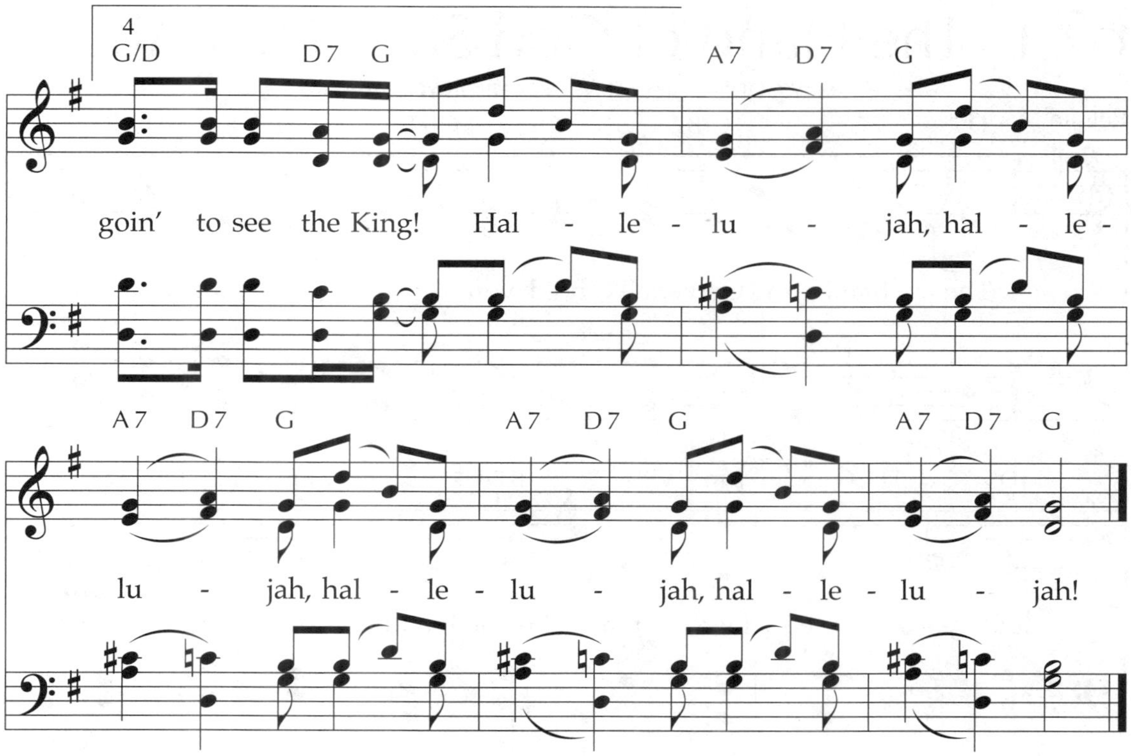
4
G/D D7 G A7 D7 G
goin' to see the King! Hal - le - lu - jah, hal - le -
A7 D7 G A7 D7 G A7 D7 G
lu - jah, hal - le - lu - jah, hal - le - lu - jah!

In the Bulb There Is a Flower 670

PROMISE 8.7.8.7 D

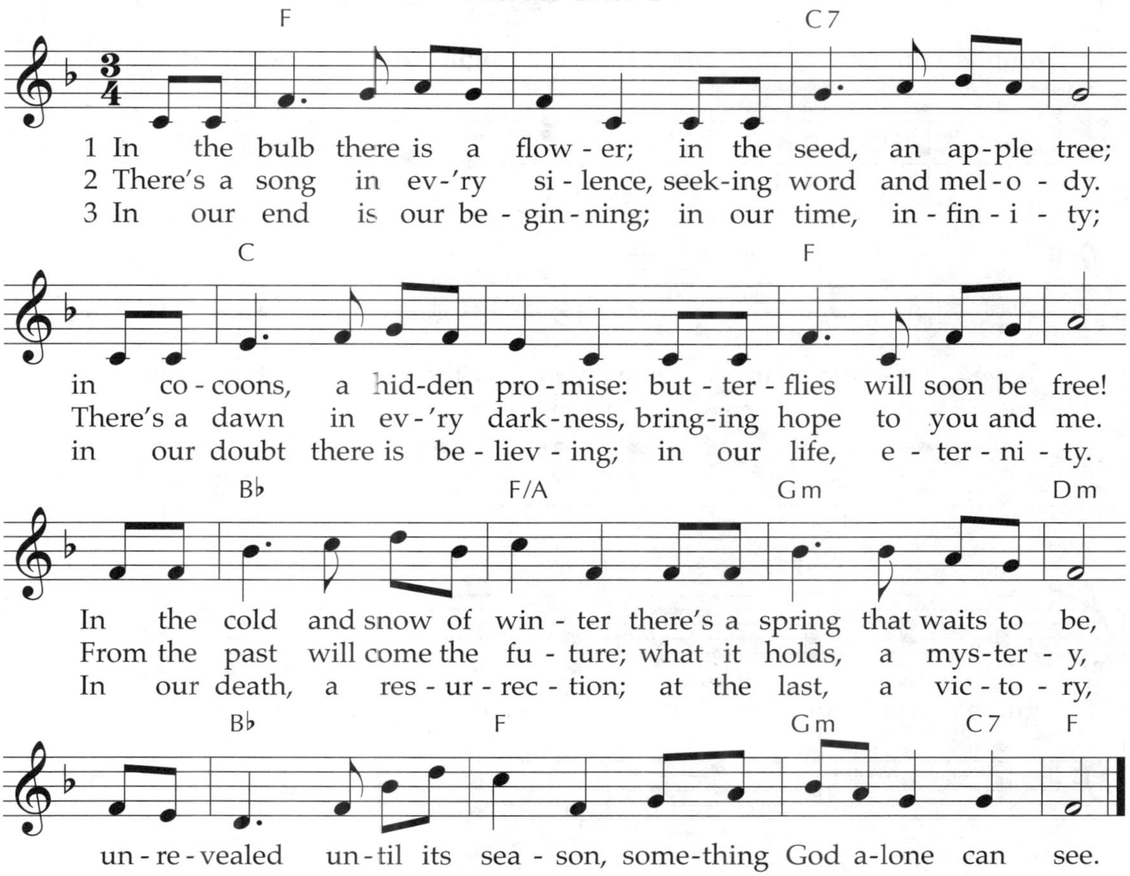
F C7
1 In the bulb there is a flow - er; in the seed, an ap-ple tree;
2 There's a song in ev-'ry si - lence, seek-ing word and mel-o - dy.
3 In our end is our be - gin-ning; in our time, in - fin - i - ty;
C F
in co - coons, a hid-den pro - mise: but - ter - flies will soon be free!
There's a dawn in ev-'ry dark-ness, bring-ing hope to you and me.
in our doubt there is be - liev - ing; in our life, e - ter - ni - ty.
B♭ F/A Gm Dm
In the cold and snow of win - ter there's a spring that waits to be,
From the past will come the fu - ture; what it holds, a mys-ter - y,
In our death, a res - ur - rec - tion; at the last, a vic - to - ry,
B♭ F Gm C7 F
un - re - vealed un - til its sea - son, some-thing God a - lone can see.

Text: Natalie Sleeth (USA), 1985
Music: Natalie Sleeth, 1985

671 The Hand of God Shall Hold You

MAY GOD'S LIGHT SHINE EVER UPON YOU Irregular

Refrain
D7 G G/B C G6/B Am Am/C
The hand of God shall hold you, the peace of God en -
D D7/C Bm B7/D♯ Em Em7/D
fold you, the love that dreamed and formed you still sur -
A7 C/D D7 G G/B C G6/B
rounds you here to - day; the light of God be - side you, a -
Am Am/C D D7/C Bm B7/D♯
bove, be - neath, in - side you, the light that shines to
Em Em7/D Am7 C/D D7 C/G G
guide you home to the lov - ing hand of God.

Text: Marty Haugen (USA)
Music: Marty Haugen

For All the Saints 672

SINE NOMINE 10.10.10 with alleluias

G C D7 G
1 For all the saints, who from their la - bors rest, who
2 Thou wast their rock, their ref - uge, and their might, thou,
3 Oh, bless'd com - mun - ion, fel - low - ship di - vine! We
4 The gold - en eve - ning bright-ens in the west.
5 But lo! There breaks a yet more glo - rious day; the
6 From earth's wide bounds, from o - cean's far - thest coast, through
A D2 G A7 D
thee by faith be - fore the world con - fessed, thy
Christ, the hope that put their fears to flight; 'mid
feeb - ly strug - gle, they in glo - ry shine, yet
Soon, soon to faith - ful ser - vants com - eth rest. Sweet
saints tri - um - phant rise in bright ar - ray, as
gates of pearl streams in the count - less host, *all
G C G D
name, O Je - sus, be for - ev - er bless'd.
gloom and doubt, their true and shin - ing light.
all are one in thee, for all are thine.
is the calm of par - a - dise the bless'd.
God to glo - ry calls them all a - way.
prais - ing Fa - ther, Son, and Ho - ly Ghost.
G7 C G Em Am D7 G
Al - le - lu - ia, al - le - lu - ia!

*Alternate phrase: to praise Creator, Christ, and Holy Ghost

Text: William W. How (England), *Hymns for Saints' Days, and Other Hymns*, 1864, alt.
Music: Ralph Vaughan Williams (England), *The English Hymnal*, 1906

673 Our God in Heaven

LORD'S PRAYER (MILLER) Irregular

C F C
Our God in heav-en, ho - ly is your
Am G C F/A C/G
name, your reign come, your will done, on earth as in
B♭ F B♭ F Em Am D7/A G/B
heav-en. Give us to-day our dai - ly bread, and
C/B♭ F/A Fm/A♭ C/G D/F♯ Fm
help us for-give, as we have been for - giv - en.
C F/A Em/G Dm/F E Am
In the time of tri-al, lead us in - to light, for yours is the
C F Dm7 Gsus
king-dom, and the pow-er, and the glo-ry, for - ev -

Text: based on Matthew 6:9–13; adapt. Mark A. Miller (USA) and Laurie Zelman (USA)
Music: Mark A. Miller

C F C
er. Our God in heav-en, ho - ly is your
Gsus G F/A C/G B♭ F B♭ F C
name, ho - ly is your name.

Our Father, Who Art in Heaven 674

OUR FATHER WHO ART IN HEAVEN Irregular

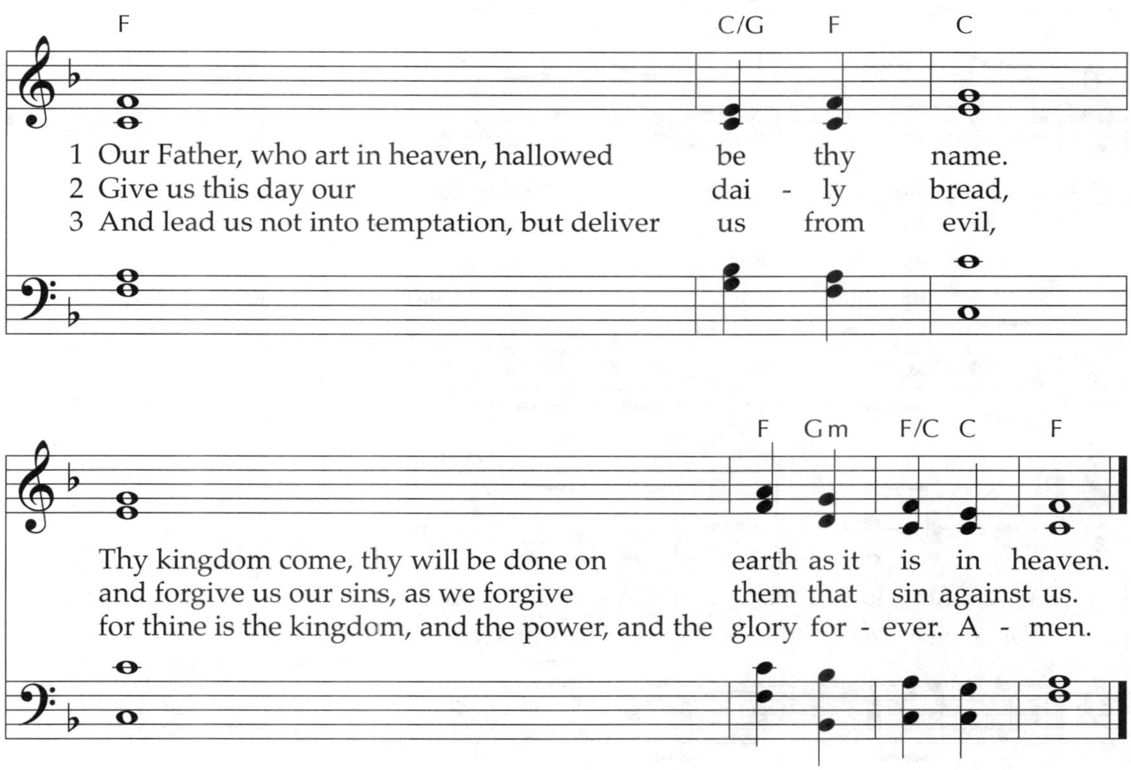
F C/G F C
1 Our Father, who art in heaven, hallowed be thy name.
2 Give us this day our dai - ly bread,
3 And lead us not into temptation, but deliver us from evil,
F Gm F/C C F
Thy kingdom come, thy will be done on earth as it is in heaven.
and forgive us our sins, as we forgive them that sin against us.
for thine is the kingdom, and the power, and the glory for - ever. A - men.

Text: Matthew 6:9–13
Music: anon. Anglican chant (Scotland)

675 أبانا الذي في السماءِ

Abana alathi (Abana in Heaven)

ABANA ALATHI FI SSAMA / ABANA IN HEAVEN Irregular

Am Dm Am Am/C E Dm Am Dm Am E/G#
A - ba-na‿al - a - thi fi‿s - sa - ma li ya - ta - qad das is - mu - ka
Li - ya'- ti - ma la - ku - tu ka li - ta - kun ma shi - a - tu - ka
A - ba - na in heav - en, hal - low - ed be your ho - ly name.
Your king - dom come, your will be done, in all the earth as in heav'n.
Ka - ma - fi‿s - sa - ma - i ka - tha - li - ka 'a - la‿al - ar - di
Wa khub - za - na ka - fa - fa - na 'a - ti - na fi ay - a - mi - na.
Your king - dom come, your will be done, in all the earth as in heav'n.
And give to us, give us this day, our dai - ly bread, O God, we pray.
Wagh - fer la - na thu - nu - ba - na ka - ma na - nu
For - give our sins as we for - give those who have sinned

Text: Arabic; based on Matthew 6:9–13; Laila Constantine (Lebanon); trans. and adapt. Anne Emile Zaki (Egypt), Emily Brink (USA), and Greg Scheer (USA), trans. and adapt. © 2008 Faith Alive Christian Resources

Music: Laila Constantine

Am
E
li-ghay-ri na La tud-khil-na fi taj-ri-
Bal naj-ji-na min ash-shir-
a-gainst us. And save us in time of
De-liv-er us from e-
Am
E
Am
ba Li-an-na la k‿al mu-l-ka
rer Wal quw-wa-ta wal ma-j-da
trial. Yours is the king-dom, yours the pow-er,
vil. yours is the glo-ry, now and ev-er.
Dm
Am
E7/B
Am
Min al-a-zal i-la‿al-a bad. A-min.
A-ba-na in heav-en. A-men.

أبانا الذي في السما ليتقدس اسمكَ
ليأت ملكوتك لتكن مشيئتكَ
كما في السماءِ كذلك على الأرضِ
وخبزنا كفافنا أعطنا في أيامنا
واغفر لنا ذنوبنا كما نحن لغيرنا
لا تدخلنا في تجربهْ بل نجنا من الشرير
لأن لك الملك والقوةَ والمجدَ
من الأزل إلى الأبدْ آمين

676 On Silken, Soft Wings

SILKEN WINGS 5.5.5.5.7.5.5.6

D G D A
1 On silk - en, soft wings our first prayers a - rise,
2 Where yearn - ing hearts dream, though no joy ap - pears,
3 When mourn - ing doves call as shad - ows in - crease,
D G D E7 A
as sil - ver dawn sings through lu - mi - nous skies:
and burn - ing hopes gleam through crys - tal - line tears:
and wan - ing life draws to long - prom - ised peace:
Bm F♯m G D
O Spir - it, pray for us now, in fath - om-less sighs.
O Spir - it, pray for us still, give wings to our fears.
O Spir - it, pray for us yet, to bless and re - lease.
G D/A A D
And all shall be well. And all things shall be well.

Text: Mary Louise Bringle (USA), 2002; refrain based on Julian of Norwich (England), 14th c., © 2006 GIA Publications, Inc.
Music: William P. Rowan (USA), © 2006 William P. Rowan (admin. GIA Publications, Inc.)

Through Our Fragmentary Prayers 677

WORDLESS 7.7.7.7

D D6 A Bm Asus A Bm Em Bm Asus A D A/C# F/A Am Dm A Asus A D
1 Through our frag - men - tar - y prayers and our si - lent,
2 Deep - er than the pul - se's beat is the Spir - it's
3 Let our jab - ber - ings give way to the hum - mings
4 Search and sound our mind and heart, Breath and Flame and
heart - hid sighs, word - less - ly the Spir - it bears our pro -
speech - less groan, mak - ing hu - man prayers com - plete through the
in the soul, as we yield our lives this day to the
Wind and Dove, let your prayer in us im - part strength to
found - est needs and cries: (hum)
prayer that is God's own:
God who makes us whole:
do the work of love. (Alleluia or Amen on last stanza)
(hum)

Text: Thomas H. Troeger (USA), 1985, *New Hymns for the Life of the Church*, 1991
Music: Carol Doran (USA), 1985, *New Hymns for the Life of the Church*, 1991

Kyrie eleison 678

KYRIE 1 Irregular

G D Em Bm C D G
Ky - ri - e, Ky - ri - e, e - le - i - son.

Translation: Lord, have mercy.

Text: from Greek liturgy Κύριε, ἐλέησον (Kyrie eleison) (Eastern Mediterranean), 4th c.
Music: Jacques Berthier (France),

679 Woza nomthwalo wakho (Come, Bring Your Burdens to God)

WOZA NOMTHWALO WAKHO 7.7.7.8

Leader
(hay.) Wo - za nom - thwa - lo, oh,
(no.) Come, bring your bur - dens, oh,
D G D
Wo - za nom - thwa - lo wa - kho; wo - za nom-
Come, bring your bur - dens to God; come, bring your
wo - za nom - thwa - lo, oh, wo - za nom - thwa - lo,
come, bring your bur - dens, oh, come, bring your bur - dens,
A D G
thwa - lo wak - ho; wo - za nom - thwa - lo wak - ho, u
bur - dens to God; come, bring your bur - dens to God, for
(Omit last time)
Je - su‿a - ka so za thi
Je - sus will nev - er say
A A7 D
Je - su‿a - ka so za thi hay.
Je - sus will nev - er say no.

Text: Xhosa; from the singing of the Mooiplaas congregation (South Africa); trans. Barbara Clark (Scotland), Mairi Munro (Scotland), and Martine Stemerick (Scotland)
Music: from the singing of the Mooiplaas congregation; transcr. Welile Sigabi (South Africa)

Calm Me, Lord

680

CALM ME, LORD 8.7.9.7

D A/C♯ Bm G
Calm me, Lord, as you calmed the storm; still me,
D Em7 Asus A D A/C♯
Lord, keep me from harm. Let all the tu - mult with -
Bm7 G/B D/A
in me cease: en - fold
Repeat as desired
Bm Em7 Asus A
me, Lord, in your peace.
Last time
Bm Em7 Asus A D
Lord, en - fold me in your peace.

Text: David Adam (Scotland), © SPCK
Music: Margaret Rizza (England), © 1998 Kevin Mayhew, Ltd. (admin. GIA Publications, Inc.)

681 Every Time I Feel the Spirit

FEEL THE SPIRIT 9.8.9.8 with refrain

Refrain
D G D G D Bm
Ev - 'ry time I feel the Spir - it mov - ing in my heart,
A D G
I will pray. Yes, ev - 'ry time I feel the
D G D Bm A7 D
Spir - it mov - ing in my heart, I will pray.
Fine
1 Up - on the moun - tain when my God spoke, out of God's
2 Jor - dan Riv - er, chil - ly and cold, it chills the
A D
mouth came fire and smoke. All a - round me, it looked so
bod - y, but not the soul. There ain't but one train that's on this
A7 D
fine, I asked my Lord if all was mine.
track, it runs to heav - en and runs right back.
To refrain

Text: African American spiritual (USA)
Music: African American spiritual; arr. Joseph T. Jones (USA); adapt. Melva Wilson Costen (USA), adapt.

Lord, Listen to Your Children 682

CHILDREN PRAYING 9.8.9.9

D D7 C/G G
Lord, lis-ten to your chil-dren pray - ing,
E7 A7
Lord, send your Spir-it in this place.
D D7 C/G G G♯dim7
Lord, lis-ten to your chil-dren pray - ing, send us
D/A A7 G7 D
love, send us pow'r, send us grace.

Text: Ken Medema (USA), 1970
Music: Ken Medema, 1970

683 Ô toi, Seigneur / O God, We Call

O GOD WE CALL Irregular

Dsus2 D G2 Dsus2 D G2
Ô toi, Sei - gneur, nous t'ap - pe - lons. Du
O God, we call, O God, we call. From
Bm G2 Bm G2
fond de no - tre cœur, nous t'ap - pe - lons, Sei - gneur.
deep in - side, we yearn, from deep in - side, we yearn,
Bm G2 Dno3
Oui, nous te dé - si - rons, Sei - gneur.
from deep in - side, we yearn for you.

Text: French and English; Linnea Good (Canada)
Music: Linnea Good

I Love the Lord

I LOVE THE LORD CM

C F/C D/C G/B G C
1 I love the Lord, who heard my cry
2 I love the Lord; who heard my cry
F Em7 G/D C
and pit - ied ev - 'ry groan.
and chased my grief a - way.
C/E F F7/E♭ D D/F♯ G G/F E
Long as I live and trou - bles rise,
O let my heart no more de - spair
Am Dm C/E Gsus G C
I'll has - ten to God's throne.
while I have breath to pray.

Text: based on Psalm 116:1–2; Isaac Watts (England), 1719, alt.
Music: Richard Smallwood (USA), 1975, © 1990 Century Oak/Richwood Music (admin. Conexion Media Group, Inc); arr. Nolan Williams (USA), © 2000 GIA Publications, Inc.

685 O Lord, Hear My Prayer

HEAR MY PRAYER 5.5.6 D

Em Am/C D
O Lord, hear my prayer. O Lord, hear my prayer.
G/B C Am/C B Em
When I call, an - swer me. O Lord, hear my prayer. O
Am/C D Em/G Am B Em
Lord, hear my prayer. Come and lis - ten to me.

Text: based on Psalm 102:1-2; *Music from Taizé*, vol. 2, 1982, 1983, 1984
Music: Jacques Berthier (France), *Music from Taizé*, vol. 2, 1982, 1983, 1984

686 Let Us Pray

LET US PRAY (Byzantine) Irregular

G D G Am D G
Leader
All
A: Let us pray to our God. God, hear our prayer.
B: Let us pray to the Lord. Lord, have mer - cy.

Text: traditional
Music: Byzantine chant; arr. © 1984 GIA Publications, Inc.

Amen 687

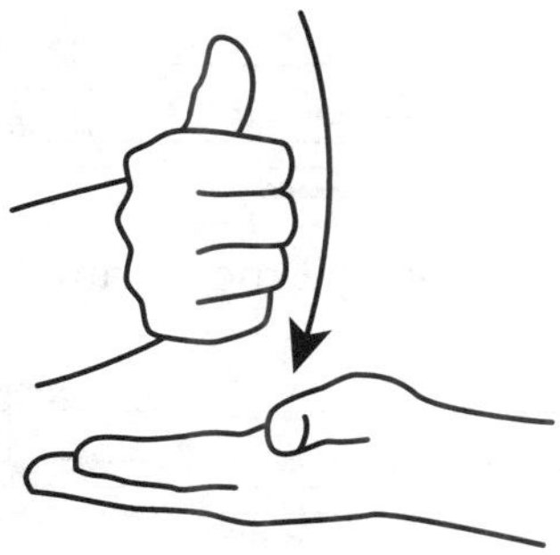

Text: Hebrew traditional, אָמֵן (Amen) (Mediterranean), ca. 4th c. BC American Sign Language; Mennonite Worship and Song Committee, 2020; illustration by Merrill Miller (USA)

Amen (Dresden) 688

DRESDEN AMEN Irregular

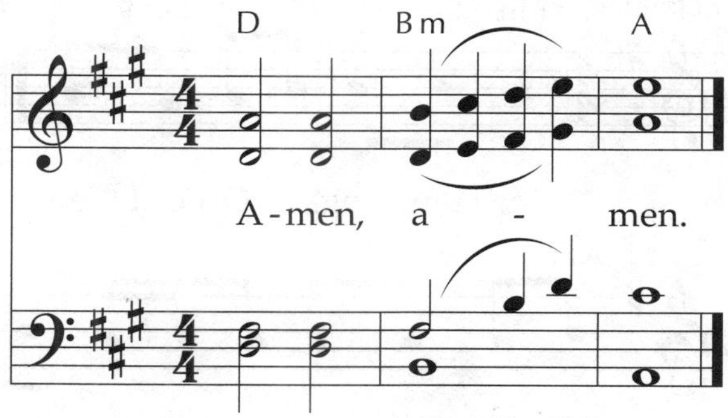

Text: Hebrew traditional, אָמֵן (Amen) (Mediterranean), ca. 4th c. BC
Music: attr. Johann G. Naumann (present-day Germany), 18th c.

Amen 689

AMEN Irregular

Text: Hebrew traditional, אָמֵן (Amen) (Mediterranean), ca. 4th c. BC
Music: African American traditional (USA); arr. Nelsie T. Johnson (USA), 1988

Amen (Threefold) 690

THREEFOLD AMEN Irregular

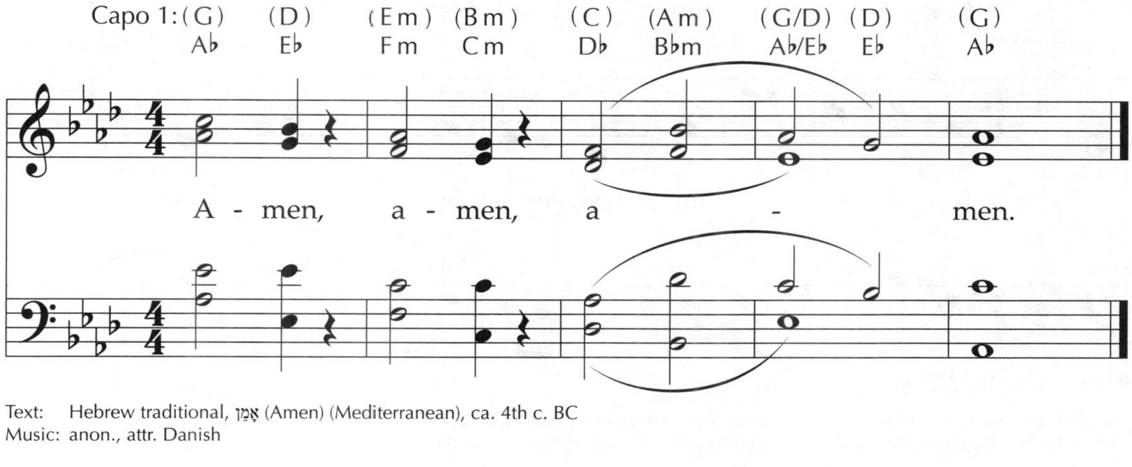

Text: Hebrew traditional, אָמֵן (Amen) (Mediterranean), ca. 4th c. BC
Music: anon., attr. Danish

691 How Long, O Lord

LAMENT Irregular

Refrain
Em D/F♯ G
How long, O Lord, how long? Will you for-get me, am I for-
Am Bsus B
sak-en? How long will you hide your face? O Lord, I am
1 Em D/F♯ 2 Em To verses D Fine
shak - en. How long, O Lord, how shak - en.

1 See how I pass my weary days
in sighs and groans; and when it's night,
my bed is watered with my tears;
my grief consumes, and dims my sight. *Refrain*

2 Look, how the pow'rs of nature mourn!
How long, how long, Almighty God, how long?
When shall your hour of grace return?
When shall I make your grace my song? *Refrain*

3 I feel my flesh so near the grave,
O my soul, my soul is tempted to despair;
but graves can never praise the Lord,
for all is dust and silence there. *Refrain*

Text: based on Psalm 13:1-4 and 30:8-10; Isaac Watts (England), *The Psalms of David*, 1719, alt.; refrain Seth Crissman (USA), 2014
Music: The Walking Roots Band (USA)

692 Kyrie eleison

KYRIE 13 Irregular

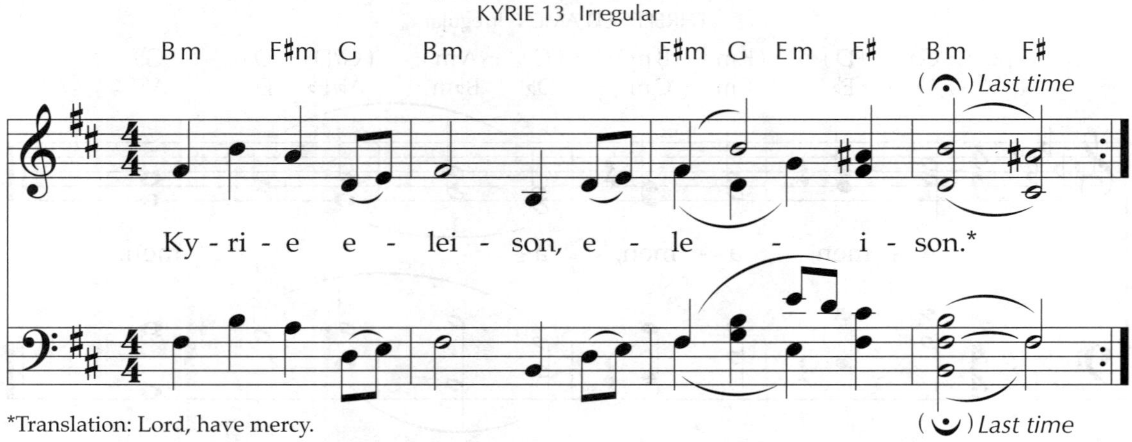
Bm F♯m G Bm F♯m G Em F♯ Bm F♯
Last time
Ky-ri-e e-lei-son, e-le-i-son.*
Last time

*Translation: Lord, have mercy.

Text: from Greek liturgy Κύριε, ἐλέησον (Kyrie eleison) (Eastern Mediterranean), 4th c.
Music: Jacques Berthier (France), © 1991 Le Presses de Taizé (admin. GIA Publications, Inc.)

Khudaya, rahem kar (Have Mercy on Us, Lord) 693

KHUDAYA, RAHEM KAR 6.5.6.5.6.5

Unison, unaccompanied
1, 3 Khu - da - ya, ra - hem kar. Khu - da - ya ra - hem,
1, 3 Have mer - cy on us, Lord, have mer - cy on us.
khu - da - ya, ra - hem kar. Khu - da - ya ra - hem.
Have mer - cy on us, Lord, have mer - cy on us.
Fine
Khu - da - ya ra - hem kar, khu - da - ya ra - hem.
Have mer - cy on us, Lord, have mer - cy on us.
2 Ma - si - ha, ra - hem kar, ma - si - ha, ra - hem.
2 Have mer - cy on us, Christ, have mer - cy on us.
Ma - si - ha ra - hem kar, ma - si - ha, ra - hem.
Have mer - cy on us, Christ, have mer - cy on us.
To verse 3
Ma - si - ha, ra - hem kar, ma - si - ha, ra - hem.
Have mer - cy on us, Christ, have mer - cy on us.

The symbol ◦ indicates when finger cymbals may be played.

Text: Urdu; from Greek liturgy Κύριε, ἐλέησον (Kyrie eleison) (Eastern Mediterranean), 4th c.
Music: R. F. Liberius (Pakistan)

694 Tears of Suffering

JEFFERSON 8.7.8.7 D

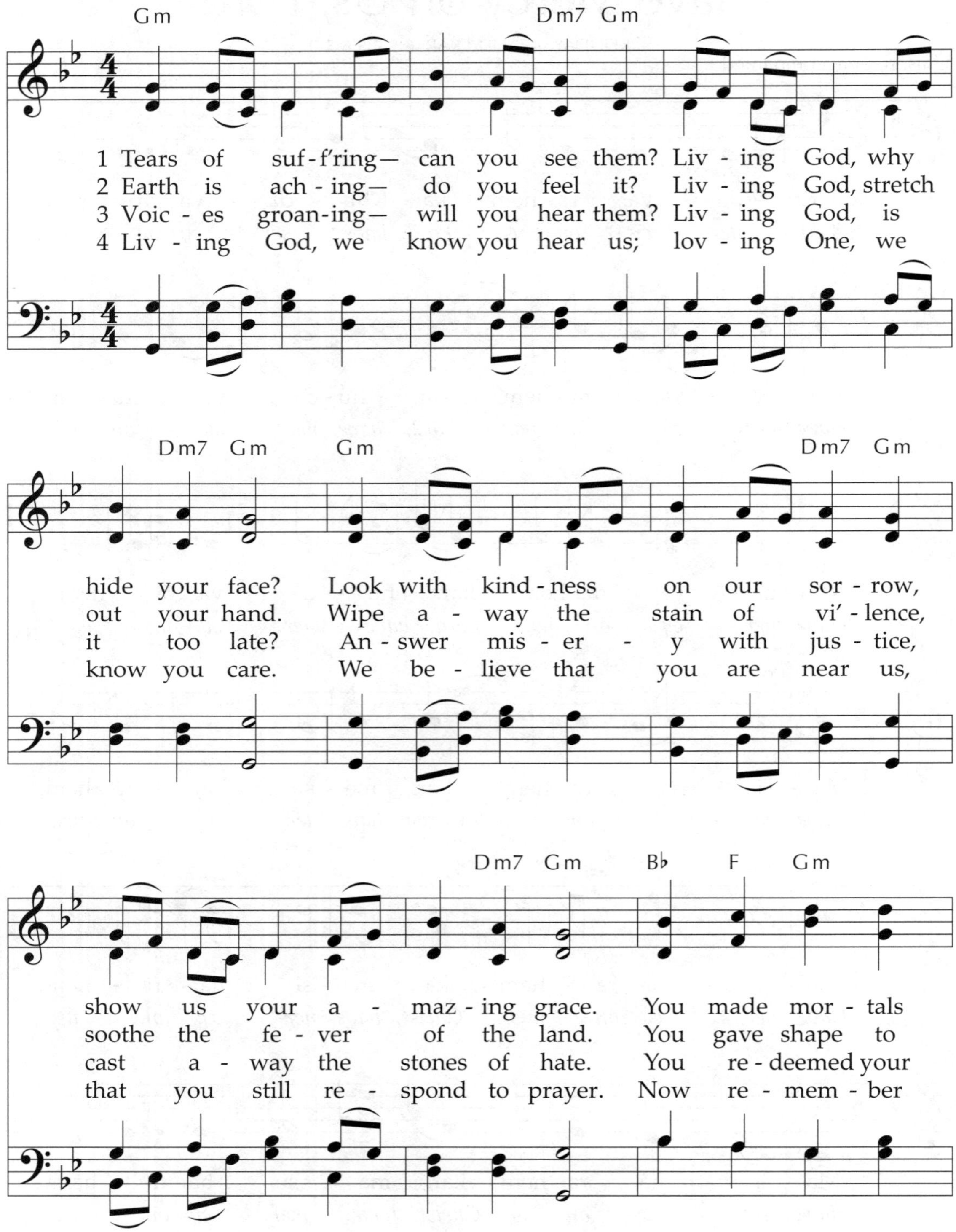
Gm Dm7 Gm
1 Tears of suf-f'ring— can you see them? Liv - ing God, why
2 Earth is ach - ing— do you feel it? Liv - ing God, stretch
3 Voic - es groan-ing— will you hear them? Liv - ing God, is
4 Liv - ing God, we know you hear us; lov - ing One, we
Dm7 Gm Gm Dm7 Gm
hide your face? Look with kind - ness on our sor - row,
out your hand. Wipe a - way the stain of vi'-lence,
it too late? An - swer mis - er - y with jus - tice,
know you care. We be - lieve that you are near us,
Dm7 Gm B♭ F Gm
show us your a - maz - ing grace. You made mor - tals
soothe the fe - ver of the land. You gave shape to
cast a - way the stones of hate. You re - deemed your
that you still re - spond to prayer. Now re - mem - ber

Text: David Gambrell (USA), 2008
Music: Walker's *Southern Harmony* (USA), 1835; arr. Randall Sensmeier (USA)

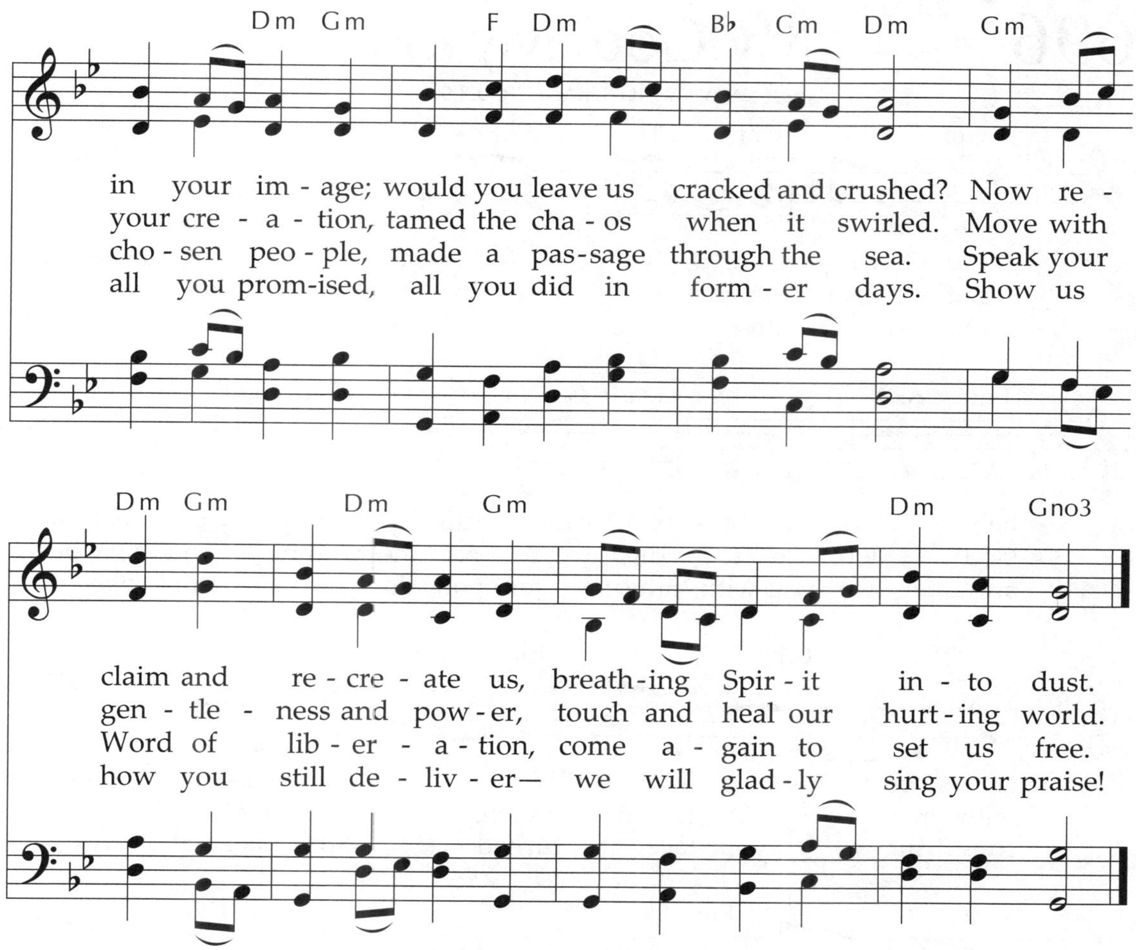
Dm Gm F Dm B♭ Cm Dm Gm
in your im - age; would you leave us cracked and crushed? Now re -
your cre - a - tion, tamed the cha - os when it swirled. Move with
cho - sen peo - ple, made a pas - sage through the sea. Speak your
all you prom-ised, all you did in form - er days. Show us
Dm Gm Dm Gm Dm Gno3
claim and re - cre - ate us, breath-ing Spir - it in - to dust.
gen - tle - ness and pow - er, touch and heal our hurt - ing world.
Word of lib - er - a - tion, come a - gain to set us free.
how you still de - liv - er— we will glad - ly sing your praise!

By the Waters of Babylon 695

BY THE WATERS Irregular

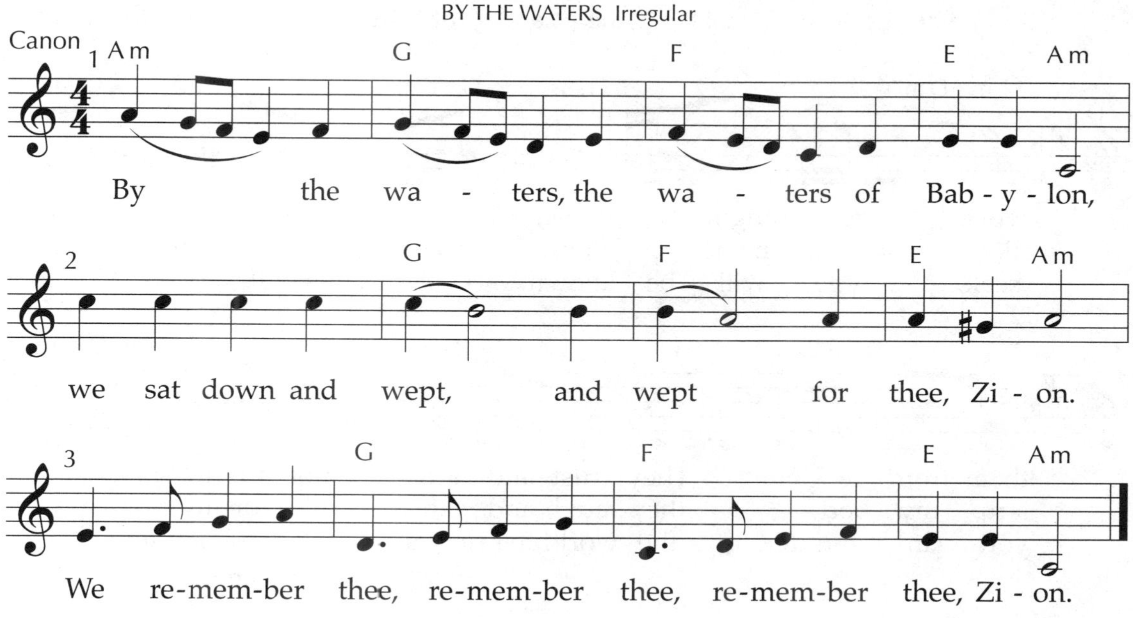
Canon
1 Am G F E Am
By the wa - ters, the wa - ters of Bab - y - lon,
2 G F E Am
we sat down and wept, and wept for thee, Zi - on.
3 G F E Am
We re-mem-ber thee, re-mem-ber thee, re-mem-ber thee, Zi - on.

Text: Psalm 137:1
Music: traditional; adapt. Philip Hayes (England), *The Muses' Delight: Catches, Glees, Canzonets, and Canons*, 1786, alt.

696 My God, My God

WAYFARING STRANGER 9.8.9.8 D

Cm G Cm G/D C m/E♭ C 7/E
1 My God, my God, would you for - sake me? Why keep your
2 But I am shunned— de - spised by mock - ers who say that
3 O God, de - liv - er me from e - vil, and I will
Fm A♭ Gsus G Cm G Cm G/D
help so far a - way? I call by day and hear no
God left me to die. Yet from the womb, you have been
an - swer you with praise; for you do not for - sake the
C m/E♭ C/E Fm G7 F m/C
an - swer. At night I groan; who hears me pray?
with me; at my first breath, you heard my cry.
suf - f'ring— your face is turned to us al - ways.
Cm Fm B♭7 E♭ C 7/E
Yet you are ho - ly, throned in prais - es. Your saints in -
Still, ter - rors lurk and cir - cle round me; my ver - y
The poor will taste the end of hun - ger; by those who
Fm Dm7(♭5) Gsus G Cm G Cm G/D
voke your might - y name, and you de - liv - er
life their schemes op - pose. They scorn my faith and
seek, you will be known. All souls will cry to
C m/E♭ C 7/E Fm G7 F m/C C m
them from e - vil. They trust and are not put to shame.
strip my bod - y; they laugh and gam - ble for my clothes.
you in won - der: the world be - longs to God a - lone.

For capo chords, see the accompaniment edition.

Text: based on Psalm 22; Adam M. L. Tice (USA), 2012,
Music: American traditional (USA); arr. Horace Clarence Boyer (USA),

Loving Spirit

697

OMNI DIE 8.7.8.7

Capo 3: (D) (A) (D) (Em) (D)
F C F Gm F
1, 5 Lov - ing Spir - it, lov - ing Spir - it, you have
2 Like a moth - er you en - fold me, hold my
3 Like a fa - ther you pro - tect me, teach me
4 Friend and lov - er, in your close - ness I am
(E7/B) (A) (D) (Bm) (D)
G7/D C F Dm F
cho - sen me to be; you have drawn me to your
life with - in your own, feed me with your ver - y
the dis - cern - ing eye, hoist me up up - on your
known and held and blest: in your prom - ise is my
(A) (F♯) (Bm) (D) (Asus) (A) (D)
C A Dm F Csus C F
won - der, you have set your sign on me.
bod - y, form me of your flesh and bone.
shoul - der, let me see the world from high.
com - fort, in your pres - ence I may rest.

Text: Shirley Erena Murray (Aotearoa New Zealand), © 1987 The Hymn Society (admin. Hope Publishing Company)
Music: *Gross Catholische Gesängbuch* (present-day Austria), 1631; harm. William Smith Rockstro (England), 19th c.

698 Somebody Prayed for Me

SOMEBODY PRAYED FOR ME Irregular

1 Some-bod-y prayed for me, had me on their
2 The peo-ple prayed for me, had me on their
3 My Je-sus prayed for me, had me on his

mind, took the time to pray for me.
mind, took the time to pray for me.
mind, took the time to pray for me.

I'm so glad they prayed, I'm so glad they prayed,
I'm so glad they prayed, I'm so glad they prayed,
I'm so glad he prayed, I'm so glad he prayed,

I'm so glad they prayed for me.
I'm so glad they prayed for me.
I'm so glad he prayed for me.

Additional verses may be improvised.

Text: African American spiritual (USA)
Music: African American spiritual

شكرو يسوع

699 Shukuru, Yesu (We Thank You, Jesus)

SHUKURU YESU Irregular

Leader D A D
Arabic: Shu-ku - ru. Shu - ku - ru.
English: We thank you. We thank you.
All
Arabic: Shu - ku - ru, Ye - su. Shu - ku - ru, Ye - su.
English: We thank you, Je - sus. We thank you, Je - sus.
D7 G A D Em/D D
Shu - ku - ru. Shu - ku - ru, shu - ku - ru, Ye - su.
We thank you. We thank you, we thank you, Je - sus.
Shu - ku - ru, Ye - su. Shu - ku - ru, shu - ku - ru, Ye - su.
We thank you, Je - sus. We thank you, we thank you, Je - sus.

شكرو يسوع

Swahili: Asanti, asanti, Yesu.

Text: Arabic; Sudanese worship chorus,
Music: unknown (Sudan); arr. Greg Scheer (USA),

700 O God of Blessings

SOLI DEO GLORIA 9.9.9.9.9 with refrain

F Bb C
1 O God of bless - ings, all praise to you! Your
2 All praise for wis - dom, great gift sub - lime, through
3 All praise for proph - ets, through grace in - spired to
4 All praise for mu - sic, deep gift pro - found, through
5 All praise for Je - sus, best gift di - vine through
6 A bil - lion voic - es in one great song, now
Dm G7 C A
love sur - rounds us our whole life through. You are the free - dom of
words and teach - ers of ev - 'ry time; for sto - ries an - cient and
preach and wit - ness with hearts on fire. Your Spir - it choos - es the
hands and voic - es in ho - ly sound: the psalms of Da - vid and
word and wit - ness, in bread and wine; in - car - nate love song of
soft and gen - tle, now deep and strong, in ev - 'ry cul - ture and
Dm C
those op - pressed; You are the com - fort of all dis -
knowl - edge new, for coach - es, men - tors, and coun - selors
weak and small to sing the new reign where might - y
Ma - ry's praise, in word - less splen - dor and lyr - ic
bound - less grace, priest, teach - er, proph - et in time and
style and key, from hill and val - ley, with sky and
F F7 Bb C7 F
tressed. Come now, O ho - ly and wel - come guest:
true whose life of ser - vice brought us to you:
fall; with them may we live your gos - pel call:
phrase, with all cre - a - tion one song we raise:
space, your stead - fast kind - ness with hu - man face:
sea, with Christ we praise you e - ter - nal - ly:
Gm Dm Eb Dm7 Gm F Bb F
*So - li De - o glo - ri - a, so - li De - o glo - ri - a!

*Latin: To God alone be glory!

For capo chords, see the accompaniment edition.

Text: Marty Haugen (USA)
Music: Marty Haugen

You Are All We Have 701

PROTECT ME, LORD; I COME TO YOU FOR SAFETY 5.6.8.6

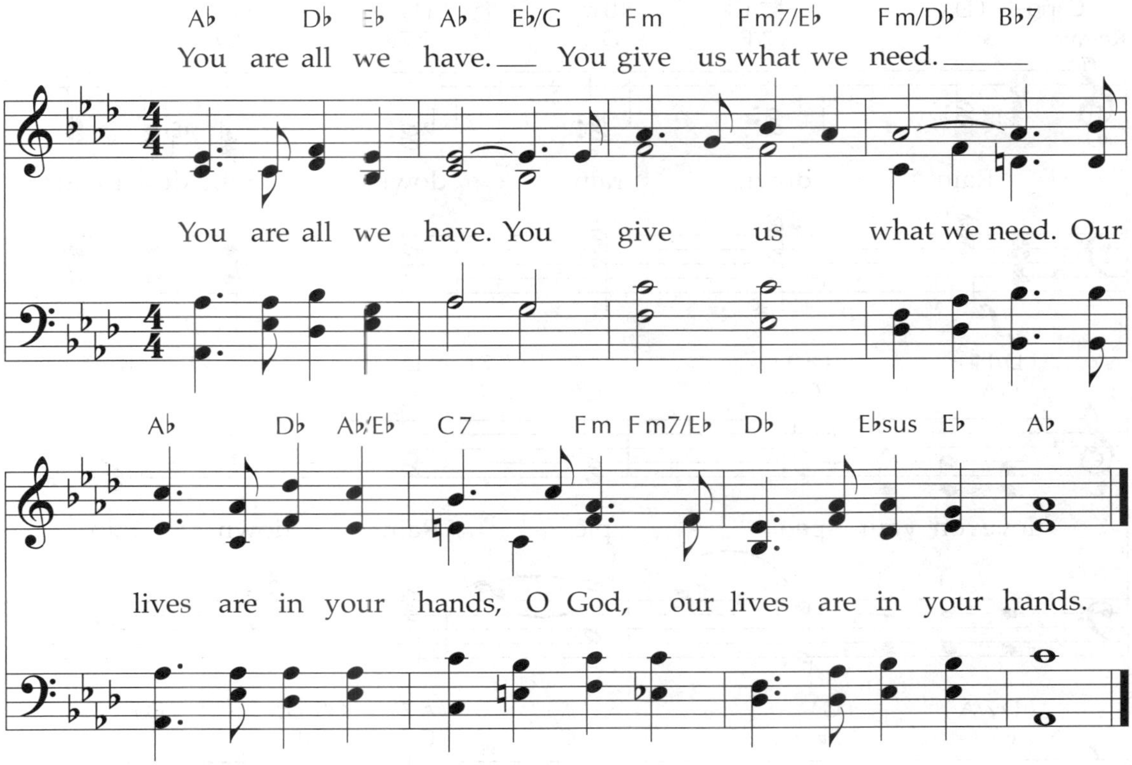
Ab Db Eb Ab Eb/G Fm Fm7/Eb Fm/Db Bb7
You are all we have. You give us what we need.
You are all we have. You give us what we need. Our
Ab Db Ab/Eb C7 Fm Fm7/Eb Db Ebsus Eb Ab
lives are in your hands, O God, our lives are in your hands.

Verses can be found in the accompaniment edition.
For capo chords, see the accompaniment edition.

Text: based on Psalm 16; Francis Patrick O'Brien (USA), alt.
Music: Francis Patrick O'Brien

Hallelujah 702

SYRIAN HALLELUJAH Irregular

Hal - le, hal - le - lu - jah. Hal - le, hal - le - lu - jah.
Hal - le-lu - jah, hal - le-lu - jah, hal - le - lu - jah.
Hal - le-lu - jah, hal - le-lu - jah, hal - le - lu - jah!

Text: Hebrew traditional; הַלְלוּ יָהּ (Hallelujah) (Mediterranean), ca. 4th c. BC
Music: Syrian traditional, as taught by Metropolitan Mar Gregorios Yohanna Ibrahim (Syria)

703 Rain Down

FAITHFUL AND TRUE Irregular

Capo 3: (D) (F♯7/C♯) (Bm) (D7/A) (G)
Refrain
F A7/E Dm F7/C B♭
Rain down, rain down, rain down your
(D/F♯) (E9) (A) (A7) (D) (F♯7/C♯) (Bm)
F/A G9 C C7 F A7/E Dm
love on your peo - ple. Rain down, rain
(D7/A) (G) (A) (A7) (G/D) (D)
F7/C B♭ C C7 B♭/F F
down, rain down your love, God of life.
Fine
(D) (F♯7/C♯) (Bm) (D7/A)
F A7/E Dm F7/C
1 Faith - ful and true is the word of our God.
2 We who re - vere and find hope in our God
3 God of cre - a - tion, we long for your truth;
1–3 Ooh,

Text: Jaime Cortez (USA), 1991
Music: Jaime Cortez, 1991

(G) (D/F♯) (E9) (A) (A7)
B♭ F/A G9 C C7
All of God's works are so wor - thy of trust.
live in the kind - ness and joy of God's wing.
you are the wa - ter of life that we thirst.
ooh,
(D) (F♯7/C♯) (Bm) (D7/A)
F A7/E Dm F7/C
God's mer - cy falls on the just and the right;
God will pro - tect us from dark - ness and death;
Grant that your love and your peace touch our hearts,
ah,
(G) (A7) (D) (A7)
B♭ C7 F C7
To refrain
full of God's love is the earth.
God will not leave us to starve.
all of our hope lies in you.
mf
To refrain
1 full of God's love is the earth.
2 God will not leave us to starve.
3 all of our hope lies in you.
mf

704 Demos gracias / Let Us Give Thanks

DEMOS GRACIAS / LET US GIVE THANKS Irregular

A E/G♯ F♯m D maj7
De-mos gra - cias al Se - ñor,
Let us give thanks, thanks to the Lord,
B m7 C♯m7 F♯sus F♯m/E A/C♯ E/G♯
gra - cias al Se - ñor. De-mos gra - cias al Se -
thanks to the Lord, our God. Let us give thanks,
F♯m D maj7 B m7 E A
ñor, gra - cias al Se - ñor.
thanks to the Lord, thanks to the Lord, our God.

Text: Spanish and English; Tony E. Alonso (USA)
Music: Tony E. Alonso

For the Healing of the Nations 705

REGENT SQUARE 8.7.8.7.8.7

1 For the heal - ing of the na - tions, Lord, we pray with
2 Lead us for - ward in - to free - dom; from de - spair your
3 All that kills a - bun - dant liv - ing, let it from the
4 You, Cre - a - tor God, have writ - ten your great name on
one ac - cord, for a just and e - qual shar - ing
world re - lease, that, re - deemed from war and ha - tred,
earth be banned: pride of sta - tus, race, or school - ing,
hu - man - kind. For our grow - ing in your like - ness,
of the things that earth af - fords. To a life of
all may come and go in peace. Show us how through
dog - mas that ob - scure your plan. In our com - mon
bring the life of Christ to mind that by our re -
love in ac - tion help us rise and pledge our word.
care and good - ness fear will die and hope in - crease.
quest for jus - tice may we hal - low life's brief span.
sponse and ser - vice, earth its des - ti - ny may find.

For a higher key, see "Angels from the Realms of Glory" (#265).
*Alternate tune: FROM THE DEPTHS (#157)

Text: Fred Kaan (England), 1965, alt.,
Music: Henry T. Smart (England), *Psalms and Hymns for Divine Worship*, 1867

706 O Healing River

HEALING RIVER Irregular

Capo 3: (C) E♭ (G) B♭ (C) E♭ (G) B♭ (C) E♭
Echo*
1 O heal - ing riv - er, (O heal - ing riv - er) send down your
2 This land is parch - ing, this land is
3 Let the seed of free - dom a - wake and
(G) B♭ (C) E♭ (G) B♭ (C) E♭ (G) B♭ (C) E♭
wa - ters, send down your wa - ters
burn - ing, no seed is grow - ing
flour - ish, let the deep roots nour - ish,
(Am) Cm (D) F (G) B♭ (D) F
up - on this land. O heal - ing
in the bar - ren ground. O heal - ing
let the tall stalks rise. O heal - ing
(G) B♭ (C) E♭ (G) B♭ (C) E♭ (G7/C) B♭7/E♭ C E♭
riv - er, send down your wa - ters, and wash the
riv - er, send down your wa - ters, O heal - ing
riv - er, send down your wa - ters, O heal - ing
(G) B♭ (D) F (C) E♭ (G) B♭ (C) E♭ (G) B♭
blood from off the sand.
riv - er, send your wa - ters down.
riv - er, from out of the skies.

*An echo can be sung after each phrase.

Text: Frances Minkoff (USA)
Music: Fred Hellerman (USA)

Dona nobis pacem 707

DONA NOBIS PACEM Irregular

Text: Latin traditional "grant us peace" (Rome), ca. 7th c.; Arabic traditional, ٱلسَّلَامُ عَلَيْكُمْ (May peace be upon you) (Eastern Mediterranean); Hebrew traditional, שִׂים שָׁלוֹם טוֹבָה וּבְרָכָה (Grant peace, goodness, and blessing) (Eastern Mediterranean)
Music: traditional liturgical

708 As the Waters Rise around Us

BRYN CALFARIA 8.7.8.7 with refrain

Gm D Gm D Gm
1 As the wa - ters rise a - round us, and the
2 Numb with grief, our hearts are heav - y, seek - ing
3 Homes and cit - y streets are rav - aged, man - y
4 Gra - cious God, your strong com - pas - sion stilled the
B♭ Cm D Gm D Gm
winds rage o - ver - head; as de - struc - tion's wake con -
cour - age to en - dure, as the harsh - est cost is
lost be - yond re - pair. Brood-ing Spir - it, help us
storm and part - ed seas. Free and lead us till we
D Gm B♭ Cm D Gm
founds us with its mount - ing toll of dead:
lev - ied on the poor - est of the poor.
sal - vage signs of life from such de - spair.
fash - ion worlds of jus - tice, hope, and peace.
Refrain
Gm D7
Christ, have mer - cy. Christ, have mer - cy. Christ, have
Christ, have mer - cy. Christ, have mer - cy.

Text: Mary Louise Bringle (USA), 2005,
Music: William Owen (Wales), *Y Perl Cerddorol (The Pearl of Music)*, vol. 2, 1886; version from *Welsh Hymns and Their Tunes*, 1990

Gm Cm Gm D
mer - cy.
Christ, have mer - cy. Hear your peo - ple's yearn - ing
Gm B♭ Cm D7 Gm
cry. Hear your peo - ple's yearn-ing cry.

Agios o Theos (Holy, Holy, Holy God) 709

AGIOS, O THEOS 6.6.7.6

Dm A Dm C F
A - gi - os o The - os, a - gi - os is - chi - ros,
Ho - ly, ho - ly, ho - ly God, ho - ly al - might - y God,
C7 F Dm A Dm
a - gi - os a - tha - na - tos, e - le - i - son i - mas.
ho - ly and im - mor - tal God, have mer - cy up - on us.

Text: Greek; Byzantine rite (present-day Turkey), ca. 5th c., Τρισάγιον (Trisagion) "Thrice Holy"
Music: traditional Orthodox liturgy (Russia); harm. Alfred V. Fedak (USA),

710 This Is My Song

FINLANDIA 10.10.10.10.10.10

F C7/G F B♭ C F
1 This is my song, O God of all the na - tions,
2 My coun-try's skies are blu - er than the o - cean,
3 This is my prayer, O God of all earth's king-doms,
C7/G F B♭ F
a song of peace for lands a - far and mine.
and sun-light beams on clo - ver leaf and pine.
Your king-dom come; on earth your will be done.
Dm F C Gm
This is my home, the coun - try where my heart is:
But oth - er lands have sun-light too, and clo - ver,
O God, be lift - ed up till all shall serve you,
F/C B♭ A
here are my hopes, my dreams, my ho - ly shrine;
and skies are ev' - ry - where as blue as mine.
and hearts u - nit - ed learn to live as one.

For capo chords, see #649.

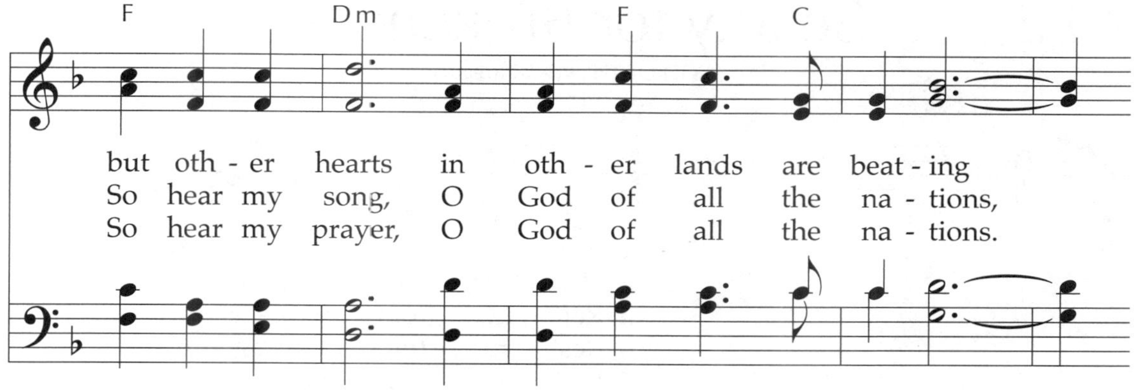
F
Dm
F
C
but oth - er hearts in oth - er lands are beat - ing
So hear my song, O God of all the na - tions,
So hear my prayer, O God of all the na - tions.

F/C
C7
F
with hopes and dreams as true and high as mine.
a song of peace for their land and for mine.
my - self I give you; let your will be done.

يا رب السلام Ya Rab as-salami 711
(God of Peace and Justice)

YA RAB AS-SALAMI Irregular

Em
B/D♯
Em
B7
Ya Rab as - sa - la - mi, am - ter al-ay - na‿as - sa - lam.
God of peace and jus - tice, rain down up-on us your peace.

Em
B/D♯
Em
Am
B7
Em
Ya Rab as - sa - la - mi, Im - la' qu - lu - ba - na‿as - sa - lam.
God of peace and jus - tice, let ev - 'ry heart be filled with peace.

يا رب السلام، أمطر علينا السلام.
يا رب السلام، املأ قلوبنا السلام.

Text: Arabic; Palestinian and Lebanese traditional; trans. John L. Bell (Scotland)
Music: Palestinian and Lebanese traditional; arr. John L. Bell

712 Beauty for Brokenness

GOD OF THE POOR Irregular

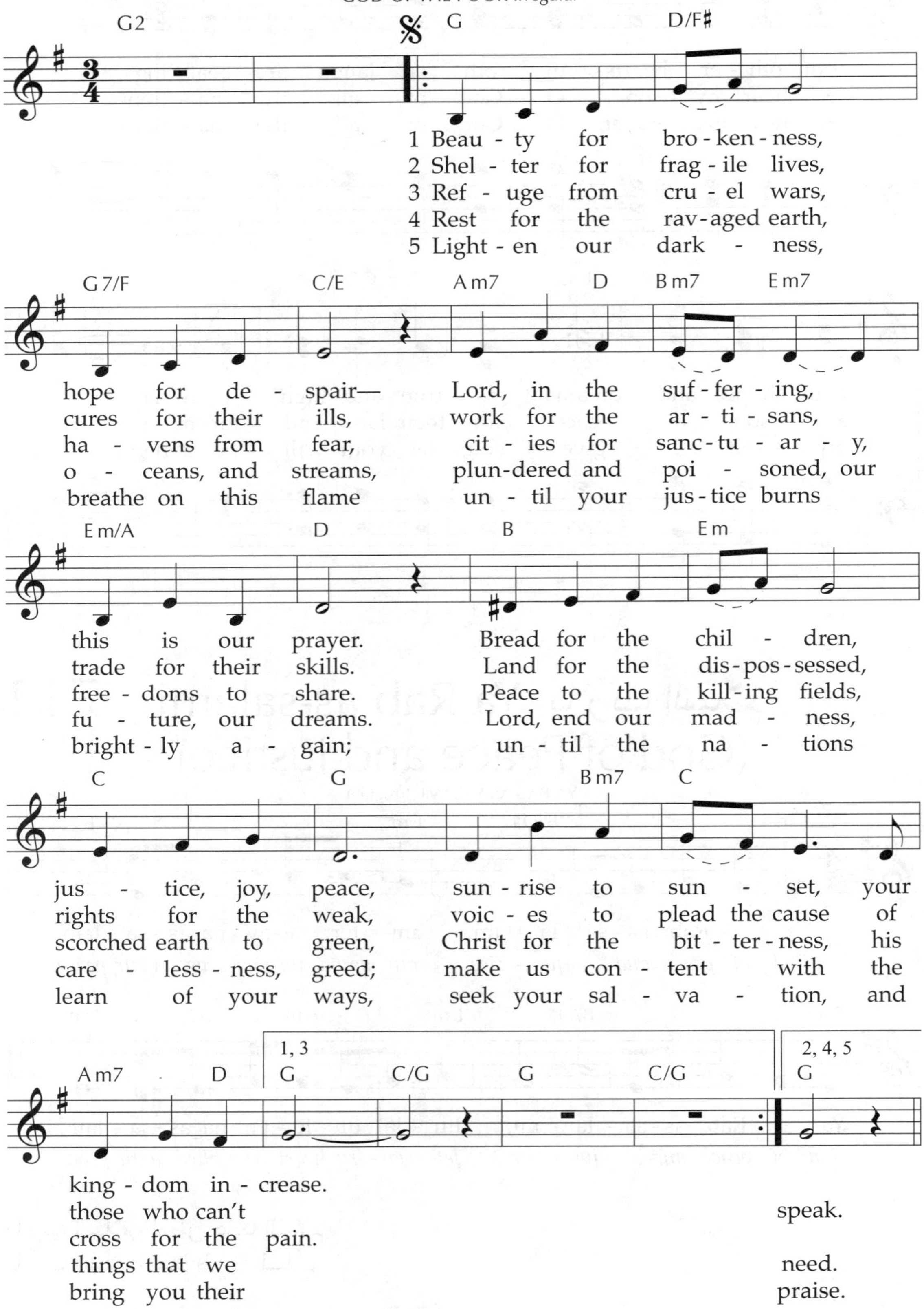
G2 G D/F♯
1 Beau - ty for bro - ken - ness,
2 Shel - ter for frag - ile lives,
3 Ref - uge from cru - el wars,
4 Rest for the rav - aged earth,
5 Light - en our dark - ness,
G7/F C/E Am7 D Bm7 Em7
hope for de - spair— Lord, in the suf - fer - ing,
cures for their ills, work for the ar - ti - sans,
ha - vens from fear, cit - ies for sanc - tu - ar - y,
o - ceans, and streams, plun - dered and poi - soned, our
breathe on this flame un - til your jus - tice burns
Em/A D B Em
this is our prayer. Bread for the chil - dren,
trade for their skills. Land for the dis - pos - sessed,
free - doms to share. Peace to the kill - ing fields,
fu - ture, our dreams. Lord, end our mad - ness,
bright - ly a - gain; un - til the na - tions
C G Bm7 C
jus - tice, joy, peace, sun - rise to sun - set, your
rights for the weak, voic - es to plead the cause of
scorched earth to green, Christ for the bit - ter - ness, his
care - less - ness, greed; make us con - tent with the
learn of your ways, seek your sal - va - tion, and
Am7 D 1, 3 G C/G G C/G 2, 4, 5 G
king - dom in - crease.
those who can't speak.
cross for the pain.
things that we need.
bring you their praise.

Text: Graham Kendrick (England), 1993, alt.
Music: Graham Kendrick, 1993

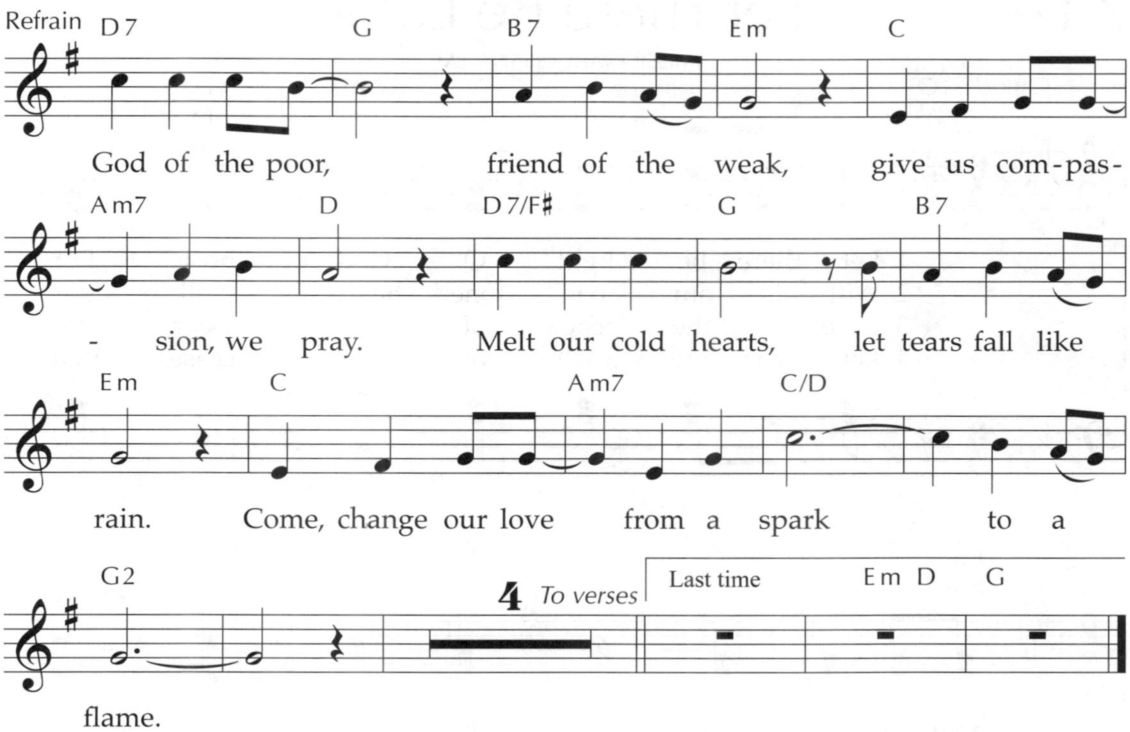
Refrain
D7 G B7 Em C
God of the poor, friend of the weak, give us com-pas-
Am7 D D7/F♯ G B7
-sion, we pray. Melt our cold hearts, let tears fall like
Em C Am7 C/D
rain. Come, change our love from a spark to a
G2
flame.
4 To verses
Last time
Em D G

Make Me an Instrument of Your Peace 713

BERGOGLIO Irregular

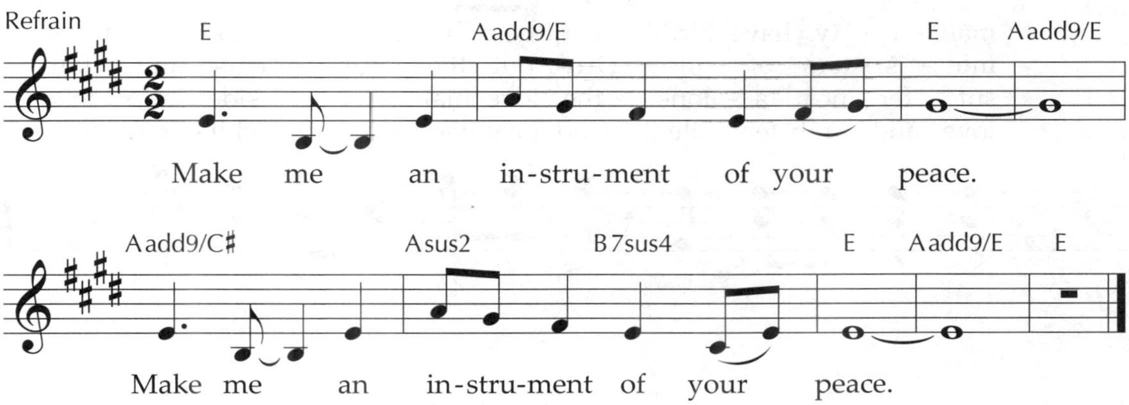
Refrain
E Aadd9/E E Aadd9/E
Make me an in-stru-ment of your peace.
Aadd9/C♯ Asus2 B7sus4 E Aadd9/E E
Make me an in-stru-ment of your peace.

Verses can be found in the accompaniment edition.

Text: based on the Prayer of St. Francis; attr. Francis of Assisi (present-day Italy), 13th c.; trans. anon., alt.
Music: Tony Alonso (USA),

714 Let There Be Light

MISSIONARY CHANT LM

Capo 1: (G) A♭ (Am) B♭m (D) E♭
1 Let there be light, O God of hosts! Let
2 With - in our pas - sioned hearts in - still the
3 Give us the peace of vi - sion clear to
4 Let woe and waste of war - fare cease, that
(Em) Fm (G) A♭ (D) E♭ (G) A♭
there be wis - dom on the earth! Let broad hu -
calm that end - eth strain and strife. Make us your
see each oth - er's good, our own, to joy and
use - ful la - bor yet may build its homes with
(C) D♭ (G) A♭ (D7) E♭7 (G) A♭
man - i - ty have birth! Let there be deeds in - stead of boasts.
min - is - ters of life. Drive out the urge to curse and kill.
suf - fer not a - lone: the love that casts a - side all fear.
love and laugh - ter filled! God, give your way - ward chil - dren peace!

Alternate tune: OLD HUNDREDTH (#71)

Text: William M. Vories (Japan), 1908, *Advocate of Peace*, 1909, alt.
Music: Charles H. C. Zeuner (USA), *American Harp*, 1832

Longing for Light

715

CHRIST, BE OUR LIGHT 9.8.9.6 with refrain

Em Am7 Bm7 Esus Em
1 Long-ing for light, we wait in dark-ness. Long-ing for
2 Long-ing for peace, our world is troub-led. Long-ing for
3 Long-ing for food, man-y are hun-gry. Long-ing for
4 Long-ing for shel-ter, man-y are home-less. Long-ing for
5 Man-y the gifts, man-y the peo-ple, man-y the
Am7 Bm7 Esus Em Am7
truth, we turn to you. Make us your own,
hope, man-y de-spair. Your word a-lone
wa-ter, man-y still thirst. Make us your bread,
warmth, man-y are cold. Make us your build-ing,
hearts that yearn to be-long. Let us be ser-vants
D G C Am7 Dsus D
your ho-ly peo-ple, light for the world to see.
has pow'r to save us. Make us your liv-ing voice.
bro-ken for oth-ers, shared un-til all are fed.
shel-ter-ing oth-ers, walls made of liv-ing stone.
to one an-oth-er, mak-ing your king-dom come.
Refrain
G C/G G Em Bm Em Am7 D
Christ, be our light! Shine in our hearts. Shine through the dark-ness.
Christ, be our light! Shine in our hearts. Shine through the dark-ness.
G Dsus D Em Em7/D C Am7 G Am7/G G
Last time
Christ, be our light! Shine in your church gath-ered to-day.
Last time

Text: Bernadette Farrell (England)
Music: Bernadette Farrell

716 God of Grace and God of Glory

CWM RHONDDA 8.7.8.7.8.7 extended

G D G C G D7
1 God of grace and God of glo - ry, on thy peo-ple pour thy
2 Lo! the hosts of e - vil round us scorn thy Christ, as - sail his
3 Cure thy chil-dren's war - ring mad-ness; bend our pride to thy con -
4 Save us from weak res - ig - na-tion to the e - vils we de -
G D G Am7/C
pow'r. Crown thine an - cient chur - ch's sto - ry, bring its bud to
ways! From the fears that long have bound us, free our hearts to
trol; shame our wan - ton, self - ish glad-ness, rich in things and
plore. Let the search for thy sal - va-tion be our glo - ry
G/D D G D7 G
glo - rious flow'r. Grant us wis - dom, grant us cour - age, for the
faith and praise. Grant us wis - dom, grant us cour - age, for the
poor in soul. Grant us wis - dom, grant us cour - age, lest we
ev - er - more. Grant us wis - dom, grant us cour - age, serv - ing
D7 G Am7/C G/D D7 G
fac - ing of this hour, (of this hour) for the fac - ing of this hour.
liv - ing of these days, (of these days) for the liv - ing of these days.
miss thy king-dom's goal, (king-dom's goal) lest we miss thy king-dom's goal.
thee whom we a - dore, (we a - dore) serv-ing thee whom we a - dore.

Text: Harry Emerson Fosdick (USA), 1930, *Praise and Service*
Music: John Hughes (Wales), 1905, *The Voice of Thanksgiving* no. 4, 1928

Renew Your Church 717

ALL IS WELL 10.6.10.6.8.8.8.6

1 Re - new your church, its min - is - tries re - store, both to serve and a - dore.
2 Teach us your word, re - veal its truth di - vine; on our path let it shine.
3 Teach us to pray, for you are al - ways near. Your still voice let us hear.
4 Teach us to love with heart and mind and soul. You, O Christ, be our goal.
Make it a - gain as salt through - out the land, and as light from a stand.
Tell of your works, your might - y acts of grace; from each page show your face.
Our souls are rest - less till they rest in you, where we find strength a - new.
Break down old walls of prej - u - dice and hate. Leave us not to our fate.
'Mid som - ber shad - ows of the night, where greed and ha - tred spread their
As you have loved us, sent your Son, and our sal - va - tion now is
Be - fore your pres - ence keep us still, that we may find for us your
As you have loved and giv'n your life to end hos - til - i - ty and
blight, O send us forth with pow'r en - dued. Help us, God, be re - newed.
won, O let our hearts with love be stirred. Help us, God, know your word!
will, and seek your gui - dance ev - 'ry day. Teach us, Christ, how to pray!
strife, O share your grace from heav'n a - bove. Teach us, Christ, how to love!

Text: K. L. Cober (USA), 1960, alt., © 1960 K. L. Cober, renewed 1985 Judson Press
Music: American traditional (USA), 1842, adapt. *Sacred Harp*, 1844

718 Gentle Shepherd, Come and Lead Us

GENTLE SHEPHERD Irregular

Capo 3: (D) F (E7) G7
Gen-tle Shep - herd, come and lead us, for we
(Em) Gm (A7) C7 (D) F (G/D) B♭/F (D) F
need you to help us find our way. Gen-tle Shep - herd,
(E7) G7 (Em) Gm (A7) C7
come and feed us, for we need your strength from day to
(D) F (G/D) B♭/F (D) F (F♯m) Am (D7) F7 (G) B♭
day. There's no oth - er we can turn to who can
(E7) G7 (Em) Gm (A7) C7 (D) F
help us face an - oth - er day. Gen-tle Shep-herd, come and

Text: Gloria Gaither (USA)
Music: William J. Gaither (USA)

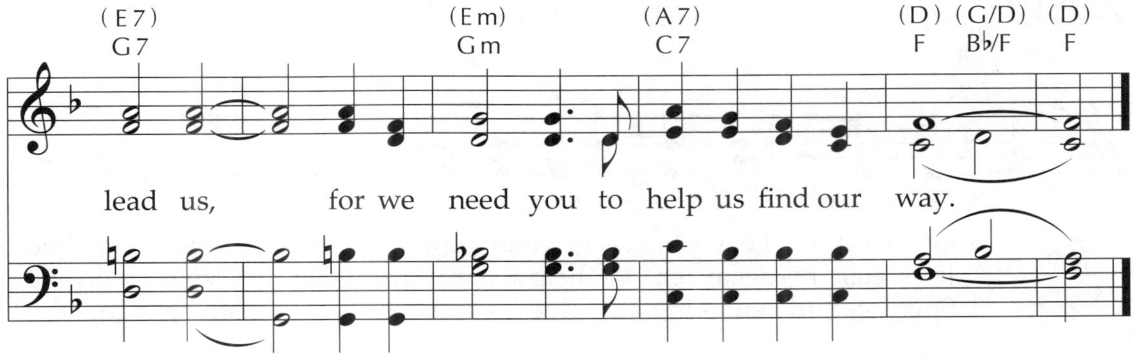
(E7) (Em) (A7) (D) (G/D) (D)
G7 Gm C7 F B♭/F F
lead us, for we need you to help us find our way.

Jesus, Help Us Live in Peace 719

UNITY 7.7.7.7

E B C♯m B
Refrain: Je - sus, help us live in peace,
1 Man - y times we don't a - gree
2 How we long for pow'r and fame,
A E B
from our blind - ness set us free.
on what's right or wrong to do.
seek - ing ev - 'ry earth - ly thing.
E E7 A
Fill us with your heal - ing love.
It's so hard to real - ly see
We for - get the one who came
E F♯m
To verses and refrain
A E A/E
Last time
E
Help us live in u - ni - ty. ty.
from the oth - er's point of view.
as a ser - vant, not a king.

Text: Jerry Derstine (JD Martin) (USA)
Music: Jerry Derstine (JD Martin)

720 O God in Heaven

HALAD 5.5.5.5.5.5.5.4

Em
1 O God in heav - en, grant to your chil-dren mer - cy and
2 Je - sus, re-deem - er, help us re - mem - ber your pain and
3 Spir - it un - end - ing, give us your bless-ing: strength for the
B7 Em Am D7
bless-ing, songs nev-er ceas-ing, grace to in - vite us, peace to u -
pas - sion, your res - ur - rec - tion, your call to fol - low, your love to -
wea - ry, help for the need - y, hope for the scorn-ful, peace for the
G Am D B7 Em
nite us— O God in heav - en, auth - or of love.
mor - row— Je - sus, re - deem - er, sav - ior, and friend.
mourn - ful— Spir - it un - end - ing, com-fort and guide.

Christ Be in Your Senses 721

APPALACHIAN FALL 6.5.6.5 D

D G Bm D Asus A
1 Christ be in your sens - es, marked with sa - cred sign.
2 Christ be in your vis - ion, guard you day and night;
3 Christ be in your breath - ing, con - stant - ly im - part
D G Bm E Asus A
In the In - car - na - tion flesh be - came di - vine.
keep your feet from stum - bling, shine God's ho - ly light.
grace to ev - 'ry move - ment, peace with - in your heart.
Bm D G D A D A D
Christ be in your hear - ing, tune you to re - joice;
Christ be in your speak - ing, train your ev' - ry word.
Christ be in your sens - es marked with sa - cred sign.
G Bm D A Bm D A G/D D
in each shout or whis - per, hear God's call - ing voice.
In your dai - ly wit - ness let God's truth be heard.
In the Spir - it's pres - ence, flesh be - comes di - vine.

722 Help Us to Help Each Other

MARTYRDOM (AVON) CM

G C G D G
1 Help us to help each oth - er, Lord, each
2 Help us to build each oth - er up, your
3 Je - sus, u - nit - ed by your grace, and
4 Drawn by the mag - net of your love, we
D G Em G D G D Em
oth - er's load to bear, that all may live in
strength with - in us prove. In - crease our faith, con -
each to each en - deared, with con - fi - dence we
find our hearts made new. Near - er each oth - er
C G D G Em G/D D7 G
true ac - cord, our joys and pains to share.
firm our hope and fill us with your love.
seek your face and know our prayer is heard.
let us move, and near - er still to you.

Text: Charles Wesley (England), *Hymns and Sacred Poems,* 1742, alt.; stanzas 1, 2, and 4 rev. in *Hymns for Today's Church,* 1982,

Music: Hugh Wilson (Scotland); adapt. Robert A. Smith (Scotland), *Sacred Music,* 1825

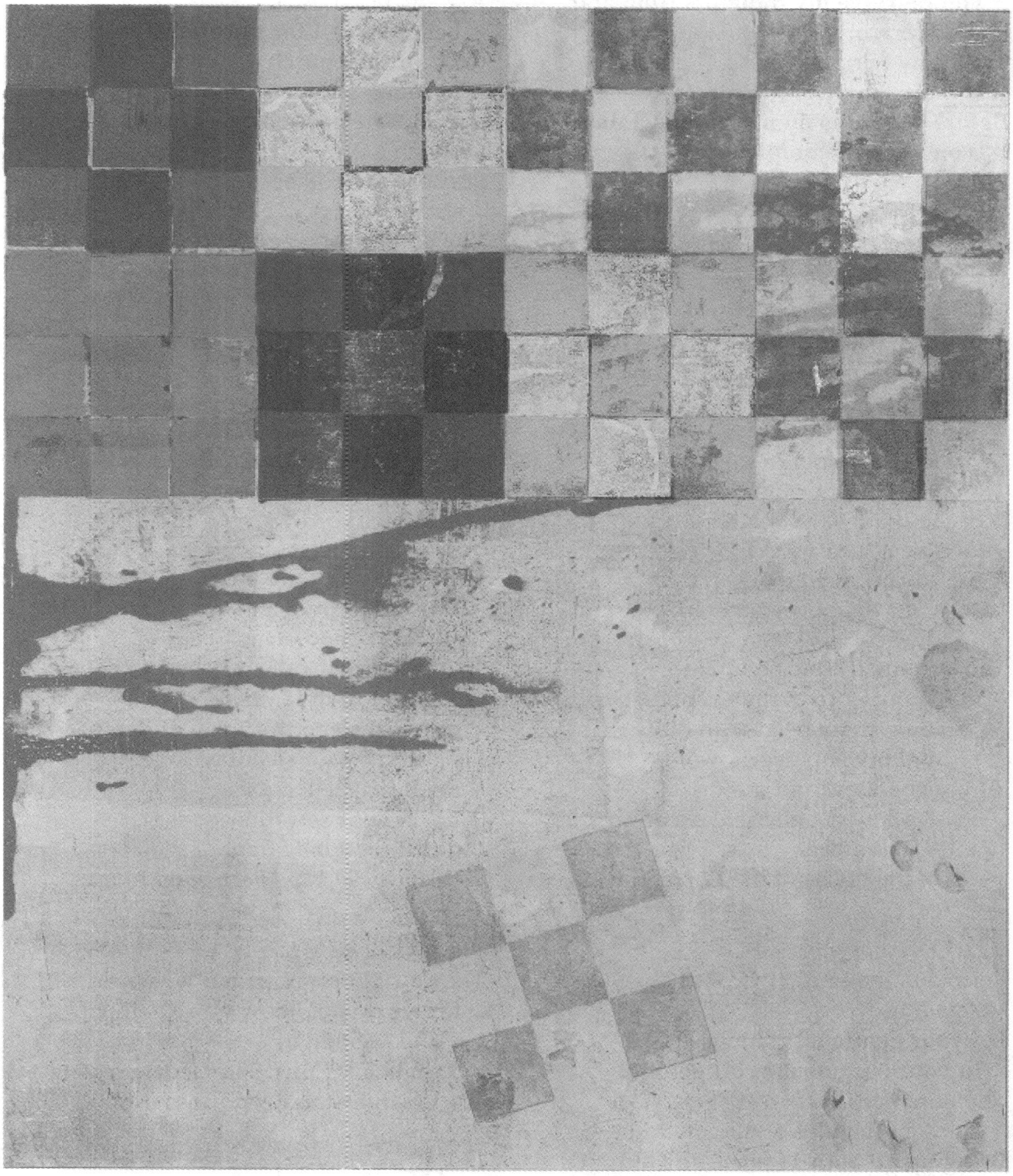

724 *Psalm 139:1-4*

O LORD, you have searched me
and known me.
You know when I sit
and when I rise;
you perceive my thoughts from afar.
You discern my going out
and my lying down;
you are familiar with all my ways.
Before a word is on my tongue, LORD,
you know it completely.

725 *Psalm 23*

The LORD is my shepherd;
I lack nothing.
The LORD makes me lie down
in green pastures
and leads me beside still waters.
You restore my soul, O LORD,
and guide me along right pathways
for your name's sake.
Though I walk through the valley
of the shadow of death,
I shall fear no evil;
for you are with me;
your rod and your staff,
they comfort me.
You prepare a table before me
in the presence of my enemies;
you anoint my head with oil,
and my cup overflows.
Surely goodness and mercy
shall follow me all the days of my life,
and I will dwell
in the house of the LORD forever.

726 *Philippians 4:4-7*

Rejoice in the Lord always!
Again I say, rejoice!
Let your gentleness show
in your treatment of all people.
The Lord is near.
Don't be anxious about anything.
Bring up all your requests to God
in your prayers and petitions,
along with giving thanks.
Then the peace of God
that exceeds all understanding
will guard your hearts and minds
in Christ Jesus.

727 *James 5:13-16*

Are any of you suffering hardships?
Let them pray.
Are any of you happy?
Let them sing praises.
Are any of you sick?
Let them call for the elders
of the church
to come, pray, and anoint with oil
in the name of the Lord.
Let such a prayer be offered in faith.
Pray for each other
so that you may be healed.
The earnest prayer of the righteous
is powerful and effective.

728 *Psalm 13 (excerpts)*

How long, O LORD?
Will you forget me forever?
How long will you hide
your face from me?
How long must I bear pain in my soul,
and have sorrow
in my heart all day long?
How long shall my enemy
be exalted over me?
Look on me and answer,
O LORD my God!
Give light to my eyes,
or I will sleep the sleep of death.
I trusted in your steadfast love;
my heart shall rejoice
in your salvation.
I will sing to the LORD,
because God has been good to me.

729 *Romans 8:26*

The Spirit helps us in our weakness;
for we do not know how to pray
as we ought,
but that very Spirit intercedes
with sighs too deep for words.

730 *Psalm 46:10*

Be still
and know
that I am God.

Previous page: 723. *Nine Patch #8*, Brenton Good (USA), 2015, monotype ⓦ

Open My Heart / Abre mi corazón 731

OPEN MY HEART Irregular

Capo 3: (D)
F
(Asus) (A)
Csus C
(Bm)
Dm
(A)
C
O - pen my heart, o - pen my heart.
A - bre mi co-ra - zón. A - bre mi co - ra - zón.
O - pen my heart, o - pen my heart.
A - bre mi co - ra - zón.
O - pen my heart, o - pen my heart.
A - bre mi co - ra - zón.
(G)
B♭
(F♯m7)
Am7
(Bm)
Dm
(A)
C
O - pen my heart, o - pen my heart.
A - bre mi co-ra - zón. A - bre mi co - ra - zón.
O - pen my heart, o - pen my heart.
A - bre mi co - ra - zón.
O - pen my heart, o - pen my heart.
A - bre mi co - ra - zón.

Text: English and Spanish; Ana Hernández (USA)
Music: Ana Hernández

732 Open My Eyes (Abre mis ojos)

ABRE MIS OJOS Irregular

Verses
E A E/G♯ F♯m7 B7 E B/D♯ C♯m7
1, 5 O - pen my eyes, Lord. Help me to see your face.
2 O - pen my ears, Lord. Help me to hear your voice.
3 O - pen my heart, Lord. Help me to love like you.
1, 5 A - bre mis o - jos, que quie - ro ver co - mo tú.
2 A - bre mis o - í - dos, que quie-ro o - ír co - mo tú.
3 A - bre mi co - ra - zón, que quie-ro a - mar co - mo tú.
C♯m7/B A E/G♯ F♯m7 B7 E A E Fine
O - pen my eyes, Lord. Help me to see. [To verse 2]
O - pen my ears, Lord. Help me to hear. [To verse 3]
O - pen my heart, Lord. Help me to love. [To verse 4]
A - bre mis o - jos, a - yú - da - me a ver.
A - bre mis o - í - dos, a - yú - da-me a o - ír.
A - bre mi co - ra - zón, a - yú - da-me a a-mar.
Verse 4
E/G♯ A
4 And the first shall be last, and our
4 Da - me la a - le - grí - a de tu
E/G♯ F♯m7 B7sus
eyes are o - pened, and we'll hear like nev-er be -
sal - va - ción, cre - a en mí un co - ra - zón pu -
E A G♯m7
fore. And we'll speak in new ways, and we'll see God's
ro. No me a - rro - jes le - jos de tu ros - tro, Se -
C♯m7 F♯sus F♯7 F♯m7 B7sus
To verse 5
face in plac - es we've nev - er known.
ñor, no me qui - tes tu san - to es - pí - ri - tu.

O Everlasting Love 733

O EVERLASTING LIGHT SM

Capo 1: (G) Ab (C) Db (D) Eb (G) Ab (C) Db (G) Ab
1 O ev - er - last - ing Love, well - spring of
2 O ev - er - last - ing Fount from which the
3 O ev - er - last - ing Health from which all
4 O ev - er - last - ing Rest, lift off life's
5 O ev - er - last - ing Strength, up - hold me
(A7) Bb7 (D) Eb (G) Ab
grace and peace, pour down your full - ness
wa - ters burst, the streams of the e -
heal - ing springs, my bliss, my treas - ure,
load of care! Re - lieve, re - vive this
in the way; bring me, in spite of
(C) Db (G) Ab (D7) Eb7 (G) Ab
from a - bove, bid doubt and trou - ble cease.
ter - nal mount that quench time's sor - est thirst.
and my wealth, to you my spir - it clings.
bur - dened breast, and ev' - ry sor - row bear.
foes, at length to joy, and light, and day!

Text: Horatius Bonar (Scotland), *Hymns of Faith and Hope*, 1861, alt.
Music: Eli S. Hallman (Canada), ca. 20th c.

734 For Those with Whom Our Lives Are Bound

ALL WHO LABOR 8.5.8.5 D with refrain

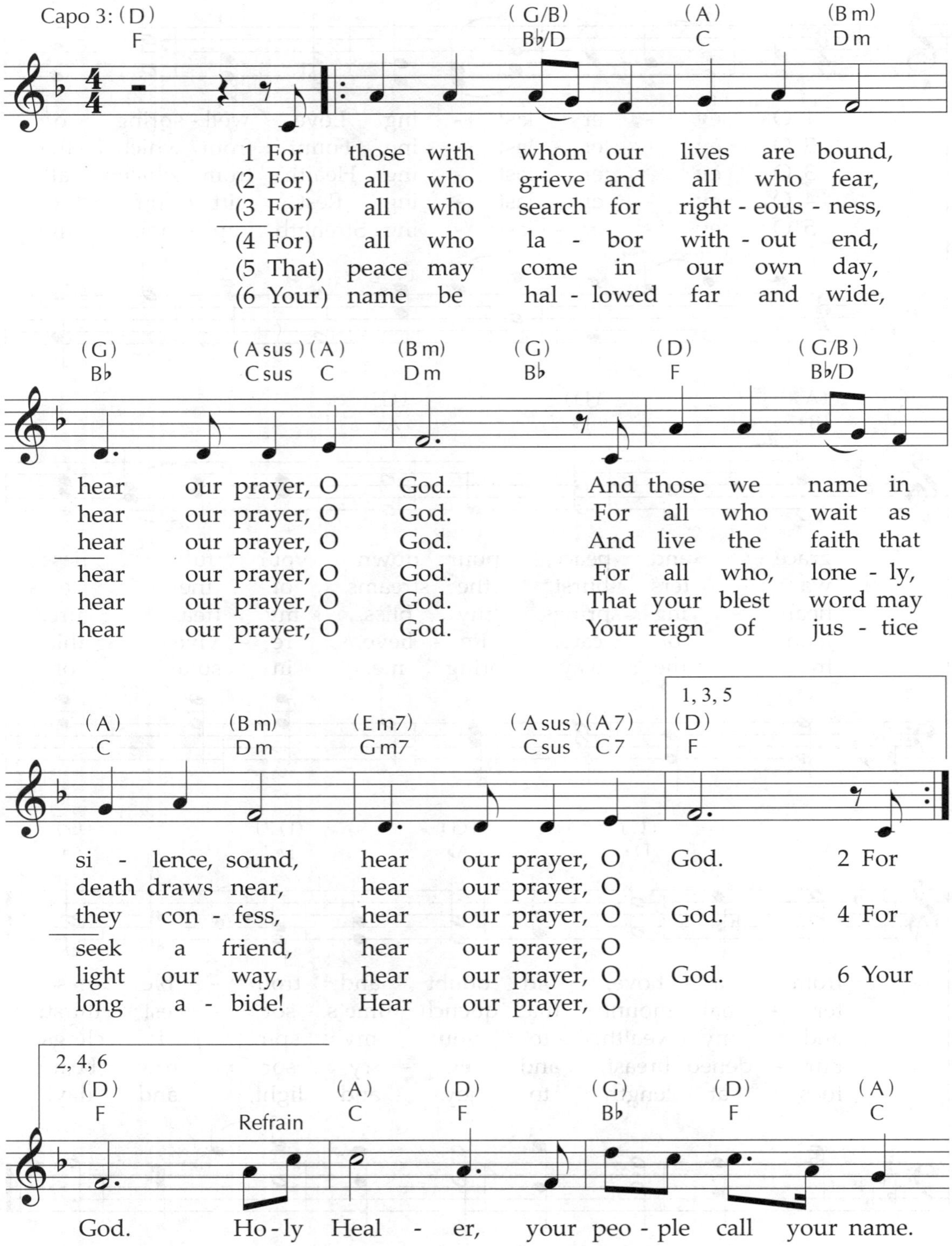
Capo 3: (D) F
1 For those with whom our lives are bound, hear our prayer, O God. And those we name in silence, sound, hear our prayer, O God. 2 For
(2 For) all who grieve and all who fear, hear our prayer, O God. For all who wait as death draws near, hear our prayer, O
(3 For) all who search for right-eous-ness, hear our prayer, O God. And live the faith that they con-fess, hear our prayer, O God. 4 For
(4 For) all who la-bor with-out end, hear our prayer, O God. For all who, lone-ly, seek a friend, hear our prayer, O
(5 That) peace may come in our own day, hear our prayer, O God. That your blest word may light our way, hear our prayer, O God. 6 Your
(6 Your) name be hal-lowed far and wide, hear our prayer, O God. Your reign of jus-tice long a-bide! Hear our prayer, O
1, 3, 5
2, 4, 6
God.
Refrain
Ho-ly Heal-er, your peo-ple call your name.

Text: Ruth Duck (USA)
Music: Mark A. Miller (USA)

(D) F (E7) G7 (A) C (D) F
Send your Spir - it. Hear our prayer. Ho-ly Heal - er, your
(G) B♭ (F♯/A♯) A/C♯ (Bm) Dm (G) B♭ (Asus) Csus (A) C
peo - ple call your name. Send your Spir - it. Hear our
2, 4 (D) F
prayer. 3 For
5 That
6 (Bm) Dm (G) B♭ (Asus) Csus (A) C (D) F
prayer. Send your Spir-it. Hear our prayer.

When We Must Bear Persistent Pain 735

PROSPECT LM

C F Dm Gm B♭ Am C7 Dm F B♭ Dm
1 When we must bear per - sis - tent pain, and suf - fer
2 Sup - port us as we learn new ways to care for
3 We thank you for the bet - ter days when we may
4 In ease or pain, in life and death, to you our
Gm B♭ Am C7 F C7
with no cure in sight, come, Ho - ly Pres - ence,
bod - ies new - ly frail. Help us en - dure and
smile to greet the sun, to do your work with
frag - ile lives be - long, and so we trust you
F Gm Dm F B♭ Gm B♭ Am C7 F
breathe your peace with gifts of warmth and heal - ing light.
live and love. Hear our com - plaint when pa - tience fails.
clear - ing mind, and bless your name when day is done.
in all things. You are our hope, our health, our song.

For capo chords, see the accompaniment edition.

Text: Ruth Duck (USA), 2004, © 2005 GIA Publications, Inc.
Music: Walker's *Southern Harmony* (USA), 1835; harm. David N. Johnson (USA), © 1968 Augsburg Publishing House (admin. Augsburg Fortress)

736 Hold Us in Your Mercy

HOLD US IN YOUR MERCY (Daigle) Irregular

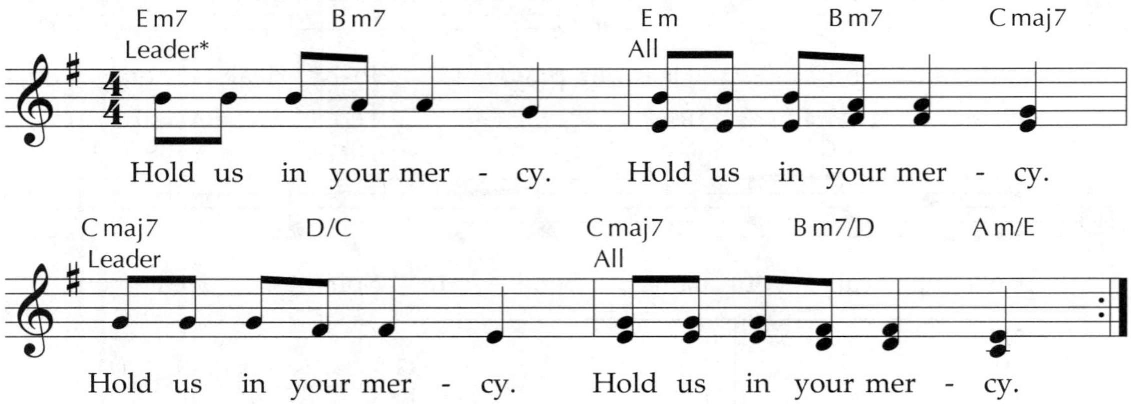
Em7 Bm7 Em Bm7 Cmaj7
Leader*
All
Hold us in your mer - cy. Hold us in your mer - cy.
Cmaj7 D/C Cmaj7 Bm7/D Am/E
Leader
All
Hold us in your mer - cy. Hold us in your mer - cy.

*Stanzas may be found in the accompaniment edition.

Text: Rory Cooney (USA)
Music: Gary Daigle (USA)

737 Breathe on Me, Breath of God

TRENTHAM SM

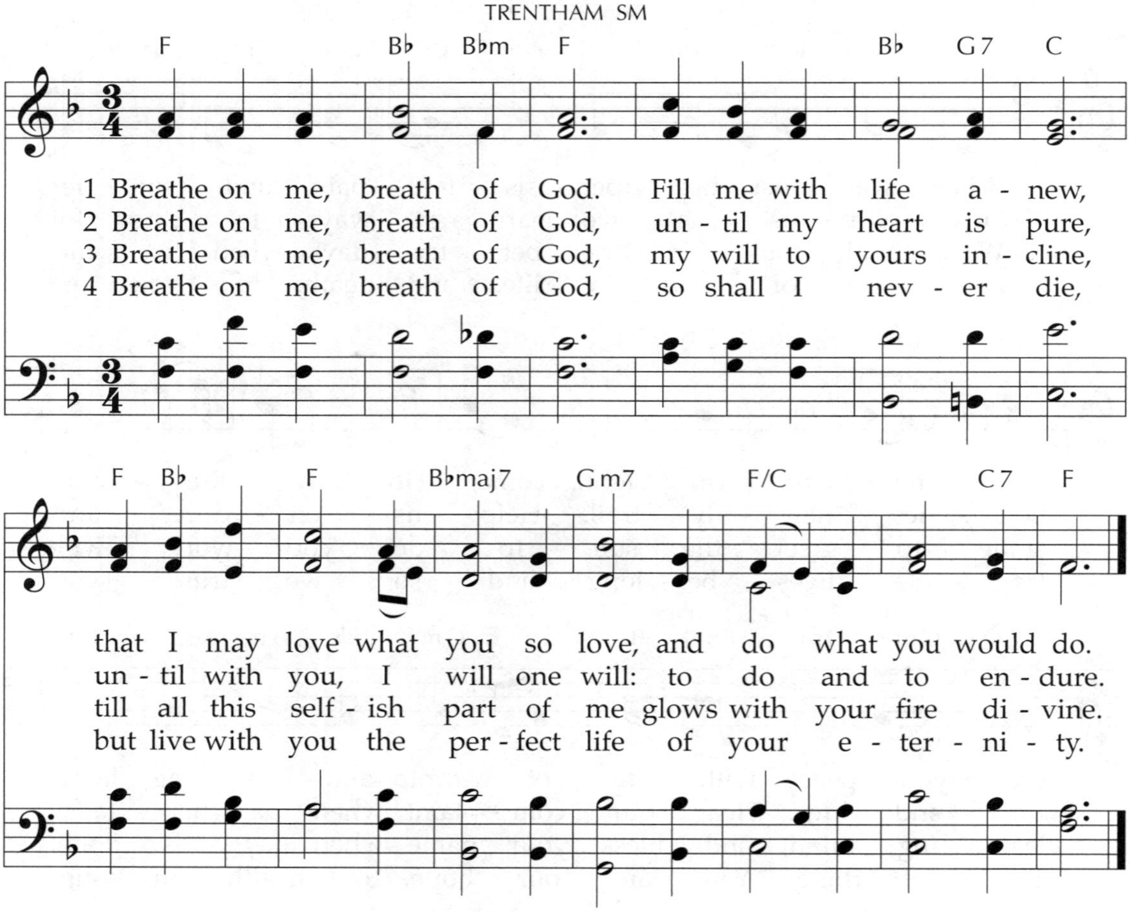
F B♭ B♭m F B♭ G7 C
1 Breathe on me, breath of God. Fill me with life a - new,
2 Breathe on me, breath of God, un - til my heart is pure,
3 Breathe on me, breath of God, my will to yours in - cline,
4 Breathe on me, breath of God, so shall I nev - er die,
F B♭ F B♭maj7 Gm7 F/C C7 F
that I may love what you so love, and do what you would do.
un - til with you, I will one will: to do and to en - dure.
till all this self - ish part of me glows with your fire di - vine.
but live with you the per - fect life of your e - ter - ni - ty.

Text: Edwin Hatch (England), *Between Doubt and Prayer*, 1878, alt.
Music: Robert Jackson (England), *Fifty Sacred Leaflets*, 1888

Open My Eyes That I May See 738

OPEN MY EYES 8.8.9.8.8.8.8.4

Capo 1: (G) Ab (D7) Eb7 (G) Ab
1 O-pen my eyes that I may see glimps-es of truth thou hast for me.
2 O-pen my ears that I may hear voic-es of truth thou send-est clear,
3 O-pen my mouth and let me bear glad-ly the warm truth ev-'ry-where.
(B7) C7 (Em) Fm (B7) C7 (Em) Fm (A7) Bb7
Place in my hands the won-der-ful key that shall un-clasp and
and while the wave notes fall on my ear, ev-'ry-thing false will
O-pen my heart and let me pre-pare love with thy chil-dren
(D) Eb (G) Ab (D7) Eb7
set me free. Si-lent-ly now I wait for thee, read-y, my God, thy
dis-ap-pear. Si-lent-ly now I wait for thee, read-y, my God, thy
thus to share. Si-lent-ly now I wait for thee, read-y, my God, thy
(G) Ab (G7) Ab7 (C) Db (D7) Eb7 (G) Ab
will to see. O-pen my eyes, il-lu-mine me, Spir-it di-vine!
will to see. O-pen my ears, il-lu-mine me, Spir-it di-vine!
will to see. O-pen my mouth, il-lu-mine me, Spir-it di-vine!

Text: Clara H. Scott (USA), *Best Hymns*, No. 2, 1895
Music: Clara H. Scott, *Best Hymns*, No. 2, 1895

739 Herr, füll mich neu (Fill Me Anew)

HERR, FÜLL MICH NEU 4.8.4.8 with refrain

C Am Dm7 G C
1 Herr, füll mich neu, füll mich neu mit dei-nem Gei-ste,
2 Herr, füll mich neu, füll mich neu mit dei-ner Lie-be,
3 Herr, füll mich neu, füll mich neu mit dei-nem Glau-ben,
4 Herr, füll mich neu, füll mich neu mit dei-ner Freu-de,
1 Fill me a-new, fill me with your Ho-ly Spir-it.
2 Fill me a-new, fill me with your lov-ing kind-ness.
3 Fill me a-new, with a con-stant faith a-bid-ing.
4 Fill me a-new, fill me now with joy and glad-ness,
Em Am D G
der mich be-lebt und zu dir, mein Gott, hin-zie-het!
die bei dir bleibt und mit Freu-den Las-ten trä-get!
der auf dich schaut und in an-dern Glau-ben we-cket!
die ü-ber-strömt und in Lob und Preis dich rüh-met!
God, you give life, and you draw me to your pres-ence.
Those who stay close car-ry joy-ful-ly their bur-dens.
Look-ing to you will a-wak-en faith in oth-ers.
so that my heart o-ver-flows with joy-ous prais-es!
Refrain
C Am E Am D G D7 G
Hier bin ich vor dir. Leer sind mei-ne Hän-de.
Here be-fore you now; see, my hands are emp-ty.

Text: German; Jesus-Bruderschaft, Gnadenthal (Germany); trans. Jean Janzen (USA), Kenneth Nafziger (USA), and Randall Spaulding (USA), 2006, rev. 2019, trans. © 2006 Jean Janzen, Kenneth Nafziger, and Randall Spaulding

Music: Jesus-Bruderschaft, Gnadenthal; harm. Klaus Heizmann (Germany), 2004, harm. © Haus der Musik, Wiesbaden, Germany

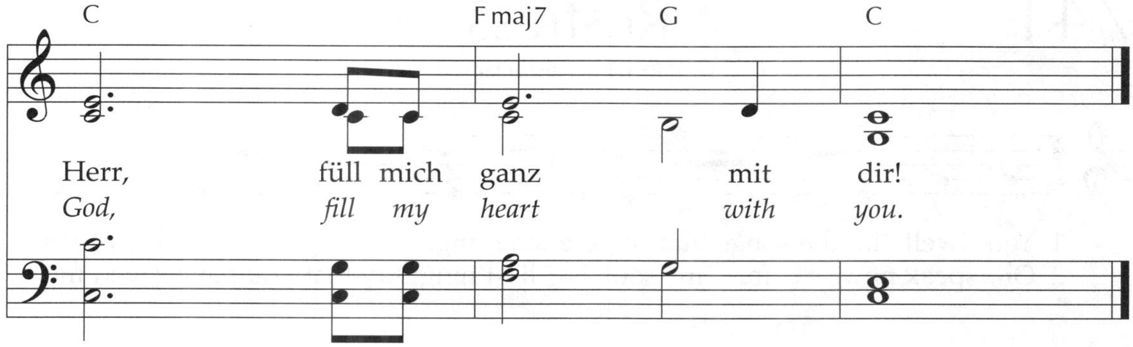
C
Fmaj7
G
C
Herr, füll mich ganz mit dir!
God, fill my heart with you.

Spirit of the Living God 740

IVERSON Irregular

Capo 3:
(D) F
(A7) C7
(D) F
(A) C
(D) F
Spir - it of the liv-ing God, fall a-fresh on me. Spir - it of the
(A7) C7
(D) F
(A7) C7
(D) F
(G) B♭
(D) F
(Bm) Dm
(E7) G7
liv-ing God, fall a-fresh on me. Melt me, mold me, fill me,
(A) C
(A7) C7
(D) F
(Em) Gm
(D/A) F/C
(Em7) Gm7
(A7) C7
(D) F
use me. Spir - it of the liv - ing God, fall a-fresh on me.

Text: Daniel Iverson (USA), *Revival Songs*, 1929
Music: Daniel Iverson, *Revival Songs*, 1929; arr. Herbert G. Tovey (USA)

741 Restless

RESTLESS Irregular

C2
C2/B
Am7
1 You dwell in the songs that we are sing-ing, ris-ing to the heav-ens,
2 Oh, speak now, for my soul is lis-t'ning; say that you have saved me,
Em
G
C2
ris - ing to your heart, your heart. Our prais - es, fill - ing up the
whis-per in the dark, the dark. 'Cause I know you're more than my sal-
C2/B
Am7
spac - es in be-tween our frail - ty and ev - 'ry - thing you
va - tion; with-out you I am hope - less. Tell me who you
Em
G
Dm7
Am7
Gsus
are. You are the keep - er of my heart. And I'm
are. You are the keep - er of my heart.
Refrain
C2
Dm7
C2/E
F2
rest - less; I'm rest - less till I rest in you, till I
Am7
G
C2
Dm7
rest in you. I am rest - less; I'm rest - less till I
C2/E
F2
1, 3
Am7
G
C2
Last time
rest in you, till I rest in you. O God.

Text: Audrey Assad (USA) and Matt Maher (Canada)
Music: Audrey Assad and Matt Maher

2
Am7 G Fmaj9 C2/E Fmaj9
rest in you. Oh.
Bridge
Am7 Gsus/B Fmaj9 C2/E Fmaj9
Oh, still my heart, hold me close; let me hear a
Am7 Gsus/B Fmaj9 C2/E Fmaj9
still, small voice. Let it grow; let it rise in - to a shout, in -
1
Am7 Gsus/B
2
Am7 Gsus/B F2
To refrain
to a cry. Oh, to a cry. And I am

Way way way

742

WAY WAY WAY Irregular

Way way way way way. Way way way way
way. Way way way way way.

Other traditional prayers may be used, such as "Alleluia," "Christ have mercy," "Kyrie eleison," or "Holy Spirit, come."

Text: Ojibwe traditional (Red Lake Nation, USA), *Chippewa Music*, 1913; additional phrases as suggested by Mark MacDonald (First Nations, Canada), as sung in Ojibwe communities (Minnesota, USA)
Music: traditional Ojibwe lullaby; transcr. Frances Densmore (USA), *Chippewa Music*, 1913

743 Just a Closer Walk with Thee

CLOSER WALK Irregular

Capo 3: (G) B♭ (Am7) Cm7 (D) F (D7) F7
1, 5 Just a clos - er walk with thee, grant it,
2 I am weak but thou art strong: Je - sus,
3 Through this world of toil and snares, if I
4 When my fee - ble life is o'er, time for
(G) B♭ (G7) B♭7
Je - sus, is my plea; dai - ly walk-ing close to
keep me from all wrong; I'll be sat - is - fied as
fal - ter, Lord, who cares? Who with me my bur - den
me will be no more; guide me gen - tly, safe - ly
(C) E♭ (A♯dim7) C♯dim7 (G/D) B♭/F (D7) F7 (G) B♭
thee, let it be, dear Lord, let it be.
long as I walk, let me walk close to thee.
shares? None but thee, dear Lord, none but thee.
o'er to thy king - dom shore, to thy shore.

Text: African American traditional (USA), ca. 20th c.
Music: African American traditional, ca. 20th c.; acc. David Berry (USA), 2019

Shepherd Me, O God

744

SHEPHERD ME Irregular

Capo 1: (Em) (C) (G) (D)
Refrain
Fm Db Ab Eb
Shep-herd me, O God, be - yond my wants, be -
Shep-herd me be - yond my wants, be -
(Bm7) (C) (Am7) (Bm7) (Em) (Am/E) (Em)
Cm7 Db Bbm7 Cm7 Fm Bbm/F Fm
yond my fears, from death in - to life.
yond my fears, from death to life.

1 God is my shepherd, so nothing shall I want,
I rest in the meadows of faithfulness and love,
I walk by the quiet waters of peace. *Refrain*

2 Gently you raise me and heal my weary soul,
you lead me by pathways of righteousness and truth;
my spirit shall sing the music of your name. *Refrain*

3 Though I should wander the valley of death,
I fear no evil, for you are at my side,
your rod and your staff, my comfort and my hope. *Refrain*

4 You have set me a banquet of love in the face of hatred,
crowning me with love beyond my power to hold. *Refrain*

5 Surely your kindness and mercy follow me
all the days of my life;
I will dwell in the house of my God forevermore. *Refrain*

Text: based on Psalm 23; Marty Haugen (USA), 1985, *Gather*, 1988
Music: Marty Haugen, *Gather*, 1988

745 God, Whose Giving

HYFRYDOL 8.7.8.7 D

F C F Gm/F C F C
1 God, whose giv - ing knows no end - ing from your
2 Skills and time are ours for press - ing toward the
3 Trea - sure, too, you have en - trust - ed, gain through
F Gm/B♭ C F C F Gm/F
rich and end - less store— na - ture's won - der, Je - sus'
goals of Christ your Son: all at peace in health and
pow'rs your grace con-ferred— ours to use for home and
C F C F Gm/B♭ C F
wis - dom, cost - ly cross, grave's shat - tered door—
free - dom, ra - ces joined, the church made one.
kin - dred, and to spread the gos - pel word.
Am Dm7 Gm7 C7 F
gift - ed by you, we turn to you, of - f'ring
Now di - rect our dai - ly la - bor, lest we
O - pen wide our hands in shar - ing, as we

For capo chords, see #218.

Text: Robert L. Edwards (USA), *Ten New Stewardship Hymns*, 1961,
Music: Rowland H. Prichard (Wales), ca. 1830, *Cyfaill y Cantorion*, 1844; arr. Ralph Vaughan Williams (England), *The English Hymnal*, 1906; adapt. 1951, *BBC Hymn Book*,

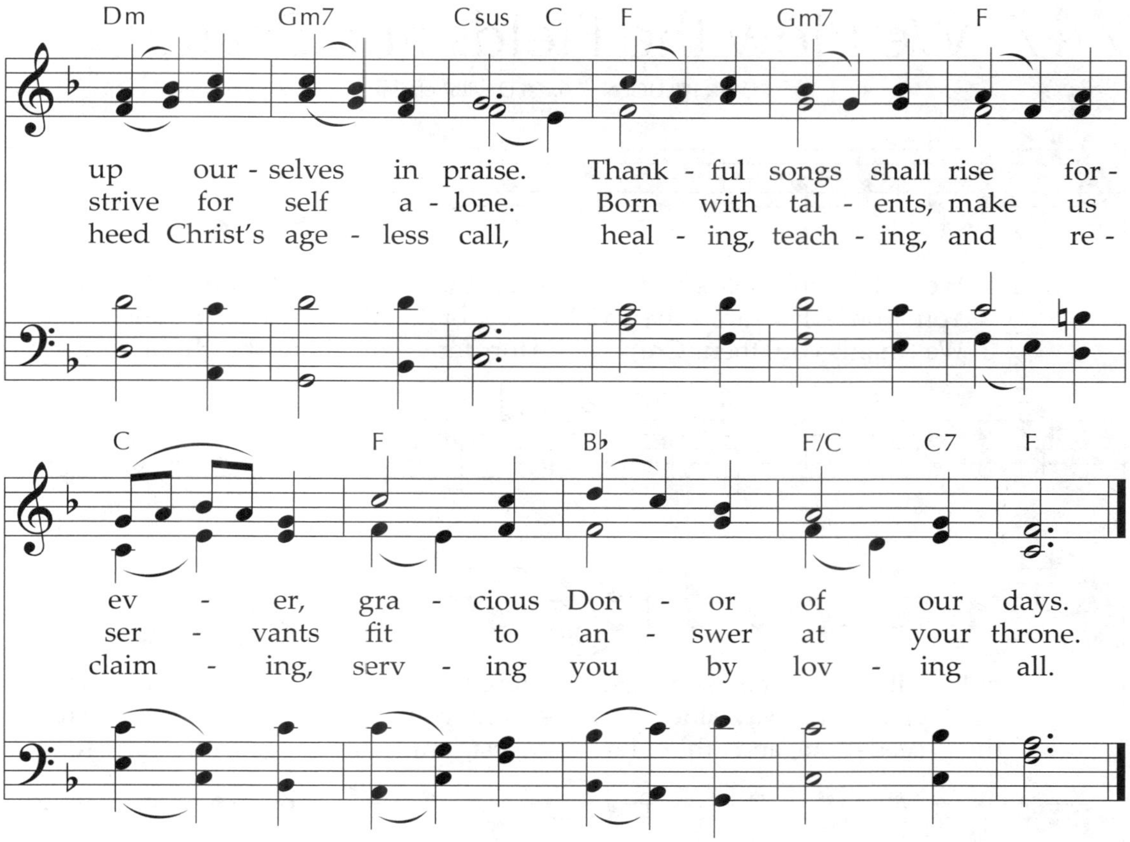
Dm Gm7 Csus C F Gm7 F
up our - selves in praise. Thank - ful songs shall rise for -
strive for self a - lone. Born with tal - ents, make us
heed Christ's age - less call, heal - ing, teach - ing, and re -
C F B♭ F/C C7 F
ev - er, gra - cious Don - or of our days.
ser - vants fit to an - swer at your throne.
claim - ing, serv - ing you by lov - ing all.

Grant Us, God, the Grace 746

STUTTGART 8.7.8.7

G Em D G C D G
Grant us, God, the grace of giv - ing with a spir - it large and free,
Em B Em D G D7 G
that our - selves and all our liv - ing we may of - fer un - to thee.

Chord symbols represent a simplified harmony.

Text: Robert Murray (Canada), from "Lord, Thou Lov'st the Cheerful Giver," *Hymnal of the Presbyterian Church in Canada*, 1880, alt.
Music: attr. Christian Friedrich Witt (present-day Germany), *Psalmodia Sacra*, 1715; adapt. Henry J. Gauntlett (England), *Hymns Ancient and Modern*, 1861

747 We Plow the Fields and Scatter

WIR PFLÜGEN 7.6.7.6 D with refrain

1 We plow the fields and scat - ter the good seed on the land,
2 You on - ly are the Mak - er of all things near and far.
3 We thank you, then, Cre - a - tor, for all things bright and good,
but it is fed and wa - tered by God's al - might - y hand.
You paint the way-side flow - er, you light the eve - ning star.
the seed-time, and the har - vest, our life, our health, our food.
God sends the snow in win - ter, the warmth to swell the grain,
The winds and waves o - bey you, by you the birds are fed;
Ac - cept the gifts we of - fer for all your love im - parts,
the breez - es, and the sun - shine, and soft re - fresh - ing rain.
much more to us, your chil - dren, you give our dai - ly bread.
and what you most would wel - come: our hum - ble, thank - ful hearts.

Text: Matthias Claudius (present-day Germany), *Wir pflügen und wir streuen, Fest*, 1782; trans. Jane M. Campbell (England), *Garland of Song*, 1861, alt.
Music: attr. Johann A. P. Schulz (present-day Germany), *Lieder für Volksschulen mit Musik*, 1800

Refrain
All good gifts a - round us are sent from heav'n a - bove.
We thank you, God, we thank you, God, for all your love.

Take, O Take Me as I Am 748

GIVING 7.7.7.4

Capo 1: (C) (F/C) (Dm/C) (G/C) (C) (F/A)
D♭ G♭/D♭ E♭m/D♭ A♭/D♭ D♭ G♭/B♭
Take, O take me as I am; sum-mon out what I shall
(Gsus) (G) (F) (G/F) (C/E) (Am) (Dm7) (Gsus) (G)
A♭sus A♭ G♭ A♭/G♭ D♭/F B♭m E♭m7 A♭sus A♭
be; set your seal up-on my heart and live in me.

Text: John L. Bell (Scotland)
Music: John L. Bell

749 Jesus Christ Is Love Divine

JESUS CHRIST IS LOVE DIVINE 7.7.7.7 with refrain

G D/A A7sus D
D A Bm
1 Je - sus Christ is love di - vine,
2 By God's grace, love finds our heart;
3 In our weak-ness, love per - sists.
4 We give thanks for all the ways
Em D A D A Bm
love a - live e - ter - nal - ly. Mea-sure-less in space and time,
we re-ceive it grate-ful - ly. Yet the love that we im-part
In our fail-ures, love re-stores. Love in-vites when we re - sist.
love is shap-ing us to - day. Hum-bly we re - turn our praise:
Em D A D
Refrain
G D
be - yond words, a mys - ter - y.
re - flects back im - per - fect - ly.
We build walls; love o - pens doors.
ev - 'ry - thing we do and say.
When we love, we
F♯ Bm G D A D
move with Christ; love in us has come a - live.

Text: based on the writings of Pilgram Marpeck (present-day Germany), 16th c.; Nathan Grieser (USA), 2019
Music: Nathan Grieser, 2019

750 God of the Fertile Fields

ITALIAN HYMN 6.6.4.6.6.6.4

G Am D G D7
1 God of the fer - tile fields, shap-er of earth that yields
2 We would be stew - ards true, hold-ing in trust from you
3 As grows the hid - den seed to fruit that serves our need,
4 God of the coun - try-side, dear to the Christ who died

Text: Georgia Harkness (USA), *Fourteen New Rural Hymns,* 1955, alt., © 1955, renewed 1983 The Hymn Society (admin. Hope Publishing Co.)
Music: Felice de Giardini (England), *Collection of Psalm and Hymn Tunes,* 1769

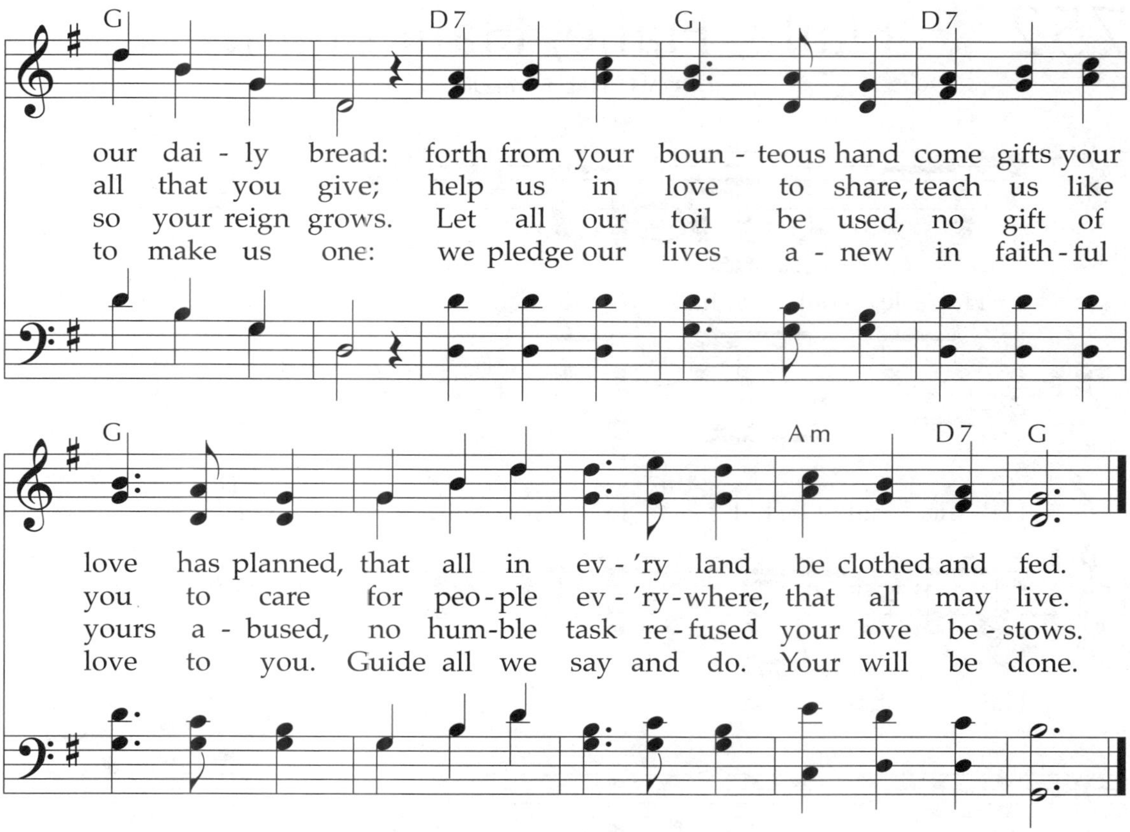
G D7 G D7
our dai - ly bread: forth from your boun - teous hand come gifts your
all that you give; help us in love to share, teach us like
so your reign grows. Let all our toil be used, no gift of
to make us one: we pledge our lives a - new in faith - ful
G Am D7 G
love has planned, that all in ev - 'ry land be clothed and fed.
you to care for peo - ple ev - 'ry - where, that all may live.
yours a - bused, no hum - ble task re - fused your love be - stows.
love to you. Guide all we say and do. Your will be done.

There Is in Every Person 751

REGINALDA 7.6.4.4.4.4.8.4

Capo 3: (Em) Gm (Bm/D) Dm/F (C) E♭ (G/B) B♭/D
1 There is in ev - 'ry per - son ca - pa - ci - ty for love.
2 There is in ev - 'ry per - son ca - pa - ci - ty for grace.
3 There is in ev - 'ry per - son ca - pa - ci - ty for trust.
4 There is in ev - 'ry per - son ca - pa - ci - ty for hope.
(C) E♭ (G/B) B♭/D (C) E♭ (D) F
If not to give, then to re - ceive. If not to grasp, then to be - lieve.
(D/F♯) F/A (G) B♭ (D) F (Bsus) Dsus (B) D (C) E♭ (Dsus) Fsus (Em) Gm
God's im - age marks each one of us, and God is love.
God's mer - cy seeks each one of us and of - fers grace.
God's sto - ry shapes each one of us and teach - es trust.
God's vi - sion calls each one of us and leads to hope.

Text: Adam M. L. Tice (USA), © 2015 GIA Publications, Inc.
Music: Benjamin Brody (USA), 2015, © 2017 GIA Publications, Inc.

752 Halle, Halle, Hallelujah!

HALLE HALLE Irregular

G D G D/F♯ Em
Hal - le, hal - le, hal - le - lu - jah!
C Am7 D
Hal - le, hal - le, hal - le - lu - jah!
Hal - le, hal - le, hal - le - lu, hal - le - lu - jah!
Hal - le, hal - le, hal - le - lu - jah!
G D G D/F♯ Em
Hal - le, hal - le, hal - le - lu - jah! Hal - le -
To repeat
Last time
Am G/D D7 G C/G G Am/G G
Hal - le - lu - jah! jah!
lu - jah! Hal - le - lu, hal - le - lu - jah! jah!
Hal - le - lu - jah! jah!

Text: Hebrew traditional; הַלְלוּ יָהּ (Hallelujah) (Mediterranean), ca. 4th c. BC
Music: Caribbean traditional; arr. John L. Bell (Scotland),

तन मन धन प्रभू तव चरणी 753

Tana mana dhana prabhū tava caraṇī (Heart and Mind, Possessions, God)

TANA MANA DHANA Irregular

1 Ta - na ma - na dha - na pra - bhū ta - va ca - ra - ṇī.
2 Ta - na ma - na dha - na pra - bhū ta - va ca - ra - ṇī.
1 Heart and mind, pos - ses - sions, God, I of - fer un - to you;
2 Heart and mind, pos - ses - sions, God, I of - fer un - to you;
Sa - ka - la tu - jhē hē tū - ci di - lē - sī
Śa - ra - ṇā - ga - ta mī pa - ti - ta tu - lā gā
all these were yours, God, and you gave them all to me.
you are the way, the truth, you are the life.
a - gha - ṭi - ta ta - va ka - ra - ṇī. Bē - ta vi - cā - ra - hī
ja - ya dē bha - va ta - ra - ṇī. Mā - jhē hē tē
Won - drous are the gifts you give to me. Plans and my thoughts and
Sin - ful, I com - mit my - self to you. Je - sus Christ is fill - ing
ha - ra ma - ma ka - ra - ṇē av - a - lam - bē ic -
mī - ca mi - ḷa - vi - lē sa - ma - ja - ta - sē a - bhi -
ev - 'ry - thing I ev - er do are de - pend - ent on your
all my heart and soul. He can give me vic - t'ry o'er
chē - va - ra ta - va bā ka - ri - tō ma - na - dha - ra - ṇī.
mā - nē pūr - vī ā - tā khē - da ma - nī.
will and love a - lone. I com - mit my spir - it un - to you.
all that threat - ens me. Je - sus Christ is fill - ing all my heart.

1 तन मन धन प्रभू तव चरणी
सकल तुझे हे तूचि दिलेसी
अघटित तव करणी
बेत विचारही हर मम करणे
अवलंबे इच्छेवर तव बा
करितो मनधरणी

2 तन मन धन प्रभू तव चरणी
शरणागत मी पतित तुला गा
जय दे भव तरणी
माझे हे ते मीच मिळविले
समजतसे अभिमाने पूर्वी
आता खेद मनी

Text: Marathi; Krishnarao Rathnaji Sangle (India), 19th c.; trans. Alden H. Clark (USA)
Music: Indian traditional; adapt. Marion Jean Chute (USA), alt.

754 In My Life, Lord, Be Glorified

LORD BE GLORIFIED Irregular

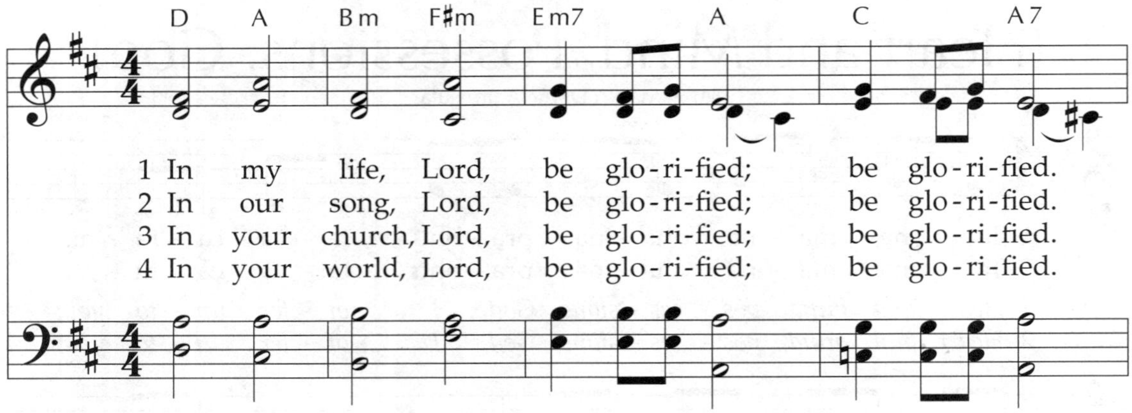
D A Bm F♯m Em7 A C A7
1 In my life, Lord, be glo-ri-fied; be glo-ri-fied.
2 In our song, Lord, be glo-ri-fied; be glo-ri-fied.
3 In your church, Lord, be glo-ri-fied; be glo-ri-fied.
4 In your world, Lord, be glo-ri-fied; be glo-ri-fied.

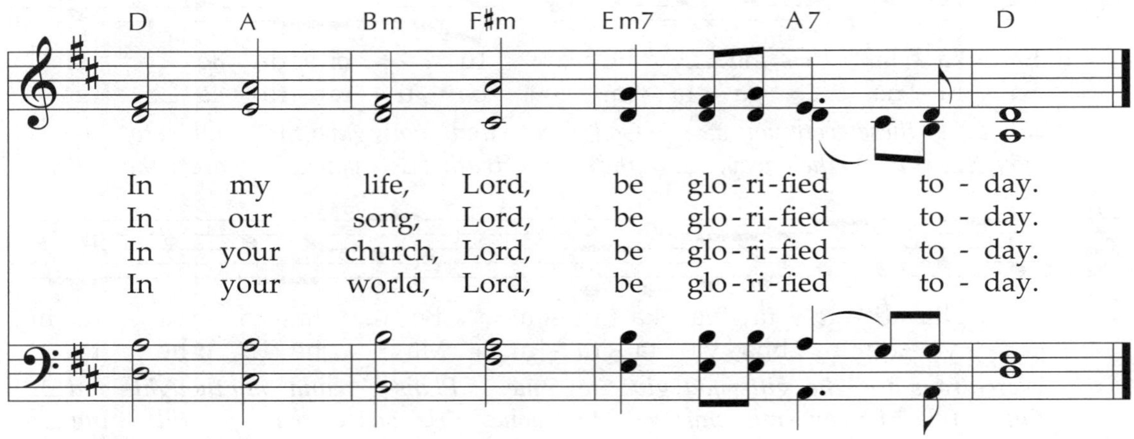
D A Bm F♯m Em7 A7 D
In my life, Lord, be glo-ri-fied to - day.
In our song, Lord, be glo-ri-fied to - day.
In your church, Lord, be glo-ri-fied to - day.
In your world, Lord, be glo-ri-fied to - day.

Text: Bob Kilpatrick (USA), 1978
Music: Bob Kilpatrick

755 내게 있는 향유 옥합 Naege itneun hyangyu (To My Precious Lord)

TO MY PRECIOUS LORD Irregular

Refrain
D A/C♯ Bm F♯m G Em E7 A
내 게 있 는 향 유 옥 합 주 께 가 져 와
Nae - ge it - neun hyang - yu ok - hap ju - kke ga - jyeo wa
To my pre - cious Lord I bring my flask of fra - grant oil;

Text: Korean; Chung Kwan Park (Korea); English trans. Edward Poitras (USA), rev. Mary Louise Bringle (USA), 2011, English trans.
Music: Chung Kwan Park; arr. Paul Junggap Huh (USA) and Alfred V. Fedak (USA), 2012

D A/C♯ Bm F♯m G A D
그 발 위 에 입 맞 추 고 깨 뜨 립 니 다
Geu bal we - ae ip ma - chu - go kkae - tteu - rip - ni - da
kneel - ing down, I kiss his feet, a - noint them with the oil.
D F♯m Bm F♯m Em E7 A
1 Je - sus, who for my sake walked the road to Cal - va - ry,
2 Je - sus, who for my sake had his feet nailed to the cross,
3 When in clouds of glo - ry you come back to earth a - gain,
D A/C♯ Bm F♯m G A D
with each step has marked the im - print of his love for me.
with his blood has washed and healed me, paid the heav - y cost.
Je - sus, with your love em - brace and claim me as your friend.

1 나를 위해 험한 산 길
오르신 그 발
걸음 마다 크신 사랑
새겨 놓았네

2 나를 위해 십자가에
달리신 그 발
흘린 피로 나의 죄를
대속 하셨네

3 주님 다시 이 땅 위에
임하실 그 때
주의 크신 사랑으로
날 받아 주소서

1 Nareul wihae heomhan san gil
oreushin geu bal
Georeum mada keushin sarang
saegyeo nohatneh

2 Nareul wihae shipjagaeh
dallishin geu bal
Heullin piro naeh joehreul
daesok hashutneh

3 Junim dashi ee ttang wieh
imhasil geu ttae
Jueh keushin sarangeuro
nal bada jusoseo

756 God, We Pause This Moment

WEM IN LEIDENSTAGEN 6.5.6.5

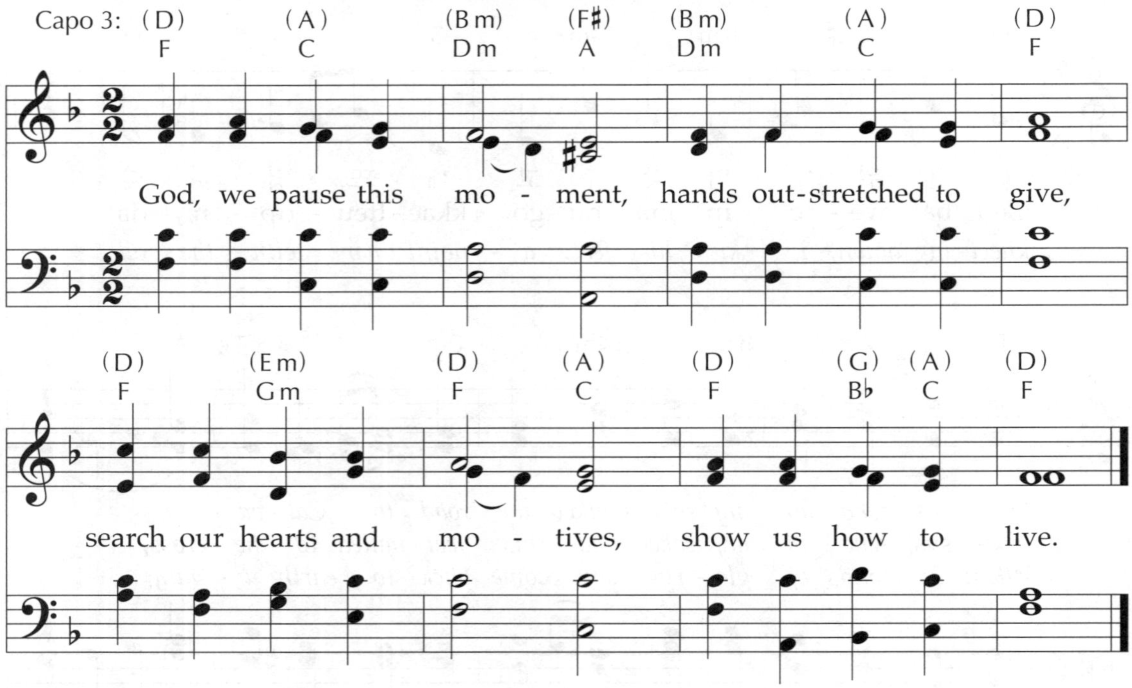
Capo 3: (D) (A) (Bm) (F♯) (Bm) (A) (D)
F C Dm A Dm C F
God, we pause this mo - ment, hands out-stretched to give,
(D) (Em) (D) (A) (D) (G) (A) (D)
F Gm F C F B♭ C F
search our hearts and mo - tives, show us how to live.

Text: Merle Good (USA), © 2018 Merle Good
Music: Friedrich Filitz (Germany), *Vierstimmiges Choralbuch*, 1847

757 There's Enough for All

ENOUGH FOR ALL Irregular

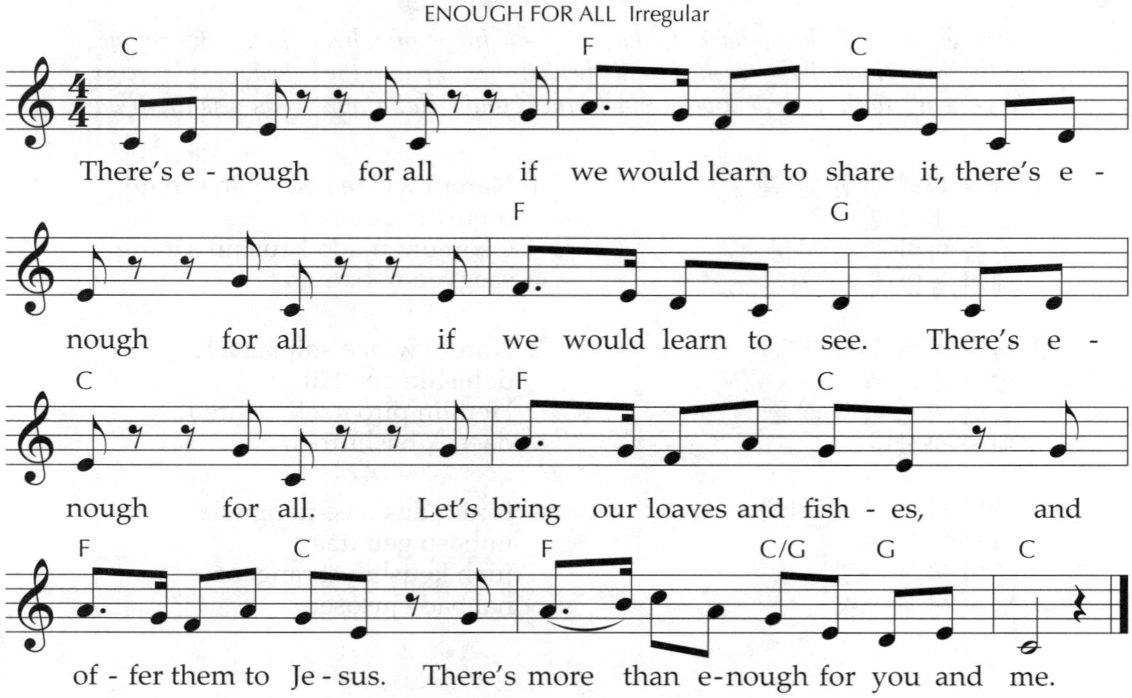
C F C
There's e - nough for all if we would learn to share it, there's e -
F G
nough for all if we would learn to see. There's e -
C F C
nough for all. Let's bring our loaves and fish - es, and
F C F C/G G C
of - fer them to Je - sus. There's more than e-nough for you and me.

Text: Bryan Moyer Suderman (Canada)
Music: Bryan Moyer Suderman; acc. Charlene Nafziger (Canada), 2008

Who Will Speak a Word of Warning 758

CHURCH UNITED 8.7.8.7 D

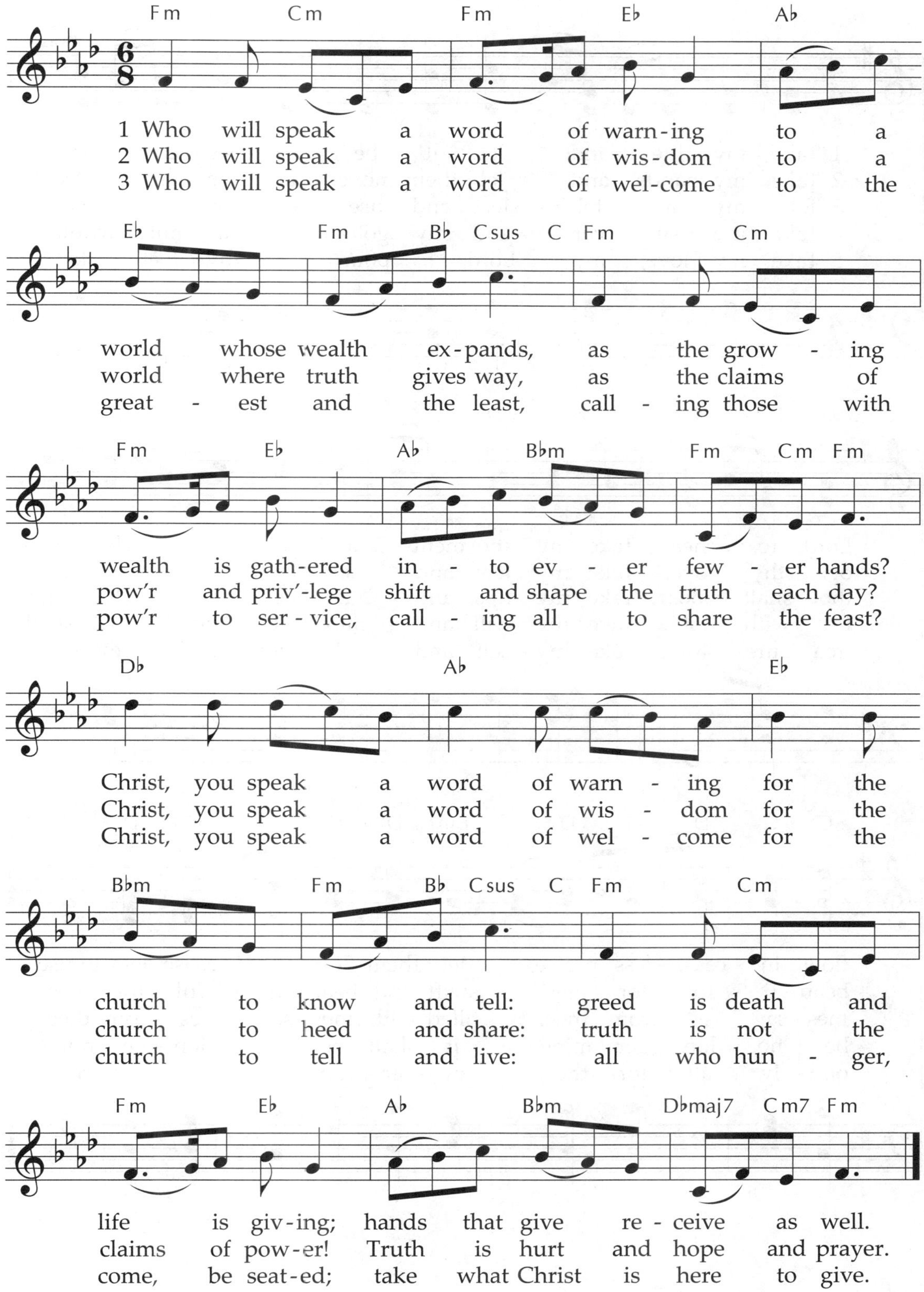
Fm Cm Fm E♭ A♭
1 Who will speak a word of warn-ing to a
2 Who will speak a word of wis-dom to a
3 Who will speak a word of wel-come to the
E♭ Fm B♭ Csus C Fm Cm
world whose wealth ex-pands, as the grow - ing
world where truth gives way, as the claims of
great - est and the least, call - ing those with
Fm E♭ A♭ B♭m Fm Cm Fm
wealth is gath-ered in - to ev - er few - er hands?
pow'r and priv'-lege shift and shape the truth each day?
pow'r to ser - vice, call - ing all to share the feast?
D♭ A♭ E♭
Christ, you speak a word of warn - ing for the
Christ, you speak a word of wis - dom for the
Christ, you speak a word of wel - come for the
B♭m Fm B♭ Csus C Fm Cm
church to know and tell: greed is death and
church to heed and share: truth is not the
church to tell and live: all who hun - ger,
Fm E♭ A♭ B♭m D♭maj7 Cm7 Fm
life is giv-ing; hands that give re - ceive as well.
claims of pow-er! Truth is hurt and hope and prayer.
come, be seat-ed; take what Christ is here to give.

For capo chords, see the accompaniment edition.

Text: Richard Leach (USA), © 2000 Selah Publishing Co., Inc.
Music: Alfred V. Fedak (USA), 1988, © 1989 Selah Publishing Co., Inc.

759 Take My Life, and Let It Be

HENDON 7.7.7.7 extended

G D G Em C Am
1 Take my life, and let it be con - se - crat - ed,
2 Take my hands, and let them move at the im - pulse
3 Take my in - tel - lect and use ev - 'ry pow'r as
4 Take my sil - ver and my gold; not a mite would
5 Take my love; my Lord, I pour at thy feet its
G D7 G D G
Lord, to thee. Take my mo-ments and my days; let them
of thy love. Take my feet, and let them be swift and
thou shalt choose. Take my lips, and let them be filled with
I with - hold. Take my will and make it thine; it shall
trea - sure store. Take my - self, and I will be ev - er,
C G D G D Em D G C G/D D G
flow in cease - less praise, let them flow in cease - less praise.
beau - ti - ful for thee, swift and beau - ti - ful for thee.
mes - sag - es from thee, filled with mes - sag - es from thee.
be no lon - ger mine, it shall be no lon - ger mine.
on - ly, all for thee, ev - er, on - ly, all for thee.

Text: Frances R. Havergal (England), *Songs of Grace and Glory*, Appendix, 1874
Music: Henri Abraham César Malan (Switzerland), 1827; harm. Lowell Mason (USA), *Carmina Sacra*, 1841

Take My Life, That I May Be (Que mi vida entera esté) 760

TOMA MI VOLUNTAD 7.7.7.7 with refrain

Refrain
E A B7
Take my life, that I may be con-se-crat-ed, God,
To-ma, oh Dios, mi vo-lun-tad, y haz-la tu-ya, na-
E A
to thee. Take my mo-ments and my days;
-da más; to-ma, sí, mi co-ra-zón
B7 E To verses Last time A B E
let them flow in cease-less praise.
y tu tro-no en él ten-drás.
A B7
1 Take my hands, and let them move at the
2 Take my sil-ver and my gold; not a
3 Take my will, and make it thine; it shall
1 Que mi vi-da en-te-ra es-té con-sa-
2 Que mis ma-nos pue-dan dar el im-
3 Que mis bie-nes o-fren-dar se-pa
E
im-pulse of thy love. Take my feet, and let
mite would I with-hold. Take my love; my God,
be no lon-ger mine. Take my heart, it is
gra-da a ti, Se-ñor; Que mis dí-as al
pul-so de tu a-mor; que mis pies al ca-
siem-pre a ti, Se-ñor; y mi a-mor a ti
A B7 E B7 To refrain
them be swift and beau-ti-ful for thee.
I pour at thy feet its trea-sure store.
thine own, it shall be thy roy-al throne.
co-rrer ma-ni-fies-ten tu lo-or.
-mi-nar lle-ven siem-pre ben-di-ción.
lo doy, mi te-so-ro, lo que soy.

Text: Frances R. Havergal (England), *Songs of Grace and Glory*, Appendix, 1874; Spanish trans. Vicente Mendoza (Mexico), *El Nuevo Himnario Evangélico*, 1914, alt.

Music: William Dexheimer-Pharris (USA); arr. Mark Sedio (USA),

761 I Love to Tell the Story

HANKEY 7.6.7.6 D with refrain

A♭ D♭ A♭
1 I love to tell the sto - ry of un - seen things a - bove:
2 I love to tell the sto - ry. 'Tis pleas - ant to re - peat
3 I love to tell the sto - ry, for those who know it best
E♭7 A♭ E♭
of Je - sus and his glo - ry, of Je - sus and his love.
what seems, each time I tell it, more won - der - ful - ly sweet.
seem hun - ger - ing and thirst - ing to hear it, like the rest.
E♭7 A♭ Fm C
I love to tell the sto - ry be - cause I know 'tis true.
I love to tell the sto - ry, for some have nev - er heard
And when, in scenes of glo - ry, I sing the new, new song,
D♭ A♭ E♭7 A♭
It sat - is - fies my long - ings as noth - ing else could do.
the mes - sage of sal - va - tion from God's own ho - ly word.
'twill be the old, old sto - ry that I have loved so long.

Text: Catherine Hankey (England), 1866, *Joyful Songs Nos. 1–3 Combined*, 1869
Music: William G. Fischer (USA), *Joyful Songs Nos. 1–3 Combined*, 1869

Refrain
E♭ A♭ D♭ A♭
I love to tell the sto - ry, 'twill be my theme in glo - ry,
D♭ A♭ E♭7 A♭
to tell the old, old sto - ry of Je - sus and his love.

This Little Light of Mine 762

THIS LITTLE LIGHT OF MINE (civil rights song) Irregular

Swing:
G
This lit - tle light of mine, I'm gon - na let it shine!
C G
This lit - tle light of mine, I'm gon - na let it shine!
Em
This lit - tle light of mine, I'm gon - na let it shine!
G D G
Let it shine, let it shine, let it shine!

Additional stanzas:

Everywhere I go, I'm gonna let it shine!
Jesus gave it to me . . .
Shine, shine, shine . . .

Text: African American traditional (USA), ca. 20th c.
Music: African American traditional, ca. 20th c.

763 Waterfall

WATERFALL Irregular

O my Sav - ior, I give you glo - ry, my Re -
deem - er, my God and Friend. There is no one, oh so
ho - ly, and this love will nev - er end.
Fine
1 I can't think of an-y-where, an-y-where I would want to be more
2 See the pow'r of e-vil in - jus - tice: cap - tive peo - ple,
3 I am here to speak a mes - sage, tell the truth that will
than with you. I can't think of an - y - thing, an-y-thing
fam - 'lies, and dreams. See the cit - y in the des - ert,
set you free. I pro - claim, "Free - dom to the cap - tives,
I would rath - er do than give you glo - ry. Come, my Sav - ior,
va - cant now with - out a stream. God will come
free-dom to you in Je - sus' name!" By the pow - er
on the clouds; Ho - ly Spir - it, speed the hour.
in a whis - per; love and hope the wa - ter God brings.
of the Spir - it, com - fort comes to the peo - ple who mourn.
I will shout out loud the mes - sage:
Watch the stream be - come a riv - er
In the Ju - bi - lee that's ris - ing,

Text: Jonathan Reuel (USA), 1995, 2013, rev. 2019
Music: Jonathan Reuel; acc. Anneli Loepp Thiessen (Canada)

C G
"Free - dom is com - ing and the mo - ment is now."
bring - ing life where death has been.
good news comes to the suf - fer - ing poor.
Bm G D
Let your rain come down all a - round. Let the thun - der
A Bm G
sound, shake the ground. Let the wa - ter - fall pound, break - ing down
D A Bm
all the lies you found un - der me. Let the sight - less
G D A
see, let them see. Set the bound ones free, set them free.
Bm G D
Wa - ter fall on me, wa - ter - fall, I have sought your
A G D Bm A
heart, hear me call. Re - veal who you are;
G D Asus A G D
set things right in this world. Re - veal who you are;
Bm A G D Asus A
Last time D.C. al Fine
teach us how to re - build.

764 Oh, for a Thousand Tongues

AZMON CM

A E A F♯m E
1 Oh, for a thou - sand tongues to sing my
2 Je - sus! the name that charms our fears, that
3 He speaks, and list'n - ing to his voice new
4 My gra - cious Sav - ior and my God, as -
5 Glo - ry to God and praise and love be
A E7 A E A
great Re-deem - er's praise, with glo - ries ev - er
bids our sor - rows cease, 'tis mu - sic to the
life the dead re - ceive, the mourn - ful, bro - ken
sist me to pro - claim, to spread through all the
ev - er, ev - er giv'n by saints be - low and
D A/E E7 A
ech - o - ing the tri - umphs of God's grace.
sin - ner's ears, 'tis life and health and peace.
hearts re - joice, the hum - ble poor be - lieve.
earth a - broad the hon - ors of thy name.
saints a - bove, the church in earth and heav'n.

Text: Charles Wesley (England), 1739, *Hymns and Sacred Poems*, 1740, alt.
Music: Carl G. Glaser (Germany); arr. Lowell Mason (USA), *Modern Psalmist*, 1839

Neno lake Mungu (Listen, God Is Calling) 765

NENO LAKE MUNGU 6.4.6.4 with refrain

Refrain
Leader, freely
All, in tempo
G D
Ne - no, ne - no la - ke Mu-ngu la - ku - i - ta
Lis - ten: lis - ten, God is call - ing, through the Word in -
G Em D7/A G Em D7 G
Fine
we - we, ne - no la wo - ko - vu, te - na je - ma.
vit - ing, of - fer - ing for - give - ness, com - fort, and joy.
Leader
All
D Em
Ye - su a - li - se - ma, Mka - hu - bi - ri.
1 Je - sus tells his peo - ple: share the good news
2 Let none be for - got - ten through - out the world.
3 Help us to be faith - ful, stand - ing stead - fast,
Leader
All
G Em D G
To refrain
Ne - no la - ke Mu - ngu la - wo - ko - vu.
that he came to save us, and sets us free.
In the tri - une name of God, go and bap - tize.
walk - ing in your pre - cepts, led by your Word.

Text: Swahili; Tanzanian traditional; trans. Howard S. Olson (USA), alt., trans.

Music: Tanzanian traditional; arr. Austin C. Lovelace (USA),

766 Go in Grace and Make Disciples

IN BABILONE 8.7.8.7.7.7.8.7

G D G Am G
1 Go in grace and make dis - ci - ples. Bap - tize in God's
2 Go and fol - low Christ's ex - am - ple, not to van - quish,
3 Go in Pen - te - cos - tal spir - it, man - y tongues and
D7 G G D G Am
ho - ly name. Tell of death and res - ur - rec - tion; Eas - ter's
but to heal. Mend the wounds of sin's di - vi - sions. Ser - vant
man - y gifts. Feed the hearts of hun - gry peo - ple. Spread the
G D7 G Em Am E Am
vic - t'ry now pro - claim. Christ's com - mis - sion sends us forth
love to all re - veal. Roles and ranks shall be re - versed;
gos - pel that up - lifts. Till the day of Christ's re - turn,
D G D A D G
to the na - tions of the earth. Go in grace and
jus - tice poured for all who thirst. Go and fol - low
as dis - ci - ples, teach and learn. Go in Pen - te -

Text: Mary Louise Bringle (USA), 2001,
Music: Dutch traditional (present-day Netherlands), *Oude en Nieuwe Hollantse Boerenlieties en Contradansen*, ca. 1710

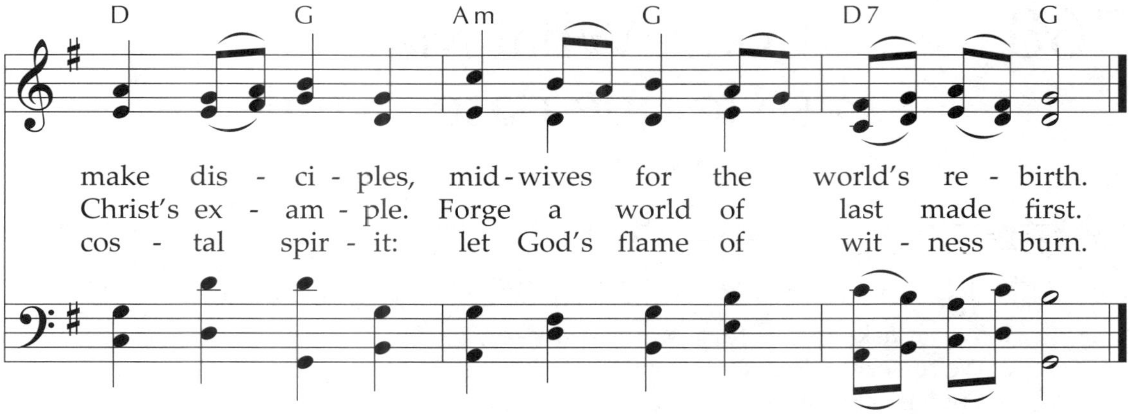
D G Am G D7 G
make dis - ci - ples, mid - wives for the world's re - birth.
Christ's ex - am - ple. Forge a world of last made first.
cos - tal spir - it: let God's flame of wit - ness burn.

Nzambi wakatamba (God Loves All His Many People) 767

COME, RECEIVE HIS JOY Irregular

Capo 3: (D) F (G) B♭ (D) F (A7) C7
1 Nzam - bi wa - ka - tam - ba ku - swa ba - pa - bu - lo - ba
2 U - di mu - swe we - we u - lwe bu mwa - na wan - di
3 Ye - ye u - di ne lu - pan - du ye - wa de - nan - ga;
1 God loves all his man - y peo - ple with sur - pass - ing love,
2 God wants you to come to him now, wants you as his child.
3 In the Lord is our sal - va - tion, in the Lord is love.
(D) F (G) B♭ (D) F (A7) C7 (D) F
Ye - ye u - twen - ze - la bim - pe bu ba - na ben - di.
ku - ben - gi, lwa - ku mu - lun - da ye u - di Mfu - mu.
u - ben - gi, lua ku mu - lun - da u - pe te di - san - ka.
bless - es all as his own chil - dren, cares for ev - 'ry one.
Come, my friend, his arms are o - pen; he is Lord of all.
Come, my friend, his arms are o - pen; come, re - ceive his joy.
Refrain
(A7) C7
Lwa mu - lun - da, lwa mu - lun - da, u - pe - te di - san - ka;
Come to him, friend, come to him, friend, come, re - ceive his joy.
(D) F (G) B♭ (D) F (A7) C7 (D) F
bin - tu bia pa - bu - lo - ba ka - bi - na nshi - ki - di - lu.
Earth - ly things don't last for - ev - er; come, re - ceive his joy.

Text: Tshiluba; Lubunda Mukungu (present-day Democratic Republic of the Congo); trans. rev. Anna Juhnke (USA), *International Songbook*, Mennonite World Conference, 1978, alt.,

Music: Tshiluba traditional (present-day Democratic Republic of the Congo), *International Songbook*, Mennonite World Conference, 1978, alt.

768 Come What May / Pase lo que pase, ¡ven!

PASE LO QUE PASE VEN Irregular

D G A7 D
1 We ask you for your pow-er,
2 We're serv - ing you with glad-ness, pa-se lo que pa - se, ¡ven!
3 The threats will cir - cle round us,
A7 D
strength for ev - 'ry hour,
chal - leng - ing the mad - ness, pa-se lo que pa - se, ¡ven!
your peace will sur - round us,
G A7 D
Though the path be lone - ly,
Just for Je - sus' glo - ry, pa-se lo que pa - se, ¡ven!
We will spread your bless - ing,
A7 D
we will o - bey you on - ly,
we're liv - ing out his sto - ry, pa-se lo que pa - se, ¡ven!
your might-y word pro - fess - ing,
Refrain
G A D
Come what may, let us speak with bold-ness,
Pa - se lo que pa - se, ¡ven! Ha - ble-mos con va - lor,

Text: Doug Krehbiel (USA) and Jude Krehbiel (USA); Spanish Gilberto Flores (USA)
Music: Doug Krehbiel and Jude Krehbiel

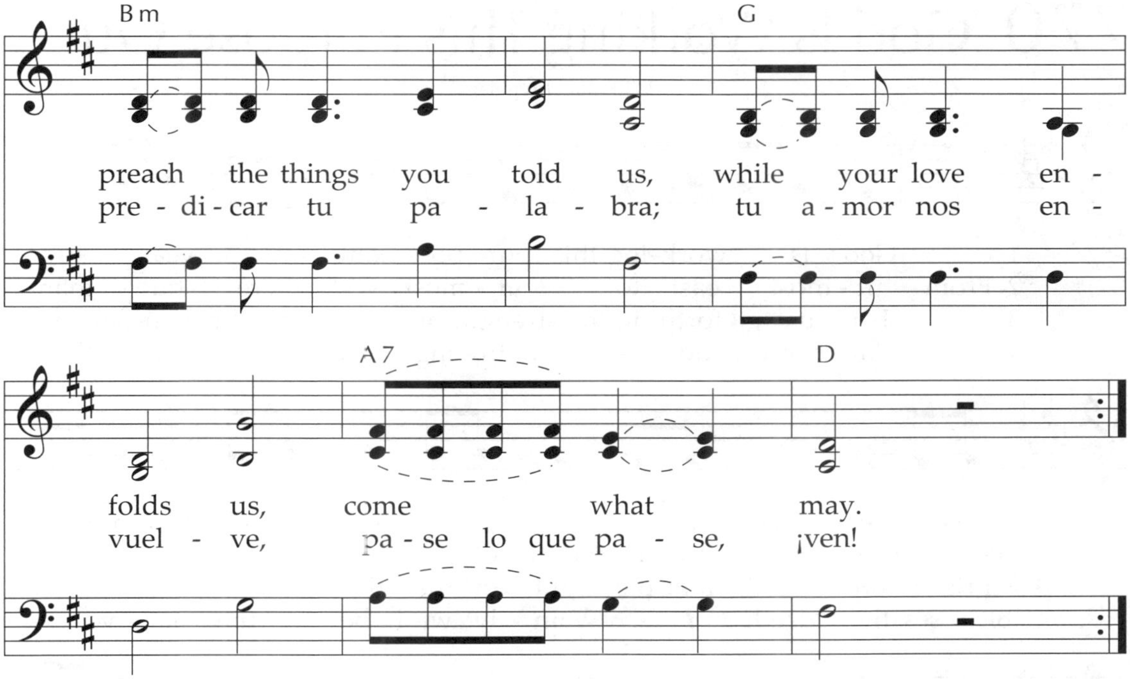
Bm
G
preach the things you told us, while your love en -
pre - di - car tu pa - la - bra; tu a - mor nos en -
A7
D
folds us, come what may.
vuel - ve, pa - se lo que pa - se, ¡ven!

Ey lou nis (Now I Know) 769

EY LOU NIS Irregular

Dm
Leader
All
Leader
Am
All
1 Ey lou nis Ey lou nis knhom dang hoeille tha, knhom
2 Dou chnes jou Dou chnes jou nom knea janh tou, nom
1 Now I know, Now I know, by God's own grace, by
2 Now with hope, Now with hope, go out in peace, go
Dm
Leader
All
Leader
dang hoeille tha, Neak koe chea Neak koe chea mnous som
knea janh tou, Bom ploe nou Bom ploe nou a - wai
God's own grace, all of you all of you are the
out in peace, bring good news bring good news to all
All
nop Preas poet. mnous som nop Preas poet.
chea ka poet. a - wai chea ka poet.
chil - dren of God. are the chil - dren of God.
peo - ple on earth. to all peo - ple on earth.

1 កឡូវនេះ ខ្ញុំដឹងហើយថា
អ្នកក៏ជាមនុស្ស សំណព្វព្រះពិត

2 ដូច្នេះចូរនាំគ្នាចេញទៅ
បន្លឺនូវអ្វីជាការពិត

Text: Khmer; based on Philippians 4:7; Barnabas Mam (Cambodia); stanza 2 Eang Chhun (Cambodia); trans.
Music: Cambodian traditional

770 God Is Working This Purpose Out

PURPOSE Irregular

1 God is work-ing this pur-pose out, as year suc-
2 From ut-most east to ut-most west, where hu-man
3 Let us go forth in the strength of God, with the ban-ner of
4 All we can do is noth-ing worth un-less God

ceeds to year; God is work-ing this pur-pose
feet have trod, by the mouth of man-y mes-sen-
Christ un-furled, that the light of the glo-rious gos-pel of
bles-ses the deed. Vain-ly we hope for the har-vest-

out, and the time is draw-ing near; near-er and
gers goes forth the voice of God: "Give ear to
truth may shine through-out the world. Let us all
tide till God gives life to the seed. Yet near-er and

near-er draws the time, the time that shall sure-ly be:
me, ye con-ti-nents, ye isles, give ear to me,
fight with sor-row and sin to set the cap-tives free,
near-er draws the time, the time that shall sure-ly be,

when the earth shall be filled with the glo-ry of God
that the earth may be filled with the glo-ry of God
that the earth may be filled with the glo-ry of God
when the earth shall be filled with the glo-ry of God

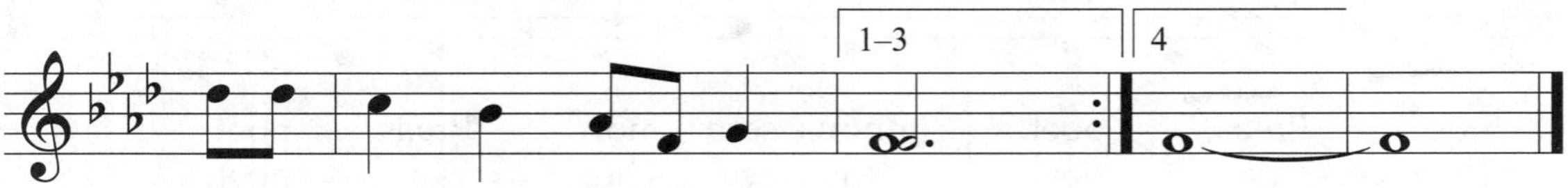

as the wa-ters cov-er the sea.
as the wa-ters cov-er the sea."
as the wa-ters cov-er the sea.
as the wa-ters cov-er the sea.

Text: Arthur C. Ainger (England), 1894, *Church Missionary Hymn Book*, 1899, alt.
Music: Martin Shaw (England), *Enlarged Songs of Praise*, 1931, © Oxford University Press

Enviados somos de Dios (We Have Been Sent by God) 771

ENVIADO 12.12.12.12.12.12

Em B Em B
En - via - dos so-mos de Dios. Nues-tras ma - nos lis-tas es -
We have been sent by God, with our hands pre-pared to
Em Am B7 Em
tán, pa - ra cons-tru - ir con Dios un mun-do co - mu - nal.
serve, and we build a - long with God a fam - 'ly here on earth.
Am D G C
Los án - gel - es no son en - via - dos a cam - biar un
The an - gels are not sent to change this world of pain in -
Am B7 Em
mun - do de do - lor por un mun - do de paz; nos
to a world of love where peace and jus - tice reign; it
Am D G C
ha to - ca - do hoy ha - cer - lo rea - li - dad. A -
falls to each of us to do this work to - day. We
Am B7 Em
yú - da - nos, oh Dios, a ha - cer tu vo - lun - tad.
seek to do your will. Oh, help us, God, we pray.

772 God of Justice

GOD OF JUSTICE Irregular

1 God of jus - tice, Sav-ior to all, came to res - cue the weak and the poor; chose to serve and not be served. Je - sus, you have called us.
2 To act just - ly ev - e - ry day, lov - ing mer - cy in ev - e - ry way; walk - ing hum - bly be - fore you, God. You have shown us what you re - quire.
Free - ly we've re - ceived, now free - ly we will give. We must
Refrain
go, live to feed the hun - gry, stand be - side the bro - ken, we must go. Step - ping for - ward, keep us from just sing - ing, move us in - to ac - tion, we must go.
Last time to Coda
1

Text: Tim Hughes (England)
Music: Tim Hughes

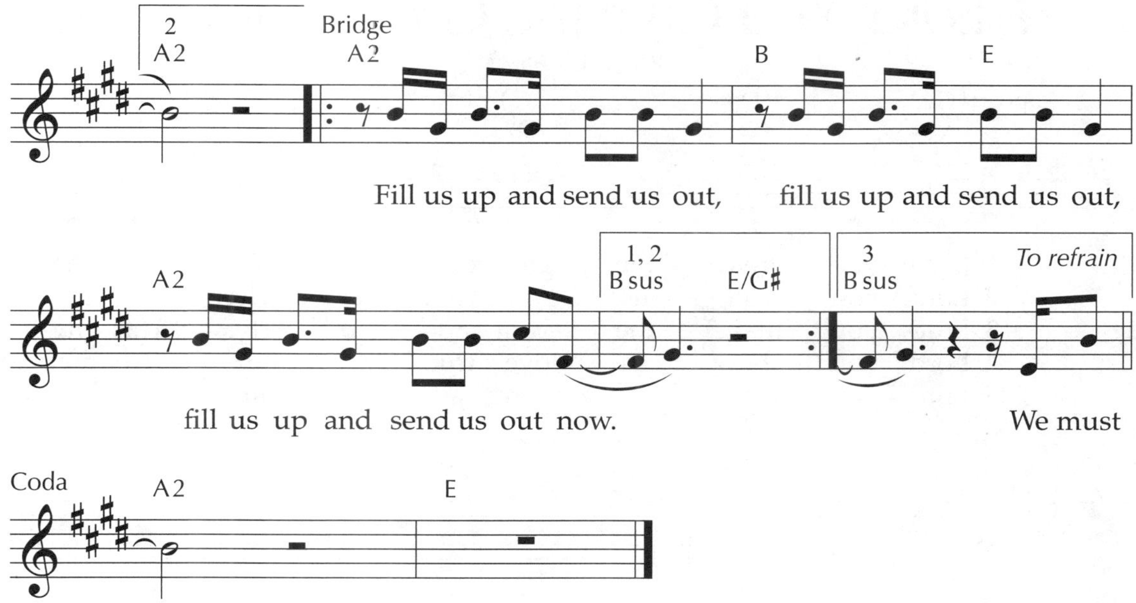
2
A2
Bridge
A2
B
E
Fill us up and send us out, fill us up and send us out,
A2
1, 2
B sus
E/G♯
3
B sus
To refrain
fill us up and send us out now.
We must
Coda
A2
E

Ubi caritas et amor

773

TAIZÉ UBI CARITAS Irregular

Capo 3: (D) F (A) C (Bm) Dm (G) B♭ (B) D (E) G (A) C
U - bi ca - ri - tas et a - mor,
(D) F (A) C (Bm) Dm (Em) Gm (A) C (D) F
u - bi ca - ri - tas, De - us i - bi est.

Translation: Where charity and love are found, God is there.

Verses can be found in the accompaniment edition.

Text: Latin; "Ubi caritas et amor," 8th–9th c.
Music: Jacques Berthier (France), *Music from Taizé*, vol. 1, 1978, 1980, 1981,

774 Lord, You Give the Great Commission

RAQUEL 8.7.8.7 D

Capo 1: (G2) Ab2 (D) Eb (C) Db (G) Ab
1 Lord, you give the great com - mis - sion: "Heal the
2 Lord, you call us to your ser - vice: "In my
3 Lord, you make the com-mon ho - ly: "This my
4 Lord, you show us love's true mea - sure: "Fa - ther,
5 Lord, you bless with words as - sur - ing: "I am
(Em7) Fm7 (G) Ab (D) Eb (G) Ab
sick and preach the word." Lest the church ne - glect its
name, bap - tize and teach." That the world may trust your
bod - y, this my blood." Let us all, for earth's true
what they do, for - give." Yet we hoard as pri - vate
with you to the end." Faith and hope and love re -
(Am7) Bbm7 (C) Db (D) Eb
mis - sion, and the gos - pel go un - heard, help us wit - ness
prom - ise, life a - bun - dant meant for each, give us all new
glo - ry, dai - ly lift life hea - ven - ward, ask - ing that the
trea - sure all that you so free - ly give. May your care and
stor - ing, may we serve as you in - tend and, a - mid the
(G) Ab (D) Eb (G) Ab
to your pur - pose with re - newed in - teg - ri - ty:
fer - vor, draw us clos - er in com - mun - i - ty:
world a - round us share your chil - dren's lib - er - ty:
mer - cy lead us to a just so - ci - e - ty:
cares that claim us, hold in mind e - ter - ni - ty:
Refrain
(A sus) Bbsus (G) Ab (A m7) Bbm7 (C) Db (D) Eb (G) Ab
With the Spir - it's gifts em - pow'r us for the work of min - is - try.

Chord symbols represent a simplified harmony.

Alternate tune: BEACH SPRING (#57 or #179)

I Will Follow

775

WHERE YOU GO I'LL GO Irregular

Verse
C Em7 D
1 All your ways are good, all your ways are sure;
2 Light in - to the world, light in - to my life,
G2 D/F♯ C Em7
I will trust in you a-lone. High - er than my sight,
I will live for you a-lone. You're the one I seek,
D G2 D/F♯ C
high a-bove my life; I will trust in you a-lone.
know-ing I will find all I need in you a-lone.
D
Refrain
Em7 C2
Where you go, I'll go; where you stay, I'll stay;
G D Em7
when you move, I'll move. I will fol-low you. Whom you
C2 G
love, I'll love; how you serve, I'll serve; if this life I lose,
D Em7 C2 G D
Last time
I will fol-low you. I will fol-low you.
Bridge
C2 G D C2 G D
In you, there's life ev-er-last-ing. In you, there's free-dom for my soul.
C2 G D C2 G D
To refrain
In you, there's joy, un-end-ing joy; and I will fol-low.

Text: Chris Tomlin (USA), Jason Ingram (USA), and Reuben Morgan (Australia)
Music: Chris Tomlin, Jason Ingram, and Reuben Morgan

776 Teach Me Thy Truth

GOSHEN CM

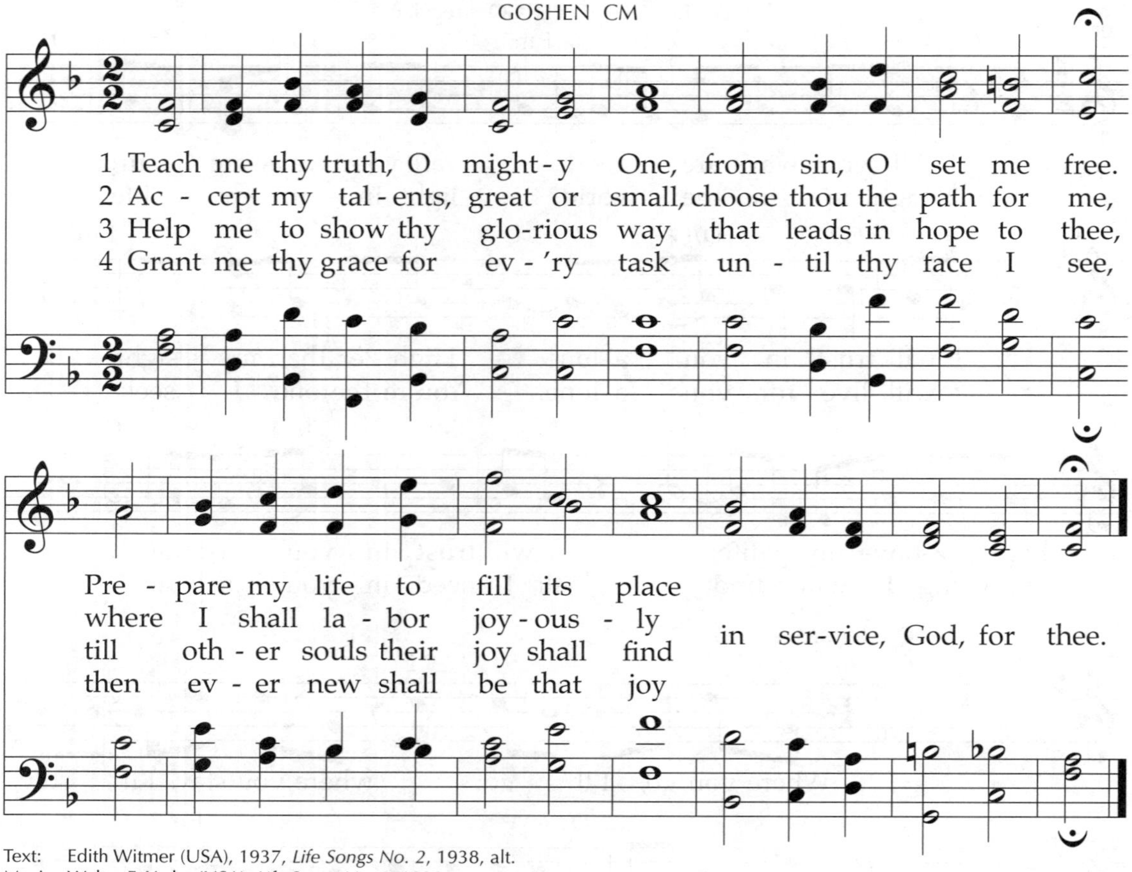
1 Teach me thy truth, O might-y One, from sin, O set me free.
2 Ac-cept my tal-ents, great or small, choose thou the path for me,
3 Help me to show thy glo-rious way that leads in hope to thee,
4 Grant me thy grace for ev-'ry task un-til thy face I see,
Pre-pare my life to fill its place
where I shall la-bor joy-ous-ly
till oth-er souls their joy shall find
then ev-er new shall be that joy
in ser-vice, God, for thee.

Text: Edith Witmer (USA), 1937, *Life Songs No. 2*, 1938, alt.
Music: Walter E. Yoder (USA), *Life Songs No. 2*, 1938

777 Seeds

SEEDS Irregular

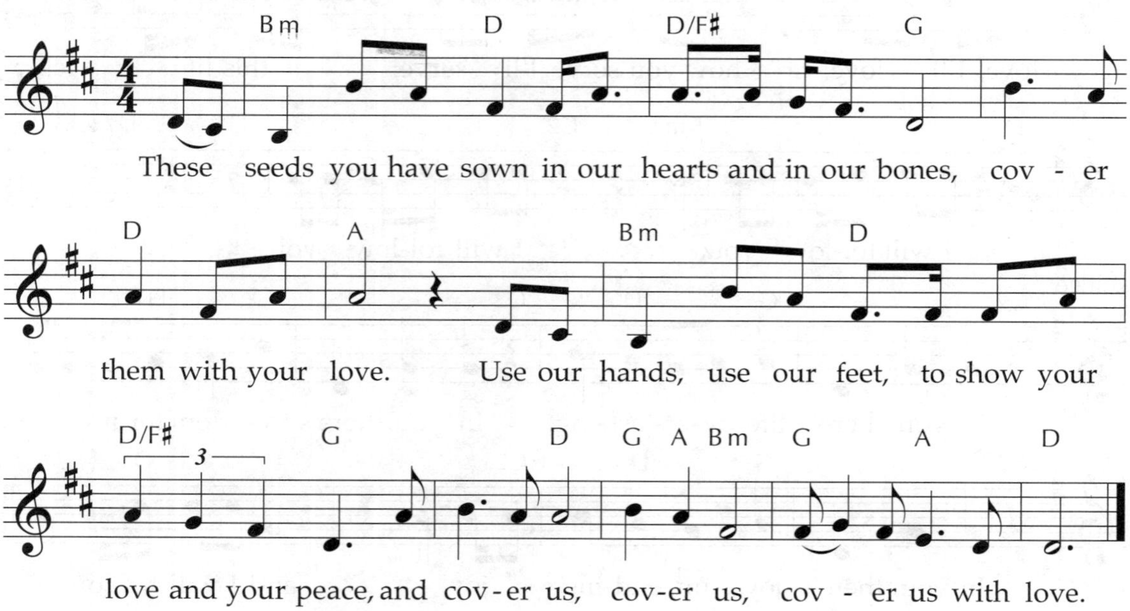
Bm
D
D/F♯
G
These seeds you have sown in our hearts and in our bones, cov-er
D
A
Bm
D
them with your love. Use our hands, use our feet, to show your
D/F♯
3
G
D
G
A
Bm
G
A
D
love and your peace, and cov-er us, cov-er us, cov-er us with love.

Text: Seth Crissman (USA) and Greg Yoder (USA), 2017
Music: Seth Crissman and Greg Yoder, 2017

Will You Let Me Be Your Servant 778

THE SERVANT SONG 8.7.8.7

Capo 1: (D) E♭ (G) A♭ (A7) B♭7 (D) E♭ (Bm) Cm
1, 6 Will you let me be your ser - vant— let me be as
2 We are pil - grims on a jour - ney; we are trav - 'lers
3 I will hold the Christ-light for you in the night-time
4 I will weep when you are weep - ing; when you laugh I'll
5 When we sing to God in hea - ven, we shall find such
(Em) Fm (A) B♭ (G) A♭ (D) E♭ (G) A♭ (A7) B♭7 (Bm) Cm
Christ to you? Pray that I may have the grace to
on the road. We are here to help each oth - er
of your fear. I will hold my hand out to you,
laugh with you. I will share your joy and sor - row
har - mon - y, born of all we've known to - geth - er
(Em) Fm (G) A♭ (A7) B♭7 (D) E♭
let you be my ser - vant too.
walk the mile and bear the load.
speak the peace you long to hear.
till we've seen this jour - ney through.
of Christ's love and a - gon - y.

Text: Richard Gillard (Aotearoa New Zealand), 1976, alt.
Music: Richard Gillard, 1976; adapt. Betty Pulkingham (USA)

779 You're Not Alone

ONE BODY Irregular

Refrain
You're not a-lone, we are one bod-y.
You're not a-lone, we stand with you.
You're not a-lone, your time of suf-f'ring is our
suf-f'ring too, and I know the day is com-ing when
we will be re-joic-ing a-new.
Fine
Verses
1 Man-y mem-bers in this bod-y that we know,
2 One bod-y, Spir-it formed and Spir-it fed,
some are great and some are small:
dif-f'rent gen-ders, rich and poor;
eyes and ears and hands and just a lit-tle toe,
a ban-quet where the least sit at the head:
one God who ac-ti-vates them all.
one bod-y bro-ken for the world.
To refrain

Text: based on 1 Corinthians 12:4–26, Bryan Moyer Suderman (Canada)
Music: Bryan Moyer Suderman; acc. Charlene Nafziger (Canada), 2010

781 *Isaiah 52:7*

How beautiful on the mountains
are the feet of the messengers
who proclaim peace,
who bring good news,
who proclaim salvation,
who say to Zion,
"Your God reigns!"

782 *Isaiah 56:1-7 (excerpts)*

Thus says the LORD:
Maintain justice,
and do what is right.
Do not let the foreigner say,
"The LORD will surely separate me
from God's people";
and do not let the eunuch say,
"I am just a dry tree."
For thus says the LORD:
To the eunuchs who
keep my sabbaths,
and hold fast my covenant,
I will give them an everlasting name
that shall not be removed.
And to the foreigners
who join themselves to the LORD,
all who keep the sabbath
and hold fast my covenant—
I will bring you to my holy mountain,
and make you joyful
in my house of prayer,
for my house shall be called
a house of prayer for all peoples.

783 *Jeremiah 29:4-11 (excerpts)*

Thus says the LORD, the God of Israel:
Build houses and live in them;
plant gardens
and eat what they produce.
Seek the welfare of the city
where I have sent you into exile,
and pray to the LORD on its behalf,
for in its welfare
you will find your welfare.
For surely I know the plans
I have for you, says the LORD,
plans for your welfare
and not for harm,
to give you a future with hope.

784 *Micah 6:8*

The LORD told you what is good
and what God seeks from you:
do justice,
love mercy,
and walk humbly
with your God.

785 *2 Corinthians 5:17-20*

Anyone who is joined to Christ
is a new creation;
the old is gone, the new has come.
All this is done by God,
who reconciled us through Christ,
changing us from enemies into friends
and giving us the ministry
of reconciling others also.
Our message is that God was making
the world friends through Christ.
God did not keep an account of their sins
and has given us the message
of reconciliation.
Here we are, then, speaking for Christ,
as though God were making
an appeal through us.
We plead on Christ's behalf:
let God reconcile us.

786 *Ephesians 2:13-18*

Now, thanks to Christ Jesus,
you who once were so far away
have been brought near
by the blood of Christ.
Christ is our peace,
the one uniting opposing groups
and breaking down the barrier
of hatred that divided us.
Christ made the law
of the commandments barren
so as to create one new person
out of the two groups, making peace.
Christ reconciled them both
as one body to God by the cross,
which ended hostility.
Upon arriving, Christ announced
the good news of peace
to those who were far away from God
and to those who were near.
We both have access to God
through Christ by the one Spirit.

Previous page: 780. *At the Impulse of God's Love: A Re-envisioning of Dirk Willems Saving His Captor's Life (1685) by Jan Luykens,* Michelle L. Hofer (USA), 2018, mixed media ⓦ

O Day of Peace

787

JERUSALEM LMD

Unison
1 O day of peace that dim - ly shines through all our
2 Then shall the wolf dwell with the lamb, nor shall the
hopes and prayers and dreams, guide us to jus - tice,
fierce de - vour the small. As beasts and cat - tle
truth, and love, de - liv - ered from our self - ish schemes.
calm - ly graze, a lit - tle child shall lead them all.
Harmony
May swords of hate fall from our hands, our hearts from
Then en - e - mies shall learn to love, all crea - tures
en - vy find re - lease, till by God's grace our war - ring
find their true ac - cord. The hope of peace shall be ful -
world shall see Christ's prom - ised reign of peace.
filled, for all the earth shall know the Lord.

788 The Garden Needs Our Tending Now

UNE JEUNE PUCELLE 8.6.8.6.8.8 with refrain

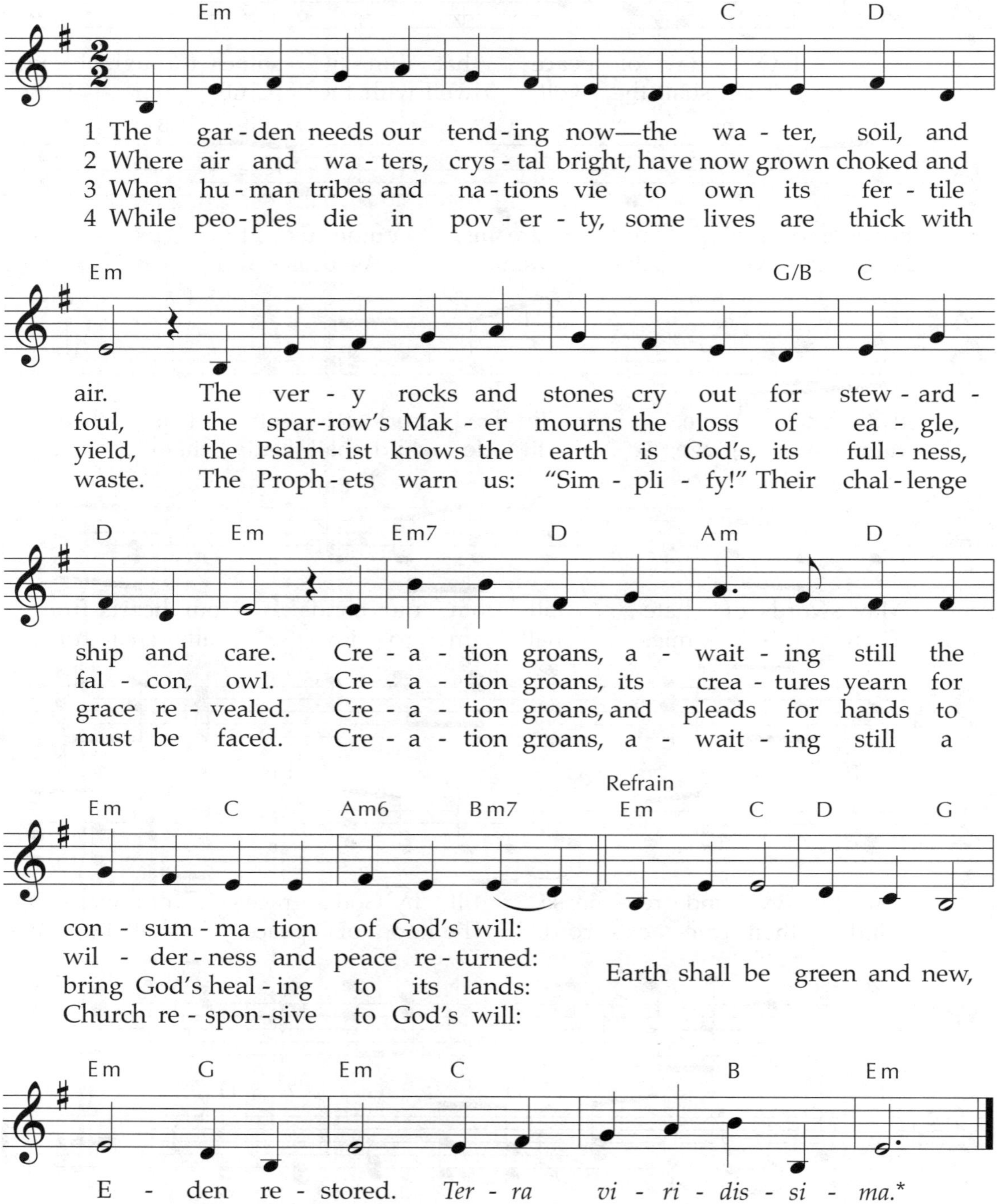
Em C D
1 The gar - den needs our tend - ing now—the wa - ter, soil, and
2 Where air and wa - ters, crys - tal bright, have now grown choked and
3 When hu - man tribes and na - tions vie to own its fer - tile
4 While peo - ples die in pov - er - ty, some lives are thick with
Em G/B C
air. The ver - y rocks and stones cry out for stew - ard -
foul, the spar-row's Mak - er mourns the loss of ea - gle,
yield, the Psalm - ist knows the earth is God's, its full - ness,
waste. The Proph - ets warn us: "Sim - pli - fy!" Their chal - lenge
D Em Em7 D Am D
ship and care. Cre - a - tion groans, a - wait - ing still the
fal - con, owl. Cre - a - tion groans, its crea - tures yearn for
grace re - vealed. Cre - a - tion groans, and pleads for hands to
must be faced. Cre - a - tion groans, a - wait - ing still a
Em C Am6 Bm7
con - sum - ma - tion of God's will:
wil - der - ness and peace re - turned:
bring God's heal - ing to its lands:
Church re - spon - sive to God's will:
Refrain
Em C D G
Earth shall be green and new,
Em G Em C B Em
E - den re - stored. Ter - ra vi - ri - dis - si - ma.*

*Latin: Greenest earth. (The writer drew inspiration for this phrase from Hildegard of Bingen's *Viridissima Virga*.)

Text: Mary Louise Bringle (USA), 1999, © 2002 GIA Publications, Inc.
Music: French traditional, 16th c.; acc. Andrew Donaldson (Canada), 2010

Be a Sower 789

BE A SOWER Irregular

D A G A D A G A D
1 Be a sow - er, plant a seed, let it grow in - to a tree. Give it wat - er, watch it grow, and give it the love that it needs.
2 Be a lis - t'ner; lis - ten close when you find a friend in need. Talk to Je - sus; Je - sus knows, and he'll give you com - fort and peace.
3 Be a dream - er; work for peace— turn your sword in - to a plow. With our neigh - bors, we will seek to make change as God shows us how.
Refrain
Em Em/G A
Be hum-ble, and gen - tle, and al - ways keep look - ing for peace.
G D A Bm
God makes the sun rise on the good and the e - vil,
G D A G D
rain fall on the rocks and the weeds. Let's be lov - ing
A D G A D
to one an - oth - er. Join in God's cir - cle of peace.

Text: Camps with Meaning (Canada)
Music: Camps with meaning, 2013; acc. Anneli Loepp Thiessen (Canada), 2020

790 How Can We Be Silent

HOW CAN WE BE SILENT Irregular

Capo 3: (Am) Cm (D) F (Am) Cm
1 How can we be si-lent when we know our God is near, bring-ing
2 How can we be si-lent when our God has con-quered death, stretch-ing
3 How can we be si-lent as we turn our eyes a - way, and ig -
4 How can we be si-lent, not give praise with all our hearts, for Christ
5 How can we be si-lent when our souls are filled with awe at the
(D) F (Am/C) Cm/E♭ (F) A♭ (E7sus) G7sus (E7) G7
light to those in shad-ows, to the worth-less, end - less worth?
out his arms to suf - fer so that we might have new life?
nore the poor and bro - ken who lie bleed-ing in the street?
Je - sus is our Sav - ior, and com - pas-sion is our king?
beau - ty of cre - a - tion, and the mer - cy of our Lord?
(Am) Cm (D) F (Am) Cm
How can we be si-lent when we are the voice of Christ, speak-ing
How can we be si-lent when we know that Je - sus rose, and will
How can we be si-lent when we're called to heal and serve in the
How can we be si-lent when God gave us life to be vi-brant
How can we be si-lent when we yearn to sing new songs? In our
(D) F (Am/C) Cm/E♭ (F) A♭ (Esus) Gsus (E) G
jus - tice to the na-tions, breath-ing love to all the earth?
come a-gain in glo - ry, end - ing suf - fer - ing and strife?
im - age of Lord Je - sus, who has stooped to wash our feet?
in - stru-ments of wor-ship, made to laugh and dance and sing?
hearts a fire is burn-ing, and it will not be ig-nored!
Refrain*
1 (F) A♭ (G) B♭ (Am) Cm 2 (F) A♭ (G) B♭ (Am) Cm
None can stop the Spir - it burn-ing now in-side us.
3 (F) A♭ (G) B♭ (Am) Cm 4 (Dm7) Fm7 (Em7) Gm7 (Fmaj7) A♭maj7 (G2) B♭2 (Am) Cm (Em7) Gm7 (A2) C2
We will shape the fu-ture. We will not be si - lent!

*May be sung as a canon.

Text: Michael Mahler (USA)
Music: Michael Mahler

Let Justice Flow Down 791

LET JUSTICE FLOW Irregular

Refrain
G C D G
Let jus-tice flow down, down like a riv-er, down to the
C D G C
val-leys where the help-less cry. Let right-eous-ness flow
D G Em7 C
through us for-ev-er; lead us to the stream that will
D7 G Fine Em Gmaj7 Dsus Em
nev-er run dry.
1 Flow to the mouths of the hun-gry;
2 Flow to the streets of the home-less,
3 Flow through the courts of our na-tion,
C Bm7 Em C
flow to the hands of the poor. Flow to the
find-ing no place they can go. Flow to the
guide us in love's de-crees. Lead us to
Bm Dsus Em C D G To Refrain
hearts of the or-phans, heal the wounds of war.
cells of the pris-on-ers, fac-ing each day a-lone.
streams of sal-va-tion; fill our lands with peace.

Text: Douglas Romanow (Canada)
Music: Douglas Romanow

How Can Our Anger Give Life 792

MARY HAMMOND Irregular

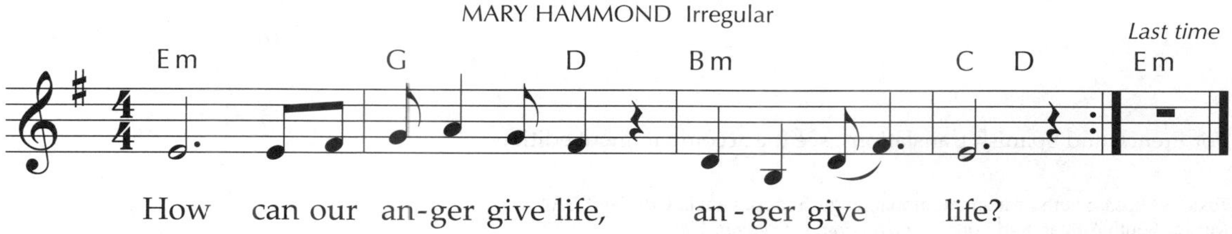
Em G D Bm C D
Last time Em
How can our an-ger give life, an-ger give life?

Text: Rachael Weasley (USA), 2015
Music: Rachael Weasley

793 Siyahamba (We Are Marching)

SIYAHAMBA Irregular

G D G C
Si - ya - hamb' e - ku-kha - nyen' kwen - khos', si - ya -
We are march - ing in the light of God; we are
D G D
hamb' e - ku - kha-nyen' kwen - khos'. Si - ya - hamb' e - ku-kha -
march-ing in the light of God. We are march - ing in the
nyen' kwen - khos'.
light of God.
G C D G
nyen' kwen - khos', si - ya - hamb' e - ku - kha - nyen' kwen, kha -
light of God; we are march-ing in the light of, the
nyen' kwen - khos'.
light of God.

For French and Spanish translations, see the accompaniment edition.

Text: Xhosa; South African traditional; English trans. Gracia Grindal (USA)
Music: South African traditional; arr. *Freedom Is Coming*, 1984

G7 C
nyen' kwen-khos'. Si-ya-ham-ba, ham-ba, si-ya-
light of, God. We are march-ing, march-ing, we are
nyen' kwen - khos'.
light of God.
G Oh! C D G
ham-ba, ham-ba, si-ya-hamb' e-ku-kha-nyen' kwen, kha-
march-ing, march-ing, we are march-ing in the light of, the
nyen' kwen - khos'.
light of God.
G7 C
nyen' kwen-khos'. Si-ya-ham-ba, ham-ba, si-ya-
light of God. We are march-ing, march-ing, we are
G Oh! C D G
ham-ba, ham-ba, si-ya-hamb' e-ku-kha-nyen' kwen-khos'.
march-ing, march-ing, we are march-ing in the light of God.

794 If the War Goes On

THE ROAD TO BASRAH 5.8.5.7.5.8.5

1 If the war goes on, and the chil - dren die of hun - ger,
2 If the war goes on, and the truth is tak - en hos - tage,
3 If the war goes on, and the dai - ly bread is ter - ror,
4 If the war goes on, and the rich in - crease their for - tunes,
5 If the war goes on, will we close the doors to heav - en?

and the old men weep, for the young men are no more,
and new hor - rors lead to the need to eu - phe - mize;
and the voice - less poor take the road as ref - u - gees;
and the arms sales soar as new weap - ons are dis - played;
If the war goes on, will we breach the gates of hell?

and the wom - en learn how to dance with - out a part - ner,
when the calls for peace are de - clared un - pa - tri - ot - ic,
when a na - tion's pride des-tines mil - lions to be home - less,
when a fer - tile field turns to no - man's-land to - mor - row,
If the war goes on, will we ev - er be for - giv - en?

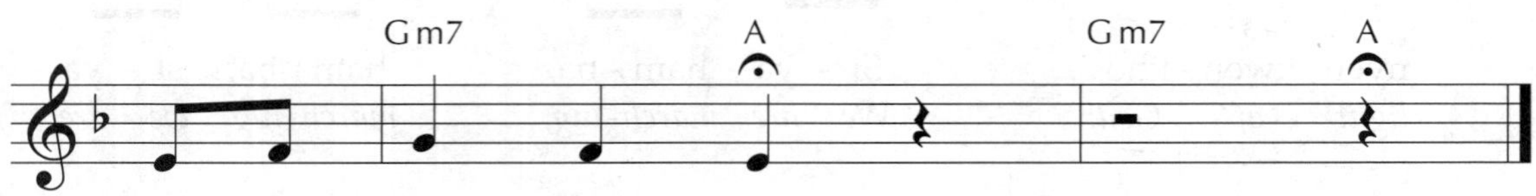

who will keep the score?
who'll ex - pose the lies?
who will heed their pleas?
who'll ap - prove such trade?
If the war goes on . . .

Text: John L. Bell (Scotland) and Graham Maule (Scotland)
Music: John L. Bell; acc. Marilyn Houser Hamm (Canada), 2003

Kyrie eleison

795

KYRIE (Reindorf) 7.7.7.7

3 Soprano
Ky - ri - e e - lei - son. Ky - ri - e e - lei - son.
1 Alto (melody)
Ky - ri - e e - le - i - son. Ky - ri - e e - le - i - son.
4 Tenor
Ky - ri - e e - lei - son. Ky - ri - e e - lei - son.
2 Bass
Ky-ri - e, Ky-ri - e, Ky-ri-
Ky - ri - e e - lei - son. Ky - ri - e e - lei - son.
Ky - ri - e e - le - i - son. Ky - ri - e e - le - i - son.
Ky - ri - e e - lei - son. Ky - ri - e e - lei - son.
e, Ky - ri - e e - lei - son. Ky - ri -

Translation: Lord, have mercy.

Voices can enter in this order: alto, bass, soprano, tenor.

Text: from Greek liturgy Κύριε, ἐλέησον (Kyrie eleison) (Eastern Mediterranean), 4th c.
Music: Dinah Reindorf (Ghana), © 1987 Dinah Reindorf

796 Kyrie eleison, Have Mercy

HAVE MERCY Irregular

Refrain
Ky-rie e-lei-son, have mer-cy, Chris-te e-lei-son, have mer-cy. Ky-rie e-lei-son, have mer-cy, Chris-te e-lei-son, have mer-cy.
1 As we come be-fore you with the needs of our world, we con-fess our fail-ures and our sin; for our words are man-y, yet our deeds have been few; fan the fire of com-pas-sion once a-gain.
2 When the cries of vic-tims go un-heard in the land, and the scars of war re-fuse to heal, will we stand for jus-tice to em-pow-er the weak, till their bonds of op-pres-sion are no more?
3 If we love our God with all our heart, mind, and strength, and we love our neigh-bors as our-selves, then this law of love will heal the na-tions of earth, and the glo-ry of Christ will be re-vealed.
4 God, re-new our vi-sion to be Christ where we live, to reach out in mer-cy to the lost; for each cup of kind-ness to the least in our midst is an of-f'ring of wor-ship to the throne.
To refrain

Text: Stuart Townend (England) and Keith Getty (Ireland); refrain from Greek liturgy Κύριε, ἐλέησον (Kyrie eleison) (Eastern Mediterranean), 4th c., trans. traditional
Music: Stuart Townend and Keith Getty

We Are People of God's Peace 797

AVE VIRGO VIRGINUM (GAUDEAMUS PARITER) 7.6.7.6 D

G D Em D G C D C D G
1 We are peo - ple of God's peace as a new cre - a - tion.
2 We are her - alds of God's peace for the new cre - a - tion,
3 We are chil - dren of God's peace in this new cre - a - tion,
4 We are ser - vants of God's peace, of the new cre - a - tion.
G D Em D G C D C D G
Love u - nites and strength - ens us at this cel - e - bra - tion.
and by grace the word of peace reach - es ev - 'ry na - tion.
spread - ing joy and hap - pi - ness through God's great sal - va - tion.
Choos - ing peace, we faith - ful - ly serve with heart's de - vo - tion.
G C D G D G A D
Sons and daugh - ters of the Lord, ser - ving one an - oth - er,
Though we fal - ter and we fail, Christ will still re - new us.
Hope we bring in spir - it meek, in our dai - ly liv - ing.
Je - sus Christ, the Prince of Peace, con - fi - dence will give us.
Em D Em D G C G C D G
a new cov - e - nant of peace binds us all to - geth - er.
By the Ho - ly Spir - it's pow'r, God is work - ing through us.
Peace with ev - 'ry - one we seek, good for e - vil giv - ing.
Christ the Lord is our de - fense; Christ will nev - er leave us.

Text: based on Menno Simons (present-day Netherlands), *Reply to False Accusations*, 1552; stanzas 1, 3, 4 vers. David Augsburger (USA), 1978; adapt. Esther Bergen (Canada), 1990; stanza 2 vers. Mennonite Worship and Song Committee, 2017 © Mennonite World Conference

Music: Johann Horn (present-day Germany), *Ein Gesangbuch der Brüder im Behemen und Merherrn*, 1544; rev. in *Catholicum Hymnologium Germanicum*, 1584

798 Sword into a Plowshare

SWORD INTO A PLOUGHSHARE Irregular

Am C G Am
Dai dai dai dai dai dai Dai dai dai dai dai dai
C G Am Fine
Dai dai dai dai dai dai Dai dai dai dai dai dai
Verses
C G
1 We share the ho - ly im - age of God, yet
2 In Je - sus we are giv - en a guide who
3 For - give, and make your en - e - mies friends; to
4 The call of God, it ech - oes through time for
D G C
choose who we will be: to walk a path that
teach - es us sha - lom: the thirst - y giv - en
vi' - lence do not fall, for peace and jus - tice
all hu - man - i - ty— each race, age,
G D G
leads in - to hate, or live in har - mo - ny.
some-thing to drink, the stran - ger wel - comed home.
are the good gifts the Spir - it gives us all.
gen - der, and class— to stand in u - ni - ty!
Refrain
Am C G
A rust - y sword is the way of a world whose pain can on - ly in -
Am C G
crease. We fight for pow-er and kill for fear our stat - us

Text: Darryl Neustaedter Barg (Canada), 1996, rev. 2019
Music: Darryl Neustaedter Barg

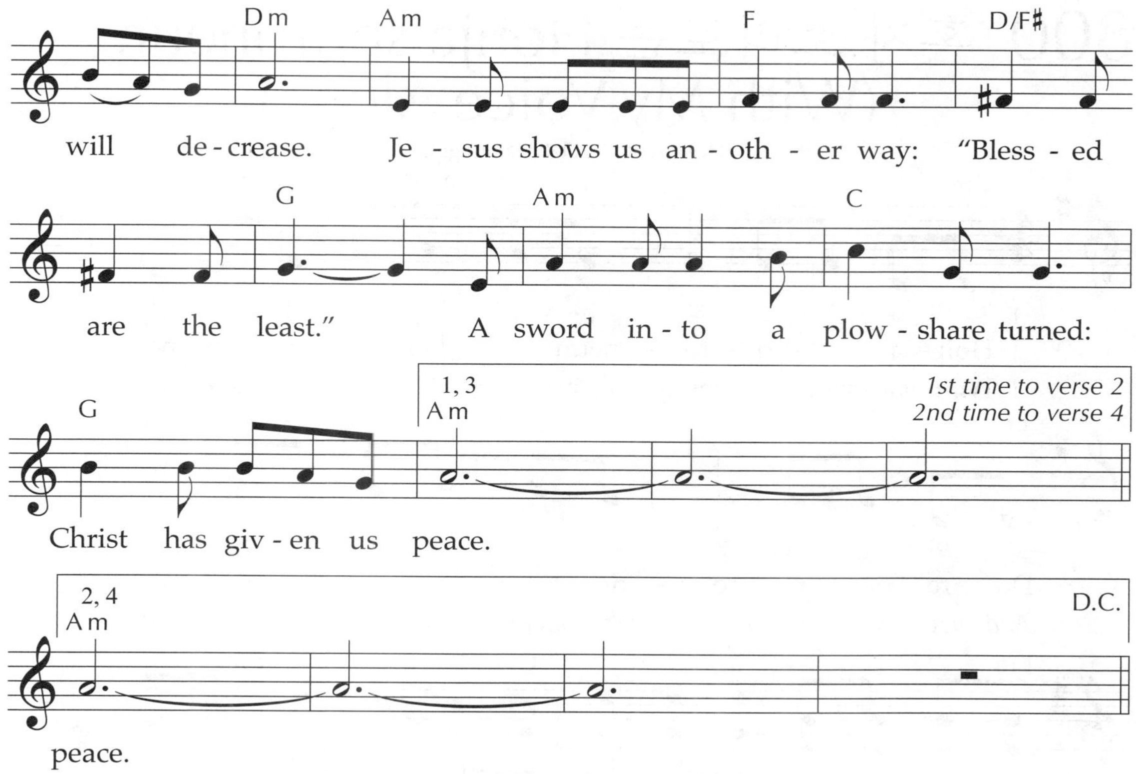
Dm Am F D/F♯
will de-crease. Je - sus shows us an - oth - er way: "Bless - ed
G Am C
are the least." A sword in - to a plow - share turned:
G
1, 3
Am
1st time to verse 2
2nd time to verse 4
Christ has giv - en us peace.
2, 4
Am
D.C.
peace.

The Kingdom of God (El reino de Dios) 799

THE KINGDOM OF GOD IS JUSTICE AND PEACE Irregular

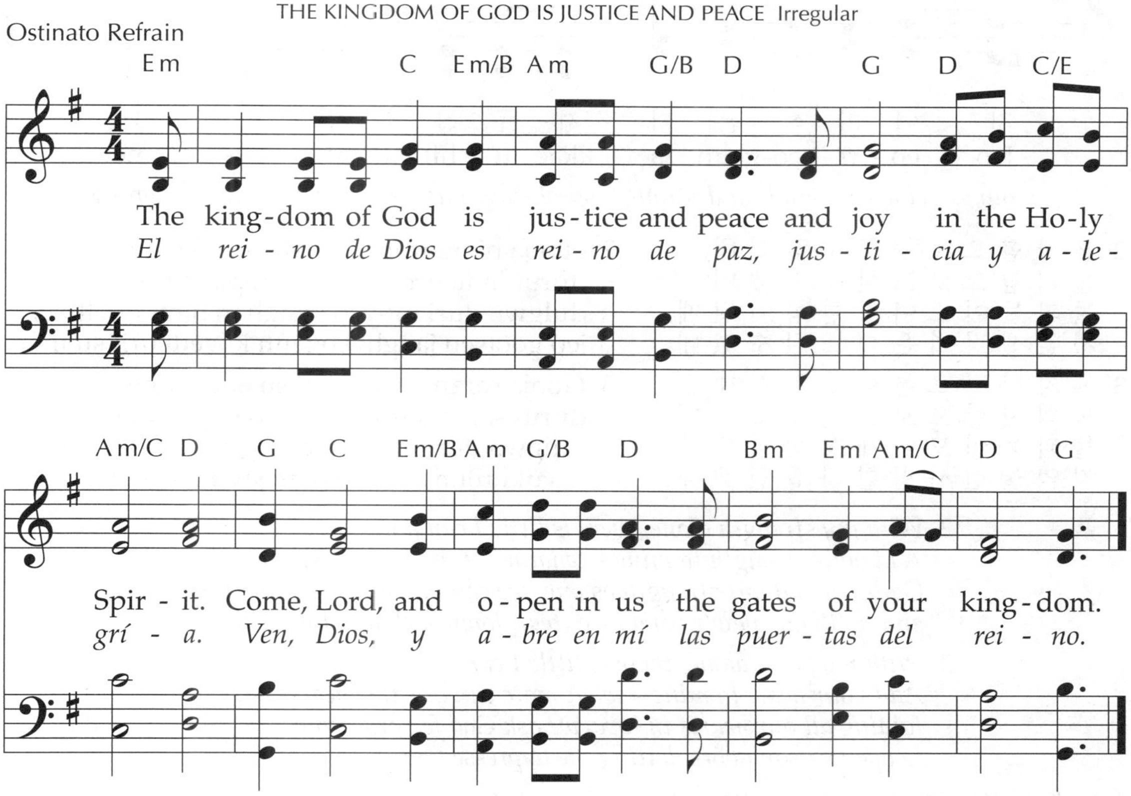
Ostinato Refrain
Em C Em/B Am G/B D G D C/E
The king-dom of God is jus-tice and peace and joy in the Ho-ly
El rei - no de Dios es rei - no de paz, jus - ti - cia y a - le -
Am/C D G C Em/B Am G/B D Bm Em Am/C D G
Spir - it. Come, Lord, and o - pen in us the gates of your king-dom.
grí - a. Ven, Dios, y a - bre en mí las puer - tas del rei - no.

Text: based on Romans 4:17; Taizé Community (France); Spanish trans. Taizé Community
Music: Taizé Community

800 혼자 소리로는 Honja sorironeun (With My Voice Alone)

HONJA SORIRONEUN Irregular

Em Am7 B
1 혼 자 소 리 로 는 할 수 없 겠 네,
1 Hon - ja so - ri - ro - neun hal su eop - gen - ne.
1 With my voice a - lone, there is lit - tle I can do.
Em G
둘 의 소 리 로 도 할 수 없 겠 네,
Du - re so - ri - ro - do hal su eop - gen - ne.
Add your voice to mine— what more can two voic - es do?
Em G Em
둘 과 둘 이 모 여 서 커 단 함 성 될 때,
Dul - gwa du - ri mo - yeo - seo keo - dan ham - seong doel - ttae.
If we gath - er more and more, we be - come a might - y roar,
B Em B7 Em
저 어 리 석 은 자 깨 우 칠 수 있 네.
Jeo eo - ri - seo - geun ja kkae - u - chil su in - ne.
our voic - es loud and strong speak - ing out a - gainst all wrong.

2 혼자힘으로는할수없겠네,
둘의힘으로도할수없겠네,
둘과둘이모여강한힘이될때,
저굳센장벽은깨뜨릴수있네.

3 혼자사랑으론할수없겠네,
둘의사랑으로도할수없겠네,
둘과둘이모여세상하나될때,
저억눌린사람참자유얻겠네.

2 Honja himeuroneun hal su eopgenne,
durui himeurodo hal su eopgenne,
dulgwa duri moyeo kanghan himi doelttae,
jeo gootsen jangbyeogeun kkaetteuril su inne.

3 Honja sarangeuron hal su eopgenne,
durui sarangeurodo hal su eopgenne,
dulgwa duri moyeo sesang hana doelttae,
jeo uknullin saram cham jayu eotgenne.

2 *With my strength alone, there is little I can do.*
Add your strength to mine—what more can our forces do?
Gath'ring all our strength as one, we can move a stubborn stone,
and, with our pow'r combined, tear down each dividing wall.

3 *With my heart alone, there is little I can do.*
Add your heart to mine—what more can our two hearts do?
Joining all our hearts in love, we ask God for grace enough
to open prison doors, letting the oppressed go free.

Text: Korean; unknown; trans. Andrew Donaldson (Canada), trans. © 2013 Andrew Donaldson
Music: Moon Seong Mo (Korea)

I'm Gonna Eat at the Welcome Table 801

WELCOME TABLE Irregular
Swing: ♫ = ♩ ♪ (triplet 3)
G
1 I'm gon-na eat at the wel-come ta - ble.
2 God's gon-na set this _ world on fire. ___
3 I'm gon-na walk and _ talk with Je - sus.
4 I'm gon-na drink at the crys-tal foun - tain.
C
I'm gon-na eat at the wel - come ta - ble some of these
God's gon-na set this _ world on fire ___ some of these
I'm gon-na walk and _ talk with Je - sus some of these
I'm gon-na drink at the crys - tal foun - tain some of these
G
days. Hal - le - lu - jah! I'm gon-na
days. Hal - le - lu - jah! God's gon-na
days. Hal - le - lu - jah! I'm gon-na
days. Hal - le - lu - jah! I'm gon-na
Em C
eat at the wel-come ta - ble. I'm gon - na
set this _ world on fire. ___ God's gon - na
walk and _ talk with Je - sus. I'm gon - na
drink at the crys - tal foun - tain. I'm gon - na
G C D G C G
eat at the wel - come ta - ble some of these days.
set this ___ world on fire ___ some of these days.
walk and ___ talk with Je - sus some of these days.
drink at the crys - tal foun - tain some of these days.

Text: African American spiritual (USA); stanzas 1–3 as recorded by the Florida Normal and Industrial Quartette (USA), 1922; stanza 4 transcr. Mary Allen Grissom (USA), *Tne Negro Sings a New Heaven*, 1930

Music: African American spiritual

802 Draw the Circle

DRAW THE CIRCLE Irregular

D G/D D G/D
Draw the cir - cle, draw the cir - cle wide. Draw the cir - cle,
G A D G A
draw the cir - cle wide. No one stands a-lone, we'll stand side by
Bm E Em A 1 D 2 D D/C
side. Draw the cir-cle, draw the cir-cle wide. wide.
Bm7 Gmaj7 A D
Draw the cir-cle wide, draw it wid-er still. Let this
Bm7 Gmaj7 E A D G D/F#
be our song: no one stands a-lone. Stand-ing side by side,
F# Bm G A7 1 D D/C# 2 D
draw the cir-cle, draw the cir-cle wide. wide.

G/D D A/D D
Draw the cir - cle wide, draw it wid - er still. Let this
G D E A D G D/F♯
be our song: no one stands a - lone. Stand - ing side by side,
Repeat as desired
F♯ Bm G A D
draw the cir - cle, draw the cir - cle wide.
Last time
F♯ Bm D/A F♯ Bm E
draw the cir - cle, draw the cir - cle wide. Draw the
Em G A D
molto rit.
cir - cle, draw the cir - cle wide.

803 We Shall Overcome

WE SHALL OVERCOME Irregular

C F C F C Am
We shall o - ver - come, we shall o - ver - come, we shall o - ver -
Refrain
D G D7 G G7 C/E F C
come some - day! Oh, deep in my heart
F C Am Ddim C7 F C/G G7 C
I do be - lieve we shall o - ver - come some - day!

We'll walk hand in hand . . . some day!
We shall live in peace . . . some day!
We are not afraid . . . today!
God will see us through . . . today!

Text: African American traditional (USA); adapt. Zilphia Horton (USA), Frank Hamilton (USA), Guy Carawan (USA), and Pete Seeger (USA); inspired by Charles Tindley, "I'll Overcome Some Day," 1900, members of the Food & Tobacco Workers Union, Charleston, South Carolina, and the civil rights movement in the American South (USA), 20th c.
Music: African American traditional (USA); adapt. Zilphia Horton, Frank Hamilton, Guy Carawan, and Pete Seeger

There Is More Love Somewhere 804

BIKO 6.6.9.6

D A7 D
There is more love* some - where.
G D A
There is more love some - where.
D7 G D Bm
I'm gon-na keep on till I find it.
D/A A7 D
There is more love some - where.

*Additional verses: hope, peace, joy

Text: African American traditional (USA)
Music: African American traditional

Peace, Salaam, Shalom 805

BEERSHEBA 5.5.5.5

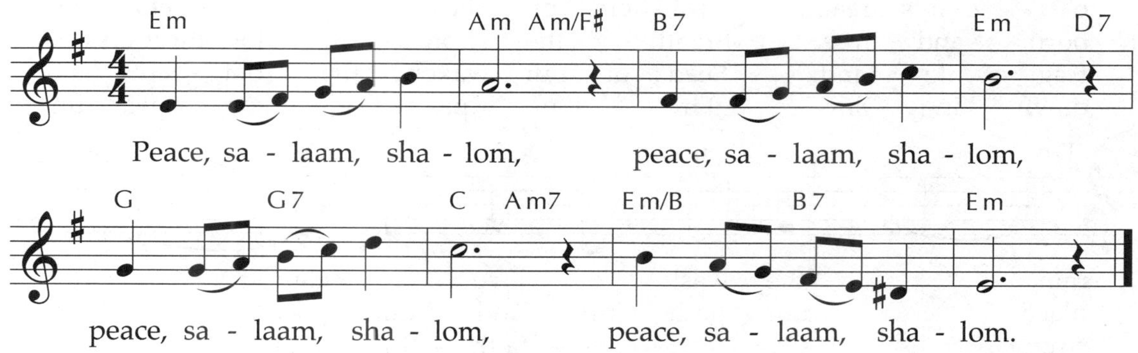
Em Am Am/F♯ B7 Em D7
Peace, sa - laam, sha - lom, peace, sa - laam, sha - lom,
G G7 C Am7 Em/B B7 Em
peace, sa - laam, sha - lom, peace, sa - laam, sha - lom.

Text: English, Arabic, Hebrew; traditional
Music: Dean McIntyre (USA), © 2004 General Board of Discipleship of the United Methodist Church

806 Called by Earth and Sky

CALLED 8.4.5.9.6 with refrain

Refrain
Called by earth and sky, prom-ise of hope held high,
this is our sa - cred liv - ing trust, treas - ure of life
sanc - ti - fied,
To verses
called by earth and sky.
Last time
called by earth and sky. called by earth and sky.
Verses
1 Pre - cious, these wa - ters, end - less seas, deep
2 Pre - cious this gift, the air we breathe; wind
3 Pre - cious these moun - tains, an - cient sands; vast
4 Pre - cious the fire that lights the way, bright
o - cean's dream, wa - ters of heal - ing, riv - ers of
born and free. Breath of the Spir - it, blow through this
frag - ile land. Seeds of our waken - ing, root - ed and
dawn - ing day. Fire of pas - sion, sor - rows un -
rain, the wash of love a - gain.
place, our gath - 'ring and our grace.
strong, Cre - a - tion's faith - ful song.
done, our faith and jus - tice one.
To refrain

Text: Pat Mayberry (Canada)
Music: Pat Mayberry; acc. Marg Stubington (Canada)

Hope of Abraham and Sarah 807

CIVILITY 8.7.8.7 D

1 Hope of A - bra - ham and Sa - rah, friend of Ha - gar, God of Ruth, you de - sire that ev - 'ry peo - ple wor - ship you in spir - it, truth. Meet us in our sa - cred plac - es, mosque and syn - a - gogue and church. Show us paths of un - der - stand - ing; bless us in our com - mon search.
2 Root us in our own tra - di - tions, faith our fore - bears hand - ed down. Grow us in your grace and knowl - edge; plant our feet on sol - id ground. Cul - ti - vate the seeds of shar - ing in this world of man - y creeds. Keep us op - en, wise in learn - ing, bear - ing fruit in lov - ing deeds.
3 Hope of those who came be - fore us, sov'-reign God whom we a - dore, form in us your new cre - a - tion free of vio - lence, hate, and war. So may star, and cross, and cres - cent, each a sign of life made new, point us toward your love and jus - tice, earth at peace and one in you.

For a four-part setting of this tune, see "Come Away from Rush and Hurry" (#9).

Alternate tune: HYFRYDOL (#218 or #745)

808 Between Darkness and Light

BETWEEN DARKNESS AND LIGHT Irregular

Bm A Bm F♯m
Hebrew: Bein ha - cho-shekh la' - or ___ e - lekh ___ ta - mid;
Arabic: Bay - nal at - ma wal nur ___ sa - am - shi da'i - man;
English: Be - tween dark - ness and light I will al - ways walk;
G A F♯7
u' - v' - khol ma - kom she'-e - lekh, ef -
wa bi - kul ma - kan sa - am - shi, sa -
and wher - ev - er I will ___ go, I will
G D F♯7 Bm Gmaj7
tach ___ cha - lon, cha - lon ___ shel or v' - ez - ra ___ zir' -
af - tach shu - bak, shu - bak ___ a - nur, wa sa - az - ra bu -
o - pen a win - dow of light, and will plant ___ the
A F♯7 G D
ei a - ha - va. Ef - tach ___ cha - lon, cha -
zur - a ___ hoob. Sa - af - tach shu - bak, shu -
seeds of ___ love. I will o - pen a
F♯7 Bm Gmaj7 A Bsus Bm
lon ___ shel or v' - ez - ra ___ zir' - ei a - ha - va.
bak ___ a - nur, wa sa - az - ra bu - zur - z ___ hoob.
win - dow of light, and will plant ___ the seeds of ___ love.

בין החושך לאור אלך תמיד
ובכל מקום שאלך
אפתח חלון חלון של אור
ואזרע זרעי אהבה

بين العتمة والنور سأمشي دائما
وبكل مكان سأمشي
سأفتح شباك ..شباك نور
وسأزرع بذور حب

Text: Hebrew and Arabic; Manal Hreib (Palestine), © 2006 Manal Hreib; English trans. Daphna Rosenberg (Israel)
Music: Daphna Rosenberg; acc. Benjamin Bergey (USA), 2019

Sing a New World into Being 809

HYMN TO JOY 8.7.8.7 D

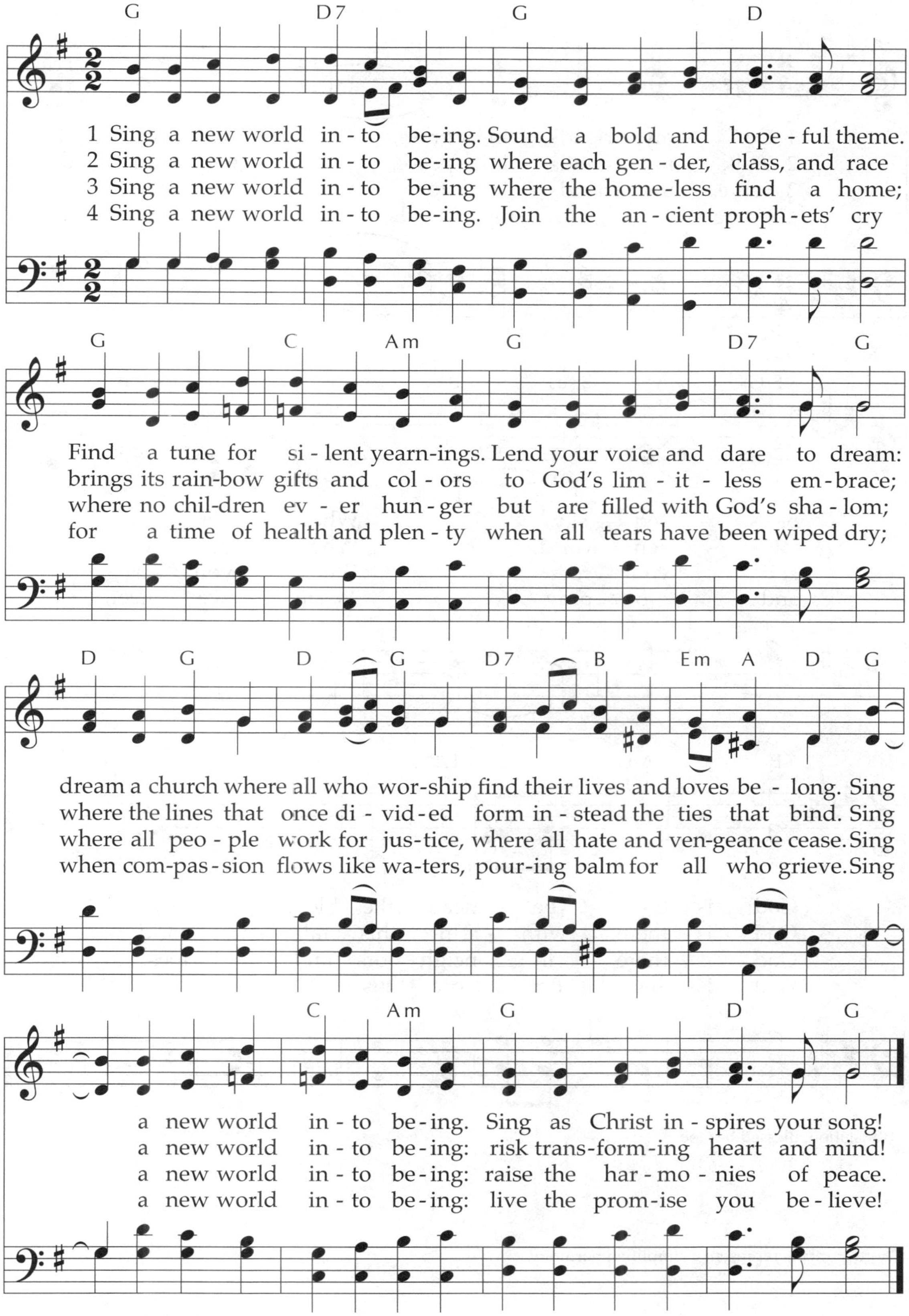
G D7 G D
1 Sing a new world in - to be-ing. Sound a bold and hope - ful theme.
2 Sing a new world in - to be-ing where each gen - der, class, and race
3 Sing a new world in - to be-ing where the home-less find a home;
4 Sing a new world in - to be-ing. Join the an - cient proph - ets' cry
G C Am G D7 G
Find a tune for si - lent yearn-ings. Lend your voice and dare to dream:
brings its rain-bow gifts and col - ors to God's lim - it - less em - brace;
where no chil-dren ev - er hun - ger but are filled with God's sha - lom;
for a time of health and plen - ty when all tears have been wiped dry;
D G D G D7 B Em A D G
dream a church where all who wor-ship find their lives and loves be - long. Sing
where the lines that once di - vid-ed form in - stead the ties that bind. Sing
where all peo - ple work for jus-tice, where all hate and ven-geance cease. Sing
when com-pas - sion flows like wa-ters, pour-ing balm for all who grieve. Sing
C Am G D G
a new world in - to be-ing. Sing as Christ in - spires your song!
a new world in - to be-ing: risk trans-form-ing heart and mind!
a new world in - to be-ing: raise the har - mo - nies of peace.
a new world in - to be-ing: live the prom-ise you be - lieve!

Text: Mary Louise Bringle (USA), © 2006 GIA Publications, Inc.
Music: Ludwig van Beethoven (Germany), 1823; adapt. Edward Hodges (England), *Trinity Collection of Church Music*, 1864, alt.

810 Go, My Friends, in Grace

BENEDICTUS DEUS 5.6.6.6

E Esus E Esus E
1 Go, my friends, in grace, be - neath the
2 Walk, my friends, in peace, with - in this
3 Serve, my friends, in love, your neigh - bors
4 Come a - gain, my friends, to wor - ship
E/G♯ Bsus B E Esus
bless - ed sky. Where you go,
fall - en world. Where you walk,
and your foes. Where you serve,
and to pray. When we meet,
E A/C♯ E/B A E
God is there, be - neath the bless - ed sky.
God is there, with - in this fall - en world.
God is there, in neigh - bors and in foes.
God is here, Ben - e - dic - tus De - us.*

*Translation: Blessed be God

Chord symbols represent a simplified harmony.

Text: David Wright (USA), 2004, *A Field of Voices,* 2007, © 2004 David Wright
Music: James E. Clemens (USA), 2004, *A Field of Voices,* 2007, © 2004 James E. Clemens

Use Us, God

USE US GOD 6.7.8.5 D

D Em D/F♯ G D Em
1 Bless our eyes, Je - sus Christ, o - pen them to
2 Bless our ears, help us hear cries of those in
3 Bless our hands, God a - bove, may they car - ry
D/F♯ G A/C♯ Em
see your light. Help us see the ways you're work - ing.
doubt and fear. Give us time to hear their sto - ries,
out your love. May they reach to all our neigh - bors,
D/F♯ G A/C♯
Meet us where we are.
let us be your ears.
reach to them in love.
Refrain
D Em D/F♯ G
Use us, God, as we go.
D Em D/F♯ G A
Let us rep - re - sent your love. E - ven though we're
Em D/F♯ G A
Last time
far from per - fect, use us as we go.

Text: Jeremy Kempf (USA)
Music: Jeremy Kempf

812 Sent Forth by God's Blessing

ASH GROVE 6.6.11.6.6.11 D

Unison
1 Sent forth by God's bless-ing, our true faith con - fess-ing, the
2 With praise and thanks - giv - ing to God ev - er liv - ing, the
peo-ple of God from this dwell-ing take leave. The sup-per is end-ed. Oh,
tasks of our ev'-ry-day life we will face. Our faith ev - er shar-ing, in
now be ex - tend-ed the fruits of this ser-vice in all who be - lieve.
love ev - er car-ing, em - brac-ing the chil-dren of each tribe and race.
Harmony
The seed of Christ's teach-ing, re - cep - tive souls reach-ing,
With your feast you feed us, with your light now lead us,
shall blos - som in ac - tion for God and for all.
u - nite us as one in this life that we share.
Unison
Your grace did in - vite us, your love shall u - nite us to
Then may all the liv - ing, with praise and thanks - giv - ing, give
work for your reign and to an - swer your call.
hon - or to Christ and his name that we bear.

Text: Omer Westendorf (USA), *People's Mass Book*, alt., © 1964 World Library Publications, Inc.
Music: Welsh traditional; harm. anon.

Heart with Loving Heart United 813

O DU LIEBE MEINER LIEBE 8.7.8.7 D

G Am D G Em D G
1 Heart with lov - ing heart u - nit - ed, met to know God's ho - ly will.
2 May we all so love each oth - er and all self - ish claims de - ny,
3 Since, O Lord, you have de-mand-ed that our lives your love should show,
Am D G Em D G
Let this love, in us ig - nit - ed, more and more our spir - its fill.
so that each one for the oth - er will not hes - i - tate to die.
so we wait to be com-mand-ed forth in - to your world to go.
D A D A D C G D
He the head, we are his mem-bers, we re - flect the light he is.
E - ven so our Lord has loved us, for our lives he gave his life.
Kin-dle in us love's com - pas - sion so that ev - 'ry - one may see
G Am D G Em D G
He the mas - ter, we dis - ci - ples, he is ours and we are his.
Still he grieves and still he suf - fers, for our self - ish - ness and strife.
in our fel - low - ship the prom - ise of a new hu - man - i - ty.

Chord symbols represent a simplified harmony.

Text: Nicolaus L. von Zinzendorf (Germany), *Herz und Herz vereint zusammen,* 1723, *Die letzien Reden unseres Herrn,* 1725; trans. Walter Klaassen (Canada), 1965, alt., © 1969, 1983 Walter Klaassen

Music: *Manuscript Chorale Book* (USA), 1735; adapt. from "Sollen nun die grünen Jahre" (present-day Germany), ca. 1700

814 O God beyond All Praising

THAXTED 13.13.13.13.13.13

Capo 3: (G) B♭ (C) E♭ (D7/A) F7/C (G) B♭ (C) E♭ (D) F (Em) Gm
1 O God be-yond all prais - ing, we wor-ship you to - day,
2 The flow'r of earth - ly splen - dor in time must sure - ly die,
3 Then hear, O gra-cious Sav - ior, ac - cept the love we bring,
(C) E♭ (D7/A) F7/C (G) B♭ (Cmaj7) E♭maj7 (Am) Cm (G) B♭
and sing the love a - maz - ing that songs can-not re - pay;
its frag - ile bloom sur-ren - der to you, the Lord most high.
that we who know your fav - or may serve you as our King.
(D) F (Em) Gm (D) F (G) B♭ (D) F (G) B♭ (C) E♭
for we can on - ly won-der at ev - 'ry gift you send,
But hid - den from all na - ture, th'e - ter - nal seed is sown,
And wheth - er our to - mor-rows be filled with good or ill,
(Em) Gm (C) E♭ (G) B♭ (Am/C) Cm/E♭ (Em) Gm (D) F
at bless-ings with - out num-ber and mer-cies with - out end.
though small in mor - tal stat - ure, to heav-en's gar - den grown:
we'll tri-umph through our sor-rows and rise to bless you still:
(C) E♭ (D7/A) F7/C (G/B) B♭/D (C) E♭ (D) F (Em) Gm
We lift our hearts be - fore you and wait up-on your Word,
for Christ, your gift from heav - en, from death has set us free,
to mar - vel at your beau - ty and glo - ry in your ways,
(C) E♭ (D7/A) F7/C (G) B♭ (Cmaj7) E♭maj7 (Am) Cm (G) B♭
we hon - or and a - dore you, our great and might - y Lord.
and we through him are giv - en the fi - nal vic - to - ry.
and make a joy - ful du - ty our sac - ri - fice of praise.

Text: Michael Perry (England), © 1982 The Jubilate Group (admin. Hope Publishing Company)
Music: Gustav Holst (England), 1918, *Songs of Praise*, 1925, adapt. from *The Planets*, 1916

Sizohamba naye (We Will Walk with God)

815

SIZOHAMBA NAYE 9.6.9.6.6.6.6.6

G
Em
D
G
Si - zo-ham - ba na - ye, wo wo wo, si - zo-ham - ba na - ye.
We will walk ___ with God, wo wo wo, we will walk ___ with God.
C
G
Em
D
G
Ngom-hla wen - ja - bu - la si - zo-ham - ba na - ye.
We will go re - joic - ing till the king - dom has come.
C
G
Em
D
G
Ngom-hla wen - ja - bu - la si - zo-ham - ba na - ye.
We will go re - joic - ing till the king - dom has come.

Text: Xhosa; traditional Swazi; trans. John L. Bell (Scotland), alt.
Music: traditional Swazi; transcr. Swedish Youth Exchange project, "Meeting Swaziland"

816 Guide My Feet

GUIDE MY FEET Irregular

Capo 1: (G) A♭ (C) D♭ (G) A♭
1, 6 Guide my feet while I run this race,
yes, my Lord!
(D7) E♭7 (G) A♭
Guide my feet while I run this race,
yes, my Lord!
(C) D♭ (G) A♭ (Em) Fm
Guide my feet while I run this race, for I
(G) A♭ (D7) E♭7 (G) A♭ (C) D♭ (G) A♭
don't want to run this race in vain! (race in vain!)

2 Hold my hand . . .
3 Stand by me . . .
4 I'm your child . . .
5 Search my heart . . .

Text: African American spiritual (USA)
Music: African American spiritual; harm. Wendell Whalum (USA), ca. 1984,

818 *Colossians 3:15-17*

Let your hearts be ruled
by the peace of Christ,
to which indeed you were called
in one body.
And be thankful.
Let the word of Christ
dwell in you richly,
teaching and admonishing
one another in all wisdom,
singing psalms and hymns
and spiritual songs
with thankfulness
in your hearts to God.
Whatever you do,
in word or deed,
do everything in the name of Jesus,
giving thanks to God our Creator
through Christ.

819 *2 Thessalonians 2:16-17*

Now may our Lord Jesus Christ,
and God our Creator,
who loved us
and gave us eternal comfort
and good hope through grace,
comfort your hearts
and establish them
in every good work and word.

820 *Habakkuk 3:17-18*

Though the fig tree does not blossom
and there are no grapes on the vines,
though the olive crop fails
and the fields produce no food,
though there are no sheep in the pen
and no cattle in the stalls,
still I will rejoice in the Lord,
I will be joyful in the God
of my salvation.

821 *Psalm 126:5-6*

May those who sow in tears
reap with songs of joy.
May those who go out weeping,
carrying seed to sow,
return with songs of joy,
carrying their sheaves.

822 *Romans 15:5-6*

May the God of endurance
and encouragement
grant you to live in such harmony
with one another,
in accord with Christ Jesus,
that together you may with one voice
glorify the God
of our Savior Jesus Christ.

823 *1 Thessalonians 5:23-24*

Now may the God of peace
sanctify you completely,
and may your whole spirit
and soul and body
be kept blameless
at the coming of our Lord Jesus Christ.
The one who calls you is faithful
and will surely do it.

824 *Ephesians 3:20-21*

Now to the One who,
by the power at work within us,
is able to do exceedingly far more
than all we could ask or imagine,
to God be the glory
in the church
and in Christ Jesus
through all generations,
forever and ever. Amen.

825 *Luke 2:29-32*

Now, Lord,
you let your servant go in peace:
your word has been fulfilled.
My own eyes have seen the salvation,
which you have prepared
in the sight of every people:
a light to reveal you to the nations
and the glory of your people Israel.

826 *Numbers 6:24-26*

May God bless you and keep you.
May the very face of God shine on you
and be gracious to you.
May God's presence embrace you
and give you peace.

Previous page: 817. *Migrant Journey*, Rafael H Barahona (Canada/USA), 2018, digital ⓦ

Move in Our Midst 827

PINE GLEN 9.9.9.9

Capo 1: (C) Db (G) Ab (C) Db (F) Gb (G) Ab (Am) Bbm (Em) Fm (G) Ab
1 Move in our midst, thou Spir - it of God. Go with us
2 Touch thou our hands to lead us a - right. Guide us for -
3 Strike from our feet the fet - ters that bind. Lift from our
4 Kin - dle our hearts to burn with thy flame. Raise up thy
(C) Db (F) Gb (G7) Ab7 (C) Db
down from thy ho - ly hill. Walk with us through the
ev - er, show us thy way. Trans-form our dark - ness
lives the weight of our wrong. Teach us to love with
ban - ners high in this hour. Stir us to build new
(G) Ab (Am) Bbm (C) Db (B7/F♯) C7/G (C/G) Db/Ab (G7) Ab7 (C) Db
storm and the calm. Spir - it of God, go thou with us still.
in - to thy light. Spir - it of God, lead thou us to - day.
heart, soul, and mind. Spir - it of God, thy love makes us strong.
worlds in thy name. Spir - it of God, O send us thy pow'r!

Chord symbols represent a simplified harmony.

Text: Kenneth I. Morse (USA), 1942, 1949, *The Brethren Hymnal*, 1951
Music: Perry L. Huffaker (USA), 1950, *The Brethren Hymnal*, 1951

828 There's a Wild Hope in the Wind

WILD HOPE Irregular

1 There's a wild hope in the wind: her whis-per is heard on the breeze. The gale is her shout that is call - ing us out. There's a wild hope in the wind.
2 There's a wild hope in the skies: her gown is the blue of for-ev - er. The pur-ple of night is her heart's pure de-light. There's a wild hope in the skies.
3 There's a wild hope in the earth: her bod - y pro-vides us with nur - ture. The dark un-der-ground is where life can a-bound. There's a wild hope in the earth.
O God in the wind, come gath - er us in,
O God in the skies, come o - pen our eyes,
O God in the earth, came aid our re - birth,
be our cour-age and prom-ise. The fu - ture is dim, but we want to live in - to a wild, wild hope.

Text: Lora Braun (Canada)
Music: Lora Braun; acc. Loretta Thorleifson (Canada), 2017

Go Now in Peace, Worship Continues 829

EARTH AND ALL STARS (abridged) 4.5.10 D

G Em A D
1 Go now in peace, wor - ship con - tin - ues;
2 Go now in joy: cel - e - brate liv - ing!
3 Go now in love. Led by Christ's teach - ing,
Em G D G
ser - vice be - gins as you go from this place.
Sing and praise God with re - joic - ing each day.
share with your neigh - bor the love that you know.
D G A D
Taught by God's Word, safe in God's tend - ing,
Lift - ed in hope, filled with thanks - giv - ing,
Gifts from the heart out - ward - ly reach - ing
Em G D G
hold to the path that will run the good race.
spread the good news as you go on your way.
car - ry love's mes - sage wher - ev - er you go.

Chord symbols represent a simplified harmony.

830 Go, My Children

AR HYD Y NOS 12.12.8.8.12

G C A D C D7 G
1 "Go, my chil - dren, with my bless - ing, nev - er a - lone.
Wak - ing, sleep - ing, I am with you, you are my own.
2 Go, my chil - dren, sins for - giv - en, at peace and pure.
Here you learned how much I love you, what I can cure.
3 Go, my chil - dren, fed and nour - ished, clos - er to me.
Grow in love, and love by serv - ing, joy - ful and free.
C Am G/D D
In my love's bap - tis - mal riv - er, I have made you mine for - ev - er.
Here you heard my dear Son's sto - ry, here you touched him, saw his glo - ry.
Here my Spir - it's pow - er filled you, here my ten - der com-fort stilled you.
G C A D C D7 G
Go, my chil-dren, with my bless - ing, you are my own.
Go, my chil-dren, sins for - giv - en, at peace and pure.
Go, my chil-dren, fed and nour - ished, joy - ful and free."

Text: Jaroslav J. Vajda (USA), © 1983 Concordia Publishing House
Music: Welsh traditional, *Musical and Poetical Relics of the Welsh Bards*, 1784

Blest Be the Tie That Binds 831

DENNIS SM

Capo 3: (D) F (A7) C7 (D) F (D7) F7 (G) B♭
1 Blest be the tie that binds our hearts in
2 We share each oth - er's woes, each oth - er's
3 When we a - sun - der part, it gives us
4 From sor - row, toil, and pain, and sin we
(D) F (A) C (A7) C7 (D) F (A) C (A7) C7
Chris - tian love. The fel - low - ship of kin - dred
bur - dens bear, and of - ten for each oth - er
in - ward pain, But we shall still be joined in
shall be free, and per - fect love and friend - ship
(D) F (G/D) B♭/F (D) F (G) B♭ (D/A) F/C (A7) C7 (D) F
minds is like to that a - bove.
flows the sym - pa - thiz - ing tear.
heart, and hope to meet a - gain.
reign through all e - ter - ni - ty.

Text: John Fawcett (England), *Hymns Adapted to the Circumstances of Public Worship . . .*, 1782, alt.
Music: Johann G. Nägeli (Switzerland), *Christliches Gesangbuch*, 1828; arr. Lowell Mason (USA), *The Psaltery*, 1845

832 The Lord Lift You Up

BENEDICTION 5.5.5.5.5.4.5.5

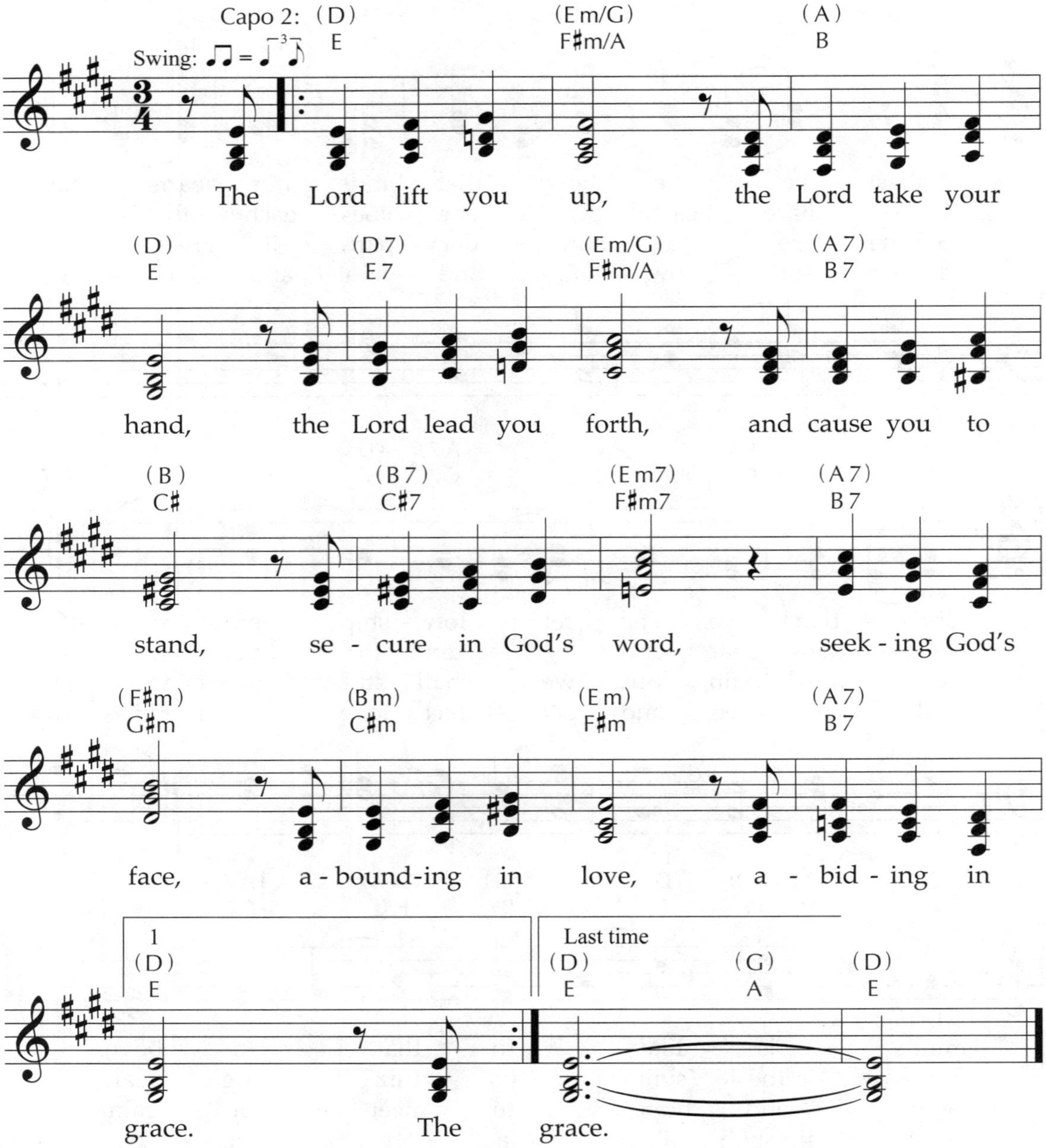
Capo 2:
Swing:
(D) E
(Em/G) F♯m/A
(A) B
The Lord lift you up, the Lord take your
(D) E
(D7) E7
(Em/G) F♯m/A
(A7) B7
hand, the Lord lead you forth, and cause you to
(B) C♯
(B7) C♯7
(Em7) F♯m7
(A7) B7
stand, se - cure in God's word, seek - ing God's
(F♯m) G♯m
(Bm) C♯m
(Em) F♯m
(A7) B7
face, a - bound - ing in love, a - bid - ing in
1
(D) E
grace. The
Last time
(D) E
(G) A
(D) E
grace.

Text: Patricia J. Shelly (USA)
Music: Patricia J. Shelly; arr. Dennis Friesen-Carper (USA)

Sálvanos, Señor (Save Us, O Lord) 833

SÁLVANOS SEÑOR, DESPIERTOS Irregular

Refrain
Am Dm E7
Sál - va - nos, Se - ñor, des - pier - tos, pro - té - ge - nos dor -
Evening: Save us, O Lord, in our wak - ing; pro - tect us in our
Sending: Let us de - part with your bless - ing till once a - gain we
Am F Dm
mi - dos, pa - ra ve - lar jun - to‿a Cris - to,
sleep - ing. Christ, keep us watch - ing and wait - ing
gath - er. Christ, keep us watch - ing and wait - ing
E E7 Am Fine
y des - can - sar en su paz.
till we can rest in your peace.
for ev - 'ry sign of your peace.
Verses
Am
1 A‿ho - ra, se - gún tu pro -
2 A quien, Se - ñor, pre - sen -
3 Glo - ria‿al Pa - dre, glo - ria‿al
1 Lord, to ful - fill what you
2 This is your gift of Sal -
3 Glo - ry to God in the
Dm G C F
me - sa, vas a de - jar a tu sier - vo‿ir en paz, por - que mis
tas - te an - te to - das las na - cio - nes, luz pa - ra‿a -
Hi - jo, glo - ria‿al Es - pí - ri - tu San - to, en un prin -
prom - ised, grant that your ser - vant may go now in peace. I have be -
va - tion, giv - en to all of the na - tions: light for the
high - est, and to the Son and the Spir - it, as it was
Dm Am/E E7 Am To refrain
o - jos han vis - to a tu Sal - va - dor.
lum - brar al mun - do y glo - ria de‿Is - ra - el.
ci - pio,‿a‿ho - ra‿y siem - pre por los si - glos, a - mén.
held my sal - va - tion with my wea - ry eyes.
world veiled in dark - ness shines from Is - ra - el.
in the be - gin - ning, now and ev - er - more, a - men.

Text: Spanish; based on Luke 2:29–32, Latin "Nunc Dimittis;" Juan José Sosa (USA); English trans. and additional refrain Adam M. L. Tice (USA)
Music: Juan José Sosa; arr. Ivette Herryman Rodríguez (USA)

834 Thuma mina (Send Me, Lord)

THUMA MINA Irregular

Leader
All
B C♯m B E C♯m
1 Thu-ma mi-na. Thu-ma mi-na, thu-ma mi-na,
2 Send me, Je-sus, send me, Je-sus,
3 Lead me, Je-sus, lead me, Je-sus,
4 Fill me, Je-sus, fill me, Je-sus,
1–3
Leader
4
2 Send me, Lord.
3 Lead me, Lord.
4 Fill me, Lord.
E F♯m E/B B
1–3
E
4
E
thu-ma mi-na, So-man-dla.
send me, Je-sus, send me, Lord.
lead me, Je-sus, lead me, Lord.
fill me, Je-sus, fill me,
Lord.

Text: Zulu; anon. (South Africa); trans. anon.
Music: South African traditional; arr. © 1984 Peace of Music Publishing AB (admin. Walton Music Corp., a division of GIA Publications, Inc.)

835 Go Now in Peace

GO NOW IN PEACE Irregular

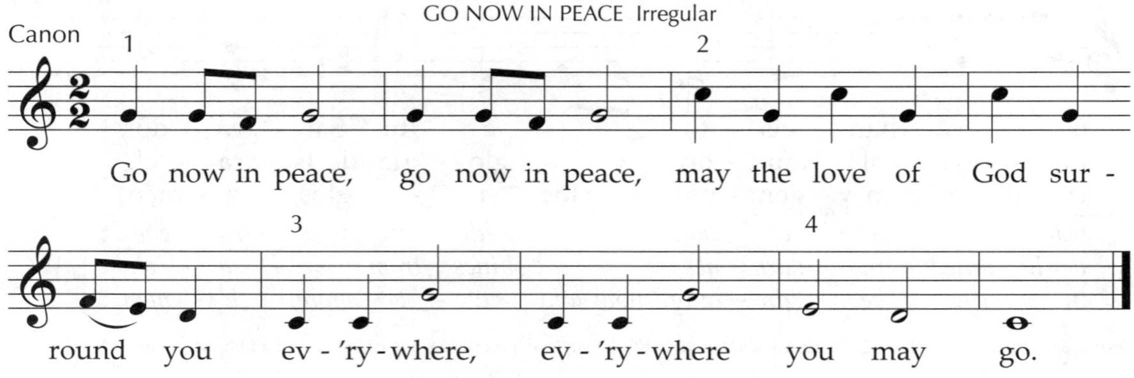
Canon
1
2
Go now in peace, go now in peace, may the love of God sur-
3
4
round you ev-'ry-where, ev-'ry-where you may go.

Text: Natalie Sleeth (USA), *Sunday Songbook*
Music: Natalie Sleeth, *Sunday Songbook*

Hey ney yana
(I Walk in Beauty)

HEY NEY YANA Irregular

Refrain
Hey ney ya - na, hey ney ya - na, hey ney
ya - na, hey ya hey yo, hey ya hey yo.
Fine
1 I walk in beau - ty, yes I do, yes I do, I
2 I leave in beau - ty, yes I do, yes I do, I
talk in beau - ty, yes I do, yes I do, I
sleep in beau - ty, yes I do, yes I do, I
sing of beau - ty, hey ya hey yo, hey ya hey yo.
dream of beau - ty, hey ya hey yo, hey ya hey yo.
To refrain

Text: Ute children's song (First Nations, USA); as taught by Brooke Medicine Eagle (First Nations, USA)
Music: Ute children's song; as taught by Brooke Medicine Eagle

837 Lead Me Forth

LEAD ME, LORD Irregular

Lead me forth. Lead me in thy right-eous-ness.
Make thy way plain be - fore my face. For it is
thou, God, thou, God, on - ly that mak - est me
dwell in safe - ty. A - men.

Text: based on Psalms 5:8 and 4:8
Music: Samuel S. Wesley (England), 1861

La paz de la tierra (The Peace of the Earth Be with You) 838

LA PAZ DE LA TIERRA 8.7.9.7.7.6

Am F
La paz de la tie - rra es - té con - ti - go, la
The peace of the earth be with you, the
G Esus E Am
paz de los cie - los tam - bién. La paz de los rí - os es -
peace of the heav - ens too; the peace of the riv - ers
F G Esus E
té con - ti - go, la paz de los ma - res tam - bién. La
be with you, the peace of the o - ceans too.
C G Am Em Am
paz pro - fun - da ca - yen - do so - bre ti. La
Deep peace fall - ing o - ver you.
C G Am Em A
paz pro - fun - da cre - cien - do en ti.
God's peace grow - ing in you.

Text: Spanish; Guatemalan traditional; trans. Christine Carson (Scotland),
Music: Guatemalan traditional

839 Go Ye Now in Peace / Go, My Friends, in Peace

GO YE NOW IN PEACE Irregular

A: Go ye now in peace, and know that the love of
B: Go, my friends, in peace, and know that the love of
God will guide you. Feel his pres - ence here be - side you
God will guide you. Feel the Spir - it here be - side you,
Feel
show-ing you the way. In your time of trou - ble when
show-ing you the way. In your time of trou - ble when
hurt and de-spair are there to grieve you, know that the Lord will
hurt and de-spair are there to grieve you, know that your God will

Text: text A Joyce Elaine Eilers (USA); text B adapt. Mennonite Worship and Song Committee
Music: Joyce Elaine Eilers

nev - er leave you. He will bring you cour - age.
nev - er leave you. God will bring you cour - age.
Know that the God who sent his Son to die that you might
Know that the Christ who came to us to die that you might
live will nev - er leave you lost and a-lone in his be-lov - ed
live will nev - er leave you lost and a-lone in his be-lov - ed
world. Go ye now in peace. Go ye now in peace.
world. Go, my friends, in peace. Go, my friends, in peace.

840 God Be with You Till We Meet Again

GOD BE WITH YOU 9.8.8.9 with refrain

1 God be with you till we meet a - gain; lov - ing coun - sels guide, up - hold you, may the Shep - herd's care en - fold you; God be with you till we meet a - gain.
2 God be with you till we meet a - gain; un - seen wings, pro - tect - ing, hide you, dai - ly man - na still pro - vide you; God be with you till we meet a - gain.
3 God be with you till we meet a - gain; when life's per - ils thick con - found you, put un - fail - ing arms a - round you; God be with you till we meet a - gain.
4 God be with you till we meet a - gain; keep love's ban - ner float - ing o'er you, smite death's threat - 'ning wave be - fore you; God be with you till we meet a - gain.
Refrain
Till we meet, Till we meet, till we meet, a - gain, till we meet at Je - sus' feet. till we meet.
Till we meet, Till we meet, till we meet, a - gain, God be with you till we meet a - gain.

Text: Jeremiah E. Rankin (USA), *Gospel Bells,* 1880, alt.
Music: William G. Tomer (USA), *Gospel Bells,* 1880

As You Go Out from Here 841

SENDING SONG Irregular

Capo 3: (D) F (D/F♯) F/A (G) B♭
As you go out from here, may the Lord go
(D) F (D/F♯) F/A (G) B♭ (A) C
with you. The face of God shine on you ev - 'ry day.
(D) F (D/F♯) F/A (G) B♭ (D) F
We are sent by God wher - ev - er we are liv - ing,
(Em) Gm (D) F (A7) C7 (G/D) B♭/F (D) F
salt and light as peo - ple of the Way.

Text: Bryan Moyer Suderman (Canada), 2001
Music: Bryan Moyer Suderman, 2001; acc. Charlene Nafziger (Canada)

שלום חברים Shalom chaverim 842
(Shalom, My Friends)

SHALOM Irregular

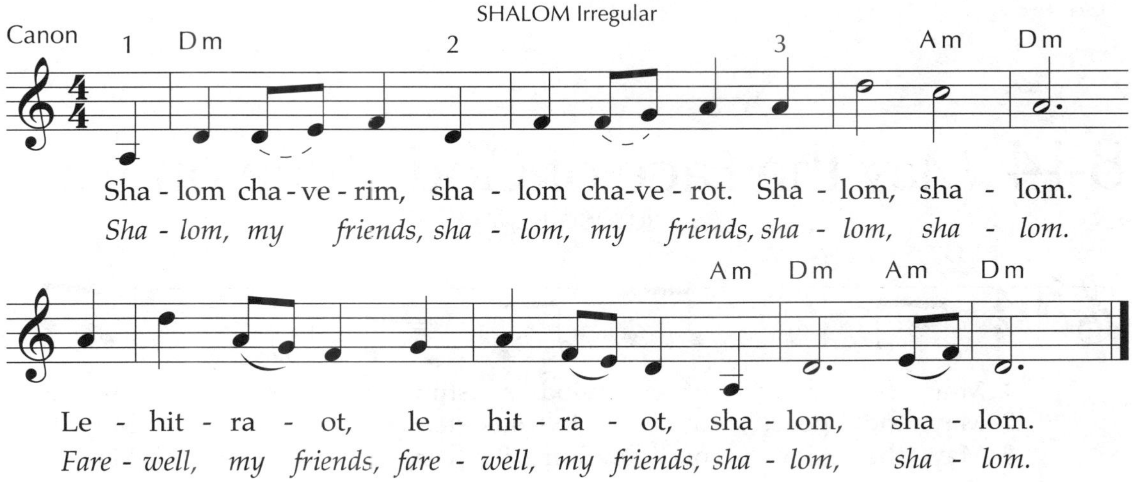
Canon 1 Dm 2 3 Am Dm
Sha - lom cha - ve - rim, sha - lom cha-ve - rot. Sha - lom, sha - lom.
Sha - lom, my friends, sha - lom, my friends, sha - lom, sha - lom.
Am Dm Am Dm
Le - hit - ra - ot, le - hit - ra - ot, sha - lom, sha - lom.
Fare - well, my friends, fare - well, my friends, sha - lom, sha - lom.

שלום חברים שלום חברות שלום שלום
להתראות להתראות שלום שלום

Text: Hebrew traditional
Music: Israeli traditional

843 キリストの平和が
Kirisuto no heiwa ga
(May the Peace of Christ)

KI RI SU TO NO Irregular

Capo 3: (C) E♭ (Em7) Gm7 (F) A♭
*キ リ ス ト の 平 和 が わ た し た
Ki - ri - su - to no hei - wa ga, wa - ta - shi - ta -
May the peace of Christ be with you. May the love of
(Em7) Gm7 (Dm7) Fm7 (G2) B♭2 (C) E♭
ち の こ こ ろ の す み ず み に ま
chi no ko - ko - ro no su - mi - zu - mi ni ma -
Christ dwell deep in your heart. May the Spir - it en-light - en your
(Em7) Gm7 (Dm/F) Fm/A♭ (G7) B♭7 (C) E♭
で ゆ き わ た り ま す よ う に
de yu - ki - wa - ta - ri - ma - su - yo - u - ni.
way. May you live in the com-fort of God's care.

*Translation: May the peace of Christ enter every corner of our hearts.

Text: Japanese; Izumi Shiota (Japan); English stanza Lori True (USA), 2008
Music: Izumi Shiota; arr. Lori True, 2008; acc. Mary Howarth (USA)

844 May the Face of God Shine on You

BLESSING Irregular

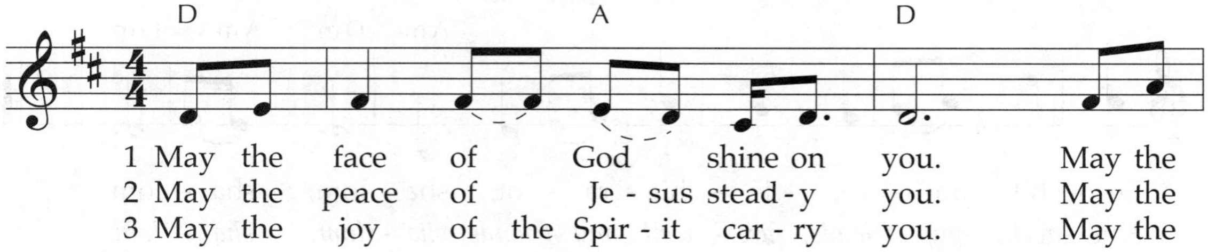
D A D
1 May the face of God shine on you. May the
2 May the peace of Je - sus stead - y you. May the
3 May the joy of the Spir - it car - ry you. May the

Text: Jerry L. Holsopple (USA)
Music: Jerry L. Holsopple

Bm A G D
face of God shine on you, with the words of prom - ise
peace of Je - sus stea - dy you when the world is shak - ing and
joy of the Spir - it car - ry you. May the laugh - ter pour wash - ing
G Bm D A D
whis - pered in your ear. May the face of God shine on you.
chal - leng - es come. May the peace of Je - sus stead - y you.
o - ver ev - 'ry day. May the joy of the Spir - it car - ry you.

Bwana awabariki (May God Grant You a Blessing) 845

BWANA AWABARIKI Irregular

G Em C D
Bwa - na a - wa - ba - ri - ki, Bwa - na a - wa - ba - ri - ki,
May God grant you a bless - ing, may God grant you a bless - ing,
G Em C G/D D7 G
Bwa - na a - wa - ba - ri - ki mi - le - le.
may God grant you a bless - ing ev - er - more.

Text: Swahili; Kenyan traditional; trans. anon.
Music: Kenyan traditional

846 The Lord Bless You and Keep You

FAREWELL ANTHEM Irregular

The Lord bless you and keep you; the Lord lift his coun-te-nance up-
May God may God lift her
on you,
and give you peace,
and give you peace, and give you
the Lord make his
may God make her
and give you peace; the Lord make his face to shine up-
may God make her
peace;
and be gra - cious un-to you, be gra-cious,
on you, and be gra-cious, and be gra-cious,

Text: based on Numbers 6:24–26, Peter C. Lutkin (USA), 1900; alternate text Mennonite Worship and Song Committee, 2019
Music: Peter C. Lutkin, 1900

the Lord
may God
be gra-cious, gra - cious un - to
A -
you.
A - men, a -
A - men, a - men, a -
A - men, a - men, a -
men, a - men, a -
- men, a - men, a - men,
men, a - men, a -
men, a - men, a -
men, a - men, a - men.
a - men, a - men.
- men, a - men, a - men.
men, a - men, a - men.

847 You Shall Go Out with Joy

THE TREES OF THE FIELD Irregular

Em
You shall go out with joy and be led forth with peace.
D7/F♯ G C/G G D/F♯ D7
The moun-tains and the hills will break forth be -
B/D♯ Em
fore you. There'll be shouts of joy and all the
Em/B B7 Em/B B7 Em
trees of the field will clap, will clap their hands.
D7 G C/G G D
And all the trees of the field will clap their hands,
*
G
the trees of the field will clap their hands.
C/G G D
The trees of the field will clap their hands,
B7 Am/C C♯dim7 B7/D♯ Em
while you go out with joy.

*Clap hands

Text: based on Isaiah 55:12; Steffi Geiser Rubin (USA), 1975
Music: Stuart Dauermann (USA), 1975

Christ, Be All around Me 848

AS I RISE Irregular
A C♯m F♯m7 D A C♯m F♯m7 D A2 C♯m7 F♯m7 D Esus E D2 A F♯m7 E D2 A F♯m7 E D2
1 As I rise, strength of God, go be-fore, lift me up; as I wake, eyes of God, look on me, be my sight.
2 As I wait, heart of God, sat-is-fy and sus-tain; as I hear, voice of God, lead me on, be my guide,
3 As I go, hand of God, my de-fense, by my side; as I rest, breath of God, fall on me, bring me peace,
1
2, 3
2 be my guide.
3 bring me peace.
Refrain
A-bove and be-low me, be-fore and be-hind me; in ev-'ry eye that sees me, Christ, be all a-round me; a-bove and be-low me, be-fore and be-hind me; in ev-'ry eye that sees me, Christ, be all a-round me.

Text: based on the "Prayer of St. Patrick" (Ireland), 5th c.; David Leonard (USA), Jack Mooring (USA), Leeland Mooring (USA), and Leslie Jordan (USA)
Music: David Leonard, Jack Mooring, Leeland Mooring, and Leslie Jordan

849 We, Your People, Sing Your Praises (Bon Berger, ton peuple t'adore)

ENDSLEIGH NEW 8.7.8.7 D

Capo 3: (D) (A) (D) (Bm) (G) (D) (A) (D)
F C F Dm B♭ F C F
We, your peo-ple, sing your prais - es as to-geth-er we are sent
Bon Ber - ger, ton peu-ple t'a - do - re i-ci en mis-sion pour toi.
(A) (D) Bm (G) (D) (A) (D)
C F Dm B♭ F C F
to re-veal your new cre - a - tion in the shad-ows of la - ment.
À tra-vers les la-men - ta - tions vient la nou-velle cré - a - tion.
(G) (D) (A)
B♭ F C
Give us cour-age for the jour - ney, shep-herd Je-sus, be our guide;
Gui - de - nous sur ce voy - a - ge, et nous au-rons la pas - sion,
(G) (A) (D) (Bm)(D/A) (G) (D) (A) (D)
B♭ C F Dm F/C B♭ F C F
help us lead with hope and pas - sion till all things are re-con-ciled.
le cou - ra - ge, et l'es - pé - ran - ce pour la ré - con - ci - lia - tion.

Text: Rebecca Mosley (USA) and Josephine Munyeli (Rwanda),

Music: Salvatore Ferretti (Italy), as sung in East Africa, 20th–21st c.; harm. Mennonite Worship and Song Committee, 2019

GATHERING

850

1 **damai besertamu**
Da-ma-ee beh-ser-ddá-moo

2 平和がありますように
Heh-yi-wa-ga Ah-ri-mah-soo-yo-oo-ni

3 **Hodesyelt nihit ooh loodo**
Hod-es-yelt ne-hit ooh loo-do

4 ความสันติสุขอยู่กับคุณ
Kwam San-dti-suk yoo-kap khun

5 **Nagaa isiniif haata'u**
Na-gan in-si-fu ha-ta-u

6 **que la paix soit avec toi**
Kuh lah paih swah ta͡ ahvek twah

7 ሰላም ለእናንተ ይሁን
Salem lenante YE-hun

8 **Kev kaj siab nyob nrog koj**
Keh KKa shia nyo nJoh KKo

9 **friede sei mit dir**
Free-deh zai mit dir

10 ຄວາມສະຫງົບສຸກຢູ່ກັບເຈົ້າ
Khuaam san gob suk yu ka chao

11 **kimia ezala na bino**
Kee-me-ah Ee-za-la Na Bino

12 **amani iwe kwenu**
Ah-mah-nee ee-weh kweh-nu

13 **la paz sea contigo**
Lah pahz SEH-ah cohn-TEE-go

14 السلام لكم
Assa-lamu lakom

15 peace be with you

16 **Na cung ah deih nak umko seh**
Na-cong-ah dat-nak om koe sah

17 평화를 빕니다
Pyoung-hwa-leul Bim-ni-dah

18 **pace vouă**
Pa-che voe-uh

19 平安与你同在
Ping an yu ni tongzai

20
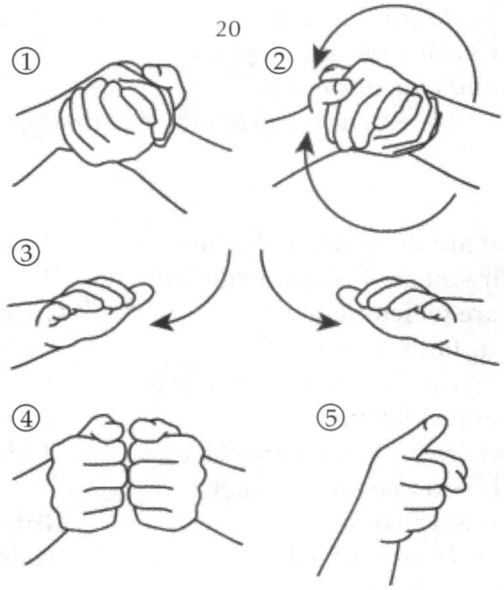

21 शान्ति मिलोस।
Shanti meel-los

22 願你平安
Yun nayee ping mon

Languages: 1. Indonesian, 2. Japanese, 3. Navajo, 4. Thai, 5. Oromiffa, 6. French, 7. Amharic, 8. Hmong, 9. German, 10. Lao, 11. Lingala, 12. Swahili, 13. Spanish, 14. Arabic, 15. English, 16. Chin, 17. Korean, 18. Romanian, 19. Mandarin, 20. American Sign Language, 21. Nepali, 22. Cantonese.

850. Mennonite Worship and Song Committee, 2020; illustration by Merrill Miller (USA)

Gathering Scripture worship resources are found at 13–21.

851

Leader: Jesus calls us
to praise and prayer,
to song and silence;
People: Jesus calls us to worship.
Leader: Jesus calls us
to hearing and healing,
to service and solidarity;
People: Jesus calls us to love.
Leader: Jesus calls us
to advocacy and action,
to protest and provision;
People: Jesus calls us to justice.
Leader: We hear the call of Christ.
All: We worship together with joy.

852

Leader: In the beginning
when it was very quiet,
the Word was with God,
All: and the Word was God.
(*here a Bible may be placed centrally*)
Leader: In the beginning
when it was very dark,
God said, "Let there be light,"
All: and there was light.
(*here a lit candle may be placed centrally*)
Leader: When the time was right,
God sent the Son;
***All: Christ came among us
and was one of us.***
(*here a cross may be placed centrally*)

853

Leader: If you are delighted to be here,
and if you are tired or troubled,
People: you are welcome.
Leader: If your faith is strong,
and if your faith is battered or frail,
People: you are welcome.
Leader: If you are eager to praise God,
and if you need to be quiet,
People: you are welcome.
***All: God welcomes us all
to worship today
and promises to meet us here.***

Spanish

Líder: Si se siente muy a gusto aquí,
o si está cansado o preocupado,
Grupo: ¡Bienvenido!
Líder: Si su fé es fuerte,
o si su fé está maltratada o frágil,
Grupo: ¡Bienvenido!
Líder: Si está ansioso por adorar a Dios,
o si necesita estar en silencio,
Grupo: ¡Bienvenido!
***Todos: Dios nos da la bienvenida a todos
para adorarle y nos promete estar
con nosotros aquí hoy.***

851. Joanna Harader (USA), 2017, alt.
852. Wild Goose Worship Group (Scotland), 2014, alt.
853. Marlene Kropf (USA), 2007; Spanish trans. Andrea De Ávila (Canada), 2019

854

Leader: Some of us are exhausted.
People: We come to rest.
Leader: Some of us are curious about Jesus.
People: We come to learn.
Leader: Some of us are hungry.
People: We come to be fed.
Leader: Some of us are disoriented.
People: We come to pray.
Leader: Some of us are broken.
People: We come to be healed.
Leader: We gather around you today, O Christ.
People: Teach us, feed us, hear us, heal us.
All: Grant us your peace. Amen.

855

Voice 1: To worship is to stand in awe under a heaven of stars,
before a flower, a leaf in sunlight, or a grain of sand.
Voice 2: To worship is to be silent, receptive,
before a tree astir with the wind, or the passing shadow of a cloud.
Voice 1: To worship is to work with dedication and with skill;
it is to pause from work and listen to a strain of music.
Voice 2: To worship is to sing with the singing beauty of the earth;
it is to listen through a storm to the still small voice within.
Voices 1&2: Worship is the mystery within us
reaching out to the Mystery beyond.

856

Leader: Christ is like a single body
that has many parts.
All: It is still one body
though every part is different.

Leader: Therefore the foot cannot say,
Part 1: I am not part of the body;
Leader: nor can the ear say,
Part 2: I am not part of the body.

Leader: The eye cannot say to the hand,
Part 1: I don't need you;
Leader: nor can the head say to the feet,
Part 2: I don't need you.

Leader: If one part suffers,
All: all parts share the pain;
Leader: if one part is praised,
All: all parts share the joy.

Leader: Together, we are Christ's body:
All: each one of us is a part of it.

854. Joanna Harader (USA), 2012
855. Jacob Trapp (USA), 20th c., adapt.
856. Wild Goose Worship Group (Scotland), 2014 ⓦ

857

Holy God,
you call us together
  to reflect on your Word
  and our life in your world.
Be with us now
  as we sing and pray together,
that we may hear your voice
  and understand your way.
This we pray
  through Jesus, the Christ. Amen.

858

Come, Holy One,
work upon us,
  set us on fire and clasp us close;
be fragrant to us,
  draw us to your loveliness;
let us love,
  let us run to you. Amen.

859

God of every place,
some of us see you today
  from mountains of joy and confidence,
  mountains of gratitude and praise.
Some of us seek you today
  from valleys of grief or doubt,
  valleys of loss or exhaustion.
And in all places,
  there you are with us,
  nudging us onward.
When we descend from the heights,
  show us your presence on the ground.
When we rise from the depths,
  show us the light of your way.
Meet us all on the path made by Jesus.

860

Almighty God,
  to you all hearts are open,
  all desires are known,
  and from you no secrets are hidden.
Cleanse the thoughts of our hearts
  by the inspiration of your Holy Spirit,
  that we may perfectly love you
  and worthily magnify your holy name,
  through Christ, our Lord. Amen.

861

Creator,
we give you thanks for all you are
  and all you bring to us
  for our visit within your creation.
In Jesus, you place the gospel
  in the center of this sacred circle
  through which all creation is related.
You show us the way to live
  a generous and compassionate life.
Give us your strength to live together
  with respect and commitment
  as we grow in your Spirit,
for you are God, now and forever. Amen.

862

You who open doors and dismantle barriers,
open our hearts to praise you,
  that we might live the full truth
    of who we are,
  that we might live as neighbors and friends,
    no longer strangers and enemies;
open our hearts to the transforming power
    of your love,
  that we might forgive and reconcile,
    making peace and learning war no more,
  that we might be your people,
    one body in one Spirit,
    to tell your grace to all the world.
We pray in the name of the One
  who walked among us
  as brother and friend. Amen

863

Source of all hope and holiness,
  we gather today to be church.
Bless those who are absent,
  but not from our hearts.
Bless those who are distant,
  but not from our love.
Bless each of us here,
  that we may choose justice by your Spirit,
  draw kindness from the well of your mercy,
  and walk humbly in your path, O God.

857. United Church of Canada, *Voices United*, 2007
858. Augustine of Hippo (present-day Algeria), 4th-5th c.
859. Alissa Bender (Canada), 2015
860. attr. Alcuin (England), 8th c.; trans. Thomas Cranmer from Sarum Rite (England), 1549
861. Anglican Council of Indigenous Peoples (Canada), 2017
862. Scott Haldeman (USA), 2012
863. Maren C. Tirabassi (USA) and Joan Jordan Grant (USA), 1998

864

Leader: We offer thanksgiving to our Creator,
recalling that Christ is the center of creation
and our lives as Christians.

As we face east, the direction of the rising sun,
we offer thanks for the gifts of the tree world
and for new beginnings.

All: ***Help us to be honest with you and others***
and to be wise and just in our use of the resources of the earth.
We give thanks to you, O God.

Leader: As we face south, where we receive warmth,
we offer thanks for the gifts of the animal world
and for the call to be humble.

All: ***Enable us to walk good paths,***
to live as family should,
and, with you, to renew the face of the earth.
We give thanks to you, O God.

Leader: As we face west, where we receive teachings of faith,
we offer thanks for the gifts of the rock world
and the purifying and fruitful waters.

All: ***Sustain us and the earth through your Holy Spirit,***
and give us faith as strong as the rock.
We give thanks to you, O God.

Leader: As we face north, the direction of wind and snow,
we offer thanks for the plant world,
and for kindness and wisdom.

All: ***Breathe your strength and endurance into us,***
and give us wisdom to treat each other with kindness.
We give thanks to you, O God.

Leader: As we face center:
From above comes the unconditional love of God.
from the earth comes the gift of life.

All: ***We give thanks for love like the wings of the eagle.***
We dedicate our lives to you, our Creator and Savior.
As we walk on this earth,
may we learn together
and celebrate the way of peace, harmony, and tranquility.
We give thanks to you, O God.

865

We light a light
in the name of the God who creates life,
in the name of the Savior who loves life,
in the name of the Spirit who is the fire of life.

864. adapt. from an Ojibwe six directions prayer by Barb Daniels (Manitoba, Canada) and Neill von Gunten (Manitoba, Canada) for Riverton Fellowship Circle, 2002 Ⓦ
865. Philip J. Newell (Scotland), 2005

866

French

Leader: Open our ears
People: to hear your word.
Leader: Open our eyes
People: to see your presence.
Leader: Open our arms
People: to the embrace of community.
Leader: Open our minds
People: to the beauty of truth.
Leader: Open our hearts
People: to the joy of new life.

Officiant: Ouvre nos oreilles
Assemblée: pour entendre ta parole.
Officiant: Ouvre nos yeux
Assemblée: pour discerner ta présence.
Officiant: Ouvre nos bras
Assemblée: à l'accueil de la communauté.
Officiant: Ouvre nos esprits
Assemblée: à la beauté de la vérité.
Officiant: Ouvre nos cœurs
Assemblée: à la joie de la nouvelle vie.

867

1: I will light a light
in the name of the Maker,
who lit the world
and breathed the breath of life for me.
(*a candle is lit and placed centrally*)

2: I will light a light
in the name of the Son,
who saved the world
and stretched out his hand to me.
(*a candle is lit and placed centrally*)

3: I will light a light
in the name of the Spirit,
who encompasses the world
and blesses my soul with yearning.
(*a candle is lit and placed centrally*)

All: ***We will light three lights for the Trinity of love:***
God above us,
God beside us,
God beneath us;
the Beginning,
the End,
the Everlasting One.

868

Leader: As a shepherd seeks a lost sheep,
People: so God seeks and saves the lost.
Leader: Like a woman who searches for a lost coin until it is found,
People: so God rejoices over one soul restored to wholeness.
Leader: As a father receives a returning wayward son,
People: so God welcomes us and lets the past be the past.
Leader: Therefore let us praise God in thanksgiving that we are received.
People: Let us receive and welcome and rejoice over one another
in the name of Jesus Christ. Amen.

866. Carol Penner (Canada) 2019; French trans. Sylvie Gudin (USA), 2019
867. Wild Goose Resource Group (Scotland), 1999
868. Ruth Duck (USA), 1981

869

Group 1: We are a covenant people,
called to God by God,
generation through generation.
Group 2: We are a covenant people,
called to Jesus by Jesus,
losing our life to gain our life.
Together: We are a covenant people,
called to church by the church,
weaving together the strong and the weak,
the stranger and the friend.
Group 1: Renamed.
Group 2: Reborn.
Together: Renewed.
We gather ourselves in the community of believers.
We gather ourselves unto you.

870

Leader: We gather in preparation,
People: for good news is about to be proclaimed.
Leader: We gather in expectation,
People: for joy is about to break forth in our midst.
Leader: We gather in celebration,
People: for we are people who say
yes to the manger,
yes to the One incarnate for others,
yes to the wholeness of God.
All: In preparation and expectation, let us celebrate!

871

Barely midnight. All of us hunkered down
around ashes of a fire. The animals
asleep. Our companions: hunger, nagging doubt.
Our wants are reasonable: provisions for the family,
better health, a better bed than this hard slope,
good grazing, sturdy lambs, and death to predators
whose hostile howls invade our restless dreams.
But let's be honest: let's admit right now:
what we want most is foolproof evidence
that God exists and knows we're here. We want
our sorrows noted, our frantic labors recognized.
We want the Holy One, although it's dark (and late
the hour) to hunker with us at the fire's glow
and speak with us—Right here. Right now.

872

Lord, your coming is still miraculous.
Your joining the family of the poor and displaced
still baffles and convicts us.
Keep us by your manger
until we learn the way of love. Amen.

869. LeAnne Zook (USA), 2017
870. William B. Oden (USA), 1976
871. Sarah Klassen (Canada), "The Shepherd's Wish List," 2012, alt.
872. Shane Claiborne (USA), Jonathan Wilson-Hartgrove (USA), and Enuma Okoro (USA), 2010

873

Leader: The dust that shapes the journey,
the cross that guides it,
the color that surrounds it,
the light that fades through it,
the Word that foretells it,
the wilderness that invites it—
All:* *this is Lent,
and into its wilderness
God calls us.
Leader: Come,
friends,
Christ is heading for Jerusalem.

874

One: From Bethlehem to Nazareth,
from Jordan to Jericho,
from Bethany to Jerusalem,
from then to now,
All: come, Lord Jesus.
One: To heal the sick,
to mend the brokenhearted,
to comfort the disturbed,
to disturb the comfortable,
to cleanse the temple,
to liberate faith from convention,
All: come, Lord Jesus.
One: To carry the cross,
to lead the way,
to shoulder the sin of the world and take it away,
All: come, Lord Jesus.
One: Today,
in this place,
to us,
All: come, Lord Jesus. Amen.

875

Leader: Alleluia! Christ is risen!
People: Christ is risen indeed! Alleluia!

876

Living God,
for whom no door is closed,
no heart is locked,
draw us beyond our doubts,
till we see your Christ
and touch his wounds
where they bleed in others. Amen

873. Roddy Hamilton (Scotland), 2008, alt. Ⓦ
874. Wild Goose Resource Group (Scotland), 1998
875. anon. (Eastern Mediterranian) Χριστὸς ἀνέστη! Ἀληθῶς ἀνέστη! Ⓦ
876. The Anglican Church in Aotearoa, New Zealand and Polynesia, *A New Zealand Prayer Book*, 1989

877

All: ***Come, Holy Spirit,***
Leader: enter our silences.
All: ***Come, Holy Spirit,***
Leader: into the depths of our longing.
All: ***Come, Holy Spirit,***
Leader: unmask our pretending.

Enter our trusting,
enter our fearing,
enter our letting go,
enter our holding back.

All: ***Come, Holy Spirit,***
Leader: embrace and free us.

878

Land Acknowledgement

We acknowledge that we are gathering
on the traditional territory of Indigenous peoples.
We affirm that settlers have specific responsibilities
in the journey of reconciliation with Indigenous peoples.

(*Name specific peoples indigenous to the region*
and treaties between Indigenous peoples and settlers.)

We give thanks to Creator,
and to those peoples who have stewarded this land for generations.
We are grateful for the opportunity to live, work, and worship here,
as we witness the reconciling movement of the Spirit
and seek to live into right relations with our Indigenous neighbors
and all of creation.

879

Prayer Before a Time of Worship or Preparation for Worship

Life-giving God,
may your Holy Spirit inspire
our praise and our prayers.
Open our hearts and minds to your presence
among us and within us.
Come alive in our words and actions
as we lead in worship.
To you alone belongs all praise and honor
and glory and blessing,
now and to the end of time. Amen.

PRAISING

Praising Scripture worship resources are found at 105–110.

880

Leader: Glory to God in the highest,
and peace to God's people on earth.
People: Glory to God!
Leader: Holy, holy, holy God,
eternal Love and majesty,
source, guide, and goal
of all that is.
People: Glory to God!
Leader: Holy, holy, holy God,
eternal Word, enfleshed among us,
showing the way of life,
the way of truth and love.
People: Glory to God!
Leader: Holy, holy, holy God,
eternal Spirit, giver of life,
abiding within and all around us,
guiding us in all our ways.
People: Glory to God!
Leader: Glory to God,
in whom we live
and move
and have our being.
People: Glory to God!
Leader: Glory to God in the highest,
and peace to God's people on earth.
People: Glory to God!

881

God of cosmos and quarks,
God of rainbows and roly-polies,
God of electricity and enzymes—
you created the earth and proclaimed it good.
The galaxies and planets are known to you,
yet also the hairs on our heads.
You cradle all things in the palm of your hand,
supporting us with love.
We magnify your name for our creation
and for all the blessings of this life.
Sustain in us a spirit of awe
for how you continue to be present in the world,
and help us to act with love
for all that you have created. Amen.

880. Harold M. Daniels (USA), 2003
881. Joelle Friesen (USA), 2016

882

We are people who must sing you,
for the sake of our very lives.
You are a God who must be sung by us,
for the sake of your majesty and honor.
And so we thank you,
for lyrics that push us past our reasons,
for melodies that break open our givens,
for cadences that locate us home,
beyond all our safe places,
for tones and tunes that open our lives beyond control
and our futures beyond despair.
We thank you for the long parade of mothers and fathers
who have sung you deep and true;
we thank you for the good company
of artists, poets, musicians, cantors, and instruments
that sing for us and with us, toward you.
We are witnesses to your mercy and splendor;
we will not keep silent . . . ever again. Amen.

883

Sing and sing. And when you cannot raise a note of song,

the rocks will cry out. And when the echoing stones go still,
in the dangerous crevice that is your heart, if you lie still,

there remains an altar, a way to enter
a terrible holiness, a lush and delicate calm.

884

Leader: In the beginning,
before time, before people,
before the world began,
All: God was.
Leader: Here and now,
among us, beside us,
clearer than air, closer than breathing,
All: God is.
Leader: In all that is to come,
when we have turned to dust
and human knowledge has been completed,
All: God will be.
Leader: Not despairing of earth, but delighting in it,
not condemning the world, but redeeming it
through Jesus Christ,
by the power of the Holy Spirit,
All: God was, God is, God will be.

882. Walter Brueggemann (USA), 2002
883. David Wright (USA), excerpted from "A Liturgy for Stones," 2003
884. Wild Goose Resource Group (Scotland), 2015

885

Leader: Hosanna!
People: Hosanna!
Leader: Blessed is the One who comes in the name of God!
People: Blessed are we, for we have been created by that same God.
Leader: Blessed is the sound of our voices, lifted up in praise.
People: Blessed are the hands that clap and strum and pluck,
joining together in one glorious hosanna.
Leader: Blessed are the bodies that move and wave and march and dance
in a tapestry of motion, embodying your love.
People: Blessed is the breath that enlivens us, animates us, and sustains us
in singing our ceaseless praise to you, O God.
Leader: Hosanna!
People: Hosanna!

886

I praise you, God—
in the sanctuary
and under the stars;
for your greatness
and for your goodness;
with loud hymns
and quiet prayers;
with helping hands
and dancing feet;
with all my breath
and with all creation;
I praise you, God. Amen.

887

Leader: Holy God, Holy One, Holy Three!
Left: Before all that is, you were God.
Right: Outside all we know, you are God.
Left: After all is finished, you will be God.

Leader: Holy God, Holy One, Holy Three!
Left: Our Life, our Mercy, our Might,
Right: our Table, our Food, our Server,
Left: our Rainbow, our Ark, our Dove,
Right: our Sovereign, our Water, our Wine,
Left: our Light, our Treasure, our Tree,
Right: our Way, our Truth, our Life.

Leader: Holy God, Holy One, Holy Three!
All: Praise now,
praise tomorrow,
praise forever.
Amen!

885. Laura Jaquith Bartlett (USA), 2009
886. Presbyterian Church (USA), *Book of Common Worship*, 2018
887. Gail Ramshaw (USA), excerpted from "Triple Praise," 2017

RECONCILING

888

Leader: Friends in Christ,
God knows our needs before we ask
and in our asking
prepares us to receive the gift of grace.

We open our lives to God's healing presence,
seeking peace with God
and reconciliation with our neighbors.

We are mindful not only of personal evil
but also of our communal sins
of family, class, race, and nation.

We confess to God whatever has wounded us
or brought injury to others,
that we may receive mercy
and become for each other
ministers of God's grace.

(*silence*)

Leader: Hear the good news!
Who is in a position to condemn?
Only Christ,
and Christ died for us,
Christ rose for us,
Christ reigns in power for us,
Christ prays for us.
People: Anyone who is in Christ is a new creation.
The old life has gone; a new life has begun.
Leader: Know that you are forgiven,
and be at peace.
People: Amen.

889

Psalm 51:1-3, 10-12

Have mercy on me, O God,
according to your steadfast love;
according to your great compassion,
blot out my transgressions.
Wash me thoroughly from my iniquity,
and cleanse me from my sin.
For I know my transgressions,
and my sin is ever before me.
Create in me a pure heart, O God,
and put a new and steadfast spirit within me.
Do not cast me away from your presence,
and do not take your holy spirit from me.
Restore to me the joy of your salvation,
and sustain in me a willing spirit.

888. based on Luke 11:9-10; Romans 8:34; 2 Corinthians 5:17; Presbyterian Church (USA), *Book of Common Worship*, 2018

890

Leader: Let us confess our sin in the presence of God and one another.

All: ***Most merciful God,***
we confess that we are captive to sin
and cannot free ourselves.
We have sinned against you in thought, word, and deed,
by what we have done and by what we have left undone.
We have not loved you with our whole heart;
we have not loved our neighbors as ourselves.
Forgive us, renew us, and lead us,
so that we may delight in your will and walk in your ways,
to the glory of your holy name. Amen.

Leader: God, who is rich in mercy,
loved us even when we were dead in sin,
and made us alive together with Christ.
By grace we have been saved.
In the name of Jesus Christ,
our sins are forgiven.
Almighty God
strengthen us with power
through the Holy Spirit,
that Christ may live in our hearts
through faith. Amen.

891

Leader: For the times we have lied to one another
and the times we have been lied to,
People: heal us, Jesus, Savior of the world.

Leader: For the times we have laughed at another's pain
and the times we have been laughed at,
People: heal us, Jesus, Savior of the world.

Leader: For the times we have betrayed a friend
and the times we have been betrayed,
People: heal us, Jesus, Savior of the world.

Leader: For the times we have spoken when we should have remained silent
and the times we have remained silent when we should have spoken,
People: heal us, Jesus, Savior of the world.

892

Jesus, Lamb of God,
have mercy on us.
Jesus, bearer of our sins,
have mercy on us.
Jesus, redeemer of the world,
give us peace.

890. adapt. from Evangelical Lutheran Church in Canada and Evangelical Lutheran Church in America (USA), *Evangelical Lutheran Worship*, 2006, Mennonite Worship and Song Committee, 2019
891. Anne Macksoud (USA), 1981
892. traditional, pre-7th c., introduced into Roman mass 7th c., Ὁ ἀμνὸς τοῦ Θεοῦ (Greek); Agnus Dei (Latin); trans. English Language Liturgical Consultation, 1998

893

For failing to love others as you have loved us . . .
God of grace, **forgive us.**
For wasting your gifts and hoarding our goods . . .
God of grace, **forgive us.**
For plundering the earth and abusing the planet . . .
God of grace, **forgive us.**
For fearing those who are strange to us and ignoring those in need . . .
God of grace, **forgive us.**
For losing heart and abandoning hope . . .
God of grace, **forgive us.**
For all the ways we turn from you . . .
God of grace, **forgive us.**
We offer our prayers in the name
of the One who saves us, Jesus Christ. **Amen.**

894

Leader: O Prince of Peace,
from peace that is no peace,
from the grip of all that is evil,
from a violent righteousness . . .
People: deliver us.
Leader: From paralysis of will,
from lies and misnaming,
from terror of truth . . .
People: deliver us.
Leader: From hardness of heart,
from trading in slaughter,
from the worship of death . . .
People: deliver us.

(*silence*)

Leader: By the folly of your gospel,
by your choosing our flesh,
by your nakedness and pain . . .
People: heal us.
Leader: By your weeping over the city,
by your refusal of the sword,
by your facing of horror . . .
People: heal us.
Leader: By your bursting from the tomb,
by your coming in judgment,
by your longing for peace . . .
People: heal us.
All: Grant us peace. Amen.

893. Presbyterian Church (USA), *Book of Common Worship*, 2018
894. source unknown, 20th c., alt.

895

Gracious God,
our sins are too heavy to carry,
too real to hide,
and too deep to undo.
Forgive what our lips tremble to name,
what our hearts can no longer bear,
and what has become for us
a consuming fire of judgment.
Set us free from a past
that we cannot change;
open to us a future
in which we can be changed;
and grant us grace to grow more and more
in your likeness and image;
through Jesus Christ,
the light of the world.

896

God of the foolish cross,
you are not the savior we expect.
Your power does not look like the power
we want our God to demonstrate.
Your wisdom makes no sense to us.
We are happy to join the crowd,
waving branches,
but not so sure we want to follow you
into the temple courts
into the upper room
into the garden of Gethsemane
to the foot of the cross.
Forgive our false assumptions.
Clarify our clouded vision.
Free us to relax into the foolishness
of your love and grace.

897

God of mercy,
we are sorry that
we have not always done
what you wanted us to do.
We have not loved you
with all our heart,
and we have not cared enough
for other people.
Forgive us through Jesus. Amen.

898

Christ our companion,
you came not to humiliate the sinner
but to disturb the righteous.
Welcome us when we are put to shame,
but challenge our smugness,
that we may truly turn from what is evil
and be freed even from our virtues,
in your name.

899

Our lives are cluttered, O Christ,
by too many things
and too much to do.
We are driven by the need to succeed
and distracted by our service.
We have often lost our way.
Forgive us.

Let us, like Mary,
find the one thing that is needed
and sit at your feet. Amen.

900

Most loving, most strong God,
who is able to fight against you?
The ancient serpent, the diabolical dragon,
is not able to oppose you.
I want you to help me fight against
the fiery dragon within me
that eats away my soul.
I want to be like the strongest sword,
fashioned by you,
with the sharpest blade
that will cut through the dragon's scales.
And as I slay the dragon within myself,
I want to offer a safe refuge for all,
who like me are frail and vulnerable,
so they may slay their own dragons,
and together we may live in peace. Amen.

895. United Church of Christ (USA), 2012
896. Joanna Harader (USA), 2012
897. The Anglican Church in Aotearoa, New Zealand and Polynesia, *A New Zealand Prayer Book*, 1988
898. Janet Morley (England), 1992
899. Marlene Kropf (USA), 1992
900. Hildegard of Bingen (present-day Germany), 1151

901

Spanish

Confesemos nuestro pecado contra Dios
y su creación respondiendo a la frase,
En tu misericordia, **escucha nuestra oración**.

Perdónanos, Dios,
por nuestra indiferencia
ante la destrucción de la naturaleza;
por nuestra ambición
por las ganancias desmedidas,
sin respeto a la vida.
En tu misericordia, **escucha nuestra oración**.

Perdónanos, Dios,
por nuestra violencia contra la tierra;
por nuestro silencio
ante los bosques devastados
y los ríos contaminados.
En tu misericordia, **escucha nuestra oración**.

Perdónanos, Dios,
por nuestra sed voraz de consumir,
sin tener en cuenta
a las generaciones futuras;
por nuestra fijación en el presente,
sin tener en cuenta el mañana.
En tu misericordia, **escucha nuestra oración**.

Perdónanos, Dios,

(*Añadir oraciones específicas para su context.*)

En tu misericordia, **escucha nuestra oración**.

Dios, perdónanos por nuestra arrogancia
en pensar que somos
el centro del universo.
Perdónanos por olvidar
nuestro lugar en la creación.
En tu misericordia,
enséñanos a amar a tus criaturas,
y cuidar de la vida
en todas sus manifestaciones. Amén.

Let us confess our sin against God
and creation, saying,
In your mercy, **hear our prayer**.

Forgive us God,
for our indifference
to the destruction of wildlife,
for the greedy search
for profit
with no respect for life.
In your mercy, **hear our prayer**.

Forgive us God,
for the violence against the earth,
for our silence
before devastated forests
and contaminated rivers.
In your mercy, **hear our prayer**.

Forgive us God,
for our voracious thirst to consume
without a thought
of future generations,
for our fixation on the present
without thinking of tomorrow.
In your mercy, **hear our prayer.**

Forgive us God,

(*Add prayers specific to local context.*)

In your mercy, **hear our prayer**.

Forgive our arrogance, God,
when we place ourselves
at the center of your universe.
Forgive us when we forget
our place in creation.
In your mercy,
teach us to love your creatures
and to care for life
in all its forms. Amen.

902

Leader: Praise to God who has given us life.
People: Blessed be God for the gift of love.
Leader: Praise to God who forgives our sin.
People: Blessed be God who sets us free.
Leader: Praise to God who kindles our faith.
People: Blessed be God, our strength, our hope.

901. anon. (Latin America), 20th c.; trans. Presbyterian Church (USA), *Book of Common Worship*, 2018, adapt. Mennonite Worship and Song Committee, 2019
902. The Anglican Church in Aotearoa, New Zealand and Polynesia, *A New Zealand Prayer Book*, 1988

903

A. Do not fear, says God,
I have redeemed you.
I have called you by name;
you are mine.

God is doing a new thing;
now it springs forth!
By the grace of Jesus Christ,
we are forgiven! **Amen.**

B. Our righteousness is found
in Christ alone,
a gift of God by faith.

Beloved people of God,
believe the good news:
through the grace of Jesus Christ,
we are forgiven. **Thanks be to God.**

C. If we have died with Christ,
we believe that
we will also live with him.
Therefore, consider yourselves
dead to sin and alive to God
in Christ Jesus.

In the name of Jesus Christ,
we are forgiven. **Alleluia.**

D. Hear the good news!
Hope does not disappoint us,
for God's love has been poured
into our hearts through the Holy Spirit
given to us in baptism.

Believe this good news and give thanks:
In Jesus Christ, we are forgiven! **Amen.**

904 *Sharing the Peace of Christ*

Hear the words of Jesus:
"Peace I leave with you,
my peace I give to you.
I do not give to you as the world gives.
Do not let your hearts be troubled,
and do not let them be afraid."
Now we share a sign of peace
with one another.

905

May almighty God have mercy on us,
forgive us our sins,
and bring us to everlasting life. Amen.

903. based on A. Isaiah 43:1, 19; B. Philippians 3:9; C. Romans 6:8, 11; D. Romans 5:5; Presbyterian Church (USA), *Book of Common Worship*, 2018

906

May the Love
which overcomes all differences,
which heals all wounds,
which puts to flight all fears,
which reconciles all who are separated,
be in us and among us
now and always.

907

Christ—
the Joy,
the Truth,
and the Light of All,
the Life of the World
and the Resurrection—
has appeared in goodness to those on earth.
Christ has become
the Image of our Resurrection,
granting divine forgiveness to all.

908

From all that is broken,
let there be beauty.
From what is torn, jagged,
ripped, frayed,
let there be
not just mendings
but meetings unimagined.
May the God in whom
nothing is wasted
gather up every scrap,
every shred and shard,
and make of them
new paths,
doorways,
worlds.

909

God forgives you.
Forgive others.
Forgive yourself.
(*silence*)

Be at peace.

904. John 14:27. See 850 for "Peace be with you" in many languages.
905. Mass of the Roman Rite, *Misereatur*, alt.
906. Frederick E. Gillis (USA), 1993
907. attr. Romanos the Melodist (Constantinople, present-day Turkey), c.490-c.556, Ἡ πάντων χαρά, Χριστός (Kontakion for Lazarus Saturday), trans. unknown
908. Jan Richardson (USA), 2010
909. The Anglican Church in Aotearoa, New Zealand and Polynesia, *A New Zealand Prayer Book*, 1988, alt.

TELLING GOD'S STORY

Scripture worship resources are available for the following themes: creation and covenant (184–189); advent and birth of Jesus (231–235); life, teaching, and ministry of Jesus (292–296); death and resurrection of Jesus (335–339); Holy Spirit, Pentecost, and church (379–385).

910

Speak to us, living God,
as you have spoken to our ancestors:
through the voices of your prophets,
the breath of your Spirit,
and the life of your Son,
so that we may live according to your word,
through Jesus Christ our Savior. Amen.

911

Living God,
by the power of your Spirit,
help us to hear your holy word,
that we may truly understand;
that, understanding, we may believe;
and believing, we may follow
in faithfulness and obedience,
seeking your honor and glory in all that we do,
through Jesus Christ. Amen.

912

Dear God,
let your Word shine in our hearts
by your Holy Spirit.
Make it so bright and warm
that we always find
our comfort and joy in it. Amen.

913 *Words to Follow the Reading of Scripture*

A. Word of God. Word of Life.

B. Holy Wisdom. Holy Word.

C. Hear what the Spirit
is saying to the church.

D. May God bless to our understanding
this reading from the Word.

E. The Word of God
for the people of God.
Thanks be to God.

F. God's Word is a lamp to our feet
and a light to our path.
Thanks be to God.

G. For the Word of God in Scripture,
for the Word of God among us,
for the Word of God within us:
Thanks be to God.

910. Presbyterian Church (USA), *Book of Common Worship*, 2018
911. Ulrich Zwingli (present-day Switzerland), 16th c.
912. Martin Luther (present-day Germany), 16th c., trans. Paul C. Stratman (USA), 2017
913. adapt. Mennonite Worship and Song Committee, 2019 C. based on Revelation 2:7, 11, 17, 29; 3:6, 13, 22; F. based on Psalm 119:105; G. Wild Goose Worship Group (Scotland), 2015 ⓦ

914

Reader: Hear the Word of God.
All:* *Our ears and hearts are open.

(*reading*)

Reader: Give thanks to the One whose Word is life.
All:* *Blessed be God forever.

915

Leader: Praise and thanks to you, holy God,
for by your Word you made all things:
you spoke light into darkness,
called forth beauty from chaos,
and brought life into being.
For your Word of life, O God,
People: we give you thanks and praise.

Leader: By your Word you called your people Israel
to tell of your wonderful gifts:
freedom from captivity,
water on the desert journey,
a pathway home from exile,
wisdom for life with you.
For your Word of life, O God,
People: we give you thanks and praise.

Leader: Through Jesus, your Word made flesh,
you speak to us and call us to witness:
forgiveness through the cross,
life to those entombed by death,
the way of your self-giving love.
For your Word of life, O God,
People: we give you thanks and praise.

Leader: Send your Spirit of truth, O God;
rekindle your gifts within us:
renew our faith,
increase our hope,
and deepen our love,
for the sake of a world in need.
Faithful to your Word, O God,
draw near to all who call on you,
through Jesus Christ. **Amen.**

916

Advent Candle Lighting

Leader: We light a candle for *hope*:
hope in our hearts,
hope in our homes,
hope in our world.
People: May the light of *hope* shine through our lives.

(*Change the focus each week: hope, peace, joy, love, Christ.*)

914. Wild Goose Worship Group (Scotland), 2015
915. Evangelical Lutheran Church in Canada and Evangelical Lutheran Church in America (USA), *Evangelical Lutheran Worship*, 2006, alt.
916. Sarah Kathleen Johnson (Canada), 2018 Ⓦ

917

Advent Candle Lighting

Leader: We light *this candle/these candles* as a sign
of our waiting and hope for the coming Christ.

Hear the Word of God:
(*leader reads the Scripture verse for the week*)

Week 1: In the beginning when God created the heavens and the earth,
God said: "Let there be light"; and there was light.
And God saw that the light was good.

Week 2: God is my light and my salvation, whom shall I fear?
Wait for God;
be strong, and let your heart take courage.

Week 3: People who walked in darkness have seen a great light.
Those who live in a land of deep darkness—
on them light has shined.

Week 4: Arise, shine; for your light has come,
and the glory of God has risen upon you.
God will be your everlasting light.

Christmas: In the beginning was the Word,
and the Word was with God, and the Word was God.
In the Word was life, and the life was the light of all people.

All: The light shines in the darkness,
and the darkness shall not overcome it!

918

Leader: Remember:
we are earth,
People: and to earth we shall return;
Leader: we are ashes,
People: and to ashes we shall return;
Leader: we are dust,
People: and to dust we shall return;
Leader: earth to earth, ashes to ashes, dust to dust.

(*silence or the imposition of ashes accompanied by the phrase*
"from dust you came, and to dust you shall return")

Leader: Remember:
the One who breathed life into dust
recreates us;
the One whose feet walked the earth
journeys with us;
the One whose embers glow in ashes
becomes in us a living flame.

917. Week 1: Genesis 1:1, 3-4; Week 2: Psalm 27:1, 14; Week 3: Isaiah 9:2; Week 4: Isaiah 60:1, 19; Christmas: John 1:1, 4; All: John 1:5; adapt. Sarah Kathleen Johnson (Canada), 2019 ⓦ
918. Sarah Kathleen Johnson (Canada), 2019 ⓦ

919

In his hands
the iron nails.
In his side
the iron spear.
On his head
a crown of thorns.
In his arid mouth the final words.
In his long-suffering the first offering.
In his slow death the first redemption.
In his sight
the standing mother.
In his nostrils
the whiff of Rome.
In his ears
the babbling mob.
In his mouth
the sour drink.
In his dying
the wind of eternity.
In his burial
the promise of life.
In his resurrection the sign we all awaited.
In his ascension the rising of our souls.

920

Eternity Sunday/Memorial Sunday/All Saints' Day

Leader: O Ancient of Days,
you have been our dwelling place
from generation to generation.
Here, in your Ground of Love,
even death becomes a time of seed planting,
from which new life eternally springs forth.

All: We give thanks, O God,
for your life and love that have no end.

Leader: On this day we remember those
who have gone before us in faith, hope, and love.
We remember those who have joined us
in the communion of the church
and others we have joined in the communion of life . . .

(*Names may be shared aloud at this time.*)

Leader: O God, in their death we feel the pain of absence.
In their death, through the unity of Christ,
we also know the joy of continued presence.
May the great cloud of witnesses
bless and sustain our daily living.

All: We give thanks, O God,
for your life and love that have no end. Amen.

919. Dallas Wiebe (USA), "INRI," 2008
920. Eric Massanari (USA), 2019 ⓦ

CONFESSING FAITH

921

Together: ***True evangelical faith cannot lie dormant***
but spreads itself out in all kinds of righteousness
and fruits of love;

Part 1: **it dies to flesh and blood;**

Part 2: it destroys all forbidden lusts and desires;

it seeks, serves, and fears God in its inmost soul;

it clothes the naked;

it feeds the hungry;

it comforts the sorrowful;

it shelters the destitute;

it aids and consoles the sad;

it does good to those who do it harm;

it serves those who harm it;

it prays for those who persecute it;

it teaches, admonishes, and judges us with the Word of God;

it seeks those who are lost;

it binds up what is wounded;

it heals the sick;

it saves what is strong;

it becomes all things to all people.

Together: ***The persecution, suffering, and anguish***
that come to it for the sake of the truth of Christ
have become a glorious joy and comfort to it.

922

We are not alone;
we live in God's world.
We believe in God:
who has created and is creating,
who has come in Jesus,
the Word made flesh,
to reconcile and make new,
who works in us and others
by the Spirit.
We trust in God.
We are called to be the Church:
to celebrate God's presence,
to live with respect in Creation,
to love and serve others,
to seek justice and resist evil,
to proclaim Jesus, crucified and risen,
our judge and our hope.
In life, in death, in life beyond death,
God is with us.
We are not alone.
Thanks be to God.

921. Menno Simons (present-day Netherlands), 1539
922. United Church of Canada, 1968, rev. 1980, 1995

923 *Apostles' Creed*

I believe in God, the Father almighty,
creator of heaven and earth.
I believe in Jesus Christ, God's only Son, our Lord,
who was conceived by the Holy Spirit,
born of the virgin Mary,
suffered under Pontius Pilate,
was crucified, died, and was buried;
he descended to the dead.
On the third day he rose again;
he ascended into heaven,
he is seated at the right hand of the Father,
and he will come to judge the living and the dead.
I believe in the Holy Spirit,
the holy catholic Church,
the communion of saints,
the forgiveness of sins,
the resurrection of the body,
and the life everlasting. Amen.

924 *Nicene Creed*

We believe in one God,
the Father, the Almighty,
maker of heaven and earth,
of all that is, seen and unseen.
We believe in one Lord, Jesus Christ,
the only Son of God,
eternally begotten of the Father,
God from God, Light from Light, true God from true God,
begotten, not made, of one Being with the Father;
through him all things were made.
For us and for our salvation
he came down from heaven,
was incarnate of the Holy Spirit and the Virgin Mary
and became truly human.
For our sake he was crucified under Pontius Pilate;
he suffered death and was buried.
On the third day he rose again
in accordance with the Scriptures;
he ascended into heaven
and is seated at the right hand of the Father.
He will come again in glory to judge the living and the dead,
and his kingdom will have no end.
We believe in the Holy Spirit, the Lord, the giver of life,
who proceeds from the Father [and the Son],
who with the Father and the Son is worshiped and glorified,
who has spoken through the prophets.
We believe in one holy catholic and apostolic Church.
We acknowledge one baptism for the forgiveness of sins.
We look for the resurrection of the dead,
and the life of the world to come. Amen.

923. traditional (Mediterranean basin), 2nd–8th c.; trans. English Language Liturgical Consultation, 1988
924. traditional (Mediterranean basin), 4th c.; trans. English Language Liturgical Consultation, 1988

925

Shared Convictions of Mennonite World Conference

By the grace of God,
we seek to live and proclaim
the good news of reconciliation
in Jesus Christ.
As part of the one body of Christ
at all times and places,
we hold the following to be central
to our belief and practice:

1. God is known to us as Father, Son,
and Holy Spirit,
the Creator who seeks to restore
fallen humanity
by calling a people to be faithful
in fellowship, worship, service,
and witness.

2. Jesus is the Son of God.
Through his life and teachings,
his cross and resurrection,
he showed us how to be faithful disciples,
redeemed the world,
and offers eternal life.

3. As a church, we are a community
of those whom God's Spirit calls
to turn from sin,
acknowledge Jesus Christ as Lord,
receive baptism upon confession of faith,
and follow Christ in life.

4. As a faith community,
we accept the Bible
as our authority for faith and life,
interpreting it together
under Holy Spirit guidance,
in the light of Jesus Christ
to discern God's will for our obedience.

5. The Spirit of Jesus empowers us
to trust God in all areas of life,
so we become peacemakers
who renounce violence,
love our enemies,
seek justice,
and share our possessions
with those in need.

6. We gather regularly to worship,
to celebrate the Lord's Supper,
and to hear the Word of God
in a spirit of mutual accountability.

7. As a worldwide community
of faith and life
we transcend boundaries
of nationality, race, class, gender,
and language.
We seek to live in the world
without conforming to the powers of evil,
witnessing to God's grace
by serving others,
caring for creation,
and inviting all people to know
Jesus Christ as Savior and Lord.

In these convictions we draw inspiration
from Anabaptist forebears
of the sixteenth century,
who modeled radical discipleship
to Jesus Christ.

We seek to walk in his name
by the power of the Holy Spirit,
as we confidently await Christ's return
and the final fulfillment of God's kingdom.

926

Dear Jesus,
I confess my need of you.
I am sorry for my sin, and I trust that you forgive me.
I accept your love and grace for me
and welcome you into my heart and into my life.
Help me believe in you and love you every day,
and help me show the world how great your love is.
I commit my life into your hands. Amen.

927

Spanish

Creemos en Dios Padre todopoderoso,
creador de los cielos y de la tierra;
creador de los pueblos y las culturas;
creador de los idiomas y de las razas.

Creemos en Jesucristo,
su Hijo, nuestro Señor,
Dios hecho carne en un ser humano
para todos los humanos;
Dios hecho carne en un momento
para todas las edades;
Dios hecho carne en una cultura
para todas las culturas;
Dios hecho carne en amor y gracia
para toda la creación.

Creemos en el Espíritu Santo,
por quien el Dios, encarnado en Jesucristo
se hace presente en nuestro pueblo
y nuestra cultura;
por quien el Dios creador
de todo cuanto existe
nos da poder para ser nuevas criaturas;
quien con sus infinitos dones,
nos hace un solo pueblo:
el cuerpo de Jesucristo.

Creemos en la Iglesia, que es universal
porque es señal del reino venidero;
que es más fiel mientras más
se viste de colores;
donde todos los colores pintan
un mismo paisaje;
donde todos los idiomas cantan
una misma alabanza.

Creemos en el reino venidero,
el día de la gran fiesta,
cuando todos los colores de la creación
se unirán en un arcoíris de armonía;
cuando todos los pueblos de la tierra
se unirán en un banquete de alegría;
cuando todas la lenguas del universo
se unirán en un coro de alabanza.

Y porque creemos,
nos comprometemos
a creer por los que no creen,
a amar por los que no aman,
a soñar por los que no sueñan,
hasta que lo que esperamos se torne realidad.

We believe in God, the Father almighty,
Creator of the heavens and the earth,
Creator of the all peoples and all cultures,
Creator of all tongues and races.

We believe in Jesus Christ,
his Son, our Lord,
God made flesh in a person
for all humanity,
God made flesh in an age
for all the ages,
God made flesh in one culture
for all cultures,
God made flesh in love and grace
for all creation.

We believe in the Holy Spirit
through whom God incarnate in Jesus Christ
makes his presence known in our peoples
and our cultures;
through whom God, Creator
of all that exists,
gives us power to become new creatures;
whose infinite gifts
make us one people:
the Body of Christ.

We believe in the church universal
because it is a sign of God's reign,
whose faithfulness is shown
in its many hues
where all the colors
paint a single landscape,
where all tongues sing
the same praise.

We believe in the Reign of God
—the day of the Great Fiesta
when all the colors of creation
will form a harmonious rainbow,
when all peoples
will join in joyful banquet,
when all tongues of the universe
will sing the same song.

And because we believe,
we commit ourselves:
to believe for those who do not believe,
to love for those who do not love,
to dream for those who do not dream,
until the day when hope becomes reality.

927. Justo González (USA, Cuba), 1996

928

No one can truly know Christ
unless they follow after him in daily life,
and no one can follow Christ in daily life
unless they truly know him.

929

I pledge allegiance to Jesus Christ,
and to God's reign for which he died—
one Spirit-led people the world over, indivisible,
with love and justice for all.

CELEBRATING BAPTISM

Baptism Scripture worship resources are found at 446–451.

930

Introduction to Baptism

Baptism with water in the name of the triune God
unites believers with Christ and the church.
Through the power of the Spirit,
we repent and turn to God in faith
and live as transformed people.
Through the waters of baptism,
God cleanses and renews us
as we commit to following Jesus
and become members of the church,
the body of Christ,
dying and rising to new life.

931

Leader: God of grace, creator of waters,
your Spirit hovered over the deep.
**Left: We remember that you separated the land from the waters
and provided rain to freshen the ground.**
Right: We remember that you flooded the earth
and held creatures and people above the waters.
**Left: We remember that you parted the waters
as your people fled from bondage in Egypt.**
Right: We remember Jesus your Son,
who, like all of us, arrived in the waters of childbirth.
**Left: We remember John baptizing in the waters of the Jordan
and the Spirit descending like a dove.**
Right: We remember that Jesus shared our thirst
and a Samaritan woman shared water from a well.
***All: Living Water,
pour your Spirit upon us.
Wash us and free us from sin,
make us fruitful in every way,
and renew your world with showers of blessing.***

928. Hans Denck (present-day Germany), 16th c.
929. June Alliman Yoder (USA) and Nelson Kraybill (USA), 2004, alt. Ⓦ
930. Mennonite Worship and Song Committee, 2020 Ⓦ
931. Mennonite Worship and Song Committee, 2020

932 *Congregational Commitment at Baptism*

As we now receive you into the fellowship of the church,
we make this covenant with you,
and we renew our own covenant with God.
We pledge to bear each other's burdens,
to assist in times of need,
to share our gifts and possessions,
to forgive as Christ has forgiven,
to support each other in times of joy and sorrow,
and in all things to work for the common good,
thus proclaiming the presence of Christ among us
so that our lives may glorify God.
Holy Spirit, make us one body,
part of the church worldwide,
united in its diversity,
now and in every age. Amen.

933 *Prayer for the Baptized*

Leader: Faithful God,
we give thanks for those who have committed their lives to you.
We ask for your guidance as they journey in faith.
We pray that they may be a blessing in our community
and in our world.
We join our hearts and voices in praise:

People: For your unending grace,
for your example and sacrifice,
for your sustaining presence,
and for the gift of the newly baptized—
we give you thanks, faithful God!

934 *Prayer for Those Preparing for Baptism*

Leader: God of wanderers and seekers,
we pray for those who are exploring faith
and those preparing for baptism.
Be with them in their questioning,
in their doubting,
and in their wondering.
Be with them in their confidence,
in their desires,
and in their hopes.

People: Be with us in discerning our common life
and guide our counsel.
Open us to faith as it grows
in ways both familiar and new
so that we may journey together
as your beloved children.
We ask this in the name of Jesus,
who prayed that we might be one
by the power of the Holy Spirit. Amen.

932. *Mennonite Hymnal*, 1969; *Hymnal: A Worship Book*, 1992; adapt. Mennonite Worship and Song Committee, 2020
933. Mennonite Worship and Song Committee, 2020
934. Mennonite Worship and Song Committee, 2020 ⓦ

935 *Reaffirmation of Baptismal Commitments*

Leader: God of covenant,
when Jesus came up from the waters of baptism,
you claimed him as your beloved child.
Through Jesus
you claim everyone who comes to you as your beloved.

Baptized: As at baptism,
we confess our faith in you today.

By your Spirit,
I will abide in your Word
as wisdom for my life.

By your Spirit,
I will give and receive counsel
in the circle of your church.

By your Spirit,
I will live without giving in to violence
and take risks for what is good.

By your Spirit,
I will share in your mission for the world
with courage and hope.

Strengthen us, God of love,
bind us together as your baptized people,
through Jesus Christ,
who lives and reigns with you and the Holy Spirit,
one God, now and forever. Amen.

CELEBRATING COMMUNION

Communion Scripture worship resources are found at 469–472.

936 *Introduction to Communion*

At the table of Christ,
we eat this bread and drink this cup
to remember the life and death and resurrection of Jesus,
to be united with Christ and with one another as the church,
and to look toward a time when all will be one.
As we eat and drink with thanksgiving,
Jesus Christ is present with us
and we are empowered by the Spirit
to follow Jesus' way of love
as the body of Christ,
broken and blessed for the life of the world.

935. Mennonite Worship and Song Committee, 2020 Ⓦ
936. Mennonite Worship and Song Committee, 2020 Ⓦ

937 *Preparation for Communion—Pledge of Love*

Leader: Friends,
as we gather to eat the bread and drink the cup,
let us respond with the pledge of love.

Will you love God before all things,
in the power of God's living Word,
and join yourself to God's way?
All: ***By the grace of God, I will.***

Leader: Will you love and serve our neighbors,
and lay down your life through the power of Jesus Christ,
who laid down his life for us?
All: ***By the grace of God, I will.***

Leader: Will you support and challenge one another,
speak and hear the truth,
cease what causes harm to our neighbors,
and do good to our enemies?
All: ***By the grace of God, I will.***

Leader: May the Spirit of God
who calls the church to Christ's Supper
give us the grace, strength, and patience
to live this pledge of love.
All: ***Amen.***

938 *Preparation for Communion*

A participant may read Matthew 5:23-24 or 2 Corinthians 5:18-20.

(*silent prayer*)

Leader: Trusting in God's grace, let us confess our sin.
All: ***Have mercy on me, O God,***
according to your steadfast love.
For I know my transgressions,
and my sin is ever before me.
Create in me a clean heart, O God,
and put a new and right spirit within me.
Leader: Anyone who is in Christ is a new creation.
The old life has gone; a new life has begun.
In the name of Jesus,
we are forgiven, loved, and free.

937. adapt. from Balthasar Hubmaier (present-day Germany), *A Form for Christ's Supper*, 1527; Mennonite Worship and Song Committee, 2020
938. based on Psalm 51:1, 3, 10 and 2 Corinthians 5:17; *Minister's Manual*, 1998; adapt. Mennonite Worship and Song Committee, 2020

939 *Invitation to the Communion Table*

Leader: The table has been prepared,
as Jesus requested,
and we are invited to the meal.
People: Come to the table—
Leader: like Peter, with more enthusiasm than resolve,
like James and John, dismayed by the priorities of God's reign.
People: Come to the table—
Leader: like Martha, hosting and leading with confidence,
like Mary, full of love and grief.
People: Come to the table—
Leader: like Judas, disillusioned and rebellious,
like Mary Magdalene, faithful to the end.
People: Come to the table—
Leader: Jesus offers the bread and the cup.
People: Come to the table of Christ!

940 *Invitation to the Communion Table*

Leader: As John baptized Jesus in the Jordan,
the Holy Spirit baptized the body of Christ.
God now gathers us at this table as the body of Christ
to hear the voice of heaven,
spoken over the waters of baptism,
saying "You are my beloved."
People: Water, bread, and wine,
the gifts of the earth,
the gifts of the church,
reveal that we belong
with God and one another.
Leader: Come with your hunger.
Come with your thirst.
All: This is Christ's table.
This is our feast.
Come, Holy Spirit!

941 *Communion Prayer—Common Practice*

Leader: O God, Ancient of Days,
your love brought galaxies into being,
summoned water and sky, earth and all creatures,
and made us in your image.
Through the ages you have cared for all you created.
When we wandered, you called us to return to you.
In the fullness of time, you sent us the Messiah, Jesus Christ,
to teach the law of love.
He lived what he taught
and loved his enemies to the end.
In wonder, we remember the life Jesus lived,
laid down, and took up again for us.

(continued)

939. Mennonite Worship and Song Committee, 2020
940. Mennonite Worship and Song Committee, 2020
941. Mennonite Worship and Song Committee, 2020; "Words of institution for the bread model 1," developed by MCUSA with attention to the experience of survivors of abuse, *Leader*, Summer 2016

Send your Spirit upon us
so that the bread we break and the cup we share
may be the communion of the body of Christ.
Send your Spirit upon us
so that we can live, conformed to Christ,
who taught us to pray . . .

Prayer Jesus Taught (989)

Leader: Jesus, on the night when he was betrayed,
took a loaf of bread,
and when he had given thanks,
he broke it and said,
"When you share bread together,
remember me."

All:* *Blessed are you, abundant God,
for you made bread to strengthen us;
you gave us this bread as a sign of your body.
Let our sharing be a taste
of the bread of heaven that feeds the world. Amen.

(*The bread may be distributed.*)

Leader: The gifts of God for the people of God.
All: Thanks be to God.

(*Participants may eat together.*)

Leader: Jesus took the cup after supper, saying,
"This cup is the new covenant.
When you drink it together,
remember me."

All: Blessed are you, bountiful God,
for you made the fruit of the vine to nourish us;
you gave us this cup as a sign of your blood.
Let our sharing be a taste of the wine we shall drink
in your joyful feast. Amen.

(*The cup may be distributed.*)

Leader: The gifts of God for the people of God.
All: Thanks be to God.

(*Participants may drink together. Alternatively, the bread and cup may be distributed and received at this time.*)

942

Prayer after Communion—Common Practice

All: Blessed are you, Eternal God;
through this holy meal
you have joined us to yourself
and to one another.
Blessed are you, Incarnate God;
you have put your life into our hands;
now we put our lives into yours.
Blessed are you, Breath of God;
as we go forth, set us free
to follow where you lead. Amen.

942. Mennonite Worship and Song Committee, 2020

943 *Communion Prayer—Global Celebration*

Leader: At this table, we receive the bread of life,
a worldwide communion with Christ and one another.
¡Gracias a Dios!
All:* *¡Gracias a Dios!
Leader: Rendons grâce à Dieu!
All:* *¡Rendons grâce à Dieu!
Leader: Thanks be to God!
All:* *Thanks be to God!
(*Add other languages spoken in the community.*)

Leader: At this table, we receive the cup,
the life of Jesus that binds us together.
¡Gracias a Dios!
All:* *¡Gracias a Dios!
Leader: Rendons grâce à Dieu!
All:* *Rendons grâce à Dieu!
Leader: Thanks be to God!
All:* *Thanks be to God!
(*Add other languages spoken in the community.*)

944 *Communion Prayer—Inspired by Early Christian Practice*

Leader: May God be with you!
People: And also with you.
Leader: Lift up your hearts!
People: We lift them up to God.
Leader: Let us give thanks to God.
People: It is good to give thanks and praise.

Leader: It is a good and joyful thing
always and everywhere to give thanks to you, Holy One.
With your people on earth
and all the company of heaven
we praise your name
and join their unending hymn:
All:* *Holy, holy, holy,
God of power and might,
heaven and earth are full of your glory.
Hosanna in the highest.
Blessed is the one who comes in your name.
Hosanna in the highest.

Great Thanksgiving

Leader: And so we proclaim this mystery of faith:
All:* *Christ has died. Christ is risen. Christ will come again.

Prayer for the Work of the Spirit

(*continued*)

943. Mennonite Worship and Song Committee, 2020 Ⓦ
944. based on the early church documents *Apostolic Tradition* (Mediterranean basin), 4th c., and Addai and Mari (Mediterranean basin), 3rd c.; elements adapt. from United Church of Canada and United Church of Christ, *Celebration of Full Communion*, 2015; *The United Methodist Worship Book*, 1992; United Church of Canada, *Voices United*, 1996; Gail Ramshaw (USA), *Pray, Praise, and Give Thanks*, 2017 Ⓦ

Leader: We praise you, all-holy God,
the Father, the Son, the Holy Spirit,
(*three trinitarian images appropriate to the occasion or biblical readings*),
today, tomorrow, and forever. Amen!
All: Amen!

Prayer Jesus Taught (989)

Share the peace of Christ

Leader: The gifts of God for the people of God.
People: Thanks be to God.

Share the bread and cup

945

Prayer after Communion—World Council of Churches

Leader: In peace let us pray:
All: O God, we give you thanks
for uniting us as the body of Christ
and for filling us with joy at this table.
Lead us toward the unity of your church,
and help us treasure signs of reconciliation.
Now that we have tasted the banquet you have prepared for us,
may we one day feast together in your heavenly city.
Through Jesus Christ,
who lives and reigns with you in the
unity of the Holy Spirit,
ever one God, world without end. Amen.

946

Prayer after Communion—Iona Community

In deep gratitude
for this moment,
this meal,
these people,
we give ourselves to you.

Send us
to live as changed people
because we have shared the Living Bread
and cannot remain the same.

Ask much of us,
expect much from us,
enable much by us,
encourage many through us.

So, God, may we glorify you
as inhabitants of earth
and citizens of heaven. Amen.

945. adapt. from World Council of Churches, *Lima Liturgy*, 1982; Mennonite Worship and Song Committee, 2020
946. Wild Goose Worship Group (Scotland), 1999 ⓦ

947 *Table Prayer for a Community Meal*

Leader: Come,
with your faith and your doubts,
with your hopes and your questions,
with your joy and your sadness.
You belong here.
Come,
if you love God and have failed your neighbor,
if you are a disciple of Jesus and have betrayed him.
You belong here.
Come,
for this is the table of Jesus,
who welcomes strangers
and shares his life with old and new friends.
All:* *We belong here.

Leader: This meal is filled with life:
All:* *the warmth of the sun,
the kindness of the rain,
the mysteries of the soil,
and the grace of human labor.

Leader: As we eat and drink, we give thanks:
All:* *for the goodness of food,
the delight of friendship,
and the love of Christ in this meal.

Leader: Come, Holy Spirit,
feast with your people.
All:* *Amen.

948 *Table Grace*

God of mystery and wonder,
at this and every table
you dissolve the distance between
the ordinary and the holy;
you break the barrier separating
the common and the sacred.
We thank you for this thin place,
this holy space,
this well of grace. Amen.

949 *Table Grace*

Receive our thanks
for night and day,
for food and shelter,
rest and play,
Be here our guest
and with us stay. Amen.

947. Mennonite Worship and Song Committee, 2020 ⓦ
948. William Kervin (Canada), 2004
949. anon. "Refugee Blessing"

950

Introduction to Footwashing

Jesus washed the feet of his disciples—
a leader unexpectedly kneeling before his followers.
We wash the feet of others
to commit ourselves to follow Jesus' example
of powerfully humble service.
We welcome the washing of our feet
to receive this act of loving service from Jesus
through one another as the body of Christ.

951

Footwashing Institution Narrative

Leader: Eternal Love, gentle God,
you invite us into the mysteries of your presence
as we bow before one another with devotion.

People: As you have loved us,
let us love one another.
As you have washed us with grace,
we wash one another.

Leader: Blessed is our brother Jesus,
who on the night he shared a final meal with friends,
rose from the table, laid aside his outer robe,
then took a towel and washed the feet of his disciples.
Having loved his own who were in the world,
he loved them to the end, saying,
"I have washed your feet
and you also ought to wash one another's feet."

People: With our hands we offer God's tenderness.
With our feet we receive Christ's abundant care.

Leader: Jesus said to his disciples,
"This is my commandment,
that you love one another as I have loved you.
No one has greater love than this,
to lay down one's life for one's friends."

All: Come, Holy Spirit,
wash us with your mercy,
pour your grace over our lives,
and flood the world with the gentleness of your love. Amen.

(*Participants wash one another's feet.*)

952

Prayer after Footwashing

Leader: Jesus Christ, our Savior,
you did not regard equality with God as something to be grasped,
but emptied yourself, taking the form of a servant.
Humbling yourself before your disciples,
you washed their feet and named them as your friends.

All: With water and a towel, you befriend us.
As we kneel before one another,
we pledge ourselves to your love,
in the power of your servanthood. Amen.

950. Mennonite Worship and Song Committee, 2020 Ⓦ
951. based on John 13; 15:12–13; Mennonite Worship and Song Committee, 2020
952. based on Philippians 2:5-11; Mennonite Worship and Song Committee, 2020

SHARING OUR STORIES

953

Prayer Before a Meeting

God of life,
we thank you that in our work
as well as our worship
we gather in your presence.
Come among us and guide us
as we meet together.

In our uncertainties, give us direction;
in our differences, give us understanding;
in our reporting, give us honesty;
in our planning, give us boldness;
in our deciding, give us graciousness.

Let us never forget that we are your people,
called to proclaim the reign of God,
committed to follow Christ in life,
united as one body in the Spirit. Amen.

954

Prayer for Camps and Retreats

Creator God,
thank you for people and places that stretch us,
help us grow, and lead us to know you more.
We see you in flickering campfires
and starry nights.
We hear you in wind through the trees
and voices raised in silly songs.
We feel you in cool splashes of water
and the warm sun on our faces.
We know that you are always with us,
leading us as the great Adventure Guide. Amen.

955

Prayer for Schools and Learning Communities

Come among us, Holy Spirit,
and create a community of learning.
Help us grow
in wisdom and understanding,
in skill and strength,
in knowledge that honors you.
Teach us
to know you, ourselves, and our neighbors more fully,
to see your presence in the world more clearly,
to love more deeply—with heart, soul, mind, and strength.
Form us
as doers of justice and lovers of mercy
as we walk humbly with you and one another
on this path of learning. Amen.

956 *Prayer for Work*

God of work and rest,
you have linked our lives one with another;
all we do affects, for good or ill, all other lives.
Guide us in the work we do,
that we may do it not for self alone,
but for the common good,
and as we seek a proper return for our own labor,
make us mindful of the rightful aspirations of other workers,
and arouse our concern for all who are out of work;
through Jesus Christ,
carpenter, teacher, healer,
beloved child of God. Amen.

957 *Prayer for Service Agencies*

God, just as you sent Joseph to Egypt
to help prepare for a time of famine,
and summoned Stephen
to respond to the needs of the poor,
and inspired Lydia
to share her wealth,
you continue to call people to use their skills and abilities
to help alleviate suffering in the world today.

We pray for those who provide emergency aid,
who rebuild and repair homes,
who advocate for peace and justice,
who offer education and training,
and who work to strengthen communities.

(*Name additional forms of service specific to the setting.*)

For all who serve,
whether staff or volunteers,
at home or abroad,
in public or behind the scenes,
we give you thanks, God.
Strengthen and encourage them.
Give them the love and compassion they need to do their work well—
to be your hands and feet in our hurting world. Amen.

958 *House Blessing*

This home is yours, my God,
may it be comfortable and filled with love.
This home is yours, my God,
may it be blessed and filled with laughter.
This home is yours, my God,
may it be safe and filled with peace.

956. Episcopal Church (USA), *The Book of Common Prayer*, 1979, adapt. Mennonite Worship and Song Committee
957. Christine Longhurst (Canada), 2018 ⓦ
958. attr. Brigid of Kildare (Ireland), ca. 5th c.

CHURCH MEMBERSHIP

959

Introduction to Church Membership

The church is the body of Christ,
created by God,
and sustained by the Spirit.
The church embodies Jesus' way of life in the world,
revealing God's reign through words and actions.
When we choose to become members of the church,
we commit ourselves to Christ,
to one another,
and to God's mission of healing and hope.
When we fall short of this vision,
we commit to turning toward one another with compassion
and to turning toward Christ,
our strength and our guide.

960

Congregational Covenant Renewal

Leader: God of covenant,
your steadfast love endures forever.
In Christ, we belong to you and your people.
Participants: Today, through the Spirit,
we renew our commitment
to fellowship and worship,
service and witness,
as partners in your mission.
God, give us grace,
in this place
and for this time,
to live this covenant.

961

Welcoming New Members

Leader: We have witnessed your commitment to Christ,
And we recognize you as *a member/members* in this congregation.
All: We welcome you with joy
as companions on the journey of faith.
We commit ourselves
to fellowship and worship,
service and witness,
as partners in God's mission.
We receive you as Christ has received us.

If children are being welcomed:

Leader: (*Name/names*), we welcome you to this family of faith.
All: We will share with you,
listen to you,
care for you,
pray for you,
laugh and cry with you.
We welcome you as Christ has welcomed us.

959. Mennonite Worship and Song Committee, 2020 Ⓦ
960. Mennonite Worship and Song Committee, 2020 Ⓦ
961. *Mennonite Hymnal*, 1969; *Hymnal: A Worship Book*, 1992; adapt. Mennonite Worship and Song Committee, 2020

962 *Blessing and Farewell*

People: **God, who is Alpha and Omega,**
we thank you for your faithfulness
in all our beginnings and endings,
and for the companions you provide
for us on our journey.

Leader: We give thanks for the presence of (*name/names of those leaving*) with us.

(*prayers for those who are leaving*)

People: **Guide this time of transition;**
prepare a home in a new community
where faithfulness may continue to grow,
through Jesus Christ
who across time and place,
makes us one. Amen.

963 *For Congregational Transitions and Anniversaries*

Leader: Give thanks to God, who is good.
People: **God's love is everlasting.**
Leader: Come, let us praise God joyfully.
People: **Let us come to God with thanksgiving.**

Leader: For the church universal,
and for this congregation of your people,
People: **thank you, God.**

Leader: For this place in which we gather
for praise and prayer, witness and service,
in the name of Jesus Christ,
People: **thank you, God.**

Leader: For disciples young and old
who have been nurtured here in faith,
People: **thank you, God.**

Leader: For the faithful who have led and loved us,
and by the offering of their gifts,
equipped us all for the work of ministry,
People: **thank you, God.**

Leader: For the ministries of worship and mission,
nurture and fellowship,
and for all whose lives have been touched by them,
People: **thank you, God.**

Leader: For all the saints who have stood among us,
whose memory still enlivens our faith
and emboldens our witness,
People: **thank you, God.**

Leader: Receive our gratitude, Holy God,
for the years through which you have led us,
and open us to the future you promise.

Give thanks to God, who is good.
People: **God's love is everlasting.**

962. Mennonite Worship and Song Committee, 2020
963. Presbyterian Church (USA), *Book of Common Worship*, 2018, abridged, alt. Ⓦ

CHURCH LEADERSHIP

964 *Introduction to Church Leadership*

Every Christian is called and gifted for ministry,
in the church and in the world,
through baptism.
For some, this ministry takes the form of church leadership,
a call and commitment to the creative work
of building up the body of Christ
and witnessing to God's love in the world.
Church leaders are empowered by the Spirit and the church,
and are accountable to God and the faith community,
who support and bless their ministry.

965 *Commissioning Leaders within a Community*

Community: Empowering God,
with your people throughout the ages,
we call members of the church
to develop gifts and skills for your service.
Thank you for raising up these leaders among us.
Fill them with the love of Christ and the church.
Empower them with your Holy Spirit.
Bless them with joy in the work of ministry.
Commissioned: We pray for wisdom, patience, and hope in this calling.
May we use the authority entrusted to us
with confidence and humility.
May we grow into the mind and spirit of Christ
through our service.
All: ***For the gifts that the Spirit nurtures within us***
and the ministries to which we are each called,
thanks be to God! Amen.

966 *Sending Leaders to Serve beyond a Community*

Leader: God's Spirit calls,
the church commissions,
and servants of Christ scatter throughout the world.
Community: We join with you in seeking first the reign of God.
We bless your service as part of our congregation's witness,
and we pledge our prayers of support for your ministry.
We trust the Holy Spirit's work within you as you serve.
May you see the face of God
in every person you meet.
May you be given a deep love
for your new community,
and may your words and deeds
reflect the grace, peace, and love of Christ.

964. Mennonite Worship and Song Committee, 2020 ⓦ
965. *Hymnal: A Worship Book*, 1992, based on *Women's Prayer Services*, World Council of Churches, 1983; adapt. Mennonite Worship and Song Committee, 2020
966. *Mennonite Hymnal*, 1969, and *Hymnal: A Worship Book*, 1992; adapt. Mennonite Worship and Song Committee, 2020

967 *Receiving a New Pastor*

Pastor: I pledge with you
to seek first the reign of God
and discern the leading of the Holy Spirit,
to follow the way of Jesus
and grow into the mind of Christ,
to love God
and love our neighbors,
to study the Scriptures prayerfully
and give thanks through all things
for the steadfast love and mercy of God.

Community: We promise
to receive your wisdom
and offer you counsel for the benefit of our lives together,
to respect you as a leader in this community of faith
and endure with you in times of disagreement,
to support your leadership with prayer and resources
and bless you in gratitude, grace, and hope
for the ministry we share.

968 *Blessing for Leaders*

One: May God, who calls you to this ministry,
grant you grace, joy, and endurance.
All: Amen!
One: May Christ guide and empower you for service and leadership.
All: Amen!
One: May the Holy Spirit fill you with the gifts you need.
All: Amen!
One: May the One whose love unites us as the body of Christ
strengthen us to live and proclaim the gospel together.
All: Amen!

CHILD BLESSING

969 *Introduction to Child Blessing*

We give thanks to God for children
and entrust them to God's loving care.
As families dedicate themselves
and their children to God,
we welcome children to the church community
and commit to nurturing them as our own.
We ask for God's blessing
on these children,
their parents,
and this community
as we grow together in God's love.

967. Mennonite Worship and Song Committee, 2020
968. Mennonite Worship and Song Committee, 2020
969. Mennonite Worship and Song Committee, 2020 ⓦ

970 *Reception and Community Commitment at Child Blessing*

Leader: You have offered (*name of child/names of children*)
to the strong and tender care of God.

All: ***We rejoice with you and give thanks for the gift of your child.***
With God as our guide,
we will share in your child's nurture and well-being.
We will support, by our example and words,
your efforts to provide a loving and caring home
where trust in God grows and Christ may be known.
Our prayers are with you and for you.
May our shared life and witness
help you grow as a family in faithfulness and joy.

971 *Child Blessing*

People: God, maker of galaxies
who numbers the hairs on our heads,
we praise your name
for the goodness of creation
and for all the blessings of this life.

Leader: We give you thanks for (*name of child/names of children*).
As Jesus took children into his arms and blessed them,
each child is held
and blessed,
and belongs to your reign.
By your grace, raise (*name of child/names of children*)
and all our children to your glory.

People: Through your Spirit,
lead them to faith in Christ,
sustain them in misfortune and danger,
and let the love they give and receive abound.
In your power, grant eternal life, through Jesus Christ. Amen.

972 *Days Recognizing Parents*

God, our Creator, we give you thanks
for those who have been *mothers/fathers/parents* for us.
Help us inherit from them
that which will make us more fully your people.
Where they have offered us blessings of love,
may we incorporate those gifts into our lives.
Where they have hurt us or fallen short of our expectations,
may we learn from them,
that we might not repeat their mistakes.
May the honor we convey toward our *mothers/fathers/parents*
reflect the honor that we feel toward you. Amen.

970. *Mennonite Hymnal*, 1969; *Hymnal: A Worship Book*, 1992; adapt. Mennonite Worship and Song Committee, 2020
971. Pilgram Marpeck (present-day Germany), 1542 and John D. Rempel (Canada), 1991 in *Hymnal: A Worship Book*, 1992; adapt. Mennonite Worship and Song Committee, 2020
972. United Methodist Church, *Worship in Daily Life*, 1999, alt. Ⓦ

MARRIAGE

973

Introduction to Marriage

God created human beings for relationship—
for friendship, family, and church.
The covenant of marriage is made
in the context of a faith community
gathered in worship to witness and bless the union.
Marriage is a gift from God
and a sign of love, faithfulness, and self-giving
made possible by God's grace.

974

Prayer of Blessing for a Marriage

Leader: God of all life,
in you we live and move and have our being.
Bless (*name*) and (*name*) with the grace
to keep the promises they have made today.

All: ***Bless them with your love***
as they grow in love for one another.

Bless them with your patience
as they share each other's burdens.

Bless them with your peace
as they live in harmony with all.

Bless them with your presence
as they welcome your Spirit
to dwell in their hearts and home.

In the name of Christ, we pray. Amen.

HEALING

975

Introduction to Healing

Healing is central to the ministry of Jesus,
who restores wholeness of body, mind, and spirit,
reconciling people to God and to one another.
We turn to Christ for healing with lament, confession,
laying on of hands, and anointing with oil,
with prayer for the life-giving Holy Spirit to act within
and beyond human action,
drawing us into the fullness of God's care.

973. Mennonite Worship and Song Committee, 2020 Ⓦ
974. *Hymnal: A Worship Book*, 1992; adapt. Mennonite Worship and Song Committee, 2020
975. Mennonite Worship and Song Committee, 2020 Ⓦ

976 *Prayer for Healing*

Individuals may choose to join the leader in speaking any or all of the lines in bold.

Leader: Great Physician,
you touched the lives of the sick and the troubled;
your hands rested on bodies in crisis;
your words soothed broken hearts.
We call on you today, O God,
because we need your healing.

People: Where we have pain, bring relief.
When we are disoriented, bring clarity.
When we confront disease or brokenness, bring healing.
When we wait for tests or news, bring patience.
When we live with barriers, bring courage.
When we are bound by addiction, bring freedom.
When illness separates us from others, bring friendship.
When we cannot make ends meet, help us.

Leader: You are with us in loneliness, bringing comfort.
You are with us in despair, bringing hope.
You are the God who cares and heals.

977 *Prayer in a Healthcare Facility*

Merciful God,
we wait, we wonder, we watch, we hope.
Your love falls on those who wait:
for a word from the doctor, a test result, a surgery, a miracle.
Your peace rests on those who wonder:
about the future, about their health, about how they will endure.
Your comfort cloaks those who watch:
over friends, children, family, and strangers.
And so, God, we hope.
We hope for healing that is deep, rich, and surprising.
We hope for courage in the face of things we cannot control.
We hope for strength to walk through this shadowed valley.
We hope for a deep sense of your nearness in this place.
We are yours.
You have called us by name.
Help us now to wait, wonder, and watch in hope. Amen.

978 *Prayer for Mental Health*

Hear our prayer, O God of healing and hope,
for all who struggle with mental illness
and those who care for them,
for their families and friends, their church and community.
We pray for greater understanding, compassion, strength, endurance.
Make your presence known even when fears threaten,
when anxieties overwhelm, when thoughts fragment and accuse,
and the burden seems too heavy to carry one more step.
Almighty and merciful God, grant one more moment,
one more breath, one more foot in front of the other.
Bring healing. Restore peace. Raise up hope.

976. Mennonite Worship and Song Committee, 2020 Ⓦ
Specific resources for healing are found in the *Worship Leader Edition*, including anointing for healing for an individual or small group, and prayers for times of reproductive loss and when relationships end.
977. Ingrid Loepp Thiessen (Canada), 2018 Ⓦ
978. April Yamasaki (Canada), 2018 Ⓦ

979 *Prayer when Aging*

Gracious God, we celebrate life.
Your creation bursts with beauty and mystery,
with seasons that are both predictable and surprising.
We thank you for new lives, changing lives, busy lives, and slowing lives.
We pray for those of us who are leaning toward the end of life.
Grant us patience
when our steps are halting, painful, or impossible.
Grant us understanding
when the world is changing all around us, too much and too fast.
Grant us peace
when loss overwhelms and we feel alone.
Grant us healing
for our worn bodies, our aching hearts, and our troubled spirits.
Grant us grace
when the past bogs us down and fills us with regret.
Grant us love
when we fear for the future of the world and our loved ones.
Grant us joy
as we celebrate the gift of life
and anticipate the day when we will see you face-to-face.
Take our hands, O God, and lead us home. Amen.

FUNERALS

980 *Introduction to Funerals*

In the face of death, we worship God:
the Creator who gives life,
Jesus who died and rose again,
and the Spirit who sighs with us in our sorrow.
We gather in grief and gratitude
to release loved ones to God's care,
to comfort one another,
and to name the hope we have for this life
and the life to come.

981

Everlasting God,
you are our refuge and strength,
a shelter in this time of need.
Console us with your presence today—
ease our loneliness,
dispel our fears,
and revive our hope.
Send your Holy Spirit
to carry us through our sorrow
and into the comfort of your love,
now and forevermore
through Jesus Christ. Amen.

979. Ingrid Loepp Thiessen (Canada), 2018 ⓦ
980. Mennonite Worship and Song Committee, 2020 ⓦ
981. *Hymnal: A Worship Book*, 1992; based on *Minister's Manual*, 1983; adapt. Mennonite Worship and Song Committee, 2020

982 *Prayer of Commendation*

Leader: Eternal God
in whom we live and move and have our being,
we thank you for the unending life
offered to us by the risen Christ.
We thank you for the life of (*name*)
and all that *he/she/they* meant to us.

All:* *Loving God,
with your help
and support one another,
we release* (name) *to your tender care.
Receive this beloved one
into the arms of your mercy.

Leader: Assure us with your love,
strengthen our faith, and grant us peace
through Jesus Christ, who is alive
and reigns with you and the Holy Spirit,
one God, now and forever. Amen.

983

Eternal Strength,
hold us.
Eternal Hope,
show us new life.
Eternal Compassion,
comfort us in our grief.
Eternal Goodness,
grant us your grace
as we live, work, and pray
in this place, in this time,
and with these people
who reveal your love. Amen.

MORNING AND EVENING

984

This day, God, may I dream your dreams;
This day, God, may I reflect your love;
This day, God, may I do your work;
This day, God, may I taste your peace.

982. Mennonite Worship and Song Committee, 2020
983. *Hymnal: A Worship Book*, 1992; based on Alcuin (England), ca. 8th c.; adapt. Mennonite Worship and Song Committee, 2020
984. Angela Ashwin (England), 1996

985 *Morning Prayer*

Call to praise

A.

O God, open our lips
and our mouths will proclaim your praise.
You are good to those who wait for you,
to all who seek you.

B. *Glory*

Glory to You,
Source of All Being,
Eternal Word,
and Holy Spirit:
as it was in the beginning,
is now, and will be forever. Amen.

Psalm

C. *Thanksgiving*

It is good to give you thanks, O Most High,
to sing praises to your name.

(*free prayers of thanksgiving*)

We declare your steadfast love
in the morning
and your faithfulness by night. Amen.

Song

Call to discipleship

D.

Jesus said,
Let anyone with ears to hear listen.
You shall love the Lord your God
with all your heart,
and with all your soul,
and with all your strength,
and with all your mind;
and your neighbor as yourself.
Do this, and you will live.
Jesus, you have the words
of eternal life.

Gospel reading

Old Testament or Epistle reading

Silent or spoken reflection on the readings

Song

E. *Zechariah's song (Luke 1:68-79)*

Blessed are you, Lord, the God of Israel,
you have come to your people
and set them free.
You have raised up for us a mighty Savior,
born of the house of your servant David.
Through your holy prophets,
you promised of old
to save us from our enemies,
from the hands of all who hate us,
to show mercy to our forebears,
and to remember your holy covenant.
This was the oath you swore
to Abraham and Sarah:
to set us free from the hands
of our enemies,
free to worship you without fear,
holy and righteous before you,
all the days of our life.
And you, child, shall be called
the prophet of the Most High,
for you will go before the Lord
to prepare the way,
to give God's people knowledge
of salvation
by the forgiveness of their sins.
In the tender compassion of our God
the dawn from on high
shall break upon us,
to shine on those who dwell in darkness
and the shadow of death,
and to guide our feet
into the way of peace.

985. *Take Our Moments and Our Days: An Anabaptist Prayer Book*, 2010, developed at Anabaptist Mennonite Biblical Seminary and adapt. for *Voices Together*, 2020 Ⓦ

Call to intercession

F.

The Spirit helps us in our weakness;
for we do not know how to pray
as we ought,
but that very Spirit intercedes
with sighs too deep for words.

Gracious God, we bring our prayers to you
as acts of love for you
and for our neighbors.
God of mercy,
hear our prayer.

We pray for ourselves
and those dear to us. . .

(*open prayers*)

God of mercy,
hear our prayer.

We pray for our community
and for our neighbors. . .

(*open prayers*)

God of mercy,
hear our prayer.

We pray for the church. . .

(*open prayers*)

God of mercy,
hear our prayer.

We pray for the world. . .

(*open prayers*)

God of mercy,
hear our prayer.

We pray for other concerns
we carry in our hearts. . .

(*open prayers*)

God of mercy,
hear our prayer.

G.

God of grace and glory,
you fling the stars into the heavens;
you see every sparrow fall.
Deepen our trust in the mystery
of your power shining through
Christ Jesus,
that we may live your love for the world.
In the name of the one who taught us,
we pray:

(*Pray together the Prayer Jesus Taught (989) in whatever language and form is most familiar.*)

H. *Benediction*

God will guide us continually,
and satisfy our needs in parched places,
and we shall be like a watered garden,
like a spring of water,
whose waters never fail. Amen.

986

God,
it is night.

The night is for stillness.
Let us be still in the presence of God.

It is night after a long day.
What has been done has been done;
what has not been done has not been done;
let it be.

The night is dark.
Let our fears of the darkness of the world
and of our own lives rest in you.

The night is quiet.
Let the quietness of your peace enfold us,
all dear to us,
and all who have no peace.

The night heralds the dawn.
Let us look expectantly to a new day,
new joys,
new possibilities.

In your name we pray. Amen.

986. The Anglican Church in Aotearoa, New Zealand and Polynesia, *A New Zealand Prayer Book*, 1988

987 *Evening Prayer*

Call to praise

A.

O God, your word is a lamp to my feet
and a light to my path
The light and peace of Jesus Christ
be with us.

B. *Glory*

Glory to You,
Source of All Being,
Eternal Word,
and Holy Spirit:
as it was in the beginning,
is now, and will be forever. Amen.

Psalm

C. *Thanksgiving*

It is good to give you thanks, O Most High,
to sing praises to your name.

(*free prayers of thanksgiving*)

We declare your steadfast love
in the morning
and your faithfulness by night. Amen.

Song

D. *Confession*

Have mercy on me, O God,
according to your steadfast love;
according to your abundant mercy
blot out my transgressions.

(*silence*)

Create in me a clean heart, O God,
and put a new and right spirit within me.
Restore to me the joy of your salvation
and sustain in me a willing spirit.
Amen.

Call to discipleship

E.

Jesus said, I am the bread of life.
Whoever comes to me
will never be hungry,
and whoever believes in me
will never be thirsty.
Jesus, you have the words
of eternal life.

Gospel reading

Old Testament or Epistle reading

Silent or spoken reflection on the readings

Song

F. *Mary's song (Luke 1:46-55)*

My soul proclaims the greatness
of the Lord,
my spirit rejoices in God my Savior,
for you, Lord, have looked with favor
on your lowly servant.
From this day all generations
will call me blessed:
you, the Almighty, have done great things
for me
and holy is your name.
You have mercy on those who fear you,
from generation to generation.
You have shown strength with your arm
and scattered the proud in their conceit,
casting down the mighty from their thrones
and lifting up the lowly.
You have filled the hungry
with good things
and sent the rich away empty.
You have come to the aid
of your servant Israel,
to remember the promise of mercy,
the promise made to our forebears,
to Abraham and Sarah
and their children for ever.

987. *Take Our Moments and Our Days: An Anabaptist Prayer Book*, 2010, developed at Anabaptist Mennonite Biblical Seminary and adapt. for *Voices Together*, 2020 Ⓦ

Call to intercession

G.

Morning, noon, and night,
call out to God, who hears your cry.
Give your burden to God,
who will be your support.

Loving God, we bring our prayers to you
with confidence,
in the name of our Sovereign Jesus.
God of mercy,
hear our prayer.

We pray for ourselves
and those dear to us. . .

(*open prayers*)

God of mercy,
hear our prayer.

We pray for our community
and for our neighbors. . .

(*open prayers*)

God of mercy,
hear our prayer.

We pray for the church. . .

(*open prayers*)

God of mercy,
hear our prayer.

We pray for the world. . .

(*open prayers*)

God of mercy,
hear our prayer.

We pray for other concerns
we carry in our hearts. . .

(*open prayers*)

God of mercy,
hear our prayer.

H.

God of grace and glory,
you keep our souls,
satisfying us with living bread
and holy work.
Renew us through forgiveness
and restore us in rest,
that we may look for the coming
of your reign
on earth as in heaven.
Secure in your love,
we pray with humility and joy:

(*Pray together the Prayer Jesus Taught (989) in whatever language and form is most familiar*)

I. *Benediction*

May the God of hope
fill us with all joy and peace in believing
so that we may abound in hope
by the power of the Holy Spirit. Amen.

988

Leader: God of deep and dazzling darkness,
here on the edge of night
before we surrender our day
to silence and mystery,
we need to hear that you love us.
People: We need to hear again
your promise never to leave us;
we need to hope in you.
Leader: Hear our prayer
for all who weep tonight,
and those who wait
beside the dying. (*pause*. . .)
Hear our prayer
for frightened children,
for anxious parents
and families in distress. (*pause*. . .)
Hear our prayer for nations at war,
for hungry refugees
and those unjustly oppressed.
(*pause*. . .)
Hear all our prayers.
All: ***God of deep and dazzling darkness,***
our world is in your hands,
and so are we.
We rest in you.
In Jesus' name. Amen.

988. Marlene Kropf (USA), 1999

PRAYING

Praying Scripture worship resources are found at 724–730.

989 *Prayer Jesus Taught*

A. Our Father in heaven,
hallowed be your name,
your kingdom come,
your will be done,
on earth as in heaven.
Give us today our daily bread.
Forgive us our sins
as we forgive those who sin against us.
Save us from the time of trial
and deliver us from evil.
For the kingdom, the power,
and the glory are yours
now and forever. Amen.

B. Our Father who art in heaven,
hallowed be thy name.
Thy kingdom come.
Thy will be done
on earth as it is in heaven.
Give us this day our daily bread,
and forgive us our trespasses,
as we forgive those
who trespass against us,
and lead us not into temptation,
but deliver us from evil.
For thine is the kingdom,
and the power, and the glory,
forever and ever. Amen.

C. Blessed One,
our source and support,
holy is your name.
May your love be enacted in the world.
May your will be done
on earth as in heaven.
Give us today our daily bread
and forgive us our sins
as we forgive those who sin against us.
Save us in the time of trial
and deliver us from evil.
For all that we do in your love,
and all that your love brings to birth,
and the fullness of love that will be
are yours, now and forever. Amen.

D. Notre Père qui es aux cieux,
que ton nom soit sanctifié,
que ton règne vienne,
que ta volonté soit faite
sur la terre comme au ciel.
Donne-nous aujourd'hui
notre pain de ce jour.
Pardonne-nous nos offenses,
comme nous pardonnons aussi
à ceux qui nous ont offensés.
Et ne nous soumets pas à la tentation,
mais délivre-nous du mal.
Car c'est à toi qu'appartiennent
le règne, la puissance et la gloire,
pour les siècles des siècles. Amen.

E. Padre nuestro que estás en los cielos,
sanctificado sea tu nombre.
Venga tu reino.
Sea hecha tu voluntad,
como en el cielo,
así también en la tierra.
Danos hoy nuestro pan cotidiano.
Y perdónanos nuestras deudas,
como también nosotros perdonamos
á nuestros deudores.
Y no nos metas en tentación,
mas líbranos del mal:
porque tuyo es el reino,
y el poder, y la gloria,
por todos los siglos. Amén.

F. Vater unser im Himmel,
geheiligt werde dein Name.
Dein Reich komme
dein Wille geschehe
wie im Himmel, so auf Erden.
Unser tägliches Brot gib uns heute.
Und vergib uns unsere Schuld,
wie auch wir vergeben
unseren Schuldigern.
Und führe uns nicht in Versuchung,
sondern erlöse uns von dem Bösen.
Denn dein ist das Reich
und die Kraft
und die Herrlichkeit
in Ewigkeit. Amen

989. Matthew 6:9-15; Luke 11:2-4. A. trans. English Language Liturgical Consultation, 1988; B. trans. Episcopal Church (USA), *The Book of Common Prayer*, 1928; C. Richard D. McCall (USA), 2003, alt.; D. French; Conseil d'Eglises chrétiennes en France (France), 1966, 2016; E. Spanish; *Reina Valera*, 1995, alt; F. German; *Arbeitsgemeinschaft für liturgische Texte* (ALT) (Germany), 1971 ⓦ

990

Between the words,
beneath the words,
beyond the words,
may God meet you
in the places
where words cannot go.

(*silence*)

991

God,
make me an instrument of your peace.
Where there is hatred, let me sow love;
  where there is injury, pardon;
  where there is doubt, faith;
  where there is despair, hope;
  where there is darkness, light;
  where there is sadness, joy.
O divine Spirit,
  grant that I may not so much seek
    to be consoled as to console,
    to be understood as to understand,
    to be loved as to love.
For it is in giving that we receive;
  it is in pardoning that we are pardoned;
  it is in dying that we are born
    to eternal life. Amen.

992

Sovereign Majesty,
we pray for the continued outpouring
  of your Spirit upon the church
so that the fires of Pentecost
  may anoint us
  to take the gospel of Jesus Christ
  to all the world.
Help us to release the anointing
  of the Holy Spirit
  which dwells within us.
Let us pour your blessing
  into the lives of others.
Let us lift up the name of Jesus
  with power from on high. Amen.

993

O God, listening to us here,
  you accept also the prayers
    of our church family
    in Africa, Asia, the Pacific,
    the Americas, and Europe.
We are all one in prayer.
So may we, as one,
  rightly carry out your commission
    to witness and to love
    in the church and throughout the world.
Accept our prayers graciously,
  even when they are somewhat strange.
They are offered in Jesus' name.

994

Gracious God,
when there is nothing we can say,
we give you thanks
that your Spirit intercedes for us
with sighs too deep for words.

Loving God,
when there is nothing we can do,
we give you thanks
that you are working for good
in this world of struggle and pain.

Holy God,
when there is nothing else we know,
still we give you thanks
that nothing in life or in death,
nothing in heaven or on earth,
nothing in this world or the world to come
will ever separate us from your great love;
through Jesus Christ. Amen.

995

Praying aloud spontaneously at the same time is an important part of prayer life in some communities. Those gathered may be given a specific period of time and a common theme for prayer. Then, empowered by the Holy Spirit, all pray aloud together. Spontaneous prayer may also be offered by one person on behalf of the community.

990. Jan Richardson (USA), 2010.
991. attr. Francis of Assisi (Italy), ca. 13th c.
992. *African American Heritage Hymnal* (USA), 2001; adapt. Mennonite Worship and Song Committee, 2020
993. anon. (Ghana), 1999
994. Presbyterian Church (USA), *Book of Common Worship*, 2018
995. Mennonite Worship and Song Committee, 2019

996

Leader: Listening God,
All: ***you hear our prayers before we speak***
yet welcome our praying;
therefore we come with confidence
to lay our requests before you.
Leader: We pray for Christians everywhere,
for our denomination and congregation,
for strength to persevere in faithfulness.
We pray for the whole people of God.
People: God of grace, hear our prayer.
Leader: We pray for the nations of the world,
for all leaders,
and for those who make policy decisions.
We pray for the well-being of our global community.
People: God of grace, hear our prayer.
Leader: We pray for the earth and all living creatures,
for regions and species at risk,
and for the sharing of resources.
We pray for the wholeness of creation.
People: God of grace, hear our prayer.
Leader: We pray for those who are overcome by violence,
for victims of injustice or oppression,
and for those in poverty or pain.
We pray for all who need healing and peace.
People: God of grace, hear our prayer.
Leader: We pray for those who endure trials,
for those who are dying,
and for those who mourn.
We pray for all in need of comfort and hope.
People: God of grace, hear our prayer.

Leader: You have heard the prayers of your people, O God.
We rest in the comfort of your care,
as we pray in Jesus' name.
All: ***Amen.***

997

Leader: With the whole people of God in Christ Jesus,
let us pray for the church, those in need, and all God's creation.

We pray, holy God, for the church universal—
for the unity of the church,
for (*the national and regional church*),
for (*a church community in the news*),
for (*local leaders by name or title*),
for . . .
O God, our Sanctuary, empower the church, and in your mercy,
People: hear our prayer.

996. *Hymnal: A Worship Book*, 1992; adapt. Mennonite Worship and Song Committee, 2019
997. Gail Ramshaw (USA), 2017, alt.

Leader: We pray, omnipotent God, for the well-being of creation—
for the will and wisdom to care for the earth,
for (*lands facing climate change*),
for (*local waters*),
for (*a species of endangered animal*),
for . . .
O God, Rainbow of promise, preserve the earth, and in your mercy,

People: hear our prayer.

Leader: We pray, righteous God, for peace and justice in the world—
for efforts toward international cooperation,
for peace in (*countries in conflict or at war*),
for an increase of justice in (*a nation or a current situation*),
for (*our elected officials by name or title*),
for . . .
O God, Sovereign and Judge, guide the nations, and in your mercy,

People: hear our prayer.

Leader: We pray, benevolent God, for the poor, oppressed, sick, bereaved, lonely—
for the hungry and the homeless,
for persons without family or friends,
for (*a group of the distressed in the news*),
for (*those afflicted with a specific disease or debility*),
for . . .
O God, Shepherd and Mother, protect the needy, and in your mercy,

People: hear our prayer.

Leader: We pray, compassionate God, for all who suffer in body, mind, or spirit—
for those in hospitals and other institutions of care,
for those who have no medical care,
for those who are incarcerated,
for (*names of the sick*),
for . . .
for all who today will die.
O God, Healer and Nurse, heal the sick, and in your mercy,

People: hear our prayer.

Leader: We pray, faithful God, for our congregation
for deeper faith and stronger commitment for us all,
for our homebound members,
for (*an outreach program*),
for (*an internal matter*),
for . . .
O God, Everlasting Arms, embrace this assembly, and in your mercy,

People: hear our prayer.

Leader: We pray, loving God, for the desires of our hearts—
(*keep five seconds of silence*)
O God, our Heart's Desire, grant us peace, and in your mercy,

People: hear our prayer.

Leader: Into your hands, gracious God, we commend all for whom we pray,
trusting in your mercy, through Jesus Christ.

All: Amen.

998

Everlasting God,
in whom we live and move
and have our being:
You have made us for yourself,
so that our hearts are restless
until they rest in you.
Give us purity of heart
and strength of purpose,
that no selfish passion may hinder us
from knowing your will,
no weakness keep us from doing it,
that in your light
we may see light clearly,
and in your service
find perfect freedom,
through Jesus Christ,
who lives and reigns with you
and the Holy Spirit. One God,
now and forever. Amen.

999

God be in my head
and in my understanding;
God be in my eyes
and in my looking;
God be in my mouth
and in my speaking;
God be in my heart
and in my thinking;
God be at my end
and at my departing. Amen.

1000

Save us, God,
from being self-centered in our prayers,
and teach us to remember
to pray for others.
May we be so caught up in love
for those for whom we pray
that we may feel their needs
as keenly as our own,
and pray for them with imagination,
sensitivity, and knowledge.
We ask this in Christ's name. Amen.

998. inspired by Augustine of Hippo (present-day Algeria), ca. 397; *The Book of Common Order of the Church of Scotland*, 1940, alt.
999. Sarum Primer (England), 11th c.
1000. John Calvin (present-day Switzerland), 16th c.

1001

Loving God,
you have baptized us into one body
and made us to drink the one Spirit.
Now grant us faithful hearts
that we may serve one another
diligently in love
and find no cause to separate or divide.
Call each of us to esteem others
better than ourselves
so we may remain together
in peace and joy.
Grant these mercies to us
and all your people. Amen.

1002

Gardener God,
you have planted and protected us
by your faithful hand.
Send us the sap of your grace
from Christ, the true Vine,
and make us blossom
and bear the fruit of love
as a sign of your life in us.
Let the sweet fragrance of the shoots
you have planted
give you praise forever. Amen.

1003

Leader: Compassionate Christ,
if you are my light,
People: shine in me.
Leader: If you are my life,
People: live in me.
Leader: If you are my jewel,
People: adorn me with beauty.
Leader: If you are my joy,
People: rejoice in me.
Leader: If I am your dwelling place,
People: inhabit me.
Leader: May I fully be your instrument,
that my body,
my soul,
and my spirit may be holy.
All: Eternal Way, lead me!
Eternal Truth, teach me!
Eternal Life, revive me!

1001. Tijs Jeuriaenss (Netherlands), 1569
1002. Pilgram Marpeck (Germany), 16th c.
1003. *Die ernsthafte Christenpflicht* (*Prayer Book for Earnest Christians*) (present-day Germany), 1708; trans. Leonard Gross (USA), 1998; adapt. Mennonite Worship and Song Committee, 2018

1004

All: ***Gracious God,***
we pray for your universal church.
Fill it with all truth in all peace:
Left: where it is corrupt, purify it;
Right: where it is in error, direct it;
Left: where it is amiss in anything,
reform it;
Right: where it is right, strengthen it;
Left: where it is in want, provide for it;
Right: where it is divided, reunite it,
All: ***for the sake of Jesus Christ***
our Savior. Amen.

1005

That huge "Why?"
held deep inside us all
or spat out occasionally
isn't an intellectual question.

It's a cry of agony.

There are no answers,
only the waiting,
the walking alongside,
the being here.

Only the giving
out of what we do not have:
the love that comes
as we give it.
The incredible risk of love
demands more of us
than easy answers
and pretty prayers.

1006

Lighting a candle
is an act of defiance.

Lighting a candle
is a prayer for courage.

Lighting a candle
is a step toward God.

God of light,
out in the world,
where you are
and I live,
help me today
to light a candle,
a candle of peace.

1007

God, give me grace
to accept with serenity the things
that cannot be changed,
courage to change the things
that should be changed,
and the wisdom to distinguish
the one from the other.
Living one day at a time,
enjoying one moment at a time,
accepting hardship
as a pathway to peace,
taking, as Jesus did,
this sinful world as it is,
not as I would have it,
trusting that you will make
all things right,
if I surrender to your will,
so that I may be reasonably happy
in this life,
and supremely happy with you forever
in the next. Amen.

1008

God,
I have so few ways to pray,
but you have so many ways to answer.
Keep me alert
to your unpredictable answers,
to your unexplainable surprises,
and by your grace,
make me one of those surprises,
for the sake of the One
who taught us the surprises
of moving mountains,
healing touches,
wondrous stories,
great banquets,
first suppers,
broken bread,
crosses,
and resurrections.

1004. William Laud (England), ca. 17th c., alt.
1005. Joy Mead (England), 2017
1006. Ruth Burgess (England), 2017, alt.
1007. Reinhold Niebuhr (USA), 1937
1008. Ted Loder (USA), 1981

1009

Source and sustainer of life,
we cherish the myriad works
of your hands.
Water, earth, and sky are yours,
as are all their inhabitants,
wild and tame.
We thank you for creatures
that nourish and serve us,
befriend, enrich, entertain,
and protect us.
May we, who are made in your image,
care for them well.
And may your groaning
yet wondrous creation
rally and thrive,
revealing to all who come after us
your wise, redemptive,
transforming love,
through Jesus Christ, our Savior. Amen.

1010

O God, our deliverer:
you cast down the mighty
and lift up those of no account.
Like Elizabeth and Mary,
who embraced one another
with songs of liberation,
may we, pregnant with your Spirit,
affirm one another in hope for the world,
in the name of Jesus. Amen.

1011

A wilderness beckons us;
a desert, a barren place,
yet a place of blessing and discovery.
Jesus, steady companion,
accompany us as we enter
the hurtful places,
the frightening places,
the dangerous places deep within us.
Jesus, our wild and well-traveled guide,
lead us into this emptiness,
where all will fall away,
and we will have nothing but you.
Walk with us through the valley
of the shadow of death,
where we shall be raised
and drink of deep springs. Amen.

1012

O Tree of Calvary,
send your roots deep down
into my heart.
Gather together the soil of my heart,
the sands of my fickleness,
the mud of my desires.
Bind them all together,
O Tree of Calvary,
interlace them with your strong roots,
entwine them with the network
of your love.

1013

O Risen Christ,
you breathe your Holy Spirit on us
and you tell us:
"Peace be yours."
Opening ourselves to your peace—
letting it soften
the harsh and rocky ground
of our hearts—
means preparing ourselves to be
bearers of reconciliation
wherever you may place us.
But you know at times
we are at a loss.
So come lead us
to wait in silence,
to let a ray of hope shine forth
in our world.

1014

O God,
you withdraw from our sight,
that you may be known by our love;
help us to enter the cloud
where you are hidden,
and surrender all our certainty
to the darkness of faith
in Jesus Christ. Amen.

1009. Presbyterian Church (USA), *Book of Common Worship*, 2018, alt. Ⓦ
1010. Janet Morley (England), 1988
1011. Steve Garnaas Holmes (USA), 2011
1012. anon. (India)
1013. Brother Roger of Taizé (France), 20th c., alt.
1014. Janet Morley (England)

GIVING

1015

Generous God,
you gave us life;
now we give our lives back to you.
We present ourselves:
our work and play,
our joys and sorrows,
our thoughts and deeds,
our gifts and resources,
to be used by you
for the sake of all people everywhere,
through Jesus Christ. Amen.

1016

Jesus of love and leftovers,
we struggle with what to share
and how much is enough.
Sometimes we are the disciples,
quietly suggesting you send
the needy crowds away.
Sometimes we are the crowds,
bringing only our desire
to be close to you.
When we have little,
embolden us to share it.
When we have nothing,
welcome us to stay and eat.
In giving and receiving,
we participate in the miracle of enough.
Thank you, Jesus.

1017

God of life,
we give these offerings in gratitude,
rejoicing in the abundance
of your gifts to us.
We give these offerings in faith,
trusting that you will provide
for our needs.
We give these offerings in hope,
knowing you can use them
to spread your love in this world.
And with these offerings, we give ourselves;
may we live with generous hearts
and open hands. Amen.

1018

Creator Spirit,
you clothe the flowers of the field:
enable us to rejoice in all the gifts
with which you fill us,
and may that be enough for us. Amen.

1019

Blessed are you, O God,
maker of all things.
Through your goodness
you have blessed us with good gifts:
our selves, our time,
and our possessions.
We receive these gifts in gratitude
and offer them to the world
with your love,
through the one who gave himself for us,
Jesus Christ, our Savior. Amen.

1020

God of extravagant mercy,
with hands outstretched
you have poured out
wonder and pleasure and delight,
goodness and beauty and bounty.
So take these offerings, we pray,
as our protest against all
that is evil and ugly and impoverished,
trivial and wretched and tyrannical,
in our world and in ourselves—
that we, too, may be poured out
for the world. Amen.

1021

How silently,
how silently
the wondrous gift is given.

I would be silent now,
Lord,
and expectant . . .
that I may receive
the gift I need,
so that I may become
the gift others need.

1015. First University United Methodist Church (USA), 1969
1016. Michelle Dueck (Canada), 2019
1017. Joanna Harader (USA), 2013
1018. Brother Roger of Taizé (France), 2000, alt.
1019. Evangelical Lutheran Church in Canada and Evangelical Lutheran Church in America, (USA), *Evangelical Lutheran Worship*, 2006, alt.
1020. Terry Falla, ed. (Australia), 1994
1021. Ted Loder (USA), 1981

1022

Leader: Holy One,
as you are faithful to us,
may we be faithful to you:
**People: faithful with our time and energy,
faithful with our possessions and wealth.**
Leader: Receive these gifts by your grace.
**People: Multiply and use them
through the power of the Holy Spirit
to make real your reign
of love, justice, and peace in our world. Amen.**

1023

Leader: What will you offer the body of Christ today?
*All: Bring all that you have.
Bring all that you are.*
Left: The gifts of silence and the gifts of words are welcome.
Right: The gifts of leading and the gifts of following are welcome.
Left: The gifts of doubt and the gifts of faith are welcome.
Right: The gifts of the head and the gifts of the heart are welcome.
Left: The gifts of planning and the gifts of spontaneity are welcome.
*All: May all that we are as individuals
come together to strengthen the living body of the church,
Christ Incarnate.*

1024

Leader: There is no scarcity. There is no shortage.
No lack of love, of compassion, of joy in the world.
There is enough. There is more than enough.
Only fear and greed make us think otherwise.
No one need starve.
People: There is enough land and enough food.
Leader: No one need die of thirst.
People: There is enough water.
Leader: No one need live without mercy.
People: There is no end to grace.
Leader: And we are all instruments of grace.
**People: The more we give it, the more we share it,
the more we use it, the more God makes.**
Leader: There is no scarcity of love.

1025

Spanish

Oh Dios, dales pan
a los que tienen hambre,
y hambre de justicia
a los que tienen pan. Amén.

O God, to those who have hunger,
give bread,
and to those who have bread,
give hunger for justice. Amen.

1022. Joanna Harader (USA), 2017, alt.
1023. LeAnne Zook (USA), 2011, rev. 2020
1024. Rosemarie Freeney Harding (USA), ca. 1990
1025. traditional (Latin America); adapt. Ana Victoria Aguilera Martinez (Mexico), 2019

LIVING GOD'S STORY

Service and witness for peace Scripture worship resources are found at 781–786.

1026

Jesus Christ,
you stretched out your arms of love
on the cross
that everyone might come within the reach
of your saving embrace:
So clothe us in your Spirit, that we,
reaching forth our hands in love,
may bring those who do not know you
to the knowledge and love of you,
for the honor of your name. Amen.

1027

Convert us,
Jesus the persecuted,
as you converted Paul
and sent him as apostle to the world.
May our love, our prayers, our suffering
carry your gospel at whatever cost
to all who wait to hear it. Amen.

1028

Nurturing God,
root us in your love
and grow us up to bear
the fruit of your Spirit:
love, joy, peace,
patience, kindness,
goodness, faithfulness, gentleness,
and self-control. Amen.

1029

Christ, whose insistent call
disturbs our settled lives:
give us discernment to hear your word,
grace to relinquish our tasks,
and courage to follow empty-handed
wherever you may lead;
that the voice of your gospel
may reach to the ends of the earth.
Amen.

1030

Grow us slowly,
persistently,
and deeply, God,
to be people who watch without distraction,
listen without interruption,
and stay put without inclination to flee.
Amen.

1031

Liberating God,
prevent us from falling into the sin
of believing that the slavery of Egypt
is better than the struggle in the desert.
Amen.

1032

Gracious God, bless our cities.
Give us grace to join in creating cities
where neighborhoods remain vibrant
and whole,
where people find support
and community,
and where arts, culture,
and sports flourish.
Make the diverse fabric of the city
a delight to all who live and visit there
and a strong bond uniting people
around common goals for the good of all,
through Jesus Christ. Amen.

1033

Living Christ, in these times,
when we fear we are losing hope
or feel that our efforts are futile,
let us see in our hearts and minds
the image of your resurrection,
and let that be our source of courage
and strength.
With that, and in your company,
help us face challenges and struggles
against all that is born of injustice.
Amen.

1026. Episcopal Church (USA), *The Book of Common Prayer*, 1979
1027. The Anglican Church in Aotearoa, New Zealand and Polynesia, *A New Zealand Prayer Book*, 1988
1028. Shane Claiborne (USA), Jonathan Wilson-Hartgrove (USA), and Enuma Okoro (USA), 2010, alt.
1029. Janet Morley (England), 2005
1030. Anthony (Egypt), ca. 4th c., alt.
1031. anon. (Nicaragua), 20th c., alt.
1032. Evangelical Lutheran Church in Canada and Evangelical Lutheran Church in America, *Evangelical Lutheran Worship*, 2006, alt.
1033. anon. (Philippines), 20th c.

1034

Holy and righteous God,
you created us in your image.
Grant us grace to contend fearlessly
against evil
and to make no peace with oppression.
Help us, like your servant
(*name of biblical figure or inspiring example*),
to work for justice among people
and nations,
to the glory of your name. Amen.

1035

Christ has no body now on earth but yours;
yours are the only hands
with which Christ can do his work,
yours are the only feet
with which Christ can go about the world,
yours are the only eyes
through which Christ's compassion
can shine forth upon a troubled world.
Christ has no body on earth now but yours.

1036

Lay one brick at a time,
take one step at a time;
we can be responsible
only for the one action
of the present moment.
But we know that God will take them
and multiply them,
as Jesus multiplied
the loaves and fishes.

1037

Love cannot remain by itself—
it has no meaning.
Love has to be put into action,
and that action is service.
Whatever form we are,
whatever our abilities,
whatever our resources,
it is not how much we do,
but how much love we put in the doing;
a lifelong sharing of love with others.

1038

Spanish

La paz no es producto
del terror ni del miedo.
La paz no es el silencio
de los cementerios.
La paz no es producto de una violencia
y de una represión que calla.
La paz es la aportación generosa, tranquila,
de todos para el bien de todos.
La paz es dinamismo.
La paz es generosidad,
es derecho y es deber,
en que cada uno se sienta
en su puesto en esta hermosa familia.

English

Peace is not the product
of terror or fear.
Peace is not the silence
of cemeteries.
Peace is not the silent result
of violent repression.
Peace is the generous, tranquil contribution
of all to the good of all.
Peace is dynamic.
Peace is generous,
a right and a duty,
each one feeling in the right place
as part of this beautiful family.

1039

May we go forth into the world
with courage and confidence,
and be ready to confront evil
without retreating,
knowing that people—
young and old,
chosen and called by God—
will receive power to stand fast
against evil,
and to triumph day by day.

1034. Evangelical Lutheran Church in Canada and Evangelical Lutheran Church in America, *Evangelical Lutheran Worship*, 2006 Ⓦ
1035. Teresa of Ávila (present-day Spain), 16th c.
1036. Dorothy Day (USA), *The Catholic Worker*, 1957
1037. Teresa of Calcutta (India), 1983, alt.
1038. Oscar Romero (El Salvador), 1977
1039. M. Moran Weston (USA), 1972 Ⓦ

1040

Leader: In defiance of corruption and falsehood,
People: we commit to truth and integrity,
and we pray for honesty and uprightness
to increase in our world.
Leader: In defiance of apathy and hatred,
People: we choose to be proactive in love,
and we pray for understanding and peace
to increase in our world.
Leader: In defiance of skepticism and cynicism,
People: we embrace the mystery of faith,
and we pray for humility and wonder
to increase in our world.
Leader: In defiance of self-interest and human arrogance,
People: we celebrate God's salvation,
and we pray for compassion and faith
to increase in our world.
Leader: In defiance of all that would oppose God's purpose among us,
People: we choose again to follow Christ,
and we continue to pray,
not just now, but at all times. Amen.

1041

Leader: Jesus, servant, at supper with your disciples
you put a towel around your waist.
Like Peter, we protest and distort your simple parable of love.
People: Wash us, Lord,
that we may be ready to wash each other's feet
and to serve one another for your sake.
Leader: Jesus, servant, unless your Spirit lives in us,
we will lord it over the people and institutions in our care.
People: Come, dwell within us
and within our churches,
that we may learn how to follow you
who came not to be served
but to serve.
Leader: We pray to you,
the one who gave your life as a ransom for many.
People: Amen.

1042

Spanish

God our sanctuary,
grant us
and our neighbors
near and far
courage in our hearts,
peace in our homes,
and justice in our streets. Amen.

Dios nuestro santuario,
concédenos a nosotros
y a nuestros vecinos
cercanos y lejanos
valentía en nuestros corazones,
paz en nuestros hogares,
y justicia en nuestras calles. Amén.

1040. John van de Laar (South Africa), 2009
1041. 8th Assembly of the Christian Conference of Asia (Korea), 1985
1042. Columbus Mennonite Church (USA), 2018; adapt. Andrea de Ávila (Canada) and Cristina Horst (Argentina)

1043 *Prayer for National Occasions*

Leader: Some trust in governments
and some in borders,
All: ***but we trust in God,***
who invites all people to live in peace.
Left: For the earth belongs to God,
and all creation is in God's care:
Right: land and waters, plants and animals, sky and soil
declare the hospitality of God.
Left: The world belongs to God,
and all who live in it.
Right: We belong to one another as siblings,
all of us children of God.

Leader: With gratitude for the home God has made for us on this planet, we pray:
Left: Send your Holy Spirit
to strengthen our resolve
to strive for communities
where foreigners become neighbors
and strangers become friends.
Right: Revive our desire for the reign of Christ,
who releases prisoners
and liberates the oppressed,
who frees the world from greed
and proclaims God's peace.
All: ***Make justice roll down like a river***
and righteousness flow like an everlasting stream. Amen.

1044 *Response to Community Crisis*

In our doubt and fear, may we know the compassion of the Shepherd,
who tends us in the valley of shadows and will sit with us as long as we need.

In our anger and frustration, may we know the passion of the Prophet,
who overturns the tables of injustice and curses this fruitless age.

In our pain and despair, may we know the healing of the Comforter,
who strengthens us with hope that is stronger than death.

Make us a community of costly and courageous love,
overcoming destruction and injustice wherever we may find it.

We pray in solidarity
with those whose hearts and bodies are aching today.

(*silence*)

By the tender mercy of our God,
may the dawn from on high break upon us,
to give light to those who sit in shadows,
and to guide our feet in the way of peace.

1043. based on Psalms 20:7; 24:1; Luke 4:18-19; Amos 5:24; Isaac Villegas (USA), 2019 ⓦ
1044. based on Psalm 23, Mark 11, John 14, Luke 1; Peter Goerzen (USA), 2017 ⓦ

1045 *1 Corinthians 13:4-13 (excerpts)*

Love is patient;
love is kind;
love is not envious or boastful
or arrogant or rude.
It does not insist on its own way;
it is not irritable or resentful;
it does not rejoice in wrongdoing,
but rejoices in the truth.
It bears all things, believes all things,
hopes all things, endures all things.
Love never ends.
But as for prophecies,
they will come to an end;
as for tongues,
they will cease;
as for knowledge,
it will come to an end.
And now these three remain:
faith, hope, and love;
and the greatest of these is love.

1046

If there is to be peace in the world,
there must be peace in the nations.
If there is to be peace in the nations,
there must be peace in the cities.
If there is to be peace in the cities,
there must be peace between neighbors.
If there is to be peace between neighbors,
there must be peace in the home.
If there is to be peace in the home,
there must be peace in the heart.

1047

Come, come, whoever you are.
Wanderer, worshiper, lover of leaving.
It doesn't matter.
Ours is not a caravan of despair.
Come, even if you have broken your vow
a thousand times.
Come, yet again, come, come.

1048

Let the rain come and wash away
the ancient grudges, the bitter hatreds
held and nurtured over generations.
Let the rain wash away the memory
of the hurt, the neglect.

Then let the sun come out and
fill the sky with rainbows.
Let the warmth of the sun heal us
wherever we are broken.

Let it burn away the fog so that
we can see each other clearly,
so that we can see beyond labels,
beyond accents, gender, or skin color.

Let the warmth and brightness
of the sun melt our selfishness,
so that we can share the joys and
feel the sorrows of our neighbors.

And let the light of the sun
be so strong that we will see all
people as our neighbors.

Let the earth, nourished by rain,
bring forth flowers
to surround us with beauty.
And let the mountains teach our hearts
to reach upward to heaven. Amen.

1049

Blessed be the ones
who dance
in the corridors of death,
who sing
in the hallways of terror,
who laugh
in the prisons of fear,
who shout
across the silencing walls,
who love
beyond the borders of hatred,
who live
to welcome home freedom,
who die
never turning their heads,
who return
as the rising of hope.

1046. Lao-Tse (China), ca. 4th c. BCE
1047. attr. Jalāl ad-Dīn Muhammad Rūmī (present-day Persia), 13th c.
1048. Rabbi Harold Kushner (USA), 2003, adapt.
1049. Jan Richardson (USA), 2000

SENDING

Sending Scripture worship resources are found at 818–826.

1050

Leader: From where we are
to where you need us:
All: ***Jesus, now lead on.***
Leader: From the familiarity of what we know
to the wonder of what you will reveal:
All: ***Jesus, now lead on.***
Leader: To transform the fabric of this world
until it resembles the shape of your kingdom:
All: ***Jesus, now lead on.***
Leader: Because good things have been prepared
for those who love God:
All: ***Jesus, now lead on.***

1051

Leader: In our concerns and in our choices,
All: ***God is with us.***
Leader: In our disappointments and in our joys,
All: ***God is with us.***
Leader: In our protesting and in our serving,
All: ***God is with us.***
Leader: Now and always,
All: ***God is with us.***

1052

A. Go in peace. Christ is with you.
Thanks be to God.

B. Go in peace.
Share the good news.
Thanks be to God.

C. Go in peace.
Remember the poor.
Thanks be to God.

D. Go in peace. Go be peace.
Thanks be to God.

E. Go in peace. Prepare the way.
Thanks be to God.

F. Go in peace. Christ is risen. Alleluia!
Thanks be to God. Alleluia!

G. Go in peace.
Rejoice in the power of the Spirit.
Thanks be to God.

Spanish

A. Vayan en paz. Cristo está con ustedes.
Damos gracias a Dios.

B. Vayan en paz,
compartiendo las buenas nuevas.
Damos gracias a Dios.

C. Vayan en paz,
recordando a los pobres.
Damos gracias a Dios.

French

A. Allez en paix. Christ est avec vous.
Rendons grâce à Dieu.

B. Allez en paix.
Répandez la bonne nouvelle.
Rendons grâce à Dieu.

C. Allez en paix.
Souvenez-vous des pauvres.
Rendons grâce à Dieu.

1050. Wild Goose Worship Group (Scotland), 2000
1051. Norman Shanks (Scotland), 2017
1052. Evangelical Lutheran Church in Canada and Evangelical Lutheran Church in America (USA), *Evangelical Lutheran Worship*, 2006; Spanish and French trans. Mennonite Worship and Song Committee, 2020

1053

May the God of glory,
the Word of life,
and the Spirit of truth
bless you all,
now and forever.

1054

The peace of God,
which passes all understanding,
keep your hearts and minds
in the knowledge and love of God,
and of God's Son, Jesus Christ our Lord;
and the blessing of God almighty,
the Father, the Son, and the Holy Spirit,
remain with you always. Amen.

1055

Go, knowing you are beloved by God.
Go, praising God for the good news
in Jesus Christ.
Go, living the message
of God's grace, peace, and love. Amen.

1056

God dearly loves us,
and through Christ left us an example,
that we might follow in his footsteps.
Christ is the light
that has come into the world;
may God grant that this light
shine around you,
and that you walk in it. Amen.

1057

May the Son of God,
who is already formed in you,
grow in you
so that for you
he will become immeasurable,
and that in you he will become
laughter,
exultation,
the fullness of joy
which no one will take from you.

1053. Presbyterian Church (USA), *Book of Common Worship*, 2018
1054. based on Philippians 4:7; *Book of Common Prayer* (England), 1549
1055. Eleanor Epp-Stobbe (Canada), 2013
1056. Mayken Boosers (present-day Netherlands), 1564; adapt. Mennonite Worship and Song Committee, 2019
1057. Isaac of Stella (England), 12th c.

1058

May God bless you with a restless discomfort
about easy answers, half-truths,
and superficial relationships,
so that you may seek truth boldly
and love deep within your heart.

May God bless you with holy anger
at injustice, oppression,
and exploitation of people,
so that you may work tirelessly
for justice, freedom, and peace.

May God bless you with the gift of tears
to shed with all who suffer
from pain, rejection, and starvation,
so that you may reach out to bring comfort
and transform pain into joy.

May God bless you with enough foolishness
to believe that you really can
make a difference in this world,
so that you are able, with God's grace,
to do what others claim cannot be done.

1059

Go forth in peace, and be of good courage;
hold fast to that which is good,
rejoicing in the power of the Holy Spirit.
And may the God
who fills the hungry with good things
fill us all with Christlike love
and with a consuming hunger for justice
in our land and in our world. Amen.

1060

May the blessing of the God
of Sarah and Hagar,
the blessing of the Child
born of Mary,
and the blessing of the Spirit
who broods over us
be with you all. Amen.

1061

May the warm winds of heaven
blow softly upon you,
and may the Great Spirit
make Sunrise in your heart.

1058. Ruth Fox, OSB (USA), 1985
1059. Bread for the World, 20th c., USA
1060. Mennonite Worship and Song Committee, 2020; inspired by Lois Wilson (Canada), 1973
1061. anon. Cherokee blessing (USA), 20th c.

1062

Live without fear:
your Creator has made you holy,
has always protected you,
and loves you as a mother.
Go in peace to follow the good road,
and may God's blessing
be with you always.

1063 *Psalm 106:48*

Praise be to the LORD,
the God of Israel,
from everlasting to everlasting.
Let all the people say,
"Amen! Praise the LORD."
"Amen! Praise the LORD."

1064

When the song of the angels is stilled,
when the star in the sky is gone,
when the kings and princes are home,
when the shepherds are back
with their flock,
the work of Christmas begins:
to find the lost,
to heal the broken,
to feed the hungry,
to release the prisoner,
to rebuild the nations,
to bring peace among people,
to make music in the heart.

1065

Whatever wilderness the Spirit
has brought you to:
walk in boldness,
as a beloved child of God;
walk in peace,
under the shelter of the Most High;
walk in faith,
knowing Christ walks with you.
Amen.

1066

May the Christ who walks
on wounded feet
walk with you on the road.
May the Christ who serves
with wounded hands
stretch out your hands to serve.
May the Christ who loves
with a wounded heart
open your hearts to love.
May you see the face of Christ
in everyone you meet,
and may everyone you meet
see the face of Christ in you.

1067

God of power,
may the boldness of your Spirit
transform us,
may the gentleness of your Spirit
lead us,
may the gifts of your Spirit
be our goal and our strength,
now and always.

1068

Eternal God,
you call us to ventures
of which we cannot see the ending,
by paths as yet untrodden,
through perils unknown.
Give us faith to go out with courage,
not knowing where we go,
but only that your hand is leading us,
and your love supporting us,
through Jesus Christ. Amen.

1069

Christ be within us to keep us,
beside us to guard,
before us to lead,
behind us to protect,
beneath us to support,
above us to bless.

1062. Clare of Assisi (Italy), ca.13th c.
1064. Howard Thurman (USA), 1985
1065. Joanna Harader (USA), 2003

1066. unattributed benediction
1067. The Anglican Church in Aotearoa, New Zealand and Polynesia, *A New Zealand Prayer Book*, 1988
1068. Eric Milner-White (England), 20th c., alt.
1069. The Anglican Church in Aotearoa, New Zealand and Polynesia, *A New Zealand Prayer Book*, 1988

ACKNOWLEDGMENTS

GRATITUDE

Deep gratitude is owed each of the families at the center of committee work. Your support may not be directly visible in these pages, but it fundamentally made this work happen. A project of this scope could not have been undertaken without generous circles of personal support. Thank you!

The Mennonite Worship and Song Committee worked within these subcommittee structures:

Text committee: Katie Graber, Tom Harder, Adam M. L. Tice (chair)

Tune and accompaniment committee: Benjamin Bergey (chair), Paul Dueck, Emily Grimes, Anneli Loepp Thiessen, Cynthia Neufeld Smith

Worship resources committee: Sarah Kathleen Johnson (chair), SaeJin Lee, Anneli Loepp Thiessen, Allan Rudy-Froese, Bradley Kauffman

Intercultural worship committee: Katie Graber (chair), SaeJin Lee, Adam M. L. Tice, Allan Rudy-Froese, Cynthia Neufeld Smith, Paul Dueck

Popular idiom committee: Darryl Neustaedter Barg (co-chair), Benjamin Bergey, Mike Erb, Emily Grimes, Anneli Loepp Thiessen (co-chair), Sarah Kathleen Johnson, Tom Harder

Many hands carried the work forward throughout this endeavor. We wish to thank all who screened collections and made recommendations. Thanks also to the theologians and historians who provided timely and thoughtful analysis as the collection first began to take shape. Our gratitude also goes to the many language consultants who offered counsel and practical support. Many individuals tested these songs and worship resources in your communities and followed up with valuable responses. Thank you as well to all of the individuals and communities that held the work of *Voices Together* in prayer.

We acknowledge the broad community of support, including (and certainly not limited to) those named below, that made possible the development and production of this collection.

African American traditions consulting group: Regina Shands Stoltzfus, Vikki Pruitte-Sorrells, Michelle Armster, Shannon Dycus, Tony Brown

American Sign Language consulting group: Austin Kocher, Erica Lea-Simka, Kathy Nofziger Yeakey, Mary Schmidt, Sue Leatherman Sommers, Ardell Stauffer, Anabaptist Disabilities Network

Confessing faith worship resources consulting group: Jeremy Bergen, Malinda Elizabeth Berry, John D. Rempel, Paul M. Zehr

German chorales consulting group: Rosi Penner Kaufman, Dietrich Bartel, Kathleen King Martin, Cynthia Neufeld Smith

Indigenous traditions consulting group: Keshia Littlebear-Cetrone, Steve Heinrichs, Geraldine Balzer, Willis Busenitz, Tamara Shantz

Lead engraver: James E. Clemens

Lead proofreaders: Andrea Welty Peachey, Cynthia Neufeld Smith, Sara Versluis

Permissions and professional support: GIA Publications, Inc., Michael Boschert, permissions officer

Psalms consulting group: Adam M. L. Tice, Janeen Bertsche Johnson, Sarah Kathleen Johnson, Gerald Gerbrandt, Derek Suderman, Ron Guengerich

Research associates: Carl Bear, Joanne Gallardo, David Gonzol, William Mateer, Naomi Tice, Matthew Rissler

Resources from the Taizé Community consulting group: Laura Enns, Gwen Gustafson-Zook, Phil Kniss, Lloyd Mast

Spanish language consultants: Andrea de Avila, Cristina Horst, Byron Pellecer

Typists: Donna Darby, Karen Gingerich, Susan Gingerich, Martha Graber, Cheryl Martin Miller, Joan Tice

Visual Art Committee: Randy Horst, Sarah Kathleen Johnson (co-chair), Bradley Kauffman, SaeJin Lee (co-chair), Merrill Miller, Tom Yoder Neufeld

LEGAL

VOICES TOGETHER DONORS

FORTISSISSIMO—FOR A GIFT OF $100,000

WITH THANKS FOR THE GENEROUS SUPPORT OF

Ed and Carol Nofziger, Archbold, OH

Everence® and Mennonite Central Committee U.S.

FORTISSIMO—FOR A GIFT OF $25,000–$99,999

HONOREES:

Honoring Clarence Rich, hymn leader at Zion MC, Archbold, OH, by Kevin Sauder

DONORS:

Anonymous, ON

From an anonymous family who loves to sing

With thanks for the generous support of College Mennonite Church, Goshen, IN

With thanks for the generous support of Mennonite Church Eastern Canada

With thanks for the generous support of Mennonite Church USA

With thanks for the generous support of Mersynergy Charitable Foundation, ON

With thanks for the generous support of Shantz Mennonite Church, Baden, ON

With thanks for the generous support of United Service Foundation, Lancaster, PA

FORTE—FOR A GIFT OF $10,000–$24,999

HONOREES:

In memory of Russell and Gladys Alderfer: "Oh, for a thousand tongues to sing"

In memory of Vernon J. Hieser (1910–2011) by daughter Judy Hershberger and Lotus

Honoring John & Marian Martin, Beryl & Betty Lehman, with love Don & Barb Martin

Ever singing, Sally Roeschley White (1937–2006), with love by Donald E. White

DONORS:

Calvin Institute of Christian Worship, Vital Worship Grant, 2017–18

Central District Conference of MC USA—*Knowing Christ's love, Answering God's call*

From the MennoMedia board of directors

With thanks for the generous support of Mennonite Church Canada

With thanks for the generous support of the Schowalter Foundation, N. Newton, KS

MEZZO FORTE—FOR A GIFT OF $5,000–$9,999

HONOREES:

In honor of Harold A. & Ferne Hagey Alderfer, Lansdale, PA, with gratitude & love

In loving memory of Michelle Renee Carpenter (1984–95) by Steve and Chris

We sang you home, Dad. Now Grace, Kate, Hannah, & Julia live your legacy. *HWB* 420

Honoring Ralph V. Hirschey (1918–95), who spent his life joyfully singing hymns

"Make a joyful noise to the Lord" (Ps 100:1) Lois Yake & Clif Kenagy, Albany, OR

In memory of Marilyn L. Peifer Nolt; "Nothing is lost on the breath of God"

In honor of William D. Swartley, Franconia Conference Music Secretary (1955–68)

Ann & Byron Weber Becker honor Ann's parents, Margaret & Lewis Weber, ON

In grateful memory of Russel S. & Anna Mae Zeager, Elizabethtown, PA

DONORS:

Anonymous, Buhler, KS

Anonymous, Hutchinson, KS

Together in *Word & Sign*, on a journey with Jesus, Blooming Glen Mennonite Church

With thanks for the generosity of the Eastern VA Mission Endowment Fund

To God be the glory, may the music never end. Norman L. and Helen Keller

With thanks for Oak Grove Mennonite Church's generous support, Smithville, OH

With thanks for the generous support of Plains Mennonite Church, Hatfield, PA

Salford Mennonite Church, Harleysville, PA—*Joyfully learning to follow Jesus*

Sing for joy, praising our God! Esther & Arlin Shisler, Plains MC, Lansdale, PA

With thanks for the support of John & Erma Stutzman, Menno. Church of Normal, IL

MEZZO PIANO—FOR A GIFT OF $1,000–$4,999

HONOREES:
In honor of Howard & Phyllis Baumgartner
Honoring our parents. Phil & Evon Bergey
In memory of David Breckbill (1957–2016)
Descendants of Fred and Millie Brenneman
Sheldon & Janis Burkhalter honor parents
Elsie Ford Carpenter, 1922–2017, Cranston, RI
Jane Landes in honor of Helen G. Clemens
In memory of Esther Diener, W. Clinton MC
For those who taught me to sing
In loving memory of Jeannette Gingerich
In memory of Paul and Stella Godshall
In honor of Vernon R. Goering (1931–2017)
Honoring Lisbet Halteman & Lizzie Guntz
In memory of Margaret Beachy Hershberger
In memory of Evie Hertzler (1938–2008)
Sandra B. King—Your music is a blessing
Honoring Hannah Lapp by her husband Joe
In memory of Freeman Lehman (1932–2014)
Vesta & Verl Lehman; Hertha & Peter Kampen
The family of Constance Longacher
Descendants of Joe and Mayme Longacher
In memory of my wife Marjora M. Miller
RIP Floyd Newcomer, a joyful chorister
O come, let us sing to the Lord! Ps 95:1
Our thanks for congregational singing
To honor our parents, Roy & Carolyn Roth
Love to Jackson and Nicholas Schlegel
Ron & Barb Schlegel honor Wilfred Schlegel
Lucille Shank, musician, piano teacher
In memory of Doris L. Swartzendruber
In memory, Michael P. Yoder, ever singing
In loving memory of John Zehr, Urbana, IL

DONORS:
Anonymous, CA
Anonymous, Ephrata, PA
Anonymous, Harleysville, PA
Anonymous, Harrisonburg, VA
Anonymous, South Bend, IN
Anonymous, St. Jacobs, ON
Anonymous, Waterloo, ON
Akron Mennonite Church, Akron, PA
Doug Basinger and John Flickinger
Belmont Mennonite Church, Elkhart, IN
Benton Mennonite Church, Goshen, IN
Columbus Mennonite Church, Columbus, OH
Delaware Valley Fam. Business Ctr., PA
Roy and Charlotte Derksen
Marianne & Jim Erb family
Amy Gingerich & Ryan Claassen
Lauren R. Good and Jennifer Hiebert
Grace Mennonite Church, Pandora, OH
Ken & Sue Hochstetler
Len & Brenda Jewitt, Waterloo, ON
Ruth and Timothy Stoltzfus Jost family
Marcia and Eric Lehman, Archbold, OH
Thomas A. and Mary Jo Lehman
Lombard Mennonite Church, Lombard, IL
Jon and Rhoda Mast, Millersburg, OH
William and Marna Mateer
William F. & Phyllis J. Miller, Goshen, IN
Ohio Conference of Mennonite Church USA
Fidelia E. Plett Foundation
Praise God in worship and in daily life!
Rochester Mennonite Fellowship, NY
Walter and Vera Schmucker
David & Susan Seyler
Stepping Stones
The Gladys and Edgar Stoesz family
Mary Swartzendruber family Kay & Douglas
Waterloo North Mennonite Church, ON
Barry and Marjorie Martin Weaver
Beatrice Wideman, Elmira, ON
Christian P. Yoder & Jonathan D. Miller
LeRoy J. & Martha M. Yoder, Hartville, OH
Michael P. (d.) & Mary Lehman Yoder, Goshen
Roberta A. (Miller) Yoder, Goshen, IN
Andrea Zuercher, Lawrence, KS
William and Joyce Zuercher, Hesston, KS

PIANO—FOR A GIFT OF $500–$999

HONOREES:

In honor of Clayton R. Auernheimer
Honouring Menno M. Brubacher, 1874–1956
In memory of Etta Brubaker, 1916–2017
Memorial J. Lawrence & Harriet Burkholder
In memory of LaVonda Claassen, 1937–2008
Parents Mabel David Deckert—Sharon Cong.
Eugene Mennonite Church, Eugene, OR
For our parents, who taught us to sing
Harmonia Sacra Soc. honors Joseph Funk
How can I keep from singing: to D. Graber
In honor of pastors Tom & Lois Harder
Jay Hartzler, EMHS Choral Dir. 1981–2015
Samuel H. Horst Sr. Chambersburg, 1884–1945
In memory of Norman Hostetler Sr.
In honor of Rosanna and David Hostetler
In memory of our hymn-loving parents
"I will sing of my redeemer."
In honor of Pat Johnson, Carol & Don O.
In memory of church musician Walter Jost
In honor of Jill and Melissa Kauffman
In honor of Harold and Mary Keener
In memory of Wayne & Esther Lapp Kempf
Honoring Emery & Ruth King, Frazer, PA
Glen & Orpha King & Phyllis A. King Yoder
Rev. Abraham Kroeger, martyred—USSR, 1921
Bill Kruger, Rev. Abraham Kroeger's nephew
Honoring our parents Paul & Erma Leaman
Henry Longenecker 1913–2005 chorister
Husband Robert remembers Nancy L. Martin
In memory of Virgil L. Miller, 1940–2012
In memory of W & L Miller and M & M Nofziger
In memory of Willard Moser
Arnold & Maietta Moshier, music pioneers
In memory of Thomas J. Peachey; Spichers
In loving memory of Celia Preheim
In honour of Roma, Tristan, Mathom Quapp
Arthur & Helen (Wiens) Rempel, Winnipeg
In memory of Gwen Rich
In memory of Paul M. Schrock, 1935–2011
With thanks for Shalom Ch. musicians, KS
In loving memory of Roy & Elaine Shantz
Honoring Randy Spaulding's musical gifts
In memory of Sue Steiner by husband Sam
Frances (Gerig) Stuckey, 1908–2003
Bryan Moyer Suderman SmallTALL Ministry
Honoring Bradley Swope, Clearwater, FL
Thank God for our gifted musical family
To parents who believe in our song. JHMK
In memory of Hobert D. Yoder, 1932–2014

DONORS:

Anonymous, Apple Creek, OH
Anonymous, Archbold, OH
Anonymous, Archbold, OH
Anonymous, Bloomington, IL
Anonymous, Cincinnati, OH
Anonymous, Columbiana, OH
Anonymous, Goshen, IN
Anonymous, Goshen, IN
Anonymous, Harrisonburg, VA
Anonymous, Lancaster, PA
Anonymous, Lansdale, PA
Anonymous, Normal, IL
Anonymous, Normal, IL
Anonymous, North Newton, KS
Anonymous, Sun City, AZ
Harlan & Jean Anders, Manheim, PA
Loren & Judy Bender, New Holland, PA
Robert & Margaret Bruckhart, Richmond, VA
Russ and Jane Eanes, Harrisonburg, VA
Earl L. & Etta F. Esch
Richard and Dorothy Nickel Friesen
Firman and Susan Gingerich
James and Joan Gingrich
For all musicians, major and minor. SDG
Hilda and Elmer Hildebrand
Hillcrest Mennonite Church, ON
Wayne and Lois Hochstetler
Barry and Janeen Bertsche Johnson
Phyllis A. & the late Elton D. Lehman
"Keep on Singing" Gary & Brenda Leis
Norma Lichti, New Hamburg, ON
Ingrid and Jim Loepp Thiessen, ON
Mountain States Mennonite Conf., CO-NM
Nith Valley Mennonite, New Hamburg, ON
Rainbow Mennonite, Kansas City, KS
Henry and Charlotte Rosenberger
Ryan, Valerie, Evan, Neil, and Simon
Ronald and Leanne Schertz
George & Louise Schroeder, Stratford, ON
Larry and Marcia Shantz, ON
Gratefully, Sam & Janice Suter Showalter
Marie Kanagy Stevanus, Washington, DC
Stirling Avenue Mennonite Church, ON
Rev. Lauren Voyles & Rev. T. Wes Moore
Kyle and Tracey Weirich, Elkhart, IN
Dr. Carl and Phyllis Yoder
Chaska and Philip Yoder
Delvon and Shirley Yoder, Goshen, IN
Terry A. & Joan Gotwals Yoder

COPYRIGHT HOLDERS INDEX

1 Text: © 1993 Delores Dufner. Published by OCP, 5536 NE Hassalo, Portland, OR 97213. All rights reserved. Used by permission.
2 © 1994 Iona Community, GIA Publications, Inc., agent
3 © Phil Porter
6 © 2007 Abingdon Press (admin. Music Services)
8 Trans.: © 1982 Mennonite Indian Leaders' Council (admin. Native Mennonite Ministries)
9 Text: © 1999 Marva J. Dawn
Music: © 2008 Re:Create Music, admin. Faith Alive Christian Resources
10 © 1982 GIA Publications, Inc.
11 © 2016 Phil Campbell-Enns
12 © 2020 SaeJin Lee
20 Trans.: © 2006 Evangelical Lutheran Worship, admin. Augsburg Fortress
22 Trans.: © 1967 OCP Publications
23 Trans.: © Lutheran World Foundation
Arr.: © 1984 Utryck, admin. Walton Music Corp., a div. of GIA Publications, Inc.
24 © Jonathan Maracle, SOCAN
26 © 1978 Mennonite World Conference
27 © 1992 Hope Publishing Company, Carol Stream, IL 60188. All rights reserved. Used by permission.
29 © 1998 Vineyard Songs
30 © 1989 WGRG, Iona Community, GIA Publications, Inc., agent
32 © 2008 WGRG, Iona Community, GIA Publications, Inc., agent
33 © 2001 Integrity's Praise! Music and Sound of The New Breed, admin. CapitolCMGPublishing.com. All rights reserved. Used by permission.
35 © 2018 Carol Ann Weaver
36 © 1994 GIA Publications, Inc.
37 Music: © 1989 Hope Publishing Co.
38 Text: © 2016 GIA Publications, Inc.
39 Text: © 2005 David Wright
Music: © 2005 James E. Clemens
41 © 1982, GIA Publications, Inc.
42 Text: © 2004, rev. 2018 Becca J. R. Lachman
Arr.: © 2008 Alice Parker. Used by permission.
43 © 2004 This Here Music/Worldmaking.net
44 Text: © 2019 GIA Publications, Inc.
Harm.: © 1990 Alice Parker. Used by permission.
45 Trans.: © 2019 Mennonite Worship and Song Committee, admin. GIA Publications, Inc.
49 © 1998 Vineyard Songs
50 Text: © John Richards (admin. Renewal Servicing)
Music: © 2015 James E. Clemens
51 Adapt.: © 1994 Doreen Clellamin
52 © 1978, 1980, 1981, Les Presses de Taizé, GIA Publications, Inc., agent
53 Text: © 1971 Estate of John Webster Grant
54 Music: © 2014 Deanna Witkowski, Tilapia Tunes
55 Text: © 1995 Jody L. Caldwell
Music: © 1995 Kimberly A. Williams.
56 Text: © 1982 Hope Publishing Company, Carol Stream, IL 60188. All rights reserved. Used by permission.
Music: © 1969 Hope Publishing Company, Carol Stream, IL 60188. All rights reserved. Used by permission.
57 Text: © 1970 Anne Neufeld Rupp
Trans.: © 1988 Barbara Mink
Harm.: © 1989 Joan Fyock Norris
58 © 1998 Les Presses de Taizé, GIA Publications, Inc., agent
59 Trans.: © 1982 Mennonite Indian Leaders' Council (admin. Native Mennonite Ministries)
60 © 2016 Drink Your Tea Music (admin. at EssentialMusicPublishing.com). All rights reserved. Used by permission.
61 © Oxford University Press
63 © 1999 Borealis Music
64 Trans.: © 2019 Mennonite Worship and Song Committee, admin. GIA Publications, Inc.
Transcr.: © 1955 Gesangbuch der Mennoniten Brüdergemeinde
66 Stanzas: © 2006 Evangelical Lutheran Worship (admin. Augsburg Fortress)
Music: © 1979 Les Presses de Taizé, GIA Publications, Inc., agent
67 © 2004 Vastago Producciones
68 © 2006 Abingdon Press (admin. The Copyright Co.)
69 © 1984 Candied Jamm Music/Savgos Music (admin. BMI)
71 Text A: © The Pilgrim Press
72 Music: © 2019 Darryl Neustaedter Barg
76 Desc.: © 1971 Godfrey Hewitt
77 © 1991 Les Presses de Taizé, GIA Publications, Inc., agent
80 Text: © 1993 Selah Publishing Co., Inc.
Desc.: © 1980 Harold Flammer, Inc.
82 © 1987 Niko Njotorahardjo
83 Text: © 1972 Hope Publishing Company, Carol Stream, IL 60188. All rights reserved. Used by permission.
85 Transcr.: © 1989 United Methodist Publishing House (admin. Music Services)
86 © 1985 Mountain Spring Music; Straightway Music
87 © 1984 Oxford University Press, Inc.
88 Stanza 4 adapt.: © 2000 Augsburg Fortress
89 Trans. and arr.: © 1999, 2019 CanZion (admin. CanZion Editora)
90 Music: © 1991 Lumko Institute
92 © 2016 Karl Andrew Martin, Kaple Music; Capitol CMG Genesis; Housefires Sounds; Said And Done Music; sixsteps Music; Thankyou Music; worshiptogether.com songs; Bethel Music Publishing
93 Trans.: © 2009 Faith Alive Christian Services
Paraphr.: © 2009 Yamuger, Indonesian Institute for Sacred Music
94 Music: © 1979 Les Presses de Taizé, GIA Publications, Inc., agent
96 © 2000 Vineyard Songs
97 Music: © 1978, 1980, 1981 Les Presses de Taizé, GIA Publications, Inc., agent
99 English trans.: © English Language Liturgical Consultation, 1988
Adapt.: Mennonite Worship and Song Committee, 2019, admin. GIA Publications, Inc.
Music: © 1984 GIA Publications, Inc.
102 © 1993, 1994, 2012 GIA Publications, Inc.
104 © 2020 Meg Harder
111 © 2011 Shout! Publishing; sixsteps Music; Said and DoneMusic; ThankYou Music (PRS), admin. CapitolCMGPublishing.com. All rights reserved. Used by permission.
112 Text: © 1992 GIA Publications, Inc.
Music: © 1971 Walton Music Corp., a div. of GIA Publications, Inc.
115 Text: © 1980 Nobuaki Hanaoka
Transcr.: © 1983 Abingdon Press
116 © 2004 sixsteps Music/worshiptogether.com songs/ Wondrously Made Songs
117 © 1988 GIA Publications, Inc.
118 © 1986, 1991, 2011 Les Presses de Taizé, GIA Publications, Inc., agent
121 © 1998 Fostco Music Press
Arr.: © 2019 James E. Clemens

122 Text: © 1998, 2003 GIA Publications, Inc.
Harm.: Healey Willan
124 Text: © 1970 Hope Publishing Company, Carol Stream, IL 60188. All rights reserved. Used by permission.
Music: © 1991 Bradley P. Lehman
125 © 1993 Wondrous Worship
127 © 1998 Les Presses de Taizé, GIA Publications, Inc., agent
129 Text: © 2019 Brenda Hostetler Meyer
131 © 1975 Claude Frayssé
English trans.: © 1989 *Hymnal: A Worship Book*, Brethren Press, 1451 Dundee Ave., Elgin, IL 60120-1674, brethrenpress@brethren.org
Spanish trans.: © 2003 Mennonite World Conference
Acc.: © 1992 Marilyn Houser Hamm
132 © 2004 Integrity's Hosanna! Music, admin. CapitolCMGPublishing.com. All rights reserved. Used by permission.
134 Music and text: © 1989, 1994 Hope Publishing Company, Carol Stream, IL 60188. All rights reserved. Used by permission.
136 Arr.: © 1990 WGRG, Iona Community, GIA Publications Inc., agent
137 Trans.: © 1990 John D. Rempel
139 © 1995 Mercy/Vineyard Publishing
140 Trans.: © 1978, 2006 *Lutheran Book of Worship* (admin. Augsburg Fortress)
Harm.: © 1990 *Hymnal: A Worship Book*, Brethren Press, 1451 Dundee Ave., Elgin, IL 60120-1674, brethrenpress@brethren.org
141 © 1994 Andrew Kreider
142 Trans. and adapt.: © 2019 Katie Graber
Adapt. from transcr.: © 1996 Hildegard Publishing Company
143 Text: © 2017 GIA Publications, Inc.
144 Text: © 2005 Hope Publishing Company, Carol Stream, IL 60188. All rights reserved. Used by permission.
Music: © 2003 Zimbel Press
145 Text and music: © 1992, 2005, Hope Publishing Company, Carol Stream, IL 60188. All rights reserved. Used by permission.
146 Text: © 2015 GIA Publications, Inc.
148 Text: © 2015 GIA Publications, Inc.
Music: © SEFIM
149 Text: (c) 1996, music, 2016 Hope Publishing Company, Carol Stream, IL 60188. All rights reserved. Used by permission.
150 © 1992 Hope Publishing Company, Carol Stream, IL 60188. All rights reserved. Used by permission.
151 Music: © 2008 James E. Clemens
152 Text: © 1967 David Elton Trueblood. HarperCollins Publishers, Inc.
Music: © 1968 Esther Wiebe
153 © 1996 Abingdon Press
154 Text: © 2015 GIA Publications, Inc.
155 © 2011 sixsteps Music; Sweater Weather Music; Thankyou Music; Valley of Songs Music
157 Text: © 1991 GIA Publications, Inc.
Harm.: © 1988 Harris J. Loewen
Desc.: © 2020 Paul Dueck
161 Music: © 1969 Faith & Life Press/Mennonite Publishing House (admin. MennoMedia)
164 Text: © 1994 Susan Palo Cherwien (admin. Augsburg Fortress)
165 Trans.: © 2018 Mennonite Worship and Song Committee, admin. GIA Publications, Inc.. Attr. Evan Rohmingliana; as taught by members of Chin Emmanuel Baptist Church, Houston, TX 2017.
166 © 2015 Jaylene Johnson
167 © 2003 Thankyou Music
168 © 2017 GIA Publications, Inc.
169 © 1997 Integrity's Hosanna! Music
171 Music: © 2008 James E. Clemens
172 © 2017 LovedIntoBeing Music
173 © 1999 Nathan Stucky
Acc.: © 2020 Brian Wiebe
174 © 2011 Choristers Guild
175 Text: © 2010 Heather Josselyn-Cranson
Music: © 2016 GIA Publications, Inc.
176 Text: © 1983 Harris J. Loewen
Music: © 2019 Katie Graber
177 Harm.: © 1983 John Ribble
178 © 2000 New Spring Publishing; Never Say Never Songs, admin. New Spring Publishing/ Storm Boy Music; Meaux Mercy, admin. CapitolCMGPublishing.com. All rights reserved. Used by permission.
179 Text: © 2008 Carolyn Winfrey Gillette, www.carolynshymns.com
Harm.: © 1989 Joan Fyock Norris
181 © 2003 Doug Krehbiel and Jude Krehbiel
183 © 2020 J. Tyler Klassen
188 Trans.: © 2006 Evangelical Lutheran Worship, admin. Augsburg Fortress
190 Text: © 2019 GIA Publications, Inc.
193 Arr.: © 1990 Melva Wilson Costen
194 Text: © 1992 GIA Publications, Inc.
195 © 2014 Bethel Music Publishing. All rights reserved. Used by permission.
196 Text: © 1996
Music: © 1997 The Pilgrim Press
197 Text: © 1989 Hope Publishing Company, Carol Stream, IL 60188. All rights reserved. Used by permission.
198 Text: © 2019 Jean Janzen, The Pilgrim Press
Music: © 2008 James E. Clemens
199 © 1992 Bernadette Farrell, admin. OCP, 5536 NE Hassalo, Portland, OR 97213. All rights reserved. Used by permission.
200 Text: © 2006 Sarah Kathleen Johnson
Music: © 2019 Leonard Enns
201 Text: © 2018 Hope Publishing Company, Carol Stream, IL 60188. All rights reserved. Used by permission.
202 © 1991 Shawn Kirchner Publishing
205 Text: © 2001 GIA Publications, Inc.
Music: © 2000 William P. Rowan (admin. GIA Publications, Inc.)
206 Text: © 2004 David Wright
Music: © 2004 James E. Clemens
207 © 1986 Desert Flower Music
208 Text: © 2000 Jeannette M. Lindholm (admin. Augsburg Fortress)
209 Text: © 2009 GIA Publications, Inc.
Arr.: © 2019 Kathryn Harsha
211 Text: © 1995 Selah Publishing Co., Inc.
Acc.: © James E. Clemens
213 Text: © 2014 GIA Publications, Inc.
Arr.: © 1992 Horace Clarence Boyer
214 Stanza 3 trans.: © 2006 Augsburg Fortress
Stanza 4: © 1969 Concordia Publishing House, cph.org. Used by permission.
217 © 1969 Faith & Life Press
218 Adapt. © 1951 Oxford University Press
219 Music: © 1971 Range Road Music, Inc., Quartet Music, Inc., and New Cadenza Music, Inc., dist. Hal Leonard, Inc.
221 Text: © 2019 Sarah Kathleen Johnson
222 Text: © 1987 Hope Publishing Company, Carol Stream, IL 60188. All rights reserved. Used by permission.
Music: © 1991 *Hymnal: A Worship Book*, Brethren Press, 1451 Dundee Ave., Elgin, IL 60120-1674, brethrenpress@brethren.org.

223 Text: © 1973 Hope Publishing Company, Carol Stream, IL 60188. All rights reserved. Used by permission.
224 Trans. and arr.: © 2005 GIA Publications, Inc.
225 © 1997 Rough Stones Music
226 Stanza 1 trans.: © 1982 Hope Publishing Company, Carol Stream, IL 60188. All rights reserved. Used by permission.
227 © 2000 Thankyou Music, admin. CapitolCMGPublishing.com. All rights reserved. Used by permission.
228 © 1984 Les Presses de Taizé, GIA Publications, Inc., agent
229 Text: © 2002 Jeanette M. Lindholm (admin. Augsburg Fortress)
Music: © 1977 GIA Publications, Inc.
230 © 2020 Rachel Epp Buller
236 Text: © 1985 Church Pension Fund
237 Text: © 2006 GIA Publications, Inc.
Harm.: © 2011 Alfred V. Fedak
238 Text: © 2010, rev. 2017 Adam Michael Wood, adammichaelwood.com, adam.michael.wood@gmail.com
239 © 1990 WGRG, Iona Community, GIA Publications, Inc., agent
241 Desc.: © 1961 Oxford University Press
242 © 2003 Pigal Ediciones Musicales (admin. WB Music Corp.)
243 Harm.: © 1962 Bristol Churches Housing Association Ltd.
246 Text: © 2009, GIA Publications, Inc.
247 Desc.: © 1961 Oxford University Press
252 Arr.: © 2000 GIA Publications, Inc.
254 Trans.: © 1990 Hope Publishing Company, Carol Stream, IL 60188. All rights reserved. Used by permission.
255 Text: © 1982 Hope Publishing Company, Carol Stream, IL 60188. All rights reserved. Used by permission.
256 © 2015 Capitol CMG Publishing and Music Services, Inc.
258 Text and harm.: © 1996 LNWhymns.com (admin. Music Services)
260 Text: © 2019 GIA Publications, Inc.
262 © 1990 National Committee of Three-Self Patriotic Movement of the Protestant Churches in China / Chinese Christian Council (CCC/TSPM)
Paraphr.: © Kathleen Moody
263 Trans.: © 1978 *Lutheran Book of Worship*
264 Harm.: © 1963, 1980 Walter Ehret, Walton Music Corp., a div. of GIA Publications, Inc.
266 Music: © 1989 Joan Fyock Norris
268 © 1994 Scott Soper. Published by OCP, 5536 NE Hassalo, Portland, OR 97213. All rights reserved. Used by permission.
269 Stanzas 2–3 trans.: © 1989 Hope Publishing Company, Carol Stream, IL 60188. All rights reserved. Used by permission.
270 Text: © 2015 GIA Publications, Inc.
271 © 2007 Les Presses de Taizé, GIA Publications, Inc., agent
273 Text: © 1992 GIA Publications, Inc.
Desc.: © 1995 Diana McLeod
274 Arr.: © 2000 GIA Publications, Inc.
275 © 1940 (ren. 1967) James D. Vaughan Music Publisher (dist. Spirit Sound Music Group)
276 © 2018 Christopher Clymer Kurtz and Maria Clymer Kurtz
278 Text: © 2004 Carolyn Winfrey Gillette, www.carolynshymns.com
279 Text: © 2009 GIA Publications, Inc.
Arr.: © 1931 Oxford University Press
280 Text: © 1996 Selah Publishing Co., Inc.
Music: © 2015 Selah Publishing Co., Inc.
281 Text: © 1989 Hope Publishing Company, Carol Stream, IL 60188. All rights reserved. Used by permission.
Music: © 1991 Philip K. Clemens
282 © 1974 Marilyn Houser Hamm
283 Spanish text and music: © 1979 Cesáreo Gabaráin and Ediciones Paulinas, admin. OCP, 5536 NE Hassalo, Portland, OR 97213. All rights reserved. Used by permission.
284 © 1988 WGRG, Iona Community, GIA Publications, Inc., agent
285 Text: © 2006 GIA Publications, Inc.
287 Text: © 1995 WGRG, Iona Community, GIA Publications, Inc., agent
Harm.: © 2001 James E. Clemens
288 © 2019 Paul Zach Publishing, Integrity's Alleluia! Music, admin. CapitolCMGPublishing.com. All rights reserved. Used by permission.
289 Korean revision: © 2001 The United Methodist Publishing House (admin. Music Services)
Music: © Kyung Dong Presbyterian Church
290 © 2015 GIA Publications, Inc.
291 © 2020 Michelle Burkholder
297 © 1986 GIA Publications, Inc.
298 © 2009 GIA Publications, Inc.
299 Text: © 2020 Katie Graber
Music: © 2020 Anneli Loepp Thiessen
301 Text: © 1977, rev. 1995 Hope Publishing Company, Carol Stream, IL 60188. All rights reserved. Used by permission
Music: © 1984 Bradley P. Lehman
302 © 1994 GIA Publications, Inc.
304 Text: © 2006, 2009 GIA Publications, Inc.
Music: © 2009 GIA Publications, Inc.
307 Text: © 1993 GIA Publications, Inc.
Music: © 1943, 1961, 1985 Church Pension Fund
308 Text: © 2009 Sarah Kathleen Johnson.
Music: © 2002 Selah Publishing Co., Inc.
309 © 2005 Phil Campbell-Enns
310 Text: © 2005 David Wright
Music: © 2005 James E. Clemens
312 © 1999 Bret Hesla (admin. Augsburg Fortress)
314 © 1991 Signpost Music
316 Text: © 1982 Hope Publishing Company, Carol Stream, IL 60188. All rights reserved. Used by permission.
319 Text: © 2016 GIA Publications, Inc.
320 Text: © 1982 Hope Publishing Company, Carol Stream, IL 60188. All rights reserved. Used by permission.
321 Text and music: © 2003 Oxford University Press
324 © 2000 sixsteps Music (admin. EMI Christian Music Publishing)
326 Text: © 1990 Hope Publishing Company, Carol Stream, IL 60188. All rights reserved. Used by permission.
327 Text and music: © 1981 Les Presses de Taizé, GIA Publications, Inc., agent
328 Text: © 2019 Sisters of St. Benedict
Music: © 2019 Bradley Kauffman
Acc.: © GIA Publications, Inc.
332 © 2001 Thankyou Music
334 © 2020 Anne Hostetler Berry
341 Text: © 1968 Makumira University College (admin. Augsburg Fortress)
Trans.: © 1977 (admin. Augsburg Fortress)
342 Stanzas 2, 3, 4: © 1994, 2003 GIA Publications, Inc.
Harm.: © 2006 James E. Clemens.
343 Text: © 1986 Oxford University Press
Music: © 2019 Bradley P. Lehman
344 Text: © 2014, arr.: © 1995, GIA Publications, Inc.

345 Text: © 1993 Nigel Weaver
Music: © 2012 Richard VanOss (admin. Faith Alive Christian Resources).
347 Harm.: © 1988 Alice Parker. Used by permission.
349 © 2009 Capitol CMG Publishing, admin. CapitolCMGPublishing.com and Essential Music Publishing
351 Arr.: © 2001 James E. Clemens
352 Harm.: © 1966 Alice Parker. Used by permission.
353 Text: © 1928 Oxford University Press
Harm.: © 2001 James E. Clemens
354 Text: © 1986 Hope Publishing Company, Carol Stream, IL 60188. All rights reserved. Used by permission.
Music: © 2011, GIA Publications, Inc.
356 © 1998 Les Presses de Taizé, GIA Publications, Inc., agent
Desc.: © 2000 GIA Publications, Inc.
359 Text: © 1975, rev. 1995 Hope Publishing Company, Carol Stream, IL 60188. All rights reserved. Used by permission.
360 Ref.: © 1991 *Hymnal: A Worship Book*
Stanzas: © 2019 Brenda Hostetler Meyer
Music: © 1989 Jacek Gałuszka, OP
362 Music: © 1999 David J. Gonzol
365 © 1989 Maranatha Praise, Inc. (admin. Music Services)
366 Text: © 1972, 1997 Hope Publishing Company, Carol Stream, IL 60188. All rights reserved. Used by permission.
367 © Lutheran Theological College, Makumira
Arr.: © 2001, 2004 General Board of Global Ministries, t/a GBGMusik, 458 Ponce de Leon Ave., Atlanta, GA 30308. copyright@umcmission.org.
368 © 1981 Surtsey Publishing, ren. © 1993 Carolyn McDade
Harm.: © 1992 Unitarian Universalist Association
369 © 2011 Capitol CMG Genesis, admin. CapitolCMGPublishing.com. All rights reserved. Used by permission.
370 © 1979 Les Presses de Taizé, GIA Publications, Inc., agent
372 © 1985 Oxford University Press, Inc.
373 © 2005 Hope Publishing Company, Carol Stream, IL 60188. All rights reserved. Used by permission.
374 © Patricia Shelly
376 Text: © 1991 Jean Wiebe Janzen
Music: © 2019 Anneli Loepp Thiessen
377 © 1991 Hope Publishing Company, Carol Stream, IL 60188. All rights reserved. Used by permission.
378 © 2020 Gwen M. Stamm
385 Trans.: © 2020 Melanie A. Howard
386 © 1993 WGRG, Iona Community, GIA Publications, Inc., agent
387 © 1966 F.E.L. Publications, assigned to The Lorenz Corp., 1991, (admin. Music Services)
388 © 2001 Schaff Music Publishing, LLC, admin. CapitolCMGPublishing.com. All rights reserved. Used by permission.
389 © 2014 Nathan Grieser
391 © 2012 Geonyong Lee
392 Text: © 2005 GIA Publications, Inc.
393 © 2011 Thankyou Music, admin. CapitolCMGPublishing.com. All rights reserved. Used by permission.
394 Text: © Mennonite Church and General Conference Mennonite Church, 1995; adapt. Mennonite Church Canada and Mennonite Church USA, 2002
Music: © 2018 Darryl Neustadter-Barg
395 Text: © 1971 Hope Publishing Company, Carol Stream, IL 60188. All rights reserved. Used by permission.
Music: © 1962 Theodore Presser Co.
396 © 1994 Lisa Hubbell Mackinney
398 © 1984 Meadowgreen Music Company, Word Music, LLC
399 Text adapt.: © 1983 Harris J. Loewen
Music: © 1983 Faith & Life Press/Mennonite Publishing House (admin. MennoMedia)
400 Trans.: © 2008 General Board of Global Ministries, t/a GBGMusik, 458 Ponce de Leon Ave., Atlanta, GA 30308. copyright@umcmission.org.
401 © 1997 Integrity's Hosanna! Music
402 Trans.: © 1983 Ruth Naylor
Arr.: © 1967, ren., Lawson-Gould Music Publishers. All rights reserved. Used by permission of Alfred Music.
403 © 1988, 1994 Réveil Publications
Trans.: © 2017 Andrew Donaldson, www.andrewdonaldson.ca
404 Text: © 2015 GIA Publications, Inc.
Music: © 2019 Lee Dengler
405 Adapt.: © 2005 *Church Hymnary*, 4th ed.
406 © 2003 Wayne Leupold Editions, Inc.
407 Text: © 1994 Oxford University Press
Music: © 2002 GIA Publications, Inc.
409 Text: © 1979 Church of the Brethren General Board, Brethren Press, 1451 Dundee Ave., Elgin, IL 60120-1674, brethrenpress@brethren.org
Music: © 1979 Dianne Huffman Morningstar
410 Text: © 1991 GIA Publications, Inc.
412 © 1990 GIA Publications, Inc.
413 © 2004 Joseph Kabemba (admin. General Board of Global Ministries, t/a GBGMusik, 458 Ponce de Leon Ave., Atlanta, GA 30308. copyright@umcmission.org.
415 © 2004 Gateway Create Publishing, admin. CapitolCMGPublishing.com/Integrity Music
416 © 1970 Steve Engle and La Verne Church of the Brethren
417 © 1972 Maranatha! Music, Inc., admin. CapitolCMGPublishing.com.
418 Trans.: © 2019 Hope Publishing Company
420 Text: © 1996 Hope Publishing Company, Carol Stream, IL 60188. All rights reserved. Used by permission.
Music: © 2001 GIA Publications, Inc.
422 © 2006 Shawn Kirchner and Ryan Harrison
423 Text: © 1993 John Thornburg
424 Text: © Oxford University Press
425 English paraphr.: © Andrew Donaldson, www.andrewdonaldson.ca. Ravela Joseph, as taught by Vinita Manchala.
426 Text: © 1991 Jean Janzen
Music: © 2015 Wayne Leupold Editions, Inc.
427 Text: © 1979 The Hymn Society
428 Text: © 1987 WGRG, Iona Community, GIA Publications, Inc., agent
429 © 2008 Paul M. Vasile
430 Text A: Brian Wren © 2009 Hope Publishing Company, Carol Stream, IL 60188. All rights reserved. Used by permission.
431 © 1988 Oxford University Press
432 Text: © 1991 GIA Publications, Inc.
433 Text: © 1991 GIA Publications, Inc.
434 Text: © 2019 Brenda Hostetler Meyer
Music: © 2019 The Walking Roots Band
436 © 1949, 1953 The Stuart Hine Trust (admin. Hope Publishing Company, Carol Stream, IL 60188). All rights reserved. Used by permission.
437 © 1980 Savgos Music, Inc.
Arr.: © 2000 GIA Publications, Inc.
438 Music: © 2011 Jackson Henry
439 © 2014 Jeremy Kempf
440 Text: © 2017 GIA Publications, Inc.
Music: © 1989 Joan Fyock Norris

441 Text: © 1991 GIA Publications, Inc.
442 Text: © 2011 GIA Publications, Inc.
Music: © 2019 GIA Publications, Inc.
443 © Capitol CMG Publishing
444 Trans.: © 1966 Marion Wenger
Alt.: © 1990 Harris J. Loewen
445 © 2020 Matthew C. Regier
452 Text: © 2010 Celebrating Grace, Inc.
Music: © 2005 Wayne Leupold Editions, Inc.
455 © 2018 Anneli Loepp Thiessen
456 © 2012 Hillsong Music Publishing, admin. CapitolCMGPublishing.com. All rights reserved. Used by permission.
457 Text: © 1969 International Commission on English in the Liturgy Corp.
Music: © 1977 International Commission on English in the Liturgy Corp.
458 © 2019 GIA Publications, Inc.
459 Stanzas 1–3 trans.: © 1985 The Sisters of Saint Benedict
Stanzas 4–5 trans.: © World Library Publications, a div. of GIA Publications, Inc.
460 Text: © 2015, GIA Publications, Inc.
Music: © 2019 Heather Josselyn-Cranson
461 © 2008 Hope Publishing Company, Carol Stream, IL 60188. All rights reserved. Used by permission.
462 © 1994 GIA Publications, Inc.
464 Trans.: © 1993 The Pilgrim Press. Manuel Dávila, La Misa Popular Nicaragüense, 20th c.
465 Text: © 2000 GIA Publications Inc.
466 Text: © Selah Publishing Co.
Music: © 1996, harm.: © 2019, Hope Publishing Company, Carol Stream, IL 60188. All rights reserved. Used by permission.
467 © 1983 GIA Publications, Inc.
468 © 2020 Dona Park
473 © 1984 Utryck; admin. Walton Music Corp., a div. of GIA Publications, Inc.
474 Text: © 1991 GIA Publications, Inc.
Music: © 1993 GIA Publications, Inc.
475 © 2015 GIA Publications, Inc.
476 © 1984, trans.: © 2005, Les Presses de Taizé, GIA Publications, Inc., agent
477 © 1987 Ekklesia Music, ILP
478 Text: © 1971, rev. 1995 Hope Publishing Company, Carol Stream, IL 60188. All rights reserved. Used by permission.
Arr.: © 1989 The United Methodist Publishing House (admin. Music Services)
479 © 2009 sixsteps Music; spiritandsong.com; Thankyou Music; worshiptogether.com, admin. CapitolCMGPublishing.com. All rights reserved. Used by permission.
480 © 1970 GIA Publications, Inc.
Spanish Trans.: © 2005 GIA Publications, Inc.
481 Text: © 1996, Mandarin trans. and music: 2013, all by Hope Publishing Company, Carol Stream, IL 60188. All rights reserved. Used by permission.
483 Text: © 2016 GIA Publications, Inc.
Music: © 2019 Benjamin Bergey
484 Harm.: © 2019 Cynthia Neufeld Smith
485 Text: © 1989 Hope Publishing Company, Carol Stream, IL 60188. All rights reserved. Used by permission.
487 English trans.: © 2019 J. Nelson Kraybill
Acc.: © 2020 Marilyn Houser Hamm
488 Adapt.: © 2020 Mennonite Worship and Song Committee, admin. GIA Publications, Inc.
489 © James E. Clemens
490 © 1986 GIA Publications, Inc.
Acc.: © 1992 Randall L. Spaulding
492 Ref. and stanzas 2, 3 trans.: © 1975, 1986 GIA Publications, Inc.
Stanza 1 trans.: © 2001 Augsburg Fortress
493 © 2009 Make Way Music
494 © 1999 Integrity's Praise! Music
495 Text: © David Higham Assoc., Ltd.
Harm.: © 1931 Oxford University Press, London
498 © 1977 Chinese Christian Literature Council Ltd.
499 Arr.: © 1978 Lawson-Gould Music Publishers. All rights reserved. Used by permission of Alfred Music.
501 Text: © 1990 admin. Asian Institute for Liturgy and Music
Music: © 1990 Francisco Feliciano (admin. Asian Institute for Liturgy and Music)
Arr.: © 2006 Augsburg Fortress
504 © 1987 GIA Publications, Inc.
505 Stanza 3: © 1982 The Jubilate Group (admin. Hope Publishing Company, Carol Stream, IL 60188). All rights reserved. Used by permission.
507 Text: © 2017 Andrew Donaldson, www.andrewdonaldson.ca
Music: © 1977 GIA Publications, Inc.
508 Text: © 1981 Ronald S. Cole-Turner
Music: © 1960, ren. 1988 Hope Publishing Company, Carol Stream, IL 60188. All rights reserved. Used by permission.
509 © 2010 Celebrating Grace, Inc.
510 Text: © 2019 Brenda Hostetler Meyer
Harm.: © 1989 Joan Fyock Norris
511 © 2014 Hope Publishing Company, Carol Stream, IL 60188. All rights reserved. Used by permission.
512 © 1982 World Library Publications, a div. of GIA Publications, Inc.
513 Text: © 2001 Carolyn Winfrey Gillette, www.carolynshymns.com
514 © 1976 Word Music LLC
515 Trans. and arr.: © 1991 Alice Parker. Used by permission.
518 Text: © 1986 Daniel Bechtel
Music: © 1993 Selah Publishing Co., Inc.
519 Text and music: © 2013 GIA Publications, Inc.
520 Text: © 2016 GIA Publications, Inc.
Music: © 2011 Wayne Leupold Editions, Inc.
521 © 2013 Atlas Mountain Songs; Said And Done Music; sixsteps Music; Thankyou Music; worshiptogether.com Songs
522 Text: © 1993 Susan Palo Cherwien (admin. Augsburg Fortress)
Harm.: © 2004 James E. Clemens
523 Text: © 1986 Oxford University Press
Music: © 2019 Gregory A. Smucker
524 Text: © 1983 Hope Publishing Company, Carol Stream, IL 60188. All rights reserved. Used by permission.
Harm.: © 2004 James E. Clemens
525 © 2000 Christian Conference of Asia (admin. GIA Publications, Inc.)
526 © 1971, trans.: 2019 Mortimer Arias
527 Text: © 2001 The Hymn Society (admin. Hope Publishing Company, Carol Stream, IL 60188). All rights reserved. Used by permission.
528 Text: © 2009 John A. Dalles
Music: © 1996, 1998 Amanda Husberg, admin. Concordia Publishing House, cph.org. Used by permission.
529 Text: © 1967 Hope Publishing Company, Carol Stream, IL 60188. All rights reserved. Used by permission.
530 Text: © 1988 (admin. Hope Publishing Company, Carol Stream, IL 60188). All rights reserved. Used by permission.
Music: © 1982 Noël Tredinnick (admin. Jubilate Hymns)

531 Text: © 2008 Hope Publishing Company, Carol Stream, IL 60188. All rights reserved. Used by permission.
532 © 2008 Gord Johnson
533 Text and music adapt.: © 2007 GIA Music Publications, Inc.
534 Text: © 1989 Hope Publishing Company, Carol Stream, IL 60188. All rights reserved. Used by permission.
Music: © 2016 GIA Publications, Inc.
535 © 2014, GIA Publications, Inc.
537 © 1969 Hope Publishing Company, Carol Stream, IL 60188. All rights reserved. Used by permission.
538 Trans.: © Maggie Hamilton
Music: © 1978 Harald Lyche & Co. (admin. A/S Musikforlag)
539 Music: © 2016 Pax Ressler
540 © 1987 WGRG, Iona Community, GIA Publications, Inc., agent
Arr.: © 2015 Lilly Chapel Press, LLC
541 © 1998 Borealis Music
542 Text: © 2013 GIA Publications, Inc.
Music: © 1999 Selah Publishing Co., Inc.
543 © 1998 Les Presses de Taizé, GIA Publications, Inc., agent
545 © 1981 Daniel L. Schutte and New Dawn Music, admin. OCP
546 Text: © 2002 Iona Community, GIA Publications, Inc., agent
Music: © 2019 Charlene Nafziger
547 Text: © 1982 Hope Publishing Company, Carol Stream, IL 60188. All rights reserved. Used by permission.
548 Music: © 1991 Bradley P. Lehman
549 Harm.: © 1927 Oxford University Press
550 Music: © 1989 Sacred Music Press
551 © 2009 Capitol CMG Publishing, admin. CapitolCMGPublishing.com All rights reserved. Used by permission.
552 Stanzas 1, 2: © 1987 Faith Alive Christian Resources
Stanza 3: © 2020 Mennonite Worship and Song Committee, admin. GIA Publications, Inc.
553 Text: © 2009 Oxford University Press
Harm.: © 2020 Bradley Kauffman
554 Text: © 1982 Hope Publishing Company, Carol Stream, IL 60188. All rights reserved. Used by permission.
Music: © 2019 Irene Zacharias Moon
556 Music: © 1965 J. Randall Zercher
559 Text and music transcr.: © 2010 Côte d'Ivoire Annual Conference, United Methodist Church (admin. General Board of Global Ministries, t/a GBGMusik, 458 Ponce de Leon Ave., Atlanta, GA 30308. copyright@umcmission.org)
561 © 2001 Integrity Worship Music
562 © 1997 Daniel Smiley
564 Harm.: © 1966 Alice Parker. Used by permission.
565 Text: © 1983 Hope Publishing Company, Carol Stream, IL 60188. All rights reserved. Used by permission.
Music: © 2003 GIA Publications, Inc.
567 © 1995 Samuel Paul
English trans.: © 1990 Hope Publishing Company, Carol Stream, IL 60188. All rights reserved. Used by permission.
568 © 2007 Revolution of Hope Music Group, SESAC
Acc.: © 2019 Benjamin Bergey
569 Text: © 2015 Oxford University Press
Music: © 1958, 1986 Pilgrim Press
571 Versification © 2019 Mennonite Worship and Song Committee, admin. GIA Publications, Inc.
572 Music: © 2008 James E. Clemens
574 Music adapt.: © 1970 World Library Publications, a div. of GIA Publications, Inc.
576 Trans.: © 1969, 1983 David Augsburger
Harm.: © 1969 Faith & Life Press/ Mennonite Publishing House
578 Text: © 1990 Mennonite World Conference
579 Text: © 2015 Andrew Donaldson, www.andrewdonaldson.ca
580 Text: © 2005 Hope Publishing Company, Carol Stream, IL 60188. All rights reserved. Used by permission.
Music: © 2016 GIA Publications, Inc.
581 © 1970 Les Petites Soeurs de Jésus and L'Arche Community
Stanzas 1-3 trans.: © 1970 Estate of Stephen Somerville
Stanza 4 trans.: © 2018 Mennonite Worship and Song Committee, admin. GIA Publications, Inc.
582 © 1995 Common Cup Company
Arr.: © Andrew Donaldson, www.andrewdonaldson.ca
583 Trans.: © 1990, Myron Augsburger
584 © 1999 Vineyard Songs (admin. Music Services)
585 Text: © 1996 Hope Publishing Company, Carol Stream, IL 60188. All rights reserved. Used by permission.
Music: © 2019 David J. Gonzol
586 © 1993 World Library Publications, a div. of GIA Publications, Inc.
587 © 1993 Juliana Howard
588 Music: © 1984 GIA Publications, Inc.
589 Trans.: © 1983 Paul R. Gregory
591 © 2011 Jessica Hedrick Miller
593 Text and transcr. © 2008 General Board of Global Ministries (admin. GBGMusik)
English trans.: © 2006 GIA Publications, Inc.
French trans.: © 2013 Community of Christ
594 © 1998 WGRG, Iona Community, GIA Publications, Inc., agent
595 Arr.: © 1989 The United Methodist Publishing House (admin. Music Services)
596 © 1995 WGRG, Iona Community, GIA Publications, Inc., agent
597 © 2013 Thankyou Music
598 © 2019 Connie Johnson-Evers
599 © 1965, 1993, arr.: © 2000 GIA Publications, Inc.
600 Harm.: © 1969 Faith & Life Press/Mennonite Publishing House
601 © 1953, ren., arr. 2020 Chappell & Co., Inc. All rights reserved. Used by permission of Alfred Music.
603 Text: © 2019 Katie Graber
Music: © 2017 Charlene Nafziger
604 © 1991 Les Presses de Taizé, GIA Publications, Inc., agent
605 Arr.: © 1989 *Hymnal: A Worship Book*, alt. Mennonite Worship and Song Committee, admin. GIA Publications, Inc.
607 © Asempa Publishers
609 © 2000 Camps with Meaning
Acc.: © 2019 Anneli Loepp Thiessen
610 Text: © 1938, ren. © 2012
Arr.: © 2012 Warner-Tamerlane Publishing Corp. All rights reserved. Used by permission of Alfred Music.
612 © 2019 GIA Publications, Inc.
613 © 2017 Joanne Bender
614 Music: © 2014 Hope Publishing Company, Carol Stream, IL 60188. All rights reserved. Used by permission.
618 Arr.: © 2011 Alfred V. Fedak
620 Arr.: © 2007 United Church of Canada
622 © 1973 Jerry Derstine (JD Martin)
Harm.: © 1991 Marilyn Houser Hamm and Jerry Derstine (JD Martin)

623 Text: © 2009 GIA Publications, Inc.
Arr.: © 1992 *Hymnal: A Worship Book*, Brethren Press, 1451 Dundee Ave., Elgin, IL 60120-1674, brethren-press@brethren.org
625 © 2006 Hal Leonard Corporation
627 © 1982, 1983, 1984 Les Presses de Taizé, GIA Publications, Inc., agent
629 © 1986 Rough Stones Music
630 Text: © 2019 Susan Naus Dengler
Music: © 2019 Anneli Loepp Thiessen
632 © 1991 Les Presses de Taizé, GIA Publications, Inc., agent
633 © 1990, arr. © 2010 Bridge Building Music and T. Autumn Music, admin. CapitolCMGPublishing.com. All rights reserved. Used by permission.
634 © 2003 Santa Barbara Music Publishing, Inc.
635 Music: © 2008 James E. Clemens
636 Text: © 1996 The Pilgrim Press
Arr.: © 2014 Hope Publishing Company, Carol Stream, IL 60188. All rights reserved. Used by permission.
637 © 2002 Thankyou Music
640 Harm.: © 1969 Faith & Life Press/Mennonite Publishing House (admin. MennoMedia)
641 © 1979 New Dawn Music (admin. OCP)
642 Text: © 1996, music: © 1997, The Pilgrim Press
644 © 1987 GIA Publications, Inc.
645 © 1961 Paragon Music Corp.
Arr.: © 2000 GIA Publications, Inc.
646 Text: © 2006, music: © 2008 Hope Publishing Company, Carol Stream, IL 60188. All rights reserved. Used by permission.
648 © 2018 Stockwell Massamba
650 Transcr.: © 1990 WGRG, Iona Community (admin. GIA Publications, Inc.)
651 Music: © 2010 RUBLEMUSIC
652 Text: © 1996 Jeannette M. Lindholm (admin. Augsburg Fortress)
653 © 1996 Hope Publishing Company, Carol Stream, IL 60188. All rights reserved. Used by permission.
654 © 2007, 2011 Les Presses de Taizé, GIA Publications, Inc., agent
655 Text: © 1983 Hope Publishing Company, Carol Stream, IL 60188. All rights reserved. Used by permission.
Music: © 2019 Benjamin Bergey
656 Text: © 2002 Oxford University Press
Music: © 1998 GIA Publications, Inc.
657 Text: © 1996 WGRG, Iona Community, GIA Publications, Inc., agent
Music: © 1997 Dean McIntyre
661 Harm.: © 1969 Faith & Life Press/Mennonite Publishing House
662 Arr.: © 2019 Bradley Kauffman
663 Trans.: © Singing the Living Tradition
Arr.: © 2019 Benjamin Bergey
664 Arr.: © 1933, 1961 Presbyterian Board of Christian Education
665 Trans. and music: © 1958, arr.: 2010 GIA Publications, Inc.
669 © 1976 Bud John Songs, Inc.
670 © 1986 Hope Publishing Company, Carol Stream, IL 60188. All rights reserved. Used by permission.
671 © 1994 GIA Publications, Inc.
673 © 2008 Abingdon Press (admin. Music Services)
675 Arabic and music: © 2002 Songs of the Evangelical Presbyterian Church of Egypt (admin. Faith Alive Christian Resources)
Trans. and adapt.: © 2008 Faith Alive Christian Resources
676 © 2006, GIA Publications, Inc.
677 © 1989 Oxford University Press, Inc.
678 Music: © 1979 Les Presses de Taizé, GIA Publications, Inc., agent
679 English trans. and transcr.: © WGRG, Iona Community, GIA Publications, Inc., agent
680 Text: © SPCK
Music: © 1998 Kevin Mayhew, Ltd. (admin.GIA Publications, Inc.)
681 Music adapt.: © 1990 Melva Wilson Costen
682 © 1973 Hope Publishing Company, Carol Stream, IL 60188. All rights reserved. Used by permission.
683 © 1994 Borealis Music
684 Music: © 1990 Century Oak/Richwood Music (BMI), (admin. Conexion Media Group, Inc)
Arr.: © 2000 GIA Publications, Inc.
685 © 1982 Les Presses de Taizé, GIA Publications, Inc., agent
686 Arr.: © 1984 GIA Publications, Inc.
691 Ref. and music: © 2014 The Walking Roots Band
692 Music: © 2018 Les Presses de Taizé, GIA Publications, Inc., agent
694 Text: © 2015 GIA Publications, Inc. arr. Randall Sensmeier
696 Text: © 2013 GIA Publications, Inc.
Arr.: © 1992 Horace Clarence Boyer
697 Text: © 1987 The Hymn Society (admin. Hope Publishing Company, Carol Stream, IL 60188). All rights reserved. Used by permission.
699 Text: © 2007 East Africa Annual Conference
Arr.: © 2007 Greg Scheer
Text and arr.: admin. General Board of Global Ministries t/a GBGMusik, 458 Ponce de Leon Ave., Atlanta, GA 30308. copyright@umcmission.org
700 © 1999, GIA Publications Inc.
701 © 1992 GIA Publications, Inc.
703 © 1992 Jamie Cortez. Published by OCP, 5536 NE Hassalo, Portland, OR 97213. All rights reserved. Used by permission
704 © 2019 GIA Publications, Inc.
705 Text: © 1968 Hope Publishing Company, Carol Stream, IL 60188. All rights reserved. Used by permission.
706 © 1964 (ren.) Appleseed Music, Inc.
708 Text: © 2006 GIA Publications, Inc.
709 Harm.: © 2000 Alfred V. Fedak
710 Text: © 1934, 1962 Lorenz Publishing Company
Arr.: © 1933, 1961 Presbyterian Board of Christian Education
711 Trans. and arr.: © 2007, 2008 WGRG, Iona Community, GIA Publications, Inc., agent
712 © 1993 Make Way Music (admin. Music Services)
713 Music: © 2018 GIA Publications, Inc.
715 © 1993 Bernadette Farrell, admin. OCP, 5536 NE Hassalo, Portland, OR 97213. All rights reserved. Used by permission.
717 Text: © 1960 K. L. Cober, ren. 1985 Judson Press
718 © 1974 William J. Gaither
719 © 1971, 2004 Jerry Derstine (JD Martin)
720 Text: © 1964 Christian Conference of Asia
Adapt.: © 1961 Elena G. Maquiso
Arr.: © 1980 World Council of Churches
721 Text: © 2002 GIA Publications, Inc.
Music: © 2000 William P. Rowan (admin. GIA Publications, Inc.)
722 Stanzas 1, 2, and 4 rev.: © 1982 Hope Publishing Company, Carol Stream, IL 60188. All rights reserved. Used by permission.
723 © 2020 Brenton Good
725 Adapt.: © 2006 Evangelical Lutheran Worship, admin. Augsburg Fortress
731 © 2003 Ana Hernández
732 © 1988, 1998, 1999 Jesse Manibusan and Rufino Zaragoza. OFM, Spirit and Song, admin. OCP, 5536 NE Hassalo, Portland, OR 97213. All rights reserved. Used by permission.

734 © 2014 Hope Publishing Company, Carol Stream, IL 60188. All rights reserved. Used by permission.
735 Text: © 2005 GIA Publications, Inc.
Harm.: © 1968 Augsburg Publishing House (admin. Augsburg Fortress)
736 © 1993 GIA Publications, Inc.
739 © 1978 Jesus-Bruderschaft e.V.
Trans.: © 2006 Jean Janzen, Kenneth Nafziger and Randall Spaulding
Harm.: © 2004 Haus der Musik
740 © 1935, 1963 Birdwing Music and BWG Songs, Inc.
741 © 2010 River Oaks Music Company/Thankyou Music/Valley of Songs Music
744 © 1986 GIA Publications, Inc.
745 Text: © 1961, 1989 The Hymn Society (admin. Hope Publishing Company, Carol Stream, IL 60188). All rights reserved. Used by permission.
Music: adapt. © 1951 Oxford University Press
748 © 1995 WGRG, Iona Community, GIA Publications, Inc., agent
749 © 2019 Nathan Grieser
750 Text: © 1955, ren. 1983 The Hymn Society
751 Text: © 2015, music: © 2017 GIA Publications, Inc.
752 Arr.: © 1990 WGRG, Iona Community, GIA Publications, Inc., agent
753 © 1958 United Church Press
754 © 1978, 1986 Prism Tree Music (admin. the Lorenz Corp.)
755 Text and music: © 1983 Chung Kwan Park, music arr. Paul Junggap Huh and Alfred V. Fedak, 2012
English trans.: © 2001 Edward Poitras, rev. © 2013 The United Methodist Publishing House (admin. Music Services)
756 Text: © 2018 Merle Good
757 © 2004 SmallTall Music
758 Text: © 2000, music: © 1989 Selah Publishing Co., Inc.
760 Music: William Dexheimer-Pharris, arr. Mark Sedio, © 1999 Augsburg Fortress
763 © 1995 Jonathan Reuel
765 Trans.: © Makumira University College, Tanzania (admin. Augsburg Fortress)
Arr.: © 1995 Austin C. Lovelace (admin. Augsburg Fortress)
766 Text: © 2002 GIA Publications, Inc.
767 Trans.: © 1978, 1990 Mennonite World Conference. *International Songbook*, Mennonite World Conference, 1978
768 Doug Krehbiel and Jude Krehbiel
769 Trans.: © 1990, GIA Publications, Inc.
770 Music: © 1931 Oxford University Press
771 Text: © José Aguiar
Arr.: © 2003 Augsburg Fortress
772 © 2004 Thankyou Music, admin. CapitolCMGPublishing.com. All rights reserved. Used by permission.
773 © Les Presses de Taizé, GIA Publications, Inc., agent
774 Text: © 1978 Hope Publishing Company, Carol Stream, IL 60188. All rights reserved. Used by permission.
Music: © 1985 Skinner Chavez-Melo
775 © 2010 SHOUT! Music Publishing; sixsteps Music; Vamos Publishing; worshiptogether.com; So Essential Tunes; Spirit Nashville Three
777 © 2017 The Walking Roots Band
778 © 1977 Scripture in Song, admin. CapitolCMGPublishing.com. All rights reserved. Used by permission.
779 © 2005, acc.: © 2010 Bryan Moyer Suderman/ SmallTall Music
780 © 2020 Michelle L. Hofer
787 Text: © 1982 Hope Publishing Company, Carol Stream, IL 60188. All rights reserved. Used by permission.
Harm.: © 1986 GIA Publications, Inc.
788 Text: © 2002 GIA Publications, Inc.
Arr.: © 2010 Andrew Donaldson, www.andrewdonaldson.ca
789 © 2013 Camps with Meaning
790 © 2003 GIA Publications, Inc.
791 Text and music: © 1994 Douglas Romanow & Citizens for Public Justice
792 © 2015 Rachael Weasley
793 © 1984 Utryck, admin. Walton Music Corp., a div. of GIA Publications, Inc.
794 © 2003 WGRG, Iona Community, GIA Publications, Inc., agent
795 Music: © 1987 Dinah Reindorf; harm. as taught by Ysaye Maria Barnwell, Laurelville Mennonite Church Center
796 © 2010 Thankyou Music/Getty Music Publishing
797 Stanza 2: © Mennonite World Conference
798 © 1996 Darryl Neustaedter Barg
799 © 2001, 2011 Les Presses de Taizé, GIA Publications, Inc., agent
800 © Kyung Dong Presbyterian Church (admin. Sung Mo Moon)
Trans.: © 2013 Andrew Donaldson, www.andrewdonaldson.ca
802 Text: © 1994 Common Cup Company
Music: © 2008 Abingdon Press (admin. Music Services)
805 Music: © 2004 General Board of Discipleship of the United Methodist Church
806 © 2005 Pat Mayberry
Acc.: © 2005 Marg Stubington
807 Text: © 2005 GIA Publications, Inc.
Music: © 2008 Re:Create Music, admin. Faith Alive Christian Resources
808 Hebrew and Arabic texts: © 2006 Manal Hreib
English trans. and music: © 2006 Daphna Rosenberg
809 Text: © 2006 GIA Publications, Inc.
810 Text: © 2004 David Wright
Music: © 2004 James E. Clemens
811 © 2009 Jeremy Kempf
812 Text: © 1964 World Library Publications, a div. of GIA Publications, Inc.
813 Trans.: © 1969, 1983 Walter Klaassen
814 Text: © 1982 The Jubilate Group (admin. Hope Publishing Company, Carol Stream, IL 60188). All rights reserved. Used by permission.
815 Trans. and transcr.: © 2002 WGRG, Iona Community, GIA Publications, Inc., agent
816 Harm.: © Estate of Wendell Whalum
817 © 2020 Rafael H. Barahona
825 English trans. of Scripture: © 1998, English Language Liturgical Consultation (ELLC). Used by permission. www.englishtexts.org.
828 © 2014 Lora Braun
Arr.: © 2017 Loretta Thorleifson
829 Text: © 2004 Wayne Leupold Editions, Inc.
Music: © 1968, this arr.: © 2020 Augsburg Publishing House (admin. Augsburg Fortress)
830 Text: © 1983 Concordia Publishing House, cph.org. Used by permission.
832 © 1983 Patricia J. Shelly
834 Arr.: © 1984 Peace of Music Publishing, AB, admin. Walton Music Corp., a div. of GIA Publications, Inc.
835 © 1976 Hinshaw Music, Inc.
838 Text: © 1998 Christine Carson and Iona Community, GIA Publications, Inc., agent
839 Text A and music: © Unichappell Music, Inc.
841 © 2011 SmallTall Music
844 © 2009 Jerry L. Holsopple
847 © 1975 Lillenas Publishing Co.
848 © 2014 Jack Mooring Music, admin. CapitolCMGPublishing.com. All rights reserved. Used by permission.

849 Text: © 2013 Rebecca Mosley and Josephine Munyeli
Arr.: © Mennonite Worship and Song Committee, admin. GIA Publications, Inc.
851 © 2017 Joanna Harader
852 © 2014 Wild Goose Resource Group, Iona Community, GIA Publications, Inc., agent
853 © 2007 Marlene Kropf
Spanish trans.: © 2019 Andrea F. De Ávila Balboa
854 © 2012 Joanna Harader
855 © Jacob Trapp Estate
856 © 2014 Wild Goose Resource Group, Iona Community, GIA Publications, Inc., agent
857 From "Daily Prayer for Morning or Mid-Day Devotions Prayer," *Voices United: The Hymn and Worship Book of The United Church of Canada/L'Église Unie du Canada* © 1995 The United Church of Canada
859 © 2015 Alissa Bender
861 © 2017 The Episcopal Church
862 © 2012 W. Scott Haldeman
863 Reprinted by permission of United Church Press. From *An Improbable Gift of Blessing* by Maren C. Tirabassi and Joan Jordan Grant © 1998 Maren C. Tirabassi and Joan Jordan Grant. All rights reserved.
864 © 2002 Barb Daniels and Neill von Gunten
865 © 2005 J. Phillip Newell
866 © 2019 Carol Penner
867 © 1999 Wild Goose Resource Group, Iona Community, GIA Publications, Inc., agent
868 Reprinted by permission of United Church Press. From *Bread for the Journey*, ed. Ruth Duck © 1981 The Pilgrim Press. All rights reserved.
869 © 2017 LeAnne Zook
870 © 1976 William B. Oden
871 © 2012 Sarah Klassen, reprinted with permission from *Monstrance*, Turnstone Press (Winnipeg, MB)
872 Taken from *Common Prayer: A Liturgy for Ordinary Radicals* by Shane Claiborne, Jonathan Wilson-Hartgrove, and Enuma Okoro © 2010 The Simple Way and School for Conversion. Used by permission of Zondervan. www.zondervan.com.
873 © 2008 Roddy Hamilton
874 © 1998 Wild Goose Resource Group, Iona Community, GIA Publications, Inc., agent
876 © 1989 The Anglican Church in Aotearoa, New Zealand and Polynesia
877 Taken from *The Book of a Thousand Prayers*, compiled by Angela Ashwin © 1996, 2002 Angela Ashwin. Used by permission of Zondervan. www.zondervan.com
878 © 2020 Mennonite Worship and Song Committee, admin. GIA Publications, Inc.
879 © 2011 Christine Longhurst
880 Reprinted from the *Book of Common Worship* © 2018 Westminster John Knox Press. All rights reserved.
881 © 2016 Joelle Friesen
882 © 2002 Walter Brueggemann
883 © 2003 David Wright
884 © 2015 Wild Goose Resource Group, Iona Community, GIA Publications, Inc., agent
885 © 2009 Laura Jaquith Bartlett
886 Reprinted from the *Book of Common Worship* © 2018 Westminster John Knox Press. All rights reserved.
887 © 2017 Gail Ramshaw
888 Adapt. from the *Book of Common Worship* © 2018 Westminster John Knox Press. All rights reserved.
890 © 2006 Augsburg Fortress
891 © 1981 Anne Macksoud
892 English trans. of Agnus Dei: © 1998, English Language Liturgical Consultation (ELLC). Used by permission. www.englishtexts.org.
893 Reprinted from the *Book of Common Worship* © 2018 Westminster John Knox Press. All rights reserved.
895 Reprinted by permission of Local Church Ministries (A Covenanted Ministry of the United Church of Christ). From *Book of Worship: United Church of Christ* © 1986, 2012. All rights reserved.
896 © 2012 Joanna Harader
897 © 1989 The Anglican Church in Aotearoa, New Zealand and Polynesia
898 © 1992 Janet Morley
899 © 1992 Marlene Kropf
901 © Red Crearte. Trans. adapt. from the *Book of Common Worship* © 2018 Westminster John Knox Press. All rights reserved.
902 © 1989 The Anglican Church in Aotearoa, New Zealand and Polynesia
903 Reprinted from the *Book of Common Worship* © 2018 Westminster John Knox Press. All rights reserved.
906 © 1993 Judy Gillis
908 From Jan L. Richardson's *In the Sanctuary of Women: A Companion for Reflection & Prayer* © 2010. Used by permission of Upper Room Books. upperroombooks.com.
909 © 1989 The Anglican Church in Aotearoa, New Zealand and Polynesia
910 Reprinted from the *Book of Common Worship* © 2018 Westminster John Knox Press. All rights reserved.
912 © 2017 Paul C. Stratman
913 G.: © 2015 Wild Goose Resource Group, Iona Community, GIA Publications, Inc., agent
914 © 2015 Wild Goose Resource Group, Iona Community, GIA Publications, Inc., agent
915 © 2006 Augsburg Fortress
916 © 2018 Sarah Kathleen Johnson
917 © 2019 Sarah Kathleen Johnson
918 © 2019 Sarah Kathleen Johnson
919 From *On the Cross* (DreamSeeker Books) by Dallas Wiebe. © 2005 Cascadia Publishing House
920 © 2019 Eric Massanari
922 From *Voices United: The Hymn and Worship Book of The United Church of Canada/L'Église Unie du Canada* © 1995 The United Church of Canada
923 English trans. of the Creed © 1998, English Language Liturgical Consultation (ELLC). Used by permission. www.englishtexts.org.
924 English trans. of the Creed © 1998, English Language Liturgical Consultation (ELLC). Used by permission. www.englishtexts.org.
925 © 2006 Mennonite World Conference
926 © 2020 Mennonite Worship and Song Committee, admin. GIA Publications, Inc.
927 © 1996 The United Methodist Publishing House. All rights reserved. Used by permission.
929 © June Alliman Yoder and J. Nelson Kraybill. Used with permission.
930 © 2020 Mennonite Worship and Song Committee, admin. GIA Publications, Inc.
931 © 2020 Mennonite Worship and Song Committee, admin. GIA Publications, Inc.
932 © 2020 Mennonite Worship and Song Committee, admin. GIA Publications, Inc.
933 © 2020 Mennonite Worship and Song Committee, admin. GIA Publications, Inc.
935 © 2020 Mennonite Worship and Song Committee, admin. GIA Publications, Inc.
936 © 2020 Mennonite Worship and Song Committee, admin. GIA Publications, Inc.
937 © 2020 Mennonite Worship and Song Committee, admin. GIA Publications, Inc.
938 Excerpted from Psalm 51:1, 3, 10 and 2 Corinthians 5:17
939 © 2020 Mennonite Worship and Song Committee, admin. GIA Publications, Inc.
940 © 2020 Mennonite Worship and Song Committee, admin. GIA Publications, Inc.

941 © 2020 Mennonite Worship and Song Committee, admin. GIA Publications, Inc.
942 © 2020 Mennonite Worship and Song Committee, admin. GIA Publications, Inc.
943 © 2020 Mennonite Worship and Song Committee, admin. GIA Publications, Inc.
944 © 2020 Mennonite Worship and Song Committee, admin. GIA Publications, Inc.
945 © 2020 Mennonite Worship and Song Committee, admin. GIA Publications, Inc.
946 © 1999 Wild Goose Resource Group, Iona Community, GIA Publications, Inc., agent
947 © 2020 Mennonite Worship and Song Committee, admin. GIA Publications, Inc.
948 © 2003 William S. Kervin, *A Year of Grace: 365 Mealtime Prayers* (London/Peabody: Hendrickson/SPCK)
949 "Refuge (Saranam) Blessing" © 2003 William S. Kervin, *A Year of Grace: 365 Mealtime Prayers* (London/Peabody: Hendrickson/SPCK)
950 © 2020 Mennonite Worship and Song Committee, admin. GIA Publications, Inc.
951 © 2020 Mennonite Worship and Song Committee, admin. GIA Publications, Inc.
952 © 2020 Mennonite Worship and Song Committee, admin. GIA Publications, Inc.
953 © 2020 Mennonite Worship and Song Committee, admin. GIA Publications, Inc.
954 © 2018 Anneli Loepp Thiessen
955 © 2018 Sarah Bixler
956 © 1979 Episcopal Church (USA)
957 © 2018 Christine Longhurst
959 © 2020 Mennonite Worship and Song Committee, admin. GIA Publications, Inc.
960 © 2020 Mennonite Worship and Song Committee, admin. GIA Publications, Inc.
961 © 2020 Mennonite Worship and Song Committee, admin. GIA Publications, Inc.
962 © 2020 Mennonite Worship and Song Committee, admin. GIA Publications, Inc.
963 Adapt. from the *Book of Common Worship* © 2018 Westminster John Knox Press. All rights reserved.
964 © 2020 Mennonite Worship and Song Committee, admin. GIA Publications, Inc.
965 © 2020 Mennonite Worship and Song Committee, admin. GIA Publications, Inc.
966 © 2020 Mennonite Worship and Song Committee, admin. GIA Publications, Inc.
967 © 2020 Mennonite Worship and Song Committee, admin. GIA Publications, Inc.
968 © 2020 Mennonite Worship and Song Committee, admin. GIA Publications, Inc.
969 © 2020 Mennonite Worship and Song Committee, admin. GIA Publications, Inc.
970 © 2020 Mennonite Worship and Song Committee, admin. GIA Publications, Inc.
971 © 2020 Mennonite Worship and Song Committee, admin. GIA Publications, Inc.
972 © 1999 The United Methodist Publishing House. All rights reserved. Used by permission.
973 © 2020 Mennonite Worship and Song Committee, admin. GIA Publications, Inc.
974 © 2020 Mennonite Worship and Song Committee, admin. GIA Publications, Inc.
975 © 2020 Mennonite Worship and Song Committee, admin. GIA Publications, Inc.
976 © 2020 Mennonite Worship and Song Committee, admin. GIA Publications, Inc.
977 © 2018 Ingrid Loepp Thiessen
978 © 2018 April Yamasaki
979 © 2018 Ingrid Loepp Thiessen
980 © 2020 Mennonite Worship and Song Committee, admin. GIA Publications, Inc.
981 © 2020 Mennonite Worship and Song Committee, admin. GIA Publications, Inc.
982 © 2020 Mennonite Worship and Song Committee, admin. GIA Publications, Inc.
983 © 2020 Mennonite Worship and Song Committee, admin. GIA Publications, Inc.
984 Taken from *The Book of a Thousand Prayers*, compiled by Angela Ashwin © 1996, 2002 Angela Ashwin. Used by permission of Zondervan. www.zondervan.com.
985 © 2020 Mennonite Worship and Song Committee, admin. GIA Publications, Inc.
986 © 1989 The Anglican Church in Aotearoa, New Zealand and Polynesia
987 © 2020 Mennonite Worship and Song Committee, admin. GIA Publications, Inc.
988 © 1999 Marlene Kropf
989 A.: English trans. of Our Father © 1998 English Language Liturgical Consultation (ELLC). Used by permission. www.englishtexts.org.
C.: © 2003 Richard D. McCall
990 From Jan L. Richardson's *In the Sanctuary of Women: A Companion for Reflection & Prayer* © 2010. Used by permission of Upper Room Books. upperroombooks.com.
992 © 2001 GIA Publications, Inc.
994 Reprinted from the *Book of Common Worship* © 2018 Westminster John Knox Press. All rights reserved.
995 © 2020 Mennonite Worship and Song Committee, admin. GIA Publications, Inc.
996 © 2020 Mennonite Worship and Song Committee, admin. GIA Publications, Inc.
997 © 2017 Gail Ramshaw
1002 © 2020 Mennonite Worship and Song Committee, admin. GIA Publications, Inc.
1003 © 2020 Mennonite Worship and Song Committee, admin. GIA Publications, Inc.
1005 © 2012, 2017 Used with permission. www.ionabooks.com.
1006 © 2017 Used with permission. www.ionabooks.com.
1008 © 1981 Ted Loder
1009 © 1940 *Hymns Ancient and Modern*
1010 © 1988 Janet Morley
1011 © 2011 The United Methodist Publishing House. All rights reserved. Used by permission.
1013 © Les Presses de Taizé, GIA Publications, Inc., agent
1014 © 2006 Janet Morley
1015 © 1969 Abingdon Press/The United Methodist Publishing House. All rights reserved. Used by permission.
1017 © 2013 Joanna Harader
1018 © 2000 Les Presses de Taizé, GIA Publications, Inc., agent
1019 © 2006 Augsburg Fortress
1020 © 1994 Terry Falla
1021 © 1981 Ted Loder
1022 © 2017 Joanna Harader
1023 © 2011 LeAnne Zook
1024 Selection from "Foreword: Daughter's Precis" in *Remnants* by Rosemarie Freeney Harding and Rachel Elizabeth Harding © 2015 Duke University Press. Republished by permission.
1026 © 1979 Episcopal Church (USA)
1027 © 1989 The Anglican Church in Aotearoa, New Zealand and Polynesia
1028 Taken from *Common Prayer: A Liturgy for Ordinary Radicals* by Shane Claiborne, Jonathan Wilson-Hartgrove, and Enuma Okoro © 2010 The Simple Way and School for Conversion. Used by permission of Zondervan. www.zondervan.com.
1029 © 2005 Janet Morley

CONTRIBUTORS INDEX

AUTHORS, COMPOSERS, ARTISTS, ARRANGERS, AND TRANSLATORS

Dots (•) indicate individuals identifying as Anabaptist or otherwise connected with Anabaptism. When a text or tune is anonymous, entries can be found under culture groups or sources.

Abbington, James (b. 1960), 599
Adam, David (b. 1936), 225, 680
Adams, Sarah Flower (1805–1848), 658
Addison, Joseph (1672–1719), 119
African American Heritage Hymnal, 992
African American (USA) text and tune, 193, 252, 306, 329, 392, 453, 453, 454, 482, 499, 558, 574, 594, 647, 681, 689, 698, 743, 762, 801, 803, 804, 816
Aguiar, José, 771
Ainger, Arthur C. (1841–1919), 770
Akers, Doris M. (1923–1995), 601
Alcuin of York (ca. 735–804), 554, *860*, *983*
Alexander, Cecil F. (1818–1895), 177
Alexander, James W. (1804–1859), 325
Alford, Henry (1810–1871), 123, 588
Allen, Alejandro, 415
Allen, Chester G. (1838–1878), 100
Allen, George N. (1812–1877), 610
Alonso, Tony (b. 1980), 304, 420, 704, 713
Ambrose of Milan (340–397), 214, 500
American (USA, Euro-) hymn text, 7, 300, 488, 564
American (USA, Euro-) hymntune, 1, 37, 42, 44, 70, 163, 191, 251, 300, 347, 433, 441, 478, 529, 563, 564, 592, 600, 640, 661, 694, 717, 735
American (USA, Euro-) traditional tune (ca. 20th c.), 213, 696
Andrade, Moises (1948–2009), 501
Ángel, Chris (b. 1976), 475
Anglican Council of Indigenous Peoples, *861*
• Annelein of Freiburg (16th c.), 630
Anthony of Egypt (251–356), *1030*
Appling, William (1932–2008), 574
Aquinas, Thomas (1225–1274), 459
Arabic text and tune, 711
Arbeitsgemeinschaft für liturgische Texte, *989*
Argentine text and tune, 136
Arias, Mortimer (1924–2016), 526
Arnatt, Ronald (1930–2018), 112
Arndt, John, 494
Arpellet, Abraham, 559
Ashwin, Angela, *984*
Askins, George (d. 1816), 25
Assad, Audrey (b. 1983), 741
Assembly of the Christian Conference of Asia (Korea, 1985), *1041*
Atkinson, Frederick C. (1841–1896), 557
• Augsburger, David (b. 1938), 576, 797
• Augsburger, Myron (b. 1929), 583
Augustine of Hippo (354–430), *858*, *998*
• *Ausbund*, 45, 399, 444, 571, 576, 583, 630
Austrian hymntune, 126
Auza, Antonio (1915–1981), 526
Aydelott, Guy, 284

Babcock, Maltbie D. (1858–1901), 180
Bach, J. S. (1685–1750), 269, 325, 463, 624, 639
Baker, Theodore (1851–1934), 138, 216
Baloche, Paul (b. 1962), 401
• Barahona, Rafael H. (b. 1979), *817*
Baring-Gould, Sabine (1834–1924), 221
Barnett, Marie (b. 1960), 139
Barret, Pat (b. 20th c.), 92
Bartholomew, William (1793–1867), 616
Bartlett, Laura Jaquith (b. 20th c.), *885*
Batak traditional tune, 93
Batastini, Robert (b. 1942), 476
Bateman, Christian H. (1813–1889), 28
Bayly, Albert F. (1901–1984), 424
Bechtel, Daniel (b. 1932), 518
Bede, The Venerable (8th c.), 363

Beethoven, Ludwig van (1770–1827), 103, 513, 809
Bell, John (b. 1949), 2, 30, 32, 239, 284, 287, 386, 540, 546, 594, 596, 650, 657, 711, 748, 752, 794, 815
Bell, Maurice F. (1862–1947), 305
Bell, Steve (b. 1960), 314
ben Judah, Daniel, 204
• Bender, Alissa (b. 1979), *859*
• Bender, Joanne (b. 1950), 613
Bentley, W. Warren (1845–1926), 619
Berg, Caroline V. S. (1832–1903), 517
• Bergen, Esther C. (1921–2005), 578, *797*
Bergése, Alain, 131
• Bergey, Benjamin (b. 1988), 483, 655, 663
• Berry, Anne Hostetler (b. 1976), *334*
Berthier, Jacques (1923–1994), 52, 58, 64, 66, 77, 94, 97, 118, 127, 228, 327, 356, 370, 476, 543, 604, 627, 632, 678, 685, 692, 773
Bible, Ken (b. 1950), 258
Billings, William (1746–1800), 357
Bittner, Mary R. (1938–2007), 829
• Bixler, Sarah (b. 1980), *955*
Bjorlin, David (b. 1984), 143, 190, 319, 440
Bliss, Philip P. (1838–1876), 617
Boberg, Carl (1859–1940), 436
Bonar, Horatius (1808–1889), 536, 733
Book of Common Order of the Church of Scotland, The, 998
Book of Common Prayer, The (1979), Episcopal Church (USA), *956*, *989*, *1026*, *1054*
• Boosers, Mayken (present–day Netherlands), *1056*
Borderies, Etienne J. F. (1764–1832), 241
Borthwick, Jane (1813–1897), 497, 664
Bouknight, Lillian (d. 1990), 437
Bourgeois, Louis (1510–1559), 5, 71, 212, 424, 552
Boyce, R. Fisher (1887–1968), 275
Boyd, Robert (1771–1822), 246
Boyer, Horace Clarence (1935–2009), 213, 696
Bradbury, William B. (1816–1868), 318, 371, 516, 560, 621, 662
• Braun, Lora (b. 1971), 828
Bray, Jillian (b. 1939), 150, 646
Brazilian text and tune, 113
Bread for the World, *1059*
Bridges, Matthew (1800–1894), 408
Bridges, Robert (1844–1930), 330, 639
Brigid of Kildare (ca. 451–525), *958*
Bringle, Mary Louise (b. 1953), 205, 224, 237, 260, 285, 304, 527, 649, 675, 676, 708, 721, 755, 766, 788, 809
Brink, Emily (b. 1940), 675
Bristol, Lee H., Jr. (1923–1979), 395
Brody, Benjamin (b. 1975), 290, 354, 751
Brooks, Phillips (1835–1893), 245
Brother Roger of Taizé (1915–2005), *1013*, *1018*
Brown, Brenton (b. 1973), 49, 96
Browne, Simon (1680–1732), 371
Brüchner, Herman (1866–1942), 631
Brueggemann, Walter (b. 1933), *882*
• Brunk, J. D. (1872–1926), 40
Budry, Edmond L. (1854–1932), 355
Buley, David (b. 1958), 651
• Buller, Rachel Epp (b. 1974), *230*
Burgess, Ruth, *1006*
• Burkholder, Michelle (b. 1978), *291*
Burleigh, Harry T. (1866–1949), 392
Byrd, Marc (b. 1970), 178
Byrne, Mary Elizabeth, 549
Byzantine chant, 686

Cabrera, Juan Bautista, 346
Caldwell, Jody L. (b. 1954), 55
Calvin, John (1509–1564), *1000*
Cambodian traditional tune, 769
Cameron, Catherine (1927–2019), 529
Cameroon text and tune, 239
Campbell, Jane M. (1817–1878), 747
• Campbell-Enns, Phil (b. 1968), 11, 309
• Camps With Meaning, 609, 789
Canadian text and tune (20th c.), 405
Carawan, Guy (1927–2015), 803
Caribbean traditional tune, 593, 752
Carson, Christine, 838
Carson, Daniel (b. 20th c.), 155
Cartford, Gerhard (1923–2016), 23
Case, Joel, 195
Cash, Ed (b. 1971), 116, 256
Castañeda, Francis (b. 1968), 116
Celtic blessing, unattributed, *1066*
Chandler, John (1806–1876), 4
Chant, see plainsong
Chao, Tzu-chen (1888–1979), 498
Chapin, Aaron (18th–19th c.), 589
Chavez-Melo, Skinner (1944–1992), 774
Cherokee blessing (USA), (20th c.), *1061*
Chhun, Eang, 769
Chisholm, Thomas O. (1866–1960), 419
Choplin, Pepper (b. 1951), 509
Chute, Marion J. (1901–1995), 753
Claiborne, Shane (b. 1975), *872*, *1028*
Clare of Assisi (1194–1253), *1062*
Clark, Alden H. (1878–1960), 753
Clark, Barbara, 679
Claudius, Matthias (1740–1815), 747
Clellamin, Doreen (b. 1941), 51
• Clemens, James E. (b. 1966), 39, 50, 121, 151, 171, 198, 206, 211, 280, 287, 310, 342, 351, 353, 426, 489, 522, 524, 572, 635, 810
• Clemens, Philip K. (1941–2009), 281
• Clock, Leenaerdt (16th c.), 45
• Clymer Kurtz, Christopher (b. 1978), 276
• Clymer Kurtz, Maria (b. 1977), 276
Cober, K. L (1902–1993), 717
Coffin, Henry Sloane (1877–1954), 210
• Coffman, S. F. (1872–1954), 40
Cole, John (1774–1855), 119
Cole-Turner, Ronald S. (b. 1948), 508
Colligan, Richard Bruxvoort (b. 1967), 43
Colón, Carlos (b. 1966), 242
• Columbus Mennonite Church (USA), *1042*
Conseil d'Eglises chrétiennes en France, *989*
Constantine, Laila (b. 1959), 675
Converse, Charles C. (1832–1918), 628
Cooney, Rory (b. 1952), 412, 736
Coote, Constance (1844–1936), 484
Copes, V. Earle (1921–2014), 508
Cortez, Jaime (b. 1963), 703
Cory, Julia (1851–1934), 34
Costen, Melva Wilson (b. 1933), 193, 681
Cowper, William (1731–1800), 618
Cox, Frances E. (1812–1897), 101
Cranmer, Thomas (b. 1489), *860*
• Crissman, Seth (b. 1986), 691, 777
Crocker, Matt (b. 1987), 456
• Croegaert, Jim (b. 1946), 225, 629
Croft, William (1678–1727), 203
Croly, George (1780–1860), 557
Crosby, Fanny J. (1820–1915), 47, 84, 100, 435, 626
Crossman, Samuel (1623–1684), 320
Crouch, Andrae (1942–2015), 669
Crüger, Johann (1598–1662), 114, 330, 624
Crum, John Macleod Campbell (1872–1958), 353
Cuéllar, Guillermo (b. 1955), 102
Cummings, William H. (1831–1915), 247
Cutts, Peter (b. 1937), 56

Daigle, Gary (b. 1957), 736
Dalles, John A. (b. 1954), 528
Damon, Daniel Charles (b. 1950), 68, 636

Damon, W. (ca. 1540–1591), 465
Daniels, Andrew, 829
• Daniels, Barb (b. 1945), *864*
Daniels, Harold M. (1927–2015), *880*
Danish traditional tune, 690
Darwall, John (1731–1789), 4, 80
Dauermann, Stuart (b. 1944), 847
Dávila, Manuel (1924–2014), 464
Daw, Carl P., Jr. (b. 1944), 56, 197, 201, 222, 226, 326, 418, 534, 580, 585, 787
Dawn, Marva J. (b. 1948), 9
Day, Dorothy (1897–1980), *1036*
Day, George H. (1883–1966), 307
• de Ávila, Andrea, *853*, *1042*
de Benoît, Claire-Lise (1917–2008), 387
de Courrèges, Gaëtan (b. 1941), 403
de Giardini, Felice (1716–1796), 750
Dearmer, Percy (1867–1936), 331
Decius, Nicolaus (1485–1546), 38
DeMey, Gregg (b. 1972), 9, 807
Democratic Republic of the Congo (Tshiluba) traditional tune, 767
• Denck, Hans (1495–1527), *928*
• Dengler, Lee (b. 1949), 404, 458, 625
• Dengler, Susan Naus (b. 1949), 625, 630
Densmore, Frances (1867–1957), 742
• Derstine, Jerry (JD Martin) (b. 1947), 622, 719
DeShazo, Lynn (b. 1956), 132, 169
Dexheimer-Pharris, William (b. 1956), 102, 760
Didache, 477
Diephouse, David J. (b. 1947), 93
Dix, William C. (1837–1898), 267, 277
Doane, William H. (1832–1915), 47, 84
• Dock, Christopher (ca. 1698–1771), 515
Doddridge, Philip (1702–1751), 217
Doerksen, Brian (b. 1965), 29, 96
Donaldson, Andrew (b. 1951), 403, 425, 507, 579, 582, 800
Doran, Carol (b. 1936), 87, 372, 677
Dorsey, Thomas A. (1899–1993), 610
Draper, William H. (1855–1933), 81
Dubois, Theodore (1837–1924), 138
Duck, Ruth (b. 1947), 71, 112, 194, 196, 273, 636, 642, 734, 735, 807, *868*
• Dueck, Michelle (b. 1981), *1016*
• Dueck, Paul (b. 1956), 157
Dufner, Delores (b. 1939), 1, 38, 122, 328, 342, 459, 520
Dunstan, Sylvia G. (1955–1993), 157, 410, 432, 433, 441, 474
Dutch hymntune, 22, 34, 352, 766
Dvořák, Antonín (1841–1904), 533
Dykes, John B. (1783–1826), 76, 286, 573

Edgar, Mary S. (1889–1973), 550
Edwards, Robert L. (1915–2006), 745
Ehret, Walter (1918–2009), 264
Eilers, Joyce Elain (1941–2009), 839
Elderkin, George D. (1845–1928), 274
Ellerton, John (1826–1893), 506
Elliott, Charlotte (1789–1871), 560
Ellor, James (1819–1899), 364
Elvey, George J. (1816–1893), 123, 408
• Engle, Steve (b. 1943), 416
English hymn text (19th c.), 250
English hymntune, 74, 177, 208, 250, 303, 346, 359, 363, 695
English Language Liturgical Consultation, *892*, *989*
English traditional tune, 267, 522, 524, 536
• Enns, Leonard (b. 1948), 200
Episcopal Church (USA), *The Book of Common Prayer* (1979), *956*, *989*, *1026*, *1054*
• Epp-Stobbe, Eleanor, *1055*
Evangelical Lutheran Church in Canada and Evangelical Lutheran Church in America (USA), *890*, *915*, *1019*, *1032*, *1034*, *1052*
Evans, David (1874–1948), 28
Excell, Edwin O. (1851–1921), 163

Faber, Frederick W. (1814–1863), 156, 575
Falk, Johann D. (1768–1826), 254
Falla, Terry (b. 20th c.), *1020*
Farjeon, Eleanor (1881–1965), 495
Farrell, Bernadette (b. 1957), 199, 715
Farrington, Harry W. (1880–1930), 573
Fawcett, John (1740–1817), 831
Featherstone, William R. (1846–1873), 133
Fedak, Alfred V. (b. 1953), 237, 542, 550, 618, 709, 755, 758
Feiten, Dan (b. 1953), 477
Feliciano, Francisco (1941–2014), 501
Ferguson, Manie P. (1850–1932), 375
Ferretti, Salvatore (1817–1874), 849
Fieldes, Mia (b. 1983), 349
Filipino prayer, anon. (20th c.), *1033*
Filipino traditional tune, 720
Filitz, Friedrich (1804–1876), 756
Finnish traditional tune, 143
First University United Methodist Church, *1015*
Fischer, William G. (1835–1912), 761
Fliedner, Federico (1845–1901), 244
• Flores, Gilberto (b. 1945), 768
Fortunatus, Venantius (530–609), 331
Fosdick, Harry Emerson (1878–1969), 716
Foster, Valeria A. (b. 1935), 252
Founds, Rick (b. 1954), 365
Fox, Sister Ruth, OSB (USA), (1985), *1058*
Francis of Assisi (ca. 1181–1226), 81, 713, *991*
Franck, Johann (1618–1677), 624
Franz, Ignace (1808–1852), 126
Frayssé, Claude (1941–2002), 131
Frazier, Philip (1892–1964), 128
• Frederick, Don, 416
French hymn text, 249, 325
French hymntune, 45, 249, 287, 342, 353
French traditional tune, 65, 238, 432, 788
• Friesen, Joelle (b. 1994), *881*
Frye, Michael (b. 20th c.), 584
• Funk, Joseph (1778–1862), 402
• Fyock Norris, Joan (b. 1938), 57, 179, 266, 440, 510

Gabaráin, Cesáreo (1936–1991), 283
Gaither, Gloria (b. 1942), 718
Gaither, William J. (b. 1936), 718
Gałuszka, Jacek (b. 1965), 360
Gambrell, David (b. 1972), 146, 404, 460, 694
Ganda traditional tune (Swahili), 367
Garnaas-Holmes, Steve, (b. 1953) *1011*
Gastoldi, Giovanni G. (1582–1609), 666
Gauntlett, Henry J. (1805–1876), 746
Gebhardt, Ernst H. (1832–1899), 668
Gelineau, Joseph (1920–2008), 148
German traditional tune, 158, 216
Genevan Psalter (16th c.), 5, 71, 101, 212, 424, 552
Gerhardt, Paul (1607–1676), 215, 325
German hymn text, 130, 216, 350
German hymntune, 62, 88, 130, 146, 182, 260, 313, 358, 444, 813
German traditional tune, 216
Gesius, Bartholomäus (1562–1613), 577
Getty, Keith (b. 1974), 332, 796
Ghanaian prayer, *993*
Ghanaian text and tune (Twi), 607
Gibbons, Orlando (1583–1625), 46
Gibson, Colin (b. 1933), 27, 653
Gillard, Richard (b. 1953), 778
Gillette, Carolyn Winfrey (b. 1961), 179, 278, 513

Gillis, Frederick E. (1940–2013), *906*
Glaser, Carl G. (1784–1829), 764
Godel, Didier (b. 1945), 403
• Goerzen, Peter (b. 1984), *1044*
Gondo, Alexander (b. 1936), 2
González, Justo (b. 1937), *927*
• Gonzol, David J. (b. 1955), 362, 585
• Good, Brenton (b. 1978), *723*
Good, Linnea (b. 1962), 63, 541, 683
• Good, Merle (b. 1946), 756
Goodson, Albert A. (b. 1933), 599
Gordon, Adoniram J. (1836–1895), 133
Goss, John (1800–1880), 75, 428
Goudimel, Claude (1514–1572), 212, 424, 552
Gould, John E. (1821–1875), 340
• Graber, David (b. 1942), 8, 59
• Graber, Katie (b. 1976), 142, 176, 299, 603
• Graber, Ora (1903–1981), 577
Grant, Amy (b. 1960), 398
Grant, David (1833–1893), 660
Grant, Joan Jordan (b. 1939), *863*
Grant, John W. (1919–2006), 53
Grant, Robert H. (1779–1838), 74
Greatorex, Henry W. (1813–1858), 430
Green, Fred Pratt (1903–2000), 83, 124, 269, 395, 547
Gregory the Great (d. 604), 305
Gregory, Paul R. (1920–2012), 589
• Grieser, Nathan (b. 1986), 389, 749
Grindal, Gracia (b. 1943), 80, 140, 793
Grissom, Mary Allen, 801
• Gross, Leonard (b. 1931), *1003*
Gruber, Franz (1786–1863), 244
Guarani traditional tune, 620
Guatemalan text and tune, 838
• Gudin, Sylvie, *866*
Gungor, David (b. 1986), 494
Gungor, Lisa, 551
Gungor, Michael (b. 1980), 551
Gutiérrez-Achon, Raquel (b. 1927), 283

Haldeman, W. Scott (b. 1966), *862*
• Hallman, Eli S. (1866–1955), 733
Hamilton, Frank (b. 1934), 803
Hamilton, Maggie, 538
Hamilton, Roddy (b. 1966), *873*
Hamm, Barbara (b. 1943), 149, 461
• Hamm, Marilyn Houser (b. 1951), 282, 477, 622
Hampton, Calvin (1938–1984), 229, 507
Hanaoka, Nobuaki (1946–2011), 115
Handel, George F. (1685–1759), 253, 355
Hankey, Catherine (1834–1911), 761
• Harader, Joanna (b. 1975), *851, 854, 896, 1017, 1022, 1065*
• Harder, Meg, *104*
Harding, James P. (1850–1911), 272
• Harding, Rosemarie Freeney (1930–2004), *1024*
Harkness, Georgia (1891–1974), 710, 750
Harling, Per (b. 1948), 61
• Harrison, Ryan (b. 1974), 422
• Harsha, Kathryn (b. 1973), 209
• Hart, Phil (b. 1949), 771
Hascall, Jefferson (1816–1868), 662
Hassler, Hans L. (1564–1612), 325
Hastings, Thomas (1784–1872), 486, 643
Hatch, Edwin (1835–1889), 737
Hatton, John (1710–1793), 414
Haugen, Marty (b. 1950), 10, 36, 41, 99, 117, 297, 344, 442, 504, 588, 644, 671, 700, 744
Hausmann, Julie K. (1825–1901), 631
Havergal, Frances R. (1836–1879), 759, 760
Havergal, William (1793–1870), 316
Hawn, C. Michael (b. 1948), 367
Haydn, Franz Joseph (1732–1809), 197
Hayes, Philip (1738–1797), 695
• Heap of Birds, John (1894–1966), 8
Heber, Reginald (1783–1826), 76, 272
Hebrew traditional, 192
Hedge, Frederick H. (1805–1890), 421
• Hedrick Miller, Jessica (b. 1988), 591
Heermann, Johann (1585–1647), 330
Heizmann, Klaus (b. 1944), 739
Hellerman, Fred (b. 1927), 706
Helser, Jonathan David (b. 1978), 195
Hemy, Henri F. (1818–1888), 575
Henry, Jackson (b. 1978), 438
Herbert, George (1593–1633), 48
Hernández, Ana (b. 1957), 731
• Herr, Amos (1816–1897), 496
Herzberger, F. W. (1859–1930), 358
Hesla, Bret (b. 1957), 102, 312
Hewitt, Godfrey (1909–2002), 76
Hildegard of Bingen (1098–1179), 55, 376, 663, 788, *900*
Hindalong, Steve (b. 1959), 178
Hine, Stuart K. (1899–1989), 436
Hodges, Edward (1796–1867), 103, 809
Hodoroaba-Roberts, Sida, 593
• Hofer, Michelle (b. 1974), *780*
Hoffman, Elisha A. (1839–1929), 160, 555
Holden, Oliver (1765–1844), 364, 411
• Holliman, Lenora Hart, 181
• Holsapple, Josh (b. 1997), 332
• Holsopple, Jerry L. (b. 1957), 844
Holst, Gustav (1874–1934), 527 , 814
Holzschuher, Heinrich (1798–1847), 254
Hopp, Roy (b. 1951), 407
Hopson, Hal (b. 1933), 466
Horman, John D. (b. 1946), 144
Horn, Johann (ca. 1490–1547), 348, 797
• Horst, Cristina, *1042*
Horton, Zilphia (1910–1956), 803
• Hostetler Meyer, Brenda (b. 1957), 129, 360, 434, 510
Houghton, Israel (b. 1971), 33
Houston, Joel (b. 1979), 456
How, William W. (1823–1897), 672
Howard, Juliana (b. 20th c.), 587
• Howard, Melanie A. (b. 1986), *385*
Hoyle, Richard B. (1875–1939), 355
Hreib, Manal (b. 20th c.), 808
Hu, Te-ngai (20th c.), 498
• Hubbell, Lisa (b. 1961), 396
• Hubmaier, Balthasar (ca. 1480–1528), 402, *937*
• Huffaker, Perry Lee (1902–1982), 827
Hughes, Howard (b. 1930), 457
Hughes, John (1873–1932), 606, 716
Hughes, Tim (b. 1977), 227, 772
Huh, Paul Junggap (b. 1962), 755
Huijbers, Bernard (1922–2003), 22
Hull, Asa (1828–1907), 668
Husband, John J., 91
Husberg, Amanda (b. 1940), 452, 528, 535
• *Hymnal: A Worship Book* (1992), 360, 605, 623, *932, 961, 965, 966, 970, 971, 974, 981, 983, 996*

Ibrahim, Gregorios Yohanna, Metropolitan Mar (b. 1948), 702
Idle, Christopher (b. 1938), 537, 530, 554
Indian hymn text (Telugu), 425
Indian prayer, *1012*
Indian text and tune, 753
Indian traditional tune, 443
Infante, Pedro (1917–1957), 771
Ingram, Jason (b. 1974), 775
Iona Community (arr.), 136, 284, 428, 546, 838
Ireland, John N. (1879–1962), 154, 320
Irish hymn text, 549
Irish hymntune, 344, 485, 652
Irish traditional tune, 412, 549, 618, 636, 657

Irvine, Jessie S. (1836–1887), 660
Isaac of Stella (1100–1169), *1057*
Israeli text and tune, 842
Iverson, Daniel (1890–1977), 740

Jabusch, Willard F. (b. 1930), 283
Jackson, Robert (1840–1914), 737
Jacob, Pierre, 403
Jacobi, Johann Christian (1670–1750), 463
James, Mary Dagworthy (1810–1883), 619
James of Jerusalem (1st c.), 65
Janus, Martin (1620–1682), 639
• Janzen, Jean (b. 1933), 121, 198, 376, 426, 739
Japanese traditional tune, 115
Jarman, Thomas (1776–1861), 78
Jennings, Carolyn (b. 1936), 464
• Jeuriaenss, Tijs (16th c.), *1001*
John of Damascus (ca. 675–787), 348
Johnson, Brian (b. 1978), 195
Johnson, Christopher (b. 1962), 537
Johnson, David N. (1922–1987), 735, 829
Johnson, Gord (b. 1955), 532
Johnson, J. Rosamund (1873–1954), 611
Johnson, James W. (1871–1938), 611
Johnson, Jaylene, 166
Johnson, Joseph (1848–1926), 539
Johnson, Nelsie T. (1912–2009), 689
Johnson, Norman (1928–1983), 443
• Johnson, Sarah Kathleen (b. 1986), 200, 221, 308, *916*, *917*, *918*
• Johnson-Evers, Connie (b. 1966), 598
Joncas, Michael (b. 1951), 462, 641
Jones, David Hugh (1900–1983), see John Ribble
Jones, Jacque B. (b. 1950), 44, 213, 344, 535
Jones, Joseph T. (1902–1983), 681
Jordan, Leslie (b. 20th c.), 848
Joseph, Ravela (b. 1937), 425
Josselyn-Cranson, Heather (b. 1973), 175, 460
• Juhnke, Anna (1940–2005), *767*
Julian of Norwich (1343–ca. 1417), 426, 586, 676
Jung, Carl (1875–1961), 421

"K" in Rippon's *Selection of Hymns*, 592
Kaan, Fred (1929–2009), 366, 431, 485, 705
Kabemba, Joseph (b. 20th c.), 413
Kaple, Kirby (b. 20th c.), 92
Kappauf, Carolyn, 413
Kasbohm, Donna (b. 1933), 196
Kassia (8th c.), 142
• Kauffman, Bradley (b. 1974), 328, 553, 662
• Kauffman, Lloyd (b. 1944), 540
• Kempf, Jeremy (b. 1979), 439, 811
Ken, Thomas (1637–1711), 70, 71, 505
Kendrick, Graham (b. 1950), 493, 712
Kenyan traditional, 159, 845
Kervin, William (b. 1959), *948*
Kethe, William (d. 1594), 5
Key, Stephen (b. 1965), 437, 633
Khill, Yusuf (1931–2015), 321
Kilpatrick, Bob (b. 1952), 754
Kimbrough, S. T., 413
Kiowa text and tune, 400
• Kirchner, Shawn (b. 1970), 202, 422, 634
Kirk, James M. (1854–1945), 375
Kirkpatrick, William (1838–1921), 95, 510, 626
• Klaassen, Walter (b. 1926), 813
• Klassen, J. Tyler (b. 1958), *183*
• Klassen, Sarah (b. 1932), *871*
Knapp, Phoebe P. (1839–1908), 435
Knapp, William (1698–1768), 305
Kocher, Conrad (1786–1872), 120, 277
• Kolb, Abram B. (1862–1925), 361
Krause, Jonathan (1701–1762), 497
• Kraybill, J. Nelson (b. 1954), 487, *929*
• Krehbiel, Doug (b. 1957), 181, 768
• Krehbiel, Jude (b. 1945), 181, 768
• Kreider, Andrew (b. 1967), 141
Kremser, Eduard (1838–1914), 34
Krisman, Ronald F. (b. 1946), 224, 480
• Kropf, Marlene (b. 1943), *853*, *899*, *988*
Kushner, Rabbi Harold (b. 1935), *1048*
Kyamanywa, Bernard (b. 1938), 341

• Lachman, Becca J. R. (b. 1980), 42
Lafferty, Karen (b. 1948), 417
Landsberg, Max (1845–1927), 204
Lao-Tse (4th–6th c. BCE), *1046*
Laotian text and tune, 525
L'Arche Community, 581
Latin American text and tune, 487, *901*, *1025*
Laud, William (1573–1645), *1004*
LaValley, A. Jeffrey (b. 20th c.), 69
Layritz, Friedrich (1808–1859), 216
Leach, Richard (b. 1953), 211, 280, 466, 758
Lee, Geonyong (b. 1947), 391
• Lee, SaeJin (b. 1986), *12*
• Lehman, Bradley P. (b. 1964), 124, 301, 343, 548
Lehman, F. M. (1868–1953), 162
Lehman Mays, Claudia (1892–1973), 162
Leman, Wayne (b. 1949), 181
Leonard, David (b. 1982), 848
Leoni, Meyer (1750–1797), 190, 204
Les Petites Soeurs de Jésus, 581
Lewis-McLaren, Grace (b. 1939), 368
Liberius, R. F., 693
Light, Gordon (b. 1944), 582, 802
Ligthelm, Salomon (b. 20th c.), 456
Lillenas, Haldor (1885–1959), 170
Lindemann, Johan (1549–1631), 666
Lindholm, Jeannette M. (b. 1961), 208, 229, 652
Lockward, Jorge (b. 1965), 153, 593
Lockwood, George (b. 1946), 283, 526
Loder, Ted (b. 1930), *1008*, *1021*
• Loepp Thiessen, Anneli (b. 1995), 299, 376, 455, 630, *954*
• Loepp Thiessen, Ingrid (b. 1961), *977*, *979*
• Loewen, Harris J. (b. 1953), 157, 176, 254, 377, 399
Loh, I-to (b. 1936), 2, 262, 481
Longfellow, Samuel (1819–1892), 46, 503
• Longhurst, Christine (b. 1959), *879*, *957*
Lorenz, Edmund S. (1854–1942), 7
Lovelace, Austin C. (1919–2010), 765
Lowry, Robert (1826–1899), 31, 129, 333, 605, 667
Lubben, Dave (b. ca. 1976), 561
Lubis-Nainggolan, Tilly (1925–2002), 93
Luna, Félix César (1925–2009), 242
Luther, Martin (1483–1546), 140, 214, 263, 421, 463, 571, *912*
Lutkin, Peter C. (1858–1931), 846
Lyte, Henry F. (1793–1847), 75, 502

MacDonald, George (1824-1905), 263
• Mack, Alexander, Sr. (1679–1735), 577
MacKay, William P. (1839–1885), 91
Macksoud, Anne (b. 1942), *891*
McFarland, S. M. (18th–19th c.), 402
McLeod, Diana, 273
Maher, Matt (b. 1974), 155, 167, 349, 479, 494, 741
Mahler, Michael (b. 1981), 790
Maimonides, Moses (1138–1204), 204
Malan, Henri Abraham César (1787–1864), 488, 759
Mam, Barnabas (b. 1950), 769
Manchala, Vinita, 425
Manderfeld, Christine (b. 1938), 614
Manibusan, Jesse (b. 1958), 732
Mann, Newton (1836–1926), 204
• Manz, Felix (1498–1527), 444

Maquiso, Elena (1914–1995), 720
Maracle, Jonathan, 24
Marchionda, James V. (b. 1958), 512
• Mark, Arlene, *953*
Marlatt, Earl (1892–1976), 249
• Marpeck, Pilgram (1495–1556), 749, *971*, *1002*
Marshall, Jane (1924–2019), 406
Marshall, W. S. (probable pseudonym), 375
Martin, Karl (b. 20th c.), 92
Martinez, Ana Victoria Aguilera (b. 1950), *1025*
Martínez, Raquel Mora (b. 1940), 153
Mason, Lowell (1792–1872), 240, 259, 323, 488, 497, 658, 759, 764, 831
Mass of the Roman Rite, *905*
• Massamba, Stockwell (b. 1990), 648
• Massanari, Eric (b. 1968), *920*
Massie, Richard (1800–1887), 463
Matheson, George (1842–1906), 608
Matsikenyiri, Patrick (b. 1937), 68
Maule, Graham (1958–2019), 30, 287, 540, 794
Maurus, Rabanus (ca. 776–856), 53
Mayberry, Pat (b. 1950), 806
McCall, Richard D., *989*
McClelland Gay, Annabeth (1925–2020), 569
McCracken, Sandra (b. 1977), 60
McDade, Carolyn (b. 1935), 368
McGranahan, James (1840–1907), 590
McGuire, Jan (b. 1960), 509
McIntyre, Dean (b. 1925), 657, 805
McKay, V. Michael (b. 1952), 388
McLaren, Brian (b. 1956), 568
Mead, Joy, *1005*
Medema, Ken (b. 1943), 514, 682
Medicine Eagle, Brooke (b. 1943), 836
Medieval tune, 463, 579
Medley, Samuel (1738–1799), 347
Mendelssohn, Felix (1809–1847), 247, 616
Mendoza, Vicente (1875–1955), 760
• Mennonite Church USA, *941*
• *Mennonite Hymnal, The* (1969), *932*, *961*, *966*, *970*
• Mennonite World Conference, *925*
• Mennonite Worship and Song Committee, 45, 56, 64, 67, *73*, 86, 99, 158, 159, 165, 355, 552, 571, 581, 583, 615, 648, *687*, 797, 849, *850*, *878*, *901*, *913*, *926*, *930*, *931*, *932*, *933*, *934*, *935*, *936*, *937*, *939*, *940*, *941*, *942*, *943*, *947*, *950*, *951*, *952*, *959*, *960*, *961*, *962*, *964*, *965*, *966*, *967*, *968*, *969*, *970*, *971*, *973*, *974*, *975*, *976*, *980*, *981*, *982*, *983*, *996*, *1003*, *1052*, *1056*
Mercer, William (1811–1873), 241
Miller, Edward (ca. 1735–1807), 491
Miller, Frederick S. (1808–1895), 289
Miller, Mark A. (b. 1967), 6, 174, 673, 734, 802
• Miller, Merrill (b. 1960), *73*, *615*, *687*, *850*
Millham, W. T. T. (1880–1961), 323
Milman, Henry H. (1791–1868), 316
Milner-White, Eric (1884–1963), *1068*
Minchin, James (b. 1942), 501
• *Minister's Manual*, *938*, *981*
Mink, Barbara (b. 1937), 57
Minkoff, Frances (1915–2002), 706
Mo, Moon Seong, 800
Moen, Don (b. 1950), 125
Mohr, Joseph (1792–1848), 244
Molefe, S. C. (1917–1987), 90
Monk, William H. (1823–1889), 120, 182, 277, 313, 350, 502
Monoetius, Bartholomeus (16th c.), 576
Monsell, John S. B. (1811–1875), 122
Montgomery, James (1771–1854), 265, 317
Moody, Kathleen (b. 20th c.), 262
Mooiplaas congregation (South Africa), 679
• Moon, Irene Zacharias (b. 1955), 554
Moore, Bob (b. 1962), 474
Moore, James E. (b. 1951), 467
Moore, Thomas (1779–1852), 643
Mooring, Jack (b. 1988), 848
Mooring, Leeland (b. 1988), 848
Morgan, Mark (b. 20th c.), 511
Morgan, Reuben (b. 1975), 775
Morison, John (1750–1798), 259
Morley, Janet (b. 20th c.), *898*, *1010*, *1014*, *1029*
Morningstar, Dianne Huffman (1944–2010), 409
Morris, Sally Ann (b. 1952), 168, 175, 298, 519, 534, 580, 642, 656
• Morse, Kenneth I. (1913–1999), 131, 409, 827
• Mosley, Rebecca (b. 1972), 849
Mote, Edward (1797–1874), 159, 621
Moultrie, Gerard (1829–1885), 65
• Moyer, J. Harold (1927–2012), 161, 217, 222, 399, 576, 600, 640, 661
• Moyer Suderman, Bryan (b. 1969), 546, 757, 779, 841
Mukungu, Lubunda (b. 20th c.), 767
Munro, Mairi (?–2017), 679
Munyeli, Josephine (b. 1963), 849
Murray, James R. (1841–1905), 257
Murray, Robert (1832–1910), 746
Murray, Shirley Erena (1931–2020), 27, 144, 145, 149, 150, 373, 420, 481, 531, 567, 646, 697
Muscogee text and tune, 85
Mxadana, George (b. 20th c.), 650
Myrin, Jonas (b. 1982), 111, 521

Na, Young Soo (b. 1938), 289
• Nafziger, Charlene (b. 1972), 546, 603
• Nafziger, Kenneth (b. 1941), 739
Nägeli, Johann G. (1773–1836), 831
Naumann, Johann G. (1741–1801), 688
Naylor, Ruth (b. 1934), 402
Neale, John M. (1818–1866), 210, 236, 261, 315, 331, 342, 348
Neander, Joachim (1650–1680), 62, 88
• Neufeld Rupp, Anne (1932–2020), 57
• Neufeld Smith, Cynthia (b. 1954), 484
Neumann, Johann P. (1774–1849), 137
• Neustaedter Barg, Darryl (b. 1968), 72, 394, 798
New Zealand Prayer Book, A, *876*, *897*, *902*, *909*, *986*, *1027*, *1067*, *1069*
Newell, J. Philip (b. 1953), *865*
Newton, John (1725–1807), 163
Nicaraguan prayer, *1031*
Nicolai, Philipp (1556–1608), 226
Niebuhr, Reinhold (1892–1971), *1007*
Niles, D. T. (1908–1970), 720
Nishimura, Sugao (1871–1964), 589
Niwagila, Wilson (b. 1940), 367
Njotorahardjo, Niko (b. 1949), 82
Nockels, Christy (b. 1973), 155
Nuxalk text and tune, 51
Nyberg, Anders (b. 1955), 23, 473
Nystedt, Knut (1915–2014), 538

Oakeley, Frederick (1802–1880), 241
O'Brien, Francis Patrick (b. 1958), 701
Oden, William B. (1925–2013), *870*
Ojibwe text and tune, 742, *864*
Okoro, Enuma (b. 20th c.), *872*, *1028*
Olearius, Johannes (1611–1684), 212
Olson, Ernst (1870–1958), 517
Olson, Howard S. (1922–2010), 341, 367, 765
Oosterhuis, Huub (b. 1933), 22
Orthodox Church in America (USA), *907*
Owen, William (1813–1893), 708
Oxenham, John (1852–1941), 390
Pace, Adger M. (1882–1959), 275
Pagura, Federico J. (1923–2016), 387
Palestrina, Giovanni P. da (ca. 1525–1594), 350

Palo Cherwien, Susan (b. 1953), 164, 522
Pandopo, H. A. (b. 1935), 93
Paris, Twila (b. 1958), 86
Park, Chung Kwan (b. 1958), 755
• Park, Dona (b. 1995), *468*
Parker, Alice (b. 1925), 42, 44, 347, 352, 402, 515, 546, 564
Parker-Carver, Tamryn (b. 20th c.), 145
Parry, Charles H. H. (1848–1918), 531, 547, 787
Parry, Joseph (1841–1903), 659
Patrick of Ireland (ca. 5th c.), 43, 848
Patterson, Frederick D. (1901–1988), *992*
Paul, Samuel, 567
Pawltay (Kiowa) text and tune, 400
Peace, Albert L. (1844–1912), 608
Pearsall, Robert L. (1795–1856), 261
• Penner, Carol (b. 1960), *866*
Perera, Homero (1939–2019), 526
Perronet, Edward (1721–1792), 364, 411
Perry, Michael (1942–1996), 223, 814
Pettman, C. Edgar (1866–1943), 221, 255
Pierpoint, Folliott S. (FP 1835–1917), 120
Plains Indian traditional, 8, 59, 128
Plainsong, 53, 210, 236, 331, 418, 459, 491, 500
Poitras, Edward (b. 1932), 289, 755
Polish text and tune, 243
Pollock, Charles E. (1823–1897), 555
Polman, Bert (1945–2013), 552
Pope, Marion (b. 1928), 391
Pope, Michael (b. 20th c.), 545
Porter, Phil (b. 1953), 3
Pott, Francis (1832–1909), 350
Powell, Kathy (b. 1942), 302
Praetorius, Michael (1571–1621), 216, 427
• *Prayer Book for Earnest Christians, 1003*
Presbyterian Church (USA), *Book of Common Worship, 886, 888, 893, 901, 903, 910, 963, 994, 1009, 1053*
Price, Frank W. (1895–1974), 498
Prichard, Rowland H. (1811–1887), 218, 745
Proulx, Richard (1937–2010), 492, 787
Prudentius, Aurelius Clemens (348–410), 418
Puerto Rican text and tune, 224, 351
Pulkingham, Betty (1928–2019), 778
Purcell, Henry (1659–1695), 423

Rajkumar, Peniel Jesudason Rufus (b. 20th c.), 425
Ramírez, Ariel (1921–2010), 242
Ramshaw, Gail (b. 1947), *887, 944, 997*
Rankin, Jeremiah E. (1828–1904), 840
Redhead, Richard (1820–1901), 317
Redman, Beth (b. 1975), 637
Redman, Matt (b. 1974), 92, 111, 256, 479, 521, 637
Redner, Lewis H. (1831–1908), 245
Reed, Edith M. G. (1885–1923), 243
Reeves, Jesse (b. 20th c.), 116, 155, 324
• Regier, Matthew C., *445*
Reinagle, Alexander Robert (1756–1809), 390
Reindorf, Dinah (b. 1938), 795
• Rempel, John D. (b. 1944), 137, *971*
Rend Collective, 393, 597
Renville, Joseph R. (1779–1846), 128
• Ressler, Pax (b. 1989), 539
• Reuel, Jonathan (b. 1972), 763
Reynolds, William M. (1812–1876), 214
Ribbers, Joke (1933–2003), 431
Ribble, John (pseudonym for David Hugh Jones, 1900–1983), 177
Richards, John (b. 1939), 50
Richardson, Jan (b. 1967), *908, 990, 1049*
Riddle, Jennie Lee (b. 1967), 415
Rinckart, Martin (1586–1649), 114
Ríos, Mario (b. 1974), 116
Rippon, John (1751–1836), 364, 411
Rische, August (1819–1906), 158
Rizza, Margaret (b. 1929), 680
Robertson, Glenn, 49
Robinson, Robert (1735–1790), 563
Rockstro, William Smith (1823–1895), 697
Rodríguez, Ivette Herryman (b. 1982), 833
Rodriguez, Michael (b. 1987), 67
Röhl, Carl (19th–20th c.), 619
Rohmingliana, Evan (b. 20th c.), 165
Romanow, Douglas (b. 1966), 791
Romero, Jesús Adrián (b. 1961), 67
Romero, Oscar (1917–1980), *1038*
Romero, Toni, 456
Rosales, Luis (1910–1992), 543
Rosario, Ingrid (b. 1974), 139
Rosenberg, Daphna (b. 1967), 808
Rossetti, Christina G. (1830–1894), 255
Rowan, William P. (b. 1951), 205, 518, 676, 721
Rowthorn, Jeffery (b. 1934), 427, 774
Rubin, Steffi Geiser (b. 1950), 847
Rumi (1207–1273), *1047*
Runyan, Michael K. (b. 20th c.), 512
Runyan, William M. (1870–1957), 419
Rusbridge, Arthur E. (1917–1969), 243
Russell, Arthur T. (1806–1874), 215
• Russian Mennonite traditional tune, 64
Russian Orthodox tune, 147, 709
Russian traditional tune, 157, 484
Rutter, John (b. 1950), 264

Saboly, Nicolas (1614–1675), 258
Sadler, Gary (b. 1954), 169
Salinas, Juan (b. 1962), 89
Sammis, John H. (1846–1919), 570
Sánchez, Armando, 456
Sangle, Krishnarao Rathnaji (1834–1908), 753
• Saptojoadi (b. 1950), 26
Sarum Rite, 860, 999
• Sattler, Michael (1495–1527), 583
Scheer, Greg (b. 1966), 89, 675, 699, 755
Schein, Johann H. (1586–1630), 577
Schlottoff, Bernd, 387
• Schneider, Michael (16th c.), 571
Scholefield, Clement C. (1839–1904), 506
Scholtes, Peter (1938–2009), 387
Schop, Johann (ca. 1590 - 1667), 269, 639
Schrader, Jack (b. 1942), 37
Schubert, Franz (1797–1892), 137
Schubring, Julius (1806–1889), 616
Schulte, Anton, 387
Schultz, Larry E. (b. 1965), 452
Schulz, Johann A. P. (1747–1800), 747
Schutte, Daniel L. (b. 1947), 545
Schütz, Johann J. (1640–1690), 101
Schwartz, Stephen (b. 1948), 219
Scott, Clara H. (1841–1897), 738
Scottish hymntune, 602
Scottish traditional tune, 30, 209, 211, 495, 540
Scriven, Joseph M. (1819–1886), 628
Sears, Edmund H. (1810–1876), 220, 248
Sedio, Mark (b. 1954), 760
Seeger, Pete (1939–2014), 803
Seltz, Martin A., 88, 214
Sensmeier, Randall (b. 1948), 694
Shanks, Norman (b. 1942), *1051*
Shaw, Martin (1875–1958), 177, 495, 549, 770
• Shelly, Patricia (b. 1951), 374, 832
Shelton, Chris (b. 1978), 270
Sheppard, Franklin L. (1852–1930), 180
Shiota, Izumi (b. 1951), 843
Showalter, Anthony J. (1858–1924), 160
Shi, Qigui (b. 1929), 262
Sibelius, Jean (1865–1957), 649, 664, 710
Sicilian traditional tune, 254

Sigabi, Welile (?–2008), 679
Silcher, Friedrich (1789–1860), 631
• Simons, Menno (1496–1561), 439, 797, *921*
Simpson-Curenton, Evelyn (b. 1953). 274, 645
Skinner, John (1843–1927), 486
Sleeth, Natalie (1930–1992), 670, 835
Smallwood, Richard (b. 1948), 633, 684
Smart, Christopher (1722–1771), 266
Smart, Henry T. (1813–1879), 194, 265, 410, 705
Smilde, Bernard (b. 20th c.), 431
• Smiley, Daniel (b. 1973), 562
Smith, David, 22
Smith, H. Percy (1825–1898), 583
Smith, Michael W. (b. 1957), 398
Smith, Paul B. (20th c.), 443
Smith, Robert A. (1780–1829), 722
Smith, Walter C. (1824–1908), 98
Smith, William F. (b. 1941), 595
• Smucker, Gregory (b. 1960), 523
Somerville, Stephen, 581
Soper, Scott (b. 1961), 268
Sosa, Juan José (b. 1947), 833
Sosa, Pablo (1933–2020), 51, 136, 593, 665
South African hymn text, 23, 79, 90, 473, 793, 834
South African hymntune, 23, 79, 473, 793, 834
South African traditional tune, 32, 322
Spaeth, Harriet K. (1845–1925), 216
Spafford, Horatio G. (1828–1888), 617
Spanish hymntune, 28
Spanish traditional tune, 579
• Spaulding, Randall (b. 1965), 739
• Stamm, Gwen M. (b. 1956), *378*
Stanfill, Kristian (b. 1983), 155
Stanford, Charles V. (1852–1924), 83
Stemerick, Martine (b. 20th c.), 679
Stennett, Samuel (1727–1795), 661
Steurlein, Johann (1546–1613), 122
Stevenson, John A. (1761–1833), 503
Stone, Lloyd (1912–1993), 710
Stone, Samuel J. (1839–1900), 397
Strathdee, Jim (b. 1941), 207
Stratman, Paul C. (b. 1965), *912*
Strutt, Richard (1848–1927), 164
• Stucky, Nathan (b. 1977), 173
• Stucky, Pedro, 131
Stuempfle, Herman G., Jr. (1923–2007), 307, 465
Sudanese text and tune, 699
• Suderman, Bryan Moyer (b. 1969), 546, 757, 779, 841
Suppe, Gertrude C. (1911–2007), 283
Swain, Joseph (1761–1796), 600
Swazi (Xhosa) text and tune, 815
Swedish hymntune, 436, 517
Swee Hong, Lim (b. 1963), 145, 373
Syrian traditional tune, 702

Taizé community, 77, 118, 127, 228, 271, 327, 356, 370, 476, 543, 604, 627, 632, 654, 799, *1013*, *1018*
• *Take Our Moments and Our Days: An Anabaptist Prayer Book*, *985*, *987*
Tallis, Thomas (1505–1585), 326, 505
Tans'ur, William (1706–1783), 285
Tanzania (Haya) traditional tune, 341
Tanzanian text and tune, 765
Tappan, William B. (1794–1849), 318
Tate, Nahum (1652–1715), 253
Teresa of Ávila (1515–1582), 568, 604, *1035*
Teresa of Calcutta (1910–1997), *1037*
Tersteegen, Gerhard (1697–1769), 62
Teschner, Melchior (1584–1635), 215, 315
Theodulph of Orleans (ca. 760–821), 315
Therkelsen, Sverre (b. 1925), 538
Thew, Neill (b. 20th c.), *877*
Thomas à Kempis (1380–1471), 303
Thomas, Donn C., 645
Thompson, Will L. (1847–1909), 544
Thornburg, John (b. 1954), 400, 406, 423
Threlfall, Jeannette (1821–1880), 313
Thring, Godfrey (1823–1903), 286, 408
Thurman, Howard (1899–1981), *1064*
• Tice, Adam M. L. (b. 1979), 89, 148, 154, 168, 209, 242, 246, 279, 290, 298, 392, 442, 458, 475, 483, 519, 526, 542, 612, 623, 696, 751, 833
Tindley, Charles A. (1851–1933), 311, 595
Tirabassi, Maren C. (b. 1951), *863*
Tisserand, Jean (d. 1494), 342
Tomer, William G. (1833–1896), 840
Tomlin, Chris (b. 1972), 116, 256, 324, 775
Toolan, Suzanne (b. 1927), 480
Torrey, Richard, Jr., 668
Torwalt, Bryan (b. 1985), 369
Torwalt, Katie (b. 1988), 369
Touliatos, Diane (b. 20th c.), 142
Tourjee, Lizzie S. (1858–1913), 156
Tovey, Herbert G. (1888–1972), 740
Townend, Stuart (b. 1963), 332, 796
Towner, Daniel B. (1850–1919), 570
Trapp, Jacob (1899–1992), *855*
Tredinnick, Noël (b. 1949), 530
Troeger, Thomas (b. 1945), 5, 87, 343, 372, 407, 523, 553, 569, 656, 677
Troutbeck, John (1832–1899), 269
• Troyer, Scott, 571
True, Lori (b. 1961), 533, 565, 843
Trueblood, D. Elton (1900–1994), 152

Ukrainian Orthodox tune, 135
United Church of Canada, *857*, *922*, *944*
United Church of Christ, *895*, *944*
United Methodist Church, *944*, *972*
Ute text and tune, 836

Vajda, Jaroslav J. (1919–2008), 830
van Beethoven, Ludwig (1770–1827), 103, 513, 809
van de Laar, John (b. 1965), *1040*
van Dyke, Henry (1852–1933), 103
VanOss, Richard (b. 1953), 345
Vasile, Paul M. (b. 1976), 172, 429
Venerable Bede, The (8th c.), 363
• Villegas, Isaac (b. 1979), *1043*
Visser, Larry (b. 1962), 520
von Fallersleben, Heinrich A. H. (1798–1874), 130
• von Gunten, Neill, *864*
von Rist, Johann (1607–1667), 269
von Schlegel, Catharina A. D. (1697–1797), 664
von Zinzendorf, Nicolaus (1700–1760), 64, 813
Vories, William M. (1880–1964), 714
Vulpius, Melchior (ca. 1570–1615), 214, 366

Waddell, Chrysogonus (1930–2008), 490
Wade, John F. (1711–1786), 241
Waldmann, Andreas, 227
• Walking Roots Band, The, 434, 691, 777
Walt, J. D. (b. 20th c.), 324
Walter, William Henry (1825–1893), 273
Walther, Johann (1684–1748), 463
Walton, James G. (1821–1905), 575
Walworth, Clarence A. (1820–1900), 126
Ware, Henry (1794–1843), 340
Warner, Anna B. (1824–1915), 516
Warner, Steven C. (b. 1954), 586
Watt, Lauchlan M. (1867–1957), 556
Watts, Isaac (1674–1748), 31, 182, 203, 240, 322, 323, 414, 640, 691
• Weasley, Rachael (b. 1983), 792
• Weaver, Carol Ann (b. 1948), 35
Weaver, Nigel (b. 1952), 345

Webb, Benjamin (673–735), 303, 363
Webb, Charles H. (b. 1933), 80, 85, 300, 441
Webb, George J. (1803–1887), 223
Webbe, Samuel, Sr. (1740–1816), 643
Wehlander, Keri K. (b. 1956), 63
Weissrock, John (1938–2018), 545
Welsh hymntune, 98, 278
Welsh traditional tune, 237, 319, 812, 830
• Wenger, Marion (b. 1932), 444
Wesley, Charles (1707–1788), 78, 218, 191, 247, 274, 346, 548, 638, 659, 722, 764
Wesley, Samuel S. (1766–1837), 397, 837
West African tune, 559
Westendorf, Omer (1916–1997), 459, 812
Weston, M. Moran (1910–2002), *1039*
Wetzel, Richard D. (b. 1935), 387
Whalum, Wendell (1931–1987), 499, 816
White, B. F. (1800–1879), 57, 179
White, David Ashley (b. 1944), 308
• Whiteshield, Harvey (1860–1941), 59
Whittle, David W. (1840–1901), 590
Wiant, Bliss (1895–1975), 498
• Wiebe, Dallas (1930–2008), *919*
• Wiebe, Esther (b. 1932), 152
Wild Goose Resource Group, *852*, *856*, *867*, *874*, *884*, *913*, *914*, *946*, *1050*
Willan, Healey (1880–1968), 122
Willcocks, David (1919–2015), 241, 247
Williams, Kimberly A. (b. 1959), 55
Williams, Nolan, Jr. (b. 1969), 311, 684
Williams, Peter (1723–1796), 606
Williams, Ralph Vaughan (1872–1958), 48, 81, 208, 218, 270, 279, 433, 536, 672, 745
Williams, Thomas J. (1869–1944), 201
Williams, William (1717–1791), 606
Willis, Richard S. (1819–1900), 130, 220, 248
Wilson, Hugh (1766–1824), 722
Wilson, Lois M. (b. 1927), *1060*
Wilson-Hartgrove, Jonathan (b. 1980), *872*, *1028*
Winkworth, Catherine (1827–1878), 88, 114, 212, 226, 263, 463, 624, 666
Witkowski, Deanna (b. 1972), 54
• Witmer, Edith (1902–1982), 776
Witt, Christian Friedrich (ca. 1660–1717), 746
Wood, Adam Michael (b. 1982), 238
Woodward, George R. (1848–1934), 352, 427, *472*
Work, John W. (1871–1925), 252
World Council of Churches, *945*, *965*
Wren, Brian (b. 1936), 134, 254, 281, 301, 354, 359, 430, 478, 524, 565, 655
• Wright, David (b. 1966), 39, 206, 310, 810, *883*
Wu, Jing-ren, 262
Wunderlich, Erhardt Friedrich (1830–1895), 658

• Yamasaki, April, *978*
Yigdal (ca. 17th c.), 190, 204
• Yoder, Greg (b. 1986), 777
• Yoder, June Alliman (b. 1944), *929*
• Yoder, Lawrence M. (b. 1943), 26
• Yoder, Walter E. (1889–1964), 776
Young, Carlton (b. 1926), 134, 400
Young, Edward (1683–1765), 357
Young, John F. (1820–1885), 244
Young, Mark, 116
Younker, Brett (b. 1984), 92

Zach, Paul, 288
Zaki, Anne Emile, 675
Zambian (Tonga) text and tune, 578
Zamorano, Coalo (b. 1972), 116
Zaragoza, Rufino (b. 1957), 732
Zelman, Laurie (b. mid-20th c.), 6, 673
• Zercher, J. Randall (b. 1940), 556
Zeuner, Charles H. C. (1880–1964), 714
Zhu, Wei-yu (1890–1986), 262
Zimbabwean text and tune, 68, 566
Zimbabwean traditional tune, 322
• Zook, LeAnne (b. 1972), *869*, *1023*
Zschech, Darlene (b. 1965), 125, *926*
Zundel, John (1815–1882), 638
Zwingli, Ulrich (1484–1531), *911*

NON-ENGLISH LANGUAGES INDEX

Italic numbers refer to worship resources.

American Sign Language, *73*, *615*, *687*, *850*
Amharic, *850*
Arabic, 321, 675, 699, 707, 711, 805, 808, *850*
Cantonese, 443, *850*
Catalan, 118
Cheyenne, 8, 59, 181
Chin, 165, *850*
Cree vocables, 651
Dakota, 128
Dutch, 431
Filipino, 501
French, 71, 131, 249, 387, 401, 403, 559, 581, 593, 620, 628, 632, 683, 793, 849, *850*, *866*, *943*, *989*, *1052*
German, 45, 62, 64, 71, 88, 114, 126, 130, 137, 158, 227, 244, 254, 387, 497, 619, 624, 627, 631, 658, 668, 739, *850*, *989*
Greek, 147, 282, 620, 678, 692, 709, 795, 796
Guarani, 620
Hebrew, 192, 707, 805, 808, 842
Hmong, 628, *850*
Indonesian languages, 26, 82, 93, *850*
Japanese, 589, 843, *850*
Khmer, 769
Kiowa, 400
Korean, 289, 391, 755, 800, *850*
Lao, 525, 628, *850*
Latin, 52, 77, 94, 97, 241, 260, 271, 282, 370, 418, 492, 700, 707, 773
Lingala, 413, 648, *850*
Mandarin, 262, 481, 498, *850*
Marathi, 753
Mohawk vocables, 24
Muscogee, 85
Navajo, 443, 562, *850*
Nepali, *850*
Norwegian, 538
Nuxalk vocables, 51
Ojibwe vocables, 742
Oromiffa, *850*
Portuguese, 113, 127
Romanian, *850*
Shona, 2, 68
Sotho, 473
Spanish, 52, 57, 67, 71, 89, 102, 116, 118, 125, 127, 131, 136, 139, 151, 153, 224, 228, 242, 244, 283, 323, 346, 351, 365, 369, 387, 401, 415, 456, 464, 476, 480, 487, 526, 543, 593, 604, 620, 627, 665, 704, 731, 732, 760, 768, 771, 799, 833, 838, *850*, *853*, *901*, *927*, *943*, *989*, *1025*, *1038*, *1042*, *1052*
Swahili, 79, 159, 341, 367, 699, 765, 845, *850*
Telugu, 425
Thai, 443, *850*
Tonga, 578
Tshiluba, 767
Twi, 607
Urdu, 567, 693
Ute vocables, 836
Xhosa, 90, 679, 793, 815
Zulu, 23, 68, 79, 566, 834

TOPICS AND USES IN WORSHIP INDEX

Regular typeface indicates songs.
Regular typeface enclosed in brackets indicates worship resources.

Absolution
See: Assurance of Grace

Abuse
Calm Me, Lord, 680
Forgive, Forgive Us, Holy God, 149
God Made from One Blood, 523
In the Rifted Rock I'm Resting (Wehrlos und verlassen sehnt sich), 619
In Words of Truth, 148
Lord, Listen to Your Children, 682
Nothing Is Lost on the Breath of God, 653
[From all that is broken], 908
[Gracious God, when there is nothing], 994
[Great Physician, you touched the lives], 976
[Healing is central to the ministry of Jesus], 975
[May God bless you with a restless discomfort], 1058

Activism
See: Protest

Addiction
See also: Mental Health
Cast Out, O Christ, 285
Hold Us in Your Mercy, 736
O God, to You I Cry in Pain, 646
When Pain or Sorrow / Hold On, 612
[God, give me grace to accept], 1007
[Great Physician, you touched the lives], 976
[Most loving, most strong God], 900

Adoration
See: PRAISING: Adoration (125-139)
See also: Praise
Alleluia (Clemens), 635
Cantai ao Senhor (O Sing to the Lord), 113
Come, Now Is the Time to Worship, 29
Crown Him with Many Crowns, 408
Gott ist gegenwärtig (God Is Here among Us), 62
How Great Is Our God (Cuán grande es Dios), 116
Jesu, Joy of Our Desiring, 639
Lobe den Herren (Praise to the Lord, the Almighty), 88
Margam, satyam, jivam nive (Living, Moving, End and Beginning), 425
Naege itneun hyangyu okhap (To My Precious Lord), 755
O God, You Search Me, 199
Open the Eyes of My Heart (Ouvre les yeux / Abre mis ojos), 401
Revelation Song (Digno y santo), 415
There's Nothing Worth More (Nada vale más), 369
Tú estás aquí (My God Is Here), 67
We Long to Know Her, 44
You Dwell in the Songs / Restless, 741
Your Grace Finds Me, 521
[Come, Holy One, work upon us], 858
[Compassionate Christ, if you are my light], 1003
[I praise you, God—in the sanctuary], 886
[I saw a vast crowd], 110
[Sing the Goodness], 104
[To worship is to stand in awe], 855

Advent Candle Lighting
See also: Candle Lighting
Christe, lux mundi (Christ, You Are Light), 271
Dans nos obscurités (Within Our Darkest Night), 632
He Came Down, 239
Hope Is a Candle, 211
There Is More Love Somewhere, 804
[We light a candle for hope], 916
[We light this candle as a sign], 917

Advent of Jesus Christ
See: Jesus Christ: Advent

Affirming Faith
See: Confessing Faith

Affirming the Human Body
Christ Be in Your Senses, 721
Christ Has No Body Here but Ours, 568
God Calls You Good, 172
When Hands Reach Out, 513
[Dear ones, I plead with you], 105
[Tree of Life], 12

African American Heritage
See: Heritage: African American

Aging
Bring Many Names, 134
God Made from One Blood, 523
O Blessed Spring, 522
Time Propels Us like a Current, 507
When Aging Takes Its Toll, 520
When Memory Fades, 649
When the Storms of Life Are Raging, 595
[Gracious God, we celebrate life], 979

Agnus Dei / Lamb of God
Lamb of God / Cordero de Dios, 151
Ya hamala Allah (O Lamb of God), 321
[Jesus, Lamb of God], 892

All Saints' Day
See also: Death and Eternal Life
For All the Saints, 672
God, Be the Love, 43
Holy God, We Praise Thy Name, 126
Shall We Gather at the River, 667
So lange Jesus bleibt der Herr (As Long as Jesus' Reign Goes On), 64
Today We Sing with Thankfulness, 535
[Give thanks to God, who is good], 963
[Holy and righteous God, you created us], 1034
[O Ancient of Days, you have been our dwelling place], 920

Alleluia
Agneau de Dieu (O Lamb of God), 559
Alleluia (canon), 362
Alleluia (Clemens), 635
Alleluia (Doxology refrain), 72
Alleluia / Make a Joyful Noise (Psalm 100), 66
Alleluia (South African), 650
Alleluia (Ukrainian), 135
Halle, Halle, Hallelujah!, 752
Hallelujah (Syrian), 702
Heleluyan, 85
That Easter Morn, at Break of Day, 342
The Strife Is O'er, 350
Way way way (Ojibwe), 742
[Alleluia (ASL)], 73
[Alleluia! Christ is risen!], 875

Amen
Amen (African American), 689
Amen (Dresden), 688
Amen (Threefold), 690
God Welcomes All, 32
Masithi: amen (Sing Amen), 90
[Amen (ASL)], 687

Anabaptist Heritage: 16th Century
See: Heritage: 16th-Century Anabaptist

Angels
Let All Mortal Flesh Keep Silence, 65
My Latest Sun Is Sinking Fast, 662
[I saw a vast crowd], 110

Anger
See also: Protest
Gentle God, When We Are Driven, 150
God, Give Me Time, 144
How Can Our Anger Give Life, 792
Jesus Christ Is Waiting, 287
Lord Jesus, Come and Overturn, 146
My Soul Cries Out, 412
Strong, Peaceful Man of Galilee, 573
When I Can't Find My Way, 591
[In defiance of corruption and falsehood], 1040
[In our doubt and fear], 1044
[May God bless you with a restless discomfort], 1058
[The Lord is merciful and gracious], 186

Animals
See also: Creation
All Creatures Worship God Most High, 81
God Speaks to Us in Bird and Song, 539
Haneul naneun saeleul bora (See the Birds That Fly), 289
Light Dawns on a Weary World, 205
Morning Has Broken, 495
Ngayong nagdadapit hapon (When Twilight Comes), 501
Peace to You, 168
The Garden Needs Our Tending Now, 788
Touch the Earth Lightly, 145
We Dream of a Turning, 209
[Bless the Lord, O my soul], 185
[Confesemos nuestro pecado contra Dios], 901
[Sing the Goodness], 104
[Sing to the Lord a new song], 106
[Source and sustainer of life], 1009
[Tree of Life], 12
[We offer thanksgiving to our Creator], 864

Anniversaries
Christ Is Alive, and Goes Before Us, 565
O God, Our Help in Ages Past, 203
O God, You Search Me, 199
Time Propels Us like a Current, 507
We've Come This Far by Faith, 599
[Give thanks to God, who is good], 963
[In the beginning, before time], 884

Anointing
See also: SHARING OUR STORIES: Healing and Anointing (642-651)
See also: Church Leadership; Commissioning: Other; Healing; Vocation
All Who Are Thirsty, 49
Anointing Fall on Me, 645
Cast Thy Burden upon the Lord, 616
Christ Be in Your Senses, 721
Come Away from Rush and Hurry, 9
Hold Us in Your Mercy, 736
Kindle in Us Your Love, 54
Lord, Listen to Your Children, 682
Naege itneun hyangyu okhap (To My Precious Lord), 755
O Fiery Spirit, 55
O Holy Spirit, Root of Life, 376
Onyame wo mu o (In Your Sickness), 607
Open My Heart / Abre mi corazón, 731
Spirit of the Living God, 740
Take, O Take Me as I Am, 748
There Is a Balm in Gilead, 647
Use Us, God, 811
When Aging Takes Its Toll, 520
When We Must Bear Persistent Pain, 735

Woza nomthwalo wakho (Come, Bring Your Burdens to God), 679
[Are any of you suffering hardships], 727
[Great Physician, you touched the lives], 976
[Healing is central to the ministry of Jesus], 975
[Sovereign Majesty, we pray for the continued outpouring], 992

Ascension of Jesus Christ

See: Jesus Christ: Ascension of

Ash Wednesday

See also: Journey to the Cross; Lent
Create in Me a Clean Heart, 141
Out of the Depths I Cry to You, 140
Sign Us with Ashes, Merciful God, 304
The Glory of These Forty Days, 305
[A wilderness beckons us], 1011
[Remember: We are earth], 918
[The dust that shapes the journey], 873
[Whatever wilderness the Spirit], 1065

Assurance of Grace

See: RECONCILING: Assurance of Grace (156-174); WORSHIP RESOURCES: Reconciling (888-909)
See also: Confession of Sin; Forgiveness; Grace
All Will Be Well, 586
Balaacoolwe (Blessed Are the Persecuted), 578
Be Still and Know, 37
Blessed Assurance, 435
Christ Calls to Me, 542
Christ Has Broken Down the Wall, 174
Come, Let Us All Unite to Sing, 7
Come to Me, O Weary Traveler, 157
Come, Ye Disconsolate, 643
For All the Saints, 672
God Be with You Till We Meet Again, 840
How Firm a Foundation, 592
I Heard the Voice of Jesus Say, 536
I Love the Lord, 684
I Sing with Exultation, 444
Jesus, Lover of My Soul, 659
Make Me an Instrument of Your Peace, 713
More Than You Know, 598
Na nzela na lola (As Long as We Follow), 413
Nada te turbe, 604
No Longer Slaves to Fear, 195
Nothing Can Ever Come between Us, 654
Nothing Is Lost on the Breath of God, 653
Sometimes a Light Surprises, 618
We Walk by Faith, 588
When the Storms of Life Are Raging, 595
You Are All We Have, 701
[Christ—the Joy, the Truth], 907
[Dear Jesus, I confess my need of you], 926
[Do not fear, says God], 903.A
[Friends in Christ, God knows our needs], 888
[From all that is broken], 908
[God forgives you], 909
[Hear the good news!], 903.D
[Hear the words of Jesus: "Peace I leave with you"], 904
[If we have died with Christ], 903.C
[Let us confess our sin], 890
[May almighty God have mercy on us], 905
[May the Love which overcomes], 906
[Most loving, most strong God], 900
[Our righteousness is found in Christ alone], 903.B
[Peace be with you], 850
[Praise to God who has given us life], 902
[The Lord is merciful and gracious], 186
[Trusting in God's grace, let us confess], 938

Atonement

See also: Blood of Christ; Salvation; Sin
Ah, Holy Jesus, 330
Christ the Lord Is Risen Today (El Señor resucitó), 346
Christ, We Do All Adore Thee, 138
Come, Let Us All Unite to Sing, 7
Come, Thou Fount, 563
Dooládó' Shi Diyinda! (What a Wonderful Savior), 562
From Heaven Above to Earth I Come, 263
Go to Dark Gethsemane, 317
How Can We Worship Caesar's Cross, 308
In Christ Alone, 332
Just As I Am, without One Plea, 560
Kwake Yesu nasimama (Here on Christ the Rock I Will Stand), 159
Naege itneun hyangyu okhap (To My Precious Lord), 755
O Lord My God / How Great Thou Art, 436
O phi nong oei (Dear Friends, We're One), 525
O Sacred Head, Now Wounded, 325
Sing, My Tongue, the Song of Triumph, 331
To God Be the Glory, 84
We Praise Thee, O God, 91
We Read the Cross, 569
What Wondrous Love Is This, 564
Wonderful Grace of Jesus, 170
[From Bethlehem to Nazareth], 874
[Now, thanks to Christ Jesus], 786
[Our righteousness is found in Christ alone], 903.B

Baptism

See: CELEBRATING BAPTISM (441-458); WORSHIP RESOURCES: Celebrating Baptism (930-935); ART AND SCRIPTURE: Baptism (445-451)
All Who Are Thirsty, 49
Breathe on Me, Breath of God, 737
Come, My Way, My Truth, My Life, 48
Come, Thou Fount, 563
Count Well the Cost, 577
Every Time I Feel the Spirit, 681
Ey lou nis (Now I Know), 769
God, Be the Love, 43
Go in Grace and Make Disciples, 766
Go, My Children, 830
Holy Spirit, Truth Divine, 46
I Bind My Heart This Tide, 556
I Want Jesus to Walk with Me, 306
Lord, I Am Fondly, Earnestly Longing, 555
My Love Colors Outside the Lines, 582
New Earth, Heavens New, 377
Spirit of God! Descend, 557
Take My Life, and Let It Be, 759
Take My Life, That I May Be (Que mi vida entera esté), 760
True Evangelical Faith, 439
Who Are These, 360
Who Now Would Follow Christ, 576
[As John baptized Jesus in the Jordan], 940
[Come, all you who are thirsty], 14
[Do you not know that all who were baptized], 449
[From the River to the Wilderness], 445
[Hear the good news!], 903D
[Here is my servant, the one I uphold], 448
[I believe in God, the Father almighty], 923
[In Christ Jesus you are all children], 450
[Jesus' eleven disciples went to a mountain], 451
[Lead a life worthy of the calling], 446
[Loving God, you have baptized us], 1001
[When Flaming Dove Meets Rising Waters], 378
[While everyone was being baptized], 447

Baptism of Jesus

See: Jesus Christ: Baptism of

Benediction

See: Sending: Blessing

Benedictus / Zechariah's Song

Bless'd Be the God of Israel, 223
[Blessed are you, Lord, the God of Israel], 985.E

Bible

See: Word of God

Birth of Jesus Christ

See: Jesus Christ: Birth of

Blessing: Other

See also: Child Blessing; Sending: Blessing
Bless This Food and Bless Your People, 489
Christ Be in Your Senses, 721
God, Be the Love, 43
Life-Giver, Maker, God of All, 38
O Everlasting Love, 733
Peace to You, 168
The Lord, Your God Is with You, 173
Use Us, God, 811
[Christ be within us to keep us], 1069
[Faithful God, we give thanks], 933
[God dearly loves us], 1056
[God of all life, in you we live and move], 974
[God, who is Alpha and Omega], 962
[God will guide us continually], 985.H
[Gracious God, bless our cities], 1032
[May God bless you and keep you], 826
[May God bless you with a restless discomfort], 1058
[May God, who calls you to this ministry], 968
[May the blessing of the God of Sarah and Hagar], 1060
[May the God of endurance], 822
[May the God of glory], 1053
[May the God of hope], 987.I
[May the grace of Jesus Christ], 21
[May the Son of God], 1057
[May those who sow in tears], 821
[May we go forth into the world with courage], 1039
[Now may our Lord Jesus Christ], 819
[Now may the God of peace], 823
[Now, to the One who by the power], 824
[Some people brought children], 18
[Sovereign Majesty, we pray for the continued outpouring], 992
[The peace of God which passes all understanding], 1054
[This home is yours, my God], 958

Blessing: Sending

See: Sending: Blessing

Blood of Christ

See also: Atonement; Communion; Jesus Christ: Death of
Blessed Assurance, 435
I Am the Bread of Life (Yo soy el pan de vida), 480
In the Quiet Consecration, 484
Let All Mortal Flesh Keep Silence, 65
Let the Hungry Come to Me, 459
Remembrance, 479
Seed, Scattered and Sown, 477
So lange Jesus bleibt der Herr (As Long as Jesus' Reign Goes On), 64
When I Survey the Wondrous Cross (La cruz excelsa al contemplar), 323
When I Survey the Wondrous Cross (South Africa, Zimbabwe), 322
[Christ is the image of the invisible God], 189
[For I received from the Lord], 469
[Now, thanks to Christ Jesus], 786

Blue Christmas

See: Longest Night / Blue Christmas

Body of Christ

See also: Church; Communion; Community; Unity
Christ Has No Body Here but Ours, 568
Count Well the Cost, 577
Dhuh Pangeran (O Prince of Peace), 26
Here in This Place, 10
How Can I Say, 388
I Am the Bread of Life (Yo soy el pan de vida), 480
In Christ There Is No East or West, 390
Jésus, je voudrais te chanter (Lord Jesus, You Shall Be My Song), 581
Let All Mortal Flesh Keep Silence, 65
Let the Hungry Come to Me, 459

Longing for Light, 715
Lord, You Give the Great Commission, 774
May You Be Rooted and Grounded in Love, 396
One Is the Body, 386
Ososo (Come Now, O Prince of Peace), 391
Remembrance, 479
The Church's One Foundation, 397
We Are One in the Spirit, 387
What Is This Place, 22
When Hands Reach Out, 513
Will You Let Me Be Your Servant, 778
You're Not Alone, 779
[As John baptized Jesus in the Jordan], 940
[As we now receive you into the fellowship], 932
[At the table of Christ], 936
[By the grace of God we seek to live and proclaim], 925
[Christ has no body now on earth], 1035
[Christ is like a single body], 856
[Christ is the image of the invisible God], 189
[Creemos en Dios Padre todopoderoso], 927
[For I received from the Lord], 469
[In peace let us pray: O God, we give you thanks], 945
[Jesus washed the feet of his disciples], 950
[Lead a life worthy of the calling], 446
[Let your hearts be ruled], 818
[Now, thanks to Christ Jesus], 786
[The church is the body of Christ], 959
[What will you offer the body of Christ today], 1023
[You who open doors], 862

Call of God

See: God's Call

Call to Worship

See: Gathering; Welcome

Calling

See: God's Call

Camps and Retreats

See also: Children: Appropriate for; Creation: Beauty of; Evening; Morning; Rest
Be a Sower, 789
Be Still and Know, 37
Like a Rock, 63
Lord, You've Searched Me, 609
Sword into a Plowshare, 798
The Lord, Your God Is with You, 173
This Little Light of Mine, 762
[A wilderness beckons us], 1011
[Creator God, thank you for people and places], 954
[God of cosmos and quarks], 881
[Grow us slowly], 1030
[I praise you, God—in the sanctuary], 886
[Our lives are cluttered], 899

Candle Lighting

See also: Advent Candle Lighting; Peace Lamp Lighting
Between Darkness and Light, 808
Dans nos obscurités (Within Our Darkest Night), 632
Joyous Light of Heavenly Glory, 504
Kindle in Us Your Love, 54
This Little Light of Mine, 762
Thy Word Is a Lamp, 398
[In our doubt and fear], 1044
[In the beginning when it was very quiet], 852
[I will light a light in the name of the Maker], 867
[Lighting a candle], 1006
[We light a light], 865

Canticles

See: Benedictus / Zechariah's Song; Magnificat / Mary's Song; Nunc dimittis / Simeon's Song

Child Blessing

See: SHARING OUR STORIES: Child Blessing (508-510); WORSHIP RESOURCES: Sharing Our Stories—Child Blessing (969-972)
See also: Blessing: Other; Children / Childhood; Family; Reproductive Loss
Let the Children Come to Me, 512
Your Grace Finds Me, 521
[God, maker of galaxies, who numbers the hairs], 971
[Some people brought children], 18
[We give thanks to God for children], 969
[You have offered], 970

Child Consecration

See: Child Blessing

Child Dedication

See: Child Blessing

Children / Childhood

See also: Child Blessing; Family; Nurturing Faith
Child of Blessing, Child of Promise, 508
Children of the Heavenly Father, 517
Come On, Children, to the Gospel Feast, 511
God, Give Me Faith like a Child, 519
Helpless and Hungry, 268
Hosanna, Loud Hosanna, 313
Jesus Loves Me, 516
Let the Children Come to Me, 512
O Blessed Spring, 522
O Little Children, Gather, 515
See the Children Here Before Us, 509
Today Earth Is Singing, 510
[God, maker of galaxies, who numbers the hairs], 971
[Hear, O Israel], 187
[Some people brought children], 18
[We give thanks to God for children], 969
[You have offered], 970

Children: Appropriate for

See also: Camps and Retreats; Children / Childhood; Home: Worship and Prayer; Schools and Learning Communities
Alleluia (Clemens), 635
Alleluia (South African), 650
Amen (African American), 689
And I Will Raise You Up, 641
As You Go Out from Here, 841
Be a Sower, 789
Be Still and Know, 37
Be Thou My Vision, 549
Breathe on Me, Breath of God, 737
Christ, Be All around Me, 848
Christ Is Risen! Shout Hosanna!, 354
Come and See, 282
Come On, Children, to the Gospel Feast, 511
Come, Thou Fount, 563
Could It Be That God Is Singing, 42
Draw the Circle Wide, 802
El Senyor és la meva força (In the Lord I'll Be Ever Thankful), 118
Eternal Light, Shine in My Heart, 554
Everlasting God, on You I Call, 630
Every Time I Feel the Spirit, 681
Fill Us with Your Feast, 309
God, Be the Love, 43
God Calls You Good, 172
God Lights a Lamp, 299
God of Wonders, 178
God Speaks to Us in Bird and Song, 539
God Who Touches Earth with Beauty, 550
Guide My Feet, 816
Hacia Belén (Mary Journeyed), 224
Halle, Halle, Hallelujah!, 752
Helpless and Hungry, 268
Holy Lord, 314
How Can Our Anger Give Life, 792
I Am That Great and Fiery Force, 663
I Sing the Mighty Power of God, 182
Jesus, Be the Center, 584
Jesus, Help Us Live in Peace, 719
Jesus, Remember Me (Jesús, recuérdame), 327
Kindle in Us Your Love, 54
Kombo na Yesu (The Name of Jesus), 648
Kwake Yesu nasimama (Here on Christ the Rock I Will Stand), 159
Let's Walk Together, 6
Like a Rock, 63
Listen to the Word That God Has Spoken, 405
Lord, I Lift Your Name on High (Tu nombre levantaré), 365
Lord, Listen to Your Children, 682
Love the Lord Your God, 288
May You Be Rooted and Grounded in Love, 396
More Than You Know, 598
My Lighthouse, 597
My Love Colors Outside the Lines, 582
My Soul Cries Out, 412
Na nzela na lola (As Long as We Follow), 413
New Earth, Heavens New, 377
O Beautiful Star of Bethlehem, 275
O Lord, Hear My Prayer, 685
Ô toi, Seigneur / O God, We Call, 683
Planets Humming as They Wander, 175
Poor of the Earth, 213
Prabhoo Lay lay (Savior Jesus, Enfold Me), 567
Rain Down, 703
Sanna, sannanina, 79
Seeds, 777
Seek Ye First, 417
Segala puji syukur (All Our Praise), 82
Shepherd Me, O God, 744
Shukuru Yesu (We Thank You), 699
Solemn Stillness, Weary Streets, 276
Somebody Prayed for Me, 698
Somlandela (We Will Follow), 566
Sword into a Plowshare, 798
Take My Life, That I May Be (Que mi vida entera esté), 760
The Lord, Your God Is with You, 173
There Are Many Gifts, 374
There Is in Every Person, 751
There Were Angels Hovering Round, 251
There's a Wild Hope in the Wind, 828
There's Enough for All, 757
This Little Light of Mine, 762
Together, 389
Touch the Earth Lightly, 145
Tú has venido a la orilla (Lord, You Have Come to the Lakeshore), 283
Use Us, God, 811
Way way way (Ojibwe), 742
We Come, 225
We Dream of a Turning, 209
We Long to Know Her, 44
What a Friend We Have in Jesus, 628
What Is the World Like, 298
When at Creation's Dawn, 121
Will You Come and Follow Me, 540
You Are Holy, You Are Whole, 61
Your Love Is Washing Over Me, 166
You're Not Alone, 779
[Christ be within us to keep us], 1069
[Come among us, Holy Spirit, and create a community], 955
[Creator God, thank you for people and places], 954
[God be in my head], 999
[God forgives you], 909
[God of cosmos and quarks], 881
[God of mercy, we are sorry], 897
[God our sanctuary], 1042
[Holy God, you call us together], 857
[In our concerns and in our choices], 1051
[In the beginning when it was very quiet], 852
[I praise you, God—in the sanctuary], 886
[Lighting a candle], 1006
[Open our ears to hear your word], 866
[Peace be with you], 850
[Praying aloud spontaneously], 995
[Receive our thanks for night and day], 949
[Tree of Life], 12
[We have witnessed your commitment], 961
[We light a candle for hope], 916

Children's Time

See also: Children: Appropriate for; Children / Childhood

Come On, Children, to the Gospel Feast, 511
God Welcomes All, 32
Let the Children Come to Me, 512
Sizohamba naye (We Will Walk with God), 815
[Some people brought children], 18

Christ the King

See: Reign of Christ

Christmas

See: Jesus Christ: Birth of

Church

See: TELLING GOD'S STORY: Church (386-397); ART AND SCRIPTURE: Holy Spirit, Pentecost, Church (378-385)

See also: Body of Christ; Church Leadership; Church Membership; Community; Unity

Christ Has No Body Here but Ours, 568
Count Well the Cost, 577
Enviados somos de Dios (We Have Been Sent by God), 771
God Calls Us, 394
God of Grace and God of Glory, 716
Heart with Loving Heart, 813
Help Us to Help Each Other, 722
Here in This Place, 10
Holy Spirit, Come to Us, 58
Holy Spirit, Come with Power (Ven, Espíritu, cual viento), 57
Honja soriróneun (With My Voice Alone), 800
I Believe in God Almighty, 433
Life-Giver, Maker, God of All, 38
Lord, You Give the Great Commission, 774
Make Us One, 455
O Praise the Gracious Power, 87
Praise Be to God, 115
Somebody Prayed for Me, 698
Summoned by the God Who Made Us, 1
The Day You Gave Us, 506
What Is This Place, 22
Wind Who Makes All Winds, 372
You're Not Alone, 779
[Are any of you suffering hardships], 727
[As we now receive you into the fellowship], 932
[As you come to Christ the living stone], 381
[Baptism with water in the name of the triune God], 930
[Be sincere in your love for others], 384
[By the grace of God we seek to live and proclaim], 925
[Christ is like a single body], 856
[Creemos en Dios Padre todopoderoso], 927
[Empowering God, with your people], 965
[Every Christian is called], 964
[Friends, as we gather to eat the bread], 937
[Give thanks to God, who is good], 963
[God of covenant, when Jesus came up from the waters], 935
[God of covenant, your steadfast love], 960
[God of life, we thank you that our work], 953
[God, who is Alpha and Omega], 962
[God's Spirit calls, the church commissions], 966
[Hear what the Spirit is saying], 913.C
[How very good and pleasant it is], 17
[I believe in God, the Father almighty], 923
[I pledge with you], 967
[I was glad when they said to me], 16
[In Christ Jesus you are all children], 450
[Lead a life worthy of the calling], 446
[May God, who calls you to this ministry], 968
[Now, through the church], 385
[Now, to the One who by the power], 824
[Source of all hope and holiness], 863
[The church is the body of Christ], 959
[There are different kinds of gifts], 380
[We are a covenant people], 869
[We are not alone], 922
[We believe in one God, the Father, the Almighty], 924
[We have witnessed your commitment], 961
[What will you offer the body of Christ today], 1023
[When Flaming Dove Meets Rising Waters], 378
[When the day of Pentecost came], 379
[You are no longer foreigners], 382
[You have offered], 970

Church Leadership

See: WORSHIP RESOURCES: Sharing Our Stories—Church Leadership (964-968)

See also: Church; Commissioning: Other; Ministry; Ordination; Vocation

Anointing Fall on Me, 645
God the Spirit, Guide and Guardian, 534
How Clear Is Our Vocation, 547
Lord, You Give the Great Commission, 774
One Is the Body, 386
Spirit of the Living God, 740
Take, O Take Me as I Am, 748
Teach Me Thy Truth, 776
There Are Many Gifts, 374
Today We Sing with Thankfulness, 535
[Empowering God, with your people], 965
[Every Christian is called], 964
[God's Spirit calls, the church commissions], 966
[I pledge with you], 967
[Jesus, servant, at supper with your disciples], 1041
[May God, who calls you to this ministry], 968

Church Membership

See: WORSHIP RESOURCES: Sharing Our Stories—Church Membership (959-963)

See also: Church

Draw the Circle Wide, 802
For We Are Strangers No More, 409
Heart with Loving Heart, 813
Take, O Take Me as I Am, 748
There Are Many Gifts, 374
[As we now receive you into the fellowship], 932
[Baptism with water in the name of the triune God], 930
[Give thanks to God, who is good], 963
[God of covenant, when Jesus came up from the waters], 935
[God of covenant, your steadfast love], 960
[God, who is Alpha and Omega], 962
[The church is the body of Christ], 959
[We are a covenant people], 869
[We have witnessed your commitment], 961
[What will you offer the body of Christ today], 1023

Church of the Brethren Heritage

See: Heritage: Church of the Brethren

Church: Praying for

See: Praying: For the Church

City

See also: Rural Life

En medio de la vida (You Are the God within Life), 526
I Saw a Tree by the Riverside, 514
In the Heartbeat of the City, 530
Let's Walk Together, 6
Seek the Peace of the City, 206
You Are Salt for the Earth, 297
[Gracious God, bless our cities], 1032
[I saw a new heaven and a new earth], 339
[If there is to be peace in the world], 1046
[O Prince of Peace], 894
[Thus says the Lord, the God of Israel], 783

Clapping

See also: Music

Light Dawns on a Weary World, 205
You Shall Go Out with Joy, 847
[Clap your hands all you peoples], 108
[Hosanna! Hosanna!], 885

Comfort

See also: Suffering; Joy

Abide with Me, 502
All Will Be Well, 586
And I Will Raise You Up, 641
Be at Rest, 532
Be Still and Know, 37
Be Still, My Soul, 664
Blessed Assurance, 435
Calm Me, Lord, 680
Children of the Heavenly Father, 517
Come to Me, O Weary Traveler, 157
Come, Ye Disconsolate, 643
Comfort, Comfort, O My People, 212
El Senyor és la meva força (In the Lord I'll Be Ever Thankful), 118
Far Above the Noise of Life, 625
Far, Far Away / I Will Arise, 300
God Calls You Good, 172
Haneul naneun saeleul bora (See the Birds That Fly), 289
In the Bulb There Is a Flower, 670
In the Quiet Curve of Evening, 587
In the Rifted Rock I'm Resting (Wehrlos und verlassen sehnt sich), 619
Jesu, meine Freude (Jesus, Priceless Treasure), 624
Joys Are Flowing like a River, 375
Lord, Listen to Your Children, 682
Loving Spirit, 697
May the Face of God Shine on You, 844
My Lighthouse, 597
Nearer, My God, to Thee, 658
Nothing Can Ever Come between Us, 654
Nothing Can Separate Us, 171
Nothing Is Lost on the Breath of God, 653
Now, on Land and Sea Descending, 503
On Silken, Soft Wings, 676
Open, Lord, My Inward Ear, 548
O Thou, in Whose Presence, 600
Praise, My Soul, the King of Heaven!, 75
Precious Lord, Take My Hand, 610
Quietly, Peacefully, 533
Shepherd Me, O God, 744
Shout to the Lord (Cante al Señor),125
Still My Soul, 603
The Hand of God Shall Hold You, 671
The Lord's My Shepherd, 660
There Is a Balm in Gilead, 647
Thy Word Is a Lamp, 398
What a Friend We Have in Jesus, 628
When Grief Is Raw, 655
When Pain or Sorrow / Hold On, 612
When Peace like a River, 617
You Are All We Have, 701
Your Love Is Washing Over Me, 166
[Blessed are the poor in spirit], 295
[Dear God, let your word shine], 912
[Eternal God in whom we live], 982
[Eternal Strength, hold us], 983
[Everlasting God, you are our refuge], 981
[Great Physician, you touched the lives], 976
[I lift my eyes to the hills], 109
[In the face of death, we worship God], 980
[May God bless you and keep you], 826
[Merciful God, we wait], 977
[Now may our Lord Jesus Christ], 819
[O Lord, you have searched me], 724
[Rejoice in the Lord always], 726
[This home is yours, my God], 958

Commissioning: Other

See also: Church Leadership; Mission; Sending: Commissioning; Service; Vocation

God of Justice, 772
Here I Am, Lord, 545
How Clear Is Our Vocation, 547
Neno lake Mungu (Listen, God is Calling), 765
O Holy Spirit, by Whose Breath, 53
Spirit of Life, 368
The Church of Christ, in Every Age, 395
There Are Many Gifts, 374

You Are Salt for the Earth, 297
[As you come to Christ the living stone], 381
[Blessed be the ones who dance], 1049
[Christ has no body now on earth], 1035
[Christ is like a single body], 856
[Empowering God, with your people], 965
[Eternal God, you call us to ventures], 1068
[Every Christian is called], 964
[God dearly loves us], 1056
[God, just as you sent Joseph to Egypt], 957
[God of covenant, when Jesus came up from the waters], 935
[God's Spirit calls, the church commissions], 966
[I pledge with you], 967
[In deep gratitude for this moment], 946
[In defiance of corruption and falsehood], 1040
[Let your hearts be ruled], 818
[Love cannot remain by itself], 1037
[May God bless you with a restless discomfort], 1058
[May God, who calls you to this ministry], 968
[May we go forth into the world with courage], 1039
[Now, to the One who by the power], 824
[The Lord told you what is good], 784

Commissioning: Sending

See: Sending: Commissioning

Commitment

Breathe on Me, Breath of God, 737
Count Well the Cost, 577
Faith of the Martyrs, 575
Here I Am, Lord, 545
I Bind My Heart This Tide, 556
I Have Decided to Follow Jesus, 443
In My Life, Lord, Be Glorified, 754
In the Morning When I Rise, 499
Jesus A, Nahetotaetanome (Jesus, Lord, How Joyful), 8
Jesus Christ Is Love Divine, 749
Just As I Am, without One Plea, 560
Lo, I Am with You, 284
O Christ, Impart Your Teaching True, 583
O Splendor of God's Glory Bright, 500
Somlandela (We Will Follow), 566
Take My Life, and Let It Be, 759
Take My Life, That I May Be (Que mi vida entera esté), 760
Take, O Take Me as I Am, 748
Tana mana dhana prabhū tava caraṇī (Heart and Mind, Possessions, God), 753
Teach Me Thy Truth, 776
When I Survey the Wondrous Cross (La cruz excelsa al contemplar), 323
When I Survey the Wondrous Cross (South Africa, Zimbabwe), 322
When Love Is Found, 524
When We Walk with the Lord, 570
Who Now Would Follow Christ, 576
Will You Come and Follow Me, 540
[Amen (ASL)], 687
[Creator, we give you thanks], 861
[Dear Jesus, I confess my need of you], 926
[Friends, as we gather to eat the bread], 937
[God of covenant, when Jesus came up from the waters], 935
[God of covenant, your steadfast love], 960
[Grow us slowly], 1030
[I pledge allegiance to Jesus Christ], 929
[I pledge with you], 967
[In defiance of corruption and falsehood], 1040
[Jesus Christ, our Savior, you did not regard equality with God], 952
[The church is the body of Christ], 959
[The reign of heaven is like a treasure], 294
[Thus says the Lord, the God of Israel], 783
[We are a covenant people], 869
[We give thanks to God for children], 969
[We have witnessed your commitment], 961
[We offer thanksgiving to our Creator], 864
[You have offered], 970

Committees

See: Meetings and Committees

Communion

See: CELEBRATING COMMUNION: Meal (459-489); WORSHIP RESOURCES: Celebrating Communion (936-952); ART AND SCRIPTURE: Communion (468-472)

As We Rise, O God, to Meet You, 39
Brethren, We Have Met to Worship, 25
Christ Has Died, Christ Is Risen, 438
Christ Is Risen! Shout Hosanna!, 354
Christ, on the Night He Was Betrayed, 491
Come Away from Rush and Hurry, 9
Come, My Way, My Truth, My Life, 48
Come to the Water, 35
God the Sculptor of the Mountains, 423
Here in This Place, 10
I'm Gonna Eat at the Welcome Table, 801
In Christ There Is No East or West, 390
In the Heartbeat of the City, 530
In Thy Holy Place We Bow, 40
Let All Mortal Flesh Keep Silence, 65
Let Us Build a House, 36
Let's Walk Together, 6
Lord, You Give the Great Commission, 774
Mothering God, You Gave Me Birth, 426
Ngayong nagdadapit hapon (When Twilight Comes), 501
Sent Forth by God's Blessing, 812
Sign Us with Ashes, Merciful God, 304
Sing to the God of Harvest, 122
The Risen Christ, 345
The Water Is Ready, 458
Trinity Song, 60
What Is This Place, 22
You Are Holy, You Are Whole, 61
[Blessed are you, O God, maker of all things], 1019
[Come, all you who are thirsty], 14
[Communion], 468
[For I received from the Lord], 469
[Hear the words of Jesus: "Peace I leave with you"], 904
[Jesus, Lamb of God], 892
[Jesus said "I am the true vine"], 472
[Loaves and Fishes], 291
[Peace be with you], 850
[The crowd said to Jesus, "You must show us more miracles"], 471
[Two disciples were traveling], 470

Community

See also: Church; Unity; Unity in Diversity

Blest Be the Tie That Binds, 831
Brethren, We Have Met to Worship, 25
Draw the Circle Wide, 802
From the Waters I Will Rise, 442
Heart with Loving Heart, 813
Help Us to Help Each Other, 722
Here in This Place, 10
Hope Is a Candle, 211
I Come with Joy, 478
In the Heartbeat of the City, 530
Let Us Break Bread Together, 482
Praise with Joy the World's Creator, 428
Rain, Come Down, 634
Seed, Scattered and Sown, 477
The Church of Christ Cannot Be Bound, 392
Ubi caritas et amor, 773
We Are People of God's Peace, 797
We Place upon Your Table, 462
What a Fellowship / Leaning on the Everlasting Arms, 160
When Pain or Sorrow / Hold On, 612
Will You Let Me Be Your Servant, 778
You're Not Alone, 779
[As we now receive you into the fellowship], 932
[As you come to Christ the living stone], 381
[At the Impulse of God's Love], 780
[Be sincere in your love for others], 384
[By the grace of God we seek to live and proclaim], 925
[Christ is like a single body], 856
[Communion], 468
[Creemos en Dios Padre todopoderoso], 927
[For the Word of God in Scripture], 913.G
[Friends, as we gather to eat the bread], 937
[God created human beings for relationship], 973
[God of wanderers and seekers], 934
[God, who is Alpha and Omega], 962
[Gracious God, bless our cities], 1032
[In our doubt and fear], 1044
[Jesus of love and leftovers], 1016
[La paz no es producto del terror ni del miedo], 1038
[Lead a life worthy of the calling], 446
[Let the rain come and wash away], 1048
[Make a joyful noise to the Lord], 20
[Nine Patch #8], 723
[Open our ears to hear your word], 866
[The Word of God for the people of God], 913.E
[There are different kinds of gifts], 380
[We are people who must sing you], 882
[What will you offer the body of Christ today], 1023
[Where two or three are gathered], 19
[You are no longer foreigners], 382

Compassion

See also: Kindness; Love for Others

Beloved, God's Chosen, 164
Bless the Arms That Comfort, 527
Blest Be the Tie That Binds, 831
For Those with Whom Our Lives Are Bound, 734
Here to the House of God We Come, 27
Make Me an Instrument of Your Peace, 713
Open My Heart / Abre mi corazón, 731
Softly and Tenderly Jesus Is Calling, 544
Spirit, Open My Heart, 636
There Is in Every Person, 751
Ubi caritas (Where True Love), 492
Use Us, God, 811
When Pain or Sorrow / Hold On, 612
You're Not Alone, 779
[Blessed are you, Lord, the God of Israel], 985.E
[Christ has no body now on earth], 1035
[Compassionate Christ, if you are my light], 1003
[Creator, we give you thanks], 861
[Eternal Strength, hold us], 983
[God, just as you sent Joseph to Egypt], 957
[God, make me an instrument of your peace], 991
[Hear our prayer, O God of healing and hope], 978
[In defiance of corruption and falsehood], 1040
[In our doubt and fear], 1044
[Love cannot remain by itself], 1037
[O Tree of Calvary], 1012
[There is no scarcity], 1024

Confessing Faith

See: CONFESSING FAITH (419-440); WORSHIP RESOURCES: Confessing Faith (921-929)

See also: Creeds: Historic; Faith

All Hail the Power of Jesus' Name (CORONATION), 411
All Hail the Power of Jesus' Name (DIADEM), 364
All People That on Earth Do Dwell, 5
Bless'd Be the God of Israel, 223
Bring Many Names, 134
Christ Is Alive! Let Christians Sing, 359
Christ Is Arisen, 358
Christ Is King! Let Earthly Powers, 410
Christ Is Our Cornerstone, 4
Christ Jesus Lay, 463
Christ the Lord Is Risen Today (El Señor resucitó), 346
Christe, lux mundi (Christ, You Are Light), 271
Come, Let Us All Unite to Sing, 7
Faith Begins by Letting Go, 585
Glory to God in the Highest, 99
God Calls Us, 394

God Is Working This Purpose Out, 770
Here I Am to Worship (Ich will dich anbeten), 227
Holy God, We Praise Thy Name, 126
Holy, Holy, Holy!, 76
Hope of Abraham and Sarah, 807
How Firm a Foundation, 592
I Am the Bread of Life (Yo soy el pan de vida), 480
I Have Decided to Follow Jesus, 443
I Know Not Why God's Wondrous, 590
I Know That My Redeemer Lives, 347
I Love the Lord, 684
I Love to Tell the Story, 761
I Sing the Mighty Power of God, 182
I Sing with Exultation, 444
Ikke ved makt (Not by Your Might), 538
In Thee Is Gladness, 666
Jesus Loves Me, 516
Like a Rock, 63
Lord, You Sometimes Speak, 537
Lord, You've Searched Me, 609
My Hope Is Built on Nothing Less, 621
My Life Flows On, 605
My Shepherd Will Supply My Need, 640
O God, Great Womb, 176
O God, Our Help in Ages Past, 203
Oh, for a Thousand Tongues (AZMON), 764
Oh, for a Thousand Tongues (LYNGHAM), 78
Onyame wo mu o (In Your Sickness), 607
Shema Yisrael, 192
Shout to the Lord (Cante al Señor),125
The Church's One Foundation, 397
The Love of God, 162
The Strife Is O'er, 350
The Word of God Is Solid Ground, 399
This Little Light of Mine, 762
Wakantanka (Many and Great), 128
What a Fellowship / Leaning on the Everlasting Arms, 160
When Peace like a River, 617
Womb of Life and Source of Being, 112
Wonderful Grace of Jesus, 170
You Are All We Have, 701
[Amen (ASL)], 687
[For God so loved the world], 338
[Friends, as we gather to eat the bread], 937
[Hear, O Israel], 187
[I am convinced that neither death, nor life], 337
[In defiance of corruption and falsehood]. 1040
[Let the same mind be in you], 335

Confession of Sin

See: RECONCILING: Confession of Sin (140-155); WORSHIP RESOURCES: Reconciling (888-909)
See also: Assurance of Grace; Forgiveness; Repentance; Sin
Ah, Holy Jesus, 330
All Praise to Thee, My God, 505
Bless the Lord, My Soul (Tengo sed de ti / Bendiz o Senhor), 127
Far, Far Away / I Will Arise, 300
Just As I Am, without One Plea, 560
Khudaya, rahem kar (Have Mercy on Us, Lord), 693
Kyrie eleison (Ghanaian), 795
Kyrie eleison, Have Mercy, 796
Kyrie eleison (Taizé Kyrie 1), 678
Kyrie eleison (Taizé Kyrie 13), 692
Lord, Have Mercy (Manderfeld) 614
Lord, Have Mercy (Moosonee), 651
Lord, I Am Fondly, Earnestly Longing, 555
Mercy, Mercy, Lord, 169
My Jesus, I Love Thee, 133
Oré poriajú verekó (Kyrie eleison), 620
Sign Us with Ashes, Merciful God, 304
So nimm denn meine Hände (Take Thou My Hand), 631
Spirit, Open My Heart, 636
While I Keep Silence, 310
[Almighty God, to you all hearts are open], 860
[Blessed One, our source and support], 989.C
[Christ, have mercy (ASL)], 615
[Christ our companion, you came not to humiliate the sinner], 898
[Confesemos nuestro pecado contra Dios], 901
[Dear Jesus, I confess my need of you], 926
[For failing to love others], 893
[For the times we have lied], 891
[Friends in Christ, God knows our needs], 888
[God of mercy, we are sorry], 897
[God of the foolish cross], 896
[Gracious God, our sins are too heavy], 895
[Gracious God, we pray for your universal church], 1004
[Have mercy on me, O God], 889
[Have mercy on me, O God (Evening Prayer)], 987.D
[Let us confess our sin], 890
[Most loving, most strong God], 900
[Notre Père qui es aux cieux], 989.D
[O Prince of Peace], 894
[Our Father in heaven], 989.A
[Our Father, who art in heaven], 989.B
[Our lives are cluttered], 899
[Padre nuestro que estás en los cielos], 989.E
[Trusting in God's grace, let us confess], 938
[Vater unser im Himmel], 989.F

Conflict

See also: Peace; Peace and Justice; Peace: Conflict and War; Peace: Interpersonal; Violence
Beauty for Brokenness, 712
God, Give Me Time, 144
God Made from One Blood, 523
Healing River of the Spirit, 642
Jesus, Help Us Live in Peace, 719
[Anyone who is joined to Christ], 785
[Gracious God, we pray for your universal church], 1004
[Loving God, you have baptized us], 1001
[Most loving, most strong God], 900
[Now, thanks to Christ Jesus], 786

Conversion and New Life

See: SHARING OUR STORIES: Conversion and New Life (548-565)
See also: Commitment
Amazing Grace!, 163
As I Went Down to the River to Pray, 453
Breathe on Me, Breath of God, 737
Come, O Thou Traveler Unknown, 191
Crashing Waters at Creation, 441
El cielo canta alegría (Heaven Is Singing for Joy), 665
Far, Far Away / I Will Arise, 300
Fill Us with Your Feast, 309
From the Waters I Will Rise, 442
Herr, füll mich neu (Fill Me Anew), 739
Holy Spirit, Come with Power (Ven, Espíritu, cual viento), 57
Holy Spirit, Truth Divine, 46
I Have Decided to Follow Jesus, 443
I Heard the Voice of Jesus Say, 536
I Know Not Why God's Wondrous, 590
I Sought the Lord, 161
Jesus, Rock of Ages, 622
Lord Jesus, Come and Overturn, 146
Love Divine, All Loves Excelling, 638
My Jesus, I Love Thee, 133
Njoo kwetu, Roho mwema (Gracious Spirit), 367
No Longer Slaves to Fear, 195
O Love That Will Not Let Me Go, 608
Open My Eyes that I May See, 738
Prabhoo Lay lay, 567
Sign Us with Ashes, Merciful God, 304
There's a Wild Hope in the Wind, 828
True Evangelical Faith, 439
We Praise Thee, O God, 91
What Can I Leave Behind, 154
While I Keep Silence, 310
With Water Freely Flowing, 452
You Have Put on Christ, 457
[Alive], 334
[Anyone who is joined to Christ], 785
[Baptism with water in the name of the triune God], 930
[Convert us, Jesus the persecuted], 1027
[Dear Jesus, I confess my need of you], 926
[Dear ones, I plead with you], 105
[Do you not know that all who were baptized], 449
[Friends in Christ, God knows our needs], 888
[From all that is broken], 908
[Gracious God, our sins are too heavy], 895
[Have mercy on me, O God], 889
[Have mercy on me, O God (Evening Prayer)], 987.D
[In Christ Jesus you are all children], 450
[Open our ears to hear your word], 866
[Remember: We are earth], 918
[Two disciples were traveling], 470
[When Flaming Dove Meets Rising Waters], 378
[You who open doors], 862

Courage

A Mighty Fortress Is Our God, 421
God of Grace and God of Glory, 716
I Know Not Why God's Wondrous, 590
In Thee Is Gladness, 666
Jésus, je voudrais te chanter (Lord Jesus, You Shall Be My Song), 581
Kwake Yesu nasimama (Here on Christ the Rock I Will Stand), 159
Lift Every Voice and Sing, 611
Sometimes a Light Surprises, 618
The Lord Is My Light, 437
Wait for the Lord / Contemplaré tu vida, 228
We've Come This Far by Faith, 599
Your Love Is Washing Over Me, 166
[Come, Holy Spirit, enter our silences], 877
[Do not fear, says God], 903
[Eternal God, you call us to ventures], 1068
[God our sanctuary], 1042
[Gracious God, we celebrate life], 979
[Hear our prayer, O God of healing and hope], 978
[Hear the words of Jesus: "Peace I leave with you"], 904
[In our doubt and fear], 1044
[Lighting a candle], 1006
[Live without fear], 1062
[Living Christ, in these times], 1033
[That huge "Why?"], 1005
[The angel said "Do not be afraid!"], 234

Covenant

See: TELLING GOD'S STORY: Covenant (190-195); ART AND SCRIPTURE: Creation and Covenant (183-189)
See also: Exodus; Law
And I Will Raise You Up, 641
Bless'd Be the God of Israel, 223
Don't Be Afraid, 596
Hear the Turmoil of the Nations, 201
Here by the Water, 629
Hope of Abraham and Sarah, 807
My Soul Cries Out, 412
My Soul Proclaims with Wonder, 222
New Earth, Heavens New, 377
O Come, O Come, Immanuel, 210
Out of the Depths I Cry to You, 140
Prepare the Way! the Prophet Called, 220
Sing a New World into Being, 809
There Is a Line of Women, 546
View the Present, 407
We Are People of God's Peace, 797
We Give Thanks unto You, 117
We Praise You, O God, Our Redeemer, 34
Your Grace Is Enough, 167
Zisuh nih a zultu hna sinah (Peace Be with You! Jesus Told His Friends), 165
[Blessed are you, Lord, the God of Israel], 985.E
[God created human beings for relationship], 973
[God of covenant, your steadfast love], 960
[Hear, O Israel], 187
[Mist, Sun, Morning], 183
[Praise be to the Lord], 1063

[The crowd said to Jesus, "You must show us more miracles"], 471
[The Lord is merciful and gracious], 186
[Thus says the Lord: Maintain justice], 782
[We are a covenant people], 869

Creation

See: TELLING GOD'S STORY: Creation (175-182); ART AND SCRIPTURE: Creation and Covenant (183-189)
See also: Animals; Creation: Beauty of; Creation: Care; Creation: God as Creator; Creation: Lament
Crashing Waters at Creation, 441
From the Parent's Heart, the Firstborn (Corde natus ex parentis), 418
In the Beginning, 270
Joyful Is the Dark, 281
Spirit, Working in Creation, 50
There's a Wild Hope in the Wind, 828
When at Creation's Dawn, 121
You Shall Go Out with Joy, 847

Creation: Beauty of

See also: Creation; Creation: God as Creator
All Creatures Worship God Most High, 81
All Things Bright and Beautiful, 177
Creation Is a Song / Ho'ė enemeohe, 181
For You, O God, My Soul, 41
For the Beauty of the Earth, 120
God Speaks to Us in Bird and Song, 539
God Who Touches Earth with Beauty, 550
Here by the Water, 629
I Saw a Tree by the Riverside, 514
Joyful, Joyful, We Adore Thee, 103
La paz de la tierra (The Peace of the Earth Be with You), 838
Morning Has Broken, 495
Planets Humming as They Wander, 175
Praise Be to God, 115
Qing zao qi lai kan (Golden Breaks the Dawn), 498
Schönster Herr Jesu (Beautiful Savior), 130
This Is God's Wondrous World, 180
This Is My Song, 710
[Bless the Lord, O my soul], 185
[Come, with your faith and your doubts], 947
[Creator God, thank you for people and places], 954
[Let the rain come and wash away], 1048
[May the warm winds of heaven], 1061
[Mist, Sun, Morning], 183
[Sing the Goodness], 104
[To worship is to stand in awe], 855
[Tree of Life], 12
[We offer thanksgiving to our Creator], 864

Creation: Care

See also: Creation; Creation: Lament; Land
At the Dawn of Your Creation, 179
Beauty for Brokenness, 712
Called by Earth and Sky, 806
God of the Fertile Fields, 750
Light Dawns on a Weary World, 205
Na nzela na lola (As Long as We Follow), 413
O God, We Read the Holy Law, 571
Peace to You, 168
The Garden Needs Our Tending Now, 788
Touch the Earth Lightly, 145
[Bless the Lord, O my soul], 185
[Confesemos nuestro pecado contra Dios], 901
[For failing to love others], 893
[God of cosmos and quarks], 881
[Listening God, you hear our prayers], 996
[Mist, Sun, Morning], 183
[Source and sustainer of life], 1009
[Though the fig tree does not blossom], 820
[We offer thanksgiving to our Creator], 864
[With the whole people of God], 997

Creation: God as Creator

See also: Creation; Creation: Beauty of
At the Dawn of Your Creation, 179
Before the Waters Nourished Earth, 652
Creating God, Your Fingers Trace, 427
For You, O God, My Soul, 41
God, Bless the Work Your People Do, 528
God of Wonders, 178
God the Sculptor of the Mountains, 423
God, Who Stretched the Spangled Heavens, 529
God's Glory Fills the Heavens, 197
I Am That Great and Fiery Force, 663
I Sing the Mighty Power of God, 182
Joyful, Joyful, We Adore Thee, 103
Joyous Light of Heavenly Glory, 504
Listen to the Word That God Has Spoken, 405
Mothering God, You Gave Me Birth, 426
Now, on Land and Sea Descending, 503
Nyanyikanlah nyanyian baru (Sing to God a New Song), 93
O God, Great Womb, 176
Praise the Lord, Sing Hallelujah, 95
Sing to the God of Harvest, 122
Wakantanka (Many and Great), 128
We Long to Know Her, 44
We Worship God the Rock, 424
[Bless the Lord, O my soul], 185
[Blessed are you, O God, maker of all things], 1019
[Christ is the image of the invisible God], 189
[Creator, we give you thanks], 861
[Does not Wisdom call], 184
[God of cosmos and quarks], 881
[God of grace, creator of waters], 931
[I believe in God, the Father almighty], 923
[In the beginning was the Word], 235
[In the beginning when it was very quiet], 852
[Live without fear], 1062
[Mist, Sun, Morning], 183
[O God, Ancient of Days, your love], 941
[Praise and thanks to you, holy God], 915
[Sing to the Lord a new song], 106
[Some trust in governments], 1043
[Source and sustainer of life], 1009
[This is the day that the Lord has made], 15
[We believe in one God, the Father, the Almighty], 924
[We offer thanksgiving to our Creator], 864

Creation: Lament

See also: Creation; Creation: Care; Disaster; Lament
As the Waters Rise around Us, 708
Beauty for Brokenness, 712
O Healing River, 706
Touch the Earth Lightly, 145
[Confesemos nuestro pecado contra Dios], 901
[For failing to love others], 893
[Though the fig tree does not blossom], 820

Creation: Season of

See: Creation

Creeds: Historic

See also: Confessing Faith
I Believe in God Almighty, 433
[I believe in God, the Father almighty], 923
[We believe in one God, the Father, the Almighty], 924

Crisis: Local, National, Global

See also: Creation: Lament; Peace: Conflict and War; Protest; Service Agencies; Suffering
Amen (African American), 689
As the Waters Rise around Us, 708
Beauty for Brokenness, 712
Don't Be Afraid, 596
God of Grace and God of Glory, 716
Longing for Light, 715
O Healing River, 706
Precious Lord, Take My Hand, 610
Rain, Come Down, 634
There Is More Love Somewhere, 804
When the Storms of Life Are Raging, 595
[Eternal Strength, hold us], 983
[Everlasting God, you are our refuge], 981
[In our doubt and fear], 1044
[Let the rain come and wash away], 1048
[Lighting a candle], 1006
[O Prince of Peace], 894

Cross

See: Atonement; Jesus Christ: Death of; Journey to the Cross

Crucifixion of Jesus Christ

See: Jesus Christ: Death of

Dance

See also: Affirming the Human Body; Music
Cantai ao Senhor (O Sing to the Lord), 113
Come and Seek the Ways of Wisdom, 196
God, Give Me Faith like a Child, 519
How Can We Be Silent, 790
Jesus Christ Is Waiting, 287
Time Propels Us like a Current, 507
We Dream of a Turning, 209
With Mary Sing Magnificat, 208
[Blessed be the ones who dance], 1049
[Hosanna! Hosanna!], 885
[I praise you, God—in the sanctuary], 886

Darkness and Light

Arise, Your Light Is Come!, 273
Be Thou My Vision, 549
Between Darkness and Light, 808
Christe, lux mundi (Christ, You Are Light), 271
Dans nos obscurités (Within Our Darkest Night), 632
Darkness Is Not Dark to You, God, 200
De noche iremos (By Night, We Hasten), 543
Fill Us with Your Feast, 309
God Speaks to Us in Bird and Song, 539
Here I Am to Worship (Ich will dich anbeten), 227
Here in This Place, 10
Hope Is a Candle, 211
How Great Is Our God (Cuán grande es Dios), 116
I Will Follow, 775
In the Beginning, 270
In the Morning When I Rise, 499
Jesus, Be the Center, 584
Joyful Is the Dark, 281
Joyous Light of Heavenly Glory, 504
Let There Be Light, 714
Light Dawns on a Weary World, 205
Longing for Light, 715
Make Me an Instrument of Your Peace, 713
Move in Our Midst, 827
Nearer, My God, to Thee, 658
Now, on Land and Sea Descending, 503
Now the Heavens Start to Whisper, 237
O Beautiful Star of Bethlehem, 275
O God, Great Womb, 176
O God, You Search Me, 199
Oh, How Shall I Receive Thee, 215
Sálvanos, Señor, despiertos (Save Us, O Lord), 833
See Whose Glory Fills the Skies, 274
Siyahamba (We Are Marching), 793
The Hand of God Shall Hold You, 671
The Lord Is My Light, 437
This Little Light of Mine, 762
Thy Word Is a Lamp, 398
When I Can't Find My Way, 591
Wisdom from on High Is Dawning, 238
[Alive], 334
[Blessed are you, Lord, the God of Israel], 985.E
[God dearly loves us], 1056
[God, it is night], 986
[God, make me an instrument of your peace], 991
[God of deep and dazzling darkness], 988
[God's Word is a lamp], 913.F
[In the beginning was the Word], 235
[In the beginning when it was very quiet], 852
[I will light a light in the name of the Maker], 867
[Lighting a candle], 1006

[Now, Lord, you let your servant], 825
[O God, you withdraw from our sight], 1014
[O God, your word is a lamp to my feet], 987.A
[The people walking in darkness], 231
[We light a light], 865
[We light this candle as a sign], 917

Days Recognizing Parents

See also: Children / Childhood; Family
God Made from One Blood, 523
Like a Mother Who Has Borne Us, 518
Loving Spirit, 697
[God, our Creator, we give you thanks], 972

Death

See also: SHARING OUR STORIES: Death and Eternal Life (652-672)
See also: Death and Eternal Life; Eternal Life; Funeral / Memorial Service
For Those with Whom Our Lives Are Bound, 734
How Long, O Lord, 691
In the Morning When I Rise, 499
Thy Word Is a Lamp, 398
[Gracious God, when there is nothing], 994
[Remember: We are earth], 918

Death and Eternal Life

See: SHARING OUR STORIES: Death and Eternal Life (652-672)
See also: Death; Eternal Life; Funeral / Memorial Service; Heaven
10,000 Reasons / Bless the Lord, 111
Abide with Me, 502
All Creatures Worship God Most High, 81
Amazing Grace!, 163
Breathe on Me, Breath of God, 737
Children of the Heavenly Father, 517
Christ Is Arisen, 358
Christ Is Our Cornerstone, 4
Christ Is Risen, 349
Christ Jesus Lay, 463
Come, Christians, Join to Sing, 28
Dooládó' Shi Diyinda! (What a Wonderful Savior), 562
Eternal Light, Shine in My Heart, 554
Every Time I Feel the Spirit, 681
God Be with You Till We Meet Again, 840
Guide Me, O Thou Great Jehovah, 606
I Am the Bread of Life (Yo soy el pan de vida), 480
I Sing with Exultation, 444
Jésus, je voudrais te chanter (Lord Jesus, You Shall Be My Song), 581
Just a Closer Walk with Thee, 743
Lift Your Glad Voices, 340
Make Me an Instrument of Your Peace, 713
Mfurahini, haleluya (Christ Has Arisen, Alleluia!), 341
Now the Green Blade Rises, 353
O Beautiful Star of Bethlehem, 275
O Blessed Spring, 522
O God beyond All Praising, 814
O God, Our Help in Ages Past, 203
O Love That Will Not Let Me Go, 608
O Sacred Head, Now Wounded, 325
O Thou, in Whose Presence, 600
On Silken, Soft Wings, 676
Precious Lord, Take My Hand, 610
Quietly, Peacefully, 533
Remembrance, 479
Sálvanos, Señor, despiertos (Save Us, O Lord), 833
Shepherd Me, O God, 744
So lange Jesus bleibt der Herr (As Long as Jesus' Reign Goes On), 64
So nimm denn meine Hände (Take Thou My Hand), 631
The Lord Is Risen Indeed!, 357
The Strife Is O'er, 350
Thine Is the Glory, 355
This Joyful Eastertide, 352
To God Be the Glory, 84
Unless a Grain of Wheat, 302
We Are Often Tossed and Driven, 311
We Shall Walk through the Valley, 574
What Wondrous Love Is This, 564
When All Thy Mercies, 119
When Memory Fades, 649
Zisuh nih a zultu hna sinah (Peace Be with You! Jesus Told His Friends), 165
[A wilderness beckons us], 1011
[Alive], 334
[Do you not know that all who were baptized], 449
[Eternal God in whom we live], 982
[Everlasting God, you are our refuge], 981
[For God so loved the world], 338
[God be in my head], 999
[God, make me an instrument of your peace], 991
[God of deep and dazzling darkness], 988
[Gracious God, we celebrate life], 979
[Gracious God, when there is nothing], 994
[I am convinced that neither death, nor life], 337
[I saw a new heaven and a new earth], 339
[In the face of death, we worship God], 980
[Now, Lord, you let your servant], 825
[O Ancient of Days, you have been our dwelling place], 920
[Our physical bodies cannot inherit], 336
[Remember: We are earth], 918
[The Lord is my shepherd], 725

Death of Jesus Christ

See: Jesus Christ: Death of

Disability

Bless the Arms That Comfort, 527
God Calls You Good, 172
O God, You Search Me, 199
There Is in Every Person, 751
When Hands Reach Out, 513
[Great Physician, you touched the lives], 976
[Love cannot remain by itself], 1037

Disaster

See also: Crisis: Local, National, Global; Suffering
As the Waters Rise around Us, 708
How Firm a Foundation, 592
My Lighthouse, 597
O Healing River, 706
When the Storms of Life Are Raging, 595
[God, just as you sent Joseph to Egypt], 957

Discipleship

See also: Following Christ
Agneau de Dieu (O Lamb of God), 559
As I Went Down to the River to Pray, 453
As with Gladness, 277
Be Still, My Soul, 664
Brethren, We Have Met to Worship, 25
Christ Calls to Me, 542
Christ Has No Body Here but Ours, 568
Christ, on the Night He Was Betrayed, 491
Come to Me, O Weary Traveler, 157
Come What May / Pase lo que pase ¡ven!, 768
Count Well the Cost, 577
Dawk'yah towgyah thawy báht-awm (Take the Saving Word of God), 400
Faith of the Martyrs, 575
For the Fruit of All Creation, 124
From the Waters I Will Rise, 442
Go to Dark Gethsemane, 317
God Who Touches Earth with Beauty, 550
God, Whose Giving, 745
God, Whose Purpose Is to Kindle, 152
Gott ist gegenwärtig (God Is Here among Us), 62
Guide My Feet, 816
Heart with Loving Heart, 813
Here's My Life, I Lay It Down, 561
How Clear Is Our Vocation, 547
I Bind My Heart This Tide, 556
I Have Decided to Follow Jesus, 443
I Sing with Exultation, 444
I Will Follow, 775
Jesus A, Nahetotaetanome (Jesus, Lord, How Joyful), 8
Jesus, Be the Center, 584
Jesus Christ Is Love Divine, 749
Jésus, je voudrais te chanter (Lord Jesus, You Shall Be My Song), 581
Jesus Took a Towel, 490
Let This Mind Be in You, 572
Lo, I Am with You, 284
Lord, I Want to Be a Christian, 558
My Love Colors Outside the Lines, 582
Nearer, My God, to Thee, 658
O Christ, Impart Your Teaching True, 583
O God, We Read the Holy Law, 571
O Little Children, Gather, 515
Prabhoo Lay lay (Savior Jesus, Enfold Me), 567
Somlandela (We Will Follow), 566
Strong, Peaceful Man of Galilee, 573
Take My Life, and Let It Be, 759
Take My Life, That I May Be (Que mi vida entera esté), 760
Tana mana dhana prabhū tava caraṇī (Heart and Mind, Possessions, God), 753
The Church of Christ, in Every Age, 395
The Wonderful Cross, 324
The Word of God Is Solid Ground, 399
There Is a Line of Women, 546
Thuma mina (Send Me, Lord), 834
To Leave the Stones Unthrown, 580
Tú has venido a la orilla (Lord, You Have Come to the Lakeshore), 283
We Are People of God's Peace, 797
What Can I Leave Behind, 154
When We Walk with the Lord, 570
Who Are These, 360
Who Now Would Follow Christ, 576
Will You Come and Follow Me, 540
With Water Freely Flowing, 452
You Are Salt for the Earth, 297
You Have Put on Christ, 457
[Be sincere in your love for others], 384
[Come among us, Holy Spirit, and create a community], 955
[Dear ones, I plead with you], 105
[Jesus said "I am the true vine"], 472
[Let the same mind be in you], 335
[Let your hearts be ruled], 818
[No one can truly know Christ], 928
[Now may our Lord Jesus Christ], 819
[Source of all hope and holiness], 863
[True evangelical faith], 921
[We offer thanksgiving to our Creator], 864

Diversity: Unity in

See: Unity in Diversity

Doubt

See also: SHARING OUR STORIES: Doubt and Faith (585-604)
See also: Faith
As a Deer in Want of Water, 552
Ask the Complicated Questions, 440
Christ Has Broken Down the Wall, 174
Come Now, O God, 143
Come, O Thou Traveler Unknown, 191
God Weeps with Us, 656
How Long, O Lord, 691
How Many Times We Start Again, 553
Make Me an Instrument of Your Peace, 713
Njoo kwetu, Roho mwema (Gracious Spirit), 367
Oceans (Océanos), 456
Si tuvieras fe (If You Only Had Faith), 593
Spirit of God! Descend, 557
These Things Did Thomas Count as Real, 343
We Are Often Tossed and Driven, 311
[Barely midnight. All of us hunkered down], 871
[Come, with your faith and your doubts], 947
[Creemos en Dios Padre todopoderoso], 927
[Eternal God, you call us to ventures], 1068
[God of wanderers and seekers], 934
[Gracious God, when there is nothing], 994
[How long, O Lord], 728
[If you are delighted to be here], 853
[Living God for whom no door is closed], 876

[O God, you withdraw from our sight], 1014
[That huge "Why?"], 1005
[The table has been prepared], 939

Doxologies

See also: Gloria in excelsis / Glory to God in the Highest; Gloria Patri / Glory to the Father

All Praise to Thee, My God, 505
Praise God / Dedication anthem, 70
Praise God (Doxology), 71
Praise to the Living God, 204

Earth Day

See: Creation: Care

Easter

See: Jesus Christ: Resurrection of

Ecology

See: Creation: Care

Economic Justice

See: Justice: Economic

Education

See: Learning; Nurturing Faith; Schools and Learning Communities

Environment

See: Creation: Care

Epiphany of Jesus Christ

See: Jesus Christ: Epiphany of

Eternal life

See also: SHARING OUR STORIES: Death and Eternal Life (652-672)

See also: Death; Death and Eternal Life; Funeral / Memorial Service; Heaven

And I Will Raise You Up, 641
Come, We That Love, 31
Hallelujah! schöner Morgen (Hallelujah! Fairest Morning!), 497
Holy God, We Praise Thy Name, 126
I'm Gonna Eat at the Welcome Table, 801
My Jesus, I Love Thee, 133
Praise to the Living God, 204
Ubi caritas (Where True Love), 492
[Christ—the Joy, the Truth], 907
[May almighty God have mercy on us], 905

Eternity Sunday

See: All Saints' Day

Eucharist

See: Communion

Evangelism

See: Mission

Evening

See also: SHARING OUR STORIES: Morning and Evening (494-507); See: WORSHIP RESOURCES: Sharing Our Stories—Morning and Evening (984-988)

10,000 Reasons / Bless the Lord, 111
Abide with Me, 502
All Praise to Thee, My God, 505
De noche iremos (By Night, We Hasten), 543
God of Wonders, 178
God Speaks to Us in Bird and Song, 539
In the Morning When I Rise, 499
Joyous Light of Heavenly Glory, 504
Ngayong nagdadapit hapon (When Twilight Comes), 501
Now, on Land and Sea Descending, 503
Sálvanos, Señor, despiertos (Save Us, O Lord), 833
This Is God's Wondrous World, 180
[Bless the Lord, O my soul], 185
[Evening Prayer], 987
[God, it is night], 986
[God of deep and dazzling darkness], 988
[Hear, O Israel], 187
[I lift my eyes to the hills], 109
[It is good to give you thanks (Evening Prayer)], 987.C
[It is good to give you thanks (Morning Prayer)], 985.C
[My soul proclaims the greatness], 987.F
[Now, Lord, you let your servant], 825
[Receive our thanks for night and day], 949

Evil

A Mighty Fortress Is Our God, 421
God of Grace and God of Glory, 716
In the Rifted Rock I'm Resting (Wehrlos und verlassen sehnt sich), 619
My God, My God, 696
Rain, Come Down, 634
[Be sincere in your love for others], 384
[God of extravagant mercy], 1020
[In defiance of corruption and falsehood], 1040
[Most loving, most strong God], 900
[O Prince of Peace], 894

Exile

See also: Immigration and Refugees

By the Waters of Babylon, 695
Seek the Peace of the City, 206
Waterfall, 763
[Praise and thanks to you, holy God], 915
[Thus says the Lord, the God of Israel], 783

Exodus

See also: Covenant

All Who Hunger, Gather Gladly, 474
Come, Ye Faithful, Raise the Strain, 348
Crashing Waters at Creation, 441
God the Sculptor of the Mountains, 423
Guide Me, O Thou Great Jehovah, 606
Lead On, O Cloud of Presence, 194
No Longer Slaves to Fear, 195
Wade in the Water, 454
We Sing to You, O God, 80
When Israel Was in Egypt's Land, 193
Who Are These, 360
[God of grace, creator of waters], 931
[Liberating God, prevent us], 1031
[Praise and thanks to you, holy God], 915
[The crowd said to Jesus, "You must show us more miracles"], 471

Expanding Our Circle

See: LIVING GOD'S STORY: Expanding Our Circle (802-808)

See also: Interfaith; Unity in Diversity

Called by Earth and Sky, 806
How Can Our Anger Give Life, 792
My Love Colors Outside the Lines, 582
Shalom chaverim (Shalom, My Friends), 842
[Blessed be the ones who dance], 1049
[Come, come, whoever you are], 1047
[If there is to be peace in the world], 1046
[La paz no es producto del terror ni del miedo], 1038
[Let the rain come and wash away], 1048
[Sing and sing], 883
[That huge "Why?"], 1005
[To worship is to stand in awe], 855

Faith

See also: SHARING OUR STORIES: Doubt and Faith (585-604)

See also: Confessing Faith; Doubt; Faith Journey; Nurturing Faith

A Mighty Fortress Is Our God, 421
Akekho ofana / Hakuna wakaita (There's No One in This World like Jesus), 68
As a Deer in Want of Water, 552
Ask the Complicated Questions, 440
Blessed Assurance, 435
Build My Life, 92
Faith Begins by Letting Go, 585
Faith of the Martyrs, 575
God, Give Me Faith like a Child, 519
Haneul naneun saeleul bora (See the Birds That Fly), 289
Holy Presence, Holy Teacher, 531
How Many Times We Start Again, 553
I Believe in God Almighty, 433
I Know Not Why God's Wondrous, 590
I Know That My Redeemer Lives, 347
In the Rifted Rock I'm Resting (Wehrlos und verlassen sehnt sich), 619
I Will Follow, 775
Jesus Loves Me, 516
Kwake Yesu nasimama (Here on Christ the Rock I Will Stand), 159
Make Me an Instrument of Your Peace, 713
My Hope Is Built on Nothing Less, 621
My Life Flows On, 605
My Love Colors Outside the Lines, 582
Njoo kwetu, Roho mwema (Gracious Spirit), 367
O Worship Our God, All Glorious Above, 74
Oceans (Océanos), 456
Out of the Depths I Cry to You, 140
Rain Down, 703
Restore Our Faith, O Saving God, 198
Si tuvieras fe (If You Only Had Faith), 593
So nimm denn meine Hände (Take Thou My Hand), 631
Sometimes a Light Surprises, 618
Summoned by the God Who Made Us, 1
The Lord Is My Light, 437
There Is in Every Person, 751
These Things Did Thomas Count as Real, 343
Thy Word Is a Lamp, 398
True Evangelical Faith, 439
We Are Often Tossed and Driven, 311
We Sing to You, O God, 80
We Walk by Faith, 588
We've Come This Far by Faith, 599
When We Walk with the Lord, 570
[Come, with your faith and your doubts], 947
[Eternal God, you call us to ventures], 1068
[For God so loved the world], 338
[God of grace and glory, you fling the stars], 985.G
[God of Life, we give these offerings], 1017
[God of wanderers and seekers], 934
[Grow us slowly], 1030
[How long, O Lord], 728
[If you are delighted to be here], 853
[Let me hear what the Lord God says], 188
[Living God, by the power of your Spirit], 911
[Love is patient], 1045
[O God, you withdraw from our sight], 1014
[Praise the Lord], 107
[The table has been prepared], 939
[True evangelical faith], 921
[We are not alone], 922

Faith Journey

See also: Conversion and New Life; Faith; Nurturing Faith; Walking with God

Akekho ofana / Hakuna wakaita (There's No One in This World like Jesus), 68
As a Deer in Want of Water, 552
Blessed Be Your Name, 637
Come and Seek the Ways of Wisdom, 196
Come, We That Love, 31
De noche iremos (By Night, We Hasten), 543
Fill Us with Your Feast, 309
God, Be the Love, 43
Guide Me, O Thou Great Jehovah, 606
Guide My Feet, 816
How Many Times We Start Again, 553
I Sought the Lord, 161
Like a Mother Who Has Borne Us, 518
Njoo kwetu, Roho mwema (Gracious Spirit), 367
O Blessed Spring, 522
O God, You Search Me, 199
Qing zao qi lai kan (Golden Breaks the Dawn), 498
Somos pueblo que camina (We Are People on a Journey), 464
We Are One in the Spirit, 387
We Sing to You, O God, 80
We Walk by Faith, 588
When I Can't Find My Way, 591
Ya-ma-ji ko-e-te (In Lonely Mountain Ways), 589

Your Grace Finds Me, 521
[Faithful God, we give thanks], 933
[God of every place], 859
[God of wanderers and seekers], 934
[Migrant Journey], 817
[The Lord told you what is good], 784

Faithfulness of God
See: God: Faithfulness of

Family
See also: SHARING OUR STORIES: Family, Friendship, and Marriage (523-525)
See also: Aging; Children / Childhood; Friendship; Marriage
Bless the Arms That Comfort, 527
Child of Blessing, Child of Promise, 508
For the Beauty of the Earth, 120
God Made from One Blood, 523
Like a Mother Who Has Borne Us, 518
Loving Spirit, 697
See the Children Here Before Us, 509
When Love Is Found, 524
[Friends in Christ, God knows our needs], 888
[God created human beings for relationship], 973
[God, maker of galaxies, who numbers the hairs], 971
[God of all life, in you we live and move], 974
[God, our Creator, we give you thanks], 972
[We give thanks to God for children], 969
[We have witnessed your commitment], 961
[We Owe Them a Complicated Debt], 230
[You are no longer foreigners], 382
[You have offered], 970

Father's Day
See: Days Recognizing Parents

Fear
See: Courage

Fellowship
See: Community

Feminine Language for God
See: God: Feminine Language for

Following Christ
See: SHARING OUR STORIES: Following Christ (566-584)
See also: Discipleship; Walking with God
Agneau de Dieu (O Lamb of God), 559
Akekho ofana / Hakuna wakaita (There's No One in This World like Jesus), 68
All the Room Was Hushed and Still, 493
Be Thou My Vision, 549
Christ, Be All around Me, 848
Come and See, 282
Come to Me, O Weary Traveler, 157
Come What May / Pase lo que pase ¡ven!, 768
Enviados somos de Dios (We Have Been Sent by God), 771
From the Waters I Will Rise, 442
Gentle Shepherd, 718
Go Ye Now in Peace / Go, My Friends, in Peace, 839
God, Be the Love, 43
God Calls Us, 394
Guide My Feet, 816
Hamba nathi (Come, Walk with Us), 23
Here by the Water, 629
Here's My Life, I Lay It Down, 561
Honja sorironeun (With My Voice Alone), 800
I Have Decided to Follow Jesus, 443
I Saw a Tree by the Riverside, 514
I Sing with Exultation, 444
I Want Jesus to Walk with Me, 306
I Will Follow, 775
Jesus Calls Us, 30
Jesus Christ Is Love Divine, 749
Jesus, Tempted in the Desert, 307
Just a Closer Walk with Thee, 743
Lead Me Forth, 837
Let Us Build a House, 36
Lo, I Am with You, 284
Lord, I Want to Be a Christian, 558
May the Face of God Shine on You, 844
Na nzela na lola (As Long as We Follow), 413
Naege itneun hyangyu okhap (To My Precious Lord), 755
O Carpenter, Why Leave the Bench, 280
O God in Heaven, 720
Oceans (Océanos), 456
Prabhoo Lay lay (Savior Jesus, Enfold Me), 567
Seeking Warmth from Charcoal Blazing, 344
Sword into a Plowshare, 798
The Risen Christ, 345
The Wonderful Cross, 324
There Is a Line of Women, 546
Thy Word Is a Lamp, 398
Tú eres todopoderoso (Because You're Holy), 89
Tú has venido a la orilla (Lord, You Have Come to the Lakeshore), 283
What Can I Leave Behind, 154
Who Are These, 360
Will You Come and Follow Me, 540
Zisuh nih a zultu hna sinah (Peace Be with You! Jesus Told His Friends), 165
[Baptism with water in the name of the triune God], 930
[Blessed are you, Eternal God], 942
[Christ, whose insistent call], 1029
[From where we are], 1050
[God dearly loves us], 1056
[God of every place], 859
[Gracious God, our sins are too heavy], 895
[Holy God, you call us together], 857
[In defiance of corruption and falsehood], 1040
[Jesus said "I am the true vine"], 472
[Jesus, servant, at supper with your disciples], 1041
[Jesus washed the feet of his disciples], 950
[Let the same mind be in you], 335
[Living God, by the power of your Spirit], 911
[No one can truly know Christ], 928

Footwashing
See: CELEBRATING COMMUNION: Footwashing (490-493)
See also: Communion; Holy Thursday
Holy Spirit, Come to Us, 58
Let's Walk Together, 6
Naege itneun hyangyu okhap (To My Precious Lord), 755
The Church of Christ Cannot Be Bound, 392
Ubi caritas et amor, 773
Will You Let Me Be Your Servant, 778
[Eternal Love, gentle God, you invite us], 951
[Jesus Christ, our Savior, you did not regard equality with God], 952
[Jesus, servant, at supper with your disciples], 1041
[Jesus washed the feet of his disciples], 950
[While Jesus was in Bethany], 296

Forgiveness
See also: Assurance of Grace; Confession of Sin; Forgiveness: From God; Forgiveness: From Others; Forgiveness: From Ourselves; Grace; Mercy
Abana alathi (Abana in Heaven), 675
All Praise to Thee, My God, 505
Gentle God, When We Are Driven, 150
God, Give Me Time, 144
Make Me an Instrument of Your Peace, 713
Mercy, Mercy, Lord, 169
Our Father, who Art in Heaven, 674
Our God in Heaven, 673
Sword into a Plowshare, 798
[As a shepherd seeks a lost sheep], 868
[Blessed One, our source and support], 989.C
[Dear Jesus, I confess my need of you], 926
[God forgives you], 909
[Let us confess our sin], 890
[Notre Père qui es aux cieux], 989.D
[Our Father in heaven], 989.A
[Our Father, who art in heaven], 989.B
[Padre nuestro que estás en los cielos], 989.E
[The Lord is merciful and gracious], 186
[Trusting in God's grace, let us confess], 938
[Vater unser im Himmel], 989.F

Forgiveness: From God
See also: Forgiveness
Abana alathi (Abana in Heaven), 675
All Praise to Thee, My God, 505
Create in Me a Clean Heart, 141
Dooládó' Shi Diyinda! (What a Wonderful Savior), 562
Far, Far Away / I Will Arise, 300
Forgive, Forgive Us, Holy God, 149
From Heaven Above to Earth I Come, 263
Gentle God, When We Are Driven, 150
God, Grant Us Mercy, 142
I Know Not Why God's Wondrous, 590
Just As I Am, without One Plea, 560
Lamb of God / Cordero de Dios, 151
Let Us Break Bread Together, 482
Lord, I Need You, 155
Mercy, Mercy, Lord, 169
Mfurahini, haleluya (Christ Has Arisen, Alleluia!), 341
Oh, qué bueno es Jesús (Oh, How Great Is Christ the Lord), 351
Our Father, who Art in Heaven, 674
Our God in Heaven, 673
Out of the Depths I Cry to You, 140
Perdón, Señor, 153
There's a Wideness in God's Mercy, 156
To God Be the Glory, 84
Ya hamala Allah (O Lamb of God), 321
[Christ—the Joy, the Truth], 907
[Do not fear, says God], 903
[Friends in Christ, God knows our needs], 888
[God forgives you], 909
[God of mercy, we are sorry], 897
[Hear the good news!], 903D
[Hear the words of Jesus: "Peace I leave with you"], 904
[If we have died with Christ], 903C
[May almighty God have mercy on us], 905
[Our righteousness is found in Christ alone], 903B
[Praise to God who has given us life], 902

Forgiveness: From Others
See also: Forgiveness
Make Me an Instrument of Your Peace, 713
Mercy, Mercy, Lord, 169
Our God in Heaven, 673
[For the times we have lied], 891
[God forgives you], 909
[God, make me an instrument of your peace], 991
[Hear the words of Jesus: "Peace I leave with you"], 904

Forgiveness: From Ourselves
See also: Forgiveness
Could It Be That God Is Singing, 42
Will You Come and Follow Me, 540
[God forgives you], 909
[O Risen Christ, you breathe your Holy Spirit], 1013

Freedom
See: Liberation

Friendship
See also: SHARING OUR STORIES: Family, Friendship, and Marriage (523-525)
See also: Community; Family
Bless the Arms That Comfort, 527
Blest Be the Tie That Binds, 831
For the Beauty of the Earth, 120
For Those with Whom Our Lives Are Bound, 734

God Speaks to Us in Bird and Song, 539
O phi nong oei (Dear Friends, We're One), 525
Rain, Come Down, 634
Shalom chaverim (Shalom, My Friends), 842
When Pain or Sorrow / Hold On, 612
You're Not Alone, 779
[Anyone who is joined to Christ], 785
[Be sincere in your love for others], 384
[Come, with your faith and your doubts], 947
[For the times we have lied], 891
[How very good and pleasant it is], 17
[Jesus Christ, our Savior, you did not regard equality with God], 952

Funeral / Memorial Service

See: WORSHIP RESOURCES: Sharing Our Stories—Funerals (980-983)

See also: Comfort; Death; Death and Eternal Life; Eternal Life; Grief; Hope; Jesus Christ: Resurrection of

10,000 Reasons / Bless the Lord, 111
Abide with Me, 502
All Creatures Worship God Most High, 81
Amazing Grace!, 163
And I Will Raise You Up, 641
Before the Waters Nourished Earth, 652
Be Still, My Soul, 664
Christ Is Arisen, 358
Christ Is Risen, 349
El cielo canta alegría (Heaven Is Singing for Joy), 665
Eternal Light, Shine in My Heart, 554
For All the Saints, 672
God Weeps with Us, 656
Go, Silent Friend, 657
Guide Me, O Thou Great Jehovah, 606
I Am the Bread of Life (Yo soy el pan de vida), 480
In the Bulb There Is a Flower, 670
Jesus, Lover of My Soul, 659
Lift Your Glad Voices, 340
My Jesus, I Love Thee, 133
My Latest Sun Is Sinking Fast, 662
Nearer, My God, to Thee, 658
Nothing Is Lost on the Breath of God, 653
Now the Green Blade Rises, 353
O God, Our Help in Ages Past, 203
O Love That Will Not Let Me Go, 608
O Thou, in Whose Presence, 600
Oh, Have You Not Heard (Ich weiss einen Strom), 668
On Jordan's Stormy Banks I Stand, 661
Precious Lord, Take My Hand, 610
Quietly, Peacefully, 533
Shall We Gather at the River, 667
Shepherd Me, O God, 744
So nimm denn meine Hände (Take Thou My Hand), 631
Soon and Very Soon, 669
The Hand of God Shall Hold You, 671
The Lord's My Shepherd, 660
Today We Sing with Thankfulness, 535
We Shall Walk through the Valley, 574
When Grief Is Raw, 655
[Eternal God in whom we live], 982
[Eternal Strength, hold us], 983
[Everlasting God, you are our refuge], 981
[God be in my head], 999
[I am convinced that neither death, nor life], 337
[I saw a new heaven and a new earth], 339
[In the face of death, we worship God], 980
[May God bless you and keep you], 826
[O Ancient of Days, you have been our dwelling place], 920
[Our physical bodies cannot inherit], 336
[Remember: We are earth], 918
[The Lord is my shepherd], 725

Gathering

See: GATHERING (1-67); WORSHIP RESOURCES: Gathering (850-879); ART AND SCRIPTURE: Gathering(12-21)

See also: God: Presence of; Invocation; Welcome

All Creatures Worship God Most High, 81
All Hail the Power of Jesus' Name (CORONATION), 411
All Hail the Power of Jesus' Name (DIADEM), 364
All Who Hunger, Gather Gladly, 474
Come and See, 282
Come, Gracious Spirit, 371
Come On, Children, to the Gospel Feast, 511
For You, O God, My Soul, 41
From North and South, from East and West, 460
Hallelujah! schöner Morgen (Hallelujah! Fairest Morning!), 497
Heart with Loving Heart, 813
Herr, füll mich neu (Fill Me Anew), 739
I Come with Joy, 478
I Heard the Voice of Jesus Say, 536
I Owe the Lord a Morning Song, 496
I'm Gonna Eat at the Welcome Table, 801
Jesus, Be the Center, 584
Joyous Light of Heavenly Glory, 504
Let the Hungry Come to Me, 459
Let Us Break Bread Together, 482
Listen in the Silence, 541
Lobe den Herren (Praise to the Lord, the Almighty), 88
Morning Has Broken, 495
Nzambi wakatamba (God Loves All His Many People), 767
O Little Children, Gather, 515
O Worship Our God, 129
O Worship Our God, All Glorious Above, 74
Oh, for a Thousand Tongues (AZMON), 764
Oh, for a Thousand Tongues (LYNGHAM), 78
Praise Be to God, 115
Remembrance, 479
Sanna, sannanina, 79
Segala puji syukur (All Our Praise), 82
Shall We Gather at the River, 667
Sign Us with Ashes, Merciful God, 304
Sing Praise to God Who Reigns, 101
Sleepers, Wake, 226
Somos pueblo que camina (We Are People on a Journey), 464
Together, 389
Ubi caritas (Where True Love), 492
We Praise Thee, O God, 91
We Sing to You, O God, 80
Wind Who Makes All Winds, 372
Womb of Life and Source of Being, 112
[A wilderness beckons us], 1011
[As you come to Christ the living stone], 381
[Come, all you who are thirsty], 14
[Come, come, whoever you are], 1047
[Come, let us go up], 13
[Communion], 468
[Dear God, let your word shine], 912
[Dear ones, I plead with you], 105
[Everlasting God, in whom we live and move], 998
[Gardener God, you have planted], 1002
[Glory to God in the highest], 880
[Hear the words of Jesus: "Peace I leave with you"], 904
[Holy God, Holy One, Holy Three!] 887
[Hosanna! Hosanna!], 885
[How very good and pleasant it is], 17
[I praise you, God—in the sanctuary], 886
[I was glad when they said to me], 16
[In Christ Jesus you are all children], 450
[In the beginning, before time], 884
[Lead a life worthy of the calling], 446
[Let your hearts be ruled], 818
[Living God, by the power of your Spirit], 911
[Make a joyful noise to the Lord], 20
[May the grace of Jesus Christ], 21
[Now, thanks to Christ Jesus], 786
[O God, open our lips], 985.A
[O God, you withdraw from our sight], 1014
[O God, your word is a lamp to my feet], 987.A
[O Tree of Calvary], 1012
[Rejoice in the Lord always], 726
[Sing to the Lord a new song], 106
[Speak to us, living God], 910
[This is the day that the Lord has made], 15
[Thus says the Lord: Maintain justice], 782
[Tree of Life], 12
[What will you offer the body of Christ today], 1023
[When the day of Pentecost came], 379
[Where two or three are gathered], 19
[You are no longer foreigners], 382

Giving

See: GIVING (745-760); WORSHIP RESOURCES: Giving (1015-1025)

See also: Service; Stewardship

As with Gladness, 277
For the Fruit of All Creation, 124
God of Justice, 772
Here's My Life, I Lay It Down, 561
Lo, I Am with You, 284
Praise God (Doxology), 71
Sing to the God of Harvest, 122
Teach Me Thy Truth, 776
We Praise You, O God, Our Redeemer, 34
[Christ is like a single body], 856
[Come, all you who are thirsty], 14
[Creator, we give you thanks], 861
[Lay one brick at a time], 1036
[Loaves and Fishes], 291
[Love cannot remain by itself], 1037
[While Jesus was in Bethany], 296

Gloria in Excelsis / Glory to God in the Highest

Glory to God in the Highest, 99

Gloria Patri / Glory to the Father

Glory to God, Whose Goodness Shines on Me, 429
Sing with Joy to the Author / Glory Be to the Father, 430
[Glory to You, Source of All Being (Evening Prayer)], 987.B
[Glory to You, Source of All Being (Morning Prayer)], 985.B

Glory of God

See: God: Glory of

Glory to God in the Highest

See: Gloria in excelsis / Glory to God in the Highest

Glory to the Father

See: Gloria Patri / Glory to the Father

God: Creator

See: Creation: God as Creator

God: Faithfulness of

10,000 Reasons / Bless the Lord, 111
All People That on Earth Do Dwell, 5
Alleluia / Make a Joyful Noise (Psalm 100), 66
Amazing Grace!, 163
Be at Rest, 532
Be Still, My Soul, 664
Blessed Be Your Name, 637
Come to Me, O Weary Traveler, 157
For the Fruit of All Creation, 124
God Is Great and God Is Good, 488
God of the Bible, 420
God, Whose Giving, 745
Gravity of Love, 494
Great Is Thy Faithfulness, 419
Haneul naneun saeleul bora (See the Birds That Fly), 289
I Sought the Lord, 161
I to the Hills Will Lift My Eyes, 602
Ikke ved makt (Not by Your Might), 538
In the Quiet Curve of Evening, 587
Lord, You Sometimes Speak, 537
Nada te turbe, 604
Nun danket alle Gott (Now Thank We All Our God), 114
O Everlasting Love, 733
O God, Our Help in Ages Past, 203
O Lord My God / How Great Thou Art, 436

Oceans (Océanos), 456
Praise to the Living God, 204
Rain Down, 703
Rejoice, Rejoice Forevermore, 402
Restore Our Faith, O Saving God, 198
Seek Ye First, 417
Sometimes a Light Surprises, 618
Taste and See, 467
Tears of Suffering, 694
The God of Sarah Praise, 190
The Lord Lift You Up, 832
Time Propels Us like a Current, 507
Total Praise, 633
We Give Thanks unto You, 117
We Plow the Fields and Scatter, 747
We Sing to You, O God, 80
We Worship God the Rock, 424
We've Come This Far by Faith, 599
What a Fellowship / Leaning on the Everlasting Arms, 160
When All Thy Mercies, 119
When I Can't Find My Way, 591
When Memory Fades, 649
When the Storms of Life Are Raging, 595
Ya-ma-ji ko-e-te (In Lonely Mountain Ways), 589
You Are Good, 33
You Shall Go Out with Joy, 847
Your Grace Is Enough, 167
Your Love Is Amazing, 96
[As a shepherd seeks a lost sheep], 868
[Give thanks to God, who is good], 963
[God of Life, we give these offerings], 1017
[Holy One, as you are faithful to us], 1022
[I lift my eyes to the hills], 109
[It is good to give you thanks (Evening Prayer)], 987.C
[It is good to give you thanks (Morning Prayer)], 985.C
[Let me hear what the Lord God says], 188
[Make a joyful noise to the Lord], 20
[Merciful God, we wait], 977
[Now may the God of peace], 823
[The Lord is merciful and gracious], 186

God: Feminine Language and Images for

See also: God: Images and Names of

Bring Many Names, 134
Come and Seek the Ways of Wisdom, 196
Could It Be That God Is Singing, 42
God Lights a Lamp, 299
God of the Bible, 420
Like a Mother Who Has Borne Us, 518
Loving Spirit, 697
Mothering God, You Gave Me Birth, 426
Ngayong nagdadapit hapon (When Twilight Comes), 501
O God, Great Womb, 176
O Worship Our God, All Glorious Above, 74
One Is the Body, 386
Praise God (Doxology), 71
Sing Praise to God Who Reigns, 101
The Lord Bless You and Keep You, 846
There's a Wild Hope in the Wind, 828
Unexpected and Mysterious, 229
We Long to Know Her, 44
We Sing to You, O God, 80
Wisdom from on High Is Dawning, 238
Womb of Life and Source of Being, 112
[Does not Wisdom call], 184
[Live without fear], 1062
[Sing the Goodness], 104
[With the whole people of God], 997

God: Glory of

All Things Bright and Beautiful, 177
Glory to God, Whose Goodness Shines on Me, 429
God Is Working This Purpose Out, 770
God's Glory Fills the Heavens, 197
Holy, Holy, Holy!, 76
Praise the Lord, Sing Hallelujah, 95
Sing with Joy to the Author / Glory Be to the Father, 430
[Blessed One, our source and support], 989.C
[Glory to God in the highest], 880
[Glory to You, Source of All Being (Evening Prayer)], 987.B
[Glory to You, Source of All Being (Morning Prayer)], 985.B
[God of grace and glory, you fling the stars], 985.G
[God of grace and glory, you keep our souls], 987.H
[Notre Père qui es aux cieux], 989.D
[Our Father in heaven], 989.A
[Our Father, who art in heaven], 989.B
[Padre nuestro que estás en los cielos], 989.E
[Vater unser im Himmel], 989.F

God: Images and Names of

See also: God: Feminine Language and Images for; Jesus Christ: Images and Names of

A Mighty Fortress Is Our God, 421
And I Will Raise You Up, 641
Be Thou My Vision, 549
Before the Waters Nourished Earth, 652
Bring Many Names, 134
Come and Seek the Ways of Wisdom, 196
Come, My Way, My Truth, My Life, 48
Creating God, Your Fingers Trace, 427
Creation Is a Song / Ho'ē enemeohe, 181
Darkness Is Not Dark to You, God, 200
Ehane he'ama (Father God, You Are Holy), 59
Eternal Light, Shine in My Heart, 554
Glory to God in the Highest, 99
God Be with You Till We Meet Again, 840
God the Spirit, Guide and Guardian, 534
Hallelujah, Salvation, and Glory, 69
Holy Presence, Holy Teacher, 531
How Great Is Our God (Cuán grande es Dios), 116
I Am That Great and Fiery Force, 663
I Believe in God Almighty, 433
Immortal, Invisible, God Only Wise, 98
Life-Giver, Maker, God of All, 38
Like a Mother Who Has Borne Us, 518
Like a Rock, 63
Lobe den Herren (Praise to the Lord, the Almighty), 88
Loving Spirit, 697
Margam, satyam, jivam nive (Living, Moving, End and Beginning), 425
Mothering God, You Gave Me Birth, 426
My Lighthouse, 597
My Shepherd Will Supply My Need, 640
O Everlasting Love, 733
O God, Great Womb, 176
O Holy Spirit, Root of Life, 376
O Worship Our God, All Glorious Above, 74
Praise God / Dedication anthem, 70
Praise God (Doxology), 71
Sing Praise to God Who Reigns, 101
Sing with Joy to the Author / Glory Be to the Father, 430
There Is in Every Person, 751
There's a Wild Hope in the Wind, 828
Through Our Fragmentary Prayers, 677
Time Propels Us like a Current, 507
We Long to Know Her, 44
We Sing to You, O God, 80
We Worship God the Rock, 424
When at Creation's Dawn, 121
With Mary Sing Magnificat, 208
Womb of Life and Source of Being, 112
[Does not Wisdom call], 184
[Glory to God in the highest], 880
[Glory to You, Source of All Being (Evening Prayer)], 987.B
[Glory to You, Source of All Being (Morning Prayer)], 985.B
[Holy God, Holy One, Holy Three!] 887
[Sing the Goodness], 104
[The angel said to Mary], 233
[When the day of Pentecost came], 379
[With the whole people of God], 997

God: Judgment of

See: Judgment

God: Love of

See also: Jesus Christ: Love of

Before the Waters Nourished Earth, 652
Come, Let Us All Unite to Sing, 7
Come, O Thou Traveler Unknown, 191
Create in Me a Clean Heart, 141
Don't Be Afraid, 596
Ehane he'ama (Father God, You Are Holy), 59
Go Now in Peace, 835
God, Be the Love, 43
God Lights a Lamp, 299
God Speaks to Us in Bird and Song, 539
God Welcomes All, 32
Gott ist die Liebe (I Know God Loves Me), 158
Gravity of Love, 494
Holy Spirit, Come to Us, 58
How Shallow Former Shadows, 326
Ikke ved makt (Not by Your Might), 538
Joyful Is the Dark, 281
Joyful, Joyful, We Adore Thee, 103
Love Came Down at Christmas, 255
Love Divine, All Loves Excelling, 638
Love Has Come, 258
Loving Spirit, 697
May You Be Rooted and Grounded in Love, 396
More Than You Know, 598
Ngayong nagdadapit hapon (When Twilight Comes), 501
Nothing Can Ever Come between Us, 654
Nothing Can Separate Us, 171
Nothing Is Lost on the Breath of God, 653
Nzambi wakatamba (God Loves All His Many People), 767
O Everlasting Love, 733
O God beyond All Praising, 814
O God, We Read the Holy Law, 571
Praise to the Living God, 204
Rain Down, 703
Seeds, 777
The Love of God, 162
There Is in Every Person, 751
There's a Wideness in God's Mercy, 156
Tú estás aquí (My God Is Here), 67
Ubi caritas et amor, 773
Ubi caritas (Where True Love), 492
We Give Thanks unto You, 117
Your Love Is Amazing, 96
Your Love Is Washing Over Me, 166
[Do not fear, says God], 903
[Eternal God in whom we live], 982
[For God so loved the world], 338
[God of grace and glory, you fling the stars], 985.G
[God of grace and glory, you keep our souls], 987.H
[Go, knowing you are beloved by God], 1055
[Gracious God, when there is nothing], 994
[Have mercy on me, O God], 889
[I am convinced that neither death, nor life], 337
[I will light a light in the name of the Maker], 867
[Love is patient], 1045
[May the grace of Jesus Christ], 21
[May the Love which overcomes], 906
[Now may our Lord Jesus Christ], 819
[Nurturing God, root us in your love], 1028
[The Lord is merciful and gracious], 186
[Thus says the Lord, the God of Israel], 783
[We light a candle for hope], 916

God: Mystery and Holiness of

Agios o Theos (Holy, Holy, Holy God), 709
Because the Words We Wait to Hear, 406
Build My Life, 92
Called or Not Called, God Is There, 422
Come, O Thou Traveler Unknown, 191
Darkness Is Not Dark to You, God, 200
Every Time I Feel the Spirit, 681
Gathered Here, 3
Heilig, heilig, heilig (Holy, Holy, Holy), 137
How Great Is Our God (Cuán grande es Dios), 116
Immortal, Invisible, God Only Wise, 98
In Thy Holy Place We Bow, 40
Joyful Is the Dark, 281
Lord, You Sometimes Speak, 537

Margam, satyam, jivam nive (Living, Moving, End and Beginning), 425
O God, Great Womb, 176
O Great Spirit, 51
Open the Eyes of My Heart (Ouvre les yeux / Abre mis ojos), 401
Planets Humming as They Wander, 175
Santo (Holy), 136
Santo, santo, santo (Holy, Holy, Holy), 102
Time Propels Us like a Current, 507
Unexpected and Mysterious, 229
We Long to Know Her, 44
You Are Holy, You Are Whole, 61
You Dwell in the Songs / Restless, 741
You, Lord, Are Both Lamb and Shepherd, 432
Your Love Is Amazing, 96
[Between the words], 990
[Eternal God, you call us to ventures], 1068
[God, I have so few ways to pray], 1008
[God of mystery and wonder at this and every table], 948
[O God, you withdraw from our sight], 1014
[Sing and sing], 883
[To worship is to stand in awe], 855

God: Power of

A Mighty Fortress Is Our God, 421
Agios o Theos (Holy, Holy, Holy God), 709
And I Will Raise You Up, 641
Anointing Fall on Me, 645
Be Still, My Soul, 664
Build My Life, 92
Cantai ao Senhor (O Sing to the Lord), 113
Creating God, Your Fingers Trace, 427
Don't Be Afraid, 596
Every Time I Feel the Spirit, 681
God Is Working This Purpose Out, 770
God of Our Strength, 47
God of Wonders, 178
God, Who Stretched the Spangled Heavens, 529
Gravity of Love, 494
Hallelujah, Salvation, and Glory, 69
How Great Is Our God (Cuán grande es Dios), 116
I Am That Great and Fiery Force, 663
I Sing the Mighty Power of God, 182
Ikke ved makt (Not by Your Might), 538
I to the Hills Will Lift My Eyes, 602
Kombo na Yesu (The Name of Jesus), 648
Let Justice Flow Down, 791
O Everlasting Love, 733
O God beyond All Praising, 814
O God, Great Womb, 176
O God, Our Help in Ages Past, 203
O God, Our Refuge, 434
O Lord My God / How Great Thou Art, 436
Open the Eyes of My Heart (Ouvre les yeux / Abre mis ojos), 401
Praise Be to God, 115
Praise the Lord, Sing Hallelujah, 95
Si tuvieras fe (If You Only Had Faith), 593
The Lord Is My Light, 437
There's a Wild Hope in the Wind, 828
Tú eres todopoderoso (Because You're Holy), 89
Wade in the Water, 454
Wakantanka (Many and Great), 128
We Give Thanks unto You, 117
We Sing to You, O God, 80
We Worship God the Rock, 424
You Are Exalted, 86
[Are any of you suffering hardships], 727
[Be still and know that I am God], 730
[Clap your hands all you peoples], 108
[God of power, may the boldness of your Spirit], 1067
[God of the foolish cross], 896
[I saw a vast crowd], 110
[Lead a life worthy of the calling], 446
[Most loving, most strong God], 900
[My soul proclaims the greatness], 987.F
[Now, to the One who by the power], 824
[The Lord is merciful and gracious], 186

God: Presence of

See: GATHERING: God's Presence with Us (37-67)

See also: Invocation; Jesus Christ: Presence of

Abide with Me, 502
As You Go Out from Here, 841
Because the Words We Wait to Hear, 406
Beyond a Dying Sun, 416
Blessed Are You, 290
Bless'd Be the God of Israel, 223
Bless This Food and Bless Your People, 489
Called or Not Called, God Is There, 422
Come, Ye Disconsolate, 643
Dans nos obscurités (Within Our Darkest Night), 632
Darkness Is Not Dark to You, God, 200
El Senyor és la meva força (In the Lord I'll Be Ever Thankful), 118
En medio de la vida (You Are the God within Life), 526
Eternal Light, Shine in My Heart, 554
Everlasting God, on You I Call, 630
Go, My Children, 830
God Be with You Till We Meet Again, 840
God of Grace and God of Glory, 716
Gravity of Love, 494
Herr, füll mich neu (Fill Me Anew), 739
How Firm a Foundation, 592
I Am That Great and Fiery Force, 663
I Sing the Mighty Power of God, 182
I Sought the Lord, 161
In the Quiet Curve of Evening, 587
Listen to the Word That God Has Spoken, 405
Lord, You've Searched Me, 609
More Than You Know, 598
O God, You Search Me, 199
O Thou, in Whose Presence, 600
Onyame wo mu o (In Your Sickness), 607
Open, Lord, My Inward Ear, 548
Oré poriajú verekó (Kyrie eleison), 620
Over My Head, 594
Peace, Be Still, 202
Praise, My Soul, the King of Heaven!, 75
Praise to the Living God, 204
Rain Down, 703
The Lord, Your God Is with You, 173
There's a Wild Hope in the Wind, 828
Thy Word Is a Lamp, 398
Time Propels Us like a Current, 507
Ubi caritas et amor, 773
Wakantanka (Many and Great), 128
We Sing to You, O God, 80
We've Come This Far by Faith, 599
When I Can't Find My Way, 591
Wij geloven één voor één (We Believe as One by One), 431
Word and Sign, 483
Your Grace Finds Me, 521
Your Love Is Washing Over Me, 166
[At the Impulse of God's Love], 780
[Barely midnight. All of us hunkered down], 871
[Be still and know that I am God], 730
[Christ be within us to keep us], 1069
[Does not Wisdom call], 184
[Eternal Strength, hold us], 983
[Everlasting God, you are our refuge], 981
[For the Word of God in Scripture], 913.G
[God, it is night], 986
[God of cosmos and quarks], 881
[God of deep and dazzling darkness], 988
[God of every place], 859
[God of mystery and wonder at this and every table], 948
[Have mercy on me, O God], 889
[Hear our prayer, O God of healing and hope], 978
[I am convinced that neither death, nor life], 337
[I lift my eyes to the hills], 109
[I saw a new heaven and a new earth], 339
[I will light a light in the name of the Maker], 867
[If you are delighted to be here], 853
[In our concerns and in our choices], 1051
[In the beginning, before time], 884
[In the beginning when it was very quiet], 852
[Life-giving God, may your Holy Spirit inspire], 879
[May God bless you and keep you], 826
[May the grace of Jesus Christ], 21
[Now, to the One who by the power], 824
[O Lord, you have searched me], 724
[Open our ears to hear your word], 866
[Rejoice in the Lord always], 726
[Sing and sing], 883
[The Lord is my shepherd], 725
[The Lord told you what is good], 784
[The Spirit helps us in our weakness], 729
[This day, God, may I dream your dreams], 984
[We are not alone], 922
[When Flaming Dove Meets Rising Waters], 378
[You who open doors], 862

God: Reign of

See: Reign of God

God: Word of

See: Word of God

God: Works of

See also: Creation: God as Creator

At the Dawn of Your Creation, 179
Before the Waters Nourished Earth, 652
Crashing Waters at Creation, 441
Creating God, Your Fingers Trace, 427
For the Beauty of the Earth, 120
God of the Fertile Fields, 750
God the Sculptor of the Mountains, 423
God, Who Stretched the Spangled Heavens, 529
God Who Touches Earth with Beauty, 550
I Sing the Mighty Power of God, 182
Nyanyikanlah nyanyian baru (Sing to God a New Song), 93
O God, Great Womb, 176
O Lord My God / How Great Thou Art, 436
Planets Humming as They Wander, 175
Wakantanka (Many and Great), 128
We Give Thanks unto You, 117
We Long to Know Her, 44
[Bless the Lord, O my soul], 185
[From all that is broken], 908
[God of grace, creator of waters], 931
[Now, to the One who by the power], 824
[Praise and thanks to you, holy God], 915
[Source and sustainer of life], 1009
[There are different kinds of gifts], 380
[We are not alone], 922
[We offer thanksgiving to our Creator], 864

God's Call

See: SHARING OUR STORIES: God's Call (536-547)

See also: Vocation

All Who Are Thirsty, 49
Arise, Your Light Is Come!, 273
Called by Earth and Sky, 806
Christ Be in Your Senses, 721
Christ Has Broken Down the Wall, 174
Come and See, 282
Come, Now Is the Time to Worship, 29
Eat This Bread (Coman de este pan), 476
Enviados somos de Dios (We Have Been Sent by God), 771
Far Above the Noise of Life, 625
God Calls Us, 394
God of Justice, 772
Holy Presence, Holy Teacher, 531
Jesus A, Nahetotaetanome (Jesus, Lord, How Joyful), 8
Jesus Calls Us, 30
Neno lake Mungu (Listen, God is Calling), 765
Nzambi wakatamba (God Loves All His Many People), 767
O Carpenter, Why Leave the Bench, 280
O God in Heaven, 720
Oceans (Océanos), 456
Quietly, Peacefully, 533
Seek Ye First, 417

The Water Is Ready, 458
Tú has venido a la orilla (Lord, You Have Come to the Lakeshore), 283
What Does the Lord Require of You?, 207
[As you come to Christ the living stone], 381
[Christ, whose insistent call], 1029
[Do not fear, says God], 903
[Empowering God, with your people], 965
[Eternal God, you call us to ventures], 1068
[Every Christian is called], 964
[God's Spirit calls, the church commissions], 966
[Here is my servant, the one I uphold], 448
[Jesus calls us to praise and prayer], 851
[Lead a life worthy of the calling], 446
[The Lord told you what is good], 784
[We are not alone], 922

Good Friday

See: Jesus Christ: Death of

Government

Christ Is King! Let Earthly Powers, 410
Hear the Turmoil of the Nations, 201
Let There Be Light, 714
This Is My Song, 710
Who Will Speak a Word of Warning, 758
[Clap your hands all you peoples], 108
[I pledge allegiance to Jesus Christ], 929
[Listening God, you hear our prayers], 996
[Praise the Lord], 107
[Some trust in governments], 1043

Grace

See also: Assurance of Grace; Forgiveness; Mercy
Ah, Holy Jesus, 330
Amazing Grace!, 163
Christ Calls to Me, 542
Come, Thou Fount, 563
God, Grant Us Mercy, 142
I Know Not Why God's Wondrous, 590
Just As I Am, without One Plea, 560
Lord, I Am Fondly, Earnestly Longing, 555
Lord, I Need You, 155
Make Us One, 455
The Lord Lift You Up, 832
The Water Is Ready, 458
There's a Wideness in God's Mercy, 156
Wonderful Grace of Jesus, 170
Your Grace Finds Me, 521
Your Grace Is Enough, 167
[Come, come, whoever you are], 1047
[Friends in Christ, God knows our needs], 888
[Gracious God, we celebrate life], 979
[Let us confess our sin], 890
[May the grace of Jesus Christ], 21
[Now may our Lord Jesus Christ], 819
[The Lord is merciful and gracious], 186
[There is no scarcity], 1024
[You who open doors], 862

Grace: Assurance of

See: Assurance of Grace

Gratitude

See: Praying: Gratitude

Greatest Commandment

See also: Love for God; Love for Others
Come, Now Is the Time to Worship, 29
Je louerai l'Éternel (Praise, I Will Praise You, Lord), 131
Kyrie eleison, Have Mercy, 796
Love the Lord Your God, 288
Move in Our Midst, 827
O God, We Read the Holy Law, 571
Renew Your Church, 717
[Come among us, Holy Spirit, and create a community], 955
[God of mercy, we are sorry], 897
[Hear, O Israel], 187
[Jesus said, let anyone with ears], 985.D
[Let us confess our sin], 890

Greed

See: Justice: Economic

Grief

See also: Death; Lament; Suffering
A Voice Was Heard in Ramah, 278
Balaacoolwe (Blessed Are the Persecuted), 578
Blessed Are You, 290
By the Waters of Babylon, 695
Go, Silent Friend, 657
God Weeps with Us, 656
How Long, O Lord, 691
In the Morning When I Rise, 499
Rain, Come Down, 634
What a Friend We Have in Jesus, 628
What Comfort Can Our Worship Bring, 623
When Grief Is Raw, 655
When I Can't Find My Way, 591
When Memory Fades, 649
[A wilderness beckons us], 1011
[Blessed are the poor in spirit], 295
[Eternal Strength, hold us], 983
[Everlasting God, you are our refuge], 981
[I saw a new heaven and a new earth], 339
[In our doubt and fear], 1044
[In the face of death, we worship God], 980
[O Ancient of Days, you have been our dwelling place], 920

Guidance

See also: Walking with God
Be Thou My Vision, 549
Gentle Shepherd, 718
God, Be the Love, 43
God of Our Strength, 47
Guide My Feet, 816
How Many Times We Start Again, 553
Lead Me Forth, 837
Listen in the Silence, 541
Nun danket alle Gott (Now Thank We All Our God), 114
Oceans (Océanos), 456
Open My Eyes that I May See, 738
Shepherd Me, O God, 744
The Hand of God Shall Hold You, 671
We Give Thanks unto You, 117
[Faithful God, we give thanks], 933
[God, give me grace to accept], 1007
[God of life, we thank you that our work], 953
[God will guide us continually], 985.H
[God's Word is a lamp], 913.F
[The Lord is my shepherd], 725
[Thus says the Lord, the God of Israel], 783

Harvest

See also: Land; Rural Life; Thanksgiving
Come, Ye Thankful People, 123
For the Fruit of All Creation, 124
God of the Fertile Fields, 750
Great Is Thy Faithfulness, 419
We Place upon Your Table, 462
We Plow the Fields and Scatter, 747
[Bless the Lord, O my soul], 185
[Come, with your faith and your doubts], 947
[Go forth in peace, and be of good courage], 1059
[God of Life, we give these offerings], 1017
[May those who sow in tears], 821
[Mist, Sun, Morning], 183
[Though the fig tree does not blossom], 820

Healing

See also: SHARING OUR STORIES: Healing and Anointing (642-651); See: WORSHIP RESOURCES: Sharing Our Stories—Healing (975-979)
See also: Anointing; Health Care Facilities; Praying: For Healing
All Who Are Thirsty, 49
Calm Me, Lord, 680
Cast Out, O Christ, 285
Come, Ye Disconsolate, 643
For the Healing of the Nations, 705
For Those with Whom Our Lives Are Bound, 734
God Calls Us, 394
Healer of Our Every Ill, 644
Healing River of the Spirit, 642
Hold Us in Your Mercy, 736
Jesus Christ Is Waiting, 287
Kombo na Yesu (The Name of Jesus), 648
Lord, Listen to Your Children, 682
Lord, You Give the Great Commission, 774
O Everlasting Love, 733
O Fiery Spirit, 55
O God, to You I Cry in Pain, 646
O Healing River, 706
O Holy Spirit, Root of Life, 376
Oh, Have You Not Heard (Ich weiss einen Strom), 668
Open My Eyes (Abre mis ojos), 732
Open My Heart / Abre mi corazón, 731
Sometimes a Light Surprises, 618
Still My Soul, 603
There Is a Balm in Gilead, 647
What Can I Leave Behind, 154
When Aging Takes Its Toll, 520
When Grief Is Raw, 655
When Memory Fades, 649
When We Must Bear Persistent Pain, 735
Will You Come and Follow Me, 540
With Mary Sing Magnificat, 208
Woza nomthwalo wakho (Come, Bring Your Burdens to God), 679
[Are any of you suffering hardships], 727
[For the times we have lied], 891
[From all that is broken], 908
[God, I have so few ways to pray], 1008
[Gracious God, we celebrate life], 979
[Great Physician, you touched the lives], 976
[Healing is central to the ministry of Jesus], 975
[Hear our prayer, O God of healing and hope], 978
[I saw a new heaven and a new earth], 339
[Jesus calls us to praise and prayer], 851
[Jesus stood up to read], 292
[Let the rain come and wash away], 1048
[Merciful God, we wait], 977
[O Prince of Peace], 894
[Some of us are exhausted], 854

Health Care Facilities

See also: Healing
Bless the Arms That Comfort, 527
When Aging Takes Its Toll, 520
When Memory Fades, 649
[Great Physician, you touched the lives], 976
[Hear our prayer, O God of healing and hope], 978
[How long, O Lord], 728
[I lift my eyes to the hills], 109
[Merciful God, we wait], 977
[The Lord is my shepherd], 725

Health: Mental

See: Mental Health

Healthcare

See: Health Care Facilities

Heaven

See also: Death and Eternal Life; Eternal Life
Amazing Grace!, 163
Blessed Are You, 290
Christ Is Our Cornerstone, 4
Come, Christians, Join to Sing, 28
Come, We That Love, 31
Dooládó' Shi Diyinda! (What a Wonderful Savior), 562
El cielo canta alegría (Heaven Is Singing for Joy), 665
Every Time I Feel the Spirit, 681
God Be with You Till We Meet Again, 840
Holy God, We Praise Thy Name, 126
I'm Gonna Eat at the Welcome Table, 801
Just a Closer Walk with Thee, 743
My Jesus, I Love Thee, 133
My Latest Sun Is Sinking Fast, 662
Nearer, My God, to Thee, 658
O Beautiful Star of Bethlehem, 275

Oh, Have You Not Heard (Ich weiss einen Strom), 668
On Jordan's Stormy Banks I Stand, 661
Precious Lord, Take My Hand, 610
Shall We Gather at the River, 667
So lange Jesus bleibt der Herr (As Long as Jesus' Reign Goes On), 64
Soon and Very Soon, 669
The Lord Is Risen Indeed!, 357
Ubi caritas (Where True Love), 492
[Eternal God in whom we live], 982
[I saw a new heaven and a new earth], 339
[Let the same mind be in you], 335

Heritage: 16th-Century

All People That on Earth Do Dwell, 5
All Praise to Thee, My God, 505
A Mighty Fortress Is Our God, 421
As a Deer in Want of Water, 552
Christ Has No Body Here but Ours, 568
Christ Jesus Lay, 463
Come, Ye Faithful, Raise the Strain, 348
Comfort, Comfort, O My People, 212
From Heaven Above to Earth I Come, 263
In Thee Is Gladness, 666
I Sing with Exultation, 444
Life-Giver, Maker, God of All, 38
Lord Jesus, Come and Overturn, 146
Nada te turbe, 604
O God, We Read the Holy Law, 571
O Gott Vater (O God and Father), 45
On This Great Day of Days, 260
Out of the Depths I Cry to You, 140
Praise God (Doxology), 71
Savior of the Nations, Come!, 214
Sing Praise to God Who Reigns, 101
Sing to the God of Harvest, 122
Sleepers, Wake, 226
The Garden Needs Our Tending Now, 788
The Strife Is O'er, 350
We Are People of God's Peace, 797
We Worship God the Rock, 424
[Christ has no body now on earth], 1035
[Dear God, let your word shine], 912
[Living God, by the power of your Spirit], 911
[Save us, God, from being self-centered], 1000

Heritage: 16th-Century Anabaptist

Everlasting God, on You I Call, 630
I Sing with Exultation, 444
Jesus Christ Is Love Divine, 749
O Christ, Impart Your Teaching True, 583
O God, Our Refuge, 434
O God, We Read the Holy Law, 571
O Gott Vater (O God and Father), 45
Rejoice, Rejoice Forevermore, 402
The Church of Christ Cannot Be Bound, 392
The Word of God Is Solid Ground, 399
We Are People of God's Peace, 797
[At the Impulse of God's Love], 780
[By the grace of God we seek to live and proclaim], 925
[Friends, as we gather to eat the bread], 937
[Gardener God, you have planted], 1002
[God dearly loves us], 1056
[God, maker of galaxies, who numbers the hairs], 971
[Loving God, you have baptized us], 1001
[No one can truly know Christ], 928
[True evangelical faith], 921

Heritage: African American

See also: Justice: Racial

Amen (African American), 689
Anointing Fall on Me, 645
Every Time I Feel the Spirit, 681
Go Tell It on the Mountain, 252
Guide My Feet, 816
Hallelujah, Salvation, and Glory, 69
I Want Jesus to Walk with Me, 306
I'm Gonna Eat at the Welcome Table, 801
In the Morning When I Rise, 499
Just a Closer Walk with Thee, 743
Lead Me, Guide Me, 601
Let Us Break Bread Together, 482
Lift Every Voice and Sing, 611
Lord, I Want to Be a Christian, 558
Over My Head, 594
Precious Lord, Take My Hand, 610
Somebody Prayed for Me, 698
Soon and Very Soon, 669
The Lord Is My Light, 437
There Is a Balm in Gilead, 647
There Is More Love Somewhere, 804
This Little Light of Mine, 762
Total Praise, 633
Wade in the Water, 454
We Are Often Tossed and Driven, 311
Were You There, 329
We Shall Overcome, 803
We Shall Walk through the Valley, 574
We've Come This Far by Faith, 599
When Israel Was in Egypt's Land, 193
When the Storms of Life Are Raging, 595
[Alive], 334
[May we go forth into the world with courage], 1039
[Sovereign Majesty, we pray for the continued outpouring], 992
[There is no scarcity], 1024
[When the song of the angels is stilled], 1064

Heritage: Before 1500

See also: Agnus Dei / Lamb of God; Creeds: Historic; Gloria in excelsis / Glory to God in the Highest; Gloria Patri / Glory to the Father; Kyrie eleison / Lord, Have Mercy; Sanctus / Holy, Holy, Holy

Agios o Theos (Holy, Holy, Holy God), 709
All Creatures Worship God Most High, 81
All Glory, Laud, and Honor, 315
All Will Be Well, 586
Be Thou My Vision, 549
Christ, Be All around Me, 848
Christ Has Died, Christ Is Risen, 438
Christ Is Arisen, 358
Christ Is Our Cornerstone, 4
Christ Is Risen, 349
Christ Jesus Lay, 463
Christ, We Do All Adore Thee, 138
Come, Ye Faithful, Raise the Strain, 348
Creating God, Your Fingers Trace, 427
Creator of the Stars of Night, 236
Dona nobis pacem, 707
Eternal Light, Shine in My Heart, 554
From the Parent's Heart, the Firstborn (Corde natus ex parentis), 418
God, Be the Love, 43
God, Grant Us Mercy, 142
Good Christian Friends, Rejoice, 261
Holy God, We Praise Thy Name, 126
Holy Spirit, Come to Us, 58
I Am That Great and Fiery Force, 663
Jesus Christ Is Waiting, 287
Joyous Light of Heavenly Glory, 504
Kindle in Us Your Love, 54
Let All Mortal Flesh Keep Silence, 65
Let the Hungry Come to Me, 459
Lo, How a Rose E'er Blooming, 216
Make Me an Instrument of Your Peace, 713
Mary, Woman Weeping, 328
Mothering God, You Gave Me Birth, 426
Now the Green Blade Rises, 353
O Come, O Come, Immanuel, 210
O Fiery Spirit, 55
O Holy Spirit, by Whose Breath, 53
O Holy Spirit, Root of Life, 376
O Love, How Deep, How Broad, 303
O Sacred Head, Now Wounded, 325
O Splendor of God's Glory Bright, 500
On Silken, Soft Wings, 676
On This Great Day of Days, 260
Praise to the Living God, 204
Savior of the Nations, Come!, 214
Seed, Scattered and Sown, 477
Sing, My Tongue, the Song of Triumph, 331
Sing We Triumphant Hymns, 363
That Easter Morn, at Break of Day, 342
The Church of Christ Cannot Be Bound, 392
The Glory of These Forty Days, 305
Ubi caritas et amor, 773
Ubi caritas (Where True Love), 492
Veni Sancte Spiritus, 370
Who Are These, 360
With Astonishment, Fear, and Wonder, 579
[Alleluia! Christ is risen!], 875
[Almighty God, to you all hearts are open], 860
[Christ—the Joy, the Truth], 907
[Come, Holy One, work upon us], 858
[Eternal Strength, hold us], 983
[Everlasting God, in whom we live and move], 998
[God be in my head], 999
[God, make me an instrument of your peace], 991
[Grow us slowly], 1030
[Live without fear], 1062
[May almighty God have mercy on us], 905
[May God be with you! And also with you], 944
[May the Son of God], 1057
[Most loving, most strong God], 900
[This home is yours, my God], 958

Heritage: Church of the Brethren

Beyond a Dying Sun, 416
Called or Not Called, God Is There, 422
Count Well the Cost, 577
For We Are Strangers No More, 409
Move in Our Midst, 827
Rain, Come Down, 634

Holy, Holy, Holy

See: Sanctus / Holy, Holy, Holy

Holy Spirit

See: TELLING GOD'S STORY: Holy Spirit (367-377); ART AND SCRIPTURE: Holy Spirit, Pentecost, Church (378-385)

See also: God: Images and Names of; Holy Spirit: Gifts of; Invocation; Pentecost

Anointing Fall on Me, 645
As We Rise, O God, to Meet You, 39
Breathe on Me, Breath of God, 737
Come and Seek the Ways of Wisdom, 196
Come, Ye Disconsolate, 643
Could It Be That God Is Singing, 42
Every Time I Feel the Spirit, 681
Go, My Children, 830
Go Ye Now in Peace / Go, My Friends, in Peace, 839
God, Whose Purpose Is to Kindle, 152
Gott ist gegenwärtig (God Is Here among Us), 62
Healer of Our Every Ill, 644
Healing River of the Spirit, 642
Herr, füll mich neu (Fill Me Anew), 739
Holy Spirit, Come to Us, 58
Holy Spirit, Come with Power (Ven, Espíritu, cual viento), 57
Holy Spirit, Truth Divine, 46
How Can We Be Silent, 790
I Believe in God Almighty, 433
I Know Not Why God's Wondrous, 590
Kindle in Us Your Love, 54
Like the Murmur of the Dove's Song, 56
Listen in the Silence, 541
Loving Spirit, 697
Move in Our Midst, 827
O Fiery Spirit, 55
O Holy Spirit, by Whose Breath, 53
On Silken, Soft Wings, 676
Prabhoo Lay lay (Savior Jesus, Enfold Me), 567
Praise to the Living God, 204
Spirit, Do Your Work in Us, 475
Spirit of God! Descend, 557
Spirit of the Living God, 740
Spirit, Working in Creation, 50
The Church of Christ, in Every Age, 395
The Kingdom of God (El reino de Dios), 799
There's a Wild Hope in the Wind, 828
Through Our Fragmentary Prayers, 677
With Water Freely Flowing, 452
[Bless the Lord, O my soul], 185
[Come, Holy Spirit, enter our silences], 877

[Go in peace. Rejoice in the power], 1052.G
[God of power, may the boldness of your Spirit], 1067
[Gracious God, when there is nothing], 994
[Hear the good news!], 903.D
[Hear what the Spirit is saying], 913.C
[I believe in God, the Father almighty], 923
[Lead a life worthy of the calling], 446
[May the grace of Jesus Christ], 21
[Now, thanks to Christ Jesus], 786
[O God, Ancient of Days, your love], 941
[O Risen Christ, you breathe your Holy Spirit], 1013
[Praise and thanks to you, holy God], 915
[Praying aloud spontaneously], 995
[Sovereign Majesty, we pray for the continued outpouring], 992
[The people say: Our bones are dried up], 383
[There are different kinds of gifts], 380
[The Spirit helps us in our weakness], 729
[We believe in one God, the Father, the Almighty], 924
[When Flaming Dove Meets Rising Waters], 378
[When the day of Pentecost came], 379

Holy Spirit: Gifts of

See also: Holy Spirit

As the Wind Song through the Trees, 373
Go in Grace and Make Disciples, 766
Holy Spirit, Come with Power (Ven, Espíritu, cual viento), 57
Longing for Light, 715
Lord, You Give the Great Commission, 774
May You Be Rooted and Grounded in Love, 396
O Holy Spirit, by Whose Breath, 53
One Is the Body, 386
Summoned by the God Who Made Us, 1
There Are Many Gifts, 374
When Hands Reach Out, 513
You're Not Alone, 779
[Christ is like a single body], 856
[Empowering God, with your people], 965
[God of power, may the boldness of your Spirit], 1067
[Living God, by the power of your Spirit], 911
[May God, who calls you to this ministry], 968
[Nurturing God, root us in your love], 1028
[There are different kinds of gifts], 380
[What will you offer the body of Christ today], 1023
[When the day of Pentecost came], 379

Holy Thursday

See also: Communion; Footwashing; Journey to the Cross

All the Room Was Hushed and Still, 493
Bleibet hier (Stay with Me), 627
Christ, on the Night He Was Betrayed, 491
Go to Dark Gethsemane, 317
In the Quiet Consecration, 484
Jesus Took a Towel, 490
Ngayong nagdadapit hapon (When Twilight Comes), 501
Prepare a Room for Me, 465
Seeking Warmth from Charcoal Blazing, 344
Stay with Me, the Night Has Come, 319
'Tis Midnight, and on Olive's Brow, 318
Ubi caritas et amor, 773
Ubi caritas (Where True Love), 492
[Eternal Love, gentle God, you invite us], 951
[For I received from the Lord], 469
[God of the foolish cross], 896
[Jesus Christ, our Savior, you did not regard equality with God], 952
[Jesus, servant, at supper with your disciples], 1041
[Jesus washed the feet of his disciples], 950

Holy Week

See: Holy Thursday; Jesus Christ: Death of; Palm Sunday

Home: Worship and Prayer

See also: Children: Appropriate for; Evening; Morning; Table Graces

[Communion], 468
[Evening Prayer], 987
[God, it is night], 986
[God of deep and dazzling darkness], 988
[Hear, O Israel], 187
[Morning Prayer], 985
[This day, God, may I dream your dreams], 984
[This home is yours, my God], 958
[Where two or three are gathered], 19

Hope

Abide with Me, 502
Amazing Grace!, 163
Beautiful Things, 551
Beyond a Dying Sun, 416
Christ Is Risen! Shout Hosanna!, 354
Come, Thou Long-Expected Jesus, 218
Come, Ye Disconsolate, 643
For the Healing of the Nations, 705
God Calls Us, 394
God, Give Me Faith like a Child, 519
Gravity of Love, 494
Healer of Our Every Ill, 644
Hope Is a Candle, 211
How Firm a Foundation, 592
I Know That My Redeemer Lives, 347
In the Bulb There Is a Flower, 670
In Thee Is Gladness, 666
Lift Every Voice and Sing, 611
Make Me an Instrument of Your Peace, 713
My Hope Is Built on Nothing Less, 621
Na nzela na lola (As Long as We Follow), 413
O Little Town of Bethlehem, 245
Oh, How Shall I Receive Thee, 215
On Jordan's Stormy Banks I Stand, 661
Out of the Depths I Cry to You, 140
Sing a New World into Being, 809
Soon and Very Soon, 669
There Is More Love Somewhere, 804
There's a Wild Hope in the Wind, 828
We Shall Overcome, 803
We Shall Walk through the Valley, 574
When Grief Is Raw, 655
[Alive], 334
[As you come to Christ the living stone], 381
[Blessed be the ones who dance], 1049
[Creemos en Dios Padre todopoderoso], 927
[Great Physician, you touched the lives], 976
[Hear our prayer, O God of healing and hope], 978
[I saw a new heaven and a new earth], 339
[Lead a life worthy of the calling], 446
[Let the rain come and wash away], 1048
[Living Christ, in these times], 1033
[Love is patient], 1045
[May God bless you with a restless discomfort], 1058
[May the God of hope], 987.I
[Merciful God, we wait], 977
[Migrant Journey], 817
[O God, our deliverer], 1010
[Our physical bodies cannot inherit], 336
[The people say: Our bones are dried up], 383
[Thus says the Lord, the God of Israel], 783
[We gather in preparation], 870
[We light a candle for hope], 916

Housing

Beauty for Brokenness, 712
Forgive, Forgive Us, Holy God, 149
Helpless and Hungry, 268
Here to the House of God We Come, 27
If the War Goes On, 794
Jesus Entered Egypt, 279
Let Justice Flow Down, 791
Longing for Light, 715
Mary, Woman Weeping, 328
My Song Is Love Unknown, 320
Sing a New World into Being, 809
The Church of Christ Cannot Be Bound, 392
[God, just as you sent Joseph to Egypt], 957
[God our sanctuary], 1042
[Receive our thanks for night and day], 949
[This home is yours, my God], 958
[Thus says the Lord, the God of Israel], 783
[True evangelical faith], 921

Humility

All the Room Was Hushed and Still, 493
Christ, on the Night He Was Betrayed, 491
Come, Now Is the Time to Worship, 29
God, Give Me Time, 144
God, Grant Us Mercy, 142
Jesus Took a Towel, 490
Will You Let Me Be Your Servant, 778
[Christ our companion, you came not to humiliate the sinner], 898
[Jesus Christ, our Savior, you did not regard equality with God], 952
[Jesus, servant, at supper with your disciples], 1041
[Jesus washed the feet of his disciples], 950
[Lead a life worthy of the calling], 446
[Let the same mind be in you], 335
[The Lord told you what is good], 784

Images of God

See: God: Images and names of

Images of Jesus Christ

See: Jesus Christ: Images and Names of

Immigration and Refugees

See also: Exile

Beauty for Brokenness, 712
By the Waters of Babylon, 695
Children of the Heavenly Father, 517
Christ Has Broken Down the Wall, 174
Helpless and Hungry, 268
Here to the House of God We Come, 27
If the War Goes On, 794
Jesus Entered Egypt, 279
Seek the Peace of the City, 206
[For failing to love others], 893
[God our sanctuary], 1042
[Lord, your coming is still miraculous], 872
[Migrant Journey], 817

Incarnation

See also: Jesus Christ: Advent of; Jesus Christ: Birth of

Although Our Lord Has Left Us, 366
Away in a Manger, 257
Break Forth, O Beauteous Heavenly, 269
Christ Be in Your Senses, 721
Come, Join in Mary's Prophet-Song, 246
Creator of the Stars of Night, 236
Ehane he'ama (Father God, You Are Holy), 59
From Heaven Above to Earth I Come, 263
God the Sculptor of the Mountains, 423
Hark! the Herald Angels Sing, 247
He Came Down, 239
Helpless and Hungry, 268
Here I Am to Worship (Ich will dich anbeten), 227
I Sing with Exultation, 444
In Christ Alone, 332
In the Beginning, 270
Infant Holy, Infant Lowly, 243
Jesus Calls Us, 30
Joyful Is the Dark, 281
Let All Mortal Flesh Keep Silence, 65
Life-Giver, Maker, God of All, 38
Lo, How a Rose E'er Blooming, 216
Love Came Down at Christmas, 255
Love Has Come, 258
My Song Is Love Unknown, 320
Noche anunciada (Night Long Awaited), 242
Noel, 256
Now the Heavens Start to Whisper, 237
O Come, All Ye Faithful, 241
O du fröhliche (Oh, How Joyfully), 254
O Little Town of Bethlehem, 245
O Love, How Deep, How Broad, 303
O Splendor of God's Glory Bright, 500

Oh, How Shall I Receive Thee, 215
Savior of the Nations, Come!, 214
Sheng ye qing (Holy Night, Blessed Night), 262
The Angel Gabriel Called Mary Blessed, 221
Unexpected and Mysterious, 229
We Praise the Word of God, 404
Where Is This Stupendous Stranger, 266
Wisdom from on High Is Dawning, 238
[Christ is the image of the invisible God], 189
[How silently], 1021
[In the beginning was the Word], 235
[In the beginning when it was very quiet], 852
[Let the same mind be in you], 335
[Lord, your coming is still miraculous], 872
[Praise and thanks to you, holy God], 915
[The angel said to Mary], 233
[We gather in preparation], 870
[We Owe Them a Complicated Debt], 230

Indigenous Communities: Resources Related to

See also: Justice: Racial

Creation Is a Song / Ho'ė enemeohe, 181
Dawk'yah towgyah thawy báht-awm (Take the Saving Word of God), 400
Dooládó' Shi Diyinda! (What a Wonderful Savior), 562
Ehane he'ama (Father God, You Are Holy), 59
Heleluyan, 85
Hey ney yana (I Walk in Beauty), 836
I Have Decided to Follow Jesus, 443
Jesus A, Nahetotaetanome (Jesus, Lord, How Joyful), 8
Lord, Have Mercy (Moosonee), 651
O Great Spirit, 51
There's a River of Life, 24
Wakantanka (Many and Great), 128
Way way way (Ojibwe), 742
[Creator, we give you thanks], 861
[May the warm winds of heaven], 1061
[Peace be with you], 850
[We acknowledge that we are gathering], 878
[We offer thanksgiving to our Creator], 864

Installation

See: Commissioning: Other; Church Leadership; Ordination

Intercession

See: Praying

Interfaith

See also: Expanding our Circle

Between Darkness and Light, 808
Dona nobis pacem, 707
Hope of Abraham and Sarah, 807
Peace, Salaam, Shalom, 805
Praise to the Living God, 204
Shalom chaverim (Shalom, My Friends), 842
Shema Yisrael, 192
The God of Sarah Praise, 190
[Come, come, whoever you are], 1047
[If there is to be peace in the world], 1046
[Let the rain come and wash away], 1048

Invocation

See also: Gathering; God: Presence of; Holy Spirit; Jesus Christ: Presence of; Praying

All Who Are Thirsty, 49
Come, My Way, My Truth, My Life, 48
Confitemini Domino (Come and Fill Our Hearts), 52
Eternal Light, Shine in My Heart, 554
Gathered Here, 3
Herr, füll mich neu (Fill Me Anew), 739
Kindle in Us Your Love, 54
Njoo kwetu, Roho mwema (Gracious Spirit), 367
Rain Down, 703
Spirit of Life, 368
Trinity Song, 60
Veni Sancte Spiritus, 370
[Almighty God, to you all hearts are open], 860
[Barely midnight. All of us hunkered down], 871
[Come, Holy One, work upon us], 858
[Come, Holy Spirit, enter our silences], 877
[Creator, we give you thanks], 861
[Dear God, let your word shine], 912
[From Bethlehem to Nazareth], 874
[Gardener God, you have planted], 1002
[God of every place], 859
[God of grace, creator of waters], 931
[Holy God, you call us together], 857
[In the beginning, before time], 884
[I praise you, God—in the sanctuary], 886
[I will light a light in the name of the Maker], 867
[Living God, by the power of your Spirit], 911
[Lord, your coming is still miraculous], 872
[O God, you withdraw from our sight], 1014
[O Tree of Calvary], 1012
[Praise and thanks to you, holy God], 915
[Source of all hope and holiness], 863
[Speak to us, living God], 910
[You who open doors], 862

Jesus Christ: Advent of

See: TELLING GOD'S STORY: Advent (210-239); ART AND SCRIPTURE: Advent and Birth of Jesus (230-235)

See also: Advent Candle Lighting; Jesus Christ: Birth of; Incarnation; Reign of Christ; Second Coming

All Who Are Thirsty, 49
Come, Join in Mary's Prophet-Song, 246
Come Now, O God, 143
Ehane he'ama (Father God, You Are Holy), 59
For You, O God, My Soul, 41
From the Parent's Heart, the Firstborn (Corde natus ex parentis), 418
It Came upon a Midnight Clear, 248
Light Dawns on a Weary World, 205
Longing for Light, 715
My Soul Cries Out, 412
O Day of Peace, 787
Ososo (Come Now, O Prince of Peace), 391
View the Present, 407
We Dream of a Turning, 209
[A shoot will come up], 232
[Barely midnight. All of us hunkered down], 871
[Blessed are you, Lord, the God of Israel], 985.E
[Come, let us go up], 13
[Do not fear, says God], 903
[Go in peace. Prepare the way], 1052.E
[God dearly loves us], 1056
[Lord, your coming is still miraculous], 872
[My soul proclaims the greatness], 987.F
[O God, our deliverer], 1010
[The angel said to Mary], 233
[The people walking in darkness], 231
[Tree of Life], 12
[We gather in preparation], 870
[We light a candle for hope], 916
[We light this candle as a sign], 917
[We Owe Them a Complicated Debt], 230

Jesus Christ: Ascension of

See: TELLING GOD'S STORY: Ascension (363-366)

See also: Reign of Christ

All Hail the Power of Jesus' Name (CORONATION), 411
Christ Is King! Let Earthly Powers, 410
Crown Him with Many Crowns, 408
One Is the Body, 386
We Praise Thee, O God, 91
[In his hands the iron nails], 919
[O God, you withdraw from our sight], 1014

Jesus Christ: Baptism of

Crashing Waters at Creation, 441
O Love, How Deep, How Broad, 303
[As John baptized Jesus in the Jordan], 940
[From the River to the Wilderness], 445
[God of covenant, when Jesus came up from the waters], 935
[God of grace, creator of waters], 931
[Here is my servant, the one I uphold], 448
[Jesus, Lamb of God], 892
[When Flaming Dove Meets Rising Waters], 378
[While everyone was being baptized], 447

Jesus Christ: Birth of

See: TELLING GOD'S STORY: Birth of Jesus (240-269); ART AND SCRIPTURE: Advent and Birth of Jesus (230-235)

See also: Incarnation; Jesus Christ: Advent of; Jesus Christ: Epiphany of; Longest Night / Blue Christmas

As with Gladness, 277
From the Parent's Heart, the Firstborn (Corde natus ex parentis), 418
Gloria, 94
Hacia Belén (Mary Journeyed), 224
Hail the Bless'd Morn, 272
He Came Down, 239
Hope Is a Candle, 211
In the Beginning, 270
Joyful Is the Dark, 281
Let All Mortal Flesh Keep Silence, 65
Poor of the Earth, 213
Savior of the Nations, Come!, 214
Solemn Stillness, Weary Streets, 276
Wisdom from on High Is Dawning, 238
[Barely midnight. All of us hunkered down], 871
[Glory to God in the highest], 880
[God of grace, creator of waters], 931
[How silently], 1021
[I believe in God, the Father almighty], 923
[In our concerns and in our choices], 1051
[In the beginning was the Word], 235
[In the beginning when it was very quiet], 852
[Lord, your coming is still miraculous], 872
[Now, Lord, you let your servant], 825
[The angel said, "Do not be afraid!"], 234
[The angel said to Mary], 233
[The people walking in darkness], 231
[We believe in one God, the Father, the Almighty], 924
[We light a candle for hope], 916
[We light this candle as a sign], 917
[We Owe Them a Complicated Debt], 230
[When the song of the angels is stilled], 1064

Jesus Christ: Death of

See: TELLING GOD'S STORY: Jesus' Death (320-332); ART AND SCRIPTURE: Jesus' Death and Resurrection (334-339)

Christ, We Do All Adore Thee, 138
Go to Dark Gethsemane, 317
How Can We Worship Caesar's Cross, 308
I Believe in God Almighty, 433
Joyful Is the Dark, 281
Lord, I Lift Your Name on High (Tu nombre levantaré), 365
Low in the Grave He Lay, 333
My God, My God, 696
O Lord My God / How Great Thou Art, 436
O Love, How Deep, How Broad, 303
O phi nong oei (Dear Friends, We're One), 525
O Praise the Gracious Power, 87
Oh, qué bueno es Jesús (Oh, How Great Is Christ the Lord), 351
Praise Him, Praise Him, 100
Revelation Song (Digno y santo), 415
Sign Us with Ashes, Merciful God, 304
Unless a Grain of Wheat, 302
We Read the Cross, 569
What Wondrous Love Is This, 564
When I Survey the Wondrous Cross (La cruz excelsa al contemplar), 323

When I Survey the Wondrous Cross (South Africa, Zimbabwe), 322
You, Lord, Are Both Lamb and Shepherd, 432
[Alive], 334
[Do you not know that all who were baptized], 449
[For I received from the Lord], 469
[God of the foolish cross], 896
[God, I have so few ways to pray], 1008
[I believe in God, the Father almighty], 923
[If we have died with Christ], 903C
[In his hands the iron nails], 919
[Jesus Christ, you stretched out your arms], 1026
[Let the same mind be in you], 335
[O Tree of Calvary], 1012
[Praise and thanks to you, holy God], 915
[That huge "Why?"], 1005
[We believe in one God, the Father, the Almighty], 924

Jesus Christ: Epiphany of

See: TELLING GOD'S STORY: Jesus' Epiphany (270-279)

See also: Jesus Christ: Birth of

Angels, from the Realms of Glory, 265
Break Forth, O Beauteous Heavenly, 269
Here I Am to Worship (Ich will dich anbeten), 227
Longing for Light, 715
Love Has Come, 258
On This Great Day of Days, 260
Sálvanos, Señor, despiertos (Save Us, O Lord), 833
The First Noel, the Angel Did Say, 250
What Child Is This, 267
[Now, Lord, you let your servant], 825
[When the song of the angels is stilled], 1064

Jesus Christ: Images and Names of

See also: God: Images and Names of; Name of Jesus;

A Wonderful Savior Is Jesus, 626
Agneau de Dieu (O Lamb of God), 559
Christ Is King! Let Earthly Powers, 410
Christ Is Our Cornerstone, 4
Christ Who Left His Home in Glory, 361
Come and Seek the Ways of Wisdom, 196
Come, Christians, Join to Sing, 28
Come, My Way, My Truth, My Life, 48
Come, O Thou Traveler Unknown, 191
Come, Ye Disconsolate, 643
Comme un souffle fragile (As a Sigh Great with Yearning), 403
Gentle Shepherd, 718
God the Spirit, Guide and Guardian, 534
Hail the Bless'd Morn, 272
Haleluya! Pelo tsa rona (Hallelujah! We Sing Your Praises), 473
Hark! the Herald Angels Sing, 247
Healer of Our Every Ill, 644
Hold Us in Your Mercy, 736
I Am That Great and Fiery Force, 663
I Am the Bread of Life (Yo soy el pan de vida), 480
In the Rifted Rock I'm Resting (Wehrlos und verlassen sehnt sich), 619
Jesu, meine Freude (Jesus, Priceless Treasure), 624
Jesus on the Mountain Peak, 301
Jesus, Rock of Ages, 622
Kombo na Yesu (The Name of Jesus), 648
Kwake Yesu nasimama (Here on Christ the Rock I Will Stand), 159
Lamb of God / Cordero de Dios, 151
Lo, How a Rose E'er Blooming, 216
Love Has Come, 258
Noche anunciada (Night Long Awaited), 242
Noel, 256
Now the Heavens Start to Whisper, 237
O Come, All Ye Faithful, 241
O Come, O Come, Immanuel, 210
O Holy Spirit, Root of Life, 376
O Love That Will Not Let Me Go, 608
O Splendor of God's Glory Bright, 500
Ososo (Come Now, O Prince of Peace), 391
Praise Him, Praise Him, 100
Prepare a Room for Me, 465
Schönster Herr Jesu (Beautiful Savior), 130
Stille Nacht, heilige Nacht (Silent Night, Holy Night), 244
Thine Is the Glory, 355
To Us a Child of Hope Is Born, 259
We, Your People, Sing Your Praises (Bon Berger, ton peuple t'adore), 849
You, Lord, Are Both Lamb and Shepherd, 432
[Christ is the image of the invisible God], 189
[Christ—the Joy, the Truth], 907
[Does not Wisdom call], 184
[I saw a vast crowd], 110
[Jesus, Lamb of God], 892
[Sing the Goodness], 104
[The people walking in darkness], 231
[We believe in one God, the Father, the Almighty], 924

Jesus Christ: Life of

See also: TELLING GOD'S STORY: Life, Teaching, and Ministry of Jesus (280-303); ART AND SCRIPTURE: Life, Teaching, and Ministry of Jesus (291-296)

See also: Jesus Christ: Baptism of; Jesus Christ: Miracles of; Jesus Christ: Teachings of; Jesus Christ: Transfiguration of, Journey to the Cross

All the Room Was Hushed and Still, 493
Christ, on the Night He Was Betrayed, 491
Could It Be That God Is Singing, 42
Jesus Took a Towel, 490
Lord, I Lift Your Name on High (Tu nombre levantaré), 365
Lord Jesus, Come and Overturn, 146
My Love Colors Outside the Lines, 582
My Song Is Love Unknown, 320
Naege itneun hyangyu okhap (To My Precious Lord), 755
O Love, How Deep, How Broad, 303
Oceans (Océanos), 456
Praise with Joy the World's Creator, 428
Somlandela (We Will Follow), 566
Strong, Peaceful Man of Galilee, 573
[A wilderness beckons us], 1011
[Eternal Love, gentle God, you invite us], 951
[For I received from the Lord], 469
[From Bethlehem to Nazareth], 874
[From the River to the Wilderness], 445
[God, I have so few ways to pray], 1008
[God of work and rest], 956
[Jesus of love and leftovers], 1016
[Jesus, servant, at supper with your disciples], 1041
[Jesus stood up to read], 292
[Jesus washed the feet of his disciples], 950
[Loaves and Fishes], 291
[O God, Ancient of Days, your love], 941
[O Prince of Peace], 894
[Some of us are exhausted], 854
[Some people brought children], 18
[The table has been prepared], 939
[While everyone was being baptized], 447
[While Jesus was in Bethany], 296

Jesus Christ: Love of

See also: God: Love of

Come, O Thou Traveler Unknown, 191
I Come with Joy, 478
I Heard the Voice of Jesus Say, 536
I Love to Tell the Story, 761
Jesus Christ Is Love Divine, 749
Jesus Loves Me, 516
Jesus, Rock of Ages, 622
Jesus Took a Towel, 490
Love Divine, All Loves Excelling, 638
Love Has Come, 258
My Song Is Love Unknown, 320
Ngayong nagdadapit hapon (When Twilight Comes), 501
O God of Blessings, 700
O Love, How Deep, How Broad, 303
O phi nong oei (Dear Friends, We're One), 525
O Sacred Head, Now Wounded, 325
Prabhoo Lay lay (Savior Jesus, Enfold Me), 567
Softly and Tenderly Jesus Is Calling, 544
What Wondrous Love Is This, 564
[O Tree of Calvary], 1012

Jesus Christ: Miracles of

See also: Jesus Christ: Life of

Fierce Raged the Tempest, 286
Hold Us in Your Mercy, 736
Jesus Christ Is Waiting, 287
Kombo na Yesu (The Name of Jesus), 648
My Love Colors Outside the Lines, 582
There's Enough for All, 757
Will You Come and Follow Me, 540
[From Bethlehem to Nazareth], 874
[God, I have so few ways to pray], 1008
[Healing is central to the ministry of Jesus], 975
[Jesus of love and leftovers], 1016
[Loaves and Fishes], 291
[Some of us are exhausted], 854
[The crowd said to Jesus, "You must show us more miracles"], 471

Jesus Christ: Name of

See: Name of Jesus

Jesus Christ: Presence of

See also: God: Presence of; Invocation

Akekho ofana / Hakuna wakaita (There's No One in This World like Jesus), 68
Although Our Lord Has Left Us, 366
Christ, Be All around Me, 848
Come, My Way, My Truth, My Life, 48
From North and South, from East and West, 460
Go Ye Now in Peace / Go, My Friends, in Peace, 839
God, Be the Love, 43
God the Sculptor of the Mountains, 423
In the Morning When I Rise, 499
In the Singing, in the Silence, 481
Jesus, Be the Center, 584
Let the Hungry Come to Me, 459
Lo, I Am with You, 284
Love Has Come, 258
Oceans (Océanos), 456
Praise with Joy the World's Creator, 428
Prepare a Room for Me, 465
Somos pueblo que camina (We Are People on a Journey), 464
Spirit, Do Your Work in Us, 475
The Bread We Break Is Telling, 466
There's Nothing Worth More (Nada vale más), 369
Thy Word Is a Lamp, 398
What a Friend We Have in Jesus, 628
Word and Sign, 483
[At the table of Christ], 936
[Christ be within us to keep us], 1069
[Go in peace. Christ is with you], 1051.A
[Jesus' eleven disciples went to a mountain], 451
[O God, your word is a lamp to my feet], 987.A
[Some of us are exhausted], 854
[Two disciples were traveling], 470
[Where two or three are gathered], 19

Jesus Christ: Reign of

See: Reign of Christ

Jesus Christ: Resurrection of

See: TELLING GOD'S STORY: Jesus' Resurrection (333-362); ART AND SCRIPTURE: Jesus' Death and Resurrection (334-339)

Christ Has Died, Christ Is Risen, 438
Christ Is Alive, and Goes Before Us, 565
Christ Jesus Lay, 463
Come, Christians, Join to Sing, 28
Crown Him with Many Crowns, 408
How Can We Be Silent, 790
I Am the Bread of Life (Yo soy el pan de vida), 480
I Believe in God Almighty, 433
In Christ Alone, 332

In the Bulb There Is a Flower, 670
Lord, I Lift Your Name on High (Tu nombre levantaré), 365
Revelation Song (Digno y santo), 415
Sign Us with Ashes, Merciful God, 304
The Bread We Break Is Telling, 466
Unless a Grain of Wheat, 302
Were You There, 329
We Walk by Faith, 588
You, Lord, Are Both Lamb and Shepherd, 432
Zisuh nih a zultu hna sinah (Peace Be with You! Jesus Told His Friends), 165
[Alive], 334
[Alleluia (ASL)], 73
[Alleluia! Christ is risen!], 875
[Blessed be the ones who dance], 1049
[Christ is the image of the invisible God], 189
[Christ—the Joy, the Truth], 907
[Do you not know that all who were baptized], 449
[Eternal God in whom we live], 982
[Go in peace. Christ is risen], 1052.F
[God, I have so few ways to pray], 1008
[I believe in God, the Father almighty], 923
[If we have died with Christ], 903C
[In his hands the iron nails], 919
[Let the same mind be in you], 335
[Living Christ, in these times], 1033
[Living God for whom no door is closed], 876
[May the Christ who walks on wounded feet], 1066
[O Risen Christ, you breathe your Holy Spirit], 1013
[Our physical bodies cannot inherit], 336
[Peace be with you], 850
[Praise and thanks to you, holy God], 915
[Two disciples were traveling], 470
[We believe in one God, the Father, the Almighty], 924

Jesus Christ: Second Coming of

See also: Jesus Christ: Advent of; Judgment; Reign of Christ
A Wonderful Savior Is Jesus, 626
Christ Has Died, Christ Is Risen, 438
Come Now, O God, 143
Come, Ye Thankful People, 123
For All the Saints, 672
Hark! the Glad Sound!, 217
How Can We Be Silent, 790
I Am the Bread of Life (Yo soy el pan de vida), 480
I Believe in God Almighty, 433
I Know Not Why God's Wondrous, 590
I'm Gonna Eat at the Welcome Table, 801
It Came upon a Midnight Clear, 248
Jésus, je voudrais te chanter (Lord Jesus, You Shall Be My Song), 581
Kwake Yesu nasimama (Here on Christ the Rock I Will Stand), 159
Let All Mortal Flesh Keep Silence, 65
My Hope Is Built on Nothing Less, 621
O Lord My God / How Great Thou Art, 436
Praise Him, Praise Him, 100
Sleepers, Wake, 226
The Bread We Break Is Telling, 466
This Joyful Eastertide, 352
View the Present, 407
Wait for the Lord / Contemplaré tu vida, 228
When Peace like a River, 617
[Now may the God of peace], 823

Jesus Christ: Teachings of

See also: TELLING GOD'S STORY: Life, Teaching, and Ministry of Jesus (280-303); ART AND SCRIPTURE: Life, Teaching, and Ministry of Jesus (291-296)
See also: Greatest Commandment; Jesus Christ: Life of; Parables; Prayer Jesus Taught; Sermon on the Mount;
Abana alathi (Abana in Heaven), 675
All the Room Was Hushed and Still, 493
Balaacoolwe (Blessed Are the Persecuted), 578
Be a Sower, 789
Haneul naneun saeleul bora (See the Birds That Fly), 289
Holy Spirit, Come to Us, 58
Jesus Calls Us, 30
O God, We Read the Holy Law, 571
Our Father, who Art in Heaven, 674
Our God in Heaven, 673
Renew Your Church, 717
Seek Ye First, 417
Sleepers, Wake, 226
Strong, Peaceful Man of Galilee, 573
Sword into a Plowshare, 798
There's Enough for All, 757
This Little Light of Mine, 762
To Leave the Stones Unthrown, 580
Waterfall, 763
Who Will Speak a Word of Warning, 758
[As a shepherd seeks a lost sheep], 868
[Blessed are the poor in spirit], 295
[Blessed One, our source and support], 989.C
[Do not fight back against someone], 293
[For I received from the Lord], 469
[From Bethlehem to Nazareth], 874
[God, I have so few ways to pray], 1008
[Jesus' eleven disciples went to a mountain], 451
[Jesus said, I am the bread of life], 987.E
[Jesus said, let anyone with ears], 985.D
[Jesus stood up to read], 292
[Notre Père qui es aux cieux], 989.D
[O God, Ancient of Days, your love], 941
[Our Father in heaven], 989.A
[Our Father, who art in heaven], 989.B
[Padre nuestro que estás en los cielos], 989.E
[Praise and thanks to you, holy God], 915
[Some of us are exhausted], 854
[The crowd said to Jesus, "You must show us more miracles"], 471
[The reign of heaven is like a treasure], 294
[Vater unser im Himmel], 989.F
[Where two or three are gathered], 19
[You who open doors], 862

Jesus Christ: Transfiguration of

Jesus on the Mountain Peak, 301
You, Lord, Are Both Lamb and Shepherd, 432
[God of every place], 859

John the Baptist

See also: Jesus Christ: Baptism of
Crashing Waters at Creation, 441
Prepare the Way! the Prophet Called, 220
Prepare Ye the Way of the Lord, 219
The Glory of These Forty Days, 305
[From the River to the Wilderness], 445
[God of grace, creator of waters], 931

Journey to the Cross

See: TELLING GOD'S STORY: Journey to the Cross (304-319)
See also: Ash Wednesday; Holy Thursday; Jesus Christ: Death of; Lent; Palm Sunday
All the Room Was Hushed and Still, 493
Bleibet hier (Stay with Me), 627
Christ, on the Night He Was Betrayed, 491
In the Quiet Consecration, 484
Jesus Took a Towel, 490
My Song Is Love Unknown, 320
O Love, How Deep, How Broad, 303
Prepare a Room for Me, 465
Sanna, sannanina, 79
Sign Us with Ashes, Merciful God, 304
Who Now Would Follow Christ, 576
With Astonishment, Fear, and Wonder, 579
Ya hamala Allah (O Lamb of God), 321
[A wilderness beckons us], 1011
[From Bethlehem to Nazareth], 874
[God of the foolish cross], 896
[Jesus, Lamb of God], 892
[No one can truly know Christ], 928
[Remember: We are earth], 918
[The dust that shapes the journey], 873
[Whatever wilderness the Spirit], 1065
[While Jesus was in Bethany], 296

Joy

See also: SHARING OUR STORIES: Suffering and Joy (605-641)
See also: Comfort
A Voice Was Heard in Ramah, 278
As a Deer in Want of Water, 552
Be Not Afraid, 356
Be Still, My Soul, 664
Beautiful Things, 551
Before the Waters Nourished Earth, 652
Blessed Are You, 290
Come Now, O God, 143
Come, Thou Long-Expected Jesus, 218
Dooládó' Shi Diyinda! (What a Wonderful Savior), 562
El cielo canta alegría (Heaven Is Singing for Joy), 665
En medio de la vida (You Are the God within Life), 526
Fierce Raged the Tempest, 286
From Heaven Above to Earth I Come, 263
Good Christian Friends, Rejoice, 261
Haleluya! Pelo tsa rona (Hallelujah! We Sing Your Praises), 473
He Came Down, 239
Hope Is a Candle, 211
How Clear Is Our Vocation, 547
I Come with Joy, 478
I Heard the Voice of Jesus Say, 536
I Know That My Redeemer Lives, 347
I Love the Lord, 684
In the Bulb There Is a Flower, 670
In Thee Is Gladness, 666
Jesus, Lover of My Soul, 659
Joyful, Joyful, We Adore Thee, 103
Joys Are Flowing like a River, 375
Joy to the World, 240
Just a Closer Walk with Thee, 743
Lift Your Glad Voices, 340
My Latest Sun Is Sinking Fast, 662
Nzambi wakatamba (God Loves All His Many People), 767
O du fröhliche (Oh, How Joyfully), 254
O Thou, in Whose Presence, 600
Oh, Have You Not Heard (Ich weiss einen Strom), 668
Prabhoo Lay lay (Savior Jesus, Enfold Me), 567
Rain Down, 703
Segala puji syukur (All Our Praise), 82
Shepherd Me, O God, 744
Sizohamba naye (We Will Walk with God), 815
Solemn Stillness, Weary Streets, 276
The Lord's My Shepherd, 660
We Are Often Tossed and Driven, 311
When We Walk with the Lord, 570
You're Not Alone, 779
You Shall Go Out with Joy, 847
[Are any of you suffering hardships], 727
[Christ is like a single body], 856
[Clap your hands all you peoples], 108
[Come, with your faith and your doubts], 947
[Creemos en Dios Padre todopoderoso], 927
[Dear God, let your word shine], 912
[God of every place], 859
[God, who is Alpha and Omega], 962
[Gracious God, we celebrate life], 979
[If you are delighted to be here], 853
[In our concerns and in our choices], 1051
[Make a joyful noise to the Lord], 20
[May the Son of God], 1057
[May those who sow in tears], 821
[Rejoice in the Lord always], 726
[This is the day that the Lord has made], 15
[Though the fig tree does not blossom], 820
[We light a candle for hope], 916

Judgment

See also: Justice; Reign of Christ; Reign of God
I Believe in God Almighty, 433

I'm Gonna Eat at the Welcome Table, 801
Jesus Christ Is Waiting, 287
Kwake Yesu nasimama (Here on Christ the Rock I Will Stand), 159
Lord Jesus, Come and Overturn, 146
Mercy, Mercy, Lord, 169
We Long to Know Her, 44
When Grief Is Raw, 655
[A shoot will come up], 232
[Christ our companion, you came not to humiliate the sinner], 898
[Gracious God, our sins are too heavy], 895
[I believe in God, the Father almighty], 923
[The Lord is merciful and gracious], 186
[We are not alone], 922
[We believe in one God, the Father, the Almighty], 924

Justice

See also: LIVING GOD'S STORY: Peace and Justice (779-801)
See also: Creation: Care; Justice: Economic; Justice: Racial; Peace; Peace and Justice
Bless'd Be the God of Israel, 223
Go in Grace and Make Disciples, 766
God of Justice, 772
Gracias, Señor, por el pan (Thank You, O God, for This Bread), 487
Hark! the Glad Sound!, 217
Holy Presence, Holy Teacher, 531
Honja soriRoneun (With My Voice Alone), 800
In Words of Truth, 148
Jesus Christ Is Waiting, 287
Jesus Entered Egypt, 279
Joyous Light of Heavenly Glory, 504
Like a Mother Who Has Borne Us, 518
Mary, Woman Weeping, 328
My Soul Proclaims with Wonder, 222
Perdón, Señor, 153
Sing a New World into Being, 809
Somos pueblo que camina (We Are People on a Journey), 464
The Risen Christ, 345
There Is a Line of Women, 546
Today We Sing with Thankfulness, 535
To Us a Child of Hope Is Born, 259
True Evangelical Faith, 439
We Place upon Your Table, 462
We Praise the Word of God, 404
We Shall Overcome, 803
What Does the Lord Require of You?, 207
Who Are These, 360
[Christ our companion, you came not to humiliate the sinner], 898
[Go forth in peace, and be of good courage], 1059
[God our sanctuary], 1042
[In defiance of corruption and falsehood], 1040
[Liberating God, prevent us], 1031
[Living Christ, in these times], 1033
[O Dios, dales pan a los que tienen hambre], 1025
[O God, our deliverer], 1010
[Thus says the Lord: Maintain justice], 782
[We are not alone], 922

Justice: Economic

See also: Justice
Arise, Your Light Is Come!, 273
As the Waters Rise around Us, 708
Beauty for Brokenness, 712
Blessed Are You, 290
Forgive, Forgive Us, Holy God, 149
For the Fruit of All Creation, 124
For the Healing of the Nations, 705
Gentle God, When We Are Driven, 150
Go in Grace and Make Disciples, 766
God, Bless the Work Your People Do, 528
God of Grace and God of Glory, 716
God, We Pause This Moment, 756
Gracias, Señor, por el pan (Thank You, O God, for This Bread), 487
Haneul naneun saeleul bora (See the Birds That Fly), 289
Hark! the Glad Sound!, 217
Helpless and Hungry, 268
Here to the House of God We Come, 27
How Can We Worship Caesar's Cross, 308
Jesus Is Coming, 312
Longing for Light, 715
Lord Jesus, Come and Overturn, 146
Peace to You, 168
Somos pueblo que camina (We Are People on a Journey), 464
Strong, Peaceful Man of Galilee, 573
The Church of Christ Cannot Be Bound, 392
There's Enough for All, 757
Who Will Speak a Word of Warning, 758
[A shoot will come up], 232
[Blessed are the poor in spirit], 295
[Come, all you who are thirsty], 14
[Creator Spirit, you clothe the flowers], 1018
[For failing to love others], 893
[Go forth in peace, and be of good courage], 1059
[Go in peace. Remember the poor], 1052.C
[God of work and rest], 956
[Great Physician, you touched the lives], 976
[Jesus of love and leftovers], 1016
[Jesus stood up to read], 292
[Lay one brick at a time], 1036
[Loaves and Fishes], 291
[Lord, your coming is still miraculous], 872
[My soul proclaims the greatness], 987.F
[O Dios, dales pan a los que tienen hambre], 1025
[There is no scarcity], 1024

Justice: Racial

See also: Heritage: African American; Indigenous Communities: Resources Related to; Justice
Christ Has Broken Down the Wall, 174
Christ Is Alive! Let Christians Sing, 359
Creating God, Your Fingers Trace, 427
Dhuh Pangeran (O Prince of Peace), 26
Draw the Circle Wide, 802
For the Healing of the Nations, 705
How Can I Say, 388
Jesus Calls Us, 30
Let's Walk Together, 6
O Praise the Gracious Power, 87
Ososo (Come Now, O Prince of Peace), 391
Praise with Joy the World's Creator, 428
Sing a New World into Being, 809
Somos pueblo que camina (We Are People on a Journey), 464
Ubi caritas (Where True Love), 492
We Shall Overcome, 803
You Are Good, 33
[Alive], 334
[Creemos en Dios Padre todopoderoso], 927
[For failing to love others], 893
[In defiance of corruption and falsehood], 1040
[Let the rain come and wash away], 1048
[May God bless you with a restless discomfort], 1058
[May we go forth into the world with courage], 1039
[There is no scarcity], 1024
[We acknowledge that we are gathering], 878

Kindness

See also: Compassion; Love for Others
Bless the Arms That Comfort, 527
Christ Has No Body Here but Ours, 568
Make Me an Instrument of Your Peace, 713
Ubi caritas et amor, 773
What Does the Lord Require of You?, 207
[Love is patient], 1045
[Nurturing God, root us in your love], 1028
[Source of all hope and holiness], 863
[The Lord told you what is good], 784
[We offer thanksgiving to our Creator], 864

Kingdom

See: Reign of Christ; Reign of God

Kyrie eleison / Lord, Have Mercy

Come and See, 282
Khudaya, rahem kar (Have Mercy on Us, Lord), 693
Kyrie eleison (Ghanaian), 795
Kyrie eleison, Have Mercy, 796
Kyrie eleison (Russian Orthodox), 147
Kyrie eleison (Taizé Kyrie 1), 678
Kyrie eleison (Taizé Kyrie 13), 692
Let Us Pray, 686
Lord, Have Mercy (Manderfeld) 614
Lord, Have Mercy (Moosonee), 651
Oré poriajú verekó (Kyrie eleison), 620
Way way way (Ojibwe), 742
[Christ Have Mercy (ASL)], 615

Labor Day

See: Work

Lamb of God

See: Agnus Dei / Lamb of God

Lament

See: PRAYING: Lament (691-696)
See also: Anger; Creation: Lament, Grief; Praying; Suffering
As the Waters Rise around Us, 708
How Can Our Anger Give Life, 792
If the War Goes On, 794
In Words of Truth, 148
Kyrie eleison, Have Mercy, 796
On Silken, Soft Wings, 676
Out of the Depths I Cry to You, 140
Rain, Come Down, 634
Stay with Me, the Night Has Come, 319
The Garden Needs Our Tending Now, 788
We, Your People, Sing Your Praises (Bon Berger, ton peuple t'adore), 849
What Comfort Can Our Worship Bring, 623
When Pain or Sorrow / Hold On, 612
[A wilderness beckons us], 1011
[Alive], 334
[God of every place], 859
[Gracious God, when there is nothing], 994
[How long, O Lord], 728
[Nine Patch #8], 723
[That huge "Why?"], 1005
[The people say: Our bones are dried up], 383
[The Spirit helps us in our weakness], 729
[Though the fig tree does not blossom], 820

Land

See also: Creation; Creation: Care; Rural Life
Beauty for Brokenness, 712
Called by Earth and Sky, 806
God of the Fertile Fields, 750
O Healing River, 706
The Garden Needs Our Tending Now, 788
This Is My Song, 710
We Plow the Fields and Scatter, 747
[Mist, Sun, Morning], 183
[Some trust in governments], 1043
[There is no scarcity], 1024
[We acknowledge that we are gathering], 878
[We offer thanksgiving to our Creator], 864
[With the whole people of God], 997

Las posadas

See also: Jesus Christ: Advent of; Jesus Christ: Birth of
Hacia Belén (Mary Journeyed), 224

Last Supper

See: Communion; Holy Thursday

Law

See also: Covenant
God's Glory Fills the Heavens, 197
Holy Spirit, Truth Divine, 46
O Come, O Come, Immanuel, 210
O God, We Read the Holy Law, 571
Praise to the Living God, 204
The Word of God Is Solid Ground, 399

[Hear, O Israel], 187
[Jesus said, let anyone with ears], 985.D
[Praise and thanks to you, holy God], 915

Leadership: Church

See: Church Leadership

Learning

See also: Nurturing Faith; Schools and Learning Communities

Ask the Complicated Questions, 440
Holy Presence, Holy Teacher, 531
O Christ, Impart Your Teaching True, 583
See the Children Here Before Us, 509
Teach Me Thy Truth, 776
[Come among us, Holy Spirit, and create a community], 955
[Creator God, thank you for people and places], 954
[May God bless to our understanding], 913.D
[Some of us are exhausted], 854

Lent

See also: Baptism; Confession of Sin; Conversion and New Life; Following Jesus; Journey to the Cross

Agneau de Dieu (O Lamb of God), 559
As a Deer in Want of Water, 552
Beautiful Things, 551
Christ Has No Body Here but Ours, 568
Count Well the Cost, 577
Create in Me a Clean Heart, 141
Fill Us with Your Feast, 309
Forgive, Forgive Us, Holy God, 149
From the Waters I Will Rise, 442
God, Grant Us Mercy, 142
God Who Touches Earth with Beauty, 550
God, Whose Purpose Is to Kindle, 152
Here's My Life, I Lay It Down, 561
How Can We Worship Caesar's Cross, 308
How Many Times We Start Again, 553
I Bind My Heart This Tide, 556
I Have Decided to Follow Jesus, 443
I Sing with Exultation, 444
I Want Jesus to Walk with Me, 306
Jésus, je voudrais te chanter (Lord Jesus, You Shall Be My Song), 581
Jesus, Tempted in the Desert, 307
Just As I Am, without One Plea, 560
Lamb of God / Cordero de Dios, 151
Let This Mind Be in You, 572
Lord, I Am Fondly, Earnestly Longing, 555
Lord, I Need You, 155
Lord, I Want to Be a Christian, 558
Lord Jesus, Come and Overturn, 146
My Song Is Love Unknown, 320
O Christ, Impart Your Teaching True, 583
O Love, How Deep, How Broad, 303
Out of the Depths I Cry to You, 140
Perdón, Señor, 153
Prabhoo Lay lay (Savior Jesus, Enfold Me), 567
Sign Us with Ashes, Merciful God, 304
Somlandela (We Will Follow), 566
The Glory of These Forty Days, 305
To Leave the Stones Unthrown, 580
Unless a Grain of Wheat, 302
We Are Often Tossed and Driven, 311
We Read the Cross, 569
We Shall Walk through the Valley, 574
What Can I Leave Behind, 154
What Wondrous Love Is This, 564
While I Keep Silence, 310
Who Now Would Follow Christ, 576
Ya hamala Allah (O Lamb of God), 321
[A wilderness beckons us], 1011
[As a shepherd seeks a lost sheep], 868
[From Bethlehem to Nazareth], 874
[God of the foolish cross], 896
[Grow us slowly], 1030
[Jesus, Lamb of God], 892
[Liberating God, prevent us], 1031
[No one can truly know Christ], 928
[Our lives are cluttered], 899
[Remember: We are earth], 918
[The dust that shapes the journey], 873
[Whatever wilderness the Spirit], 1065

Liberation

See also: Salvation

Arise, Your Light Is Come!, 273
Beyond a Dying Sun, 416
Bless'd Be the God of Israel, 223
Christ Jesus Lay, 463
Come, Thou Long-Expected Jesus, 218
Come, We That Love, 31
Come, Ye Faithful, Raise the Strain, 348
Crashing Waters at Creation, 441
Creator of the Stars of Night, 236
For the Healing of the Nations, 705
God, Whose Purpose Is to Kindle, 152
Hark! the Glad Sound!, 217
Honja sorironeun (With My Voice Alone), 800
In Thee Is Gladness, 666
Jesus Is Coming, 312
Jesus Shall Reign, 414
Kyrie eleison, Have Mercy, 796
Lead On, O Cloud of Presence, 194
Lift Every Voice and Sing, 611
Move in Our Midst, 827
No Longer Slaves to Fear, 195
O Come, O Come, Immanuel, 210
O God of Blessings, 700
O Healing River, 706
Oh, How Shall I Receive Thee, 215
Praise with Joy the World's Creator, 428
Santo, santo, santo (Holy, Holy, Holy), 102
Tears of Suffering, 694
There's a River of Life, 24
Wade in the Water, 454
Waterfall, 763
We Praise the Word of God, 404
When Israel Was in Egypt's Land, 193
Who Are These, 360
With Mary Sing Magnificat, 208
Wonderful Grace of Jesus, 170
You Shall Go Out with Joy, 847
[Alive], 334
[Blessed are you, Lord, the God of Israel], 985.E
[Come, Holy Spirit, enter our silences], 877
[Gracious God, our sins are too heavy], 895
[Jesus stood up to read], 292
[Liberating God, prevent us], 1031
[Most loving, most strong God], 900
[My soul proclaims the greatness], 987.F
[O God, our deliverer], 1010
[Praise to God who has given us life], 902
[Some trust in governments], 1043

Light

See: Darkness and Light

Lighting Candles

See: Candle Lighting

Longest Night / Blue Christmas

See also: Grief; Jesus Christ: Advent of; Jesus Christ: Birth of; Lament; Suffering

All Who Are Thirsty, 49
Come Now, O God, 143
Dans nos obscurités (Within Our Darkest Night), 632
Stay with Me, the Night Has Come, 319
Wait for the Lord / Contemplaré tu vida, 228
We Come, 225
[Barely midnight. All of us hunkered down], 871
[Gracious God, when there is nothing], 994
[How silently], 1021
[In our concerns and in our choices], 1051
[In the beginning when it was very quiet], 852
[Lighting a candle], 1006
[That huge "Why?"], 1005

Lord, Have Mercy

See: Kyrie eleison / Lord, Have Mercy

Lord's Prayer

See: Prayer Jesus Taught

Lord's Supper

See: Communion

Love Feast

See: Communion

Love for God

See also: Adoration; Greatest Commandment

Flow to You, 132
Je louerai l'Éternel (Praise, I Will Praise You, Lord), 131
Love Came Down at Christmas, 255
Love the Lord Your God, 288
Magnificat, 97
My Jesus, I Love Thee, 133
O God, We Read the Holy Law, 571
Santo (Holy), 136
Shout to the Lord (Cante al Señor),125
Spirit, Open My Heart, 636
Take My Life, and Let It Be, 759
Take My Life, That I May Be (Que mi vida entera esté), 760
This Is the Air I Breathe (Eres mi respirar), 139
[Almighty God, to you all hearts are open], 860
[Come, Holy One, work upon us], 858
[Friends, as we gather to eat the bread], 937
[God of mercy, we are sorry], 897
[Hear, O Israel], 187
[Jesus said, let anyone with ears], 985.D
[Love is patient], 1045
[May the Love which overcomes], 906
[Our lives are cluttered], 899

Love for Others

See also: Compassion; Greatest Commandment; Kindness

All the Room Was Hushed and Still, 493
Between Darkness and Light, 808
Bless the Arms That Comfort, 527
Blest Be the Tie That Binds, 831
God, Give Me Faith like a Child, 519
He Came Down, 239
Help Us to Help Each Other, 722
Here I Am, Lord, 545
Holy Spirit, Come to Us, 58
Hope Is a Candle, 211
I Come with Joy, 478
Jesus Christ Is Love Divine, 749
Love Came Down at Christmas, 255
Love the Lord Your God, 288
May You Be Rooted and Grounded in Love, 396
Mercy, Mercy, Lord, 169
O God, We Read the Holy Law, 571
Put Peace into Each Other's Hands, 485
Renew Your Church, 717
Seek the Peace of the City, 206
Spirit, Open My Heart, 636
The Lord Lift You Up, 832
There Is in Every Person, 751
Trinity Song, 60
Ubi caritas et amor, 773
Ubi caritas (Where True Love), 492
Use Us, God, 811
When Love Is Found, 524
[At the Impulse of God's Love], 780
[Be sincere in your love for others], 384
[Do not fight back against someone], 293
[Eternal Love, gentle God, you invite us], 951
[For failing to love others], 893
[Friends, as we gather to eat the bread], 937
[Gardener God, you have planted], 1002
[God of all life, in you we live and move], 974
[God of mercy, we are sorry], 897
[Jesus calls us to praise and prayer], 851
[Jesus said, let anyone with ears], 985.D
[Let me hear what the Lord God says], 188
[Love cannot remain by itself], 1037
[Love is patient], 1045
[May the Christ who walks on wounded feet], 1066
[May the Love which overcomes], 906
[Nurturing God, root us in your love], 1028
[Save us, God, from being self-centered], 1000

[That huge "Why?"], 1005
[There is no scarcity], 1024
[The Spirit helps us in our weakness (Morning Prayer)], 985.F
[This day, God, may I dream your dreams], 984
[Thus says the Lord, the God of Israel], 783
[We light a candle for hope], 916

Love of God

See: God: Love of

Love of Jesus Christ

See: Jesus Christ: Love of

Magnificat / Mary's Song

Magnificat, 97
My Soul Cries Out, 412
My Soul Proclaims with Wonder, 222
[My soul proclaims the greatness], 987.F

Marriage

See also: SHARING OUR STORIES: Family, Friendship, and Marriage (523-525); See: WORSHIP RESOURCES: Sharing Our Stories—Marriage (973-974)

See also: Family; Love for Others

Jesus Christ Is Love Divine, 749
When Love Is Found, 524
Will You Let Me Be Your Servant, 778
[God created human beings for relationship], 973
[God of all life, in you we live and move], 974
[Love is patient], 1045

Mary, Mother of Jesus

Come, Join in Mary's Prophet-Song, 246
Creator of the Stars of Night, 236
Gott ist gegenwärtig (God Is Here among Us), 62
Hacia Belén (Mary Journeyed), 224
I Believe in God Almighty, 433
Jesus Entered Egypt, 279
Joyful Is the Dark, 281
Lo, How a Rose E'er Blooming, 216
Love Has Come, 258
Magnificat, 97
Mary, Woman Weeping, 328
My Soul Cries Out, 412
My Soul Proclaims with Wonder, 222
O God of Blessings, 700
O Worship Our God, 129
Savior of the Nations, Come!, 214
Still, Still, Still, 264
The Angel Gabriel Called Mary Blessed, 221
There Is a Line of Women, 546
There Were Angels Hovering Round, 251
Unexpected and Mysterious, 229
What Child Is This, 267
With Mary Sing Magnificat, 208
[I believe in God, the Father almighty], 923
[May God be with you! And also with you], 944
[May the blessing of the God of Sarah and Hagar], 1060
[My soul proclaims the greatness], 987.F
[O God, our deliverer], 1010
[The angel said to Mary], 233
[We believe in one God, the Father, the Almighty], 924
[We Owe Them a Complicated Debt], 230

Mary's Song

See: Magnificat / Mary's Song

Materialism

See: Justice: Economic

Maundy Thursday

See: Holy Thursday

Meetings and Committees

God, Bless the Work Your People Do, 528
Njoo kwetu, Roho mwema (Gracious Spirit), 367
[Eternal God, you call us to ventures], 1068
[Evening Prayer], 987
[God of life, we thank you that our work], 953
[Jesus, servant, at supper with your disciples], 1041
[Morning Prayer], 985
[What will you offer the body of Christ today], 1023

Membership: Church

See: Church Membership

Memorial Service

See: Funeral / Memorial Service

Mennonite World Fellowship Sunday

See also: Heritage: 16th-Century Anabaptist

See also: Anabaptist contributors marked with a dot in the Contributors Index

Akekho ofana / Hakuna wakaita (There's No One in This World like Jesus), 68
Cantai ao Senhor (O Sing to the Lord), 113
Dhuh Pangeran (O Prince of Peace), 26
Ehane he'ama (Father God, You Are Holy), 59
Enviados somos de Dios (We Have Been Sent by God), 771
Gracias, Señor, por el pan (Thank You, O God, for This Bread), 487
Heart with Loving Heart, 813
I Have Decided to Follow Jesus, 443
In Christ There Is No East or West, 390
Je louerai l'Éternel (Praise, I Will Praise You, Lord), 131
Jesus, Help Us Live in Peace, 719
Kirisuto no heiwa ga (May the Peace of Christ), 843
Kwake Yesu nasimama (Here on Christ the Rock I Will Stand), 159
Nyanyikanlah nyanyian baru (Sing to God a New Song), 93
Nzambi wakatamba (God Loves All His Many People), 767
Tú has venido a la orilla (Lord, You Have Come to the Lakeshore), 283
Uyai mose (Come All You People), 2
We Are One in the Spirit, 387
We Are People of God's Peace, 797
We, Your People, Sing Your Praises (Bon Berger, ton peuple t'adore), 849
What a Friend We Have in Jesus, 628
You're Not Alone, 779
[At this table, we receive the bread of life], 943
[By the grace of God we seek to live and proclaim], 925
[Creemos en Dios Padre todopoderoso], 927
[God dearly loves us], 1056
[Loving God, you have baptized us], 1001
[O God, listening to us here], 993
[True evangelical faith], 921

Mental Health

See also: Addiction; Healing

Calm Me, Lord, 680
Cast Out, O Christ, 285
O God, to You I Cry in Pain, 646
Still My Soul, 603
When Memory Fades, 649
When Pain or Sorrow / Hold On, 612
When We Must Bear Persistent Pain, 735
[God, give me grace to accept], 1007
[Gracious God, when there is nothing], 994
[Great Physician, you touched the lives], 976
[Hear our prayer, O God of healing and hope], 978
[Merciful God, we wait], 977

Mercy

See also: Forgiveness; Grace

Cast Thy Burden upon the Lord, 616
Khudaya, rahem kar (Have Mercy on Us, Lord), 693
Kyrie eleison (Ghanaian), 795
Kyrie eleison (Russian Orthodox), 147
Kyrie eleison (Taizé Kyrie 1), 678
Kyrie eleison (Taizé Kyrie 13), 692
Let Us Pray, 686
Lord, Have Mercy (Manderfeld) 614
Lord, Have Mercy (Moosonee), 651
Mercy, Mercy, Lord, 169
Oré poriajú verekó (Kyrie eleison), 620
Softly and Tenderly Jesus Is Calling, 544
The Church of Christ Cannot Be Bound, 392
The Lord Lift You Up, 832
There's a Wideness in God's Mercy, 156
When All Thy Mercies, 119
Ya hamala Allah (O Lamb of God), 321
[Blessed are the poor in spirit], 295
[Christ, have mercy (ASL)], 615
[Have mercy on me, O God (Evening Prayer)], 987.D
[Jesus, Lamb of God], 892
[Let us confess our sin], 890
[May almighty God have mercy on us], 905
[The Lord is merciful and gracious], 186
[The Lord told you what is good], 784

Ministry

See also: Church Leadership; Commissioning: Other; Service; Vocation

Bless the Arms That Comfort, 527
En medio de la vida (You Are the God within Life), 526
God, Whose Giving, 745
Lord, You Give the Great Commission, 774
One Is the Body, 386
Renew Your Church, 717
Today We Sing with Thankfulness, 535
[Anyone who is joined to Christ], 785
[Empowering God, with your people], 965
[Every Christian is called], 964
[God's Spirit calls, the church commissions], 966
[I pledge with you], 967
[May God, who calls you to this ministry], 968
[What will you offer the body of Christ today], 1023

Miracles of Jesus Christ

See: Jesus Christ: Miracles of

Mission

See: LIVING GOD'S STORY: Mission (761-770); WORSHIP RESOURCES: Living God's Story (1026-1049); ART AND SCRIPTURE: Service and Witness for Peace (780-786)

See also: Sending; Service

All the Room Was Hushed and Still, 493
As You Go Out from Here, 841
Be a Sower, 789
Blessed Assurance, 435
Christ Has No Body Here but Ours, 568
Come What May / Pase lo que pase ¡ven!, 768
Come, Ye Thankful People, 123
Dhuh Pangeran (O Prince of Peace), 26
El cielo canta alegría (Heaven Is Singing for Joy), 665
Faith of the Martyrs, 575
For the Fruit of All Creation, 124
Go Now in Peace, Worship Continues, 829
Heart with Loving Heart, 813
Here I Am, Lord, 545
How Can We Be Silent, 790
I Bind My Heart This Tide, 556
In Christ There Is No East or West, 390
Jésus, je voudrais te chanter (Lord Jesus, You Shall Be My Song), 581
Jesus Shall Reign, 414
O Praise the Gracious Power, 87
Oh, for a Thousand Tongues (LYNGHAM), 78
Prabhoo Lay lay (Savior Jesus, Enfold Me), 567
Santo, santo, santo (Holy, Holy, Holy), 102
Sing a New World into Being, 809
Siyahamba (We Are Marching), 793
The Church of Christ, in Every Age, 395
The Risen Christ, 345
The Word of God Is Solid Ground, 399
There Is a Line of Women, 546

Thuma mina (Send Me, Lord), 834
True Evangelical Faith, 439
We Are One in the Spirit, 387
You Are Salt for the Earth, 297
[Anyone who is joined to Christ], 785
[At the Impulse of God's Love], 780
[Christ, whose insistent call], 1029
[Convert us, Jesus the persecuted], 1027
[Dear Jesus, I confess my need of you], 926
[Go in peace. Share the good news], 1052.B
[God, just as you sent Joseph to Egypt], 957
[God's Spirit calls, the church commissions], 966
[How beautiful on the mountains], 781
[Jesus Christ, you stretched out your arms], 1026
[Jesus' eleven disciples went to a mountain], 451
[O God, listening to us here], 993
[Sovereign Majesty, we pray for the continued outpouring], 992
[Thus says the Lord, the God of Israel], 783
[True evangelical faith], 921
[Two disciples were traveling], 470

Morning

See also: SHARING OUR STORIES: Morning and Evening (494-507); See: WORSHIP RESOURCES: Sharing Our Stories—Morning and Evening (984-988)

10,000 Reasons / Bless the Lord, 111
God of Wonders, 178
God Speaks to Us in Bird and Song, 539
Great Is Thy Faithfulness, 419
Hallelujah! schöner Morgen (Hallelujah! Fairest Morning!), 497
Holy, Holy, Holy!, 76
I Owe the Lord a Morning Song, 496
In the Morning When I Rise, 499
Jesus Shall Reign, 414
Morning Has Broken, 495
O Splendor of God's Glory Bright, 500
Qing zao qi lai kan (Golden Breaks the Dawn), 498
This Is God's Wondrous World, 180
[Bless the Lord, O my soul], 185
[Blessed are you, Lord, the God of Israel], 985.E
[Hear, O Israel], 187
[I lift my eyes to the hills], 109
[It is good to give you thanks (Evening Prayer)], 987.C
[It is good to give you thanks (Morning Prayer)], 985.C
[Mist, Sun, Morning], 183
[Morning Prayer], 985
[Receive our thanks for night and day], 949
[This day, God, may I dream your dreams], 984
[This is the day that the Lord has made], 15

Mother's Day

See: Days Recognizing Parents

Music

See also: Clapping; Dance

Alleluia / Make a Joyful Noise (Psalm 100), 66
As We Rise, O God, to Meet You, 39
Build My Life, 92
Cantai ao Senhor (O Sing to the Lord), 113
Could It Be That God Is Singing, 42
Flow to You, 132
God Speaks to Us in Bird and Song, 539
Laudate Dominum (Sing, Praise, and Bless the Lord), 77
Margam, satyam, jivam nive (Living, Moving, End and Beginning), 425
My Life Flows On, 605
O God of Blessings, 700
Oh, for a Thousand Tongues (AZMON), 764
Oh, for a Thousand Tongues (LYNGHAM), 78
Over My Head, 594
Planets Humming as They Wander, 175
Segala puji syukur (All Our Praise), 82
The Lord, Your God Is with You, 173
Together, 389
When at Creation's Dawn, 121
When in Our Music God Is Glorified, 83
[Clap your hands all you peoples], 108
[Hosanna! Hosanna!], 885
[Let your hearts be ruled], 818
[Make a joyful noise to the Lord], 20
[May those who sow in tears], 821
[Praise the Lord], 107
[Sing and sing], 883
[Sing the Goodness], 104
[Sing to the Lord a new song], 106
[To worship is to stand in awe], 855
[We are people who must sing you], 882
[When the song of the angels is stilled], 1064

Mystery of God

See: God: Mystery and holiness of

Name of Jesus

See also: Jesus Christ: Images and Names of

All Hail the Power of Jesus' Name (CORONATION), 411
All Hail the Power of Jesus' Name (DIADEM), 364
Kombo na Yesu (The Name of Jesus), 648
My Hope Is Built on Nothing Less, 621
Oh, for a Thousand Tongues (AZMON), 764
Oh, for a Thousand Tongues (LYNGHAM), 78
Revelation Song (Digno y santo), 415
We Come, 225
Wonderful Grace of Jesus, 170
[Are any of you suffering hardships], 727
[If we have died with Christ], 903C
[Let the same mind be in you], 335
[Let us confess our sin], 890
[Let your hearts be ruled], 818
[Morning, noon, and night], 987.G
[Sovereign Majesty, we pray for the continued outpouring], 992
[Where two or three are gathered], 19

National Holidays

See also: Government

For the Healing of the Nations, 705
Let Justice Flow Down, 791
Let There Be Light, 714
This Is My Song, 710
[I pledge allegiance to Jesus Christ], 929
[Listening God, you hear our prayers], 996
[Some trust in governments], 1043

Nature

See: Creation; Creation: Beauty of

New Creation

See also: Reign of Christ; Reign of God

Beautiful Things, 551
Before the Waters Nourished Earth, 652
Beyond a Dying Sun, 416
Build Your Kingdom Here, 393
Christ Is Alive, and Goes Before Us, 565
Christ Is Risen! Shout Hosanna!, 354
Fill Us with Your Feast, 309
Go in Grace and Make Disciples, 766
Joy to the World, 240
Let's Walk Together, 6
Longing for Light, 715
Love Divine, All Loves Excelling, 638
Move in Our Midst, 827
Na nzela na lola (As Long as We Follow), 413
New Earth, Heavens New, 377
O Love That Will Not Let Me Go, 608
Peace to You, 168
Prepare the Way! the Prophet Called, 220
Sing a New World into Being, 809
The Garden Needs Our Tending Now, 788
There's a Wild Hope in the Wind, 828
Unexpected and Mysterious, 229
We Are People of God's Peace, 797
We Dream of a Turning, 209
We, Your People, Sing Your Praises (Bon Berger, ton peuple t'adore), 849
What Is the World Like, 298
[Anyone who is joined to Christ], 785
[I saw a new heaven and a new earth], 339
[Tree of Life], 12

New Year

Christ Is Alive, and Goes Before Us, 565
From Heaven Above to Earth I Come, 263
O God, Our Help in Ages Past, 203
Time Propels Us like a Current, 507
We've Come This Far by Faith, 599
[Give thanks to God, who is good], 963
[In the beginning, before time], 884

Night

See: Evening

Nonviolence

See also: Peace and Justice; Protest

Be a Sower, 789
Come, Join in Mary's Prophet-Song, 246
Gentle God, When We Are Driven, 150
God of Grace and God of Glory, 716
I Bind My Heart This Tide, 556
Ikke ved makt (Not by Your Might), 538
Let There Be Light, 714
Make Me an Instrument of Your Peace, 713
Mountain of God, 11
O Day of Peace, 787
Peace to You, 168
Strong, Peaceful Man of Galilee, 573
Sword into a Plowshare, 798
To Leave the Stones Unthrown, 580
We Are People of God's Peace, 797
We Dream of a Turning, 209
With Astonishment, Fear, and Wonder, 579
[At the Impulse of God's Love], 780
[Be still and know that I am God], 730
[By the grace of God we seek to live and proclaim], 925
[Come, let us go up], 13
[Do not fight back against someone], 293
[God of covenant, when Jesus came up from the waters], 935
[God, make me an instrument of your peace], 991
[Here is my servant, the one I uphold], 448

Nunc dimittis / Simeon's Song

Sálvanos, Señor, despiertos (Save Us, O Lord), 833
[Now, Lord, you let your servant], 825

Nurturing Faith

See: SHARING OUR STORIES: Nurturing Faith (511-522)

See also: Aging; Children / Childhood; Faith; Learning; Schools and Learning Communities

Bring Many Names, 134
Child of Blessing, Child of Promise, 508
Faith Begins by Letting Go, 585
God Made from One Blood, 523
Holy Presence, Holy Teacher, 531
Loving Spirit, 697
Mothering God, You Gave Me Birth, 426
My Shepherd Will Supply My Need, 640
See the Children Here Before Us, 509
When All Thy Mercies, 119
When Love Is Found, 524
[Come among us, Holy Spirit, and create a community], 955
[Creator God, thank you for people and places], 954
[God, maker of galaxies, who numbers the hairs], 971
[Gracious God, we celebrate life], 979
[Jesus' eleven disciples went to a mountain], 451
[You have offered], 970

Obedience

Arise, Your Light Is Come!, 273
Christ, on the Night He Was Betrayed, 491
Come and Seek the Ways of Wisdom, 196
Could It Be That God Is Singing, 42
Go to Dark Gethsemane, 317
Here I Am, Lord, 545

I Will Follow, 775
O Christ, Impart Your Teaching True, 583
The Word of God Is Solid Ground, 399
There's a Wild Hope in the Wind, 828
When We Walk with the Lord, 570
[By the grace of God we seek to live and proclaim], 925
[Hear, O Israel], 187
[Let the same mind be in you], 335
[Living God, by the power of your Spirit], 911

Offering

See: Giving

Ordination

See also: Church Leadership; Commissioning: Other; Ministry; Vocation

Be Thou My Vision, 549
God the Spirit, Guide and Guardian, 534
Here I Am, Lord, 545
How Clear Is Our Vocation, 547
Open My Eyes that I May See, 738
Santo, santo, santo (Holy, Holy, Holy), 102
Spirit of the Living God, 740
Take My Life, and Let It Be, 759
Take My Life, That I May Be (Que mi vida entera esté), 760
Take, O Take Me as I Am, 748
Tana mana dhana prabhū tava caraṇī (Heart and Mind, Possessions, God), 753
Teach Me Thy Truth, 776
There Are Many Gifts, 374
Thuma mina (Send Me, Lord), 834
Today We Sing with Thankfulness, 535
Tú has venido a la orilla (Lord, You Have Come to the Lakeshore), 283
[Empowering God, with your people], 965
[Every Christian is called], 964
[I pledge with you], 967
[May God, who calls you to this ministry], 968

Our Father

See: Prayer Jesus Taught

Palm Sunday

See also: Journey to the Cross

All Glory, Laud, and Honor, 315
Holy Lord, 314
Hosanna, Loud Hosanna, 313
Jesus Is Coming, 312
Ride On, Ride On in Majesty, 316
Sanna, sannanina, 79
With Astonishment, Fear, and Wonder, 579
[God of the foolish cross], 896
[Hosanna! Hosanna!], 885

Parables

See also: Jesus Christ: Teachings of

Be a Sower, 789
Dooládó' Shi Diyinda! (What a Wonderful Savior), 562
Far, Far Away / I Will Arise, 300
God Lights a Lamp, 299
God the Sculptor of the Mountains, 423
Seed, Scattered and Sown, 477
Seeds, 777
Si tuvieras fe (If You Only Had Faith), 593
Unless a Grain of Wheat, 302
What Is the World Like, 298
[As a shepherd seeks a lost sheep], 868
[God, I have so few ways to pray], 1008
[The reign of heaven is like a treasure], 294

Parents

See: Aging; Child Blessing; Children / Childhood; Days Recognizing Parents; Family

Patience

Be Still, My Soul, 664
In the Bulb There Is a Flower, 670
Open, Lord, My Inward Ear, 548
Out of the Depths I Cry to You, 140
Spirit of God! Descend, 557
Wait for the Lord / Contemplaré tu vida, 228
We Come, 225
[Friends, as we gather to eat the bread], 937
[Gracious God, we celebrate life], 979
[Great Physician, you touched the lives], 976
[Lead a life worthy of the calling], 446
[Love is patient], 1045
[Nurturing God, root us in your love], 1028

Peace

See also: LIVING GOD'S STORY: Peace and Justice (779-801)

See also: Justice; Nonviolence; Peace and Justice; Peace: Conflict and War; Peace: Inner; Peace: Interpersonal; Reconciliation

Between Darkness and Light, 808
Dhuh Pangeran (O Prince of Peace), 26
Dona nobis pacem, 707
Go Now in Peace, 835
He Came Down, 239
In Christ There Is No East or West, 390
Kirisuto no heiwa ga (May the Peace of Christ), 843
La paz de la tierra (The Peace of the Earth Be with You), 838
O Healing River, 706
Ososo (Come Now, O Prince of Peace), 391
Peace, Salaam, Shalom, 805
Prepare the Way! the Prophet Called, 220
Put Peace into Each Other's Hands, 485
Sálvanos, Señor, despiertos (Save Us, O Lord), 833
Shalom chaverim (Shalom, My Friends), 842
This Is My Song, 710
To Us a Child of Hope Is Born, 259
We Are People of God's Peace, 797
We Shall Walk through the Valley, 574
[Do not fight back against someone], 293
[Go in peace. Go be peace], 1052.D
[God, make me an instrument of your peace], 991
[How beautiful on the mountains], 781
[If there is to be peace in the world], 1046
[Jesus, Lamb of God], 892
[La paz no es producto del terror ni del miedo], 1038
[Let your hearts be ruled], 818
[Lighting a candle], 1006
[May God bless you and keep you], 826
[Now, Lord, you let your servant], 825
[Now may the God of peace], 823
[Peace be with you], 850
[Rejoice in the Lord always], 726
[The angel said "Do not be afraid!"], 234
[This home is yours, my God], 958
[When Flaming Dove Meets Rising Waters], 378

Peace and Justice

See: LIVING GOD'S STORY: Peace and Justice (779-801); WORSHIP RESOURCES: Living God's Story (1026-1049); ART AND SCRIPTURE: Service and Witness for Peace (780-786)

See also: Justice; Peace; Reconciliation

A Voice Was Heard in Ramah, 278
Beauty for Brokenness, 712
Beyond a Dying Sun, 416
Build Your Kingdom Here, 393
Christ Has Broken Down the Wall, 174
Christ Is Alive! Let Christians Sing, 359
Come, Join in Mary's Prophet-Song, 246
Creating God, Your Fingers Trace, 427
Forgive, Forgive Us, Holy God, 149
For the Healing of the Nations, 705
For Those with Whom Our Lives Are Bound, 734
Gentle God, When We Are Driven, 150
God of Grace and God of Glory, 716
God of the Bible, 420
God, Whose Purpose Is to Kindle, 152
Hope Is a Candle, 211
Hope of Abraham and Sarah, 807
How Can We Worship Caesar's Cross, 308
I Bind My Heart This Tide, 556
Jesus Is Coming, 312
Let There Be Light, 714
Let Us Build a House, 36
Let's Walk Together, 6
Light Dawns on a Weary World, 205
Longing for Light, 715
Mountain of God, 11
My Soul Cries Out, 412
Peace to You, 168
Praise with Joy the World's Creator, 428
Restore Our Faith, O Saving God, 198
Seek the Peace of the City, 206
Strong, Peaceful Man of Galilee, 573
Waterfall, 763
We Dream of a Turning, 209
With Astonishment, Fear, and Wonder, 579
With Mary Sing Magnificat, 208
Ya Rab as-salami (God of Peace and Justice), 711
You Are Salt for the Earth, 297
[A shoot will come up], 232
[At the Impulse of God's Love], 780
[Be sincere in your love for others], 384
[Blessed are the poor in spirit], 295
[Blessed are you, Lord, the God of Israel], 985.E
[Blessed be the ones who dance], 1049
[By the grace of God we seek to live and proclaim], 925
[Come, let us go up], 13
[Here is my servant, the one I uphold], 448
[Holy and righteous God, you created us], 1034
[Holy One, as you are faithful to us], 1022
[I pledge allegiance to Jesus Christ], 929
[In our doubt and fear], 1044
[Jesus calls us to praise and prayer], 851
[Jesus stood up to read], 292
[La paz no es producto del terror ni del miedo], 1038
[Lay one brick at a time], 1036
[Let me hear what the Lord God says], 188
[May God bless you with a restless discomfort], 1058
[My soul proclaims the greatness], 987.F
[O Prince of Peace], 894
[Some trust in governments], 1043
[Source of all hope and holiness], 863
[The Lord told you what is good], 784
[There is no scarcity], 1024
[Tree of Life], 12
[When the song of the angels is stilled], 1064

Peace: Conflict and War

See also: Conflict; Peace; Peace and Justice; Violence

Beauty for Brokenness, 712
Come, Join in Mary's Prophet-Song, 246
Comfort, Comfort, O My People, 212
Crown Him with Many Crowns, 408
Forgive, Forgive Us, Holy God, 149
For the Healing of the Nations, 705
For We Are Strangers No More, 409
Gentle God, When We Are Driven, 150
God of Grace and God of Glory, 716
Healing River of the Spirit, 642
Hope of Abraham and Sarah, 807
If the War Goes On, 794
It Came upon a Midnight Clear, 248
Kyrie eleison, Have Mercy, 796
Let Justice Flow Down, 791
Longing for Light, 715
O Holy Spirit, by Whose Breath, 53
We Dream of a Turning, 209
[Come, let us go up], 13
[If there is to be peace in the world], 1046
[La paz no es producto del terror ni del miedo], 1038
[Let the rain come and wash away], 1048
[Listening God, you hear our prayers], 996
[O Prince of Peace], 894
[We light a candle for hope], 916
[With the whole people of God], 997
[You who open doors], 862

Peace: Inner

See also: Peace

As the Wind Song through the Trees, 373
Beloved, God's Chosen, 164

Be Still and Know, 37
Calm Me, Lord, 680
Christ, Be All around Me, 848
Come Away from Rush and Hurry, 9
Confitemini Domino (Come and Fill Our Hearts), 52
Fierce Raged the Tempest, 286
Go Ye Now in Peace / Go, My Friends, in Peace, 839
Healer of Our Every Ill, 644
Healing River of the Spirit, 642
I Know Not Why God's Wondrous, 590
In the Heartbeat of the City, 530
Jesu, meine Freude (Jesus, Priceless Treasure), 624
Joys Are Flowing like a River, 375
My Shepherd Will Supply My Need, 640
O God, You Search Me, 199
O Holy Spirit, by Whose Breath, 53
Oh, Have You Not Heard (Ich weiss einen Strom), 668
Peace, Be Still, 202
Still My Soul, 603
The Lord Bless You and Keep You, 846
The Risen Christ, 345
Total Praise, 633
When Peace like a River, 617
Ya hamala Allah (O Lamb of God), 321
Zisuh nih a zultu hna sinah (Peace Be with You! Jesus Told His Friends), 165
[Friends in Christ, God knows our needs], 888
[God forgives you], 909
[God, give me grace to accept], 1007
[God, it is night], 986
[Gracious God, we celebrate life], 979
[Hear our prayer, O God of healing and hope], 978
[Hear the words of Jesus: "Peace I leave with you"], 904
[If there is to be peace in the world], 1046
[In our doubt and fear], 1044
[Merciful God, we wait], 977
[Most loving, most strong God], 900
[O Risen Christ, you breathe your Holy Spirit], 1013
[Rejoice in the Lord always], 726
[The peace of God which passes all understanding], 1054
[We light a candle for hope], 916

Peace: Interpersonal

See also: Conflict; Peace

For We Are Strangers No More, 409
Gentle God, When We Are Driven, 150
God, Give Me Time, 144
Jesus, Help Us Live in Peace, 719
Make Me an Instrument of Your Peace, 713
Put Peace into Each Other's Hands, 485
Seek the Peace of the City, 206
Together, 389
[At the Impulse of God's Love], 780
[Be sincere in your love for others], 384
[Do not fight back against someone], 293
[For the times we have lied], 891
[Friends in Christ, God knows our needs], 888
[God forgives you], 909
[God, make me an instrument of your peace], 991
[Hear the words of Jesus: "Peace I leave with you"], 904
[Jesus stood up to read], 292
[La paz no es producto del terror ni del miedo], 1038
[Most loving, most strong God], 900
[Now, thanks to Christ Jesus], 786
[O Prince of Peace], 894
[Tree of Life], 12
[We light a candle for hope], 916

Peace Lamp Lighting

See also: Peace

Arise, Your Light Is Come!, 273
Between Darkness and Light, 808
Dans nos obscurités (Within Our Darkest Night), 632
Kindle in Us Your Love, 54
Let There Be Light, 714
This Little Light of Mine, 762
[God our sanctuary], 1042
[If there is to be peace in the world], 1046
[La paz no es producto del terror ni del miedo], 1038
[Lighting a candle], 1006
[Peace be with you], 850
[We light a candle for hope], 916
[We light a light], 865

Peace Sunday

See: Peace

Pentecost

See: ART AND SCRIPTURE: Holy Spirit, Pentecost, Church (378-385)

See also: Church; Holy Spirit

All Who Are Thirsty, 49
As the Wind Song through the Trees, 373
Breathe on Me, Breath of God, 737
Come, Gracious Spirit, 371
Come, Thou Fount, 563
Confitemini Domino (Come and Fill Our Hearts), 52
Dona nobis pacem, 707
Go in Grace and Make Disciples, 766
God, Whose Purpose Is to Kindle, 152
Herr, füll mich neu (Fill Me Anew), 739
Holy Spirit, Come to Us, 58
Holy Spirit, Come with Power (Ven, Espíritu, cual viento), 57
Holy Spirit, Truth Divine, 46
Joys Are Flowing like a River, 375
Kindle in Us Your Love, 54
Like the Murmur of the Dove's Song, 56
Move in Our Midst, 827
Njoo kwetu, Roho mwema (Gracious Spirit), 367
O Holy Spirit, by Whose Breath, 53
Spirit of God! Descend, 557
Spirit of Life, 368
Spirit of the Living God, 740
Spirit, Working in Creation, 50
There Are Many Gifts, 374
There's Nothing Worth More (Nada vale más), 369
Veni Sancte Spiritus, 370
Wind Who Makes All Winds, 372
[At this table, we receive the bread of life], 943
[Come, Holy Spirit, enter our silences], 877
[Creemos en Dios Padre todopoderoso], 927
[Go in peace. Rejoice in the power], 1052.G
[God of covenant, when Jesus came up from the waters], 935
[God of power, may the boldness of your Spirit], 1067
[Gracious God, we pray for your universal church], 1004
[Hear the good news!], 903D
[Jesus Christ, you stretched out your arms], 1026
[Loving God, you have baptized us], 1001
[O God, listening to us here], 993
[Sovereign Majesty, we pray for the continued outpouring], 992
[When Flaming Dove Meets Rising Waters], 378
[When the day of Pentecost came], 379

Persecution

Balaacoolwe (Blessed Are the Persecuted), 578
Everlasting God, on You I Call, 630
Faith of the Martyrs, 575
God of Grace and God of Glory, 716
Mary, Woman Weeping, 328
My God, My God, 696
O Christ, Impart Your Teaching True, 583
O God, Our Refuge, 434
Onyame wo mu o (In Your Sickness), 607
When the Storms of Life Are Raging, 595
Who Are These, 360
[Blessed are the poor in spirit], 295
[Convert us, Jesus the persecuted], 1027
[Do not fight back against someone], 293
[True evangelical faith], 921

Pilgrimage

See also: Walking with God

Akekho ofana / Hakuna wakaita (There's No One in This World like Jesus), 68
Come, We That Love, 31
Guide Me, O Thou Great Jehovah, 606
Hamba nathi (Come, Walk with Us), 23
How Many Times We Start Again, 553
I Want Jesus to Walk with Me, 306
Lift Every Voice and Sing, 611
O Beautiful Star of Bethlehem, 275
Somos pueblo que camina (We Are People on a Journey), 464
We've Come This Far by Faith, 599
What a Fellowship / Leaning on the Everlasting Arms, 160
With Astonishment, Fear, and Wonder, 579
With Water Freely Flowing, 452
[A wilderness beckons us], 1011
[God dearly loves us], 1056
[Live without fear], 1062
[May the Christ who walks on wounded feet], 1066
[Migrant Journey], 817
[Whatever wilderness the Spirit], 1065

Power of God

See: God: Power of

Praise

See: PRAISING: Praise (68-112); WORSHIP RESOURCES: Praising (880-887); ART AND SCRIPTURE: Praising (104-110)

See also: Adoration; Thanksgiving

All Hail the Power of Jesus' Name (CORONATION), 411
All Hail the Power of Jesus' Name (DIADEM), 364
All People That on Earth Do Dwell, 5
All Things Bright and Beautiful, 177
Alleluia (canon), 362
Alleluia (Clemens), 635
Alleluia / Make a Joyful Noise (Psalm 100), 66
Alleluia (South African), 650
Alleluia (Ukrainian), 135
Be Not Afraid, 356
Bless the Lord, My Soul (Tengo sed de ti / Bendiz o Senhor), 127
Blessed Assurance, 435
Bless'd Be the God of Israel, 223
Blessed Be Your Name, 637
Christ Is Arisen, 358
Christ Is King! Let Earthly Powers, 410
Christ Is Our Cornerstone, 4
Christ Is Risen! Shout Hosanna!, 354
Christ Who Left His Home in Glory, 361
Come, Christians, Join to Sing, 28
Come, Now Is the Time to Worship, 29
Come, Thou Fount, 563
Come, We That Love, 31
Come, Ye Faithful, Raise the Strain, 348
Creation Is a Song / Ho'ė enemeohe, 181
Crown Him with Many Crowns, 408
El cielo canta alegría (Heaven Is Singing for Joy), 665
En medio de la vida (You Are the God within Life), 526
From the Parent's Heart, the Firstborn (Corde natus ex parentis), 418
Glory to God, Whose Goodness Shines on Me, 429
God of Our Strength, 47
God, Whose Giving, 745
Gravity of Love, 494
Haleluya! Pelo tsa rona (Hallelujah! We Sing Your Praises), 473
Halle, Halle, Hallelujah!, 752
Hallelujah (Syrian), 702
Here by the Water, 629
Here I Am to Worship (Ich will dich anbeten), 227
Hey ney yana (I Walk in Beauty), 836
I Know That My Redeemer Lives, 347
I Love to Tell the Story, 761
I Owe the Lord a Morning Song, 496
Jesus Christ Is Love Divine, 749
Jesus on the Mountain Peak, 301

Jesus Shall Reign, 414
Joyous Light of Heavenly Glory, 504
Let All Mortal Flesh Keep Silence, 65
Let Us Break Bread Together, 482
Lord, I Lift Your Name on High (Tu nombre levantaré), 365
Morning Has Broken, 495
Mothering God, You Gave Me Birth, 426
My Lighthouse, 597
New Earth, Heavens New, 377
Now, on Land and Sea Descending, 503
O God beyond All Praising, 814
O Lord My God / How Great Thou Art, 436
Oh, for a Thousand Tongues (AZMON), 764
Oh, qué bueno es Jesús (Oh, How Great Is Christ the Lord), 351
Over My Head, 594
Planets Humming as They Wander, 175
Praise to the Living God, 204
Praise with Joy the World's Creator, 428
Qing zao qi lai kan (Golden Breaks the Dawn), 498
Shema Yisrael, 192
Shout to the Lord (Cante al Señor),125
Sing We Triumphant Hymns, 363
Sing with Joy to the Author / Glory Be to the Father, 430
Sleepers, Wake, 226
Soon and Very Soon, 669
Taste and See, 467
The Lord, Your God Is with You, 173
Thine Is the Glory, 355
This Is God's Wondrous World, 180
Total Praise, 633
Uyai mose (Come All You People), 2
We Praise You, O God, Our Redeemer, 34
We Worship God the Rock, 424
We, Your People, Sing Your Praises (Bon Berger, ton peuple t'adore), 849
What Wondrous Love Is This, 564
You Are Good, 33
You Are Holy, You Are Whole, 61
You Dwell in the Songs / Restless, 741
Your Grace Finds Me, 521
Your Grace Is Enough, 167
[Alleluia (ASL)], 73
[Alleluia! Christ is risen!], 875
[As you come to Christ the living stone], 381
[Bless the Lord, O my soul], 185
[Blessed One, our source and support], 989.C
[Christ is the image of the invisible God], 189
[Clap your hands all you peoples], 108
[Glory to God in the highest], 880
[Glory to You, Source of All Being (Evening Prayer)], 987.B
[Glory to You, Source of All Being (Morning Prayer)], 985.B
[Holy God, Holy One, Holy Three!] 887
[Hosanna! Hosanna!], 885
[I lift my eyes to the hills], 109
[I praise you, God—in the sanctuary], 886
[I saw a vast crowd], 110
[In the beginning, before time], 884
[Lead a life worthy of the calling], 446
[Let the same mind be in you], 335
[Make a joyful noise to the Lord], 20
[May God be with you! And also with you], 944
[May the God of endurance], 822
[My soul proclaims the greatness], 987.F
[Notre Père qui es aux cieux], 989.D
[Now, to the One who by the power], 824
[O God, open our lips], 985.A
[Our Father in heaven], 989.A
[Our Father, who art in heaven], 989.B
[Padre nuestro que estás en los cielos], 989.E
[Praise and thanks to you, holy God], 915
[Praise be to the Lord], 1063
[Praise the Lord], 107
[Praise to God who has given us life], 902
[Sing and sing], 883
[Sing the Goodness], 104
[Sing to the Lord a new song], 106
[The angel said "Do not be afraid!"], 234
[This is the day that the Lord has made], 15
[Though the fig tree does not blossom], 820
[Vater unser im Himmel], 989.F
[We are people who must sing you], 882

Prayer before a Time of Worship or Preparation for Worship

[Almighty God, to you all hearts are open], 860
[Dear God, let your word shine], 912
[Life-giving God, may your Holy Spirit inspire], 879
[Living God, by the power of your Spirit], 911
[Speak to us, living God], 910

Prayer Jesus Taught

Abana alathi (Abana in Heaven), 675
Our Father, who Art in Heaven, 674
Our God in Heaven, 673
[Blessed One, our source and support], 989.C
[Notre Père qui es aux cieux], 989.D
[Our Father in heaven], 989.A
[Our Father, who art in heaven], 989.B
[Padre nuestro que estás en los cielos], 989.E
[Vater unser im Himmel], 989.F

Praying

See: PRAYING (673-744); WORSHIP RESOURCES: Praying (989-1014); ART AND SCRIPTURE: Praying (723-730)
See also: Invocation; Lament; Prayer Jesus Taught; Praying: About Prayer; Praying: Answered prayer; Praying: For One Another; Praying: For Ourselves; Praying: For the Church; Praying: For the World; Praying: Gratitude; Silence
Agios o Theos, 709
As I Went Down to the River to Pray, 453
Be Still and Know, 37
Be Thou My Vision, 549
Bleibet hier (Stay with Me), 627
Brethren, We Have Met to Worship, 25
Bwana awabariki (May God Grant You a Blessing), 845
Cast Thy Burden upon the Lord, 616
Creator of the Stars of Night, 236
Eternal Light, Shine in My Heart, 554
Flow to You, 132
God, Who Stretched the Spangled Heavens, 529
Guide My Feet, 816
Jesus, Remember Me (Jesús, recuérdame), 327
Khudaya, rahem kar (Have Mercy on Us, Lord), 693
Kyrie eleison (Ghanaian), 795
Kyrie eleison (Russian Orthodox), 147
Kyrie eleison (Taizé Kyrie 13), 692
Lead Me, Guide Me, 601
Like the Murmur of the Dove's Song, 56
Listen in the Silence, 541
Lord, Have Mercy (Manderfeld) 614
Lord, Have Mercy (Moosonee), 651
My Shepherd Will Supply My Need, 640
O Splendor of God's Glory Bright, 500
Oré poriajú verekó (Kyrie eleison), 620
Out of the Depths I Cry to You, 140
Precious Lord, Take My Hand, 610
Qing zao qi lai kan (Golden Breaks the Dawn), 498
Seek Ye First, 417
Shepherd Me, O God, 744
Si tuvieras fe (If You Only Had Faith), 593
So nimm denn meine Hände (Take Thou My Hand), 631
Spirit of God! Descend, 557
Stay with Me, the Night Has Come, 319
Teach Me Thy Truth, 776
The Day You Gave Us, 506
The Lord's My Shepherd, 660
There Is a Balm in Gilead, 647
Thuma mina (Send Me, Lord), 834
'Tis Midnight, and on Olive's Brow, 318
We Long to Know Her, 44
What Comfort Can Our Worship Bring, 623
When I Can't Find My Way, 591
When Pain or Sorrow / Hold On, 612
When the Storms of Life Are Raging, 595
Ya hamala Allah (O Lamb of God), 321
[Are any of you suffering hardships], 727
[Christ, have mercy (ASL)], 615
[Evening Prayer], 987
[God of deep and dazzling darkness], 988
[How long, O Lord], 728
[I lift my eyes to the hills], 109
[Morning, noon, and night], 987.G
[Morning Prayer], 985
[Nine Patch #8], 723
[O Lord, you have searched me], 724
[Rejoice in the Lord always], 726
[Some of us are exhausted], 854
[The Lord is my shepherd], 725
[The Spirit helps us in our weakness], 729
[The Spirit helps us in our weakness (Morning Prayer)], 985.F
[Thus says the Lord: Maintain justice], 782

Praying: About Prayer

See also: PRAYING: Prayer (673-690)
See also: Praying
Brethren, We Have Met to Worship, 25
I Love the Lord, 684
On Silken, Soft Wings, 676
Si tuvieras fe (If You Only Had Faith), 593
Through Our Fragmentary Prayers, 677
What a Friend We Have in Jesus, 628
What Comfort Can Our Worship Bring, 623
[Are any of you suffering hardships], 727
[Between the words], 990
[Every Time I Feel the Spirit, 681
[O Lord, you have searched me], 724
[Praying aloud spontaneously], 995
[Rejoice in the Lord always], 726
[That huge "Why?"], 1005
[The Spirit helps us in our weakness], 729
[Thus says the Lord, the God of Israel], 783

Praying: Answered prayer

See also: Praying
Demos gracias (Let Us Give Thanks), 704
Shukuru Yesu (We Thank You), 699
Somebody Prayed for Me, 698
[Between the words], 990
[Blessed be the ones who dance], 1049
[From all that is broken], 908
[God, I have so few ways to pray], 1008
[It is good to give you thanks (Evening Prayer)], 987.C
[It is good to give you thanks (Morning Prayer)], 985.C
[O Lord, you have searched me], 724

Praying: For Healing

See also: Healing; Health Care Facilities; Praying
Cast Out, O Christ, 285
For the Healing of the Nations, 705
For Those with Whom Our Lives Are Bound, 734
Healer of Our Every Ill, 644
Kombo na Yesu (The Name of Jesus), 648
O Healing River, 706
O Thou, in Whose Presence, 600
Onyame wo mu o (In Your Sickness), 607
When Grief Is Raw, 655
When We Must Bear Persistent Pain, 735
[Are any of you suffering hardships], 727
[Great Physician, you touched the lives], 976
[Hear our prayer, O God of healing and hope], 978
[Listening God, you hear our prayers], 996
[Merciful God, we wait], 977
[With the whole people of God], 997

Praying for Hearing the Word

See: Scripture Proclamation

Praying: For One Another
See also: PRAYING: For One Another and Ourselves (731-744)
See also: Praying; Praying: For Ourselves
Somebody Prayed for Me, 698
Use Us, God, 811
When Pain or Sorrow / Hold On, 612
Woza nomthwalo wakho (Come, Bring Your Burdens to God), 679
[Are any of you suffering hardships], 727
[Christ is like a single body], 856
[Do not fight back against someone], 293
[God of deep and dazzling darkness], 988
[God of every place], 859
[God our sanctuary], 1042
[God, just as you sent Joseph to Egypt], 957
[God, who is Alpha and Omega], 962
[Listening God, you hear our prayers], 996
[Morning, noon, and night], 987.G
[Nine Patch #8], 723
[Save us, God, from being self-centered], 1000
[Source of all hope and holiness], 863
[Sovereign Majesty, we pray for the continued outpouring], 992
[The Spirit helps us in our weakness (Morning Prayer)], 985.F
[With the whole people of God], 997

Praying: For Ourselves
See also: PRAYING: For One Another and Ourselves (731-744)
See also: Praying; Praying: For One Another
Calm Me, Lord, 680
In My Life, Lord, Be Glorified, 754
Just As I Am, without One Plea, 560
Lord, I Am Fondly, Earnestly Longing, 555
Lord, I Want to Be a Christian, 558
Make Me an Instrument of Your Peace, 713
My God, My God, 696
O God, to You I Cry in Pain, 646
O Great Spirit, 51
O Lord, Hear My Prayer, 685
Open, Lord, My Inward Ear, 548
Spirit of Life, 368
Take, O Take Me as I Am, 748
There Is More Love Somewhere, 804
What a Friend We Have in Jesus, 628
[Almighty God, to you all hearts are open], 860
[Blessed One, our source and support], 989.C
[Christ our companion, you came not to humiliate the sinner], 898
[Come among us, Holy Spirit, and create a community], 955
[Come, Holy Spirit, enter our silences], 877
[Convert us, Jesus the persecuted], 1027
[Creator God, thank you for people and places], 954
[Dear Jesus, I confess my need of you], 926
[Eternal God, you call us to ventures], 1068
[Everlasting God, in whom we live and move], 998
[Gardener God, you have planted], 1002
[God be in my head], 999
[God, give me grace to accept], 1007
[God, it is night], 986
[God, make me an instrument of your peace], 991
[God of cosmos and quarks], 881
[God of grace and glory, you fling the stars], 985.G
[God of life, we thank you that our work], 953
[God of the foolish cross], 896
[God of work and rest], 956
[God, our Creator, we give you thanks], 972
[God our sanctuary], 1042
[Gracious God, bless our cities], 1032
[Grow us slowly], 1030
[Have mercy on me, O God], 889
[Holy and righteous God, you created us], 1034
[Jesus Christ, you stretched out your arms], 1026
[Jesus, Lamb of God], 892
[Liberating God, prevent us], 1031
[Listening God, you hear our prayers], 996
[Living God for whom no door is closed], 876
[Lord, your coming is still miraculous], 872
[Morning, noon, and night], 987.G
[Most loving, most strong God], 900
[Notre Père qui es aux cieux], 989.D
[Nurturing God, root us in your love], 1028
[O God, our deliverer], 1010
[O Risen Christ, you breathe your Holy Spirit], 1013
[Our Father in heaven], 989.A
[Our Father, who art in heaven], 989.B
[Padre nuestro que estás en los cielos], 989.E
[Save us, God, from being self-centered], 1000
[Some trust in governments], 1043
[Sovereign Majesty, we pray for the continued outpouring], 992
[The Spirit helps us in our weakness (Morning Prayer)], 985.F
[This home is yours, my God], 958
[Vater unser im Himmel], 989.F
[With the whole people of God], 997

Praying: For the Church
See: PRAYING: For the Church (715-722)
See also: Church; Praying
God, Be with Us, 613
Herr, füll mich neu (Fill Me Anew), 739
In My Life, Lord, Be Glorified, 754
[Give thanks to God, who is good], 963
[Gracious God, we pray for your universal church], 1004
[Jesus, servant, at supper with your disciples], 1041
[Listening God, you hear our prayers], 996
[Loving God, you have baptized us], 1001
[Morning, noon, and night], 987.G
[O God, listening to us here], 993
[Source of all hope and holiness], 863
[Sovereign Majesty, we pray for the continued outpouring], 992
[The Spirit helps us in our weakness (Morning Prayer)], 985.F
[With the whole people of God], 997

Praying: For the World
See: PRAYING: For the World (705-714)
See also: Peace and Justice; Praying
God, Whose Purpose Is to Kindle, 152
In My Life, Lord, Be Glorified, 754
Kyrie eleison, Have Mercy, 796
Kyrie eleison (Taizé Kyrie 13), 692
Let Justice Flow Down, 791
Make Me an Instrument of Your Peace, 713
Tears of Suffering, 694
Waterfall, 763
[Confesemos nuestro pecado contra Dios], 901
[God of deep and dazzling darkness], 988
[God our sanctuary], 1042
[In defiance of corruption and falsehood], 1040
[Listening God, you hear our prayers], 996
[Morning, noon, and night], 987.G
[O God, listening to us here], 993
[O Prince of Peace], 894
[Some trust in governments], 1043
[Sovereign Majesty, we pray for the continued outpouring], 992
[The Spirit helps us in our weakness (Morning Prayer)], 985.F
[With the whole people of God], 997

Praying: Gratitude
See: PRAYING: Gratitude (697-704)
See also: Praying; Thanksgiving
Blessed Be Your Name, 637
Come, Thou Fount, 563
El Senyor és la meva força (In the Lord I'll Be Ever Thankful), 118
For the Beauty of the Earth, 120
For the Fruit of All Creation, 124
Great God, the Giver of All Good, 486
Great Is Thy Faithfulness, 419
Nun danket alle Gott (Now Thank We All Our God), 114
O God beyond All Praising, 814
On Silken, Soft Wings, 676
[Blessed are you, O God, maker of all things], 1019
[Bless the Lord, O my soul], 185
[Creator Spirit, you clothe the flowers], 1018
[God, maker of galaxies, who numbers the hairs], 971
[God of cosmos and quarks], 881
[God of every place], 859
[God of extravagant mercy], 1020
[God of Life, we give these offerings], 1017
[God of mystery and wonder at this and every table], 948
[How long, O Lord], 728
[It is good to give you thanks (Evening Prayer)], 987.C
[It is good to give you thanks (Morning Prayer)], 985.C
[Let your hearts be ruled], 818
[Nine Patch #8], 723
[Receive our thanks for night and day], 949
[Source and sustainer of life], 1009
[The Lord is my shepherd], 725
[Though the fig tree does not blossom], 820

Praying: Lament
See: Lament

Praying: Short Prayer Responses
See also: Agnus Dei / Lamb of God; Alleluia; Amen; Kyrie eleison / Lord, Have Mercy
Agios o Theos (Holy, Holy, Holy God), 709
All Will Be Well, 586
Be Still and Know, 37
Bleibet hier (Stay with Me), 627
Bless the Lord, My Soul (Tengo sed de ti / Bendiz o Senhor), 127
Christe, lux mundi (Christ, You Are Light), 271
Confitemini Domino (Come and Fill Our Hearts), 52
Dans nos obscurités (Within Our Darkest Night), 632
Demos gracias (Let Us Give Thanks), 704
Don't Be Afraid, 596
El Senyor és la meva força (In the Lord I'll Be Ever Thankful), 118
Every Time I Feel the Spirit, 681
Gloria, 94
God, Grant Us Mercy, 142
Healer of Our Every Ill, 644
Hold Us in Your Mercy, 736
Holy Spirit, Come to Us, 58
How Can Our Anger Give Life, 792
How Long, O Lord, 691
Jesus, Remember Me (Jesús, recuérdame), 327
Kindle in Us Your Love, 54
Let Us Pray, 686
Listen in the Silence, 541
Lord, Listen to Your Children, 682
Magnificat, 97
Make Me an Instrument of Your Peace, 713
Nada te turbe, 604
Njoo kwetu, Roho mwema (Gracious Spirit), 367
Nothing Can Ever Come between Us, 654
Nothing Can Separate Us, 171
O Fiery Spirit, 55
O Lord, Hear My Prayer, 685
Open My Heart / Abre mi corazón, 731
Ô toi, Seigneur / O God, We Call, 683
Peace, Salaam, Shalom, 805
Perdón, Señor, 153
Santo (Holy), 136
Seeds, 777
Shepherd Me, O God, 744
Shukuru Yesu (We Thank You), 699
Somebody Prayed for Me, 698
Stay with Me, the Night Has Come, 319

Take, O Take Me as I Am, 748
The Kingdom of God (El reino de Dios), 799
There Is More Love Somewhere, 804
Ubi caritas et amor, 773
Ubi caritas (Where True Love), 492
Veni Sancte Spiritus, 370
Wait for the Lord / Contemplaré tu vida, 228
Way way way (Ojibwe), 742
Ya Rab as-salami (God of Peace and Justice), 711
You Are All We Have, 701
Your Love Is Washing Over Me, 166

Priesthood of Believers

See also: Church; Holy Spirit: Gifts of; Ministry; Vocation;
There Are Many Gifts, 374
What Is This Place, 22
[As you come to Christ the living stone], 381
[Empowering God, with your people], 965
[Every Christian is called], 964
[May God, who calls you to this ministry], 968
[There are different kinds of gifts], 380
[What will you offer the body of Christ today], 1023
[You are no longer foreigners], 382

Prisons

See also: Liberation
Bless'd Be the God of Israel, 223
Honja sorironeun (With My Voice Alone), 800
Let Justice Flow Down, 791
O God, Our Refuge, 434
[Blessed be the ones who dance], 1049
[Jesus stood up to read], 292
[Some trust in governments], 1043
[When the song of the angels is stilled], 1064

Prophets

See: TELLING GOD'S STORY: Prophets (205-209)
Comfort, Comfort, O My People, 212
Hope Is a Candle, 211
Let Justice Flow Down, 791
Light Dawns on a Weary World, 205
Lo, How a Rose E'er Blooming, 216
Noel, 256
O Day of Peace, 787
O God of Blessings, 700
Poor of the Earth, 213
Praise to the Living God, 204
Prepare the Way! the Prophet Called, 220
Prepare Ye the Way of the Lord, 219
Spirit, Working in Creation, 50
Sword into a Plowshare, 798
There Is a Line of Women, 546
Waterfall, 763
Who Will Speak a Word of Warning, 758
[A shoot will come up], 232
[Blessed are you, Lord, the God of Israel], 985.E
[Blessed be the ones who dance], 1049
[Come, all you who are thirsty], 14
[Come, let us go up], 13
[Do not fear, says God], 903
[Here is my servant, the one I uphold], 448
[In our doubt and fear], 1044
[Jesus stood up to read], 292
[My soul proclaims the greatness], 987.F
[Praise and thanks to you, holy God], 915
[Speak to us, living God], 910
[The people say: Our bones are dried up], 383
[The people walking in darkness], 231

Protection

A Mighty Fortress Is Our God, 421
All Praise to Thee, My God, 505
And I Will Raise You Up, 641
A Wonderful Savior Is Jesus, 626
Be Still, My Soul, 664
Calm Me, Lord, 680
Children of the Heavenly Father, 517
Come What May / Pase lo que pase ¡ven!, 768
Everlasting God, on You I Call, 630
Gentle Shepherd, 718
In the Rifted Rock I'm Resting (Wehrlos und verlassen sehnt sich), 619
I to the Hills Will Lift My Eyes, 602
Jesu, meine Freude (Jesus, Priceless Treasure), 624
Jesus, Lover of My Soul, 659
Loving Spirit, 697
My Life Flows On, 605
My Lighthouse, 597
Nearer, My God, to Thee, 658
Nothing Can Ever Come between Us, 654
O God, Our Refuge, 434
Oceans (Océanos), 456
Qing zao qi lai kan (Golden Breaks the Dawn), 498
Shout to the Lord (Cante al Señor),125
Sing Praise to God Who Reigns, 101
The Lord is My Light, 437
Thy Word Is a Lamp, 398
Total Praise, 633
We Sing to You, O God, 80
What a Fellowship / Leaning on the Everlasting Arms, 160
You Are All We Have, 701
Your Love Is Amazing, 96
Your Love Is Washing Over Me, 166
[Blessed One, our source and support], 989.C
[Christ be within us to keep us], 1069
[I am convinced that neither death, nor life], 337
[I lift my eyes to the hills], 109
[Live without fear], 1062
[May God bless you and keep you], 826
[Notre Père qui es aux cieux], 989.D
[Our Father in heaven], 989.A
[Our Father, who art in heaven], 989.B
[Padre nuestro que estás en los cielos], 989.E
[The Lord is my shepherd], 725
[This home is yours, my God], 958
[Thus says the Lord, the God of Israel], 783
[Vater unser im Himmel], 989.F

Protest

See also: Anger; Peace and Justice
Amen (African American), 689
Draw the Circle Wide, 802
Hear the Turmoil of the Nations, 201
How Can Our Anger Give Life, 792
How Can We Be Silent, 790
I'm Gonna Eat at the Welcome Table, 801
Jesus Christ Is Waiting, 287
Let Justice Flow Down, 791
O Healing River, 706
Siyahamba (We Are Marching), 793
There Is More Love Somewhere, 804
We Shall Overcome, 803
Your Love Is Washing Over Me, 166
[Blessed be the ones who dance], 1049
[God of extravagant mercy], 1020
[In defiance of corruption and falsehood], 1040
[In our concerns and in our choices], 1051
[In our doubt and fear], 1044
[Jesus calls us to praise and prayer], 851
[Lay one brick at a time], 1036
[Liberating God, prevent us], 1031
[Lighting a candle], 1006
[May we go forth into the world with courage], 1039

Psalms

2: Hear the Turmoil of the Nations, 201
13: How Long, O Lord, 691
13: [How long, O Lord], 728
16: You Are All We Have, 701
19: God's Glory Fills the Heavens, 197
22: My God, My God, 696
23: My Shepherd Will Supply My Need, 640
23: Shepherd Me, O God, 744
23: The Lord's My Shepherd, 660
23: [The Lord is my shepherd], 725
30: How Long, O Lord, 691
32: While I Keep Silence, 310
34: Taste and See, 467
42: As a Deer in Want of Water, 552
46: A Mighty Fortress Is Our God, 421
46: [Be still and know that I am God], 730
47: [Clap your hands all you peoples], 108
51: Create in Me a Clean Heart, 141
51: [Have mercy on me, O God], 889
72: Jesus Shall Reign, 414
85: [Let me hear what the Lord God says], 188
85: Restore Our Faith, O Saving God, 198
90: O God, Our Help in Ages Past, 203
91: And I Will Raise You Up, 641
95: For You, O God, My Soul, 41
98: Cantai ao Senhor (O Sing to the Lord), 113
100: All People That on Earth Do Dwell, 5
100: Alleluia / Make a Joyful Noise (Psalm 100), 66
100: [Make a joyful noise to the Lord], 20
103: Praise, My Soul, the King of Heaven!, 75
104: O Worship Our God, All Glorious Above, 74
104: [Bless the Lord, O my soul], 185
106: [Praise be to the Lord], 1063
116: I Love the Lord, 684
117: Laudate Dominum (Sing, Praise, and Bless the Lord), 77
118: [This is the day that the Lord has made], 15
121: I to the Hills Will Lift My Eyes, 602
121: [I lift my eyes to the hills], 109
122: [I was glad when they said to me], 16
126: [May those who sow in tears], 821
130: Out of the Depths I Cry to You, 140
133: [How very good and pleasant it is], 17
136: We Give Thanks unto You, 117
137: By the Waters of Babylon, 695
139: Lord, You've Searched Me, 609
139: O God, You Search Me, 199
139: [O Lord, you have searched me], 724
146: [Praise the Lord], 107
148: Nyanyikanlah nyanyian baru (Sing to God a New Song), 93
148: Praise the Lord, Sing Hallelujah, 95

Racial Justice

See: Justice: Racial

Reconciliation

See also: Justice; Peace; Peace and Justice
All Praise to Thee, My God, 505
Between Darkness and Light, 808
Christ Has Broken Down the Wall, 174
Christ Is Alive! Let Christians Sing, 359
Come, Join in Mary's Prophet-Song, 246
Could It Be That God Is Singing, 42
Far, Far Away / I Will Arise, 300
For the Healing of the Nations, 705
For We Are Strangers No More, 409
Gentle God, When We Are Driven, 150
Go, My Friends, in Grace, 810
God Calls Us, 394
God, Give Me Time, 144
God Made from One Blood, 523
Healing River of the Spirit, 642
Honja sorironeun (With My Voice Alone), 800
I Come with Joy, 478
Jesus, Help Us Live in Peace, 719
Khudaya, rahem kar (Have Mercy on Us, Lord), 693
Kyrie eleison (Ghanaian), 795
Kyrie eleison (Russian Orthodox), 147
Kyrie eleison (Taizé Kyrie 1), 678
Kyrie eleison (Taizé Kyrie 13), 692
Like the Murmur of the Dove's Song, 56
Lord, Have Mercy (Manderfeld) 614
Lord, Have Mercy (Moosonee), 651
Make Me an Instrument of Your Peace, 713
O Day of Peace, 787
Oré poriajú verekó (Kyrie eleison), 620
Ososo (Come Now, O Prince of Peace), 391
Put Peace into Each Other's Hands, 485
Renew Your Church, 717
Together, 389
We Are People of God's Peace, 797
We Dream of a Turning, 209

We, Your People, Sing Your Praises (Bon Berger, ton peuple t'adore), 849
When Love Is Found, 524
[Anyone who is joined to Christ], 785
[As a shepherd seeks a lost sheep], 868
[At the Impulse of God's Love], 780
[Blessed be the ones who dance], 1049
[By the grace of God we seek to live and proclaim], 925
[Christ is the image of the invisible God], 189
[Creator, we give you thanks], 861
[For the times we have lied], 891
[Friends, as we gather to eat the bread], 937
[Friends in Christ, God knows our needs], 888
[God, make me an instrument of your peace], 991
[Have mercy on me, O God (Evening Prayer)], 987.D
[Healing is central to the ministry of Jesus], 975
[Hear the words of Jesus: "Peace I leave with you"], 904
[In peace let us pray: O God, we give you thanks], 945
[Jesus, Lamb of God], 892
[La paz no es producto del terror ni del miedo], 1038
[Let the rain come and wash away], 1048
[May the Love which overcomes], 906
[Now, thanks to Christ Jesus], 786
[O Risen Christ, you breathe your Holy Spirit], 1013
[The church is the body of Christ], 959
[Thus says the Lord: Maintain justice], 782
[Trusting in God's grace, let us confess], 938
[We acknowledge that we are gathering], 878
[We are not alone], 922
[We offer thanksgiving to our Creator], 864
[You who open doors], 862

Reconciling
See: Confession of Sin; Assurance of Grace

Refugees
See: Immigration and Refugees

Regeneration
See: Conversion and New Life

Reign of Christ
See: TELLING GOD'S STORY: Reign of Christ (407-418)
See also: Jesus Christ: Advent of; Jesus Christ: Ascension of; Judgment; New Creation; Peace and Justice;Reign of God; Second Coming;
A Wonderful Savior Is Jesus, 626
All Glory, Laud, and Honor, 315
All Hail the Power of Jesus' Name (DIADEM), 364
Arise, Your Light Is Come!, 273
Build Your Kingdom Here, 393
Cantai ao Senhor (O Sing to the Lord), 113
Christe, lux mundi (Christ, You Are Light), 271
Christ Is Risen, 349
Christ the Lord Is Risen Today (El Señor resucitó), 346
Christ, We Do All Adore Thee, 138
Christ Who Left His Home in Glory, 361
Come, Christians, Join to Sing, 28
Come Now, O God, 143
Come, Thou Long-Expected Jesus, 218
Come, Ye Thankful People, 123
Creator of the Stars of Night, 236
Dhuh Pangeran (O Prince of Peace), 26
For All the Saints, 672
For the Healing of the Nations, 705
Hallelujah, Salvation, and Glory, 69
Hark! the Glad Sound!, 217
Hosanna, Loud Hosanna, 313
How Can We Be Silent, 790
How Great Is Our God (Cuán grande es Dios), 116
I Am the Bread of Life (Yo soy el pan de vida), 480
I Believe in God Almighty, 433
I Know Not Why God's Wondrous, 590
I Sing with Exultation, 444
It Came upon a Midnight Clear, 248
Jesus Is Coming, 312
Jésus, je voudrais te chanter (Lord Jesus, You Shall Be My Song), 581
Jesus on the Mountain Peak, 301
Joy to the World, 240
Kwake Yesu nasimama (Here on Christ the Rock I Will Stand), 159
Let All Mortal Flesh Keep Silence, 65
Let's Walk Together, 6
Longing for Light, 715
Low in the Grave He Lay, 333
My Hope Is Built on Nothing Less, 621
My Soul Proclaims with Wonder, 222
New Earth, Heavens New, 377
O God beyond All Praising, 814
O Lord My God / How Great Thou Art, 436
Open My Eyes (Abre mis ojos), 732
Praise Him, Praise Him, 100
Prepare the Way! the Prophet Called, 220
Ride On, Ride On in Majesty, 316
Schönster Herr Jesu (Beautiful Savior), 130
See Whose Glory Fills the Skies, 274
Sing a New World into Being, 809
Sing We Triumphant Hymns, 363
Sleepers, Wake, 226
So lange Jesus bleibt der Herr (As Long as Jesus' Reign Goes On), 64
Soon and Very Soon, 669
The Bread We Break Is Telling, 466
The Day You Gave Us, 506
This Joyful Eastertide, 352
To Us a Child of Hope Is Born, 259
Tú eres todopoderoso (Because You're Holy), 89
Wait for the Lord / Contemplaré tu vida, 228
We Praise Thee, O God, 91
What Child Is This, 267
When Peace like a River, 617
With Astonishment, Fear, and Wonder, 579
You, Lord, Are Both Lamb and Shepherd, 432
[A shoot will come up], 232
[At the table of Christ], 936
[Creemos en Dios Padre todopoderoso], 927
[From Bethlehem to Nazareth], 874
[From where we are], 1050
[I pledge allegiance to Jesus Christ], 929
[I saw a new heaven and a new earth], 339
[I saw a vast crowd], 110
[In peace let us pray: O God, we give you thanks], 945
[Jesus stood up to read], 292
[Now may the God of peace], 823
[O God, our deliverer], 1010
[Some trust in governments], 1043
[The people walking in darkness], 231
[Tree of Life], 12
[We gather in preparation], 870

Reign of God
See also: New Creation; Peace and Justice; Reign of Christ
A Mighty Fortress Is Our God, 421
Abana alathi (Abana in Heaven), 675
Build Your Kingdom Here, 393
Haneul naneun saeleul bora (See the Birds That Fly), 289
Hear the Turmoil of the Nations, 201
Holy God, We Praise Thy Name, 126
How Great Is Our God (Cuán grande es Dios), 116
Let Justice Flow Down, 791
Let the Hungry Come to Me, 459
Mountain of God, 11
My Soul Cries Out, 412
Na nzela na lola (As Long as We Follow), 413
O Day of Peace, 787
O God of Blessings, 700
O Gott Vater (O God and Father), 45
Open the Eyes of My Heart (Ouvre les yeux / Abre mis ojos), 401
Our Father, who Art in Heaven, 674
Our God in Heaven, 673
The Kingdom of God (El reino de Dios), 799
There's a River of Life, 24
We Dream of a Turning, 209
What Is the World Like, 298
You Are Exalted, 86
You Are Salt for the Earth, 297
[At this table, we receive the bread of life], 943
[Blessed are the poor in spirit], 295
[Blessed One, our source and support], 989.C
[Clap your hands all you peoples], 108
[Come, let us go up], 13
[From Bethlehem to Nazareth], 874
[From where we are], 1050
[God of the foolish cross], 896
[Holy One, as you are faithful to us], 1022
[How beautiful on the mountains], 781
[I pledge allegiance to Jesus Christ], 929
[In deep gratitude for this moment], 946
[Jesus stood up to read], 292
[Let the same mind be in you], 335
[Notre Père qui es aux cieux], 989.D
[O God, our deliverer], 1010
[Our Father in heaven], 989.A
[Our Father, who art in heaven], 989.B
[Padre nuestro que estás en los cielos], 989.E
[Some people brought children], 18
[Some trust in governments], 1043
[The reign of heaven is like a treasure], 294
[Tree of Life], 12
[Vater unser im Himmel], 989.F

Repentance
See also: Confession of Sin; Conversion and New Life
Comfort, Comfort, O My People, 212
Far, Far Away / I Will Arise, 300
Just As I Am, without One Plea, 560
My Jesus, I Love Thee, 133
Softly and Tenderly Jesus Is Calling, 544
Spirit of God! Descend, 557
Spirit, Open My Heart, 636
To God Be the Glory, 84
[Dear Jesus, I confess my need of you], 926
[Do you not know that all who were baptized], 449
[Gracious God, our sins are too heavy], 895
[Have mercy on me, O God], 889

Reproductive Loss
Nothing Is Lost on the Breath of God, 653

Rest
See also: SHARING OUR STORIES: Vocation, Work, and Rest (526-535)
See also: Sunday / Sabbath; Work
All Praise to Thee, My God, 505
Be at Rest, 532
Beauty for Brokenness, 712
Come Away from Rush and Hurry, 9
Come to Me, O Weary Traveler, 157
Come to the Water, 35
Far Above the Noise of Life, 625
Hallelujah! schöner Morgen (Hallelujah! Fairest Morning!), 497
In the Heartbeat of the City, 530
In the Rifted Rock I'm Resting (Wehrlos und verlassen sehnt sich), 619
Lord, I Need You, 155
Now, on Land and Sea Descending, 503
O Everlasting Love, 733
Quietly, Peacefully, 533
Sálvanos, Señor, despiertos (Save Us, O Lord), 833
The Lord, Your God Is with You, 173
[God, it is night], 986
[God of deep and dazzling darkness], 988
[God of grace and glory, you keep our souls], 987.H
[Our lives are cluttered], 899
[Receive our thanks for night and day], 949
[Some of us are exhausted], 854

Resurrection of Jesus Christ
See: Jesus Christ: Resurrection of

Retreats
See: Camps and Retreats

Righteousness
See: Justice

Rural Life
See also: City; Harvest; Land
Come, Ye Thankful People, 123
En medio de la vida (You Are the God within Life), 526
For the Fruit of All Creation, 124
God of the Fertile Fields, 750
We Plow the Fields and Scatter, 747
[Bless the Lord, O my soul], 185
[Gardener God, you have planted], 1002
[May those who sow in tears], 821
[Mist, Sun, Morning], 183
[Though the fig tree does not blossom], 820

Sabbath
See: Sunday / Sabbath

Salvation
See also: Liberation
A Wonderful Savior Is Jesus, 626
Amazing Grace!, 163
Blessed Assurance, 435
Bless'd Be the God of Israel, 223
Christ Jesus Lay, 463
From Heaven Above to Earth I Come, 263
Good Christian Friends, Rejoice, 261
Gott ist die Liebe (I Know God Loves Me), 158
I Know Not Why God's Wondrous, 590
I Love to Tell the Story, 761
I Sing with Exultation, 444
In Thee Is Gladness, 666
Lord, I Am Fondly, Earnestly Longing, 555
Lord, I Lift Your Name on High (Tu nombre levantaré), 365
Love Divine, All Loves Excelling, 638
Mfurahini, haleluya (Christ Has Arisen, Alleluia!), 341
My Hope Is Built on Nothing Less, 621
O du fröhliche (Oh, How Joyfully), 254
O phi nong oei (Dear Friends, We're One), 525
O Worship Our God, 129
Oh, for a Thousand Tongues (AZMON), 764
Oh, for a Thousand Tongues (LYNGHAM), 78
Sálvanos, Señor, despiertos (Save Us, O Lord), 833
Sing, My Tongue, the Song of Triumph, 331
This Joyful Eastertide, 352
To God Be the Glory, 84
Wakantanka (Many and Great), 128
What Wondrous Love Is This, 564
When Peace like a River, 617
Wonderful Grace of Jesus, 170
[For God so loved the world], 338
[How beautiful on the mountains], 781
[I saw a vast crowd], 110
[Now, Lord, you let your servant], 825

Sanctification
See: Conversion and New Life

Sanctus / Holy, Holy, Holy
From North and South, from East and West, 460
Holy Lord, 314
[May God be with you! And also with you], 944

Schools and Learning Communities
See also: Children: Appropriate for; Nurturing Faith; Learning
Ask the Complicated Questions, 440
Holy Presence, Holy Teacher, 531
Teach Me Thy Truth, 776
[Come among us, Holy Spirit, and create a community], 955
[God of wanderers and seekers], 934

Science and Technology
At the Dawn of Your Creation, 179
God, Who Stretched the Spangled Heavens, 529
Gravity of Love, 494
Planets Humming as They Wander, 175
[Come among us, Holy Spirit, and create a community], 955
[God of cosmos and quarks], 881
[God of work and rest], 956
[Mist, Sun, Morning], 183

Scripture
See: Word of God

Scripture Proclamation
See also: Word of God
Anointing Fall on Me, 645
Because the Words We Wait to Hear, 406
Comme un souffle fragile (As a Sigh Great with Yearning), 403
Dawk'yah towgyah thawy báht-awm (Take the Saving Word of God), 400
Hallelujah! schöner Morgen (Hallelujah! Fairest Morning!), 497
Holy Spirit, Come with Power (Ven, Espíritu, cual viento), 57
Let This Mind Be in You, 572
Listen in the Silence, 541
Listen to the Word That God Has Spoken, 405
Lord, You Sometimes Speak, 537
O Gott Vater (O God and Father), 45
Open My Eyes (Abre mis ojos), 732
Open My Eyes that I May See, 738
Open My Heart / Abre mi corazón, 731
Open the Eyes of My Heart (Ouvre les yeux / Abre mis ojos), 401
Spirit of the Living God, 740
This Is the Air I Breathe (Eres mi respirar), 139
Thy Word Is a Lamp, 398
We Praise the Word of God, 404
[Dear God, let your word shine], 912
[For the Word of God in Scripture], 913.G
[God's Word is a lamp], 913.F
[Hear the Word of God], 914
[Hear what the Spirit is saying], 913.C
[Holy Wisdom. Holy Word], 913.B
[Jesus said, I am the bread of life], 987.E
[Jesus said, let anyone with ears], 985.D
[Living God, by the power of your Spirit], 911
[May God bless to our understanding], 913.D
[Open our ears to hear your word], 866
[Praise and thanks to you, holy God], 915
[Speak to us, living God], 910
[The Word of God for the people of God], 913.E
[Word of God. Word of Life], 913.A

Seasons
All Things Bright and Beautiful, 177
I Saw a Tree by the Riverside, 514
O Blessed Spring, 522
O God, Great Womb, 176
[Bless the Lord, O my soul], 185
[Gardener God, you have planted], 1002
[We offer thanksgiving to our Creator], 864

Second Coming
See: Jesus Christ: Second Coming of

Sending
See: SENDING (809-849); WORSHIP RESOURCES: Sending (1050-1069); ART AND SCRIPTURE: Sending (817-826)
See also: Mission; Sending: Commissioning; Sending: Blessing; Service
As We Rise, O God, to Meet You, 39
For We Are Strangers No More, 409
God of Justice, 772
God the Spirit, Guide and Guardian, 534
Guide Me, O Thou Great Jehovah, 606
Lead Me Forth, 837
Lead Me, Guide Me, 601
Lead On, O Cloud of Presence, 194
Life-Giver, Maker, God of All, 38
Over My Head, 594
Praise God / Dedication anthem, 70
Sanna, sannanina, 79
Sent Forth by God's Blessing, 812
Siyahamba (We Are Marching), 793
Soon and Very Soon, 669
Take My Life, and Let It Be, 759
Take My Life, That I May Be (Que mi vida entera esté), 760
The Hand of God Shall Hold You, 671
[Alleluia! Christ is risen!], 875
[Be sincere in your love for others], 384
[Blessed be the ones who dance], 1049
[Christ has no body now on earth], 1035
[Christ, whose insistent call], 1029
[Compassionate Christ, if you are my light], 1003
[Convert us, Jesus the persecuted], 1027
[Everlasting God, in whom we live and move], 998
[God be in my head], 999
[God, make me an instrument of your peace], 991
[God our sanctuary], 1042
[God, who is Alpha and Omega], 962
[God will guide us continually], 985.H
[God's Spirit calls, the church commissions], 966
[Hear the words of Jesus: "Peace I leave with you"], 904
[In deep gratitude for this moment], 946
[Jesus Christ, you stretched out your arms], 1026
[Lead a life worthy of the calling], 446
[Let your hearts be ruled], 818
[Living Christ, in these times], 1033
[Love cannot remain by itself], 1037
[May God bless you and keep you], 826
[May the God of endurance], 822
[May the God of hope], 987.I
[May the grace of Jesus Christ], 21
[May those who sow in tears], 821
[May we go forth into the world with courage], 1039
[Migrant Journey], 817
[Now may our Lord Jesus Christ], 819
[Now may the God of peace], 823
[Now, Lord, you let your servant], 825
[Now, to the One who by the power], 824
[Peace be with you], 850
[Rejoice in the Lord always], 726
[The Lord told you what is good], 784
[Though the fig tree does not blossom], 820

Sending: Blessing
See: SENDING: Blessing (830-849)
See also: Blessing: Other; Sending
Go Ye Now in Peace / Go, My Friends, in Peace, 839
God, Be with Us, 613
Light Dawns on a Weary World, 205
Sálvanos Señor Despiertos (Save Us, O Lord), 833
Sent Forth by God's Blessing, 812
The Hand of God Shall Hold You, 671
[Christ be within us to keep us], 1069
[Go in peace. Christ is risen], 1052.F
[Go in peace. Christ is with you], 1052.A
[Go in peace. Go be peace], 1052.D
[Go in peace. Prepare the way], 1052.E
[Go in peace. Rejoice in the power], 1052.G
[Go in peace. Remember the poor], 1052.C
[Go in peace. Share the good news], 1052.B
[Go, knowing you are beloved by God], 1055
[God dearly loves us], 1056
[God of power, may the boldness of your Spirit], 1067
[God, who is Alpha and Omega], 962
[God will guide us continually], 985.H
[In our concerns and in our choices], 1051
[Live without fear], 1062
[May God bless you and keep you], 826
[May God bless you with a restless discomfort], 1058
[May the blessing of the God of Sarah and Hagar], 1060

[May the Christ who walks on wounded feet], 1066
[May the God of endurance], 822
[May the God of glory], 1053
[May the God of hope], 987.I
[May the grace of Jesus Christ], 21
[May the Son of God], 1057
[May the warm winds of heaven], 1061
[May those who sow in tears], 821
[May we go forth into the world with courage], 1039
[Migrant Journey], 817
[Now may our Lord Jesus Christ], 819
[Now may the God of peace], 823
[Now, to the One who by the power], 824
[The peace of God which passes all understanding], 1054
[Whatever wilderness the Spirit], 1065

Sending: Commissioning

See: SENDING: Commissioning (809-829)
See also: Commissioning: Other; Sending
Arise, Your Light Is Come!, 273
Christ Be in Your Senses, 721
Ey lou nis (Now I Know), 769
Go in Grace and Make Disciples, 766
I Will Follow, 775
Lead On, O Cloud of Presence, 194
Lord, You Give the Great Commission, 774
Thuma mina (Send Me, Lord), 834
We, Your People, Sing Your Praises (Bon Berger, ton peuple t'adore), 849
[Blessed be the ones who dance], 1049
[Christ has no body now on earth], 1035
[Eternal God, you call us to ventures], 1068
[From where we are], 1050
[Go forth in peace, and be of good courage], 1059
[Go in peace. Christ is risen], 1052.F
[Go in peace. Christ is with you], 1052.A
[Go in peace. Go be peace], 1052.D
[Go in peace. Prepare the way], 1052.E
[Go in peace. Rejoice in the power], 1052.G
[Go in peace. Remember the poor], 1052.C
[Go in peace. Share the good news], 1052.B
[Go, knowing you are beloved by God], 1055
[God dearly loves us], 1056
[In our concerns and in our choices], 1051
[Lay one brick at a time], 1036
[Let your hearts be ruled], 818
[Love cannot remain by itself], 1037
[May God bless you with a restless discomfort], 1058
[May we go forth into the world with courage], 1039
[Now, to the One who by the power], 824
[The Lord told you what is good], 784
[When the song of the angels is stilled], 1064

Separation from the World

I Have Decided to Follow Jesus, 443
In the Morning When I Rise, 499
O Christ, Impart Your Teaching True, 583
Rejoice, Rejoice Forevermore, 402
Unless a Grain of Wheat, 302
What a Friend We Have in Jesus, 628
[Blessed are the poor in spirit], 295
[By the grace of God we seek to live and proclaim], 925
[Creator Spirit, you clothe the flowers], 1018
[Dear ones, I plead with you], 105
[Do you not know that all who were baptized], 449
[God of extravagant mercy], 1020
[Our lives are cluttered], 899
[The reign of heaven is like a treasure], 294

Sermon on the Mount

See also: Jesus Christ: Teachings of; Prayer Jesus Taught
Ask the Complicated Questions, 440
Balaacoolwe (Blessed Are the Persecuted), 578
Blessed Are You, 290
Gentle God, When We Are Driven, 150
Haneul naneun saeleul bora (See the Birds That Fly), 289
Renew Your Church, 717
Seek Ye First, 417
This Little Light of Mine, 762
To Leave the Stones Unthrown, 580
You Are Salt for the Earth, 297
[Blessed are the poor in spirit], 295
[Creator Spirit, you clothe the flowers], 1018
[Do not fight back against someone], 293

Service

See: LIVING GOD'S STORY: Service (771-778); WORSHIP RESOURCES: Living God's Story (1026-1049); ART AND SCRIPTURE: Service and Witness for Peace (780-786)
See also: Mission; Sending; Sending: Commissioning; Service Agencies
All the Room Was Hushed and Still, 493
As We Rise, O God, to Meet You, 39
Brethren, We Have Met to Worship, 25
Christ Has No Body Here but Ours, 568
Christ, on the Night He Was Betrayed, 491
Come What May / Pase lo que pase ¡ven!, 768
For the Fruit of All Creation, 124
Go in Grace and Make Disciples, 766
Go, My Children, 830
Go, My Friends, in Grace, 810
Go Now in Peace, Worship Continues, 829
Help Us to Help Each Other, 722
Holy Presence, Holy Teacher, 531
I Bind My Heart This Tide, 556
Je louerai l'Éternel (Praise, I Will Praise You, Lord), 131
Jesus Took a Towel, 490
Joyous Light of Heavenly Glory, 504
One Is the Body, 386
Sing a New World into Being, 809
Take My Life, and Let It Be, 759
Take My Life, That I May Be (Que mi vida entera esté), 760
The Church of Christ Cannot Be Bound, 392
The Church of Christ, in Every Age, 395
There Is a Line of Women, 546
True Evangelical Faith, 439
Tú has venido a la orilla (Lord, You Have Come to the Lakeshore), 283
Ubi caritas (Where True Love), 492
Use Us, God, 811
We, Your People, Sing Your Praises (Bon Berger, ton peuple t'adore), 849
[As we now receive you into the fellowship], 932
[At the Impulse of God's Love], 780
[At the table of Christ], 936
[Blessed are you, O God, maker of all things], 1019
[Christ has no body now on earth], 1035
[Empowering God, with your people], 965
[Eternal Love, gentle God, you invite us], 951
[Everlasting God, in whom we live and move], 998
[Friends, as we gather to eat the bread], 937
[Generous God, you gave us life], 1015
[Go in peace. Remember the poor], 1052.C
[God, just as you sent Joseph to Egypt], 957
[God of extravagant mercy], 1020
[God of Life, we give these offerings], 1017
[God's Spirit calls, the church commissions], 966
[Holy One, as you are faithful to us], 1022
[In our concerns and in our choices], 1051
[Jesus calls us to praise and prayer], 851
[Jesus Christ, our Savior, you did not regard equality with God], 952
[Jesus, servant, at supper with your disciples], 1041
[Jesus washed the feet of his disciples], 950
[Lay one brick at a time], 1036
[Living God for whom no door is closed], 876
[Love cannot remain by itself], 1037
[May the Christ who walks on wounded feet], 1066
[Nine Patch #8], 723
[Our lives are cluttered], 899
[There are different kinds of gifts], 380
[There is no scarcity], 1024
[True evangelical faith], 921
[While Jesus was in Bethany], 296

Service Agencies

See also: Service
Christ Has No Body Here but Ours, 568
[Christ has no body now on earth], 1035
[God, just as you sent Joseph to Egypt], 957
[Jesus, servant, at supper with your disciples], 1041
[Lay one brick at a time], 1036

Silence

All the Room Was Hushed and Still, 493
Be Still and Know, 37
Darkness Is Not Dark to You, God, 200
In the Quiet Consecration, 484
In the Quiet Curve of Evening, 587
In the Singing, in the Silence, 481
Let All Mortal Flesh Keep Silence, 65
Listen in the Silence, 541
Lord, You Sometimes Speak, 537
Open, Lord, My Inward Ear, 548
Open My Eyes that I May See, 738
Through Our Fragmentary Prayers, 677
While I Keep Silence, 310
[Be still and know that I am God], 730
[Between the words], 990
[Friends in Christ, God knows our needs], 888
[God forgives you], 909
[God, it is night], 986
[How silently], 1021
[In our doubt and fear], 1044
[O Prince of Peace], 894
[O Risen Christ, you breathe your Holy Spirit], 1013
[Sing and sing], 883
[To worship is to stand in awe], 855

Simeon's Song

See: Nunc dimittis / Simeon's Song

Sin

See also: Evil; Forgiveness; Confession of Sin
Before the Waters Nourished Earth, 652
Christ Calls to Me, 542
Come Now, O God, 143
Create in Me a Clean Heart, 141
Jesus, Lover of My Soul, 659
No Longer Slaves to Fear, 195
Sign Us with Ashes, Merciful God, 304
[Do you not know that all who were baptized], 449
[For the times we have lied], 891
[Friends in Christ, God knows our needs], 888
[Have mercy on me, O God], 889
[Let us confess our sin], 890
[Remember: We are earth], 918

Singing

See: Music

Spiritual Gifts

See: Holy Spirit: Gifts of

Stewardship

See also: Creation: Care; Giving; Justice: Economic
At the Dawn of Your Creation, 179
Blessed Are You, 290
Called by Earth and Sky, 806
Forgive, Forgive Us, Holy God, 149
God, We Pause This Moment, 756
God, Whose Giving, 745
Grant Us, God, the Grace, 746
Tana mana dhana prabhū tava caraṇī (Heart and Mind, Possessions, God), 753
The Church of Christ Cannot Be Bound, 392
There's Enough for All, 757
Who Will Speak a Word of Warning, 758

[Blessed are you, O God, maker of all things], 1019
[Generous God, you gave us life], 1015
[God of Life, we give these offerings], 1017
[Holy One, as you are faithful to us], 1022
[There is no scarcity], 1024

Suffering

See also: SHARING OUR STORIES: Suffering and Joy (605-641)
See also: Grief; Lament; Trials
A Voice Was Heard in Ramah, 278
All Who Are Thirsty, 49
As a Deer in Want of Water, 552
As the Waters Rise around Us, 708
Balaacoolwe (Blessed Are the Persecuted). 578
Be Still, My Soul, 664
Beautiful Things, 551
Before the Waters Nourished Earth, 652
Blessed Are You, 290
By the Waters of Babylon, 695
Come Now, O God, 143
Come, Ye Disconsolate, 643
En medio de la vida (You Are the God within Life), 526
Faith of the Martyrs, 575
Fierce Raged the Tempest, 286
God Weeps with Us, 656
Healing River of the Spirit, 642
How Can Our Anger Give Life, 792
How Clear Is Our Vocation, 547
How Long, O Lord, 691
I Heard the Voice of Jesus Say, 536
I Love the Lord, 684
In the Bulb There Is a Flower, 670
In the Morning When I Rise, 499
In Thee Is Gladness, 666
I Want Jesus to Walk with Me, 306
Jesus, Lover of My Soul, 659
Just a Closer Walk with Thee, 743
Lift Every Voice and Sing, 611
Lift Your Glad Voices, 340
Lo, I Am with You, 284
Mary, Woman Weeping, 328
My God, My God, 696
My Latest Sun Is Sinking Fast, 662
O God, Our Refuge, 434
O God, to You I Cry in Pain, 646
O Sacred Head, Now Wounded, 325
O Thou, in Whose Presence, 600
Oh, Have You Not Heard (Ich weiss einen Strom), 668
Oré poriajú verekó (Kyrie eleison), 620
Prabhoo Lay lay (Savior Jesus, Enfold Me), 567
Precious Lord, Take My Hand, 610
Shepherd Me, O God, 744
Still My Soul, 603
The Lord's My Shepherd, 660
The Word of God Is Solid Ground, 399
'Tis Midnight, and on Olive's Brow, 318
We Are Often Tossed and Driven, 311
What Can I Leave Behind, 154
What Comfort Can Our Worship Bring, 623
When Grief Is Raw, 655
When I Can't Find My Way, 591
When Pain or Sorrow / Hold On, 612
When the Storms of Life Are Raging, 595
When We Must Bear Persistent Pain, 735
While I Keep Silence, 310
Woza nomthwalo wakho (Come, Bring Your Burdens to God), 679
You're Not Alone, 779
[A wilderness beckons us], 1011
[Are any of you suffering hardships], 727
[Christ is like a single body], 856
[Come, with your faith and your doubts], 947
[Convert us, Jesus the persecuted], 1027
[God, give me grace to accept], 1007
[God of deep and dazzling darkness], 988
[God of every place], 859
[God, who is Alpha and Omega], 962
[Gracious God, when there is nothing], 994
[Great Physician, you touched the lives], 976
[How long, O Lord], 728
[If you are delighted to be here], 853
[In his hands the iron nails], 919
[In our concerns and in our choices], 1051
[In our doubt and fear], 1044
[Liberating God, prevent us], 1031
[May God bless you with a restless discomfort], 1058
[May those who sow in tears], 821
[That huge "Why?"], 1005
[Though the fig tree does not blossom], 820

Sunday / Sabbath

See also: Rest
God, Bless the Work Your People Do, 528
Hallelujah! schöner Morgen (Hallelujah! Fairest Morning!), 497
O God, Great Womb, 176
[Grow us slowly], 1030
[I was glad when they said to me], 16
[Our lives are cluttered], 899
[Some of us are exhausted], 854
[This is the day that the Lord has made], 15
[Thus says the Lord: Maintain justice], 782

Table Graces

All Who Hunger, Gather Gladly, 474
Bless This Food and Bless Your People, 489
Demos gracias (Let Us Give Thanks), 704
God Is Great and God Is Good, 488
Gracias, Señor, por el pan (Thank You, O God, for This Bread), 487
Great God, the Giver of All Good, 486
Praise God (Doxology), 71
[Come, with your faith and your doubts], 947
[Communion], 468
[God of mystery and wonder at this and every table], 948
[Loaves and Fishes], 291
[O Dios, dales pan a los que tienen hambre], 1025
[Receive our thanks for night and day], 949

Teachings of Jesus Christ

See: Jesus Christ: Teachings of

Technology

See: Science and Technology

Thanksgiving

See: PRAISING: Thanksgiving (113-124)
See also: Harvest; Praise; Praying: Gratitude
10,000 Reasons / Bless the Lord, 111
Ah, Holy Jesus, 330
All Things Bright and Beautiful, 177
Alleluia / Make a Joyful Noise (Psalm 100), 66
Be at Rest, 532
Beloved, God's Chosen, 164
Blessed Be Your Name, 637
Demos gracias (Let Us Give Thanks), 704
En medio de la vida (You Are the God within Life), 526
Glory to God in the Highest, 99
God of the Fertile Fields, 750
Great God, the Giver of All Good, 486
Great Is Thy Faithfulness, 419
Here by the Water, 629
I Owe the Lord a Morning Song, 496
O God beyond All Praising, 814
Taste and See, 467
Today We Sing with Thankfulness, 535
Tú eres todopoderoso (Because You're Holy), 89
We Plow the Fields and Scatter, 747
We Praise You, O God, Our Redeemer, 34
Zisuh nih a zultu hna sinah (Peace Be with You! Jesus Told His Friends), 165
[At the table of Christ], 936
[At this table, we receive the bread of life], 943
[Bless the Lord, O my soul], 185
[Creator Spirit, you clothe the flowers], 1018
[Faithful God, we give thanks], 933
[Give thanks to God, who is good], 963
[God of cosmos and quarks], 881
[In deep gratitude for this moment], 946
[It is good to give you thanks (Evening Prayer)], 987.C
[It is good to give you thanks (Morning Prayer)], 985.C
[Let your hearts be ruled], 818
[Make a joyful noise to the Lord], 20
[May God be with you! And also with you], 944
[O Ancient of Days, you have been our dwelling place], 920
[O God, Ancient of Days, your love], 941
[Praise and thanks to you, holy God], 915
[Receive our thanks for night and day], 949
[Rejoice in the Lord always], 726
[Sing the Goodness], 104
[Source and sustainer of life], 1009
[We are people who must sing you], 882
[We give thanks to God for children], 969
[We offer thanksgiving to our Creator], 864

Time

God Is Working This Purpose Out, 770
God Speaks to Us in Bird and Song, 539
O God, Great Womb, 176
O God, Our Help in Ages Past, 203
O God, You Search Me, 199
Time Propels Us like a Current, 507
[God, give me grace to accept], 1007
[Holy God, Holy One, Holy Three!] 887
[In the beginning, before time], 884
[O Lord, you have searched me], 724

Tithing

See: Giving

Transfiguration

See: Jesus Christ: Transfiguration of

Trials

See also: Suffering
Amazing Grace!, 163
Balaacoolwe (Blessed Are the Persecuted), 578
Come, O Thou Traveler Unknown, 191
Come, Ye Disconsolate, 643
Everlasting God, on You I Call, 630
Faith of the Martyrs, 575
Fill Us with Your Feast, 309
How Firm a Foundation, 592
I Want Jesus to Walk with Me, 306
Jesus, Tempted in the Desert, 307
Just a Closer Walk with Thee, 743
Lift Every Voice and Sing, 611
Lo, I Am with You, 284
Onyame wo mu o (In Your Sickness), 607
Precious Lord, Take My Hand, 610
What a Friend We Have in Jesus, 628
When Peace like a River, 617
[A wilderness beckons us], 1011
[Are any of you suffering hardships], 727
[God, give me grace to accept], 1007
[God of every place], 859
[Gracious God, when there is nothing], 994
[Great Physician, you touched the lives], 976
[How long, O Lord], 728
[Listening God, you hear our prayers], 996
[May those who sow in tears], 821
[That huge "Why?"], 1005
[Though the fig tree does not blossom], 820

Trinity

See also: God: Images and Names of
Come and Seek the Ways of Wisdom, 196
Creating God, Your Fingers Trace, 427
Eternal Light, Shine in My Heart, 554
Glory to God, Whose Goodness Shines on Me, 429
God the Spirit, Guide and Guardian, 534
Holy God, We Praise Thy Name, 126
Holy, Holy, Holy!, 76
I Believe in God Almighty, 433
Make Us One, 455
Mothering God, You Gave Me Birth, 426

Nun danket alle Gott (Now Thank We All Our God), 114
O God in Heaven, 720
O Holy Spirit, Root of Life, 376
O Worship Our God, 129
One Is the Body, 386
Praise Be to God, 115
Praise God / Dedication anthem, 70
Praise God (Doxology), 71
Praise with Joy the World's Creator, 428
Sing with Joy to the Author / Glory Be to the Father, 430
Trinity Song, 60
We Come, 225
Wij geloven één voor één (We Believe as One by One), 431
Womb of Life and Source of Being, 112
[Blessed are you, Eternal God], 942
[Creemos en Dios Padre todopoderoso], 927
[From the River to the Wilderness], 445
[Glory to God in the highest], 880
[Glory to You, Source of All Being (Evening Prayer)], 987.B
[Glory to You, Source of All Being (Morning Prayer)], 985.B
[Holy God, Holy One, Holy Three!] 887
[I believe in God, the Father almighty], 923
[I will light a light in the name of the Maker], 867
[Jesus' eleven disciples went to a mountain], 451
[May the blessing of the God of Sarah and Hagar], 1060
[May the God of glory], 1053
[May the grace of Jesus Christ], 21
[Praise to God who has given us life], 902
[The angel said to Mary], 233
[The peace of God which passes all understanding], 1054
[We believe in one God, the Father, the Almighty], 924
[We light a light], 865
[While everyone was being baptized], 447

Trinity Sunday

See: Trinity

Trust

See: Faith

Union with Christ

See also: Union with God

Agneau de Dieu (O Lamb of God), 559
Christ Has No Body Here but Ours, 568
Christ, Be All around Me, 848
God, Be the Love, 43
I Am the Bread of Life (Yo soy el pan de vida), 480
I Bind My Heart This Tide, 556
In the Rifted Rock I'm Resting (Wehrlos und verlassen sehnt sich), 619
Jesu, Joy of Our Desiring, 639
Jesus, Be the Center, 584
Jesus Christ Is Love Divine, 749
Let the Hungry Come to Me, 459
Let This Mind Be in You, 572
Lord, I Want to Be a Christian, 558
Love Divine, All Loves Excelling, 638
One Is the Body, 386
Prabhoo Lay lay (Savior Jesus, Enfold Me), 567
Take My Life, and Let It Be, 759
The Bread We Break Is Telling, 466
You Have Put on Christ, 457
[Anyone who is joined to Christ], 785
[As John baptized Jesus in the Jordan], 940
[As you come to Christ the living stone], 381
[At the table of Christ], 936
[Baptism with water in the name of the triune God], 930
[Christ has no body now on earth], 1035
[Compassionate Christ, if you are my light], 1003
[Do you not know that all who were baptized], 449
[Gardener God, you have planted], 1002
[In Christ Jesus you are all children], 450
[Jesus said "I am the true vine"], 472
[Let us confess our sin], 890
[Living Christ, in these times], 1033
[May the Christ who walks on wounded feet], 1066
[May the God of endurance], 822
[May the Son of God], 1057
[Now, thanks to Christ Jesus], 786
[O Tree of Calvary], 1012
[Rejoice in the Lord always], 726
[You are no longer foreigners], 382

Union with God

See also: Union with Christ

Be Thou My Vision, 549
Christ, Be All around Me, 848
Eternal Light, Shine in My Heart, 554
God, Be the Love, 43
Let the Hungry Come to Me, 459
Lord, You've Searched Me, 609
O God, You Search Me, 199
Open, Lord, My Inward Ear, 548
Praise, My Soul, the King of Heaven!, 75
This Is the Air I Breathe (Eres mi respirar), 139
You Are All We Have, 701
[Blessed are you, Eternal God], 942
[Everlasting God, in whom we live and move], 998
[God be in my head], 999
[Gracious God, our sins are too heavy], 895

Unity

See also: Body of Christ; Church; Community; Unity in Diversity

Blest Be the Tie That Binds, 831
Christ Has Broken Down the Wall, 174
Dhuh Pangeran (O Prince of Peace), 26
Draw the Circle Wide, 802
Enviados somos de Dios (We Have Been Sent by God), 771
For We Are Strangers No More, 409
From North and South, from East and West, 460
Heart with Loving Heart, 813
Help Us to Help Each Other, 722
Holy Spirit, Come to Us, 58
Honja sorironeun (With My Voice Alone), 800
I Come with Joy, 478
In Christ There Is No East or West, 390
Jesus, Help Us Live in Peace, 719
Let the Hungry Come to Me, 459
Like the Murmur of the Dove's Song, 56
Make Us One, 455
O Blessed Spring, 522
O Holy Spirit, by Whose Breath, 53
O phi nong oei (Dear Friends, We're One), 525
O Praise the Gracious Power, 87
One Is the Body, 386
Ososo (Come Now, O Prince of Peace), 391
Praise with Joy the World's Creator, 428
Renew Your Church, 717
Seed, Scattered and Sown, 477
Sent Forth by God's Blessing, 812
Sizohamba naye (We Will Walk with God), 815
Somos pueblo que camina (We Are People on a Journey), 464
Sword into a Plowshare, 798
The Bread We Break Is Telling, 466
The Church's One Foundation, 397
There Are Many Gifts, 374
Together, 389
Trinity Song, 60
Ubi caritas et amor, 773
Ubi caritas (Where True Love), 492
We Are One in the Spirit, 387
We Shall Overcome, 803
Will You Let Me Be Your Servant, 778
[Anyone who is joined to Christ], 785
[As John baptized Jesus in the Jordan], 940
[As you come to Christ the living stone], 381
[At the table of Christ], 936
[Blessed are you, Eternal God], 942
[Communion], 468
[Gracious God, we pray for your universal church], 1004
[How very good and pleasant it is], 17
[I saw a vast crowd], 110
[In Christ Jesus you are all children], 450
[In peace let us pray: O God, we give you thanks], 945
[Lead a life worthy of the calling], 446
[Loving God, you have baptized us], 1001
[May the God of endurance], 822
[Now, thanks to Christ Jesus], 786
[O God, listening to us here], 993
[Tree of Life], 12
[When the day of Pentecost came], 379
[You are no longer foreigners], 382
[You who open doors], 862

Unity in Diversity

See also: Unity

Christ Has Broken Down the Wall, 174
Creating God, Your Fingers Trace, 427
Dhuh Pangeran (O Prince of Peace), 26
Draw the Circle Wide, 802
For We Are Strangers No More, 409
From North and South, from East and West, 460
God Made from One Blood, 523
God Welcomes All, 32
God, Whose Giving, 745
Here in This Place, 10
How Can I Say, 388
I Come with Joy, 478
In Christ There Is No East or West, 390
Jesus Calls Us, 30
Let Us Build a House, 36
Let's Walk Together, 6
Like the Murmur of the Dove's Song, 56
O Holy Spirit, by Whose Breath, 53
O Lord My God / How Great Thou Art, 436
O Praise the Gracious Power, 87
One Is the Body, 386
Ososo (Come Now, O Prince of Peace), 391
Praise with Joy the World's Creator, 428
Renew Your Church, 717
Seed, Scattered and Sown, 477
Sent Forth by God's Blessing, 812
Sing a New World into Being, 809
Summoned by the God Who Made Us, 1
Sword into a Plowshare, 798
There Are Many Gifts, 374
Together, 389
Ubi caritas et amor, 773
We Dream of a Turning, 209
We Place upon Your Table, 462
When Hands Reach Out, 513
You Are Good, 33
You're Not Alone, 779
[As we now receive you into the fellowship], 932
[At this table, we receive the bread of life], 943
[Christ is like a single body], 856
[Creemos en Dios Padre todopoderoso], 927
[God of wanderers and seekers], 934
[Gracious God, bless our cities], 1032
[I saw a vast crowd], 110
[In Christ Jesus you are all children], 450
[Nine Patch #8], 723
[Now, Lord, you let your servant], 825
[Peace be with you], 850
[There are different kinds of gifts], 380
[Thus says the Lord: Maintain justice], 782
[Tree of Life], 12
[What will you offer the body of Christ today], 1023
[When the day of Pentecost came], 379
[You are no longer foreigners], 382

Urban Life

See: City

Violence

See also: Nonviolence; Peace; Peace: Conflict and War; Conflict; Peace: Interpersonal

How Can We Worship Caesar's Cross, 308
Ikke ved makt (Not by Your Might), 538
Mary, Woman Weeping, 328

[Confesemos nuestro pecado contra Dios], 901
[O Prince of Peace], 894

Vocation

See also: SHARING OUR STORIES: Vocation, Work, and Rest (526-535)
See also: Church Leadership; God's Call; Ministry; Ordination; Priesthood of Believers; Work
Enviados somos de Dios (We Have Been Sent by God), 771
God the Spirit, Guide and Guardian, 534
God, Who Stretched the Spangled Heavens, 529
Holy Presence, Holy Teacher, 531
How Clear Is Our Vocation, 547
O Carpenter, Why Leave the Bench, 280
Quietly, Peacefully, 533
Teach Me Thy Truth, 776
There Are Many Gifts, 374
Today We Sing with Thankfulness, 535
Tú has venido a la orilla (Lord, You Have Come to the Lakeshore), 283
[Christ is like a single body], 856
[Empowering God, with your people], 965
[Every Christian is called], 964
[God's Spirit calls, the church commissions], 966
[Here is my servant, the one I uphold], 448
[I pledge with you], 967

Walking with God

See also: Faith Journey; Following Christ; Pilgrimage
As You Go Out from Here, 841
Everlasting God, on You I Call, 630
Go, My Friends, in Grace, 810
Go Ye Now in Peace / Go, My Friends, in Peace, 839
Hamba nathi (Come, Walk with Us), 23
Hey ney yana (I Walk in Beauty), 836
How Many Times We Start Again, 553
I Want Jesus to Walk with Me, 306
I Will Follow, 775
Kirisuto no heiwa ga (May the Peace of Christ), 843
Lead Me, Guide Me, 601
Lead On, O Cloud of Presence, 194
Like a Mother Who Has Borne Us, 518
Move in Our Midst, 827
Rejoice, Rejoice Forevermore, 402
Santo, santo, santo (Holy, Holy, Holy), 1C2
Siyahamba (We Are Marching), 793
Sizohamba naye (We Will Walk with God), 815
The Lord Lift You Up, 832
Thy Word Is a Lamp, 398
True Evangelical Faith, 439
Use Us, God, 811
We Are One in the Spirit, 387
We've Come This Far by Faith, 599
What a Fellowship / Leaning on the Everlasting Arms, 160
What Does the Lord Require of You?, 207
With Astonishment, Fear, and Wonder, 579
With Water Freely Flowing, 452
Ya-ma-ji ko-e-te (In Lonely Mountain Ways), 589
You Are Salt for the Earth, 297
[God dearly loves us], 1056
[May the Christ who walks on wounded feet], 1066
[Migrant Journey], 817
[Source of all hope and holiness], 863
[The Lord told you what is good], 784
[Whatever wilderness the Spirit], 1065

War

See: Peace: Conflict and War

Wedding

See: Marriage

Week of Prayer for Christian Unity

See also: Church; Unity in Diversity
For We Are Strangers No More, 409
Here in This Place, 10
Holy Spirit, Come to Us, 58
In Christ There Is No East or West, 390
Make Us One, 455
May You Be Rooted and Grounded in Love, 396
O Praise the Gracious Power, 87
One Is the Body, 386
Ososo (Come Now, O Prince of Peace), 391
Summoned by the God Who Made Us, 1
The Church of Christ Cannot Be Bound, 392
The Church's One Foundation, 397
[Gracious God, we pray for your universal church], 1004
[How very good and pleasant it is], 17
[I believe in God, the Father almighty], 923
[In peace let us pray: O God, we give you thanks], 945
[Loving God, you have baptized us], 1001
[Make a joyful noise to the Lord], 20
[O God, listening to us here], 993
[We believe in one God, the Father, the Almighty], 924
[You are no longer foreigners], 382

Welcome

See: GATHERING: Welcome (1-36)
See also: Gathering
All Who Hunger, Gather Gladly, 474
Christ Has Broken Down the Wall, 174
Come On, Children, to the Gospel Feast, 511
Come to the Table of Grace, 461
I'm Gonna Eat at the Welcome Table, 801
Let the Hungry Come to Me, 459
Remembrance, 479
Sing a New World into Being, 809
Together, 389
We Dream of a Turning, 209
[As a shepherd seeks a lost sheep], 868
[Come, come, whoever you are], 1047
[Come, with your faith and your doubts], 947
[God of every place], 859
[If you are delighted to be here], 853
[The table has been prepared], 939

Wisdom

See: TELLING GOD'S STORY: Wisdom (196-204)
See also: Psalms
Ask the Complicated Questions, 440
Be Thou My Vision, 549
Beloved, God's Chosen, 164
Eternal Light, Shine in My Heart, 554
God of Grace and God of Glory, 716
Holy Presence, Holy Teacher, 531
In the Beginning, 270
Jesu, Joy of Our Desiring, 639
O Come, O Come, Immanuel, 210
O God of Blessings, 700
O Holy Spirit, Root of Life, 376
Quietly, Peacefully, 533
Who Will Speak a Word of Warning, 758
Wisdom from on High Is Dawning, 238
[Be still and know that I am God], 730
[Come among us, Holy Spirit, and create a community], 955
[Does not Wisdom call], 184
[God, give me grace to accept], 1007
[God of the foolish cross], 896
[Holy Wisdom. Holy Word], 913.B
[Now, through the church], 385
[Praise and thanks to you, holy God], 915
[Thus says the Lord: Maintain justice], 782
[We offer thanksgiving to our Creator], 864

Witness

See: Mission

Women of the Bible

See also: Mary, Mother of Jesus
A Voice Was Heard in Ramah, 278
Bless the Arms That Comfort, 527
Brethren, We Have Met to Worship, 25
Christ Who Left His Home in Glory, 361
God Lights a Lamp, 299
Hope of Abraham and Sarah, 807
O God, Our Refuge, 434
That Easter Morn, at Break of Day, 342
The God of Sarah Praise, 190
There Is a Line of Women, 546
Unexpected and Mysterious, 229
With Mary Sing Magnificat, 208
[As a shepherd seeks a lost sheep], 868
[God, give me grace to accept], 1007
[God, just as you sent Joseph to Egypt], 957
[God of grace, creator of waters], 931
[Holy and righteous God, you created us], 1034
[May God be with you! And also with you], 944
[May the blessing of the God of Sarah and Hagar], 1060
[My soul proclaims with wonder]
[O God, our deliverer], 1010
[Our lives are cluttered], 899
[The table has been prepared], 939
[While Jesus was in Bethany], 296

Word of God

See: TELLING GOD'S STORY: Word of God (398-406); WORSHIP RESOURCES: Telling God's Story (910-920)
See also: Scripture Proclamation
Come and Seek the Ways of Wisdom, 196
Dooládó' Shi Diyinda! (What a Wonderful Savior), 562
God of the Bible, 420
God's Glory Fills the Heavens, 197
Holy Spirit, Come with Power (Ven, Espíritu, cual viento), 57
How Firm a Foundation, 592
Jesus Loves Me, 516
Lord, You Sometimes Speak, 537
O God of Blessings, 700
Open My Eyes that I May See, 738
Praise to the Living God, 204
Renew Your Church, 717
There Is a Line of Women, 546
This Is the Air I Breathe (Eres mi respirar), 139
What Is This Place, 22
When We Walk with the Lord, 570
[Come, let us go up], 13
[Dear God, let your word shine], 912
[For the Word of God in Scripture], 913.G
[God's Word is a lamp], 913.F
[Hear the Word of God], 914
[Hear what the Spirit is saying], 913.C
[Holy Wisdom. Holy Word], 913.B
[In the beginning was the Word], 235
[In the beginning when it was very quiet], 852
[Jesus said, I am the bread of life], 987.E
[Jesus stood up to read], 292
[Let your hearts be ruled], 818
[Living God, by the power of your Spirit], 911
[May God bless to our understanding], 913.D
[Now, Lord, you let your servant], 825
[O God, your word is a lamp to my feet], 987.A
[Open our ears to hear your word], 866
[Praise and thanks to you, holy God], 915
[Speak to us, living God], 910
[The Word of God for the people of God], 913.E
[Two disciples were traveling], 470
[Word of God. Word of Life], 913.A

Work

See also: SHARING OUR STORIES: Vocation, Work, and Rest (526-535)
See also: Rest; Vocation
Beauty for Brokenness, 712
Bless the Arms That Comfort, 527
En medio de la vida (You Are the God within Life), 526
For the Fruit of All Creation, 124
For Those with Whom Our Lives Are Bound, 734
God, Bless the Work Your People Do, 528
God of the Fertile Fields, 750
Haneul naneun saeleul bora (See the Birds That Fly), 289

[God of grace and glory, you keep our souls], 987.H
[God of life, we thank you that our work], 953
[God of work and rest], 956
[Our lives are cluttered], 899
[This day, God, may I dream your dreams], 984
[To worship is to stand in awe], 855

World Communion

See also: Church; Communion; Unity in Diversity

Eat This Bread (Coman de este pan), 476
From North and South, from East and West, 460
Gracias, Señor, por el pan (Thank You, O God, for This Bread), 487
Haleluya! Pelo tsa rona (Hallelujah! We Sing Your Praises), 473
In Christ There Is No East or West, 390
In the Singing, in the Silence, 481
Ngayong nagdadapit hapon (When Twilight Comes), 501
Somos pueblo que camina (We Are People on a Journey), 464
[At this table, we receive the bread of life], 943
[By the grace of God we seek to live and proclaim], 925
[Communion], 468
[Creemos en Dios Padre todopoderoso], 927
[For I received from the Lord], 469
[In peace let us pray: O God, we give you thanks], 945
[Jesus said "I am the true vine"], 472
[May God be with you! And also with you], 944
[O God, listening to us here], 993
[The crowd said to Jesus, "You must show us more miracles"], 471

World: Praying for

See: Praying: For the World

Worship

All Creatures Worship God Most High, 81
All People That on Earth Do Dwell, 5
Alleluia / Make a Joyful Noise (Psalm 100), 66
As We Rise, O God, to Meet You, 39
Brethren, We Have Met to Worship, 25
Build My Life, 92
Christ Is Our Cornerstone, 4
Come Away from Rush and Hurry, 9
Come, Now Is the Time to Worship, 29
Darkness Is Not Dark to You, God, 200
Flow to You, 132
For You, O God, My Soul, 41
From North and South, from East and West, 460
God of Justice, 772
Go Now in Peace, Worship Continues, 829
Hallelujah! schöner Morgen (Hallelujah! Fairest Morning!), 497
Here I Am to Worship (Ich will dich anbeten), 227
Here in This Place, 10
Hope of Abraham and Sarah, 807
I'm Gonna Eat at the Welcome Table, 801
In Thy Holy Place We Bow, 40
Let Us Build a House, 36
Lobe den Herren (Praise to the Lord, the Almighty), 88
Lord Jesus, Come and Overturn, 146
Love Divine, All Loves Excelling, 638
O Gott Vater (O God and Father), 45
O Worship Our God, 129
Open the Eyes of My Heart (Ouvre les yeux / Abre mis ojos), 401
Remembrance, 479
Revelation Song (Digno y santo), 415
Segala puji syukur (All Our Praise), 82
Shout to the Lord (Cante al Señor),125
Summoned by the God Who Made Us, 1
The Day You Gave Us, 506
What Comfort Can Our Worship Bring, 623
When in Our Music God Is Glorified, 83
You Dwell in the Songs / Restless, 741
[Almighty God, to you all hearts are open], 860
[As you come to Christ the living stone], 381
[Dear ones, I plead with you], 105
[For I received from the Lord], 469
[Holy God, you call us together], 857
[I saw a vast crowd], 110
[I was glad when they said to me], 16
[Jesus calls us to praise and prayer], 851
[Life-giving God, may your Holy Spirit inspire], 879
[Make a joyful noise to the Lord], 20
[Some of us are exhausted], 854
[Thus says the Lord: Maintain justice], 782
[To worship is to stand in awe], 855

Zechariah's Song

See: Benedictus / Zechariah's Song

SCRIPTURAL ALLUSIONS AND REFERENCES INDEX

Italic numbers refer to worship resources. Numbers in brackets indicate Scripture worship resources.

GENESIS

1 . . . 176, 177, 178, 182, 405, 507, 694, 806, 864, *881*
1–2 . . . 179, *884*
1–3 . . . *183*, 652
1:1–2 . . . 50, 281, 373, *1060*
1:1–5 . . . 121, 129, *235*, 270, 441, *852*, *867*, *917*
1:1–10 . . . *931*
1:1–19 . . . 423, 426, 495, 529
1:1–25 . . . 436
1:11–13 . . . 750
1:14–19 . . . 504
1:26–31 . . . 1, 134, 145, 172, 246, 705, 751, *901*, *1009*
2–3 . . . *12*
2:1–3 . . . 528
2:4–15 . . . 531, 694, 788, 806
2:4–25 . . . 209
2:7 . . . 39, 737, *867*, *918*
3:19 . . . 304, 657, *918*
3:20 . . . 546
6–9 . . . *887*
7–8 . . . 708, *931*
8:21–22 . . . 419, 652
12:1–3 . . . 553
15–16 . . . 190, 190, 807, *1060*
18:1–8 . . . *949*
18:1–15 . . . 190, 546
18:1–21 . . . 553
21:1–21 . . . 190, 309
22:1–14 . . . 165
25:19–34 . . . *891*
28:10–22 . . . 589, 589, 658
32:1–15 . . . *891*
32:24–30 . . . 191
33:1–17 . . . 144, 389, 523, *891*
35:1–15 . . . 658
37–50 . . . *957*
38 . . . 546
45:1–15 . . . 144, 389, 523

EXODUS

1:8–22 . . . 208, 546
3:1–15 . . . 663, *871*
5 . . . 193
7–12 . . . *1031*
11 . . . 193
12:1–20 . . . 463, 624
13:17–22 . . . 194, 606, 632, 793
13:17–14:31 . . . 423
14 . . . 193, 194, 348, 441, 454, 694, *931*
15:1–21 . . . 195, 348, 441
15:20–21 . . . 208, 579
16 . . . 309, *471*, 474, 606, 840
17:1–7 . . . 606
19:5 . . . 570
19:16–18 . . . 681
20:8–11 . . . 528
20:12 . . . *972*
20:21 . . . 200
30:22–33 . . . 645
32:6 . . . 832
33:21–22 . . . 619, 626
[Exodus 34:6–7] . . . *186*
34:6–7 . . . 156

LEVITICUS

19:18 . . . 288, 571, 796, *890*, *897*, *985.D*
25 . . . 217, *1024*

NUMBERS

[Numbers 6:24–26] . . . *826*
6:24–26 . . . 829, 830, 832, 835, 838, 839, 841, 842, 844, 845, 846
9:15–17 . . . 632, *1031*
14:18–19 . . . 156
21:4–9 . . . *1031*
21:4–20 . . . 309
35:34 . . . 145

DEUTERONOMY

4:7 . . . 118
4:29–31 . . . 161
5:12–15 . . . 528
5:22–27 . . . 116, 200
6:4 . . . 192, 431
6:4–5 . . . 59, 288, 796
[Deuteronomy 6:4–7] . . . *187*
6:5 . . . 29, 131, 571, 717, 827, *890*, *897*, *955*, *985.D*
7:9–10 . . . 832
8 . . . 637
8:3 . . . 139
10:17–20 . . . 279, 556, 774
11:8–12 . . . 662
15:7–8 . . . 750
24:14–22 . . . 124
26:1–11 . . . 122, 747, *1015*, *1017*, *1019*
28:1–6 . . . 750
30:14 . . . 400, 405
32:1–12 . . . 101
32:11–12 . . . 80, 88, 376
32:18 . . . 80
34:1–4 . . . 661

JOSHUA
1:7–9 . . . . . *910, 911*
2 546
3 . . . . . 454, 606
4:1–9 629
6:1–20 579
24:15 443

JUDGES
4:1–7 . . . . . 74, 195

RUTH
1:14–18 . . . . . 527, *775*

1 SAMUEL
1:11 546
2:1–10 . . . . . 142, 222, 412, 487, *987.F*
3:3–10 . . . . . 545, 765
7:12 . . . . . 563, 599
18–20 . . . . . *862*

2 SAMUEL
12:1–15 . . . . . 141, 208, *889*, *987.D*
22:2–7 . . . . . 125, 421, 424, 605

1 KINGS
6 . . . . . 22, 36
8 . . . . . *16*
8:27–30 36
8:37–40 145
19:11–13 . . . . . 537, 541, 548, 741, *855*

2 KINGS
2:11 305
4:42–44 . . . . . *471*, *757*, *1016*
5:10–15 642
22:8–13 406

1 CHRONICLES
16:8–36 103
16:23–36 116
16:28–36 129
16:29–33 . . . . . 125, 594, 847
16:34–36 . . . . . 114, 118, 704
29:10–13 . . . . . 86, 436

2 CHRONICLES
3–7 . . . . . *16*
5:13 . . . . . 83, 117

EZRA
9:4 406

NEHEMIAH
1:9 304
5 . . . . . *1024*
8 . . . . . *910, 911*
8:6 90
9 611
9:15–21 . . . . . *186*, 606

ESTHER
1–10 546
4:14 716

JOB
1–42 . . . . . *728*
1:20–22 637
2:13 634
9:7–10 . . . . . 175, 529
12:7–10 81
14:1–2 . . . . . 98, 203
19:25–27 . . . . . 347, 801
23:12 139
26:7–14 . . . . . 182, 436
38 . . . . . 112, 176
38–40 . . . . . 537, 828
38:1–3 406
38:8–11 456
38:31–33 175
42:6 . . . . . *918*

PSALMS
1 . . . . . *12*, *911*
1:1–3 . . . . . 142, 399, 571, 807
1:3 514
2 201
4:1 . . . . . 682, 686, 736
4:1–3 646
4:8 837
5:1–3 497
5:8 . . . . . 601, 837
6 . . . . . 646, 735, 736
7:1–10 434
8 . . . . . 101, 116, 179, 180, 436, 529
8:3–4 . . . . . *985.H*
8:5–9 145
9:1–2 131
10:14–18 791
[Psalm 13 (excerpts)] *728*
13 . . . . . 148, 691, 794
15 148
16 . . . . . 616, 701
16:7–11 136
17:1 . . . . . 682, 686
17:6–7 434
18:1–3 . . . . . 47, 125, 421, 424, 630, 733
18:1–6 605
18:1–13 . . . . . 44, 74
18:1–19 434
18:7–15 663
19 197
19:1–6 . . . 103, 175, 178, 180, 181, *183*, 427, 436, 495, 498, 503, 504, 539, 581, 594, 806, *855*, *954*
19:7–11 571
19:14 45
20:7 . . . . . *1043*
22 696
22:1 . . . . . *1005*
22:3 741
[Psalm 23] *725*
23 . . . . . 9, 35, 574, 600, 639, 640, 660, 718, 744, 840, *1011*, *1044*
23:1 604
23:1–4 . . . . . 167, 601, 602, 630, 834
23:5 645
24 799
24:1–2 . . . . . 180, 788, *1009*, *1043*
25 . . . . . 155, 156, 631
25:1–3 616
25:4–10 . . . . . 398, 402, 601
26:6–7 . . . . . *889*
27 . . . . . 160, 437, 595, 603
27:1 . . . . . *47*, *917*
27:7–9 . . . . . 51, 502, 832
27:14 . . . . . 41, 228
28:7–9 630
29 44
29:1–2 129
30 591
30:4–5 618
30:8–10 691
30:8–12 143
30:11–12 . . . . . 6, 666
31 434
31:5 . . . . . *926*
31:14–16 671
31:24 228
32 42
32:3–5 . . . . . 310, *889*
32:6–7 . . . . . 437, 456, 603
32:10–11 494
33:1–3 82
33:1–9 120
33:5–9 . . . . . 441, 703
33:20–22 591
34:1–10 467
34:4 161
34:8 . . . . . 474, 475, *943*
34:9–10 604
36:5–10 . . . 96, 434, 563, 659, 667, 668, *998*
37:1–7 664
37:7 . . . . . 202, 286
37:23–24 610
39:12 685
40:5 128
40:5–10 . . . . . *860*
40:7–10 . . . . . 399, 545, 761
40:13–17 . . . . . 595, 694
42 . . . . . 49, 543, 552, 586, 623
42–43 591
42:1–2 . . . . . 139, 683
42:8 506
43 . . . . . 552, 623
43:3 . . . . . 398, 714
45:2–7 . . . . . 201, 259, 408, 410
45:6 126
46 . . . . . 47, 421, 633, 664, 714, *730*
46:1–4 . . . . . 203, *981*
46:4–5 . . . . . 667, 668
[Psalm 46:10] *730*
46:10 . . . . . 9, 37, 202
47 101
[Psalm 47:1, 6–7] *108*
47:1–2 . . . . . 69, 125
48 31
48:9–14 34
51 . . . . . 42, 153, 169, 555, 796, *889*, *938*
[Psalm 51:1–3, 10–12] *889*
51:1–12 . . . . . 141, *987.D*
51:6–12 . . . . . *860*
51:10–12 . . . . . 550, 557
51:12 198
51:12–14 732
51:15 . . . . . 738, *985.A*
51:15–17 731
55:1 . . . . . 682, 686
55:17 . . . . . *987.G*
55:22 . . . . . 616, *987.G*
56 654
57:1–3 . . . . . 80, 736
57:9–11 86
59:16–17 . . . . . 496, 497, 498
61:1 . . . . . 682, 686
61:1–4 . . . . . 619, 626
62 646
62:1–2 . . . . . 92, 619, 626, 741
62:1–8 . . . . . 41, 591
62:7–8 47
63:1 . . . . . 161, 458, 543, 683
63:1–8 . . . . . 139, 610
63:4 365
65 . . . . . 122, 125
65:9–13 . . . . . 710, 747, 750, 847
66:1–4 82
67 26
69:1–2 456
69:13–15 456
70 . . . . . 595, 694
71 . . . . . *104*, 520, 649, 979
71:5–6 554
71:14–24 . . . . . 496, 761
72 . . . . . 217, 414
73:21–26 . . . . . 369, 610, 624
73:28 658
77:10–19 182
78:1–4 34
78:23–25 . . . . . *471*, 474
82:1–4 791
84 38
84:1–4 . . . . . 63, 204, 517, 539, 683, 788
84:8 685
85:4–7 91
85:6–13 . . . . . 36, 198
[Psalm 85:8–11] *188*
85:10 . . . . . 196, 278
85:11–12 122
86:1–7 . . . . . 682, 685, 686, 736
86:5–15 . . . . . *186*
86:8 92
86:11 549
86:15–16 . . . . . 156, 832
87 31
88 646
89:1–2 96
89:1–18 119
89:8–9 . . . 128, 286, 375, 595, 597, 659, 664, 680, 708
89:15–17 793
89:46–52 . . . . . *728*
90:1 . . . . . 416, *920*
90:1–8 203
90:14 497
91 . . . . . 47, 101, 160, 641, 840
91:1–2 . . . . . 421, *1065*

91:1–6 .505
91:11 .589
92:1–2 . 420, 505, *985.C*, *987.C*
92:1–5 .496, 497, 504, 506
92:12–15 .514
93 .125
95:1–2 .28, 29, 100
95:1–7 .41, 101, 701, *963*
95:6–7 .2, 29, 227
96 .*106*, 113, 116
96:1–2 .80
96:8–12 .129, 747, 847
97 .663
98 .93, *104*, *106*, 113, 240, 611
98:1–2 .80
98:7–8 .747, 847
99:1–5 .86
[Psalm 100] .*20*
100 .2, 5, 28, 29, 33, 36, 66, 82
102:1–2 .682, 685, 686
102:17–20 .791
102:26–27 .502
103 .75, 101, *185*, *186*, 616, 644
103:1 .127
103:1–8 .88, 111, 646
103:6–14 .156, 832
103:13–14 .517, 518, 697
[Psalm 104] .*185*
104 . 74, 111, 122, 128, 180, *183*, 423, 637, 747
104:1–4 .116, 539
104:1–9 .490
104:1–14 .436
104:14–15 .462, 477
104:19 .522
104:24–35 .182
104:27–28 .488
104:31–34 .119
105 .535, 606
106:1–2 .96
106:8 .*1063*
106:47–48 .90
107:1–9 .80, *864*
107:8–9 .459, 487
107:10–16 .217
107:23–30 . 128, 286, 375, 595, 597, 659, 664, 680, 708
107:28–32 .633
107:35–38 .763
108:3–5 .86
111:1 .88
112:4–8 .498
113 .*1010*
113:1–5 .86, 414, 506
114:1–8 .441, 454
116:1–2 .684
116:7 .532
116:8–19 .694, 696
117 .77, 96
117:1–2 .419
118:1–4 .96
118:8–9 .*107*
118:19–29 .4, 312, 313, 315
118:22–23 .*381*
[Psalm 118:24] .*15*
118:26 .460, *885*
119:1–5 .399
119:18 .738
119:25–40 .816
119:33–36 .776
119:64 .703
119:105 . 403, 717, *912*, *913.F*, *987.A*
119:105–112 .398
119:129–136 .398, 403
[Psalm 121] .*109*
121 .602, 609, 633
121:1–2 .494
122 .36
[Psalm 122:1] .*16*
124 .595
126 .36, 397, 416, *1057*
126:4–6 .664
[Psalm 126:5–6] .*821*
127:1–2 .770
130 .140, 225
130:1–2 .456
131 .664
[Psalm 133:1] .*17*
133:1 .390
133:2 .645
136 .32, 33, 96, 117, 419, *963*
136:1–3 .704
136:1–9 .114
136:1–15 .441
137 .794
137:1 .695
138:7 .306, 595
139 .587, *724*
[Psalm 139:1–4] .*724*
139:1–4 .43, 533, *996*
139:1–12 .609
139:1–18 .199, 494, 521
139:7–10 .182, 422
139:7–12 .526, 610, 631
139:11–12 .200, 632, 808
139:13–16 .172, 195, 513
139:23–24 .731, 756
141:1–2 .132
141:8 .228
142:5–7 .434
143:1 .682, 685, 686
144:1–2 .421
145 .78, 92, *186*, 701, 761, 764
145:1–7 .86
145:1–13 .116
145:14–19 .118, 488
146 .170
[Psalm 146:1–3] .*107*
146:5–9 . 11, 217, 223, 273, 312, 393, 404, 414, 420, 428, 487, 540, 645, 700, 763, 791, 800, *870*, *1043*
147 .637
147:1–6 .217
147:4–8 .427
148 . 70, 71, 81, 93, 95, 103, 120, 121, 175, 177, 181, 427, 814
148:1–6 .594
148:7–10 .847
148:13–14 .86
149 .*106*, 113
149:1–5 .31
150 .83, 88, *882*, *885*, *886*
150:6 .121

PROVERBS

1–9 .*183*
4:4–14 .196
8 .196
[Proverbs 8:1–30] .*184*
8:22–36 .200, 376
14:31 .712
16:20 .570

ECCLESIASTES

3:1–8 .522, 670
8:12 .586
12:1–7 .520, 649

SONG OF SOLOMON

2:10–13 .*1048*
8:6 .54, 748

ISAIAH

1:16–17 .153
1:21–23 .149
2:2–4 . 11, *12*, 209, 391, 402, *782*, 789, 798, *943*
2:2–5 .87
[Isaiah 2:3–4] .*13*
2:5 .793, *1056*
4:5–6 .632
5 .*472*
6:1–3 . 61, 76, 102, 126, 136, 137, 460, 709, *880*, *944*
6:1–5 .401
6:1–10 .40, 65, 226
6:6–8 .45
6:6–13 .758
6:8 .540, 545, 771, 834
6:9–10 .*866*
7:14 .210, 213, 216, 245, 246, 247, 270
9:2 .269, 808, *917*
[Isaiah 9:2, 6] .*231*
9:2–7 .218, 712
9:6–7 .247, 256, 259, 278, *894*
10:1–2 .149
11:1 .210, 237
[Isaiah 11:1–4] .*232*
11:1–5 .213, *292*, *955*
11:1–10 .216
11:6–9 .*12*, 209, 787
12:2 .304, 437
12:2–6 . *108*, 118, 597, *985.I*
25:1 .86
25:6–10 .225, 416, 460, 463, 634, 669
26:3–4 .52
26:8–9 .139, 683
29:16 .44
30:19–21 .811
32:1–2 .619, 626
32:3 .811
35 .205
35:3–4 .268
35:5–7 .732, 738, 763
35:8–10 .31, *339*
40:1–5 .212, 223
40:3–5 .219, 220, 228, *1052.E*
40:9 .252, 268
40:11 .100, 517, 718, 840
40:21–26 .128
40:28–31 .80, 176, 437, 603, *864*, *981*
41:4 .204, 507
41:8–13 .592
41:17–20 .205, 763, 809
[Isaiah 42:1–3] .*448*
42:1–3 .*292*, *445*, *447*
42:6–7 .*292*, 665
[Isaiah 42:10–11] .*106*
42:10–13 .113
42:16 .808
42:18–20 .732, 738
43:1–5 .166, 456, 592, 596, *903.A*, *977*
43:1–13 .586
43:18–21 .309, 551, *903.A*
44:23 .847
45:11–12 .513
45:23 .29
46:3–4 .520, 649
48:17–18 .617, 832, 838
49:1 .195
49:15 .*230*
49:5–6 .271, 504, 825, 833
50:4–9 .150, *293*, 325, 580
51:3 .788
51:4 .504
51:10–15 .454
51:11 .31, *339*
[Isaiah 52:7] .*781*
52:7 .102, 836
53:1–9 .330, 432, *892*
[Isaiah 55:1–2] .*14*
55:1–2 .9, 35, 49, 459, 461, 464, 476, 758
55:6–9 .161
55:12 .815, 847
55:12–13 .205
56:1–2 .528
[Isaiah 56:1–7 (excerpts)] .*782*
58:5–11 .*784*
58:6–7 .487, 800
58:7–9 .715
58:8 .269, 644, 733
58:8–10 .504
58:11 .*985.I*
59:1–15 .149
60:1–3. . . 134, 237, 238, 271, 273, 274, 277, 500, 715, *917*
60:1–5 .825
60:17–18 .707, 711, 712
60:19–20 .98, 500, 504, 554
60:19–22 .549
61 .414, 712
[Isaiah 61:1–2] .*292*
61:1–3 . .11, 50, 273, 393, 404, 420, 428, 540, 645, 700, 763, 791, *821*, *870*, *1043*, *1064*
61:1–6 .217

61:1–9 . . . 170
62 . . . 530, 611
62:1–2 . . . 223
64:1–4 . . . 226
64:1–12 . . . 143
64:8 . . . 403, *908*
65:17–25 . . . *12*, 377, 530, 608, 652, 787, 809
66:2 . . . 406
66:12–13 . . . 229, 426, 518, 671, 697, *1062*
66:22–23 . . . *377*

JEREMIAH
1:4–8 . . . 195, 834
5:22 . . . 456
7:5–7 . . . 149
8:22 . . . 647
10:10–13 . . . 128, 204
17:7–8 . . . 514
18:1–6 . . . 403
23:9 . . . 406
23:23–24 . . . 587
29:4–7 . . . 206, 530, 841, *1032*
[Jeremiah 29:4–11 (excerpts)] . . . *783*
29:11 . . . *817*
31 . . . 31
31:15 . . . 278
31:31–34 . . . 377, 636, *869*
32:36–41 . . . 550
33:9 . . . 530

LAMENTATIONS
3:18–26 . . . 111, 618
3:22–24 . . . 419, 420, 814
5:21–22 . . . 198

EZEKIEL
1 . . . 663
11:17–21 . . . *383*, 636
22:23–29 . . . 149
34:11–16 . . . 718
34:11–31 . . . 432, *725*
34:24–27 . . . 747
36:26–27 . . . 636, 731, 740
36:35 . . . 788
37 . . . 372
37:1–14 . . . *383*, 550
37:9 . . . 370
[Ezekiel 37:11, 14] . . . *383*
47:6–12 . . . 642, 667, 668, 706

DANIEL
6:16–28 . . . 305
6:26–27 . . . 204
7:9 . . . 134
7:13–14 . . . 69
9:3–19 . . . 153, 685

HOSEA
4:1–3 . . . 145
11:1 . . . 279
11:1–9 . . . 518, 697

JOEL
2:12–13 . . . *186*, 304, 533, *860*
2:28–32 . . . 36, 369, *379*, 716
3:18 . . . 801

AMOS
5:8 . . . 128, 175, 236
5:21–24 . . . *772*, *784*, 791, *1043*

OBADIAH
17 . . . 31, 212

JONAH
2 . . . 456
3–4 . . . *898*
4:1–11 . . . *186*
4:2 . . . 832

MICAH
4:1–4 . . . 11, *13*, 391, *782*, 789, 798, *943*
4:1–7 . . . *12*
5:2–5 . . . 213, 245
6:6–8 . . . 11, 207, 458, 772, *863*, *955*
[Micah 6:8] . . . *784*
7:7 . . . 225, 591
7:8 . . . 437, 603
7:14 . . . 304

NAHUM
1:5–8 . . . 125
1:15 . . . *781*

HABAKKUK
1:2–4 . . . 149
2:14 . . . 770
2:20 . . . 62, 65
[Habakkuk 3:17–18] . . . *820*
3:17–18 . . . 618, 637

ZEPHANIAH
3:17 . . . 42, 173

HAGGAI
2:1–9 . . . 74, 369, 763

ZECHARIAH
2:13 . . . 65, 202, 286
4:6 . . . 538
8 . . . *12*
9:9 . . . 316
9:16–17 . . . 836
13:9 . . . 304, 583

MALACHI
3:1 . . . *1052.E*
3:1–4 . . . 592
4:2 . . . 238, 274, 618

MATTHEW
1 . . . 546, *870*
1–2 . . . *230*, *872*
1:18–25 . . . 210, 214, *233*, 245, 266, *1060*
1:18–2:12 . . . 256, 258
1:20–23 . . . 143, 246, 270, 553
2:1–12 . . . 244, 250, 260, 265, 266, 267, 272, 275, 276, 277, *1064*
2:13–15 . . . 279
2:13–23 . . . 278
3:1–3 . . . 212, 219, 220, *1052.E*
3:1–17 . . . 453, *931*
3:11–17 . . . *378*, 452
3:13–17 . . . 303, 371, 441, *445*, *447*, *448*, *935*, *940*
4:1–2 . . . 305, *873*
4:1–11 . . . 303, 307, *1011*, *1065*
4:4 . . . 45, 139
4:16 . . . *231*
4:18–22 . . . 283, 540, 573, *1029*
[Matthew 5:3–12] . . . *295*
5:3–12 . . . 149, 290, 360, 578, 607, 712, 734, 798, *921*, *1049*
5:3–16 . . . 10, 284
5:4 . . . 634, 656
5:5 . . . 142
5:6 . . . 393, 464
5:9 . . . 485
5:10–12 . . . 576, 630
5:13–16 . . . 297, 717, 754, 841
5:14–16 . . . 665, 762, *916*, *1006*
5:21–26 . . . 150
5:23–24 . . . *938*
5:38–48 . . . 150, 713, *780*
5:39–42 . . . 573, 580
[Matthew 5:39–42, 44] . . . *293*
5:43–45 . . . 789, *937*
5:44 . . . 798, *921*
5:45 . . . 521, 703
6:1–6 . . . *879*, *1000*
6:8 . . . *888*
6:9–13 . . . 45, 673, 674, 675, *989.A*, *989.B*, *989.C*, *989.D*, *989.E*, *989.F*
6:10 . . . 149, 710
6:11 . . . 488, 498
6:12 . . . 505
6:16–18 . . . 305
6:19–21 . . . 62
6:25–34 . . . 177, 289, 618, 653, *726*, 757, 788, *1018*, *1024*
6:33 . . . 228, 393, 400, 417
7:1–5 . . . 389
7:7–8 . . . 161, 228, 417
7:7–11 . . . 440, 486, *862*
7:13–14 . . . 45
7:15–20 . . . *472*
7:24–27 . . . 63, 92, 159, 332, 399, 621
8:3 . . . *867*
8:8 . . . 644
8:11 . . . 26
8:18–22 . . . 27, 287, 443, 775, *1029*
8:23–27 . . . 128, 286, 375, 595, 597, 659, 664, 680, 708
8:28–34 . . . 285
9:9–13 . . . 544, 566, *947*
9:27–33 . . . 736
10:5–15 . . . 771, 772, 774, *1029*
10:29–31 . . . 653, *971*, *985.H*
10:34–39 . . . 152, 432
10:37–39 . . . 154, 575, 576, 577, 664
10:40–42 . . . 237, 279, 796, *853*
11:2–6 . . . 102, 217, *292*, *975*
11:28–30 . . . 9, 23, 35, 157, 503, 536, 547, 560, 570, 625, 628, 643, 679, 733, 743, *895*
12:9–13 . . . 287
12:15–21 . . . *448*
12:33 . . . *472*
12:46–50 . . . 390
13:3–9 . . . 297, 477, 789
13:3–23 . . . *777*
13:10–17 . . . *866*
13:17 . . . 418
13:18–23 . . . 812
13:23 . . . 403
13:24–30 . . . 123, 423
13:31–32 . . . 298
13:36–43 . . . 123, 423
[Matthew 13:44–46] . . . *294*
13:44–46 . . . 68, 369, 624, 639
13:55–56 . . . 280
14:13–21 . . . *291*, 757, *854*, *1016*, *1036*
14:19 . . . 488, 489
14:22–33 . . . 161, 456, 582, 595, 610
15:22–28 . . . 736
15:29–39 . . . *854*
15:32–38 . . . *291*, *757*, *1016*, *1036*
15:36 . . . 488, 489
16:13–20 . . . 397
16:19 . . . 673, 674, 675
16:21–28 . . . 873
16:24 . . . 580, 583, 658, *928*
16:24–26 . . . 443, 561, 566, 575, 576, 577, 608
16:24–28 . . . 569, 664
17:1–8 . . . 301, *859*
17:14–19 . . . 736
17:20 . . . 531, 593, *1008*
18:1–5 . . . 6, *18*, 518, 519
18:10–14 . . . 718, *725*, *868*
18:19–20 . . . 460
[Matthew 18:20] . . . *19*
18:20 . . . 465
18:21–22 . . . 144
19:4–6 . . . 524
19:13–15 . . . 18, 508, 509, 510, 512, 515, 516, *969*, *971*
19:16–21 . . . 775
20:1–16 . . . 124
20:17–19 . . . *873*
20:20–28 . . . *1041*
20:26–28 . . . *772*, 778
20:30–34 . . . 736
21:1–11 . . . 312, 313, 315, 316, 320, 579, *896*
21:9 . . . 79, 100, 314, 460, *885*, *944*
21:12–17 . . . 146, 287, 423, 573, *874*, *1044*
21:23–27 . . . 582
21:42–44 . . . 4, *381*, 410
22:1–10 . . . 209, 458
22:1–14 . . . 511
22:8–10 . . . 462, 464
22:15–22 . . . 753, *929*
22:34–40 . . . 255, 288, 388, 571, 717, 753, 796, 827, *890*, *897*, *955*, *985.D*
22:36–37 . . . 29, 131, *187*
23 . . . 758
23:1–36 . . . *898*

23:37 10, 426, 501
23:39 460
24:29–31 436, 755
24:36 590
24:42–44 407
25:1–13 226, 298
25:14–30 745
25:20–23 562
25:31–46 27, 268, 487, 715, 772, *876, 921, 1066*
25:34–40 124, 279, 392, 439, 518, 798
26:6–13 *296*
26:17–29 465, 501, *939*
26:20–25 330, 480
26:26 464, 485
26:26–29 10, 65, 459, 461, 462, *468, 469,* 473, 476, 478, 479, 481, 482, 484, *887, 936, 941*
26:30 83
26:36–46 318, 319, 627
26:36–75 317
26:69–75 344
27:11–54 317, 320
27:27–54 322, 323, 331
27:28–30 325
27:32–54 569
27:32–28:10 329, *919*
27:35 696
27:45–54 326
27:46 696, *1005*
27:55–61 546
27:57–28:10 333, 353
27:59–60 281
28:1–10 340, 341, 346, 348, 350, 354, 355, 358, 359, 361, 546, 565, *875*
28:5–6 356, *1052.F*
[Matthew 28:16, 18–20] *451*
28:16–20 395, 765, 766, *966, 993*
28:19 *923*
28:19–20 455, 769, 774, 834, *930*
28:20 43, 284, 398, 848

MARK
1:1–8 223
1:1–11 453, *931, 935*
1:1–13 305
1:2–3 212, 219, 220, *1052.E*
1:8–11 *378*, 452
1:9–11 441, *445, 448, 940*
1:9–13 303
1:10 371
1:12–13 307, *873, 1011, 1065*
1:15 413
1:16–20 283, 566, 573, *1029*
1:21–45 285
1:29–45 287, 644, 648
1:41 *867*
2:1–12 527, 830
2:15–17 544, *947*
3:1–5 287
3:31–35 390
4:2–20 777
4:3–9 297, 477, 789
4:10–12 *866*
4:14–20 812
4:20 403
4:26–29 123, 423
4:30–34 298
4:35–41 128, 286, 375, 595, 597, 659, 664, 680, 708
4:39 202
5:1–20 285
5:21–43 287, 644, 648, *1008*
5:36 596
6:3 280
6:6–13 *1029*
6:13 645
6:30–34 *854*
6:30–44 *291*, 757, *1016, 1036*
6:41 488, 489
6:45–52 456, 595
6:56 287
7:14–23 141, *1020*
7:24–37 287, 644, 648
8:1–9 *291, 854, 1016, 1036*
8:6 488, 489
8:22–25 732
8:31–38 575, 577
8:34 580, 583, 658, *928*
8:34–38 154, 443, 561, 569, 576, 664
9:1 413
9:2–13 301, *859*
9:24 588
9:33–37 *18*, 508, 509, 510, 518
9:35 778
9:50 485
10:7–8 524
[Mark 10:13–16] *18*
10:13–16 508, 509, 510, 512, 515, 516, 519, *969, 971*
10:17–21 775
10:32–34 *873*
10:35–45 *1041*
10:43–45 772, 778
10:46–52 736
11:1–10 100, 312, 313, 315, 316, 320, *579, 896*
11:9–10 79, 314, 460, *885, 944*
11:15–19 146, 287, 423, 573, *874, 1044*
12:10–11 4, *381*, 410
12:28–34 59, 192, 255, 288, 388, 431, 571, 717, 796, 827, *890, 897, 955, 985.D*
12:29–30 29, 131, *187*
12:32–34 *784*
12:41–44 753, 756
13:1–13 159, 621
13:2 412
13:24–27 218, 407, 436, 755
[Mark 14:3–9 (excerpts)] *296*
14:12–25 465, 501, *939*
14:17–19 330
14:22 464, 485
14:22–25 10, 65, 459, 461, 462, *468, 469,* 473, 476, 478, 479, 480, 481, 482, 484, *887, 936, 941*
14:26–27 83
14:32–42 318, 319, 627
14:32–72 317
14:66–72 344
15:1–39 317
15:6–47 320
15:16–20 325
15:16–39 322, 323
15:21–39 569
15:22–16:8 329, *919*
15:22–39 331
15:24 696
15:33–39 326
15:33–47 546
15:34 696, *1005*
15:42–16:8 333, 353
15:46 281
16:1–8 340, 341, 346, 354, 355, 358, 359, 565, *875*
16:1–11 348, 350, 361, 546, 582
16:6 356, *1052.F*
16:15–16 *451*, 765, 766, 834
16:19–20 363, 365, 366, 386

LUKE
1–2 *230*, *870, 872*
1:26–38 216, 221
1:26–56 229
1:32–33 256
[Luke 1:35] *233*
1:39–56 *1010*
1:42–43 62
1:46–55 97, 142, 208, 222, 246, 412, 700, *987.F*
1:50–53 33, 487
1:53 *1059*
1:68–79 195, 215, 223, *985.F*
1:68–80 210, 218
1:78–79 227, *231*, 237, 238, 271, 272, 273, 274, 398, 601, *1044*
2:1–7 224, 268, 281, 546, *931, 1060*
2:1–20 214, 243, 244, 245, 251, 252, 254, 256, 257, 258, 261, 262, 263, 264, 265, 266, 269
2:6–20 260, 267
2:8 213
2:8–20 241, 247, 248, 249, 250, 253, 259, 276, *871, 1064*
2:10–11 240
[Luke 2:10-14 (excerpts)] *234*
2:14 94, 99, 242, *880*
[Luke 2:29–32] *825*
2:29–32 218, 833
2:35 328
2:36–38 208, 546
2:41–52 423
3:1–22 453, *931*
3:2–6 212, 223, *1052.E*
3:16–22 *378*, 452
[Luke 3:21–22] *447*
3:21–22 371, 441, *445, 447, 448, 935, 940*
4:1–2 305, *873*
4:1–13 303, 307, *1011, 1065*
[Luke 4:16–19, 21] *292*
4:16–21 102, 170, 217, 404, 414, 428, *1064*
4:18–19 11, 223, 273, 312, 393, 420, 540, 645, 700, 763, 791, 800, *870, 1043*
4:21–30 330, *921*
5:1–11 283, 540, 573, *1029*
5:13 *867*
5:27–32 544, *947*
6:1–10 287
6:18–19 287
6:20–23 578, 607, 712, 734, 798, *1049*
6:20–26 142, 168, 284, 290, *295*
6:21 634
6:22–23 630
6:27–36 *293, 780*, 798, *937*
6:27–38 713
6:29 573
6:41–42 389
6:43–45 *472*
6:46–49 63, 92, 332, 399
7:6–7 644
7:11–17 353, 764
7:18–23 102, *292, 975*
7:36–38 755, 759, 760
7:36–50 *296*
8:1–3 546
8:5–15 297, 477, 777, 789, 812
8:10–11 *866*
8:15 403
8:19–21 390
8:22–25 128, 286, 375, 595, 597, 659, 664, 680, 708
8:26–39 285
9:1–6 *1029*
9:10–17 *291*, 757, *854, 1016, 1036*
9:16 488, 489
9:23 580, 583, 658, *928*
9:23–27 443, 561, 569, 575, 576, 608, 664
9:28–36 301, *859*
9:46–48 *18*, 518
9:57–62 443, 566, 577, 775, *1029*
9:58 27, 287
10:1–11 771, *966, 1029*
10:25–28 29, 131, *187*, 288, 388, 571, 717, 796, 827, *890, 897, 955, 985.D*
10:25–37 298, 790
10:38–42 527, 546, *899, 939*
10:42 434
11:2 710
11:2–4 45, 673, 674, 675, *989.A, 989.B, 989.C, 989.D, 989.E, 989.F*
11:3 488, 498
11:4 505
11:9–13 417, 440, *862*
11:11–13 486, 682
11:37–54 758, *898*
12:6–7 653, *881, 971, 985.H*
12:13–21 142, 561, 759, 760, *1017, 1018*
12:22–31 177, 289, 618, 757
12:22–34 *1018*
12:31 417
12:32–34 759, 760, 561
12:35–40 226, 228, 298
12:49–51 152
12:51–53 432
13:1–5 159, 621
13:1–9 *820*

13:10–13 . . . . .287, 644, 648
13:18–19 298
13:29–30 . . . . .26, 32, 460, 484
13:34 . . . . .426, 501
14:7–24 209
14:15 484
14:15–24 . . . . .36, 458, 511
14:21–23 . . . . .462, 464
14:26–33 . . . . .576, 577
14:27 154
15 . . . . .653, *868*
15:1–7 . . . . .563, 718, *725*, *947*
15:1–24 300
15:8–10 . . . . .172, 299
15:10 665
15:11–32 . . . . .298, 544, 562
15:18 155
15:32 347
16:13–15 . . . . .290, 573, 758
16:22 662
17:4 144
17:6 . . . . .531, 593
17:11–19 . . . . .287, 644, *985.C*, *987.C*
18:1–8 628
18:9–14 . . . . .142, *890*, *898*, *898*
18:13 141
18:15–17 . . . . . . *18*, 508, 509, 510, 512, 515, 516, 519, *969*, *971*
18:18–30 . . . .*775*
18:31–34 . . . .*873*
18:35–43 736
19:1–10 . . . . .540, 802
19:11–27 745
19:17 562
19:28–40 . . . . .312, 313, 315, 579, *896*
19:28–44 . . . . .316, 320
19:38 . . . . .460, *885*
19:40 . . . .*883*
19:41–44 . . . .*894*
19:45–48 . . . . .146, 423, 573, *874*, *1044*
20:17–18 . . . . .4, *381*, 410
20:27–38 . . . .*973*
21:1–4 . . . . .753, 756, 759, 760
21:5–19 . . . . .159, 621, *921*, *1027*
21:6 412
21:25–36 407
22:7–20 . . . . .465, 501
22:7–34 . . . .*939*
22:14–20 . . . 10, 65, 459, 461, 462, *468*, *469*, 473, 476, 478, 479, 480, 481, 482, 484, *887*, *936*, *941*
22:19 . . . . .464, 485
22:39–46 . . . . .318, 319, 627
22:39–71 317
22:55–62 344
23:1–49 317
23:13–56 320
23:26–49 569
23:32–49 . . . . .322, 323
23:32–56 331
23:32–24:12 . . . . .329, *919*
23:33 . . . .*1012*
23:34 774
23:42 327
23:44–45 326
23:49–56 546
23:50–24:12 . . . . .333, 353
23:53 281
24:1–12 . . . . . . 340, 341, 346, 348, 350, 354, 355, 358, 359, 361, 546, 565, *875*
24:5 . . . . .356, *1052.F*
[Luke 24:13–35 (excerpts)] *470*
24:13–35 . . . . .23, 464, *468*, *1066*
24:13–49 345
24:22–24 546
24:28–35 . . . . .465, 466, 482, 489
24:29 502
24:30–32 . . . . .403, 481, 486, 732, 738
24:34 . . . .*875*
24:36 . . . .*850*, *904*
24:45–48 765
24:50–53 . . . . .363, 365, 366, 386, *1014*

JOHN

1:1 . . . .*917*
1:1–4 . . . .*71*, 241, 402, 405, 430
1:1–5 . . . .*189*, 200, 236, 425, 495
1:1–9 . . . . .238, 271
[John 1:1–5, 10–14]. *235*
1:1–14 . . . . . . .227, 239, 269, 270, 500, *1056*
1:1–18 . . . . .211, 256, 418, *852*
1:3–4 584
1:3–14 715
1:5 . . . .*917*
1:5–14 214
1:10–14 . . . . .30, *335*
1:14 . . .59, 196, 247, 281, 376, 404, 537, 721
1:14–18 . . . . .223, 262
1:19–34 . . . .*378*, 453
1:23 212
1:29 . . . . .99, 151, 321
1:29–34 . . . . . . 441, *445*, *447*, *448*, 452, *931*, *935*, *940*
1:29–36 . . . . .559, *892*
1:31–34 371
1:35–51 282
1:43–46 566
2:1–12 . . . . .582, *887*
2:13–22 . . . . . .146, 287, 423, 573, *874*, *1044*
3:1–10 . . . . .439, 442
3:1–17 112
3:2 543
3:3–6 452
3:5–8 . . . . .129, 367, 368
3:8 . . . . .373, 790
3:13 263
3:14–21 . . . . .418, 436
[John 3:16]. *338*
3:16 . . . . .115, 737
3:16–18 . . . . .84, 128, 158, *338*, 638
3:19–21 148
3:19–30 . . . .*235*
4:1–42 . . . .*14*, *931*
4:7–15 49
4:10 . . . . .424, 543
4:13–15 . . . . . . .441, 452, 455, 536, 555, 622
4:23 807
4:35–38 123
5:2–9 454
6 . . . .*471*, *1025*
6:1–14 . . . .*291*, *757*, *1016*, *1036*
6:11 . . . . .488, 489
6:15–21 . . . . .456, 595
6:25–58 . . . . .460, 464, 477, 479
[John 6:30–35]. *471*
6:30–35 25
6:30–58 . . . . .39, 40, 459
6:35 . . . . .476, *987.E*
6:35–58 . . . . . . .465, 473, 474, 480, 484, *946*
6:48–51 463
6:68 . . . .*985.D*, *987.E*
7:15–17 583
7:37–39 . . . . *14*, 49, 424, 441, 458, 536, 543, 622, 659, 733
8:7 580
8:12 . . . . . 227, *235*, 269, 271, 274, 500, 536, 584, *895*, *907*, *1056*
8:34–36 143
9 811
9:5 274
10:1–18 . . .583, 600, 639, 640, 660, 718, 744
10:1–30 432
10:11–18 . . . . .100, 534, *725*, 849
10:17–18 . . . . .478, 484
11:1–45 . . . . .480, 655, *907*
11:25–26 . . . . .663, *907*
11:31–35 634
11:31–45 25
12:1–8 . . . .*296*, 527, 546
12:12–15 . . . . . .312, 313, 315, 320, 579, *896*
12:13 . . . . .79, 100, 314, 460, *885*, *944*
12:24–26 . . . . .302, 353, 608, 670, 814
12:35–36 . . . . .274, 793, *1056*
13:1–17 . . . . .6, 392, 490, 493, *950*, *951*, *952*
13:1–30 491
13:1–35 . . . .*468*, *1041*
13:14–15 . . . . .558, 790
13:34–35 . . . . . . 58, 169, 255, 288, 387, 492, 493, 524, 665, 811, 813, *893*
14 567
14:1 604
14:1–4 . . . . .133, 562, 657
14:6–7 . . . . 8, 48, 84, 89, 282, 402, 425, 584, 753, *887*, *907*, *1003*
14:13–14 . . . . .628, 648
14:15–17 . . . . .58, *729*
14:15–27 . . . . . .112, 367, 372, 643, 697, 839
14:15–31 .60, *379*, *1044*
14:19–23 . . . . .43, 848
14:25–27 . . . . .375, 431, 714, 720
14:25–31 . . . . .46, 53, 56, 533
14:27 . . . . . 52, 166, 168, 596, 604, 707, 711, 844, *850*, *904*
[John 15:1–5]. *472*
15:1–17 . . . . .30, 56, 522, *1002*
15:4–5 502
15:8 754
15:9–14 .133, 638, 813
15:10–11 570
15:12–13 . . . . .58, *951*
15:12–17 . . . . .493, 525, *937*
15:15 628
15:26–27 . . . .*379*, 839
16:4–15 . . . . .367, *379*
16:12–14 46
16:20–22 666
16:23–24 648
16:33 581
17:1–3 554
17:1–10 698
17:11 . . . . .87, 390, 455
17:13 8
17:20–26 . . . . . .389, 428, 455, 525, 598, 720
18:15–18 344
18:25–27 344
18:36 413
18:39–40 320
19 320
19:1–5 325
19:1–30 317
19:16–30 . . . . .331, 569
19:16–37 . . . . .322, 323
19:16–20:18 . . . . .329, *919*
19:25–30 328
19:34 267
19:38–20:18 353
19:41–42 281
20 348
20:1–10 . . . . . . 333, 340, 341, 346, 354, 355, 358, 359, 361, 565
20:1–18 . . . . .342, 546
20:1–20 350
20:19–23 . . . . .50, 52, 57, 112, 165, 375, 830
20:19–31 . . . . .343, 345, *850*, *876*, *904*
20:21–23 . . . . . .55, 395, 737, 739, 771, *1013*
20:24–29 . . . . .67, 588, *1066*
20:31 648
21:1–14 . . . .*291*
21:9–17 344

ACTS

1:1–5 . . . .*966*
1:1–11 . . . . .365, 366, 386, *919*
1:6–11 . . . . .363, *1014*
1:8 . . . . .39, 46, 367, 395, 769, 827, *992*
2 . . . .*378*, *379*, *992*
[Acts 2:1–4]. *379*
2:1–4 . . . . 46, 53, 54, 55, 56, 57, 58, 91, 369, 373, 375, 563, 739, 766, *858*
2:1–13 .370, 372, *877*
2:1–21 50
2:17–21 . . . . .36, 369, 716
2:22–36 463
2:23–24 . . . . .331, 333
2:37–42 . . . . .160, 431, 453, 458
2:43–47 . . . . .482, *932*, *960*, *961*
4:8–12 . . . . .4, 410
4:23–33 768
4:29–31 716
4:32–35 . . . . .753, 831
6 . . . .*957*
6:1–7 . . . .*965*

8:26–40 ... 453
9:1–22 ... *1027*
10:34–35 ... 710
10:44–48 ... 740, *877*
13:1–3 ... *966*
16:11–15 ... *957*
16:22–34 ... 25, 434, 575
16:25–26 ... 579
17:22–31 ... 422, 433
17:26 ... 523
17:28 ... 553, *880*, *998*
20:28 ... 534
20:35 ... 713
22:3–21 ... *1027*
26:2–23 ... *1027*

ROMANS

3:21–26 ... 84, 163, 170, 365, 436, 590
4:17 ... 799
5:1–5 ... 637
5:5 ... 54, 58, 370, *903.D*
5:5–11 ... 332, *338*, 436, 767
5:6–21 ... 330, 564
6:1–11 ... 408, 439, 442, *449*, 522, 548, 555
6:3–5 ... 359, 452, 455, 657, *930*
[Romans 6:3–4, 10–11] ... *449*
6:3–11 ... 347, 350, 577, 713
6:5–14 ... 349, 460, 564, *903.C*
6:15–23 ... 155, 554
7:23–25 ... *890*
8 ... 542
8:1–4 ... 304, 564
8:1–25 ... 435
8:1–30 ... 53, 368, 827
8:9–11 ... 62, 349, 567, 740, *879*
8:12–17 ... 376, 720, 830
8:18–25 ... 236, 407, 551, 670, 715, 766, 828
8:18–30 ... 112, 694, 770
8:22 ... *1009*
8:22–28 ... 420, 557, 591, 612, 623
[Romans 8:26] ... *729*
8:26–27 ... 56, 541, 676, 677, 681, *877*, *985.G*, 990
8:26–39 ... *994*
8:28 ... *1050*
8:28–39 ... *337*, 586, 607, 624, 666
8:32–34 ... 174, 436, *888*
8:35–39 ... 162, 590, 592, 803
[Romans 8:38–39] ... *337*
8:38–39 ... 64, 171, 332, 422, 517, 654
9:20–21 ... 403
10:9–13 ... *450*, *926*
10:12–18 ... *781*, *1029*
11:33–36 ... 422
[Romans 12:1–2] ... *105*
12:1–2 ... 550, 753, 759, 760
12:1–8 ... 526
12:1–13 ... 531
12:4–8 ... 22, 374, *380*, 396, 568, 856
12:9 ... *1059*
12:9–13 ... 492
12:9–18 ... 778, 813
[Romans 12:9–21 (excerpts)] ... *384*
12:9–21 ... 168, 713, 719, *780*
12:11 ... 776
12:14–21 ... 803
12:15 ... 636, 656
12:18 ... 485
13:1–10 ... *929*
13:8–10 ... 288, 571, 796, *890*, *897*, *985.D*
14:7–8 ... 735
14:11 ... 29
[Romans 15:5–6] ... *822*
15:5–7 ... 390, 665, *853*, *961*
15:5–9 ... 719
15:13 ... 39, 52, 394, 613, 829, 843, 844, *987.I*, *1052.G*, *1059*
15:33 ... 838, 842

1 CORINTHIANS

1:10 ... 492, 813
1:10–18 ... 87
1:17–18 ... 324
1:18–25 ... *896*
1:25 ... 440
1:26–31 ... 700, 743
1:30 ... 155
2:1–13 ... 3
2:2 ... 499
2:6–16 ... 44, 639
2:9 ... 226
3:5–11 ... *1036*
3:9–11 ... 36, 332
3:10–15 ... 92, 397, 592
3:10–19 ... *381*, *382*
3:11 ... 4, 622
3:16–17 ... 62
3:19–23 ... 428
5:7–8 ... 463
6:11 ... 562
9:24–27 ... 804, 816
10:13 ... 607
10:16–17 ... 386, 459, 464, 466, 475, 477, 478, 480, 481, 482, 484, 485, *715*, *773*, *812*
11:17–29 ... 462, 478, 481, 484
[1 Corinthians 11:23–26] ... *469*
11:23–26 ... 10, 36, 65, 459, 460, 461, 464, *466*, *468*, 473, 476, 479, 480, 482, 483, 485, *887*, *936*, *941*, *944*
12 ... 1, *380*, 386, 396, 715, *856*, *932*, *959*, *964*, *965*, *1023*, *1035*
[1 Corinthians 12:4–7] ... *380*
12:4–11 ... 53, 374, 766, 774
12:4–26 ... 779
12:4–31 ... 513
12:12–13 ... 174, 387, 442, 455
12:12–26 ... 391
12:12–31 ... 38, *450*
12:13 ... 32, 802, *930*, *1001*
12:27–28 ... 534, 568
13 ... 492, 524, 749, *973*, *991*
13:4–7 ... *906*
13:4–13 ... *1045*
13:12 ... 311
13:12–13 ... 804
13:13 ... 374, 519, 751, *915*, *1017*
14:12 ... 374
15 ... *336*, 340, 347, 350, 352
15:1–11 ... 433
15:3–4 ... 351
15:9–11 ... 163, *1027*
15:12–20 ... 354
15:12–28 ... 357, 358, 463, 479
15:20–28 ... 460
15:35–58 ... 302
[1 Corinthians 15:50–57 (excerpts)] ... *336*
15:50–58 ... 346, 357, 463, 617, 790
15:51–52 ... *334*
15:54–56 ... 165, 341, 355, 416, 502
15:54–58 ... 48, 331, 332, 333, 349, 408, 670
15:58 ... 776
16:14 ... 396

2 CORINTHIANS

1:3 ... *819*
1:3–7 ... 613, 643, 656, 843
1:21–22 ... 748, *992*
3:17–18 ... 638, *895*
4:1–6 ... 437, 603
4:1–15 ... 768
4:6 ... 401, 500, 632, 714
4:7–18 ... 630, *908*
4:16–5:10 ... 743
4:18 ... 422
5:5 ... 697
5:6–10 ... 67, 435, 562
5:7 ... 585, 588
5:14 ... 647
5:14–21 ... 638
5:16–17 ... 377
5:16–21 ... 389, 391, 394, 797, 809
5:17 ... *334*, 439, 605, *888*, *938*
[2 Corinthians 5:17–20] ... *785*
5:17–21 ... 25, 652, *786*, 849
5:18–21 ... 535, *888*, *938*
6:3–10 ... 560
7:1 ... 558
9:6–15 ... 122, 124, 745
9:7–8 ... 746, 756, *819*
9:8–10 ... 486
10:3–5 ... 768
12:1–10 ... *1027*
12:9–10 ... 167, 743
13:3–4 ... 167
13:11–12 ... 485, 719
13:11–14 ... 598, 613, 810, 835, 843
[2 Corinthians 13:13] ... *21*
13:13–14 ... 60, 428, 429, *1053*

GALATIANS

1:13–24 ... *1027*
2:10 ... *1052.C*
2:19–20 ... 556
3:19–29 ... *786*
[Galatians 3:26–28] ... *450*
3:26–29 ... 32, 174, 390, 455, 769
3:27 ... 457, *930*
3:28 ... 30, 428, 798, 802
4:1–7 ... 195, 769
4:4–5 ... *852*
5:1 ... 304
5:14 ... 288, 571, 796, *890*, *897*, *985.D*
5:16–26 ... 827
5:22–23 ... 239, *1028*
5:22–26 ... 53, 396, 557
6:1–2 ... 154, 722, 831, *932*
6:14 ... 308, 322, 323, 324, 443
6:15 ... 849

EPHESIANS

1:3 ... 845
1:3–14 ... 7, 99, 429, 430, 521, 720
1:7 ... 304
1:7–14 ... 770
1:17–23 ... 116, 397, 401
2:1–10 ... 163, 170, 767, 814
2:4–5 ... *890*
2:4–10 ... 349, 521
2:8 ... 322, 323
2:11–22 ... 26, 30, 36, 87, 390, 391, 409, *862*
[Ephesians 2:13–18] ... *786*
2:13–20 ... 168, 174, 308, 485, 717, *785*, 797
[Ephesians 2:19–21] ... *382*
2:19–22 ... 1, *381*, 397
3:7–13 ... *385*, 770
[Ephesians 3:10] ... *385*
3:14–15 ... 523
3:14–21 ... 162, 396, 492, 749
3:16–21 ... 43, 848
3:17 ... *890*, *1028*
3:18–19 ... 303
[Ephesians 3:20–21] ... *824*
4:1–3 ... 485
[Ephesians 4:1–6] ... *446*
4:1–6 ... 30, 60, 387, 433, 455
4:1–16 ... 374, 396, 779, *856*
4:4–6 ... 397
4:4–13 ... 386, *964*
4:8–10 ... 366
4:11–13 ... 534, 774
4:15–16 ... *937*
4:26–27 ... 792
5:1–2 ... 365, 773
5:15–20 ... 39, *818*
5:19–20 ... 83, 486, 699
6:1–4 ... *972*
6:10–18 ... 549, *900*
6:18 ... 628

PHILIPPIANS

1:20–26 ... 499
1:21–22 ... 584
2:1–2 ... 478, 665
2:1–4 ... 284, 722, *1001*
2:1–8 ... 395, 719
2:4–11 ... *926*
2:5 ... 572
2:5–8 ... 215
[Philippians 2:5–11] ... *335*
2:5–11 ... 142, 227, 236, 263, 303, 410, 432, 444, 490, 564, *952*
2:9–11 ... 29, 86, 92, 116, 125, 130, 363, 364, 411, 431, 648
2:12–13 ... 713
2:15 ... 665

3:7–9 . . . 548, 624, *903.B*
3:7–11 . . . 322, 323, 499
4:4–6 . . . 118, 228
[Philippians 4:4–7] . . . *726*
4:6 . . . 396, 679
4:6–7 . . . 619, *1052.A*, *1052.B*, *1052.C*, *1052.D*, *1052.E*, *1052.F*, *1052.G*
4:7 . . . 52, 617, *1054*
4:13 . . . 159

COLOSSIANS
1:9–12 . . . 716
1:15–17 . . . 130, 236, 260
[Colossians 1:15–20] . . . *189*
1:15–20 . . . 68, 138, 242
1:15–23 . . . 89, 444, *785*, *786*, *861*
2:13–15 . . . 617
3:9–12 . . . *450*
3:11 . . . 390, 798, 802
3:11–15 . . . 30, 36, 164, 485, 717
3:12–17 . . . *446*, *973*
3:14 . . . *723*
3:15 . . . *1052.A*, *1052.B*, *1052.C*, *1052.D*, *1052.E*, *1052.F*, *1052.G*
[Colossians 3:15–17] . . . *818*
3:16 . . . 83
3:17 . . . 699
3:20–21 . . . *972*

1 THESSALONIANS
3:12–13 . . . 558
4:13–14 . . . 351, *980*
4:13–18 . . . 352, 407, 436, 438, 626
5:1–11 . . . 407
5:11–15 . . . 613, 722
5:13 . . . 485
5:18 . . . 704
[1 Thessalonians 5:23–24] . . . *823*

2 THESSALONIANS
2:14 . . . 765
[2 Thessalonians 2:16–17] . . . *819*
3:16 . . . 707, 711

1 TIMOTHY
1:12–16 . . . 542
1:15–16 . . . *338*
1:17 . . . 98
2:1–2 . . . 168
2:1–7 . . . *929*, *996*, *997*
2:5 . . . 361
3:16 . . . 438
4 . . . *965*
6:6–10 . . . 758

2 TIMOTHY
1:6–14 . . . 590, 768
1:9–10 . . . 129
3:16–17 . . . 399, 537
4:6–8 . . . 275, 662, 816

TITUS
2:11–14 . . . 62
3:4–8 . . . 435, 452, 542, 830

PHILEMON
. . . 195, *1027*

HEBREWS
1:1–2 . . . 537, *910*
1:1–8 . . . 99, 126, 130, 418
2:1–13 . . . 129
2:6–9 . . . 408
2:10–18 . . . 159, 479
2:14–15 . . . 347, 350
4:12 . . . 404
4:14–16 . . . 444, 628, 643, 666
4:14–5:10 . . . 112
6:17–18 . . . 420
7:20–28 . . . 361
8:10 . . . *869*
9:11–14 . . . 548, 560
9:11–22 . . . 617
10:1–10 . . . 332, 426, 525, *919*
10:15–16 . . . *869*
10:24–25 . . . 22
11 . . . 535, *1068*
11:1 . . . 585, 804, *817*
11:1–3 . . . 599
11:8–12 . . . 807
11:17–19 . . . 165
12:1–3 . . . 43, 443, 672, 816, *858*, *920*
12:1–15 . . . 804
12:14–15 . . . 485
12:18–29 . . . 801
13:2 . . . 279
13:15 . . . 814
13:20–21 . . . 810, 829

JAMES
1:2–4 . . . 547
1:2–8 . . . 585
1:19 . . . 580
1:21 . . . 400
1:27 . . . 395
2:1–18 . . . 392
2:8 . . . 288, 571, 796, *890*, *897*, *985.D*
2:14–26 . . . 439
3 . . . 144
[James 5:13–16] . . . *727*
5:13–18 . . . 612, 698
5:14 . . . 645, *975*

1 PETER
1:3–9 . . . 115, 435
1:3–12 . . . 211
1:6–9 . . . 67, 666
1:19–21 . . . *912*
[1 Peter 2:4–5, 9–10] . . . *381*
2:4–10 . . . 1, 4, 36, *382*, 420
2:12 . . . 754
2:13–17 . . . *929*
2:21 . . . 306, 558, *1056*
2:21–25 . . . 303
3:8–14 . . . 168
4:1–4 . . . 62
4:5–6 . . . 433
4:8–11 . . . 6, 745, 754
4:10–14 . . . 647
5:1–5 . . . 534, *1041*
5:7 . . . 598, 616

2 PETER
1:11 . . . 562
1:20–21 . . . 50
3:8–13 . . . 377, 407, 638, 801

1 JOHN
1:1–4 . . . *913.A*
1:5 . . . 671
1:6–7 . . . 793
1:8–10 . . . 796
2:1–2 . . . 84
2:15–17 . . . 402
2:20–27 . . . 645
3:1–2 . . . 166, 172, 517, 596, 625, 769
3:1–6 . . . 435
3:11–24 . . . 493, 571
3:16–24 . . . 58
3:23 . . . 431
4:7–16 . . . 58, 158, 387, 493, 751
4:7–21 . . . 7, 191, 255, 258, 388, 425, 492, 638, 749, 773, *906*
4:9–10 . . . *338*
4:10–16 . . . 67, 539, 598
4:16–21 . . . 133, 169, 714, 733, 813
4:18 . . . 195
5:1–12 . . . 439
5:2–3 . . . 570
5:14–15 . . . 682, 686
5:20 . . . 581

2 JOHN
4–6 . . . 815, *951*, *1056*

3 JOHN
5–8 . . . 32, 409, 810

JUDE
2 . . . 810, 835

REVELATION
1:4–8 . . . *884*, *887*
1:8 . . . 114, 238, 309, 418, 425, 430, 507
1:17–18 . . . 347, 596
2–3 . . . *913.C*
2:8–11 . . . 166, 311, 434
4 . . . 40, 65, 76, 102, 126, 175, 415
4–5 . . . 64, *110*
4:1–8 . . . 401
4:8 . . . 61, 136, 137, 460, 709, *880*, *944*
4:8–11 . . . 204, *335*, *884*, *887*
5 . . . 116
5:6–14 . . . 65, 151, 226, 408, 410, 415, 564
5:9–14 . . . 89, *104*, 138, 432, 525, 767, *892*
5:13–14 . . . 70, 71, 78, *335*, 764
6:9–10 . . . 265
6:15–17 . . . 162
7:1–12 . . . 364, 411
7:4–17 . . . 313
[Revelation 7:9–12] . . . *110*
7:9–12 . . . 33, 427
7:9–17 . . . 65, 76, 91, *104*, 126, 360, 560
7:13–17 . . . 6, 49, 432, 559, 801
8:3 . . . 203
11:15–18 . . . 414, 672
12:1–17 . . . *900*
12:10–12 . . . 611
14:12–13 . . . 672
15:2–4 . . . 28, 136
17:14 . . . 410
19 . . . 69
19:1–10 . . . 65, 110
19:9 . . . 459, 484
[Revelation 21:1–5] . . . *339*
21:1–5 . . . 416, 669, 809
21:1–7 . . . 31, 49, 205, 377, 459, 638, 652
21:3–5 . . . 38, 551, 574, 608, 655
21:3–7 . . . 425
21:5 . . . 25, *334*, 460, 507, 565
21:6 . . . 962
21:22–27 . . . *104*, 215, 793
22 . . . *12*
22:1–2 . . . 441, 522, 705, 706
22:1–5 . . . 24, 424, 500, 642, 661, 667, 668, 763
22:5 . . . 504
22:13 . . . 116
22:16 . . . 237
22:17 . . . *14*
22:17–20 . . . 49
22:20 . . . *874*

METRICAL INDEX

Short Meter
SM 6.6.8.6
DENNIS 831
FESTAL SONG 273
GOLDEN HILL 589
O EVERLASTING LIGHT 733
SOUTHWELL 465
TRENTHAM 737

SM with refrain
CHRISTPRAISE RAY 87

SM extended
MIKTAM 520

SM extended with refrain
WE'RE MARCHING TO ZION 31

SM Double
SMD 6.6.8.6.6.6.8.6
DIADEMATA 408
MARIANNE 580
TERRA BEATA 180

Common Meter
CM 8.6.8.6
AFFLICTION 646
AWFUL MAJESTY 402
AZMON 764
BANGOR 285
CARPENTER 280
CHRISTMAS 253
CRIMOND 660
DUNDEE 602
GENEVA (Cole) 119
GOSHEN 776
GRATITUDE 496
I LOVE THE LORD 684
LUCILE 308
MARTYRDOM (AVON) 722
MCKEE 392
MORNING SONG (CONSOLATION) 623
NEW BRITAIN 163
SHANTI 588
ST. ANNE 203
ST. PETER 390

CM with refrain
ANGEL BAND 662
BOUND FOR THE PROMISED LAND 661
EL NATHAN 590

CM extended
ANTIOCH 240
CORONATION 411
DIADEM 364
DOVE OF PEACE 478
LYNGHAM 78
ZERAH 259

CM Double
CMD 8.6.8.6.8.6.8.6
CAROL 220, 248
COMMUNION 217
ELLACOMBE 182
FOREST GREEN 208
JONES 535
KINGSFOLD 536
MOSHIER 656
RESIGNATION 640
SALVATION 246
SARAH-ELIZABETH 528
SEACHRIST 144
SHEPHERD'S PIPES 569
THE ROWAN TREE 553
THIRD MODE MELODY 326
THREE IN ONE 460

Long Meter
LM 8.8.8.8
ALSACE 513
ARMS OF PATIENCE 426
BRIGHTNESS 343
CONDITOR ALME SIDERUM 236
DE NOCHE IREMOS 543
DE SPIRITU SANCTO 663
DEO GRACIAS 303, 363
DICKINSON COLLEGE 395
DUKE STREET 414
ERHALT UNS, HERR 146
HAMBURG 323
HILDEGARD 376
LEAVENING 176
MARYTON 583
MISSIONARY CHANT 714
O WALY WALY see THE WATER IS WIDE
OLD HUNDREDTH 5, 71
OLIVE'S BROW 318
OUR REFUGE 434
PROSPECT 735
PUER NOBIS NASCITUR 427
RETREAT 486
ROCKINGHAM OLD 491
ROUGH SEAS 149
SANDELL 517
SENZENINA 322
SERENA 554
SO LANGE JESUS BLEIBT 64
SPLENDOR PATERNAE 500
TALLIS' CANON 505
THE WATER IS WIDE 522, 524
TRURO 359
VENI CREATOR SPIRITUS 53
VOM HIMMEL HOCH 263
WAREHAM 305
WINCHESTER NEW 316
WOODWORTH 560

LM with alleluias
LASST UNS ERFREUEN 81, 270

LM with refrain
ALEGRÍA, ALEGRÍA, ALEGRÍA 224
GOD OF OUR STRENGTH 47
INDIGO 304
SOLID ROCK 621
ST. CATHERINE 575
VENI EMMANUEL 210

LM extended
BACA 371
SHOUT ON, PRAY ON 347

LM Double
LMD 8.8.8.8.8.8.8.8
CREATION 197
IN CHRIST ALONE 332
JERUSALEM 787

3.3.3.3.3.3.3.3
LYDIA 483

3.6.9.8.3.6
STILL, STILL, STILL 264

4.4.7.5
BOUND 171

4.4.8 D
BE NOT AFRAID 356

4.4.8.4.4.4 D
AUTUMN 635

4.5.10 D
EARTH AND ALL STARS (abridged) 829

4.5.10.6.5.5.4
WESTCHASE 134

4.7.4.7.4
CONFESIÓN 153

4.8.4.8 with refrain
HERR, FÜLL MICH NEU 739

4.11.5.11
IKKE VED MAKT 538

5.4.8.5.8.5 with refrain
CHILD OF THE POOR 268

5.5.5.4 D
BUNESSAN 495

5.5.5.4.5.5.5.4 with refrain
FRESH AS THE MORNING 420

5.5.5.5
BEERSHEBA 805

5.5.5.5 D
LE P'ING 498

5.5.5.5.5.4.5.5
BENEDICTION 832

5.5.5.5.5.5.4.4
ASSAM 443

5.5.5.5.5.5.5.4
HALAD 720

5.5.5.5.7.5.5.6
SILKEN WINGS 676

5.5.6.5.6.5.6.5 with refrain
JUDAS MACCABEUS 355

5.5.7.4.4.7
O SANCTISSIMA 254

5.5.10 D
AI HU 145

5.5.10.6.5.10
JOYFUL DARK 281

5.6.5.6.5.6 with refrain
ALEXANDRA 377

5.6.5.6.5.6.5.5
CANTAI AO SENHOR 113

5.6.5.6.5.6.7
UYAI MOSE 2

5.6.6.6
BENEDICTUS DEUS 810

5.6.7.5.5.8
CRUSADERS' HYMN 130

5.6.8.6
PROTECT ME, LORD; I COME TO YOU FOR SAFETY 701

5.7.5.5.5.5
HEAR, O ISRAEL 192

5.8.5.7.5.8.5
THE ROAD TO BASRAH 794

6.4.6.4 with refrain
NENO LAKE MUNGU 765

6.4.6.4.6.6.4
BETHANY (Mason) 658

6.4.10.6.6.4.11.4
JE LOUERAI L'ÉTERNEL 131

6.5.5.6
O-SO-SO 391

6.5.6.5
WEM IN LIEDENSTAGEN 756

6.5.6.5 D
APPALACHIAN FALL 721
CRANHAM 527
KING'S WESTON 279
LOCKLEY 168
SANCTUS (Schubert) 137

6.5.6.5.6.5
KHUDAYA, RAHEM KAR 693

6.5.6.5.7.5.6.3
LET US STAND 328

6.6.4.6.6.6.4
ITALIAN HYMN 750

6.6.5.6.6.5.7.8.6
JESU MEINE FREUDE 624

6.6.6.4 with refrain
GIVE ME JESUS 499

6.6.6.5 D
STILLWATER 458

6.6.6.6 D
MADRID 28

6.6.6.6.4.4.8
LOVE UNKNOWN 154, 320

6.6.6.6.6 with refrain
PERSONENT HODIE 260

6.6.6.6.8.8
DARWALL'S 148th 4, 80

6.6.6.7
SERVANT 572

6.6.7.6
AGIOS, O THEOS 709

6.6.7.7.7.8.5.5
IN DULCI JUBILO 261

6.6.8
LAUDATE DOMINUM 77

6.6.8.4 D
LEONI 190, 204
WORD OF GOD 404

6.6.8.6.6.8.3.3.6.6
WUNDERBARER KÖNIG 62

6.6.9 D with refrain
TRUST AND OBEY 570

6.6.9.6
BIKO 804

6.6.10.6.6.10.14.14.6.6.10
ANTHEM 611

6.6.11.6.6.11 D
ASH GROVE 812

6.7.6.7 with refrain
LOVE INCARNATE 255
VRUECHTEN 352

6.7.6.7.6.6.6.6
NUN DANKET ALLE GOTT 114

6.7.7.7
UNION 556

6.7.8.5 D
USE US GOD 811

6.7.8.9.8
SHENG YE JING 262

6.7.9.5
ARGENTINE SANTO 136

6.8.8 with refrain
MALEMBE 413

7.3
KAB 655

7.4.6.8 with refrain
ALEGRÍA (Sosa) 665

7.4.6.8.8.8
GREATOREX 430

7.4.7.4 D
SO NIMM DENN MEINE HÄNDE 631

7.4.8.4
KLEIN CREDO 431

7.5.7.5
RISE 442

7.5.7.5.7.6.7.6
NUN WEND IHR HÖREN SAGEN 444

7.5.8.5
SEEK THE PEACE 206

7.5.8.7.8.6 with refrain
SINGING JOY TO THE WORLD 276

7.5.8.8 with refrain
NO WORDS 634

7.6.4.4.4.4.8.4
REGINALDA 751

7.6.6.7.8 with refrain
TEMPLE OF PEACE 205

7.6.7.6
CHRISTUS, DER IST MEIN LEBEN 366
MARPECK 475

7.6.7.6 D with refrain
BOLIVIANO 526
HANKEY 761
REESE 290
WIR PFLÜGEN 747

7.6.7.6 D
AURELIA 397
AVE VIRGO VIRGINUM (GAUDEAMUS PARITER) 348, 797
CLIMBING VINE 546
ELLACOMBE 313
HERZLICH TUT MICH VERLANGEN 325
JONATHAN'S TUNE 466
LANCASHIRE 194
LLANGLOFFAN 278
OPEN HEART 452
SALLY GARDENS 618
ST. THEODULPH (VALET WILL ICH DIR GEBEN) 215
WALNUT 222
WEBB 223
WIE LIEBLICH IST DER MAIEN 122

7.6.7.6 with refrain
COMME UN SOUFFLE FRAGILE 403
GO TELL IT ON THE MOUNTAIN 252
ROYAL OAK 177
ST. THEODULPH (VALET WILL ICH DIR GEBEN) 315

7.6.7.6.6.7.6
ES IST EIN ROS' 216

7.6.7.6.7.6.7.7.6 with refrain
WE COME TO YOUR FEAST 462

7.6.7.6.7.6.12 with refrain
WONDERFUL GRACE 170

7.6.7.6.7.7.7.6
KELVINGROVE 540
WHISPER 548

7.6.7.6.8.6 with refrain
ST. BRENDAN'S 387

7.7.7.4
GIVING 748

7.7.7.4 D with refrain
HERE I AM, LORD 545

7.7.7.6 with refrain
OH, QUÉ BUENO 351

7.7.7.7
BROKEN WALLS 174
KYRIE (Reindorf) 795
NUN KOMM, DER HEIDEN HEILAND 214
SONG 13 46
THE CALL 48
UNITY 719
WORDLESS 677

7.7.7.7 with alleluias
EASTER HYMN 346

7.7.7.7 with refrain
GLORIA 249
JESUS CHRIST IS LOVE DIVINE 749
JESUS LOVES ME 516
TOMA MI VOLUNTAD 760
WE'LL WALK IN THE LIGHT 274

7.7.7.7 extended
HENDON 488, 759

7.7.7.7 D
ABERYSTWYTH 659
FALCONE 372
MENDELSSOHN 247
ST. GEORGE'S WINDSOR 123

7.7.7.7.7
CYSGA DI FY MHLENTYN TLWS 319

7.7.7.7.7.7
DIX 120, 277
EZRA D 519
FIDES INCIPIT 585
REDHEAD NO. 76 (GETHSEMANE) 317

7.7.7.7.8.7.8.7
IN THY HOLY PLACE WE BOW 40

7.7.7.8
WOZA NOMTHWALO WAKHO 679

7.7.7.8.7.7 with refrain
NOEL 256

7.7.9
DAWK'YAH TOWGYAH 400

7.7.10.7
TABLE OF GRACE 461

7.7.15.7.7.11
BY AND BY 311

7.8.6.8 with refrain
WILD MOUNTAIN THYME 636

7.8.7.8 with alleluia
MOUNTAIN PEAK 301

7.8.7.8.7.7
GROẞER GOTT, WIR LOBEN DICH 126

8.3.8.3.7.7.8.3
STAND BY ME 595

8.3.8.3.8.8.8.4 with refrain
GOD IS LOVE 7

8.4.5.9.6 with refrain
CALLED 806

8.4.8.4.8.8.8.4
FIRSTFRUITS 124

8.5.8.5
EARTHRISE 550

8.5.8.5 with refrain
GO DOWN MOSES 193

8.5.8.5 D with refrain
ALL WHO LABOR 734

8.5.8.5.8.8.8.5
FRANKLIN PARK 407

8.5.8.5.10.12.5.5.5
I WILL SING WITH YOU 389

8.6
TABLE GRACE 489

8.6.6.6 with refrain
CREATION IS A SONG 181

8.6.8.6.6
HEAVEN'S RAIN 198

8.6.8.6.7.6.7.6
ST. LOUIS 245

8.6.8.6.7.7 with refrain
WELCOME 6

8.6.8.6.8.6
SILENCE 310

8.6.8.6.8.8 with refrain
UNE JEUNE PUCELLE 788

8.6.8.8.6.6
REPTON 547

8.7 with refrain
SOMOS PUEBLO 464

8.7.7.7.7.8.6
SAKURA 115

8.7.8.3.8.7.8.3 with refrain
YOU ARE THERE 587

8.7.8.7
AUSTIN 518
FROM THE DEPTHS 157
KINGDOM (Copes) 508
McRAE 266, 440
OMNI DIE 697
RESTORATION (I WILL ARISE) 441
STENKA RAZIN 484
STUTTGART 746
SUN AND THUNDER 50
THE SERVANT SONG 778
WELLESLEY 156

8.7.8.7 iambic
ST. COLUMBA 485, 652

8.7.8.7 with refrain
BEAUTIFUL RIVER 667
BLESSED QUIETNESS 375
BRYN CALFARIA 708
CHRIST IS RISEN 361
HOW CAN I KEEP FROM SINGING 605
RIFTED ROCK 619
SPIRIT, FILL US 39

8.7.8.7 D
ALL WHO HUNGER 474
BAPTISM BY FIRE 152
BEACH SPRING 57, 179
BEECHER 638
CHURCH UNITED 758
CIVILITY 9, 807
COLBERT 354
COLUMCILLE 344
CONVERSE 628
DEANNA 509
EBENEZER 201
ENDSLEIGH NEW 849
GENEVA (Day) 307
HOLY MANNA 25, 529
HYFRYDOL 218, 745
HYMN TO JOY 103, 809
INVITATION NEW 42
JEFFERSON 694
JESUS CALLS US 30
JOEL 642
JOYOUS LIGHT 504
LADUE CHAPEL 112
NETTLETON 1, 563
O DU LIEBE MEINER LIEBE 813
PLEADING SAVIOR 433
PROMISE 670
RAQUEL 774
RUSTINGTON 531
ST. HELENA 229, 507

SUO GAN 237
TREASURED 175, 534

8.7.8.7 D iambic
THE WORD OF GOD 399

8.7.8.7 D with refrain
PRAISE JEHOVAH 95

8.7.8.7.6
BRIDEGROOM 56

8.7.8.7.6.6.6.6.7
EIN FESTE BURG 421, 571

8.7.8.7.6.8.6.7
GREENSLEEVES 267

8.7.8.7.7.7
TAWA 150

8.7.8.7.7.7 with refrain
HARWELL 497

8.7.8.7.7.7.8.7
IN BABILONE 766

8.7.8.7.7.7.8.8
GENEVA 42 (FREU DICH SEHR) 212, 552

8.7.8.7.7.8.7.4
CHRIST LAG IN TODESBANDEN 463

8.7.8.7.8.6.8.7
VESPER HYMN 503

8.7.8.7.8.7
BENEDIC ANIMA 428
EYES CLOSED 200
IRBY 410
LAUDA ANIMA 75
MADELEINE 196
PANGE LINGUA 331
PICARDY 65, 432
REGENT SQUARE 265, 705
WESTMINSTER ABBEY 423

8.7.8.7.8.7 extended
CWM RHONDDA 606, 716

8.7.8.7.8.8
MACH'S MIT MIR / EISENACH 577

8.7.8.7.8.8.7
ALLEIN GOTT IN DER HÖH 38
AUS TIEFER NOT (DE PROFUNDIS) 140
AUS TIEFER NOT (HERR WIE DU WILLST) 45
MIT FREUDEN ZART 101

8.7.8.7.8.8.7.7
ERMUNTRE DICH 269
W ZLOBIE LEZY 243
WERDE MUNTER 639

8.7.8.7.9
CLEVELAND 537

8.7.9.7
CALM ME, LORD 680

8.7.9.7.7.6
LA PAZ DE LA TIERRA 838

8.7.10
JOURNEY 613

8.7.12.7
BEAUTIFUL FLOWER 515

8.8
PREPARE YE THE WAY 219

8.8.6.8.6
WARUM BETRÜBST DU DICH, MEIN HERZ 576

8.8.8
BE STILL AND KNOW 37

8.8.8 with alleluias
O FILII ET FILIAE 342
VICTORY 350

8.8.8.3
ST. AËLRED 286

8.8.8.6
EVENING LIGHT 539

8.8.8.7
OLD YEAVERING 530

8.8.8.8 with refrain
CHUNG CHI 481

8.8.8.8.6
ST. MARGARET 608

8.8.8.8.8.6.8.6 with refrain
LOVE OF GOD 162

8.8.8.8.8.8
KHAO I DANG 27
MELITA 573
VERNON 191

8.8.8.8.8.8.7.8
UNRAVELED 603

8.8.8.9
SOJOURNER 306

8.8.9.8.8.8.8.4
OPEN MY EYES 738

8.8.10.8.8
BORN BELOVED 172

8.9.8.8.9.8.6.6.4.8.8
WACHET AUF 226

8.10.8.10 with refrain
GRAVITY OF LOVE 494

8.10.10 with refrain
PESCADOR DE HOMBRES 283

8.12.8.12.8.10
SPIRIT OF LIFE 368

9.6.8.6.8.7.10 with refrain
TWO OAKS 36

9.6.9.6.6.6.6.6
SIZOHAMBA NAYE 815

9.7.8.8.8.7.8.7
SEE THE BIRDS 289

9.7.8.9.9
IN THE LORD I'LL BE EVER THANKFUL 118

9.8.8.8
ANNELEIN'S PRAYER 630

9.8.8.9 with refrain
GOD BE WITH YOU 840

9.8.9.5.5
GREEN TYLER 43

9.8.9.6 with refrain
CHRIST, BE OUR LIGHT 715

9.8.9.8
ST CLEMENT 506

9.8.9.8 D
WAYFARING STRANGER 213, 696

9.8.9.8 with refrain
CHRIST IS ALIVE 565
FEEL THE SPIRIT 681

9.8.9.8.9.6.6
KOMT NU MET ZANG 22

9.8.9.9
CHILDREN PRAYING 682

9.8.10.8 D with refrain
STAR OF THE COUNTY DOWN 412

9.8.10.9.8.10 with refrain
BEAUTIFUL STAR OF BETHLEHEM 275

9.8.12.9.8.12 with refrain
JEHOVAH JIREH 165

9.9.9.9
EL NACIMIENTO 242
PINE GLEN 827

9.9.9.9 D with refrain
COMO PODEN PER SAS CULPAS 579

9.9.9.9 with refrain
MFURAHINI, HALELUYA 341

9.9.9.9.9 with refrain
SOLI DEO GLORIA 700

9.9.10.9.9.8
UN FLAMBEAU (BRING A TORCH) 258

9.9.11.11
O GOD, YOU SEARCH ME 199

9.10.9.9 with refrain
BLESSED ASSURANCE 435

10.6.10.6.8.8.8.6
ALL IS WELL 717

10.8.8.7
RESTORATION (I WILL ARISE) 300

10.9 with refrain
GOTT IST DIE LIEBE 158

10.9.10.9 with refrain
OPEN THE WELLS 555
SHOWALTER 160

10.9.10.10
SOMLANDELA 566

10.9.10.10 D
GATHER US IN 10

10.10 with refrain
BREAK BREAD TOGETHER 482

10.10.9.10
SLANE 549

10.10.10 with alleluias
CREATION'S DAWN 121
SINE NOMINE 672

10.10.10.4
ENGELBERG 83

10.10.10.6
FAITH 161

10.10.10.10
EVENTIDE 502
MORECAMBE 557
NEW WORLD 298
O PRINCE OF PEACE 26
TAKE UP THE SONG 542
UPPER ROOM 345

10.10.10.10.10
GENEVA 124 (OLD 124th) 424

10.10.10.10.10.10
FINLANDIA 664

10.10.11.10
LISTEN 405

10.10.11.11
LYONS 74

10.10.11.8 with refrain
ERB 612

10.10.12
PEACOCK 386

10.10.12.7.3
GABRIEL'S MESSAGE 221

10.11.11.11.12.11.10.11
RESURRECTION 340

11.7.11.6 with refrain
FILL US WITH YOUR FEAST 309

11.7.11.7 with refrain
THE BEAUTIFUL RIVER 668
THOMPSON 544

11.8.11.8 D
ZION'S PILGRIM 600

11.8.11.8 with refrain
KIRKPATRICK 626
PAVE THE WAY WITH BRANCHES 312

11.8.11.9 with refrain
VILLE DU HAVRE 617

11.10 with refrain
CHRIST AROSE 333

11.10.10 with refrain
O LORD OF LIGHT 41

11.10.11.8
GALLOWAY TAM 211

11.10.11.10
CONSOLATOR (CONSOLATION) 643
LE CÉNACLE 148
MORNING STAR 272

11.10.11.10 D

LONDONDERRY AIR 657
STAR IN THE EAST 44

11.10.11.10 with refrain

FAITHFULNESS 419
HOW GREAT THOU ART 436
STRANGERS NO MORE 409

11.10.11.10.11.10

FINLANDIA 649, 710

11.10.13.10 with refrain

LOCH LOMOND 209

11.11 with refrain

REVIVE US AGAIN 91

11.11.10.11

NOËL NOUVELET 287, 353
PRESENCE 284

11.11.11 with refrain

LOST IN THE NIGHT 143

11.11.11.5

HERZLIEBSTER JESU 330

11.11.11.11

CRADLE SONG 510
FOUNDATION (BELLEVUE) 592
GOD MADE 523
GORDON 133
MUELLER 257
ST. DENIO (JOANNA) 98

11.11.11.11 with refrain

TO GOD BE THE GLORY 84

11.12.12.10

NICAEA 76

12.9.12.12.9

WONDROUS LOVE 564

12.10.12.10.11.10 with refrain

ALLEN 100

12.11.12.11

KREMSER 34
ST. CATHERINE'S COURT 164

12.12.8.8.12

AR HYD Y NOS 830

12.12.11.11

ADORO TE DEVOTE 459

12.12.12.12 with refrain

UBI CARITAS 492

12.12.12.12.12.12

ENVIADO 771

12.14.12.12

LES PETITES SOEURS 581

13.13.13.13.13.13

THAXTED 814

14.10.14.10 with refrain

ENGLE 416

14.14.4.7.8

LOBE DEN HERREN 88

Irregular

ABANA ALATHI FI SSAMA / ABANA IN HEAVEN 675
ABRE MIS OJOS 732
ACCLAMATION (Henry) 438
ADESTE FIDELES 241
ADORE THEE 138
AGNEAU DE DIEU 559
ALL WHO ARE THIRSTY 49
ALLELUIA 7 66
ALLELUIA SOUTH AFRICA 650
AMEN 689
AMEN SIAKUDUMISA 90
AMEN THEMBA 32
ANGELS HOVERING ROUND 251
ANOINTING FALL ON ME 645
AS I RISE 848
AS I WENT DOWN TO THE RIVER 453
BALM IN GILEAD 647
BAPTIZED IN CHRIST 457
BE A SOWER 789
BE AT REST 532
BE THE CENTRE 584
BEAUTIFUL THINGS 551
BEAUTY OF HOLINESS 129
BERGOGLIO 713
BETWEEN DARKNESS AND LIGHT 808
BIRMINGHAM (Mendelssohn) 616
BLEIBET HIER 627
BLESS THE LORD (TEN THOUSAND REASONS) 111
BLESS THE LORD , MY SOUL 127
BLESSED BE YOUR NAME 637
BLESSING 844
BREATHE 139
BRING FORTH THE KINGDOM 297
BUILD YOUR KINGDOM HERE 393
BWANA AWABARIKI 845
BY THE WATERS 695
CHILD OF GOD 195
CHRIST IS RISEN (Maher/Fieldes) 349
CHRIST IST ERSTANDEN 358
CHRISTE, LUX MUNDI 271
CLEAN HEART 141
CLOSER WALK 743
COME AS A CHILD 282
COME, NOW IS THE TIME TO WORSHIP 29
COME, RECEIVE HIS JOY 767
CONFITEMINI DOMINO 52
CUÉLLAR 102
DANS NOS OBSCURITÉS 632
DAPIT HAPON 501
DEDICATION ANTHEM 70
DEMOS GRACIAS / LET US GIVE THANKS 704
DESERT ALLELUIA 35
DISTURB 406
DIVINUM MYSTERIUM 418
DON'T BE AFRAID 596
DONA NOBIS PACEM 707
DON'T BE DISCOURAGED WHEN TROUBLE'S IN YOUR LIFE 599
DOOLÁDÓ' SHI DIYINDA 562
DOXOLOGY REFRAIN 72
DRAW THE CIRCLE 802
DRESDEN AMEN 688
DU ÄR HELIG 61
EASTER ANTHEM 357
EAT THIS BREAD 476
EHANE HE'AMA 59
EKKLESIA 477
ENOUGH FOR ALL 757
EY LOU NIS 769
FAITHFUL AND TRUE 703
FAREWELL ANTHEM 846
FLOW TO YOU 132
GATHERED HERE IN THE MYSTERY 3
GENTLE SHEPHERD 718
GENTLE VOICE 625
GLORIA (Mass of Creation) 99
GLORIA III 94
GLORY TO GOD (Vasile) 429
GO NOW IN PEACE 835
GO YE NOW IN PEACE 839
GOD OF JUSTICE 772
GOD OF THE POOR 712
GOD OF WONDERS 178
GRACIAS SEÑOR 487
GREAT IS YOUR FAITHFULNESS 167
GREEN LANE 653
GUIDE MY FEET 816
HAKUNA WAKAITA 68
HALELUYA! PELO TSA RONA 473
HALLE HALLE 752
HALLELUJAH, SALVATION, AND GLORY 69
HAMBA NATHI 23
HAVE MERCY 796
HE CAME DOWN 239
HE IS EXALTED 86
HEALER OF OUR EVERY ILL 644
HEALING RIVER 706
HEAR MY PRAYER 685
HELELUYAN 85
HERE I AM TO WORSHIP 227
HEY NEY YANA 836
HINCKS 455
HOLD US IN YOUR MERCY (Daigle) 736
HOLY LORD 314
HOLY SPIRIT 369
HONJA SORIRONEUN 800
HOW CAN WE BE SILENT 790
HOW GREAT IS OUR GOD 116
I AM THE BREAD OF LIFE 480
I WON'T BE FRIGHTENED ANYMORE 166
IN DIR IST FREUDE 666
IVERSON 740
JESUS A, NAHETOTAETANOME 8
JESUS TOOK A TOWEL 490
JESUS, ROCK OF AGES 622
JUNG'S LINTEL 422
KI RI SU TO NO 843
KIEV ALLELUIA 135
KINDLE IN US 54
KOINONIA 388
KOMBO NA YESU 648
KWAKE YESU NASIMAMA 159
KYRIE 1 678
KYRIE 13 692
LACQUIPARLE 128
LAFFERTY 417
LAMB OF GOD 151
LAMENT 691
LAY IT DOWN 561
LEAD ME, GUIDE ME 601
LEAD ME, LORD 837
LET JUSTICE FLOW 791
LET THE CHILDREN COME 512
LET US PRAY (Byzantine) 686
LIKE A ROCK 63
LISTEN IN THE SILENCE 541
LORD BE GLORIFIED 754
LORD I LIFT 365
LORD, I WANT TO BE A CHRISTIAN 558
LORD, YOU'VE SEARCHED ME 609
LORD'S PRAYER 673
LOVE EACH OTHER 493
MAGNIFICAT 97
MANDERFELD KYRIE 614
MANY GIFTS 374
MARGAM, SATYAM, JIVAM NIVE 425
MARY HAMMOND 792
MAY GOD'S LIGHT SHINE EVER UPON YOU 671
MERCY MERCY 169
MOON 207
MOUNTAIN OF GOD 11
MY LIGHTHOUSE 597
MY LOVE COLOURS OUTSIDE THE LINES 582
NADA TE TURBE 604
NEVER THE BLADE SHALL RISE 302
NEW HOPE 598
NEW WORLD (Dvořák) 533
NINA 299
NJOO KWETU, ROHO MWEMA 367
NOTHING CAN EVER 654
NYANYIKANLAH 93
O FIERY SPIRIT 55
O GOD WE CALL 683
O GREAT SPIRIT 51
O PHARISEOS 142
O PHI NONG OEI 525
OH HOW COULD IT BE 479
ON EAGLE'S WINGS 641
ONE BODY 779
ONYAME WO MU 607
OPEN MY HEART 731
OPEN THE EYES 401
ORÉ PORIAJÚ VEREKÓ (KYRIE ELEISON) 620
ORTHODOX KYRIE 147
OTO SA BARANKI 360
OUR FATHER WHO ART IN HEAVEN 674
OUR LORD SAID THAT ALL WOULD BE WELL 586
OVER MY HEAD 594
OWEN 511
PASE LO QUE PASE VEN 768
PEACE PILGRIM'S PRAYER 202
PICARDY 238
PRABHOO LAY LAY 567
PRECIOUS LORD 610
PURPOSE 770
REMEMBER ME 327
RESTLESS 741
REVELATION SONG 415
RIVER OF LIFE 24
ROOTED AND GROUNDED 396
ROTHLISBERGER 362
SÁLVANOS SEÑOR, DESPIERTOS 833
SANNANINA 79
SEEDS 777
SENDING SONG 841
SHALOM 842
SHEPHERD ME 744
SHOUT FOR JOY 82
SHOUT TO THE LORD 125
SHUKURU YESU 699
SI TUVIERAS FE 593
SIYAHAMBA 793
SOFT FIELD OF CLOVER 629
SOMEBODY PRAYED FOR ME 698
SOON AND VERY SOON 669
STILLE NACHT 244
SWORD INTO A PLOUGHSHARE 798
SYRIAN HALLELUJAH 702
TAIZÉ UBI CARITAS 773
TANA MANA DHANA 753
TASTE AND SEE 467
TEACH MY SONG 155
THE FIRST NOEL 250
THE GREATEST COMMANDMENT 288
THE KINGDOM OF GOD IS JUSTICE AND PEACE 799
THE LORD IS MY LIGHT 437
THE MOOSONEE SERVICE 651
THE TREES OF THE FIELD 847
THIS LITTLE LIGHT OF MINE (civil rights song) 762
THREEFOLD AMEN 690
THUMA MINA 834
THY WORD 398
TO MY PRECIOUS LORD 755
TO THE ONE 591
TONGA MELODY 578
TOTAL PRAISE 633
TREE SONG 514
TRINITY SONG 60
TÚ ERES TODOPODEROSO 89

TÚ ESTÁS AQUÍ 67
TUI AMORIS IGNEM 58
VENI SANCTE SPIRITUS 370
VISION: HEALING AND HOPE 394
WADE IN THE WATER 454
WAIRUA TAPU 373
WAIT FOR THE LORD 228
WATERFALL 763
WAY WAY WAY 742
WE COME 225
WE GIVE THANKS UNTO YOU 117
WE SHALL OVERCOME 803
WE SHALL WALK THROUGH THE VALLEY IN PEACE 574
WE WILL WALK 439
WELCOME TABLE 801
WERE YOU THERE 329
WHERE FEET MAY FAIL 456
WHERE YOU GO I'LL GO 775
WILD HOPE 828
WILD MOUNTAIN THYME 636
WITH KINDNESS 568
WONDERFUL CROSS 324
WORTHY OF EVERY SONG 92
YA HAMALALLAH 321
YA RAB AS-SALAMI 711
YOU ARE GOOD 33
YOUR GRACE FINDS ME 521
YOUR LOVE IS AMAZING 96
ZEPHANIAH 3:17 173

TUNE INDEX

ABANA ALATHI FI SSAMA / ABANA IN HEAVEN 675
ABERYSTWYTH 659
ABRE MIS OJOS 732
ACCLAMATION (Henry) 438
ADESTE FIDELES 241
ADORE THEE 138
ADORO TE DEVOTE 459
AFFLICTION 646
AGIOS, O THEOS 709
AGNEAU DE DIEU 559
AI HU 145
AJALON, see REDHEAD NO. 76
ALEGRÍA (Sosa) 665
ALEGRÍA, ALEGRÍA, ALEGRÍA 224
ALEXANDRA 377
ALL IS WELL 717
ALL WHO ARE THIRSTY 49
ALL WHO HUNGER 474
ALL WHO LABOR 734
ALLEIN GOTT IN DER HÖH 38
ALLELUIA 7 66
ALLELUIA SOUTH AFRICA 650
ALLEN 100
ALSACE 513
AMAZING GRACE, see NEW BRITAIN
AMEN 689
AMEN SIAKUDUMISA 90
AMEN THEMBA 32
ANGEL BAND 662
ANGELS HOVERING ROUND 251
ANNELEIN'S PRAYER 630
ANOINTING FALL ON ME 645
ANTHEM 611
ANTIOCH 240
APPALACHIAN FALL 721
AR HYD Y NOS 830
ARGENTINE SANTO 136
ARMS OF PATIENCE 426
ARNSBERG, see WUNDERBARER KÖNIG
AS I RISE 848
AS I WENT DOWN TO THE RIVER 453
ASH GROVE 812
ASSAM 443
AURELIA 397
AUS TIEFER NOT (DE PROFUNDIS) 140
AUS TIEFER NOT (HERR WIE DU WILLST) 45
AUSTIN 518
AUTUMN 635
AVE VIRGO VIRGINUM (GAUDEAMUS PARITER) 348, 797
AVON 722
AWFUL MAJESTY 402
AZMON 764

BACA 371
BALM IN GILEAD 647
BANGOR 285
BAPTISM BY FIRE 152
BAPTIZED IN CHRIST 457
BE A SOWER 789
BE AT REST 532
BE NOT AFRAID 356
BE STILL AND KNOW 37
BE THE CENTRE 584
BEACH SPRING 57, 179
BEAUTIFUL FLOWER 515
BEAUTIFUL RIVER 667
BEAUTIFUL STAR OF BETHLEHEM 275
BEAUTIFUL THINGS 551
BEAUTY OF HOLINESS 129
BEECHER 638
BEERSHEBA 805
BENEDIC ANIMA 428
BELLEVUE 592
BENEDICTION 832
BENEDICTUS DEUS 810
BERGOGLIO 713
BETHANY (Mason) 658
BETWEEN DARKNESS AND LIGHT 808
BIKO 804
BIRMINGHAM (Mendelssohn) 616
BLEIBET HIER 627
BLESS THE LORD (TEN THOUSAND REASONS) 111
BLESS THE LORD, MY SOUL 127
BLESSED ASSURANCE 435
BLESSED BE YOUR NAME 637
BLESSED QUIETNESS 375
BLESSING 844
BOLIVIANO 526
BORN BELOVED 172
BOUND 171
BOUND FOR THE PROMISED LAND 661
BREAK BREAD TOGETHER 482
BREATHE 139
BRIDEGROOM 56
BRIGHTNESS 343
BRING A TORCH 258
BRING FORTH THE KINGDOM 297
BROKEN WALLS 174
BRYN CALFARIA 708
BUILD YOUR KINGDOM HERE 393
BUNESSAN 495
BWANA AWABARIKI 845
BY AND BY 311
BY THE WATERS 695

CALLED 806
CALM ME, LORD 680
CANTAI AO SENHOR 113
CAROL 220, 248
CARPENTER 280
CHILD OF GOD 195
CHILD OF THE POOR 268
CHILDREN PRAYING 682
CHRIST AROSE 333
CHRIST IS ALIVE 565
CHRIST IS RISEN 361
CHRIST IS RISEN (Maher/ Fieldes) 349
CHRIST IST ERSTANDEN 358
CHRIST LAG IN TODESBANDEN 463
CHRIST, BE OUR LIGHT 715
CHRISTE, LUX MUNDI 271
CHRISTMAS 253
CHRISTPRAISE RAY 87
CHRISTUS, DER IST MEIN LEBEN 366
CHUNG CHI 481
CHURCH UNITED 758
CIVILITY 9, 807
CLEAN HEART 141
CLEVELAND 537
CLIMBING VINE 546
CLOSER WALK 743
COLBERT 354
COLUMCILLE 344
COME AS A CHILD 282
COME, NOW IS THE TIME TO WORSHIP 29
COME, RECEIVE HIS JOY 767
COMME UN SOUFFLE FRAGILE 403
COMMUNION 217
COMO PODEN PER SAS CULPAS 579
CONDITOR ALME SIDERUM 236
CONFESIÓN 153
CONFITEMINI DOMINO 52
CONSOLATOR (CONSOLATION) 643
CONVERSE 628
CORONATION 411
CRADLE SONG 510
CRANHAM 527
CREATION 197
CREATION IS A SONG 181
CREATION'S DAWN 121
CRIMOND 660
CRUSADERS' HYMN 130
CUÉLLAR 102
CWM RHONDDA 606, 716
CYSGA DI FY MHLENTYN TLWS 319

DANS NOS OBSCURITÉS 632
DAPIT HAPON 501
DARWALL'S 148th 4, 80
DAWK'YAH TOWGYAH 400
DE NOCHE IREMOS 543
DE SPIRITU SANCTO 663
DEANNA 509
DEDICATION ANTHEM 70
DEMOS GRACIAS / LET US GIVE THANKS 704
DENNIS 831
DEO GRACIAS 303, 363
DESERT ALLELUIA 35
DIADEM 364
DIADEMATA 408
DICKINSON COLLEGE 395
DISTURB 406
DIVINUM MYSTERIUM 418
DIX 120, 277
DON'T BE AFRAID 596
DON'T BE DISCOURAGED WHEN TROUBLE'S IN YOUR LIFE 599
DONA NOBIS PACEM 707
DOOLÁDÓ' SHI DIYINDA 562
DOVE OF PEACE 478
DOXOLOGY REFRAIN 72
DRAW THE CIRCLE 802
DRESDEN AMEN 688
DU ÄR HELIG 61
DUKE STREET 414
DUNDEE 602
EARTH AND ALL STARS (abridged) 829
EARTHRISE 550
EASTER ANTHEM 357
EASTER HYMN 346
EAT THIS BREAD 476
EBENEZER 201
EHANE HE'AMA 59
EIN FESTE BURG 421, 571
EISENACH 577
EKKLESIA 477
EL NACIMIENTO 242
EL NATHAN 590
ELLACOMBE 182, 313
ENDSLEIGH NEW 849
ENGELBERG 83
ENGLE 416
ENOUGH FOR ALL 757
ENVIADO 771
ERB 612
ERHALT UNS, HERR 146
ERIE , see CONVERSE
ERMUNTRE DICH 269
ES IST EIN ROS' 216
EVENING LIGHT 539
EVENTIDE 502
EY LOU NIS 769
EYES CLOSED 200
EZRA D 519

FAITH 161
FAITHFUL AND TRUE 703
FAITHFULNESS 419
FALCONE 372
FAREWELL ANTHEM 846
FEEL THE SPIRIT 681
FESTAL SONG 273
FIDES INCIPIT 585
FILL US WITH YOUR FEAST 309
FINLANDIA 649, 664, 710
FIRSTFRUITS 124
FLOW TO YOU 132
FOREST GREEN 208
FOUNDATION (BELLEVUE) 592
FRANKLIN PARK 407
FRESH AS THE MORNING 420
FREU DICH SEHR 212, 552
FROM THE DEPTHS 157

GABRIEL'S MESSAGE 221
GALLOWAY TAM 211
GATHER US IN 10
GATHERED HERE IN THE MYSTERY 3
GAUDEAMUS PARITER 348, 797
GENEVA (Cole) 119
GENEVA (Day) 307
GENEVA 42 (FREU DICH SEHR) 212, 552
GENEVA 124 (OLD 124th) 424
GENTLE SHEPHERD 718
GENTLE VOICE 625
GETHSEMANE 317
GIVE ME JESUS 499
GIVING 748
GLORIA 249
GLORIA (Mass of Creation) 99
GLORIA III 94
GLORY TO GOD (Vasile) 429
GO DOWN MOSES 193

GO NOW IN PEACE 835
GO TELL IT ON THE MOUNTAIN 252
GO YE NOW IN PEACE 839
GOD BE WITH YOU 840
GOD IS LOVE 7
GOD MADE 523
GOD OF JUSTICE 772
GOD OF OUR STRENGTH 47
GOD OF THE POOR 712
GOD OF WONDERS 178
GOLDEN HILL 589
GORDON 133
GOSHEN 776
GOTT IST DIE LIEBE 158
GRACIAS SEÑOR 487
GRATITUDE 496
GRAVITY OF LOVE 494
GREAT IS YOUR FAITHFULNESS 167
GREATOREX 430
GREEN LANE 653
GREEN TYLER 43
GREENSLEEVES 267
GROßER GOTT, WIR LOBEN DICH 126
GUIDE MY FEET 816

HAKUNA WAKAITA 68
HALAD 720
HALELUYA! PELO TSA RONA 473
HALLE HALLE 752
HALLELUJAH, SALVATION, AND GLORY 69
HAMBA NATHI 23
HAMBURG 323
HANKEY 761
HARWELL 497
HAVE MERCY 796
HE CAME DOWN 239
HE IS EXALTED 86
HEALER OF OUR EVERY ILL 644
HEALING RIVER 706
HEAR MY PRAYER 685
HEAR, O ISRAEL 192
HEAVEN'S RAIN 198
HELELUYAN 85
HENDON 488, 759
HERE I AM TO WORSHIP 227
HERE I AM, LORD 545
HERR, FÜLL MICH NEU 739
HERZLICH TUT MICH VERLANGEN 325
HERZLIEBSTER JESU 330
HEY NEY YANA 836
HILDEGARD 376
HINCKS 455
HOLD US IN YOUR MERCY (Daigle) 736
HOLY LORD 314
HOLY MANNA 25, 529
HOLY SPIRIT 369
HONJA SORIRONEUN 800
HOW CAN I KEEP FROM SINGING 605
HOW CAN WE BE SILENT 790
HOW GREAT IS OUR GOD 116
HOW GREAT THOU ART 436
HYFRYDOL 218, 745
HYMN TO JOY 103, 809

I AM THE BREAD OF LIFE 480
I LOVE THE LORD 684
I WILL ARISE 300, 441
I WILL SING WITH YOU 389
I WON'T BE FRIGHTENED ANYMORE 166
IKKE VED MAKT 538
IN BABILONE 766
IN CHRIST ALONE 332
IN DIR IST FREUDE 666
IN DULCI JUBILO 261
IN THE LORD I'LL BE EVER THANKFUL 118
IN THY HOLY PLACE WE BOW 40
INDIGO 304
INVITATION NEW 42

IRBY 410
ITALIAN HYMN 750
IVERSON 740

JE LOUERAI L'ÉTERNEL 131
JEFFERSON 694
JEHOVAH JIREH 165
JERUSALEM 787
JESU MEINE FREUDE 624
JESUS A, NAHETOTAETANOME 8
JESUS CALLS US 30
JESUS CHRIST IS LOVE DIVINE 749
JESUS LOVES ME 516
JESUS TOOK A TOWEL 490
JESUS, ROCK OF AGES 622
JOEL 642
JONATHAN'S TUNE 466
JONES 535
JOURNEY 613
JOYFUL DARK 281
JOYOUS LIGHT 504
JUDAS MACCABEUS 355
JUNG'S LINTEL 422

KAB 655
KELVINGROVE 540
KHAO I DANG 27
KHUDAYA, RAHEM KAR 693
KI RI SU TO NO 843
KIEV ALLELUIA 135
KINDLE IN US 54
KING'S WESTON 279
KINGDOM (Copes) 508
KINGSFOLD 536
KIRKPATRICK 626
KLEIN CREDO 431
KOINONIA 388
KOMBO NA YESU 648
KOMT NU MET ZANG 22
KREMSER 34
KWAKE YESU NASIMAMA 159
KYRIE (Reindorf) 795
KYRIE 1 678
KYRIE 13 692

LE CÉNACLE 148
LA PAZ DE LA TIERRA 838
LACQUIPARLE 128
LADUE CHAPEL 112
LAFFERTY 417
LAMB OF GOD 151
LAMENT 691
LANCASHIRE 194
LASST UNS ERFREUEN 81, 270
LAUDA ANIMA 75
LAUDATE DOMINUM 77
LAY IT DOWN 561
LE P'ING 498
LEAD ME, GUIDE ME 601
LEAD ME, LORD 837
LEAVENING 176
LEONI 190, 204
LES PETITES SOEURS 581
LET JUSTICE FLOW 791
LET THE CHILDREN COME 512
LET US PRAY (Byzantine) 686
LET US STAND 328
LIKE A ROCK 63
LISTEN 405
LISTEN IN THE SILENCE 541
LLANGLOFFAN 278
LOBE DEN HERREN 88
LOCH LOMOND 209
LOCKLEY 168
LONDONDERRY AIR 657
LORD BE GLORIFIED 754
LORD I LIFT 365
LORD, I WANT TO BE A CHRISTIAN 558
LORD, YOU'VE SEARCHED ME 609
LORD'S PRAYER (Miller) 673
LOST IN THE NIGHT 143
LOVE EACH OTHER 493
LOVE INCARNATE 255

LOVE OF GOD 162
LOVE UNKNOWN 154, 320
LUCILE 308
LYDIA 483
LYNGHAM 78
LYONS 74

MACH'S MIT MIR / EISENACH 577
MADELEINE 196
MADRID 28
MAGNIFICAT 97
MALEMBE 413
MANDERFELD KYRIE 614
MANY GIFTS 374
MARGAM, SATYAM, JIVAM NIVE 425
MARIANNE 580
MARPECK 475
MARTYRDOM (AVON) 722
MARY HAMMOND 792
MARYTON 583
MAY GOD'S LIGHT SHINE EVER UPON YOU 671
MCKEE 392
McRAE 266, 440
MELITA 573
MENDELSSOHN 247
MERCY MERCY 169
MFURAHINI, HALELUYA 341
MIKTAM 520
MISSIONARY CHANT 714
MIT FREUDEN ZART 101
MOON 207
MORECAMBE 557
MORNING SONG (CONSOLATION) 623
MORNING STAR 272
MOSHIER 656
MOUNTAIN OF GOD 11
MOUNTAIN PEAK 301
MUELLER 257
MY LIGHTHOUSE 597
MY LOVE COLOURS OUTSIDE THE LINES 582

NADA TE TURBE 604
NENO LAKE MUNGU 765
NETTLETON 1, 563
NEVER THE BLADE SHALL RISE 302
NEW BRITAIN 163
NEW HOPE 598
NEW WORLD 298
NEW WORLD (Dvořák) 533
NICAEA 76
NINA 299
NJOO KWETU, ROHO MWEMA 367
NO WORDS 634
NOEL 256
NOËL NOUVELET 287, 353
NOTHING CAN EVER 654
NUN DANKET ALLE GOTT 114
NUN KOMM, DER HEIDEN HEILAND 214
NUN WEND IHR HÖREN SAGEN 444
NYANYIKANLAH 93

O DU LIEBE MEINER LIEBE 813
O EVERLASTING LIGHT 733
O FIERY SPIRIT 55
O FILII ET FILIAE 342
O GOD WE CALL 683
O GOD, YOU SEARCH ME 199
O GREAT SPIRIT 51
O LORD OF LIGHT 41
O PHARISEOS 142
O PHI NONG OEI 525
O PRINCE OF PEACE 26
O SANCTISSIMA 254
O WALY WALY, see THE WATER IS WIDE
O-SO-SO 391
ODE TO JOY, see HYMN TO JOY
OH HOW COULD IT BE 479

OH, QUÉ BUENO 351
OLD HUNDREDTH 5, 71
OLD YEAVERING 530
OLIVE'S BROW 318
OMNI DIE 697
ON EAGLE'S WINGS 641
ONE BODY 779
ONYAME WO MU 607
OPEN HEART 452
OPEN MY EYES 738
OPEN MY HEART 731
OPEN THE EYES 401
OPEN THE WELLS 555
ORÉ PORIAJÚ VEREKÓ (KYRIE ELEISON) 620
ORTHODOX KYRIE 147
OTO SA BARANKI 360
OUR FATHER WHO ART IN HEAVEN 674
OUR LORD SAID THAT ALL WOULD BE WELL 586
OUR REFUGE 434
OVER MY HEAD 594
OWEN 511

PANGE LINGUA 331
PASE LO QUE PASE VEN 768
PASSION CHORALE, see HERZLICH TUT MICH VERLANGEN
PAVE THE WAY 312
PEACE PILGRIM'S PRAYER 202
PEACOCK 386
PERSONANT HODIE 260
PESCADOR DE HOMBRES 283
PETRA, see REDHEAD NO. 76
PICARDY 65, 238, 432
PINE GLEN 827
PLAINSONG MODE VIII, see VENI CREATOR SPIRITUS
PLEADING SAVIOR 433
PRABHOO LAY LAY 567
PRAISE JEHOVAH 95
PRECIOUS LORD 610
PREPARE YE THE WAY 219
PRESENCE 284
PROMISE 670
PROSPECT 735
PROTECT ME, LORD; I COME TO YOU FOR SAFETY 701
PUER NOBIS NASCITUR 427
PURPOSE 770

RAQUEL 774
REDHEAD NO. 76 (GETHSEMANE) 317
REESE 290
REGENT SQUARE 265, 705
REGINALDA 751
REMEMBER ME 327
REPTON 547
RESIGNATION 640
RESTLESS 741
RESTORATION (I WILL ARISE) 300, 441
RESURRECTION 340
RETREAT 486
REVELATION SONG 415
REVIVE US AGAIN 91
RIFTED ROCK 619
RISE 442
RIVER OF LIFE 24
ROCKINGHAM OLD 491
ROOTED AND GROUNDED 396
ROTHLISBERGER 362
ROUGH SEAS 149
ROYAL OAK 177
RUSTINGTON 531

ST. AËLRED 286
ST. ANNE 203
ST. BRENDAN'S 387
ST. CATHERINE 575
ST. CATHERINE'S COURT 164
ST. CLEMENT 506
ST. COLUMBA 485, 652
ST. DENIO (JOANNA) 98

ST. ELIZABETH, see CRUSADERS' HYMN
ST. GEORGE'S WINDSOR 123
ST. HELENA 229, 507
ST. LOUIS 245
ST. MARGARET 608
ST. PETER 390
ST. THEODULPH (VALET WILL ICH DIR GEBEN) 215, 315
SAKURA 115
SALLY GARDENS 618
SÁLVANOS SEÑOR, DESPIERTOS 833
SALVATION 246
SANCTUS (Schubert) 137
SANDELL 517
SANNANINA 79
SARAH-ELIZABETH 528
SEACHRIST 144
SEE THE BIRDS 289
SEEDS 777
SEEK THE PEACE 206
SENDING SONG 841
SENZENINA 322
SERENA 554
SERVANT 572
SHALOM 842
SHANTI 588
SHENG YE JING 262
SHEPHERD ME 744
SHEPHERD'S PIPES 569
SHOUT FOR JOY 82
SHOUT ON, PRAY ON 347
SHOUT TO THE LORD 125
SHOWALTER 160
SHUKURU YESU 699
SI TUVIERAS FE 593
SILENCE 310
SILKEN WINGS 676
SINE NOMINE 672
SINGING JOY TO THE WORLD 276
SIYAHAMBA 793
SIZOHAMBA NAYE 815
SLANE 549
SO LANGE JESUS BLEIBT 64
SO NIMM DENN MEINE HÄNDE 631
SOFT FIELD OF CLOVER 629
SOJOURNER 306
SOLI DEO GLORIA 700
SOLID ROCK 621
SOMEBODY PRAYED FOR ME 698
SOMLANDELA 566
SOMOS PUEBLO 464
SONG 13 46
SOON AND VERY SOON 669
SOUTHWELL 465
SPIRIT OF LIFE 368
SPIRIT, FILL US 39
SPLENDOR PATERNAE 500
STAND BY ME 595
STAR IN THE EAST 44
STAR OF THE COUNTY DOWN 412
STENKA RAZIN 484
STILL, STILL, STILL 264
STILLE NACHT 244
STILLWATER 458
STRANGERS NO MORE 409
STUTTGART 746
SUN AND THUNDER 50
SUO GAN 237
SWORD INTO A PLOUGHSHARE 798
SYRIAN HALLELUJAH 702

TABLE GRACE 489
TABLE OF GRACE 461
TAIZÉ UBI CARITAS 773
TAKE UP THE SONG 542
TALLIS' CANON 505
TANA MANA DHANA 753
TASTE AND SEE 467
TAWA 150
TEACH MY SONG 155
TEMPLE OF PEACE 205
TERRA BEATA 180
THAXTED 814
THE BEAUTIFUL RIVER 668
THE CALL 48
THE FIRST NOEL 250
THE GREATEST COMMANDMENT 288
THE KINGDOM OF GOD IS JUSTICE AND PEACE 799
THE LORD IS MY LIGHT 437
THE MOOSONEE SERVICE 651
THE ROAD TO BASRAH 794
THE ROWAN TREE 553
THE SERVANT SONG 778
THE TREES OF THE FIELD 847
THE WATER IS WIDE 522, 524
THE WORD OF GOD 399
THIRD MODE MELODY 326
THIS LITTLE LIGHT OF MINE (civil rights song) 762
THOMPSON 544
THREE-IN-ONE 460
THREEFOLD AMEN 690
THUMA MINA 834
THY WORD 398
TO GOD BE THE GLORY 84
TO MY PRECIOUS LORD 755
TO THE ONE 591
TOMA MI VOLUNTAD 760
TONGA MELODY 578
TON-Y-BOTEL, see EBENEZER
TOTAL PRAISE 633
TREASURED 175, 534
TREE SONG 514
TRENTHAM 737
TRINITY SONG 60
TRURO 359
TRUST AND OBEY 570
TÚ ERES TODOPODEROSO 89
TÚ ESTÁS AQUÍ 67
TUI AMORIS IGNEM 58
TWO OAKS 36

UBI CARITAS 492
UN FLAMBEAU (BRING A TORCH) 258
UNE JEUNE PUCELLE 788
UNION 556
UNITY 719
UNRAVELED 603
UPPER ROOM 345
USE US GOD 811
UYAI MOSE 2

VALET WILL ICH DIR GEBEN 215, 315
VENI CREATOR SPIRITUS 53
VENI EMMANUEL 210
VENI REDEMPTOR GENTIUM, see NUN KOMM, DER HEIDEN HEILAND
VENI SANCTE SPIRITUS, see NUN KOMM DER HEIDEN HEILAND
VERNON 191
VESPER HYMN 503
VICTORY 350
VILLE DU HAVRE 617
VISION: HEALING AND HOPE 394
VOM HIMMEL HOCH 263
VRUECHTEN 352

W ZLOBIE LEZY 243
WACHET AUF 226
WADE IN THE WATER 454
WAIRUA TAPU 373
WAIT FOR THE LORD 228
WALNUT 222
WAREHAM 305
WARUM BETRÜBST DU DICH, MEIN HERZ 576
WATERFALL 763
WAY WAY WAY 742
WAYFARING STRANGER 213, 696
WE COME 225
WE COME TO YOUR FEAST 462
WE GIVE THANKS UNTO YOU 117
WE SHALL OVERCOME 803
WE SHALL WALK THROUGH THE VALLEY IN PEACE 574
WE WILL WALK 439
WE'LL WALK IN THE LIGHT 274
WE'RE MARCHING TO ZION 31
WEBB 223
WELCOME 6
WELCOME TABLE 801
WELLESLEY 156
WEM IN LIEDENSTAGEN 756
WERDE MUNTER 639
WERE YOU THERE 329
WESTCHASE 134
WESTMINSTER ABBEY 423
WHERE FEET MAY FAIL 456
WHERE YOU GO I'LL GO 775
WHISPER 548
WIE LIEBLICH IST DER MAIEN 122
WIE SOLL ICH DICH EMPFANGEN, see ST. THEODULPH (VALET WILL ICH DIR GEBEN)
WILD HOPE 828
WILD MOUNTAIN THYME 636
WINCHESTER NEW 316
WIR PFLÜGEN 747
WITH KINDNESS 568
WONDERFUL CROSS 324
WONDERFUL GRACE 170
WONDROUS LOVE 564
WOODWORTH 560
WORD OF GOD 404
WORDLESS 677
WORTHY OF EVERY SONG 92
WOZA NOMTHWALO WAKHO 679
WUNDERBARER KÖNIG 62
YA HAMALALLAH 321
YA RAB AS-SALAMI 711
YIGDAL, see LEONI
YOU ARE GOOD 33
YOU ARE THERE 587
YOUR GRACE FINDS ME 521
YOUR LOVE IS AMAZING 96

ZEPHANIAH 3:17 173
ZERAH 259
ZION'S PILGRIM 600

FIRST LINES AND COMMON TITLES INDEX OF WORSHIP RESOURCES

Titles proceeded by a † are passages of Scripture. Italic first lines are given for translations when the original language also appears.

† A shoot will come up 232
A wilderness beckons us 1011
Advent Candle Lighting (Hope, Peace, Joy, Love) . 916
Advent Candle Lighting (The Light Shines) 917
Alive (visual art) 334
Alleluia (ASL) 73
Alleluia! Christ is risen! 875
Allez en paix 1052.A–C
Almighty God, to you all hearts are open 860
Amen (ASL) 687
† Anyone who is joined to Christ 785
Apostles' Creed 923
† Are any of you suffering hardships? 727
As a shepherd seeks a lost sheep 868
As John baptized Jesus in the Jordan 940
As we now receive you into the fellowship 932
† As you come to Christ, the living stone 381
At the Impulse of God's Love (visual art) 780
At the table of Christ 936
At this table, we receive the bread of life 943

Baptism with water in the name of the triune God 930
Barely midnight. All of us hunkered down 871
† Be sincere in your love for others 384
† Be still and know that I am God 730
Between the words 990
† Bless the Lord, O my soul 185
† Blessed are the poor in spirit 295
Blessed are you, Eternal God 942
† Blessed are you, Lord, the God of Israel 985.E
Blessed are you, O God, maker of all things . . . 1019
Blessed be the ones who dance 1049
Blessed One, our source and support 989.C
Blessing and Farewell 962
Blessing for Leaders 968
By the grace of God, we seek to live and proclaim 925

Call to Discipleship (Evening Prayer) 987.E
Call to Discipleship (Morning Prayer) 985.D
Call to Intercession (Evening Prayer) 987.G
Call to Intercession (Morning Prayer) 985.F
Call to Praise (Evening Prayer) 987.A
Call to Praise (Morning Prayer) 985.A
Child Blessing 971
Christ be within us to keep us 1069
Christ has no body now on earth 1035
Christ, Have Mercy (ASL) 615
Christ is like a single body 856
† Christ is the image of the invisible God 189
Christ our companion, you came not to humiliate the sinner 898
Christ—the Joy, the Truth 907
Christ, whose insistent call 1029
† Clap your hands, all you peoples 108
† Come, all you who are thirsty 14
Come among us, Holy Spirit, and create a community 955
Come, come, whoever you are 1047
Come, Holy One, work upon us 858
Come, Holy Spirit, enter our silences 877
† Come, let us go up 13
Come, with your faith and your doubts 947
Commissioning Leaders within a Community . . 965
Communion (visual art) 468
Communion Prayer—Common Practice 941
Communion Prayer—Global Celebration 943
Communion Prayer—Inspired by Early Christian Practice 944
Compassionate Christ, if you are my light 1003
Confesemos nuestro pecado contra Dios 901
Confession (Evening Prayer) 987.D
Congregational Commitment at Baptism 932
Congregational Covenant Renewal 960
Convert us, Jesus the persecuted 1027
Creator God, thank you for people and places . . 954
Creator Spirit, you clothe the flowers 1018
Creator, we give you thanks 861
Creemos en Dios Padre todopoderoso 927

Days Recognizing Parents 972
Dear God, let your word shine 912
Dear Jesus, I confess my need of you 926
† Dear ones, I plead with you 105
Dios nuestro santuario 1042
Do not fear, says God 903.A
† Do not fight back against someone 293
† Do you not know that all who were baptized . . . 449
† Does not Wisdom call 184

Empowering God, with your people 965
Eternal God in whom we live 982
Eternal God, you call us to ventures 1068
Eternal Love, gentle God, you invite us 951
Eternal Strength, hold us 983
Eternity Sunday/Memorial Sunday/All Saints' Day 920
Evening Prayer 987.A–I
Everlasting God, in whom we live and move . . . 998
Everlasting God, you are our refuge 981
Every Christian is called 964

Faithful God, we give thanks 933
Footwashing Institution Narrative 951
For Congregational Transitions and Anniversaries 963
For failing to love others 893
† For God so loved the world 338
† For I received from the Lord 469
For the times we have lied 891
For the Word of God in Scripture 913.G
Friends in Christ, God knows our needs 888
Friends, as we gather to eat the bread 937

From all that is broken 908
From Bethlehem to Nazareth................. 874
From the River to the Wilderness (visual art) ... 445
From where we are 1050

Gardener God, you have planted 1002
Generous God, you gave us life.............. 1015
Give thanks to God, who is good 963
Glory (Evening Prayer).................... 987.B
Glory (Morning Prayer) 985.B
Glory to God in the highest 880
Glory to You, Source of All Being (Evening Prayer)............................... 987.B
Glory to You, Source of All Being (Morning Prayer)............................... 985.B
Go forth in peace, and be of good courage 1059
Go in peace 1052.A–G
Go, knowing you are beloved by God 1055
God be in my head......................... 999
God created human beings for relationship 973
God dearly loves us....................... 1056
God forgives you 909
God, give me grace to accept 1007
God, I have so few ways to pray 1008
God, it is night 986
God, just as you sent Joseph to Egypt.......... 957
God, make me an instrument of your peace 991
God, maker of galaxies who numbers the hairs............................... 971
God of all life, in you we live and move........ 974
God of cosmos and quarks................... 881
God of covenant, when Jesus came up from the waters 935
God of covenant, your steadfast love 960
God of deep and dazzling darkness........... 988
God of every place......................... 859
God of extravagant mercy 1020
God of grace and glory, you fling the stars ... 985.G
God of grace and glory, you keep our souls .. 987.H
God of grace, creator of waters 931
God of life, we give these offerings.......... 1017
God of life, we thank you that in our work 953
God of mercy, we are sorry 897
God of mystery and wonder, at this and every table 948
God of power, may the boldness of your Spirit 1067
God of the foolish cross...................... 896
God of wanderers and seekers................ 934
God of work and rest........................ 956
God, our Creator, we give you thanks 972
God our sanctuary......................... 1042
God, who is Alpha and Omega 962
God will guide us continually 985.H
God's Spirit calls, the church commissions 966
God's Word is a lamp to our feet........... 913.F
Gracious God, bless our cities 1032
Gracious God, our sins are too heavy.......... 895
Gracious God, we celebrate life............... 979
Gracious God, we pray for your universal church 1004
Gracious God, when there is nothing.......... 994
Great Physician, you touched the lives 976
Grow us slowly 1030

† Have mercy on me, O God................... 889
Have mercy on me, O God (Evening Prayer)............................... 987.D
Healing is central to the ministry of Jesus 975
† Hear, O Israel 187
Hear our prayer, O God of healing and hope ... 978
Hear the Word of God....................... 914
Hear the words of Jesus: "Peace I leave with you" 904
Hear what the Spirit is saying to the church 913.C
† Here is my servant, the one I uphold 448
Holy and righteous God, you created us 1034
Holy God, Holy One, Holy Three! 887
Holy God, you call us together 857
Holy One, as you are faithful to us........... 1022
Holy Wisdom. Holy Word. 913.B
Hosanna! Hosanna!......................... 885
House Blessing............................ 958
† How beautiful on the mountains.............. 781
† How long, O Lord?......................... 728
How silently 1021
† How very good and pleasant it is 17

† I am convinced that neither death, nor life 337
I believe in God, the Father almighty 923
† I lift my eyes to the hills 109
I pledge allegiance to Jesus Christ............. 929
I pledge with you.......................... 967
I praise you, God—in the sanctuary 886
† I saw a new heaven and a new earth 339
† I saw a vast crowd......................... 110
† I was glad when they said to me............... 16
I will light a light in the name of the Maker 867
If there is to be peace in the world 1046
If you are delighted to be here............... 853
† In Christ Jesus you are all children........... 450
In deep gratitude for this moment 946
In defiance of corruption and falsehood 1040
In his hands the iron nails 919
In our concerns and in our choices 1051
In our doubt and fear 1044
In peace let us pray: O God, we give you thanks 945
In the beginning, before time................. 884
† In the beginning was the Word 235
In the beginning when it was very quiet 852
In the face of death, we worship God.......... 980
Introduction to Baptism 930
Introduction to Child Blessing................ 969
Introduction to Church Leadership 964
Introduction to Church Membership 959
Introduction to Communion 936
Introduction to Footwashing 950
Introduction to Funerals..................... 980
Introduction to Healing 975
Introduction to Marriage 973
Invitation to the Communion Table (Come to the Table).............................. 939
Invitation to the Communion Table (Waters of Baptism) 940
It is good to give you thanks (Evening Prayer)............................... 987.C
It is good to give you thanks (Morning Prayer)............................... 985.C

Jesus calls us to praise and prayer 851
Jesus Christ, our Savior, you did not regard equality with God 952
Jesus Christ, you stretched out your arms 1026
† Jesus' eleven disciples went to a mountain 451
Jesus, Lamb of God 892
Jesus of love and leftovers 1016
† Jesus said, I am the bread of life 987.E
† Jesus said, "I am the true vine" 472
Jesus said, Let anyone with ears 985.D
Jesus, servant, at supper with your disciples . . . 1041
† Jesus stood up to read 292
Jesus washed the feet of his disciples 950

La paz no es producto del terror ni del miedo . . 1038
Land Acknowledgement 878
Lay one brick at a time 1036
† Lead a life worthy of the calling 446
† Let me hear what the LORD God says 188
Let the rain come and wash away 1048
† Let the same mind be in you 335
Let us confess our sin 890
Let us confess our sin against God 901
† Let your hearts be ruled 818
Liberating God, prevent us 1031
Life-giving God, may your Holy Spirit inspire . . 879
Lighting a candle 1006
Listening God, you hear our prayers 996
Live without fear 1062
Living Christ, in these times 1033
Living God, by the power of your Spirit 911
Living God, for whom no door is closed 876
Loaves and Fishes (visual art) *291*
Lord, your coming is still miraculous 872
Love cannot remain by itself 1037
† Love is patient 1045
Loving God, you have baptized us 1001

† Make a joyful noise to the LORD 20
† Mary's Song/Magnificat 987.F
May almighty God have mercy on us 905
May God be with you! And also with you 944
May God bless to our understanding 913.D
† May God bless you and keep you 826
May God bless you with a restless discomfort . . 1058
May God, who calls you to this ministry 968
May the blessing of the God of Sarah and Hagar 1060
May the Christ who walks on wounded feet . . . 1066
† May the God of endurance 822
May the God of glory 1053
May the God of hope 987.I
† May the grace of Jesus Christ 21
May the Love which overcomes 906
May the Son of God 1057
May the warm winds of heaven 1061
† May those who sow in tears 821
May we go forth into the world with courage . . 1039
Merciful God, we wait 977
Migrant Journey (visual art) 817
Mist, Sun, Morning (visual art) 183
Morning, noon, and night 987.G
Morning Prayer 985.A–H
Most loving, most strong God 900
† My soul proclaims the greatness 987.F

Nicene Creed 924
Nine Patch #8 (visual art) 723
No one can truly know Christ 928
Notre Père qui es aux cieux 989.D
† Now may our Lord Jesus Christ 819
† Now may the God of peace 823
† Now, thanks to Christ Jesus 786
† Now, through the church 385
† Now, to the One who, by the power 824
Nurturing God, root us in your love 1028

O Ancient of Days, you have been our dwelling place 920
O Dios, dales pan a los que tienen hambre 1025
O God, Ancient of Days, your love 941
O God, listening to us here 993
O God, open our lips 985.A
O God, our deliverer 1010
O God, to those who have hunger 1025
O God, you withdraw from our sight 1014
O God, your word is a lamp to my feet 987.A
† O LORD you have searched me 724
O Prince of Peace 894
O Risen Christ, you breathe your Holy Spirit . . 1013
O Tree of Calvary 1012
Open our ears to hear your word 866
Our Father in heaven 989.A
Our Father who art in heaven 989.B
Our lives are cluttered 899
† Our physical bodies cannot inherit 336
Ouvre nos oreilles pour entendre ta parole 866

Padre nuestro que estás en los cielos 989.E
Peace be with you 850
Peace is not the product of terror or fear 1038
Praise and thanks to you, holy God 915
† Praise be to the LORD 1063
† Praise the LORD 107
Praise to God who has given us life 902
Prayer after Communion—Common Practice . . 942
Prayer after Communion—Iona Community . . . 946
Prayer after Communion—World Council of Churches 945
Prayer after Footwashing 952
Prayer Before a Meeting 953
Prayer Before a Time of Worship or Preparation for Worship 879
Prayer for Camps and Retreats 954
Prayer for Healing 976
Prayer for Mental Health 978
Prayer for National Occasions 1043
Prayer for Schools and Learning Communities 955
Prayer for Service Agencies 957
Prayer for the Baptized 933
Prayer for Those Preparing for Baptism 934
Prayer for Work 956
Prayer in a Healthcare Facility 977
Prayer Jesus Taught 989.A–F
Prayer of Blessing for a Marriage 974
Prayer of Commendation 982
Prayer when Aging 979
Praying aloud spontaneously 995
Preparation for Communion 938
Preparation for Communion—Pledge of Love . . 937

Reaffirmation of Baptismal Commitments 935
Receive our thanks for night and day. 949
Receiving a New Pastor 967
Reception and Community Commitment at Child Blessing. 970
† Rejoice in the Lord always!. 726
Remember: we are earth 918
Response to Community Crisis 1044

Save us, God, from being self-centered 1000
Sending Leaders to Serve beyond a Community. 966
Shared Convictions of Mennonite World Conference 925
Sharing the Peace of Christ (Assurance of Grace). 904
Si se siente muy a gusto aquí 853
Sing and sing 883
Sing the Goodness (visual art). 104
† Sing to the LORD a new song 106
Some of us are exhausted 854
† Some people brought children. 18
Some trust in governments. 1043
Source and sustainer of life 1009
Source of all hope and holiness 863
Sovereign Majesty, we pray for the continued outpouring 992
Speak to us, living God. 910

Table Grace (God of Mystery) 948
Table Grace (Receive Our Thanks) 949
Table Prayer for a Community Meal. 947
That huge "Why?". 1005
† The angel said, "Do not be afraid!". 234
† The angel said to Mary 233
The church is the body of Christ 959
† The crowd said to Jesus, "You must show us more miracles" 471
The dust that shapes the journey. 873
† The LORD is merciful and gracious 186
† The LORD is my shepherd 725
† The LORD told you what is good 784
The peace of God, which passes all understanding 1054
† The people say: Our bones are dried up 383
† The people walking in darkness 231
† The reign of heaven is like a treasure 294
† The Spirit helps us in our weakness 729
The Spirit helps us in our weakness (Morning Prayer) 985.F
The table has been prepared 939
The Word of God for the people of God 913.E
† There are different kinds of gifts 380
There is no scarcity 1024
This day, God, may I dream your dreams 984
This home is yours, my God 958
† This is the day that the LORD has made 15
† Though the fig tree does not blossom. 820
† Thus says the LORD: Maintain justice 782
† Thus says the LORD, the God of Israel. 783
To worship is to stand in awe 855
Tree of Life (visual art) 12
True evangelical faith 921
Trusting in God's grace, let us confess 938
† Two disciples were traveling 470

Vater unser im Himmel. 989.F
Vayan en paz 1052.A–C

We acknowledge that we are gathering 878
We are a covenant people. 869
We are not alone. 922
We are people who must sing you 882
We believe in God, the Father almighty 927
We believe in one God, the Father, the Almighty 924
We gather in preparation 870
We give thanks to God for children 969
We have witnessed your commitment 961
We light a candle for hope 916
We light a light 865
We light this candle as a sign 917
We offer thanksgiving to our Creator 864
We Owe Them a Complicated Debt (visual art) . 230
Welcoming New Members. 961
What will you offer the body of Christ today? . 1023
Whatever wilderness the Spirit 1065
When Flaming Dove Meets Rising Waters (visual art). 378
† When the day of Pentecost came. 379
When the song of the angels is stilled. 1064
† Where two or three are gathered. 19
† While everyone was being baptized 447
† While Jesus was in Bethany 296
With the whole people of God. 997
Word of God. Word of Life 913.A
Words to Follow the Reading of Scripture 913.A–G

† You are no longer foreigners 382
You have offered 970
You who open doors 862

† Zechariah's Song/Benedictus 985.E

FIRST LINES AND COMMON TITLES INDEX OF SONGS

Regular typeface indicates the original language of a hymn. Italic first lines are given for translations of hymns when the original language also appears. Upper case is used for titles when the tune name stands in for a common title.

10,000 Reasons . . . 111

A Dios alabaré . . . 131
A Mighty Fortress Is Our God . . . 421
A Rusty Sword . . . 798
A Voice Was Heard in Ramah . . . 278
A Wonderful Savior Is Jesus . . . 626
Abana alathi . . . 675
Abana in Heaven . . . 675
Abide with Me . . . 502
Abre mi corazón . . . 731
Abre mis ojos, oh Cristo . . . 401
Abre mis ojos, que quiero ver . . . 732
ADESTE FIDELES . . . 241
Agios o Theos . . . 709
Agneau de Dieu . . . 559
Ah, Holy Jesus . . . 330
Akekho ofana . . . 68
All Are Welcome . . . 36
All Creatures of Our God and King . . . 81
All Creatures, Worship God Most High . . . 81
All Glory, Laud, and Honor . . . 315
All Hail the Power of Jesus' Name (CORONATION) . . . 411
All Hail the Power of Jesus' Name (DIADEM) . . . 364
All Our Praise . . . 82
All People That on Earth Do Dwell . . . 5
All Praise to Thee, My God . . . 505
All the Room Was Hushed and Still . . . 493
All Things Bright and Beautiful . . . 177
All This Pain . . . 551
All Who Are Thirsty . . . 49
All Who Hunger, Gather Gladly . . . 474
All Will Be Well . . . 586
All Your Ways Are Good . . . 775
Alleluia (Canon) . . . 362
Alleluia (Clemens) . . . 635
Alleluia (Doxology Refrain) . . . 72
Alleluia (South African) . . . 650
Alleluia (Taizé) . . . 66
Alleluia (That Easter Morn) . . . 342
Alleluia (Ukrainian) . . . 135
Although Our Lord Has Left Us . . . 366
Amazing Grace! . . . 163
Amen (African American) . . . 689
Amen (Dresden) . . . 688
Amen (God Welcomes All) . . . 32
Amen (Threefold) . . . 690
And I Will Raise You Up . . . 641
Angels, from the Realms of Glory . . . 265
Angels We Have Heard on High . . . 249
Anointing Fall on Me . . . 645
Arise, Your Light Is Come! . . . 273
As a Deer in Want of Water . . . 552
As a Sigh Great with Yearning . . . 403
AS I RISE . . . 848
As I Went Down to the River to Pray . . . 453
As Long as Jesus' Reign Goes On . . . 64
As Long as We Follow . . . 413
As the Waters Rise around Us . . . 708
As the Wind Song through the Trees . . . 373
As We Rise, O God, to Meet You . . . 39
As with Gladness . . . 277
As You Go Out from Here . . . 841
Asalaam aleikum . . . 707
Ask the Complicated Questions . . . 440
At the Dawn of Your Creation . . . 179
Aunque mis ojos . . . 67
Away in a Manger . . . 257

Balaacoolwe . . . 578
Be a Sower . . . 789
Be at Rest . . . 532
Be Not Afraid . . . 356
Be Still and Know . . . 37
Be Still, My Soul . . . 664
Be Thou My Vision . . . 549
Beautiful Savior . . . 130
Beautiful Things . . . 551
Beauty for Brokenness . . . 712
Because of You I Raise . . . 89
Because the Words We Wait to Hear . . . 406
Because You're Holy . . . 89
Before the Waters Nourished Earth . . . 652
Beloved, God's Chosen . . . 164
Bendiz o Senhor . . . 127
Between Darkness and Light . . . 808
Beyond a Dying Sun . . . 416
Bleibet hier . . . 627
Bless Our Eyes . . . 811
Bless the Arms That Comfort . . . 527
Bless the Lord . . . 111
Bless the Lord, My Soul . . . 127
Bless This Food and Bless Your People . . . 489
Blessed Are the Persecuted . . . 578
Blessed Are You . . . 290
Blessed Assurance . . . 435
Bless'd Be the God of Israel . . . 223
Blessed Be Your Name . . . 637
BLESSED QUIETNESS . . . 375
Blest Be the Tie That Binds . . . 831
Bon Berger, ton peuple t'adore . . . 849
Break Forth, O Beauteous Heavenly Light . . . 269
Breathe on Me, Breath of God . . . 737
Brethren, We Have Met to Worship . . . 25
Brightest and Best . . . 272
Brillando el Rey está . . . 116
Bring Many Names . . . 134
Build My Life . . . 92
Build Your Kingdom Here . . . 393
Bwana awabariki . . . 845
By Night, We Hasten . . . 543
By the Waters of Babylon . . . 695

Called by Earth and Sky . . . 806
Called or Not Called, God Is There . . . 422
Calm Me, Lord . . . 680
Cantai ao Senhor . . . 113

Cante al Señor 125
Cast Out, O Christ. 285
Cast Thy Burden upon the Lord 616
C̄hạn tạds̄incı lǣw ca tāmph ra yesū 443
Child of Blessing, Child of Promise 508
Children of the Heavenly Father 517
Christ, Be All around Me 848
Christ Be in Your Senses. 721
Christ Calls to Me 542
Christ Has Arisen, Alleluia! 341
Christ Has Broken Down the Wall 174
Christ Has Died, Christ Is Risen 438
Christ Has No Body Here but Ours 568
Christ Is Alive, and Goes Before Us 565
Christ Is Alive! Let Christians Sing. 359
Christ Is Arisen 358
Christ Is King! Let Earthly Powers 410
Christ Is Our Cornerstone 4
Christ Is Risen 349
Christ Is Risen! Shout Hosanna! 354
Christ Jesus Lay 463
Christ, on the Night He Was Betrayed 491
Christ the Lord Is Risen Today 346
Christ Upon the Mountain Peak 301
Christ, We Do All Adore Thee. 138
Christ Who Left His Home in Glory 361
Christ, You Are Light 271
Christe, lux mundi 271
Coman de este pan 476
Come All You People 2
Come and Fill Our Hearts 52
Come and See 282
Come and Seek the Ways of Wisdom. 196
Come Away from Rush and Hurry 9
Come, Bring Your Burdens to God 679
Come, Christians, Join to Sing. 28
Come, Gracious Spirit. 371
Come, Holy Spirit, Kindle 54
Come, Join in Mary's Prophet-Song. 246
Come, Let Us All Unite to Sing 7
Come, Let Us Go 11
Come, My Way, My Truth, My Life 48
Come, Now Is the Time to Worship. 29
Come Now, O God 143
Come Now, O Prince of Peace 391
Come, O Thou Traveler Unknown 191
Come On, Children, to the Gospel Feast 511
Come, Rain, Come Down. 634
Come Set Your Rule 393
Come, Thou Fount 563
Come, Thou Long-Expected Jesus 218
Come to Me, O Weary Traveler 157
Come to the Table of Grace 461
Come to the Water. 35
Come, Walk With Us 23
Come, We That Love. 31
Come What May 768
Come, Ye Disconsolate 643
Come, Ye Faithful, Raise the Strain 348
Come, Ye Thankful People. 123
Comfort, Comfort, O My People. 212
Comme un souffle fragile. 403
Confitemini Domino. 52
Contemplaré tu vida. 228
Corde natus ex parentis 418
Cordero de Dios 151
Could It Be That God Is Singing 42
Count Well the Cost 577
Crashing Waters at Creation 441
Create in Me a Clean Heart 141
Creating God, Your Fingers Trace 427
Creation Is a Song 181
Creator of the Stars of Night 236
Crown Him with Many Crowns. 408
Cuán grande es Dios 116

Dans nos obscurités 632
Darkness Is Not Dark to You, God 200
Dawk'yah towgyah thawy báht-awm 400
De noche iremos 543
Dear Friends, We're One 525
DEDICATION ANTHEM 70
Demos gracias 704
Dhuh Pangeran 26
Digno y santo 415
Dona nobis pacem. 707
Don't Be Afraid 596
DON'T BE DISCOURAGED 599
Dooládó' Shi Diyinda 562
Draw the Circle 802

EASTER ANTHEM. 357
Eat This Bread 476
Ehane he'ama 59
El cielo canta alegría 665
El reino de Dios 799
El Señor es mi fortaleza 118
El Señor resucitó 346
El Senyor és la meva força 118
En medio de la vida 526
Enviados somos de Dios 771
Eres mi respirar 139
Eternal Light, Shine in My Heart 554
Everlasting God, On You I Call. 630
Every Time I Feel the Spirit 681
Ey lou nis 769

Fairest Lord Jesus 130
Faith Begins by Letting Go. 585
Faith of the Martyrs 575
Far Above the Noise of Life. 625
Far, Far Away. 300
Father God, You Are Holy 59
Feed Us and Guide Us, Merciful God 304
Fierce Raged the Tempest 286
Fill Me Anew 739
Fill Us with Your Feast 309
Flow to You 132
For All the Saints 672
For God so Loved Us 158
For the Beauty of the Earth 120
For the Fruit of All Creation 124
For the Healing of the Nations 705
For Those with Whom Our Lives Are Bound 734
For We Are Strangers No More. 409
For You, O God, My Soul 41
Forgive, Forgive Us, Holy God 149
FRESH AS THE MORNING 420
From Heaven Above to Earth I Come 263
From North and South, from East and West. 460
From the Parent's Heart, the Firstborn 418
From the Waters I Will Rise 442

Gather Your People, Merciful God (Lent) 304

Gathered Here . . . 3
Gentle God, When We Are Driven . . . 150
Gentle Shepherd . . . 718
Gloria (Canon) . . . 94
GLORIA (Mass of Creation) . . . 99
Glory Be to the Father . . . 430
Glory to God in the Highest . . . 99
Glory to God, Whose Goodness Shines . . . 429
Go in Grace and Make Disciples . . . 766
Go Now in Peace . . . 835
Go Now in Peace, Worship Continues . . . 829
Go Tell It on the Mountain . . . 252
Go to Dark Gethsemane . . . 317
Go Ye Now in Peace . . . 839
Go, My Children . . . 830
Go, My Friends, in Grace . . . 810
Go, My Friends, in Peace . . . 839
Go, Silent Friend . . . 657
God, Be the Love . . . 43
God, Be with Us . . . 613
God Be with You Till We Meet Again . . . 840
God, Bless the Work Your People Do . . . 528
God Calls Us . . . 394
God Calls You Good . . . 172
God–Creator, Christ the Son . . . 455
God, Fill Me Now . . . 793
God, Give Me Faith like a Child . . . 519
God, Give Me Time . . . 144
God, Grant Us Mercy . . . 142
God Is Great and God Is Good . . . 488
God Is Here among Us . . . 62
God Is Working This Purpose Out . . . 770
God Lights a Lamp . . . 299
God Loves All His Many People . . . 767
God Made from One Blood . . . 523
God of Grace and God of Glory . . . 716
God of Justice . . . 772
God of Our Strength . . . 47
God of Peace and Justice . . . 711
God of the Bible . . . 420
God of the Fertile Fields . . . 750
GOD OF THE POOR . . . 712
God of Wonders . . . 178
God Speaks to Us in Bird and Song . . . 539
God the Sculptor of the Mountains . . . 423
God the Spirit, Guide and Guardian . . . 534
God, We Pause This Moment . . . 756
God Weeps with Us . . . 656
God Welcomes All . . . 32
God, Who Stretched the Spangled Heavens . . . 529
God Who Touches Earth with Beauty . . . 550
God, Whose Giving . . . 745
God, Whose Purpose Is to Kindle . . . 152
God's Glory Fills the Heavens . . . 197
Golden Breaks the Dawn . . . 498
Good Christian Friends, Rejoice . . . 261
Gott ist die Liebe . . . 158
Gott ist gegenwärtig . . . 62
Gracias, Señor, por el pan . . . 487
Gracious Spirit . . . 367
Grant Us, God, the Grace . . . 746
Gravity of Love . . . 494
Great God, the Giver of All Good . . . 486
Great Is Thy Faithfulness . . . 419
GREAT IS YOUR FAITHFULNESS . . . 167
Guide Me, O Thou Great Jehovah . . . 606
Guide My Feet . . . 816
Hacia Belén . . . 224
Hail the Bless'd Morn . . . 272
Hakuna wakaita . . . 68
Haleluya! Pelo tsa rona . . . 473
Halle, Halle, Hallelujah! . . . 752
Hallelujah! Fairest Morning! . . . 497
Hallelujah, Salvation, and Glory . . . 69
Hallelujah! schöner Morgen . . . 497
Hallelujah (Syrian) . . . 702
Hallelujah! We Sing Your Praises . . . 473
Hamba nathi . . . 23
Haneul naneun saeleul bora . . . 289
Hark! the Glad Sound! . . . 217
Hark! the Herald Angels Sing . . . 247
HAVE MERCY . . . 796
Have Mercy on Us, Lord . . . 693
He Came Down . . . 239
Healer of Our Every Ill . . . 644
Healing River of the Spirit . . . 642
Hear the Turmoil of the Nations . . . 201
Heart and Mind, Possessions, God . . . 753
Heart with Loving Heart United . . . 813
Heaven Is Singing for Joy . . . 665
Heilig, heilig, heilig . . . 137
Heleluyan . . . 85
Help Us to Help Each Other . . . 722
Helpless and Hungry . . . 268
Here by the Water . . . 629
Here I Am, Lord . . . 545
Here I Am to Worship . . . 227
Here in This Place . . . 10
Here on Christ the Rock I Will Stand . . . 159
Here to the House of God We Come . . . 27
Here's My Life, I Lay It Down . . . 561
Herr, füll mich neu . . . 739
Hey ney yana . . . 836
Hodiyingo hazą́ągi hinínáa doo . . . 562
Ho'ė enemeohe . . . 181
Hold On . . . 612
Hold Us in Your Mercy . . . 736
Holy . . . 136
Holy Father, Son, and Spirit . . . 60
Holy God, We Praise Thy Name . . . 126
Holy, Holy, Holy! . . . 76
Holy, Holy, Holy (German) . . . 137
Holy, Holy, Holy God . . . 709
Holy, Holy, Holy (Spanish) . . . 102
Holy, Holy, Holy Lord . . . 314
Holy Lord . . . 314
Holy Night, Blessed Night . . . 262
Holy Presence, Holy Teacher . . . 531
Holy Spirit, Come to Us . . . 58
Holy Spirit, Come with Power . . . 57
HOLY SPIRIT (Torwalt) . . . 369
Holy Spirit, Truth Divine . . . 46
Honja sorironeun . . . 800
Hope Is a Candle . . . 211
Hope of Abraham and Sarah . . . 807
Hosanna, Loud Hosanna . . . 313
HOW CAN I KEEP FROM SINGING . . . 605
How Can I Say . . . 388
How Can Our Anger Give Life . . . 792
How Can We Be Silent . . . 790
How Can We Worship Caesar's Cross . . . 308
How Clear Is Our Vocation . . . 547
How Firm a Foundation . . . 592
How Great Is Our God . . . 116

How Great Thou Art . . . 436
How Long, O Lord . . . 691
How Many Times We Start Again . . . 553
How Shallow Former Shadows . . . 326

I Am That Great and Fiery Force . . . 663
I Am the Bread of Life . . . 480
I Am Weak and I Need Thy Strength . . . 601
I Believe in God Almighty . . . 433
I Bind My Heart This Tide . . . 556
I Cannot See You . . . 67
I Come with Joy . . . 478
I Have Decided to Follow Jesus . . . 443
I Heard the Voice of Jesus Say . . . 536
I Know God Loves Me . . . 158
I Know Not Why God's Wondrous . . . 590
I Know That My Redeemer Lives . . . 347
I Lift My Eyes . . . 494
I Love the Lord . . . 684
I Love to Tell the Story . . . 761
I Owe the Lord a Morning Song . . . 496
I Saw a Tree by the Riverside . . . 514
I Sing the Mighty Power of God . . . 182
I Sing with Exultation . . . 444
I Sought the Lord . . . 161
I, the Lord of Sea and Sky . . . 545
I to the Hills Will Lift My Eyes . . . 602
I Walk in Beauty . . . 836
I Want Jesus to Walk with Me . . . 306
I Will Arise . . . 300
I Will Follow . . . 775
I WILL SING WITH YOU . . . 389
Ich weiß einen Strom . . . 668
Ich will dich anbeten . . . 227
If the War Goes On . . . 794
If You Only Had Faith . . . 593
Ikke ved makt . . . 538
I'm Gonna Eat at the Welcome Table . . . 801
Immortal, Invisible, God Only Wise . . . 98
In Christ Alone . . . 332
In Christ There Is No East or West . . . 390
In Lonely Mountain Ways . . . 589
In My Life, Lord, Be Glorified . . . 754
In My Wrestling . . . 597
In the Beginning . . . 270
In the Bulb There Is a Flower . . . 670
In the Heartbeat of the City . . . 530
In the Lord I'll Be Ever Thankful . . . 118
In the Morning When I Rise . . . 499
In the Quiet Consecration . . . 484
In the Quiet Curve of Evening . . . 587
In the Rifted Rock I'm Resting . . . 619
In the Singing, in the Silence . . . 481
In the Word, God Is Speaking . . . 562
In Thee Is Gladness . . . 666
In Thy Holy Place We Bow . . . 40
In Words of Truth . . . 148
In Your Sickness . . . 607
Infant Holy, Infant Lowly . . . 243
It Came upon a Midnight Clear . . . 248
It Is Well with My Soul . . . 617
It's There in the Newborn . . . 521

Je louerai l'Éternel . . . 131
Jesu, Joy of Our Desiring . . . 639
Jesu, meine Freude . . . 624
Jesus A, Nahetotaetanome . . . 8
Jesus, Be the Center . . . 584
Jesus Calls Us . . . 30
Jesus Christ Is Love Divine . . . 749
Jesus Christ Is Waiting . . . 287
Jesus Entered Egypt . . . 279
Jesus, Help Us Live in Peace . . . 719
Jesus Is Coming . . . 312
Jésus, je voudrais te chanter . . . 581
Jesus, Lord, How Joyful You Have Made Us . . . 8
Jesus, Lover of My Soul . . . 659
Jesus Loves Me . . . 516
Jesus on the Mountain Peak . . . 301
Jesus, Priceless Treasure . . . 624
Jesús, recuérdame . . . 327
Jesus, Remember Me . . . 327
Jesus, Rock of Ages . . . 622
Jesus Shall Reign . . . 414
Jesus, Tempted in the Desert . . . 307
Jesus, the Light of the World . . . 274
Jesus Took a Towel . . . 490
Joy to the World . . . 240
Joyful Is the Dark . . . 281
Joyful, Joyful, We Adore Thee . . . 103
Joyous Light of Heavenly Glory . . . 504
Joys Are Flowing like a River . . . 375
Just a Closer Walk with Thee . . . 743
Just As I Am, without One Plea . . . 560

Khudaya, rahem kar . . . 693
Kindle in Us Your Love . . . 54
Kirisuto no heiwa ga . . . 843
KOINONIA . . . 388
Kombo na Yesu . . . 648
Kuv tug kwvluag yog Tswv Yesxus . . . 628
Kwake Yesu nasimama . . . 159
Kyrie eleison (Ghanaian) . . . 795
Kyrie eleison (Oré poriajú verekó) . . . 620
Kyrie eleison (Russian Orthodox) . . . 147
Kyrie eleison (Taizé KYRIE 1) . . . 678
Kyrie eleison (Taizé KYRIE 13) . . . 692
Kyrie eleison, Have Mercy . . . 796
Kyrie (Moosonee) . . . 651

La cruz excelsa al contemplar . . . 323
La paz de la tierra . . . 838
La única razón . . . 89
Lamb of God . . . 151
Laudate Dominum . . . 77
Lay it Down . . . 561
Lead Me Forth . . . 837
Lead Me, Guide Me . . . 601
LEAD ME, LORD . . . 837
Lead On, O Cloud of Presence . . . 194
Leaning on the Everlasting Arms . . . 160
Les anges dans nos campagnes . . . 249
Let All Mortal Flesh Keep Silence . . . 65
Let Justice Flow Down . . . 791
Let the Children Come to Me . . . 512
Let the Hungry Come to Me . . . 459
Let There Be Light . . . 714
Let This Mind Be in You . . . 572
Let Us Break Bread Together . . . 482
Let Us Build a House . . . 36
Let Us Give Thanks . . . 704
Let Us Pray . . . 686
Let's Walk Together . . . 6
Licht deiser Velt . . . 227

Life-Giver, Maker, God of All . . . 38
Lift Every Voice and Sing . . . 611
Lift Your Glad Voices . . . 340
Light Dawns on a Weary World . . . 205
Light of the World, You Stepped Down . . . 227
Like a Mother Who Has Borne Us . . . 518
Like a Rock . . . 63
Like a Tender Breath, Stirring . . . 403
Like the Murmur of the Dove's Song . . . 56
Listen, God Is Calling . . . 765
Listen in the Silence . . . 541
Listen to the Word That God Has Spoken . . . 405
Living, Moving, End and Beginning . . . 425
Llénanos Señor, de tu paz . . . 52
Lo, How a Rose E'er Blooming . . . 216
Lo, I Am with You . . . 284
Lobe den Herren . . . 88
Longing for Light . . . 715
Lord, Have Mercy (Manderfeld) . . . 614
Lord, Have Mercy (Moosonee) . . . 651
Lord, I Am Fondly, Earnestly Longing . . . 555
Lord, I Come, I Confess . . . 155
Lord, I Lift Your Name on High . . . 365
Lord, I Need You . . . 155
Lord, I Want to Be a Christian . . . 558
Lord, I Will Lift Mine Eyes . . . 633
Lord Jesus, Come and Overturn . . . 146
Lord Jesus, You Shall Be My Song . . . 581
Lord, Listen to Your Children . . . 682
Lord of All Creation . . . 178
Lord, You Are Good . . . 33
Lord, You Give the Great Commission . . . 774
Lord, You Have Come to the Lakeshore . . . 283
Lord, You Sometimes Speak . . . 537
Lord, You've Searched Me . . . 609
LORD'S PRAYER . . . 673
Love Came Down at Christmas . . . 255
Love Divine, All Loves Excelling . . . 638
Love Has Come . . . 258
Love Incarnate, Love Divine . . . 256
Love the Lord Your God . . . 288
Loving Spirit . . . 697
Low in the Grave He Lay . . . 333

Magnificat . . . 97
Make a Joyful Noise (Psalm 100) . . . 66
Make Me an Instrument of Your Peace . . . 713
Make Us One . . . 455
Many and Great . . . 128
Margam, Satyam, Jivam nive . . . 425
Mary Journeyed . . . 224
Mary, Woman Weeping . . . 328
Masithi: Amen . . . 90
May God Grant You a Blessing . . . 845
May the Face of God Shine on You . . . 844
May the Peace of Christ . . . 843
May You Be Rooted and Grounded . . . 396
Mercy, Mercy, Lord . . . 169
Mfurahini, haleluya . . . 341
Mi Cristo, mi rey . . . 125
Mid sahaihaokheu phrayesu . . . 628
More Than You Know . . . 598
Morning Has Broken . . . 495
Mothering God, You Gave Me Birth . . . 426
Mountain of God . . . 11
Move in Our Midst . . . 827
My God Is Here . . . 67
My God, My God . . . 696
My Hope Is Built . . . 621
My Jesus, I Love Thee . . . 133
My Jesus, My Savior . . . 125
My Latest Sun Is Sinking Fast . . . 662
My Life Flows On . . . 605
My Lighthouse . . . 597
My Love Colors Outside the Lines . . . 582
My Shepherd Will Supply My Need . . . 640
My Song Is Love Unknown . . . 320
My Soul Cries Out . . . 412
My Soul Proclaims with Wonder . . . 222

Na nzela na lola . . . 413
Nada te turbe . . . 604
Nada vale más . . . 369
Naege itneun hyangyu . . . 755
Näher, mein Gott, zu dir . . . 658
Nearer, My God, to Thee . . . 658
Neno lake Mungu . . . 765
New Earth, Heavens New . . . 377
Ngayong nagdadapit hapon . . . 501
Ngo ji ging kyut ding jiu gan ceoi je sou . . . 443
Night Long Awaited . . . 242
Njoo kwetu, Roho mwema . . . 367
No Longer Slaves to Fear . . . 195
Noche anunciada . . . 242
Noche de paz, noche de amor . . . 244
Noel . . . 256
Not by Your Might . . . 538
Nothing Can Ever Come between Us . . . 654
Nothing Can Separate Us . . . 171
Nothing Is Lost on the Breath of God . . . 653
Now I Know . . . 769
Now, on Land and Sea Descending . . . 503
Now Thank We All Our God . . . 114
Now the Green Blade Rises . . . 353
Now the Heavens Start to Whisper . . . 237
Nun danket alle Gott . . . 114
Nyanyikanlah nyanyian baru . . . 93
Nzambi wakatamba . . . 767

O Beautiful Star of Bethlehem . . . 275
O Blessed Spring . . . 522
O Carpenter, Why Leave the Bench . . . 280
O Christ, Impart Your Teaching True . . . 583
O Come, All Ye Faithful . . . 241
O Come, O Come, Immanuel . . . 210
O Day of Peace . . . 787
O du fröhliche . . . 254
O Everlasting Love . . . 733
O Fiery Spirit . . . 55
O God and Father . . . 45
O God beyond All Praising . . . 814
O God in Heaven . . . 720
O God of Blessings . . . 700
O God, Great Womb . . . 176
O God, Our Help in Ages Past . . . 203
O God, Our Refuge . . . 434
O God, to You I Cry in Pain . . . 646
O God, We Call . . . 683
O God, We Read the Holy Law . . . 571
O God, You Search Me . . . 199
O Gott Vater . . . 45
O Great Spirit . . . 51
O Healing River . . . 706
O Holy Spirit, by Whose Breath . . . 53

O Holy Spirit, Root of Life . . . 376
O Lamb of God (Arabic) . . . 321
O Lamb of God (French) . . . 559
O Little Children, Gather . . . 515
O Little Town of Bethlehem . . . 245
O Lord, Hear My Prayer . . . 685
O Lord My God . . . 436
O Love, How Deep, How Broad . . . 303
O Love That Will Not Let Me Go . . . 608
O My Savior . . . 763
O phi nong oei . . . 525
O Praise the Gracious Power . . . 87
O Prince of Peace . . . 26
O Sacred Head, Now Wounded . . . 325
O Sing to the Lord . . . 113
O Splendor of God's Glory Bright . . . 500
O Thou, in Whose Presence . . . 600
Ô toi, Seigneur . . . 683
O Worship Our God (BEAUTY OF HOLINESS) . . 129
O Worship Our God, All Glorious Above . . . 74
Océanos . . . 456
Oceans . . . 456
Of the Father's Love Begotten . . . 418
Oh, for a Thousand Tongues (LYNGHAM) . . . 78
Oh, for a Thousand Tongues (AZMON) . . . 764
Oh, Have You Not Heard . . . 668
Oh, How Could It Be . . . 479
Oh, How Great Is Christ the Lord . . . 351
Oh, How Joyfully . . . 254
Oh, How Shall I Receive Thee . . . 215
Oh, qué bueno es Jesús . . . 351
Oh, The Wonderful Cross . . . 324
ON EAGLE'S WINGS . . . 641
On Jordan's Stormy Banks I Stand . . . 661
On Silken, Soft Wings . . . 676
On this Day Earth Shall Ring . . . 260
On This Great Day of Days . . . 260
One Is the Body . . . 386
Onyame wo mu o . . . 607
Open, Lord, My Inward Ear . . . 548
Open My Eyes . . . 732
Open My Eyes That I May See . . . 738
Open My Heart . . . 731
Open the Eyes of My Heart . . . 401
Oré poriajú verekó . . . 620
Ososo . . . 391
Our Father God, Thy Name We Praise . . . 45
Our Father, Who Art in Heaven . . . 674
Our God in Heaven . . . 673
Our Hearts Are Empty . . . 225
Out of the Depths I Cry to You . . . 140
Ouvre les yeux . . . 401
Over My Head . . . 594

Pase lo que pase, ¡ven! . . . 768
PAVE THE WAY . . . 312
Peace, Be Still . . . 202
Peace Be with You! Jesus Told His Friends . . . 165
Peace, Salaam, Shalom . . . 805
Peace to You . . . 168
Perdón, Señor . . . 153
Planets Humming as They Wander . . . 175
Poor of the Earth . . . 213
Prabhoo Lay lay . . . 567
Praise Be to God . . . 115
Praise God (Dedication Anthem) . . . 70
Praise God (Doxology) . . . 71
Praise Him, Praise Him . . . 100
Praise, I Will Praise You, Lord . . . 131
Praise, My Soul, the King of Heaven! . . . 75
Praise the Lord (SAKURA) . . . 115
Praise the Lord, Sing Hallelujah . . . 95
Praise to the Living God . . . 204
Praise to the Lord, the Almighty . . . 88
Praise with Joy the World's Creator . . . 428
Precious Lord, Take My Hand . . . 610
Prepare a Room for Me . . . 465
Prepare the Way! the Prophet Called . . . 220
Prepare Ye the Way of the Lord . . . 219
Put Peace into Each Other's Hands . . . 485

Qing zao qi lai kan . . . 498
Que mi vida entera esté . . . 760
Quietly, Peacefully . . . 533

Rain Down . . . 703
Rain, Come Down . . . 634
Rejoice, Rejoice Forevermore . . . 402
Remembrance . . . 479
Renew Your Church . . . 717
Restless . . . 741
Restore Our Faith, O Saving God . . . 198
Revelation Song . . . 415
Ride On, Ride On in Majesty . . . 316
ROOTED AND GROUNDED . . . 396

Sálvanos Señor . . . 833
Sanna, sannanina . . . 79
Santo . . . 136
Santo, santo, santo . . . 102
Save Us, O Lord . . . 833
Savior Jesus, Enfold Me . . . 567
Savior of the Nations, Come! . . . 214
Schönster Herr Jesu . . . 130
See the Birds That Fly . . . 289
See the Children Here before Us . . . 509
See Whose Glory Fills the Skies . . . 274
Seed, Scattered and Sown . . . 477
Seeds . . . 777
Seek the Peace of the City . . . 206
Seek Ye First . . . 417
Seeking Warmth from Charcoal Blazing . . . 344
Segala puji syukur . . . 82
Seigneur, prends pitié . . . 620
Send Me, Lord . . . 834
Señor, ten piedad . . . 620
Sent Forth by God's Blessing . . . 812
Shall We Gather at the River . . . 667
Shalom chaverim . . . 842
Shalom, My Friends . . . 842
Shema Yisrael . . . 192
Sheng ye qing . . . 262
Shepherd Me, O God . . . 744
Shí k'ad Jesus bikéé' yishááł doo . . . 443
SHOUT ON, PRAY ON . . . 347
Shout to the Lord . . . 125
Shukuru, Yesu . . . 699
Si tu avais foi . . . 593
Si tuvieras fe . . . 593
Sign Us with Ashes, Merciful God . . . 304
Silent Night, Holy Night . . . 244
Sim Shalom . . . 707
Sing a New World into Being . . . 809
Sing Amen . . . 90

Sing, My Tongue, the Song of Triumph 331
Sing, Praise, and Bless the Lord 77
Sing Praise to God Who Reigns 101
Sing to God a New Song 93
Sing to the God of Harvest 122
Sing We Triumphant Hymns 363
Sing with Joy to the Author 430
Siyahamba 793
Sizohamba naye. 815
Sleepers, Wake. 226
So lange Jesus bleibt der Herr 64
So nimm denn meine Hände. 631
SOFT FIELD OF CLOVER. 629
Softly and Tenderly Jesus Is Calling. 544
Solemn Stillness, Weary Streets. 276
Somebody Prayed for Me 698
Sometimes a Light Surprises 618
Somlandela. 566
Somos pueblo que camina 464
Somos uno en espíritu 387
Soon and Very Soon 669
Spirit, Do Your Work in Us 475
Spirit of God! Descend 557
Spirit of Life 368
Spirit of the Living God 740
Spirit, Open My Heart 636
Spirit, Working in Creation 50
Stay with Me 627
Stay with Me, the Night Has Come 319
Still My Soul 603
Still, Still, Still. 264
Stille Nacht, heilige Nacht 244
Strong, Peaceful Man of Galilee 573
Summoned by the God Who Made Us 1
Sword into a Plowshare 798

Take My Life, and Let It Be 759
Take My Life, That I May Be 760
Take the Saving Word of God 400
Take Thou My Hand 631
Take, O Take Me as I Am 748
Tana mana dhana prabhū tava caraṇī 753
Taste and See 467
Teach Me Thy Truth 776
Tears of Suffering 694
Tengo sed de ti 127
Thank You, O God, for This Bread 487
That Easter Morn, at Break of Day 342
The Angel Gabriel Called Mary Blessed 221
The Bread We Break Is Telling 466
The Church of Christ Cannot Be Bound 392
The Church of Christ, in Every Age 395
The Church's One Foundation 397
The Day You Gave Us. 506
The First Noel, the Angel Did Say 250
The Garden Needs Our Tending Now. 788
The Glory of These Forty Days 305
The God of Abraham Praise 204
The God of Sarah Praise. 190
The Hand of God Shall Hold You. 671
The Kingdom of God 799
The Lord Bless You and Keep You 846
The Lord Is King 64
The Lord Is My Light 437
The Lord Is Risen Indeed! 357
The Lord Lift You Up 832
The Lord Your God Is with You 173
The Lord's My Shepherd 660
The Love of God 162
The Name of Jesus 648
The Peace of the Earth Be with You 838
The Risen Christ 345
The Splendor of the King. 116
The Strife Is O'er 350
The Water Is Ready. 458
The Wonderful Cross 324
The Word of God Is Solid Ground 399
There Are Many Gifts. 374
There Is a Balm in Gilead. 647
There Is a Line of Women 546
There Is in Every Person 751
There Is More Love Somewhere 804
There Were Angels Hovering Round. 251
There's a River of Life. 24
There's a Wideness in God's Mercy 156
There's a Wild Hope in the Wind. 828
There's Enough for All 757
There's No One in This World like Jesus 68
There's Nothing Worth More 369
These Seeds You Have Sown. 777
These Things Did Thomas Count. 343
Thine Is the Glory 355
This is a Day of New Beginnings
This Is God's Wondrous World 180
This is My Father's World 180
This Is My Song. 710
This Is the Air I Breathe 139
This Joyful Eastertide 352
This Little Light of Mine. 762
Through Our Fragmentary Prayers 677
Thuma mina. 834
Thy Word Is a Lamp. 398
Time Propels Us like a Current. 507
'Tis Midnight, and on Olive's Brow 318
To God Be the Glory 84
To Leave the Stones Unthrown. 580
To My Precious Lord 755
To the One 591
To Us a Child of Hope Is Born 259
Today Earth Is Singing. 510
Today We Sing with Thankfulness. 535
Together 389
Total Praise. 633
Touch the Earth Lightly 145
Tous unis dans l'Esprit 387
Trinity Song 60
True Evangelical Faith 439
TRUST AND OBEY. 570
Tú eres todopoderoso. 89
Tú estás aquí 67
Tú has venido a la orilla 283
Tu nombre levantaré 365
Tu voz me llama a las aguas 456

Ubi caritas. 492
Ubi caritas et amor 773
Unexpected and Mysterious 229
UNITY. 719
Unless a Grain of Wheat 302
Use Us, God 811
Uyai mose. 2

Velaré contigo 627
Ven, Espíritu, cual viento 57

Veni Sancte Spiritus 370
View the Present 407

Wade in the Water 454
Wait for the Lord 228
Wakantanka 128
Waterfall 763
Way way way 742
We Are Marching 793
We Are Often Tossed and Driven 311
We Are One in the Spirit 387
We Are People of God's Peace 797
We Are People on a Journey 464
We Ask You for Your Power 768
We Believe, as One by One 431
We Come 225
WE COME TO YOUR FEAST 462
We Dream of a Turning 209
We Give Thanks unto You 117
We Have Been Sent by God 771
We Long to Know Her 44
We Place upon Your Table 462
We Plow the Fields and Scatter 747
We Praise the Word of God 404
We Praise Thee, O God 91
We Praise You, O God, Our Redeemer 34
We Read the Cross 569
We Remember You 479
We Shall Overcome 803
We Shall Walk through the Valley 574
We Sing to You, O God 80
We Thank You, Jesus 699
We Walk by Faith 588
We Will Follow 566
We Will Walk with God 815
We Worship God the Rock 424
We, Your People, Sing Your Praises 849
We've Come This Far by Faith 599
Weary and Tempted 309
Wehrlos und verlassen sehnt sich 619
WELCOME TABLE 801
Were You There 329
What a Fellowship 160
What a Friend We Have in Jesus 628
What a Wonderful Savior 562
What Can I Leave Behind 154
What Child Is This 267
What Comfort Can Our Worship Bring 623
What Does the Lord Require of You? 207
What Is the World Like 298
What Is This Place 22
What Wondrous Love Is This 564
When Aging Takes Its Toll 520
When All Thy Mercies 119
When at Creation's Dawn 121
When Grief Is Raw 655
When Hands Reach Out 513
When I Can't Find My Way 591
When I Survey the Wondrous Cross 323
When I Survey the Wondrous Cross (South African, Zimbabwean) 322
When in Our Music God Is Glorified 83
When Israel Was in Egypt's Land 193
When Love Is Found 524
When Memory Fades 649
When Pain or Sorrow 612
When Peace like a River 617
When the Storms of Life Are Raging 595
When Twilight Comes 501
When We Must Bear Persistent Pain 735
When We Walk with the Lord 570
WHERE FEET MAY FAIL 456
Where Is This Stupendous Stranger 266
Where True Love 492
While I Keep Silence 310
While Shepherds Watched Their Flocks 253
Who Are These 360
Who Now Would Follow Christ 576
Who Will Speak a Word of Warning 758
Wij geloven één voor één 431
Will You Come and Follow Me 540
Will You Let Me Be Your Servant 778
Wind Who Makes All Winds 372
Wir sind einig im Geiste 387
Wisdom from on High Is Dawning 238
With Astonishment, Fear, and Wonder 579
With Mary Sing Magnificat 208
With My Voice Alone 800
With Water Freely Flowing 452
Within Our Darkest Night 632
Womb of Life and Source of Being 112
Wonderful Grace of Jesus 170
Word and Sign 483
Worthy Is the Lamb 415
Worthy of Every Song 92
Woza nomthwalo wakho 679

Ya hamala Allah 321
Ya Rab as-salami 711
Yamaji koete 589
Yo soy el pan de vida 480
You Are All We Have 701
You Are Exalted 86
You Are Good 33
You Are Holy, You Are Whole 61
You Are Salt for the Earth 297
You Are the God within Life 526
You Call Me Out upon the Waters 456
You Dwell in the Songs 741
You Have Put on Christ 457
You, Lord, Are Both Lamb and Shepherd 432
You Shall Go Out with Joy 847
You Unravel Me with a Melody 195
Your Grace Finds Me 521
Your Grace Is Enough 167
Your Love Is Amazing 96
Your Love Is Washing Over Me 166
You're Not Alone 779

Zai gechang Zhong 481
ZEPHANIAH 3:17 173
Zisuh nih a zultu hna sinah 165